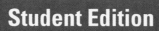
Student Edition

History Alive!®
Pursuing American Ideals

Equality

Rights

Liberty

Opportunity

Democracy

TCi™

Chief Operating Officer: Amy Larson
Director of Product Development: Maria Favata
Editorial Project Manager: Nancy Rogier
Production Manager: Jodi Forrest

TCi™ Teachers' Curriculum Institute
P.O. Box 1327
Rancho Cordova, CA 95741

Customer Service: 800-497-6138
www.teachtci.com

ISBN 978-1-934534-88-5
3 4 5 6 7 8 9 10 11 -WC- 17 16 15 14 13
Manufactured by Webcrafters, Inc., Madison, WI
United States of America, April 2013, Job # 105143

SUSTAINABLE FORESTRY INITIATIVE
Certified Sourcing
www.sfiprogram.org
SFI-00617

Program Director
Bert Bower

Program Author

Diane Hart is a nationally recognized author and assessment consultant. She has written textbooks on U.S. history, world history, geography, American government, and economics, most of which are still used in elementary, middle, and high schools across the country. She also authored the first civics text for Palau, a newly emerging nation in the South Pacific.

Ms. Hart has consulted with a wide range of clients on curriculum and instructional design issues. She had also worked with the departments of education in several states on the development of standards-based social studies assessments. Her most recent project has been the development of cross-cultural competency training programs to prepare military service personnel to work effectively with people from cultures very different from their own. She is also an active member of the National Council for the Social Studies, serving on the board of directors and contributing to *Social Education*.

As a writer, Ms. Hart is passionate about engaging all students in the compelling drama of human development across time and space. As an educator, she is equally passionate about preparing young people to deal successfully with life in an increasingly complex world.

Senior Writer
Brent Goff

Contributing Writers
Kate Connell
David Fasulo
Andrew Goldblatt
Holly Melton
Linda Scher
Ellen Todras
Julie Weiss

Lead Program Developer
Steve Seely

Curriculum Developers
Nicole Boylan
Terry Coburn
Julie Cremin
Erin Fry
Amy George
Colleen Guccione
Kelly Shafsky

Teacher and Content Consultants
Suzy Allione
Betty Carroll
Loyal Frazier
Karl Grubaugh
Thomas Johnson
Lindsay Petrie
Michael Radcliffe
Deb Schneider
Kathy Taylor

Scholars
Dr. James Banner
Independent Scholar

Dr. Dan Dupre
Department of History
University of North Carolina, Charlotte

Dr. Richard R. John
Department of History
University of Illinois at Chicago

Dr. Robert Johnston
Department of History
University of Illinois at Chicago

Dr. Jeff Jones
Department of History
The University of North Carolina, Greensboro

Dr. Ben Keppel
Department of History
University of Oklahoma

Dr. Delores McBroome
Department of History
Humboldt State University

Dr. Paula A. Michaels
Department of History
The University of Iowa

Dr. Carol Petillo
History Department
Boston College

Dr. Bruce Schulman
Department of History
Boston University

Dr. Timothy Thurber
Department of History
Virginia Commonwealth University

Dr. Stanley Underdal
Department of History and American Studies Program
San Jose State University

Dr. Wyatt Clinton Wells
Department of History
Auburn University, Montgomery

Music Consultant
Melanie Pinkert
Music Faculty
Montgomery College, Maryland

Cartographer
Mapping Specialists
Madison, Wisconsin

Researchers
Jessica Efron
Carla Valetich

Establishing an American Republic
1492–1896

Industrialism and Reform
1840–1920

Expanding American Global Influence
1796–1921

The Roaring Twenties and the Great Depression
1914–1944

World War II and the Cold War
1917–1960

The Search for a Better Life
1945–1990

Tumultuous Times
1954–1980

The Making of Modern America
1980–Present

Resources

Political Cartoons

Selected Primary Source Quotations

History Alive!®
Pursuing American Ideals

Chapter 1

What Is History?

What is history, and why should we study it?

1.1 Introduction

More than 200,000 people gathered at the Lincoln Memorial in Washington, D.C., on a hot August day in 1963. There they heard Reverend Martin Luther King Jr. give one of the most powerful speeches in U.S. history. His "I have a dream" speech was a watershed event of the civil rights movement.

By speaking on the steps of the memorial, King underscored the historical connection between the civil rights movement and President Abraham Lincoln's efforts to end slavery. In 1863, at the height of the Civil War, Lincoln had signed the Emancipation Proclamation, freeing slaves in Confederate states. Later that year, in his famous Gettysburg Address, Lincoln reminded the nation why slavery must end: "Fourscore and seven years ago," he began, "our fathers brought forth, upon this continent, a new nation, conceived in liberty and dedicated to the proposition that all men are created equal." The words of the Gettysburg Address are carved on a wall of the Lincoln Memorial.

Speaking a century later, King echoed Lincoln's words:

> Five score years ago, a great American, in whose symbolic shadow we stand today, signed the Emancipation Proclamation. This momentous decree came as a great beacon light of hope to millions of Negro slaves who had been seared in the flames of withering injustice. It came as a joyous daybreak to end the long night of their captivity. But one hundred years later, the Negro still is not free . . . Now is the time to rise from the dark and desolate valley of segregation to the sunlit path of racial justice.
> —Martin Luther King Jr., "I have a dream" speech, 1963

By beginning his speech with a reference to the past, King made the point that history matters. What happened long ago shapes how we live today. What he said next made another point: We are not prisoners of the past. If we can dream of a better tomorrow, it lies in our power to shape the history to come.

Abraham Lincoln, the 16th president of the United States, remains one of the most honored leaders in American history. Lincoln is best remembered for holding the nation together through the Civil War and helping end slavery.

1.2 History: The Past and the Stories We Tell About It

The term *history* can mean several related things. It can refer to events in the past, as in the history of a family. It can also refer to the stories we tell about the past. In this way, just about anyone can be a historian, or someone who reconstructs and retells stories of the past. History is also an academic, or scholarly, discipline—like economics, physics, or mathematics—and is taught and studied in schools.

This chapter considers history in each of these dimensions: as the past, as stories about the past, and as an academic subject. Its main focus, however, is on the writing, or reconstruction, of history and on how historians do their work.

History Begins with a Question or Problem Historians begin their work with a question they hope to answer or a problem they wish to solve. For example, a historian might start with the question, *Was the Civil War inevitable?* Next, he or she gathers facts and information related to the question. This material becomes the evidence the historian uses to reconstruct the past. Evidence is information that can be used to prove a statement or support a conclusion.

Historical evidence can come in many forms. It might be an old letter or manuscript. Or it might be an **artifact**—a human-made object—such as a tool, a weapon, or part of a building. Evidence can also be found in photographs, recorded music, and old movies. And, of course, it can be found in books, magazines, and newspapers, as well as in interviews with experts or historical figures.

Historians refer to these various forms of information as sources. There are two basic types of sources on which historians typically rely when writing history. A **primary source** is a document or other record of past events created by people who were present during those events or during that period. An eyewitness account, such as a Civil War soldier's diary, is an example of a primary source.

In the 1850s, *Uncle Tom's Cabin* was a best seller. Today it is read as a historical novel and a primary source of that time.

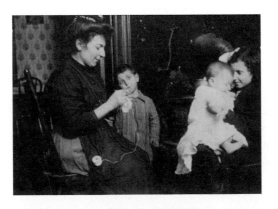

Photographs are visual primary sources that show what life was like in the past.

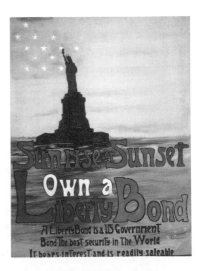

Posters from the past are today's historical artifacts.

Examples of a **secondary source** include a book or commentary from someone who was not present at the events or perhaps not even alive during that period. Many secondary sources are created long after the events in question. One example is a book about the Civil War written in the 1990s.

Historians Select and Weigh Evidence All historical evidence, whether primary or secondary, must be critically evaluated. Historians carefully examine each source for the creator's **point of view,** perspective, or outlook on events. This outlook may be shaped by many factors, such as the person's age, gender, religion, occupation, or political views. For example, a historian would expect that a southern plantation owner in the 1850s would have had a point of view different from that of a northern factory worker.

Sometimes a source contains information or conclusions that reflect a distinct point of view. This is not necessarily a bad thing, but historians are careful to look for signs of **bias** when analyzing evidence. In general, bias is any factor that might distort or color a person's observations. Bias takes many forms, ranging from a simple friendship or preference for someone to an unfair dislike of a person or group. Whatever its form, bias can make a source less than trustworthy.

Historians Reconstruct and Interpret the Past Once their evidence is selected and evaluated, historians begin to reconstruct what happened. They often begin by establishing a **chronology,** or sequence of events in time. Once historians are certain of the correct order of events, they are better able to make connections among those events. They can identify causes and effects. They can also begin to look for long-range changes and trends that may have developed over many years or even decades. For example, in considering whether the Civil War was inevitable, a historian would examine the events leading up to the war. He or she would also look for points at which war might have been averted.

Newspapers provide historians with eyewitness accounts of past events.

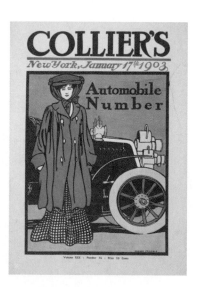
Magazine covers can reveal a lot about the cultural values of the years in which they were created.

Everyday artifacts, like John Wilkes Booth's boot, help connect us to the lives of historical figures.

When writing history, historians do not focus only on facts or chronologies. If they did, history books would be little more than a **chronicle,** or a simple listing, of what happened year by year. The more challenging part of a historian's task is to interpret the past—to weave together the evidence and produce a story that helps readers understand and draw meaning from history.

The process of finding the meaning or significance of historical events is called historical interpretation. By interpreting history, historians add their analysis of events to the facts they have judged to be true. They consider not only what happened, but also how and why it happened and what effect it had on the people involved. They also consider how those events may have shaped the world today. Each historian brings a particular point of view to this task. At the same time, historians try to ensure that their interpretations are faithful to the facts of history and are supported by the evidence.

History Is Never Finished History is not science, and it cannot be rigorously tested and proved. Much of history is still open to interpretation. Because historians have their own distinct backgrounds and points of view, their historical interpretations will often differ. They publish their work with the understanding that it will be reviewed, and often criticized, by other historians.

In this way, history continues to be debated and revised. In fact, some people describe history as an ongoing argument about the past. Differences of opinion about how to interpret the past make the academic study of history interesting and vital. This public debate also makes it possible for mistakes made by one historian to be corrected by later historians.

With each new generation of historians come new arguments. As historian Frederick Jackson Turner once wrote, "Each age tries to form its own conception of the past. Each age writes the history of the past anew with reference to the conditions uppermost in its own time." In other words, our understanding of the past is always being shaped by what we, in the present day, bring to it. In that sense, history is never finished.

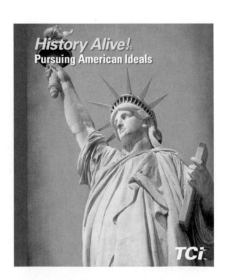

General histories like this book help readers develop a broad view of the past.

Historical interpreters bring history to life at living museums, such as Colonial Williamsburg.

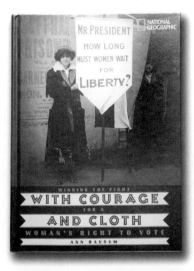

Specialized histories, such as this book, provide in-depth information about a specific subject.

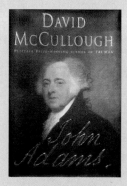

How Do Historians Reconstruct the Past?

When Pulitzer Prize–winning historian David McCullough set out to write a biography of John Adams, he gathered evidence from a variety of primary and secondary sources. He also examined artifacts and visited places frequented by Adams during his lifetime. The result was a compelling biography of one of our nation's least-well-known founders.

In writing his biography of Adams, McCullough built on the works of earlier historians. Such secondary sources fill the bookshelves in his office.

Historic drawings show what Boston was like when Adams practiced law there.

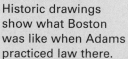

Artifacts like Adams's cradle help historians re-create scenes from the past. This cradle had been used for five generations and held both President Adams and President John Quincy Adams.

Primary sources, including letters Adams sent to Congress, reveal details about government affairs at the time.

Historic sites associated with Adams, such as his birthplace and childhood home in Quincy, Massachusetts, show how he and his family lived.

1.3 Why Study History?

"History is more or less bunk!" said automobile industrialist Henry Ford in a 1916 interview. They were words he would live to regret. Not only was Ford making history by putting Americans into cars they could afford, but he also discovered that learning about the past was fun. Ultimately, he used much of his fortune to create a collection of historic buildings and everyday objects from his era. "We're going to build a museum that is going to show industrial history," he announced when he began his collection, "and it won't be bunk." The result was the largest indoor-outdoor museum in the world.

For the more than 1 million people who visit the Henry Ford Museum and Greenfield Village in Dearborn, Michigan, each year, history is anything but bunk. As visitors wander through Greenfield Village, they can imagine what life was like more than a century ago. Re-creations of Thomas Edison's workshop and the Wright brothers' bicycle shop bring visitors face to face with the excitement and frustration of inventing a light bulb or an airplane. By touring the automobile collection, visitors learn how this machine has changed our world. Just as Ford had hoped, seeing the past his way is highly entertaining. But that is only one reason to study history.

History Helps Us Develop Empathy for Others Studying history can help us develop **empathy** for others. Empathy is the ability to imagine oneself in another's place and to understand that person's feelings, desires, ideas, and actions. It involves more than just feeling sympathy for other people. Empathy also enables one to "walk in other people's shoes"—to feel "with" them or "as one" with them.

History makes us aware of problems, sorrows, joys, and hardships faced by people in other times and places. As that awareness grows, we have a better chance of understanding our own experiences—both good and bad. We also become more skilled at empathizing with people whose lives are different from our own. As we mature, empathy becomes a useful guide in our relations with other people. As the American writer Robert Penn Warren observed,

> History cannot give us a program for the future, but it can give us a fuller understanding of ourselves, and of our common humanity, so that we can better face the future.
>
> —Robert Penn Warren, *The Legacy of the Civil War,* 1961

History Makes Us Better Thinkers "*History* is a Greek word," wrote British historian Arnold Toynbee, "which means, literally, just *investigation*." The process of investigating what happened long ago involves analyzing evidence and making judgments about what sources are credible. It also requires evaluating different points of view about what is important and why.

These are all essential critical-thinking skills, not just in the history classroom but also in life. You will need to exercise these skills whenever you make an important decision about your own future. These skills will also help you make more informed decisions about public issues as a citizen and voter.

Voting may not seem like making history, but each time Americans cast ballots, they are shaping the history their grandchildren will read about in school. Studying history can develop the critical-thinking skills that will help you make good decisions when you vote.

History Teaches Us to Avoid Errors of the Past A century ago, Spanish philosopher George Santayana proposed another reason for studying history: "Those who cannot remember the past are condemned to repeat it." History is full of examples of failed peoples and nations, and the study of history can reveal what they did—or did not do—that contributed to their doom. Looking at the failures of the past, novelist Maya Angelou wrote, "History, despite its wrenching pain, cannot be unlived, but if faced with courage, need not be lived again."

The more we learn today about the errors of the past, the better chance we have of avoiding them in the future. Viewed in this way, observed writer Norman Cousins, "history is a vast early warning system."

History Is Interesting "At the heart of good history," wrote screenwriter and journalist Stephen Schiff, "is a naughty little secret: good storytelling." And he should know. For decades, screenwriters and moviemakers have mined history for good stories and brought them to life on screen. Even movies that do not seem particularly historical are often based in part on historical events or settings. Knowing about the history behind these stories can increase your enjoyment of such films.

At a deeper level, figuring out the what and why of historical events is a lot like solving a puzzle or a mystery. Figuring out what happened can be challenging enough. Deciding what is important and why is even more of a challenge. Even so, anyone can do this detective work. And the more of the mystery of history you solve, the more alive the past will become for you.

As Henry Ford discovered when he set out to create a history museum, learning about the past can be fun. It can also help you develop empathy by introducing you to a wide range of human experiences. In this history classroom, students are learning what it was like to be an immigrant trying to enter the United States through Ellis Island around 1900.

Summary

History can refer to the past. It can be a reconstruction of the past. It is also an academic subject. Historians use various tools and techniques to reconstruct history. They try to make their accounts faithful to historical facts and events, as they understand them, while also interpreting those events.

Evidence Historians gather facts and information about people and events in history. A selection of this information becomes the evidence on which they base their historical accounts.

Primary sources Historians use primary sources, including written documents, photographs, films, and other records created by people who took part in historical events.

Secondary sources Historians use secondary sources, such as written documents and other information created by people who were not involved in the historical events in question.

Point of view Historians consider the points of view and the biases of the people who created their sources.

Historical interpretation While recounting the facts of history, historians also interpret the evidence. They assign meaning or significance to historical events. Historians often differ in their interpretations of history, which can lead to lively debates over historical issues.

Why study history The study of history can help people develop greater empathy for others, become better thinkers, and avoid repeating the mistakes of the past.

A Declaration by the Representatives of the UNITED STATES
OF AMERICA, in General Congress assembled.

When in the course of human events it becomes necessary for one people to
dissolve the political bands which have connected them with another, and to
~~assume among the powers of the earth the~~ assume among the powers of the earth the separate and equal ~~station to~~ station to
which the laws of nature & of nature's god entitle them, a decent respect
to the opinions of mankind requires that they should declare the causes
which impel them to ~~the~~ the separation.

We hold these truths to be self-evident; ~~sacred & undeniable~~ that all men are
created equal ~~& independent,~~ that ~~from that equal creation they derive~~ they are endowed by their creator with ~~equal~~
~~rights, some of which are~~ inherent & inalienable, rights, that among ~~which~~ these are ~~the preservation of life, & liberty,~~
life, & liberty, & the pursuit of happiness; that to secure these rights ~~ends~~, go-
-vernments are instituted among men, deriving their just powers from
the consent of the governed; that whenever any form of government
~~shall~~ becomes destructive of these ends, it is the right of the people to alter
or to abolish it, & to institute new government, laying it's foundation on
such principles & organising it's powers in such form, as to them shall
seem most likely to effect their safety & happiness. prudence indeed
will dictate that governments long established should not be ~~changed~~ for
light & transient causes: and accordingly all experience hath shewn that
mankind are more disposed to suffer while evils are sufferable, than to
right themselves by abolishing the forms to which they are accustomed. but
when a long train of abuses & usurpations [begun at a distinguished period
&] pursuing invariably the same object, evinces a design to ~~subject~~ reduce

Chapter 2

Defining and Debating America's Founding Ideals

What are America's founding ideals, and why are they important?

2.1 Introduction

On a June day in 1776, Thomas Jefferson set to work in a rented room in Philadelphia. His task was to draft a document that would explain to the world why Great Britain's 13 American colonies were declaring themselves to be "free and independent states." The Second Continental Congress had appointed a five-man committee to draft this declaration of independence. At 33, Jefferson was one of the committee's youngest and least experienced members, but his training in law and political philosophy had prepared him for the task. He picked up his pen and began to write words that would change the world.

Had he been working at home, Jefferson might have turned to his large library for inspiration. Instead, he relied on what was in his head to make the declaration "an expression of the American mind." He began,

> We hold these truths to be self-evident, that all men are created equal, that they are endowed by their Creator with certain unalienable Rights, that among these are Life, Liberty and the pursuit of Happiness.—That to secure these rights, Governments are instituted among Men, deriving their just powers from the consent of the governed.
> —Thomas Jefferson, Declaration of Independence, 1776

In these two sentences, Jefferson set forth a vision of a new nation based on **ideals**. An ideal is a principle or standard of perfection that we are always trying to achieve. In the years leading up to the Declaration, the ideals that Jefferson mentioned had been written about and discussed by many colonists. Since that time, Americans have sometimes fought for and sometimes ignored these ideals. Yet, throughout the years, Jefferson's words have continued to provide a vision of what it means to be an American. In this chapter, you will read about our nation's founding ideals, how they were defined in 1776, and how they are still being debated today.

In many ways Thomas Jefferson, shown here with his fellow committee members Benjamin Franklin and John Adams, was an odd choice to write the Declaration of Independence. Not only was Jefferson young and inexperienced, he was also a slaveholder. For all his fine words about liberty and equality, Jefferson proved unwilling to apply his "self-evident" truths to the men and women he held in bondage.

2.2 The First Founding Ideal: Equality

"We hold these truths to be self-evident, that all men are created equal."

When Jefferson wrote these words, this "truth" was anything but **self-evident,** or obvious. Throughout history, almost all societies had been divided into unequal groups, castes, or **social classes.** Depending on the place and time, the divisions were described in different terms—patricians and plebeians, lords and serfs, nobles and commoners, masters and slaves. But wherever one looked, some people had far more wealth and power than others. **Equality,** or the ideal situation in which all people are treated the same way and valued equally, was the exception, not the rule.

Defining Equality in 1776 For many Americans of Jefferson's time, the ideal of equality was based on the Christian belief that all people are equal in God's eyes. The colonists saw themselves as rooting this ideal on American soil. They shunned Europe's social system, with its many ranks of nobility, and prided themselves on having "no rank above that of freeman."

This view of equality, however, ignored the ranks below "freeman." In 1776, there was no equality for the half million slaves who labored in the colonies. Nor was there equality for women, who were viewed as inferior to men in terms of their ability to participate in society.

Debating Equality Today Over time, Americans have made great progress in expanding equality. Slavery was abolished in 1865. In 1920, a constitutional amendment guaranteed all American women the right to vote. Many laws today ensure equal treatment of all citizens, regardless of age, gender, physical ability, national background, and race.

Yet some people—both past and present—have argued that achieving equal rights does not necessarily mean achieving equality. Americans will not achieve equality, they argue, until we address differences in wealth, education, and power. This "equality of condition" extends to all aspects of life, including living standards, job opportunities, and medical care.

Is equality of condition an achievable goal? If so, how might it best be achieved? These and other questions about equality are likely to be hotly debated for years to come.

In 1848, a group of women used the Declaration of Independence as a model for their own Declaration of Sentiments on women's rights. They declared that "all men and women are created equal." Achieving equality, however, has been a tremendous struggle. This photograph shows a woman, some 60 years later, still marching for the right to vote.

For much of our history, African Americans were treated as less than equal to whites. No one knew that better than the participants of this civil rights march in Washington, D.C., in 1963. Their signs reminded the nation that each person in our society should be treated with equal respect.

2.3 The Second Founding Ideal: Rights

"They are endowed by their Creator with certain unalienable Rights."

The idea that people have certain **rights** would have seemed self-evident to most Americans in Jefferson's day. Rights are powers or privileges granted to people either by an agreement among themselves or by law. Living in British colonies, Americans believed they were entitled to the "rights of Englishmen." These rights, such as the right to a trial by jury or to be taxed only with their consent, had been established slowly over hundreds of years. The colonists believed, with some justice, that having these rights set them apart from other peoples in the world.

Defining Rights in 1776 Jefferson, however, was not thinking about specific legal or political rights when he wrote of "unalienable rights." He had in mind rights so basic and so essential to being human that no government should take them away. Such rights were not, in his view, limited to the privileges won by the English people. They were rights belonging to all humankind.

This universal definition of rights was strongly influenced by the English philosopher John Locke. Writing a century earlier, Locke had argued that all people earned certain **natural rights** simply by being born. Locke identified these natural rights as the rights to life, liberty, and property. Locke further argued that the main purpose of governments was to preserve these rights. When a government failed in this duty, citizens had the right to overthrow it.

Debating Rights Today The debate over what rights our government should preserve began more than two centuries ago, with the writing of the U.S. Constitution and the Bill of Rights, and continues to this day. The Constitution (and its amendments) specifies many basic rights, including the right to vote, to speak freely, to choose one's faith, and to receive fair treatment and equal justice under the law. However, some people argue that the government should also protect certain economic and social rights, such as the right to health care or to a clean environment.

Should our definition of rights be expanded to include new privileges? Or are there limits to the number of rights a government can protect? Either way, who should decide which rights are right for today?

This celebration of the Bill of Rights was painted by Polish American artist Arthur Szyk in 1949. It includes a number of Revolutionary War-era symbols, such as flags, Minutemen, and America's national bird, the bald eagle. Szyk wanted his work to promote human rights. "Art is not my aim," he maintained, "it is my means."

Every year, millions visit the Liberty Bell in Philadelphia's Independence National Historic Park. The huge bell was commissioned by the Pennsylvania Assembly in 1753. Its every peal was meant to proclaim "liberty throughout all the land." Badly cracked and battered, the bell is now silent. But it remains a beloved symbol of freedom.

2.4 The Third Founding Ideal: Liberty

"That among these [rights] are Life, Liberty and the pursuit of Happiness."

By the time Jefferson was writing the Declaration, the colonists had been at war with Britain for more than a year—a war waged in the name of **liberty,** or freedom. Every colony had its liberty trees, its liberty poles, and its Sons and Daughters of Liberty (groups organizing against the British). Flags proclaimed "Liberty or Death." A recently arrived British immigrant to Maryland said of the colonists, "They are all liberty mad."

Defining Liberty in 1776 Liberty meant different things to different colonists. For many, liberty meant political freedom, or the right to take part in public affairs. It also meant civil liberty, or protection from the power of government to interfere in one's life. Other colonists saw liberty as moral and religious freedom. Liberty was all of this and more.

However colonists defined liberty, most agreed on one point: the opposite of liberty was slavery. "Liberty or slavery is now the question," declared a colonist, arguing for independence in 1776. Such talk raised a troubling question. If so many Americans were so mad about liberty, what should this mean for the one fifth of the colonial population who labored as slaves? On the thorny issue of slavery in a land of liberty, there was no consensus.

Debating Liberty Today If asked to define liberty today, most Americans would probably say it is the freedom to make choices about who we are, what we believe, and how we live. They would probably also agree that liberty is not absolute. For people to have complete freedom, there must be no restrictions on how they think, speak, or act. They must be aware of what their choices are and have the power to decide among those choices. In all societies, there are limits to liberty. We are not, for example, free to ignore laws or to recklessly endanger others.

Just how liberty should be limited is a matter of debate. For example, most of us support freedom of speech, especially when it applies to speech we agree with. But what about speech that we don't agree with or that hurts others, such as hate speech? Should people be at liberty to say anything they please, no matter how hurtful it is to others? Or should liberty be limited at times to serve a greater good? If so, who should decide how, why, and under what circumstances liberty should be limited?

2.5 The Fourth Founding Ideal: Opportunity

"That among these [rights] are Life, Liberty and the pursuit of Happiness."

Something curious happened to John Locke's definition of natural rights in Jefferson's hands. Locke had included property as the third and last right in his list. But Jefferson changed property to "the pursuit of Happiness." The noted American historian Page Smith wrote of this decision,

> The change was significant and very American . . . The kings and potentates, the powers and principalities of this world [would not] have thought of including "happiness" among the rights of a people . . . except for a select and fortunate few. The great mass of people were doomed to labor by the sweat of their brows, tirelessly and ceaselessly, simply in order to survive . . . It was an inspiration on Jefferson's part to replace [property] with "pursuit of happiness" . . . It embedded in the opening sentences of the declaration that comparatively new . . . idea that a life of weary toil . . . was not the only possible destiny of "the people."
>
> —Page Smith, *A New Age Now Begins*, 1976

The destiny that Jefferson imagined was one of endless **opportunity,** or the chance for people to pursue their hopes and dreams.

Horatio Alger, author of *Strive and Succeed,* wrote more than 100 "dime novels" in the late 1800s. Many of these inexpensive books were about opportunity. They showed how a poor boy might achieve the American dream of success through hard work, courage, and concern for others.

Defining Opportunity in 1776 The idea that America was a land of opportunity was as old as the colonies themselves. Very soon after colonist John Smith first set foot in Jamestown in 1607, he proclaimed that here "every man may be master and owner of his owne labour and land." Though Jamestown did not live up to that promise, opportunity was the great lure that drew colonists across the Atlantic to pursue new lives in a new land.

Debating Opportunity Today More than two centuries after the Declaration of Independence was penned, the ideal of opportunity still draws newcomers to our shores. For most, economic opportunity is the big draw. Here they hope to find work at a decent wage. For others, opportunity means the chance to reunite families, get an education, or live in peace.

Many foreigners come to America looking for the opportunity to achieve the American dream. The American dream is the concept that poor could become successful through hard work, courage, and concern for others.

For all Americans, the ideal of opportunity raises important questions. Has the United States offered equal opportunity to all of its people? Or have some enjoyed more opportunity to pursue their dreams than have others? Is it enough to "level the playing field" so that everyone has the same chance to succeed in life? Or should special efforts be made to expand opportunities for the least fortunate among us?

The right to vote is so basic to a democracy that most Americans today think little about it. For much of our history, however, that right was denied to women and most African Americans. Their "consent" was not considered important to those who governed.

2.6 The Fifth Founding Ideal: Democracy

"That to secure these rights, Governments are instituted among Men, deriving their just powers from the consent of the governed."

In these few words, Jefferson described the basis of a **democracy**—a system of government founded on the simple principle that the power to rule comes from the consent of the governed. Power is not inherited by family members, as in a **monarchy**. Nor is it seized and exercised by force, as in a **dictatorship**. In a democracy, the people have the power to choose their leaders and shape the laws that govern them.

Defining Democracy in 1776 The colonists were familiar with the workings of democracy. For many generations, the people had run their local governments. In town meetings or colonial assemblies, colonists had learned to work together to solve common problems. They knew democracy worked on a small scale. But two questions remained. First, could democracy be made to work in a country spread over more than a thousand miles? In 1776, many people were not sure that it could.

The second question was this: Who should speak for "the governed"? In colonial times, only white, adult, property-owning men were allowed to vote or hold office. This narrow definition of voters did not sit well with many Americans, even then. "How can a Man be said to [be] free and independent," protested citizens of Massachusetts in 1778, "when he has not a voice allowed him" to vote? As for women, their voices were not yet heard at all.

Debating Democracy Today The debate over who should speak for the governed was long and heated. It took women more than a century of tenacious struggle to gain voting rights. For many minority groups, democracy was denied for even longer. Today, the right to vote is universal for all American citizens over the age of 18.

Having gained the right to vote, however, many people today do not use it. Their lack of participation raises challenging questions. Why do so many Americans choose not to make their voices heard? Can democracy survive if large numbers of citizens decide not to participate in public affairs?

2.7 In Pursuit of America's Ideals

"Ideals are like stars," observed Carl Schurz, a German American politician in the late 1800s. "You will not succeed in touching them with your hands, but like the seafaring man on the ocean desert of waters, you choose them as your guides, and, following them, you reach your destiny." In this book, the ideals found in the Declaration of Independence will serve as your guiding stars. You will come upon these ideals again and again—sometimes as points of pride, sometimes as prods to progress, and sometimes as sources of sorrow.

Living up to these ideals has never been a simple thing. Ideals represent the very highest standards, and human beings are far too complex to achieve such perfection. No one illustrates that complexity more clearly than Jefferson. Although Jefferson believed passionately in the Declaration's ideals, he was a slaveholder. Equality and liberty stopped at the borders of his Virginia plantation. Jefferson's pursuit of happiness depended on depriving the people who labored for him as slaves the right to pursue happiness of their own.

Soon after the Continental Congress approved the Declaration of Independence, it appointed a committee to design an official seal for the United States. The final design appears on the back of the one-dollar bill. One side shows an American eagle holding symbols of peace and war, with the eagle facing toward peace. The other shows an unfinished pyramid, symbolizing strength and endurance. Perhaps another reason for the unfinished pyramid was to show that a nation built on ideals is a work in progress. As long as our founding ideals endure, the United States will always be striving to meet them.

The front of the Great Seal features a bald eagle and a shield with 13 red and white stripes, representing the original 13 states. The scroll in the eagle's beak contains our national motto, *E Pluribus Unum,* which means "Out of Many, One." The motto refers to the creation of one nation out of 13 states.

Summary

Throughout their history, Americans have been inspired and guided by the ideals in the Declaration of Independence—equality, rights, liberty, opportunity, and democracy. Each generation has struggled with these ideals. The story of their struggles lies at the heart of our nation's history and who we are as Americans.

Equality The Declaration of Independence asserts that "all men are created equal." During the past two centuries, our definition of equality has broadened to include women and minority groups. But we are still debating the role of government in promoting equality today.

Rights The Declaration states that we are all born with "certain unalienable Rights." Just what these rights should be has been the subject of never-ending debates.

Liberty One of the rights mentioned in the Declaration is liberty—the right to speak, act, think, and live freely. However, liberty is never absolute or unlimited. Defining the proper limits to liberty is an unending challenge to a free people.

Opportunity This ideal lies at the heart of the "American dream." It also raises difficult questions about what government should do to promote equal opportunities for all Americans.

Democracy The Declaration of Independence states that governments are created by people in order to "secure these rights." Governments receive their "just powers" to rule from the "consent of the governed." Today we define such governments as democracies.

Chapter 3

Setting the Geographic Stage

How has geography influenced the development of the United States?

3.1 Introduction

In late 1606, three small ships crammed with about 105 men and boys set sail from England across the Atlantic. These colonists sought, in the words of a song, "to get the pearl and gold" in "Virginia, Earth's only paradise." They were lured by visions of riches—gold, silver, gems—and the promise of adventure.

Four months later, the travel-weary settlers finally sailed into Chesapeake Bay on the eastern coast of North America. Their first impressions of Virginia exceeded expectations. One voyager wrote of "fair meadows and goodly tall trees, with such fresh waters running through the woods as I was almost ravished at [carried away by] the first site thereof." The settlers chose a site on the James River, which they named for their king, where they established Jamestown, the first permanent English colony in North America.

One of the colony's leaders, John Smith, declared the site "a very fit place for the erecting of a great city." Smith could not have been more wrong. The swampy ground swarmed with mosquitoes. It also lacked good drinking water. By the first winter, more than half the settlers had died of sickness and starvation. To top it all off, the "gold" they found turned out to be iron pyrite, a common mineral also known as "fool's gold." The hoped-for "land of opportunity" had turned out to be a land of daunting challenges. Yet the infant colony survived, due in large part to Smith's leadership and the help of local Indians, who brought the settlers food.

The story of Jamestown's struggle for survival illustrates how geography can affect human events. The North American continent, with its abundant resources, held out the promise of opportunity to all who migrated to its shores. But at the same time, as the Jamestown colonists discovered, this new land also presented those who came with countless obstacles to overcome. In this chapter, you will start to see how geography has helped shape the course of American history, from the arrival of the first Americans to the present day.

This picture shows the wives of settlers arriving at the low, swampy peninsula of Jamestown. Today, the original site of Jamestown sits no longer on a peninsula, but on an island. The site was cut off from the mainland by tidal currents of the James River.

The Mississippi River is a major north-south transportation route. Ships that travel along it carry farm products, raw materials, and factory goods, among other products.

For centuries, the Rocky Mountains, with their tall peaks and rugged passes, blocked east-west movement across the continent.

Although today the Great Plains support agricultural activity, early pioneers would not have believed it possible. They called the grassy, dry region the Great American Desert. Americans did not significantly develop or inhabit the Great Plains until railroads were extended across the country in the late 1800s.

3.2 A Vast, Varied Land: Physical Features of the United States

The United States today measures more than 3 million square miles in area. Within this vast land lie extremely varied **physical features**. The country includes almost all types of **landforms**, from mountains and valleys to plains and plateaus. It also has many bodies of water, from enormous lakes and major rivers to tidewater marshes and swampy bayous. Since humans first arrived, these physical features have influenced patterns of migration and settlement.

Blessings and Barriers The land and its resources have attracted people and helped shape their ways of life. America's earliest people came to the continent tens of thousands of years ago by following animals they hunted. Their descendants spread across the continent and developed ways of life suited to the land's varied environments. Some groups also shaped their environment to meet their needs—for example, by using fire to keep cleared areas of forest open.

Like these early Indians, settlers from Europe found that the nation's physical features influenced where and how they lived. In the 1500s, the Spanish began settling the Southwest and Southeast in search of gold. Once there, they stayed to run farms and mines. Starting in the 1600s, English colonists adapted to the land and its climate as they began their new lives in North America. For example, the Southeast's broad coastal plain, with its plentiful rainfall and warm temperature, was ideal for farms. By contrast, the Northeast's natural harbors developed into centers of trade and commerce. Because water was the fastest way to transport goods and people in the nation's early days, cities sprang up along internal waterways—such as New Orleans on the Mississippi River and Chicago on Lake Michigan.

Although the land has lured people for thousands of years, it has also posed challenges. For example, the Appalachian Mountains in the East, the Rocky Mountains in the West, and the deserts in the Southwest have been natural barriers to travel and settlement. Harsh climate conditions, poor soil, and lack of water have made living difficult or even impossible in some areas of the country. As you study American history, look for the effect the land has had on the nation's development.

The elevation profile at right shows a cross-section of the United States. How do you think the physical features of the United States affected settlement patterns?

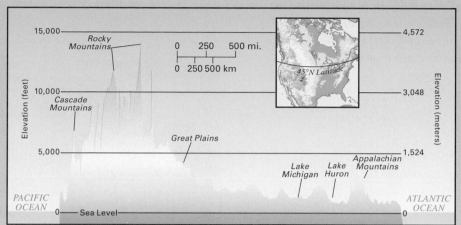

Elevation

Feet	Meters
Over 10,000	Over 3,050
5,001–10,000	1,526–3,050
2,001–5,000	611–1,525
1,001–2,000	306–610
0–1,000	0–305
Below sea level	Below sea level

When colonists arrived in North America, most of England had already been deforested. Colonists set up logging operations to provide wood for shipbuilding, home construction, and furniture making. American forests today still provide lumber for these purposes, as well as for export to other countries.

3.3 A Land of Plenty: Natural Resources of the United States

The abundance of **natural resources** in the United States has long made it a land of opportunity. Soil, forests, wildlife, and minerals have provided the basis for economic activity since the ancient peoples migrated to North America from Asia. Their descendants developed ways of life suited to local resources. Some tribes followed buffalo on the Great Plains. Others developed economies based on woodland game, marine mammals, or fish from rivers or oceans. Still others relied on the land itself, clearing trees and diverting waterways to farm the land.

In 1848, the discovery of gold in California set off a worldwide "gold fever." Treasure hunters from as far away as Europe and China, like the ones shown above, raced to the gold fields in hopes of striking it rich.

Using the Land Itself: Farming Dazzled by stories of gold in Mexico and silver in Peru, the Jamestown colonists expected to find these precious metals in Virginia too. To their surprise, they discovered none. They reluctantly turned to farming, growing crops for both subsistence and export.

The first colonists' inability to find these precious minerals had a profound effect on the historical development of the United States. One historian argued,

> One of the greatest factors in making land in North America so important was that settlers along the Atlantic Coast failed to find sources of quick mineral riches; consequently they turned to the slower processes of agriculture to gain livelihoods. Farming, from the beginning, became the main way of American frontier life.
>
> —Thomas D. Clark, *Frontier America,* 1969

By *frontier,* Clark was referring to the land still unknown to, and undeveloped by, the colonists. Once colonists began to prosper by farming, the lure of western farmland drew explorers and then settlers across the Appalachians to the fertile interior plains. Even today, commercial agriculture in this part of the United States produces a significant portion of the world's crops.

Resources of the Woods, Seas, and Subsoil Parts of our nation that do not have good farmland are rich in other resources. New England's rocky soil and cold winters limited farming to a small scale. Instead, New Englanders built their economy on the resources of the forest and sea. They exported dried fish and whale oil and used their abundant timber to build fishing boats and merchant ships. This successful shipbuilding industry, as well as the area's sheltered harbors, made New England the center of trade with other countries.

Though Virginia did not have the precious metals the colonists had hoped for, other parts of the country did contain mineral resources. As the United States expanded across the continent in the 1800s, settlers found copper, lead, gold, silver, nickel, and zinc far beneath the soil. These minerals became a source of wealth, as well as the raw materials for American factories to produce an astonishing array of goods. Today, every state has an active mining industry, even tiny Rhode Island and tropical Hawaii.

The energy resources of the United States have played a critical role in the country's economic development. Large reserves of **fossil fuels,** such as coal, oil, and natural gas, helped the United States become an industrial giant in the 1800s. These fuels continue to provide energy for industry and transportation. Water is another important source of energy. Today about 7.5 percent of the country's electric power is generated by waterpower in hydroelectric dams. Energy resources will continue to play a vital part in the nation's future.

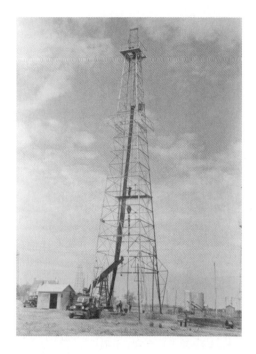

Oil prospectors erected derricks to hold the equipment to drill oil wells. Oklahoma's oil reserves are among the largest in the nation.

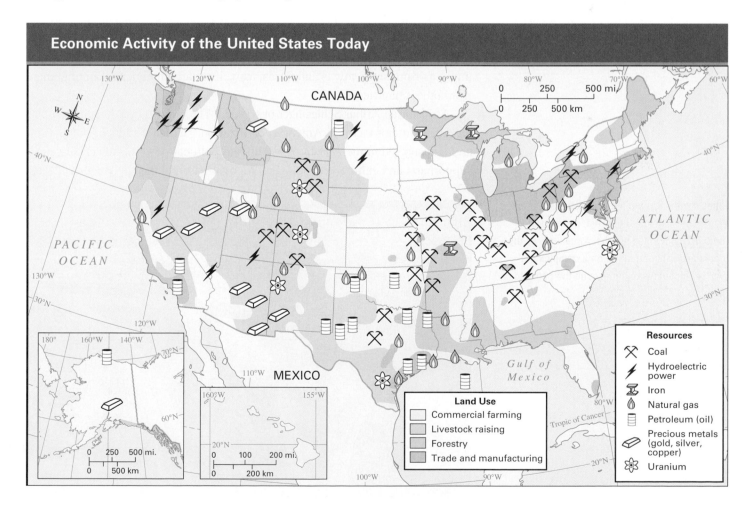

Economic Activity of the United States Today

Resources
- ⚒ Coal
- ⚡ Hydroelectric power
- Iron
- ◊ Natural gas
- ▯ Petroleum (oil)
- Precious metals (gold, silver, copper)
- ⚛ Uranium

Land Use
- Commercial farming
- Livestock raising
- Forestry
- Trade and manufacturing

St. Louis, Missouri, owed its early growth to its location near the confluence of the Mississippi and Missouri rivers. In the early 1800s, St. Louis served as the gateway to the West for explorers, fur traders, and settlers.

3.4 A Growing Population: From Farms to Cities

In 1790, the United States held its first **census,** or official count of its population. Census takers counted about 3.9 million people that year. Of that total, only about 5 percent—roughly 195,000—lived in towns or cities that had more than 2,500 people. The rest lived spread out on farms or in small villages. This seemed just right to Thomas Jefferson, whose ideal was a nation of independent farmers.

Growth of Cities Despite Jefferson's high opinion of farmers, the United States would not remain a strictly rural nation. Colonial cities like Boston and Philadelphia began as trading centers at transportation crossroads. As they grew, they became centers of wealth, attracting skilled artisans, professional people, and workers from near and far.

As American settlers moved west, cities developed across the landscape. Physical features influenced where cities sprouted, and ease of access was one key to the birth of cities. St. Louis, Missouri, for example, developed at the juncture of the Mississippi and the Missouri rivers. Its location made it a logical place for the exchange and shipment of farm products, raw materials, and finished products. In the 1800s, improvements to transportation—such as roads, canals, steamships, and railroads—linked cities to the outside world and contributed to their expansion.

In the late 1800s, better transportation encouraged the concentration of industries in cities. These new industries, fueled by abundant natural resources, increased the population of cities. The economic opportunity in cities drew migrants from small towns and farms, as well as large numbers of immigrants from other countries.

As historian Arthur Schlesinger observed, "The city, no less than the frontier, has been a major factor in American civilization." Urban centers of population and industry led to the growth of wealth and political power. Such centers also support arts and culture, technological innovations, and the exchange of ideas.

Cities respond to population growth in various ways. Los Angeles, California, has sprawled outward in lowrise suburbs. Angelinos, as the locals are called, depend on a complex network of highways to get around their spread-out city.

Chicago, Illinois, has responded to population growth by building up as well as out. Downtown Chicago is famous for its soaring skyscrapers. Hundreds of thousands of people stream into this area on weekdays to work and shop. Many arrive on elevated trains, like the one shown here.

U.S. Population Today From 1870 to 1920, the number of people living in U.S. cities increased from 10 million to more than 50 million. Population growth continued over the next 100 years. By 2010, the U.S. Census Bureau estimated the nation's population at 308.7 million. About 83 percent of the population lived in metropolitan areas. The commerce and industry that these city populations generate contribute significantly to the status of the United States as one of the world's economic giants.

Population density is a measure of the number of people who live in a given unit of area. In the United States, metropolitan areas, or large cities and their neighboring cities and towns, are areas with a population of 2,500 or more.

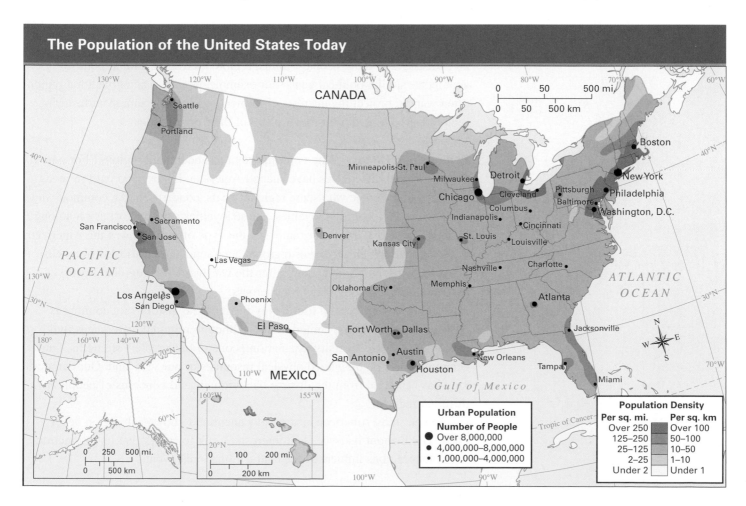

The Population of the United States Today

Urban Population Number of People	
●	Over 8,000,000
●	4,000,000–8,000,000
•	1,000,000–4,000,000

Population Density	
Per sq. mi.	Per sq. km
Over 250	Over 100
125–250	50–100
25–125	10–50
2–25	1–10
Under 2	Under 1

3.5 United and Divided: Regions and American History

The United States is made up of 50 separate states, each with its own government. The divisions between states are political boundaries—government-defined borders with exact locations. Yet when Americans think about their country, they also divide it into unofficial regions. A region is a geographic area defined by one or more characteristics that set it apart from other areas. A region may be as large as a continent or as small as a city neighborhood characterized by a distinct economic activity, style of home, food or culture, or ethnic group.

Regional Identity A quick glance over the American landscape today reveals remarkable similarities. From coast to coast, you see the same restaurants, stores, highways, movies, and television programs. A closer look, however, reveals that each region of the country has its own identity. Physical features, climate, and natural resources have shaped each region's economy and settlement patterns. Arid and semiarid regions, for instance, tend to be thinly settled, because they lack adequate water for farming and industry.

A region's "personality" also reflects its population. The traditions and culture of the people living in a region give it its own particular flavor. For example, each region has its own characteristic foods, such as spicy burritos in the Southwest and clam chowder in the Northeast. Each region also has its own speech patterns, building styles, and festivals, to name but a few elements of regional identity.

A region's geographic, economic, and cultural factors also shape its needs and wants. As a result, people within a region often share similar points of view and pursue similar political goals. For example, people in an agricultural region often want to protect the interests of farmers, while those in a manufacturing region tend to look out for the interests of their industries.

Regions and History Why is it important to understand regions? For one thing, regional differences have shaped American history and culture in significant ways. People who share regional goals, concerns, and a common way of life can develop strong loyalties. These loyalties can cause division among regions. The most dramatic example of this type of division was the American Civil War, which erupted over regional economic and political differences between North and South. Long after the war was over, regional loyalty remained strong among many Southerners.

Regions also give us a useful way to study the history of a country as large and diverse as the United States. Although regional differences may cause tension, our diversity as a nation is one of our greatest strengths. Our economy relies on the varied physical resources of our vast land. Our democracy has benefited from the diverse backgrounds and concerns of people in different regions.

As you study American history, pay attention to how each region developed. Think about its issues and interests. Look for ways that its interaction with other regions influenced the course of national events.

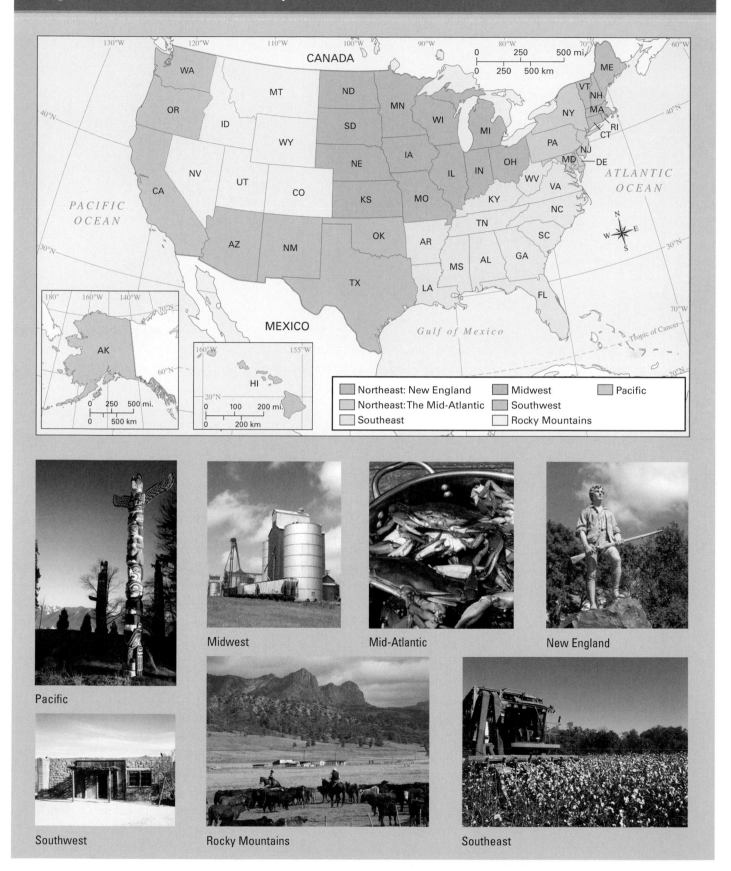

Northeast: New England

Northeast: The Mid-Atlantic

Southeast

Midwest

Southwest

Rocky Mountains

Pacific

Pacific

Midwest

Mid-Atlantic

New England

Southwest

Rocky Mountains

Southeast

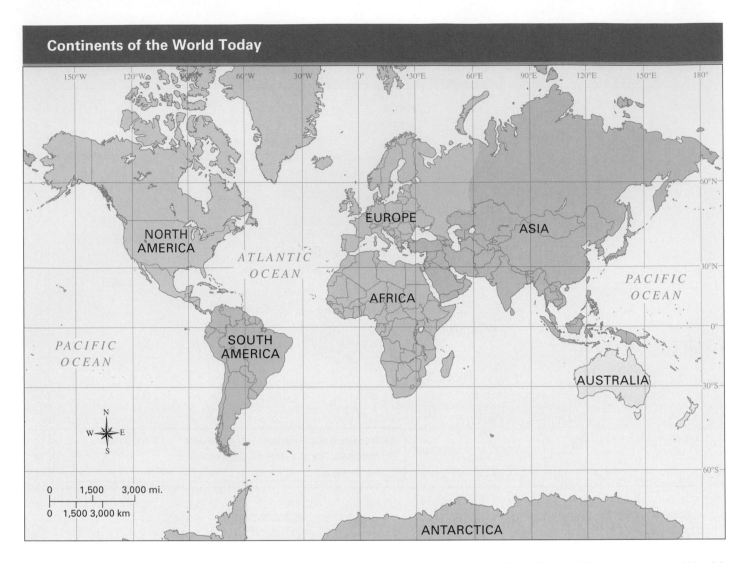

3.6 One Continent, Two Oceans: The United States and the World

Geography has played a significant role in how Americans interact with the rest of the world. More than 3,000 miles of Atlantic Ocean separate the United States from Europe. The distance across the Pacific Ocean to Asia is twice as far. In the nation's early years, it took weeks or even months for news to travel across these seas. As a result, to most Americans, what happened beyond their own country's shores was of little interest. They well understood George Washington's farewell advice to "steer clear of permanent alliances with any portion of the foreign world."

Territorial Expansion President Washington wanted no part of political intrigues abroad. However, he foresaw that the new nation would have to interact with the world beyond its borders in other ways. In order to grow, the United States, at various times, negotiated with other countries for more territory. In 1803, the United States purchased enough land from France to double the country's size. Within several decades, it had acquired Florida from Spain and the Oregon Territory from Great Britain. In 1867, the United States agreed to purchase Alaska from Russia. The Hawaiian Islands became U.S. territory three decades later.

Not all territories became part of the United States peacefully. The original 13 states had their birth in the American Revolution against Great Britain. Winning a war with Mexico in the mid-19th century added Texas and the American Southwest to the United States. With the addition of this land, the United States spanned the continent of North America, from the Atlantic Ocean to the Pacific.

Foreign Trade Despite the country's isolated location between these two oceans, Americans have always engaged in international commerce. Even the original colonists traded products across the Atlantic. The first settlers at Jamestown eventually built their economy around shipping tobacco to England for sale. By 1750, the colonies were producing a variety of cash crops for sale overseas. Soon after the American Revolution, Americans began trading with Asia.

As the country industrialized during the 1800s, foreign trade also expanded. Agricultural products still led U.S. exports, but manufactured goods and natural resources, such as iron ore, were shipped abroad for sale too. Americans were also buying a wide array of imported goods, from Chinese tea to English teapots.

During the 1900s, the United States developed trade relationships with countries around the world. By the second half of the 20th century, **globalization**—the process by which cultures, economies, and politics of nations around the world become integrated—had taken hold. Today, the United States is a leader of the global economy and maintains trade relationships with most other countries of the world.

Summary

North America's physical geography has played various roles in the course of U.S. history. The land's size, landforms, natural resources, and location have all influenced the nation's historical, cultural, and economic development.

Physical features Almost every type of landform and body of water exists in the United States. Some have stood as barriers to movement. Others have proved to be suitable locations for settlement, offering a variety of economic opportunities.

Natural resources The lands of the United States offer an abundance of natural resources, which have helped the country establish and sustain itself. Resources such as fertile soil, forests, minerals, and fossil fuels have shaped the economies and cultures of the United States.

Regions Different parts of the United States have developed their own regional identities. At times, regional differences have threatened national unity, but they have also enriched American life and culture.

Population Over more than two centuries, the U.S. population has grown from fewer than 4 million to nearly 300 million. Urbanization has rapidly turned the nation into a country of cities.

World leader The Atlantic and Pacific oceans could have isolated the United States from events elsewhere in the world. However, interactions with other nations, through territorial expansion, immigration, and globalization, have helped make the United States a world leader.

Chapter 4

The Colonial Roots of America's Founding Ideals

How did the colonial period help to shape America's five founding ideals?

4.1 Introduction

The year was 1620. A group of 102 passengers were gathered on the *Mayflower,* a small ship anchored off the coast of Massachusetts. They had traveled from England to join the colony already established in Virginia. However, storms had blown their ship off course, carrying them hundreds of miles north to Cape Cod. Worn out by their journey, they decided to settle in Massachusetts.

About one third of the passengers were English Protestant Separatists who had come seeking religious freedom. These Separatists had broken away from the Church of England. Fearing persecution because they had formed their own church, they had fled to Holland. Later they received permission to settle in Virginia.

Other *Mayflower* passengers were simply seeking the opportunity to own land in America. According to Separatist leader William Bradford, some of these "strangers" became rebellious as the ship neared Cape Cod. They said no one "had the power to command them" as they were no longer bound by Virginia laws.

Fearing that a revolt could destroy the colony before it began, the Separatist leaders drew up an agreement known as the **Mayflower Compact**. The Separatists and the other passengers agreed to live in a "Civil Body Politic." They further agreed to obey "just and equal Laws" enacted by representatives of their choosing "for the general good of the Colony." This was the first written framework for self-government in what is now the United States.

The *Mayflower* passengers established Plymouth Colony, the second English foothold in North America, after Jamestown. Bradford, who became Plymouth's governor, described the Separatists as pilgrims, or people on a religious journey, which is how they are known today. Over the next century and a half, thousands of people would follow them across the Atlantic. For many, though not for all, this settlement would offer liberty, opportunity, and the chance for a new life.

In this painting, colonists step ashore at Plymouth after disembarking from the *Mayflower.* They brought few possessions with them and would have to find or create almost everything they needed to survive. Their settlement would become part of the Massachusetts Bay Colony.

◀ Signing of the Mayflower Compact, 1620

4.2 Limited Liberty, Opportunity, and Equality

The planting of colonies on the Atlantic shore triggered great changes. It brought together people from three continents—North America, Europe, and Africa—in ways that none of them were prepared for. For many, it opened up a bright new age of liberty, equality, and opportunity. For others, it brought a dark period of suffering and enslavement.

The Lure of the American Colonies: Land and Liberty The 13 colonies that eventually became the United States were founded in different ways and for different reasons. Virginia was founded by a private trading company. Some colonies, such as Pennsylvania, were founded by individual **proprietors,** or owners, who received large land grants from the king. New York was originally founded by the Dutch and later captured by the British. The New England colonies were started by English Protestants called Puritans because they wanted to purify the Church of England. They wanted to create "a city upon a hill," a more perfect society based on their religious beliefs. Georgia began as a home for the poor and for criminals found guilty of not paying their debts.

Like the Jamestown settlement, almost all of the colonies faced hardships in the beginning. By 1700, however, most were thriving, although not always in ways that their founders had hoped. Most proprietors had expected to transplant the society they knew in England. In English society, a small upper class held most of the wealth and power, while the lower classes did most of the work but had few of the rights and received few of the rewards. Most colonists, however, wanted more opportunity. John Smith, a leader of the Jamestown settlement, observed that "no man will go from [England] to have less freedom" in America.

The key to a better life was the abundance of land in the colonies. Land ownership increased economic opportunity and enabled colonists to escape a life of rigid inequality. Historian Eric Foner notes, "Land, English settlers believed, was the basis of liberty. Owning land gave men control over their own labor and, in most colonies, the right to vote." The colonists' access to land, however, also meant a loss of liberty for American Indians and enslaved Africans.

William Penn, the founder of Pennsylvania, was one of the few colonial leaders who treated American Indians fairly. This painting shows him signing a treaty with a tribe. Penn's conduct ensured good relations with Indians in the colony.

American Indians Suffer from Colonization The land that drew colonists to America was, of course, already occupied. At first, relations between native peoples and colonists were mutually beneficial. American Indians taught colonists to cultivate native crops like corn, tomatoes, potatoes, and tobacco. They introduced colonists to useful inventions like canoes and snowshoes. In return, American Indians acquired goods from the colonists, such as iron tools, metal pots, guns, and woven cloth. But the Europeans also unwittingly brought diseases that wiped out entire tribes and left others severely weakened.

In addition, settlers eventually stripped eastern tribes of most of their land through purchase, wars, and unfair treaties. A treaty is a formal agreement between two or more peoples or nations. The loss of land deprived Indians of control over resources they needed to maintain their way of life. Also, settlers rarely treated them as equals. Only a few colonial leaders, notably William Penn, founder of Pennsylvania, treated them fairly and paid them for their land.

Freedom for Some, Slavery for Others Land was the main source of wealth in the American colonies. But without labor to work it, land had little value. Many colonists bought small plots of land of their own rather than working for others. Therefore, large landowners faced a severe labor shortage.

At first, some landowners met their labor needs through contracts with **indentured servants**. These were poor English settlers who voluntarily gave up their freedom for three to seven years in exchange for passage to America. At the end of their contract, they were released and given a payment known as "freedom dues." However, employers complained that these servants were disrespectful and likely to run away—behavior they blamed on a "fondness for freedom."

In 1619, a Dutch ship captain sold 20 captive Africans to colonists in Virginia. For the next several decades, small numbers of Africans were brought to the colonies. At first, they worked side by side with white indentured servants. A few were even treated as indentured servants, working to earn their freedom. The vast majority, however, were enslaved. Gradually landowners came to depend more and more on slaves to meet their labor needs. Eventually every colony legalized slavery, but most slaves toiled on **plantations** in the southern colonies. These were huge farms that required a large labor force to grow cash crops—crops sold for profit.

Although slavery in the colonies began for economic reasons, it became firmly rooted in **racism**. Skin color became the defining trait of a slave. As one colonial government declared, "All Negro, mulatto [of mixed black and white ancestry], and Indian slaves within this dominion . . . shall be held to be real estate." Laws established slavery as a lifetime condition, unless an owner granted freedom, and also defined children born of enslaved women as slaves.

Phillis Wheatley, a former slave who became one of the colonies' best-known poets, wrote of the yearning for freedom: "In every human Breast, God has implanted a Principle, which we call Love of Freedom; it is impatient of Oppression, and pants for Deliverance." Although some African Americans escaped the bonds of slavery, freedom did not bring equality. Like American Indians, blacks were viewed as inferior to whites.

This Dutch ship carried slaves to colonists in Virginia. Though landowners initially bought small numbers of slaves, soon colonists depended on slaves to help plantations profit.

In the first half of the 1700s, the number of slaves brought to the English colonies rose from 5,000 to 45,000 a year. As these graphs indicate, the percentage of Africans in the colonial population greatly increased during this period.

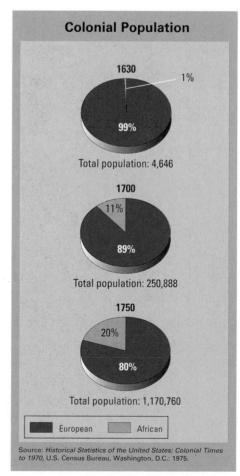

Colonial Population

1630
1%
99%
Total population: 4,646

1700
11%
89%
Total population: 250,888

1750
20%
80%
Total population: 1,170,760

■ European ■ African

Source: *Historical Statistics of the United States: Colonial Times to 1970*, U.S. Census Bureau, Washington, D.C.: 1975.

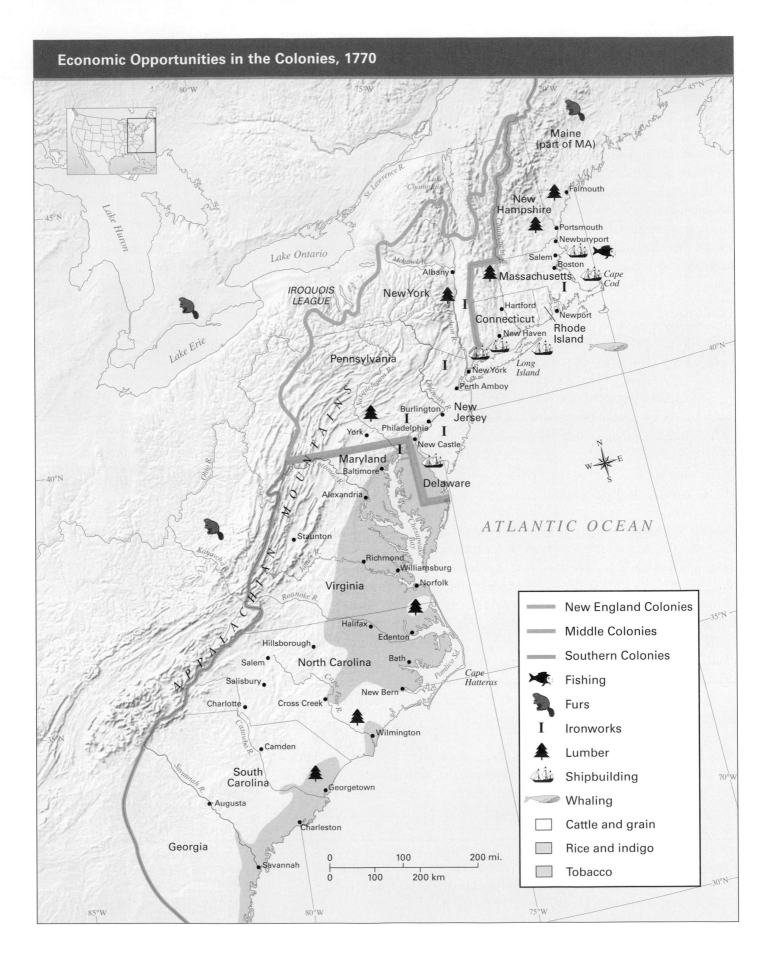

Maine
(part of MA)

Falmouth

New
Hampshire

Portsmouth

Newburyport

Salem

Boston

Cape
Cod

Albany

Massachusetts

New York

Hartford

Newport

Connecticut

Rhode
Island

New Haven

IROQUOIS
LEAGUE

St. Lawrence R.

Lake
Champlain

Lake Ontario

Mohawk R.

Hudson R.

Connecticut R.

New York

Long
Island

Lake Huron

Lake Erie

Pennsylvania

Susquehanna R.

Perth Amboy

Delaware R.

Burlington

New
Jersey

York

Philadelphia

New Castle

Maryland

Baltimore

Delaware

Alexandria

Ohio R.

Potomac R.

Kanawha R.

Staunton

James R.

Richmond

Williamsburg

Virginia

Norfolk

Chesapeake Bay

ATLANTIC OCEAN

Roanoke R.

Halifax

Edenton

Hillsborough

Bath

Salem

North Carolina

Pamlico Sd.

Cape
Hatteras

Salisbury

New Bern

Charlotte

Cross Creek

Cape Fear R.

Catawba R.

Wilmington

Camden

Savannah R.

South
Carolina

Georgetown

Augusta

Charleston

Georgia

Savannah

APPALACHIAN MOUNTAINS

80°W
75°W
70°W
45°N
45°N
40°N
40°N
35°N
35°N
85°W
80°W
75°W
70°W
30°N

N
W E
S

0   100   200 mi.
0   100   200 km

Legend	
New England Colonies	
Middle Colonies	
Southern Colonies	
Fishing	
Furs	
Ironworks	
Lumber	
Shipbuilding	
Whaling	
Cattle and grain	
Rice and indigo	
Tobacco	

The New England Colonies

The fertile valleys, the forests, and the sea supplied resources for New England's mixed economy of farming, lumbering, fishing, shipbuilding, and trade.

Massachusetts	New Hampshire	Connecticut	Rhode Island
Founded in 1620 by English Puritans seeking religious liberty (included Plymouth)	Settled in 1623 by English fishermen and farmers	Founded in 1636 by Puritan colonists from Massachusetts	Founded in 1636 by Roger Williams as a haven for all faiths
Contribution to American ideals	*Contribution to American ideals*	*Contribution to American ideals*	*Contribution to American ideals*
Mayflower Compact (1620): First written framework for self-government in North America	**Town meetings:** Served as training grounds for democratic self-government	**Fundamental Orders of Connecticut (1638):** First written constitution in the colonies	**Charter of Rhode Island and Providence Plantations (1663):** Gave religious freedom to people of all faiths

The Middle Colonies

The rich soil of the Middle Colonies provided the foundation for an economy based on farming and livestock raising. Trade was important to such port cities as Philadelphia and New York.

New Jersey	New York	Delaware	Pennsylvania
First settled by Dutch colonists around 1630	Founded in 1625 by Dutch colonists as New Amsterdam	Founded in 1638 by Swedish colonists as New Sweden	Founded in 1682 by William Penn as a haven for English Quakers
Contribution to American ideals	*Contribution to American ideals*	*Contribution to American ideals*	*Contribution to American ideals*
Religious diversity: Showed that a colony could thrive with many religious sects	**Zenger trial (1735):** Established the right of freedom of the press in the colonies	**Ethnic diversity:** Showed that peoples from many ethnic groups could live together as equals	**Resolutions of the Germantown Mennonites (1688):** First public protest against slavery in the colonies

The Southern Colonies

The warm, wet climate of the Southern Colonies made this region ideal for growing cash crops such as tobacco, rice, and indigo.

Virginia	Maryland	North and South Carolina	Georgia
Founded in 1607 by English colonists seeking economic opportunity	Founded in 1634 by English colonists as a haven for Catholics	Founded in 1663 by eight English proprietors; became two separate colonies in 1729	Founded in 1732 by James Edward Oglethorpe as a haven for debtors and the poor
Contribution to American ideals	*Contribution to American ideals*	*Contribution to American ideals*	*Contribution to American ideals*
Ordinance for Virginia (1619): Created the House of Burgesses, the first colonial legislative body	**Act of Religious Toleration (1649):** First colonial act allowing religious freedom for Christians	**Revolt of 1719:** An uprising against the rule of proprietors, leading to self-government in South Carolina	**Georgia Charter (1732):** Created opportunity for English debtors and prisoners to start new lives in Georgia

The Magna Carta, signed by King John in 1215, limited the power of the English king. It guaranteed the rule of law and ensured that people could not be taxed without their consent. It helped establish the principle of basic rights for the English people.

4.3 Colonial Rights and the Growth of Self-Government

In 1744, a doctor touring the colonies wrote of dining at a tavern with

> a very mixed company of different nations and religions. There were Scots, English, Dutch, Germans, and Irish; there were Roman Catholics, Churchmen, Presbyterians, Quakers, Newlightmen, Methodists, Seven Day men, Moravians, Anabaptists, and one Jew.
> —*Hamilton's Itinerarium: Being a Narrative of a Journey from May to September,* 1744

For all the differences observed by the doctor, these people shared a deep attachment to their rights and freedoms.

The "Rights of Englishmen" For the majority of colonists, the idea that people were entitled to certain rights and freedoms was rooted in English history. They traced that idea back to the signing of the Magna Carta, or Great Charter, in 1215. This agreement between King John and his rebellious barons listed rights granted by the king to "all the freemen of our kingdom." Some of these rights established a system of justice based on **due process of law**. Under such a system, a government cannot deprive a person of life, liberty, or property except according to rules established by law.

Furthermore, the king agreed to make no special demands for money without the consent of his barons. This provision later led to the establishment of a **legislature,** a group of people chosen to make laws. This English lawmaking body was called **Parliament**. The Magna Carta also laid the foundation for the principle that people cannot be taxed except by their representatives in a legislature. Most importantly, the agreement made it clear that the monarch was not above the law. In contrast, rulers elsewhere typically had unlimited power over their people.

Over time, the "rights of Englishmen" were expanded, but not without conflict. One such conflict was a bitter struggle between King James II and Parliament for control of the English government. In 1688, the king was forced to flee England after a bloodless change of power called the Glorious Revolution. The throne was offered to a Dutch prince, William of Orange, husband of Princess Mary of England. Parliament then enacted the English Bill of Rights, which further limited the power of the monarch. Passed in 1689, this act confirmed that the power to tax rested only with Parliament. The act set forth individual rights, including the right to have a trial by jury and to petition the government for redress of wrongs. It also protected English citizens from "cruel and unusual punishments."

The Right to Self-Government English colonists brought these ideas about good government with them to America. Separated from England by 3,000 miles of ocean, they needed to make laws suited to life in the colonies. At New England town meetings, for example, townspeople got together to discuss local issues and solve problems by themselves. Such meetings helped lay the early foundations for self-government in the colonies.

Over time, each colony elected a legislature. The first was Virginia's **House of Burgesses,** formed in 1619. The colonial legislatures were hardly models of democracy, for only white, male landowners could elect representatives. In many colonies, a person had to own a certain amount of property in order to vote. Nevertheless, the legislatures reflected a belief in self-government. These assemblies also affirmed the principle that the colonists could not be taxed except by their elected representatives in the legislatures.

For the colonists, self-government was local, with each colony operating independently of the others. In fact, the colonies were reluctant to work together even to face a common threat. In 1754, after war broke out in the Ohio Valley over rival French and British claims to land, Benjamin Franklin drafted the **Albany Plan of Union.** It proposed a **confederation,** or alliance, of the colonies for their own defense. The idea was as old as ancient Greece, and Franklin could also point to an alliance of six American Indian tribes known as the Iroquois League. Tribal representatives met as a Grand Council to make laws, settle disputes, and plan military strategy. However, Franklin's plan for a colonial Grand Council with the powers to tax and raise an army was quickly rejected. Parliament saw a colonial confederation as a potential threat to its authority, and the colonies were unwilling to pursue the matter.

Seeking Freedom of Religion Although colonists shared a belief in their right to self-government, they were divided by religion. In the early 1600s, the governments of most countries saw religious diversity as a danger. The Puritans were not the only people who came to America to escape harassment in England for their unorthodox beliefs. Religious persecution also led to the founding of Maryland as a haven for Catholics and Pennsylvania as a refuge for Quakers. Some colonies, such as New Jersey and Pennsylvania, had more religious diversity than others.

Experience with religious persecution did not, however, lead to tolerance. Although the Puritans sought religious freedom for themselves, they refused to grant it to those who did not share their beliefs. In 1635, Puritan leaders in Massachusetts banished Roger Williams, a preacher, for holding "newe and dangerous opinions." Williams went on to found the colony of Rhode Island, where he welcomed colonists of all faiths. He firmly believed that freedom of religion, which he called "liberty of conscience," was compatible with law and order. To make his point, Williams used the example of a society aboard a ship at sea:

> There goes many a ship to sea, with . . . Papists [Catholics] and Protestants, Jews and Turks [Muslims] . . . I affirm, that all the liberty of conscience, that ever I pleaded for, turns on these two hinges—that none of the Papists, Protestants, Jews, or Turks be forced to come to the ship's prayers or worship, nor compelled [kept] from their own particular prayers or worship, if they practice any. I further add that I never denied, that notwithstanding this liberty, the commander of this ship ought to command the ship's course, yea, and also command that justice, peace, and sobriety be kept and practiced, both among the seamen and all the passengers.
>
> —Roger Williams, Letter to the Town of Providence, 1655

This drawing by Benjamin Franklin is considered the first political cartoon in American history. In it, Franklin compares the colonies' lack of unity to a snake cut into pieces. He drew the cartoon to promote the Albany Plan of Union, but the plan failed to win support.

Like Roger Williams, Anne Hutchinson was banished from Massachusetts for her religious views. Her belief that people did not need the Puritan church to worship God angered church leaders. Seeking religious freedom, she moved to Rhode Island and later to New York.

Elsewhere, religious prejudice was slow to fade. When Quakers came to Virginia, the House of Burgesses tried to drive them out by making it illegal to be "loving to Quakers." In 1649, the proprietor of Maryland tried to end quarreling between Catholics and Protestants by enacting the **Act of Religious Toleration**. This law declared that no Christian could be in any way "troubled" because of practicing his or her religion. However, it did not apply to non-Christians. Indeed, Jews suffered from prejudice in most colonies and generally did not have the right to vote or hold office. But they were usually allowed to worship and work in peace.

The Right to Free Expression: The Zenger Trial Governments on both sides of the Atlantic also feared freedom of expression. Even though colonies had their own legislatures, they were also subject to rule by governors appointed by the king. Following English practice for royal officials, these governors did not support freedom of expression. In the colonies, newspaper publishers who criticized governors risked being jailed. In their defense, publishers argued that "there can be . . . no such thing as public liberty, without freedom of speech."

In 1734, John Peter Zenger, a New York printer, was arrested for publishing "seditious libels"—rebellious statements that are false or damaging— about the governor of New York. At the trial, the judge instructed the jury to consider only whether Zenger had published the damaging remarks without regard to their truthfulness. Zenger's attorney, Andrew Hamilton, asked the jury to consider whether the remarks were true, arguing that a free people should "have a right publicly to remonstrate against the abuses of power in the strongest terms." The jury found Zenger not guilty, and he was freed. The verdict in the 1735 **Zenger trial** helped promote the idea that the press should have the freedom to print the truth, and that this freedom is a right that should be protected.

This etching shows the trial of John Peter Zenger, in New York. Zenger, the printer of the *New York Weekly Journal,* was accused of libel. His eloquent lawyer, Andrew Hamilton, got him acquitted and, in the process, established a precedent for freedom of the press.

The Right to Think Freely: The Great Awakening The Zenger trial took place during a period of religious revival known as the Great Awakening. Beginning in the 1730s, traveling preachers toured the colonies, attracting huge crowds to their emotional gatherings. Critics of this revival declared that the preachers were encouraging disrespect for "the established church and her ministers." They were right. As historian Curtis Nettels observed in 1963,

> The Great Awakening popularized the idea that the truth was to be found by each person in the Bible—not in man-made laws, sermons, or creeds. Authorities who violated the divine law did not merit respect . . . here were the seeds of revolution.

Although the Great Awakening was concerned mainly with spiritual matters, it had a broader impact, as Nettels suggests. It encouraged people to question authority and think for themselves. One revival preacher proclaimed, "The common people claim as good a right to judge and act for themselves in matters of religion as civil rulers or the learned clergy." As the colonists became more comfortable thinking freely about religious matters, they would also begin to think and speak more freely about political matters.

Many colonists were swept up by religious fervor during the Great Awakening. Preachers like George Whitefield, shown here, gave emotional sermons and encouraged people to seek God on their own terms. This movement also led people to think for themselves and helped undermine political authority.

Summary

Between 1607 and 1733, English settlers established 13 colonies in North America. The development of colonial economies and governments showed that the ideals on which the United States would be founded had begun to take root. However, those ideals were still far from being realized.

Land and liberty Many settlers were attracted to the colonies by the opportunity to acquire land. They saw land ownership as the basis of liberty. Those who could acquire enough land could enjoy the rewards of their labor and gained the right to vote.

American Indians Opportunity for colonists came at a high cost for Indians. They lost their land and suffered from diseases brought from Europe by the colonists.

Slavery The first African slaves were brought to Virginia in 1619. Over time, slavery spread to every colony. However, the majority of slaves worked on southern plantations.

The Rights of Englishmen English colonists were deeply attached to their rights as Englishmen. These rights were rooted in the Magna Carta and the English Bill of Rights.

Self-government Beginning with the Virginia House of Burgesses, each colony established its own government with an elected legislature. Rejection of the Albany Plan of Union showed that each colony cherished running its own affairs.

Freedom of religion Many religious groups, such as Puritans, Quakers, Catholics, and Jews, came in search of religious freedom. The Maryland Act of Religious Toleration recognized the need to accept religious differences.

Freedom of expression and thought The Zenger trial was a victory for freedom of the press in the colonies. The Great Awakening encouraged people to question authority and think for themselves.

Chapter 5

Americans Revolt

Were the American colonists justified in rebelling against British rule?

5.1 Introduction

In 1770, the colonists of New York City erected a large statue of King George III on horseback. The 4,000-pound statue stood in Bowling Green, a public park near the southern tip of Manhattan. It was made of lead and was gilded to shine like pure gold. Over the next few years, the statue dominated the green, symbolizing loyalty to the king.

On July 9, 1776, the newly written **Declaration of Independence** was read aloud at a public gathering in New York City. The reading of the Declaration spelled doom for the King George statue. In a burst of patriotism, angry New Yorkers swarmed Bowling Green. They flung ropes around the statue and pulled it down. They cut off the king's head and set it aside, planning to impale it on a spike later. Then they chopped the rest of the statue into pieces. In the midst of all the chaos, someone stole the head; to this day, it has never been found. Many of the remaining lumps of lead were melted down to make bullets to fire at British soldiers.

What caused the conversion of these colonists from loyal British subjects to unruly vandals? Actually, their change in attitude was gradual and cumulative. Trouble had been brewing in the colonies for years.

By 1776, most colonists belonged to one of three groups, based on their views of British rule. One group was the Loyalists, who staunchly supported the British government. A second group was the Patriots, who opposed British rule and believed the colonists should separate from Britain immediately and by any means necessary. These were the people who tore down the statue of the king. The third group was the Moderates. The Moderates were unhappy with aspects of British rule, but they were cautious about the possible effects of severing ties with Britain. They hoped that the problems could be resolved peacefully. A peaceful solution was a tall order, though, given the growing antagonism between Britain and the colonies.

George III was king of Great Britain from 1760 to 1820. He was only 22 when he came to the throne and lacked many of the qualities of a good leader. He was said to be immature, stubborn, and unsure of himself. Nevertheless, he was determined to be a strong ruler.

◀ New Yorkers pull down the statue of King George III, 1776

5.2 The Road to Revolution

The toppling of the King George statue came on the eve of the American Revolution. But there had been discontent in the colonies for more than two decades. Some problems dated back to a war that took place in North America from 1754 to 1763. That war was part of a worldwide struggle between France and Britain for territory and power. Because many American Indians fought on the side of France, colonists called it the French and Indian War. Britain won the war, but that victory set it on a collision course with its 13 American colonies.

Britain Imposes New Regulations and Taxes Britain now had to control a much larger empire in North America and wanted to prevent further conflict with the tribes who had been France's allies. Therefore, Parliament passed the Proclamation of 1763, which declared that colonists could not settle west of the Appalachian Mountains. However, many colonists continued to move west.

To help keep peace on the western frontier, Britain built a long chain of forts and sent more troops. It thought the colonies should help pay for this protection, but the colonists believed they could defend themselves. They also mistrusted having a large British army in their midst during peacetime.

Nevertheless, Parliament decided to raise revenue from the colonies to pay for the troops. At the time, citizens in Britain paid heavier taxes than they did in the colonies, and Parliament thought the colonists should pay their share. In 1764, it passed the Sugar Act, which placed customs duties on sugar and other non-British imports. In the past, such sales taxes were designed to regulate trade and encourage colonists to buy British goods. Also, these taxes were not enforced. The Sugar Act was the first tax by Parliament that was enforced by Britain. Colonial protests were limited, though, because the law mainly affected merchants in New England and the Middle Colonies.

In 1765, however, Parliament caused an uproar throughout the colonies by taking a new step to raise revenue. It passed the **Stamp Act,** which required colonists to buy a stamp for every piece of paper they used. Newspapers and documents had to be printed on stamped paper. Even playing cards had to carry a stamp. Stamp taxes were already common in Britain, but this was the first stamp tax that Parliament levied on the colonists. Furthermore, unlike the Sugar Act, the Stamp Act affected a wide range of people throughout the colonies.

The colonists argued that as British citizens they could be directly taxed only by their elected representatives. They were represented in the colonial legislatures but not in Parliament. They recognized that Parliament could regulate trade, but they saw its direct taxes as **tyranny,** or unjust use of government power. Patrick Henry, a Virginia lawyer and legislator, railed about "dying liberty." "No taxation without representation!" became the rallying cry for colonial protests.

After months of colonial unrest, Parliament repealed the Stamp Act in 1766. At the same time, however, it passed the Declaratory Act reaffirming its right to govern the colonies. The act stated that the colonies "have been, are, and of right ought to be, subordinate unto, and dependent upon the imperial crown and Parliament of Great Britain." Parliament declared that it could make laws binding the colonies "in all cases whatsoever." Over the next several years, it imposed new taxes and regulations, causing colonial resentment to rise.

Colonists protested the passage of the Stamp Act in 1765. The law placed a tax on every piece of paper sold in the colonies. To organize protests against the law, colonial leaders formed the Sons of Liberty, a group dedicated to resisting British rule.

The Colonies Increasingly Resist British Authority The colonists were not used to Parliament asserting its authority. For 150 years, Britain had maintained an unofficial policy of salutary neglect, or healthy disregard, letting the colonies pretty much run themselves. While each colony had a royal governor, it also had its own legislature, laws, and taxes. Although the colonists were subject to British laws, they often ignored the inconvenient ones. During this long period, they had come to believe that they had the ability and right to manage their own affairs.

In 1767, Parliament passed the Townshend Acts, a set of customs duties on British glass, lead, paints, paper, and tea. Since the colonists had admitted Britain's right to regulate trade, Parliament thought they had little reason to protest. However, these duties were intended to raise revenue, so the colonists saw them as direct taxes in disguise. Samuel Adams of Boston was one of the key leaders who rallied colonists to defy the British.

One main form of protest was a **boycott**. This was a peaceful protest in which people refused to buy or use British goods. By boycotting British goods, the colonists hoped to influence British merchants to put pressure on Parliament to change its policies.

Relations with the British were very tense in Boston. On March 5, 1770, a group of residents confronted British soldiers on the street. A fight broke out, and the soldiers opened fire, killing five colonists. Samuel Adams called the killings a massacre. Paul Revere, a local silversmith, made an engraving that showed soldiers firing at peaceful, unarmed citizens. Prints were distributed throughout the colonies, and the event became known as the Boston Massacre.

On the same day as the Boston Massacre, Parliament repealed most of the Townshend duties, partly in response to colonial boycotts. Parliament retained the tea tax, though, to reaffirm its authority. The repeal of most of the Townshend duties appeased many colonists, so tensions died down. Adams tried to keep the spirit of protest alive, however, by organizing groups of letter writers—known as **committees of correspondence**—to spread news about British actions to towns throughout Massachusetts. Eventually, committees of correspondence formed in every one of the colonies.

American newspapers protested the Stamp Acts by printing an image of a skull and cross-bones to represent the British tax stamp.

The Boston Massacre of March 5, 1770, began with a street fight and ended with the deaths of five colonists. The incident was sparked by public anger over the Townshend Acts and other British policies.

In 1773, Parliament unintentionally sparked new protests by passing the Tea Act, which gave the British East India Company the sole right to sell tea in the colonies. The act was intended to help the struggling company, but angry colonists saw this complete control of the tea trade as a threat to colonial merchants. Committees of correspondence spread the word to boycott the company's tea. Some colonists took stronger action by destroying tea shipments, most famously in Boston. On the night of December 16, men dressed as Mohawk Indians boarded three British tea ships in Boston Harbor. They broke open the tea chests and threw about 90,000 pounds of tea into the water.

This protest, which became known as the **Boston Tea Party,** brought down the wrath of the British government. In 1774, Parliament passed a series of laws so harsh that the colonists called them the **Intolerable Acts.** These laws closed Boston Harbor, shut down the civilian courts, and placed Massachusetts under firm British control. More troops were sent to Boston.

These measures prompted anger throughout the colonies. George Washington, a Virginian, called the policies "repugnant to every principle of natural justice." Many men and women throughout the colonies began to think of themselves firmly as Patriots working together to oppose British rule.

Why Were the Intolerable Acts So Intolerable?

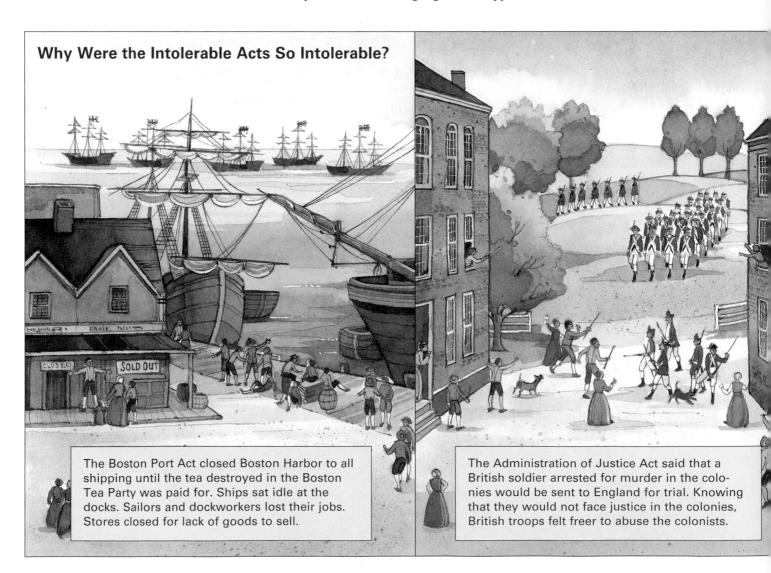

The Boston Port Act closed Boston Harbor to all shipping until the tea destroyed in the Boston Tea Party was paid for. Ships sat idle at the docks. Sailors and dockworkers lost their jobs. Stores closed for lack of goods to sell.

The Administration of Justice Act said that a British soldier arrested for murder in the colonies would be sent to England for trial. Knowing that they would not face justice in the colonies, British troops felt freer to abuse the colonists.

The Fighting Begins After the Intolerable Acts, the colonists organized another boycott of British goods. They also began to set up **militias**. These were groups of men, mostly local farmers and laborers, who volunteered to be soldiers during emergencies. In New England, the militias called themselves Minutemen because they claimed that they could be ready to fight in 60 seconds.

On the evening of April 18, 1775, the Minutemen were called into action. About 700 British soldiers were marching from Boston to seize a stockpile of Patriot munitions in Concord, Massachusetts. In the early morning, they reached the village of Lexington, where 70 to 80 Minutemen were waiting for them. No one is sure who fired first, but a shot rang out. The British then unleashed a volley of bullets, killing 8 colonists and wounding 10.

The British continued six miles to Concord, where they ran into several hundred Minutemen. In a short battle at Concord's North Bridge, the colonists routed the British and sent them fleeing back to Boston. During their retreat, the British were constantly assaulted, losing over 200 men. News of the battles quickly spread throughout the colonies. Within days, militia troops by the thousands were camped around Boston, daring the British to fight again.

The Quartering Act required colonists to feed and house British troops in their homes. No one's property was safe from an invasion by the despised British troops.

The Massachusetts Government Act put the colony under the control of an appointed governor. The elected assembly was closed down, and town meetings were banned. Colonists lost the right to govern themselves.

5.3 Declaring Independence

As the conflict between Britain and the colonies escalated, colonial leaders came together in Philadelphia to discuss options. The first meeting of this Continental Congress, in 1774, had recommended boycotts and other actions to protest the Intolerable Acts. At the Second Continental Congress, held in 1775 after the battles at Lexington and Concord, delegates decided to form a new Continental Army. As a commanding general, they chose George Washington, a leading officer in the Virginia militia. The colonies had not declared independence, however. Most colonists still hoped for a peaceful solution.

Colonists Extend an Olive Branch While the Second Continental Congress was in session, the war around Boston continued. In June 1775, the two sides clashed at the Battle of Bunker Hill. The British won the battle, but they paid a heavy price. More than 1,000 British troops were killed or wounded, while the colonial forces suffered 450 casualties. To some colonists, the high British casualties were proof that the British were not invincible.

Still, Congress hesitated to break with Britain. In July 1775, it sent a petition to King George III affirming loyalty to him, asking for help in addressing their grievances, and expressing hope for a peaceful settlement. This letter came to be called the Olive Branch Petition because olive branches symbolize peace. However, the king refused to receive the petition, having heard the news of Bunker Hill. He proclaimed that the colonists were in "open and avowed rebellion" and that Britain would "bring the traitors to justice."

In his revolutionary pamphlet *Common Sense,* Thomas Paine made the case for independence. "Everything that is right or reasonable pleads for separation," he wrote. "The blood of the slain, the weeping voice of nature cries, 'TIS TIME TO PART.''

Thomas Paine Writes *Common Sense* Not all colonists supported the Olive Branch Petition. To some, it made no sense to ask for peace while colonists in New England were being killed. This was certainly the opinion of Thomas Paine, a recent immigrant from Britain. Early in 1776, Paine published *Common Sense,* a 47-page pamphlet that made a fervent case for independence. It declared that nobody should be ruled by a king. Paine wrote, "Monarchy and succession have laid . . . the world in blood and ashes."

Paine mocked the idea that Britain should rule the American continent. He argued that British rule had only brought harm to the colonies, declaring that colonial trade had suffered under British control and that the colonies had been dragged into Britain's conflicts with other European countries.

Paine even proposed the kind of government Americans should set up: a representative democracy giving roughly equal weight to each colony. His pamphlet was hugely influential. Within three months, 120,000 copies of *Common Sense* had been sold. Paine's persuasive words fired up the colonists and hastened the movement toward independence.

Enlightenment Ideas Inspire Change Paine's pamphlet helped spread ideas that were already popular among Patriot leaders. Those ideas stemmed from the Enlightenment, an intellectual movement of the 1600s and 1700s that greatly influenced the colonies. Enlightenment thinkers stressed the value of science and reason, not only for studying the natural world, but also for improving human society and government.

John Tumbull's depiction of the signing of the Declaration of Independence shows the drafting committee presenting the document. Actually, there was no formal presentation or signing ceremony. Trumbull's purpose was to memorialize the members of Congress. He took great care to craft their faces accurately. This is one of four revolutionary scenes he created for the Capitol.

The writings of English philosopher John Locke particularly influenced Patriot thinking. Locke believed that people enjoyed natural rights to life, liberty, and property. Furthermore, he said that governments and citizens are bound by a social contract. People agree to obey their government if it respects their natural rights. If the government fails to do so, people have the right to overthrow it.

The Colonies Declare Independence As their meeting continued in Philadelphia, many members of the Second Continental Congress had these Enlightenment ideas in mind. On June 7, 1776, Richard Henry Lee of Virginia introduced a resolution proposing independence for the colonies. The Lee Resolution led to formation of a committee to draft a declaration of independence. This committee was made up of Thomas Jefferson of Virginia, Roger Sherman of Connecticut, Benjamin Franklin of Pennsylvania, Robert R. Livingston of New York, and John Adams of Massachusetts.

The task of crafting the words went to Thomas Jefferson. A gifted writer, Jefferson was also a strong believer in natural rights. The Declaration of Independence reflects this thinking when it lists "life, liberty, and the pursuit of happiness" as "unalienable rights" that governments were created to protect.

The Declaration of Independence also states that governments should derive their powers from the consent of the governed, that is, from the people. It asserts that people have the right to alter or abolish a government when it becomes "destructive" of their rights. To illustrate how destructive Britain's rule had been, the Declaration includes a long list of abuses by the king and his government over the years. It then concludes,

> These United Colonies are and of Right ought to be Free and Independent States; that they are Absolved from all Allegiance to the British Crown, and that all political connection between them and the State of Great Britain, is and ought to be totally dissolved . . . And for the support of this Declaration, with a firm reliance on the protection of divine Providence, we mutually pledge to each other our Lives, our Fortunes and our sacred Honor.

On July 2, Congress voted for independence by passing the Lee Resolution. Then on July 4 it formally approved the Declaration of Independence. The Declaration was later written on parchment for delegates to sign. In effect, they were signing a formal declaration of war against Britain.

George Washington and his troops crossed the icy Delaware River on December 25, 1776. In Trenton, German mercenaries were sleeping off a Christmas feast. Taking them by surprise, Washington and his men captured 918 Germans and killed 30, while suffering only 4 casualties.

5.4 Fighting for Independence

At the war's start, the Patriots' prospects were not promising. Britain had a professional, well-trained army of about 40,000 soldiers. It also employed 30,000 German **mercenaries,** professional soldiers for hire. The Continental Army, on the other hand, was constantly short of soldiers. General Washington seldom had more than 20,000 troops at one time. He had to supplement his regular troops with militia forces. Many of them would fight for a while and then go home to take care of their farms and families.

The Americans Get Off to a Shaky Start In the summer of 1776, it looked as if Britain might force a quick end to the war. Soon after the Declaration of Independence was signed, the British massed their forces for an attack on New York City. Washington's army tried to hold them off, but the outnumbered, inexperienced Americans were no match for the British professionals. Suffering heavy losses, the Continental Army was forced to retreat.

The battle for New York City was the first of many American losses in the weeks that followed. Time and again, the Americans had to pull back as British forces pursued them out of New York, through New Jersey, and across the Delaware River into Pennsylvania.

By December 1776, Congress had fled Philadelphia in despair. Many of Washington's troops had gone home. Of the few thousand who were left, many were weak and ill. But Washington would not give up. Instead, he planned a surprise attack on German mercenaries wintering in Trenton, New Jersey.

Late on December 25, about 4,000 Americans crossed the ice-choked Delaware River to march on Trenton. There they took the 1,400-man force of Germans by surprise. The mercenaries surrendered after only a brief fight. A week later, the Americans defeated a British force at Princeton, New Jersey. Nathanael Greene, one of Washington's most trusted officers, wrote modestly to Thomas Paine, "The two late actions at Trenton and Princeton have put a very different face upon affairs." Indeed, the two victories gave Americans hope that the cause of liberty was not dead.

Military Strategies Evolve As the war continued, military leaders on both sides developed new strategies. After his losses around New York, Washington avoided large battles that could put his army at risk. He fought a defensive war by trying to wear out the British rather than soundly defeat them.

The new British strategy was to cut New England off from the rest of the colonies by taking control of New York's Hudson River valley. To do this, Britain sent General John Burgoyne with about 8,000 men south from Canada to Albany, New York. Burgoyne's troops were supposed to join up there with a second British column of about 2,000 men sent to Albany from the west.

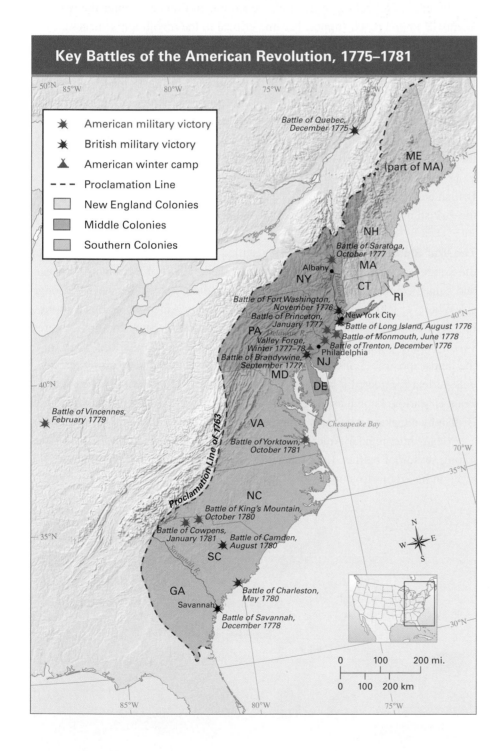

Key Battles of the American Revolution, 1775–1781

* American military victory
* British military victory
▲ American winter camp
- - - Proclamation Line
☐ New England Colonies
☐ Middle Colonies
☐ Southern Colonies

Battle of Quebec, December 1775
ME (part of MA)
NH
Battle of Saratoga, October 1777
Albany
NY
MA
CT
RI
Battle of Fort Washington, November 1776
Battle of Princeton, January 1777
New York City
Battle of Long Island, August 1776
PA
Battle of Monmouth, June 1778
Valley Forge, Winter 1777–78
Battle of Trenton, December 1776
Battle of Brandywine, September 1777
Philadelphia
NJ
MD
DE
Battle of Vincennes, February 1779
VA
Chesapeake Bay
Proclamation Line of 1763
Battle of Yorktown, October 1781
NC
Battle of King's Mountain, October 1780
Battle of Cowpens, January 1781
Battle of Camden, August 1780
SC
GA
Savannah
Battle of Charleston, May 1780
Battle of Savannah, December 1778

0   100   200 mi.
0   100   200 km

Victory at Saratoga Brings Foreign Assistance Burgoyne's march was dogged by problems. The army's route crossed rugged terrain, and the heavily laden troops had to chop down trees, build bridges, and lay out log roads through swamps. Along the way, there were several battles with militias.

When the British reached Saratoga Springs 30 miles north of Albany, militia troops were there to meet them. Meanwhile, British reinforcements from New York had failed to arrive. Finding himself surrounded, Burgoyne surrendered on October 17, 1777. This decisive American victory in the **Battle of Saratoga** was a major turning point in the revolution. Until then, the Americans had fought alone. The defeat of Burgoyne encouraged France to enter the war against Britain. French support became critical to the revolution's success.

Washington's Army Winters at Valley Forge In the winter of 1777–78, the British still occupied Philadelphia. Washington and his army made camp at nearby Valley Forge, Pennsylvania. During that harsh winter, about one fourth of Washington's troops—2,500 men—died from disease and exposure.

Still, Washington held his ragtag army together and continued to train them for battle. When the British abandoned Philadelphia to return to New York City, Washington's forces were ready. In June 1778, they attacked the British at Monmouth, New Jersey. The battle was an American victory, and the British escaped to New York. This was the last major clash in the North.

The War Shifts to the South Having stalled in the North, the British turned to the South. In December 1778, they captured the key port of Savannah, Georgia, and gained control over the Carolinas. But they did not keep their grip for long.

Wherever they went, the British were harried by American troops fighting in a style that later came to be called **guerrilla warfare**. Such fighting features small, mobile groups of soldiers who attack swiftly and then shrink back into the landscape. The South, with its tangle of deep woods and swampy terrain, was perfect for guerrilla warfare. The most successful of these fighters was Francis Marion, known as the Swamp Fox. His band of guerrillas frustrated the British by attacking without warning and quickly fading back into the swamps.

Meanwhile, regular American forces in the South engaged the British. After a long season of battles, Lord Charles Cornwallis, the British commander, brought his troops to Yorktown, Virginia.

Women played an active role in the war. The legend of Molly Pitcher is often used to illustrate the bravery of women during the revolution. Molly Pitcher became known as the heroine of the Battle of Monmouth Court House, which took place in New Jersey in 1778. According to legend, Mary Hays, the wife of an artilleryman, carried water to soldiers during the battle, thus earning the nickname "Molly Pitcher." Legend also holds that when her husband was wounded, she took her husband's place in the gun crew.

In the fall of 1781, American troops converged on Yorktown, joined by French soldiers and naval forces. In total, more than 16,000 troops surrounded the 8,000-man British army. The Battle of Yorktown began on October 6 and lasted about two weeks. On October 19, 1781, Cornwallis surrendered.

The War Ends Yorktown was the last battle of the war, but it took Britain several months to accept defeat. Peace talks began in Paris in 1782, and in September 1783, American and British representatives signed the Treaty of Paris, ending the war. In this treaty, Britain recognized American independence. It also gave up its claims to all lands between the Atlantic coast and the Mississippi River, from Canada south to Florida.

Victory had come at a great cost. At least 6,500 Americans were killed in combat, while another 10,000 died from disease. An additional 8,500 died as British prisoners.

Even so, most Americans savored their victory and looked forward to healing the nation's wounds. That was a big challenge in itself. But Americans faced an even larger and more daunting task: to begin creating a society that embodied the ideals of liberty, equality, and opportunity set forth in the Declaration of Independence. As a first step, they would struggle with the practical issues of forming a government based on the consent of the governed.

In 1817, Congress commissioned John Trumbull to create this depiction of the British surrender at Yorktown. At the center is American general Benjamin Lincoln leading the British troops. On the right are General Washington and his troops. On the left are French, Polish, and Prussian soldiers. Foreign allies were critical to the American victory.

Summary

Beginning in the 1760s, many American colonists grew increasingly unhappy with British rule. Eventually they rebelled and declared independence. During the revolution, American forces wore down and defeated the larger and more experienced British army. In 1783, the United States became an independent country.

The Stamp Act After the French and Indian War, Britain passed the Stamp Act to raise revenue in the colonies. Protests against "taxation without representation" led to its repeal.

Differing loyalties Patriots like Samuel Adams resisted all efforts by the British to exert more control over the colonies. Loyalists, in contrast, supported British rule. Moderates had mixed feelings but hoped the differences with Britain could be settled peacefully.

The Intolerable Acts Following the Boston Tea Party, Britain cracked down on resistance with laws known in the colonies as the Intolerable Acts. Boston became an occupied city.

Lexington and Concord Tensions between colonists and British troops in Massachusetts led to armed conflict in Lexington and Concord. These battles helped spark a wider war.

Declaration of Independence On July 4, 1776, the Continental Congress approved the Declaration of Independence. It asserted that the colonies were "free and independent states."

Saratoga The Continental Army suffered defeats in the early days of the war. But victory at Saratoga in 1777 turned the tide and brought France into the war as an American ally.

Yorktown The British defeat at Yorktown in 1781 ended the long war. Two years later, Britain recognized American independence in the Treaty of Paris.

Chapter 6

Creating the Constitution

What is the proper role of a national government?

6.1 Introduction

In 1782, an army officer wrote a letter to George Washington. In it, he expressed his hope, shared by many of his fellow officers, that the independent American states would be joined into "a kingdom with Washington as the head." The general was appalled. He had spent years in bloody battle working to sever ties with a monarchy. Washington wrote back, "Be assured Sir, no occurrence in the course of the War, has given me more painful sensations than your information of there being such ideas existing in the Army . . . banish these thoughts from your mind."

Like Washington, most Americans did not want to be ruled by a monarch. What they did want, though, was an effective government. In the minds of many, that was not what they had under the **Articles of Confederation,** the nation's first constitution. Troops who wanted Washington to be king were suffering from Congress's inability to meet the army's basic needs. "On the general subject of supplies," wrote a member of Congress, "we need hardly inform you that our Army is extremely clamorous, we cannot pay them—we can hardly feed them."

Over the next few years, many Americans believed that things were going from bad to worse for the new nation. In 1786, a group of rebellious farmers who could not pay their debts shut down several courthouses in Massachusetts. Congress could not help the state government deal with the rebellion. Some Americans saw this as a sign that the nation was sliding into anarchy.

If a more effective government was needed, how should it be structured? That was the question facing delegates called to a special convention in Philadelphia in 1787. This **Constitutional Convention** took place in the room on the facing page, in a building now known as Independence Hall. Presiding over the convention was none other than George Washington, the man who would *not* be king.

This statue in the Virginia State Capitol shows George Washington as an American "Cincinnatus." Cincinnatus was a legendary Roman patriot, a citizen-farmer who turned soldier and leader in a time of crisis, just as Washington did. And like Washington, he returned to farming after the crisis was over.

The Granger Collection, New York

Prior to 1807, the constitution of New Jersey allowed African Americans and unmarried women to vote if they owned property. Married women were denied the vote because by law their property belonged to their husbands. Thousands of women voted in New Jersey between 1776 and 1807—before the law was changed to restrict the vote to white men.

6.2 A Confederation of States

In 1776, the Declaration of Independence had asserted that the colonies were independent states. Even as the war got underway, the legislatures of the 13 states began to write their own constitutions. Within a year, almost all of them had new plans of government reflecting the principles in the Declaration of Independence. In fact, the words of the Declaration were written right into the New York state constitution. However, it was not until almost the end of the war that the states agreed to form a loose confederation.

Comparing State Constitutions The state constitutions were similar in many ways. They all began with a statement of rights. These rights were guided by three founding ideals expressed in the Declaration of Independence: equality, freedom, and democracy. Each state constitution separated the powers of government into executive, legislative, and judicial branches.

However, the state constitutions were far from being completely democratic. They did not establish governments by consent of all of the governed. They typically limited voting rights to white men who paid taxes or owned a certain amount of property. Only New Jersey gave voting rights to women and African Americans who owned property. None of the original 13 states' constitutions outlawed slavery, and all states south of Pennsylvania denied slaves equal rights as human beings.

Decisions in Forming a National Government While the states were writing their constitutions, the Continental Congress was trying to decide how the nation as a whole should be governed. When Congress first met in 1774 to resolve disputes with Britain, it had no authority over the colonial legislatures. Even when directing the war effort, it had no authority over the states, often begging them for soldiers and supplies. Therefore, many members of Congress wanted to form a national government, one that had powers to govern the states. However, they knew this would be a tricky undertaking. After being controlled by Britain for so long, Americans were not inclined to hand over power to another central government—even one they elected.

When Congress drafted the nation's first constitution in 1777, it knew that many Americans feared a powerful national government. For that reason, the proposed Articles of Confederation created a framework for a loose confederation of states. Within this alliance, each state would retain "sovereignty, freedom, and independence." Any power not specifically given to Congress was reserved for the states. This meant that each state could often develop its own policies.

On paper at least, the Articles did give Congress several key powers. Only Congress could declare war, negotiate with foreign countries, and establish a postal system. It could also settle disputes between states. But it had no power to impose taxes, which explains why the Continental Army was so starved of funds. In addition, the Articles did not set up an executive branch to carry out the laws or a judicial branch to settle legal questions.

But even with the war still raging, some states were hesitant to approve a plan of government that would give Congress any control over their affairs. It took three and a half years for **ratification** of the Articles by all 13 states.

Two Ordinances Lay the Foundation for Land Policy Despite its limited power, Congress recorded some notable achievements under the Articles of Confederation. Perhaps its most important success was the creation of policies for the settlement of western lands.

In the Treaty of Paris ending the Revolutionary War, Britain gave up control of a region known as the Northwest Territory. No government had yet been established for this large territory that stretched west from the Appalachian Mountains, north of the Ohio River, and east of the Mississippi River. Congress wanted to organize this land and sell it to raise revenue. To do so, it passed the Land Ordinance of 1785. An **ordinance** is a law that sets local regulations.

The Land Ordinance of 1785 set up a system for surveying and dividing land in the new territory. After being surveyed, the land was to be divided into 36-square-mile townships. Each township would be divided into 36 numbered sections of 1 square mile each. Each section would then be divided for sale to settlers and land dealers. Section 16, however, was always set aside for schools.

In 1787, Congress passed the Northwest Ordinance to specify how these western lands would be governed. This ordinance declared that the region would be divided into three to five territories. When a territory had 5,000 free adult men, those men could elect a legislature. When the population reached 60,000 free inhabitants, the legislature could write a constitution and form a government. If Congress approved both, the territory would become a state.

A number of the ordinance's provisions reflected the principle of equality. Each new state would have equal standing with the original states, and its people would enjoy the same freedoms and rights. Furthermore, slavery would be banned in any state formed from the region.

The Northwest Ordinance set up a system that became a general guide for admission of future states. For that reason alone, it is considered the most important law passed during the period of confederation.

Under the Articles of Confederation, Congress set two key land policies for the Northwest Territory. The Land Ordinance of 1785 organized the region into townships. The Northwest Ordinance of 1787 set rules for the formation of new states. Within a half century of its passage, enough people had settled in the Northwest Territory to create five new states.

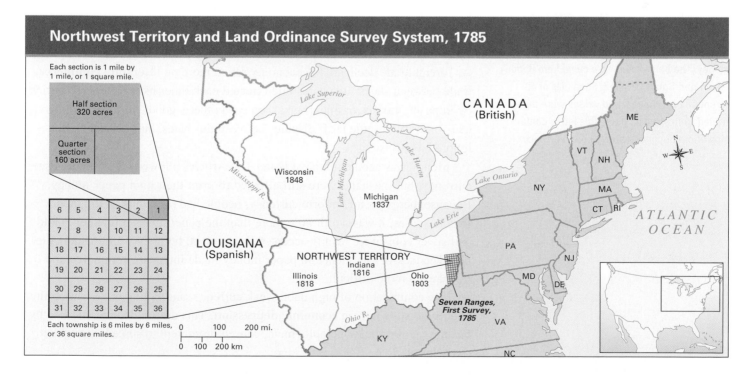

Northwest Territory and Land Ordinance Survey System, 1785

Each section is 1 mile by 1 mile, or 1 square mile.

Half section 320 acres

Quarter section 160 acres

6	5	4	3	2	1
7	8	9	10	11	12
18	17	16	15	14	13
19	20	21	22	23	24
30	29	28	27	26	25
31	32	33	34	35	36

Each township is 6 miles by 6 miles, or 36 square miles.

0   100   200 mi.
0 100 200 km

Lake Superior

CANADA (British)

ME

Mississippi R.

Wisconsin 1848

Lake Michigan

Lake Huron

Michigan 1837

Lake Ontario

VT

NH

NY

MA

CT RI

ATLANTIC OCEAN

Lake Erie

PA

NJ

LOUISIANA (Spanish)

NORTHWEST TERRITORY

Illinois 1818

Indiana 1816

Ohio 1803

MD

DE

Seven Ranges, First Survey, 1785

VA

Ohio R.

KY

NC

6.3 The Confederation in Crisis

Although Congress under the Articles of Confederation had notable successes, many Americans saw problems with the confederation. Most of these problems stemmed from the fact that the Articles gave so much authority to the states and so little to Congress. George Washington declared that the Articles were no more effective at binding the states together than "a rope of sand."

Trouble with Foreign Countries Congress's weaknesses were recognized not only at home but also abroad. The lack of central authority made relations with foreign countries more difficult. For example, one British official said it would be better to negotiate with each state than to do business with Congress. When Congress tried to reach a trade agreement with Britain in 1785, Britain refused because it knew the states wouldn't agree to be bound by the accord.

Many foreign countries also questioned the nation's financial stability. The United States had accumulated a huge war debt, mostly to foreign lenders. But Congress lacked funds to pay its debts. The Articles directed the state legislatures to pay taxes to the national treasury based on the value of each state's land. However, Congress could not force the states to pay.

To make matters worse, overseas trade shrank under the confederation. Britain restricted American trade by closing some of its ports to American vessels. These actions hurt the American economy, which depended heavily on the British market. Meanwhile, the United States had little success boosting trade with other countries.

Another problem was national defense. In the Treaty of Paris, Britain had agreed to withdraw troops from the Northwest Territory. Once it saw how weak Congress was, however, it refused to pull them out. Britain and Spain supplied arms to American Indians and urged them to attack settlers. Having disbanded the Continental Army after the war, Congress had no military force to counteract this threat.

Quarrels Between the States There were troubles between the states, too. As foreign trade declined, the economy relied more on **interstate commerce,** trade between states. But states often treated each other like separate countries by imposing **tariffs,** or import taxes, on each other's goods. In theory, Congress had authority to settle tariff disputes between the states, but the states often ignored its decisions.

Money was another divisive issue. The Articles allowed Congress to issue currency, but the states were still allowed to print their own paper money. Because there was no uniform currency, people had little faith in the money. In some cases, it was worth little more than the paper it was printed on. Gold and silver coins were readily accepted as payment, but they were in short supply. The lack of confidence in paper money made interstate commerce and travel even more difficult.

The combination of high debt, weak currency, and falling trade caused the country to slide into an **economic depression**. This drastic decline, marked by business failures and unemployment, caused discontent to spread throughout the country.

The country had serious money problems under the Articles of Confederation. After the war, each state began printing its own paper money. The bills shown here came from Rhode Island and South Carolina. Soon bills of different colors, shapes, and values were being traded from state to state. This led to confusion and a decline in the value of currency.

Daniel Shays led a rebellion in Massachusetts to protest harsh economic conditions for farmers. Shays, at top right, is shown with his followers as they shut down a Massachusetts courthouse. Because Congress did not have the funds to help Massachusetts, the state had to put down the rebellion by itself. This incident highlighted the weakness of the confederation.

Discontent Fuels Shays' Rebellion in Massachusetts Farmers were among those who suffered most from the economic depression. Falling crop prices and the loss of foreign markets left many farmers with crippling debts they could not repay. Farmers in western Massachusetts were hit especially hard. Some had their property auctioned off by local courts for nonpayment of debts and taxes. Others were sent to debtors' prison when they could not pay their debts.

In the summer of 1786, armed and angry farmers occupied a courthouse to prevent the court from doing business. In the following weeks, these rebels took over other Massachusetts courts, hoping to prevent trials and imprisonment of debtors. This uprising, known as Shays' Rebellion after its main leader, Daniel Shays, quickly mushroomed. In September 1786, Shays led hundreds of farmers to occupy the courthouse in Springfield, Massachusetts. A few months later, he led about 1,200 farmers to try to seize a weapons stockpile in the same city. This time, the Massachusetts militia stopped them, and the rebellion collapsed.

To face the threat of Shays' Rebellion, Massachusetts had needed funds to hire and supply a larger militia. But Congress had been unable to send money. Instead, private donations from wealthy people had helped the state militia put down the revolt. In the aftermath of Shays' Rebellion, rich businesspeople and landowners were particularly worried about Congress's weakness. They feared that anarchy would engulf the nation. Many Americans were not so pessimistic but did agree that the government should be strengthened.

A Call for a Constitutional Convention While Shays' Rebellion was erupting in Massachusetts, delegates were gathering at a convention in Annapolis, Maryland. This formal assembly was called to fix trade problems between the states. But the delegates knew they had more serious problems to address.

Two important political leaders, Alexander Hamilton of New York and James Madison of Virginia, were among the delegates. They drafted a request that all states send representatives to a constitutional convention to be held in Philadelphia in May 1787. The purpose would be to revise the Articles of Confederation to create a stronger, more effective system of government.

6.4 The Constitutional Convention

The Constitutional Convention opened on May 25, 1787. Delegates from every state but Rhode Island gathered in the room where the Declaration of Independence had been signed 11 years before. Congress had instructed them to revise, not replace, the Articles of Confederation. However, many delegates were already convinced that a new constitution was needed. Through months of debate, the delegates would work out this plan of government and then set it forth in a document called the **Constitution of the United States**.

A Distinguished Group of Delegates The 55 delegates were the cream of American political life. Historian James McGregor Burns has described them as the "well-bred, the well-fed, the well-read, and the well-wed." All were white men. Among them were former soldiers, governors, members of Congress, and men who had drafted state constitutions. Their average age was 42.

The delegates represented a wide range of personalities and experience, and many were eloquent speakers. At 81, Benjamin Franklin was the senior member. The wisdom and amicable wit of this writer, inventor, and diplomat enlivened the proceedings. George Washington, hero of the Revolution, lent dignity to the gathering. Alexander Hamilton, his former military aide, brought intellectual brilliance. Other delegates, like Roger Sherman of Connecticut, contributed law and business experience. James Madison of Virginia was perhaps the most profound political thinker and the best prepared of all the delegates.

A few key leaders of the Revolution did not attend. Thomas Jefferson and John Adams were serving as representatives of the United States in Europe. Reading a list of the delegates in Paris, Jefferson described them as "an assembly of demigods." Other leaders, like Samuel Adams, were not there because they opposed efforts to strengthen the national government. Patrick Henry was named as a Virginia delegate but chose to stay home, saying he "smelt a rat." Indeed, many Americans remained fearful of giving a central government too much power.

The Ideas Behind the Constitution No one had a greater role than Madison. He worked tirelessly to develop and promote the new plan. For his role in shaping the new framework, he is called "the Father of the Constitution."

The delegates' political views were strongly influenced by Enlightenment thinkers. English philosopher John Locke's ideas about natural rights and the social contract helped shape the Declaration of Independence. They would also be guiding principles for drafting the Constitution.

The delegates also looked to the ideas of the Baron de Montesquieu, another Enlightenment thinker. He favored a three-part government with **separation of powers** between executive, legislative, and judicial branches. These branches would work together in a system of **checks and balances,** each branch limiting the power of the others. This would prevent tyranny by keeping each branch from seizing excessive power.

The delegates discussed these and other ideas for almost four months. Day after day, through a long, sweltering summer, they would debate, argue, write, revise, and debate some more. As they met, they knew that, once again, they were making history.

Delegates to the Constitutional Convention of 1787 met at the Pennsylvania State House, in Philadelphia, to write the Constitution. Although the weather was brutally hot that summer, the windows of the meeting hall were nailed shut to keep the proceedings a secret. This is the same building in which the Declaration of Independence was adopted in 1776. Today it is called Independence Hall.

Four Key Voices

Roger Sherman

Roger Sherman of Connecticut proposed the compromise that broke the deadlock over representation in Congress. Under his scheme, more populous states would have greater representation in the House, but each state would have two senators regardless of population.

Gouverneur Morris

Gouverneur Morris of Pennsylvania, "the penman of the Constitution," played a key role in crafting the final wording. His own view was that the government should represent the wealthy and be led by a strong president elected for life.

John Rutledge

John Rutledge of South Carolina defended the interests of southern planters by supporting slavery. He was an effective speaker and an advocate for a strong central government. He favored dividing society into classes as a means to determine representation in Congress.

James Madison

James Madison of Virginia is known as the "father" and "chief architect" of the Constitution. An expert on political theory and history, he took a leading role in debates and in planning the framework. He pushed for a strong central government.

State Delegates

Every state but Rhode Island sent representatives to the Constitutional Convention. Of the 55 delegates, 9 left early for personal reasons, and 4 walked out in protest. Of the remaining 42 delegates, 39 signed the Constitution.

Delaware
Richard Bassett
Gunning Bedford Jr.
Jacob Broom
John Dickinson
George Read

Massachusetts
Elbridge Gerry*
Nathaniel Gorham
Rufus King
Caleb Strong*

Maryland
Daniel Carroll
Luther Martin*
James McHenry
John F. Mercer*
Daniel of St. Thomas Jenifer

Connecticut
Oliver Ellsworth*
William Samuel Johnson
Roger Sherman

Virginia
John Blair
James Madison
George Mason*
James McClurg*
Edmund C. Randolph*
George Washington
George Wythe*

Georgia
Abraham Baldwin
William Few
William Houston*
William L. Pierce*

North Carolina
William Blount
William R. Davie*
Alexander Martin*
Richard Dobbs Spaight
Hugh Williamson

New Jersey
David Brearley
Jonathan Dayton
William C. Houston*
William Livingston
William Paterson

South Carolina
Pierce Butler
Charles Cotesworth Pinckney
Charles Pinckney
John Rutledge

Pennsylvania
George Clymer
Thomas FitzSimons
Benjamin Franklin
Jared Ingersoll
Thomas Mifflin
Gouverneur Morris
Robert Morris
James Wilson

New York
Alexander Hamilton
John Lansing Jr.*
Robert Yates*

New Hampshire
Nicholas Gilman
John Langdon

*Delegate did not sign the Constitution.

For months, delegates to the Constitutional Convention debated how the government of the United States should be structured. This 19th century engraving depicts Benjamin Franklin presenting an argument to the convention.

The Convention Begins with a Plan from Virginia The first thing the delegates did was to elect George Washington as presiding officer. Next, they adopted rules of procedure. One was the rule of secrecy. The delegates needed to speak freely and frankly, and they could not do so if the public were watching. So despite the intense summer heat, they shut the windows, drew the drapes, and posted a sentry outside.

The Virginia delegates wanted to establish a strong national government and promptly proposed a plan. The Virginia Plan, written mainly by James Madison, was clearly meant to replace the Articles, not revise them. It called for a national government with three branches, just as Montesquieu had described. The legislative branch would make laws, the executive branch would carry out the laws, and the judicial branch would interpret the laws.

Under the Virginia Plan, the new government would have a **bicameral legislature,** a lawmaking body made up of two houses. In contrast, the Articles of Confederation had established Congress as a unicameral, or one-house, legislature. The Virginia Plan proposed that representation in the two houses of Congress should be based on the population of each state. This would give the more populous states more delegates, and therefore more influence, than states with smaller populations.

New Jersey Introduces a Rival Plan For about two weeks, the delegates discussed the Virginia Plan. Some thought it gave too much power to the national government. Some opposed a bicameral legislature. Moreover, smaller states did not like their representation in Congress being limited by population.

On June 13, William Paterson of New Jersey introduced an alternative to the Virginia Plan. The New Jersey Plan proposed a series of amendments to the Articles of Confederation. It called for a less powerful national government with a unicameral Congress in which all states had equal representation.

Delegates of the smaller states welcomed the New Jersey Plan. But after several days of debate, the convention voted to reject this proposal and return to discussion of the Virginia Plan.

Discontent, Debate, and the Great Compromise For the next month, the delegates debated the Virginia Plan point by point. They continued to argue about the critical issue of representation in the legislature. Debate grew so heated that delegates from some states threatened to leave the convention.

Finally, Roger Sherman of Connecticut came forward with a compromise designed to satisfy all sides. His plan called for a bicameral legislature with a different form of representation in each house. In the Senate, the states would have equal representation. In the House of Representatives, states would have representation based on their populations. Sherman's plan, known as the **Great Compromise,** resolved the thorny issue of representation in Congress.

Slavery and Commerce Issues Divide the States Other issues also divided the delegates. Those from northern and southern states differed strongly on questions of slavery and commerce. A number of northern states wanted to include a provision for abolishing slavery. But most southerners opposed ending a system of labor on which their agricultural economy depended.

Differences over slavery generated strong debate on representation and taxes. Since most slaves lived in the South, southern states wanted slaves to be counted in determining representation in the House of Representatives. Yet they did not want them counted when determining each state's share of taxes to support the national government. In contrast, the northern states wanted slaves to be counted for taxation but not when determining representation.

In the end, the delegates reached another important compromise. For representation in the House, every five slaves would be counted as equal to three whites. The Three-Fifths Compromise settled the dispute, but the contradiction between the ideals of the Declaration of Independence and the practice of slavery would haunt the country in the decades to come.

North and South also argued over commerce. Northerners favored giving Congress broad powers to control trade. Southerners worried that Congress might outlaw the slave trade and place heavy taxes on southern exports of crops such as cotton and tobacco. Again, the delegates reached a compromise. Congress would have the power to regulate foreign and interstate commerce, but it could not tax exports and it could not outlaw the slave trade until 1808.

Creating the Executive Branch Another major issue concerned the formation of the executive branch. Some delegates wanted a single executive to head the government. Others were concerned that giving power to a single leader might lead to monarchy or tyranny. They favored an executive committee made up of at least two members. In the end, though, the delegates voted for a single president.

The next question was how to elect the president. Some delegates thought Congress should do it, while others favored popular elections. They finally decided to set up a special body called the **Electoral College**. This body would be made up of electors from each state who would cast votes to elect the president and vice president. Each state would have as many electors as the number of senators and representatives it sent to Congress.

On September 17, 1787, after months of hard work, the Constitution was signed by 39 of the 42 delegates present. The Constitutional Convention was over, but the Constitution still needed to be ratified by the states. The document began with the ringing words, "We the people of the United States, in order to form a more perfect union . . ." Now each state would decide whether this plan of government was indeed "more perfect" and thus worthy of becoming the law of the land.

Delegates signed the Constitution on September 17, 1787. But support for the Constitution was not unanimous. A few delegates left the convention early in protest, and three of those present refused to sign. Nevertheless, most delegates seemed to believe that they had achieved a historic result.

6.5 Ratifying the Constitution

The proposed Constitution included a provision for ratification. To go into effect, the plan of government would need to be approved by 9 out of the 13 states. Ratification would take place at state conventions, but it was by no means assured. Many Americans were concerned that the Constitution gave too much power to the national government. As a result, supporters of the Constitution would have to work hard to win its ratification.

Federalists and Anti-Federalists The people who supported the Constitution called themselves Federalists. They favored a federal government—a strong central government that shared power with the states. Those who preferred a loose association of states with a weaker central government were called Anti-Federalists. The battle between Federalists and Anti-Federalists would be played out in the press, in state legislatures, and at the state ratifying conventions.

Alexander Hamilton, James Madison, and John Jay led the Federalist campaign. Using the pen name "Publius," they wrote a series of 85 essays designed to win support for the Constitution. These essays, known as *The Federalist Papers,* were published over the course of several months and made a strong case for the new plan of government. Some historians have called their publication one of the most powerful public relations campaigns in history.

In *The Federalist Papers,* Hamilton, Madison, and Jay provided detailed explanations of key parts of the Constitution. On the issue of central power, for example, Madison explained how the system of checks and balances would ensure that no one branch of government would have control over the other two. He also explained why such a system was needed:

> If men were angels, no government would be necessary. If angels were to govern men, neither external nor internal controls on government would be necessary. In framing a government which is to be administered by men over men, the great difficulty lies in this: you must first enable the government to control the governed; and in the next place oblige it to control itself.
> —James Madison, *The Federalist* No. 51, 1788

Because *The Federalist Papers* explain the purpose of the Constitution, people who read these essays today can gain insight into the intentions of the Constitution's original drafters.

The Call for a Bill of Rights By January 1788, Delaware, Pennsylvania, and New Jersey had ratified the Constitution. Georgia and Connecticut soon followed. But a bitter debate in Massachusetts brought to the forefront a major Anti-Federalist concern about the Constitution: the lack of a bill of rights.

Anti-Federalists in Massachusetts complained that the Constitution did not adequately protect individual rights and freedoms against encroachment by the national government. They argued that it should be altered to include such rights as the freedoms of speech, religion, and the press. They also wanted guarantees that every citizen would have such rights as the right to trial by jury and protection against unreasonable seizure of property. The lack of such guarantees became a sticking point in many states as the ratification process wore on.

One of the places the battle between the Federalists and Anti-Federalists played out was in the press. This allegorical engraving, published in a magazine in 1788, shows the figure of cupid holding a copy of the Constitution, in front of a temple with thirteen columns, representing the thirteen states. The engraving associates harmonious government with the Constitution, and therefore represents a Federalist point of view.

After much debate, Massachusetts agreed to ratify if amendments were added after ratification to protect fundamental rights. A number of other states ratified the Constitution with the same understanding. By the summer of 1788, all but two states had ratified. North Carolina joined the new union in 1789 and Rhode Island in 1790.

With James Madison leading the way, the first Congress of the new government framed the proposed amendments. Madison himself believed that individual rights were already protected by the Constitution, making the amendments unnecessary. However, his friend Thomas Jefferson helped change his mind. Jefferson wrote from France that "a bill of rights is what the people are entitled to against every government on earth, general or particular, and what no government should refuse." He argued that the great strength of such a bill of rights was "the legal check which it puts into the hands of the judiciary."

On December 15, 1791, enough states had ratified 10 amendments to make them part of the Constitution. These 10 amendments are known collectively as the Bill of Rights. Over the course of the nation's history, 17 more amendments have been added to the Constitution.

Today the Constitution is the oldest written framework of national government in use anywhere in the world. Forged over the course of a few months in the summer of 1787, the Constitution of the United States has more than stood the test of time.

Summary

After the Revolution, the states first formed a loose confederation. However, many Americans thought this arrangement did not satisfy the need for a strong central authority. Delegates from the various states came together to write a new constitution that would provide the basis for a durable and balanced government.

The Articles of Confederation The nation's first constitution established a governing framework that gave the states more power than the national government. This lack of central authority contributed to various problems, including a poor economy and weak national defense.

The Northwest Ordinance This land policy established rules for the creation of governments in the Northwest Territory and the eventual admission of western states.

The Constitution of the United States Frustrated by weaknesses of the confederation, delegates met in Philadelphia in 1787 for the Constitutional Convention. Instead of revising the Articles, they wrote a new constitution that established a national government with three branches.

The Electoral College After much debate, the delegates decided that a single executive, a president, should lead the executive branch. A body called the Electoral College, made up of electors from each state, would elect the president and vice president.

Ratification After the Constitution was completed in September 1787, it was sent to the states for ratification. During the debate over ratification, supporters agreed to add amendments to guarantee basic freedoms. With this assurance, the Constitution was ratified in 1788 and became law. The first 10 amendments, known as the Bill of Rights, were ratified in 1791.

Chapter 7

An Enduring Plan of Government

Does the Constitution support the ideals in the Declaration of Independence?

7.1 Introduction

On September 17, 2003, the nation's leaders met in the Rotunda of the National Archives building in Washington, D.C. The heads of the three branches of the national government were there. The leaders of the Senate and the House of Representatives represented the legislative branch. The president represented the executive branch. The chief justice represented the judicial branch.

These leaders were attending a ceremony to celebrate the unveiling of some newly restored historical documents. The documents had been carefully preserved with the latest tools and technology. They rested on cushions of handmade paper and were encased in frames of titanium and aluminum. They were further protected by sapphire windows, traveling light beams, and precisely positioned mirrors set up to detect any changes that could harm the documents.

Why were these documents given such importance? They are the "Charters of Freedom" upon which our government was founded: the Declaration of Independence, the Constitution, and the Bill of Rights. In a speech at the unveiling ceremony, President George W. Bush said, "The courage of America's first leaders gave us the Declaration. Their patience and wisdom gave us the Constitution . . . The supreme law of this land is the work of practical minds addressed to practical questions."

When the president spoke of "the supreme law of this land," he was referring to the Constitution. Although this plan of government was written over 200 years ago, its rules and principles still guide our political system. The Constitution has weathered the centuries because it is a flexible, "living document" that can be interpreted and amended to meet changing needs.

An archivist at the ceremony noted why more than a million people a year come to see the Charters of Freedom. It is "not just because they are historical documents," he said, "but because they are a living part of the democracy we live in today."

The Capitol, home of the legislative branch

The White House, center of the executive branch

The Supreme Court, head of the judicial branch

◀ The Declaration of Independence, the Constitution, and the Bill of Rights are all housed in the Charters of Freedom Hall at the National Archives in Washington, D.C.

The Preamble to the Constitution sets certain broad goals for the government. One of these is to "establish justice." The Supreme Court is the highest authority in matters of justice. The nine Supreme Court Justices hear cases in this room.

The government should also "provide for the common defense." Here midshipmen from the U.S. Naval Academy walk in formation.

Another goal for government is to "promote the general welfare." This includes providing funds for public works, such as this bridge in Boston.

7.2 A Strong Yet Balanced Government

In 1789, Benjamin Franklin wrote, "Our new Constitution is now established, and has an appearance that promises permanency; but in this world nothing can be said to be certain except death and taxes." Franklin's words were prophetic, but they also sounded a note of caution. While our constitutional government has survived for more than two centuries, there is no guarantee that it will continue to endure. Its survival depends on our upholding the principles of the Constitution.

The framers of the Constitution worked hard to set up a political system that would last. They wanted a government that was strong enough to govern, but not so strong that it endangered citizens' freedoms. They also wanted ordinary Americans to understand and support the Constitution. For this reason, they organized it very carefully.

The Constitution has three parts. The first part, the **Preamble,** describes the purpose of the document and the government it creates. The second part, the articles, establishes how the government is structured and how the Constitution can be changed through amendments. The third part, the amendments, includes the Bill of Rights and other changes to the Constitution.

The Preamble Establishes the Purposes of the Government A preamble is an introduction explaining the purpose of a document, typically a legal document. The Preamble to the Constitution begins with the phrase, "We the people . . ." These words announce that the Constitution's authority is based on the people themselves. The power to form the government did not come from an existing government, or the states, or a supreme being. "We the people" echoes the idea in the Declaration of Independence that governments should derive "their just powers from the consent of the governed."

The next phrase, "in Order to form a more perfect Union," shows the framers' determination to improve upon the government established under the Articles of Confederation. They wanted the union of states to become stronger so that the states would work together, rather than fight among themselves.

The rest of the Preamble lists goals for the new government. The framers wanted to "establish justice" by creating a government that would establish and carry out fair laws that applied equally to all people. They wanted to "insure domestic Tranquility." In this phrase, "domestic" refers to the internal affairs of the nation. By insuring domestic tranquility, the framers hoped to establish a country of peace and order. They also wanted the government to "provide for the common defense," the protection of the country as a whole against foreign enemies.

The framers wanted the United States to have a society and an economy in which people could thrive and prosper. So they declared that the government should "promote the general Welfare." They also wanted to "secure the Blessings of Liberty to ourselves and our Posterity." By posterity, they meant future generations.

The framers knew that achieving these goals required a strong central government. However, they recognized that the Constitution must also limit that government's powers.

The Articles Define the Powers of Government The Constitution has seven articles. The first three lay out the structures and powers of the three parts of the government: the legislative, executive, and judicial branches.

Dividing the government into three branches sets up a strong central government, yet also distributes power. The system of checks and balances ensures that no branch becomes too powerful. Each branch can limit the power of another. For example, the president can veto a bill, but the bill can still become law if a two-thirds majority of Congress votes to override the veto. In this example, the executive branch checks the power of the legislative branch, which then checks the power of the executive branch.

To give another example, when the Supreme Court rejects a law as unconstitutional, it is checking the power of the legislative and executive branches. Checks and balances also extend to the appointment of key officials. For example, the president's nominations of Supreme Court justices are subject to the Senate's approval.

Through the system of checks and balances, Congress has the power to impeach and convict the president, vice president, and any civilian official of the United States. To **impeach** an official is to charge that person with an offense committed while in office. Only the House of Representatives can vote to impeach—to accuse an official of committing what the Constitution calls "Treason, Bribery, or other High Crimes and Misdemeanors." However, only the Senate can convict. If the Senate votes by a two-thirds majority to convict, the official is removed from office. Two presidents have been impeached, but neither was convicted.

The Constitution does not only divide power among the three branches of the national, or federal, government. As you will see, it also divides power between the federal government and state governments.

Provisions for checks and balances are a key feature of the Constitution. Checks and balances help prevent any one branch of government from wielding too much power.

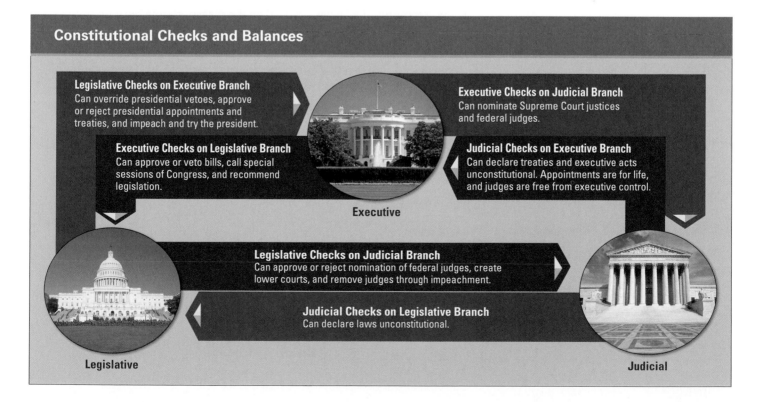

Constitutional Checks and Balances

Legislative Checks on Executive Branch
Can override presidential vetoes, approve or reject presidential appointments and treaties, and impeach and try the president.

Executive Checks on Legislative Branch
Can approve or veto bills, call special sessions of Congress, and recommend legislation.

Executive

Executive Checks on Judicial Branch
Can nominate Supreme Court justices and federal judges.

Judicial Checks on Executive Branch
Can declare treaties and executive acts unconstitutional. Appointments are for life, and judges are free from executive control.

Legislative Checks on Judicial Branch
Can approve or reject nomination of federal judges, create lower courts, and remove judges through impeachment.

Judicial Checks on Legislative Branch
Can declare laws unconstitutional.

Legislative

Judicial

7.3 The Legislative Branch Makes the Laws

The framers wanted to establish a fair way to make laws and to ensure that lawmakers are accountable to the people. Therefore, Article I of the Constitution defines the basic structure, procedures, and powers of Congress.

The Structure of Congress To balance the powers of small and large states, the framers set up Congress as a bicameral, or two chamber, legislature. The two chambers are the Senate and the House of Representatives.

The membership of the Senate is based on equal representation of the states. It is made up of 100 senators, two from each state. Senators serve a six-year term.

Representation in the House is based on state population. There are 435 members. Every 10 years, a census determines how that number is apportioned by state. Each state is then divided into congressional districts. As of the 2010 census, the most populous state, California, had 53 districts. In contrast, some states consist of only one district. The people of each district elect one House representative, who serves a two-year term.

How Congress Does Its Job The main function of Congress is to make laws. Most laws begin as bills, proposals for new laws. Tax bills must begin in the House. Other bills can be initiated in either chamber. If the House and Senate pass a bill, it goes to the president, who has 10 days to sign or veto it. Congress can override a veto with a two-thirds majority vote in each house.

Congressional Powers Article I grants certain powers to Congress. For example, Congress can coin and regulate money, collect taxes, maintain an army and navy, declare war, pay government debts, and regulate foreign trade. In addition, it may "make all laws which shall be necessary and proper" to carry out such powers. This clause has been called the **elastic clause** because it gives Congress flexibility to fulfill its duties. In 1791, for example, Congress created a national bank to help collect taxes, pay debts, and regulate trade. Some people, however, think that Congress sometimes "stretches" its powers too far.

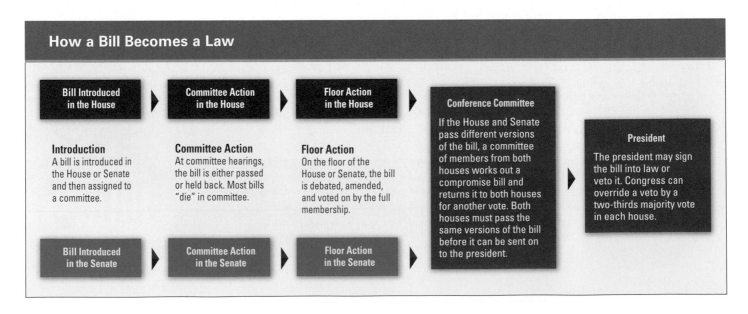

How a Bill Becomes a Law

Bill Introduced in the House → **Committee Action in the House** → **Floor Action in the House** →

Conference Committee
If the House and Senate pass different versions of the bill, a committee of members from both houses works out a compromise bill and returns it to both houses for another vote. Both houses must pass the same versions of the bill before it can be sent on to the president.

→ **President**
The president may sign the bill into law or veto it. Congress can override a veto by a two-thirds majority vote in each house.

Introduction
A bill is introduced in the House or Senate and then assigned to a committee.

Committee Action
At committee hearings, the bill is either passed or held back. Most bills "die" in committee.

Floor Action
On the floor of the House or Senate, the bill is debated, amended, and voted on by the full membership.

Bill Introduced in the Senate → **Committee Action in the Senate** → **Floor Action in the Senate** →

U.S. Capitol Building

Bicameral Legislature

House of Representatives
(435 members)

- Each member represents a district
- Two-year terms

Qualifications:
- 25 years old
- Citizen for 7 years

Powers:
- Proposes tax laws
- Can impeach the president

Senate
(100 members)

- Each member represents a state
- Six-year terms

Qualifications:
- 30 years old
- Citizen for 9 years

Powers:
- Approves presidential appointments
- Ratifies treaties
- Conducts trial of the president after impeachment

House of Representatives and Senate Together

- Propose and pass laws
- Declare war
- Override the president's veto with a two-thirds vote
- Propose amendments to the Constitution with a two-thirds vote

George Washington (left) is shown with members of his first cabinet (left to right): Secretary of War Henry Knox, Secretary of the Treasury Alexander Hamilton, Secretary of State Thomas Jefferson, and Attorney General Edmund Randolph. The Constitution does not mention a cabinet, but Washington set the precedent by using his secretaries as advisors.

Presidents meet with members of the cabinet on a regular basis. Here, President Barack Obama confers with Secretary of State Hillary Clinton.

7.4 The Executive Branch Enforces the Laws

Article II describes the election, powers, and duties of the president. As **chief executive,** the president is the head of the largest branch of the federal government. Under the Constitution, the president and the rest of the executive branch must "take Care that the Laws be faithfully executed."

Powers of the Chief Executive In addition to enforcing laws, the president proposes legislation, including the annual federal budget. As commander in chief, the president is head of the military and has considerable authority in war. The president also oversees foreign relations, a power that includes making treaties and appointing ambassadors with the Senate's consent. The president's judicial powers include appointing Supreme Court justices, again with Senate approval, and granting pardons to people who have broken federal laws.

The Role of Other Executive Officials, Departments, and Agencies Many other officials help carry out executive duties. The vice president, the White House staff, and other close advisors help the president make key policy decisions. The president also gets advice from the cabinet, a group that consists mainly of the heads of executive departments that enforce the laws. These department heads, such as the secretary of state and attorney general, are appointed by the president and approved by the Senate. Their number has risen from four in George Washington's first cabinet to 15 today.

Cabinet members advise the president on policy matters relating to their departments. For example, the secretary of state gives advice on foreign affairs, and the secretary of labor advises on polices relating to the workplace. Some other executive departments are those of defense, education, agriculture, transportation, and energy. One of the newest is the Department of Homeland Security, created to prevent terrorism and respond to natural disasters.

Within each executive department are agencies that address different issues. For example, the Centers for Disease Control and Prevention (CDC), the Food and Drug Administration (FDA), and the National Institutes of Health (NIH) are three agencies within the Department of Health and Human Services.

There are also independent agencies outside the executive departments. Some are executive agencies that report to the president, such as the National Aeronautics and Space Administration (NASA). Others are regulatory commissions formed by Congress, such as the Consumer Product Safety Commission (CPSC). Other semi-governmental agencies, such as the U.S. Postal Service, provide specific services.

White House

President of the United States

- Four-year term

Qualifications:

- 35 years old
- Native-born citizen

Powers of the President:

- Approves or vetoes laws
- Conducts U.S. foreign relations and makes treaties with foreign governments
- Nominates cabinet members, ambassadors, and federal judges
- Serves as commander in chief of the U.S. armed forces
- Prepares the federal government's budget

Vice President

- Serves as president of the Senate
- Assumes the presidency if the president dies, resigns, or is removed from office

Other Executive Officials, Departments, and Agencies

- Advise the president
- Enforce laws

In this room, the nine justices of the Supreme Court hear cases and interpret the Constitution. Charles Evans Hughes, chief justice from 1930 to 1941, described the task this way: "We are under a Constitution, but the Constitution is what the judges say it is." This does not mean judges make their own laws. It means they rule on whether a law conforms to the Constitution.

In *Marbury v. Madison,* Chief Justice John Marshall noted in his ruling that "a law repugnant to the constitution is void." This was the first time the Supreme Court had held an act of Congress to be unconstitutional. In this and other rulings, Justice Marshall left a powerful imprint on the court and on the nation.

7.5 The Judicial Branch Interprets the Laws

The judicial branch interprets the Constitution, the "supreme Law of the Land." Article III establishes the Supreme Court and gives Congress authority to set up "inferior," or lower, federal courts. The Supreme Court and lower federal courts make up the **federal judiciary,** or federal court system.

The Federal Judiciary The federal courts have been called "the guardians of the Constitution" because they judge whether laws and actions conform to constitutional principles. However, a court may address a legal issue only if a relevant case comes before it. It cannot try to solve legal problems on its own.

Most legal disputes involve state and local laws and are addressed in the state court systems. The federal court system hears cases involving issues that are not limited to one state, such as violations of the U.S. Constitution or federal laws. Other examples are cases in which the United States, a state, or a foreign nation is a named party.

Most federal cases are first heard in the lower courts, starting with a U.S. district court. That court's decision can be appealed to a U.S. court of appeals. The final appeal is to petition the Supreme Court to hear the case. The Supreme Court may also choose to hear an appeal of a state supreme court decision involving a state or local law. Such cases usually raise an important constitutional issue affecting the nation as a whole.

Higher courts agree to hear an appeal only when they believe that a lower court may have incorrectly applied the law. The appeal process does not involve witnesses or juries. Instead, an appeals court reviews a case based on court records and oral arguments from attorneys and then makes its decision.

The Supreme Court The U.S. Supreme Court is the highest court in the land. It consists of nine justices, including a chief justice. Like other federal judges, they are appointed for life, and their salaries cannot be lowered. The framers wanted to ensure an **independent judiciary**—a system in which judges cannot be removed or have their salaries reduced for making unpopular decisions.

The Supreme Court is the last stop in the judicial system. Its decisions are final and binding on lower federal courts and on state courts. Every year, it receives about 7,000 petitions to hear cases and accepts about 100 to 150. Its rulings become **precedents,** court decisions used as guides in deciding similar cases. State courts, lower federal courts, and the Supreme Court itself are guided by precedents set by Supreme Court decisions.

The Power of Judicial Review A key authority exercised by the Supreme Court is **judicial review,** the power to review an action of the legislative or executive branch and declare it unconstitutional. This power stems from an 1803 Court case, *Marbury v. Madison,* in which the Court overturned an act of Congress. In that case, Chief Justice John Marshall ruled that Congress, in passing the law, had acted outside the bounds of its constitutional power. Judicial review has sparked debate over the years. Some argue that the Court should take an active role in making policy by overturning laws, whereas others urge restraint.

The Supreme Court

**Federal judges serve for life,
unless removed for misconduct.**

State Supreme Courts

Lower State Courts

U.S. Court of Appeals

A case appealed from a U.S. District Court goes to a U.S. Court of Appeals. These appellate courts do not have juries or hear testimony, and no new evidence is submitted. Each case is heard by a panel of three judges who review the lower court's decision to determine whether an error was made.

Other Federal Courts

Other federal courts include U.S. bankruptcy courts, the U.S. Court of Appeals for the Armed Forces, the U.S. Court of Federal Claims, and the U.S. Tax Court.

U.S. District Courts

The U.S. District Courts are the trial courts for the federal judiciary. Here the parties argue their cases, usually in front of one judge and a jury.
These are the only federal courts to hear testimony in a trial.

Printing money is one of the delegated powers of the national government. Every day, the Bureau of Engraving and Printing prints 35 million banknotes, with a total value of about $635 million.

7.6 Federalism: A System of Divided Powers

As you have seen, the Constitution defines different powers for the legislative, executive, and judicial branches of the federal government. The Constitution also establishes the principle of federalism, the division of power between the federal and state governments. Both the federal and state governments have some exclusive powers of their own, while sharing others.

The Powers of the National Government Article I, Section 8, lists the powers granted to Congress and therefore to the national government. Among these **delegated powers** are the powers to borrow money, coin money, raise an army and navy, declare war, make treaties, establish post offices, and protect patents and copyrights. The elastic clause enables Congress to make laws necessary to carry out these and other delegated powers.

Some of the delegated powers are given to the national government alone and specifically denied to the states. For example, only Congress has the power to coin or print money. The framers wanted to avoid the monetary confusion that existed under the Articles of Confederation, when many states produced their own currency. Also, it is appropriate that only the national government can declare war or make treaties with other nations. Another example is the power to regulate trade with other nations and between the states. By regulating interstate commerce, Congress helps to create a national market with few internal barriers to trade and finance.

The Powers of the States The Constitution is much less specific about state powers. In fact, the only power specifically granted to the states, in Article V, is the power to ratify amendments. On the other hand, Article I specifies those powers that are denied to the states, including taxing imports or exports without the consent of Congress, coining money, and making treaties.

During the ratification debates, many Americans expressed concern that the lack of delegated state powers in the Constitution might leave the federal government with too much power. This concern resulted in ratification of the Tenth Amendment, which declares, "The powers not delegated to the United States by the Constitution, nor prohibited by it to the States, are reserved to the States respectively, or to the people." In other words, any power not expressly granted to the national government would remain with the states and the people. These powers are called **reserved powers**.

Reserved powers include those that are appropriately handled at the state or local level. Providing police and fire protection, establishing schools, and regulating businesses within the state are all reserved powers. So are issuing marriage and driver's licenses, conducting elections, and establishing local governments.

Article IV says that states must give "full Faith and Credit" to the laws and decisions of other states. This means that states, for the most part, must accept the legal documents and actions of other states. States also have certain responsibilities to each other. For example, they must allow a child born in another state to attend their public schools. They must also help each other track down criminals.

Shared Powers of the Federal and State Governments Some of the powers delegated to Congress are not denied to the states. These are called **concurrent powers** because the federal government and the state governments can independently exercise them at the same time. For example, the federal and state governments both collect taxes. Both build roads, establish courts, borrow money, make and enforce laws, and spend money for the general welfare.

Their overlapping responsibilities often require the state and federal governments to work together. For example, Congress sets the date for national elections, and the states register voters and run the elections. The states count the ballots, and Congress organizes the Electoral College vote. Federal and state officials also coordinate efforts to provide such services as law enforcement and disaster relief.

The sharing of power can also create conflict between the federal and state governments. The Constitution provides the general framework for concurrent powers, but it does not spell out every one of them. Nor does it resolve all the issues that arise when powers are shared. Through the years, the system of shared powers has evolved through new laws, amendments to the Constitution, and court decisions.

The Law of the Land Article VI contains a very important clause that declares, "This Constitution, and the Laws of the United States . . . shall be the supreme Law of the Land; and the Judges in every State shall be bound thereby, any Thing in the Constitution or Laws of any State to the Contrary notwithstanding." Since this clause affirms that the Constitution and federal laws are the supreme law of the land, it is often called the supremacy clause.

The supremacy clause establishes that federal law must be followed in cases involving a conflict between federal and state law. A state's constitution, laws, and judicial decisions cannot conflict with the U.S. Constitution or with the laws and treaties of the United States.

Law enforcement is an example of a concurrent power shared by the states and the federal government. State police often work with federal officers to investigate crimes and handle emergencies.

The establishment of local government is a reserved power granted to the states by the Constitution. Holding town meetings is a way for residents to discuss local issues.

7.7 Amending the Constitution

The framers knew that the Constitution would have to change over time to remain relevant and useful to succeeding generations. As Thomas Jefferson wrote, the Constitution "belongs to the living and not to the dead."

Changing the Constitution Even before the Constitution was ratified, there were calls for amendments, especially in the form of a bill of rights. Article V sets up a procedure for amending the Constitution. The framers wanted to keep the government long lasting and stable, though, so they made changing the Constitution difficult.

There are two ways to propose amendments to the Constitution. Congress can propose an amendment with a two-thirds vote in each house. Alternatively, two thirds of state legislatures can ask Congress to call a national convention to draft an amendment. Either way, an amendment must have the approval of three fourths of the states to become part of the Constitution.

The Bill of Rights When ratifying the Constitution in 1788, five states included a list of amendments they wanted added to the document. Many other states and individuals also agreed that certain amendments were necessary. The main demand was for the explicit protection of individual liberties and freedoms.

The new Congress listened to the concerns of the states and the people. James Madison then put together a set of constitutional amendments. By 1791, 10 amendments protecting rights had been ratified, becoming part of the "supreme Law of the Land." They are known as the Bill of Rights.

Many people consider the First Amendment to be the most important amendment in the Bill of Rights. It protects five freedoms: the freedoms of religion, speech, the press, and assembly, and the right to petition the government.

The Constitution can be amended in four ways. All the successful amendments but one—the Twenty-first—were proposed in Congress and ratified by state legislatures. The vast majority of suggested amendments fail to win ratification.

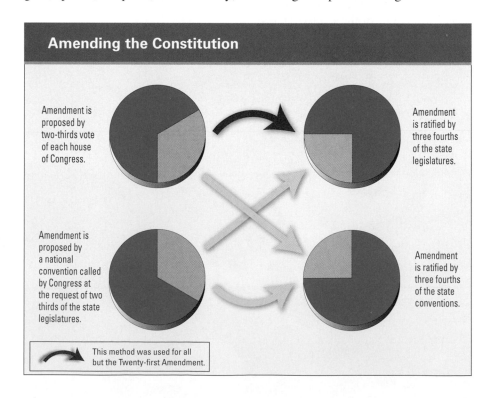

Amending the Constitution

Amendment is proposed by two-thirds vote of each house of Congress.

Amendment is ratified by three fourths of the state legislatures.

Amendment is proposed by a national convention called by Congress at the request of two thirds of the state legislatures.

Amendment is ratified by three fourths of the state conventions.

This method was used for all but the Twenty-first Amendment.

The next three amendments are designed to protect citizens from abuses of power by the federal government. The Second Amendment refers to the necessity of a "well-regulated militia" and to "the right of the people to keep and bear arms." Debate continues over whether this right was meant to apply to individuals or to members of a state militia. The Third Amendment states that homeowners cannot be forced to provide room and board to members of the military in times of peace. The Fourth Amendment guards against unreasonable searches, seizures of property, and arrests.

The next four amendments lay out rights and protections for people who are accused of crimes or are involved in other legal disputes. The Fifth Amendment is the longest one in the Bill of Rights. It says that people cannot be held for committing a crime unless they are properly indicted, or charged. It states that no person can be tried twice for a crime if the punishment is "loss of life or limb." People cannot be forced to testify against themselves, and they cannot be deprived of life, liberty, or property without "due process of law." Finally, it says that the government cannot take private property without paying a fair price for it.

The Sixth Amendment guarantees the right to a speedy and fair trial in criminal cases. The Seventh Amendment ensures the right to trial by jury in certain types of federal civil cases, those involving disputes between people or businesses. The Eighth Amendment prohibits cruel and unusual punishments and forbids courts to impose excessive bail or fines.

The last two amendments are quite general. The Ninth Amendment says that the people have other rights in addition to those listed, and that those rights must not be violated. The Tenth Amendment says that powers not delegated to the federal government belong to the states or to the people.

Further Amendments Thousands of additional amendments have been proposed over the years, but only 17 have been ratified, bringing the total number of amendments to 27. One amendment—the Eighteenth, which banned the making and selling of alcohol—was ratified and then later repealed by the Twenty-first Amendment.

Four of the additional amendments—the Twelfth, Seventeenth, Twentieth, and Twenty-second—concern the election and terms of office of public officials. Many of the other amendments stem from efforts to expand civil rights and the right to vote. The Thirteenth Amendment abolished slavery. The Fourteenth Amendment confers citizenship on all persons born or naturalized in the United States, thereby barring states from denying citizenship to blacks. This amendment also affirms that all citizens have "equal protection of the laws." The Fifteenth Amendment states that race, color, and previous condition of servitude cannot be used to deny voting rights. The Nineteenth Amendment says that gender cannot be used to deny the vote. Finally, the Twenty-sixth Amendment sets the voting age at 18.

On August 28, 1963, more than 200,000 people took part in the March on Washington. They were exercising their First Amendment rights to assemble and speak freely. This protest brought pressure on the government to pass civil rights legislation.

The right to vote is a key element of American democracy. Over the years, various constitutional amendments have expanded citizens' voting rights.

7.8 Popular Participation in Government

Our nation was founded on the ideal that government should be based on the will of the people. In the early years, "We the People" did not include all members of American society. Today there are many ways for all citizens to have a say in government. Participation is the key to an effective democracy.

"We the People," Past and Present The U.S. government exists to serve its citizens. By electing our local, state, and national representatives and leaders, "we the people" have a say in government.

When "we the people" vote, we are using the principle of majority rule to make decisions. In our early history, with very few exceptions, only white property-owning males could vote. As a result, they were the ones who made the decisions. Today "we the people" includes all citizens, regardless of race, culture, or gender. The diversity of voters now makes the government much more representative of the people.

One of the main roles of political parties is to nominate candidates for public offices. Presidential candidates are chosen at national party conventions attended by delegations from each state. Here you see Mel Martinez, who was a candidate for the U.S. Senate from Florida, addressing the 2004 Republican National Convention.

The Role of Political Parties in Government A political party is an organized group of people who have similar ideas about government. The first two American political parties emerged during the 1790s. One party, led by Thomas Jefferson, wanted to give the states more power, help small farmers, and reduce the size of the federal government. The other, led by Alexander Hamilton, favored a strong federal government that could help businesses. These parties drew more citizens into the electoral process.

Over the years, the names and beliefs of political parties have changed, but typically two parties have been dominant. Since the mid-1800s, the two parties have been the Republican and Democratic parties. Today they largely control American politics, especially at the state and national levels. Even those who consider themselves "independents" often show loyalty to one of the two parties. A candidate has a better chance of winning an election if he or she is a member of one of the two major political parties, rather than a small third party. The two-party system is so dominant that it plays a significant role in shaping public policy.

Americans also participate in the political process through marches, protests, and other group actions. These demonstrators are calling for immigrant rights in Washington, D.C., in 2006.

Political Participation Beyond Voting Despite the dominance of political parties, Americans also participate in the political process as individuals. They campaign for candidates they support or run for office themselves. They volunteer with public service organizations. They attend town meetings, public hearings, and demonstrations. They write and promote ballot measures, which are proposed laws or amendments initiated and voted on by the public, not the legislature. They also join committees, organizations, and professional societies.

Some people join **special interest groups** to make their feelings known to the government. Special interest groups are organizations whose members share a specific interest or concern and want to influence policymaking. Groups like the American Medical Association (AMA), the National Wildlife Federation (NWF), the National Rifle Association (NRA), and the American Civil Liberties Union (ACLU) spend a lot of time and money lobbying the government on behalf of their causes.

Lobbying is one way to influence decisions that the governement makes. Here, four female lobbyists attempt to influence two senators to support their cause.

Summary

The framers of the Constitution wanted to create a strong yet balanced government that guaranteed individual freedoms.

The "supreme Law of the Land" The Constitution is the supreme legal document of the United States. It consists of three parts: the Preamble, the Articles, and the amendments.

Three branches of government The first three articles establish the legislative, executive, and judicial branches of government. A system of checks and balances ensures that powers are distributed among the branches.

The legislative branch The main function of this branch of government is to enact laws. Congress consists of two houses, the Senate and the House of Representatives. The elastic clause of the Constitution gives Congress the flexibility it needs to carry out its duties.

The executive branch The main task of this branch is to enforce the laws. The president is the chief executive, or head of the executive branch. This branch also includes many other executive officials, departments, and agencies.

The judicial branch The federal judiciary is made up of the Supreme Court and many lower courts across the country. These courts interpret and apply laws in cases that come before them. The power of judicial review allows the Supreme Court to judge whether acts of Congress are constitutional.

Federalism The Constitution establishes a federal system that balances national and state powers, but it grants controlling authority to the national government in its supremacy clause.

The amendment process As a "living document," the Constitution can be amended. The first 10 amendments make up the Bill of Rights. Seventeen more amendments have been added over the years.

Political participation Citizens can participate in government in many ways. They can vote, join political parties, run for office, and exert political influence through public meetings, interest groups, and other means.

Chapter 8

Changes in a Young Nation

Did changes in the young nation open the door to opportunity for all Americans?

8.1 Introduction

In 1803, two army officers, Captain Meriwether Lewis and Lieutenant William Clark, arrived in the frontier outpost of St. Louis, Missouri. The two men were on a mission from President Thomas Jefferson to explore western rivers for a route to the Pacific Ocean. On the way, they were to collect information about the Louisiana Territory, a huge expanse of land the United States had just purchased from France.

At the time, St. Louis was a sleepy town of around 200 houses, perched on a bluff above the Mississippi River. There were no shops or hotels. The town's residents were mainly French settlers who lived by farming, fur trapping, and trading along the river. Traders would dock their boats by the river's edge and travel the grid of dirt roads that led away from the river.

Very likely, no one in St. Louis in 1803 thought much about what Lewis and Clark's arrival would mean for the little town. However, by opening the West to settlement, Lewis and Clark's expedition brought big changes to St. Louis.

By 1850, St. Louis had grown to a bustling city of more than 70,000. Its ideal location near the junction of the Mississippi and Missouri rivers made St. Louis a center of trade and commerce. Along the waterfront, wharves and brick warehouses replaced the sandy beach where small boats once landed. Dozens of large, paddle-wheel steamboats lined the docks. One visitor wrote, "The whole of the levee is covered as far as the eye can see, with merchandise landed or to be shipped; thousands of barrels of flour and bags of corn, hogsheads of tobacco, and immense piles of lead."

The makeup of St. Louis's population also changed. Once a town of trappers and fur traders, St. Louis now had prosperous merchants and bankers who rubbed shoulders with farmers and workers. Between 1840 and 1860, a wave of immigration from Germany and Ireland reshaped the ethnic mix of the city. St. Louis had become a cosmopolitan city and the "gateway to the West."

Lewis and Clark left St. Louis, Missouri, in 1804 and returned two years later, having traveled overland to the Pacific Ocean and back. Along the way, a French fur trapper and his wife, Sacajawea, joined the expedition. Sacajawea, a captive Shoshone Indian, made this epic journey carrying her young son on her back. When the expedition reached her people, she proved invaluable as a translator.

◀ The town of St. Louis, Missouri, in 1832 (top) and 1854 (bottom)

The United States in 1800

States

Territories

By 1800, the United States had expanded from 13 to 16 states. As settlers pushed west across the Appalachians, lack of good transportation became a growing problem. Many western farmers relied on the Mississippi River to ship their crops to Eastern cities.

8.2 The First Years of the New Nation

In 1790, the United States was beginning its new life as a nation. It had a Constitution and its first president, George Washington. That year, the government took its first national census and learned that the country had nearly 4 million people. Most Americans were still clustered along the eastern seaboard, but some hardy pioneers had begun to move inland.

The Country Expands Beyond Its Colonial Borders In these early years, the United States was predominantly a rural nation. However, it did have a number of flourishing cities, including the old colonial centers of Philadelphia, New York, and Boston.

The country was also expanding beyond its original 13 states. Between 1790 and 1800, three new states entered the Union: Vermont, Kentucky, and Tennessee. Many settlers were migrating west across the Appalachian Mountains into the area known as the Northwest Territory. This territory would later become the states of Ohio, Indiana, Illinois, Michigan, and Wisconsin. Settlers were also moving into the area of present-day Mississippi and Alabama. By the early 1800s, American settlements were scattered across a large territory, from the Atlantic Ocean in the east to the Mississippi River in the west.

Agriculture Is the Center of the Nation's Economy In states old and new, farming was the nation's most important economic activity. Most Americans farmed on small plots, producing food for themselves and their families. If they produced a surplus, they might sell it in nearby towns or cities.

The United States had little industry at this time. Most farmers made their own clothing and tools. In urban areas, artisans produced manufactured goods by hand in small workshops. In the Northeast, there were a few small textile mills that spun cotton by machine, but large factories did not yet exist.

Lack of good transportation kept most states and regions remote from each other. Moving people or goods across great distances was expensive and difficult. The few roads linking towns and cities were deeply rutted in dry weather and treacherous swamps in wet weather. Most long-distance travel took place on rivers or the ocean.

George Washington Gives Shape to the Office of President When George Washington took the oath of office as the nation's first president in 1789, he faced a delicate task. On the one hand, as he said in his inaugural speech, he was determined to provide Americans with "the benefits of an united and effective government." On the other hand, he had to reassure those "fellow-citizens" who feared a strong president could mean the return of a monarchy. President Washington had no road map, other than the Constitution, to guide him. "I walk on untrodden ground," he said. "There is scarcely any part of my conduct which may not hereafter be drawn into precedent."

The first test of Washington's authority as president came in 1791, when Congress passed a tax on whiskey to raise money. Western farmers, who turned their grain into whiskey for sale, were outraged. Many refused to pay the tax. Angry farmers in western Pennsylvania rose up in rebellion, attacking tax collectors and setting buildings on fire. Washington saw the Whiskey Rebellion as a threat to the federal government's authority. In 1794, President Washington sent a militia force across the Appalachians to stamp out the protests. In doing so, he made it clear that the federal government would enforce its laws.

One of Washington's first official actions was to sign Congress's Federal Judiciary Act into law. This act created the federal court system, with its district and circuit courts, that we still live under today. Washington also created the first cabinet, or group of department heads that meets to advise the president.

Political Parties Emerge Washington's most prominent cabinet members were Treasury Secretary Alexander Hamilton and Secretary of State Thomas Jefferson. Both were brilliant thinkers, but their ideas often clashed. "Hamilton and myself were daily pitted . . . like two fighting cocks," Jefferson wrote of their growing hostility. These differences led to the creation of the country's first political parties, the Federalists and the Democratic-Republicans.

Hamilton's Federalist Party supported a strong central government with wide powers. The Federalists believed that a powerful government was needed to keep order among the states. They had little faith in the wisdom of the average citizen and thought that a capable, educated elite should run the country.

In contrast, Jefferson's Democratic-Republican Party favored a small central government with limited powers. The party believed that states had the right to judge whether Congress was overstepping its constitutional powers, a view known as the states' rights theory. The Democratic-Republicans had great confidence in the ability of ordinary people to make good decisions. They also believed that political power should lie with the majority of voters rather than with a wealthy elite.

In general, Washington favored Federalist ideas. Nonetheless, in his Farewell Address, delivered near the end of his second term in 1796, he warned of "the danger of parties" and spoke of "the immense value of your national union to your collective and individual happiness." Once Washington left office, however, debates between the two parties grew increasingly acrimonious.

John Adams, a Federalist, succeeded Washington as president. In 1800, Adams ran for a second term against Thomas Jefferson. During the campaign, partisan feelings ran so high, some worried the new nation might self-destruct. Nevertheless, the 1800 election took place without serious disturbance. Thomas Jefferson won the presidency, and power shifted peacefully from one party to the other. The country had survived a major political test.

In the early 1800s, most Americans lived on farms. Thomas Jefferson and his Democratic-Republicans believed that ordinary farmers formed the backbone of American society and its democratic way of life. Federalists put more faith in educated city dwellers to run the new nation's political affairs.

During the mid-1800s, many settlers migrated west. They were driven by the desire for land and opportunity. They were also inspired by their belief in manifest destiny. According to this idea, Americans had a God-given right and duty to expand across the continent.

8.3 Geographic Changes

In May 1804, Lewis and Clark set out from St. Louis on their journey to the Pacific Ocean. They paddled up the Missouri River and into the unexplored world of the American West, crossing vast plains and snowcapped mountains. They discovered plants and animals they had never seen before. They encountered American Indian tribes and learned about their ways of life. They even found the remains of a prehistoric dinosaur. Two years and four months later, they were back in St. Louis. The news of their expedition thrilled Americans and helped promote western settlement.

From Sea to Shining Sea: Acquiring the West Much of the area that Lewis and Clark explored was part of the Louisiana Purchase. In 1803, Jefferson had bought the Louisiana Territory from France for $15 million, which was a large sum of money at the time. The Louisiana Purchase Treaty pushed the western boundary of the United Sates from the Mississippi River to the distant Rocky Mountains, at a cost of about four cents an acre.

Many people criticized Jefferson's action. Some thought the country did not need any more undeveloped land. Others protested that the purchase was unconstitutional, because the Constitution did not give the president the power to buy foreign territory. But Jefferson could not pass up an opportunity to double the size of the United Sates. The Louisiana Purchase furthered his vision of an "empire for liberty" stretching from sea to sea.

Many Americans had good reasons for supporting national expansion. The country's population was growing rapidly. Good farmland in the settled, eastern part of the country was becoming less plentiful. As a result, more and more people were moving west in search of cheap land. Many also believed expansion would make the country safer by reducing the threat of foreign invasion from the west. The idea of a larger, more powerful country also appealed to the American sense of nationalism.

This combination of nationalism and expansionism gave rise in the 1840s to a belief known as **manifest destiny**. The term means "obvious fate," and it seemed obvious to many Americans that the United States was meant to spread its founding ideals and democratic way of life across the continent and beyond. One politician at the time wrote, "Nothing less than a continent can suffice as the basis and foundation for that nation whose destiny is involved in the destiny of mankind."

The idea of manifest destiny inspired further expansion. Spain was persuaded to cede Florida to the United States in 1819. In 1845, Texas joined the Union as a state, after first gaining independence from Mexico. The United States and Great Britain signed a treaty in 1846 giving the United States control over about half of Oregon Country. That same year, the United States went to war with Mexico over a border dispute in Texas. At the end of the Mexican War, the United States gained most of the American Southwest in the Treaty of Guadalupe Hidalgo. The Gadsden Purchase of 1853, which added a portion of present-day southern Arizona and New Mexico, completed the nation's continental expansion at that time.

Settlers Find Opportunity and Liberty in the West As the United States expanded, American settlers moved into the newly acquired territories. Some traveled by wagon along the Santa Fe Trail, which was an old trade route from the Missouri River to Santa Fe, New Mexico. Many more headed west on the Oregon Trail, which stretched from Independence, Missouri, to Portland, Oregon. The journey along the Oregon Trail, across the Great Plains and the Rocky Mountains, took many months and cost countless settlers their lives. Those who made it found fertile farmlands in the green valleys of Oregon.

One group that made the journey west in the 1840s was made up of the Mormons. This religious group traveled over the Oregon Trail to Utah to escape persecution. They settled on the desert lands surrounding Great Salt Lake and created a thriving, prosperous community.

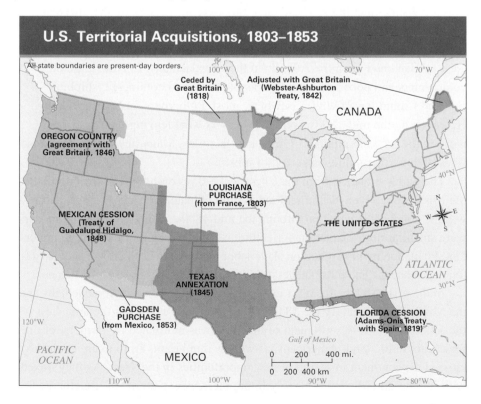

U.S. Territorial Acquisitions, 1803–1853

All state boundaries are present-day borders.

Ceded by Great Britain (1818)

Adjusted with Great Britain (Webster-Ashburton Treaty, 1842)

CANADA

OREGON COUNTRY (agreement with Great Britain, 1846)

LOUISIANA PURCHASE (from France, 1803)

MEXICAN CESSION (Treaty of Guadalupe Hidalgo, 1848)

THE UNITED STATES

TEXAS ANNEXATION (1845)

GADSDEN PURCHASE (from Mexico, 1853)

FLORIDA CESSION (Adams-Onis Treaty with Spain, 1819)

ATLANTIC OCEAN

PACIFIC OCEAN

MEXICO

Gulf of Mexico

0 200 400 mi.
0 200 400 km

Between 1803 and 1853, the continental United States doubled in size. Each new territorial acquisition opened up land for settlers while bringing hardship to American Indians.

In this 1839 image of Davy Crockett, the West is portrayed as a wild, uncharted frontier. Crockett, a trail guide and former congressman from Tennessee, embodied the traits of strength and independence that many Americans valued. These qualities were considered essential for life in the American West.

American Indians Face a Forced Westward Migration Although westward expansion provided new opportunities for settlers, it spelled tragedy for many American Indians. As the United States added new territories, it also brought many Indian homelands within its national borders. Settlers who coveted these lands agitated for the removal of tribes to less desirable areas.

In 1830, Congress passed the Indian Removal Act to clear Indians from lands east of the Mississippi River. The plan was to move the tribes west to Indian Territory, which later became the state of Oklahoma. In a message to Congress entitled "On Indian Removal," President Andrew Jackson praised the act for placing "a dense and civilized population in large tracts of country now occupied by a few savage hunters."

Although most tribes reluctantly went along with removal, some resisted. The Cherokees attempted a legal defense, claiming they were protected from removal by earlier treaties. When Georgia refused to recognize the treaty rights, the Cherokees appealed to the Supreme Court. In *Worcester v. Georgia*, the Court upheld the Cherokees' treaty rights. President Jackson, however, refused to enforce the Court's decision. Other tribes, such as the Seminoles of Florida and the Sauk and Fox Indians of Wisconsin Territory, turned to armed resistance. These tribes were nearly wiped out by army troops.

In the end, the tribes that resisted removal were moved by force. The most famous forced migration was that of the Cherokees in 1838. On the journey to Indian Territory, about 4,000 of the more than 17,000 Cherokees died from starvation, disease, and harsh winter weather. This tragic journey is remembered today as the Trail of Tears.

The Country Develops Sectional Identities As the United States expanded, the three main sections of the country—North, South, and West—began to develop distinct identities. These identities were influenced by the different geographic characteristics of each section and by the people who settled there.

The North included the states that stretched from Pennsylvania north to New England and from the Atlantic to the Appalachians. In New England, cold winters and poor soil led many people to turn to commerce, shipbuilding, and fishing for a living. Elsewhere, most northerners farmed for a living. However, by the mid-1800s, some northerners were leaving their farms to work in the growing number of mills and factories. Many new immigrants also flocked to northern cities in search of jobs.

The South stretched from the Chesapeake Bay south to Florida and west to the Mississippi River. With the South's mild climate and rich soil, agriculture was the dominant occupation through the mid-1800s. Although most southerners were small farmers, plantation agriculture was becoming more and more important. Plantation owners relied on slave labor to cultivate cash crops, such as cotton and tobacco. The most successful planters lived lives of great affluence.

In the early 1800s, the West meant the lands between the Appalachians and the Mississippi River. By the 1840s, however, the West meant the area west of the Mississippi. Early settlement of the West was motivated by farmers' desire for cheap, fertile land. Americans, as well as immigrants from many countries, crossed the continent in search of new opportunities in the West. As they mixed with Indians and Mexicans already living there, new patterns of life emerged.

8.4 Political Changes in an Emerging Democracy

From 1790 to 1830, there was an expansion of democracy in the United States. Few Americans represented this change better than Andrew Jackson. Born into poverty in the Carolina backcountry, Jackson managed to prosper as a planter, buying land and slaves. He went on to become a judge, a U.S. senator, and a military hero. Despite his wealth and fame, Jackson maintained a common, man-of-the-people image. This image and a new spirit of democracy in the country helped sweep Jackson to the presidency in 1828.

Democracy for the Common Man—But Not Woman Jackson owed his victory in part to an expansion of **suffrage,** or voting rights. By 1828, most states had dropped the requirement that voting citizens must own property. The number of popular votes increased from around 350,000 in 1824 to some 1,155,000 the year Jackson was elected president. Although these changes marked an expansion of democracy, many Americans were still denied this most basic political right. No states allowed women, American Indians, or slaves to vote. Only a few granted suffrage to free African American men.

Other changes were also making the election process more democratic. In many states, secret paper ballots were replacing the more public voice-vote system. This change encouraged people to vote without fear of intimidation at the polls. By 1832, open national conventions had replaced private party meetings, called caucuses, to nominate candidates for president and vice president.

Political parties made politics more democratic by involving more people in election campaigns. By the 1820s, parties were using newspapers, campaign songs, and get-out-the-vote rallies to drum up interest in voting. The percentage of eligible voters who actually went to the polls increased sharply as campaigns became more interesting.

While running for president in 1828, Andrew Jackson pioneered the use of political rallies and other lively campaign events to reach voters. Other politicians soon followed his lead. Jackson's inauguration in 1829 brought a flood of admirers to Washington, D.C. The celebration became a near riot as supporters poured into the White House. As one observer put it, "It was the people's day and the people's president, and the people would rule."

Jackson Loses, Then Wins, the Presidency Jackson first ran for president in 1824. That year, four candidates ran for president, all of them claiming to be Democratic-Republicans. Each candidate represented the interests of a different section of the country. Jackson managed to attract enough voters in all sections to win the popular vote. However, he did not have enough votes in the Electoral College to win the presidency. In accordance with the Constitution, the election went to the House of Representatives, which chose John Quincy Adams to be president. Jackson's supporters vowed revenge in the next election.

Jackson knew there would be many new voters in 1828, most of them "common people." To gain their support, he formed a new political party known as the Democratic Party. Democrats claimed to speak for ordinary farmers and workers, rather than for the wealthy and privileged few. This new party supported a decentralized government and states' rights.

The Alien and Sedition Acts were signed into law by President John Adams, father of John Quincy Adams, in 1798 as the country prepared for war with France. These acts authorized the president to deport noncitizens who were considered "dangerous to the peace and safety of the United States." The acts also restricted speech that was critical of the government.

Jackson's opponent, John Quincy Adams, also headed a new party, the National Republican Party. The National Republicans represented business, shipping, and banking interests in the Northeast. This party favored a strong central government that would fund internal improvements, such as roads and canals, to grow the economy. Southerners feared that they would be taxed in the form of high tariffs to pay for these improvements. They also worried that a stronger federal government might be tempted to interfere with slavery.

Both parties tried to win voters by avoiding sectional issues and flinging nasty charges at one another. When the mudslinging was over, Jackson's "common man" appeal won him a landslide victory. At his inauguration, Jackson threw open the White House doors to his followers. They tromped through the residence with muddy boots and spilled punch on the furniture. It was a raucous celebration of popular democracy.

Once in office, Jackson rewarded his loyal supporters with government jobs. Those who lost their jobs to make way for Jackson supporters denounced this practice as a **spoils system**. The name comes from the ancient wartime saying, "To the victor belong the spoils [prizes] of war." Jackson, however, defended "rotation in office" as a democratic reform. Government jobs, he argued, were not the property of an elite few but should be open to all.

Nullification: Defining the Limits of State and Federal Powers A key issue facing the young republic was the balance between state and federal power. This issue first came up in 1798, when Congress passed two controversial laws known as the Alien and Sedition Acts. Believing the laws to be unconstitutional, Thomas Jefferson and James Madison penned protests known as the Virginia and Kentucky resolutions. The resolutions called on states to nullify, or declare void, any federal law that violates the Constitution. This principle of **nullification** would become a flash point in a later battle over states' rights.

Meanwhile, the Supreme Court under Chief Justice John Marshall made a number of rulings that affirmed federal power. The first ruling came in 1819 in *McCulloch v. Maryland,* which arose when Maryland tried to tax the Baltimore branch of the Bank of the United States, a national bank created by an act of Congress. The **Marshall Court** ruled that "the power to tax involves the power to destroy." Under the Supremacy Clause, no state had the right to destroy or in any way nullify what Congress had enacted. In *Gibbons v. Ogden,* the Supreme Court reaffirmed the power of Congress to regulate interstate commerce. The case arose when the New York legislature granted two men the exclusive right to run steamboats on the Hudson River. New Jersey, which shares the river with New York, protested. The Court rejected New York's effort to control boat traffic on the river, on the ground that it interfered with interstate commerce.

The issue of states' rights reached a boiling point in 1832, when South Carolina tried to nullify two federal tariff laws. Like many southern states, South Carolina relied on imports of cheap manufactured goods, and tariffs raised the prices on these goods. As the nullification crisis heated up, state leaders threatened to withdraw from the Union if the tariff laws were enforced. President Jackson stood his ground, preparing to use force if necessary. At the same time, he rushed a lower tariff bill through Congress. The crisis passed, but the tension between states' rights and federal power did not go away.

8.5 Economic Changes in a Developing Nation

In 1789, a young Englishman named Samuel Slater came to the United States looking for opportunity. Unlike most immigrants, however, he was not seeking land to farm. Instead, he came to set up a cotton-spinning mill using the latest technology. While working in an English textile mill, Slater had memorized the designs for machines that spun cotton fiber into thread. Soon after arriving in the United States, he built a mill in Rhode Island and was on his way to fame and fortune. Slater's mill marked the beginning of **industrialization** in the United States. Industrialization is the move from producing goods by hand to producing them by machine.

New Inventions Make Production More Efficient Slater was not alone. Other inventors in the United States were working on new machines that would spur industrialization. One of the most successful of these inventors was a New Englander named Eli Whitney. While visiting a Georgia plantation in 1793, Whitney observed how slaves spent hours cleaning the seeds from cotton. Within days, he had invented the **cotton gin,** a machine that could clean 50 pounds of cotton in the time it took to clean one pound by hand.

Whitney's cotton gin revolutionized cotton production, making cotton the nation's leading cash crop. The cotton gin also revolutionized slavery. Until then, many had expected slavery to die out in the South, as it had in the North. Instead, as cotton production increased, so did the demand for slave labor.

Whitney also introduced the idea of interchangeable parts. Until then, musket parts were made by hand, and each part was slightly different. Whitney showed how muskets could be put together using identical parts that could be made in quantity and interchanged from one gun to another. Whitney's system made musket manufacturing much faster and paved the way for the **mass production** of goods. Mass production is the making of goods on a large scale in factories.

In the 1830s, new machines increased **productivity**—the rate at which goods can be produced—in agriculture. John Deere invented the steel-tipped plow, which drastically reduced the labor required to plow a field. Around the same time, Cyrus McCormick created a mechanical reaper that could harvest grain much faster than traditional methods with less labor. In response, farmers began to focus on cash crops, using the money they made to buy the expensive new machines and other goods they needed.

The Factory System Changes How People Work New technology brought new ways of working. Boston merchant Francis Cabot Lowell, father of the **factory system,** opened his first cotton mill in 1814. Lowell's factory used a series of machines, housed in one building, that turned raw cotton into finished cloth. He hired young women from local farms to tend his machines. Many of these "mill girls" were happy to leave their unpaid farm work for a factory job with wages.

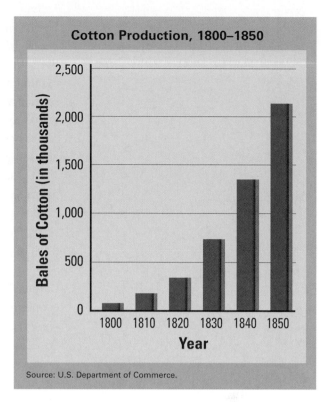

Cotton production soared with the introduction of the cotton gin in 1793. Because cotton planters relied on slave labor, the slave system also became deeply entrenched. By 1860, one of every three people living in the South was enslaved.

The new factory system was a far cry from the old system of handmade goods produced at home or in small workshops for local use. Factories churned out large quantities of goods for consumption across the country. The mass production of goods helped bring about a change from a traditional to a **market economy**. This change was known as the **market revolution**. In a **traditional economy,** people make most of the things they use. Goods are often traded by barter or other informal types of exchange. In a market economy, people buy and sell goods for money, rather than producing them for themselves.

These economic developments had positive and negative effects. As productivity increased, living standards usually improved. Americans with cash in their pockets had more goods to choose from when they shopped. However, many factory workers had to work for low wages in unsafe, unhealthy conditions to produce these goods.

Canals, Roads, and Rails: Connecting the Country The growth of the market economy sparked a transportation revolution. In the early 1800s, good roads were hard to find anywhere in the United States. By the mid-1800s, however, American engineers had built all-weather roads that had stone surfaces and proper drainage. The most ambitious project was the National Road, which stretched across the Appalachians from Maryland to the Mississippi River. On this road, a trip from Maryland to Illinois that once took weeks could be completed in days.

Traveling by river was cheaper than building roads, but traveling upstream was a problem. In 1807, Robert Fulton attached a steam engine to two huge paddle wheels mounted on a raft. This steam-powered riverboat, the *Clermont*, chugged up the Hudson River from New York to Albany, launching a steamboat craze. By 1830, approximately 200 steamboats were traveling the nation's waterways, hauling freight and passengers.

Canals extended water travel to places rivers did not run. In 1817, when construction of the Erie Canal began, most canals were 2 or 3 miles long. In contrast, the Erie Canal, which linked the Hudson River to Lake Erie, stretched 363 miles. Once the canal was completed, goods could travel from New York City to the Midwest by river, through the canal, and onto the Great Lakes. The canal helped make New York City the country's biggest and most prosperous city. The success of the Erie Canal prompted dozens of other canal projects throughout the country.

Railroads were another key element in the transportation revolution. Inspired by steamboats, engineers built steam-powered locomotives that hauled freight and passenger cars along railroad lines, even in winter when rivers and canals froze. By the mid-1800s, thousands of miles of track stretched across the nation.

Henry Schenck Tanner created this map of the eastern United States around 1830. The map shows both railroad lines and canals, as well as state boundaries. Railroad construction was just beginning, but many canals had already been built across the country. The most famous, the Erie Canal, allowed farmers in the Ohio Valley to ship their crops directly to New York City, rather than using the much longer route down the Mississippi River.

8.6 Social Changes in the Young Republic

The first half of the 19th century was a time of great change in American life. The country was expanding, the economy was growing, and the political system was becoming more democratic. These developments filled many people with hope for the future. But not all Americans benefited from these changes. Many continued to suffer from poverty, limited opportunity, and a lack of rights. As a result, various reform movements arose to tackle problems in American society.

The Second Great Awakening Inspires Reformers

The reform efforts of the early 1800s found inspiration in a religious revival known as the Second Great Awakening. Preachers traveled from town to town, holding revival meetings and calling on people to embrace the Christian faith. These preachers urged people to turn from the sins of their selfish lives and receive God's love and forgiveness. Revivalists preached an egalitarian message: God's love and redemption were open to everyone. They taught that Christians could transform society by working for justice. This optimism and outpouring of religious fervor helped fuel the reform movements of the early 1800s.

Few reformers accomplished more than Dorothea Dix. Deeply religious, Dix found her calling after visiting a Boston jail. She was shocked to see inmates locked in small, dark, unheated cells. Among the inmates were mentally ill women who had not committed any crime. Dix made a two-year study of other jails and found the same inhumane conditions. Children, debtors, and the mentally ill were all treated like hardened criminals. Her reform efforts brought substantial change in the penal system and in mental health care across the United States.

The spirit of reform and Jacksonian democracy affected education. In the early 1800s, few children had the chance to go to school. Horace Mann, an early American educator, believed that free, public education would strengthen democracy and help young people escape poverty. Mann pushed for a public school system in Massachusetts. His idea soon caught on in other states as well. By 1850, many states were promoting public education.

Another reform effort fueled by the Second Great Awakening was the temperance movement. Many reformers blamed crime, poverty, and mental illness on alcohol abuse. They called for temperance, or moderation in drinking habits. The American Temperance Union attracted more than a million members within a year of its formation. It also became a training ground for leaders in other areas of reform.

After witnessing the inhumane treatment of prison inmates, Dorothea Dix researched jails and mental insitution for years. Dix's research and advocacy helped reform the penal system and mental institutions throughout the country.

Abolitionists, like Frederick Douglass, waged a fierce campaign against slavery during the first half of the 1800s. They gave speeches and tried to win support for abolition.

Reformers Push to Abolish Slavery One reform movement came to overshadow all others: the movement to end slavery. Opposition to slavery had existed since the first Africans were brought to Virginia in the early 1600s. Congress banned the importation of slaves in 1808, and opponents of slavery hoped slavery would eventually just die out. Instead, the rise in cotton production that followed the invention of the cotton gin fueled a dramatic expansion of slavery.

In the early 1800s, free African Americans in the North formed several antislavery societies. Their efforts got a big boost from the religious fervor at revival meetings. Revivalists attacked slavery on the grounds that it was immoral. They also helped people see that slavery went against such ideals as liberty and equality, which lay at the heart of American democracy. Although some antislavery reformers believed slavery should be ended gradually, others called for immediate **abolition,** or the end of slavery, everywhere.

Abolitionists gave speeches, wrote pamphlets, and lobbied government officials in an effort to end slavery. The abolitionist movement gained power and public attention in the 1830s through a newspaper called *The Liberator,* published by William Lloyd Garrison. Garrison advocated not only an immediate end to slavery but also full equality for African Americans, a radical idea at the time. Another important abolitionist was Frederick Douglass, a former slave whose autobiography recounted his own struggle for freedom. Douglass's personal story and his dynamic stage presence made him a powerful spokesman for abolition.

As the abolition movement grew, supporters of slavery—both northern and southern—went on the attack. Mobs attacked abolitionists, burned their homes, and destroyed their printing presses. In spite of these attacks, abolitionists continued their work, making slavery the most crucial issue of their time.

Women Demand Equal Rights A number of abolitionist leaders also joined the growing movement for women's rights. One was a former slave named Sojourner Truth. A tall, striking woman who knew how to stand up for herself, Truth was not afraid to speak out. At one gathering, after hearing men portray women as being weak, she exclaimed, "Look at my arm! I have plowed and planted and gathered into barns, and no man could head [outdo] me—and ain't I a woman?"

In the mid-1800s, women were still second-class citizens in America. They were denied many of the rights and privileges given to men, including the right to vote and to control their own money or property. Most women were expected to stay at home and not try to "better" themselves by pursuing an education or a career. But a growing number of women began to challenge these restrictions. Their efforts gave rise to the first women's movement.

In 1848, supporters of women's rights gathered for the **Seneca Falls Convention,** in Seneca Falls, New York. There they drafted a statement called the Declaration of Sentiments, which was based on the Declaration of Independence. It began, "We hold these truths to be self-evident: that all men and women are created equal." The statement went on to list various acts of tyranny by men against women.

In the years after the Seneca Falls Convention, reformers like Elizabeth Cady Stanton and Susan B. Anthony continued to struggle for women's rights. Progress was slow, but over time, states began to change their laws. New York, for example, gave women control over their property and wages. Other states passed more liberal divorce laws. Getting the right to vote would take much longer, but eventually, in 1920, that barrier to women's rights would also fall.

Women's rights reformer Elizabeth Cady Stanton spoke to supporters at the first Women's Rights Convention in 1848. The convention was held in Seneca Falls, New York, where Stanton lived with her husband. At the time, women were denied many basic rights, including the right to vote. Many men, and some women, believed that women already enjoyed political rights through their husbands and should stay focused on home and family.

Summary

The United States experienced political, geographic, economic, and social changes in the first half of the 1800s. During this time, the nation expanded from 13 states along the Atlantic coast to a huge nation that spanned a continent.

Manifest destiny Inspired by the belief that their nation was destined to expand, Americans acquired vast western lands and began a movement to settle these new territories.

Indian Removal Act As settlers moved westward, they pushed Indians out of their homelands and forced their removal to lands set aside as Indian Territory in present-day Oklahoma.

Jacksonian democracy As voting rights expanded, the United States became more democratic. In 1828, Andrew Jackson was elected president as the champion of the common man.

Marshall Court In the ongoing struggle between states' rights and federal power, the Marshall Court made key decisions that strengthened the federal government's power.

Factory system New machines and ways of organizing work in factories made production more efficient and changed the way Americans worked. A market economy began to develop.

Second Great Awakening A major religious revival movement inspired reform movements in many areas of American life, including prison reform, temperance, public education, and the abolition of slavery.

Seneca Falls Convention At an 1848 meeting in Seneca Falls, New York, a women's movement was launched that would last for decades. Its goal was equality under the law for both men and women.

Chapter 9

A Dividing Nation

Was the Civil War inevitable?

9.1 Introduction

On May 22, 1856, Senator Charles Sumner of Massachusetts was savagely beaten on the floor of the Senate. The attack followed a speech Sumner had given entitled "The Crime Against Kansas." Sumner was an ardent abolitionist, and in his speech, he had blasted fellow senators for passing a law that would allow slavery in Kansas Territory.

Sumner heaped particular scorn on one of the law's authors, Senator Andrew P. Butler of South Carolina. Sumner sneered at Butler for his proslavery beliefs and his tendency to drool when he spoke. Butler was an aged but distinguished member of the Senate. Many senators found Sumner's speech offensive, and Southerners were outraged.

Two days later, Preston Brooks, Butler's nephew and a member of the House, approached Sumner, who was seated at his desk. Declaring Sumner's speech a "libel on South Carolina and Mr. Butler," Brooks began to beat Sumner over the head with his gold-tipped cane. Brooks eventually broke his cane, but not before he had left Sumner bloody and unconscious on the Senate floor. Sumner survived the attack, but it was three years before he recovered from his injuries and returned to the Senate.

The incident underscored the country's deep divisions over the issue of slavery. Southerners praised Brooks for defending the South and his family's honor. Many Southerners sent Brooks new canes to replace the one he had broken on Sumner's head. The city of Charleston, South Carolina, even sent a cane with the inscription, "Hit him again."

In contrast, many Northerners were appalled by the incident. They saw it as another example of the same Southern brutality that was responsible for slavery. Many in the North who had previously rejected the antislavery movement as too radical now found themselves more sympathetic to limiting slavery—and more hostile toward the South.

Charles Sumner spent his life working for equal rights for African Americans. Shortly before his death in 1874, the Charles Sumner School opened in Washington, D.C. It was one of the first public schools erected for educating Washington's black community. Today the school is a museum, with a permanent exhibit on one of Sumner's friends—fellow abolitionist Frederick Douglass.

◀ Preston Brooks assaulting Charles Sumner on the floor of the Senate

9.2 Sectional Differences Divide the Union

The Ohio River meanders for nearly 1,000 miles from its origins in western Pennsylvania to the Mississippi River, at Cairo, Illinois. The Ohio has played a significant role in American history. It served as the main route for westward migration into the old Northwest Territory. It also served as a boundary between North and South. The Northwest Ordinance of 1787 declared that all lands north of the Ohio would be free of slaves, leaving slavery allowable in lands to the south. This law helped make the creation of new western states easier for a time. But it did not solve the problem of slavery. As the country expanded, sectional differences over slavery increasingly divided the country.

Slavery Comes to the National Stage: The Missouri Compromise In the early 1800s, Ohio, Indiana, and Illinois applied for statehood. Because they were all north of the Ohio River, they entered the Union as free states. During the same period, Louisiana, Mississippi, and Alabama—all south of the Ohio—entered as slave states.

By 1819, the number of slave states and free states was balanced at 11 each. That meant neither North nor South had a controlling majority in the Senate. But that year, Missouri, which lay to the west of the Ohio River, applied for admission as a slave state. If admitted, Missouri would tip the balance of power in the Senate toward the South.

Suddenly, slavery became a national issue. Northerners in Congress protested that most of Missouri lay north of the point where the Ohio River met the Mississippi. By all rights, they said, it should be a free state. They also worried that making Missouri a slave state might turn the rest of Louisiana Territory toward slavery. So they insisted that Missouri could only enter as a free state. Southern senators disagreed. Congress was deadlocked.

When the Senate took up the matter again in 1820, however, things had changed. Maine was asking to join the Union as a free state. This opened the way for a deal known as the **Missouri Compromise,** which was sponsored by Speaker of the House Henry Clay. Under the terms of the compromise, Missouri would enter the Union as a slave state and Maine as a free state, preserving the balance of power in the Senate. In addition, the law drew a line across the Louisiana Territory at latitude 36° 30′. North of that line, slavery would be banned. South of the line, it would be permitted.

The Missouri Compromise broke the deadlock in the Senate, but it pleased no one. Northerners were angry about the extension of slavery to Missouri. Southerners disliked the ban on slavery in much of the Louisiana Territory.

The Missouri Compromise kept the balance between slave and free states by admitting Missouri into the Union as a slave state, while Maine entered as a free state. It also set a line at the 36° 30′ parallel. North of this line, slavery was banned. South of the line, it was permitted.

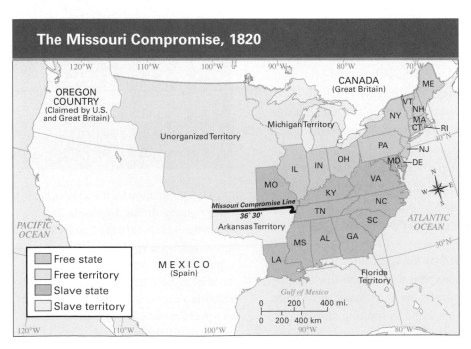

The Missouri Compromise, 1820

Legend:
- Free state
- Free territory
- Slave state
- Slave territory

Enslaved African Americans, 1790–1860

Year	Slave Population
1790	697,681
1800	893,602
1810	1,191,362
1820	1,538,022
1830	2,009,043
1840	2,487,355
1850	3,204,313
1860	3,953,760

Source: U.S. Census Bureau.

The compromise eased tensions temporarily, but it was not a permanent solution. Meanwhile, nothing had been settled about the future of slavery. Reflecting on this failure, John Quincy Adams wrote in his diary,

> I have favored this Missouri compromise, believing it to be all that could be effected [accomplished] under the present Constitution, and from extreme unwillingness to put the Union at hazard [risk] . . . If the Union must be dissolved, slavery is precisely the question on which it ought to break. For the present however, the contest is laid asleep.
>
> —John Quincy Adams, 1820

Two Ways of Life: The North and the South The dispute between North and South over Missouri was more than a battle over slavery. It was a conflict over different ways of life. **Sectionalism,** or a strong attachment to regional interests, had become a major issue in American politics.

By midcentury, the North was becoming increasingly **urban,** as people migrated from farms to cities in search of economic opportunities. In the Northeast, between 1800 and 1860, the percentage of the population living in cities grew from 9 to 35 percent. Some cities grew very fast. The population of New York City, for example, soared during that time from 60,000 to more than 800,000. Waves of immigration, mostly from Ireland and Germany, helped swell populations.

In contrast, the South was still predominantly rural in 1860. Most of the population lived on small farms or large plantations scattered across the countryside. The largest Southern city, New Orleans, had a population of only 169,000 people.

The Missouri Compromise put the slavery issue to rest for a time. But it also allowed the buying and selling of human beings, as shown here, to continue in half of the states. As a result, the number of enslaved African Americans more than doubled after 1820, reaching almost 4 million by 1860.

The economies of the two regions were also different. Although agriculture was still a significant part of the North's economy, workshops, factories, and mills also churned out large amounts of manufactured goods. Most of the immigrants entering the country in the 1840s and 1850s settled in the North because that was where the jobs were.

A growing network of canals and railroad lines in the North helped carry the products of mills and factories to customers. By 1860, more than 20,000 miles of rail lines crisscrossed the northern half of the country. These lines connected the cities and factories of the Northeast with the farming regions of the Midwest. In contrast, the South invested much less in transportation and had only half as many rail lines. Instead, it relied on rivers for transportation.

Unlike the North, the South had little industry in 1860. Its economy continued to be based on the export of agricultural products. Rice, corn, and cotton all grew well in the South, with cotton being the most important of the three crops. Some white Southerners owned large plantations worked by large numbers of slaves. But most were small farmers who depended on family members for labor. Only one in four Southern households owned slaves.

Still, plantation agriculture and slave labor formed the basis of the Southern economy. Without slavery, the plantation system would collapse, causing great economic harm to the South. For that reason, most Southerners saw abolitionism as a threat to their economy and way of life.

This map reveals differences in the economies of the North and South in 1860. Although farming was still the main activity in both regions, trade and industry were growing rapidly in the North. In contrast, the economy of the South was dependent on the export of rice, corn, and cotton.

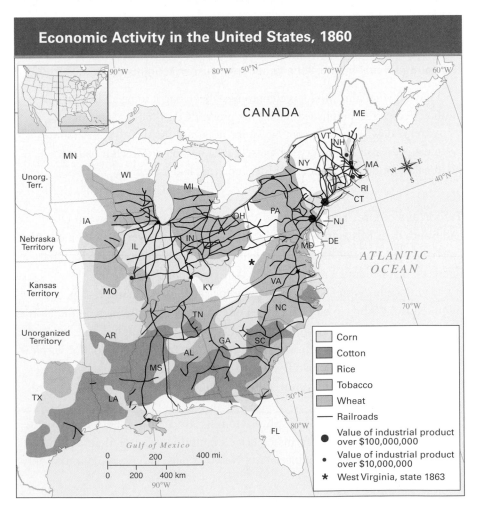

Economic Activity in the United States, 1860

Corn
Cotton
Rice
Tobacco
Wheat
— Railroads
● Value of industrial product over $100,000,000
• Value of industrial product over $10,000,000
★ West Virginia, state 1863

9.3 The Ongoing Debate over Slavery: 1850–1856

It was 1850, and Senator Henry Clay of Kentucky was once again trying to save the Union. Clay was one of the country's leading statesmen, spending much of his political career trying to mend sectional differences. His efforts to win passage of the Missouri Compromise in 1820 had earned him the title "The Great Compromiser." Now, 30 years later, North and South were once again on the brink of dividing the Union over the issue of slavery. The elderly Clay was tired and ill, but he would make one last effort to hold the country together.

The Growing Divide over Slavery In both the North and the South, people had mixed views on slavery. Many moderates in the North accepted slavery where it already existed. They did, however, object to extending slavery into new territories and states, an opinion known as the Free-Soil position.

More radical abolitionists wanted to end slavery everywhere. Until that happened, many stood ready to help slaves liberate themselves. They did so by establishing a network of secret escape routes and safe houses for runaways that became known as the Underground Railroad. An escaped slave-turned-abolitionist named Harriet Tubman was the best-known "conductor" on the Underground Railroad. Tubman risked her life many times by returning to the South to guide slaves to freedom in the North.

In the South, moderates saw slavery as a necessary evil that would eventually die out as more and more slaves were freed. Southern radicals, however, held that slaves were property and that limiting the expansion of slavery into new territories deprived Southerners of their property rights.

Territorial expansion became the flash point in the ongoing debate over slavery. Just how divided the country was became clear in 1846, when President James K. Polk asked Congress for money to negotiate with Mexico for the acquisition of California. David Wilmot, a representative from Pennsylvania, attached an amendment to the funding bill known as the Wilmot Proviso. The amendment would have banned slavery from any territory that the United States might acquire. Wilmot's objective, he said, was "to preserve for free white labor a fair country." The Wilmot Proviso passed several times in the House, which had a majority from the North. Its passage was blocked, however, in the Senate, where the South had more senators—and thus, more power.

The debate over the expansion of slavery was renewed after the United States acquired vast lands in the Southwest in its war with Mexico. Moderates in both the North and the South proposed settling these new territories on the basis of **popular sovereignty,** or rule by the people. This meant allowing voters in the territories to decide whether to permit slavery. But popular sovereignty did not address the problem of keeping a balance of power in Congress if and when these territories became states.

This problem came front and center when California applied for admission to the Union as a free state in 1849. California's entry as a free state would tip the balance of power toward the North. Of course, Northerners welcomed this idea, while Southerners strongly opposed it. Congress was deadlocked again, and some Southerners spoke of withdrawing from the Union.

Born into slavery, Harriet Tubman escaped to Philadelphia in 1849 via the Underground Railroad. She made her first trip back to the South to help others escape just after the Fugitive Slave Law made it a federal crime to help runaway slaves. She made 19 rescue trips during the 1850s, never losing a fugitive. At one time, rewards for her capture totaled about $40,000.

The Compromise of 1850 allowed California to enter the Union as a free state. The rest of the Southwest was left open to slavery, depending on a vote of the people who settled there. This compromise held the country together for a time, but it did not satisfy either side in the slavery dispute.

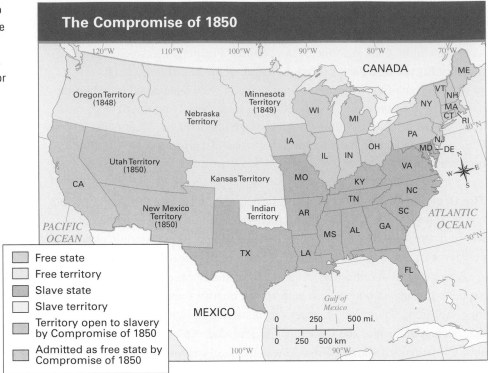

The Compromise of 1850

Free state
Free territory
Slave state
Slave territory
Territory open to slavery by Compromise of 1850
Admitted as free state by Compromise of 1850

A Compromise with Something for Everyone At this point, Henry Clay stepped forward with a plan known as the **Compromise of 1850**. Clay's plan had something for everyone. It admitted California into the Union as a free state, which pleased the North. It divided the rest of the Southwest into two territories—New Mexico and Utah—and opened both to slavery, which pleased the South. It ended the slave trade in Washington, D.C., but allowed existing slaveholders there to keep their slaves, making both sides happy.

The Compromise of 1850 also included a strong **Fugitive Slave Law**. The new law required the return of escaped slaves to their owners, something slaveholders had been demanding for years. "All good citizens," it added, "are hereby commanded to aid and assist in the prompt and efficient execution of this law." Those who did not could be fined or jailed.

To get his plan through Congress, Clay persuaded Senator Daniel Webster of Massachusetts to lend his support. Webster opposed slavery, but he agreed to support Clay's compromise in an effort to end the crisis. In a speech before Congress, Webster urged his fellow senators to unite for the good of the nation. "I wish to speak today, not as a Massachusetts man, nor as a Northern man, but as an American," he said. "I speak today for the preservation of the Union." The debate went on for months, but Congress finally approved Clay's compromise.

The Compromise Satisfies No One Clay and Webster hoped the Compromise of 1850 would placate both sides and help ease tensions over slavery. Instead, the compromise pleased almost no one. The Fugitive Slave Law caused particular friction. The law allowed Southern "slave catchers" to come north to retrieve escaped slaves and required Northerners to come to the aid of these slave catchers or face fines, even imprisonment. Many Northerners felt the law was immoral and refused to obey it. Their resistance outraged Southerners.

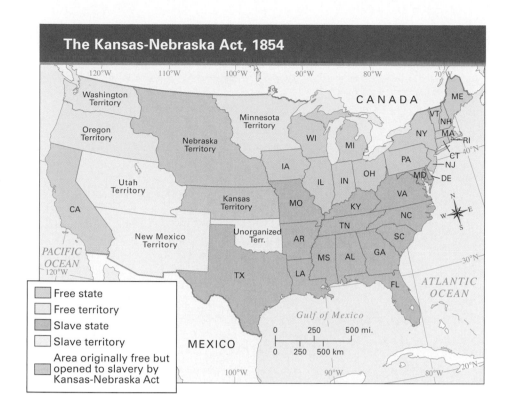

The Kansas-Nebraska Act, 1854

Free state
Free territory
Slave state
Slave territory
Area originally free but opened to slavery by Kansas-Nebraska Act

The Kansas-Nebraska Act overturned the Missouri Compromise by organizing Kansas and Nebraska territories on the basis of popular sovereignty. The law angered Free-Soilers in the North, who feared that slavery would soon spread across the Great Plains.

Friction between the sections was further intensified by publication in 1852 of *Uncle Tom's Cabin*. In this best-selling novel, Harriet Beecher Stowe described the cruelties of slavery through the story of a dignified slave named Uncle Tom. The novel describes Tom's experiences with three slaveholders. Two of them treat Tom kindly. The third, Simon Legree, abuses Tom and has Tom beaten to death for refusing to tell where two escaped slaves are hiding.

Stowe hoped her novel would help bring slavery to a quick and peaceful end. Instead, the book increased the hostility of many Northerners toward the South. Southerners, in turn, saw Stowe's description of slavery as both inaccurate and an insult to their way of life.

Let the People Decide: The Kansas-Nebraska Act In 1854, another act of Congress set the North and the South on a collision course. That year, Senator Stephen Douglas of Illinois introduced a bill to organize the Great Plains for settlement. Because this area lay north of the Missouri Compromise line, the bill did not mention slavery. Southerners in Congress agreed to vote for the bill if the two new territories—Kansas and Nebraska—were organized on the basis of popular sovereignty. With Southern support, the **Kansas-Nebraska Act** made it through Congress. "The true intent and meaning of this act," it said, was "not to legislate slavery into any Territory or State, nor to exclude it therefrom."

The Kansas-Nebraska Act dismayed many Northerners. They thought the Missouri Compromise had put most of the Great Plains off-limits to slavery. Now they feared slavery would spread like a plague across the country. To prevent that from happening, antislavery activists and settlers, or Free-Soilers, united to form a new political party in 1854. The new **Republican Party** took a firm stand against the Fugitive Slave Law and the Kansas-Nebraska Act.

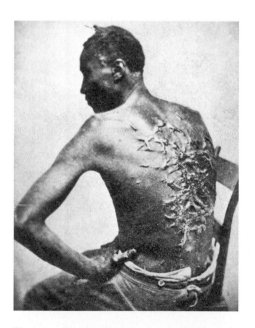

Photographs, like this one of a cruelly treated slave, added fuel to the fire lit by *Uncle Tom's Cabin*. As Northerners became more aware of the inhumanity of slavery, many refused to cooperate with the Fugitive Slave Law. Some Northern states even passed personal liberty laws, which prohibited state and local officers from cooperating with slave catchers.

In an attempt to keep Kansas "free soil," John Brown led a group of antislavery enthusiasts to wreak havoc in proslavery towns across the state. During the settlement of Kansas, supporters and opponents of slavery came into deadly conflict. Newspapers called their violent struggle "Bleeding Kansas." Kansas finally joined the Union as a free state in 1861.

Kansas Becomes a Battleground over Slavery By 1855, settlers were pouring into Kansas. Most were peaceful farmers seeking good land to farm. But the territory also attracted **agitators,** or protesters, who wanted to influence the vote on slavery. Abolition societies in the North sent in Free-Soilers, while groups in the South recruited proslavery settlers to occupy Kansas.

It was not long before these two opposing groups came into conflict. From Missouri, armed agitators called "border ruffians" crossed into Kansas and threatened the Free-Soilers. On May 21, 1856, proslavery forces raided the Free-Soil town of Lawrence, Kansas. They burned buildings, looted stores, and destroyed two printing presses. Northern newspapers called the border ruffians' rampage the "Sack of Lawrence."

Antislavery activists led by John Brown met violence with violence. Brown was an antislavery zealot who had dedicated his life to ending slavery by any means necessary. He urged his followers to "fight fire with fire" and "strike terror in the hearts of the proslavery people." Two days after the Lawrence raid, Brown and seven of his supporters attacked the proslavery town of Pottawatomie. They dragged five men out of their homes and killed them with their swords.

Brown's massacre prompted still more bloodshed in Kansas, as proslavery and antislavery forces battled for control of the territory. But the violence was not restricted to Kansas. It was also infecting the nation's capital. The day after the Lawrence raid, Preston Brooks attacked and beat Charles Sumner on the Senate floor. Despite efforts at compromise, the struggle over slavery was getting more violent.

9.4 From Compromise to Crisis: 1857–1861

Like many slaves, Dred Scott and his wife, Harriet, wanted their freedom. But rather than run away, they tried to win it legally. In 1846, they sued for their freedom in a St. Louis, Missouri, court. The Scotts had lived with their owner for several years in the free territory of Wisconsin. They based their suit on the argument that living in a free territory had made them free people. What began as a simple lawsuit led to one of the most notorious Supreme Court decisions in the history of the nation.

Missouri slave Dred Scott, pictured above beside his wife, Harriet, sued for his freedom by arguing that having lived with his owner in free territory, he should be a free man. The case was decided by the Supreme Court in 1857. By a majority of 7–2, the Court ruled that Scott could not bring a suit in a federal court because African Americans were not U.S. citizens. Shortly after this decision, Scott was sold. His new owner gave him the freedom the Court had denied.

The Dred Scott Decision Outrages the North In 1856, the case of *Scott v. Sandford* reached the Supreme Court. The Court, led by Chief Justice Roger Taney, faced two key questions. First, did slaves have the right to bring a case before a federal court? Second, did the Scott's stay in Wisconsin make them free? Taney, however, saw in this case the opportunity to resolve the slavery issue once and for all. He asked the Court to consider two additional questions. Did Congress have the power to make laws concerning slavery in the territories? If so, was the Missouri Compromise a constitutional use of that power?

The Court issued the **Dred Scott decision** in 1857. It began by reviewing the Declaration of Independence's words that "all men are created equal." Writing for majority, Taney said,

> The general words . . . seem to embrace the whole human family . . . But it is too clear for dispute, that the enslaved African race were not intended to be included, and formed no part of the people who framed and adopted this declaration.
>
> —Chief Justice Roger Taney, *Scott v. Sandford,* 1857

To this Taney added, "Dred Scott was not a citizen of Missouri within the meaning of the Constitution . . . and [is] not entitled as such to sue in its courts."

The Court also rejected the idea that Scott's stay in Wisconsin had made him a free man. Taney reasoned that giving Scott his freedom would be like taking property from his owner. The Fifth Amendment to the Constitution protects private property. Thus, the Missouri Compromise was unconstitutional by establishing territories "which prohibited a citizen from holding or owning property of this kind."

The ruling struck the nation like a bombshell. Southerners were thrilled. They believed the Court had settled the slavery question in their favor. Northerners were stunned. The Court's decision had invalidated the whole idea of "free soil" and opened all territories to slavery. "The decision," wrote a New York newspaper, "is the moral assassination of a race and cannot be obeyed."

John Brown's Raid on Harpers Ferry Shocks the South The Dred Scott decision helped convince radical abolitionists like John Brown that slavery would never be ended by legal means. In 1859, Brown decided to try a different approach—he provoked an armed uprising of slaves to free themselves.

With 21 other men, Brown seized the federal **arsenal** at Harpers Ferry, Virginia. An arsenal is a place where guns and ammunition are stored. Brown intended to distribute the weapons to slaves in the area and spark a slave revolt.

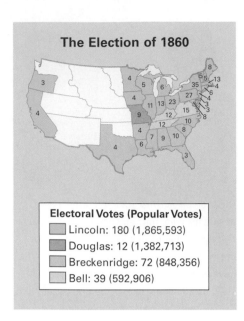

The Election of 1860

Electoral Votes (Popular Votes)
- Lincoln: 180 (1,865,593)
- Douglas: 12 (1,382,713)
- Breckenridge: 72 (848,356)
- Bell: 39 (592,906)

In the presidential election of 1860, the country was divided along party lines. Lincoln and the Republicans took the Northern states and the far west. The Southern Democrats took most of the South. Lincoln won in the electoral college with less than 40 percent of the popular vote.

The Civil War began on April 12, 1861, when Southern troops opened fire on Fort Sumter. After 34 hours of shelling, Major Robert Anderson sent a telegram to Lincoln's secretary of war, announcing the surrender of the fort. The Union troops left, he reported, "with colors flying and drums beating."

Brown's plan was thwarted when federal troops stormed the arsenal and captured him and his men. Brown was tried for treason, convicted, and executed. Even so, **John Brown's raid** on Harper's Ferry shocked the South and prompted widespread fears of a slave rebellion. Most Southerners saw Brown as a lunatic whose extreme views were representative of the antislavery movement.

Many Northerners, on the other hand, saw Brown as a hero and martyr to the cause of abolition. Poet and philosopher Ralph Waldo Emerson declared that Brown would make the gallows "as glorious as a cross." When the Civil War began a few months later, Union troops marched into battle singing, "John Brown's body lies a-mouldering in the grave, His soul goes marching on."

The Election of 1860 Splits the Nation The presidential election of 1860 drove a final wedge between North and South. Sectional strains had split the Democratic Party into northern and southern **factions,** or competing groups. Northern Democrats nominated Stephen Douglas of Illinois and backed popular sovereignty in the territories. Southern Democrats picked John C. Breckinridge of Kentucky, who wanted slavery to be allowed in all territories. John Bell of Tennessee, who ran as the candidate of the Constitutional Union Party, tried to avoid the divisive issue of slavery.

It was the fourth candidate, however, who polarized the nation. He was Abraham Lincoln, the Republican Party nominee. Lincoln, an Illinois lawyer, was a moderate but firm opponent of slavery who had first gained national attention during a run for the Senate in 1858. In a famous series of debates against his opponent, Stephen Douglas, Lincoln had condemned slavery as "a moral, social, and political wrong."

Lincoln lost the Senate race to Douglas, but his campaign had won him strong antislavery support in the North. This support, as well as the split in the Democratic Party, helped sweep Lincoln to victory in 1860. Lincoln won the presidency with less than 40 percent of the votes, all of them cast in the North. His name did not even appear on the ballot in many Southern states.

Lincoln's victory raised the cry of **secession,** or withdrawal from the Union, in the South. Southerners feared that with a Republican in the White House, Congress would try to abolish slavery. Lincoln tried to calm Southern fears. He said he would not interfere with slavery in the South. He also said he would support enforcement of the Fugitive Slave Law. But he refused to support the

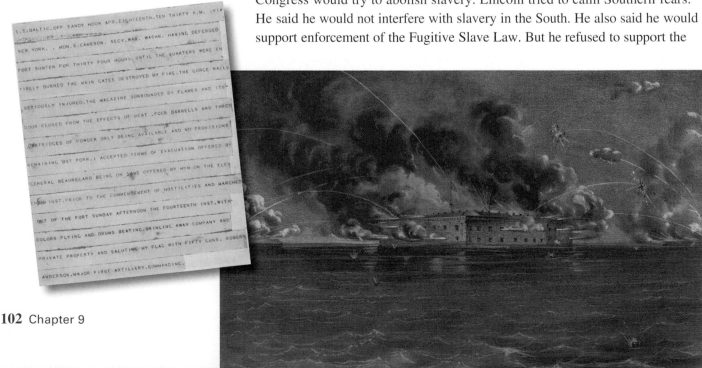

extension of slavery to the western territories. On that question, he said, there could be no compromise.

Secession Spreads Across the South On December 20, 1860, South Carolina seceded from the Union. Over the next several weeks, six more Southern states pulled out. Together they formed the Confederate States of America, with Jefferson Davis as president.

Lincoln was sworn into office as the nation's 16th president on March 4, 1861. In his inaugural address, President Lincoln declared that secession was both wrong and unconstitutional. He added that he had no legal right to interfere with slavery in the states where it existed, but he expressed his determination to keep the Union together. He appealed to the rebellious states to return. "In your hands, my fellow dissatisfied countrymen, and not in mine," he said, "is the momentous issue of civil war."

On April 12, 1861, Southern forces opened fire on **Fort Sumter**, a federal fort in Charleston harbor. After a day and a half of bombardment, the troops in the fort surrendered. The attack on Fort Sumter provoked fury in the North. "There is no more thought of bribing or coaxing the traitors who have dared to aim their cannon balls at the flag of the Union," wrote one newspaper. There could be no more compromise. The Civil War had begun.

Summary

In the mid-1800s, the United States was deeply divided over slavery. By 1860, a series of events had widened this gulf to the breaking point. The election of Abraham Lincoln as president that year triggered a secession crisis that led to the Civil War.

Missouri Compromise This 1820 compromise banned slavery from much of the Louisiana Territory while maintaining the balance of power between slave and free states in the Senate.

Compromise of 1850 Henry Clay hoped this compromise on slavery in the West would please everyone. But its inclusion of the Fugitive Slave Law deeply angered many Northerners.

Uncle Tom's Cabin This best-selling novel touched the hearts of Northerners with its story of a kind slave who was mistreated by a brutal owner, turning many against slavery.

Kansas-Nebraska Act This 1854 act opened Kansas and Nebraska to settlement under the banner of popular sovereignty. Kansas erupted in violence as proslavery and antislavery settlers battled for control of the territory.

Republican Party Antislavery activists and Free-Soilers came together in 1854 to form the Republican Party, which was committed to stopping the spread of slavery.

Dred Scott decision This 1858 Supreme Court decision denied citizenship to African Americans and opened all western territories to slavery. Northerners were appalled and Southerners pleased.

Election of 1860 Republican candidate Abraham Lincoln won election in 1860 with a minority of the popular votes. Fearing that Republicans would try to interfere with slavery, several slave states seceded. On April 10, 1861, Southern forces attacked Fort Sumter, beginning the Civil War.

Chapter 10

The Civil War

How did the Civil War affect the United States and its people?

10.1 Introduction

Wilmer McLean was about to sit down to lunch with a group of Confederate officers on July 18, 1861, when a cannonball ripped through his roof. It landed in the stewpot, scattering stew all over the kitchen.

This was more than McLean had bargained for when he moved his family to a farm in the country. McLean had been a prosperous merchant in Alexandria, Virginia, just outside Washington, D.C. When he retired, he decided to move to the countryside for some peace and quiet. He bought a farm outside the small village of Manassas Junction, Virginia. The farm was comfortable and pleasant, with fields, woods, and a small stream called Bull Run. Unfortunately for McLean, Manassas was also the site of an important railroad junction. These rail lines made Manassas a strategic location in the Civil War—one that both the North and the South wanted to control.

Since the shelling of Fort Sumter in April 1861, the North and the South had been in a state of war. However, there had been no major combat since that first engagement. Then, in mid-July, the two opposing armies gathered their forces near McLean's farm.

Three days after the cannonball landed in McLean's kitchen, the First Battle of Bull Run began. The fighting raged across McLean's land for hours, but by afternoon, the Union forces were in full retreat. In the Union army, this embarrassing flight would be remembered as "the great skedaddle." A year later, another battle took place on McLean's farm. At that point, McLean decided to leave Manassas and find a safer place to live.

The McLean family relocated to the south in a small Virginian town called Appomattox Court House. McLean hoped that the town's remote location would keep the war away from his doorstep. But as you will read later in this chapter, he did not get his wish. Wilmer McLean had one more important role to play in the Civil War.

The First Battle of Bull Run, shown here, was the first major conflict of the Civil War. The battle was fought on Wilmer McLean's farm in Manassas Junction, Virginia. Interestingly, McLean's next home, in Appomattox Court House, Virginia, would play a key role at the end of the war.

◀ Confederate soldiers before the First Battle of Bull Run in 1861

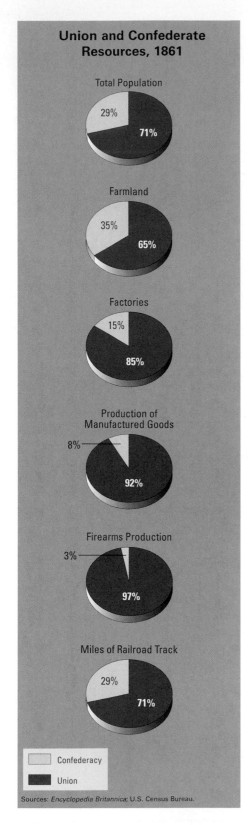

Union and Confederate Resources, 1861

Total Population

29%
71%

Farmland

35%
65%

Factories

15%
85%

Production of Manufactured Goods

8%
92%

Firearms Production

3%
97%

Miles of Railroad Track

29%
71%

☐ Confederacy
■ Union

Sources: *Encyclopedia Britannica*; U.S. Census Bureau.

When the Civil War began, the Union had clear advantages over the Confederacy in terms of resources. In a short war, these advantages might not have mattered. In a long war, they would prove decisive.

10.2 Four Long Years of War

At the time of the Confederate attack on Fort Sumter in April 1861, seven states had seceded from the Union. In the months that followed, the eight slave states in the Upper South faced a difficult decision—to secede or not. Finally, four of them—Maryland, Delaware, Kentucky, and Missouri—remained in the Union, but not without serious reservations. The country, now formally divided between the Union and the Confederacy, braced for war.

The Advantages of the Union and the Confederacy As the war began, both sides were confident of a quick victory. Northerners were certain they could overwhelm the South with their superior resources. Not only did the Union have more than twice as many people than the South, but it also had a much more diverse economy. The North outstripped the South in farm production, factories, naval force, and railroad lines, which were crucial for moving troops and supplies.

Yet Southerners were optimistic. They had the advantage of fighting a defensive war on their own soil, as well as outstanding military leadership. All they had to do to win was push back invading Union forces. Before long, they believed, the Union would tire of battle and leave the Confederacy in peace.

Believing their cause was just, volunteers on both sides rushed to enlist. The 70,000 new troops that marched into battle on Wilmer McLean's farm in 1861 were certain the other side would collapse at the first whiff of gunpowder. The realities of the First Battle of Bull Run, however, destroyed such illusions. Although the South won the day, their victory did not come easily. For the North, the defeat at Bull Run was a harsh wake-up call.

The Anaconda Plan Begins to Squeeze the Confederacy After Bull Run, President Abraham Lincoln realized he had to plan for a long war. With General Winfield Scott, he devised a strategy that came to be known as the Anaconda Plan. As the name suggests, the idea was to surround the South and squeeze it to death, like an anaconda snake crushing its prey.

To accomplish this goal, the Union planned to set up a **naval blockade**— a line of ships stopping sea traffic in and out of Southern ports. The blockade would keep the South from trading its cotton in Europe for the war supplies it needed. Next, the Union navy would take control of the Mississippi River, separating Texas, Louisiana, and Arkansas from the rest of the South. From there, the Union army would move east to squeeze the life out of the Deep South. Finally, Union forces would invade Virginia and lop off the enemy's head, in this case the Confederate capital of Richmond.

The Union enjoyed early success with the first two steps in the plan. The navy blockaded Southern ports and stopped most trade. It also seized New Orleans and began to move up the Mississippi River. At the same time, Union forces commanded by General Ulysses S. Grant fought their way south toward the Mississippi. Along the way, Grant won decisive battles that brought much of Tennessee under Union control.

Not everything went the North's way, however. The Union navy's push up the Mississippi was blocked at Vicksburg, a key city on the river. Union armies also failed to take Richmond, despite a major offensive in the summer of 1862. The Confederate capital remained safe from Union forces for two more years.

Antietam: The Bloodiest Day of the War After Union forces failed to capture Richmond, the South tried to turn the tables on the North. The top Confederate general, Robert E. Lee, decided to invade Union territory by crossing into Maryland. He hoped this show of strength would persuade Maryland to join the Confederacy. He also hoped that major victories on Union soil would encourage Great Britain and France to give aid to the Confederacy.

After crossing the Potomac River, Lee's army clashed with Union forces on September 17, 1862, at Antietam Creek, near Sharpsburg, Maryland. The Battle of Antietam was the bloodiest one-day battle in American history, with more than 20,000 soldiers killed or wounded. One soldier recalled, "I have never in my soldier['s] life seen such a sight. The dead and wounded covered the ground." Despite the enormous human cost, the battle ended in a stalemate, and Lee retreated back across the Potomac into Virginia.

Although the Battle of Antietam was not decisive, it was a turning point in the war. Not only had Lee's invasion of the North failed, but he had also lost a quarter of his army in the effort. European countries remained reluctant to recognize or assist the Confederacy. Furthermore, Lee's failure gave Lincoln the chance to take a step that would change the course of the war.

The Emancipation Proclamation Changes Union War Aims Although Lincoln opposed slavery, he refused at first to make abolition a war aim. "My paramount object in this struggle is to save the Union," he wrote, "and is not either to save or destroy slavery." But as the war dragged on, Lincoln decided that tying the war effort to **emancipation**—freeing the slaves—made sense.

Calling for the end of slavery, Lincoln knew, would link the war to a moral cause in the North. It would also win support in Europe, where opposition to slavery was strong. Freeing the slaves could also deprive the South of part of its workforce. In fact, since the start of the war, thousands of slaves had freed themselves by running away to the Union lines. News of these runaways may have influenced Lincoln's decision to call for the emancipation of all slaves.

A few days after Antietam, Lincoln issued a warning to the Confederate states: Return to the Union by January 1, 1863, or he would free their slaves. The Confederacy ignored the warning, and on January 1, Lincoln signed the **Emancipation Proclamation,** which declared all slaves living in states "in rebellion against the United States" to be "thenceforward, and forever free." Slaves living in areas loyal to or under Union control were not affected.

The Emancipation Proclamation had little immediate effect, because the Confederacy ignored it. Nevertheless, it gave the Union a great moral purpose and signified that a Union victory would mean the end of slavery.

The one-day Battle of Antietam in September 1862 was the bloodiest single day of the Civil War. Civil War photographer Mathew Brady shocked Americans by displaying photographs of battlefield corpses in his New York gallery. *The New York Times* wrote that Brady had brought "home to us the terrible reality and earnestness of war."

The Battle of Gettysburg was the deadliest conflict of the Civil War. It climaxed with Pickett's Charge, a Confederate assault on Union forces dug in on Cemetery Ridge. The Confederates suffered heavy losses and were forced to retreat. Today, Gettysburg National Military Park and the Gettysburg National Cemetery attract more than a million tourists each year.

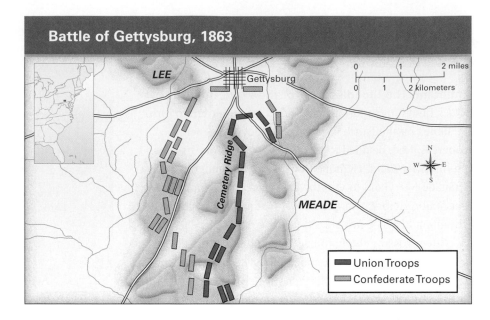

Battle of Gettysburg, 1863

LEE

Gettysburg

Cemetery Ridge

MEADE

0   1   2 miles
0   1   2 kilometers

■ Union Troops
▢ Confederate Troops

Turning the Tide: Vicksburg and Gettysburg To hasten that victory, General Grant continued to battle his way toward the Mississippi River. In May 1863, he arrived at the Confederate stronghold of Vicksburg, Mississippi, and settled in for a long siege. For six weeks, his troops shelled the city from one side, while Union gunboats battered it from the other. The Confederates dug caves into the hillsides and tried to ride it out. But eventually, they gave in. On July 4, the Confederate army at Vicksburg surrendered, and the Union finally gained control of the Mississippi.

Meanwhile, another great battle was underway in the village of Gettysburg, Pennsylvania. It began when General Lee invaded the North a second time. On July 1, 1863, his army of approximately 75,000 troops met a Union force of about 95,000 just west of the town. The Battle of Gettysburg lasted for three terrible days. At first, Lee's troops held their position, but on July 3, they suffered devastating losses and were forced to retreat. More than 50,000 soldiers were killed or wounded. Having lost a third of his army, Lee would not attack the North again but would fight a defensive war only. For the North, this victory marked a major turning point in the war.

Several months later, President Lincoln visited Gettysburg. There he gave one of the most stirring speeches in American history, the Gettysburg Address. Lincoln noted that the war was testing whether a nation "conceived in liberty, and dedicated to the proposition that 'all men are created equal' . . . can long endure." He then declared that the nation would endure and that out of war would come a "new birth of freedom."

Total War Forces the South to Surrender After the defeats at Gettysburg and Vicksburg, Southerners continued to defend their land fiercely, despite dwindling resources. To force a Confederate surrender, General Grant adopted a policy known as **total war,** which called for doing whatever was necessary to undermine the enemy's willingness or capacity to fight. To implement this policy, Grant adopted a two-pronged strategy. He would lead his forces into Virginia to engage Lee's army and take the Confederate capital of Richmond.

Meanwhile, another Union general, William Tecumseh Sherman, would wage a campaign of destruction through Georgia and the Carolinas.

Sherman was a battle-hardened veteran who believed in total war. "We cannot change the hearts of these people of the South," he said, "but we can make war so terrible . . . and make them so sick of war that generations [will] pass away before they again appeal to it." In May 1864, he marched his troops southward from Tennessee with orders to inflict "all the damage you can."

In September, Sherman captured Atlanta and burned much of it to the ground. He then continued toward the coast. During **Sherman's March to the Sea,** his troops destroyed everything they found of value. They looted houses, burned fields, and killed livestock. After taking the port city of Savannah, Georgia, Sherman turned north and swept through the Carolinas.

While Sherman waged total war, Grant and Lee were locked in fierce combat in Virginia. Despite heavy losses, Grant continued on toward Richmond. On April 3, 1865, he captured the capital. With his army surrounded, Lee was finally forced to surrender.

On April 9, Lee and Grant met at the village of Appomattox Court House. Oddly enough, their meeting took place in the house of Wilmer McLean, the same man whose farm in Manassas had been the site of the first real battle of the war. As McLean later said, "The war started in my front yard and ended in my parlor." The terms of surrender Grant offered Lee were generous. Confederate officers could keep their weapons. Any officers or troops who claimed their own horses could keep them. Most important, "Each officer and man will be allowed to return to his home, not to be disturbed by the United States authorities." At long last, the Civil War was over.

In 1864, General William Tecumseh Sherman waged total war on the South in an effort to bring the Confederacy to its knees. During his infamous March to the Sea through Georgia, his troops burned farms and towns, leaving a path of destruction 60 miles wide. When criticized for his actions, Sherman replied, "War is cruelty, and you cannot refine it."

Sherman's March to the Sea, 1864

10.3 Challenges Facing Government Leaders

While the war raged, leaders in both the Union and the Confederacy faced enormous challenges. Not only did they have to mount a huge military effort, but they also had to find ways to pay for a long war. In addition, they had to shore up public support for an increasingly unpopular struggle.

Lincoln's Balancing Act President Lincoln was elected in 1860 without getting a majority of the popular vote. Because his base of support was so thin, he faced daunting political problems as he tried to hold the Union together. His every move was criticized by political opponents and an often-hostile press.

Early in the war, one of Lincoln's top priorities was to keep the border states of Maryland, Delaware, Kentucky, and Missouri in the Union. Maryland, in particular, was crucial, because it surrounded Washington, D.C., on three sides. At the start of the war, pro-secession mobs attacked a Union regiment as it passed through Baltimore. Lincoln sent in troops and suspended the constitutional right of **habeas corpus**—the right of a person to appear in court so a judge can determine whether the person is being imprisoned lawfully. Suspending this right allowed the Union to jail suspected opponents without charge and to hold them indefinitely. Lincoln's policy was harsh, but he saw it as necessary to keep Maryland and neighboring Delaware from seceding.

The question of emancipation posed even more challenges for Lincoln. Although abolitionists pressured him to end slavery immediately, he resisted for fear of alienating the border states or angering those in the Union who did not support abolition. After it became apparent to him that emancipation was necessary, he waited until he could make his announcement from a position of strength. Even then, he made sure that his proclamation did not cover slaves in states loyal to the Union. Although that decision upset the abolitionists, they still regarded the Emancipation Proclamation as a major step forward.

As the war dragged on, Lincoln faced other difficulties. One was finding enough men to fight. Lacking sufficient volunteers, Congress enacted a **military draft** in 1863. The draft law required all white men between the ages of 20 and 45 to report for military duty. However, the law had loopholes. For $300, a man who did not want to serve could buy his way out of the draft, or he could hire a replacement to serve in his place. This meant that affluent Northerners could avoid service, while the poor went off to war.

Anger over the new law triggered rioting in New York and other cities. Bitter about being drafted to free slaves,

This map shows Union and Confederate states at the outbreak of the Civil War in 1861. Two years later, a new state, West Virginia, was created when part of Virginia split from the Confederacy and joined the Union.

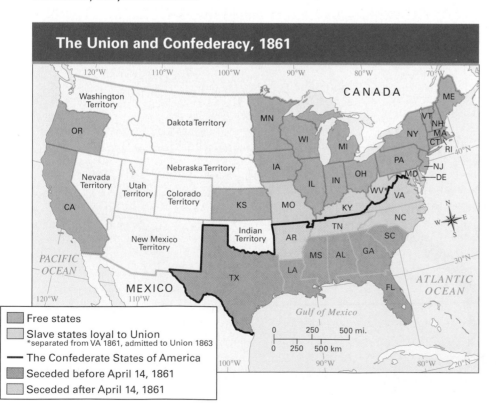

The Union and Confederacy, 1861

Free states

Slave states loyal to Union
*separated from VA 1861, admitted to Union 1863

The Confederate States of America

Seceded before April 14, 1861

Seceded after April 14, 1861

the New York City rioters directed their rage at African Americans. Estimates of casualties in the New York City **draft riots** ran as high as 1,000 killed and wounded.

President Lincoln also faced the challenge of leading a Union that was far from united. One wing of the Democratic Party did not believe the cost of the war—in lives, money, and civil liberties—was justified. These Democrats also did not see emancipation as a worthy war objective. Republicans nicknamed these critics **Copperheads,** after a poisonous snake. "Every victory of the government they lament as a defeat of their party," wrote a Philadelphia observer. "In every success of the rebels they see a party victory and hail it with triumph."

Challenges for Southern Leaders Confederate president Jefferson Davis also faced challenges in raising an army. In 1862, the South had passed America's first draft law. Like the Northern version that came later, this law included a loophole that allowed rich plantation owners to avoid military service. This issue prompted complaints of it being a "rich man's war but a poor man's fight." Some Southern states tried to evade the law, calling it an assault on states' rights.

The main challenge for Davis and other Confederate leaders, however, was figuring out how to pay for the war while keeping the Southern economy afloat. Prior to the war, the South had relied on cotton sales for most of its income. Much of that cotton was shipped to Europe, especially to Great Britain, where it played a key role in the textile industry. When the war began, the South placed an **embargo** on cotton exports in an attempt to force Great Britain and other European countries to recognize the Confederacy and assist it with arms and money. But Southern leaders failed to realize that Great Britain already had a surplus of cotton and was developing new sources of supply. Thus, the cotton embargo failed to prompt European action, and the South lost valuable export income.

Without income from cotton sales, the South could not import the goods it needed to fight a long war. That problem was exacerbated by the Union naval blockade. Shortages of goods soon led to rising prices. Between 1860 and 1863, food prices in the South rose by more than 1,000 percent. Bacon went from 12 cents a pound to $1.50 and butter from 23 cents a pound to $3.00. With their purchasing power eroding day by day, Southerners lost faith in the Confederate currency. "An oak leaf," said a Georgian in 1863, "will be worth just as much as the promise of the Confederate treasury to pay one dollar."

As these economic problems hit home, Southerners began to show signs of discontent. They complained about high prices and a lack of food for the poor. They also accused wealthy Southerners of hoarding goods. At times, their anger erupted into violence.

In April 1863, a **bread riot** broke out in Richmond, Virginia. Hundreds of women rampaged through downtown, breaking windows and stealing food, shoes, and other goods. According to one account, President Davis confronted the women. "You say you are hungry and have no money," he said. "Here is all I have." He dug into his pockets and flung coins into the crowd. Then he threatened to have troops open fire if the rioters did not leave. The women went home, but other similar riots broke out in towns and cities across the South.

In 1863, draft protests broke out in many Northern cities. The riot in New York City, shown here, was the most violent. The mostly working-class Irish American mob burned buildings and attacked African Americans. Order was finally restored by Union troops, who were rushed to New York from the Battle of Gettysburg.

Angered by food shortages and rising prices, hundreds of women staged a bread riot in Richmond, Virginia, in April 1863. They looted stores and stole food and other goods. By this time, the Southern economy was in dire straits. However, newspapers denied reports of hunger and blamed the riot on criminals.

Medical care was shockingly poor during the Civil War. Doctors did not know what caused infections or how diseases spread. A North Carolina soldier wrote, "These Big Battles is not as Bad as the fever." He was right. More soldiers died of disease than from injuries.

10.4 The Effect of the War on Soldiers

Around 3 million men fought in the Civil War. As many as a third of these soldiers died or were wounded in battle. Even for those who escaped without injury, the war exacted a tremendous cost. Soldiers had to leave their homes and families for up to four years while enduring numerous hardships.

New Weapons Make Battle More Deadly The Civil War was an extremely brutal and destructive conflict. One reason for this was the development of new and deadlier weapons, such as the **rifled musket**. Unlike the old smoothbore musket, this gun had grooves on the inside of the barrel that caused the bullet to spin, allowing it to travel much faster, farther, and with greater accuracy. Improved cannons with explosive shells also allowed armies to unleash a hail of artillery fire on their opponents.

These new weapons were deadly enough, but poor battlefield tactics exacerbated their effects. Instead of spreading troops out to make them difficult to target, generals massed the soldiers together for large frontal assaults on enemy lines. This tactic had worked well enough in previous wars, when guns were less accurate. But in the Civil War, snipers who were dug into defensive positions could mow down a line of charging troops with ease, even at great distances. This mismatch of new weapons with old tactics led to incredibly bloody battles, like the one at Antietam.

Civil War battles were typically chaotic, terrifying events. Fifty years later, a former soldier could still recall the awful sound of battle:

> The screaming and bursting of shells, . . . the death screams of wounded animals, the groans of their human companions, wounded and dying and trampled underfoot by hurrying batteries, riderless horses and the moving lines of battle . . . a perfect hell on earth.
>
> —Unknown Union soldier, describing the Battle of Gettysburg

Battles often took place in open fields. But sometimes, as the following soldier describes, the battles occurred in wooded areas, where the enemy was hard to spot:

> No one could see the fight fifty feet from him. The lines were very near each other, and from the dense underbrush and the tops of trees came puffs of smoke, the "ping" of the bullets and the yell of the enemy. It was a blind and bloody hunt to the death, in bewildering thickets, rather than a battle.
>
> —Unknown Union soldier, describing the Battle of the Wilderness, 1864

Although men on both sides fought with courage, it was the rare soldier who eagerly sought conflict. As one put it, "When bullets are whacking against tree trunks and solid shots are cracking skulls like egg-shells, the consuming passion in the breast of the average man is to get out of the way."

Medical Care on the Battlefield Many soldiers who were wounded in battle died where they fell. Those who were rescued often faced a grim fate in the hands of military doctors. In the 1860s, medical knowledge was quite limited. Doctors did not know how to treat many diseases, nor did they understand the causes of infection and the need for sanitary procedures in surgery.

Battlefield surgeons often worked in clothes covered with blood. They wiped their hands and surgical tools on their jackets or dipped them in dirty water between operations. One of their most common tools was the bone saw, which was used to perform amputations. Because musket balls typically shattered bones on impact, doctors had little recourse but to remove whole limbs, often without anesthesia. Piles of arms, legs, and feet would stack up outside medical tents.

Poor hygiene was another major problem in camp. Soldiers often pitched their tents near open latrines and bathed in the same water that they used for drinking. These practices encouraged the spread of disease. For every soldier who died in battle, an estimated two or three more died of disease from unsanitary conditions in camp.

Keeping Busy Between Battles The life of soldiers was not all about the horrors of war. Most of their time was spent away from combat. On average, for every day of battle, they spent 50 days hanging around the camp. When they were not marching or drilling, the men usually had a lot of time on their hands.

To stay occupied in camp, soldiers on both sides pursued various pastimes. Reading was a common activity. Many soldiers were particularly interested in newspapers from home. Soldiers also wrote letters to their loved ones, played cards, and went swimming. Hunting and fishing were popular, as were sports like baseball and wrestling. Soldiers even performed magic shows, skits, and plays for their campmates. One Confederate production, called "Medical Board," satirized army doctors and their fondness for amputation.

Music played a special part in the lives of soldiers. To raise their spirits before battle, they sang patriotic songs like "The Battle Cry of Freedom" and "Dixie." Most of the time, however, they preferred traditional folk songs and sentimental ballads. They also made up songs about the hardships of war and the tedium of camp life. One mournful song, "Weeping Sad and Lonely," was a favorite among homesick troops on both sides.

> Weeping, sad and lonely,
> Hopes and fears how vain! . . .
> When this cruel war is over,
> Praying that we meet again.
> —Henry Tucker, 1863

When Union and Confederate forces were camped near each other, as sometimes happened, troops from both armies might even join in songs together, their voices echoing across the distance between their camps.

With plenty of time between battles, soldiers passed some of the time playing card games and sports. Baseball was popular among both Confederate and Union troops. Abner Doubleday, the man often credited with inventing baseball in 1839, became a major general in the Union army during the Civil War. He commanded the troops at Fort Sumter when it was first fired on, and he later fought heroically at Gettysburg.

10.5 The Effect of the War on African Americans

Although the war started as a conflict over states' rights and a fight to preserve the Union, at heart it was a struggle over the future of slavery. As former slave and abolitionist leader Frederick Douglass wrote,

> The Negro is the key to the situation, the pivot upon which the whole rebellion turns . . . This war, disguise it as they may, is virtually nothing more or less than perpetual [everlasting] slavery against universal freedom.
>
> —Frederick Douglass, 1861

The Promise of Freedom Stirs African Americans Although the Emancipation Proclamation did not free any slaves when it was issued, it did cause great rejoicing among African Americans in the North. Many saw emancipation as the first step toward gaining equal rights for blacks. One man described the ecstatic response he saw at a public reading of the proclamation in Washington, D.C.:

> Men squealed, women fainted, dogs barked, white and colored people shook hands, songs were sung, and by this time cannons began to fire . . . and follow in the wake of the roar that had . . . been going on behind the White House . . . The President came to the window and made responsive bows, and thousands told him, if he would come out of that palace, they would hug him to death . . . It was indeed a time of times, . . . nothing like it will ever be seen again in this life.
>
> —Henry M. Turner, *The Negro in Slavery, War, and Peace,* 1913

African Americans and the War Effort Even before the Emancipation Proclamation, thousands of slaves had fled to Union lines. Because there was no government policy on the fugitives, Union commanders were left to make their own decisions about what to do with them. Some tried to return fugitives to their former owners or to keep them out of Union camps. Others paid the fugitives wages for noncombat work as cooks, carpenters, guides, and drivers.

Black leaders and abolitionists had favored the idea of African American recruitment since the start of the war. But Lincoln had sidestepped offers by free blacks in the North to raise African American regiments, fearing the effect black troops might have on the border states. Widely held prejudices also played a role in his reluctance to recruit blacks. Many Northerners doubted that African Americans would make good soldiers. Frederick Douglass complained, "Colored men were good enough to fight under Washington, but they are not good enough to fight under [General George] McClellan."

The Union army emancipated many slaves as it moved through the South. Thousands of these freed slaves followed the troops and became a key source of labor for the Union army. But other freedmen stayed behind on abandoned Southern plantations. With their owners gone, they split up the land and established their own farms.

As the war wore on, public opinion began to change. Congress authorized African American recruitment in 1862. The next year, the War Department issued General Order 143, which authorized the "organization of Colored Troops." The most famous black unit was the **54th Massachusetts Regiment,** which played a critical role in winning acceptance for black soldiers. On July 18, 1863, the 54th stormed the Confederate defenses at Fort Wagner, South Carolina. The assault failed, and more than 40 percent of the regiment was killed. But the troops fought valiantly and earned the praise of the nation. One newspaper wrote that without the 54th, "two hundred thousand troops for whom it was a pioneer [first experience] would never have put into the field."

Other black regiments also showed great courage under fire. Several were made up of **freedmen**—freed slaves—in the Union Army, including the 1st South Carolina Volunteers and the 1st and 3rd Louisiana regiments. After seeing the Louisiana troops in battle, one white officer wrote, "You have no idea how my prejudices with regard to negro troops have been dispelled . . . [They] behaved magnificently and fought splendidly . . . They are far superior in discipline to the white troops, and just as brave."

Racism and Discrimination Persist Despite their contributions to the war effort, African Americans still faced racism and hostility. During the New York City draft riots, dozens of African Americans were killed. In the military, black soldiers were usually assigned menial tasks, like digging ditches. They were often given poor weapons and did not receive the same training for battle as did white soldiers. As a result, they suffered higher casualty rates. In addition, black soldiers who were captured in the South faced the risk of being enslaved or executed rather than imprisoned, as white soldiers were.

African American troops were also paid as laborers, not soldiers. While white soldiers earned $13 a month, African Americans were paid just $10. Some black regiments protested by refusing to accept any pay at all. Others took a more militant approach. In November 1863, a company of black soldiers stacked their weapons and refused to pick them up again until they received equal pay. Their leader, a black sergeant named William Walker, was charged with mutiny and executed by firing squad. Finally, in June 1864, Congress agreed to equalize pay for white and black soldiers, including all back pay.

Some 186,000 African Americans served in the Union army and another 10,000 in the navy. Although African Americans made up 1 percent of the North's population, they accounted for nearly 10 percent of the troops. They fought bravely and earned the respect of their white officers. But they were often given the worst jobs, and scarcely 100 of them rose to the rank of officer.

10.6 The Contributions of Women to the War Effort

Women on both sides of the conflict played a vital role in the war effort. One of these women was Clara Barton. When the war began, Barton volunteered for war relief on the Union side. "While our soldiers stand and fight," she said, "I can stand and feed and nurse them." She began by gathering food and other supplies for the troops. Later she became a nurse and cared for hundreds of wounded soldiers. At Antietam, when the field hospital came under artillery attack, she steadied the operating table while the doctor completed his surgery. The doctor later called her "the angel of the battlefield."

Clara Barton was one of thousands of women who served as nurses in the Civil War. Most worked for little pay and under difficult conditions. Barton sometimes brought care to wounded soldiers in the battlefield, even while bullets were still flying. Her wartime experiences led her to found the American Red Cross in 1881.

Rose Greenhow worked as a Confederate spy. She was caught and tossed into prison, along with her daughter "Little Rosie." To Southerners, her treatment was yet more proof of Yankee brutality. Greenhow seemed to relish the role of the martyr who suffers for her beliefs. A fellow prisoner wrote, "Greenhow enjoys herself amazingly."

Women Soldiers and Spies Though women were not allowed in the armed forces, some saw combat on the front lines. As many as 400 women disguised themselves as men and enlisted in the Union and Confederate armies. One woman, "Franklin Thompson" of Michigan, had to desert on her way to a hospital in order to keep her secret.

Other women served behind the lines in the dangerous role of spy. Women made good spies, in part because they were not suspected as quickly as men. If caught, they were also less likely to be punished severely. One of the most famous Confederate spies was Rose Greenhow. A well-connected member of Washington society, she used her contacts to learn about Union troop movements and passed this information along to the Confederate army. Her reports helped the Confederates win the First Battle of Bull Run in 1861. Eventually, Greenhow was discovered, arrested, and banished to the South.

Elizabeth Van Lew, a resident of Richmond, was a successful spy for the Union. She even managed to plant one of her assistants, a former slave named Mary Elizabeth Bowser, as a maid in the home of Jefferson Davis. In that way, Bowser and Van Lew gained access to Confederate war plans. Van Lew managed to divert suspicion and avoid arrest by pretending to be mentally unbalanced. In public, she muttered to herself and looked confused. The locals called her "Crazy Bet," but when Union troops took Richmond in 1865, she dropped the act and was honored as a hero.

Women Provide Medical Care Other women, like reformer Dorothea Dix, played a crucial role by providing medical care to wounded and sick soldiers. Sojourner Truth and Harriet Tubman served as Union nurses as well, dividing their time between medical work and scouting for the Union army. In the end, more than 3,000 women served as nurses to the Union army.

Southern women also worked as nurses, and because almost all of the fighting took place on Southern soil, many turned their homes into medical shelters. After the First Battle of Bull Run, for instance, Sally Tompkins established a hospital in a private home and began caring for wounded Confederate soldiers. Altogether, she treated more than 1,300 men over the course of the war, while registering just 73 deaths. In honor of her achievements, Jefferson Davis made Tompkins a captain in the army. She was the only woman to become an officer in the Confederate army.

Women often had to overcome prejudice in order to serve. At the start of the war, many men viewed caring for wounded soldiers as "unladylike." Others believed the presence of women nurses in hospitals would distract the soldiers or that women would prove too delicate for battlefield conditions.

Women doctors faced even greater obstacles. Surgeon Mary Walker tried but failed to get approval to join the Union army as a doctor. Instead, she volunteered as an assistant surgeon in a Washington hospital. Throughout the war, she worked as a battlefield doctor and later received the congressional Medal of Honor for her services.

Women Hold Down the Home Front With thousands of men fighting in the war, women—black and white—stepped in to perform crucial jobs to support their families and the war effort. They took over family farms and businesses. They also organized aid societies to raise money for war supplies and to collect and distribute food to soldiers.

Northern women had already been a part of the prewar workforce in the textile industry. As the war dragged on, rising demand for military uniforms led to more women working in textile mills and garment factories. Women in the South also made clothes, though most worked at home as private contractors.

The war also provided new job opportunities for women. For the first time, women filled a significant number of government positions. They worked in offices copying documents, for the Treasury Department minting money, and for the postal service. Women also took dangerous jobs in munitions factories, making bullets and artillery shells for the Union and the Confederate armies. Accidents in these factories were common, and many women lost their lives.

Summary

The Civil War lasted four years and cost 620,000 lives. It was by far the most destructive conflict ever waged on American soil.

Anaconda Plan Once it became clear that the war would not be quickly won, President Lincoln prepared for a long conflict with a plan to slowly crush the Confederacy.

Emancipation Proclamation By 1863, Lincoln issued a proclamation freeing all slaves in the rebellious states. However, freedom for most slaves did not come until the end of the war.

Gettysburg Address In his dedication of a cemetery for the men who died in the Battle of Gettysburg, Lincoln reminded the Union that it was fighting to preserve a nation "conceived in liberty and dedicated to the proposition that all men are created equal."

Sherman's March to the Sea The Union won the war in 1865 after General William T. Sherman waged total war across Georgia and General Ulysses S. Grant captured Richmond, Virginia.

Copperheads Both Abraham Lincoln and Jefferson Davis had to deal with opposition groups that did not support their war aims. In the North, Copperheads urged an immediate end to the war. In the South, part of Virginia seceded and joined the Union as West Virginia.

Draft riots and bread riots The leaders of the Union and the Confederacy faced challenges in managing the war effort. In the North, protesters rioted over draft laws. In the South, women protested severe shortages of food and supplies.

54th Massachusetts Regiment African Americans welcomed emancipation and the chance to fight for the Union. Although they showed great courage, blacks continued to suffer from racism and inequality.

Women's service Women made great contributions to the war effort. They collected supplies and served as soldiers, spies, medical personnel, and farm and factory workers.

Chapter 11

Reconstruction

How was the nation's commitment to its founding ideals tested during Reconstruction?

11.1 Introduction

How could a nation torn apart by civil war put itself back together? That was the question facing all Americans in 1865. In his second inaugural address, Abraham Lincoln spoke of healing the wounds on both sides of the conflict:

> With malice [hatred] toward none; with charity for all; with firmness in the right, as God gives us to see the right, let us strive on to finish the work we are in; to bind up the nation's wounds; to care for him who shall have borne the battle, and for his widow and his orphan; to do all which may achieve and cherish a just and lasting peace among ourselves and with all nations.
> —Abraham Lincoln, Second Inaugural Address, March 1865

But Lincoln would not have the chance to put his plan into action. A little more than a month after his inauguration, he was assassinated while attending a play at Ford's Theater in Washington, D.C. Northerners were deeply grieved by his murder. Young Caroline Cowles Richards wrote in her diary, "I have felt sick over it all day and so has every one that I have seen. All seem to feel as though they had lost a personal friend, and tears flow plenteously."

Lincoln's assassin, an actor named John Wilkes Booth, believed he was saving the Confederacy by murdering the president. Although few Southerners rejoiced at Lincoln's death, many Northerners blamed the South for his murder, as well as for the war. They wanted the South punished.

With Lincoln gone, the task of bringing these two sides together fell to his vice president, Andrew Johnson. A large part of healing the nation's wounds would be to rebuild the devastated South. This undertaking, called Reconstruction, was an enormous task. But it was also an enormous opportunity to extend the ideals of liberty, equality, and opportunity to the almost 4 million African Americans who had just been freed from slavery.

President Abraham Lincoln was one of the last casualties of the Civil War. By the time of his death on April 15, 1865, more than half a million people had died in the struggle. Moreover, much of the South lay in ruins. Rebuilding cities like Charleston, South Carolina, would be hard enough. Reconstructing a nation after such a long and bitter war would be even more difficult.

◀ The ruins of Charleston, South Carolina, after the Civil War, April 1865

'Take it quietly UNCLE ABE and I will draw it closer than ever!!

A few more stitches ANDY and the good old UNION will be mended!

THE "RAIL SPLITTER" AT WORK REPAIRING THE UNION.

This 1864 cartoon shows Abraham Lincoln and Andrew Johnson trying to repair a torn map of the Union. Lincoln, once a rail-splitter, is using a rail to push the South and the North closer to one another. Johnson, once a tailor, is using the needle and thread to stitch together the two sides. After Lincoln was assassinated, the job of reconstructing the South fell to Johnson.

11.2 Andrew Johnson Begins Presidential Reconstruction

"The queerest character that ever occupied the White House"—that is how one observer described Andrew Johnson. Certainly, Johnson's path to the presidency was unusual. When the war broke out, Johnson was a senator from Tennessee. Even though his state seceded, he kept his senate seat—the only senator from a Southern state to do so. A lifelong Democrat, Johnson was nonetheless nominated by Republicans to run for vice president in 1864. True to his party roots, Johnson saw himself as a champion of the common man. But though he condemned former slaveholders as a "pampered, bloated, corrupted aristocracy," he had little concern for former slaves. They would have no role in his plans for reconstructing the South.

Johnson's Reconstruction Plan: A Smooth Return for Southern States Fewer than two months after taking office, Johnson announced his Reconstruction plan. A former Confederate state could rejoin the Union once it had written a new state constitution, elected a new state government, repealed its act of secession, canceled its war debts, and ratified the Thirteenth Amendment to the Constitution. The first of three Reconstruction-era amendments, the Thirteenth Amendment abolished slavery. Republicans in Congress urged Johnson to add a requirement that Southern states must grant freedmen the right to vote. Johnson, however, resisted their pleas. "White men alone," he insisted, "must manage the South."

Former Slaves Test Their New Freedom As Presidential Reconstruction got underway, former slaves were testing the meaning of freedom. For many, it meant freedom to travel. Before emancipation, slaves could not leave their homes without a travel pass from their masters. Now they took to the road, often in search of loved ones who had been sold in slavery times. For others, freedom meant the right to wed, knowing that the marriage was not only legal but could also last "until death do us part." "Weddings, just now, are very popular and abundant among the colored people," wrote an army chaplain. "I have married during the month twenty-five couples, mostly those who have families, and have been living together for years."

Freedom also meant the right to pursue something else long denied to slaves—an education. Freedmen flocked to schools set up by various groups. Booker T. Washington, a freedman who became a leading educator, observed,

It was a whole race trying to go to school. Few were too young, and none too old, to make the attempt to learn. As fast as any kind of teachers could be secured, not only were day-schools filled, but night-schools as well. The great ambition of the older people was to try to learn to read the Bible before they died.

—Booker T. Washington, *Up from Slavery: An Autobiography,* 1901

Along with education, freedmen were desperate to acquire land to farm. During the war, Congressman Thaddeus Stevens had advocated breaking up Southern plantations to give freed slaves "forty acres and a mule" in return for their years of unpaid labor. "We have turned, or are about to turn, loose four million slaves without a hut to shelter them or a cent in their pockets," he argued. "If we do not furnish them with homesteads . . . we had better have left them in bondage." Congress, however, refused to implement Stevens's plan, arguing that to take planters' land without payment would violate their property rights.

Before the end of the war, the Union government had established the **Freedmen's Bureau** to assist former slaves and poor whites living in the South. The bureau provided food, clothing, education, and medical care. It also gave legal assistance to former slaves and acted as a court of law in some situations. But its attempts to solve the problem of farmland for freedmen were thwarted by Johnson, who pardoned former Confederates and returned the land to them.

Congress established the Freedmen's Bureau in 1865 to give relief to former slaves and poor whites. The bureau provided food and medical care, as well as legal assistance. The bureau also helped set up more than 4,300 schools for African Americans of all ages. One of these schools is pictured above.

Black Codes Restrict the Freedom of Former Slaves As new Southern governments were formed, Johnson withdrew Union troops from the South. Many Northerners did not share Johnson's willingness to let the South reconstruct itself. Congressman Benjamin Flanders warned of former Confederate leaders: "Their whole thought and time will be given to plans for getting things back as near to slavery as possible."

Sadly, Flanders was right. Across the South, state legislatures passed **black codes**—laws intended to restrict the freedom and opportunities of African Americans. The black codes served three purposes. The first was to spell out the rights of African Americans. They could own property, work for wages, marry, and file lawsuits. But other **civil rights,** or rights of citizenship, such as the right to vote or to serve on juries, were denied them. The second purpose was to ensure a workforce for planters who had lost their slaves. The codes required freedmen to sign yearly labor contracts each January. Those who did not could be arrested and sent to work for a planter.

The final purpose of the black codes was to maintain a social order in the South that limited the upward mobility of African Americans. The codes barred blacks from any jobs but farm work and unskilled labor, making it impossible for them to rise economically or to start their own businesses. Such restrictions led a Northern journalist touring the South to write,

> The whites seem wholly unable to comprehend that freedom for the negro means the same thing as freedom for them. They readily enough admit that the Government has made him free, but appear to believe that they still have the right to exercise over him the same old control.
> —Sidney Andrews, *Atlantic Monthly,* 1866

Tensions between President Andrew Johnson and the Radical Republicans escalated when Congress called for Johnson's impeachment. Here, Thaddeus Stevens, a Radical Republican who served on the House committee that reccommended Johnson's impeachment, presents the final speech during the Senate trial. In the end, Johnson was acquitted by just one vote.

11.3 Congress Takes Control of Reconstruction

By the end of 1865, every Southern state had formed a new government. The Thirteenth Amendment had been added to the Constitution. In President Andrew Johnson's view, Reconstruction was over. After looking at the black codes enacted across the South, many in the North disagreed with Johnson. One Republican newspaper wrote,

> We tell the white men of Mississippi that the men of the North will convert the state of Mississippi into a frog pond before they will allow such laws to disgrace one foot of soil in which the bones of our soldiers sleep and over which the flag of freedom waves.
>
> —*Chicago Tribune*, December 1865

Radical Republicans Challenge Johnson's Reconstruction When Congress met in December 1865, many lawmakers were of the opinion that Reconstruction had hardly begun. A group of **Radical Republicans,** led by Thaddeus Stevens and Charles Sumner, were especially critical of Johnson's plan. The Radicals had been abolitionists before the war. Now they were determined to reconstruct the nation on the basis of equal rights for all. Their commitment to racial equality put them on a collision course with the president.

Early in 1866, the Radical Republicans joined with more moderate lawmakers to enact two bills designed to help former slaves. The first extended the life of the Freedmen's Bureau beyond its original one-year charter and gave the bureau greater powers. The second, the Civil Rights Act of 1866, took direct aim at the black codes. It declared that African Americans were entitled to "equal benefit of all laws . . . enjoyed by white citizens."

To Congress's surprise, President Johnson vetoed both bills. The continuation of the Freedmen's Bureau, he argued, was too costly and would encourage freedmen to lead a "life of indolence [laziness]." He rejected the Civil Rights Act as a violation of states' rights. In one of his veto messages, Johnson claimed to be representing the will of the people. "This [claim] is modest," quipped one Republican, "for a man made president by an assassin."

Republicans gathered the two-thirds majority in each house needed to override Johnson's veto of the Civil Rights Act. This was the first time in American history that a major piece of legislation became law over a president's veto. Next, they enacted a new Freedmen's Bureau bill. When Johnson vetoed it, Congress overrode his action once again.

To further protect the rights of freedmen, Congress passed the **Fourteenth Amendment** to the Constitution. The basic principle underlying this amendment, Stevens said, was that state laws "shall operate *equally* upon all." The amendment reversed the Dred Scott decision by defining "all persons born or naturalized in the United States" as citizens. It further prohibited any state from denying its citizens "due process" or "the equal protection of the laws."

The Fourteenth Amendment became a major issue in the election of 1866. President Johnson toured the North, making fiery speeches against the amendment and its Republican supporters. His tour did the president more harm than good. Republicans won a veto-proof, two-thirds majority in both houses of Congress. From that point on, Congress would control Reconstruction.

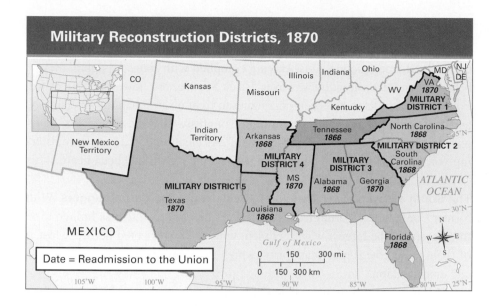

Military Reconstruction Districts, 1870

Date = Readmission to the Union

VA *1870* MILITARY DISTRICT 1

North Carolina *1868*

MILITARY DISTRICT 2

South Carolina *1868*

Tennessee *1866*

Arkansas *1868*

MILITARY DISTRICT 4

MILITARY DISTRICT 3

MS *1870*

Alabama *1868*

Georgia *1870*

MILITARY DISTRICT 5

Texas *1870*

Louisiana *1868*

Florida *1868*

The congressional plan for the reconstruction of the South was based on the belief that the South had no legal governments. Until such governments could be established, the South was divided into five military districts. Each was run by a major general supported by federal troops. Tennessee met the standards for readmission before the military districts were established in 1867.

Congress Puts the South Under Military Rule In 1867, Congress laid out its plan for Reconstruction in a series of laws known as the Reconstruction Acts. These acts outlined a process for admitting Southern states back into the Union. The South was to be divided into five districts, each controlled by federal troops. Election boards in each state would register male voters—both black and white—who were loyal to the Union. Southerners who had actively supported the Confederacy would not be allowed to vote. The voters would elect conventions to write new state constitutions. The constitutions had to grant African Americans the right to vote. The voters would then elect state legislatures, which were required to ratify the Fourteenth Amendment.

In addition, Congress enacted two laws designed to keep Johnson from interfering with its Reconstruction plan. The Command of the Army Act limited the president's power as commander in chief of the army. The Tenure of Office Act barred the president from firing certain federal officials without the "advice and consent" of the Senate.

President Johnson Faces Impeachment President Johnson blasted both of these laws as unconstitutional restrictions on his power. To prove his point, he fired Secretary of War Edwin Stanton, a Radical Republican appointed to office by President Lincoln. Two days later, the House of Representatives voted to impeach Johnson for violating the Tenure of Office Act. The House further charged that "Andrew Johnson had brought the high office of the President of the United States into contempt, ridicule, and disgrace, to the great scandal of all good citizens." Johnson then faced trial in the Senate. If two thirds of the senators found him guilty of any charge, he would be removed from office.

During his Senate trial, the president's lawyers argued that Johnson's only "crime" had been to oppose Congress. Were he to be removed for that reason, "no future President will be safe who happens to differ with a majority of the House and . . . Senate." They also quietly spread the word that if acquitted, Johnson would no longer oppose Congressional Reconstruction. When the votes were cast, Johnson escaped removal by a vote of 35 to 19, just one vote short of the two-thirds majority required.

Southerners scorned Northerners who moved to the South after the war as "carpetbaggers." In their eyes, these newcomers were worthless fortune hunters whose few possessions could fit in a single carpetbag. In this cartoon, President Ulysses S. Grant is portrayed as the ultimate "carpetbagger," riding on the back of the "solid South."

This portrait shows some of the 16 African Americans who represented Southern states in Congress between 1869 and 1880. The last black Congressman from the South in this era was George Henry White of North Carolina. Elected in 1897, his term ended in 1901. For the next 28 years, no African Americans served in Congress.

11.4 Living Under Congressional Reconstruction

White Southerners were shocked by the return of federal troops to the South under the Reconstruction Acts. Having complied with Johnson's plan, they believed that Reconstruction was over. Black Southerners, however, were elated. For months, freedmen had been organizing to fight discrimination. "We simply ask," one group declared in a petition to Congress, "that the same laws that govern white men shall govern black men." As election boards began registering voters across the South in 1867, it seemed their pleas had been heard.

The South's New Voters: Freedmen, Scalawags, and Carpetbaggers With former Confederates barred from registering, the right to vote was limited to three groups. The largest was freedmen, who had never voted before. Most of them joined the Republican Party, which they saw as the party of Lincoln and emancipation.

The next largest group consisted of white Southerners who had opposed secession. Many were poor farmers who also had never voted before. Because they viewed the Democratic Party as the party of secession, they, too, registered as Republicans. Southern Democrats, who viewed these new Republicans as traitors to the South, scorned them as "scalawags," or worthless scoundrels. The last group of voters was made up of Northerners, most of them former soldiers, who were attracted to the South after the war. Yankee-hating Southerners called them "carpetbaggers," a term for a piece of luggage travelers often carried. They despised carpetbaggers as fortune hunters who invaded the South to profit from the misfortunes of Southerners.

The newly registered voters cast their first ballots in the 1868 presidential election. The Republican candidate for president was the Union war hero Ulysses S. Grant. He supported Congressional Reconstruction and promised to protect the rights of freedmen in the South. His democratic opponent, Horatio Seymour, promised to end Reconstruction and return the South to its traditional leaders—white Democrats.

The election was marred by violence in several Southern states. A white Republican in Georgia wrote, "We cannot vote without all sorts of threats and intimidations. Freedmen are shot with impunity [no punishment]." Even so, the Republican Party swept every Southern state except for Louisiana and Georgia, where attacks on Republicans had made campaigning impossible. Nationwide, Seymour won a majority of white votes. Grant, however, won the popular vote with the help of half a million black voters. For Republicans, the lesson of the election was clear: Their party needed the black vote in order to remain in power.

Grant's victory helped persuade Congress to pass the last of the Reconstruction amendments. The **Fifteenth Amendment** states that "the right of citizens . . . to vote shall not be denied or abridged [limited] by the United States or by any State on account of race, color, or previous condition of servitude." "Nothing in all history," wrote abolitionist William Lloyd Garrison, equaled "this wonderful, quiet, sudden transformation of four millions of human beings from . . . the auction-block to the ballot box."

New State Governments Begin to Rebuild the South

Across the South, voters chose delegates—about one fourth of them African Americans—to state constitutional conventions. These delegates wrote constitutions that not only banned racial discrimination but also guaranteed blacks the right to vote and to hold public office. Elections were then held to form governments. To the dismay of white Democrats, a majority of those elected were Republicans and about a fifth of them freedmen. The new governments quickly ratified the Fourteenth and Fifteenth amendments, the last step of the Reconstruction process. By 1870, every Southern state had been readmitted to the Union.

The most enduring accomplishment of these Reconstruction governments was the creation of the South's first public, tax-supported school systems. At first, whites stayed away rather than mix with blacks. To attract white students, most states segregated their schools by race, even where doing so was prohibited by law. **Segregation**—the forced separation of races in public places—was not the rule in other areas of life. In fact, several of the Reconstruction governments outlawed segregation in transportation, places of entertainment, and other businesses. But these laws were hard to enforce.

The South's Economic Recovery Remains Slow

The new state governments undertook ambitious programs to strengthen the Southern economy. They hoped economic growth would alleviate poverty and racial tensions. Unfortunately, money intended to rebuild roads and bridges and to expand railroads often fell into the hands of corrupt government officials. Although industry and trade led to the rebirth of some Southern cities, most of the South remained dependent on agriculture.

The plight of Southern farmers became increasingly desperate. The South was still suffering the staggering costs of the war. During the conflict, many whites had lost all they had—their homes, farms, and businesses. Taxes and debts led some to sell their land. Even once-wealthy planters were struggling. They had land but no money to hire workers to produce crops. Many planters divided their land into small plots that they rented to workers who would grow crops, a system known as **tenant farming**. In some cases, tenant farmers would pay a share of their crop as rent instead of cash.

At first, **sharecropping** looked promising to both black and white landless farmers. They hoped that in time they would earn enough money to buy land for themselves. In reality, these farmers often experienced a new form of bondage: debt. Most sharecroppers had to borrow money from planters to buy the food, tools, and supplies they needed. Few ever earned enough from the sale of their crops to repay these debts. As a result, sharecropping usually led to a life of **debt peonage** rather than one of economic independence. Under this system, debtors were forced to work for the person they owed money to until they paid off their debts. "We make as much cotton and sugar as we did when we were slaves," noted one Texas sharecropper, "and it does us as little good now as it did then."

Sharecropping grew out of the needs of planters who had no workforce and of former slaves and white farmers who had no land. Freedmen often preferred sharecropping to working as paid farmhands because it gave them independence. As sharecroppers, they did not have to answer to an overseer about how they used their time.

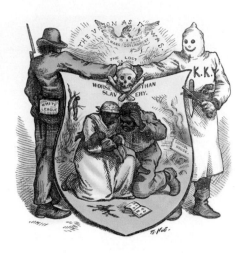

Between 1882 and 1903, white supremacists murdered nearly 2,000 African Americans in the South. This Thomas Nast cartoon depicts a Klan member and another white supremacist holding the threat of death in the form of a skull over an African American family.

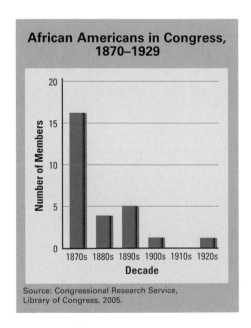

African Americans in Congress, 1870–1929

Source: Congressional Research Service, Library of Congress, 2005.

At the beginning of Reconstruction, there were a significant number of African Americans in Congress. After the Jim Crow laws were enacted, the numbers dwindled quickly.

11.5 Reversing Reconstruction

The South's experiment with Reconstruction governments was short. Thomas Miller, a black lawmaker in South Carolina, would later recall,

> We were eight years in power. We had built schoolhouses, established charitable institutions, built and maintained the penitentiary system, provided for the education of the deaf and dumb . . . rebuilt the bridges and reestablished the ferries. In short, we had reconstructed the state and placed it on the road to prosperity.
>
> —Thomas Miller

Former Confederates, however, saw this period of biracial government quite differently. For them, it was a time of struggle to return the South to "white man's rule."

White Resistance to Reconstruction Most Southern whites refused to support Reconstruction governments for a number of reasons. Many considered the governments illegal, because so many former Confederates had been prevented from voting or running for office. Others were angry at the governments for raising taxes to pay for schools and other improvements. Some had even lost their land when they were unable to pay taxes on it. Still others were upset by the corruption in the new governments.

Underlying all of these complaints was the fact that most Southern whites could not accept the idea of former slaves voting and holding office. Many were white supremacists who believed in the superiority of the white race. The most radical turned to violence, forming terrorist groups with names like the White Brotherhood and the Knights of the White Camelia. Members of the best-known terror group, the **Ku Klux Klan,** had to swear that they were "opposed to negro equality, both social and political." These groups terrorized blacks and white Republicans to keep them from voting. Their tactics included the burning of African American schools, attacks on Freedmen's Bureau officials, and even outright murder.

Northerners Grow Tired of Reconstruction In 1870 and 1871, Congress took action to end the wave of terror by passing the Enforcement Acts. These laws made it a federal crime to deprive citizens of their civil rights. President Grant sent federal marshals into the South to crush the terror groups. These officials arrested hundreds of men and sent a few to prison. The result was a temporary reduction in terrorism.

After passage of the Enforcement Acts, however, Northerners seemed to lose interest in reconstruction of the South. In 1872, Congress closed the Freedmen's Bureau. That same year, it passed an amnesty act. This act granted **amnesty,** or a general pardon, to most former Confederates, allowing them to vote and hold office once again. Even President Grant had grown tired of the South and its problems. In 1875, the governor of Mississippi asked Grant for help in protecting freedmen's voting rights during the state's November election. Grant refused the request by saying, "The whole public are tired out with these annual autumnal [election season] outbreaks in the South."

By this time, Grant had other things to worry about. Leading members of his administration had been accused of corruption. The economy had crashed. Moreover, a new generation of Republican leaders had come to power and recognized that voters in the North no longer cared about Reconstruction.

The Election of 1876 Brings an End to Reconstruction President Grant did not run for reelection in 1876. Instead, the Republicans nominated Ohio's Rutherford B. Hayes, a former Union general. The Democratic candidate for president was New York governor Samuel Tilden, a crusader for clean government. Tilden won the popular vote, but his 184 electoral votes were one shy of the 185 needed to win.

The electoral votes of South Carolina, Florida, and Louisiana were disputed. Republican leaders claimed that Hayes won the most votes in those states. Democrats said Tilden won more votes. With no clear resolution, the election went to the House of Representatives.

After weeks of secret dealing, leaders of both parties in the House arrived at an agreement known as the Compromise of 1877. Under this agreement, Hayes received the electoral votes from the three disputed states and became president. In return, he agreed to name a Southerner to his cabinet, remove the last remaining federal troops from the South, and give federal aid to Southern railroad construction. Much of the deal fell apart after Hayes took office, but the troops were removed, and Reconstruction was officially over.

African Americans Lose Ground Under Redeemer Governments By the time Reconstruction ended, white supremacists calling themselves Redeemers had regained power in every Southern state. Their goal was to redeem, or save, the South by returning it to "white man's rule." "The whole South," commented a freedman, "had got into the hands of the very men who held us as slaves."

Once in office, the Redeemers reversed improvements made in education by cutting spending for public schools. As the governor of Virginia explained, "Schools are a luxury . . . to be paid for, like any other luxury, by the people who wish their benefits." As public funding dried up, schools either closed their doors or began to charge fees. By the 1880s, only about half of all black children in the South attended school.

The Redeemers put even more effort into reversing the political gains made by freedmen during Reconstruction. Many states passed laws requiring citizens who wanted to vote to pay a **poll tax**. The tax was set high enough to make voting, like schooling, a luxury most blacks could not afford. Some states also required potential voters to pass a **literacy test**. The tests were made so difficult that almost nobody could pass, no matter how well educated.

During and after Reconstruction, African Americans in the South created their own schools and colleges. The most famous was Booker T. Washington's Tuskegee Institute. Washington stressed practical skills over book learning. He believed learning trades and succeeding economically would help African Americans gain civil rights.

In theory, poll taxes and literacy tests applied equally to both black and white citizens, as required by the Fifteenth Amendment. In practice, however, whites were excused from both by a **grandfather clause** inserted in voting laws. This clause exempted citizens whose ancestors had voted before January 1, 1867. Because no African Americans could vote in the South before that day, the grandfather clause applied only to whites.

The Redeemer governments also reversed laws that had outlawed segregation in public places. New legislation drew a "color line" between blacks and whites in public life. Whites called these new acts **Jim Crow laws,** an insulting reference to a black character in a popular song. African Americans were not allowed to sit with whites in buses or rail cars. Restaurants and other businesses served whites only or served black customers separately. These are just a few of the examples of how blacks were discriminated against.

African Americans Struggle to Protect Their Rights Blacks resisted attacks on their rights in many ways. The boldest protested openly. This put them at risk of being **lynched**—killed by hanging—by white mobs.

Homer Plessy, a black man arrested for sitting in a whites-only railroad car in Louisiana, looked to the courts for help. Plessy argued that Jim Crow laws violated the equal protection clause of the Fourteenth Amendment. In 1896, his case, *Plessy v. Ferguson,* reached the Supreme Court. The majority of the justices ruled that segregation was constitutional as long as the facilities

How Far Could Jim Crow Go?

Not all Southerners supported segregation. When a law to separate blacks and whites in railway cars was proposed in South Carolina in 1898, the *Charleston News and Courier* tried to show how silly the idea was by taking segregation to ridiculous extremes. Except for Jim Crow witness boxes, however, all of the newspaper's "silly" suggestions were eventually put into practice and continued through the 1900s, as shown here.

If there must be Jim Crow cars on railroads, there should be Jim Crow cars on the street railways. Also on all passenger boats . . . If there are to be Jim Crow cars, moreover, there should be Jim Crow waiting saloons [rooms] at all stations, and Jim Crow eating houses . . . There should be Jim Crow sections of the jury box, and a separate Jim Crow dock and witness stand in every court—and a Jim Crow Bible for colored witnesses to kiss.

—*Charleston News and Courier*

COLORED MUST SIT IN BALCONY

GRAND THEATER Birmingham

ACE SIGN COMPANY

14 JULY '31

COLORED

provided to blacks were equal to those provided to whites. This "separate but equal" doctrine was soon applied to almost every aspect of life in the South. However, the facilities set apart for African Americans in Southern states were seldom equal to those labeled "whites only."

Some African Americans chose to move to the North rather than endure the humiliation of forced segregation. Most African Americans, however, remained in the South and got by as best they could. With participation in politics closed to them, they focused on their families, churches, and communities. The majority farmed for a living, often as sharecroppers or tenant farmers. A growing number of African Americans started their own businesses. The number of black-owned businesses in the South soared from 2,000 in 1865 to nearly 25,000 by 1903.

African Americans also banded together to build schools and colleges for their children. By 1900, more than a million and a half black children were attending school. As a result, literacy rates for Southern blacks rose from near zero to 50 percent. The South's new black colleges offered vocational training in such fields as farming and carpentry, as well as professional training in law, medicine, and teaching.

For the next half century, segregation would rule life in the South. But the Fourteenth and Fifteenth amendments, with their promise of equal rights, were not completely forgotten. In time, they would be reawakened as part of a new struggle for racial equality.

Summary

The Reconstruction era lasted from 1865 to 1877. During these years, biracial governments were established across the South. These governments expanded the rights and opportunities of former slaves. But when Reconstruction ended, the South returned to "white man's rule."

Reconstruction amendments During Reconstruction, three amendments were added to the Constitution. The Thirteenth Amendment outlawed slavery, the Fourteenth Amendment made former slaves citizens, and the Fifteenth Amendment gave African American men the right to vote.

Presidential Reconstruction In 1865, President Johnson allowed the Southern states to reconstruct themselves. Most enacted black codes that severely restricted the rights of former slaves.

Congressional Reconstruction Congress took control of Reconstruction in 1867. Federal troops were sent to the South to oversee the establishment of state governments that were more democratic.

Reconstruction governments The South's first biracial state governments established a public school system and outlawed racial segregation. But these governments were bitterly opposed by white terrorist groups like the Ku Klux Klan.

Jim Crow laws Reconstruction ended as part of the Compromise of 1877. Once Democrats regained control of the state governments in the South, they passed Jim Crow laws that segregated blacks from whites in public life. In 1896, the Supreme Court ruled in *Plessy v. Ferguson* that segregation was constitutional under the doctrine of "separate but equal."

Chapter 12

Change and Conflict in the American West

What opportunities and conflicts emerged as Americans moved westward?

12.1 Introduction

By the mid-1800s, many Americans felt the need for a change, for a fresh start. Like the early settlers who crossed the Appalachians, they migrated westward in search of opportunity.

Entire families packed their belongings into covered wagons and hit the westward trail. Sooner or later, they crossed the Mississippi River. From their perspective, this mighty river was the frontier, or boundary, marking the beginning of wilderness. "I do remember my emotions after we were all landed on the [other] side of the river," one traveler recalled. "I felt as if we had left all civilization behind us."

In many ways, they had. Overland travelers would spend weeks or months on what amounted to a long and challenging expedition. They would have to adapt themselves to the demands of living on the trail, such as repairing wagons and handling oxen and other livestock. They also had to learn to cook and clean under tough circumstances.

The travelers had to survive with limited resources. Water and wood were scarce on the plains, and food was also difficult to find. They brought very little to eat besides flour, bacon, beans, salt, and coffee. One woman wrote in her journal, "About the only change we have from bread and bacon is bacon and bread."

Many of the new migrants were farmers, but other people also sought opportunity in the West. Miners searched for gold, silver, and other minerals in the hills and mountains. On the grassy plains, ranchers hired cowboys to herd their cattle. Immigrant workers found jobs laying rail lines, and railroad owners made profits shipping western goods to market. However, this rising tide of migration brought further conflict with American Indians. The tribes of the Great Plains, in particular, would fight long and hard against the massive invasion of their lands and destruction of their way of life.

Thousands of Americans moved west in the late 1800s. They packed their goods in covered wagons for the long overland journey. Many hoped to reach Oregon or California, but others settled on the Great Plains.

◀ Engraving of westward migration pushing Indians from their land

131

Some miners panned for gold using the simple placer method. They shoveled soil from a streambed into a shallow pan and then washed away the sand and gravel with stream water. This left the heavier gold particles in the pan. Other placer miners used more sophisticated washing methods.

12.2 Mining and Ranching Opportunities in the West

The first settlers heading west from the Mississippi Valley had a distant objective. They wanted to reach the rich farmlands of the Far West. They moved as fast as they could across the Great Plains. Then they struggled to get over the Rocky Mountains. Most of them stopped for good only when they reached the fertile fields and valleys of Oregon and California. By 1848, 14,000 people had made this journey. This trickle of migration changed quickly in the mid-1800s, however, after settlers found gold in California.

Miners: In Search of the Big Strike In 1848, a landowner named John Sutter was building a sawmill on the American River, in California's Central Valley. This river flowed down from the Sierra Nevada range to the east. In January of that year, Sutter's workers found gold near the mill. Sutter tried to keep the gold a secret, but eventually word got out. Up and down the Pacific Coast, men deserted their work to head for Sutter's Mill. By the year's end, gold fever gripped the whole nation and even spread abroad. The California gold rush was on.

In the spring of 1849, some 40,000 migrants from the East headed overland to California. That same year, about 40,000 more people boarded steamships bound for San Francisco. Soon California swarmed with "forty-niners," as these miners were called. About nine out of ten were men, most of them young. Many came from Mexico, and thousands more arrived from as far away as Europe and China. All of them were motivated by one great hope—to strike it rich.

Few of these prospectors and treasure hunters knew anything about mining. Luckily, much of California's gold was not locked up in solid rock. Over time, water erosion had dislodged much of the gold and washed it down into streambeds. Miners called this placer gold, which they could mine using simple tools, such as pans and shovels. Other prospectors looked for veins of gold and silver in solid rock. Often working in groups, they used hand tools and weak explosives to extract the metal. Miners called a thick vein a lode. Every prospector's dream was to find the "mother lode" that would produce untold riches.

Between 1850 and 1860, California's population jumped from about 93,000 to over 380,000. Prospectors set up tent camps near their claims. Merchants of all kinds followed close on their heels. As stores, banks, saloons, and restaurants opened up, some camps swelled into towns. When a site no longer produced much metal, most prospectors moved on.

For three decades after the California gold rush, hordes of miners chased their dream of riches from Mexico to Alaska and east as far as the Black Hills of Dakota. They endured backbreaking work and conditions that were dismal and sometimes dangerous. However, very few prospectors ever struck it rich. After years of searching, most would have agreed with the familiar saying, "Gold is where I ain't!"

By the early 1850s, most of the ore that could be easily mined in California had been found. Individual prospectors eventually gave way to large mining companies that used hydraulic machines to wash away whole hillsides in search of gold. In the process, they damaged the environment, destroying habitat, polluting rivers, and leaving behind large piles of debris on which nothing could grow.

Cowboys spent a lot of time outdoors, working with cattle. One of their jobs was to round up calves and use a hot branding iron to mark them with the special insignia of their ranch. Another job was to herd mature cattle to market on the long drive.

Ranchers and Cowboys Find a Home on the Range While miners uncovered the West's valuable stores of gold, silver, and other minerals, cattle ranchers found opportunity in a different kind of natural resource: grass. Their beef cattle thrived on the abundant grasses and open range of the Great Plains.

Plains cattle ranching had started in Texas before the Civil War. The region had a long tradition of ranching going back to the first Spanish settlers. Mexican **vaqueros** started many cowboy customs. They rode horses and wore boots with pointed toes and wide-brimmed hats. They rounded up cattle and branded them.

Many Texas ranchers went off to fight in the Civil War and never returned. Untended, their cattle multiplied. By the mid-1860s, several million tough longhorn cattle roamed wild on the open plains. Many lacked the brands that showed ownership. Some Texans began to round up unbranded cattle with an eye toward driving, or herding, them north to market.

Their timing was good. The growing populations of eastern cities had raised the demand for beef. In the East, ranchers could get $40 a head for cattle that sold for $5 or less back in Texas. Also, railroad companies had begun extending rail lines west from Missouri into Kansas. Cowhands could drive their herds to "cow towns" that sprang up along the rail lines. The potential for large profits made a long cattle drive to one of these cow towns seem well worth the effort.

The era of the long drive began in 1867, when cowboys following the **Chisholm Trail** drove longhorns north from San Antonio, Texas, to Abilene, Kansas. From Abilene and other cow towns, live cattle were shipped in rail cars to meatpacking centers like Chicago. Working as a team, a dozen cowboys could drive more than a thousand cattle at a time along the trail. African Americans and Mexican Americans made up at least a quarter of all cowboys on the long drives.

Cowboys led rough lives, working outdoors and sleeping on the ground in all types of weather. They had to be prepared to defend the herd against people who wanted to steal the cattle, as well as against Indian attacks. There was also the constant threat of a stampede.

The long drives ended once rail lines reached into cattle country during the 1880s. The new lines not only transported cattle to market but also brought farmers to the plains. The newcomers sparked conflict with the cattle ranchers by fencing off their farms with barbed wire, effectively closing the open range. Nature dealt cattle ranching an even harsher blow when the blizzards of 1886 and 1887 killed thousands of cattle, forcing many ranchers into bankruptcy. Those who survived decided to fence in their ranches and raise only as many cattle as their land could support.

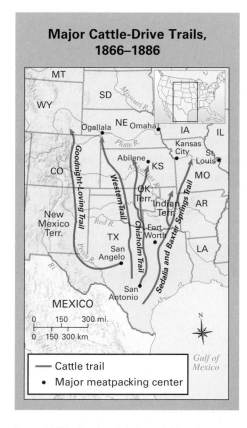

Major Cattle-Drive Trails, 1866–1886

In 1866, Charles Goodnight and Oliver Loving blazed a cattle trail from south Texas to Denver. They sold their herd and cleared a large profit. Soon other Texans were driving herds of cattle to various cow towns located on railroad lines. From there, the cattle were shipped to meatpacking plants in Chicago and other eastern cities.

12.3 Railroads Open the West to Rapid Settlement

An easterner bound for the California goldfields in 1849 could not have made it halfway to the Mississippi River by train alone. Before the 1850s, most railroads were short lines, connecting cities and towns in just one region. A flurry of rail building in the 1850s changed that. By 1860, rail lines extended from the Atlantic Coast across the Mississippi. This expansion set the stage for opening up western lands to settlement and for linking the East and West coasts by rail.

The gold rush had produced a population explosion in the Far West. Yet this growing region remained in isolation, essentially separated from the rest of the nation. During the 1850s, many people pointed out the need for better transportation and communication between East and West. In particular, merchants demanded a faster way to transport goods across the Great Plains and the Rockies. They wanted a transcontinental railroad, one that spanned the continent. This need presented a great opportunity to railroad builders.

The First Transcontinental Railroad Creates Huge Challenges In 1861, four wealthy merchants in Sacramento, California, founded the Central Pacific Railroad Company. Known as the "Big Four," they sought government support for a transcontinental railroad. One of them, C. P. Huntington, went to Washington to act as a **lobbyist** to push for a railroad bill. Lobbyists try to persuade legislators to pass laws favorable to groups they represent.

Plans for a transcontinental railroad had been stalled by debate in Congress over whether to follow a northern or southern route. However, the South's secession and the onset of the Civil War led Congress to approve a northern route that would unite California and Oregon with the rest of the Union. The Pacific Railway Act, passed in 1862, directed the Central Pacific and the newly created Union Pacific Railroad Company to construct railway and telegraph lines from the Missouri River to the Pacific Ocean. The Union Pacific would start in Omaha, Nebraska, and work its way west. The Central Pacific would start in Sacramento and head east.

Building the first transcontinental railroad posed tremendous challenges. One problem was raising enough funds. Under the Pacific Railway Act, the government pledged to help each company by granting it 6,400 acres of land and up to $48,000 in loans for each mile of track laid. Once the laying of rails began, the owners could sell the land to settlers to help pay for construction costs. But they needed startup money. The Union Pacific had trouble raising funds and did not lay its first rails until 1865.

The Union Pacific also faced conflicts with some of the tribes that lived on the Great Plains. Its route followed the Platte River through territory controlled by the Cheyenne, Arapaho, and Lakota Sioux.

By 1900, there were more than 200,000 miles of railroad track in the country, including four transcontinental lines. Long-distance rail travel called for better ways of keeping time. In 1883, the railroads adopted a system that divided the nation into the four time zones shown here.

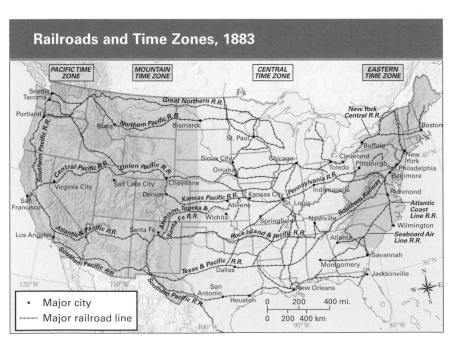

Railroads and Time Zones, 1883

PACIFIC TIME ZONE   MOUNTAIN TIME ZONE   CENTRAL TIME ZONE   EASTERN TIME ZONE

- Major city
- ┼┼┼┼ Major railroad line

All three tribes had been battling the U.S. Army for years, and their attacks on railroad workers sometimes stopped construction.

For the Central Pacific, rough terrain was a major challenge. Crossing the Sierra Nevada was an epic engineering feat. The rail line had to pass over, and sometimes through, high mountain passes. It also had to bridge deep canyons. On some days, progress was measured in inches. Beyond the Sierra Nevada lay the Great Basin, a vast, dry region where summers are blistering hot.

Working on the Railroad: Jobs and Hardships for Immigrants In meeting these construction challenges, the two railroad companies owed much of their success to immigrant labor. At first, both companies faced a severe labor shortage. They needed thousands of workers, but the Civil War and the gold rush had siphoned off a large part of the labor pool.

The end of the Civil War in 1865 solved part of the Union Pacific's labor problem. Ex-soldiers and former slaves eagerly joined company crews. So did immigrants from Europe. In fact, the bulk of its 12,000-man workforce was made up of Irish immigrants. Large numbers of Irish began immigrating to the United States after a potato disease brought famine to Ireland in 1845. Many first settled in eastern cities, where they were looked down on for being Catholic and poor. In the face of such discrimination, railroad jobs seemed like an attractive opportunity.

When the Central Pacific began construction in 1865, it also faced a shortage of workers. In desperation, it decided to hire workers from China, despite widespread prejudice against the Chinese. The company advertised in China, promising impoverished workers good pay. By 1868, the Central Pacific was employing about 10,000 Chinese workers, who made up four fifths of its labor force. Chinese workers were paid lower wages than white workers and were targets of racism.

Working on the railroad was both strenuous and dangerous. Some workers were killed in Indian attacks. The use of dynamite to blast tunnels through the Sierra Nevada also resulted in injuries and deaths. Extreme cold in winter left many workers with frostbite, and snow avalanches killed others. Yet the workers who survived had money in their pockets.

Railroads Become Lifelines in the West Both companies overcame all obstacles, and on May 10, 1869, their lines met at Promontory Point, Utah. That day marked a turning point in the history of the West. With the completion of the railroad, travel time between the Pacific and Atlantic coasts shrank from 4 months to 10 days. To mark the occasion, two officials, one from each company, drove ceremonial spikes of gold and silver into the railroad ties.

Once the first transcontinental railroad had been completed, railroad construction continued elsewhere with a fury. This rapid expansion made many "railroad barons," like the Big Four, very rich. It also encouraged settlement by making land available to farm families. Towns sprang up along the routes. In addition, railroads served the transportation needs of new industries, such as mining and lumbering. Perhaps most importantly, they united East and West.

For many people in the West, the railroads became lifelines. But because farmers depended on them, the railroads could charge excessive rates to ship their crops to market. Such policies led to growing demands for some government control over the railroad companies.

In this photograph, Chinese laborers do the dangerous work of creating a tunnel at the summit of the Sierra Nevada mountains. Chinese laborers made up four fifths of the labor force for the construction of the Central Pacific railway line, which stretched from San Francisco to Utah.

On May 10, 1869, workers completed the first railroad to span the continent. This picture shows the celebration that took place as the Union and Central Pacific lines were joined together at Promontory Summit, Utah, allowing for the beginning of passenger service from Omaha to San Francisco.

12.4 Indian Wars Shatter Tribal Cultures

To many people, the railroad represented progress. But for the Indians on the Great Plains, it was a threat to their very existence. The railroad cut through their hunting grounds, disturbing the buffalo, their main source of food, clothing, and shelter. It also brought ranchers, farmers, and soldiers to the hunting grounds. In response, many tribes fought the railroad, waging war to stop the rush of settlement that jeopardized their ways of life. Their battle for survival represented the latest round of what are known as the Indian Wars.

Cultures Clash on the Great Plains From the perspective of a nation bent on expanding westward, the many Indian tribes in the West presented a problem. They refused to change their customs to conform to the settlers' culture. For example, they believed that tribes or villages had rights to areas of land. However, they did not believe that land could be owned, bought, or sold.

Differences between Indians and settlers over land had led to conflict early in the nation's history. Conflicts continued as settlers crossed the Appalachians and laid claim to tribal lands in the Ohio and Mississippi river valleys. To end such conflicts, the Indian Removal Act of 1830 had forced the largest tribes living east of the Mississippi to move west to Oklahoma Territory on the Great Plains. When settlers began to populate the West after the Civil War, they again clashed with native peoples. The Indians were once more viewed as "an obstacle to the progress of settlement and industry," as one government official put it.

A complex clash of cultures occurred on the Great Plains. Nomadic tribes had roamed the plains freely for centuries in pursuit of buffalo. They had little in common with eastern tribes, who had been conquered and "removed" to the plains in the 1830s. These differences led to conflict between nomadic tribes that wanted more open land and settled tribes that wanted to protect their farmland.

By the early 1870s, the U.S. Army had forced the Apache of Arizona and New Mexico onto reservations. Chief Geronimo, shown here, refused to settle down and kept fighting until 1886 to protect his homeland. He finally surrendered, though, and took up farming in Oklahoma Territory.

In 1850, Indians roamed freely over the western half of the United States. Over time, the federal government forced them onto smaller and smaller reservations. Many tribes fought to save their lands. President Rutherford B. Hayes admitted in 1877, "Many, if not most, of our Indian wars have had their origin in broken promises and acts of injustice upon our part."

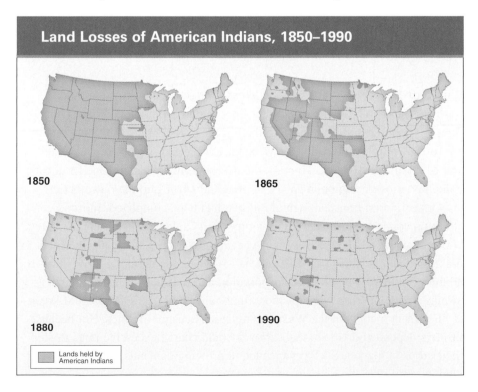

Land Losses of American Indians, 1850–1990

1850

1865

1880

1990

Lands held by American Indians

Larger conflicts arose with the advance of white civilization. As settlers moved westward, they slaughtered millions of buffalo, endangering a vital element of tribal cultures. Many tribes refused to give up their homelands and ways of life without a fight. Their warriors began attacking settlers.

The U.S. Army responded with attacks on the plains tribes. In 1864, troops raided a party of Cheyennes and Arapahos who had camped at Sand Creek, Colorado, with permission from the commander of a nearby fort. More than 150 people, many of them women and children, were killed. The Sand Creek Massacre sparked a general uprising among the plains tribes.

In an effort to end conflict and open up land for settlers, the federal government tried to confine most western tribes to **reservations**. A reservation is an area of federal land reserved for an Indian tribe. Federal officials promised to protect these tribes. However, instead of protecting Indians, the government far too often helped prospectors and settlers who invaded a reservation. For example, a gold strike in the Black Hills of the Dakota Territory brought hordes of miners onto the Sioux reservation in the 1870s. The government ignored the invasion, even though the Treaty of Fort Laramie, signed in 1868, guaranteed the Sioux exclusive rights to the land.

Many tribes, from the Apaches and Comanches in the south to the Sioux, Cheyennes, and Arapahos in the north, refused to stay on reservations. Bands of raiders moved out onto the plains, where they fought to stop the expansion of settlements. In 1876, Sioux and Cheyennes who were camped near the Little Bighorn River in Montana came under attack by U.S. Cavalry troops under George Armstrong Custer. The much larger Indian force, led by Sioux chiefs Sitting Bull and Crazy Horse, wiped out Custer's troops.

After the Battle of the Little Bighorn, also known as "Custer's Last Stand," federal forces hunted down and captured about 3,000 Sioux warriors. Over the next few years, the army subdued the other major tribes of the Great Plains.

As part of its assimilation policy, the federal government set up boarding schools for Indian children. The director of the Carlisle Indian Industrial School in Pennsylvania said that his goal was to "kill the Indian and save the man."

Adaptation and Efforts to Assimilate American Indians The settlement of the West was disastrous for large numbers of American Indians. Many died as a result of violence, disease, and poverty. Others clung to a miserable existence on reservations.

The survivors struggled to adapt to their changed circumstances. Some Indians tried agriculture. The eastern tribes that had been removed to Oklahoma became successful farmers. Many tribes established their own government and schools.

At the same time, the U.S. government adopted policies aimed at speeding the **assimilation,** or absorption, of Indians into the dominant culture. Federal officials set up about two dozen boarding schools to educate American Indians in "white men's ways." Congress furthered the assimilation push by enacting the Dawes Act of 1887. Under this law, a tribe could no longer own reservation lands as a group. Instead, the government began distributing land to individuals within a tribe. Each family was granted its own plot of land, which it could hold or sell. This change eroded a cornerstone of American Indian cultures—the belief that land could not be bought or sold. Land sales, both free and forced, greatly decreased the amount of Indian-owned land.

New farm machinery, like this threshing machine, helped to turn the Great Plains into the nation's breadbasket. But to pay for such machines, most farmers had to borrow money. Rising debt, along with years of drought on the plains, led to many bankruptcies. By the 1890s, tens of thousands of homesteaders had "gone bust."

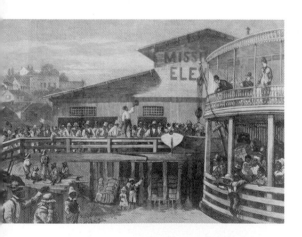

In 1879, a rumor caused a surge in black migration to Kansas. The rumor held that the federal government would give free land and $500 to every black family that moved there. About 6,000 African Americans made the trek. The rumored aid never came through. This image depicts African Americans at Mississippi preparing to move west.

12.5 Settling the Great Plains

Despite resistance from tribes of the Great Plains, settlers continued to migrate there during the second half of the 19th century. They ventured on foot, on horseback, and in ox-drawn wagons. Later they came by rail. Most had one goal: the opportunity to turn a plot of grassland into a farm.

Opportunities and Challenges on the Great Plains Several factors transformed the Great Plains from a place to pass through en route to the West Coast into a land of opportunity. Perhaps the most important was the steady expansion of the railroads. The railroads carried settlers onto the plains, and the railroad companies sold settlers land that the companies had been granted by the government. Another factor was that families felt much safer migrating to the West because the army had reduced the threat of attack by plains tribes. A third factor was the passage in 1862 of two federal laws that encouraged settlement.

The two new laws were the **Homestead Act** and the Morrill Land-Grant Act. The Homestead Act was designed to provide tracts of land called homesteads to settlers in the West. The act offered 160 acres of public land for a small fee to anyone who agreed to work the land and live on it for five years. This law attracted about 600,000 farmers who claimed more than 80 million acres of land by the end of the 19th century. The Morrill Land-Grant Act gave each state large tracts of public land to help finance the establishment of agricultural colleges. To raise funds to build colleges, states sold homesteads to settlers.

The plains offered settlers a fresh start. The settlers knew by the look and smell of the rich soil that crops would thrive in this land. To be successful, however, they had to overcome some difficult challenges. The first was building houses on the largely treeless plains. Lacking lumber, some homesteaders simply dug a hole in the side of a hill as a shelter. Other settlers fashioned houses out of the tough plains turf, or sod. They called these houses "soddies." Sod blocks, cut out of the ground with a shovel or an ax, formed the walls. Most roofs were made of sod as well. Once farmers could afford lumber delivered by train, they replaced their dugouts and soddies with wood-frame houses.

Another challenge was the environment. The Great Plains region typically has an arid climate. The settlers who flocked there in the 1870s and 1880s arrived during an abnormally wet period. The unusual amounts of rain helped crops flourish. Still, farmers had to deal with winter's deep cold, piercing winds, and blizzard snows. By the early 1890s, drought conditions had returned, especially in Kansas, Nebraska, Colorado, and the Dakotas. As the soil dried up, wheat, corn, and other crops failed. Farmers also had to contend with grasshoppers. Great clouds of these pests, thick enough to darken the sky, descended on fields with little warning. They chewed for days on everything edible, destroying entire crops.

In the face of these hardships, many farmers left the plains. The sides of their covered wagons bore the words "In God We Trusted, In Kansas We Busted." Others worked to overcome the harsh conditions by using dry-farming techniques. To conserve soil moisture, they plowed and planted a field one year and left it uncultivated the next. Also, tools had made farm life easier. The steel plow, invented in 1837, had made it easier to cut through the thick

prairie sod and prepare it for planting. The mechanical reaper neatly cut and bound sheaves of grain at harvesttime. Windmills pumped water from deep wells for household use and irrigation.

African Americans See the Plains as the "Promised Land" The women and men who settled the West represented a broad range of Americans. Many were native-born white farm families from the Midwest. Some had moved at least once before. Other settlers were immigrants from Europe. Often they were lured by the claims of railroad agents skilled at stretching the truth. Still others were former slaves searching for the opportunity to own their own land.

After the Civil War, many African Americans fled the South in search of better lives elsewhere. Thousands joined the westward movement. Freedmen worked as cowboys in Texas. They also joined the army, helping to protect settlers. However, most African Americans who headed west became farmers.

Former slaves such as Henry Adams and Benjamin "Pap" Singleton encouraged African Americans to build farm communities on the Great Plains. These leaders helped organize a postwar migration to Kansas and beyond. The migrants became known as **Exodusters,** a reference to Exodus, the second book of the Bible, which recounts the Israelites' escape from slavery in Egypt, the beginning of their journey to the "Promised Land."

Offered the opportunity to succeed or fail on their own terms, as independent farmers, thousands of African Americans made the trek to Kansas. Some bought farmland and formed new communities, such as Nicodemus, a town of about 700 black settlers from Kentucky. Others found work in towns and on farms in Texas, Oklahoma, and other plains states.

Despite their rising numbers and the independence that came with owning land, African Americans in the West still faced racism. For example, when a group of black migrants from Mississippi tried to settle in Lincoln, Nebraska, white townspeople drove them away. The migrants persisted, however, and Lincoln eventually accepted black residents into the community.

On April 22, 1889, about 50,000 people lined up on the Oklahoma border. The federal government had decided to open nearly 2 million acres of Indian Territory to settlement. At the signal, the Oklahoma land rush began. The homesteaders, known as "boomers," raced to stake their claims. By nightfall they had claimed nearly all the available land. Settlers who had entered the territory illegally days earlier were called "sooners."

This promotional print for the National Grange organization depicts idealized scenes of farm life. The Grange movement, founded in 1867 by Oliver Hudson Keeley, helped give a political voice to farmers.

12.6 Farmers Rise Up in Protest

Farmers transformed the grasslands of the Great Plains into bountiful croplands. Their hard work, aided by improved farm machinery, greatly increased agricultural productivity. Yet many of them failed to prosper. To buy costly new machinery, many had taken out bank loans, often at high interest rates. They also owed money to merchants for the seeds they bought on credit every year, and to railroads, which kept raising shipping rates. Crop prices, however, dropped as supply outstripped demand at home and in the world market. With their incomes reduced, farmers found it difficult to pay their debts. As their debts mounted, so did their anger.

Farmers' Frustrations Give Rise to Populism In 1867, Oliver Hudson Kelley started an educational and social organization to help farmers in Minnesota. Known as the National Grange, it soon spread throughout the country. The Grange helped farmers find their political voice. They channeled their anger into a protest movement based on **populism,** a political philosophy that favors the common person's interests over those of wealthy people or business interests.

In the early 1870s, several states passed "Granger laws" to regulate railroad rates. In 1886, the Supreme Court ruled in the case *Wabash, St. Louis and Pacific R.R. v. Illinois* that the federal government, not the states, had the power to regulate railroads because railroads were a form of interstate commerce. In response, Congress passed the Interstate Commerce Act in 1887. This law established the Interstate Commerce Commission to ensure that railroads set "reasonable and just" rates.

Farmers also took action through other organizations. One of these groups, the Greenback Party, was formed in the mid-1870s with a plan to raise crop prices and relieve farmers' debts. The Greenbackers' goal was to increase the amount of greenbacks, or paper money, in circulation by changing the **monetary policy** of the government. Monetary policy is aimed at controlling the supply and value of a country's currency.

At that time, the amount of money flowing through the U.S. economy was controlled by a monetary policy known as the **gold standard**. According to this policy, every paper dollar in circulation had to be backed by a dollar's worth of gold in the U.S. Treasury. The gold standard ensured the value of U.S. currency but limited the amount of money the government could print.

The Greenbackers wanted the government to increase the money supply by issuing greenbacks backed by both gold and silver. By increasing the money supply, Greenbackers hoped to fuel inflation, or a general rise in prices, including crop prices. Higher crop prices would give farmers more income with which to pay off their debts. The Greenback Party failed to achieve its main goal, but it did open many Americans' eyes to the farmer's plight.

In the 1880s, farmers in the South and Midwest formed local organizations called Farmers' Alliances. These groups later led protests against railroads, banks, and other powerful interests centered in the East. In the 1890 election, many Democratic and Republican candidates claiming to support policies proposed by Farmers' Alliances won elections at the state level and seats in Congress. Yet they enacted only a few Alliance proposals into law. In response, disappointed Alliance members vowed to create their own national political party.

The Rise and Fall of the Populist Party By 1892, populism had broadened its appeal beyond farmers to include industrial workers. That year, farm and labor leaders met in Omaha, Nebraska, to launch the People's Party, also known as the **Populist Party**. Populist candidate James B. Weaver ran for president that year on a platform that called for government ownership of railroads, the coinage of silver to increase the money supply, and other reforms designed to help working people. More than a million Americans voted for Weaver, about 8.5 percent of the total vote.

The money supply remained a major issue during the 1890s. The opposing sides of the debate became known as "silverites" and "gold bugs." The Republicans generally favored the gold standard. The Democrats were deeply divided, but the silverites prevailed as the election of 1896 approached. William Jennings Bryan won the Democratic presidential nomination with a moving speech that condemned the gold standard. In a booming voice he declared, "You shall not crucify mankind upon a cross of gold."

Instead of running their own candidate, the populists endorsed Bryan. The Democrats lost the election, and the Populist Party soon faded from the political scene. But the anger and idealism that had given rise to populism did not fade with it. During the party's short life, many Americans had begun to rethink what government could and should do to promote opportunity for all. "The power of government—in other words the power of the people—should be expanded," declared the populists' Omaha Platform, to end "oppression, injustice, and poverty." This vision would soon inspire a new generation of reformers.

At the 1896 Democratic convention, William Jennings Bryan gave his "Cross of Gold" speech to populist acclaim. Bryan demanded an end to the gold standard to increase the money supply.

Summary

Settlement of the West in the mid- and late 1800s brought opportunities for many Americans. This migration also sparked conflict as settlers invaded Indian homelands.

Mining Gold-rush fever sparked a rush of prospectors to the West. Though few fortunes were made, this migration helped populate California and other western regions.

Ranching Riding along the Chisholm Trail and other routes, cowboys herded cattle north to be shipped to meatpacking plants.

Transcontinental railroad Building the first rail line to California was a huge undertaking that relied on government support and immigrant labor. The spread of railroads across the West brought wealth to railroad barons and opened the region to settlement.

Indian wars The tribes on the Great Plains fought to preserve their way of life. To prevent conflict and open lands for settlement, the government moved tribes onto reservations. Through the Dawes Act, it tried to assimilate Indians into white culture.

Homestead Act The Homestead Act brought more farmers to the Great Plains, including African Americans who called themselves Exodusters. Farmers faced such challenges as crop-eating insects and drought.

Protests by farmers Burdened by falling crop prices and large debts, farmers formed political organizations such as the Grange. Their protest movements gave rise to the Populist Party.

Chapter 13

The Age of Innovation and Industry

Was the rise of industry good for the United States?

13.1 Introduction

In September 1878, a young inventor from Menlo Park, New Jersey, went to see a set of experimental arc lights. The lights were too hot and bright for practical use, but they fascinated him. The more he studied the lights and the generator that powered them, the more excited he became.

The inventor, Thomas Alva Edison, knew he could invent a better lighting system, one that could be used anywhere. At the age of 31, he was already known as the "Wizard of Menlo Park." Among his many inventions were the phonograph and a highly efficient automated telegraph system. Now Edison vowed to invent a practical incandescent lamp—what we would call a light bulb.

Edison and his team of scientists and mechanics set to work. Other inventors had tried for decades to produce a practical light bulb. The main problem was finding a filament—a thin fiber or wire—that would heat to a bright glow when electric current passed through it, but would not melt. Edison tried thousands of materials, from platinum to twine to human hair. Finally, around 1879, he tried bamboo fibers that he had pulled from a Japanese fan. After carbonization—the process of converting a fiber to pure carbon—the bamboo filament burned and burned without melting. Edison finally had his light bulb.

That major success did not end Edison's quest. He was already hard at work on other components of a complete electric lighting system. He and his team were designing generators, meters, and cables. They were making plans for distributing electricity. They were installing lighting displays to promote the benefits of the electric lamp. Edison did not simply invent the light bulb. He envisioned the future of electricity, and he acted to make his vision a reality.

Inventions like Edison's light bulb helped spur a new age of innovation and industry after the Civil War. This period also saw the rise of big businesses that created great wealth. This chapter explores how industrialization affected the nation as a whole. The next chapter examines its effects on workers.

Thomas Edison set up his first laboratory when he was just 10 years old. He would eventually become the most productive inventor in American history, with more than 1,000 inventions to his name.

◀ Edison's laboratory in New Jersey, around 1900

13.2 New Inventions and Technologies

Edison was one of thousands of ingenious inventors, mechanics, and scientists working to create new products and machines in the late 1800s. Thanks in part to their work, American life changed dramatically. The United States evolved from a largely agricultural nation into a complex industrial society.

This shift brought modern conveniences to many consumers. In 1865, Americans still lived in the "horse and buggy" era. They lit their homes with candles or oil lamps. They kept fresh foods in an icebox, a cabinet cooled by a large block of ice. And they waited a month or more for letters to cross the country. By 1900, many Americans illuminated their homes with electric lights. They kept foods cold in an electric refrigerator. They could send news across the continent in an instant by telegraph or telephone. A few could even afford to replace their horse and buggy with a new automobile.

Americans Invest in New Technology These innovations captured the imagination of investors who were willing to finance, or fund, the development of new products. Without this financial backing, many inventions would never have reached the market. Some would never have been built at all.

This willingness to risk money on new businesses lies at the heart of **capitalism**. Capitalism is an economic system in which factories, equipment, and other means of production are privately owned rather than being controlled by government. Capitalists in the late 1800s provided the funds to build railroads and factories and furnish them with machinery and supplies. They put money into new technology and scientific research. In return for risking their money, they hoped to reap rewards if the new business proved profitable.

Edison, for example, received generous financial support from a group of capitalists led by the wealthy banker J. P. Morgan. Together they formed the Edison Electric Light Company. In 1880 alone, this group provided the inventor with $150,000. In return, Edison gave the company the rights to his lighting inventions for a five-year period. The investors helped Edison pursue his vision, and they profited handsomely as a result.

Thomas Edison's light bulb was one of many innovations that dramatically changed the daily lives of Americans. By the early 1900s, many people had electricity and refrigeration in their homes. They could travel and communicate more rapidly. This print from 1882 shows workers laying tubes for electric wires on the streets of New York City.

Financial backers often protected their investments by making sure inventors acquired patents. A patent gives an inventor the sole legal right to make or sell an invention for a specified period of time. The federal government began issuing patents in 1790. By 1860, only 36,000 had been granted. Between 1860 and 1900, the number skyrocketed to more than 600,000. Edison holds the record for patents issued to one person, with 1,093 in all.

Revolutionary Changes in Communication and Transportation The use of electricity had brought dramatic progress in communications even before the Civil War. Artist and inventor Samuel F. B. Morse created the first practical telegraph by 1837. To send messages by electrical signal, he used a dot-and-dash system later known as Morse code. In 1843, Morse set up an experimental telegraph line linking Washington, D.C., with Baltimore, Maryland. He opened this line to commercial use the following year.

Telegraph lines soon crisscrossed the countryside, mainly following railroad tracks. The railroads relied on the telegraph to keep track of their trains. Newspapers also used the telegraph to gather information and send stories to local newspapers. Several companies established telegraph networks. By the 1870s, however, the Western Union Telegraph Company dominated the industry. By 1900, nearly a million miles of telegraph wires were carrying more than 60 million messages a year.

The next revolution in communications came with the telephone. For nearly 12 years, the inventor Alexander Graham Bell had pursued the idea of sending speech over wires. He finally succeeded on March 10, 1876. According to popular legend, the first telephone message was the result of an emergency—with Bell calling out to his lab assistant, Watson, after accidentally spilling acid. However, in a letter to his father, Bell made no mention of any accident:

> I was in one room at the Transmitting Instrument and Mr. Watson at the Receiving Instrument in another room—out of ear shot. I called out into the Transmitting Instrument, "Mr. Watson—come here—I want to see you"—and he came! He said he had heard each word perfectly . . . I feel that I have at last struck the solution of a great problem—and the day is coming when telegraph wires will be laid on to houses just like water or gas—and friends converse with each other without leaving home.

Bell's invention attracted plenty of financial support. In 1877, he founded the Bell Telephone Company. That same year, the first commercial telephone line was strung in Boston, where Bell lived. By 1893, more than 250,000 phones were in use. That year, Bell's patent ran out, allowing others to profit from his invention. Independent telephone companies formed across the country, helping create a surge in home use of the new technology. By 1920, the number of telephones had grown to at least 13 million.

Two other inventions changed how Americans moved. The first, the automobile, came to the United States from Europe. The second, the airplane, was home grown. In 1903, the brothers Orville and Wilbur Wright made the first successful powered-airplane flights in history, near Kitty Hawk, North Carolina. After that first success, inventors worked continually to improve airplane design.

In this illustration from 1863, soldiers set up an army telegraph line. The first telegraph lines went up in 1843. By 1866, companies had installed over 75,000 miles of wire. At first, railroads and newspapers took the greatest advantage of this high-speed means of communication. Soon many others benefited. By 1911, the nation had 1.5 million miles of telegraph wire. Someone could send a telegram from almost anywhere in the United States to almost anywhere else.

Oilfields like this one in Pennsylvania marked the birth of a huge new industry. Drilling companies took petroleum out of the ground. Refiners turned it into kerosene for lamps and into oil for lubricating machinery. Later they refined it into gasoline for automobiles.

"Rock Oil" Provides a New Source of Fuel The development of new fuels gave rise to another new industry. Before the Civil War, lamps mainly burned whale oil, which was very expensive. In the mid-1800s, a Canadian scientist discovered how to refine crude oil that seeped out of the ground into a lamp oil called kerosene. But the supply of surface oil was limited. Then a former railroad conductor named Edwin Drake made an important discovery.

In 1858, Drake went to Titusville, Pennsylvania, on business. He had bought stock in the Pennsylvania Rock Oil Company, which gathered surface oil for use in medicine. While in Titusville, Drake studied the techniques of drilling salt wells. Drake decided to lease land from the company for oil drilling. In August 1859, after several weeks of drilling, he struck oil.

Countless more wells were drilled in Pennsylvania and 13 other states. Oil drilling and refining became a huge industry, supplying fuel for lamps, lubricating oils for machinery, and later, gasoline for automobiles.

The Bessemer Process Revolutionizes Steelmaking A new technology for turning iron into steel gave rise to another major industry. Iron is a useful metal, but it is brittle and fairly soft. Steel is a purified form of iron mixed with carbon. Engineers prefer steel for most purposes because it is harder, stronger, and lighter than iron. Before the 1850s, however, the process for making steel out of iron was time-consuming and expensive.

The skyscraper relied on two technologies developed in the 1850s. The Bessemer process produced cheap steel, which was lighter and stronger than iron or brick. Engineers could now build tall structures that didn't collapse under their own weight. Invention of the passenger elevator provided easy access to the higher floors.

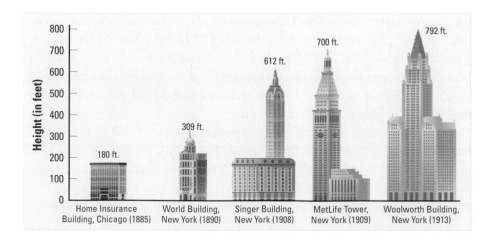

In 1855, a British inventor named Henry Bessemer patented a new method of making steel. The **Bessemer process** involved blowing air through molten iron. The blast of air removed impurities. Using this process, steel could be produced far more cheaply and quickly than in the past. After seeing the process at work in England, Andrew Carnegie decided to invest heavily in steel production in the United States. In 1873, he began to form the Carnegie Steel Company, which later built the largest and most modern steel mill of its time near Pittsburgh, Pennsylvania.

As the steel industry grew, steel became the metal of choice for heavy construction. Railroads switched to steel rails. Builders began using steel to construct longer bridges and taller buildings. In 1883, the longest suspension bridge in the world opened. This towering structure, the Brooklyn Bridge, stretched for 6,700 feet across the East River in New York City. Two years later, builders erected the world's first skyscraper, a 10-story building in downtown Chicago. Neither of these structures could have been built without the use of steel.

Electricity Lights Up America A single invention can have far-reaching effects. Edison's light bulb, for example, gave birth to the electric power industry. In 1882, Edison built a central generating station in New York City. Its wiring electrified a section of lower Manhattan. Before long, the demand for electricity became too great for the Edison Electric Light Company to meet on its own. Throughout the country, other companies built their own central generating stations to meet customers' needs. By 1891, there were more than 1,300 stations, providing enough electricity to power about 3 million light bulbs.

Access to electricity had a huge impact on American industry. Artificial light allowed businesses to stay open longer. Factories could run through the night. Electricity changed home life too. Americans could not only work and read at night but also plug in electric refrigerators and other appliances. Electricity was costly at first, though, and power companies built stations mainly in the cities. Many Americans, especially in rural areas, had to wait decades more for electric transmission lines to reach them.

The Electricity Building brightened the Pan-American Exposition of 1901 in Buffalo, New York. This site illuminated recent advances in the field of electricity. Displays included a variety of innovations in typesetting technology and electric machinery.

Men, women, and children operated the new machines that powered the industrial age. Workers often stood at their machines for 10 to 12 hours a day, with few breaks. For reasons of efficiency, they did the same task over and over again. This system boosted productivity, but it made the work dull and exhausting.

13.3 An Explosion of Industrial Growth

The growth of technology and the creation of communication and electric power networks helped fuel the expansion of American industry in the late 1800s. Companies that had once served mainly local markets expanded to sell their goods nationwide. To meet the needs of this growing national market, companies developed new ways of operating.

New Ways to Manage Work Farsighted business owners realized they could profit from serving customers nationwide. But to do this, they had to create systems of mass production that would enable them to supply a much larger market. The basic elements of this system already existed. By the early 1800s, factories were using interchangeable parts to produce goods in large quantities.

After the Civil War, factory owners improved these methods of mass production. They built specialized machinery that could produce identical parts for quick assembly into finished products. They no longer needed skilled artisans to craft individual parts. Instead, they could use unskilled workers to run the machines and hire supervisors to manage the day-to-day operations.

Engineers reorganized factory work to increase productivity, dividing up the production process so that each worker did a single task. One engineer, Frederick W. Taylor, used scientific techniques to analyze these tasks. He watched workers and timed them with a stopwatch. Through these time-and-motion studies, he determined the most efficient way to perform each task. He trained workers to work faster by reducing wasted motion. Speed boosted productivity, which increased profits.

How Did Ford's Assembly Line Work?

Henry Ford pioneered the use of the moving assembly line to make a complex product with hundreds of parts. This innovation cut the time needed to assemble a Model T Ford from more than 12 hours to less than 6 hours. By making production so efficient, Ford could produce a "motor car for the multitudes."

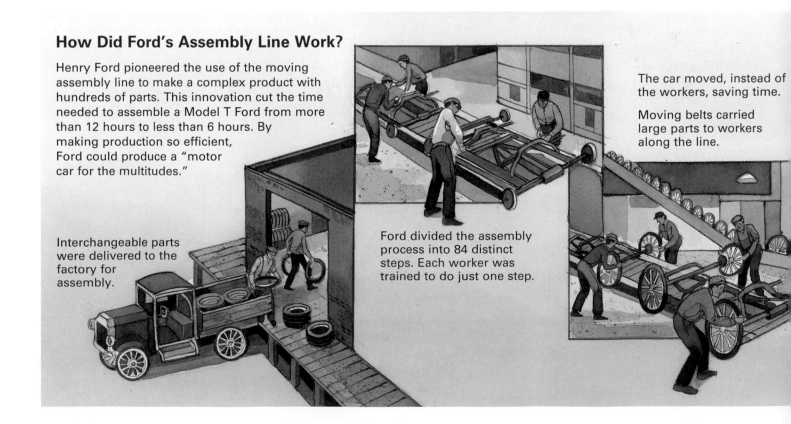

Interchangeable parts were delivered to the factory for assembly.

Ford divided the assembly process into 84 distinct steps. Each worker was trained to do just one step.

The car moved, instead of the workers, saving time.

Moving belts carried large parts to workers along the line.

Taylor later published his findings in a book called *The Principles of Scientific Management*. The book had a profound effect on industry in the early 1900s. One person who took it seriously was Henry Ford, who pioneered the moving assembly line to mass-produce automobiles. In a Ford plant, there was no wasted motion. Workers stood in one place all day, while a conveyor belt brought the work to them. Each worker did one or two small tasks, and then the belt moved the car to the next worker's station. One worker might put bolts in the frame while the next worker tightened them down. The process continued, part by part, until the car rolled off the assembly line, ready to be driven away.

Increased productivity resulted in cheaper goods. But it also meant that a factory could operate with fewer workers. Those who remained had to perform the same dull task all day long, but at a faster pace. Many assembly-line workers felt as though they had become machines. As you will read in Chapter 14, workers often protested for better working conditions.

New Ways to Finance and Organize Businesses Before the Civil War, individual owners ran most businesses. As businesses grew larger, however, their need for the three basic **factors of production**—land, labor, and capital—grew as well. Land, which includes resources such as soil, forests, and minerals, was still abundant. Labor was plentiful as well thanks to a steady stream of immigrants into the country during this period. **Capital,** however, was a problem. Capital is any asset that can be used to produce an income. Money, buildings, tools, and machinery are all forms of capital.

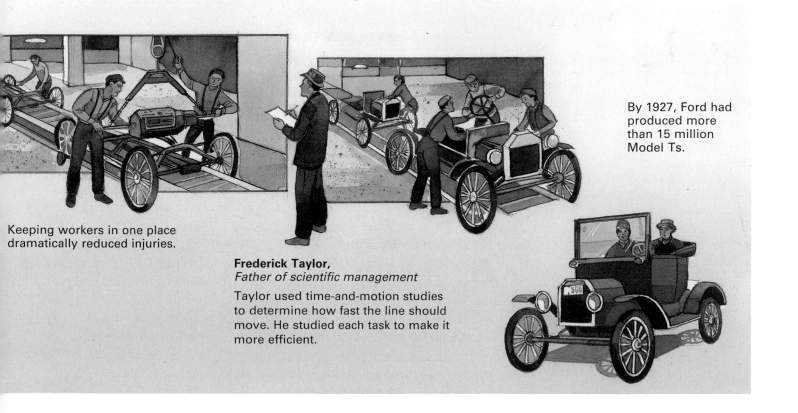

Keeping workers in one place dramatically reduced injuries.

Frederick Taylor,
Father of scientific management
Taylor used time-and-motion studies to determine how fast the line should move. He studied each task to make it more efficient.

By 1927, Ford had produced more than 15 million Model Ts.

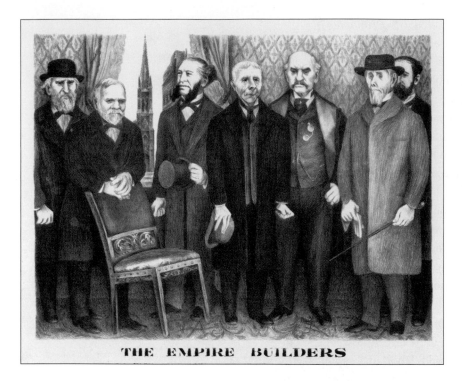

THE EMPIRE BUILDERS

Industrialists profited from new ways of financing and organizing businesses. Andrew Carnegie (second from left) used efficient business practices and new technology in his steel plants. Carnegie and other "captains of industry" also set up trusts and built monopolies. These forms of big business brought them great personal wealth.

Small business owners did not have all the capital they needed to expand. For this reason, many of them formed **corporations**.

A corporation is a company that is recognized by law as existing independently from its owners. A corporation can own property, borrow money, sue, or be sued. People invest in corporations by buying stock, or a share in the ownership of the business. By buying stock, investors became owners of the company. The money they paid for their stock helped to finance the corporation. Wealthy capitalists controlled corporations by buying huge amounts of stock.

As owners of a corporation, stockholders could profit from its success. Unlike the owners of small businesses, however, investors were not liable for a corporation's debts. The most they could lose was the amount they invested. Also, these owners did not run the daily operations. The corporation hired managers, accountants, engineers, and others to keep production going.

Competition among corporations provided consumers with a wide choice of new products, but it caused headaches for business owners. In the battle to sell products, companies slashed prices. Profits fell, debts rose, and many companies went bankrupt. Cutthroat competition threatened to drag down even the best-run companies. As a result, some powerful capitalists decided that to stay in business, they would have to limit competition.

Business owners began devising ways to reduce competition. One method was to buy or bankrupt competitors. John D. Rockefeller had great success with this approach in the oil industry. During the 1860s, he earned a fortune refining oil in Cleveland, Ohio. In 1870, he formed a corporation called Standard Oil. Standard Oil expanded by buying out or merging with other companies. Rockefeller's company also undercut its competitors by making deals with railroads, which agreed to ship its oil at discount prices. The savings on shipping allowed Standard Oil to cut its oil prices. These price cuts forced smaller oil companies to reduce prices too, causing many of them to either be sold to Standard Oil or go bankrupt. Rockefeller told one independent oil refiner, "You can't compete with the Standard . . . If you refuse to sell, it will end in your being crushed."

By 1882, Standard Oil had become a **monopoly,** a company that completely dominates a particular industry. It controlled 90 percent of the nation's oil production. With its competitors out of the way, Standard Oil could raise its prices and reap great profits.

Another approach to reducing competition was to form business **trusts**. A trust is a set of companies that are managed by a small group known as trustees. The trustees have the power to prevent companies in the trust from competing with each other.

13.4 Big Business and the Government

Trusts and monopolies concentrated capital—and power—in the hands of a few people. With less competition, companies grew larger and more profitable. Americans began to refer to these industrial giants as "big business." Unlike owners of small, traditional businesses, those who ran huge corporations seldom knew their workers. Big business was impersonal, extremely profit-driven, and responsive mainly to investors.

Businesses Grow Larger and More Powerful Corporations generally expanded in one of two ways. The first strategy was **horizontal integration**. This approach called for joining together as many firms from the same industry as possible. An example was Standard Oil's practice of buying up refineries to gain control of the oil-refining industry.

A second strategy was known as **vertical integration**. This approach involved taking control of each step in the production and distribution of a product, from acquiring raw materials to manufacturing, packaging, and shipping. Carnegie expanded his steel company through vertical integration. He bought the iron mines and coalfields that sent raw materials to his company's mills. He bought the ships and railroads that transported supplies and finished products. Vertical integration gave Carnegie complete control of the production process and the power to dominate the steel industry.

The Government Leaves Business Alone By the late 1800s, many Americans realized that big business was limiting competition. Lack of competition allowed prices to rise, which helped producers but hurt consumers. However, lawmakers were unwilling to stop such business practices. Most politicians had long favored a policy of **laissez-faire**. This doctrine held that the market, through supply and demand, would regulate itself if government did not interfere. The French phrase *laissez-faire* translates as "allow to do." To political leaders, this meant "leave business alone."

Another influential idea at the time, **social Darwinism,** also discouraged government regulation of business practices. Based on Charles Darwin's theory of evolution, social Darwinism held that the best-run businesses led by the most capable people would survive and prosper. This doctrine's most avid supporter, Herbert Spencer, coined the phrase "survival of the fittest." Social Darwinists argued that government should leave businesses alone to succeed or fail on their own.

Some industrialists, like John Rockefeller, expanded their business through horizontal integration. They worked to buy up every company they could in the same business. In Rockefeller's case, horizontal integration led to monopoly. Others, like Andrew Carnegie, expanded through vertical integration. They worked to bring every process of their business—from generating raw materials to marketing the finished product to consumers—under their control.

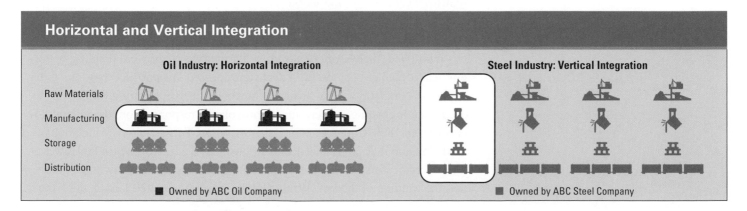

Horizontal and Vertical Integration

Oil Industry: Horizontal Integration

Raw Materials
Manufacturing
Storage
Distribution

■ Owned by ABC Oil Company

Steel Industry: Vertical Integration

■ Owned by ABC Steel Company

This cartoon, titled "The Protectors of Our Industries," shows four wealthy industrialists—Marshall Field, Cornelius Vanderbilt, Jay Gould, and Russell Sage—sitting on their moneybags. These "protectors" amassed huge fortunes while paying their workers, seen below, as little as possible. Gould was widely viewed as the most corrupt of the robber barons. He considered himself the most hated man in 19th-century America.

In reality, the federal government did not leave businesses alone, but actually helped many of them. It gave the railroads hundreds of millions of dollars worth of land. It sold natural resources such as forests and minerals at very low prices to companies that were prepared to exploit them. It also imposed protective tariffs on foreign goods to make them more expensive than American-made goods. Tariffs forced consumers to pay higher prices than they would have in a free market.

During the late 1800s, some businesses bribed legislators to pass laws favoring their companies. Much of the free land handed out to the railroads, for example, came in return for cash payments to politicians. In 1904, journalist Lincoln Steffens wrote, "Our political leaders are hired, by bribery . . . to conduct the government of city, state, and nation, not for the common good, but for the special interests of private business."

Tariffs and other government aid did help industry prosper. In the late 1800s, the American economy grew rapidly. From 1877 to 1900, the value of American exports doubled. By 1900, the United States had the strongest industrial economy in the world.

Government Takes Some Action to Limit Business As trusts and monopolies multiplied, many Americans grew alarmed that they were denying opportunities to smaller businesses. A few states passed laws or filed lawsuits to try to restore competition. Big business, however, just kept getting bigger.

Increasing public concern finally provoked a response from the federal government. In 1890, Congress passed the **Sherman Antitrust Act,** which outlawed trusts, monopolies, and other forms of business that restricted trade. However, the government made only feeble attempts to enforce the new law. One problem was the wording of the law. Written by lawyers who favored laissez-faire, the

Sherman Antitrust Act was full of vague language. Congress left it to the courts to clarify the law, but the courts were not impartial, or unbiased. They often interpreted the law in favor of big business. For example, in 1895 the Supreme Court blocked government efforts to break up a sugar trust that controlled most of the nation's sugar manufacturing. In *United States v. E.C. Knight Co.,* the Court ruled that the Sherman Act applied only to trade, not to manufacturing.

13.5 The Gilded Age

In 1873, the writer Mark Twain coauthored a book about rich industrialists and corrupt politicians called *The Gilded Age*. Something that is gilded looks like gold, but only on the outside. The title described American society in this period well. Industrialists who had made great fortunes led glittering lives. But beneath that glitter, this period was marked by political corruption and social unrest.

From Industrialists to Philanthropists During the Gilded Age, the growth of three industries fueled a rapid expansion of the American economy. From 1870 to 1900, steel production rose from 77,000 tons to more than 11 million tons. Oil production swelled from around 5 million barrels annually to more than 63 million barrels. Railroad track expanded from 53,000 to around 200,000 miles. From these industries, three towering figures emerged: Carnegie, Rockefeller, and Cornelius Vanderbilt. All three started as **entrepreneurs**—bold risk-takers who established new businesses. Along the way, they amassed huge fortunes.

Wealthy industrialists lived in grand style during the Gilded Age. Many "captains of industry" built lavish homes, such as the Vanderbilt Breakers mansion in Newport, Rhode Island. Meanwhile, many of their workers lived in poverty.

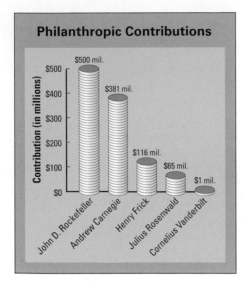

Philanthropic Contributions

Contribution (in millions)

- $500 mil. — John D. Rockefeller
- $381 mil. — Andrew Carnegie
- $116 mil. — Henry Frick
- $65 mil. — Julius Rosenwald
- $1 mil. — Cornelius Vanderbilt

Some successful industrialists used their wealth to promote the common good. Rockefeller and Carnegie gave away huge sums. Henry Clay Frick, Carnegie Steel's chairman of the board, followed his boss's example. Julius Rosenwald, head of Sears, Roebuck and Company, was also a generous philanthropist. Vanderbilt willed most of his $100 million fortune to his son, but did give away $1 million to found Vanderbilt University.

In 1890, Carnegie earned $25 million. That year, the average industrial worker made about $440. Carnegie lived in a 4-story, 64-room mansion on Millionaires' Row in New York City. Workers near his Pittsburgh mill lived in cramped, poorly ventilated rooms with primitive sanitation. This huge gap in living standards did not bother most industrialists. Some would have explained it as social Darwinism in action. Others might have said that by working hard and following Carnegie's example, anyone could be rich.

Carnegie's rags-to-riches story supported such views. After arriving from Scotland in 1848 at the age of 12, he worked in a Pennsylvania cotton mill earning $1.20 a week. His thrift and shrewd investments gave him a $50,000 annual income by the time he was 30. Through a combination of daring business tactics and technological innovation, Carnegie prospered and gained control of several steel plants. In 1889, the year before his income hit $25 million, he published an article titled "Wealth." In it, he declared that rich people had a duty to use their surplus wealth for "the improvement of mankind." He added, "A man who dies rich dies disgraced."

Carnegie set a splendid example by using his fortune to benefit society. In 1911, he established the Carnegie Corporation of New York. This charitable foundation offered grants of money to promote the advancement of knowledge. It focused on education, especially libraries. Carnegie helped build more than 2,500 free public libraries throughout the world. He also used his money to support cultural institutions and to promote international peace.

Like Carnegie, Rockefeller had the foresight to get in on the ground floor of an industry with a bright future. He started with one oil refinery, which he built into a huge corporation, Standard Oil. Rockefeller's monopolistic approach to business brought him fabulous wealth—and a terrible reputation. In an era of tough competition, he stood out for his ruthless tactics. However, like Carnegie, he became a **philanthropist,** a person who gives money to support worthy causes. He used his fortune to help establish the University of Chicago in 1892. He also started several charitable organizations, including the Rockefeller Foundation. Through these organizations, he supported medical research, education, and the arts.

Cornelius Vanderbilt followed a similar path to wealth. In 1810, at the age of 16, he started a ferry business in New York Harbor. Later he built up a fleet of steamships. By upgrading his ships and cutting shipping rates, he prospered. Ambitious and clever, Vanderbilt mastered the world of trade and transportation. He set up a profitable route from New York to San Francisco in time to carry many forty-niners to the goldfields. In 1862, he sold his steamer business and invested in railroad stock. He soon owned several rail lines, opening the first direct service from New York City to Chicago. Unlike Carnegie and Rockefeller, however, Vanderbilt never believed he had a duty to use his wealth to benefit society. Nevertheless, in 1873, he donated $1 million to found Vanderbilt University in Nashville, Tennessee.

Robber Barons or Captains of Industry? History is not quite sure how to judge the business giants of the Gilded Age. Critics call them robber barons for the way they gained their wealth and the lordly style in which they lived. Supporters call them captains of industry who, despite some shady dealings, helped usher in our modern economy.

From the critics' point of view, the industrialists prospered for mostly negative reasons. They ruthlessly drove rivals out of business and raised prices by limiting competition. They robbed the nation of its natural resources and bribed officials to ensure their success. They kept wages low and imposed dreadful working conditions, while trying to squeeze every ounce of work out of their employees.

Supporters argue, however, that industrialists prospered for mostly positive reasons. They worked hard and took advantage of new technology. Industrialists found new ways to finance and organize businesses for greater efficiency and productivity. And their success created jobs for millions of Americans. Shopkeepers, doctors, lawyers, and others in the growing middle class profited from the up-surge in business. Their living standards climbed along with the rising economy. But it would take years of struggle before workers shared in these benefits, as you will read in the next chapter. Perhaps the greatest inequality in American history occurred during the Gilded Age.

This debate about the overall impact of the industrialists may never be resolved. But one thing is clear. The industrial expansion of the late 1800s helped give rise to a vibrant economy and consumer society. Americans had access to an unprecedented abundance of goods and services—and they kept demanding more. By the early 1900s, economic growth had helped make the United States one of the most powerful nations in the world.

Much of the philanthropy of a century ago still provides benefits today. Charitable foundations established in the Gilded Age continue to support worthy causes. Libraries like this one, built through a Carnegie grant, remain vibrant institutions in many communities.

Summary

Innovations in technology and business boosted American industry in the late 1800s. Large steel, oil, and railroad corporations dominated the economy, with little governmental control. Industrial expansion produced greater access to goods and services, and it improved standards of living for many Americans, but not all.

Innovations and inventions Innovations, such as the electric light bulb and kerosene, spurred the growth of new industries. The telegraph and telephone brought modern communications to homes and businesses. The Bessemer process lowered the cost of steel and encouraged new forms of construction.

New business techniques Business leaders formed corporations to attract capital from investors, who became owners by buying stock. They improved production methods in order to mass-produce more goods in less time. By promoting horizontal or vertical integration, some leaders gained control of major industries. They also sought to reduce competition by forming monopolies and trusts.

Laissez-faire The federal government generally adopted a laissez-faire policy toward business. This hands-off approach reflected a belief in social Darwinism. The Sherman Antitrust Act was only feebly enforced.

The Gilded Age While industrialists amassed great fortunes, society was tainted by political corruption and a huge gap between rich and poor. Carnegie, Rockefeller, and Vanderbilt used some of their wealth to promote the common good. Historians debate their overall impact, noting increased industrial productivity but also unfair business practices.

Chapter 14

Labor's Response to Industrialism

Was the rise of industry good for American workers?

14.1 Introduction

In 1898, a young woman named Rose Schneiderman was hired at a factory in New York City. Her job was to sew the linings into men's caps. But she would soon take on a much larger role in the story of American labor.

Like most factory workers at the time, Schneiderman worked long hours under difficult conditions. At night, she returned home to a crowded, run-down apartment. But Schneiderman was determined to improve these conditions. She began to organize the workers at the cap factory. Before long, she had become a leader of the New York City branch of the Women's Trade Union League, a national labor organization.

In 1909, Schneiderman helped organize a major labor action known as the "Uprising of 20,000." In this event, thousands of young women walked off their jobs making clothing at garment factories in New York. The women were demanding higher wages and better working conditions. Some companies made settlements with the workers. However, demands for unlocked factory doors and working fire escapes were never met. Although their walkout failed to achieve all of their goals, it did set the stage for more labor actions to come.

Two years later, a tragedy at a garment factory helped focus even more attention on the plight of workers. In 1911, the Triangle Shirtwaist Factory caught fire. Because the doors to the factory were locked, many of the women couldn't escape. One hundred forty-six workers died in the fire. Afterward, on April 2, Schneiderman gave an impassioned speech. In it, she said,

> This is not the first time girls have been burned alive in the city. Every week I must learn of the untimely death of one of my sister workers . . . The life of men and women is so cheap and property is so sacred . . . It is up to the working people to save themselves. The only way they can save themselves is by a strong working-class movement.

Over the years, Schneiderman continued her efforts on behalf of American workers. She became one of the key figures in the American labor movement.

In the fall of 1909, some 20,000 garment workers in New York City went on strike in what was called the "Uprising of 20,000." Strikers stood on picket lines outside factories, where many were arrested by the police or beaten by hired thugs. The strike lasted for 14 weeks but produced only modest gains for workers.

◀ Triangle Shirtwaist Fire, March 25, 1911

In textile factories, coal mines, or steel mills like the one shown here, workers labored under harsh conditions. Steelworkers put up with noise, heat, and dust. They also faced the ongoing threat of injury or death from heavy machinery or molten steel.

14.2 Conditions of the Working Class

Americans have long cherished the ideal of equality. Unlike European countries, the United States has never had monarchs or noble families who held economic and political power just because they were part of an upper class. In the Gilded Age, however, a class system started to emerge in the United States. That is, society began to divide into unequal groups based on wealth and power.

In 1879, the economist Henry George described this change as an "immense wedge" being forced through society. "Those who are above the point of separation are elevated, but those who are below are crushed down." The people being crushed belonged to the working class.

Many Workers Labored Under Terrible Conditions The working class included men, women, and children. They provided the skill and the muscle that helped push American productivity to new heights and made employers rich. Yet those same employers often treated their workers—their human resources—as if they were merely parts of the machinery.

Industrial workers had an exhausting schedule. They typically worked 6 days a week, for 10 or more hours a day. For their efforts, workers earned about $1 a day. The work itself was repetitive and boring. Unlike farming or craft work, in which a worker did a variety of tasks, the factory system relied on a **division of labor**. This meant that production was divided into separate tasks, with one task assigned to each worker. Factory owners designed the system this way for the sake of efficiency.

Workers often performed their tasks in hazardous environments. A priest described a steel plant as "the slaughterhouse; they kill them [workers] there every day." Whirling shafts, slippery floors, spinning blades, and molten steel all had the potential to injure or kill. Unlike today, worker safety was not a major concern. Workers were not given helmets or safety glasses, and those who were hurt or disabled received little or no financial compensation for their injuries. Factory owners believed that paying wages fulfilled their obligation to workers.

Industrial processing often created toxic gases and dust. Workers in textile mills, for example, inhaled cotton dust all day. Worse yet was the situation of coal miners. Mary Harris ("Mother") Jones, a labor activist, described the "wretched work" that miners did. Their lungs "breathe coal dust," she wrote, and "coal dust grinds itself into the skin, never to be removed." Textile workers and miners suffered from lung diseases. Workers in cramped, unventilated **sweatshops** faced the constant threat of contagious diseases such as tuberculosis. A sweatshop is a small factory where employees work long hours under poor conditions for low wages.

Laborers put up with such adversity, or hardship, because they could lose their jobs if they protested. With immigrants pouring into the country, employers had little trouble replacing a complaining worker.

Widespread Child Labor Children worked in industry for two main reasons. First, even with both parents employed, a typical family could barely survive. The child's wages, though meager, made a crucial difference. Secondly, children earned less than adults, so factory owners were happy to employ them. At the same time, children were expected to do the same amount of work as their parents.

Throughout the 1800s, critics voiced concerns about child labor. Some states enacted laws setting a minimum age for workers, often 14 or 15 years. However, these laws led to little change. Where child-labor laws existed, companies often ignored them, and states often failed to enforce them. As a result, 6-year-olds worked in Georgia's cotton mills, and boys as young as 8 worked in the coal mines of Pennsylvania. In 1907, poet Edwin Markham described a typical street scene in New York's garment district: "Nearly any hour on the East Side of New York City you can see them—pallid boy or spindling girl—their faces dulled, their backs bent under a heavy load of garments piled on head and shoulders."

Child workers experienced some of the most dangerous working conditions. Because they were small, they could squeeze inside running machinery to make repairs. Young miners driving mules through tunnels risked being crushed by loads of coal. In January 1876, a Pennsylvania newspaper noted, "During the past week nearly one boy a day has been killed" in the mines.

Unsanitary Living Conditions When their shifts finally ended, worn-out industrial workers headed home. For most, however, home offered little comfort. The great mass of workers, especially immigrants, lived in slums—heavily populated parts of a city marked by filth and squalor. Jane Addams, a social reformer, described a typical slum in Chicago:

> The streets are inexpressibly dirty, the number of schools inadequate, sanitary legislation unenforced, the street lighting bad, the paving miserable and altogether lacking in the alleys and smaller streets, and the stables foul beyond description.
> —Jane Addams, *Twenty Years at Hull-House,* 1910

In the slums, workers lived in **tenements,** run-down apartment buildings of four to six stories, usually housing four families on each floor. A New York commission noted that these families "cook, eat, and sleep in the same room, men, women, and children together." Disease flourished in such cramped and often airless quarters, and fire was an ever-present danger.

Children often ran the machines in factories like this one, photographed in 1908. They worked under the same dangerous, unhealthy conditions as adults. Only a few states had laws regulating child labor. As a result, children under 10 years of age worked long hours in cotton mills, mines, and factories into the early 1900s.

Conditions in tenement buildings were crowded and dirty. In this tenement room, the family slept, ate, and hung their laundry. At the table the mother and children work at making trimings for hats to earn extra money.

14.3 The Labor Movement

In the late 1800s, workers in American industry faced a set of painful facts. Their pay was low, and they worked in dangerous and unhealthy conditions. Their homes were often equally dismal, and their children had little opportunity to go to school. Whenever the economy slumped, life got even worse. Employers cut workers' pay or eliminated their jobs. Perhaps most distressing of all, individual workers had little power to change their circumstances. They could not bargain with employers. Nor could they seek help from the government, which did little to regulate working conditions.

American workers joined together in labor unions as early as the 1790s. Few strikes, however, took place before the Civil War. One early strike, in 1860, pitted women shoe-makers against factory owners in Lynn, Massachusetts.

Workers Unite for Better Conditions In the early years of the Industrial Revolution, some workers developed a strategy for improving their lives. They formed **labor unions**. A labor union is a group of workers organized to protect the interests of its members. Historically, most labor unions have focused on three primary goals: higher wages, shorter hours, and better working conditions.

The first worker organizations in the United States appeared in the late 1700s in New York City and Philadelphia. By the mid-1800s, local unions had formed in many other cities. Much of a union's power came from the threat of a **strike,** a labor action in which workers simply refuse to go to work. A strike could easily shut down a factory, railroad, or mine. Unions generally used the strike as a last resort, when owners would not sit down to discuss the issues.

A Difficult Start for National Labor Organizations After the Civil War, local unions began to realize that they might benefit from cooperating with each other to achieve their goals. As a result, a number of unions joined forces to form a national labor federation, or group of unions. This federation focused on efforts to establish an eight-hour workday. But poor leadership and lack of unity led to its collapse in 1872.

In the mid-1870s, an economic depression inflicted more damage on efforts to create national labor unions. In times of economic crisis, high unemployment intensified the competition for jobs.

Some business owners used this competition to undermine unions. They pressured workers to sign "yellow-dog contracts," written pledges not to join a union. Owners would not hire workers who did not sign a pledge. They also exchanged lists of union members and organizers, refusing jobs to any worker whose name was on these blacklists. Yellow-dog contracts and blacklists discouraged workers from joining unions.

Common Goals, Different Strategies During the depression of the 1870s, business owners' tactics succeeded in smashing many labor unions. After the economy regained its strength, however, the labor movement also revived. A series of new national labor organizations arose, bringing together various unions under one banner.

One of these new federations was the Knights of Labor. It attracted many members in the late 1870s with a policy of accepting both skilled and unskilled workers, including women and African Americans. However, the Knights declined after 1886, in part because of competition from another federation.

That rival group was the **American Federation of Labor (AFL)**. Unlike the Knights, the AFL concentrated mainly on organizing skilled workers. It also had a more narrow focus on "bread-and-butter" worker objectives, such as higher wages and shorter workdays. Founded in 1886, the AFL became the only major national labor organization in the 1890s.

In the early 1900s, another labor organization arose, the Industrial Workers of the World (IWW). Its members were nicknamed Wobblies. IWW leaders introduced radical ideas into the union movement, adopting the socialist theories of the German political philosopher Karl Marx. **Socialism** is a political theory that advocates ownership of the means of production, such as factories and farms, by the people rather than by capitalists and landowners. Its goals are the elimination of private property and the fair treatment of workers. IWW members saw socialism as the path to a better life for workers.

In practice, each of these national labor organizations acted as a union. They engaged in **collective bargaining**—negotiations between employers and employee representatives concerning wages, working conditions, and other terms of employment. They also called strikes when collective bargaining failed.

These three national labor organizations had a huge impact on the labor movement. Each had its own policies and strategies for improving workers' lives, and each attracted a different set of workers.

Three National Labor Organizations

Union	Year Formed, Key Leaders	Goals	Members	Peak Membership	Strategies
Knights of Labor	1869, Terence Powderly	• eight-hour workday • abolition of child labor • regulation of trusts • equal pay for men and women • education for the working class	• skilled and unskilled workers • women • African Americans	700,000 members in 1886	• arbitration • boycotts • strikes
American Federation of Labor	1886, Samuel Gompers	• increased wages • improved working conditions • limitation of work hours • recognition of the AFL	only skilled workers in a particular trade	1 million members in 1900	• negotiation • boycotts • strikes
Industrial Workers of the World	1905, William Haywood, Eugene V. Debs, Daniel De Leon	• organization of all workers into a single union • overthrow of capitalism	• lumbermen • miners • textile workers • dockworkers	100,000 members between 1912 and 1917	• boycotts • strikes • sabotage

The Railroad Strike of 1877 started in West Virginia after the B & O Railroad cut wages. The strike spread rapidly, and strikers soon shut down most of the nation's rail lines. Several governors called in their state militias to restore order. Violent clashes like the one shown here, in Pittsburg, killed more than 100 people nationwide.

14.4 Strikes Erupt Nationwide

As labor unions gained strength in the late 1800s, workers showed a greater willingness to strike. At the same time, business owners stubbornly opposed union demands. As a result, confrontations between unions and owners increased. These struggles intensified after a bitter railroad strike in 1877.

Violence Marks the Railroad Strike of 1877 The railroad strike began during the depression of the mid-1870s. The government, holding to its laissez-faire policy, did nothing to boost the economy or help suffering workers. As families starved and children died, rage boiled up in working-class communities.

Meanwhile, railroad companies responded to the depression by slashing wages. In 1877, rail workers in West Virginia went on strike. The strike soon spread across the country. Before long, strikers had shut down at least half of the nation's rail lines. It was the largest labor uprising in U.S. history.

To keep the tracks closed, strikers battled police and state militias. Meanwhile, riots broke out in various cities as strike supporters expressed their anger by burning and looting railroad property. Police and militia forces could not control the chaos. Finally, President Rutherford B. Hayes called in the army. He used federal troops to restore order and get the trains rolling again. It was the first time the U.S. Army had been used to break a strike, but it would not be the last.

Two weeks of turmoil had left about 100 people dead and millions of dollars worth of property destroyed. The violence and destruction alarmed many Americans. They feared a working-class revolution, perhaps led by socialists or other radical groups. Such a revolution did not take place, but the stage was set for even larger and more violent strikes.

More Strikes, More Violence The Railroad Strike of 1877 boosted union membership and gave members a greater sense of their own power. In the years that followed, national labor organizations tried to harness that power to change working conditions. Strikes became more numerous during this time. Three major events during this period underscored the growing struggle between owners and workers: the **Haymarket Affair,** the **Homestead Strike,** and the **Pullman Strike.**

The Haymarket Affair took place in Chicago in 1886. It started when strikers fought with "scabs," nonunion workers brought in to replace striking workers. Police trying to break up the fight shot into the crowd, killing at least one striker and wounding others. A group of **anarchists**—people who reject all forms of government—called for a protest meeting the next day in Haymarket Square.

More than a thousand people showed up for the meeting, including the city's mayor. Several speakers addressed the crowd. The mayor noted that the crowd remained calm. Near the end of the speeches, however, a force of about 180 Chicago police stormed in to break up the gathering. In the confusion that followed, someone threw a bomb that exploded among the police. Panicked, the police fired into the crowd, killing at least four protesters. Several officers died.

The bomber was never identified, but four radical anarchists were tried and executed for their part in the demonstration. The Haymarket Affair divided and confused the labor movement. Many workers backed the anarchists, but union

leaders feared that supporting the radicals might further inflame public fears.

The Homestead Strike came several years later, in 1892. It involved iron- and steelworkers at the Carnegie Steel plant in Homestead, Pennsylvania. Andrew Carnegie was away in Europe at the time and had left his manager, Henry Frick, in charge. Frick hired 300 private guards from the Pinkerton Agency to protect the plant against the strikers. Industrialists had hired Pinkerton agents before. They often worked as spies, joining unions to discover their plans and identify union members. Though not police officers, the Pinkerton men carried guns.

When the Pinkerton agents arrived at the plant, the strikers were armed and ready. After a daylong gun battle in which nine strikers died, the Pinkerton agents gave up and the strikers took control of the town. Pennsylvania's governor then called out the state militia, and the strikers scattered. Frick brought in nonunion workers to run the plant, and the union was shut out for the next four decades.

In the Pullman Strike of 1894, the government again supported management against striking workers. The Pullman Palace Car Company, in the southern part of Chicago, made fancy railcars for long-distance travelers. Its employees all lived in the company town of Pullman. In company towns, workers rented company-owned housing and bought food and other goods at company stores, often at inflated prices. As a result, many workers owed large debts to the company. Often all of their wages went toward paying off bills at the company store.

In the spring of 1894, during another depression, Pullman cut wages, but not rents or other charges, by about 25 percent. Frustrated, the workers went on strike. The American Railway Union supported the Pullman Strike. Its members shut down most rail traffic in the Midwest by refusing to handle trains with Pullman cars. Some of those trains included mail cars, and interfering with the mail was a federal offense. Therefore, President Grover Cleveland sent federal troops into Chicago to break the strike. After a violent encounter between troops and strikers, the strike collapsed, and the troops withdrew.

A bomb exploded among police in Chicago's Haymarket Square in 1886 during a rally held by local anarchists. Several officers and civilians died. By the time the Haymarket Affair ended, four anarchists had been executed for the crime.

14.5 Mixed Success for Unions

The union struggles of the late 1800s brought mixed results for organized labor. Unions generally experienced more setbacks than gains and failed to get government support or the backing of most Americans. Through collective bargaining and strikes, however, they made some advances, especially on the issues of hours and wages.

Setbacks: Government Favors Owners over Workers Although the Railroad Strike of 1877 helped boost union membership, it prompted the federal government to take the side of business owners in most labor disputes. Unions needed government support to improve the lives of workers, but the federal government generally opposed union activities. It sent troops to break up strikes and used legal means to undermine unions.

The Pullman Strike revealed one way the federal government could intervene to favor employers over unions. To end the strike, a federal court issued an injunction against the American Railway Union and its head, Eugene V. Debs. An injunction is a court order that prohibits a specific action. The court based the injunction on a broad interpretation of the Sherman Antitrust Act. This act was designed to prohibit trusts and monopolies. Now it was being used against striking workers, on the grounds that their strike limited trade and commerce.

When Debs and other railway union leaders ignored the injunction, they were arrested and sent to jail. Later the Supreme Court ruled, in the case *In re Debs,* that such a broad, or "blanket," injunction was legal. After that decision,

Heroes of the Labor Movement

Rose Schneiderman

Rose Schneiderman was born in Poland and became a union leader in New York City in the early 1900s. After the 1911 fire at the Triangle Shirtwaist Factory, she worked as a leader with the International Ladies Garment Workers Union to lobby for fire-safety laws and other union-backed reforms.

Samuel Gompers

Samuel Gompers started out as a cigar maker and local union leader in New York City. He later helped found the American Federation of Labor and served as its president for almost 40 years. A moderate, he favored cooperation over strikes and resisted efforts to introduce socialist ideas into the AFL.

Mary Harris "Mother" Jones

Mother Jones roamed the country helping coal miners, textile workers, and others to form unions. A fiery and persuasive speaker, she called herself a "hell-raiser." She wrote, "Injustice boils in men's hearts as does steel in its cauldron, ready to pour forth, white hot, in the fullness of time."

Eugene V. Debs

As a young man, Eugene Debs worked as a locomotive fireman. He later helped found the American Railway Union and the Industrial Workers of the World. As a leader of the Socialist Party of America, Debs ran for president five times between 1900 and 1920, the last time while in prison.

federal judges could and did shut down any strikes or boycotts that they ruled to be "conspiracies in restraint of trade."

To thrive, unions needed the support and respect of the American people. They failed to win either. The violent nature of strikes and of events like the Haymarket Affair caused many Americans to view union members as dangerous radicals. Violence and radicalism also weakened unions by scaring away potential union members.

Gains: Unions Win Small Bread-and-Butter Victories Most unions remained relatively small in the late 1800s. Only about 10 percent of the employed labor force joined unions. Yet for that minority, work hours and wages improved steadily. From 1890 to 1915, average work hours per week for union employees fell from 54 to 49. At the same time, weekly pay rose from $17.60 to $21.30.

Wages and hours for nonunion workers also improved, though not to the same degree. Skilled laborers, whether union or nonunion, made the greatest gains. Most unskilled laborers, consisting largely of white women, African Americans, and new immigrants, still struggled to make ends meet.

Unions achieved more than just better wages, hours, and working conditions. They also won some recognition of workers' rights. They challenged an economic system in which owners could treat their workers no better than machines. Unions insisted that workers should be able to sit down with owners, as equals, at the bargaining table. This in itself gave some power to the working class, where it had little or none before.

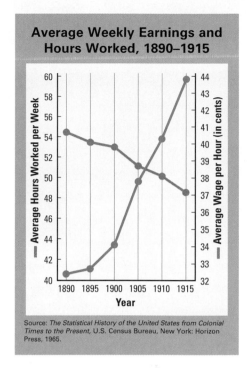

Average Weekly Earnings and Hours Worked, 1890–1915

Source: *The Statistical History of the United States from Colonial Times to the Present*, U.S. Census Bureau, New York: Horizon Press, 1965.

This graph shows that, by 1915, workers were making an average of $3.70 more per week than in 1890. At the same time, they were working almost six fewer hours per week.

Summary

The efforts of industrial workers in the late 1800s helped boost the American economy. Yet factory owners often treated their workers poorly, imposing low wages, long hours, and poor working conditions. Many workers joined labor unions to fight for better treatment and to raise their standard of living. But hostility between unions and employers sometimes led to violence.

Working-class conditions The working class suffered greatly during the Gilded Age. Industrial workers accepted low pay and dangerous conditions because they could not afford to lose their jobs. Many working-class families occupied run-down tenements in poor city slums.

Child labor American industry relied on the labor of whole families, including children, who often worked longer hours than adults.

Labor unions Workers united to form labor unions and to negotiate better wages and working conditions. Union membership increased with the rise of national unions and labor federations, such as the American Federation of Labor.

Strikes Failed negotiations led often to strikes and sometimes to violence. The government generally took the side of business and industry and often helped to break strikes.

Losses and gains for workers Periodic depressions shrank union membership, while violent incidents like the Haymarket Affair, Homestead Strike, and Pullman Strike helped turn public opinion against unions. However, unions gained wage increases and reductions in work hours.

Chapter 15

Through Ellis Island and Angel Island: The Immigrant Experience

What was it like to be an immigrant to the United States around the turn of the century?

15.1 Introduction

In 1886, the Statue of Liberty, a gift from France, was unveiled on an island in New York Harbor. The colossal statue, with its torch of freedom held high, made a strong impression on the hundreds of thousands of immigrants who passed by it each year. One of those newcomers, Edward Corsi, recalled what it was like seeing Lady Liberty for the first time:

> I looked at that statue with a sense of bewilderment, half doubting its reality. Looming shadowy through the mist, it brought silence to the decks of the *Florida*. This symbol of America—this enormous expression of what we had all been taught was the inner meaning of this new country we were coming to—inspired awe in the hopeful immigrants. Many older persons among us, burdened with a thousand memories of what they were leaving behind, had been openly weeping ever since we entered the narrower waters on our final approach toward the unknown. Now somehow steadied, I suppose, by the concreteness of the symbol of America's freedom, they dried their tears.
>
> —Edward Corsi, *In the Shadow of Liberty,* 1935

Corsi understood the symbolism of the Statue of Liberty for freedom-seeking immigrants. So did poet Emma Lazarus, who grew up in an immigrant family. These words she wrote about the statue are inscribed on its base:

> "Give me your tired, your poor,
> Your huddled masses yearning to breathe free,
> The wretched refuse of your teeming shore.
> Send these, the homeless, tempest-tost to me,
> I lift my lamp beside the golden door!"
>
> —Emma Lazarus, "The New Colossus," 1883

Millions of immigrants came to the United States at the turn of the century. Many arrived with few possessions and little money. They faced many challenges adapting to life in their new home.

15.2 Why Europeans Immigrated to the United States

Lazarus's poem suggests that the United States was a land of opportunity for the world's poor and downtrodden masses. By the 1880s, this had already been true for decades. Great waves of immigration had washed over the country since at least the 1840s. Some immigrants who chose to come to the United States were from Asia, Mexico, and Canada, but the vast majority crossed the Atlantic Ocean from Europe. They entered the country mainly through the port of New York City.

From the 1840s until the 1890s, most of these Europeans came from northern and western Europe. Millions of Irish, British, Germans, and Scandinavians crossed the ocean to become Americans. In the late 1800s, however, immigration from southern and eastern Europe steadily increased. Italians, Greeks, Hungarians, Poles, and Russians began to dominate the steamship passenger lists. For all of these immigrants, the reasons for moving can be divided into **push factors** and **pull factors**. Push factors are problems that cause people to move, whereas pull factors are attractions that draw them to another place.

Difficulties Push People from Europe Population growth and hunger were two major push factors that caused Europeans to emigrate, or leave their homeland. Much of Europe experienced rapid population growth in the 1800s. This growth resulted in crowded cities, a lack of jobs, and food shortages. Crop failures added to people's woes. Potato rot left many Irish starving in the 1840s. The Irish potato famine led to a wave of Irish emigration to the United States.

Another push factor was scarcity of **arable** land, or land suitable for growing crops. In the 1800s, mechanization of agriculture led to the growth of commercial farming on large tracts of land in Europe. In the process, common lands, traditionally available to all, were combined and enclosed by fences. Many peasants were suddenly thrown off the land and into poverty. Even families with large estates faced land shortages. In parts of Europe, landholdings were divided among all children at the death of their parents. After a few generations of such divisions, the resulting plots were too small to support a family. A hunger for land drove many Europeans across the Atlantic.

Some immigrants planned to go to the United States, make their fortune, and return to their homelands. Others had no wish to go back. Many of those people emigrated because of the fourth major push factor: religious persecution. Russian and Polish Jews, for example, fled their villages to escape deadly attacks by people who abhorred their religion. Lazarus wrote her Statue of Liberty poem with this group of immigrants in mind. Lazarus

In the late 1800s, many Jews in Europe faced persecution for their culture and beliefs. This hostility was very strong in Russia. The first Russian pogrom, or organized massacre of Jews, occurred in 1881. Attacks like this reflected a brutal anti-Semitism that caused more than a million Jews to leave Russia for the United States.

The Granger Collection, New York

had heard stories told by Jewish refugees from Russia. They described the **pogroms,** or organized anti-Jewish attacks, that had forced them to leave their country. Armenian immigrants, many of them Catholics, told similar stories about persecution and massacres at the hands of Turks in the largely Muslim Ottoman Empire.

Opportunities Pull Europeans to the United States
One of the great pull factors for European immigrants was the idea of life in a free and democratic society. They longed to live in a country where they had the opportunity to achieve their dreams. Less abstract, or more concrete, factors such as natural resources and jobs also exerted a strong pull.

The United States had ample farmland, minerals, and forests. Germans, Scandinavians, and eastern Europeans brought their farming skills to the rolling hills and plains of the Midwest. They introduced new types of wheat and other grains that would help turn this region into the country's breadbasket. European immigrants also pros-pected for gold and silver. They mined iron and coal. They chopped down forests and sawed the trees into lumber.

Booming industries offered jobs to unskilled workers, like the Irish, Italian, Polish, and Hungarian peasants who poured into the cities in the late 1800s. These new immigrants also worked on the ever-expanding rail system, sometimes replacing Irish and Chinese laborers. American railroad companies advertised throughout Europe. They offered glowing descriptions of the Great Plains, hoping to sell land they received as government grants.

An even greater lure, however, came in the form of personal communications from friends and relatives who had already immigrated. Their letters back to the old country, known as **America letters,** might be published in newspapers or read aloud in public places. Sometimes the letters overstated the facts. Europeans came to think of the United States as the "land of milk and honey" and a place where the "streets are paved with gold." America letters helped persuade many people to immigrate to the United States.

Improvements in Transportation Make Immigration Easier After the Civil War, most European immigrants crossed the Atlantic by steamship, a technological advance over sailing ships. What had once been a three-month voyage now took just two weeks. Some passengers could afford cabins in the more comfortable upper decks of the ship. But most had to settle for **steerage,** the open area below the main deck.

In steerage, hundreds of strangers were thrown together in huge rooms, where they slept in rough metal bunks. The rolling of the ship often made them ill. Seasickness, spoiled food, and filthy toilets combined to create an awful stench. During the day, steerage passengers crowded onto the main deck for fresh air.

Most European immigrants came to this country on steamships. The poorer ones crossed the Atlantic in steerage—the open space below the main deck that once housed the steering mechanism of sailing ships. Conditions there were so cramped that many passengers spent most of their time on deck.

Ellis Island processed millions of immigrants between 1892 and 1954, when it finally closed. In the 1980s, the main buildings were restored, and a museum was established on the site. Ellis Island is now part of the Statue of Liberty National Monument.

15.3 To Ellis Island and Beyond

At the turn of the century, European immigrants arrived in New York Harbor by the thousands every day. After all they had been through, they looked forward to stepping onto dry land. First-class and second-class passengers—those on the upper decks—did just that. After a brief onboard examination, they disembarked at the Hudson River piers. Steerage passengers, however, had to face one last hurdle: Ellis Island.

The **Ellis Island Immigration Station,** built in 1892 on a small piece of land in the harbor, was the port of entry for most European immigrants arriving in New York. Steerage passengers passed through a set of buildings staffed by officers of the Bureau of Immigration. This was a time of high anxiety for the immigrants. An array of officials would examine them closely to make sure they were fit to enter the country. Some of them would not pass inspection.

Medical Inspections at Ellis Island Outside the main building at Ellis Island, officials attached an identification tag to each immigrant. The medical inspection began after the immigrants entered the building. Public Health Service doctors watched as people crossed through the baggage room and climbed the steep stairs to the enormous Registry Room, or Great Hall. This brief observation period became known as the "six-second exam." People who limped, wheezed, or otherwise showed signs of disease or disability would be pulled aside for closer inspection.

In the Great Hall, the immigrants underwent a physical examination and an eye test. During the brief physical, the doctor checked for a variety of health problems, using chalk to mark the immigrant's clothing with a symbol for the suspected disease or other problem. For example, an *L* stood for lameness, an *H* meant a possible heart condition, and an *X* indicated a mental problem. Disabled individuals or those found to have incurable illnesses would face **deportation,** a forced return to their home country.

The most dreaded mark was an *E* for eye condition. The doctor would check for trachoma, a contagious infection that could lead to blindness. Anyone with trachoma would certainly be rejected. In fact, this disease accounted for the most deportations by far.

Legal Interviews in the Great Hall Immigrants with medical problems would be sent to a detention area. The rest got in line and slowly worked their way to the back of the Great Hall for the legal interview. One by one, they stood

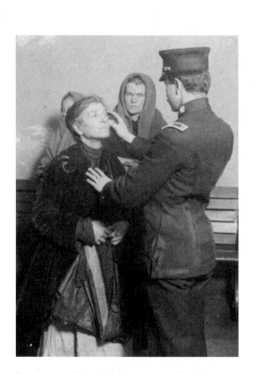

Immigrants dreaded the eye examination because failure often meant being deported. Doctors lifted the immigrant's eyelids for inspection. Some used their fingers, while others used tools such as a buttonhook. They looked for infection, especially the highly contagious disease trachoma, which could lead to blindness.

before the primary inspector, who usually worked with an interpreter. The inspector asked a list of 29 questions, starting with "What is your name?"

It was once thought that many names were shortened or respelled at Ellis Island, but actually such changes were rare. Passenger lists, including the 29 questions and answers, were created at the port of departure in Europe. Immigrants provided their name, age, sex, race, marital status, occupation, destination, and other information. Steamship officials wrote the answers on the passenger list. In most cases, Ellis Island inspectors merely asked the questions again to verify that the answers matched those on the passenger list.

The trickiest question was, "Do you have work waiting for you in the United States?" Those immigrants who wanted to show they were able to succeed in their new country sometimes answered yes. However, the Foran Act, a law passed by Congress in 1885, made it illegal for U.S. employers to import foreigners as **contract laborers**. The law's main purpose was to prevent the hiring of new immigrants to replace striking workers. Any immigrant who admitted to signing a contract to work for an employer in the United States could be detained.

About 20 percent of immigrants failed either the medical examination or the legal interview. This does not mean they were denied entry. Those with treatable illnesses were sent to a hospital on Ellis Island for therapy. There they might stay for days or weeks until a doctor pronounced them fit. Other detained immigrants had to await a hearing in front of a Board of Special Inquiry. These immigrants stayed in dormitories on the second and third floors of the main building, sleeping in iron bunks that resembled those in steerage.

The Granger Collection, New York

Along with receiving a medical exam, immigrants lined up for a legal interview. An inspector asked a series of questions to verify that immigrants could enter the country legally. Immigrants who passed the medical and legal tests would be free to go. Those who failed would be held for days, or even weeks, until their cases were decided.

The board members reviewed the details of each immigrant's case and listened to testimony from the detainee's friends and relatives, if any lived nearby. The board voted to accept almost all of the immigrants who came before it. In the end, about 2 percent of all immigrants were deported.

Most of the immigrants who passed through Ellis Island spent a very short time undergoing medical and legal examination. Yet the whole process, including the waiting time, lasted for several agonizing hours. It ended with the legal interview. Immigrants who passed that final test were free to go. Relieved that the long ordeal was over, they boarded a ferry bound for New York City and a new life.

The crowded tenements and dirty streets of this poor ethnic neighborhood suggest the rough life of the urban immigrant. This scene, however, also reveals why these areas were so appealing. The smells, sounds, and ethnic vitality served to sustain the new Americans in a difficult time of transition.

Beyond Ellis Island: Life in the Cities Some new European immigrants quickly found their way to the farm country of the Midwest. However, the majority of the jobs were in the cities, so most immigrants stayed in New York or boarded trains bound for Boston, Cleveland, Chicago, or other industrial centers. As a result, urban populations exploded. From 1870 to 1920, the proportion of Americans who lived in cities jumped from about 25 percent to 50 percent.

Newly arrived urban immigrants tended to live in the least desirable districts, where housing was cheapest. Such areas often contained the factories and shops that provided their livelihoods. Amid the city's din and dirt, immigrants crowded into tenement buildings and other run-down, slum housing. In 1914, an Italian immigrant described such an area of Boston:

> Here was a congestion the like of which I had never seen before. Within the narrow limits of one-half square mile were crowded together thirty-five thousand people, living tier upon tier, huddled together until the very heavens seemed to be shut out. These narrow alley-like streets of Old Boston were one mass of litter. The air was laden with soot and dirt. Ill odors arose from every direction . . . A thousand wheels of commercial activity whirled incessantly day and night, making noises which would rack the sturdiest of nerves.
> —Constantine M. Panunzio, *The Soul of an Immigrant,* 1969

Immigrants generally settled among others from their home country. They felt comfortable among people who spoke the same language, ate the same foods, and held the same beliefs. As a result, different areas of the city often had distinctive ethnic flavors. Jacob Riis, a writer and photographer, imagined a map of New York's ethnic communities. "A map of the city," he wrote in 1890, "colored to designate nationalities, would show more stripes than on the skin of a zebra, and more colors than any rainbow."

15.4 Responses to New European Immigrants

Immigrants typically came to the United States with little money and few possessions. Because of their general poverty and lack of education, most were not welcomed into American society. Without much support, they had to work hard to get ahead. In time, some saved enough to move out of the slums and perhaps even buy a home. A few opened small businesses, such as a grocery store or a tailor's shop. But many remained stuck in dangerous, low-wage factory jobs that barely paid their bills. An accident on the job or an economic downturn might leave them without work and possibly homeless and hungry.

Immigrants Receive Aid from Several Sources In the late 1800s, the government did not provide aid or assistance to unemployed workers. They were expected to fend for themselves. But needy immigrants did have several places to turn for help. The first sources of aid were usually relatives or friends, who might provide housing and food.

If necessary, the needy might seek assistance from an immigrant aid society. These ethnic organizations started as neighborhood social groups. They met mainly in churches and synagogues, groceries, and saloons—the centers of immigrant community life. They might pass the hat to collect money for a family in need. In time, local immigrant aid societies joined together to form regional and national organizations, such as the Polish National Alliance and the Sons of Italy in America.

During the 1890s, a type of aid organization called a **settlement house** arose in the ethnic neighborhoods of many large cities. A settlement house was a community center that provided a variety of services to the poor, especially to immigrants. It might offer daytime care for children, as well as classes, health clinics, and recreational opportunities for the entire community.

While adult immigrants often found it hard to assimilate, their children made a much smoother transition. Education was the key to their Americanization. As they learned to speak English and studied American history and civics, they quickly adapted to their new homeland.

Opponents of immigration claimed that the "garbage" of Europe was being dumped on American shores. Political parties included anti-immigration statements in their platforms. The Immigration Act of 1917 instituted a literacy test in an attempt to keep out uneducated immigrants. What view of the law does this cartoon express?

Immigrants might also turn to **political bosses** for help. These bosses were powerful leaders who ran local politics in many cities. They were in a position to provide jobs and social services to immigrants in exchange for the political support of immigrants who could vote. These supporters often voted for the boss and his slate of candidates in local elections.

The Assimilation of Immigrants Many immigrants held on to their old customs and language as they gradually adapted to American life. This was especially true for older immigrants living in ethnic neighborhoods. The children of immigrants, however, typically found assimilation into American society much easier than their parents did.

Education was the main tool of assimilation. Immigrant children in public schools studied American history and civics, and they learned to speak English. Yearning to fit in, they more eagerly adopted American customs.

Some patriotic organizations pushed for the Americanization of immigrants, fearing that increased immigration posed a threat to American values and traditions. Through efforts such as the publishing of guides for new citizens, they promoted loyalty to American values.

Some Americans Reject Immigrants Many Americans disliked the recent immigrants, in part because of religious and cultural differences. Most of the earlier immigrants were Protestants from northern Europe. Later waves of immigrants came from southern and eastern Europe and were often Catholics or Jews. Their customs seemed strange to Americans of northern European ancestry, who often doubted that these more recent immigrants could be Americanized. Many people also blamed them for the labor unrest that had spread across the country in the late 1800s. They especially feared that foreign anarchists and socialists might undermine American democracy.

Dislike and fear provoked demands to limit immigration and its impact on American life. This policy of favoring the interests of native-born Americans over those of immigrants is called nativism. Nativism had a long history in the United States. Before the Civil War, nativists had opposed the immigration of Irish Catholics. In the 1850s, they formed a secret political party known as the Know-Nothings, because when asked a question about the group, members were told to answer, "I don't know."

As the main source of immigration shifted to southern and eastern Europe in the late 1800s, nativism flared up again. Nativists were not only bothered by religious and cultural differences, but also saw immigrants as an economic threat. Native workers worried that immigrants were taking their jobs and lowering wages. Immigrants often worked for less money and sometimes served as scabs, replacement workers during labor disputes.

In 1894, a group of nativists founded the Immigration Restriction League. This organization wanted to limit immigration by requiring that all new arrivals take a literacy test to prove they could read and write. In 1897, Congress passed such a bill, but the president vetoed it. Twenty years later, however, another literacy bill became law. Meanwhile, efforts to slow immigration continued. During the 1920s, Congress began passing quota laws to restrict the flow of European immigrants into the United States.

15.5 Immigration from Asia

Although immigration after the Civil War was mainly from Europe, many immigrants also arrived each year from Asia. They made important contributions to the country. They also provoked strong reactions from nativists.

Chinese Immigrants Seek Gold Mountain You have read about the thousands of Chinese railroad workers who laid track through the Sierra Nevada for the Central Pacific Railroad. Thousands more joined the swarms of prospectors who scoured the West for gold. In fact, the Chinese referred to California, the site of the first gold rush, as Gold Mountain.

The vast majority of Chinese immigrants were men. They streamed into California, mainly through the port of San Francisco. Most expected to work hard and return home rich. However, they usually ended up staying in the United States.

Besides finding employment in mining and railroad construction, Chinese immigrants worked in agriculture. Some had first come to Hawaii as contract laborers to work on sugar plantations. There they earned a reputation as reliable, steady workers. Farm owners on the mainland saw the value of their labor and began bringing the Chinese to California. The Chinese were willing to do the "stoop labor" in the fields that many white laborers refused to do. By the early 1880s, most harvest workers in the state were Chinese.

Many businesses hired the Chinese because they were willing to work for less money. This allowed owners to reduce production costs even further by paying white workers less. As a result, friction developed between working-class whites and Chinese immigrants.

Mob violence against Chinese immigrants broke out in several American cities in the late 1800s. This engraving shows an anti-Chinese riot in Denver in 1880. Anti-immigrant forces blamed the Chinese for economic problems at the time. As a result, Chinese immigration was banned for 10 years.

The Exclusion Act: Shutting the Doors on the Chinese During the 1870s, a depression and drought knocked the wind out of California's economy. Seeking a scapegoat, many Californians blamed Chinese workers for their economic woes. The Chinese made an easy target. They looked different from white Americans, and their language, religion, and other cultural traits were also very different. As a result, innocent Chinese became victims of mob violence, during which many were driven out of their homes and even murdered.

Anti-Chinese nativism had a strong racial component. The Chinese were seen as an inferior people who could never be Americanized. Economist Henry George reflected this racist point of view in characterizing the Chinese as "utter heathens, treacherous, sensual, cowardly, cruel."

Nativists demanded that Chinese immigration be curtailed, or reduced. Their outcries led to the passage of the **Chinese Exclusion Act** in 1882. This law prohibited the immigration of Chinese laborers, skilled or unskilled, for a period of 10 years. It also prevented Chinese already in the country from becoming citizens. For the first time, the United States had restricted immigration based solely on nationality or race.

The Chinese Exclusion Act still allowed a few Chinese to enter the country, including merchants, diplomats, teachers, students, and relatives of existing citizens. But the act did what it was supposed to do. Immigration from China fell from a high of nearly 40,000 people in 1882 to just 279 two years later.

Starting in 1910, immigration officials processed Asian immigrants at Angel Island in San Francisco Bay. Some newcomers faced lengthy detention. Here a Chinese immigrant endures a legal interview.

Angel Island: The Ellis Island of the West Although the Chinese Exclusion Act was highly effective, some Chinese managed to evade the law by using forged documents and false names. In response, federal officials developed tougher procedures for processing Asian immigrants. They also decided to replace the old immigrant-processing center in San Francisco with a new, more secure facility located on Angel Island in San Francisco Bay.

Completed in 1910, the **Angel Island Immigration Station** became known as the "Ellis Island of the West." It was designed to enforce the exclusion act by keeping new Chinese arrivals isolated from friends and relatives on the mainland and preventing them from escaping. At Angel Island, immigrants underwent a thorough physical exam. Then they faced an intense legal interview, more involved and detailed than the Ellis Island version. Officials hoped to exclude Chinese who falsely claimed to be related to American citizens.

Interviewers asked applicants specific questions about their home village, their family, and the house they lived in. They also questioned witnesses. The process could take days. Those who failed the interviews could enter an appeal, but additional evidence took time to gather. Applicants were often detained for weeks, months, or even years.

Chinese detained at Angel Island stayed locked in wooden barracks. These living quarters were crowded and unsanitary. Detainees felt miserable and frustrated to be stopped so close to their goal. From their barracks, they could see across the water to the mainland. Some carved poems onto the walls to express their feelings. One Chinese detainee wrote,

> Imprisoned in the wooden building day after day,
> My freedom withheld; how can I bear to talk about it?
> —from Ronald Takaki, *Strangers from a Different Shore,* 1989

Many Chinese never made it to the mainland. About 10 percent were put on ships and sent back to China after failing the medical exam or legal interview.

Some Asian immigrants detained at Angel Island carved poems into the walls of the barracks there. The poems described both the misery and the determination of the detainees.

State laws barred Japanese men from marrying non-Asian women. In the picture-bride system, families arranged marriage between a son living in the United States and a daughter in Japan. The prospective bride and groom exchanged photographs and personal information.

Other Asian Groups Immigrate to the United States The Chinese Exclusion Act created a shortage of farm laborers. Large-scale farmers looked to Japan and later to Korea and the Philippines for workers. These other Asian immigrants had experiences similar to those of the Chinese. Many first emigrated to work on Hawaiian sugar plantations. They came to the United States through Angel Island to work in orchards, in vineyards, and on farms in California, Oregon, and Washington. Some worked for railroads and other industries.

A number of Japanese immigrants leased farmland and had great success growing fruits and vegetables. They formed ethnic neighborhoods that provided for their economic and social needs. Koreans had less success. Only a small number moved from Hawaii to the mainland in the early 1900s, and they led more isolated lives. Immigrants from the Philippines migrated up and down the West Coast, taking part in fruit and vegetable harvests. In the winter, many of these Filipinos worked in hotels and restaurants.

Despite their contributions, all Asian immigrants faced prejudice, hostility, and discrimination. In 1906, anti-Asian feelings in San Francisco caused the city to segregate Asian children in separate schools from whites. When Japan's government protested, President Theodore Roosevelt got involved. Hoping to avoid offending East Asia's most powerful nation, the president persuaded San Francisco's school board to repeal the segregation order. In return, hc got a pledge from Japan to discuss issues related to immigration.

In 1907 and 1908, the American and Japanese governments carried out secret negotiations through a series of notes. These notes became known as the Gentlemen's Agreement. In the end, Japanese officials agreed not to allow laborers to emigrate to the United States. They did, however, insist that wives, children, and parents of Japanese in the United States be allowed to immigrate.

15.6 Immigration from North and South

The East and West coasts were the main gateways for immigrants to the United States in the late 1800s and early 1900s. But immigrants also crossed the country's northern and southern borders. Before 1900, people passed back and forth across these land borders largely unchecked. Even later, the length and isolation of the country's borders made enforcement of immigration laws almost impossible. Europeans and Asians sometimes crossed by land to avoid immigration restrictions. However, most who came this way were either French Canadians from the north or Mexicans from the south.

Crossing the Southern Border: Immigrants from Mexico In the late 1800s and early 1900s, legal restrictions on Chinese and Japanese immigration mounted. As they did, the population of Asian farmworkers in the United States shrank. Commercial farmers in the West began to rely on a different source of labor: Mexico. By the late 1920s, Mexicans constituted a large portion of California's agricultural workers. Many Mexicans also became migrant farmworkers and construction workers in Texas.

Mexicans had lived in the area of Texas, New Mexico, Arizona, and California since the earliest Spanish settlements. In the late 1800s, more Mexicans moved to this area, in part to escape poverty and civil unrest in Mexico. By 1890, many Mexicans were migrating into the Southwest. Around this time, railroads began extending their lines across the border, which made travel faster and easier.

A demand for low-wage labor in the late 1800s contributed to a surge of immigration from Mexico. Mexican immigrants worked in various industries, from railroads and steel mills to canneries. Hundreds of thousands labored in the fields as migrant farmworkers. In this image, Mexican migrant workers pick beets in Minnesota.

Higher wages in the United States attracted many Mexicans. Some came to work on the railroads. Others labored in the copper mines of Arizona. Still others worked on the farms and in the citrus groves that blossomed throughout the region with the expansion of irrigation. The Mexican Revolution, which began in 1910, pushed even more Mexicans across the border.

Like other immigrant groups, the Mexicans often suffered at the hands of native-born Americans. They might be welcomed as cheap labor, but they were commonly scorned as inferior to white Americans. Racist attitudes toward Mexicans, especially those with dark skin, led to discrimination. They were kept in low-level jobs and commonly denied access to public facilities, including restaurants. Many Mexican children were only allowed to attend segregated schools.

Crossing the Northern Border: The French Canadians Many Canadians also came to the United States after the Civil War. Between 1865 and 1900, more than 900,000 immigrants arrived from Canada. Some of these were English-speaking Protestants, but a larger number were French-speaking Catholics. They arrived mainly from the province of Quebec.

Like other immigrants, the French Canadians were seeking greater opportunities than they had at home. Typically, they traveled by train across the border to the United States. But most did not go too far south. The majority settled in New England and around the Great Lakes. There they worked chiefly in textile mills and lumber camps.

With their language, religion, and customs, the French Canadians differed from the English-speaking society around them. At first, they resisted Americanization, preferring to maintain their cultural and historical ties to Quebec. In part because of their apparent unwillingness to assimilate, French Canadians came under attack by nativists. In 1881, a Massachusetts official declared,

> The Canadian French are the Chinese of the Eastern States. They care nothing for our institutions . . . Their purpose is merely to sojourn [stay temporarily] a few years as aliens . . . They are a horde of industrial invaders, not a stream of stable settlers.
>
> —Massachusetts Bureau of Statistics of Labor,
> Twelfth Annual Report, 1881

European, Asian, Mexican, and French Canadian immigrants all faced accusations that they were unwilling to become members of American society. In time, all would prove the nativists wrong. They would establish vibrant ethnic communities, and their cultures would become vital pieces of the American mosaic.

Summary

In the late 1800s and early 1900s, large numbers of immigrants came to the United States. Most emigrated from Europe, but many also arrived from Asia and from other parts of North America. They all saw the United States as a land of opportunity, but they faced challenges entering the United States and assimilating into American culture.

Push and pull factors Overcrowded cities, civil unrest, and shortages of food, land, and jobs pushed immigrants out of their homelands. The promise of wealth, jobs, land, and freedom pulled them to the United States.

Through Ellis Island In the late 1800s, Europeans crossed the Atlantic on steamships, many of them in steerage. In New York Harbor, steerage passengers underwent a medical inspection and a legal interview at the Ellis Island Immigration Station. Most of these new immigrants found homes in the ethnic neighborhoods of large cities or on farms in the Midwest.

Through Angel Island Asians immigrated to the United States in smaller numbers than Europeans. Chinese, Japanese, Koreans, and Filipinos found work mainly on the commercial farms of the West Coast. After 1910, Asians had to pass a rigorous inspection at the Angel Island Immigration Station before entering the country.

Across the northern and southern borders Other immigrants came from Mexico and French Canada. Mexican immigrants tended to settle in the Southwest and California. Immigrants from French Canada settled mainly in New England and the Great Lakes states. Both ethnic groups faced many of the same challenges as immigrants from other countries.

Nativism Some Americans objected to mass immigration, especially from Asia and southern and eastern Europe. Strong opposition from nativists led to the persecution of immigrants and restrictions on immigration.

Chapter 16

Uncovering Problems at the Turn of the Century

What social, political, and environmental problems did Americans face at the turn of the 20th century?

16.1 Introduction

Jacob Riis, a photographer and journalist, took the picture of three homeless boys sleeping in an alley that you see on the opposite page. It is one of many arresting photographs that made Riis one of the most respected journalists in New York City in the late 1800s.

Homeless boys were a common sight in New York at the time. In his book *How the Other Half Lives,* Riis wrote about the conditions of the urban poor. In one passage, he described the boys who lived on the streets:

> Like rabbits in their burrows, the little ragamuffins sleep with at least one eye open, and every sense alert to the approach of danger: of their enemy, the policeman, whose chief business in life is to move them on, and of the agent bent on robbing them of their cherished freedom. At the first warning shout they scatter and are off. To pursue them would be like chasing the fleet-footed mountain goat . . . There is not an open door, a hidden turn or runway, which they do not know, with lots of secret passages and short cuts no one else ever found.
>
> —Jacob Riis, *How the Other Half Lives: Studies Among the Tenements of New York,* 1890

Jacob Riis was a Danish immigrant who became a photographer and journalist in New York City in the late 1800s. He documented conditions of urban poverty and published his work in the book *How the Other Half Lives.* Riis was one of a group of journalists known as muckrakers, who exposed the nation's problems at the turn of the 20th century.

Riis was no stranger to poverty himself. He had arrived in New York as a poor immigrant in 1870 and had suffered through hard times. When he became a reporter, he dedicated himself to exposing the conditions of the poor.

Riis was one of a group of journalists known as **muckrakers**. President Theodore Roosevelt gave them that name because they "raked the mud of society." They uncovered the nation's problems and wrote about them.

In this chapter, you will read about the social, environmental, and political problems Americans faced in the early 1900s. In the next two chapters, you will see how reformers worked to solve these problems.

◀ New York City homeless, 1889 (photograph by Jacob Riis)

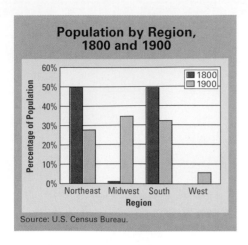

Population by Region, 1800 and 1900

Source: U.S. Census Bureau.

The U.S. population shifted to the West during the 1800s. As this graph shows, the percentage of people living in the Midwest and West increased substantially, while percentages in the North and South declined. Westward migration contributed to this shift, as did the rise of midwestern cities like Chicago and Cleveland.

Chicago was founded as a small trading post on Lake Michigan in the 1840s. By 1900, it had grown into a bustling center of commerce and industry. With its lakeside location, Chicago was an ideal hub for railroad lines and shipping. This transport network made it easy to bring raw materials to factories and finished products to markets.

16.2 The State of the Union in 1900

In 1900, the United States looked very different from a century before. Westward expansion had added vast new territory to the country. In addition, the rise of industry had stimulated rapid **urbanization**—the growth of cities—by creating jobs that drew rural residents and new immigrants to American cities. The United States had moved far beyond Thomas Jefferson's vision of a nation of small farmers. It was becoming an urban, industrial society with an increasingly diverse population from around the world.

Settlement in the West: The Closing of the Frontier By 1900, the nation included 45 states and stretched across the North American continent. Americans had fulfilled what many saw as their "manifest destiny"—their right to expand across the continent from the Atlantic to the Pacific.

This expansion was so successful that in 1890 a report from the Census Bureau announced that the "American frontier" was closed. This report said that most of the land beyond the Appalachian Mountains had been settled. Of course, there was still land available to settlers after 1890, but the popular notion of the "wide-open spaces" of the West was becoming an idea of the past.

Factories Increase Production Industrialization also brought changes to American life. Advances in technology, transportation, and communications helped fuel rapid industrial growth after the Civil War. American factory workers produced more goods much faster than anyone had ever thought possible. The numbers tell the story. In 1865, American industry produced $2 billion worth of products. By 1900, that figure had risen to $13 billion. In only 35 years, production had grown by more than six times.

More efficient machines and production methods made this increase possible. The textile industry was one of the first to mechanize. Mass production

of textiles had begun in New England before the Civil War. After the war, the industry spread to the South, where the use of modern machinery produced a boom in textile production. The iron and steel industry also thrived in the late 1800s. Between 1870 and 1900, production rose from about 3 million tons to more than 29 million tons.

As factory production increased, businesses looked for new ways to sell their products. One method was the mail-order catalog. Companies like Montgomery Ward and Sears, Roebuck and Company published and distributed catalogs offering goods of all kinds, from hardware and tools to clothes and appliances. They took orders by mail and shipped the products by railroad and canal to customers around the country.

Other companies, like Macy's and Marshall Field's, opened department stores in major cities. These large stores sold a variety of goods and even offered services, like childcare, all under one roof. Smaller chain stores like Woolworths established branches across the country to serve more Americans in the towns and cities where they lived.

Cities Attract Masses of Newcomers The United States was becoming an increasingly urban nation. In 1800, only 6 percent of Americans had lived in cities. By 1900, nearly 40 percent lived in urban areas.

City residents included many newcomers. Most immigrants settled in cities because they could find work and mingle with others from their homelands. African Americans were also beginning to move from the South to northern cities, seeking equality and opportunity. Other new arrivals were rural residents from the North, who moved to cities in large numbers in the late 1800s.

Jobs were the most important attraction in cities, but other features also drew migrants. Cities had many amusements for people to enjoy when not working. Theaters presented popular dramas and musical comedies. A type of theater called vaudeville was especially popular for its lively combination of music, comedy, and dance. Circuses were another common form of entertainment, as were spectator sports like baseball and football.

Cities had other modern attractions. Department stores took up whole city blocks and were so impressive that people called them "palaces of merchandise." Cities also boasted broad avenues lined with the mansions of wealthy residents. In some cities, steel-framed skyscrapers rose above downtown streets, reaching heights of 10 stories or more. These modern buildings become symbols of American progress and prosperity.

The Census Reveals an Increasingly Diverse People Between 1870 and 1920, at least 12 million immigrants arrived in the United States. By 1910, a majority of the population in key cities like New York, Chicago, and Cleveland consisted of foreign-born residents and their children. Over half of the nation's industrial labor force was foreign born.

By the turn of the century, immigration from different parts of the world was changing the face of American culture and society. New waves of immigrants from southern Europe and Asia were joined by immigrants from Mexico and Canada. All of these newcomers added their customs and languages to the nation's mix of cultures.

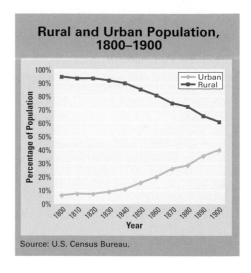

Rural and Urban Population, 1800–1900

Source: U.S. Census Bureau.

In the 1800s, many Americans moved from rural areas to urban centers. They were drawn by jobs and other opportunities in the cities. As the graph shows, the percentage of Americans living in urban areas rose from 6 percent in 1800 to almost 40 percent in 1900.

16.3 Poor Living and Working Conditions

While many Americans enjoyed the benefits of urban life in 1900, cities and city dwellers also suffered from serious problems. Many urban residents lived in poverty and labored under backbreaking conditions. They may have been tempted by the many goods generated by mass production, but most could not afford them. Even those who did have the money had no guarantee that the products were safe or reliable. Through their writings, muckrakers like Jacob Riis sought to expose these and other problems of urban life.

What Were Tenements Like in 1900?

Tenements lined the streets of poor neighborhoods in New York City in the late 1800s. Tenement residents lived in very cramped conditions. A typical tenement might house 200 people, with 9 or more residents in each small apartment.

Conditions in the Slums Many of the urban poor lived in slum tenements. They were crammed together in shoddy apartment buildings that housed four families on each floor. Each family had a very small living space. In Jacob Riis's book, a typical tenement is described as "one or two dark closets, used as bedrooms, with a living room twelve feet by ten."

Not only was each tenement crowded, but the buildings themselves were packed together. Some slum neighborhoods were among the most densely populated areas in the world. New York's Lower East Side, for example, housed 450,000 people in 1900. That amounted to more than 300,000 people per square mile. In contrast, New York City as a whole housed around 90,000 people per square mile.

One reason for poor living conditions in cities like New York was that the urban **infrastructure** was inadequate for such a large population. Infrastructure refers to the facilities and equipment required for an organization or community to function. It includes roads, sewage and power systems, and transportation. A number of muckrakers blamed city governments for failing to provide adequate infrastructure and services.

Lack of fire protection was one serious problem. At the turn of the century, many city roads and sidewalks were constructed of wood, making cities virtual firetraps. One historian described American cities of the day as "long lines of well-laid kindling." Much of Chicago burned to the ground in 1871, and much of San Francisco burned after the 1906 earthquake.

Cities also suffered from sanitation problems. By 1900, many middle-class homes had running water and indoor plumbing. These amenities reduced the incidence of disease in some neighborhoods, but they increased the amount of wastewater that cities had to remove. City engineers developed sewer systems to do the job. In poorer neighborhoods that lacked indoor plumbing, however, the waste often ended up on the streets. As a result of poor sanitation, contagious diseases such as tuberculosis and pneumonia often spread quickly through crowded slums.

Problems in the Workplace Muckrakers also exposed terrible working conditions. By 1900, unskilled factory work had replaced most skilled manufacturing jobs. Many factory workers found their work boring and strenuous. One worker said, "Life in a factory is perhaps, with the exception of prison life, the most monotonous life a human being can live."

Factory work was also dangerous. Sharp blades threatened meatpackers. Cotton dust plagued textile workers. And fire posed a risk to nearly everyone who worked in close quarters in factories. Injuries could put workers out of jobs and throw their families into dire poverty.

Other workers, especially in the garment industry, worked at home for companies that paid them for each piece of work they completed. Many employers squeezed their workers by reducing the rate they paid per piece. Workers then had to work harder and faster to earn the same amount. It was common among immigrants for entire families, including children, to do piecework so that the family could make enough money to survive.

Unsafe Products: Buyer Beware Increased production meant that more products were available, but buying them was not always a good idea. Consumers often did not know what was in the products because the government did not regulate product quality.

Meat was one example. In his 1906 novel *The Jungle,* muckraker Upton Sinclair wrote about unsanitary conditions in meatpacking plants: "There would be meat stored in great piles in rooms; and the water from leaky roofs would drip over it, and thousands of rats would race about on it." Sinclair reported that rat droppings, and even the rats themselves, often become part of processed meat. Canned goods were not regulated either. Toxic chemical preservatives like borax and formaldehyde contaminated many processed foods.

Many common medicines, like cough syrup, were also unregulated. Some products made ridiculous claims for curing illnesses, with the "cures" often involving narcotics. Medicine labels boasted such ingredients as morphine, opium, and cocaine. These substances were not prohibited, but their risks were becoming more apparent. Popular magazines told stories of consumers who believed that these medicines would cure their illnesses, only to fall prey to drug addiction.

Meanwhile, the growth of big businesses went largely unregulated, as monopolies took over many industries. Many Americans worried that small companies were being driven out of business and that monopolies were stifling opportunity. Muckrakers protested that big businesses were growing richer, while small businesses and the poor struggled even harder to survive.

The government did not regulate product quality or safety at the turn of the century. As a result, many medicines contained dangerous substances and made outrageous claims for curing illnesses.

16.4 Problems with the Environment

By the turn of the century, urbanization and industrialization were transforming not only American society but also the natural environment. Alexis de Tocqueville, a Frenchman who had visited the United States in 1831, noted that Americans seemed to think nothing of remaking nature for the sake of progress. He observed that in the process of building towns, they could destroy forests, lakes, and rivers and "not see anything astonishing in all this. This incredible destruction, this even more surprising growth, seems to [them] the usual process of things in this world." By 1900, Americans had settled much of the country and exploited many of its natural resources. Doing so enabled tremendous economic growth, but it also came at a cost to the environment.

Changing the Landscape As the 20th century began, economic activities had significantly changed the landscape. Forests were one example. Farmers cleared trees to plant crops, and loggers cut down large areas of woodland. The government encouraged logging by selling large plots of land in the Northwest for the lumber they could provide. By 1900, only a fraction of the country's virgin, or original, forests were still standing.

Ranching also transformed the landscape. Before settlers moved onto the Great Plains, buffalo had roamed across the region and grazed on its abundant grasslands. By the time the buffalo returned to places they had grazed before, the grass had grown back. But the cattle and sheep brought in by ranchers grazed the same area over and over, without moving on. As a result, they stripped the land of its natural vegetation and left it more vulnerable to erosion.

Extracting Natural Resources The landscape was also transformed by **extractive industries,** businesses that take mineral resources from the earth.

The United States had a mixed and growing economy by 1900. Most industry was concentrated in the East and the Great Lakes region. Mining and agriculture, however, were spread across the country.

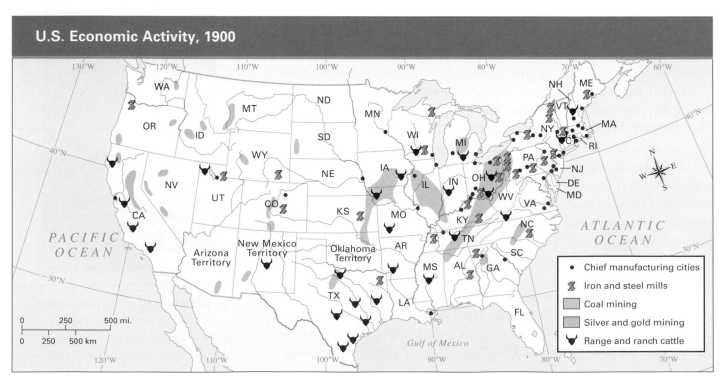

U.S. Economic Activity, 1900

- Chief manufacturing cities
- Iron and steel mills
- Coal mining
- Silver and gold mining
- Range and ranch cattle

By 1900, mining companies were using explosives and drilling equipment to extract silver, copper, gold, iron, coal, and other minerals. Meanwhile, oil companies drilled deep to pump petroleum out of the ground.

Coal and other minerals were required to fuel industry. Factories burned coal to heat water to make the steam that powered machinery. The country was particularly rich in coal. Between 1860 and 1884, the amount of coal mined per year increased from 14 million tons to 100 million tons.

Mining was dangerous and also harmed the environment. Workers risked being buried alive if a mine caved in, and many got black-lung disease from breathing coal dust day after day. Mining scarred the land, leaving open shafts, slag heaps, and polluted streams behind. Unlike today, the government imposed no environmental regulations on mining companies.

Oil drilling also took its toll on the land. The first commercial oil wells were drilled in Pennsylvania. By 1900, oil extraction was underway in Texas and California as well. But finding oil was difficult. Developers often drilled deep in search of black gold, only to come away empty-handed. Whether successful or not, they left the earth torn behind them.

One historian explained that most Americans in the 1800s believed that "the river was waiting to be dammed . . . the prairie was waiting to be farmed, the woodlands to be cut down, and the desert to be irrigated." In other words, most people saw no problem with exploiting the environment and took no notice of the harm being done to the natural landscape.

Polluting Water and Air Economic activities were also polluting the air and water in urban areas. In some cities, factories belched so much black smoke that it was difficult for people to breathe. In 1881, angry residents of New York City reported that the air smelled like sulfur, ammonia, kerosene, acid fumes, and phosphate fertilizer.

Pittsburgh, a steelmaking city, was known for being particularly filthy. The air was so polluted that it soiled everything. The people who lived closest to the steel plants suffered the worst of the pollution, but it affected those living outside the industrial center as well. One historian has written, "People's hands and faces were constantly grimy, clean collars quickly acquired a thin layer of soot, and the . . . coal dust gave clothes hung out in the weekly wash a permanent yellow tinge."

Another pollutant came from animals that lived in cities. Horses pulled carriages, and pigs roamed the streets eating garbage. Animal waste was often left where it landed, producing a foul stench and a serious disposal problem. According to one estimate, the 15,000 horses in Rochester, New York, left enough waste in a year to cover an acre of land with a layer 175 feet high.

City water was also polluted. In some cities, household sewage and industrial pollutants were simply released into nearby water sources without regard for the consequences. Other cities did try to avoid contaminating their drinking water. In Chicago, for example, engineers reversed the flow of the Chicago River so that sewage and factory waste would not flow into Lake Michigan. Some cities developed reservoirs to keep drinking water separate from wastewater. In some cases, rivers that were in the way or became too much of a health hazard were simply paved over.

In most American cities at the turn of the century, factories released their smoke directly into the air. There were no government controls on air pollution. Here, factories belch smoke in Pittsburgh. In Chicago, the smoke grew so thick at times that people could see only one block ahead of them.

In American cities, political leaders called bosses handed out favors and money to their supporters. "Boss" Tweed of the Tammany Hall political machine in New York City was the most famous of these political bosses. The power of the Tammany Hall machine was often represented as the "Tammany Tiger," as shown here.

16.5 The Politics of Fraud and Bribery

Another problem at the turn of the century was political corruption. In 1902, the muckraking journalist Lincoln Steffens published *The Shame of the Cities*, a book on corruption in city government. The book exposed the rampant fraud that plagued cities throughout the nation. Steffens reported that politicians spoke openly about accepting bribes. "I make no pretensions to virtue," one politician said, "not even on Sunday."

Corruption served the interests of dishonest politicians and those who bribed them, while weakening the political influence of average Americans. In short, it distorted and undermined democracy.

Political Machines and Bosses By 1900, many cities were controlled by **political machines**. These organizations consisted of full-time politicians whose main goal was to get and keep political power and the money and influence that went with it. Machines were usually associated with a political party. Party politicians joined forces to limit competition, while increasing their own power and wealth. At the top of this corrupt structure was the political boss, who controlled the machine and its politicians. Perhaps the most infamous of these bosses was William "Boss" Tweed of New York's Tammany Hall machine, who in the early 1870s cheated the city out of as much as $200 million.

Political machines exercised control at all levels of city government, down to the wards and precincts that subdivided most cities. Ward bosses and precinct captains got to know local residents and offered them assistance in exchange for political support. They helped immigrants who were sick or out of work. As one New York City ward boss said, "I never ask a hungry man about his past; I feed him, not because he is good, but because he needs food." This aid could take a wide variety of forms, including supplying a Christmas turkey or helping a grieving family by paying for a funeral. In exchange, residents agreed to vote for machine politicians at election time.

In some ways, the political machines worked for the good of city dwellers, particularly immigrants. At a time when the national and state governments did not provide such benefits as welfare for unemployed workers, local political machines filled the void.

Corruption in Local and State Politics Although political machines provided aid, they also stifled opportunity for many citizens. Political bosses controlled access to city jobs, such as employment in the police and fire departments or on construction projects. With a good word from a boss, a poorly qualified person could land a job in place of a capable applicant.

The political machine also controlled business opportunities. To get a city work contract, a company often had to donate to the machine's reelection campaign. Many businesses also paid politicians to keep the city government from interfering with their activities. Such payoffs became part of the cost of doing business. Muckrakers called them bribery.

The political machines profited from urban entertainment, both legal and illegal. In exchange for a payoff, the boss could clear the way for such illegal activities as gambling. Even legal businesses such as baseball teams and vaudeville theaters paid the machine. Some political bosses saw these payments as informal taxes. They used some of the revenue to help those in need, but they made sure they profited themselves.

To keep control, political machines rigged local elections. Average citizens had little influence in choosing candidates, and the machine frequently used fraud to win at the polls. Candidates might pay citizens for their votes or stuff the ballot box with phony votes. By controlling elections, political machines maintained their grip on American cities.

At the state level, corrupt politicians tied to powerful industries, such as railroads and mining, controlled many state governments. In passing laws that favored big business, states often ignored the needs of average citizens.

Corruption on the National Level The national government also suffered from corruption. For example, the Constitution gave state legislatures the power to choose senators, but corporations often bribed state legislators to elect their favored candidates to the Senate. The Senate became known as the Millionaires Club because many of its members were wealthy men with close ties to powerful industries.

In both the House and the Senate, politicians received campaign contributions from big business in exchange for passing favorable legislation. The railroad monopolies, for example, frequently gave company stock to members of Congress who passed laws that strengthened the railroads. Other businesses also gave money to lawmakers who worked to limit competition.

Politicians frequently engaged in **patronage**—giving jobs to friends and supporters. Some of these jobs went to unqualified people. This practice became a national issue after President James Garfield was assassinated in 1881 by a deranged office seeker. In 1883, Congress passed the Pendleton Civil Service Reform Act to limit patronage. The **Pendleton Act** set guidelines for hiring **civil service** employees—nonmilitary government workers. It set up a civil service commission to administer exams to new applicants for government jobs. The jobs covered by this test had to be specified by the president. Over the years, most presidents have agreed to expand the number of specified jobs. Most civil service jobs are now based on merit.

THE BOSSES OF THE SENATE

In the late 1800s, the Senate became known as the Millionaires Club because so many senators got rich on contributions from big business. This 1890 cartoon, titled "The Bosses of the Senate," shows tiny senators completely overshadowed by bloated trusts and monopolies. The sign at the back of the chamber reads, "This is a Senate of the Monopolists by the Monopolists and for the Monopolists!"

16.6 Social Tensions

American cities in 1900 brought together many types of people in crowded and often difficult circumstances. As a result, social tensions increased. Many poor city dwellers resented the comfortable lives of the rich, while the rich often looked down on the poor as the source of urban problems. Many African Americans faced racism and violence as they struggled to improve their lives and claim their democratic rights. Women were also demanding greater opportunities and rights. Meanwhile, many American families feared that the stresses and strains of urban life were eroding traditional values.

Growing Differences Between Social Classes During the late 1800s, the gap between rich and poor grew wider. Between 1865 and 1900, a small percentage of Americans grew fabulously wealthy. By 1891, according to one estimate, there were 120 Americans who were worth at least $10 million, an enormous sum at the time.

At the same time, the arrival of many immigrants swelled the ranks of the working class. Many workers found it nearly impossible to get ahead. Although wages increased gradually, the cost of living rose faster. So while the rich got richer, the poor continued to live in harsh circumstances. Many took lodgers into their tiny flats to help share the cost of rent.

Between the two extremes, the middle class expanded as a result of the rising productivity of the American economy. The growing middle class included doctors, lawyers, ministers, small business owners, merchants, and mid-level company managers.

Ethnic neighborhoods were common in American cities in 1900. Immigrants often clustered together, either out of choice or necessity. This map shows Boston's North End neighborhood in 1895. Note that four primary ethnic groups were crammed into this small area, each group occupying its own section.

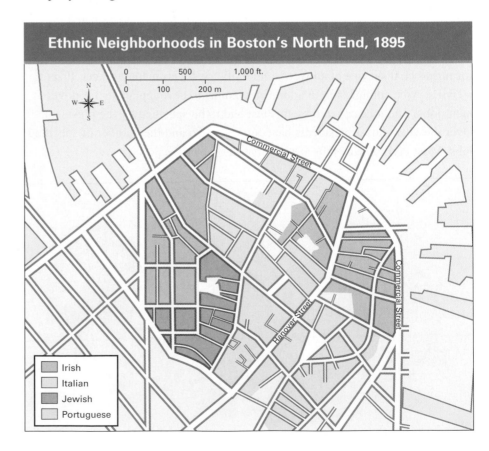

Ethnic Neighborhoods in Boston's North End, 1895

Irish
Italian
Jewish
Portuguese

By 1900, American cities were organized in ways that reflected class, race, and ethnic differences. The rich lived in mansions on streets like New York's elegant Fifth Avenue. Many Fifth Avenue residents also owned summer homes in places like Newport, Rhode Island. Their summer "cottages" were actually mansions resembling European palaces.

During this period, many middle-class families moved to comfortable homes in newly built suburbs. The men often commuted on streetcars, part of new urban transit systems. Members of the middle class tried to make their homes appear as elegant as the homes of the wealthy. Their houses often featured stained glass windows and fine furniture. Many also had reproductions of famous paintings hanging on their walls.

Working-class people remained in the cities. Immigrants tended to cluster together in ethnic neighborhoods, where they could maintain many of their old customs. Some immigrants, however, stayed in these areas because they were not allowed to live anywhere else. The Chinese in San Francisco were jammed together in one district known as Chinatown because they were barred from other areas. In cities like San Antonio and Los Angeles, Mexican immigrants lived in neighborhoods called *barrios*. African American migrants, too, generally lived in neighborhoods separated from other city residents.

Jim Crow laws in the South segregated African Americans. This photograph shows a segregated drinking fountain. Such laws made it almost impossible for southern blacks to advance by isolating them and denying them opportunities to participate fully in American life.

Life for African Americans In the 35 years since the end of the Civil War and the abolition of slavery, African Americans had made few gains in their struggle for equality. Many southern states had passed Jim Crow laws that segregated blacks from whites in trains, schools, hospitals, and other public places. Signs saying "White Only" and "Colored Only" told black Americans which waiting rooms they could enter, which bathrooms they could use, and where they could sit in theaters. Segregation affected nearly every aspect of public life in the South at the beginning of the 20th century.

In addition, by 1900 most African Americans in the South had been disenfranchised. Although the Fifteenth Amendment declared that voting rights could not be denied on the basis of "race, color, or previous condition of servitude," southern states found ways to bypass the law. Some state laws required potential voters to prove that they could read and write. These literacy tests often kept African American men from voting. So did poll taxes and property requirements. "Grandfather clauses" were another way to deny African American men the vote. Such clauses limited voting only to those men whose fathers or grandfathers had had the right to vote in 1867.

Violence against blacks was also common. Between 1882 and 1900, about 70 lynchings took place every year, mostly in the South. The victims were typically hanged or burned to death. In some cities, in both the North and the South, large-scale mob violence broke out against African Americans.

In response to racism, many African Americans fled from the South in the late 1800s. By 1900, more than 30 northern cities had 10,000 or more black residents. The number of black migrants from the South increased even more dramatically in the years that followed.

New appliances changed the way women did housework in the early 1900s. These laborsaving devices gave many middle-class women more free time to devote to pursuits outside the home. This advertising photo from 1908 shows a young woman heating food in an electric serving dish made by General Electric.

Children often worked long hours for low wages. Lewis Hine, who documented conditions of child labor in the early 20th century, took this photograph of a four year old boy picking cotton.

The Changing Role of Women Life for American women was changing, too. One trend was the growing number of women working outside the home. The number of women in the labor force nearly tripled between 1870 and 1900. At the start of the 20th century, women made up around 18 percent of the workforce. Many of these new workers were native-born, single white women. Some performed unskilled labor in textile, food-processing, and garment factories. Those with a high school education found skilled positions such as telephone operators, typists, department store clerks, nurses, and teachers. Meanwhile, many immigrant women did unskilled factory labor. Opportunities for African American women consisted mainly of working as domestic cooks or housekeepers.

New appliances made available through mass production changed the lives of many middle-class and upper-class women. Washing machines, gas stoves, carpet sweepers, and other conveniences made housework easier. For some women, however, these appliances also gave rise to new homemaking expectations. Gas stoves, for example, were far easier to use than wood stoves. But as they became available, cookbooks began to feature more time-consuming recipes. Nonetheless, the new appliances helped many women find more time for social causes and charitable activities outside the home.

Some women had the chance to attend college, too. A number of women's colleges, like Vassar, Wellesley, and Bryn Mawr, had opened after the Civil War. By 1890, nearly half of all American colleges accepted women. But the number of women in college was still fairly small compared with the number training for such occupations as teaching and nursing.

As the 20th century began, most American women did not have the right to vote. Although a few western states had granted voting rights to women, there was still no women's suffrage at the national level. Women known as suffragists actively pursued voting rights.

Challenges for the American Family The American family also faced challenges at the turn of the century, most notably around the issue of child labor. By 1900, roughly one out of every five children between the ages of 10 and 15 was a wage worker. About 1.7 million children toiled in factories, sweatshops, and mines or worked in other nonfarm jobs such as shining shoes and selling newspapers. "Breaker boys" in coal mines often worked 14 to 16 hours a day separating slate rock from coal. Grueling workweeks could stretch to 72 hours, leaving child workers little time for anything else.

Lack of education was another problem. Although public education expanded in the late 1800s, working for wages kept many children out of school. By and large, African Americans had even fewer educational opportunities than whites. In the segregated South, schools for blacks were often of inferior quality. Some African Americans, however, gained useful vocational training at all-black colleges such as Alabama's Tuskegee Institute.

Many people saw alcohol as another obstacle to improving family life and society as a whole. Since the early 1800s, there had been calls for temperance, or moderation in drinking habits. By the late 1800s, the temperance movement had grown significantly. While some reformers emphasized moderation in drinking, a growing number wanted to ban alcohol altogether. Men who did not drink, they argued, were more likely to keep their jobs and to work hard to support their families. Many reformers believed that making alcohol illegal would help lift poor families out of poverty and improve social conditions in the cities.

In addition, many parents worried that city life was corrupting the morals of their children. They believed that urban entertainments such as vaudeville theaters, dance halls, and amusement parks contributed to immoral behavior by bringing young people together in questionable surroundings, unsupervised by adults. Many parents hoped that strong bonds within families and neighborhoods might protect children from the temptations of city life.

Summary

Americans faced social, political, and environmental problems at the turn of the century. Many of these problems were the result of rapid changes brought on by industrialization, urbanization, and immigration.

Industrialization The rapid growth of industry resulted in poor working conditions for many workers. Monopolies took over industries, squeezing out competition. Some companies also made unsafe products. Muckraking journalists like Upton Sinclair, author of *The Jungle,* worked to expose these problems.

Urbanization Cities grew rapidly with the rise of industry and increased immigration. The infrastructure in many cities could not meet the demands of a growing population. Many immigrants were crammed into poor ethnic neighborhoods, such as New York's Lower East Side, where they had few services.

Environmental damage Industry and urbanization produced air and water pollution. Ranching, logging, and extractive industries also damaged the natural environment.

Political corruption Political machines, like New York's Tammany Hall, fueled corruption in city government. Big businesses influenced state and national governments. Congress passed the Pendleton Act to clean up the federal government by creating a professional civil service.

Tensions in society A growing gap between rich and poor fueled social tensions. African Americans suffered racism and mob violence, while women also faced discrimination. The temperance movement tried to limit or even ban alcohol consumption. Social changes strained American families, and many people feared the loss of traditional family bonds.

Chapter 17

The Progressives Respond

Who were the progressives, and how did they address the problems they saw?

17.1 Introduction

Garbage was a big problem in American cities at the start of the 20th century. Most cities did not have decent garbage collection, so trash just piled up. One historian described the garbage problem in a poor neighborhood in Chicago called the 19th Ward:

> In some of its alleys putrefying rubbish was piled a story and more high; its rotting wooden streets were clogged with manure, decaying garbage, and the bloated corpses of dogs and horses; and its plank-board sidewalks were lined with large uncovered garbage boxes filled to overflowing because of erratic pickup service by city-licensed scavengers.
>
> —Donald Miller, *City of the Century,* 1996

Jane Addams was a cofounder of Chicago's Hull House, a settlement house that provided support for poor urban residents, including many new immigrants. Hull House was one of a number of settlement houses founded in American cities around the turn of the century. Addams also worked to keep Chicago's streets free of garbage.

Jane Addams, a social worker and cofounder of **Hull House,** the city's first settlement house, lived in the 19th Ward. Addams knew that rats bred in the trash and that children played there. Garbage heaps, she wrote, "were the first objects that the toddling children learned to climb." She worried that these conditions promoted the spread of disease in Chicago's poor neighborhoods.

Addams decided to take action. She badgered Chicago's leaders about the trash problem. When she got no response, she applied for the job of garbage collector for her ward. Instead, she was appointed garbage inspector. In that position, Addams made sure that garbage collectors did their job.

Addams was one of many social and political reformers of the early 1900s. These reformers called themselves **progressives** because they were committed to improving conditions in American life. Cleaning up city streets was just one of the reforms that progressives supported.

In this chapter, you will learn who the progressives were and what they believed. You will read about their efforts to improve urban life, eliminate government corruption, and expand American democracy.

◀ Garbage collectors in New York City, around 1900

Many progressives were women. They also tended to be white, middle class, and college educated. Progressives believed that government should actively address the problems caused by the rapid growth of industry and cities. The women in this photograph were factory inspectors in 1914. The third woman from the left is Florence Kelley, a noted reformer and colleague of Jane Addams.

17.2 The Origins of Progressivism

By 1900, industrialization, urbanization, and immigration were contributing to great changes in American life. These changes brought new opportunities but also created new problems, particularly in cities. The progressives took action in response to these problems. They wanted to improve society by promoting social welfare, protecting the environment, and making government more efficient and democratic. The progressives had great faith in the future and a strong belief in the nation's founding ideals. They wanted to put those ideals into practice. President Woodrow Wilson described these goals in a speech in 1913:

> We have been refreshed by a new insight into our own life . . . We have made up our minds to square every process of our national life again with the standards we so proudly set up at the beginning and have always carried at our hearts. Our work is a work of restoration.
>
> —Woodrow Wilson, inaugural address of 1913

Progressives See Problems and Seek Solutions Progressives worried about the growing problems they saw in society and were determined to solve them. Until then, responsibility for addressing such issues did not lie with the government. Taking a new approach, the progressives became **activists** who were prepared to use political action to achieve reforms. They wanted government to solve society's problems.

Most progressives were urban, middle class, and college educated. The great majority were white, and many were women. The progressives included people with many different ideas about what to reform, how to reform it, and how far reforms should go. They represented many smaller reform movements rather than joining together as a single movement. But they all shared a commitment to progress and the belief that they could improve society.

The Political and Religious Roots of Progressivism The progressives were inspired by two reform movements of the late 1800s. One was the political movement called populism. The other was the religious movement called the **Social Gospel**.

Progressivism and populism had much in common, though their social origins were different. Populism was primarily a rural movement, whereas progressivism was born mainly among the urban middle class. Despite this difference, progressives embraced many populist goals. They wanted to improve conditions for farmers and industrial workers. They wanted to curb the power of big business and make government more accessible to average citizens. They also sought to expand economic opportunity and make American society more democratic.

Many progressives were also inspired by the religious ideals of the Social Gospel movement. This movement was based on the idea that social reform and Christianity went hand in hand. Followers of the Social Gospel applied Christian teachings to social and economic problems. They believed, for example, that the single-minded pursuit of wealth had taken some Americans down the wrong moral path. Walter Rauschenbusch, a Social Gospel minister, described the problem this way:

> If a man sacrifices his human dignity and self-respect to increase his income . . . he is . . . denying God. Likewise if he uses up and injures the life of his fellow-men to make money for himself, he . . . denies God. But our industrial order . . . makes property the end, and man the means to produce it.
>
> —Walter Rauschenbusch, *Christianity and the Social Crisis*, 1907

Followers of the Social Gospel believed that society must take responsibility for those who are less fortunate. Many progressives embraced this ideal and infused their reform efforts with a strong emphasis on Christian morality.

The Progressive Challenge to Social Darwinism Progressives strongly opposed social Darwinism, the social theory based loosely on Charles Darwin's theory of natural selection. Darwin had written that in nature only the fittest survive. Social Darwinists believed that in human society the fittest individuals—and corporations—would thrive, while others would fall behind. They asserted that the concentration of wealth and power in the hands of business owners and monopolies reflected the natural order.

In rejecting social Darwinism, progressives argued that domination by the rich and powerful was a distortion of democracy. They declared that most Americans were harmed when monopolies controlled the economy and corrupted politics. Progressives believed that government should play an active role in defending the political and economic rights of average citizens against the power of big business. They also wanted government to promote social reforms to clean up the cities and help those in need.

Although progressives criticized big business, most were not radicals. Unlike many socialists, they believed in private enterprise. They thought that government should balance the interests of business owners and workers, while promoting order and efficiency. They favored helping the needy but also believed that aid should go to those willing to help themselves. Although some radical reformers worked with the progressives, the progressives generally pursued moderate political goals.

Some progressives volunteered their time to provide services and solve problems in poor urban neighborhoods. In this photo, two female volunteers hand out loaves of bread to the poor.

Progressives worked to improve run-down tenements. A New York law said that tenements must be built around an open courtyard to give residents light and fresh air. It also required that there be at least one toilet for every three rooms. The illustrations above show tenement housing before and after progressive reforms.

17.3 Progressives Fight for Social Reforms

In 1904, social worker Robert Hunter wrote a book about the poverty that trapped millions of city dwellers. He described the plight of urban workers: "In the main, they live miserably, they know not why. They work sore, yet gain nothing. They know the meaning of hunger and the dread of want." Along with other progressives, Hunter worked to improve conditions for the poor.

Improving Living Conditions in Cities Living conditions for the urban poor were terrible during the early 1900s. Many city dwellers were jammed into tenements and lived in unsanitary conditions. The streets were often filled with garbage, as Jane Addams knew well.

Progressives took on the challenge of making cities cleaner and more livable. Under pressure from progressives, the state of New York passed the Tenement House Act in 1901. This law required each new tenement to be built with a central courtyard and to have a bathroom in each apartment.

Progressives like Addams also wanted the government to take responsibility for getting rid of trash. In New York, the Department of Street Cleaning took charge of garbage collection. Their collectors were called the White Wings because they wore clean, white uniforms. Muckraker Jacob Riis wrote that because of the White Wings, "Streets that had been dirty were swept. The ash barrels which had befouled the sidewalks disappeared." By cleaning up unhealthful conditions, Riis said, the White Wings "saved more lives in the crowded tenements than a squad of doctors."

Fighting to Keep Children out of Factories and in School Progressives also addressed the problem of child labor. Since many children worked in factories and sweatshops to help support their families, they could not attend school. In 1890, only 4 percent of American teenagers went to school.

Progressives pushed for laws to restrict or ban child labor. Florence Kelley, a colleague of Addams at Hull House, persuaded the Illinois state legislature to outlaw child labor in 1893. In 1904, she helped found the National Child Labor Committee. Addams also served as a board member of this organization. By 1912, the committee had convinced 39 states to pass child labor laws. These laws prohibited children under age 14 from working. Some also limited the number of hours that older children could work.

The decline in child labor meant that more children could get an education, thus creating a demand for more schools. In 1870, there were only 500 high schools throughout the nation. By 1910, that number had grown to 10,000. By 1930, almost half of all high-school-aged youth were attending school.

Progressives wanted children not only to be educated but also to be "Americanized." They believed in pressuring immigrant schoolchildren to give up their cultural traditions and become assimilated into American society.

Progressives also protested the treatment of children by the criminal justice system. In many places, the law required juvenile offenders to be sentenced to reform school, but accused children did not always get a trial. Even if the children were not convicted, they might be sent away for rehabilitation. In addition, destitute children living on the streets were often treated as juvenile offenders.

A number of progressives tried to identify and address the causes of juvenile delinquency. One of these reformers was Judge Ben Lindsey of Denver, Colorado. Like many progressives, Lindsey believed that juvenile offenders were basically good but that their surroundings led them astray. If their living environment were improved, he argued, the delinquency would disappear. Lindsey also thought that promoting good relationships between troubled youths and fair-minded judges would help young delinquents.

Lindsey and other progressives advocated creating a separate court system for juveniles. In 1905, only about 10 states had juvenile courts. By 1915, all but two states had them.

Improving Conditions in the Workplace Progressives had mixed success in helping adult workers. A law passed in New York to limit the number of hours bakers could work in a week was struck down by the Supreme Court in 1905. In *Lochner v. New York,* the Court ruled that such laws interfere with freedoms protected by the Fourteenth Amendment. "The right to purchase or to sell labor is part of the liberty protected by this amendment," wrote Justice Rufus Peckam, "unless there are circumstances which exclude the right."

Efforts to protect women fared better, perhaps because most men believed the "weaker sex" needed special protection. In 1908, the Supreme Court ruled in *Muller v. Oregon* that states could limit work hours for women. "As healthy mothers are essential to vigorous offspring," the Court ruled, "the physical well-being of woman is an object of public interest . . . [and] does not conflict with the due process or equal protection clauses of the Fourteenth Amendment."

Reformers also pushed for legislation to provide benefits to workers who were injured on the job. By 1916, almost two thirds of the states had **workers' compensation** laws. Under these laws, workers who were hurt at work still received some pay, even if their injuries prevented them from working.

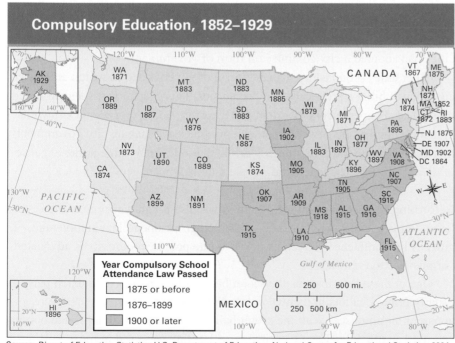

Compulsory Education, 1852–1929

Year Compulsory School Attendance Law Passed
- 1875 or before
- 1876–1899
- 1900 or later

Source: *Digest of Education Statistics,* U.S. Department of Education, National Center for Educational Statistics, 2004.

Reformers supported efforts to get children out of the workforce and into school. As this map shows, by 1900 many states required school attendance, even though child labor was still legal in many places. Southern states were among the last to pass compulsory school attendance laws.

Tom Johnson was the reform mayor of Cleveland, Ohio, from 1901 to 1909. As mayor, he worked to clean up government and help average citizens. He reduced streetcar fares to 3¢, despite strong opposition from business leaders. This collage celebrates Johnson's achievement. It is entitled *Tom L. Johnson and Incidents in the Building of the Three-cent Streetcar Line.*

17.4 Progressives Push for Political Reforms

Journalist Lincoln Steffens was among the muckrakers who exposed urban corruption at the turn of the century. Like many progressives, he did more than just expose and criticize. He proposed a solution. He said that citizens could improve city government by making demands on local politicians. He wrote, "If our political leaders are to be always a lot of political merchants, they will supply any demand we may create. All we have to do is to establish a steady demand for good government."

Fighting for Honest, Effective Local Government At the start of the 20th century, corrupt political machines ran many local governments. Bribery was commonplace. Businesses paid politicians to cast votes that favored their interests, and people who wanted public service jobs often had to buy their way in. Getting a job as a teacher in Philadelphia, for example, was costly. New teachers had to pay the political machine $120 of the first $141 they earned.

With the goal of improving democracy, progressives took aim at corruption in city governments. One strategy was to elect progressive mayors who would support reform. In Toledo, Ohio, Mayor Samuel M. Jones reformed the police department, set a minimum wage for city workers, and improved city services. In Cleveland, Ohio, Mayor Tom Johnson reduced streetcar fares, set up public baths, and increased the number of parks and playgrounds.

Progressives also wanted to reform the structure of local governments. In the early 1900s, a typical city was run by an elected mayor, and elected city councilors represented each of the city's wards, or districts. The system made it easy for political machines to control local government.

A devastating hurricane in Galveston, Texas, in 1900 set the stage for one type of reform. Unable to solve the problems of rebuilding, Galveston's government handed control to a five-person city commission appointed by the governor. Each commissioner was an expert in a field, such as finance or public safety. The positions later became elected offices. The Galveston city commission's work was so successful that by 1913 more than 350 American cities had adopted a city commission form of government.

Other cities set up a city manager form of government, in which an elected city council hired a professional city manager. This official was selected based on skills and experience rather than party loyalty. Some progressives saw this system as limiting the power of political machines and making city governments more competent. However, others worried that efficiency came at the expense of democracy because voters did not elect the city manager.

Reforming State Government Progressives also fought corruption at the state level. In many states, big business controlled government, leaving average citizens little influence. To return power to the people, progressives advocated various election reforms.

One of these reforms was the secret ballot. In the early 1900s, each party usually printed ballots in its own color, which meant voters' choices were apparent for all to see. With the secret ballot, citizens voted in a private booth and used an official ballot. Over time, secret voting was used in most elections.

Another reform was the direct primary, in which voters hold elections to choose candidates from each party to run for office in general elections. Direct primaries replaced a system in which party leaders picked the candidates.

A third reform was the **recall,** the process by which voters can remove an elected official before his or her term expires. For a recall to be placed on the ballot, enough voters must sign a petition to demand a special election.

A fourth reform was the direct **initiative**. This is a lawmaking reform that enables citizens to propose and pass a law directly without involving the state legislature. Enough voters must first sign a petition to place the proposal on the ballot. It then becomes law if voters approve it on election day. This reform was more common in western states, where many progressives inherited a populist distrust of state legislatures.

Another lawmaking reform favored in western states was the **referendum**. In this process, a law passed by a state legislature is placed on the ballot for approval or rejection by the voters. The referendum is similar to the initiative, but less commonly used.

In addition to pressing for election reforms, progressives elected reform-minded governors. One famous progressive was Robert La Follette, governor of Wisconsin from 1900 to 1906. Under his guidance, the state passed laws to limit lobbying, conserve forests and other natural resources, and support workers.

Known as "Fighting Bob," La Follette took a strong stand against the railroads, which controlled the distribution of many products, including meat and grain. By charging favored customers lower rates for carrying freight, the railroads made it hard for other businesses to compete. With reduced competition, consumers paid more for many products. La Follette responded by forming a commission to regulate railroad rates. He also convinced the legislature to increase taxes on the railroads.

Governor Hiram Johnson of California also promoted progressive reforms. Like La Follette, he wanted to limit the power of the railroads. His campaign slogan was "Kick the Southern Pacific Railroad Out of Politics." Johnson also regulated utilities, limited child labor, and signed into law an eight-hour work-day for women.

17.5 Progressives Confront Social Inequality

Although progressives faced issues of poverty, workers' rights, and corrupt government, many did not address the inequality confronting women and African Americans. However, progressive activism prompted many women and African Americans to struggle for their rights.

Women Fight for the Right to Vote Many progressive women saw themselves as "social housekeepers." They defined their public work as an extension of the work they did at home. If they could clean up their homes, they believed, they could clean up society, too. But without the right to vote, their chances for success were limited. After the Triangle Shirtwaist fire, for example, a journalist asked a New York machine politician why women factory workers had no fire protection. "That's easy," he replied. "They ain't got no votes!"

Progressive state governors, like Wisconsin's Robert La Follette, used their positions to advance reform. This cartoon highlights La Follette's success in controlling railroad monopolies. He won three terms as governor and was later elected to the U.S. Senate.

Hiram Johnson was a two-term governor of California and later served nearly 30 years in the U.S. Senate. A lawyer by training, Johnson had never held public office before his election as governor in 1910. He was a strong supporter of progressive reform and a staunch opponent of corruption in public life.

Women had demanded the right to vote as early as 1848, when a group of 300 women and men met at Seneca Falls, New York, to discuss women's rights. At the Seneca Falls Convention, Elizabeth Cady Stanton argued that "the power to make laws was the right through which all other rights could be secured." Progress toward that goal, however, was painfully slow. Women continued to agitate for women's suffrage throughout the late 1800s. During this period, leading suffragists joined together to form the **National American Woman Suffrage Association,** or **NAWSA,** with Stanton as its first president. This group helped organize the suffrage movement into a powerful political force at the state and national levels.

The first victories in the struggle for women's suffrage came at the state level. By 1898, four western states had granted women the right to vote. By 1918, women had voting rights in 15 states. As a result, they began to influence elections. In Montana, they helped elect Jeannette Rankin to the House of Representatives in 1916, four years before women had the right to vote nationwide. Rankin was the first woman to serve in Congress.

African Americans Struggle for Equality African Americans faced an even tougher battle for their rights. In the early 1900s, four fifths of African Americans lived in the South. Most struggled to make a living as farmers and were subjected to strict segregation. Southern blacks were also disenfranchised, as literacy tests, poll taxes, and other methods denied them the right to vote. Nevertheless, many African Americans were inspired by progressive ideals and worked to improve their conditions.

One leading proponent of advancement was Booker T. Washington, an African American educator. Washington founded the **Tuskegee Institute,** a vocational college for African Americans in Alabama. He encouraged blacks to gain respect and status by working their way up in society.

Western states were the first to grant women voting rights. By 1918, women had full voting rights in 15 states, many of them in the West. Women also had partial voting rights in another 23 states. Partial voting rights usually meant that women could vote in state and local elections but not in national elections.

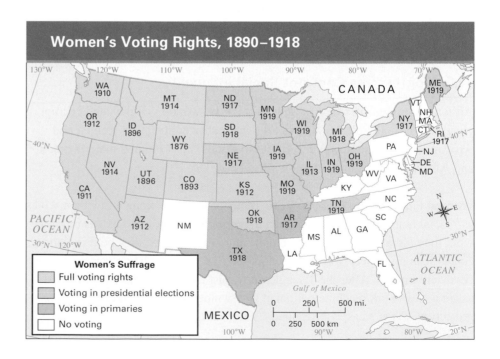

Women's Voting Rights, 1890–1918

Women's Suffrage
- Full voting rights
- Voting in presidential elections
- Voting in primaries
- No voting

Some progressives favored confronting racism. In 1909, one group formed the **National Association for the Advancement of Colored People,** or **NAACP.** The NAACP fought through the courts to end segregation. It also tried to ensure that African American men could exercise voting rights under the Fifteenth Amendment.

One of the founding members of the NAACP was W. E. B. Du Bois, a distinguished African American scholar and activist. Between 1910 and 1934, he edited *The Crisis,* an NAACP journal that focused on issues important to African Americans.

In addition to its legal work, the NAACP protested lynching and other racist violence. Between 1894 and 1898, about 550 African Americans were lynched. Among the progressives who spoke out against this violence was Ida B. Wells-Barnett, a cofounder of the NAACP. In 1892, Wells-Barnett protested the lynching of three African American grocers in Memphis, Tennessee. She expressed her outrage in *The Memphis Free Speech,* a newspaper she co-owned and edited. She also urged African Americans to leave Memphis. In response, a mob ransacked her offices.

Based on systematic research, Wells-Barnett concluded that lynching had an economic motive. She argued that whites used lynching "to get rid of Negroes who were acquiring wealth and property." Despite the efforts of Wells-Barnett and other progressives, the federal government did not pass any laws against lynching.

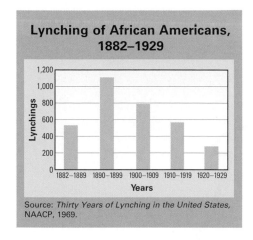

Source: *Thirty Years of Lynching in the United States,* NAACP, 1969.

This graph shows the number of African Americans lynched between 1880 and 1930. Lynchings rose sharply in the 1890s but declined after that. Although activists like Ida B. Wells-Barnett protested, the federal government did not pass antilynching laws.

Summary

In the early 1900s, progressives worked to reform American society. Inspired by reform movements like populism and the Social Gospel, progressives tackled a variety of problems. They tried to improve living and working conditions in cities, clean up state and local government, and advance the rights of women and minorities.

Urban living conditions Progressives like Jane Addams, the cofounder of Hull House, worked to fix up poor city neighborhoods. They tried to improve tenement housing, sanitation, and garbage collection.

Worker protection Progressives fought to improve working conditions. They promoted laws limiting work hours and guaranteeing workers' compensation. They formed the National Child Labor Committee to campaign against child labor and get more children into school.

Clean, responsive government Progressives sought to end government corruption at the local level. They worked to curb the power of political machines and restructure local government. They also worked to expand democracy at the state level. They supported reform governors like Robert La Follette and passed electoral reforms like the secret ballot, direct primary, recall, initiative, and referendum.

Struggle for equal rights Women and African Americans sought to advance their rights. Reform goals included voting rights for women and an end to lynching and segregation. NAWSA led the struggle for women's suffrage, while the NAACP tried to secure equality for African Americans.

Chapter 18

Progressivism on the National Stage

How well did Presidents Roosevelt, Taft, and Wilson promote progressive goals in national policies?

18.1 Introduction

On February 22, 1902, the rich financier J. P. Morgan went to the White House to see President Theodore Roosevelt. Morgan had a dispute to resolve with the president. Roosevelt had recently ordered the Justice Department to file a lawsuit against Northern Securities Company, of which Morgan was part owner, for antitrust violations.

Northern Securities was a holding company, a business that controls other companies by buying up a majority of their stock. Morgan and other business-men had created this holding company to control the long-distance railroad lines from Chicago to California. By the time the Roosevelt administration filed suit against him, Morgan held a monopoly on rail service in the Northwest.

Morgan believed it would be easy for the two men to settle their differences. "If we have done anything wrong, send your man to my man and they can fix it up," he told Roosevelt. But Roosevelt disagreed. He didn't like it when big business treated government as an equal, or worse, as its servant. "That can't be done," he told Morgan. Two years later, in 1904, the Supreme Court ruled against Northern Securities.

"Trustbusting" was one of a number of progressive reforms enacted at the national level in the early 1900s. In addition to local and state issues, progres-sives were also concerned about problems in the country as a whole. Many of them believed that the national government no longer served the interests of all Americans. In an age when big business seemed all-powerful, many reformers felt the United States was abandoning its promise of freedom and opportunity for all. They wanted the government to play a stronger role in promoting democracy and solving national problems.

Three presidents—Theodore Roosevelt, William Howard Taft, and Woodrow Wilson—worked to advance the progressive reforms. Their efforts helped change how Americans thought, and continue to think, about the role of government.

Theodore Roosevelt was the first progressive in the White House. He was a strong president who believed in using his position to influence the nation. During his two terms in office, he expanded presidential power.

◄ President Theodore Roosevelt tames the trusts

After overcoming childhood illnesses, Teddy Roosevelt led a vigorous life, which included a great love of the outdoors. As president, he put millions of acres of wilderness under government protection. Here he is shown in Yosemite National Park, which he visited in 1903.

William Howard Taft was the second progressive president. Although Taft backed reform, he lacked Roosevelt's political skill and lost the support of many progressives. He later became chief justice of the United States, the job he had wanted all along.

18.2 Three Progressive Presidents

The framers of the Constitution wanted the president to have prestige but not too much power. Many feared what might happen if the chief executive became too powerful. As the presidency evolved during the Progressive Era, Americans began to change not only their ideas about what the national government should do, but also their views about how strong the president should be.

The three presidents of the Progressive Era—Roosevelt, Taft, and Wilson—held office between 1901 and 1921. Although differing in many ways, they shared a commitment to reform. They challenged the economic and political power of the industrial giants and worked to end government corruption. In the process, all three of these leaders expanded the power of the presidency.

Theodore Roosevelt Promises a Square Deal Theodore Roosevelt was vice president under President William McKinley and became president after McKinley was assassinated in 1901. At the age of 42, he was the youngest president in American history. Also known as Teddy or TR, he was a colorful character. He was short and stout with big teeth, and he had a passion for physical fitness. As a member of New York's state assembly in the 1890s, he was known for being impulsive, but he was a shrewd politician who knew how to get things done.

Roosevelt believed that businesses, workers, and consumers should all receive a "square deal"—fair and honest treatment. His program of reform, which became known as the **Square Deal,** focused on regulating big business and protecting workers and consumers.

Roosevelt believed the country needed a strong president. "I believe in power," he once said. But he thought that presidential power should be used to benefit all Americans. Describing himself as "the steward [caretaker] of public welfare," he asserted that a president should take any actions necessary for the common good, as long as the Constitution did not forbid them.

Taft Continues Reforms After Roosevelt served two terms, he supported William Howard Taft, a member of his cabinet and a former judge from Ohio, to succeed him in 1908. Roosevelt was confident that Taft would continue his reform program.

The two men could not have been more different. Roosevelt was outspoken and loved the limelight, while Taft was quiet and reserved. Whereas Roosevelt took bold actions, Taft was cautious. In short, Taft was a reluctant, lackluster campaigner. Nevertheless, Roosevelt's support helped him sail to victory.

As president, Taft continued reform efforts. He fought to limit the power of big corporations and added land to the national forest system. However, on other issues Taft parted company with progressive reformers. Progressives wanted lower tariffs on imported goods. Lower tariffs would make foreign products less expensive for American consumers. They would also increase competition, so that American producers would have to lower prices. Big business favored high tariffs. Taft had campaigned for president on a low-tariff platform, but in 1909 he agreed to sign the Payne-Aldrich Bill, which raised tariffs. This action tarnished Taft's record as a progressive.

THE TARIFF TRIUMPH OF PHARAOH WILSON.

In the 1912 election, Taft and Roosevelt divided the Republican vote. The result was victory for Woodrow Wilson, the Democrat. In this political cartoon, entitled "The Triumph of Pharaoh Wilson," Wilson is shown as an ancient Egyptian pharaoh riding in a chariot being pulled by the Democratic donkey. The elephant and the bull moose behind him represent the Republican and Bull Moose Party.

The Election of 1912 The presidential campaign of 1912 centered on progressive reform. Roosevelt believed that Taft had betrayed progressive ideals. For that reason, he decided to run for president again in 1912. When the Republicans chose Taft as their candidate, Roosevelt decided to run as the candidate of a **third party,** a political party outside the two-party system. Roosevelt's party was called the Progressive Party but was nicknamed the Bull Moose Party after he declared his readiness by exclaiming, "I feel as fit as a bull moose."

The 1912 election also featured two other candidates. Woodrow Wilson, a man of strong progressive ideals, represented the Democratic Party. Labor leader Eugene V. Debs, running on the socialist ticket, advocated more radical change, calling on voters to make "the working class the ruling class."

The split between Taft and Roosevelt helped Wilson win the 1912 election. Wilson received 42 percent of the popular vote. Roosevelt had 27.5 percent, and Taft had 23 percent. Debs was a distant fourth with 6 percent but received almost a million votes, a strong showing for the Socialist Party.

Wilson Promises New Freedom As governor of New Jersey, Wilson had supported progressive reforms to regulate big business and clean up machine politics. As president, this idealist and scholar set out to implement a national reform program that he called New Freedom. Wilson wanted to eliminate all trusts because he believed they were denying economic freedom to small businesses and ordinary citizens. He was unable to remove the trusts, but he did further limit their power.

Wilson pushed through other progressive reforms to give a greater voice to the average citizen, restrict corporate influence, and reduce corruption in the federal government. Among his most notable achievements were laws on banking and tariff reform and the creation of the Federal Trade Commission.

Wilson was the first president since George Washington to speak before Congress, introducing and lobbying for legislation. Like Roosevelt, he also tried to influence, and utilize, public opinion to further his reform goals.

Woodrow Wilson, the last progressive president, was a scholar and idealist. The president, he wrote in 1907, "is the only voice in national affairs. Let him once win the admiration and confidence of the country, and no other single force can withstand him, no combination of forces will easily overpower him."

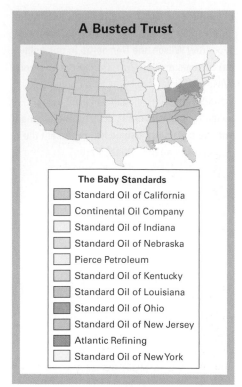

A Busted Trust

The Baby Standards

- Standard Oil of California
- Continental Oil Company
- Standard Oil of Indiana
- Standard Oil of Nebraska
- Pierce Petroleum
- Standard Oil of Kentucky
- Standard Oil of Louisiana
- Standard Oil of Ohio
- Standard Oil of New Jersey
- Atlantic Refining
- Standard Oil of New York

Trustbusting broke large monopolies into many smaller, competing companies. This map shows how the Standard Oil Trust was divided into smaller companies, nicknamed the Baby Standards, in 1911. Each of the new companies took over Standard Oil operations in its assigned region of the country. Standard Oil was one of the biggest trusts to be broken up by a progressive president.

18.3 Addressing the Effects of Industrialization

Rapid industrialization gave rise to a number of problems in American society, including unsafe products, environmental damage, and corruption in public life. The three progressives in the White House—Roosevelt, Taft, and Wilson—sought to correct these negative effects. As Roosevelt put it, "The man who holds that every human right is secondary to his profit must now give way to the advocate of human welfare." The progressive presidents worked to reduce the harmful effects of industrialization, starting with the power of the trusts.

Busting Trusts Roosevelt began the progressive trustbusting movement. To regulate monopolies, he used the Sherman Antitrust Act. This law made illegal "every contract, combination in the form of trust or otherwise, or conspiracy, in restraint of trade or commerce." The law had been passed in 1890 but had been ineffective. Its language was vague, and enforcement was weak.

Roosevelt believed that government should regulate monopolies to make sure they operated for the good of the nation. Sometimes he had to break up trusts rather than regulate them. Such actions gained him a reputation as a trustbuster. However, he was not opposed to big business. "We do not wish to destroy corporations," he said, "but we do wish to make them subserve the public good."

In addition to breaking up J. P. Morgan's Northern Securities Company, Roosevelt limited the power of railroads to set rates and stifle business competition. In 1906, he signed the Hepburn Act, which gave the federal government the authority to set maximum rail shipping rates.

Under Taft, the Justice Department brought 90 lawsuits against trusts—more than twice the number under Roosevelt. Taft supported a stricter interpretation of the Sherman Act. Roosevelt distinguished between good and bad trusts, trying to break up only trusts created specifically to squash competition. In contrast, Taft did not think a court could determine a trust's motives, so he prosecuted any trusts that had the effect of limiting trade, regardless of intent.

Wilson took even stronger action by helping to push the Clayton Antitrust Act through Congress. Passed in 1914, the Clayton Act extended the power of the Sherman Act by laying out rules that made it harder for trusts to form and to squeeze out competition. For example, the law made it illegal for a company to lower prices in one market but not others to try to force out local competitors.

The Clayton Act also protected labor unions from antitrust regulation. Courts had ruled that unions could be prosecuted for restraining commerce under the Sherman Act, but the Clayton Act made unions exempt from antitrust laws. Congress also created the Federal Trade Commission in 1914 to enforce the Clayton Act's provisions.

Progressives who wanted to eliminate trusts were displeased that the antitrust reforms left many trusts intact. Meanwhile, pro-business conservatives thought that the government should not have interfered at all with businesses. Nevertheless, the moderate reforms that were typical of progressivism produced real benefits for society.

Protecting Consumers and Workers In addition to busting trusts, the progressive presidents tried to protect consumers. Two key laws were passed in 1906 during Roosevelt's presidency: the Meat Inspection Act and the Pure Food and Drug Act.

The Meat Inspection Act required the Department of Agriculture to inspect packaged meat. This law was a response to muckraker accounts of unsanitary meatpacking plants. For example, one passage in Upton Sinclair's novel *The Jungle* described how rats often became part of the ground meat: "The packers would put poisoned bread out for them; they would die, and then rats, bread, and meat would go into the hoppers together." Sinclair later said of reaction to his book, "I aimed at the nation's heart, but hit it in the stomach."

The Pure Food and Drug Act established a new agency, the Food and Drug Administration, to test and approve drugs before they went on the market. This law addressed the calls for the regulation of patent medicines. These nonprescription medicines often promised magical cures, but many contained little more than alcohol or opium.

Roosevelt also helped improve working conditions for coal miners. In 1902, he pressured coal mine owners and the striking United Mine Workers to submit to **arbitration,** a legal process in which a neutral outside party helps resolve a dispute. A government commission decided that the miners should have higher wages and shorter hours. However, it also declared that the owners did not have to recognize the union or hire only union workers. This arbitration pleased Roosevelt and many other progressives, who believed that government should be impartial in labor disputes and stronger than either big business or unions.

Taft and Wilson expanded worker protection. Under Taft, the Department of Labor established the Children's Bureau to "investigate and report upon all matters pertaining to the welfare of children." Wilson went further to push for a ban on child labor. In 1916, he signed the Keating-Owen Child Labor Act, which prohibited companies involved in interstate commerce from hiring workers under 14 years of age. Although the law protected fewer than 10 percent of children in the labor force, it set minimum protections and a precedent for future action.

Taft and Wilson also supported an eight-hour workday—at least for some workers. For years, companies had resisted this demand by unions. Under Taft, the eight-hour day became the rule for government employees. Wilson later helped secure the same benefit for railroad workers.

Congress passed the Meat Inspection Act in 1906 to ensure that meat was safe for consumers. This law was prompted by reports that meat was often tainted by rat droppings and even poison. Federal inspectors made regular visits to meatpacking plants to enforce the law.

Protecting the Environment Progressives also wanted to protect the natural environment. They saw how industry and urban growth had polluted the air and water and devastated the landscape. They believed that government should remedy these problems, but they sometimes disagreed on the solutions.

Some progressives supported **preservation,** the protection of wilderness lands from all forms of development. John Muir, a preservationist who co-founded the Sierra Club in 1892, believed that the government must preserve the environment. "Any fool can destroy trees," he wrote. "God . . . cannot save them from fools—only Uncle Sam can do that."

Other progressives supported **conservation,** the limited use of resources. Conservationists believed that government should take a middle position between preservation and exploitation. They wanted to preserve some wilderness while also allowing some use of natural resources.

The progressive presidents, especially Roosevelt, were sympathetic to the preservationist view. Roosevelt, a great outdoorsman, once commented, "We are prone to think of the resources of this country as inexhaustible. This is not so." In practice, however, the government tended to favor the more moderate conservationist approach.

In 1905, Roosevelt backed the creation of the U.S. Forest Service. Its mission was to protect forests and other natural areas from excessive development. Roosevelt appointed Gifford Pinchot, a noted conservationist, to head the Forest Service. Like Roosevelt, Pinchot advocated a "wise use" policy of balancing the demands of economic development with the need to conserve the natural environment. Under Roosevelt, the federal government set aside nearly 150 million acres of national forests.

Taft added 2.7 million acres to the National Wildlife Refuge System. However, he angered Roosevelt and many conservationists by firing Pinchot for criticizing the government's sale of some wilderness areas in Wyoming, Montana, and Alaska.

In 1916, Wilson supported the creation of the National Park Service (NPS). Congress had founded the first national park, Yellowstone, in 1872. Later, more lands were set aside for national parks. The NPS was created to manage all these parks for preservation and public use. This mandate reflected a shift in preservationist thinking. Preservationists no longer argued that all wilderness areas should be left untouched. Instead, they accepted the idea that tourism, and thus economic development, could help protect the natural landscape.

The national park system expanded under progressive leadership. This map shows the national parks established by the end of Wilson's presidency. The first national park, Yellowstone, was established in 1872. The National Park Service was created in 1916, under Wilson, to manage and protect the park system.

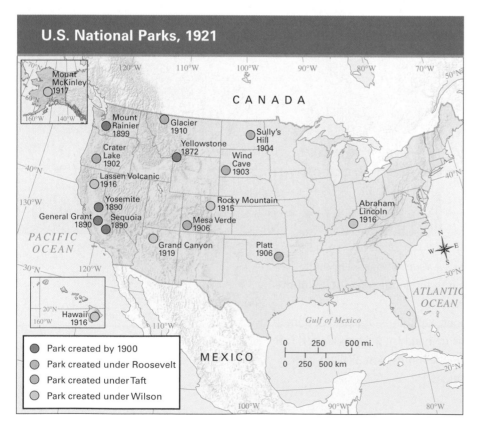

U.S. National Parks, 1921

- Mount McKinley 1917
- Mount Rainier 1899
- Glacier 1910
- Sully's Hill 1904
- Crater Lake 1902
- Yellowstone 1872
- Wind Cave 1903
- Lassen Volcanic 1916
- Yosemite 1890
- Rocky Mountain 1915
- Abraham Lincoln 1916
- General Grant 1890
- Sequoia 1890
- Mesa Verde 1906
- Grand Canyon 1919
- Platt 1906
- Hawaii 1916

CANADA

PACIFIC OCEAN

ATLANTIC OCEAN

Gulf of Mexico

MEXICO

0   250   500 mi.
0   250 500 km

- ● Park created by 1900
- ● Park created under Roosevelt
- ● Park created under Taft
- ● Park created under Wilson

18.4 Reforming the National Government

Progressives also sought to reform the federal government and its policies. They favored a range of financial reforms that would improve government funding and the banking system. They also worked for constitutional reforms, including the direct election of senators, a ban on alcohol, and women's suffrage.

Reforming the Banking System Progressives wanted government to stabilize the banking system. Since the early 1800s, the nation had been shaken by financial panics, periods when people withdrew their money from banks after losing confidence in the economy. Panics caused banks and businesses to collapse and sometimes triggered economic depressions.

Taft urged Congress to reform the banking system, but Americans differed over the proper solution. Progressives wanted government control over the system, while business leaders favored private control. In 1913, Wilson backed a proposal for a government-controlled but decentralized banking system. Congress responded by passing the Federal Reserve Act in 1913.

The Federal Reserve Act divides the country into 12 regions, each with a Federal Reserve Bank. Together, these banks and their operating rules make up the Federal Reserve System, or central bank of the United States. Under this system, private banks remain independent but agree to operate under the rules of the Federal Reserve System, which is also called the Federal Reserve or "the Fed." The Fed offers a safety net to private banks by lending them money if they are short of funds. It also sets monetary policy to regulate the amount of money in circulation, including setting interest rates and regulating how much banks can lend. The Fed has made the financial system much more stable.

The Federal Reserve Act, passed in 1913, established 12 regional banks around the country. These banks can loan money to private banks and thus help to stabilize the banking system.

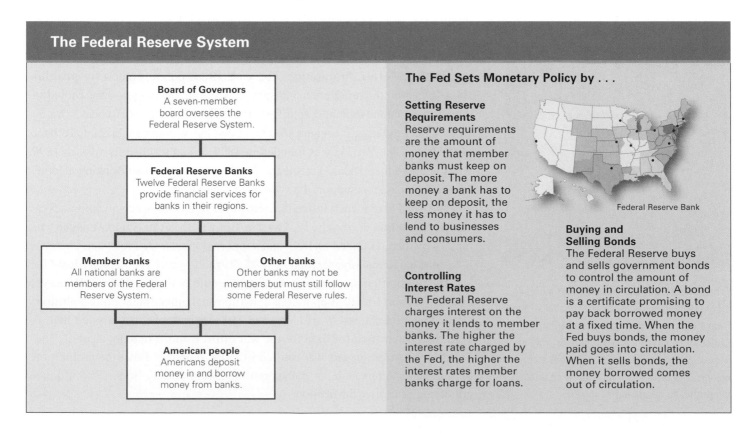

The Federal Reserve System

Board of Governors
A seven-member board oversees the Federal Reserve System.

Federal Reserve Banks
Twelve Federal Reserve Banks provide financial services for banks in their regions.

Member banks
All national banks are members of the Federal Reserve System.

Other banks
Other banks may not be members but must still follow some Federal Reserve rules.

American people
Americans deposit money in and borrow money from banks.

The Fed Sets Monetary Policy by . . .

Setting Reserve Requirements
Reserve requirements are the amount of money that member banks must keep on deposit. The more money a bank has to keep on deposit, the less money it has to lend to businesses and consumers.

Federal Reserve Bank

Controlling Interest Rates
The Federal Reserve charges interest on the money it lends to member banks. The higher the interest rate charged by the Fed, the higher the interest rates member banks charge for loans.

Buying and Selling Bonds
The Federal Reserve buys and sells government bonds to control the amount of money in circulation. A bond is a certificate promising to pay back borrowed money at a fixed time. When the Fed buys bonds, the money paid goes into circulation. When it sells bonds, the money borrowed comes out of circulation.

This is a copy of the first federal tax form, from 1913. The Sixteenth Amendment legalized the federal income tax. Progressives backed the tax as a way to eliminate tariffs. They also liked that it was a graduated tax, which placed higher taxes on those who could afford to pay.

Prohibition supporters believed that a ban on alcohol would improve society. This illustration from 1874 shows members of the Women's Christian Temperence Movement praying and protesting against the sale of alcohol at a saloon. The Eighteenth Amendment establishing prohibition was ratified in 1919.

Reforming Taxes and Tariffs As the role of the federal government expanded, its need for revenue to fund its programs increased. Big business favored raising tariffs, but progressives wanted to raise taxes. Tariffs on imports had long been used to boost government revenue. However, progressives believed that they were unfair to consumers. By raising the cost of imported goods, tariffs increased the cost of living for average Americans. A national income tax could be imposed more fairly on all citizens.

Under strong pressure from progressives, and with some support from Taft, Congress proposed the Sixteenth Amendment, which would allow the federal government to impose an income tax. After the amendment was ratified in 1913, during Wilson's presidency, Congress made the tax a graduated income tax, requiring people with higher incomes to pay a larger percentage of their earnings than those with lower incomes. Progressives were pleased because a **graduated income tax** placed a higher burden on those who had more money. Meanwhile, Wilson pressured Congress to reduce tariffs. Congress put both measures—the graduated income tax and reduced tariffs—into a single bill, the Underwood Tariff Act. Wilson signed it in 1913.

Electing Senators Directly For progressives, reform also meant giving citizens a greater say in their government. One key issue was the election of U.S. senators. The Constitution required that senators be elected by state legislatures. However, state lawmakers and the senators they elected often had close ties to large corporations.

Progressives wanted senators to respond to the will of the people, not the power of big business. Therefore, they pushed Congress to propose the Seventeenth Amendment. Proposed in 1912 and ratified in 1913, the amendment required the direct election of senators by popular vote. This procedure gave average citizens more influence in the Senate.

Legislating Morals: Prohibition The widespread public support for **prohibition**—a ban on the production and sale of alcoholic beverages—was rooted in the temperance movement dating from the early 1800s. Most advocates were women, and the largest organization had been the Women's Christian Temperance Union. The WCTU was founded in 1874. It had reached its peak in 1890, boasting more than 150,000 members. The WCTU argued that drinking alcohol made men unable to support their wives and children.

The WCTU remained influential. However, the leading organization advocating prohibition during the Progressive Era was the Anti-Saloon League, run mainly by men. Founded in 1893 and supported mostly by Protestant churches, it became a national organization in 1895. Its motto was "The Saloon Must Go."

The prohibition movement gained momentum without help from Roosevelt or Taft. Wilson finally supported a constitutional amendment on prohibition after the nation entered World War I in 1917. Proponents had argued that grain was better used for food for the war effort than for making alcohol. The Eighteenth Amendment was ratified in 1919. It declared that the prohibition of "the manufacture, sale, or transportation of intoxicating liquors" would take effect one year after ratification.

Establishing Women's Suffrage Women had been trying to win the right to vote since before the Civil War. Many temperance activists also supported women's suffrage. They argued that women were more moral than men and that women's involvement would help cleanse the corrupt world of politics.

Like prohibition, the struggle for women's suffrage was a grassroots effort that succeeded without much presidential support. Roosevelt was sympathetic but did not push for the cause until his 1912 campaign. After the nation entered World War I, leading suffragists such as Carrie Chapman Catt emphasized that giving women the right to vote would help them carry out their duties on the home front. Wilson eventually accepted their arguments. He urged Congress to propose an amendment to give women the right to vote as "a vitally necessary war measure." Meanwhile, 26 states had petitioned Congress to propose it.

In 1919, Congress proposed the amendment by decisive votes in both the House and Senate. The Nineteenth Amendment was ratified in 1920. It declared that "the right of citizens of the United States to vote shall not be denied or abridged by the United States or by any state on account of sex."

Suffragists, women who sought voting rights, faced many obstacles, including threats and harassment from angry men. However, women won the vote through ratification of the Nineteenth Amendment in 1920.

Summary

Three progressive presidents—Theodore Roosevelt, William Howard Taft, and Woodrow Wilson—held office from 1901 to 1921, during the Progressive Era. Their goals and styles of leadership differed, but they all worked to bring about reforms on the national level.

Three distinct leaders Despite their varying leadership styles, the progressive presidents believed in using government to improve society. In carrying out reform programs, such as Roosevelt's Square Deal and Wilson's New Freedom, they increased the power of the presidency.

Addressing the effects of industrialization Reformers passed laws to break up monopolies and help workers. They tried to protect consumers through such laws as the Pure Food and Drug Act. They also tried to preserve the environment by conserving resources.

Sixteenth Amendment This amendment established a federal income tax, which progressives favored as a means to fund government programs. Congress made the tax a graduated income tax, which placed a heavier tax burden on the wealthy.

Seventeenth Amendment This amendment established the direct election of U.S. senators, another progressive goal. It replaced the election of senators by state legislatures.

Federal Reserve System Congress set up the Federal Reserve to bring stability to the banking system and prevent financial panics. The Fed, which consists of 12 federal banks, lends money to private banks and sets policies that govern interest rates and the amount of money in circulation.

Eighteenth Amendment This amendment established prohibition, or a ban on alcohol. Many progressives believed that alcohol consumption was a serious social ill.

Nineteenth Amendment This amendment guaranteed women the right to vote. This was an important progressive goal designed to advance democratic rights.

Chapter 19

Foreign Policy: Setting a Course of Expansionism

Was American foreign policy during the 1800s motivated more by realism or idealism?

19.1 Introduction

On July 8, 1853, Commodore Matthew Perry led a small fleet of American warships into Edo Bay, in Japan. Edo is now called Tokyo. Perry had come to open up Japan to American shipping and trade.

For over 200 years, Japan had been almost a closed country. Fearing that foreign influence would threaten its power, the government had restricted trade to a few Chinese and Dutch merchants. As a result, most Japanese knew nothing of the Industrial Revolution. For example, they had never seen a train or steamship. So they were astonished when the black-hulled American warships steamed into Edo Bay, bristling with cannons and belching smoke. The vessels, which the Japanese called "black ships," posed a threat to Japan's isolation.

The United States had tried, but failed, to open up Japan before. This time, however, the United States had sent one of its top naval officers, Commodore Perry, with a letter from President Millard Fillmore addressed to the Japanese emperor. The letter was an offer of peace and friendship, but the warships were a sign that the United States might be willing to use force in the future. The letter asked that shipwrecked American sailors be protected and that American ships be allowed to stop for water, fuel, and other supplies. It also proposed the opening of trade between the United States and Japan.

The Japanese government promised to consider the president's letter. Perry returned with a larger fleet in 1854 to negotiate a treaty. The Japanese did not agree to trade, but they did agree to the other requests. This treaty paved the way for an 1858 treaty that opened Japan to trade with the United States.

These treaties with Japan were part of a broader effort to advance American interests in Asia. They were key victories for American **foreign policy**. Foreign policy is the set of goals, principles, and practices that guide a nation in its relations with other countries. In this chapter, you will learn how both realists and idealists shaped American foreign policy during the 1800s.

Commodore Matthew Perry led a fleet of four American warships to Japan in 1853 in an effort to open the island nation to U.S. trade. The painting on the facing page depicts one of the American "black ships" in Edo Bay during Perry's visit to Japan.

◀ A Japanese view of Commodore Perry's ship and officers

George Washington's Farewell Address was published in newspapers in 1796. As part of his advice to the nation, he urged neutrality in foreign relations. He feared that forming alliances would lead to harmful entanglements in European affairs.

19.2 Early Developments in U.S. Foreign Policy

In 1796, late in his second term as president, George Washington presented his final message to the nation. Although known as Washington's Farewell Address, it was not delivered as a speech but instead appeared in newspapers. While Washington focused mainly on domestic issues, he ended with a discussion of foreign affairs. "It is our true policy," he said, "to steer clear of permanent alliances with any portion of the foreign world." These words would shape American foreign policy for more than a century to come.

Fundamentals of U.S. Foreign Policy From Washington's time to the present, the president has led the way in formulating the nation's foreign policy. The State Department, led by the secretary of state, advises the president and carries out the details of U.S. policy. Congress also plays a role by debating and voting on foreign policy issues. A treaty with another nation does not become legally binding unless the Senate approves it by a two-thirds vote.

Presidents have a variety of tools to use in pursuing foreign policy goals. One is **diplomacy,** the art of conducting negotiations with other nations. Diplomacy may lead to informal agreements as well as treaties. A second tool is financial aid in the form of grants or loans. Such aid can be used to support friendly nations or influence their policies. A third tool is the threat or the use of armed force.

Over the past two centuries, two schools of thought, known as realism and idealism, have shaped U.S. foreign policy. **Realism** is based on the belief that relations with other countries should be guided by national self-interest. From this perspective, foreign policy should pursue practical objectives that benefit the American people. Such objectives might include national security, increased trade with other nations, and access to overseas resources.

Idealism in foreign policy is based on the belief that values and ideals should influence how countries relate to one another. From this point of view, foreign policy should be used to promote America's founding ideals—particularly democracy, liberty, and rights—to ensure a better world not just for Americans, but for all people.

At any given time, realism or idealism may dominate this country's relations with other nations. But most of the time, U.S. foreign policy reflects a blend of the two schools of thought.

Washington Advocates Neutrality and Unilateralism George Washington established two key principles of U.S. foreign policy. The first, **neutrality,** was a response to the outbreak of war between France and Great Britain in 1793. Neutrality is the policy of refusing to take sides among warring nations.

Idealists were eager to side with France, pointing out that the United States and France had signed a treaty of alliance during the War of Independence. It was now time, they argued, for the United States to stand by its ally. They were also enthralled by the French Revolution. In 1789, French leaders had issued a statement of revolutionary ideals known as the Declaration of the Rights of Man and of the Citizen. Two years later, they had abolished France's monarchy and established a republic. Many Americans were eager to support the French in their struggle for liberty.

Realists argued against taking sides. They warned that with a tiny army, the United States was ill prepared for war. Moreover, a British blockade of its ports would cripple an already wobbly economy. Convinced that war would be disastrous for the young nation, Washington issued a proclamation of neutrality. It stated that the policy of the United States was to "pursue a conduct friendly and impartial toward the belligerent [warring] powers."

In his Farewell Address, Washington took neutrality a step further. "The great rule of conduct for us in regard to foreign nations is," he advised, ". . . to have with them as little political connection as possible." This advice was translated by the presidents who followed Washington into a policy of **unilateralism**. Under this policy, the United States "went it alone" in its relations with other countries. It did not seek either military or political alliances with foreign powers.

During the War of 1812, the British bombarded Fort McHenry, near Baltimore, Maryland, which is depicted here in the background. But the defenders prevented the city from being captured. The sight of the fort's flag still waving inspired Francis Scott Key to write "The Star-Spangled Banner." In 1931, it was officially named the national anthem.

Defending Neutrality: The War of 1812 As a neutral nation, the United States had both rights and duties. It could not give aid to either side in a conflict. Nor could it allow a warring nation to use its harbors or territories as a base of operations. In return, the United States also claimed certain rights. One was the right of its citizens to live in peace without fear of attack. A second was the right to trade freely with other nations, including those at war.

The seemingly endless war in Europe tested Americans' commitment to neutrality. Both France and Britain seized U.S. ships to prevent goods from reaching the other's ports. Even more alarming, the British began kidnapping American sailors from U.S. ships, claiming they were deserters from the British navy. Both the ship seizures and the kidnappings violated what Americans saw as their rights as citizens of a neutral nation.

Presidents John Adams and Thomas Jefferson used every foreign policy tool short of war to defend the right of American ships to trade freely without being attacked. Neither had much success.

In 1809, President James Madison took up the challenge of defending neutrality. For a time, he seemed to be making some progress with France. When the British still refused to end attacks on neutral ships, Madison asked Congress for a declaration of war.

The senators and representatives who voted for war did so for a mix of reasons. Those motivated more by idealism cast their votes to defend "free trade and sailors' rights." Those motivated mainly by realism believed that a war with Great Britain would give the United States the opportunity to expand its borders into Canada.

The War of 1812 lasted more than two years. With no victory in sight, peace talks began in Ghent, Belgium, in mid-1814.

The Treaty of Ghent called for "a firm and universal Peace between His Britannic Majesty and the United States." But it left the issues that caused the war unresolved. Still, the young nation had stood up to Britain. "Not one inch of territory ceded or lost" boasted Americans as the war drew to a close.

The Monroe Doctrine declared the Americas off limits to European colonization and interference. This 1896 cartoon portrays the United States as having the power to keep European nations out. The doctrine was also used to justify the spread of U.S. influence in the region.

The Monroe Doctrine Bans Colonization When James Monroe took office as president in 1817, he faced new challenges. One came from Russia, which already controlled Alaska. In 1821, Russia issued a decree extending its colony south into territory claimed jointly by the United States and Great Britain.

Meanwhile, revolutions were sweeping across Latin America. Americans cheered as one colony after another freed itself from Spain, but rumors soon emerged that Spain meant to recolonize the region. Britain then invited the United States to join it in warning European leaders against taking such action.

Monroe chose a more unilateral approach. In a speech to Congress in 1823, he warned that "the American continents" were closed to "future colonization by any European powers." He also stated that the United States would consider European interference in the new Latin American republics "as dangerous to our peace and safety." These twin policies of **non-colonization** and **non-interference** in the Western Hemisphere became known as the **Monroe Doctrine**.

The United States invoked the Monroe Doctrine only a few times during the 1800s. One of those occasions came about when Venezuela asked for help in settling a long-standing dispute with Britain over its border with British Guiana, a British colony in South America. Venezuela appealed to the United States in the name of the "immortal Monroe" to intervene. Siding with the Venezuelans, Senator Henry Cabot Lodge of Massachusetts warned,

> If Great Britain is to be permitted to . . . take the territory of Venezuela, there is nothing to prevent her taking the whole of Venezuela or any other South American state . . . The supremacy of the Monroe Doctrine should be established and at once—peacefully if we can, forcibly if we must.
> —Henry Cabot Lodge, *North American Review,* 1895

Britain agreed to negotiate with Venezuela, but only after deciding that it was not worth going to war with the United States over a few thousand square miles of mosquito-infested jungle. Still, Americans saw the settlement of the Venezuelan boundary dispute as a victory for the Monroe Doctrine. "Never again," crowed the *Chicago Journal,* "will a European nation put forth claims to American territory without consulting the government of the United States."

19.3 The U.S. Pursues a Policy of Territorial Expansion

In 1803, President Thomas Jefferson arranged for American diplomats to attempt to buy New Orleans, a port city at the mouth of the Mississippi River. At the time, New Orleans was part of the French colony of Louisiana. Jefferson feared that French control of the port would pose a threat to American trade flowing down the Mississippi.

Much to Jefferson's surprise, the French offered to sell all of Louisiana. For the price of $15 million, less than 3 cents an acre, the United States could double its territory. Jefferson agreed to the offer. Senate approval of the Louisiana Purchase Treaty late that year signaled a new goal for U.S. foreign policy: expansionism.

Jefferson was able to secure the French colony of Lousiana for just $15 million. This transaction helped double the territory of the United States. The map above shows the land acquired through the Lousiana Purchase.

Expansion Through Diplomacy The new policy of territorial expansion was motivated by both idealism and realism. Idealists were inspired by the idea of manifest destiny—the belief that the United States was meant to spread its founding ideals and democratic way of life across the continent and beyond. Realists believed that expansion made the nation more secure by removing foreign threats on its borders. Adding new lands also gave the new nation growing room. If possible, expansionists hoped growth could come about through diplomacy. Louisiana, after all, had been acquired through diplomatic means.

Diplomacy worked well in some cases. In 1819, U.S. diplomats persuaded Spain to **cede** Florida to the United States. Expansionists then looked west to Oregon, an area that included what is now known as the Pacific Northwest. Oregon, however, was also claimed by Great Britain. The two nations had jointly occupied Oregon since 1818, and Britain had repeatedly refused U.S. attempts to extend the boundary to the 54th parallel.

Tensions increased in 1845 when President James K. Polk declared that the United States had a "clear and unquestionable" claim to the entire area. Some expansionists even called for war if Britain refused to leave. Their rallying cry of "Fifty-four forty or fight" referred to the latitude 54'40°, the northern limit of the region. Unwilling to go to war over Oregon, Britain signed a treaty in 1846 dividing the region at the 49th parallel. The United States now stretched to the Pacific Ocean.

Diplomacy also brought about the purchase of Alaska in 1867. Faced with the choice of pouring money into Alaska to defend it or of making money by selling it, Russia decided to offer this huge region to the United States. Secretary of State William Seward jumped at the chance, negotiating a price of $7.2 million and signing a treaty early the next day. Many Americans made fun of "Seward's Icebox," but later it became clear that Alaska had vast natural resources, including gold.

The Alamo was built as a mission but was occasionally used as a fort. In 1836, a force of about 180 Texans held the Alamo for several days against a large Mexican army. Their leader, William Travis, sent out a plea for help, saying, "I shall never surrender or retreat." The Texans died in battle or were executed before help could arrive.

The Annexation of Texas Diplomacy did not work as smoothly when Americans looked south to Texas. In 1821, a businessman named Moses Austin received permission from Spain to found a colony in Texas, which at that time was part of Mexico. When Austin died suddenly, his son Stephen took over the enterprise. Stephen Austin arrived in Texas just as Mexico declared its independence from Spain. Mexican officials agreed to let Austin begin his colony, but only if the settlers he attracted consented to learn Spanish, become Mexican citizens, and join the Catholic Church.

By 1830, there were about 25,000 Americans living in Texas. As their numbers grew, tensions between the Americans and the Mexican government began to rise. The Americans disliked taking orders from Mexican officials. They resented having to deal with official documents in Spanish, a language most of them were unwilling to learn. Those who had brought slaves with them to Texas were upset when Mexico ended slavery in 1829. American slaveholders in Texas ignored the law and kept their slaves in bondage.

Hoping to reduce these tensions, Stephen Austin traveled to Mexico City in 1833. Instead of negotiating with Austin, General Santa Anna, the dictator of Mexico, threw him in jail. Santa Anna also amended Mexico's constitution to increase the power of the central government. Faced with the prospect of losing the right to run their own affairs, the Texans revolted. Early in 1836, they declared Texas to be an independent country and named Sam Houston as their commander in chief.

Determined to crush the **Texas Revolution,** Santa Anna marched north with an army of several thousand troops. On reaching San Antonio, Texas, he found a band of Texas volunteers defending an old mission called the Alamo. The defenders included the famous frontiersman Davy Crockett, crack rifleman Jim Bowie, and a group of Texas freedom fighters led by William Travis. Santa Anna raised a black flag that meant, "Expect no mercy." Travis answered with a defiant cannon shot. After a 13-day siege, the Mexicans overran the Alamo and executed all of the defenders who had survived the assault.

Two weeks later, a force of three or four hundred Texan volunteers led by James Fannin was captured by Mexican troops near Goliad. Badly outnumbered, the Texans surrendered. On orders from Santa Anna, hundreds of prisoners of war were executed. Their bodies were stacked in piles and burned.

A few weeks later, the Texans had their revenge. After luring Santa Anna deep into Texas, Sam Houston sprang a trap beside the San Jacinto River.

Shouting, "Remember the Alamo! Remember Goliad!" as their war cry, the Texas volunteers overran the Mexican army. To win his freedom, Santa Anna signed two treaties agreeing to an independent Texas with the Rio Grande as its southern border. On his return to Mexico, however, the general declared that his country was not bound by any agreement on Texas.

Now an independent country, Texas became known as the Lone Star Republic because of the single star on its flag. Most Texans and many Americans wanted Texas to become part of the United States. The issue was complicated, however, by the fact that Texas allowed slavery. Whenever the question of annexing Texas came up in the Senate, Northerners who opposed slavery voted no. Not until 1845 was Texas finally admitted to the Union as a slave state.

Polk Provokes a War with Mexico The annexation of Texas by the United States angered Mexico, which had never accepted the loss of this territory. The two nations also disagreed on where to draw the Texas-Mexico border. The United States recognized the Rio Grande as the dividing line. Mexico put the border much farther north. President Polk sent a diplomat to Mexico City to try to settle the border dispute. He also instructed the diplomat to offer to buy New Mexico and California. The Mexican government refused to negotiate.

Polk then decided to provoke a clash with Mexico. In 1846, he sent troops to occupy the north bank of the Rio Grande, deep inside what Mexico considered its territory. As Polk expected, the Mexican army attacked. He then called for war, claiming that Mexico had "invaded our territory and shed American blood." Congress declared war two days later.

The Mexican army fought bravely, but it had little success. Aided by superior weapons and leadership, U.S. troops moved quickly through northern Mexico. At the same time, other U.S. forces seized New Mexico and California. The **Mexican War** finally ended after Americans captured Mexico City in 1847.

This painting shows American troops defeating the Mexican army at the Battle of Buena Vista. This battle gave the United States control of northern Mexico. As a result of the war, the United States gained almost all of the present American Southwest, from Texas west to California.

The Treaty of Guadalupe Hidalgo, which ended the Mexican War in 1848, resulted in Mexico losing half its territory. This cartoon from 1847 comments on Mexico's loss of power. The eagle is a traditional symbol of Mexico that appears on the country's flag.

PLUCKED:

THE MEXICAN EAGLE BEFORE THE WAR!   OR.   THE MEXICAN EAGLE AFTER THE WAR!

In 1848, the United States and Mexico signed the Treaty of Guadalupe Hidalgo. Mexico formally recognized the annexation of Texas, with the Rio Grande as its border. It also ceded a huge region stretching from Texas to California to the United States. In return for the Mexican Cession, the United States paid Mexico $15 million. While idealists worried that the war had been an unjust land grab, realists cheered the results. The United States had increased its territory by about one third. Mexico, in contrast, had lost half of its territory.

The Beginnings of Imperialism The acquisition of California from Mexico and Oregon from Britain gave the United States a new window on the Pacific Ocean. Business leaders were eager to open up new markets for American goods across the Pacific in China and Japan. The question was how best to do this. Many European nations, they observed, were expanding their overseas

Germany, Britain, and the United States competed for influence in the Samoan Islands in the late 1800s. As a result, the islands seethed with bitter rivalries and civil wars. King Mataafa seen here, front row, second from left, gained and lost the kingship three times in this troubled period.

markets by acquiring colonies in Africa and Asia. This new wave of colonization was inspired by a policy known as **imperialism,** or empire building. The colonies acquired by the imperialist powers supplied resources for their industries and served as markets for their manufactured goods.

While some Americans were reluctant to join this rush for empire, many were happy to acquire islands that could serve as supply stations for U.S. ships in the Pacific. In 1867, the United States claimed the uninhabited Midway Islands. It was hoped that these tiny islands, located northwest of the Hawaiian Islands, could serve as a coaling station for steamships.

The Samoan Islands were even more attractive as a way station for U.S. ships. This island group lies about halfway between Hawaii and Australia. In the 1870s, the United States, Germany, and Britain signed treaties with the Samoan king giving them access to the islands. Later the three countries made Samoa a **protectorate**—a nation protected and controlled by a stronger nation. Later Britain gave up its claim to Samoa. In 1899, the islands were divided between Germany and the United States. American Samoa provided U.S. ships with an excellent harbor at the port of Pago Pago and also became an important military post. It has remained a territory of the United States to this day.

Summary

During the 1800s, U.S. foreign policy was guided by two goals. The first was to keep the United States free of foreign alliances and out of foreign conflicts. The second was to expand the United States across the North American continent. As Americans began to look outward in the late 1800s, they debated the nation's proper role in world affairs.

Realism and idealism U.S. foreign policy is generally a blend of realism and idealism. With realism, the focus is on practical concerns and national self-interest. With idealism, the focus is on moral values and the spread of American ideals.

Neutrality and unilateralism Following the advice given by Washington in his Farewell Address, the United States tried to stay neutral in foreign wars and avoid alliances with other countries. The War of 1812 was fought in part to defend American rights as a neutral nation.

The Monroe Doctrine The Monroe Doctrine warned European powers that the United States would view efforts to establish colonies in the Americas or interfere with new Latin American republics as hostile to its interests.

Continental expansion Following a policy of expansion through diplomacy, the United States acquired the Louisiana Territory, Florida, Oregon Territory, and Alaska. By winning the Mexican War, it gained vast lands in the Southwest.

Overseas expansion In the late 1800s, the United States began to look overseas for new territory and influence. At the same time, Americans began to debate the role and value of overseas expansion.

Chapter 20

The Spanish-American War

Why did the United States go to war against Spain in 1898, and why was the outcome significant?

20.1 Introduction

In the late 1800s, one of the best-known New Yorkers was not a person at all. He was the Yellow Kid, a character in a wildly popular newspaper comic. For a time, the Yellow Kid appeared in two newspapers at once, the *New York World* and the *New York Journal,* which competed to own the comic.

The struggle over the Yellow Kid was part of a larger "newspaper war" in New York City during the 1890s. Joseph Pulitzer, the publisher of the *World,* faced off against William Randolph Hearst, the publisher of the *Journal,* in a battle to dominate the city's newspaper market. Their struggle over newspaper sales helped to provoke a real war, the Spanish-American War.

The artist who created the Yellow Kid, R. F. Outcalt, first sold his comic in 1895 to Pulitzer's *World.* The comic was set in New York's poor, rough-and-tumble ethnic neighborhoods and featured a bald-headed street urchin dressed in a bright yellow nightshirt. The Yellow Kid was an instant success. Newspaper comics were new at the time, and Pulitzer's *World* enjoyed a huge jump in sales.

Not to be outdone, Hearst lured Outcalt to the *Journal* by promising him more money. In response, Pulitzer hired another cartoonist to draw his own version of the cartoon. Before long, the two newspapers were flooded with images of the Yellow Kid and became known as the "Yellow Kid Papers" or "Yellow Papers."

The rivalry between the *World* and the *Journal* extended beyond the Yellow Kid cartoons. In their struggle to attract readers, the two "Yellow Papers" developed an exaggerated style of reporting. Their sensational news stories soon became known as **yellow journalism**. Among these stories were news reports about other countries. One favorite subject was the brutal suppression of a rebellion in Cuba against Spanish rule. Yellow journalism helped inflame public support for going to war against Spain. In this chapter, you will learn why the United States went to war against Spain and why this conflict was a significant event in American foreign relations.

The popular Yellow Kid cartoons were featured in the *New York Journal* and the *New York World*. In competing to attract readers, these papers often exaggerated the facts. Sensationalized reporting on the brutal suppression of the revolt in the Spanish colony of Cuba increased public anger against Spain.

◀ Newspapers helped push the country toward war in the 1890s.

20.2 Trouble Brewing in Cuba

The island of Cuba lies just 90 miles off the coast of Florida, in the Caribbean Sea. It was founded as a Spanish colony by Christopher Columbus in 1492 and later became one of the world's leading sugar producers. Hundreds of thousands of slaves worked on its plantations. For over three centuries, Cuba was part of Spain's vast empire. But by the late 1800s, there were just two Spanish colonies in the Americas: the islands of Puerto Rico and Cuba. A growing independence movement was threatening Spanish rule in Cuba.

Cubans Struggle for Independence During the 1800s, many Cubans had voiced a desire for self-rule. In 1868, a revolutionary group largely made up of poor whites, free blacks, and slaves demanded independence from Spain, the establishment of a republic, and the end of slavery. When Spain rejected these demands, bitter fighting followed. Spain eventually crushed the revolt but then tried to ease tensions by agreeing to limited reforms. It gave Cubans some representation in the government, and it abolished slavery in 1886.

Meanwhile, Cuba was coming under the economic influence of the United States. American business interests saw it as a good place to trade and invest. By the mid-1890s, American investment in Cuba's sugar plantations had reached many millions of dollars. American investors were therefore nervous about the island's political instability.

Despite some reforms, the political situation did not improve significantly. In 1895, Cubans again rebelled. This second struggle for independence was led by José Martí, a Cuban poet, journalist, and statesman. Forced to leave Cuba because of his revolutionary activities, Martí lived in the United States from 1881 to 1895. Even while he was living abroad, Martí inspired his fellow Cubans with calls for liberty. He wrote, "Like bones to the human body . . . so is liberty the essence of life. Whatever is done without it is imperfect." Martí sailed to Cuba in 1895 to lead the revolt but was soon killed in combat. Nevertheless, the rebellion continued.

The Cuban rebels engaged in guerrilla warfare, launching surprise attacks against Spanish forces and fading back into the countryside. In 1896, Spain sent a new commander, General Valeriano Weyler, to put down the uprising. To eliminate support for the rebels, Weyler forced tens of thousands of Cubans into reconcentration camps. These overcrowded, unsanitary prison camps provided little food or shelter, causing thousands of deaths from disease and starvation.

Cuba's proximity to the United States led to close economic ties in the late 1800s and a growing American presence on the island. Cubans living in the United States helped fund efforts to win Cuba's independence. Here, Cuban rebels await the Spanish.

Many Americans sympathized with the rebellion, seeing it as a struggle for freedom, like the American Revolution. Meanwhile, American investors feared that the political unrest was putting their Cuban investments and property at risk. Despite public calls for the United States to intervene in Cuba, President Grover Cleveland followed a policy of strict neutrality. When William McKinley was elected president in 1896, he hoped to maintain neutrality. But that would become more difficult as the public increasingly called for the United States to help the rebels.

American Newspapers React Most Americans learned about the events in Cuba through newspapers and magazines. At that time, these were the only forms of **mass media**—methods of communicating to a mass audience.

Newspapers were very popular in the late 1800s. With the yellow journalism of the time, however, many papers were not as careful in their reporting as they are today. To sell newspapers, publishers like Joseph Pulitzer and William Randolph Hearst sensationalized the news. Both the *New York World* and the *New York Journal* saw reporting on the Cuban rebellion as a good way to gain new readers. Reporters and artists were encouraged to stretch the truth about the bravery of Cuban rebels and the horrors of Spanish rule, especially "Butcher" Weyler's brutality. Many readers were shocked by these reports. Some demanded that the United States help Cuba win independence. In this way, yellow journalism helped stir public support for U.S. intervention to aid the rebels.

José Martí was an accomplished writer and the father of Cuban independence. He spent many years in exile in New York, planning the overthrow of Spanish rule. Today José Martí's image is featured on the Cuban Peso.

Political cartoons helped shape public opinion about events in Cuba. This cartoon from 1898 depicts the island suffering from Spanish misrule. The fearsome figure in the center is labeled "Spain," and he is shown stepping over a dead American sailor and a starving Cuban.

The Spanish-American War **227**

20.3 Americans Call for War with Spain

In 1897, the Spanish government promised greater self-rule in Cuba. It also removed General Weyler from his post and ordered him to return to Spain. As a result, the Cuban crisis cooled down. In February 1898, however, two events aroused American anger and led to increasing calls for war.

The de Lôme Letter Incites the Public On February 9, 1898, Hearst's *New York Journal* published a letter written by Enrique Dupuy de Lôme, the Spanish ambassador to Washington. The de Lôme letter was addressed to a friend in Cuba but was somehow stolen from the mail and sent to the *Journal* for publication.

In the letter, de Lôme called President McKinley "weak and catering to the rabble and, besides, a low politician." Americans were offended by this criticism of their president. De Lôme offered his resignation, but the damage was done. The publishing of this letter intensified anti-Spanish feelings in the United States and underscored the power of the press to inflame public opinion.

Newspapers Decry the *Maine* Incident Not long after the de Lôme affair, a much more alarming incident occurred: the sinking of the battleship **USS *Maine*** in Havana harbor. Newspapers around the country responded with calls for vengeance.

The *Maine* had sailed to Cuba in January after riots broke out in the streets of Havana. Spaniards who opposed government reforms in Cuba led the riots. Fearing harm to American citizens and property, President McKinley had sent the *Maine* to Cuba to protect American interests.

Inflammatory articles and illustrations about the sinking of the USS *Maine* helped rouse public support for war with Spain. The *New York Journal* offered a reward for evidence in the sinking. To this day, however, historians are not sure what caused the blast.

For two weeks, the *Maine* sat in Havana harbor. Then, on the night of February 15, a tremendous explosion rocked the battleship. The captain reported hearing "a bursting, rending, and crashing roar of immense volume." Then the ship began to sink. More than 260 sailors died from the blast.

An official navy investigation began immediately, but the *Journal* and other newspapers immediately blamed Spain. The Hearst paper published bellicose articles under such headlines as "The *Maine* Was Destroyed by Treachery" and "The Whole Country Thrills with War Fever!" Across the country, "Remember the *Maine*" became a rallying cry for war.

The United States Responds In March, the navy issued its report on the sinking of the *Maine*. Though the evidence was sketchy, navy investigators concluded that the explosion was caused by an underwater mine. Their report did not suggest who was responsible. In 1976, navy researchers who studied the incident again concluded that heat from a fire in a coal bin exploded a nearby supply of ammunition.

Four days before the report was completed, Senator Redfield Proctor of Vermont gave a compelling speech on the Senate floor. Proctor had just returned from Cuba and described the appalling conditions there. Although General Weyler was no longer in charge, the reconcentration camps were still in operation, and the Cuban people were still suffering. Proctor concluded,

> To me the strongest appeal is not the barbarity practiced by Weyler nor the loss of the *Maine* . . . but the spectacle of a million and a half of people, the entire native population of Cuba, struggling for freedom and deliverance from the worst misgovernment of which I ever had knowledge.
>
> —Redfield Proctor, speech before the Senate, March 17, 1898

The *Maine* report and Proctor's speech helped turn opinion in Congress and the public toward war. But President McKinley, still hoping to avoid conflict, gave Spain one last chance. He called for an **armistice,** a cessation of hostilities, until a permanent peace could be discussed. He also called on Spain to close the reconcentration camps and to take steps to grant Cuba its independence. Spain agreed to an armistice and to closing the camps, but was unwilling to give up control of Cuba.

Under great public pressure, McKinley asked Congress to declare war on Spain. Congress passed a **resolution,** a formal statement about a course of action, recognizing Cuban independence and authorizing military force, if necessary, to liberate Cuba. Congress also passed the Teller Amendment, which said that after Cuba was liberated and peace was restored, the United States would "leave the government and control of the Island to its people." Spain then passed a declaration of war against the United States. On April 25, Congress formally declared war on Spain.

On April 25, 1898, Congress declared war on Spain after the Spanish government rejected American demands for Cuban independence. Newspapers trumpeted the news and called for a quick victory over Spanish forces.

The first battle of the Spanish-American War took place in the Philippines. On May 1, 1898, the U.S. Navy under Commodore George Dewey destroyed the Spanish fleet in Manila Bay. Dewey finally took the islands on August 13. He did not know that Spain and the United States had declared peace the day before.

20.4 A "Splendid Little War" with Spain

The Spanish-American War lasted only a few months, but it had dramatic results. The United States won the conflict convincingly, demonstrating military power in overseas combat, with few American battle casualties. John Hay, who served as U.S. ambassador to Britain and later as secretary of state, described it as "a splendid little war, begun with the highest motives, carried on with magnificent intelligence and spirit, favored by that Fortune which loves the brave."

Fighting Begins in the Philippines Even though the war was sparked by problems in Cuba, the first battle took place much farther away, in the Philippines. A large group of islands southeast of China, the Philippines were Spain's largest remaining colony. As in Cuba, a revolt against Spain had been brewing. Emilio Aguinaldo, a young Filipino, led this resistance. When the Spanish-American War began, he was living in exile in Hong Kong.

At least two months before war was declared, the United States began preparing for battle in the Philippines. If war broke out, it wanted to strike a quick blow against the Spanish fleet in Manila Bay. Theodore Roosevelt, the assistant secretary of the navy at the time, instructed the commander of the Pacific squadron, Commodore George Dewey, to sail to Hong Kong and await further orders.

On May 1, just days after the declaration of war, Dewey's squadron steamed into Manila Bay and opened fire on the Spanish fleet. Taken by surprise, the fleet was entirely destroyed. Dewey did not lose a single ship and suffered only a few battle casualties.

Dewey had scored a stunning victory but did not have sufficient troops to land in Manila and take the city. In the meantime, Aguinaldo returned to the Philippines with his rebel forces to fight the Spanish on his own. American reinforcements finally arrived near the end of July. On August 13, the Philippines fell to a combined force of American soldiers and Filipino rebels.

Fighting Moves to Cuba Meanwhile, fighting had begun in Cuba. The U.S. Navy quickly set up a blockade of Havana and the north coast of Cuba. At the eastern end of the island, however, a Spanish squadron slipped into the harbor at Santiago de Cuba. President McKinley ordered troops to sail for Santiago. The plan was to join the navy there and engage the Spanish. The American troops, led by General William Shafter, arrived outside Santiago on June 20.

The U.S. Army in Cuba consisted of various forces. Among them were four regiments of African American soldiers, many of whom had fought in the Indian Wars in the American West. The army also relied on volunteer regiments, including one led by Theodore Roosevelt. When the war began, Roosevelt quit his post as assistant secretary of the navy so that he could join the fighting. Together with Colonel Leonard Wood, he helped form the First U.S. Volunteer Cavalry, better known as the **Rough Riders**. Handpicked by Roosevelt, this regiment was a mix of college athletes and western cowboys.

On July 1, General Shafter launched his assault on Santiago, moving against Spanish troops dug in along a ridge. Roosevelt and the Rough Riders charged up Kettle Hill, while other U.S. forces fought the even tougher battle for **San Juan Hill**. By nightfall, the U.S. Army had taken the ridge.

The rest of the war went quickly. The American navy destroyed the Spanish squadron as it tried to leave Santiago harbor, and on July 17, Santiago surrendered. The following week, the United States captured Puerto Rico. With no prospect of success, Spain agreed to a peace settlement on August 12. Four months after the start of the conflict, the war was over.

Despite their quick victory, not everything went well for the U.S. forces. About 5,500 Americans died in the war, mostly from tropical diseases like malaria and yellow fever. As regiments were formed on short notice, many soldiers lacked proper equipment and supplies. Most had heavy wool uniforms, a severe liability in Cuba's tropical heat, and food was often of poor quality. Despite these difficulties, the United States had won a major victory in its first overseas war.

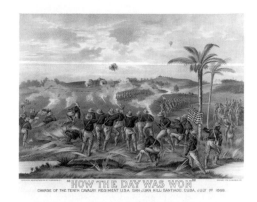

"HOW THE DAY WAS WON" CHARGE OF THE TENTH CAVALRY REGIMENT USA SAN JUAN HILL SANTIAGO, CUBA, JULY 1st 1898.

Black and white troops fought together in the assault on San Juan Hill. The 10th Cavalry Regiment, shown here, was an all African American unit. By taking the hill, American forces broke Spain's main line of defense for the city of Santiago. First Lieutenant John J. Pershing wrote of that battle: "White regiments, black regiments . . . fought shoulder to shoulder, unmindful of race or color . . . and mindful of only their common duty as Americans."

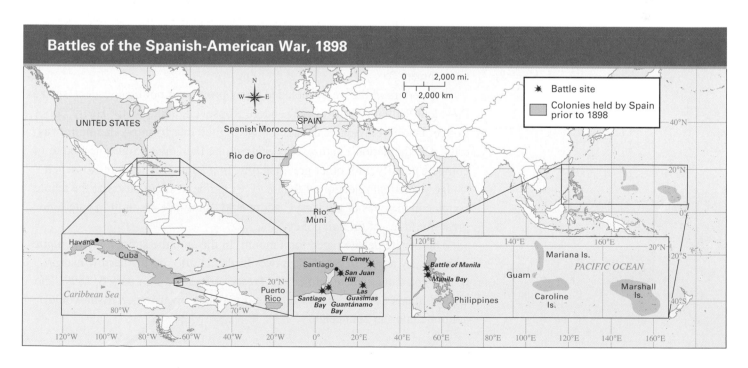

Battles of the Spanish-American War, 1898

Battle site

Colonies held by Spain prior to 1898

This cartoon refers to clashing views on the Philippines in the presidential election of 1900. Democrat William Jennings Bryan argued that the islands should be independent. President McKinley and the Republicans declared that American control was needed to keep law and order.

20.5 A New Power on the World Stage

With its victory in the Spanish-American War, the United States emerged as a new world power. It had defeated a European nation and won control of overseas territories. In the peace treaty, the United States solidified its new position in world affairs.

The Treaty of Paris The war ended on August 12, 1898, with the signing of a peace **protocol,** a first draft of a treaty to be submitted for ratification. In October, Spanish and American officials met in Paris to finalize the terms.

On December 10, the United States and Spain signed the Treaty of Paris. Spain agreed to three main points. First, it granted independence to Cuba. Second, it ceded Puerto Rico and the Pacific island of Guam to the United States. And third, it ceded the Philippines to the United States in exchange for a payment of $20 million. Under the treaty, Puerto Rico, Guam, and the Philippines became American possessions. The United States was now a colonial empire.

The Senate Debate over the Treaty For the treaty to take effect, the Senate would have to ratify it by a two-thirds vote. This vote prompted a fierce debate over imperialism. While some Americans supported creating an American empire, others were strongly opposed. The debate over the treaty raged not only in the Senate but also across the entire country.

Leading opponents were the members of the Anti-Imperialist League, an organization formed during the war to oppose the establishment of U.S. colonies. Its membership was diverse, ranging from union leader Samuel Gompers to millionaire industrialist Andrew Carnegie. Social worker Jane Addams joined, as did author Mark Twain. Although the motives and political views of league members varied widely, they all believed that imperialism violated the country's founding principles of freedom and democracy. As the league's platform stated, "We hold that the policy known as imperialism is hostile to liberty . . . We insist that the subjugation of any people is 'criminal aggression' and open disloyalty to the distinctive principles of our Government."

Supporters of the treaty included many prominent political leaders, such as President William McKinley, Theodore Roosevelt, and Senator Henry Cabot Lodge. During the Senate debate, Lodge argued that forming an empire was critical to the nation's future. He declared that the United States needed to compete equally with other great nations. In a letter to Theodore Roosevelt, Lodge wrote that rejection of the treaty would be a "humiliation of the whole country in the eyes of the world" and would "show we are unfit to enter into great questions of foreign policy."

The Senate debate raged for a month. In the end, the supporters of empire won out. By a vote of 57 to 27, a two-thirds majority by the narrow margin of two votes, the Senate ratified the Treaty of Paris on February 6, 1899. The United States now had its empire. But the debate over imperialism would continue into the 20th century.

The United States Stays in Cuba Cuba also remained an issue in American foreign policy. Although the Treaty of Paris granted Cuba independence, the island was in ruins. President McKinley decided that the United States should remain in Cuba to restore order and assist in the island's recovery.

For four years, the United States ruled Cuba under a military government. This government improved sanitation and built schools and roads. But many Cubans resented American control. They believed that the occupation violated the spirit of the Treaty of Paris and the Teller Amendment, which had pledged that the United States would leave the island after the war was over.

The United States finally withdrew its troops in 1902, but only after Cuba added provisions to its constitution to protect American interests. These provisions, called the Platt Amendment, allowed the United States to intervene in Cuban affairs and to buy or lease land for naval bases. In the years to come, U.S. troops reoccupied Cuba on several occasions. The United States finally agreed in 1934 to repeal the Platt Amendment. However, a U.S. naval base at Guantánamo Bay, on Cuba's southeastern coast, still operates under a permanent lease.

American companies also gained significant control over the Cuban economy. By 1913, American investment on the island had quadrupled from prewar levels to $220 million. U.S. business interests owned 60 percent of Cuba's rural lands and controlled many of the island's industries.

Summary

As a result of its victory in the Spanish-American War, the United States became a world power with overseas possessions. In the eyes of many, the United States had become an imperialist nation.

Cuban revolt Cubans rose up against Spanish rule in the late 1800s, and many were imprisoned in reconcentration camps. Many Americans sympathized with the Cubans' plight.

Role of the press American newspapers exaggerated stories about the Cuban revolt to play on American sympathies and sell papers. Yellow journalism helped push the country toward war.

The de Lôme Letter and the USS *Maine* Two incidents increased tensions between the United States and Spain. A letter from the Spanish ambassador criticizing President McKinley, followed by the sinking of the USS *Maine* in Havana harbor, incited American anger.

A "splendid little war" After negotiations failed, Congress declared war on Spain. The war, which lasted just four months, began in the Philippines and ended in Cuba and Puerto Rico. Many volunteers fought with the U.S. forces, including Theodore Roosevelt's Rough Riders. The most important battle of the war took place on San Juan Hill, outside Santiago.

Arguing over imperialism The Treaty of Paris recognized the U.S. victory and left the United States in possession of Puerto Rico, Guam, and the Philippines. Members of the Anti-Imperialist League spoke out against the treaty, but it was eventually ratified by the Senate.

Cuba and the Platt Amendment Although the Treaty of Paris granted independence to Cuba, the United States maintained control over the island. The Platt Amendment allowed the United States to intervene in Cuban affairs and establish military bases in Cuba.

Chapter 21

Acquiring and Managing Global Power

Were U.S. interventions abroad between 1890 and 1917 motivated more by realism or idealism?

21.1 Introduction

On May 1, 1901, the Pan-American Exposition opened in Buffalo, New York. The exposition was designed to highlight the achievements of the nations of the Western Hemisphere. But coming just three years after the Spanish-American War, it also heralded the emergence of the United States as a great power. A Triumphal Bridge served as the entrance to the fair and a symbol of American triumph.

The exposition presented a glowing demonstration of progress at the dawn of the 20th century. It showcased new developments in transportation, agriculture, and industry. It also featured performances of Buffalo Bill's Wild West Show, which reminded spectators of the vanishing "western frontier." The main attraction was the Electric Tower. Nearly 400 feet high, it was built to celebrate the relatively new invention of electricity. Visitors thrilled when the tower's many thousands of light bulbs blinked on every night, creating a magical atmosphere.

Most of the exhibits focused on advances in the United States. Latin American countries were not as well represented. Nevertheless, the exposition was meant to promote a spirit of cooperation and goodwill between the United States and the other nations of the hemisphere. The fair's logo symbolized this spirit. It showed two young women in the forms of North and South America. Their arms were extended in friendly embrace across Central America.

The exposition did not end on a positive note. On September 5, 1901, President William McKinley visited the fair and gave a speech. The following day, a young anarchist approached the president and shot him twice at point-blank range. McKinley died a week later, and Vice President Theodore Roosevelt assumed office. Under Roosevelt and the next two presidents, William Howard Taft and Woodrow Wilson, the United States embarked on a new era in foreign policy marked by increased intervention in Latin America and other parts of the world.

The Electric Tower was the centerpiece of the Pan-American Exposition, held in Buffalo in the summer of 1901. Dotted with 44,000 light bulbs, the tower cast a dazzling glow at night. Despite its impressive architecture, however, the tower—along with most other buildings at the fair—was not a permanent structure. Built rapidly out of wood, wire, and plaster, many of the buildings began to decay during heavy rains in Buffalo that year.

◀ Illustration of the 1901 Pan-American Exposition

21.2 Three Presidents, Three Foreign Policies

By going to war with Spain and acquiring overseas possessions, President McKinley had set the stage for a more aggressive foreign policy. The next three presidents—Roosevelt, Taft, and Wilson—pursued their own policies. But all three gave the United States an even greater role in world affairs.

Although their foreign policies differed, each president intervened abroad to pursue American goals. Some goals were realist, such as controlling access to foreign resources. Other goals were idealist, such as promoting democracy. In developing foreign policy, the guiding principle for all three presidents was to serve the **national interest**. This is the set of goals—political, economic, military, and cultural—that a nation considers important. Roosevelt, Taft, and Wilson carried out foreign policies they believed would advance American interests.

Roosevelt Expands U.S. Involvement Overseas Theodore Roosevelt applied an energetic spirit to foreign policy. He wanted to make the United States a great power that could exert influence around the world. He believed that the country must meet any challenge to its national interest abroad.

Roosevelt once wrote, "I have always been fond of the West African proverb: 'Speak softly and carry a big stick; you will go far.'" He believed in working quietly and patiently to achieve goals overseas but using force if necessary. Roosevelt's strong-arm approach to foreign affairs became known as the **Big Stick Policy**.

In 1904, Roosevelt formalized this policy in a major address to Congress. He reminded his audience that the Monroe Doctrine was designed to prevent European meddling in the Americas. Yet he noted that nearly a century later many countries in the hemisphere were still too weak to defend themselves. He asserted that the United States therefore must use "international police

President Roosevelt believed that the United States should act as an international police force to protect its interests. His Big Stick Policy was designed to bring order and stability to the hemisphere.

THE BIG STICK IN THE CARIBBEAN SEA

The Granger Collection, New York

power" to preserve peace and order in the hemisphere and protect American interests. He claimed that this power would help protect weak nations and was a direct extension of the Monroe Doctrine. For that reason, his statement became known as the **Roosevelt Corollary** to the Monroe Doctrine. A corollary is a proposition that is a logical extension of a principle.

Over the next several decades, the United States intervened repeatedly in Latin America and the Caribbean. It sent troops to suppress unrest and prop up rulers who supported U.S. interests. Roosevelt and his successors claimed that these actions were necessary to promote stability in the region, but many critics saw them as an exercise of imperial power.

Roosevelt also used diplomacy to help bring peace to a foreign region. In 1905, he mediated a conflict between Japan and Russia, which were fighting to control Korea and Manchuria. For his efforts in ending the war, he won the Nobel Peace Prize in 1906. However, the treaty left both Japan and Russia dissatisfied and resentful of the United States.

Taft Advances U.S. Economic Interests After becoming president in 1909, William Howard Taft continued the main thrust of Roosevelt's foreign policy but shifted to economic goals. His policy, which became known as **Dollar Diplomacy,** was to encourage and protect American trade and investment in Latin America and Asia. Taft believed that a strong economic presence abroad would advance American interests.

Taft claimed that Dollar Diplomacy would limit the use of force overseas. But the United States continued to intervene militarily. In Nicaragua, for example, it supported a revolt that brought a pro-U.S. leader into power in 1911. American banks then provided loans to the new government. The government was corrupt and unpopular, however, and a new revolt broke out in 1912. Taft sent marines to put it down and to protect American business interests. The United States kept troops in Nicaragua almost continuously until 1933.

Wilson Champions Democracy Around the Globe When Woodrow Wilson became president in 1913, he tried to take a moral approach to foreign relations. He called this policy **Moral Diplomacy**. It was based on democratic ideals, rather than on economic investment or the use of force. The United States should use its power to aid "the development of constitutional liberty in the world," Wilson said, by basing its foreign policy on "human rights, national integrity, and opportunity, as against national interests."

Wilson also introduced a concept called **self-determination** into American foreign policy. By this he meant the right of other peoples to determine their own government, free of outside influence.

In dealing with the countries of Latin America, Wilson said, "We must prove ourselves their friends and champions upon terms of equality and honor . . . whether it squares with our own interest or not." His principles were tested by more turmoil in Latin America. In 1915, a revolt in Haiti prompted him to send marines to protect American lives and investments. It was not until 1934 that the United States withdrew its troops from Haiti. In 1916, Wilson sent troops to the Dominican Republic, where they stayed for 12 years. Wilson eventually intervened more than either Taft or Roosevelt.

Beginning in the early 1900s, the United States intervened regularly in Latin America and the Caribbean. It sent troops to support friendly rulers and protect U.S. interests. Here, American marines fight antigovernment rebels in Nicaragua in 1912. U.S. forces trained the Nicaraguan army and helped establish a dictatorship that ruled that country for more than 40 years.

The construction of the Panama Canal was an enormous task. Workers toiling in tropical heat had to remove tons of soil and rock and erect massive concrete structures. The three major challenges were cutting through the hills, building a dam to create Gatún Lake, and constructing the locks.

21.3 U.S. Involvement in Latin America

In the early 1900s, Latin America and the Caribbean were a special focus of U.S. foreign policy. The United States viewed this region as its own "backyard" and therefore a good place to exert its power and influence. In addition to Nicaragua, Haiti, and the Dominican Republic, the United States intervened in other Latin American countries, notably Panama, Mexico, and Puerto Rico.

The U.S. Helps Panama Overthrow Colombian Rule The United States became interested in Panama in the mid-1800s. Various nations wanted to build a canal across Central America as a shortcut between the Atlantic and Pacific oceans. Such a canal would have enormous commercial and military value. During the Spanish-American War, the battleship USS *Oregon* had to travel almost 14,000 miles around the tip of South America to get from California to Cuba. A canal would shorten the journey to just under 5,000 miles.

The narrow Isthmus of Panama was part of Colombia. The Roosevelt administration tried to lease land in Panama for a canal, but the Colombian government turned down the offer. In 1903, the United States encouraged a revolt in Panama. Roosevelt sent warships to prevent Colombian troops from intervening. The revolt succeeded, and the United States quickly recognized Panama as an independent nation.

The Panama Canal: An Engineering Feat The new government soon signed a treaty allowing the United States to build the **Panama Canal**. The 51-mile canal was a marvel of engineering. At least 40,000 workers carved the "Big Ditch" through mountains, rainforests, and swamps. Thousands of workers fell prey to tropical diseases such as malaria and yellow fever. One worker complained that the mosquitoes were so thick "you get a mouthful with every breath."

Before the Panama Canal was built, ships traveling between the east and west coasts of the United States had to make the long journey around South America, as shown at the bottom left of this map. The Panama Canal created a shortcut for ships through Central America. The route chosen for the canal took advantage of natural lakes and rivers. Ships traveling by canal from the Atlantic to the Pacific Ocean move in a southeasterly direction across the Isthmus of Panama.

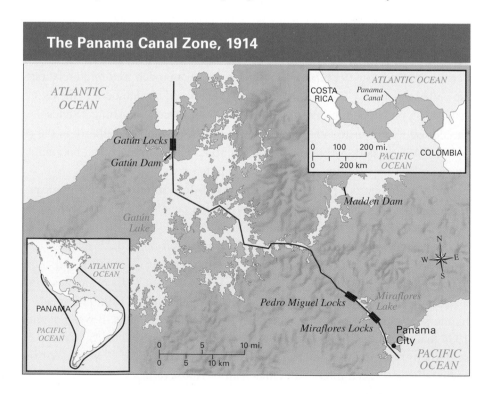

The Panama Canal Zone, 1914

After 10 years of construction, the canal opened to great fanfare on August 15, 1914. Roosevelt called it "the most important action I took in foreign affairs."

Although the canal helped to improve international trade, Roosevelt's actions in Panama angered many Latin Americans. In 1921, the United States tried to undo some of this damage by paying Colombia $25 million. Colombia's government also had special access to the canal. For most of the 1900s, however, the United States treated the canal as its own property. Not until 1999 did it return control of the canal to Panama.

How Does the Panama Canal Work?

The Panama Canal uses a series of locks to lift and lower ships over the Isthmus of Panama. By using the canal, ships sailing between the Atlantic and Pacific oceans avoid an 8,000-mile voyage around South America.

Elevation Profile

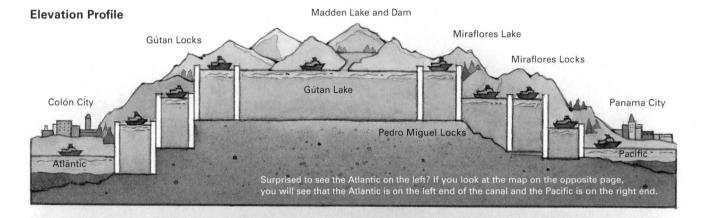

Surprised to see the Atlantic on the left? If you look at the map on the opposite page, you will see that the Atlantic is on the left end of the canal and the Pacific is on the right end.

Lifting and Lowering Ships

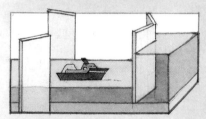

Once a ship moving up the canal enters a lock, the gates are closed behind it.

Water is released into the lock to raise the ship to the level of the next lock.

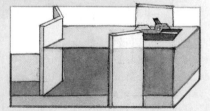

Once the water levels are equal, the gates open and the ship moves to the next lock. This operation is reversed when ships exit the canal.

Fitting Through the Locks

The largest ships that can use the Panama Canal are known as Panamax vessels. Their maximum size is determined by the dimensions of the locks and the depth of the water in the canal. Many modern ships, known as post-Panamax vessels, are too large to use the canal. Examples include supertankers and larger container ships.

WOODROW ON TOAST.

President Woodrow Wilson, U.S.A. "IF YOU DON'T TAKE CARE, I SHALL HAVE TO TREAT YOU THE SAME WAY AS EUROPE TREATS THE TURK."
Mexico. "AND HOW'S THAT?"
President Woodrow Wilson. "WELL, I SHALL HAVE TO—TO GO ON WAGGING MY FINGER AT YOU."

President Wilson tried to support the growth of democracy in Mexico. This 1913 cartoon depicts Wilson scolding Mexico. In the caption, Wilson threatens to keep wagging his finger if Mexico does not behave.

U.S. Businesses Invest Heavily in Mexico The United States also played a strong role in Mexico in the early 1900s. Since 1884, the dictator Porfirio Díaz had ruled the country with a heavy hand. Most Mexicans remained poor, while a handful of landowners, businesspeople, and foreign investors grew very rich. Americans were among the chief investors. By 1910, U.S. businesses had invested around $2 billion in Mexico, buying up land, banks, mines, and other properties.

Revolution was brewing, though. In 1910, Francisco Madero attempted to lead a revolt. Madero failed to gain enough support, but another uprising ousted Díaz in 1911. Madero took power but could not control the country. One of his generals, Victoriano Huerta, overthrew him and had him killed. Other countries then recognized the Huerta government. American business interests wanted President Wilson to do the same. They believed that Huerta would stabilize the country and protect their investments.

Wilson was horrified by Madero's murder, however. He wanted to promote democracy in Mexico and refused to recognize what he called "a government of butchers." Instead, he backed Huerta's chief opponent, General Venustiano Carranza, who he hoped would support democratic reform.

The U.S. Nearly Goes to War with Mexico Tensions between Wilson and the Huerta government almost led to war. In 1914, Wilson sent troops to Veracruz, a port on the Gulf of Mexico, to keep weapons from reaching Huerta's army. In the battle with Huerta's soldiers in the streets of Veracruz, about 90 Americans and at least 300 Mexicans were killed or wounded. Much to Wilson's surprise, most Mexicans—including Carranza—opposed the U.S. action. Other Latin American countries also criticized the intervention. Wilson hastily pulled the forces out, saying that he was only trying to help Mexico. Several months later, Huerta resigned and Carranza gained power.

But the Mexican Revolution continued. Two rebel leaders, Emiliano Zapata and Francisco "Pancho" Villa, rose up against Carranza. Villa, in particular, aroused American concern. Hoping to force a U.S. intervention, he ordered attacks on American citizens in Mexico and the United States. In one cross-border raid in 1916, Villa was responsible for the killing of 17 Americans in New Mexico. Wilson sent troops to capture him, but Villa eluded the American forces, drawing them deeper into Mexico. This military action alarmed the Mexican people, who feared a U.S. invasion. Carranza insisted that the American troops leave. At that point, the United States was nearing entry into World War I. Recognizing the failure of the intervention, Wilson withdrew from Mexico.

San Juan, the main port and the largest city in Puerto Rico, was nearly 400 years old when the United States occupied the city in 1898. This photograph shows San Juan harbor a few years later, after American rule was established. San Juan has grown enormously since then, though portions of the old Spanish city still remain.

Puerto Rico Remains a U.S. Possession The United States also became deeply involved in Puerto Rico. After the Spanish-American War, it instituted a military government that began to develop Puerto Rico's infrastructure. It set up schools and a postal service. It also built roads and improved sanitation. In 1900, the United States established a civilian government led by an American governor. Puerto Ricans formed political parties and organized a legislature. But the island remained an American possession.

Over the next two decades, Puerto Ricans grew increasingly frustrated with American rule. They were neither U.S. citizens nor an independent nation. The United States recognized Puerto Rico's strategic value in the Caribbean, however, and wanted to maintain control over the island.

In 1917, President Wilson signed the Jones Act, making Puerto Rico a U.S. territory. Puerto Ricans became citizens but were not granted all the rights of citizenship. They could not elect their own governor or vote in U.S. elections.

Puerto Rico's Status Evolves Over time, Puerto Rico became more integrated into the U.S. economy. At first, American investors poured money into sugar production, which became the island's main economic activity. The sugar industry produced great wealth for a small minority but left most Puerto Ricans in poverty. In 1930, the average annual income was just $122, one fifth of the U.S. average. Later on, Americans would make large investments in manufacturing plants. Still, many Puerto Ricans migrated to the United States. Many moved to the East Coast, seeking opportunity in New York and other cities.

A series of reforms brought political change. In 1948, Puerto Ricans elected their governor for the first time. In 1952, the island became a U.S. commonwealth. This status gave Puerto Rico control over its own laws and finances but left decisions on defense and tariffs in U.S. hands. Although most Puerto Ricans welcomed this change, some wanted more control over their affairs. They argued that the island would be better off as either a U.S. state or an independent nation. In several elections held after 1967, however, voters chose to remain a commonwealth.

Members of the U.S. Army of Occupation in Puerto Rico during the Spanish-American War received a medal for their service. The medal features a Spanish castle on one side and the American eagle on the other.

Emilio Aguinaldo led the Filipino independence struggle. The United States captured him in 1901 and ended the rebellion. He retired to private life and died in 1964.

In this cartoon, President McKinley is trying to swat a mosquito labelled "Insurgent Aguinaldo." The original caption read, "Mosquitos seem to be worse here in the Phillipines than they were in Cuba."

21.4 U.S. Involvement in Asia and the Pacific

After the Spanish-American War, the United States became a colonial power in Asia. Less than 500 miles of open sea separated the American-controlled Philippines from China, the largest country in Asia. By holding on to the Philippines, the United States would have greater access to Chinese trade and more influence in Chinese affairs. The United States wanted to ensure free trade in the Asia-Pacific region.

The Philippines Fight for Independence from the U.S. During the Spanish-American War, the United States captured the Philippines with the help of Filipino leader Emilio Aguinaldo. After the war, Aguinaldo called for independence. He claimed that the United States had promised freedom for the islands.

The United States decided not to grant independence, however. President McKinley believed that the Filipinos were not ready for self-government. He said that he wanted to "uplift and civilize and Christianize" the Filipino people. He also wanted to maintain American control over the islands to prevent another nation from seizing power.

Still, the Filipinos moved ahead with their plans for independence by writing a constitution and electing Aguinaldo president. But the United States refused to recognize the new government. In February 1899, fighting broke out between Filipino and American forces. The United States sent hundreds of thousands of soldiers to the Philippines to put down the revolt. In battle after battle, the Filipino army was defeated.

Aguinaldo then switched to guerrilla tactics, launching quick strikes on American troops. The United States responded with brutal force, destroying villages and herding civilians into prison camps. Mark Twain, one of many Americans who opposed the U.S. policy toward the Philippines, wrote bitterly, "We have pacified . . . the islanders and buried them; destroyed their fields; burned their villages; and turned their widows and orphans out-of-doors . . . And so . . . we are a World Power."

In 1901, the United States finally captured Aguinaldo. A year later, the fighting was over. The war had lasted more than three years, at great human cost. More than 200,000 Filipinos and about 5,000 Americans had died.

After the war, the United States set up a central government for the islands. The United States built schools and made improvements to Philippine harbors. It also established local governments and encouraged Filipinos to participate in them. The United States controlled the Philippines for the next half-century, finally granting independence on July 4, 1946.

U.S. Businesses Prosper in Hawaii

The Hawaiian Islands had been a focus of American interest long before the Spanish-American War. Known as the "Crossroads of the Pacific," Hawaii was an important stop for ships crossing the Pacific Ocean. In 1820, Protestant missionaries arrived in Hawaii. Within decades most Hawaiians had converted to Christianity.

By the late 1800s, the United States regarded Hawaii as an economic asset. The economy of the islands centered on the export of tropical crops, especially sugarcane and pineapple. White American planters controlled the industry, shipping most of their crops to the United States and becoming wealthy and powerful in the process.

Queen Liliuokalani was the last monarch of Hawaii. She was overthrown with U.S. support in 1893 and withdrew from public life. Seated to her left is Sanford B. Dole, the first head of government after Hawaii became a U.S. territory.

At the time, Hawaii was still a kingdom ruled by a constitutional monarch. In 1891, Liliuokalani became queen of Hawaii. She was a strong leader who resented the dominance of the wealthy white minority on the islands. She established a new constitution that gave more power to native Hawaiians. But a small group of white planters refused to accept the constitution and called on the American government for help. In 1893, U.S. military forces landed and helped the planters overthrow the queen.

The U.S. Annexes the Hawaiian Islands After the revolt, the white planters controlled the government. They applied to Congress for **annexation,** hoping to make Hawaii part of the United States. President Benjamin Harrison agreed to the islands' annexation. Then a new president, Grover Cleveland, assumed office. After discovering the circumstances of the revolt, Cleveland withdrew the annexation treaty and called on the planters to return Queen Liliuokalani to her throne. The planters refused and instead proclaimed Hawaii an independent republic.

Throughout the 1890s, Americans continued to debate the question of annexing Hawaii. Those in favor stressed the importance of Hawaii's location and the value of controlling the islands. They also hoped to continue spreading Christianity and the American way of life in Hawaii. Those opposed to annexation pointed out that colonization often caused problems. Some feared the introduction of new races and cultures into the United States. Others thought it was un-American to deprive a people of their sovereignty.

The American intervention in Hawaii produced deep resentment among native Hawaiians. Nevertheless, during the Spanish-American War in 1898, Hawaii was annexed as Congress recognized its importance as a port for the navy. Hawaii became a U.S. territory two years later. In 1959, it became a state, the only one that is not part of North America.

U.S. Interest in China In the late 1800s, the United States also focused its attention on China. This huge nation was rich in resources and offered a potentially large market for American goods.

In the 1890s, the United States and other foreign powers watched with interest as China and Japan engaged in a war over Korea. This war revealed that China was neither strong nor stable. Russia, France, and Germany supported China at the war's end and demanded favors in return. These powers, along with Britain and Japan, began to carve out spheres of influence from Chinese territory. These were areas in which a single nation controlled trading rights. In some cases, the foreign powers also demanded land for military bases. As a result, much of China was soon carved into pieces of foreign-dominated territory.

The United States wanted to prevent foreign colonization of China in order to maintain its own access to Chinese markets. With this goal in mind, Secretary of State John Hay issued several foreign policy statements, which became known collectively as the Open Door Policy. The first statement, in 1899, called on foreign nations to allow free trade in China. Although some foreign powers gave vague replies, Hay boldly announced that the Open Door Policy was "final and definitive."

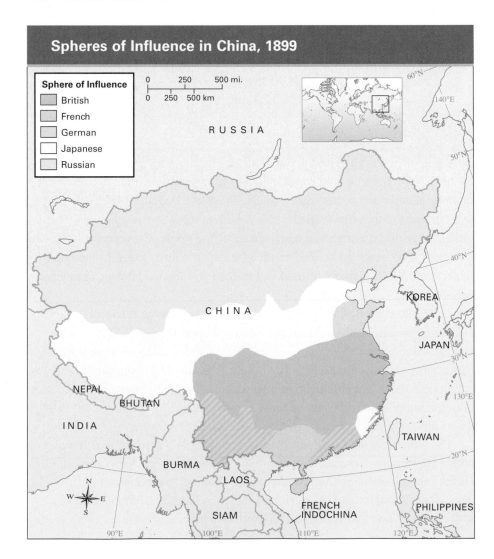

Spheres of Influence in China, 1899

Sphere of Influence
- British
- French
- German
- Japanese
- Russian

The U.S. Fights to Keep an Open Door to China The Chinese were deeply ashamed of their nation's weakness. They were proud of their ancient heritage and furious with other countries for controlling China and undermining Chinese traditions. Some Chinese tried to persuade their government to implement reforms so that China could compete in the modern world and resist western influence.

One Chinese group eventually took up arms in an effort to restore national control. This group, called the Righteous and Harmonious Fists, was commonly known as the Boxers. In 1900, the Boxers led an **insurrection,** rising up to try to expel the "foreign devils" from China. The Boxers killed hundreds of foreigners, including Christian missionaries, along with thousands of Chinese Christians. Within a few months, however, the United States, Japan, and European powers had banded together to crush the uprising.

Secretary of State Hay feared that foreign powers would attempt to use the Boxer Rebellion as an excuse to take stronger control over China. He therefore issued a firmer statement of the Open Door Policy, insisting that foreign nations not only allow free trade, but also respect Chinese independence. The other nations did not object, mainly because they did not want to fight each other over China. As a result, China remained open to American trade and influence.

This cartoon emphasizes the importance of keeping China under the influence of other countries. It portrays Uncle Sam, Japan, and Britain as dogs keeping the door open to Chinese trade.

Summary

At the start of the 20th century, the United States was an imperialist nation with overseas possessions. Three presidents—Roosevelt, Taft, and Wilson—developed foreign policies designed to expand American power and protect American interests.

Roosevelt Corollary President Roosevelt followed the Big Stick Policy in foreign affairs. In 1904, he issued the Roosevelt Corollary to the Monroe Doctrine. This policy called on the United States to use "international police power" to promote order and security in the Western Hemisphere. The use of force became a key element of foreign policy.

Dollar Diplomacy President Taft's Dollar Diplomacy focused on economic goals overseas. He emphasized the spread of American influence through economic activity. But he also sent troops to protect American interests.

Moral Diplomacy President Wilson favored a moral approach to foreign policy. He wanted to spread democratic ideals overseas. Yet he also used force to uphold American interests.

Latin America The United States became deeply involved in Latin America in the early 1900s. It helped Panama gain independence and built the Panama Canal. It intervened in Mexico. It made Puerto Rico a U.S. possession.

Asia and the Pacific The Philippines became a U.S. possession, and the United States put down an independence movement there. It annexed Hawaii after white planters overthrew the native monarchy. In China, it applied its Open Door Policy to limit foreign control and maintain access to Chinese markets.

Chapter 22

From Neutrality to War

Was it in the national interest of the United States to stay neutral or declare war in 1917?

22.1 Introduction

In the spring of 1914, President Woodrow Wilson sent "Colonel" Edward House, his trusted adviser, to Europe. House's task was to learn more about the growing strains among the European powers. After meeting with government officials, House sent Wilson an eerily accurate assessment of conditions there. "Everybody's nerves are tense," he wrote. "It needs only a spark to set the whole thing off."

That spark was not long in coming. On June 28, 1914, Archduke Franz Ferdinand and his wife, Sophie, made an official visit to Sarajevo, the capital of Austria-Hungary's province of Bosnia. Ferdinand was heir to the throne of the Austro-Hungarian Empire. A few years earlier, Bosnia had been taken over by Austria-Hungary, a move that angered many Bosnians who wanted closer ties to nearby Serbia and other Slavic ethnic groups. On the day of the visit, several terrorists, trained and armed by a Serbian group, waited in the crowd.

Early in the day, as the royal couple rode through the city in an open car, a terrorist hurled a bomb at their car. The bomb bounced off the hood and exploded nearby. Unharmed, the couple continued their visit. Another terrorist, Gavrilo Princip, was waiting farther down the route. When the car came into view, Princip fired several shots into the car, killing the royal couple.

Their murders set off a chain reaction. Within weeks, Austria-Hungary declared war on Serbia. When the Russian foreign minister learned that Austrian soldiers had begun shelling the Serbian capital of Belgrade, the stunned diplomat warned the Austrian ambassador, "This means a European war. You are setting Europe alight." He was right. A local quarrel in the Balkans quickly became far more dangerous. Russia sided with Serbia and declared war on Austria-Hungary. To help Austria-Hungary, Germany declared war on Russia and its ally France. Britain came to France's defense and declared war on Germany. Dozens of countries took sides.

In 1914, during a visit to Sarajevo, Archduke Franz Ferdinand of Austria-Hungary and his wife (shown here with their children in 1909) were gunned down by a terrorist. Although this assassination sparked the outbreak of World War I, the conflict had deeper causes.

◀ Soldiers in the trenches during World War I

22.2 The United States Tries to Stay Neutral

For most Americans, the war was a distant conflict that did not concern them. Few felt alarmed by its outbreak. In September 1914, Theodore Roosevelt smugly observed that the United States was lucky to be almost "alone among the great civilized powers in being unshaken by the present worldwide war."

Europe: A Powder Keg Waiting to Ignite How did the murder of the archduke in little-known Bosnia turn into a global conflict? The interaction of many factors led to war. One cause was the system of alliances that linked the European nations to each other. This system required member nations to come to one another's aid in case of attack. When the conflict started, these ties led to the division of Europe into two camps. Germany sided with Austria-Hungary, and they headed the **Central powers**. They were later joined by the Ottoman Empire. France, Britain, and Russia led the **Allied powers**.

In Europe, **nationalism** also created tensions. Nationalism is a strong feeling of pride in and loyalty to a nation or ethnic group. Nationalism led some European powers to put national interests first, regardless of the consequences for other countries. For example, pride in Germany's rapid growth and military power led Kaiser Wilhelm II to seek an overseas empire for his country. He wanted Germany to be a world leader. Smaller ethnic groups expressed their nationalism by seeking independence from rule by foreign countries. For example, Serbs in Bosnia who resented Austro-Hungarian rule wanted to unite with other Slavic peoples in Serbia.

As World War I began, a system of alliances divided Europe into two camps. France, Great Britain, and Russia—called the Allies—backed Serbia. They were opposed by Austria-Hungary and Germany, known as the Central powers. Other nations joined the Allies or the Central powers as the war expanded to engulf most of Europe.

European Alliances in World War I

Allied powers
Central powers
Neutral nations
Farthest advance by Central powers
Area of German U-boat activity
British blockade

Another key factor was **militarism,** a policy of glorifying military power and values. When Germany modernized its army and added to its navy, Britain felt it had to do the same. Other major powers followed their lead. Soon the nations of Europe were in a full-scale military buildup.

Imperialism added more fuel to the fire. By the 1880s, Britain and France had colonies in Africa and Asia that provided raw materials and markets for their products. Germany wanted its own colonies and a share of this lucrative trade. The only way for Germany to get the territory it wanted was to take it from someone else. Competition for trade and colonies further strained relations.

Wilson Adopts a Policy of Neutrality Soon after the war began, Woodrow Wilson declared a policy of neutrality. The United States would not take sides in the conflict. It would offer loans and sell weapons and supplies to both sides. In a message to Congress on August 19, 1914, Wilson urged Americans to remain "impartial in thought, as well as action." The European war, he said, is one "with which we have nothing to do, whose causes cannot touch us."

Wilson's decision to stay out of the war pleased many Americans. Ever since George Washington had warned the nation to avoid "entangling alliances," American presidents had tried to steer clear of European infighting. A Mississippi senator asserted, "There is no necessity for war with Germany—there is no necessity for war with any of the **belligerent** [warring] powers. Three thousand miles of water make it impossible for us to be drawn into that vortex of blood and passion and woe." As a neutral nation, the United States could make loans and sell supplies to both sides. U.S. leaders were also happy to have a way of helping American bankers, farmers, and businesses recover from a painful economic slowdown. Finally, members of the peace movement, who spoke out strongly against war, were in favor of this policy of neutrality.

Yet the situation was more complicated than America's neutrality policy expressed. In 1914, more than 32 million Americans—a full one third of the population—were either foreign born or the children of foreign-born parents. Many of these Americans had strong emotional ties to their homelands and found it hard to remain neutral. Germans and Austrian Americans were sympathetic to the Central powers. Irish Americans also sided with the Central powers out of their long-standing hatred of the British. The majority of Americans, however, favored the Allies. Many felt connected by ancestry, language, culture, and democratic values. Still others had economic ties to Britain or France.

While Americans debated neutrality, the war raged on two fronts in Europe. On the eastern front, Russia quickly advanced into Germany and Austria-Hungary. A German counterattack, however, stopped the Russian advance. In two key battles, the number of Russian casualties—soldiers killed, captured, wounded, or missing—totaled about 250,000.

On the western front, German troops easily rolled across Belgium and into France. Intense fighting by British, French, and Belgian armies finally stopped the German advance, but not until German troops were within 30 miles of Paris. By the end of 1914, the war on the western front had turned into a long and bloody **stalemate,** or deadlock. Neither side was able to knock out its enemies, and yet neither side was willing to sue for peace.

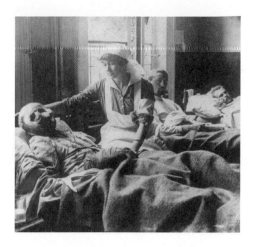

By late November 1914, the war reached a stalemate. The lines of battle stretched across Belgium and northeastern France to the border of Switzerland. Month by month, casualties mounted in what, to many Americans, looked like senseless slaughter.

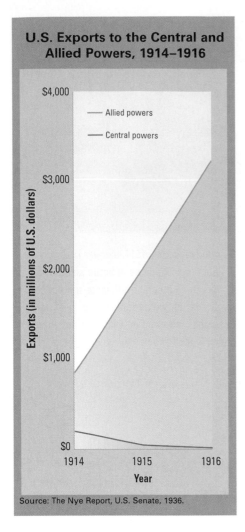

U.S. Exports to the Central and Allied Powers, 1914–1916

Exports (in millions of U.S. dollars)

$4,000

—— Allied powers

—— Central powers

$3,000

$2,000

$1,000

$0

1914   1915   1916

Year

Source: The Nye Report, U.S. Senate, 1936.

Although the United States may have declared itself neutral, American businesses and banks were anything but. Between 1914 and 1916, the value of American trade with the Allies soared from $800 million to $3 billion. U.S. banks loaned the Allies $2 billion to pay for these purchases.

22.3 Challenges to the U.S. Policy of Neutrality

As the land war dragged on, both sides sought to break the stalemate. Unable to defeat their enemy on land, both Britain and Germany looked for ways to starve their enemies into submission. To do this, they needed to win control of the seas.

Britain Stops U.S. Ships Heading for Germany The war at sea started with a British blockade of ships headed for Germany. British ships turned back any vessels carrying weapons, food, and other vital supplies to the Central powers—even ships from neutral nations such as the United States.

President Wilson complained to the British about the policy of stopping neutral ships, but he did not threaten to take action. His hesitancy came in part from the strong economic ties between Britain and the United States. Trade with Britain had given a boost to the sagging American economy, and U.S. banks and businesses were earning millions of dollars from loans and exports to the Allies. These same banks and businesses made fewer loans and sold fewer supplies and weapons to the Central powers. Moreover, many businesspeople in the United States openly supported the Allies. An officer at the Morgan bank recalled, "Our firm had never for one moment been neutral . . . We did everything we could to contribute to the cause of the Allies."

U-Boat Attacks Increase Tensions with Germany In February 1915, Germany found a way to challenge the British blockade: submarine attacks. Their deadly new weapon was the **U-boat,** short for *Unterseeboot* ("undersea boat"). The German navy hoped this new weapon would break the British blockade and at the same time stop vital supplies from reaching the Allies.

Early in 1915, Germany declared the waters around Britain a war zone. Within this zone, German U-boats could sink enemy ships without warning. Because British ships sometimes disguised themselves by flying the flags of neutral nations, neutral ships going into this zone were also at risk.

By international law and custom, warships had the right to stop and search merchant ships that they suspected of breaking a naval blockade. Such vessels could even be sunk, but only if the passengers and crew were removed first. This practice worked for warships, which could take on extra passengers, but not for submarines, which were small and cramped. In theory, a U-boat could allow the ship's crew and passengers to launch lifeboats before sinking the ship. But in practice, this strategy made no sense. A U-boat that surfaced to warn a merchant ship of an attack would become an easy target, foiling its surprise attack.

Wilson protested that sinking merchant ships without protecting the lives of passengers and crews violated international law. He warned that the United States would hold Germany to "strict accountability" for any American casualties in such attacks.

The policy of "strict accountability" was soon put to a test. On May 7, 1915, a U-boat sank the British liner *Lusitania* without warning. Among the 1,198 dead were 128 Americans. Germany tried to absolve itself from blame by arguing that the ship was armed and was carrying weapons and ammunition. The second charge was true. Nonetheless, former president Theodore Roosevelt denounced Germany's actions as "murder on the high seas."

Within the State Department, a debate raged about how to respond to the sinking of the *Lusitania*. Secretary of State William Jennings Bryan believed Americans had a "higher mission" than helping "one European monarch fight out his quarrels with another." He argued that the United States should accept the reality of submarine warfare and warn its citizens that they traveled on British ships at their own risk. State Department lawyer Robert Lansing opposed this view. He argued not only that Americans had a right to travel on British ships, but also that the United States should vigorously protect that right.

Wilson sided with Lansing and sent Germany a series of notes demanding that it stop **unrestricted submarine warfare**. Afraid that the notes violated neutrality and might involve the United States in war, Bryan resigned. Wilson chose Lansing to replace Bryan as Secretary of State. Lansing was anything but neutral. "The Allies must *not* be beaten," he wrote. "War cannot come too soon to suit me."

Four months later, in August 1915, Germany sank a second British ship, the *Arabic,* killing two Americans. Wilson sent another, more sharply worded protest to Germany. German officials promised that Germany would sink no more passenger ships without warning. In March 1916, they broke that promise by sinking the French liner *Sussex,* an attack that left several Americans injured. Wilson threatened to break off diplomatic relations with Germany if it did not stop surprise attacks. In an agreement called the *Sussex* **pledge,** Germany promised to spare all lives in any future U-boat attacks on merchant ships. But it attached a condition: The United States must force Britain to end its illegal blockade. Wilson accepted the pledge but would not accept the condition.

The *Lusitania,* a British passenger ship, sank near Ireland after being torpedoed by a German U-boat. Of the 1,198 people who died, 128 were American. The American public was outraged, and the incident helped strengthen American support for the Allies.

In 1916, Woodrow Wilson held a preparedness parade. Though he had orginally been the target of the preparedness movement, his eventual efforts to increase the nation's readiness for war helped elect him to a second term.

Preparedness, Promises, and Propaganda Concern over President Wilson's handling of the war fueled a growing preparedness movement. This movement was led by former president Theodore Roosevelt, who pointed out that the United States was ill-prepared for war should it need to fight. In 1915, the army had only 80,000 men and lacked equipment.

At the outbreak of the war, Roosevelt had not sided with either the Allies or the Central powers. Even so, he was not impressed by Wilson's policy of neutrality. He was even more put off by Wilson's statement after the sinking of the *Lusitania* that "there is such a thing as a man being too proud to fight." Roosevelt had long believed preparedness for war, not talk of neutrality, was the best guarantor of peace. As he toured the country promoting preparedness, many newspapers took up his cause. Advocates of preparedness called for an army of a million trained men and a navy larger than Great Britain's.

For a time, Wilson resisted calls to strengthen the military, but the submarine menace persuaded him that he had to increase the nation's readiness for war. With an election coming up, he launched his own nationwide tour, talking about preparedness and promising a "navy second to none." Back in the capital, he pressed Congress to allocate money to double the size of the army and begin construction of the world's largest navy. Enough Americans saw Wilson's efforts as preparedness for peace, not war, to elect him to a second term. He won reelection by a paper-thin majority on the slogan, "He kept us out of war."

MEN OF BRITAIN!
WILL YOU STAND THIS?

Nº 2 Wykeham Street, SCARBOROUGH, after the German bombardment
on Decr 16th. It was the Home of a Working Man. Four People were killed in
this House including the Wife, aged 58, and Two Children, the youngest aged 5.

78 Women & Children were killed and 228 Women
& Children were wounded by the German Raiders
ENLIST NOW

Wir dulden keine Anarchie!

Wir werden Frauen und Kinder schützen!

While Wilson tried hard to keep the nation out of war, both the Allies and the Central powers launched **propaganda** campaigns designed to whip up support for their side. Propaganda is information or rumor spread by a group or government to promote its own cause or ideas or to damage an opposing cause or idea. The information in the propaganda may or may not be accurate. Either way, the intention of propaganda is not to inform, but rather to persuade others to adopt the view or to take the action supported by the propagandist.

The Allies waged the most successful campaign. Early in the war, the British circulated stories about alleged atrocities committed by German soldiers in Belgium. The British government appointed a special commission headed by Lord James Bryce, a well-respected historian, to investigate these "outrages." Published just days after the attack of the *Lusitania*, the Bryce commission's report was filled with stories of German soldiers torturing innocent women and children and using civilians as "human shields" during combat.

The German government angrily denied these stories, as did American reporters traveling with the German army. Later study proved many of the stories to be exaggerated or invented. Nonetheless, the British government made sure the Bryce report was sent to nearly every newspaper in the United States. The more horrible the story, the more likely it was to be reprinted in the American press. As a result, neutrality "in thought" gave way to anti-German feeling in the minds of many Americans.

Both the Allies and the Central powers used propaganda posters to drum up support for the war at home. The British poster (above left) uses alleged German atrocities for this purpose. The German poster reminds German soldiers that they are fighting to resist the forces of anarchy while protecting their women and children. (Translation of the German text: "We will not bear [put up with] anarchy. We will protect women and children.")

22.4 The United States Declares a "War to End All Wars"

In a speech to the Senate on January 22, 1917, Wilson declared that he wanted to find a way to end the stalemated war in Europe. He called on the warring powers to accept a "peace without victory." He also spoke of forming a "league of honor" to help nations settle conflicts peacefully. Germany's response to Wilson's peace efforts was to launch an all-out effort to win the war, including a return to unrestricted submarine warfare. Keeping to the *Sussex* pledge, Wilson broke off diplomatic relations with Germany.

The Zimmermann Note Stirs Up Anti-German Feelings Wilson had hoped the Germans would back down, but his hopes were dashed in late February 1917. Britain had gotten hold of a note sent in code by the German foreign minister, Arthur Zimmermann, to the German minister in Mexico. Zimmermann suggested that if the United States entered the war, Mexico and Germany should become allies. Germany would then help Mexico regain "lost territory in New Mexico, Texas, and Arizona." The Zimmermann note created a sensation in the United States and stirred anti-German feeling across the nation.

Events in Russia removed another barrier to the United States joining the Allies. In March 1917, a revolution toppled the autocratic Czar Nicholas II and replaced him with a democratic government. At the start of the war, Wilson had not wanted to be allied to a dictator. With the hope of democracy in sight, the United States could now see Russia as "a fit partner" in a war against German aggression.

The United States Enters the War On April 2, 1917, Wilson spoke to a special session of Congress. He reminded lawmakers of the loss of life caused by German U-boats and how these attacks hurt the nation's ability to trade freely with other countries. Then he turned to his main theme:

> Neutrality is no longer feasible [practical] . . . where the peace of the world is involved . . . The world must be made safe for democracy. Its peace must be planted upon the tested foundations of political liberty . . . The right is more precious than peace, and we shall fight for the things which we have always carried nearest our hearts—for democracy, for the right of those who submit to authority to have a voice in their own governments.
>
> —Woodrow Wilson's War Message, address to Congress, 1917

Written in code, the Zimmermann note was deciphered by British cryptographers. The British waited to release the telegram to American newspapers until relations between the United States and Germany were at an all-time low. The threat in the telegram to help Mexico regain territory lost to the United States further inflamed public opinion against Germany.

In 1917, President Woodrow Wilson asked Congress to declare war. "It is a fearful thing to lead this great peaceful people into . . . the most terrible and disastrous of all wars," he said. "Civilization itself seems to be hanging in the balance."

When Wilson finished, lawmakers cheered. Later Wilson said sadly, "Think what it was they were applauding. My message today was a message of death for our young men."

Critics reacted strongly to Wilson's war message. Nebraska Senator George Norris argued that the United States was going to war for economic reasons only. "We have loaned many hundreds of millions of dollars to the Allies," he said. He saw American involvement in the war as a way of "making . . . payment of every debt certain and sure." Wisconsin Senator Robert LaFollette argued that the nation had gotten itself into the war by failing to treat the "belligerent nations of Europe alike." He urged the government to remain neutral and "enforce our rights against Great Britain as we have enforced our rights against Germany."

In spite of such protests, on April 4, 1917, the Senate voted 82 to 6 to declare war on Germany. The House followed on April 6 by a vote of 373 to 50. The United States was going to war.

Summary

The assassination of Archduke Franz Ferdinand sparked the outbreak of World War I. However, the war had many underlying causes, including the European alliance system and the growth of nationalism and imperialism, which led to military buildups. The United States remained neutral until events in 1917 convinced Americans to fight on the side of the Allies.

The Allied and Central powers When World War I began, the nations of Europe divided into two alliances—the Allied powers and the Central powers.

U-boats The war at sea started with a British blockade of German ports. Germany fought back by introducing a new weapon called a U-boat, or submarine. German U-boats sank both neutral and enemy vessels, often without warning.

Lusitania The German sinking of the British ship the *Lusitania* killed 128 Americans. The United States strongly protested U-boat attacks on merchant ships carrying American passengers.

Sussex **pledge** Germany agreed in the *Sussex* pledge to stop sinking merchant ships without warning but attached the condition that the United States help end the illegal British blockade. Wilson rejected that condition, and Germany did not keep the pledge.

Preparedness movement As anger over American deaths at sea grew, some Americans called for the country to prepare for war. Although Wilson won reelection on the slogan "He kept us out of war," he was already preparing the country to fight by building up the army and navy.

Unrestricted submarine warfare In a desperate bid to end the conflict, Germany announced early in 1917 that it would resume unrestricted submarine warfare.

Zimmermann note The disclosure of the Zimmermann note, calling for cooperation between Mexico and Germany to take back U.S. territory, outraged Americans. Soon after its publication, the United States declared war on Germany.

Chapter 23

The Course and Conduct of World War I

How was World War I different from previous wars?

23.1 Introduction

In 1917, many Americans viewed the nation's entry into World War I as the commencement of a great adventure. Others saw it as a noble or heroic cause that would give the country a chance to demonstrate its courage. President Woodrow Wilson's call to help make the world safe for democracy appealed to Americans' sense of idealism. Many shared the president's belief that this would be "the war to end all wars."

A young recruit named William Langer enlisted to fight in the war because, as he described it, "Here was our one great chance for excitement and risk. We could not afford to pass it up." Henry Villard felt the same. He eagerly followed incidents on the battlefields of Europe, reading newspapers and discussing events with friends. "There were posters everywhere," he recalled. "'I want you,' . . . 'Join the Marines,' 'Join the Army.' And there was an irresistible feeling that one should do something . . . I said to myself, if there's never going to be another war, this is the only opportunity to see it."

In 1917, Villard got his chance when a Red Cross official visited his college looking for volunteers to drive ambulances in Italy. Many of Villard's friends signed up. Although he knew his family would protest, Villard said, "I couldn't just stand by and let my friends depart." After securing his family's reluctant consent, Villard enlisted and soon headed out for combat duty.

Very soon after arriving in Italy, Villard discovered how little he knew about war. "The first person that I put into my ambulance was a man who had just had a grenade explode in his hands." Bomb fragments had severed both of the soldier's legs. As Villard sped from the front lines to the hospital, the wounded soldier kept asking him to drive more slowly. By the time the ambulance reached the hospital, the young man was dead. "This was a kind of cold water treatment for me, to realize all of a sudden what war was like," explained Villard. "And it changed me—I grew up very quickly . . . It was the real world."

More than 2 million Americans served in Europe during World War I. Eager to promote democracy around the world, many entered the war with great enthusiasm. But their first taste of battle left them more realistic about the horrors of war.

◀ An American soldier shares an emotional goodbye, 1917

This famous World War I recruiting poster helped entice tens of thousands of young American men to register for the draft in 1917. Once they did, it took weeks of training to prepare them for combat.

23.2 A War of Firsts for the United States

For the United States, World War I was a war of firsts. To start, it was the first time the government had agreed to commit large numbers of American soldiers to a distant war across the sea. In fact, when Congress first declared war, many Americans thought the nation would provide money, food, and equipment to the war effort—but not troops. Learning that military officials planned to expand the army, Virginia Senator Thomas Martin cried out in surprise, "Good Lord! You're not going to send soldiers over there, are you?"

That was indeed Wilson's plan. Still, with Germany preparing for a final assault, many Americans wondered whether the United States could set up military camps, train large numbers of troops, and transport these soldiers to Europe quickly enough to make a difference.

The Nation's First Selective Service System Prior to American entry into the war, the United States had a volunteer army of about 200,000 soldiers. These forces received low pay and lacked equipment. Few soldiers had ever seen combat. To enter the war, the military would need tens of thousands more soldiers—and quickly. In May 1917, Congress passed the Selective Service Act, which created a national draft. The act required all men ages 21 to 30 to register for military service at local polling stations.

To encourage Americans to comply with the draft, the government launched a major propaganda campaign. Secretary of War Newton Baker hoped tens of thousands would register on the assigned day. He urged mayors, governors, and other local leaders to make the day a "festival and [a] patriotic occasion." These efforts paid off. Nearly 10 million young men registered. Across the nation, many towns and cities held parades and celebrations honoring their draftees.

Within months, officers at camps around the country were training more than 500,000 draftees. While the new soldiers marched and drilled, the Allies grew more anxious. In a message to U.S. officials, British prime minister David Lloyd George stressed the Allies' urgent need for troops. He asked that American troops "be poured into France as soon as possible." In his view, "the difference of even a week in the date of arrival may be absolutely vital."

The First Americans Reach French Soil American troops first landed in France in June 1917. Their official name was the American Expeditionary Force (AEF), but they were nicknamed "the doughboys." The AEF fought under the command of General John J. Pershing, and most were infantry—soldiers who fight on foot. Although few in number, the American infantry bolstered the Allies' morale.

By the time the Americans reached France, the war was going badly for the Allies. Their armies had suffered several major defeats and lost many men. Even victories were deadly. The battle at Passchendaele in November 1917 cost the Allies 300,000 soldiers. For all that bloodshed, the Allied forces had regained control of barely 5 miles of German-held territory.

The Russian Revolution of 1917 added to the Allies' woes. Until then, Russian troops had kept the Central powers busy with fighting on the eastern front. As soon as Russia's new revolutionary leaders took control of the government, they began making plans to withdraw Russia from the war.

Early in 1918, Russian peacemakers met with German and Austrian officials to hammer out the treaty of Brest-Litovsk. For Russia, the terms were very harsh. The treaty forced Russia to give up large amounts of territory, including Finland, Poland, Ukraine, as well as the Baltic States—Estonia, Latvia, and Lithuania. The Central powers gained not only territory but, more important, an end to the fighting on the eastern front. Germany was free to throw all its troops into the war on the western front.

To counter the increase in German troops on the western front, the Allies asked General Pershing to assign American soldiers to Allied units to replace men killed or wounded in action. With Wilson's backing, Pershing resisted this request, insisting that most of his soldiers remain in the AEF. Pershing had two main reasons for doing so. First, he disagreed with Allied military strategy. He did not think the Allies could end the stalemate by fighting a defensive war from the trenches. Instead, he advocated tactics that were more forceful and offensive. Second, both Wilson and Pershing felt that if the AEF did well as a separate army, the United States could demand a greater role in the peacemaking process after the war. Pershing got his way. By war's end, some 2 million Americans had served overseas as part of the AEF.

Major Battles of World War I

World War I began on two main battlefronts. The western front stretched across Belgium and northern France. The eastern front spread across much of present-day Poland. Russia's withdrawal from the war in early 1918 closed down the eastern front.

The First African American Officer Training Camp During the course of the war, nearly 400,000 African Americans joined the armed forces. The military strictly segregated black and white troops in training camps and overseas. At first, it did not allow black soldiers to become officers. However, people across the country held mass meetings to push for officer training for African Americans. In 1917, the military set up a separate camp to train black soldiers as officers. Later that year, the camp graduated its first class, including 106 captains, 329 first lieutenants, and 204 second lieutenants.

Most black soldiers served under white officers in labor or supply units in France or the United States. The all-black **369th Regiment** had a different experience. As an exception to Pershing's rule about American soldiers not fighting in Allied units, the 369th operated under French command. They took part in active combat, for which they earned high praise. The soldiers of the 369th fought so fiercely, Germans called them the "Hell Fighters." After the war, France awarded the 369th the country's highest military honors.

African American soldiers of the 369th Infantry Regiment came from Harlem and other neighborhoods in New York City. While fighting at Sechault, France, the enemy named these persistent soldiers the "Hell Fighters."

In 1883, American inventor Hiram Maxim developed the first entirely automatic machine gun to become widely used by both the Allies and the Central powers. The new weapon's heavy firepower made mass assaults across open ground suicidal. As a result, both sides retreated into a vast network of trenches to fight a defensive war.

23.3 New Technologies Change the Way War Is Fought

World War I proved to be unlike previous wars in many ways. For example, for centuries, opposing forces had conducted combat face-to-face and hand-to-hand. During the American Civil War, **combatants**—those physically fighting the war—had faced off against their enemies with handguns or rifles, supported by cannons. Troops fired only at targets they could see clearly. New technology made World War I a more impersonal war, as well as a far deadlier one.

Combatants Introduce More Effective Killing Machines Weapons such as the machine gun, an improved flamethrower, and large cannons known as **howitzers** changed how and where war was fought. Unlike rifles and pistols, the machine gun was a rapid-firing weapon—the first truly automatic gun. A soldier using a machine gun, which spit out 600 bullets per minute, did not have to stop as often to reload. In time, military commanders realized that machine guns could make a greater effect when grouped together. In fact, the Germans created separate machine gun companies to support the infantry.

The invention of the machine gun had a major impact on military strategy. Armies accustomed to taking the offensive and attacking head-on were now at a disadvantage. A group of well-placed machine gunners could stop the advance of a much larger force. German forces learned this lesson quickly, but the British and French did not. Allied armies charged across open fields toward enemy lines, only to be mowed down by machine gun fire, leading to thousands of casualties. In September 1915, British infantry units, each comprising about 10,000 men, charged a well-protected German position. In four hours, more than 8,000 men were killed, almost all by machine gun fire.

At first, machine guns were used mostly for defense, because soldiers found them too heavy and bulky to carry in an offensive attack. Over time, both sides found ways to mount these weapons on aircraft and to use them on warships.

Unlike the machine gun, the flamethrower was an old weapon. In the days of the Roman Empire, soldiers had hurled these tubes filled with burning fuel at one another. During World War I, Germany developed a small, lightweight flamethrower that a single person could carry. It sprayed burning fuel on the victims. This weapon was effective in attacks on nearby trenches but could not be fired long distances.

For long-range bombings, both sides used large, heavy artillery, or "big guns." Before firing these weapons, gunners loaded them with shells that often contained dozens of small lead balls. Soldiers also used big guns to deliver poison gas. A new type of loading, firing, and recoil mechanism made these guns very useful. Gunners used them to blast through barbed wire, knock out enemy machine gun nests, and lob poison gas shells at enemy trenches.

The best known of these powerful guns were Germany's Big Berthas. Each weighed about 75 tons and could fire a 2,100-pound shell a distance of more than 9 miles. Big Berthas were the largest mobile guns ever used on the battlefield. At the beginning of the war, Big Berthas helped Germany sweep through Belgium on its drive west toward France. Unable to withstand the assault of these guns, concrete Belgian forts crumbled. In total, heavy artillery inflicted more than half of all battle casualties in World War I.

Despite such technological advances, the rifle remained the most widely used weapon on the battlefield. Soldiers found rifles to be lighter and easier to carry than bigger guns when advancing toward the enemy. Soldiers with good aim trained to be sharpshooters, who are specialists at hitting an exact target, or snipers, who fire from a concealed position. Both played a key role in a new type of combat called **trench warfare**.

Both Armies Seek Safety in Trenches The introduction of new weapons such as rapid-firing machine guns and powerful, long-range big guns made the old style of ground attack far too dangerous. Soldiers could no longer charge each other across an open field. If they did, they could be killed instantly. Instead, both sides dug trenches in the ground for protection. The result was a new kind of defensive war known as trench warfare.

Each side dug multiple lines of trenches, often in zigzag patterns to make it hard for enemy sharpshooters to hit soldiers. Closest to the enemy's trenches lay the frontline trenches. From opposing frontline trenches, soldiers hurled grenades and fired machine guns at one another. Behind the frontline trenches, soldiers dug a line of supply trenches. These held ammunition, other supplies, and communication equipment. In a third line of reserve trenches, weary soldiers rested before returning to the front lines. In the course of trench duty, soldiers rotated through the frontline, supply, and reserve trenches.

In World War I, typical frontline trenches were six to eight feet deep and wide enough for two people to stand side by side. Short trenches connected the front lines to the others. Each trench system had kitchens, bathrooms, supply rooms, and more. However, living in and doing combat from the trenches was not pleasant. Even when they were not fighting, soldiers had to relax in cramped environments.

Both the Allies and the Central powers developed new weapons in hopes of breaking the deadlock in the trenches. In April 1915, the Germans first released poison gas over Allied lines. The fumes caused vomiting and suffocation. Both sides soon developed gas masks to protect troops from such attacks.

Large barriers of barbed wire circled each side's front line and extended into the open area between the opposing trenches. This area, called no-man's land, was typically about 250 yards wide, but crossing its short distance was usually lethal. Soldiers venturing into no-man's land risked being shot or blown up. In this treeless space, any moving object was an easy target for sharpshooters and machine gunners. Water-filled craters made by bombs and artillery shells soon speckled no-man's land. Because neither side could find a way to get its troops safely across no-man's land, the war ground to a stalemate.

Conditions in the trenches were horrible. The muddy trenches smelled of rotting bodies, sweat, and overflowing latrines. Soldiers often caught fevers or suffered from painful foot infections called trench foot, which resulted from standing in the mud and cold water that pooled in the bottom of the trenches. In addition, lice, frogs, and rats surrounded the men. An Allied soldier recalled:

> One got used to many things, but I never overcame my horror of the rats. They abounded in some parts, great loathsome beasts gorged with flesh . . . About the same time every night the dug-out was invaded by swarms of rats. They gnawed holes in our haversacks [backpacks] and devoured our . . . rations.
>
> —Harold Saunders, quoted in *Everyman at War,* 1930

One of the most terrifying threats soldiers faced was the use of **chemical weapons,** which utilize toxic agents such as poison gas to kill or harm many people. Germany was the first to use poison gas in World War I. In time, the British and French did as well. The deadliest chemical used was odorless mustard gas. This caused huge, painful blisters, blindness, and lethal damage to the lungs. Those who survived a mustard gas attack often had lifelong injuries.

Early on, soldiers simply released mustard gas from cylinders and relied on the wind to carry it across no-man's land to the enemy. However, shifting winds often blew the gas back on the sender's trenches. Both sides eventually found ways to put poison gas into the shells they fired at each other. In time, both sides developed gas masks to protect their troops from these attacks.

Another new weapon, the tank, finally helped end the stalemate in the trenches. Soldiers could drive tanks over barbed wire and crush the otherwise treacherous material. They could also steer the tanks up steep embankments and across ditches to attack enemy trenches. Unsure of how effective this weapon would be, Germany was slow to develop tanks of its own. The Allies were more proactive with their use of this new technology. During the final Allied advance in the summer of 1918, tanks rolled across no-man's land ahead of Allied troops, protecting them from enemy gunfire and weakening enemy defenses.

The Sky Is the New Battlefield Improvements to airplanes brought war into the sky. The top speed for early airplanes was about 40 miles per hour. But by 1917, powerful motors allowed airplanes to travel more than three times that fast. Planes also became easier to fly and could travel farther than ever before.

From the start of the war, both sides used airplanes to scout enemy territory. But the war challenged inventors to create airplanes for more specialized uses, such as fighting and bombing. At first, pilots would lean out of the cockpit and shoot at enemy pilots with a pistol or drop bombs by hand over the side of the plane. Then Dutch inventor Anthony Fokker, working for Germany, built a device that timed the firing of a machine gun with the rotation of a plane's propeller. This allowed a pilot to safely fire a machine gun mounted on the front of his aircraft. Fokker's invention made in-air combat a serious new threat.

The Germans also created high-flying, gas-filled airships called zeppelins. These cigar-shaped aircraft were first used for scouting enemy positions. In 1915, German pilots used zeppelins in bombing raids over London. Although the German airships terrified British civilians and alarmed the Allies, they often missed their targets.

By 1916, the British had found a way to counter the airship threat. They built fighter planes that could fly as high as a zeppelin and developed bullets sharp enough to pierce the airship's outer skin, causing it to explode. The various roles of the airplane in World War I showed its usefulness and versatility. Indeed, it would play an even greater role in later conflicts.

World War I was the first war in which planes were used as weapons. Early in the war, when enemy planes met, pilots exchanged smiles and waves. Soon they were throwing bricks and grenades or shooting pistols at one another. Once guns were mounted on planes, the era of air combat began.

Waging a Savage War at Sea When World War I started, most naval experts had already predicted that the greatest sea battles would take place between heavily armed and armored **battleships**. In 1906, Britain had introduced the world's first modern battleship, the HMS *Dreadnought*. It was larger, more powerfully armed, and more heavily armored than earlier warships. Faced with this threat, the major naval powers had scrapped their old fleets and began replacing them with similar battleships. In 1916, the German and British navies fought a major naval battle with their battleships. Each side sank many ships, but neither side won a clear victory.

After that battle, Germany changed its approach to naval warfare. Its new strategy resulted from Germany's development of armed submarines, or U-boats. Moving silently under the sea, U-boats went undetected until it was too late to stop their torpedoes from reaching their targets. In the first four months of 1917,

The U-boat changed naval warfare forever. To combat U-boats, the Allies developed hydrophones. These "underwater ears" helped ships sense the approach of a U-boat and take defensive action.

German U-boats sank more than 1,000 ships carrying supplies and weapons to Allied ports. British Admiral John Jellicoe warned, "It is impossible to go on with the war if losses like this continue."

The effectiveness of U-boat attacks was greatly reduced by the development of the **convoy** system. Under this system, Allied warships protected merchant ships by escorting groups of them across the Atlantic Ocean. The number of Allied shipping losses quickly decreased. From April 1917 to November of that year, the material lost to U-boat attacks dropped from more than 850,000 tons to just over 200,000 tons. In 1918, the Allies further reduced the submarine menace by laying an underwater barrier of mines across the North Sea and the English Channel.

Meuse-Argonne Offensive, 1918

Sedan railroad

BELGIUM

GERMANY

Meuse R.

Paris

Meuse-Argonne
Offensive

LUXEMBOURG

FRANCE

The Meuse-Argonne Offensive was the last major battle of World War I. More than a million American troops helped the Allies capture the railroad that served as Germany's main supply line to France. With defeat all but certain, Germans demanded an end to the fighting. Kaiser Wilhelm abandoned his throne and fled to the Netherlands as the German government agreed to a truce.

Estimated World War I Casualties

Country	Total Casualties
Allied Powers	
Russia	9,150,000
France	6,160,800
British Empire	3,190,235
Italy	2,197,000
United States	323,018
Japan	1,210
Other Allied nations	1,040,164
Central Powers	
Germany	7,142,558
Austria-Hungary	7,020,000
Turkey	975,000
Bulgaria	266,919

Source: U.S. Department of Justice.

23.4 The War Comes to a Close

As 1918 began, the Allies knew Germany would soon launch a final offensive to end the war in the west. Every day, more troops arrived on the front lines as the Germans raced to defeat the war-weary Allies before the Americans arrived. "We should strike," General Erich Ludendorff told Kaiser Wilhelm II, the German emperor, "before the Americans can throw strong forces into the scale."

The Meuse-Argonne Offensive Leads to an Armistice In early spring 1918, the Germans began their final push. Their troops advanced rapidly to within 50 miles of Paris. By this time, however, American forces were arriving in Europe at the rate of 300,000 soldiers per month. This was enough to make a difference in the war's outcome.

Between July 15 and August 5, 1918, American forces joined French and British forces in the Second Battle of the Marne. Soon after the Allied forces counterattacked, the German troops fell back. "August 8 was the black day of the German army," General Ludendorff reported to the Kaiser. "It put the decline of our fighting power beyond all doubt . . . The war must be ended."

In late September, the Allies launched the **Meuse-Argonne Offensive**. The AEF's goal was to break through the German line to reach the Sedan railroad in northern France. This rail line was the German army's main line of supply and communication with Germany. More than 1 million U.S. troops took part in this final assault. After six weeks of hard fighting through the Argonne Forest, the Americans achieved their objective. On November 11, 1918, Germany agreed to an armistice—a truce. By then, the other Central powers had also surrendered. The long war was finally over.

Counting the Costs and Casualties For all involved, the costs of the war in human life and suffering were immense. More than 8 million soldiers had died. Another 21 million were injured, and many would never fully recover or be able to work. An English veteran and poet named Siegfried Sassoon wrote bitterly of their sacrifice:

Does it matter?—losing your legs? . . .
For people will always be kind,
And you need not show that you mind
When the others come in after hunting
To gobble their muffins and eggs.

Does it matter?—losing your sight? . . .
There's such splendid work for the blind;
And people will always be kind,
As you sit on the terrace remembering
And turning your face to the light.

—Siegfried Sassoon, "Does It Matter?", 1918

In addition, millions of civilians throughout Europe died from starvation, disease, and other war-related causes. The United States suffered far fewer casualties, with about 116,000 soldiers killed and twice that many wounded or missing.

The war had also caused horrific damage to farms, forests, factories, towns, and homes throughout Europe. An Allied soldier described the villages he saw:

They are utterly destroyed, so that there are not even skeletons of buildings left—nothing but a churned mass of debris, with bricks, stones and . . . bodies pounded to nothing. And forests! There are not even tree trunks left— not a leaf or a twig. All is buried and churned up again and buried again.
—John Raws, letter to a friend, August 4, 1916

The war had also destroyed roads, bridges, railroad lines, and other transportation facilities. Countries already severely burdened by the financial cost of war withered under the weight of these additional losses. For Europe, economic recovery would come very slowly in the years ahead.

Another cost of the war was hard to measure but very real—damage to the human spirit. Many men and women who had eagerly joined the war effort now felt deeply disillusioned by what they had experienced. They questioned long-held beliefs about the glories of Western civilization and the nobility of war. American poet Ezra Pound spoke for war-weary populations in both the United States and Europe when he wrote of the "myriad," or vast number, who had died "for a botched civilization."

Summary

World War I was the world's first truly modern war. New inventions and technological advances affected how the war was fought and how it ended. The United States provided soldiers, equipment, and finances, which contributed to the Allied victory.

Selective Service Act Before the United States could join the Allies, tens of thousands of troops had to be recruited and trained. As part of this process, Congress passed the Selective Service Act to create a national draft.

369th Regiment Hundreds of thousands of African Americans served in segregated military units during World War I. The all-black 369th Regiment received France's highest military honors for its service in Europe.

American Expeditionary Force President Woodrow Wilson and General John J. Pershing, commander of the American Expeditionary Force, insisted that most American troops fight as a force separate from the Allied army. Two million Americans fought in the AEF during the war.

The land war New weapons made land warfare much deadlier than ever before. The result was trench warfare, a new kind of defensive war.

The air war Both sides first used airplanes and airships for observation. Technological improvements allowed them to make specialized planes for bombing and fighting.

The sea war Early in the war, ocean combat took place between battleships. The Germans then used U-boats to sink large numbers of ships. To protect merchant ships, the Allies developed a convoy system. Later, the Allies laid a mine barrier across the North Sea and English Channel.

Meuse-Argonne Offensive In 1918, close to 1 million U.S. soldiers took part in the Meuse-Argonne Offensive. Their success helped bring about an armistice with Germany.

Chapter 24

The Home Front

How did Americans on the home front support or oppose World War I?

24.1 Introduction

As "doughboys" left for France, Americans at home **mobilized**—organized the nation's resources—for war. Years after the war ended, popular stage and film star Elsie Janis recalled this time as the most exciting of her life. "The war," said Janis, "was my high spot, and I think there is only one real peak in each life."

Along with many other movie stars, Janis eagerly volunteered for war work. She had a beautiful singing voice and a gift for impersonating other actors. She used both talents to raise money for the war. Janis later went overseas to become one of the first American performers to entertain U.S. troops. She gave more than 600 performances over 15 months, sometimes performing as many as nine shows a day. Before her arrival in Europe, no other woman entertainer had been permitted to work so close to the front lines.

While only a few women like Janis helped the war effort publicly, thousands found more prosaic but just as useful ways to do their part. Many women joined the workforce. With so many men overseas, a serious labor shortage developed. Eager for workers, employers across the nation put large-print "Women Wanted" notices in newspapers. In the final months of the war, a Connecticut ammunition factory was so frantic for workers that its owners hired airplanes to drop leaflets over the city of Bridgeport listing their openings.

Although the number of women in the workforce stayed about the same throughout the war, the number of occupations in which they worked rose sharply. Many who were already in the workforce took new jobs in offices, shops, and factories. They became typists, cashiers, salesclerks, and telephone operators. Women worked in plants, assembling explosives, electrical appliances, airplanes, and cars. Many took jobs in the iron and steel industry—jobs once open only to men. Most had to give up these jobs when the war ended, but they had shown the public just how capable they were.

Entertainer Elsie Janis became a tireless supporter of the war effort and used her talents to work as a fundraiser. Janis also took her act on the road, entertaining troops stationed near the front lines.

The most popular song of World War I was George M. Cohan's "Over There." Its upbeat refrain announced "the Yanks are coming" and promised "we won't come back 'til it's over over there." The song was an instant hit, selling 2 million copies by war's end. The U.S. goverment used "Over There" to inspire patriotic spirit at fundraisers and recruitment drives. Cohan was later awarded the congressional Medal of Honor for his contribution to the war effort.

A number of peace groups formed after 1914, many headed by women. Wanting a greater say in matters of war, women quite naturally linked the issues of suffrage and peace. Some even hoped that once all American women won the right to vote, they would use that power to end war.

24.2 Mobilizing Public Opinion in Favor of War

When President Woodrow Wilson called the nation to war, he knew that not all Americans would respond with enthusiasm. Opposition to the war had surfaced almost as soon as the first shots were fired. In the fall of 1914, automaker Henry Ford had financed the sailing of a "peace ship" to Europe. The passengers were **pacifists,** people who for political, moral, or religious reasons oppose all wars. They hoped to get leaders of neutral countries like Sweden to act as peacemakers. Although their trip did little good, Ford and his fellow passengers came back determined to let the American public know their views.

Peace Groups and Pacifists Oppose Entry into the War As the war raged in Europe, pacifists, progressives, and other activists joined forces to keep the United States out of the conflict. Some were simply opposed to all wars. This was true of Congresswoman Jeannette Rankin of Montana, the first woman to serve as a member of Congress. A lifelong pacifist, Rankin wanted the United States to set an example by refusing to fight. Other opponents claimed they were willing to fight to defend the United States but were opposed to getting involved in what they saw as a European conflict.

In January 1915, a group of women led by Jane Addams held a peace conference in Washington, D.C. They called for limitation of arms and mediation of the European conflict rather than combat. They believed that progressive social reforms would help eliminate the economic causes of war, and they feared that U.S. entry into the war would diminish support for their reform efforts. Conference leaders formed the **Woman's Peace Party,** which grew quickly but broke into smaller factions after the United States entered the war.

Pacifists also protested the war in other ways. Some young men acted on their beliefs by declaring themselves **conscientious objectors**. A conscientious objector is someone who opposes war for religious or moral reasons and therefore refuses to serve in the armed forces. Despite the objections of these men, military officials drafted many pacifists into the armed forces. Those who refused to serve risked going to prison.

The Government Uses Propaganda to "Sell" the War Although pacifists and peace groups represented a minority of Americans, government officials feared those groups could become a serious obstacle to a united war effort. "It is not an army that we must shape and train for the war," said Wilson. "It is a nation."

To help the government "sell" the war to the public, the president created a government propaganda agency known as the **Committee on Public Information (CPI)**. He chose reporter George Creel to head the CPI. Creel saw the CPI's work as a way of fighting war critics and preserving "American ideals."

Creel hired reporters, artists, movie directors, writers, and historians to create a massive propaganda campaign. The CPI churned out press releases supporting the war effort. It also produced films with such titles as *The Kaiser, Beast of Berlin,* and *Claws of the Hun.* These movies showed Germans as evil savages out to take over the world. Posters urged Americans to join the army and buy bonds. CPI printing presses also produced leaflets and books on topics such as German war practices. Many CPI books were printed in foreign languages, so immigrants could read *How the War Came to America* in Polish, German, Swedish, or Spanish, for example.

One of the CPI's most successful propaganda campaigns was carried out by its "Four-Minute Men." In cities and towns across the country, CPI officials recruited 75,000 men to make short, four-minute speeches at civic and social clubs, movie theaters, churches, farmhouses, and country stores. Written by CPI writers in Washington, these patriotic speeches addressed such topics as why the United States was fighting or the need to conserve fuel. About every 10 days, new speeches arrived. In places with large numbers of immigrants, speakers gave their talks in Italian, Yiddish, Serbian, and other languages.

Patriotic Fervor Sweeps the Country In small towns and large, people of all ages found ways to show their support for the war effort. At loyalty parades, families waved flags and wore patriotic costumes. Marchers shouted slogans like "Keep the flag flying" and "Down with the Kaiser."

In schools, children saved tin cans, paper, and old toothpaste tubes for recycling into war materials. Families collected peach and apricot pits for use in making gas masks. Women met in homes or at churches to knit blankets and socks for soldiers. Many people joined local Red Cross chapters, where they rolled bandages and packed supplies to send overseas.

Propaganda and patriotism sometimes had the unfortunate effect of stirring up anti-German hysteria. Almost all German American communities supported the war effort once the United States entered the conflict. However, they often suffered as the result of the suspicions of others. Employers in war industries fired German American workers, fearing they might sabotage machinery or report plans to the enemy. Karl Muck, the German-born conductor of the Boston Symphony Orchestra, was arrested as an enemy alien after refusing to conduct the "Star Spangled Banner" and protesting the wartime ban on German music.

For many Americans, all things German became associated with disloyalty. Symphonies stopped playing music by German composers. Libraries removed books by German authors. Many schools proscribed the teaching of German as a foreign language. German foods were given more patriotic names—sauerkraut became "liberty cabbage" and liverwurst, "liberty sausage."

Four-Minute Men made short speeches to build support for the war wherever they could find an audience. George Creel, head of the Committee on Public Information, claimed that his 75,000 orators delivered more than 7.5 million speeches to more than 314 million people.

During the war, women took over many jobs traditionally done by men. A Seattle newspaper reported "a sudden influx of women into such unusual occupations as bank clerk, ticket seller, elevator operator, chauffeur, street car conductor," as well as factory worker and farmer.

24.3 Transforming the Economy for the War Effort

Like Elsie Janis, movie idol Douglas Fairbanks was a top fundraiser for the war effort. At a New York rally, thousands cheered as he fought a mock boxing match against the German Kaiser. Fairbanks wore boxing gloves labeled "Victory" on one hand and "Liberty Bonds" on the other. He followed his knockout punch to the Kaiser with a rousing speech, urging the crowd to back the war effort.

Americans Buy Liberty Bonds to Fund the War World War I cost the United States about $35.5 billion. About one fourth of that cost came from taxes, which increased drastically during the war. In October 1917, Congress passed the War Revenue Act, which raised income tax rates and taxes on excess profits. It also reduced the level of taxable income to $1,000. As a result, the number of Americans paying income tax increased from 437,000 in 1916 to 4.4 million in 1918.

The government raised the rest of the money through the sale of **bonds**. A bond is a certificate issued by a government or company that promises to pay back the money borrowed at a fixed rate of interest on a specific date. Throughout the war, the government held rallies to promote the sale of Liberty Bonds. In big cities, movie stars and sports heroes urged people to buy bonds, quoting slogans such as "Come across or the Kaiser will!" and "A bond slacker is a Kaiser backer." Composer John Philip Sousa even wrote the "Liberty Bond March."

Thousands of ordinary citizens worked tirelessly selling war bonds in their hometowns. Employers gave workers time off to attend local bond rallies. In some places, those who were reluctant to buy bonds faced pressure from self-appointed patriot groups. Many foreign-born citizens felt they had to buy bonds—even if they were poor—or risk being thought un-American.

New Government Agencies Organize Industry for War As the nation geared up for war, industries began to shift from consumer goods to war production. In the past, the government had left businesses alone to make this transition. World War I was different. For the first time, government officials worked closely with industries to make sure they met the military's needs.

In July 1917, Woodrow Wilson created the War Industries Board (WIB) to direct industrial production. The WIB, headed by stockbroker Bernard Baruch, coordinated the work of government agencies and industry groups to make sure supplies and equipment were produced and delivered to the military. Baruch had the authority to tell factories what goods to produce and how much to make.

Some WIB decisions affected women's fashion. After being told to use less material in clothes, fashion designers began making shorter skirts. Women's corsets, with their metal hooks and stays, also came under scrutiny. To reduce the use of metal, women were urged to give up wearing corsets. Many were glad to comply, donating these tight-fitting undergarments to scrap drives.

The government also worked to ensure the cooperation of unions in the war effort, and labor leaders readily agreed. The National War Labor Board worked to settle any labor disputes. The War Policies Board set standards for wages, hours, and working conditions in war industries. As a result, labor unrest subsided for the duration of the war. The booming wartime economy created many jobs, and union membership rose rapidly.

Food and Fuel Help Win the War The United States faced the huge responsibility of feeding the armed forces, as well as Allied troops and civilians. To meet the challenge, Wilson set up the Food Administration to oversee production and distribution of food and fuel. To head the effort, Wilson chose Herbert Hoover, an engineer who had led relief efforts in Belgium. Hoover raised crop prices to encourage farmers to produce more food and began a campaign that urged Americans to conserve food and reduce waste.

Although he could punish people for hoarding food, Hoover relied on Americans' voluntary "spirit of self-sacrifice." Using the slogan "Food will win the war," he urged families to participate in Meatless Mondays and Wheatless Wednesdays. Hoover also called on Americans to increase the food supply by planting "victory gardens." Across the country, schoolyards, vacant lots, and public parks sprouted seeds. The Wilsons set an example by having a victory garden planted on the White House lawn.

The Fuel Administration met the nation's energy needs through a combination of increased production and conservation. To conserve energy, Americans turned down their heaters and wore sweaters on "heatless Mondays." On "gasless Sundays," they went for walks instead of driving their cars. The Fuel Administration also introduced daylight savings time. By adding an extra hour of daylight at day's end, households used less electricity for lighting.

With all of these new boards and agencies, the size of the federal government grew rapidly during the war years. The number of federal employees more than doubled between 1916 and 1918.

Conserving food was part of the war effort. In 1917, the secretary of agriculture issued an appeal to housewives: "Every woman can render important service to the nation . . . She can help to feed and clothe our armies and help to supply food to those beyond the seas by practicing effective thrift in her own household."

In 1917, the American Red Cross put out an urgent call for knitted wristlets, mufflers, sweaters, and pairs of socks. The greatest need was for socks. Soldiers stuck in wet trenches desperately needed dry socks to ward off a condition known as trench foot. Americans of all ages answered the call.

African Americans in New York City staged a peaceful march in 1917 to protest the mistreatment of blacks.

24.4 Fighting for Democracy on the Home Front

President Wilson asked Americans to help make the world "safe for democracy," but many African Americans wondered more about democracy at home. With lynchings, Jim Crow laws, and segregated army units, some were not sure what they should be fighting for.

African American Leaders Have a Mixed Response to the War Although most African Americans supported the war, black leaders disagreed about how they should respond to the war effort. W. E. B. Du Bois urged blacks to serve in the military to show their loyalty and help gain greater equality. In the National Association for the Advancement of Colored People (NAACP) journal *The Crisis,* Du Bois wrote, "Let us, while this war lasts, forget our special grievances and close our ranks shoulder to shoulder with our own white fellow citizens and the allied nations that are fighting for democracy."

The outspoken black newspaper editor William Monroe Trotter disagreed. He argued that the federal government should be working to end discrimination at home before fighting for democracy overseas. Trotter did not believe serving in the armed forces would lead to better treatment for African Americans.

African Americans Migrate North for New Opportunities On the home front, the war had a major impact on African Americans in the South. As production of war materials rose, thousands of new jobs opened up in the North at the nation's steel and auto factories. The mining and meatpacking industries also needed more workers. At the same time, the flood of new immigrants from Europe had stopped, contributing to a growing labor shortage. Employers in northern cities desperately needed workers.

Black newspapers urged southern blacks to leave home and take advantage of these opportunities in the North. Many southern blacks packed up and headed north. Once settled, they wrote letters home filled with glowing reports of their new lives:

> I just begin to feel like a man. It's a great pleasure in knowing that you have got some privilege. My children are going to the same school as whites and I don't have to umble to no one. I have registered—Will vote the next election and there isn't any "yes sir" and "no sir."
> —Author unknown, from *Letters of Negro Migrants of 1916–1918*

What began as a trickle soon turned into a mass movement of African Americans known as the **Great Migration.** Chicago, New York City, Cleveland, and other cities saw an explosion of black residents. Whites suddenly found themselves competing with blacks for jobs and housing. In some places, racial tensions sparked riots. During the "red summer" of 1919, blood flowed in many cities, including the nation's capital. One of the worst race riots broke out in East St. Louis, Illinois, after a factory owner brought in black workers to break a strike. At least 39 African Americans and 9 whites died before peace could be restored. Unlike in the past, blacks surprised their attackers by fighting back. "The Washington riot gave me the thrill that comes once in a life time," wrote a black woman. "At last our men had stood like men, [and] struck back."

Early on the morning of July 30, 1916, a huge fire destroyed the Black Tom pier on the New Jersey waterfront. Most windows within 25 miles of the pier blew out. Warehouses filled with weapons and explosives awaiting shipment to the Allies in Europe went up in flames. In time, officials figured out that the fire had been set by German agents. Such incidents were few in number, but they fed the fears of a nervous public that German spies threatened the nation.

Immigrants Face Forced "Americanization" Most immigrants, like most Americans, supported the war. They wanted a chance to show their loyalty to their adopted country. They bought war bonds, participated in conservation efforts, and worked in wartime industries.

Nevertheless, rumors of enemy agents sparked anti-immigrant sentiments. Recent immigrants became targets of self-appointed patriot groups like the American Protective League. These groups tried to enforce what they called "100 percent Americanism." Their members sometimes walked around immigrant neighborhoods looking for signs of disloyalty. They also sent the Federal Bureau of Investigation (FBI) names of people they suspected of disloyalty. Many of those people named belonged to political and labor groups.

Intolerance also led to attacks on German Americans. In April 1918, Robert Prager, a German-born citizen, was lynched by a mob near St. Louis, Missouri. His only crime was being born in Germany. Prager had tried to enlist, but officials had turned him down for medical reasons. Immigrants were not the only victims of unwarranted attacks by patriot groups. Anyone who spoke out against the war became a target. For instance, a mob whipped an Ohio minister for giving what was considered to be an antiwar speech.

The Government Cracks Down on Dissent
Fear of **espionage,** or spying, motivated Congress to pass the Espionage Act in 1917. This law made it a crime to try to interfere with the military draft. It also set severe penalties for spying, sabotage, and vaguely defined "obstruction of the war effort." The Espionage Act also gave the postmaster general broad powers to refuse mail delivery of any materials that might encourage disloyalty.

This poster urged immigrants to buy government bonds and show their support for the country. Though many immigrants showed loyalty to America, self-appointed patriotic groups scrutinized them for any activity that was not "American."

Remember Your First Thrill of AMERICAN LIBERTY

YOUR DUTY-*Buy* United States Government *Bonds* 2nd Liberty Loan of 1917

Eugene Debs was a colorful and eloquent speaker. During World War I, he publicly condemned both the war and the government's crackdown on dissent. As a result, he was convicted under the Espionage Act and jailed. While in prison, Debs ran for president as the candidate of the Socialist Party, winning nearly 1 million votes.

Posters like this one discouraged Americans from speaking out against the war. People who did speak out risked being branded as disloyal.

Americans soon felt the impact of the Espionage Act. Postmaster General Albert Burleson used his new power to ban Socialist newspapers and magazines from the mail. Popular magazines began asking readers to spy on their neighbors and coworkers. The *Literary Digest* invited readers to send in news items they thought "treasonable." The CPI ran magazine ads warning people not to "wait until you catch someone putting a bomb under a factory. Report the man who spreads pessimistic stories . . . cries for peace, or belittles our efforts to win the war."

In 1918, Congress further cracked down on dissent by enacting the **Sedition Act**. This act made it a crime to say anything that was "disloyal, profane, scurrilous, or abusive" about the government. Hundreds of people were arrested for offenses such as criticizing the draft or wartime taxes. California Senator Hiram Johnson complained that the law meant "You shall not criticize anything or anybody in the government any longer or you shall go to jail."

Socialists and Wobblies Speak Out Against the War When the war began, many members of the Socialist Party spoke out strongly against it. They viewed the war as a fight among capitalists for wealth and power. As Eugene V. Debs, head of the Socialist Party, told his followers,

> Wars throughout history have been waged for conquest and plunder . . . that is war in a nutshell. The master class has always declared the wars; the subject class has always fought the battles. The master class has had all to gain and nothing to lose, while the subject class has had nothing to gain and all to lose—especially their lives.
> —Eugene Debs, "The Canton, Ohio, Speech," June 16, 1918

Members of the Industrial Workers of the World (IWW), better known as **Wobblies**, also spoke out against the war. "Capitalists of America, we will fight against you, not for you," declared the *Industrial Worker*, the IWW newspaper, in 1917. "There is not a power in the world that can make the working class fight if they refuse." The Wobblies' antiwar views gave their enemies a chance to attack them as disloyal. In Montana, a mob hanged an IWW organizer. In September 1917, federal agents raided 48 IWW meeting halls, seizing letters and publications. Later that month, 165 IWW leaders were arrested.

In all, the government arrested and tried more than 1,500 people under the Espionage and Sedition acts. Approximately 1,000 were convicted, including Debs, who was sentenced to a 10-year prison term for urging young men to refuse to serve in the military. More than 100 Wobblies were also sent to prison, a blow from which the IWW never recovered.

The Espionage and Sedition acts made many Americans uneasy. In 1919, *Schenck v. United States,* a case involving the Espionage Act, reached the Supreme Court. Charles Schenck, a socialist, was charged with distributing leaflets to recent draftees, urging them to resist the military draft. He was convicted of interfering with recruitment. His lawyer appealed Schenck's conviction on the grounds that his right to free speech had been denied.

In a unanimous opinion, written by Justice Oliver Wendell Holmes Jr., the Court held that Schenck's conviction was constitutional. "The most stringent protection of free speech would not protect a man in falsely shouting fire in a theatre and causing a panic," Holmes wrote. Schenck's publications created "a clear and present danger" to a nation engaged in war. "When a nation is at war," wrote Holmes, "things that might be said in time of peace . . . will not be endured so long as men fight."

Summary

During World War I, the federal government worked to mobilize the country for war. At the same time, tensions arose as the need for national unity was weighed against the rights of Americans to express their opposition to the war.

Woman's Peace Party For religious or political reasons, some Americans opposed the war. Among the leading peace activists were members of the Woman's Peace Party.

Committee on Public Information During the war, the government created this propaganda agency to build support for the war. Although CPI propaganda helped Americans rally around the war effort, it also contributed to increased distrust of foreign-born citizens and immigrants.

Liberty Bonds The purchase of Liberty Bonds by the American public provided needed funding for the war and gave Americans a way to participate in the war effort.

Great Migration During the war, hundreds of thousands of African Americans migrated out of the South. They were attracted to northern cities by job opportunities and hopes for a better life.

Espionage and Sedition acts The Espionage and Sedition acts allowed the federal government to suppress antiwar sentiment. The laws made it illegal to express opposition to the war.

Socialists and Wobblies Socialists and Wobblies who opposed the war became the targets of both patriot groups and the government for their antiwar positions. Many were jailed under the Espionage and Sedition acts.

Schenck v. United States The Supreme Court upheld the constitutionality of the Espionage Act in this 1918 case. It ruled that the government could restrict freedom of speech in times of "clear and present danger."

Chapter 25

The Treaty of Versailles: To Ratify or Reject?

Should the United States have ratified or rejected the Treaty of Versailles?

25.1 Introduction

On December 13, 1918, President Woodrow Wilson's ship, the *George Washington,* slipped into the dock at Brest, France. The war was over. The Allies and the Central powers had put down their guns and signed an armistice. Wilson was going to France to participate in writing the peace treaty that he believed would "make the world safe for democracy."

As the ship made its way to the pier, its passengers could hear the sounds of warships firing their guns in Wilson's honor. On the dock, bands played the "Star Spangled Banner" as French soldiers and civilians cheered. It was a stirring beginning to the president's visit.

Once on shore, Wilson made his way through cheering throngs to the railway station. There he and the other members of the American peace delegation boarded a private train bound for Paris. In the French capital, a crowd of 2 million people greeted the Americans. They clapped and shouted their thanks to the man hailed as "Wilson the Just." One newspaper observed, "Never has a king, never has an emperor received such a welcome."

Many Europeans shared in the excitement of Wilson's arrival. They were grateful for the help Americans had given in the last months of the war. Moreover, they believed Wilson sincerely wanted to help them build a new and better world. Wherever Wilson went, people turned out to welcome him. Everyone wanted to see the man newspapers called the "Savior of Humanity" and the "Moses from across the Atlantic." Throughout Allied Europe, wall posters declared, "We want a Wilson peace."

President Wilson arrived in Europe with high hopes of creating a just and lasting peace. The warm welcome he received could only have raised his hopes still higher. Few watching these events, including Wilson himself, could have anticipated just how hard it would be to get leaders in both Europe and the United States to share his vision.

In 1918, huge crowds greeted President Woodrow Wilson (on the left) as a hero. He offered hope to millions who had been left deeply disillusioned by the war.

◀ Europeans welcoming President Woodrow Wilson to Paris, 1918

Woodrow Wilson unveiled his Fourteen Points in a speech to Congress on war aims and peace terms. In his 1918 address, he talked about the causes of the war. Then he laid out his plans for preventing future wars.

25.2 Wilson's Vision for World Peace

On January 8, 1918, Wilson went before Congress to explain his war aims. Although the war was still raging, he boldly stated an ambitious program to make the world "fit and safe to live in." He called his blueprint for peace the **Fourteen Points**. It was designed to protect "every peace-loving nation" and peoples from "force and selfish aggression."

Fourteen Points to End All Wars The first goal of Wilson's peace plan was to eliminate the causes of wars. He called for an end to secret agreements and the web of alliances that had drawn the nations of Europe into war. Recalling the deadly submarine warfare that brought the United States into the war, he wanted **freedom of the seas**. By this, he meant the right of merchant ships to travel freely in international waters in times of peace and war. He also wanted European countries to reduce their **armaments,** or weapons of war, instead of competing to make their military forces bigger and better.

A second key goal was to ensure the right to self-determination for ethnic groups so they could control their own political future. With the defeat of the Central powers, the Austro-Hungarian and Ottoman empires were falling apart. Many different ethnic groups lived within these lands. Wilson hoped to see these groups living in newly formed nations under governments of their choosing.

For Wilson, the last of his Fourteen Points was the most important. It called for setting up an international organization called the **League of Nations** to ensure world peace. Member nations would agree to protect one another's independence and **territorial integrity**. Under the principle of territorial integrity, nations respect one another's borders and do not try to gain another country's territory by force. Working together, League members would resolve conflicts before those conflicts escalated into wars.

Wilson's Unusual Decisions As the end of the war approached, President Wilson made an unusual decision. Up to that time, no president had traveled to Europe while in office. Wilson broke with tradition by deciding to lead the American delegation to the peace conference in France. He wanted to make sure his goal of a lasting peace became a reality.

As Wilson prepared for his trip, Democrats and Republicans were getting ready for the 1918 midterm elections. At that time, Democrats controlled both houses of Congress. Wilson called on the American public to show their support for his peace plan by keeping the Democrats in power. But his appeal did not work. The Republicans won a majority in both the Senate and the House. The voters' repudiation of Wilson's appeal weakened his position just as he was about to seek the support of European leaders for his peace plans.

Wilson made matters worse by his choice of other American delegates to the peace conference. Although they were competent diplomats, only one was a Republican. Upon reading the names, former president William Taft griped that Wilson wanted to "hog the whole show." Moreover, not one of the delegates had the confidence of key Republican leaders in the Senate. Because the Senate would have to ratify whatever treaty came out of the negotiations, this oversight would come back to haunt the president.

	The Points	Support of World Peace
	**Point 1** "Open covenants of peace, openly arrived at, . . . [so that] diplomacy shall proceed always frankly and in the public view"	Countries would not make secret treaties and alliances. Secret alliances had been a cause of World War I.
	**Point 2** "Absolute freedom of navigation upon the seas . . . in war and peace"	Ships would be able to travel freely in times of war. U-boat attacks on shipping had drawn the United States into World War I.
	**Point 3** "The removal, so far as possible, of all economic barriers and the establishment of an equality of trade conditions among all the nations"	Free trade among countries would promote economic growth and reduce trade conflicts that could draw nations into war.
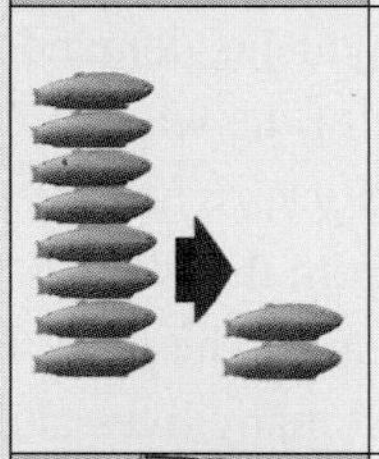	**Point 4** "National armaments will be reduced to the lowest point consistent with domestic safety."	Countries would reduce their stockpiles of weapons. Militarism had been a cause of World War I.
	**Point 5** "Impartial adjustment of all colonial claims[;] . . . the interests of the populations concerned must have equal weight with the equitable claims of the [colonial] government."	The desires of colonial peoples would be taken into consideration in creating a more peaceful world. Imperialism and competition for colonies had been a cause of World War I.
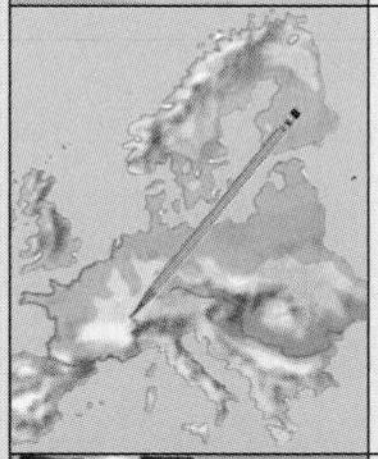	**Points 6 to 13** These points deal with the restoration of "occupied territory" to Russia, Belgium, France, Serbia, Romania, and Montenegro. They also call for drawing new borders based on "historically established lines of allegiance and nationality."	Restoring land taken from countries by war would restore respect for international law. Redrawing some borders on the basis of self-determination would reduce conflicts among ethnic groups. Frustrated nationalism in the Balkans had triggered World War I.
	**Point 14** "A general association of nations must be formed."	Countries would work together in the League of Nations to resolve conflicts before those conflicts escalated into war.

On May 27, 1919, the Big Four met at Paris to attend a peace conference. There, they hammered out the details for a peace treaty. The Treaty of Versailles was signed on June 28, 1919 and upset many people with its harsh treatment of Germany. "We came to Paris convinced that the new order was about to be established," remarked an unhappy British official. "We left it convinced that the new order had merely fouled the old."

25.3 Ideals Versus Self-Interest at Versailles

The Paris peace conference opened with great ceremony at the Palace of Versailles. The leaders of the four largest victorious nations made almost all the decisions. This group, known as the **Big Four,** included President Wilson and three prime ministers—David Lloyd George of Great Britain, Georges Clemenceau of France, and Vittorio Orlando of Italy. Representatives of Germany and the other defeated nations took no part in the talks. Russia, which had made a separate peace with Germany after its revolution, did not attend.

Peace Without Victory Gives Way to War Guilt and Reparations Wilson came to the talks eager to share his Fourteen Points with other world leaders. His hopes for easy acceptance of his goals were quickly dashed. Although the other leaders liked Wilson's vision of a peaceful world, they were more interested in protecting the interests of their own countries.

First among Clemenceau's concerns was French security. He hoped to weaken Germany to the point that it could never threaten France again. He insisted that the German army be reduced to 100,000 men. He further insisted that Germany be stripped of its coal-rich Saar Valley.

Lloyd George, who had recently won reelection on the slogan "Hang the Kaiser," insisted that Germany accept responsibility for starting the war. The inclusion of a **war-guilt clause** in the treaty demolished Wilson's earlier hope for "peace without victory." In addition, the treaty required Germany to pay $33 billion in **reparations** to the Allies. Reparations are payments demanded of a defeated nation by the victor in a war to offset the cost of the war. Germans resented both the war-guilt clause and the reparations, rightly fearing that the payments would cripple their economic recovery from the war.

Wilson tried to restrain these efforts at punishing Germany. The other leaders, however, would not back down. Their countries had lost many lives and property, and they expected compensation. They also argued that although the United States was not to receive reparations, it would benefit from them. The Allies had borrowed huge sums from American banks to finance the war. They hoped to repay these debts with reparations from Germany. Wilson reluctantly agreed to the harsh treatment of Germany in order to gain support for what he saw as most important: the League of Nations.

Self-Determination Survives, but Only in Europe Wilson also clashed with the other Allied leaders over territorial claims. In the Fourteen Points, he had called for self-determination for the peoples of Europe. The collapse of the Austro-Hungarian Empire had left unclear the fate of many ethnic groups. Wilson wanted these peoples to be free to determine their own political futures.

Wilson's commitment to self-determination helped some ethnic groups form their own nations. Yugoslavia, Czechoslovakia, Poland, and the former Russian states of Estonia, Latvia, and Lithuania all gained independence. However, other territorial decisions went against Wilson's views. For example, parts of Germany were given to France, Poland, Denmark, and Belgium, with little thought about the desires of the people living there. Italy gained territory that was home to Austrians.

In other areas, the Allies ignored self-determination. Britain, France, Italy, and Japan grabbed German colonies in China, the Pacific, and Africa. Britain and France took over areas in Southwest Asia that had once been controlled by the collapsing Ottoman Empire. They were to govern these areas as **mandates,** or territories controlled by the League of Nations, until each mandate was ready for self-rule. These mandates included Iraq, Syria, Lebanon, and Palestine, as well as some former German colonies in Africa and the Pacific Islands.

Wilson Pins His Peace Hopes on the League of Nations President Wilson had not been able to preserve all of his goals. He did, however, get the other leaders to include a charter for the League of Nations in the final agreement. Wilson hoped that, in time, the League would be able to correct the peace treaty's many flaws. More important, he believed the League would maintain peace by providing **collective security** for its members. Collective security is a commitment by many countries to join together to deal with a nation that threatens peace.

The Big Four formally signed the Treaty of Versailles on June 18, 1919. But Wilson's fight for the treaty was just beginning.

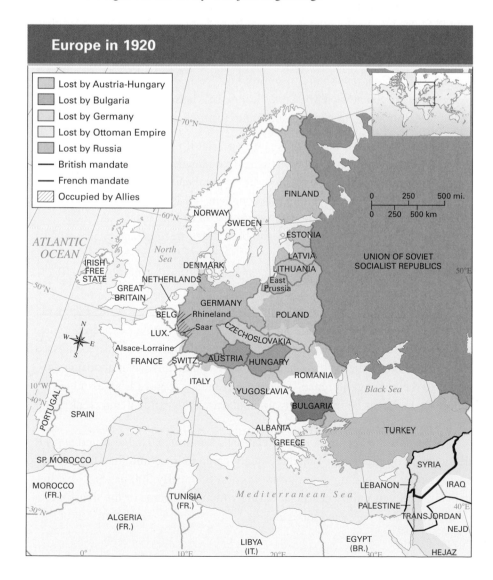

Europe in 1920

Lost by Austria-Hungary
Lost by Bulgaria
Lost by Germany
Lost by Ottoman Empire
Lost by Russia
— British mandate
— French mandate
Occupied by Allies

World War I and the Treaty of Versailles created new countries and redrew the borders of old ones. Germany and Russia both lost territory. The Austro-Hungarian and Ottoman empires ceased to exist, and their territories became new countries or mandates of Allied nations.

25.4 The Great Debate About Ratification

Two days after President Wilson returned home, he called on the Senate to ratify the Treaty of Versailles with U.S. membership in the League of Nations. Wilson had strong public support. More than 30 state legislatures and governors endorsed League membership. Still, Wilson had yet to win the necessary two-thirds vote of the Senate needed to ratify a treaty. The question was whether he could get enough Republican votes in the Senate to reach that magic number.

Massachusetts Senator Henry Cabot Lodge, shown here on the right, led the reservationists, who wanted the Treaty of Versailles changed. Idaho Senator William Borah, on the left, led the irreconcilables, who opposed the treaty in any form. Together, these two groups defeated the treaty in the Senate.

Reservationists Seek Changes Before Approving Treaty

Many Republicans in the Senate were reluctant to approve the treaty as it was written. Known as **reservationists**, they said they would vote yes, but only with a number of reservations, or changes, added to it.

The reservationists were mostly concerned with Article 10 of the League's charter. This article focused on collective security. It required member nations to work together—and even supply troops—to keep the peace. Reservationists feared this would draw the United States into wars without approval from Congress. They demanded that Article 10 be changed to read, "The United States assumes no obligation to preserve the territorial integrity or political independence of any other country . . . unless . . . Congress shall . . . so provide."

Republican Senator Henry Cabot Lodge of Massachusetts was the leader of the reservationists. In a speech outlining his views, he warned,

> The United States is the world's best hope, but if you fetter her in the interests and quarrels of other nations, if you tangle her in the intrigues of Europe, you will destroy her power for good and endanger her very existence . . . Strong, generous, and confident, she has nobly served mankind. Beware how you trifle with your marvellous inheritance, this great land of ordered liberty, for if we stumble and fall freedom and civilization everywhere will go down in ruin.
> —Henry Cabot Lodge, "On the League of Nations," August 12, 1919

Here, the "Anti-Treaty Storm" prevents Uncle Sam from rolling his "Peace Treaty" eggs on the White House lawn. This cartoon illustrates how the opposition against the treaty in Congress puts a damper on President Wilson's plans to form a League of Nations.

Lodge had both personal and political reasons for opposing the Treaty of Versailles. He and Wilson had long been bitter foes. "I never expected to hate anyone in politics with the hatred I feel toward Wilson," Lodge once confessed. He was also angry that Wilson had snubbed Republicans when choosing delegates to the peace conference. The ratification debate gave Lodge and his fellow Republicans an opportunity to embarrass the president and weaken the Democratic Party.

As head of the Senate Foreign Relations Committee, Lodge found ways to delay action on the treaty. When the treaty came to his committee for study, he spent two weeks reading aloud every word of the nearly 300 pages. Next, he held six weeks of public hearings, during which opponents of the treaty were given ample time to speak out against it.

Irreconcilables Reject the Treaty in Any Form A group of 16 Senate Republicans firmly opposed the Treaty of Versailles. Known as **irreconcilables,** their "no" vote was certain. They were completely opposed to any treaty that included an international organization that might draw the nation into war.

Republican Senator William Borah of Idaho was one of the more outspoken irreconcilables. The world, he declared, could "get along better without our intervention." He scoffed at the reservationists' position. Recalling George Washington's Farewell Address, he asked, "Where is the reservation . . . which protects us against entangling alliances with Europe?"

Internationalists Support the Treaty of Versailles Most Senate Democrats strongly supported the treaty. This group, known as **internationalists,** believed that greater cooperation among nations could work for the benefit of all. They argued that the United States had already become a major world power. As such, it should take its rightful place in the world community by becoming a member of the League of Nations. Rather than worry about the United States being dragged into another war by the League, the internationalists focused on the League's role in keeping the peace.

President Wilson Takes His Case to the People As the ratification hearings dragged on, the public began to lose interest. Upset by Lodge's delaying tactics, Wilson decided to go directly to the public for support. On learning the president was planning a speaking tour of the country, his doctor warned that it could damage his already failing health. Wilson is reported to have replied,

> [My] own health is not to be considered when the future peace and security of the world are at stake. If the Treaty is not ratified by the Senate, the War will have been fought in vain, and the world will be thrown into chaos. I promised our soldiers, when I asked them to take up arms, that it was a war to end wars.
>
> —Woodrow Wilson, August 27, 1919

The president embarked on a grueling, 8,000-mile speaking tour of the West. He spoke up to four times a day, giving about 40 speeches in 29 cities. Two irreconcilables, Borah and California Senator Hiram Johnson, followed Wilson on their own tour. Despite their attacks, the campaign for the treaty seemed to be picking up speed when disaster struck. On September 25, 1919, the president collapsed with a severe headache in Pueblo, Colorado. His doctor stopped the tour, and Wilson's train sped back to Washington.

Here, Woodrow Wilson speaks to 50,000 people at San Diego, California, to raise public support for the League of Nations. The president's speaking tour of the country was cut short when he suffered a collapse.

Edith Wilson managed the president's daily affairs after he collapsed from a stroke while touring the nation in 1919. She later said she made "the very important decision of when to present matters to my husband." But she denied making policy decisions for him.

25.5 A Divided Senate Decides the Treaty's Fate

A few days after returning to the White House, Wilson had a major stroke that left him partly paralyzed. For months, the president remained very ill. Hoping to restore his health, his wife, Edith Galt Wilson, became a gatekeeper. She decided what news he would hear and chose his few visitors.

At first, the public had no idea just how sick Wilson was. When the extent of his illness became clear, Wilson's critics accused Edith of making decisions for the country. Some called her the "assistant president." In her own account of this time, she said she had "never made a single decision regarding . . . public affairs." Still, in her role as caregiver, Edith Wilson became caught up in the nasty political fighting that marked the debate on the Versailles Treaty.

Partisanship Defeats the Treaty From the start, bitter **partisanship,** or rivalry between political parties, marked the treaty ratification process. During the months of debate, senators on both sides put loyalty to their party above all else.

By the time the treaty came to the Senate for a vote late in 1919, the reservationists had added 14 amendments to it. Most of the changes had little impact on the League of Nations. Despite this, Wilson rejected them all. He refused to accept any agreement that did not have the precise language he had agreed to in Paris. When Nebraska Senator Gilbert Hitchcock advised Wilson to work with Republicans, Wilson barked, "Let Lodge compromise!" The president called on his supporters to vote down the amendments and then pass the treaty in its original form.

The plan backfired. On the first vote, Democrats loyal to Wilson joined the irreconcilables to defeat the amended treaty. When the Senate voted on the unamended treaty, Democrats voted yes, but reservationists and irreconcilables joined forces to defeat it.

Under strong public pressure to try again, the Senate reconsidered the treaty four months later. Once again, Wilson opposed any changes. "Either we should enter the League . . . not fearing the role of leadership which we now enjoy," he told his supporters, "or we should retire . . . from the great concert of powers by which the world was saved."

Not all Senate Democrats agreed with this point of view. Fearing that the nation might be left with no treaty at all, 21 Democrats voted to accept the 14 amendments. But even with their support, the final count fell seven votes short of the two thirds needed for treaty ratification.

The 1920 Election Becomes a Referendum on the Treaty As the 1920 presidential election heated up, Wilson struggled to save the treaty. The Democratic candidate for president, Governor James M. Cox of Ohio, declared himself firmly in favor of the League of Nations. His running mate, Franklin Delano Roosevelt, supported it as well. "If you want . . . another war against civilization," Roosevelt warned, "then let us go back to the conditions of 1914. If you want the possibility of sending once more our troops and navies to foreign lands, then stay out of the League." The Republican Party straddled the issue, favoring "an international association" to prevent war but opposing the League. Its candidate, Warren G. Harding, lacked conviction either way.

Wilson called for the election to be a "great and solemn referendum" on the League of Nations. By this time, however, Americans were losing interest in the partisan debate over ratification. Issues closer to home, such as inflation and unemployment, appeared more pressing. Most people seemed to think, observed Secretary of State Robert Lansing, that Americans should "attend to our own affairs and let the rest of the nations go to the devil if they want to."

When the votes were in, Cox received just 9.1 million votes, compared with Harding's 16.1 million. "It was not a landslide," said Wilson's private secretary, Joseph Tumulty, of the Democratic defeat. "It was an earthquake." The great referendum on the treaty had gone terribly wrong.

In October 1921, the United States, which had fought separately from the Allies, signed a separate peace treaty with Germany. The League of Nations had begun operations by that time, but the nation whose president had created it was not a member.

Two decades would pass before Americans would rethink the idea of collective security. By then, the nation was engaged in a second global war. Looking back, people could not help but wonder: Could that next war have been avoided if the United States had joined the League of Nations?

Summary

After World War I, President Woodrow Wilson hoped to create a lasting peace. He insisted that the treaty ending the war should include a peacekeeping organization called the League of Nations. Many Americans feared that membership in the League could involve the United States in future wars.

The Fourteen Points Wilson outlined his goals for lasting peace in his Fourteen Points. Key issues included an end to secret agreements, freedom of the seas, reduction of armaments, self-determination for ethnic groups, and collective security through creation of an international peacekeeping organization.

The Big Four When the heads of the four major Allies—France, Great Britain, Italy, and the United States—met in Paris for peace talks, they were more focused on self-interest than on Wilson's plan.

Treaty of Versailles The treaty negotiated in Paris redrew the map of Europe, granting self-determination to some groups. Some Allies sought revenge on Germany, insisting on a war-guilt clause and reparations from Germany.

League of Nations Wilson hoped that including the League of Nations in the final treaty would make up for his compromises on other issues. He believed that by providing collective security and a framework for peaceful talks, the League would fix many problems the treaty had created.

The ratification debate The treaty ratification debate divided the Senate into three groups. Reservationists would not accept the treaty unless certain changes were made. Irreconcilables rejected the treaty in any form. Internationalists supported the treaty and the League.

Rejection of the treaty Partisan politics and Wilson's refusal to compromise led to the treaty's rejection and ended Wilson's hopes for U.S. membership in the League of Nations.

In January 1919, nearly every worker in Seattle, Washington, went on strike over wages and working conditions. For five days, most economic activity in the city halted. Despite public fear of food shortages and revolution, neither came to pass.

26.3 Rising Labor Tensions

Like many workers after World War I, Sacco and Vanzetti were union men. Sacco and his wife, Rosina, acted in plays to raise money for striking workers. Vanzetti helped organize a strike at the Plymouth Cordage Company, where he worked as a rope maker. He urged immigrant groups to support labor unions. The dedication of the two men to the union movement was one reason working-class communities later raised money for their legal defense.

Businesses Return to Prewar Labor Practices After World War I, workers struggled to keep the gains they had made during the war years. As the war had raged, the federal government had encouraged business and labor to cooperate. The National War Labor Board had settled labor disputes on generous terms to keep factories humming. Wages went up as the number of unemployed workers decreased and unions gained more clout.

After the war, however, the government stepped aside, and the struggle between business and labor over wages and working conditions resumed. Corporations fought unionization. They reduced wages and paid less attention to employee safety. Some businesses tried to increase the workday to 12 hours, whereas eight hours had been typical during the war.

Workers Respond by Organizing and Striking Working-class Americans reacted to deteriorating working conditions in several ways. Many joined unions for the first time. At this time, the American Federation of Labor (AFL) dominated the union movement. The AFL was a group of unions representing skilled workers, such as machinists or mechanics, organized by their craft. The AFL was best known for "bread and butter" unionism. It concentrated on improving wages and working conditions for its union members.

In contrast, the more radical Industrial Workers of the World (IWW), whose members were known as Wobblies, saw socialism as the solution to workers' problems. According to the preamble of the IWW constitution, "There can be no peace so long as hunger and want are found among millions of the working people and the few, who make up the employing class, have all the good things of life." The goal of the IWW, proclaimed its leader, Bill Haywood, was to put the working class "in control of the machinery of production and distribution, without regard to the capitalist masters."

In 1919, unions staged more than 3,600 strikes across the country, creating the greatest wave of labor unrest in the nation's history. One out of every 10 workers walked off the job at some point during that year. The most dramatic strike took place in Seattle, Washington. When 35,000 shipyard workers were refused a wage increase, the Seattle Central Labor Council called on all city workers to walk off their jobs. Approximately 100,000 people joined Seattle's **general strike**—a strike by workers in all industries in a region. The strike paralyzed the city. Nearly all economic activity came to a sudden halt. Mayor Ole Hanson condemned the walkout as "an attempted revolution" and called in federal troops to take control of the city. As fears of chaos mounted, Seattle's middle class turned against the workers. After five days, the unions were forced to call off their strike.

Strike-related violence, such as shown here, fueled some Americans' fears that radical union activity might lead to revolution. Public fear of radicals contributed to unions' decline.

The most controversial strike of 1919 involved the Boston police force. The police walked off the job after city officials cut their wages and refused to negotiate with their union. At first, Boston's citizens felt sympathy for the police. But that sympathy vanished as the city lapsed into anarchy. Residents set up citizen patrols to fight rising crime. Governor Calvin Coolidge called in National Guard troops to keep order. In his view, "There is no right to strike against the public safety by anybody, anywhere, any time." He fired the striking policemen and hired new ones. His firm stand made Coolidge a national hero. The next year, the Republican Party nominated him as its candidate for vice president.

Unions Lose Public Support and Membership As the strikes persisted, middle-class Americans began to view unionism as a threat to their way of life. Strike-related violence added to fears that radical union activity could lead to anarchy. Public hostility was one reason that overall union membership declined in the 1920s. A second was the failure of many strikes to achieve workers' goals. A third reason was the exclusive politics of many unions. The AFL, for example, limited its membership by refusing to organize unskilled employees. It also excluded women, African Americans, and most immigrants. In response, African Americans organized their own unions. The best known, the Brotherhood of Sleeping Car Porters, was a union of black railroad workers led by A. Philip Randolph.

In addition, a number of Supreme Court decisions weakened unions. First, the Court restricted unions' right to boycott a business that fought unionization. Then, in 1922, the Court declared unconstitutional a federal child labor law. A year later, the Court rejected a Washington, D.C., law that established a minimum wage for women workers. These decisions hurt labor unions by making it easier for companies to hire children and women at low wages.

The diminishing power of unions had a negative effect on workers. Even after the postwar recession ended, many working-class Americans gained little economic ground. Their average income remained well below $1,500 per year at a time when families needed more than that to get by.

26.4 Growing Political Tensions

Nicola Sacco became an anarchist while working in a shoe factory. Bartolomeo Vanzetti learned about anarchism while working at a rope factory. The two met in 1917, when they fled to Mexico to escape the military draft. When they returned to Massachusetts, they joined an East Boston anarchists' group. Vanzetti later boasted, "Both Nick and I are anarchists—the radical of the radical." On the night of their arrest, both were carrying guns. Sacco also had a pamphlet advertising an anarchist rally at which Vanzetti would speak. After their trial, many came to believe that Sacco and Vanzetti had been convicted because of their radical politics.

A Bomb Scare Fuels Fear of Radical Groups On April 28, 1919, a mysterious package arrived in Seattle mayor Ole Hanson's office. The package contained a bomb. The next day, a similar package sent to former Georgia Senator Thomas Hardwick exploded, injuring his maid. Acting on a tip from a New York City postal worker, the post office found 34 more bombs. The addressees included capitalists like John D. Rockefeller and political figures like Supreme Court Justice Oliver Wendell Holmes. No one ever learned who mailed the bombs.

Many Americans saw the bomb scare as another sign that **radicalism** was threatening public order. Radicalism is a point of view favoring extreme change, especially in social or economic structures. At this time, it referred to the ideas of socialist, communist, and anarchist groups. Socialists called for public ownership of the means of production, including land and factories. They believed such changes could be brought about through peaceful reforms.

Communists followed the economic theories of the German philosopher Karl Marx (1818–1883). Similar to socialism, **communism** called for public ownership of the means of production. The result would be a classless society in which all people shared equally in the wealth produced by their labor. Communists, however, believed such change could only be brought about through a revolution by the working class.

American communists drew inspiration from the Russian Revolution of 1917. During that time of unrest, a small group of communists called Bolsheviks, led by Vladimir Lenin, had seized control of the country. The Bolsheviks hoped

On September 16, 1920, a bomb exploded on Wall Street in New York City. Windows shattered throughout a half-mile radius, showering glass onto busy streets. Forty people were killed. It "turned into a shamble the busiest corner of America's financial center," said a reporter who witnessed the blast.

their success would spark communist revolutions in other countries. When that did not happen, Lenin established the Comintern (Communist International). The Comintern united radical groups throughout the world who accepted Lenin's views on the need for revolution to create a communist state.

Anarchists opposed all systems of government. They wanted a society based on freedom, mutual respect, and cooperation. Most anarchists were peaceful, but they had been associated with violence since the Chicago Haymarket Square bombing of 1886. In that incident, seven policemen were killed as they broke up an anarchist rally. None of these radical groups was very large. Combined, their membership came to less than 1 percent of the adult population. Nor were they very effective. They argued constantly among themselves. Still, many Americans viewed them with suspicion and alarm. This postwar fear of radicals became known as the **Red Scare**. Red was slang for communist.

During the Red Scare, fear of radicalism led to the deportation of hundreds of immigrants. One of the best known was Emma Goldman. She was deported to the Soviet Union in 1919.

The Red Scare Leads to Raids on "Subversives" On June 2, 1919, the intensity of the Red Scare increased. Eight bombs exploded in eight cities at the same time. One target was Attorney General Mitchell Palmer's house in Washington, D.C. In response, Palmer launched a campaign against subversives, or people who sought to overthrow the government.

Palmer and his assistant, J. Edgar Hoover, conducted raids on homes, businesses, and meeting places of people they thought might be subversives. The **Palmer Raids** sought weapons, explosives, and other evidence of violent activity. Officials entered buildings without warrants and seized records without permission. With little or no cause, they arrested 6,000 suspected radicals. Foreign-born suspects were deported, many without a court hearing. The only evidence of violent activity they found was three pistols.

Civil Liberties Suffer Palmer's tactics trampled **civil liberties,** basic rights guaranteed by law. Newspaper editor Walter Lippmann wrote of the abuses: "It is forever incredible that an administration announcing the most spacious ideals in our history should have done more to endanger fundamental American liberties than any group of men for a hundred years."

Yet for some Americans, the fear of radicalism overshadowed concerns about abuses of civil liberties. Some 30 states passed sedition laws, which made stirring up opposition to the government a crime. Books considered subversive were removed from public libraries. A mob broke into the offices of a socialist newspaper in New York City and beat up the staff. Another mob seized a Wobbly out of a jail in Washington, hanged him from a bridge, and used his body for target practice.

Palmer had hoped to ride the wave of public alarm about radicals all the way to the White House. But he went too far when he announced that a plot to overthrow the government would begin in New York City on May 1, 1920. As that day drew near, the city's police force was put on 24-hour duty. Politicians were given armed guards for protection. When nothing happened, Palmer's political ambitions were shattered.

After this false alarm, the country worried less about subversion. Most of the people arrested in the Palmer Raids were released without being accused of a crime. Still, the campaign had crippled the nation's radical movements.

26.5 Increasing Social Tensions

The police investigating the South Braintree robbery had little to go on except eyewitness accounts of two bandits who "looked Italian." Three weeks later, the police arrested Sacco and Vanzetti. When searched, the suspects were found to be carrying pistols and ammunition. When questioned, they lied about where they had been and how they had obtained their guns. Their behavior made them look suspicious to the police and, later, to a jury. But during this troubled time, some native-born Americans eyed many immigrants—especially those who were poor and spoke little English—with suspicion.

Increased Immigration Causes a Revival of Nativism Between 1905 and 1914, a million people a year immigrated to the United States. Most came from southern and eastern Europe. Immigration dipped sharply during World War I and then picked up again afterward. In 1920, about 430,000 foreigners entered the country. A year later, that number almost doubled.

The rising tide of immigrants triggered a resurgence of nativism along with calls for immigration restriction. Many nativists feared that the latest immigrants would never become "100 percent American." As one nativist warned, "There are vast communities in the nation thinking today not in terms of America, but in terms of Old World prejudices, theories, and animosities." Others argued that reducing immigration would relieve urban crowding and reduce ethnic conflicts. Union members favored restrictions because they worried that immigrants were taking jobs from union workers. Even some large employers supported immigration restriction. For this group, fear of immigrant radicalism had come to outweigh their desire for cheap immigrant labor.

Notice the two big dips in this graph. The first one follows passage of the Emergency Immigration Act of 1921. The second shows the impact of the Immigration Act of 1924.

New Laws Close the Nation's "Open Door" to Immigrants Congress responded to anti-immigrant pressure by passing the Emergency Immigration Act of 1921. This new law capped the number of people allowed into the country each year at 375,000. It also introduced a quota system to limit the number of immigrants from each country. The quota, or maximum number, was set at 3 percent of a country's residents in the United States in 1910. The quota system was intended to be a temporary measure until Congress could study immigration more closely.

Three years later, Congress passed the Immigration Act of 1924. This law reduced the number of immigrants allowed into the country each year to 164,000. It also cut quotas to 2 percent of a country's residents in the United

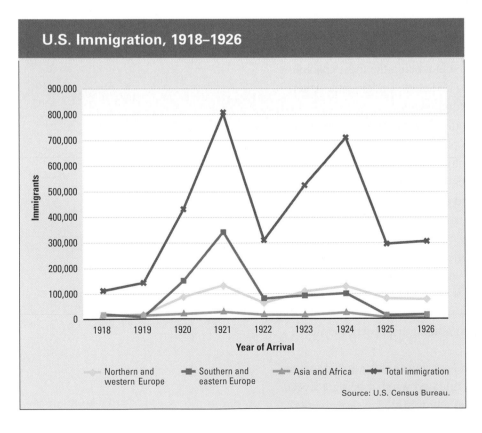

U.S. Immigration, 1918–1926

Year of Arrival

Immigrants

- Northern and western Europe
- Southern and eastern Europe
- Asia and Africa
- Total immigration

Source: U.S. Census Bureau.

States in 1890. That had been a time when most immigrants came from northern Europe. By moving the date back, the law severely reduced immigration from southern and eastern Europe. The new law also banned all immigration from Asia. When the Japanese government heard this news, it declared a national day of mourning.

By the end of the decade, immigration was more than one quarter of what it had been in 1921. But even that was not enough of a reduction for many nativists. In 1929, they persuaded Congress to lower the number of immigrants each year to 150,000.

A Revived Ku Klux Klan Targets "Alien" Influences Anti-immigrant feelings played a role in the revival of the Ku Klux Klan. The Klan was reborn in Atlanta, Georgia, in 1915 after the lynching of Leo Frank, a Jewish factory manager. Frank had been condemned to death for killing a young girl named Mary Phagan. Convinced that Frank was innocent, the governor of Georgia reduced Frank's sentence to life imprisonment. At that point, armed men, calling themselves the Knights of Mary Phagan, broke Frank out of jail and hanged him. The Knights then re-formed themselves as the new invisible order of the Ku Klux Klan.

The revived Ku Klux Klan portrayed itself as a defender of American values. It restricted membership to native-born white Protestants and set itself against African Americans, immigrants, Catholics, and Jews. "The Klan is intolerant," bragged its Imperial Wizard, Hiram Wesley Evans, "of the people who are trying to destroy our traditional Americanism . . . aliens who are constantly trying to change our civilization into something that will suit themselves better."

In the early 1920s, the Klan swelled to between 3 and 4 million members and gained considerable political power throughout the country. Lawmakers supported by the Klan won control of state legislatures in Oregon, Oklahoma, Texas, and Indiana. To demonstrate their power, Klan members held massive marches in Washington, D.C., and other major cities. Yet the Klan's violence and intimidation remained secretive. They often struck at night, wearing hoods that concealed their faces and using whippings, kidnappings, cross burnings, arson, and murder to terrorize entire communities.

The American Civil Liberties Union Defends Unpopular Views The views of nativists and the Klan did not go unchallenged. In 1920, a group of pacifists and social activists founded the American Civil Liberties Union (ACLU) to protect freedom of speech. The ACLU specialized in the defense of unpopular individuals and groups, including Nicola Sacco and Bartolomeo Vanzetti.

In the first year of the ACLU, its lawyers fought to protect immigrants who had been rounded up in the Palmer Raids for their radical beliefs from being deported. The ACLU also defended the right of trade unions to hold meetings and organize workers. ACLU lawyers helped win the release of hundreds of Wobblies and other pacifists who had been jailed during the war for expressing antiwar sentiments. The ACLU opposed censorship by fighting efforts by the Customs Office and the Post Office to ban certain books from the mail. As you will read in Chapter 29, the ACLU would later play a leading role in one of the most controversial trials of the 1920s.

The first Ku Klux Klan arose during Reconstruction to intimidate freedmen. It faded away after Reconstruction but was reborn in 1915. This new KKK targeted African Americans, immigrants, Jews, Catholics, and anyone with values that Klan members saw as "un-American."

26.6 Enduring Racial and Religious Tensions

On July 27, 1927, six years after Sacco and Vanzetti were convicted of murder, the Lowell Committee concluded that the trial of the two men had been fair. On August 23, 1927, the two men were executed. Decades after their executions, doubts remain about their guilt. Modern analysis of the evidence has confirmed that the gun found on Sacco at the time of his arrest was one of the murder weapons. This suggests that Sacco was guilty of the crime. But no one has found proof to link Vanzetti to the murders. "I have suffered because I was an Italian," Vanzetti wrote from prison.

Asians and African Americans Face Discrimination Italians were not the only victims of such prejudice. Asian immigrants also faced severe legal discrimination. Asians were barred from becoming citizens and, in several states, from owning land. Many states also banned marriages between whites and Asians.

African Americans faced continuing discrimination as well. At the end of World War I, returning black soldiers had high hopes that their service to the country would lessen prejudice. These hopes proved illusory. Black veterans had problems finding jobs. In some places, lynching made an ugly comeback. More than 70 blacks were murdered by lynch mobs in 1919.

In the summer of 1919, tensions between whites and blacks erupted into race riots. The most serious riot occurred in Chicago when whites killed a black swimmer who had strayed into the white section of a Lake Michigan beach. Some 38 people were killed and 500 injured in the riots that followed. The African American poet Claude McKay wrote of the summer of 1919:

> If we must die, let it not be like hogs
> Hunted and penned in an inglorious spot,
> While round us bark the mad and hungry dogs,
> Making their mock at our accursed lot.
> If we must die, O let us nobly die, . . .
> Like men we'll face the murderous, cowardly pack,
> Pressed to the wall, dying, but fighting back!
> —Claude McKay, "If We Must Die," 1919

In this climate of violence, many African Americans responded to the message of a leader named Marcus Garvey. The Jamaican-born Garvey believed blacks would never be treated fairly in a white-dominated country. "Our success educationally, industrially, and politically is based upon the protection of a nation founded by ourselves," he argued. "And the nation can be nowhere else but in Africa."

Garvey's **Back-to-Africa movement** attracted up to 2 million followers. He also collected enough money to start several businesses, including a steamship line intended to transport his followers to Africa. In 1925, however, Garvey was imprisoned for mail fraud connected with the sale of stock in one of his businesses. After that, his Back-to-Africa movement faded away. Yet Garvey had raised a critical issue: Should African Americans create a separate society or work for an integrated one?

Born in Jamaica, Marcus Garvey traveled widely throughout the Americas. Everywhere he went, he saw discrimination against blacks and the need to restore black pride in people of African heritage. "Up, you mighty race," he told his followers. "You can accomplish what you will." In 1920, while addressing a crowd of 25,000 in New York City, he outlined a plan to build a new black nation in Africa.

Jews and Catholics Battle Religious Prejudice The influx of 2.4 million Jewish immigrants from eastern Europe stirred up **anti-Semitism**—prejudice against Jews. In some communities, landlords refused to rent apartments to Jewish tenants. Colleges limited the number of Jewish students they accepted. Many ads for jobs stated "Christians only."

The Leo Frank case, which gave birth to the new Ku Klux Klan, also led to the founding of the Anti-Defamation League (ADL) in 1913. The organization's immediate goal was "to stop the defamation [false accusation] of the Jewish people." Its longer-term mission was "to secure justice and fair treatment to all citizens alike." Throughout the 1920s, the ADL battled discrimination against Jews in all areas of life.

Catholics were also targets of religious prejudice. In 1928, the Democratic Party nominated New York Governor Al Smith, a Catholic, for president. Soon, rumors swept the country that if Smith were elected, the Catholic pope would run the United States. Smith spent most of the campaign trying to persuade voters that his religious beliefs did not present a threat to the nation.

Smith was not convincing enough to overcome strong anti-Catholic sentiment in many parts of the country. For the first time since the end of Reconstruction, the Republican Party carried several states in the South. More than 30 years would pass before another Catholic candidate would be nominated for the nation's highest office.

Summary

Rising economic, political, and social tensions marked the years just after World War I. This tense atmosphere affected the murder trial of Nicola Sacco and Bartolomeo Vanzetti. Both men were sentenced to death, despite weak evidence. Some Americans saw Sacco and Vanzetti as victims of prejudice against immigrants and radicals.

Recession A poorly planned demobilization resulted in an economic recession after World War I. As unemployment rose, living standards for all but the richest Americans declined.

Labor unrest Unions staged thousands of strikes for better wages and working conditions. Despite these efforts, unions began to lose strength, and their membership declined.

Red Scare Fear of socialists, communists, and anarchists fueled the Red Scare. Attorney General Mitchell Palmer led raids against suspected subversives, often violating their civil liberties.

Immigration restriction Congress responded to anti-immigrant pressure by restricting immigration. A quota system also limited the number of immigrants from each country.

Back-to-Africa movement African Americans were disappointed that their service to the country in World War I did not reduce racial prejudice. Marcus Garvey's Back-to-Africa movement appealed to blacks who had given up hope for equality in the United States.

Discrimination Nativism surged in the postwar years. A revived Ku Klux Klan targeted blacks, immigrants, Jews, and Catholics as un-American. The Anti-Defamation League began in response to anti-Semitism. The American Civil Liberties Union formed to protect freedom of speech.

Chapter 27

The Politics of Normalcy

Did the Republican Era of the 1920s bring peace and prosperity to all Americans?

27.1 Introduction

Between 1917 and 1920, the United States experienced war, strikes, recession, and race riots. Ohio Senator Warren G. Harding knew what most Americans wanted next: peace and quiet. In May 1920, he told a Boston audience,

> America's present need is not heroics, but healing; not nostrums [ineffective remedies], but normalcy; . . . not agitation, but adjustment; not surgery, but serenity; not the dramatic, but the dispassionate [calm]; not experiment, but equipoise [balance]; not submergence in internationality, but sustainment in triumphant nationality.
>
> —Senator Warren G. Harding, speech in Boston, 1920

It was a typical Harding speech in the puffed-up, pompous style he called "bloviating." Pennsylvania Senator Boies Penrose jokingly warned Republican leaders, "Keep Warren at home. Don't let him make any speeches. If he goes out on a tour, somebody's sure to ask him questions, and Warren's just the sort of . . . fool that'll try to answer them."

For all of its wordiness, Harding's speech captured the public mood perfectly. Later that year, he was nominated to be the Republican candidate for president. Taking Penrose's advice, Harding campaigned from his front porch and gave short speeches, promising to bring America "back to **normalcy**." That promise won him more than 60 percent of the vote.

For Harding, normalcy meant a return to life as it was in prewar America. Wilson's concentration on world affairs would be replaced by a focus on prosperity at home. In his inaugural address, Harding declared, "We want less government in business and more business in government." Afterward, a woman in the audience observed, "We have had Wilson for eight years, and I have not understood him. I understand Harding already." Harding's inauguration began the Republican Era, which lasted through the 1920s.

Famous for leading his presidential campaign from his porch, Warren G. Harding took office in 1921. On inauguration day, the handsome, people-loving Harding was a striking contrast to the frail Woodrow Wilson. No one would have guessed that Harding's health would quickly fail. He died in office in 1923.

◀ President Warren Harding throws first ball of the baseball season, 1922

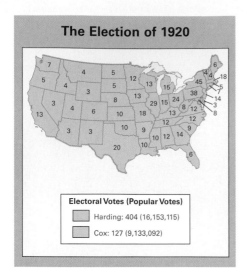

The Election of 1920

Electoral Votes (Popular Votes)

Harding: 404 (16,153,115)

Cox: 127 (9,133,092)

Republican Warren G. Harding defeated Democrat James M. Cox by a wide margin in 1920. This was the first election in which women were allowed to vote everywhere in the country.

27.2 A Republican Era Begins

The contrast between the aged, sickly Woodrow Wilson and the robust Warren Harding was proof enough that a new era had arrived. But there was more. Harding was the first president to have his inauguration speech amplified through loudspeakers. After speaking, he walked to the Senate to personally nominate his cabinet members. No president had done that since George Washington. On entering the White House, he opened the front gates, raised the blinds, and welcomed the public. Ordinary Americans had not been allowed on the White House grounds since the beginning of World War I.

Harding Cuts Taxes and Spending Before going into politics, Harding had owned a small newspaper in his hometown of Marion, Ohio. "He looks like a president," thought Harry Daugherty when he first met Harding in 1899. For the next 21 years, Daugherty managed Harding's political career all the way to the White House.

By his own admission, Harding was "a man of limited talents from a small town." But his cheerful, gregarious nature kept him popular with the public. So did his commitment to the free enterprise system. Such an economic system is characterized by private ownership of property, including land and resources. It relies on competition for profits and the forces of supply and demand to determine what goods and services should be produced and at what price.

With the support of a Republican Congress, Harding set to work to end the postwar recession. He repealed taxes that had been raised under Wilson to fund the war effort. Harding also reduced federal spending. His budget director, Chicago banker Charles Dawes, made the government operate in a more efficient way. Dawes's efforts were believed to have saved at least a billion tax dollars annually at a time when the federal government's yearly spending came to less than $5 billion. The resulting surplus was used to pay down the national debt.

Harding's **fiscal policy,** or approach to taxes and government spending, brought renewed prosperity. Prices plunged in 1921, so Americans could afford more goods and services. Unemployment dropped from nearly 12 percent when Harding took office to just above 2 percent in 1923.

Harding's Friends Betray Him: The Teapot Dome Scandal A loyal friend, Harding filled several government positions with old pals from Ohio. The leading member of this "Ohio Gang" was Harding's former campaign manager and now attorney general, Harry Daugherty. Another old friend, New Mexico Senator Albert Fall, became Harding's secretary of the interior.

But the Ohio Gang betrayed Harding's trust. Daugherty, for example, took bribes from suspects accused of crimes. The worst instance of corruption was the Teapot Dome Scandal, which began when Secretary of the Interior Fall persuaded Harding to give him control over national oil reserves in Elk Hills, California, and Teapot Dome, Wyoming. Fall then leased the oil reserves to two companies that had paid him $360,000 in bribes. When the bribes became public, Fall resigned. But the scandal left the public wondering whether any other national properties had been offered up for sale.

Harding stood by his friends, saying, "If Albert Fall isn't an honest man, I am not fit to be president of the United States." In fact, Harding was not all that physically fit. While on a "bloviating" tour of the West, Harding suffered a heart attack in San Francisco. He died on August 2, 1923.

Calvin Coolidge Promotes Business On August 3, 1923, Vice President Calvin Coolidge took the oath of office in a Vermont farmhouse. Nicknamed "Silent Cal," Coolidge was a small man of few words. Americans saw in him the quiet virtues of small-town New England: integrity, hard work, and thriftiness.

Like Harding, Coolidge believed "the chief business of the American people is business." But for Coolidge, business was more than a way to make a living. It was a worthy calling. "The man who builds a factory builds a temple," he wrote. "And the man who works there worships there."

Coolidge coasted to an easy victory in the election of 1924. Working closely with Treasury Secretary Andrew Mellon, Coolidge worked to cut taxes and eliminate unnecessary spending. He pushed for reductions in corporate taxes, income taxes, and **inheritance taxes**—taxes on assets received from people who have died. Coolidge even cut his own White House budget, economizing in little ways, such as reducing the number of towels in the bathrooms.

Under Coolidge, the nation continued to prosper. Americans assumed he would run for reelection in 1928. But in August 1927, while on vacation, he shocked reporters by handing them a statement that simply said, "I do not choose to run for president in 1928." Silent Cal had spoken.

Calvin Coolidge was at his family's dairy farm in Vermont when President Harding died. His father administered the presidential oath, using a family Bible. Although Coolidge had a very different personality from Harding, his policies were similar. He easily won reelection in 1924.

Herbert Hoover Promises to "End Poverty as We Know It" In 1928, the Republican Party turned to Herbert Hoover as its presidential nominee. Hoover was an American success story. Born in West Branch, Iowa, in 1874, he was orphaned at a young age. Despite this, he worked his way through college and became a very wealthy mining engineer. Hoover's success, along with his Quaker upbringing, inspired him to write a book titled *American Individualism*. In it, he wrote of his "abiding faith in the intelligence, the initiative, the character, the courage, and the divine touch in the individual."

At the age of 40, Hoover decided to leave engineering and devote his life to public service. During World War I, he headed President Woodrow Wilson's Food Administration. When the war ended, Hoover gained fame by setting up programs to feed the hungry in Europe. In 1921, President Harding made Hoover his secretary of commerce.

Like Harding and Coolidge, Hoover believed in promoting business. He encouraged what he called "associationalism." This involved bringing industry leaders together to improve economic efficiency. Hoover hoped that as businesses flourished, poverty would disappear. In accepting the Republican nomination for president in 1928, he said,

> We in America today are nearer to the final triumph over poverty than ever before in the history of any land. The poor-house is vanishing from among us. We have not yet reached the goal, but given a chance to go forward with the policies of the last eight years, we shall soon with the help of God be in sight of the day when poverty will be banished from this nation.
>
> —Herbert Hoover, speech accepting the Republican nomination, 1928

Before running for president, Herbert Hoover directed the Food Administration. Hoover was an American success story. Orphaned at age 9, he became a millionaire by age 40. He then turned to public service. When Hoover became president in 1929, he pledged to end poverty in the United States.

27.3 Engaging the World in an Era of Isolationism

The horrors of World War I had left many Americans yearning for a withdrawal from international affairs, a policy that became known as **isolationism**. Isolationist attitudes had been strong in the Senate when it had voted down the Treaty of Versailles. At heart, however, Harding, Coolidge, and Hoover were not isolationists. They recognized that foreign trade connected American farmers and businesspeople to the rest of the world.

In 1921, the date of this cartoon, the United States, along with other nations, had agreed to reduce the number of weapons in and size of their military. This cartoon highlights the dispute between those who support and oppose disarmament. Here, a figure representing the world bitterly remarks to Uncle Sam that "ninety thousand of your tax-payers just spent a fortune to see a fight!"

Avoiding Involvement in Europe Isolationist feeling was strongest toward Europe. Although in his campaign, Harding had favored entry into the League of Nations, upon taking office, he declared, "We seek no part in directing the destinies of the Old World." During his presidency, the State Department did not even open mail from the League.

American distrust of the League of Nations softened with time. The United States sent delegates to several League conferences in the 1920s. Presidents Harding and Coolidge also supported U.S. membership in an international court of justice known as the World Court. Established by the League in 1921, the World Court's purpose was to settle international disputes before they turned into wars. By the time the Senate approved membership in 1926, it had attached so many reservations that the other member nations refused to approve U.S. membership.

Promoting Peace Through Disarmament Although public opinion leaned toward isolationism, Americans also longed for world peace. President Harding responded by inviting representatives of Great Britain, France, Italy, and Japan to Washington to discuss naval **disarmament,** or weapons reduction. When the **Washington Naval Conference** opened in 1921, Secretary of State Charles Evan Hughes shocked the delegates by offering to scrap 30 U.S. warships. The other nations soon agreed to limit the size of their navies as well.

Supporters of the naval disarmament agreement hoped it would discourage future wars. Naysayers, however, feared that military ambitions would not be so easily contained. They were right. The Washington Naval Conference did limit the construction of large warships, but it did not affect smaller ships and submarines. Soon Japan, Great Britain, and the United States were adding cruisers and other small ships to their fleets.

Using Diplomacy to Outlaw War Efforts to negotiate an end to warfare peaked in 1928, when the United States signed the **Kellogg-Briand Pact.** This treaty began with an agreement between the United States and France to outlaw war between their countries. Eventually 62 nations signed the pact, which rejected war as "an instrument of national policy."

Americans cheered the Kellogg-Briand Pact as an important step toward world peace. "It is a thing to rejoice over," gushed the Boston *Herald*. More practical-minded realists sneered that this "international kiss" was not worth much, because it still permitted defensive wars. But the Senate approved the treaty by a vote of 85 to 1.

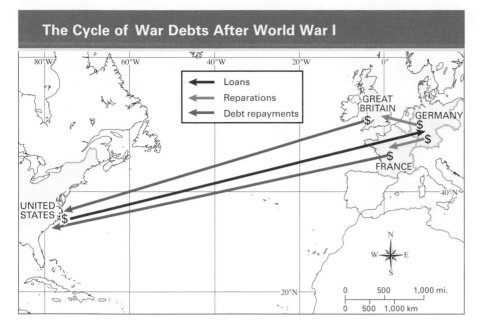

The Cycle of War Debts After World War I

Loans
Reparations
Debt repayments

GREAT BRITAIN
GERMANY
FRANCE
UNITED STATES

Europe's war debt threatened American prosperity. Charles Dawes developed a "circular loan" program to reduce the war debt. The United States loaned money to Germany, which used the money to pay back Great Britain and France. Great Britain and France then paid back the United States.

Settling Europe's War Debts In addition to worrying about the next war, the Republican presidents worked to clean up debts from the last one. At the end of World War I, Great Britain and France owed U.S. lenders $11 billion. With their economies in shambles, these countries relied on reparations from Germany to make their loan payments. The German economy, however, was in even worse shape. By 1923, Germany had stopped making reparation payments.

Charles Dawes, a banker who had served as Harding's budget director, came up with a solution to the debt crisis. American banks would loan money to Germany. Germany would use that money to pay reparations to Great Britain and France. Great Britain and France would then repay what they owed American lenders. The circular flow of money in the **Dawes Plan** worked for a while. But it also increased the amount of money Germany owed the United States, an issue that would cause problems later.

Reducing Involvement in Latin America Isolationist sentiment also had an impact on U.S. policy toward Latin America. When Harding took office in 1921, U.S. troops were stationed in Nicaragua, the Dominican Republic, and Haiti. Harding and Coolidge both tried to reduce such entanglements. In 1921, Harding settled a long dispute with Colombia over the Panama Canal. Three years later, Coolidge withdrew troops from the Dominican Republic. Still, business ties and American investments continued to pull the United States into Latin American affairs. After withdrawing the marines from Nicaragua in 1925, Coolidge sent them back in 1927 to counter a revolution.

Hoover, however, embraced a policy of nonintervention. Immediately after his election in 1928, he embarked on a goodwill tour of Latin America. In 1930, he signaled his rejection of the Roosevelt Corollary by announcing that the United States did not have the right to intervene militarily in Latin America. Even when revolutions shook Panama, Cuba, and Honduras in 1931, Hoover did not send troops. "I have no desire," he said, "for representation of the American government abroad through our military forces."

Under the economic policies of the Republican presidents, the post-World War I recession faded away. Businesses began to expand. Productivity increased dramatically. Unemployment dropped and wages rose to double what they had been before the war. By 1929, the United States was producing 40 percent of the world's manufactured goods. "Big business in America," reported muckraking journalist Lincoln Steffens, "is providing what the socialists held up as their goal—food, shelter, clothing for all."

After the debut of airplanes as weapons in World War I, Boeing Airplane Company began building them to deliver mail and transport passengers. In 1926, U.S. airlines carried only around 6,000 passengers. In 1930, the number soared to more than 400,000. Anticipating this growth, Congress passed the Air Commerce Act in 1926. The act called for the licensing of pilots and provided for a system of navigation aids across the country to make passenger service safer.

Henry Ford Pioneers a New Age of Mass Production The automobile industry led this new age of productivity. In 1910, U.S. automakers built fewer than 200,000 cars a year at prices that only the wealthy could afford. By 1929, at least half of all American families owned a car. The credit for this transformation of the car from luxury item to consumer good goes to Detroit automaker Henry Ford.

Ford's goal was to mass-produce cars in order to lower their prices. "The public should always be wondering how it is possible to give so much for the money," he wrote. He accomplished his goal by designing a revolutionary moving assembly line that cut production time from 14 to six hours. He then could cut the price of his cars from $950 in 1908 to under $290 in 1926.

When he unveiled his assembly line in 1914, Ford made a stunning announcement. He was more than doubling his workers' pay from the $2.40 per nine-hour day common in his industry to $5.00 per eight-hour day. The public loved him for it. Business leaders hated him, saying that he was ruining the labor market. Looking back, historian Frederick Lewis Allen observed,

> What Ford had actually done—in his manufacturing techniques, his deliberate price cutting, and his deliberate wage raising—was to demonstrate . . . one of the great principles of modern industrialism . . . This is the principle that the more goods you produce, the less it costs to produce them; and the more people are well off, the more they can buy, thus making this lavish and economical production possible.
>
> —Frederick Lewis Allen, *The Big Change,* 1952

Ford sold so many cars that by the mid-1920s his Detroit, Michigan, factory complex had 19 buildings covering 2 square miles. A new car rolled off his assembly lines every 10 seconds. By 1930, Ford had produced 20 million cars.

Innovations Give Birth to New Industries The automobile industry's rapid expansion fueled growth in other industries, such as steel, rubber, and oil. Highway construction boomed. Restaurants and hotels sprang up along new roads to meet the needs of motorists. The popularity of cars also created new service industries, such as gas stations and repair shops. By the mid-1920s, one of every eight American workers had a job related to the auto industry.

The airplane industry also boomed. During World War I, airplanes had become weapons. In 1927, the Boeing Airplane Company won the U.S. Post Office contract to fly mail and passengers from Chicago to San Francisco and back. By 1930, there were 38 domestic and five international airlines operating in the United States. The airplane had been transformed from novelty to vehicle.

A "plastics craze" also changed American life in the 1920s. Synthetic fibers like rayon revolutionized the clothing industry. See-through cellophane became the first fully flexible, waterproof wrapping material. Bakelite, the first plastic that would not burn, boil, melt, or dissolve in any common solvent, was vital to the production of radios. Radio had first been used for wireless communication among ships at sea. By 1920, radio stations had sprouted up in many U.S. cities. Radio production soared as a result. By 1929, radios were a big business, with Americans spending $850 million on sets and parts that year alone.

Big Businesses Get Even Bigger Businesses were not only prospering but also getting bigger due to a wave of **consolidation**. Consolidation is the merging, or combining, of two businesses. During the Progressive Era, antitrust laws had slowed business consolidation. Harding, Coolidge, and Hoover, in contrast, chose to ignore antitrust laws. The Republican presidents defended consolidation on the grounds that it made the economy more efficient.

Consolidation came early to the automobile industry. Before 1910, there were hundreds of companies building cars in the United States. By 1929, three automakers—Ford, General Motors, and Chrysler—built almost 90 percent of the cars on the market. General Motors was the brainchild of an entrepreneur named William Durant. Unlike Ford, who made just one car model, Durant offered several models at different price levels. By the end of the decade, General Motors had become the nation's leading automaker.

The story was similar in other industries. In the 1920s, a handful of **holding companies** bought up nearly 5,000 small utility companies. A holding company is a corporation that owns or controls other companies by buying up their stock. By 1929, about two thirds of American homes were wired for electricity, and consolidation led to a decline in the cost of electricity.

Consolidation also revolutionized the grocery business, as the Great Atlantic and Pacific Tea Company (A&P) launched the first grocery store chain. Mom-and-pop grocery shops were driven out of business as A&P's chain grew from fewer than 5,000 stores in 1920 to more than 15,000 by 1929. Not everyone viewed this triumph of big business as positive. An anti-chain store movement swept through a number of states and cities.

Speculators Aim to Get Rich Quick As the good times rolled on, some Americans got caught up in get-rich-quick schemes, such as Ponzi Scheme and the Florida Land Boom. In this Florida scheme, shady real estate developers sold lots along the Florida coast to eager **speculators** in other parts of the country. A speculator is someone who takes the risk of buying something in the hope of selling it for a higher price later. As long as prices were going up, no one cared that some of the lots were under water. Prices collapsed, however, after a hurricane devastated the Florida coast. Many speculators were left with nothing but near-worthless land.

During the Republican Era, ordinary Americans put money in get-rich-quick schemes, like the Florida Land Boom. Speculators bought land without seeing it in hopes of making a quick profit. Many learned later that the land they owned was under water or hard to build on, making it worthless.

How Does a Ponzi Scheme Work?

Charles Ponzi, an Italian immigrant, came up with one of the get-rich-quick schemes of the time. Ponzi advertised that he had a surefire way to double investors' money in just 90 days. He paid off a few early investors to make the scheme look legitimate. New investors, lured in by the success of others, poured money into the scheme. Eventually, Ponzi was taking in close to a million dollars a month. Unfortunately for Ponzi and his investors, a newspaper revealed that he was a fraud. By then, thousands of people had lost an estimated $10 million. Here is how his scheme worked.

1. Ponzi makes his pitch.

2. Some people invest.

3. Ponzi uses their money to reward early investors.

4. Seeing early investors double their money makes others eager to invest.

Others saw the stock market as the road to riches. In the past, only wealthy people had owned stock. During the 1920s, stock ownership had spread to the middle class. John Raskob, a General Motors executive, encouraged stock buying in a *Ladies' Home Journal* article titled "Everybody Ought to Be Rich." Raskob told his readers that if they invested a mere $15 a month in the stock market, they could expect a massive payoff of $80,000 in 20 years.

Many Americans took his advice. Housewives invested their pocket money in stocks. Barbers, cab drivers, and elevator operators bought stocks on "hot tips" they had overheard while working. As money poured into the market, stock prices soared. The **Dow Jones Industrial Average,** a measure of stock prices still used today, doubled between May 1928 and September 1929.

Left Out of the Boom: Enduring Poverty Between 1921 and 1929, the **gross national product (GNP)** of the United States rose by 40 percent. The GNP is a measure of the total value of goods and services produced within a country in a year. However, not all Americans shared in the prosperity. In 1929, a family of four needed $2,500 a year to live decently. More than half the families filing tax returns that year earned $1,500 or less.

The 1920s were hard times for farmers, many of whom were deeply in debt after the war. Surplus crops also caused farm prices to collapse. Hard times for farmers meant even harder times for farmworkers. Mexican, Mexican American, Asian, and Asian American workers earned the lowest wages and endured the worst working and living conditions.

Unskilled workers also fared poorly in the 1920s. Workers in old industries struggled to stay employed. Coal miners were laid off by the thousands as gasoline, natural gas, and electricity became more popular sources of energy. The textile industry faced heavy competition from new synthetic fabrics. Among the hardest hit were African Americans, who were often the last to be hired and the first to be fired. They were usually paid less than their white counterparts and were also barred from most unions.

Summary

The election of 1920 launched a decade-long Republican Era in national politics. During that time, three Republican presidents—Warren G. Harding, Calvin Coolidge, and Herbert Hoover—worked to return the nation to "normalcy," or peace and prosperity.

Isolationism After World War I, many Americans favored a policy of isolationism, or withdrawal from international affairs.

Free enterprise system The Republican presidents supported individual enterprise and the free enterprise system by adopting business-friendly fiscal policies. The government cut taxes and spending.

Teapot Dome Scandal The Harding administration was marred by corruption. Harding's distress over the Teapot Dome Scandal contributed to his declining health. He died in office in 1923.

Washington Naval Conference The Republican presidents turned to diplomacy to prevent another world war. The Washington Naval Conference attempted to reduce military competition by limiting the size of the world's most powerful navies.

Kellogg-Briand Pact Sixty-two nations signed this treaty, in which they agreed to outlaw war.

Dawes Plan The United States set up the Dawes Plan to help European nations pay their war debts to American lenders.

Dow Jones Industrial Average Americans hoping to "get rich quick" engaged in speculation in land and stocks. The Dow Jones Industrial Average rose as money flowed into the stock market.

Economic boom The economy prospered as businesses boomed. Business consolidation led to the domination of most major industries by just a few companies. However, poverty persisted, and many farmers and workers were left out of the boom.

28.3 Americans Take to the Air and Roads

On May 20, 1927, a little-known airmail pilot from Minnesota took off on an extraordinary journey. Charles Lindbergh was competing for the Orteig Prize—$25,000 for the first nonstop flight from New York City to Paris. He packed sandwiches, two canteens of water, and 451 gallons of gas. Lindbergh hit storm clouds and thick fog over the Atlantic that forced him at times to barely skim the ocean waves. The sun set as he drew near France. He later wrote,

> I first saw the lights of Paris a little before 10 P.M. . . .and a few minutes later I was circling the Eiffel Tower at an altitude of about four thousand feet . . . The lights of Le Bourget [airfield] were plainly visible . . . I could make out long lines of hangers, and the roads appeared to be jammed with cars.
>
> —Charles Lindbergh, *The Spirit of St. Louis,* 1953

When Lindbergh landed, 100,000 people were waiting to greet him. Overnight, he had become the biggest celebrity of the decade. That "Lucky Lindy" did not seem to care about such adulation only endeared him more to the public.

Airplanes Give Americans Wings Airplanes had proven their usefulness during World War I. After the war, the U.S. government offered thousands of surplus warplanes for sale at bargain prices. Made of wood and canvas, these planes were not all that safe. Still, many wartime pilots bought the planes and used them for an exciting but dangerous style of flying called barnstorming.

Barnstormers toured the country, putting on daring air shows at county fairs and other events. They wowed audiences by flying planes in great loops and spirals. "Wing walkers" risked death by walking from wingtip to wingtip of a plane while it was in flight. Others leaped from the wing of one flying plane to another. Many of the planes crashed, and a number of barnstormers were killed. Lindbergh was one of the lucky barnstormers to live to old age.

The U.S. Post Office also bought surplus military planes to fly mail between a few large cities. The first transcontinental airmail route was opened between New York and San Francisco in 1920. Airmail greatly aided the growth of commercial aviation. Meanwhile, engineers were working to design safer, more powerful transport planes. By 1926, Henry Ford was producing an all-metal airplane powered by three engines rather than one. The Ford Tri-Motor could carry 10 passengers at speeds of 100 miles per hour.

In the early days of flight, pilots became celebrities. Adoring fans welcomed Lindbergh back from France with a ticker-tape parade in New York City, showering him with 1,800 tons of stockbrokers' ticker tape and confetti. In 1932, Amelia Earhart became the first woman to fly solo across the Atlantic. Congress awarded her the Distinguished Flying Cross. At the medal ceremony, she said her flight had proven that men and women were equal in "jobs requiring intelligence, coordination, speed, coolness, and willpower."

Charles Lindbergh stands in front of *The Spirit of St. Louis*, the plane he flew on his solo flight across the Atlantic. The flight from New York to Paris took 33½ hours and made Lindbergh an international hero.

The skies were friendly to female pilots in the 1920s. The most famous, Amelia Earhart, was the first woman to fly solo across the Atlantic Ocean. In 1935, she became the first person to fly alone from Hawaii to California. When Earhart tried to fly around the world in 1937, her plane vanished over the Pacific Ocean.

Henry Ford inspired America's love affair with the automobile. In the 1920s, Ford's Model T's were plain but affordable. When other manufacturers began to produce better-looking cars, Ford stopped making the Model T and instead made the Model A—another great success.

Automobiles Reshape American Life By making cars affordable, automaker Henry Ford had changed the way Americans lived. Cars quickly became more than just another means of transportation. A car gave women and teenagers a new sense of freedom. It ended the isolation of farmers. It made travel to faraway places enjoyable. By the late 1920s, Americans owned more cars than bathtubs. As one woman explained, "You can't drive to town in a bathtub."

The automobile changed where Americans lived. Urban workers no longer had to live within walking distance of their workplace or near a streetcar line to get to work. Suburbs began to spread farther around cities as people found it easier to travel to and from work by car. In the 1920s, for the first time in the nation's history, suburbs grew more quickly than cities.

Before cars became popular, most roads were dirt tracks. When it rained, automobiles sometimes sank to their hubcaps in mud. Motorists often had to wait days for mud to dry before they could move on. The Federal Highway Act of 1916 encouraged states to create highway departments to address this problem. Congress passed another highway act in 1921 to support road building.

As highways crept across the continent, new businesses took root beside them. Gas stations, diners, campgrounds, and motels sprang up to serve the needs of the car traveler. Advertising billboards became common sights on roadsides. At the same time, death tolls from accidents rose. The number of people killed in automobile accidents each year increased from fewer than 5,000 before the 1920s to more than 30,000 by the 1930s. Historian Frederick Lewis Allen noted yet another change brought about by the car:

> The automobile age brought a parking problem that was forever being solved and then unsolving itself again. During the early nineteen-twenties the commuters who left their cars at the suburban railway stations at first parked them at the edge of the station drive; then they needed a special parking lot, and pretty soon an extended parking lot, and in due course, a still bigger one—and the larger the lot grew, the more people wanted to use it.
> —Frederick Lewis Allen, *The Big Change*, 1952

28.4 Mass Media Shape American Popular Culture

Adoring fans worshipped movie star Rudolph Valentino as the "Great Lover." When he died suddenly at the age of 31, more than 100,000 people lined New York City streets to witness his funeral. It was an astonishing send-off for an Italian immigrant who had come to New York as a teenager in 1913. It was also a sign that Valentino had become an important part of his adopted country's **popular culture**. Popular culture is the culture of ordinary people and includes their music, art, literature, and entertainment. Popular culture is shaped by industries that spread information and ideas, especially the mass media.

Print Media Bring Popular Culture to a National Audience Newspapers and magazines had long been sources of information for Americans. During the 1920s, the amount of printed material available expanded enormously. By 1929, Americans were buying more than 200 million copies a year of popular national magazines, such as the *Saturday Evening Post, Ladies' Home Journal, Reader's Digest,* and *Time.*

As newspaper and magazine circulation increased, more and more people read the same stories, learned of the same events, and saw the same ideas and fashions. As a result, a popular culture common to all regions of the United States began to take shape. At the same time, regional differences that had once divided Americans began to fade in importance.

Radio Gives Popular Culture a Voice Radio burst onto the American scene in the 1920s. Like newspapers and magazines, radio was a mass medium that could reach very large audiences. Suddenly, popular culture had a voice.

Radio station KDKA in Pittsburgh, Pennsylvania, is thought to be the first commercial radio station. When it broadcast the results of the 1920 presidential election, people began to have an inkling of what this new medium could do. As a result, radio sales took off.

Radio pioneer David Sarnoff had a huge impact on the development of broadcast radio. Sarnoff, a Jewish immigrant from Russia, began working for

David Sarnoff was a leader in the growth of radio and television. He pioneered the development of radio programming, bringing news, music, tears, and laughter into homes across the nation.

the Marconi Wireless Telegraph Company in 1906. Radio was first called the "wireless," because it received signals through the air rather than over wires, as the telephone did. On April 14, 1912, Sarnoff picked up a message relayed to New York City by ships at sea. It read, "*Titanic* ran into iceberg, sinking fast." For the next 72 hours, he stayed at his post, relaying the names of survivors to anxious relatives as the disaster at sea unfolded.

In 1919, Radio Corporation of America (RCA), a company that built radios, bought Marconi Wireless. Sarnoff saw that for RCA to sell many radios, it had to invest in programming that people would want to hear. But this idea was not easy to promote. "The wireless music box has no imaginable commercial value," others argued. "Who would pay for a message sent to nobody in particular?" To prove them wrong, Sarnoff arranged the broadcast of the Dempsey-Carpentier boxing match in 1921. Public response to this event confirmed the power of radio broadcasting to reach large numbers of people.

Sarnoff then proposed that RCA form a nationwide broadcasting network. He saw this network as a collection of radio stations across the country that would share programming. His proposal led to the formation of the National Broadcasting Company, or NBC. Much later, Sarnoff applied his vision to another medium—television. In 1941, NBC made the first commercial television broadcast. By then, Sarnoff was president of NBC, where he was known to all as "the General."

People soon came to expect radio stations to broadcast national news, such as elections. Many stations also brought play-by-play accounts of sports events to their listeners. In addition, stations began to broadcast regular programs of music, comedy, and drama. A situation comedy called *Amos 'n Andy* became so popular that many people would not answer their phones during its weekly broadcast.

Motion Pictures Create Movie Stars and Fans The movies, too, became a big business in the 1920s. Motion pictures were first developed in the 1890s. At that time, movies were silent. After World War I, people flocked to movie theaters, eager to escape the problems of the postwar recession. They drank in melodramatic love scenes, were thrilled by exciting fight scenes, and laughed at silly situations. Income from ticket sales rose from $301 million in 1921 to $721 million in 1929. Weekly attendance climbed from 50 million in 1920 to 90 million in 1929.

The discovery of how to add sound to movies revolutionized the motion picture industry. In 1927, *The Jazz Singer* became the first feature-length "talkie." It was an overnight hit. Dialogue became an important part of films, expanding the job of writers. While some silent-film stars adjusted to the new medium, a whole new group of stars were born.

Like radio, the movies changed popular culture in powerful ways. Movie stars became national celebrities. Fans worshipped stars such as Valentino. Actress Mary Pickford was called "America's Sweetheart." Motion pictures exposed Americans to new fashions, new hairstyles, and a loosening of the rules of social behavior. As one historian wrote, "Radio told the masses what to do, and movies showed them how to do it."

This photograph shows silent film actor Charlie Chaplin. His most iconic character is the Tramp. The Tramp's ill-fitting clothing and shuffling walk made him look like a hobo who had never owned a pair of shoes his own size. Although the Tramp was penniless and homeless, his lighthearted attitude suggested a spirit that could bounce back from the most crushing defeats.

Jeannette Rankin was the first female member of Congress. She won office in 1917 with a promise of "no war," as World War I raged in Europe. She was the only member of Congress to oppose both World War I and World War II. "You can no more win a war," she said, "than you can win an earthquake." Rankin's election opened the door to other female candidates.

28.5 Women Move Toward Greater Equality

Some of the most significant social changes of the 1920s occurred in the lives of women. In 1920, the Nineteenth Amendment granted women the right to vote. That same year, women voted on a nationwide basis in a presidential election for the first time. For suffragists, this was a dream come true. Many had hoped that because women had worked for the vote as a group, they would also vote as a group. The "woman's vote," they argued, could bring an end to war, crime, and corruption in politics. But that did not happen. Once women won the right to cast ballots, they tended to make the same choices as their male relatives made.

Women Organize and Enter Politics Many of the women who had worked so hard to gain the vote continued to be active in politics. Some formed a **grassroots organization** known as the League of Women Voters. A grassroots organization is created and run by its members, as opposed to a strong central leader. Members of the League of Women Voters worked to educate themselves and all voters on public issues.

Carrie Chapman Catt, a leader of the suffrage movement, saw that the vote alone would not gain women political power. The decisions that mattered most, she observed, were made behind a "locked door" by men. "You will have a long hard fight before you get behind that door," she warned, "for there is the engine that moves the wheels of your party machinery . . . If you really want women's votes to count, make your way there."

A few women did manage to get behind that door to run for public office. In 1917, Jeannette Rankin of Montana became the first woman elected to the House of Representatives. Two women—Nellie Tayloe Ross of Wyoming and Miriam Amanda Ferguson of Texas—became governors of their states in 1924. A year later, Representative Mae Ella Norton became the first woman to chair a congressional committee.

Women Lobby for Health Care and Equal Rights Women's groups also lobbied lawmakers to enact legislation of special interest to women. One of their concerns was the high death rate among new mothers and their infant children. In 1921, women persuaded Congress to pass the Sheppard-Towner Act. This act distributed federal funds to states to create health services for pregnant women, new mothers, and infant children. Despite fierce opposition, Congress enacted this law, in part because lawmakers wanted to appeal to new women voters.

Women's groups were less successful in other areas. In 1923, Alice Paul, representing the National Women's Party, persuaded two congressmen to introduce the equal rights amendment (ERA) to Congress. The intention of the ERA was to guarantee equal rights for all Americans, regardless of gender. It said simply, "Equality of rights under the law shall not be denied or abridged by the United States or by any State on account of sex."

Despite vigorous lobbying efforts, Congress did not approve the ERA that year. The amendment was reintroduced to Congress many times, always failing to win passage. Critics argued that the Constitution already guarantees equality under the law and that the amendment would abolish certain state and local laws

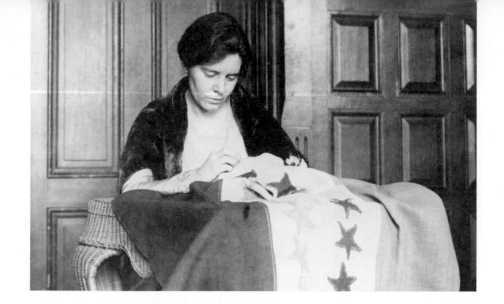

concerning women. In 1972, Congress finally approved the ERA and sent it to the states for ratification. Over the next decade, however, not enough states gave their approval to add the ERA to the Constitution. Despite this setback, Paul's amendment has been reintroduced to Congress every term since 1982.

Women Seek New Opportunities and Freedom The 1920s brought expanded educational and job opportunities for women, in addition to their greater political rights. The number of women completing high school doubled during the decade. By the 1920s, one out of every four college faculty members was a woman. Women were entering many professions once open only to men. The number of women professionals rose by 50 percent by the end of the decade.

With wider opportunities and greater incomes, women, especially young women, rebelled against old customs. They cut their hair into short "bobs," a hairstyle easier to care for than the long hair of their mothers' generation. They also wore makeup. Lipstick, rouge, and eye shadow were no longer signs of an "immoral" woman. Women also began to wear shorter dresses. In 1919, skirts hovered 6 inches above the ground. By 1927, skirts no longer covered the knees.

Women's social behavior changed as their hemlines rose. Drinking alcohol and smoking in public were no longer socially unacceptable. In fact, they were signs of a "modern" woman. Family patterns also changed. Between 1914 and 1929, the number of divorces per year more than doubled.

The decline in birth rates was due in part to the pioneering work of Margaret Sanger. As a nurse caring for poor women in New York City, Sanger saw a link between family size and human misery. "Everywhere we look," she wrote, "we see poverty and large families going hand in hand." She also came to believe that women would never achieve equality with men unless they could choose when and if to bear children. "No woman can call herself free who does not own and control her body," she said. "No woman can call herself free until she can choose consciously whether she will or will not be a mother."

In 1916, Sanger opened the country's first family planning clinic, only to be arrested and jailed. At the time, distributing birth control information was illegal in every state. Sanger dedicated her life to altering those laws. She also founded what became the nation's leading family planning organization—the Planned Parenthood Federation of America.

Margaret Sanger coined the term "birth control" to replace the older term "voluntary motherhood." In 1916, she was arrested for teaching women how to limit family size. Yet, by the 1920s, family planning clinics had begun to appear across the country.

Louis Armstrong was famous for his extended trumpet solos. People also loved Armstrong's gravelly voice. Contemporary jazz musician Wynton Marsalis has said of Armstrong, "You're talking about the deepest human feeling and the highest level of musical sophistication in the same man."

Fans called Bessie Smith the "Empress of the Blues." Orphaned at a young age, she began performing as a child. Gospel singer Mahalia Jackson remembered hearing Smith: "I feel she was having troubles like me. That's why it was such a comfort for the people of the South to hear her."

28.6 African American Musicians Launch the Jazz Age

When Louis Armstrong arrived in New York City in 1924 to join Fletcher Henderson's band, the band members were not impressed. They took one look at Armstrong's long underwear and big clumpy boots and wondered if this was really the famed cornet player. On the first night that Armstrong played a solo with the band at the Roseland Ballroom, he was nervous as well. A fellow horn player encouraged him to "close your eyes and play what you feel . . . Just let it go . . . Be yourself . . . Forget about all the people." Armstrong did as he was told, and his music soared. The audience stopped dancing to gather around him. For months afterward, the Roseland was packed with people who couldn't get enough of Armstrong's playing.

Armstrong was a master of a new kind of music called **jazz**. Unlike more formal types of music, jazz was hard to define. As Armstrong once said, "If you have to ask what jazz is, you'll never know." This new music became so popular in the 1920s that this decade is often called the Jazz Age.

Jazz Grows Out of Blues and Ragtime Jazz is a distinctly American musical form. It grew from a combination of influences, including African rhythms, European harmonies, African American folk music, and 19th-century American band music and instruments. At the turn of the 20th century, these forms began to mix and grew into blues and ragtime. The blues sprang from African American work songs, with elements of gospel and folk music. Many blues songs are about loneliness or sorrow, but others declare a humorous reaction to life's troubles. Ragtime used a syncopated, or irregularly accented, beat that gave the music a snappy, lilting feel.

Jazz combined the syncopation of ragtime with the deep feelings of the blues. To this already rich mix, jazz musicians added **improvisation**. This is a process by which musicians make up music as they play rather than relying solely on printed scores. So, to some degree, the jazz musician is his or her own composer.

Jazz was born in New Orleans. There, African American musicians were in demand to play at funeral parades, in minstrel shows, and as part of riverboat orchestras. Many gifted but untrained black musicians did not know how to read music. They began to make up melodies and expand on familiar tunes. Eventually, the improvised solo became an integral element of jazz. The jazz pianist Duke Ellington said of improvisation, "It's like an act of murder; you play with intent to commit something."

As boats and then railroads traveled away from New Orleans, they carried the new music with them. Soon jazz caught fire in Kansas City, St. Louis, Los Angeles, Chicago, and New York City. Bandleader Paul Williams remembered,

One moment, jazz was unknown, obscure—a low noise in a low dive. The next it had become a serious pastime of a hundred million people, the diversion of princes and millionaires . . . The time was ripe . . . The whole tempo of the country was speeded up . . . Americans . . . lived harder, faster than ever before. They could not go without some new outlet . . . the great American noise, jazz.
—Paul Williams, quoted in *Jazz: A History of America's Music*, 2000

Duke Ellington, shown here at the piano, was known for his good looks and elegance, as well as for his brilliant music. His band played at the Cotton Club for four years straight. "I am not playing 'jazz,'" he once told an interviewer. "I am trying to play the natural feelings of a people."

Night Clubs and Radio Bring Jazz to New Audiences In the 1920s, the black population in New York City more than doubled as a result of migration from the South. The black migrants brought their love of jazz with them to the city, and the African American neighborhood of Harlem became a magnet for jazz lovers.

The number of nightclubs and jazz clubs in Harlem in the 1920s is estimated at anywhere from 500 to several thousand. Nearly all the great jazz musicians played there at some point. Harlem's most famous jazz club was the Cotton Club. The floor show featured dancers in lavish costumes. The dancers and musicians were African American, but most of the patrons were white.

Although people could hear jazz at nightclubs in the cities, many first heard the new music on records. The first recordings of jazz were made in the 1910s. As the style gained popularity, many artists made records featuring their own work. Radio also helped spread jazz. In the late 1920s, the music of Duke Ellington and his band was broadcast nationwide from the Cotton Club. Benny Goodman, a white clarinetist, also had a popular band there. By 1929, a survey of radio stations showed that two thirds of airtime was devoted to jazz.

Jazz Becomes America's Music By then it was clear that jazz was here to stay. Jelly Roll Morton became the first musician to write the new music down. Band leader Duke Ellington composed jazz standards that are still played widely today. George Gershwin blended jazz with classical musical pieces like *Rhapsody in Blue*, which were written for full orchestras.

Young people, in particular, loved dancing to the new music. The Charleston and other dances swept the country. Unlike earlier forms of dancing, the new dances, with their kicks, twists, and turns, seemed wild and reckless. Many older Americans were shocked by jazz. They felt that its fast rhythms and improvisations were contributing to a loosening of moral standards. The *Ladies' Home Journal* even launched an anti-jazz crusade. Jazz, however, became the first uniquely American music to be played and loved around the world.

Langston Hughes published his first collection of poetry when he was only 24 years old and went on to publish more than 20 books of poetry and prose. In one of his essays, he wrote that his lifelong calling was "to explain and illuminate the Negro condition in America."

28.7 Writers and Artists in the 1920s

Young Langston Hughes had been living in Mexico with his father the year before he entered Columbia University. When he arrived in New York in 1921, his first stop was not his new college. Instead, Hughes headed to 135th Street, the heart of Harlem. He wrote of his arrival:

> I came out on the platform with two heavy bags and looked around . . . Hundreds of colored people. I hadn't seen any colored people for so long . . . I went up the steps and out into the bright September sunlight. Harlem! I stood there, dropped my bags, took a deep breath and felt happy again.
> —Langston Hughes, *The Big Sea*, 1940

For African American writers in the 1920s, Harlem was *the* place to be.

African Americans Create a "Harlem Renaissance" The word *renaissance* means a "revival" or "rebirth." It usually describes a literary or artistic movement. The **Harlem Renaissance** was the outpouring of creativity among African American writers, artists, and musicians who gathered in Harlem during the 1920s. They shared their work and encouraged each other.

Many African American writers who were part of this movement explored what it meant to be black in the United States. Langston Hughes wrote poetry, plays, and fiction that captured the anguish of African Americans' longing for equality. He composed one of his best-known poems while traveling to New York at the age of 17.

> I've known rivers:
> I've known rivers ancient as the world and older than the flow of human
>   blood in human veins.
> *My soul has grown deep like the rivers.*
>
> I bathed in the Euphrates when dawns were young.
> I built my hut near the Congo and it lulled me to sleep.
> I looked upon the Nile and raised the pyramids above it.
> I heard the singing of the Mississippi when Abe Lincoln went down to
>   New Orleans, and I've seen its muddy bosom turn all golden in the sunset.
>
> I've known rivers:
> Ancient, dusky rivers.
> *My soul has grown deep like the rivers.*
> —Langston Hughes, "The Negro Speaks of Rivers," 1920

James Weldon Johnson broke new ground with his best-known book, *The Autobiography of an Ex-Colored Man*. The novel describes an attempt by an African American to escape racial discrimination while exploring black culture in early 1900s. He also wrote the lyrics for "Lift Every Voice and Sing," which is sometimes called the Negro national anthem.

Zora Neale Hurston began her career as an anthropologist. She traveled through the South and the Caribbean, collecting the folklore of black people. She later transformed these into novels, short stories, and essays. Hurston's best-known novel is *Their Eyes Were Watching God*. It tells the story of an

African American woman living in the black town of Eaton, Florida. Hurston lets her characters, both men and women, speak in their own dialect and voices.

Literature and Art Reflect American Life White writers were also critical of American ideas and values. Sickened by the slaughter of war, some even moved to Europe, especially Paris. There they gathered at the apartment of writer Gertrude Stein, who called these young people the **Lost Generation**. They included E. E. Cummings, Ernest Hemingway, F. Scott Fitzgerald, John Dos Passos, and Sherwood Anderson. These writers developed themes and writing styles that still define modern literature.

The poet E. E. Cummings brought fresh ideas to his poetry. He used no capitalization and did not follow the usual way of presenting verse on a page. Ernest Hemingway used a direct, taut style in his novels. His first book, *The Sun Also Rises,* describes the rootless feelings of many young people after the war.

F. Scott Fitzgerald was the leading writer of the Jazz Age. His novel *The Great Gatsby* critiques the moral emptiness of upper-class American society. This passage from another Fitzgerald novel reveals the impact of the World War on the Lost Generation.

> This land here cost twenty lives a foot that summer . . . See that little stream—we could walk to it in two minutes. It took the British a month to walk it—a whole empire walking very slowly . . . leaving the dead like a million bloody rugs. No Europeans will ever do that again in this generation.
> —F. Scott Fitzgerald, *Tender Is the Night*, 1933

Writers in the United States also found fault with American life. Sinclair Lewis's novel *Main Street* looked at the tedium and narrowness of life in small-town America. Playwright Eugene O'Neill wove dark, poetic tragedies out of everyday life. Both O'Neill and Lewis won the Nobel Prize for Literature.

Artists also used their work to portray modern life. Edward Hopper's paintings of New York City and New England towns express a sense of loneliness and isolation. Rockwell Kent, one of the most popular artists of this period, used tonal contrasts to create moody scenes of nature.

Georgia O'Keeffe also found inspiration in nature. She is famous for her paintings of huge flowers and, later, desert landscapes. O'Keeffe once said of her paintings, "Nobody sees a flower—really—it is so small it takes time—we haven't time—and to see takes time, like to have a friend takes time."

Exploring Culture Becomes a Popular Pastime Americans responded to this explosion of culture with enthusiasm. Art museums displayed the works of new artists such as Hopper and O'Keeffe. Magazines also showcased popular art of the time.

The American public developed a growing interest in literature as well. Magazines and newspapers helped introduce new writers to a range of readers. In addition, two publishing innovations made books more available to readers. One was the paperback book, less expensive than hardback, clothbound books. The other was the book club. Founded in 1926, the Book of the Month Club distributed books by writers such as Hemingway to members by mail. The Book of the Month Club exposed millions of Americans to new books.

F. Scott Fitzgerald, along with his wife Zelda, were both part of the Lost Generation that rejected the consumer culture taking root in the United States. Still, the Fitzgeralds remained deeply attracted to American life and lived wildly in their youth. Both died before reaching the age of 50.

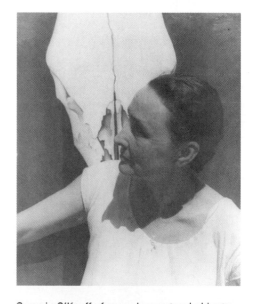

Georgia O'Keeffe focused on natural objects and painted them in pure forms and colors. Her subjects were often enlarged views of flowers, shells, rocks, or skulls. "I often painted fragments of things," she said, "because it seemed to make my statement as well as or better than the whole could."

Babe Ruth is perhaps America's most-loved athlete. He made baseball more exciting by making home runs a common part of the game. He also set many major league records, including 2,056 career bases on balls and 72 games in which he hit two or more home runs. In 1936, he was one of the first five players elected to the National Baseball Hall of Fame.

Gertrude Ederle was the first woman to swim the English Channel. Her hearing became impaired as a result of this feat. She later taught swimming to deaf children.

28.8 Sports Heroes Create a Country of Fans

The year was 1926. No woman had ever swum across the English Channel. Many people doubted that a woman could, but Gertrude Ederle, an American swimmer, was about to try. Ederle had already won Olympic medals in 1924. She had also already tried to swim the channel but had failed. In this attempt, she succeeded. Ederle not only swam 35 miles across the channel. She also beat the men's record by nearly two hours. Upon her return to the United States, Americans greeted Ederle with a ticker-tape parade through New York City.

Spectator Sports Become Big Business in the 1920s By the 1920s, the eight-hour workday, five-day workweek had become the rule in many industries. More leisure time freed Americans to pursue interests beyond work. Economist Stuart Chase estimated that Americans spent one fourth of the national income on play and recreation. Some of this money went toward **spectator sports,** or sports that attract large numbers of fans who attend games.

Sports became a big business. Professional baseball and football teams attracted legions of loyal fans. Boxing and wrestling matches also attracted crowds. The promoter of the 1921 boxing match between U.S. heavyweight champion Jack Dempsey and French challenger Georges Carpentier built a 60,000-seat stadium for the event. Ticket sales hit $1.8 million, more than any previous boxing match. When Dempsey fought to regain his title from Gene Tunney in 1927, more than 100,000 people bought tickets worth $2,658,660—a record at that time.

The mass media helped raise the public interest in sports. Millions of Americans listened to radio broadcasts of popular sporting events. One entrepreneur even figured out a way to add "live action" to a radio broadcast. He had a blow-by-blow radio broadcast of the 1927 Dempsey-Tunney match piped into a large hall while two local boxers reenacted the fight for the audience.

Sports Stars Become National Celebrities Before the 1920s, the light of publicity had never shone so brightly on sports figures. Now Americans wanted to know everything about their favorites. The media gladly fed this passion.

The most famous sports celebrity of this era was baseball slugger Babe Ruth, the legendary "Sultan of Swat." In the 1927 season, Ruth hit 60 home runs, a record that would remain unbroken for 34 years. Ruth attracted so many fans that Yankee Stadium, which opened in 1923, was nicknamed "the House That Ruth Built."

Jim Thorpe, an American Indian, was one of the greatest all-around athletes. He began his sports career as an outstanding college football player. He won fame as an Olympic track and field champion, and then went on to play professional baseball and football. In 1920, Thorpe became the first president of the group that was to become the National Football League (NFL).

Women also made their mark on sports. Gertrude Ederle broke national and world swimming records on a regular basis. Tennis star Helen Wills won many tennis championships in the United States and Europe. She was known for her ability to hit the ball harder than any woman she faced and for a calm manner that earned her the nickname "Little Miss Poker Face."

Helen Wills was the top tennis player in America for eight years. She won her first singles U.S. championship in 1923 and continued to win six more during her career. Wills also earned multiple French and Wimbledon titles and two gold medals in the 1924 Olympics.

Summary

New ideas and prosperity brought change to American popular culture in the Roaring Twenties. The creative energy of writers, artists, filmmakers, and musicians, as well as innovations by businesspeople and inventors, all contributed to new directions in American life.

Consumer culture New products and advertising encouraged a buying spree. Credit and installment buying allowed people to buy now and pay later.

Mass media National magazines, radio, and motion pictures brought news, information, and entertainment to millions of Americans. Regional differences began to fade as a new national popular culture became part of daily life.

Women voters All women gained the vote in 1920. The League of Women Voters encouraged all voters to become informed about public issues. Congress considered, but rejected, the first version of the equal rights amendment.

The Jazz Age Jazz, a new form of music, expressed the mood of the decade. Introduced by African American musicians, jazz became popular throughout the country and the world.

Harlem Renaissance Musicians and writers centered in Harlem gave voice to the experiences of African Americans in song, poetry, and novels.

Lost Generation Disillusioned by World War I and the nation's growing consumer culture, some artists and writers fled to Paris. This "Lost Generation" produced books and poetry that are still read and enjoyed today.

Spectator sports More leisure time allowed Americans to attend sporting events. Spectator sports became a big business, and athletes became national celebrities.

Chapter 29

The Clash Between Traditionalism and Modernism

How did social, economic, and religious tensions divide Americans during the Roaring Twenties?

29.1 Introduction

Norman Rockwell was born in New York City in 1894. A talented artist, he studied at a number of the city's art schools. For many young painters in the 1920s, it would have been natural to draw all the new and strange sights the city offered. But Rockwell's works had nothing to do with New York. Instead, they depicted a more traditional America, one that could be found on farms and in small towns.

In 1916, the *Saturday Evening Post,* one of the country's most popular weekly magazines, started putting Rockwell's charming pictures on its covers. By 1925, Rockwell was nationally famous. "Without thinking too much about it in specific terms," Rockwell said of his work, "I was showing the America I knew and observed to others who might not have noticed."

Most of the trends and changes that made the 1920s roar emerged in the nation's cities. Although rural life was changing as well, Rockwell's paintings appealed to a longing for the reassurance of the simple life. Some people who lived in rural areas did not approve of the changes they had witnessed since the end of World War I. They were **traditionalists,** or people who had deep respect for long-held cultural and religious values. For them, these values were anchors that provided order and stability to society.

For other Americans, particularly those in urban areas, there was no going back to the old ways. They were **modernists,** or people who embraced new ideas, styles, and social trends. For them, traditional values were chains that restricted both individual freedom and the pursuit of happiness.

As these groups clashed in the 1920s, American society became deeply divided. Many rural dwellers lined up against urbanites. Defenders of traditional morality bemoaned the behavior of "flaming youth." Teetotalers opposed drinkers. Old-time religion faced off against modern science. The result was a kind of "culture war" that in some ways is still being fought today.

The two magazine covers shown opposite and above capture the tension between traditionalism and modernism during the 1920s. The *Leslie's Illustrated Weekly Newspaper* appealed to traditionalists with nostalgic images rooted in small-town America. *Life* reached out to modernists with images of trendy fun seekers and style setters.

◀ "Fact and Fiction," a *Leslie's Illustrated Weekly Newspaper* cover by Norman Rockwell in 1917

After World War I, many Americans wanted to have fun. Performances by popular entertainment groups like Uncle Sam's Follies, shown on the right, offered freedom from traditional rules of behavior. People could dress in the latest fashions, dance the latest dances, smoke, and drink, despite prohibition.

29.2 The Growing Traditionalist-Modernist Divide

As the war ended and the doughboys began to come home from France, the title of a popular song asked a question that was troubling many rural families: "How ya gonna keep 'em down on the farm (after they've seen Paree)?" After seeing the bright lights of cities, many returning soldiers decided to leave behind the small towns they came from. The 1920 census revealed a startling statistic: for the first time ever, the United States was more than 50 percent urban. This population shift set the stage for the growing divide between traditionalists and modernists.

In the 1920s, a booming economy and high wages lured workers to urban areas such as New York City. Cities offered steady jobs and freedom to explore new ways of thinking and living.

Urban Attractions: Economic Opportunity and Personal Freedom During the 1920s, some 19 million people would move from farms to cities, largely in search of economic opportunities. Urban areas, with their factories and office buildings, were hubs of economic growth. As the economy boomed, the demand for workers increased. Wages rose as well. Between 1920 and 1929, the average per capita income rose 37 percent. At the same time, the **consumer price index,** a measure of the cost of basic necessities such as food and housing, remained steady. As a result, urban wage earners saw their standard of living improve.

Cities also offered freedom to explore new ways of thinking and living. City dwellers could meet people from different cultures, go to movies, visit museums, and attend concerts. They could buy and read an endless variety of magazines and newspapers. They could drink, gamble, or go on casual dates without being judged as immoral.

Rural Problems: Falling Crop Prices and Failing Farms The personal freedom people experienced in cities stood in strong contrast to small-town life. In rural areas, most people lived in quiet communities, where they watched out for one another. New ideas and ways of behaving were often viewed with suspicion.

In addition to losing their younger generation to cities, rural communities faced other problems during the 1920s. Farmers had prospered during the war, producing food crops for the Allies and the home front. Enterprising farmers had taken out loans to buy new machines or extra land in hopes of increasing their output and profits. After the war, however, European demand for U.S. farm products dropped sharply, as did crop prices. With their incomes shrinking, large numbers of farmers could not repay their loans. Hundreds of thousands of farmers lost their farms in the early 1920s alone. For the rest of the decade, farmers' share of the national income dropped steadily. By 1929, per capita income for farmers was less than half the national average.

Congressmen from rural states tried to reverse this downward slide with farm-friendly legislation. The most ambitious of these measures, the McNary-Haugen Bill, was first introduced in 1924. This legislation called on the federal government to raise the price of some farm products by selling surplus crops overseas. Congress passed the bill twice, in 1927 and then in 1928, but President Calvin Coolidge vetoed it both times. A strong opponent of the government's interference in markets, the president dismissed the McNary-Haugen Bill as "preposterous."

Changing Values Lead to Mutual Resentment The divide between urban modernists and rural traditionalists was not just economic. Modernists tended to view rural Americans as behind the times. Sinclair Lewis, the first American writer to win the Nobel Prize for Literature, mocked small-town values. In one of his novels, he described the residents of a small Midwestern town as

> a savorless people, gulping tasteless food, and sitting afterward, coatless and thoughtless, in rocking-chairs prickly with inane decorations, listening to mechanical music, saying mechanical things about the excellence of Ford automobiles, and viewing themselves as the greatest race in the world.
>
> —Sinclair Lewis, *Main Street,* 1920

Rural traditionalists, not surprisingly, resented such attacks on their behavior and values. In their eyes, they were defending all that was good in American life. They saw the culture of the cities as money-grubbing, materialistic, and immoral. At the same time, however, many rural people could not help but envy the comfort and excitement city life seemed to offer.

The defenders of traditional values often looked to their faith and the Bible for support in their struggle against modernism. As a result, the 1920s saw a rise in religious **fundamentalism**—the idea that religious texts and beliefs should be taken literally and treated as the authority on appropriate behavior.

Billy Sunday, a former major league baseball player, emerged as the most prominent fundamentalist preacher in the nation. His dramatic preaching style drew huge crowds. He was said to have preached to more than 100 million people in his lifetime. Sunday's largest following was in rural areas, including the South. "There is ten times more respect for God and the Bible and the Christian religion in the South," he said, "than in any other part of the United States."

Still, times were changing. A growing number of young modernists were rejecting long-accepted American values. Rural areas were losing population to the cities, and agriculture was no longer the backbone of the American economy. In addition, with improvements in mass media, country people themselves were being exposed to new ideas, music, and social values.

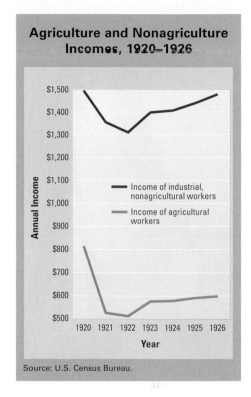

All workers saw their incomes drop during the recession that followed the war. But although the incomes of industrial workers eventually recovered, those of farm workers did not.

In the 1920s, youth were enamored by various fads such as pole-sitting, dance marathons, a game called mah-jongg, beauty contests, and crossword puzzles. Here, a daredevil completes a crossword puzzle while being hung from a building.

29.3 Generations Clash over the New Youth Culture

Before World War I, if a young man were interested in courting a young woman, he would visit her at home and meet her parents. If things went well at this first meeting, the boy would visit again. If he invited the girl to a dance or concert, an older adult would go with them as a chaperone. Eventually, the girl's parents might trust the young couple enough to let them sit by themselves on the front porch. In traditional families, these courtship patterns continued after the war. In more modern families, however, courtship changed dramatically, often confusing, if not upsetting, the older generation. Courtship was one example of how the older and younger generations clashed in the 1920s.

The Youth Perspective: The Old Ways Are Repressive During the 1920s, a growing drive for public education sent a majority of teenagers to high school for the first time in U.S. history. College enrollment also grew rapidly. As young people spent more time than ever before outside the home or workplace, a new youth culture emerged. This culture revolved around school, clubs, sports, music, dances, dating, movies, and crazy fads.

The fads young people followed were, for the most part, ephemeral. In one fad, young couples entered marathon dance competitions. The last couple left standing after many hours of dancing won a prize. Flagpole sitting, in which a participant would spend days perched atop a flagpole, was another short-lived fad. One fad from the 1920s that remains popular today is the crossword puzzle.

The most daring young women broke with the past by turning themselves into "**flappers**." They colored their hair and cut it short. Their skimpy dresses—worn without restrictive corsets—barely covered their knees. They rolled their stockings below their knees and wore unfastened rain boots that flapped around their ankles. Flappers wore makeup, which until that time had been associated with "loose" women of doubtful morals. Draped with beads and bracelets and carrying cigarette holders, they went to jazz clubs and danced the night away.

In a magazine article on the flapper, Zelda Fitzgerald wrote,

> She flirted because it was fun to flirt and wore a one-piece bathing suit because she had a good figure, she covered her face with paint and powder because she didn't need it and she refused to be bored because she wasn't boring . . . Mothers disapproved of their sons taking the Flapper to dances, to teas, to swim and most of all to heart.
> —Zelda Fitzgerald, "Eulogy on the Flapper," 1922

Modern young couples traded old-fashioned courtship for dating. Whereas the purpose of courtship had been marriage, the main point of dating was to have fun away from the watchful eyes of parents. Sedate tea parties or chaperoned dances gave way to unsupervised parties.

Older people fretted about the younger generation's "wild" ways. Many young people, however, felt free to ignore their elders. After witnessing the war's waste of life, they decided that the adults who had sent young men into battle did not deserve respect. As one young person said, "The older generation had certainly pretty well ruined this world before passing it on to us."

Easy access to cars and the mass media helped fuel the youth rebellion. Cars gave young people a means to escape the supervision of their elders.

Magazines and movies, in the meantime, spread images of a good life that was often very different from the way their parents had grown up.

Writers Ernest Hemingway and F. Scott Fitzgerald wrote about youth of the time in books with such titles as *The Beautiful and Damned*. Perhaps no one better captured the feelings of rebellious youth than poet Edna St. Vincent Millay when she wrote,

> My candle burns at both ends;
> It will not last the night;
> But ah, my foes, and oh, my friends—
> It gives a lovely light.
> —Edna St. Vincent Millay, "A Few Figs from Thistles," 1920

The Adult Perspective: Young People Have Lost Their Way Many adults considered the behavior of young people reckless and immoral. They tried to restore the old morality in a number of ways. One was censorship. Traditionalists pulled books they saw as immoral off library shelves. They also pressured filmmakers for less sexually suggestive scenes in movies. The Hays Office, named for former Postmaster General Will Hays, issued a movie code that banned long kisses and positive portrayals of casual sex. In bedroom scenes, movie couples had to follow a "two feet on the floor" rule.

Some states tried to legislate more conservative behavior. They passed laws to discourage women from wearing short skirts and skimpy swimsuits. Police with yardsticks patrolled beaches looking for offenders.

Mostly, however, the older generation restricted itself to expressing loud disapproval. When nagging did not work, many parents crossed their fingers and hoped for the best. More often than not, they were not disappointed. Most young people, even the most rebellious flappers, usually ended their dating days by getting married and raising the next generation of rebellious youth.

29.4 Wets and Drys Clash over Prohibition

On February 14, 1929, men dressed in police uniforms raided the headquarters of Chicago's Moran gang. When the officers ordered the gangsters to raise their hands and line up against the wall, the gang members thought nothing of it. The police were always annoying them. These "police officers," however, were members of Al "Scarface" Capone's rival gang in disguise. Capone's men whipped out their guns and blasted away. Seven members of the Moran gang died in what soon became known as the Saint Valentine's Day Massacre. This bloodbath was one of many unexpected consequences of what Herbert Hoover called "an experiment noble in purpose"—prohibition.

The "Dry" Perspective: Prohibition Improves Society Traditionalists and progressive reformers saw passage of the Eighteenth Amendment, which prohibited the manufacture, sale, or transport of alcoholic beverages, as a great victory. They pointed to evidence that alcoholism caused crime, violence, and the breakup of families. "Drys," as backers of prohibition were known, believed that stopping people from drinking would result in a healthier, happier society.

In this 1922 photograph, a Washington, D.C., policeman checks to see that a bathing suit hits no higher than six inches above the knee. Traditionalists in many communities passed laws designed to prevent women from appearing in public in immodest clothes. Nonetheless, modernists continued to wear revealing swimsuits.

Federal agents were fighting a losing battle as they tried to destroy stashes of illegal alcohol. The harder they tried to enforce prohibition, the more fashionable it became to flout the law. "When I sell liquor, it's called bootlegging," observed Chicago gangster Al Capone."When my patrons serve it on Lake Shore Drive, it's called hospitality."

Drys also saw prohibition as a way of taming city life. Support for prohibition centered mainly in rural areas, and many drys saw the Eighteenth Amendment as a triumph of rural over urban Americans. As one dry put it, prohibition allowed the "pure stream of country sentiment and township morals to flush out the cesspools of cities." In addition, many traditionalists were suspicious of foreigners. They associated beer drinking with immigrants of German descent and wine drinking with Italian immigrants. To them, prohibition was a way to curb such "foreign" influences.

At first, prohibition seemed to the drys to deliver its expected benefits. The national consumption of alcohol did decline, from an annual average of 2.6 gallons per capita before the war to less than 1 gallon by the 1930s. Fewer workers spent their wages at saloons, to the benefit of their families. The greatest decline in drinking probably occurred in the groups that resented prohibition the most—poor and working-class ethnic groups. In their view, prohibition was just another example of nativist prejudice toward immigrants.

The "Wet" Perspective: Prohibition Restricts Freedom and Breeds Crime

Opponents of prohibition, called "wets," were small in number at first. But as the law went into effect, their numbers grew. Opposition centered mainly in large cities and immigrant communities.

Many modernists attacked prohibition as an attempt by the federal government to legislate morality. Journalist H. L. Mencken, a champion of modernism, called drys "ignorant bumpkins of the cow states who resented the fact that they had to swill raw corn liquor while city slickers got good wine and whiskey." Another modernist, Massachusetts Senator David Walsh, rejected traditionalist arguments that drinking was sinful. He reminded drys that the first miracle performed by Jesus had been to turn water into wine. Were Jesus to perform this miracle in prohibition-era America, Walsh observed, "he would be jailed and possibly crucified again."

Prohibition seemed doomed from the start. In October 1919, Congress passed the **Volstead Act** to enforce the Eighteenth Amendment. But the federal government never gave the enforcement agency, called the Prohibition Bureau, sufficient personnel, money, or supplies. The bureau's agents were simply outnumbered by the millions of Americans who wanted to drink. Hoover later estimated that the government would need 250,000 agents to make prohibition work.

As a result, prohibition led to an increase in illegal behavior by normally law-abiding citizens. Millions of Americans simply refused to abstain from drinking. Some learned how to brew their own "bathtub gin." Others bought "bootleg" alcohol that was distilled illegally or smuggled into the United States from Canada. As thousands of bars and pubs were forced to close, they were replaced by nearly twice as many secret drinking clubs, called **speakeasies**. The term speakeasy came from the practice of speaking quietly about illegal saloons so as not to alert police. A 1929 issue of New York City's *Variety* boldly reported, "five out of every seven cigar stores, lunchrooms, and beauty parlors are 'speaks' selling gin." The number of speakeasies in New York City alone was estimated at 32,000. The widespread availability of illegal alcohol led the humorist Will Rodgers to quip, "Prohibition is better than no liquor at all."

Many Americans—such as the woman shown above—chose to ignore the ban on drinking. Bootlegging became a common trade. In 1929, Assistant U.S. Attorney General Walker Wildebrandt reported that alcohol could be bought "at almost any hour of the day or night."

The growing demand for liquor created a golden opportunity for crooks like Al Capone. **Bootlegging**—the production, transport, and sale of illegal alcohol—was a multibillion dollar business by the mid-1920s. Chicago bootlegger Capone exhibited his wealth by driving around in a $30,000 Cadillac while flashing an 11½-carat diamond ring. To keep his profits flowing without government interference, he bribed politicians, judges, and police officers. He also eliminated rival bootleggers. His thousand-member gang was blamed for hundreds of murders. In 1931, Capone finally went to jail—not for bootlegging or murder, but for tax evasion.

As lawlessness, violence, and corruption increased, support for prohibition dwindled. By the late 1920s, many Americans believed that prohibition had caused more harm than good. In 1933, the states ratified the Twenty-First Amendment, which repealed prohibition.

29.5 Modernists and Traditionalists Clash over Evolution

In 1925, Dayton, Tennessee, was a sleepy town of almost 2,000 people, plus a freethinking New York transplant named George Rappelyea. That year, the state legislature passed a law making it illegal for a public school "to teach any theory that denies the story of the Divine Creation of man as taught in the Bible."

While chatting with friends one day, Rappelyea mentioned an offer by the American Civil Liberties Union to defend any teacher who would test the law. Why not find one right here, he suggested. A trial would show how foolish the law was. It would also attract national attention to Dayton. One of his friends knew just the man for the job—a young science teacher named John Scopes, who would be willing to teach a lesson on evolution. And so the stage was set for a dramatic contest between modernists and traditionalists over the place of science and religion in public schools.

Aimee Semple McPherson, a famous fundamentalist preacher, founded the International Church of the Foursquare Gospel. In 1923, she built the Angelus Temple, which sat more than 5,000, in Los Angeles, California. She enhanced her services there with bands, choirs, and other theatrical touches. Radio broadcasts increased her audience and made her a nationally known religious figure.

The Modernist Perspective: Science Shows How Nature Works

Like many modernists, Rappelyea looked to science, not the Bible, to explain how the physical world worked. Scientists accepted as true only facts and theories that could be tested and supported with evidence drawn from nature. By the 1920s, people could see the wonders of modern science every time they turned on an electric light, listened to the radio, or visited their doctors.

One of the most controversial scientific ideas of that time was British naturalist Charles Darwin's **theory of evolution**. Darwin theorized that all plants and animals, including humans, had evolved from simpler forms of life. The evolution of one species from another took place over thousands or millions of years. It worked through a process he called "natural selection." Others called it "survival of the fittest." In this process, species that make favorable adaptations to their environment are more likely to survive than those that do not. As favorable adaptations pile up, new species evolve from old ones. In such a way, Darwin argued, human beings had evolved from apes.

The Scopes trial pitted the respected fundamentalist William Jennings Bryan, pictured above, against the brilliant defense attorney Clarence Darrow. Although Bryan won the case, he did not win his war against the teaching of evolution. Five days after the trial, Bryan died in his sleep.

John Scopes did not testify during his trial for violating Tennessee's anti-evolution law. But after being found guilty, he addressed the judge: "Your honor, I feel I have been convicted of violating an unjust statute. I will continue in the future, as I have in the past, to oppose this law in any way I can. Any other action would be in violation of my idea of academic freedom —that is, to teach the truth as guaranteed in our Constitution."

Modernists embraced the concepts of evolution and natural selection. Rather than choosing between science and religion, they believed that both ways of looking at the world could coexist. "The day is past," declared a New York City preacher, "when you can ask thoughtful men to hold religion in one compartment of their minds and their modern world view in another." By the 1920s, the theory of evolution was regularly taught in schools.

The Traditionalist Perspective: The Bible Is the Word of God Traditionalists were more likely to see science and religion in conflict. This was especially true of Christian fundamentalists, who believed the Bible was the literal word of God. They rejected the theory of evolution because it conflicted with **creationism,** the belief that God created the universe as described in the Bible.

During the early 1920s, fundamentalists vigorously campaigned to ban the teaching of evolution in public schools. They found a champion in William Jennings Bryan. A spellbinding speaker, Bryan had played a major role in American politics for 30 years. He had run for president three times and served as secretary of state under President Woodrow Wilson. Bryan toured the country, charging that modernists had "taken the Lord away from the schools."

Bryan had two reasons for taking up the creationist cause. The first was his deeply held Christian faith. The second was his fear that teaching evolution could lead young people to accept social Darwinism. This is the belief that as in nature, only the fittest members of a society will survive. Social Darwinism had been used to justify imperialism on the grounds that the fittest, or most powerful, peoples should rule the less powerful. It had also been used to promote **eugenics,** or the idea that the human species should be improved by forbidding people with characteristics judged undesirable to reproduce. Bryan saw such views as a threat to the poor and weak. He worried that widespread acceptance of social Darwinism and eugenics "would weaken the cause of democracy and strengthen class pride and power of wealth."

Creationism Versus Evolution in Tennessee Tennessee became the first state to enact a law banning the teaching of evolution in public schools. The law might not have caused a nationwide stir if Rappelyea had not decided to contest it. He sent a student to pull Scopes off a tennis court and said, "John, we've been arguing, and I said that nobody could teach biology without teaching evolution." Scopes not only agreed but also volunteered to teach a lesson on evolution the next day. Rappelyea then asked the American Civil Liberties Union to defend the young science teacher before going to the police and having Scopes arrested.

The Scopes trial, which began on July 10, 1925, brought far more attention to Dayton than Rappelyea had hoped. Bryan offered to represent the state of Tennessee. Scope's supporters added high-powered lawyer Clarence Darrow to the defense team. Although Darrow had supported Bryan for president, he disagreed with him about religion and agreed to defend Scopes for free. Some 200 reporters arrived in Dayton as the trial opened, along with tourists and hawkers selling toy monkeys. The whole country was following this contest between creationism and evolution.

In their opening statements, the opposing lawyers recognized that the issue to be decided was much more than whether Scopes had broken the law. "If evolution wins," Bryan had warned, "Christianity goes." Darrow argued, "Scopes isn't on trial; civilization is on trial." To make his point, Darrow had brought a variety of experts to Dayton to testify against the Tennessee law. After hearing one of them, the judge refused to let the rest testify because what they had to say was not relevant to the guilt or innocence of the science teacher.

For a moment, it looked like Darrow had no defense. Then he surprised everyone by calling Bryan to the stand as an expert on the Bible. "Do you claim that everything in the Bible should be literally interpreted?" Darrow asked. Bryan answered, "I believe everything in the Bible should be accepted as it is given there." However, when asked if Earth had been created in six days, Bryan answered, "I do not think it means necessarily a twenty-four-hour day." Creation, he added, "might have continued for millions of years." Darrow had tricked Bryan, the fundamentalist champion, into admitting that he himself did not always interpret each and every word in the Bible as the literal truth.

When the trial ended, it took the jury fewer than 10 minutes to find Scopes guilty, whereupon the judge fined him $100. A year later, the Tennessee Supreme Court overturned the conviction because the judge, not the jury, had imposed the fine.

Summary

Culturally, the United States became a deeply divided nation during the Roaring Twenties. Tensions arose between traditionalists, with their deep respect for long-held cultural and religious values, and modernists, who embraced new ideas, styles, and social trends.

Urban versus rural By 1920, the United States was becoming more urban than rural. Urban areas prospered as business and industry boomed. Rural areas declined economically and in population.

Youth versus adults Suspicious of the older generation after the war, many young people rejected traditional values and embraced a new youth culture. Chaperoned courting gave way to unsupervised dating. Flappers scandalized the older generation with their style of dress, drinking, and smoking.

Wets versus drys The Eighteenth Amendment launched the social experiment known as prohibition. The Volstead Act, which outlawed the sale of alcohol, was supported by drys and ignored by wets. The Twenty-First Amendment repealed prohibition in 1933.

Religion versus science Religious fundamentalists worked to keep the scientific theory of evolution out of public schools. The Scopes trial, testing Tennessee's anti-evolution law, was a legal victory for fundamentalists but a defeat in the court of public opinion. The issue of teaching creationism in biology classes is still current today.

Chapter 30

The Causes of the Great Depression

What caused the most severe economic crisis in American history?

30.1 Introduction

The door to the hotel room burst open. Groucho Marx, a wealthy, famous actor, and quite likely the funniest man in America, was breathless. He had just received a hot stock tip: shares of Union Carbide were a sure bet to go up in price.

From the doorway, Groucho shouted the news to his sleepy-eyed brother Harpo. They had to act fast, he said, before others heard the same tip. Harpo, still in his bathrobe, asked his brother to wait while he got dressed. "Are you crazy?" Groucho growled. "If we wait until you get your clothes on, the stock may jump 10 points." That day, Harpo Marx bought stock in his bathrobe.

The Marx brothers were not alone in their enthusiasm for buying stocks. In the late 1920s, many people were investing. As more and more people put money in the stock market, prices of shares kept rising. By the fall of 1929, Groucho was rich but nervous. Just how long would the good times last?

Unfortunately, Groucho's world, and that of every other American, was about to change significantly. On Tuesday, October 29, 1929, a day still remembered as **Black Tuesday,** stock prices plunged. Stocks lost their value because, all at once, many people wanted to sell their shares but very few people wanted to buy. Groucho saw his fortune evaporate that day. So did many other Americans. Suddenly the good times were over.

The 1920s were not supposed to end this way. Just the year before, President Herbert Hoover had boasted that the nation was "nearer to the final triumph over poverty than ever before in the history of any land." That triumph never happened. Instead, the nation slid into the longest economic slump Americans had ever experienced—the Great Depression.

The **stock market crash** was a key cause of the Great Depression, but it was not the only cause. Other factors contributed, too. In this chapter, you will learn how conditions of the 1920s and choices made after the stock market crash combined to bring about the worst economic crisis in American history.

Crowds gathered outside the New York Stock Exchange as the market plummeted on Black Tuesday. Many investors lost everything they owned in the crash. Ticker-tape printouts showed the prices at which stocks were being bought and sold. Record numbers of shares were traded as investors tried desperately to sell their stocks before their shares became worthless.

◀ A man selling his car after the stock market crash

30.2 A Shaky Stock Market Triggers a Banking Crisis

The purpose of the stock market is to provide businesses with the capital they need to grow. Business owners sell portions, or shares, of their companies to investors. By buying shares, investors supply money for businesses to expand. When all is well, the stock market is a useful tool in a capitalist economy. But all was not well in the 1920s.

A Speculative Boom Leads to a Spectacular Crash The stock market boom began innocently enough. Businesses thrived in the 1920s. Manufacturers were making products that consumers were eager to buy. As Americans saw business profits growing, many thought they could make a lot of money by buying shares in successful companies. The promise of financial gain drew new investors to the stock market. The result was a **bull market,** or a steady rise in stock prices over a long period of time.

But investing is not a rational science. In the late 1920s, a lot of people were swept up in the wave of speculative enthusiasm for the stock market. Like Groucho Marx, these investors believed that if prices were high today, they would go even higher tomorrow. So they bought the maximum number of shares they could afford and began counting their paper profits as the price of most stocks went up. It seemed to many Americans that there was no limit to how high the bull market could go. Investor optimism was so intense that not only did people put their savings in the stock market, but a growing number actually borrowed money to invest in stocks.

Borrowing money was easy to do in the 1920s. A buyer might pay as little as 10 percent of a stock's price and borrow the other 90 percent from a **broker,** a person who sells stock. The result was that someone with just $1,000 could borrow $9,000 and buy $10,000 worth of shares. This is called **buying on margin.** When the market was rising, brokers were happy to lend money to almost anyone.

Easy borrowing encouraged speculation, or the making of risky investments in the hope of earning large profits. Stock speculators do not necessarily buy stock to own a part of a company they believe will do well. They buy stock to make as much money as they can as quickly as possible. In a speculative market, a company's stock price does not go up because the company is growing. Prices rise because speculators want to buy a stock today and sell it for a quick profit tomorrow. As speculation drives up the price of a company's stock, the total value of the stock may become worth far more than the company itself.

Rising stock prices created a high-flying bull market without a solid foundation. When the market turned down, this borrowed-money house of cards collapsed. As prices dropped, creditors who had loaned money for buying stock on margin demanded that those loans be repaid. Unfortunately, because of falling prices, most investors could not make enough selling their stocks to repay their loans. Many had to sell their homes, cars, and furniture to pay their debts. Even businesses were affected. Many companies that had invested their profits in the stock market lost everything and had to close their doors.

Stock market prices peaked on September 3, 1929. After that, prices began dropping, sometimes in small increments, sometimes in tumbles like the huge

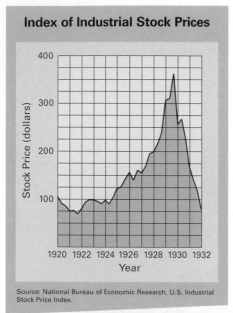

Index of Industrial Stock Prices

Source: National Bureau of Economic Research, U.S. Industrial Stock Price Index.

Frightening headlines on the stock market crash fueled public anxiety and helped contribute to the financial collapse that followed. As the graph shows, the index of industrial stocks plunged between its peak in 1929 and 1932, losing nearly two thirds of its value. A stock index measures the performance of stock prices over time.

drop on Black Tuesday in October. By then it was clear to many investors that a **bear market,** in which prices decrease steadily, had begun. Fearful of losing everything, investors rushed to sell their stocks, pushing prices down still further. By the end of the year, investors had lost more than $30 billion—an amount that exceeded the money spent by the United States to fight World War I.

A Banking Crisis Wipes Out People's Savings The stock market crash also hurt banks, triggering a crisis that unfolded over the next three years. To understand how stock losses affected banks, think about how banks operate. When people are prospering, they deposit money they do not need for day-to-day expenses in banks. The money they deposit does not just sit in the bank vault. Banks lend it out to businesses or other borrowers to earn **interest**. Interest is the charge made by a bank for the use of their money. Bank loans help people start businesses, buy homes, and plant crops.

In the 1920s, banks caught the same stock market fever that gripped the nation as a whole. Usually bankers lend money to businesses or farmers. But in the 1920s, they increasingly loaned money to stockbrokers, who in turn loaned that borrowed money to individual investors. When the stock market took a nosedive in October 1929, many investors could not repay the money borrowed from their brokers. In turn, brokers who had borrowed money from banks could not repay their loans. With bad loans piling up, banks stopped looking like a safe place to keep one's money.

People who had trusted their money to banks had good reason to worry. Even before the Depression, it was not unheard of for banks to go out of business, wiping out the savings of their depositors. During the "good times" between 1923 and 1929, banks folded at the rate of about two per day. Most of these failures were small rural banks. The stock market crash made this bad situation much worse.

As the economy continued to falter in 1930 and 1931, large numbers of depositors lost confidence in their local banks. The result was a rash of **bank runs**. In a typical bank run, panicked depositors lined up around the block to try to withdraw their money. Those first in line got their money out. But once the bank ran out of cash, it closed its doors. An appalling 3,800 banks failed in 1931 and 1932. By 1933, one fifth of the banks that were in business in the United States in 1930 had gone out of business, and millions of people had seen their savings vanish.

As news of bank failures spread, worried depositors rushed to local banks like this one in hopes of getting their money out before it was too late. Bank runs only made matters worse by forcing healthy banks to close once they ran out of funds to meet their depositors' demands. Bank failures were part of the general economic collapse brought about by the stock market crash, falling farm prices, and the decline of industry.

30.3 Too Much for Sale, Too Little to Spend

Industry had thrived in the 1920s because manufacturers were able to make a lot of merchandise very quickly. The ability to mass-produce a wide range of consumer goods started the stock boom. However, for mass production to succeed, people had to buy the goods being churned out of factories. By the late 1920s, demand for consumer goods could not keep up with production. People simply could not afford to buy all that was being produced. The resulting glut of goods in the market, combined with the stock market crash and the bank crisis, caused the economy to collapse.

A number of companies building cars established an industry in Detroit during the 1920s. However, toward the end of the decade, Americans could not afford to buy all the cars and other products that were being produced. Here, a row of new Cadillacs are fresh off the assembly line.

Overproduction Puts Too Many Goods in Stores By 1920, most American factories were using the assembly-line method of mass production. As a result, they were able to make more goods more quickly than ever before. Between 1923 and 1929, the output per worker-hour in manufacturing increased an astounding 32 percent. Farm output, too, increased throughout the 1920s. New machines and new farming techniques expanded farm production even while demand for farm products was falling.

In general, companies welcome increased production because it means increased income. A company that makes appliances, for example, wants to produce as many refrigerators as possible because the more refrigerators it makes, the more it can sell. The more refrigerators the company sells, the more money it earns. If making refrigerators costs less than it did before, so much the better.

Trouble arises when there are not enough consumers to buy all those products rolling off the assembly lines and arriving from the farms. Economists call such a predicament **overproduction**. The term refers to a situation in which more products are being created than people can afford to buy. As the 1920s came to an end, overproduction overwhelmed the American economy.

A Widening Wealth Gap Leads to Rising Debt Greater productivity led to greater profits for businesses. Some of the profits went to workers, whose wages rose steadily in the 1920s. But workers' wages did not go up nearly enough for them to consume as much as manufacturers were producing.

Most business profits went to a relatively small number of people. A wide gap separated the rich from the working class. On one side of the gap, the wealthiest 5 percent of American families received about a third of all the money earned in the country. That was more than the 60 percent of all families at the bottom on the income scale earned. Moreover, an estimated 40 percent of all Americans lived in poverty.

For a time, Americans made up for the unequal distribution of wealth by using credit to buy the radios, cars, and household appliances that flooded the market. The growing advertising industry also helped persuade people that thrift was an old-fashioned value. The more modern approach was to borrow money to buy the latest products right away. Between 1921 and 1929, personal debt more than doubled, from $3.1 billion to $6.9 billion.

Underconsumption Causes Farm Failures, Bankruptcies, and Layoffs By 1929, the buying spree was coming to an end. Many Americans found themselves deep in debt and were unwilling or unable to borrow more. Even the wealthy, who could afford to buy whatever they wanted, were buying less because they had all the goods they needed. One historian remarked that by 1929, everyone who could buy a car or radio probably already had one. The economy was showing signs of **underconsumption**. This means that people were not buying as much as the economy was producing. It is the flip side of overproduction.

Farmers were the first to experience the pain of underconsumption. Their financial difficulties began after World War I, a full decade before industry began to suffer. During the war, farmers had prospered by supplying food for American soldiers and the people of war-torn Europe. When the war ended, those markets disappeared. Consumption of farm products decreased, causing prices to drop.

Underconsumption affected farms in another way. It caused them to go further into debt. Farm incomes were falling. But farmers still wanted to buy goods made by industry, such as cars, tractors, and appliances. Like everyone else, farmers borrowed money and paid for their goods in installments. As agricultural prices continued to decline, more and more farmers had difficulty making their payments. Some farmers lost everything they owned when banks seized their farms as payment for their debts. As a result, for the first time in the nation's history, the number of farms and farmers began to decline.

By the late 1920s, the problem of underconsumption had spread to industry. Responding to the glut of products on the market, many manufacturers cut back production. In the auto and steel industries, for example, production declined by as much as 38 percent by the end of 1930. Some companies lost so much business that they were forced to declare bankruptcy and close down altogether.

Whether businesses decreased production or went bankrupt, the result was the same for workers: unemployment. As industry declined, companies laid off many workers. Those who lost their jobs also lost the ability to buy the products that industry produced. A vicious downward spiral—consisting of layoffs, reduced consumption, and then more layoffs—was set in motion. Between 1929 and 1933, the unemployment rate rose from 3 percent of the American workforce to 25 percent. Millions of Americans found themselves out of work and, as the Depression wore on, out of hope.

The pain of shrinking markets hurt agriculture years before it affected industry. Many farmers were unable to afford their land. Here, the foreclosure of a farm frustrates farmers, and police have to ensure that the auction goes smoothly.

What Caused the Great Depression?

The stock market crash triggered a long period of falling stock prices.

Bank failures wiped out depositors' savings.

Underconsumption hurt sales as people stopped buying goods. The few rich people did not buy enough, and the many poor did not spend enough, to consume all the goods being produced.

Overproduction of goods led to cutbacks and layoffs.

High tariffs hurt foreign sales.

By early 1931, the economy was a shambles. Stock prices had plunged. Bank closings were widespread. Manufacturers could not sell their products. And farmers were entering their second decade of financial distress. The federal government, under the leadership of President Herbert Hoover, took steps to improve the situation. Unfortunately, instead of minimizing the damage, many of the government's actions made things worse.

A Tight Money Supply Hobbles the Economy Many economists blame the **Federal Reserve System,** known as "the Fed," for further weakening the economy in 1930 and 1931. The Fed manages the nation's money supply. It decides how much money will be available to circulate among investors, producers, and consumers. One way it adjusts the money supply is by setting the **discount rate**. This is the rate of interest at which banks that belong to the system can borrow money from Federal Reserve banks. Member banks use the discount rate to determine the interest rates they will charge borrowers.

Before the stock market crash, the Fed had kept interest rates low. Low interest rates made borrowing easier. Easy borrowing kept money circulating. In fact, low interest rates had supported the excessive borrowing of the 1920s.

Following the crash, Federal Reserve officials kept rates low for a time. Then, in 1931, it began raising the discount rate. The immediate effect of this action was to decrease the amount of money moving through the economy. The timing of this action could not have been worse. Many people had already stopped spending, and producers had slowed production. Higher interest rates further damaged the economy by depriving businesses of the capital they needed to survive. As the amount of money dwindled, the economy slowed down, like an animal going into hibernation.

If Federal Reserve officials had concentrated on expanding the money supply after the crash, things might have gotten better. More money in circulation would have stimulated the economy to grow by making loans less expensive. Companies would have found it easier to borrow the money they needed to stay in business. This would have reduced their need to lay off so many workers. Consumers would have had more money in their pockets to spend. This would have kept factories humming. Instead, the Fed allowed the money supply to drop by a third between 1929 and 1933. This decline helped turn a nasty recession into an economic calamity.

Tariffs Cause Trade Troubles Economists also blame Congress for making decisions that further hurt the economy. To understand why, one needs to look beyond the United States. Financial problems overseas, especially in Europe, also contributed to the onset of the Great Depression.

World War I had left much of Europe in economic shambles. The Allies were having trouble paying back money borrowed from U.S. banks to finance the war. Germany was in even worse shape. The Germans were able to make their reparation payments to the Allies only by borrowing the money needed from the United States. In order to earn the dollars required to pay off these debts, these nations desperately needed to sell large amounts of goods in the United States. After the war, however, Congress enacted tariffs on many imported goods that made such sales difficult.

In 1930, Congress made a bad situation worse by passing the **Hawley-Smoot Tariff Act**. Congress meant for this law to protect American businesses from foreign competition by raising tariffs still higher. Instead, it triggered a trade war as European countries raised their tariffs on goods imported from the United States. As a result, U.S. farmers and businesses were not able to cope with overproduction by selling their excess goods to other countries.

The record-high tariffs on both sides of the Atlantic stifled international trade. This, in turn, caused a slump in the world economy. Gradually, the Great Depression spread around the globe.

Summary

The Great Depression was triggered by the stock market crash of 1929, but many other causes contributed to what became the worst economic crisis in U.S. history.

The stock market crash The stock market crash cost investors millions of dollars and contributed to bank failures and industry bankruptcies.

The financial crisis Banks made risky loans and investments in the 1920s. Some banks had to shut down when the economy collapsed, and many depositors lost their savings.

An unequal distribution of wealth The concentration of money in the hands of a few left most wage earners unable to buy all of the goods businesses were producing.

Underconsumption For a time, many consumers used credit, rather than cash, to buy such goods as cars and radios. When their level of debt grew too high, people stopped buying new products. The result was underconsumption of factory goods.

Overproduction American businesses produced more goods than people wanted or could afford. Eventually, factories had to close and workers lost their jobs.

Tight money supply After the stock market crash, Federal Reserve officials allowed the money supply to shrink. As the amount of money in circulation fell, economic activity decreased. This made it more difficult for businesses to produce and consumers to spend.

Rising interest rates After the stock market crash, Federal Reserve officials raised interest rates, making loans more expensive and limiting the amount of money in circulation. This made it more difficult for businesses to produce and consumers to spend.

Decline of international trade High import tariffs and collapsing European economies restricted international trade and deepened the Depression.

Chapter 31

The Response to the Economic Collapse

How did the federal government respond to the economic collapse that began in 1929?

31.1 Introduction

By 1932, Americans all across the country were feeling the pain of the economic collapse triggered by the stock market crash. Desperate job seekers wandered from town to town in a fruitless quest for work. Others sold apples or shined shoes to earn whatever they could. In Portland, Oregon, an unemployed veteran of World War I named Walter Waters decided it was time to take action. He persuaded a group of former soldiers to launch a protest march—all the way to Washington, D.C. There, Waters hoped to persuade Congress to accelerate payment of a long-promised bonus to World War I veterans.

The promise of a bonus for veterans dated back to 1924. Congress had voted to pay former soldiers a dollar for every day they had served during the war, plus an extra 25 cents for every day spent overseas. There was a catch, however. The government would not pay the bonus until 1945—the money was to be a retirement benefit. Veterans argued that they needed the money sooner to help them through the hard times. Members of Congress sympathetic to the cause crafted a bill that would pay the bonus right away.

In May 1932, Waters and about 250 other veterans boarded a freight train in Portland and headed east. They rode in empty boxcars and cattle cars, switching trains in various towns. Waters insisted on keeping military order: "No panhandling, no liquor, no radical talk," he told his men. The group's numbers swelled as other unemployed veterans joined this **Bonus Army**. Supportive townspeople provided them food, while some local officials, fearing violence, hurried them on their way.

At the end of May, Waters's group reached the nation's capital. By then newspapers had picked up the story, convincing veterans throughout the country to join the cause. District police set up camp for the veterans in the fields along the Anacostia River, a few blocks from the Capitol building. The veterans vowed to remain in the capital until the bonus bill was passed.

In 1932, thousands of war veterans joined the Bonus Army to demand that the government help them survive the hard times. Near the Capitol, members of the Bonus Army built a camp out of old lumber, packing boxes, scrap metal, and straw. They maintained strict discipline and required newcomers to prove they were veterans.

◀ Bonus Army marchers camping out in Washington, D.C.

31.2 Ideological Responses to the Economic Crisis

Members of the Bonus Army continued to pour into Washington for weeks. By early summer, more than 12,000 had arrived. The scraggly veterans, many with families, gave a human face to the nation's hard times. Many Americans wondered how the government would respond—not only to the frustrated veterans, but also to the economic crisis they represented.

Politicians and other public figures proposed various ways to deal with the country's economic problems. People's ideologies shaped their suggestions. An **ideology** is a set of basic ideas, beliefs, and values that form the basis of a social, economic, or political philosophy or program. While running for president in 1932, Franklin Roosevelt used a metaphor to explain three ideological responses to the Depression. "Say that civilization is a tree which, as it grows, continually produces rot and dead wood," he began. "The radical says: 'Cut it down.' The conservative says: 'Don't touch it.' The liberal compromises: 'Let's prune, so that we lose neither the old trunk nor the new branches.'"

The Conservative Response: Let the Economy Stabilize A **conservative** is someone who cherishes and seeks to preserve traditional customs and values. For conservatives in the 1930s, these values included self-reliance, individual responsibility, and personal liberty. Conservatives tend to prefer the **status quo,** or current conditions, to abrupt changes. They accept change, but only in moderation. Depression-era conservatives opposed large governmental efforts to effect change, which they felt challenged their values.

As the Depression worsened, conservatives resisted calls for radical changes to the free enterprise system. Left alone, they argued, the economy would soon stabilize and then begin to improve.

Some economists supported conservatives' hands-off approach. They insisted that economic downturns and periods of low economic activity—known as panics—were normal. They were part of the **business cycle,** a pattern in which economic growth is followed by decline, panic, and finally recovery. These lows were natural in a capitalist economy, economists argued.

This graph shows how the business cycle repeats itself over time. The cycle begins with a period of economic expansion. In time, economic activity peaks, and then the business cycle moves into a period of decline. After the downturn reaches its lowest point, a new period of economic expansion begins.

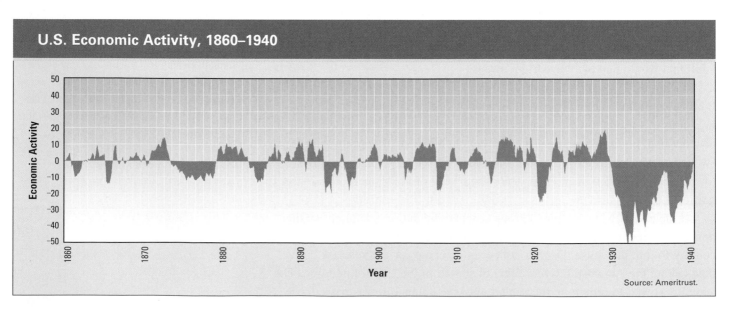

U.S. Economic Activity, 1860–1940

Source: Ameritrust.

They noted that good times followed even the severe panics of the 1870s and 1890s. The economy would also recover from this severe period.

At the start of the Depression, many Americans shared this outlook. Most preferred to suffer in silence rather than admit they needed help. But as the Depression progressed, people ran short of food and fuel. Many had no choice but to seek aid. Conservatives insisted that charities take on the growing task of providing basic necessities to the needy. If government had to step in, they argued, it should be local governments' responsibility to care for their own.

The Liberal Response: The Government Must Help A **liberal** is someone who is committed to the expansion of liberty. In the 1800s, liberals had focused on protecting individual liberty from the heavy hand of government. They favored limited government that left individuals free to exercise their rights and pursue happiness in their own way. To liberals, the government that governed the least governed the best.

With the rise of big business, liberals' views began to change. They realized that limited government could offer individuals little protection from dangerous working conditions, price-fixing monopolies, or unsafe food and drugs. By the start of the Progressive Era, many liberals believed that the government should play a role in regulating economic affairs. As the Depression set in, liberals looked to the government to expand its powers once again to protect individual liberty. However, now they defined liberty as freedom from hunger and poverty.

Liberals proposed several responses to the economic crisis. First, they called for increased spending on **public works**. These government-funded construction projects provide for such local needs as roads, bridges, and dams. They would, liberals argued, create jobs for the unemployed. Next, liberals suggested placing new taxes on corporations and the wealthy to raise money for **social welfare** programs. Such programs provide aid to those in need. They effectively redistributed money from the "haves" in a society to the "have-nots." Finally, liberals called on the government to work closely with businesses to aid in their recovery. In short, they urged the government to take on an active role within the framework of the capitalist system.

The Radical Response: Capitalism Must Go A **radical** is someone who wants to make sweeping social, political, or economic changes in a society. Radicals often have little patience for the status quo. They may seek change by democratic means or through revolution.

By the 1930s, both socialists and communists were attracting supporters with their calls for radical change. Communists, for example, proposed doing away with the market economy altogether. They wanted to replace capitalism with communism. Under that system, economic decisions would move out of the marketplace and into the hands of government planners. A totally planned economy would take the place of free markets. Wealth would be distributed to people according to their need.

Radicals viewed events like the Bonus Army protest as opportunities to spread their ideas. They encouraged working-class people to rise up against the "greedy capitalists." As the Depression wore on, such ideas began to appeal to a growing number of disillusioned Americans.

In 1931, construction began on a massive public works project: building Boulder (later renamed Hoover) Dam across the Colorado River. The government employed 21,000 workers, who completed the dam in just five years. Liberals favored increasing government spending on such projects to create jobs for the unemployed.

Here, Herbet Hoover accepts the Republican nomination for reelection in 1932. At first, he had no plans to campaign. However, as his troubles mounted, Hoover could not remain idle. By early October, he decided to take to the road in a campaign tour that included 200 speeches.

31.3 Hoover's Conservative Response to Hard Times

President Herbert Hoover strongly believed in self-reliance, rugged individualism, and hard work. His own life reflected these conservative principles. Orphaned at age nine, Hoover became a millionaire and a respected public official through his own talents and determination. Hoover was not oblivious to people's suffering. But like most conservatives, he did not believe that the federal government should give aid to the needy. Federal relief, he worried, would undermine self-reliance and encourage people to become dependent on government handouts. Instead, he supported "mutual self-help through voluntary giving."

A Cautious Approach: Limited Government Intervention Like many economists, Hoover viewed the American economy as basically sound. He felt that his job was to generate optimism and restore confidence. Optimistic business owners, he believed, would expand production. Confident consumers would spend more money. The economy would then bounce back without direct government involvement. Meanwhile, Hoover looked to local communities, mainly through churches and private charities, to take care of their citizens.

Hoover's conservative approach made sense at first. In time, however, even he could see that this depression was different from past ones. For example, unemployment continued to increase. So did the number of **Hoovervilles**—shantytowns that homeless Americans in many cities built out of crude cardboard and tarpaper. While people in cities went hungry, desperate farmers tried to boost crop prices by causing food shortages. However, it was the sharp increase in bank failures that finally caused Hoover to rethink the government's role in an economic crisis.

To deal with failing banks, Hoover at first tried his standard approach of voluntary cooperation. He prodded the owners of healthy banks to loan money to banks that were suffering. When this cooperative venture did not work, Hoover reluctantly modified his policy. In 1932, he supported the creation of a government agency to save failing banks and businesses. That agency, called the **Reconstruction Finance Corporation (RFC),** issued government loans to banks, railroads, and other big businesses.

Hoover hoped RFC loans would stimulate economic growth. Once companies began hiring again, he believed, prosperity would trickle down through the economy to those most in need. To his credit, the number of bank failures declined greatly that year. Still, conservatives criticized Hoover for putting the government in the business of saving banks. At the same time, liberals criticized what they called his **trickle-down theory** of helping the needy. The poor, they argued, could not wait for money to seep down to them from expanding businesses. They needed direct relief right away.

With a presidential election coming in the fall, Hoover knew he had to do more. In July 1932, he supported a bill authorizing the RFC to loan money to states that no longer had enough resources to help the needy. The bill also allowed the RFC to finance a variety of public works projects. This legislation stopped just short of offering direct federal relief to those in need, but it was a giant step in that direction. Hoover signed the bill into law just as the issue of the Bonus Army was about to boil over.

Hoover Battles the Bonus Army When the Bonus Army veterans first arrived in Washington, D.C., President Hoover had chosen to ignore them, hoping they would go away. They did not. However, on June 17, 1932, Congress defeated the bill that called for paying the bonuses immediately. At that point, a few thousand weary veterans gave up and headed home. But close to 10,000 Bonus Army marchers refused to leave. Walter Waters vowed to continue his protest until 1945 if necessary.

Fearful that the remaining veterans might become violent, Hoover ordered their removal. On July 28, troops used tear gas and tanks to push the veterans out of Washington. The next day, Hoover told reporters, "A challenge to the authority of the United States Government has been met, swiftly and firmly." However, reports of tanks chasing unarmed veterans out of the capital appalled many Americans.

Roosevelt Calls for a New Deal: The Election of 1932 That summer, Democrats nominated New York governor Franklin Delano Roosevelt (FDR) to be their presidential candidate. Like his distant cousin Theodore Roosevelt, FDR had a charming, magnetic personality. As he campaigned across the country, he radiated confidence in his ability to take charge of the economic crisis and lead the country to better times.

In accepting the Democratic nomination, Roosevelt promised "a new deal for the American people." While he did not yet make the details clear, FDR pledged, with this **New Deal**, to do whatever was needed to help the needy and promote recovery. "The country needs bold, persistent experimentation," he said. "It is common sense to take a method and try it. If it fails, admit it frankly and try another. But above all, try something."

A gloomy Hoover warned Americans that a Roosevelt presidency could bring disaster. Federal meddling in the economy, he claimed, would stifle free enterprise. Despite Hoover's dire warnings, Roosevelt won a landslide victory. He tallied 472 electoral votes to Hoover's 59, with a margin of victory of more than 7 million popular votes.

In 1932, Franklin Roosevelt launched an ambitious campaign tour of the country by train. Roosevelt's efforts paid off when he won the the election by a landslide. Here, Hoover and Roosevelt are travelling to Roosevelt's inauguration. There, Roosevelt delivers a speech reassuring the American people that "the only thing we have to fear is fear itself."

Roosevelt swept to victory in 1932 in most states. He attracted voters with his promise of a "new deal for the American people."

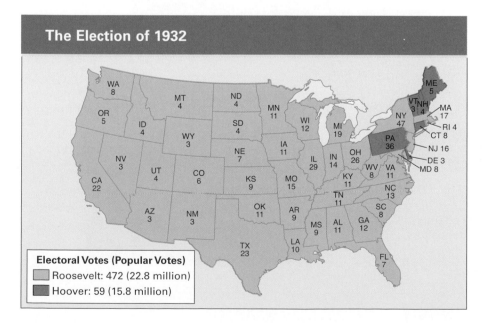

The Election of 1932

State	Electoral Votes
WA	8
MT	4
ND	4
MN	11
ME	5
OR	5
ID	4
SD	4
WI	12
MI	19
VT	3
NH	4
MA	17
NY	47
RI	4
WY	3
NE	7
IA	11
PA	36
CT	8
NV	3
IL	29
IN	14
OH	26
NJ	16
CA	22
UT	4
CO	6
KS	9
MO	15
WV	8
VA	11
DE	3
MD	8
KY	11
NC	13
AZ	3
NM	3
OK	11
AR	9
TN	11
SC	8
MS	9
AL	11
GA	12
TX	23
LA	10
FL	7

Electoral Votes (Popular Votes)
Roosevelt: 472 (22.8 million)
Hoover: 59 (15.8 million)

Laws Enacted in FDR's First Hundred Days, March 9 to June 16, 1933

During the First Hundred Days of FDR's administration, Congress passed a record number of laws. The most important of these early New Deal measures appear below.

March 9
The *Emergency Banking Act* gave the federal government broad power to help reopen the nation's banks.

March 22
The *Beer-Wine Revenue Act* legalized the sale of beer and wine.

March 31
The *Reforestation Relief Act* established the Civilian Conservation Corps, which would provide work for 250,000 young men that year.

May 12
The *Federal Emergency Relief Act* granted money to states for relief projects to help the unemployed.

May 12
The *Agricultural Adjustment Act* set prices for farm crops while trying to reduce overproduction.

May 12
The *Tennessee Valley Authority* funded construction of flood control dams and power plants in Tennessee Valley states.

May 27
The *Federal Securities Act* regulated the sale of stocks and bonds.

June 13
The *Home Owners Refinancing Act* provided aid to families in danger of losing their homes.

June 16
The *National Industrial Recovery Act* established the Public Works Administration to supervise building projects and the National Recovery Administration to encourage fair business practices.

June 16
The *Banking Act of 1933* established the Federal Deposit Insurance Corporation to insure depositors from losses when banks failed.

31.4 FDR Launches the New Deal's First Hundred Days

Franklin D. Roosevelt took office as president in March 1933. In his inaugural speech, he told Americans,

> This great nation will endure as it has endured, will revive and will prosper. So, first of all, let me assert my firm belief that the only thing we have to fear is fear itself—nameless, unreasoning, unjustified terror which paralyzes needed efforts to convert retreat into advance.

FDR presented Congress with a broad array of measures focusing on relief, recovery, and reform. Lawmakers dispensed with their usual lengthy debates to enact a record number of bills in just over three months. For that reason, this session of Congress became known as the First Hundred Days.

The relief measures that Congress passed during this remarkable session were intended to help the unemployed. For example, the Civilian Conservation Corps put young jobless men to work maintaining forests and planting trees. The recovery measures were designed to reverse the downward slide of the economy. One such law, the Agricultural Adjustment Act, tried to make farming profitable again by reducing overproduction and raising crop prices. The reform legislation passed in this session focused mainly on the financial sector. The Truth-in-Securities Act, for instance, required companies issuing stock to provide full and accurate information to investors.

As Congress finished its work, no one could say how well the new laws would work. Still, the whirlwind of activity that launched FDR's New Deal brought fresh hope to a worried nation.

Summary

Americans were anything but united in their responses to the Great Depression. Each group's political ideology shaped its approach. The election of 1932 presented voters with a choice between Republican president Herbert Hoover's conservative approach and Democratic challenger Franklin Roosevelt's promise of a New Deal.

The conservative response Conservatives thought the government should leave the economy alone. They believed that the economy would eventually stabilize itself.

The liberal response Liberals thought the government should play a more active role in the economy. They also believed the government should step in to help those in need.

The radical response Radicals advocated abolishing the free enterprise system. They believed that the government should plan economic activity and distribute wealth according to need.

Herbert Hoover At first, President Hoover relied on voluntary cooperation to ease the Depression's effects. As conditions worsened, Hoover gave government a limited role in the economy. His Reconstruction Finance Corporation, however, failed to revive the economy.

Franklin D. Roosevelt After his landslide victory in 1932, Roosevelt presented Congress with a variety of New Deal measures. During the First Hundred Days of his administration, Congress enacted many programs to provide relief, promote recovery, and enact reforms.

Chapter 32

The Human Impact of the Great Depression

How did ordinary Americans endure the hardships of the Great Depression?

32.1 Introduction

In 1933, Harry Hopkins, director of the newly formed Federal Emergency Relief Administration, hired a journalist named Lorena Hickok to travel around the country as his eyes and ears. He instructed her,

> Go talk with the preachers and teachers, businessmen, workers, farmers. Go talk with the unemployed, those who are on relief and those who aren't. And when you talk with them don't ever forget that but for the grace of God you, I or any of our friends might be in their shoes. Tell me what you see and hear. All of it.
>
> —Harry Hopkins, quoted in *One Third of a Nation: Lorena Hickok Reports on the Great Depression,* 1981

Hopkins had studied lots of statistical data. He knew what percentage of the workforce was unemployed, how much the gross national product had fallen, and how many people had lost their homes. What he could not learn from these numbers was how such realities had changed people's lives. After the 1932 election, First Lady Eleanor Roosevelt suggested that Hopkins hire Hickok—a seasoned reporter who had covered Mrs. Roosevelt as her husband Franklin campaigned for the presidency—to study this question as a roving investigator.

Once hired, Hickok traveled from West Virginia coal mines to North Dakota wheat farms, from Georgia cotton fields to western mining camps. Wherever she went, she reported to Hopkins about the hardships she observed—and there were plenty. The Depression had left many Americans hungry and homeless, and it had forced others to give up school, postpone marriage, or put off parenthood.

In this chapter, you will discover how the economic collapse of the 1930s affected workers, farmers, and families. You will consider how natural disasters intensified the suffering of many Americans. Finally, you will see how some managed to survive despite the hard times.

As Lorena Hickok traveled through 32 states, she regularly penned letters to Harry Hopkins and the Roosevelts detailing what she saw. She reported that unemployment had devastated city dwellers and farmers alike. Those without jobs endured the hardships caused by economic insecurity as best they could.

◀ Dweller living in a shantytown during the Depression

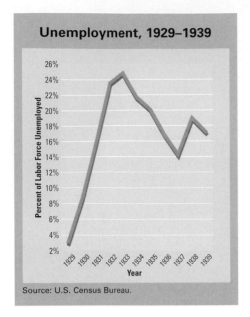

Unemployment, 1929–1939

Source: U.S. Census Bureau.

Unemployment skyrocketed after the stock market crash of 1929. At the worst point of the Depression, almost one in four workers was jobless. Unemployment most severely affected those who faced challenges finding jobs even in good times: teenagers, the elderly, minorities, and people with limited education or job skills.

32.2 A Country in Economic Distress

Living in New York City during the Depression, songwriter E. Y. Harburg saw the effects of unemployment all around him. He later recalled, "The prevailing greeting at that time, on every block you passed, by some poor guy coming up, was: 'Can you spare a dime?'" Harburg turned this observation into a song titled "Brother, Can You Spare a Dime?" It told of the sense of betrayal felt by many hardworking people who had suddenly become poor. As Harburg explained,

> This is the man who says: "I built the railroads. I built that tower. I fought your wars. I was the kid with the drum. Why . . . should I be standing in line [for a handout] now? What happened to all this wealth I created?"
> —E. Y. Harburg, quoted in Studs Turkel, *Hard Times: An Oral History of the Great Depression*, 1970

Rising Unemployment Affects Millions of Americans From 1929 to 1933, almost one in every seven businesses failed. In 1933, when Lorena Hickok began her travels, 13 million Americans were out of work. That number amounted to about 25 percent of the workforce. In comparison, only about 3.1 percent of the population had been jobless before the stock market crash in 1929.

Most unemployed Americans wanted to work. Losing their jobs was a crushing blow to people who were accustomed to providing for their families and who believed in the American ideal of opportunity for all. Those who did manage to keep their jobs often found their hours—and their pay—reduced.

When companies had to lay people off, they first let go of very young, elderly, and minority workers. African American unemployment rose as high as 50 percent in some cities during the Depression. When the New Deal began in 1933, about 20 percent of people listed on government relief rolls were African Americans, even though they made up only about 10 percent of the population.

At first, the economic collapse struck men harder than women. Men tended to work in heavy industries like automobile assembly and steelmaking, which were badly hit by the downturn. Sectors of the economy in which women tended to work declined less. Female secretaries, waitresses, maids, and telephone operators often kept their jobs, at least at first. As the Depression wore on, employers began firing women to give the jobs to men with families to support. Many states refused to hire women for government jobs if their husbands earned a **living wage,** or a wage high enough to provide an acceptable standard of living.

Unemployment had a cascading effect. The unemployed had little to spend, so many businesses lost customers and had to close—increasing unemployment. In addition to losing their jobs, many people lost their savings and their homes.

Farmers Lose Their Farms Farmers had faced economic troubles even before the Depression began. But as unemployment reduced consumers' buying power, many farmers could no longer sell their crops. As a result, they could not make mortgage payments to banks that had loaned them money. In desperation, some farmers tried to sell their farms—only to find that their **property values** had sunk along with the economy. Property value tells what a piece of real estate is worth on the market. During the Depression, many farms lost more than half their value.

Farmers who could find buyers often received far less for their land than they had paid for it. Those who could not sell their farms lost them to **foreclosure,** a legal process that allows a lender to take over the property it has helped a borrower buy. Farm families that went through foreclosure lost their homes, their livelihoods, and all the money they had invested.

Tenant farmers and sharecroppers in the South suffered the most, for these farmers, both black and white, could not afford to buy land. Instead they rented it, borrowing money from the owner to purchase seeds and other supplies. Typically, they did not earn enough selling their crops to cover their debts and rent. To make matters worse, in Mississippi the average annual income per person fell from a meager $239 in 1929 to a pathetic $117 by 1933. When tenant farmers and sharecroppers could no longer pay rent, some landowners forced them to leave.

Financial Woes Stress American Families Families suffered not only financial but also psychological stress when breadwinners lost their jobs. Many jobless men and women felt ashamed of being unemployed, believing they had brought it on themselves. Men also often felt that they lost status and authority within their families when they lost their jobs. One unemployed man put it this way: "During the depression, I lost something. Maybe you call it self-respect, but in losing it I also lost the respect of my children, and I am afraid that I am losing my wife." For some Americans, these strains were too much to take. The suicide rate reached an all-time high during the Depression.

Families struggled to stay together during the lean years. Those who could not afford rent sometimes squeezed in with relatives or friends. But when costs rose too high, thousands of people, many of them teenagers, left home. One man recalled that when he turned 16, his father told him, "Go fend for yourself. I cannot afford to have you around any longer."

The Depression affected family life in other ways as well. The marriage rate declined 22 percent from 1929 to 1933, and the birth rate also dropped. Couples were postponing getting married until their finances improved. The divorce rate also fell, since many couples could not afford to live separately or to pay the legal fees involved in a divorce.

Farm Foreclosures, 1920–1932

Year	Foreclosures per 1,000 Farms
1920	3.8
1922	11.2
1924	15.6
1926	17.0
1928	13.9
1930	18.0
1932	27.8

By the time the Depression began, farmers were used to hard times. Since 1920, the value of farm real estate had dropped more than 30 percent. At the same time, the number of farm foreclosures had been rising. Between 1920 and 1932, the number of farms taken over by banks increased by more than 700 percent.

The Works Projects Administration commissioned artists to create posters such as this one. With families struggling to stay unified during the Great Depression, this poster reminds Americans of the importance of family.

Hoovervilles sprang up on the outskirts of many American cities. People living in these shantytowns built shelters out of anything they could find. The makeshift settlements were nicknamed Hoovervilles by those who believed that President Hoover had not done enough to combat the Depression.

32.3 "Ill-Housed, Ill-Clad, Ill-Nourished"

In 1937, as Franklin Roosevelt began his second term as president and addressed the nation, he told of improvements made over the previous four years. But he also called attention to the many Americans still suffering from the Depression:

> I see millions of families trying to live on incomes so meager that the pall of family disaster hangs over them day by day . . . I see millions denied education, recreation, and the opportunity to better their lot and the lot of their children. I see millions lacking the means to buy the products of farm and factory and by their poverty denying work and productiveness to many other millions. I see one-third of a nation ill-housed, ill-clad, ill-nourished.
> —Franklin Roosevelt, second inaugural address, January 20, 1937

While the Depression affected all Americans in some way, this one third of the nation suffered the most.

Evictions Force People Out of Their Homes Without a steady income—or sometimes any income at all—many people could not pay their rent. When they failed to pay, their landlords would evict them. **Eviction** is a legal process that landlords use to remove tenants from their property. Similarly, if homeowners could not make their monthly mortgage payments, banks would foreclose on their homes, forcing families to find shelter elsewhere.

Those who became homeless did their best to get by. Some crowded into apartments with other families, huddling together against the cold when they could not afford fuel for heat. Others slept on park benches, in doorways, or, as one young homeless man reported, in haystacks, tobacco warehouses, a YMCA, a Salvation Army shelter, and jails. Once he even pried open a church window, climbed in, and pulled two seats together to make a bed.

As an increasing number of people lost their homes, Hoovervilles sprang up around many cities. Seattle's Hooverville consisted of more than 200 shacks made of tarpaper, old crates, and other scrap materials. City officials tried twice to get rid of the makeshift village by burning the shacks to the ground. When that did not work, they agreed to leave the residents alone.

Although divorce rates dropped during the 1930s, desertion rates rose. Some men, finding themselves unable to support their families, left home to live on the streets. "These are dead men," one writer observed. "They are ghosts that walk the streets by day. They are ghosts sleeping with yesterday's newspapers thrown around them for covers at night."

Teenagers also left home, often to ride the railroads in search of work. Hopping on and off moving freight trains, however, carried its own set of dangers. "I nearly was killed on my first train ride," one man who left home at 16 later recalled. "All I could think of was I shouldn't have got on this train. And if I lose my grip I'm gonna die. And what would my mother think?"

Millions Face Hunger and Starvation In addition to homelessness, loss of work often led to hunger. For many, going hungry was a new experience. One teenager who left home to find work later recalled, "I was hungry all the time, and I wasn't used to hunger. I'd never been hungry before, dreadfully hungry." In a letter to Eleanor Roosevelt, another teenager reported, "My brother and I some times even went to bed with out supper because we understand that the others [in our family] need it more than we do."

Hunger led to **malnutrition**—a physical condition that results from not getting an adequate diet of healthy food—among the poor. According to surveys conducted in the 1930s, as many as one in five children in New York endured malnutrition at the peak of the Depression. In coal-mining areas, childhood malnutrition rates may have risen as high as 90 percent.

Many families were forced to make tough choices during the Depression. This family had to sell their trailer in order to provide food for nine children.

Lack of proper nutrition left people vulnerable to diseases. One study reported that the illness rate among families of the unemployed soared to 66 percent higher than that of families with a full-time wage earner. Not surprisingly, the poor could rarely afford the medical care their sicknesses required.

People did their best to feed themselves and their families. Some picked through garbage cans looking for scraps, some stole, and still others begged. Families were known to subsist on potatoes, crackers, or dandelions. Lorena Hickok witnessed desperate mothers in South Dakota feeding their children a soup made of Russian thistle, a plant Hickok likened to barbed wire. Reporter Louis Adamic described being at home one morning when his doorbell rang. He looked out expecting to see the postman. Instead, he saw

> a girl, as we learned afterward, of ten and a boy of eight. Not very adequate for the season and weather, their clothing was patched but clean. They carried school books. "Excuse me, Mister," said the girl in a voice that sounded older than she looked, "but we have no eats in our house and my mother said I should take my brother before we go to school and ring a doorbell in some house"—she swallowed heavily and took a deep breath—"and ask you for something to eat."
>
> —Louis Adamic, *My America,* 1938

To feed the hungry, **soup kitchens** sprang up across the country. Soup was easy to prepare and could be increased in order to feed more people by adding water. **Breadlines**—long lines of people waiting for their bowl of soup and piece of bread—became a common sight in most cities. For many, that soup kitchen meal was the only food they would eat all day. At one point, New York City had 82 soup kitchens, which provided the needy with 85,000 meals a day.

In the 1930s, drought and windstorms turned much of the Great Plains into a "Dust Bowl." Farmers watched helplessly as winds picked up precious topsoil and blew it away in massive dust clouds. The drought affected much more of the country than just the Dust Bowl, but this region suffered the most.

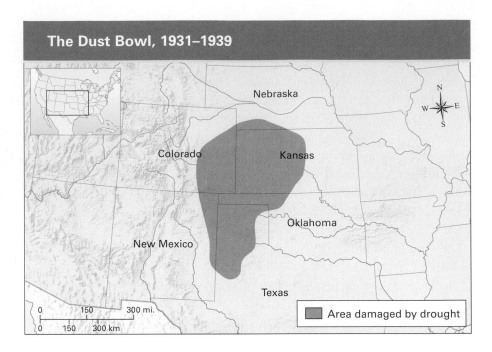

The Dust Bowl, 1931–1939

Nebraska

Colorado   Kansas

New Mexico

Oklahoma

Texas

0   150   300 mi.
0   150   300 km

■ Area damaged by drought

32.4 Natural Disasters Intensify the Suffering

As the year 1931 began, most farmers on the Great Plains were feeling optimistic. Wheat prices were holding up despite the Depression, and prospects for a record-breaking crop looked good. That summer, however, the rains abruptly stopped, and crops began to wither; then strong winds began to blow across the plains. As one wheat farmer recalled, "The winds unleashed their fury with a force beyond my wildest imagination. It blew continuously for a hundred hours and it seemed as if the whole surface of the earth would be blown away." The farmer was hardly exaggerating—he was describing the beginning of one of the worst natural disasters in the nation's history. Over the course of the next decade, drought, dust storms, and floods would add to the human misery already brought on by the hard times of the Great Depression.

Black Blizzards Plague the Great Plains At first, farmers on the Great Plains viewed the disastrous summer of 1931 as a freak of nature. The following year, they once again planted their fields and waited for the rain needed to nourish their crops. However, that rain never came—not that summer, nor the summers that followed. The prolonged drought devastated farmers, who could not get their land to produce anything but dust.

As disruptive as the drought was, the dust storms proved to be worse. Winds whipping across the plains picked up the dried-out topsoil and formed ominous black clouds. The blowing dust became so thick that people called the storms **black blizzards**. As one eyewitness recalled decades later,

> The wind kept blowing harder and harder. It kept getting darker and darker. And the old house is just a-vibratin' like it was gonna blow away. And I started trying to see my hand. And I kept bringing my hand up closer and closer and closer and closer. And I finally touched the end of my nose and I still couldn't see my hand. That's how black it was.

People tried to protect themselves by covering their faces with pieces of cloth and tacking sheets over doorways, but these efforts did little good. By the time a storm ended, one housewife reported, "Everything was full of dust."

The prolonged drought affected 100 million acres of farmland in Texas, Oklahoma, New Mexico, Colorado, and Kansas. A journalist traveling through the region at the time described it as a **Dust Bowl**—a name that stuck.

The Natural Impact of the Drought: Desertification In 1932, the weather bureau reported the occurrence of 14 dust storms. Within a year, the number nearly tripled, reaching 38. The Great Plains was experiencing **desertification,** a process in which land becomes increasingly dry and desertlike.

Several factors contributed to the desertification of the Great Plains. Drought, of course, was one, since without rain nothing would grow in farmers' fields. Decades of poor farming practices worsened the situation. During World War I, the federal government had encouraged farmers on the Great Plains to raise as much wheat as possible. After the war, as crop prices dropped, farmers had tried to increase their harvests even more to make up the difference. To do this, they had plowed and planted every tract of land they owned. By 1930, Great Plains farmers were harvesting far more wheat than they had been 10 years earlier, and they were also grazing more cattle. Such intensive use of the land depleted the soil of nutrients and left it stripped of its native drought-resistant vegetation. Once the drought came, there was no plant covering to hold the soil in place. The wind easily picked it up and blew it away.

In 1935, the federal government responded to the loss of so much valuable topsoil by establishing the Soil Conservation Service. The service promoted new farming methods designed to reduce soil erosion. It planted about 18,000 miles of trees to act as windbreaks, reducing the force of winds blowing across the plains.

Dust storms known as black blizzards made life a misery in towns like this one in rural New Mexico. "If you were cooking a meal, you'd end up with dust in your food," recalled one homemaker. "You always felt you had grit between your teeth."

Desertification is a threat whenever drought hits a semiarid area like the Great Plains. In such regions, the native vegetation is adapted to dry conditions. When this plant cover is removed, by farming or overgrazing, the soil below is exposed to sun and wind. The desertification that created the Dust Bowl was not reversed until the drought ended in 1939.

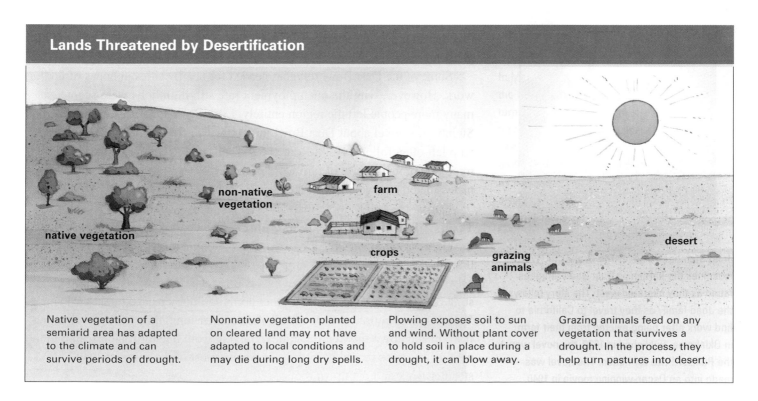

Lands Threatened by Desertification

native vegetation

non-native vegetation

farm

crops

grazing animals

desert

Native vegetation of a semiarid area has adapted to the climate and can survive periods of drought.

Nonnative vegetation planted on cleared land may not have adapted to local conditions and may die during long dry spells.

Plowing exposes soil to sun and wind. Without plant cover to hold soil in place during a drought, it can blow away.

Grazing animals feed on any vegetation that survives a drought. In the process, they help turn pastures into desert.

Chapter 33

The New Deal and Its Legacy

How did the expansion of government during the New Deal affect the nation?

33.1 Introduction

Franklin D. Roosevelt came from a wealthy New York family. He grew up on a large estate overlooking the Hudson River and attended exclusive private schools, including Harvard College. During his youth, Franklin had little contact with working-class Americans, except perhaps his parents' servants.

When Franklin fell in love with Eleanor Roosevelt, a distant cousin, she broadened his awareness. Eleanor had been taught that the wealthy have a duty to help the poor. She acted on this duty by working to improve conditions in factories and sweatshops and teaching immigrants at a settlement house in New York City. One day in 1903, while Franklin was still a college student, Eleanor took him to the home of one of her young pupils. The girl lived in a tenement in a poor neighborhood, and the dark, crowded home shocked Franklin. He declared that he "could not believe human beings lived that way." That day, Franklin Roosevelt opened his eyes to the harsh reality of life for the poorest Americans.

In the following years, Roosevelt became a skillful politician. Serving as assistant secretary of the navy and as governor of New York, he earned a reputation for being someone who could "get the job done." Spurred on by his memory of how the poor lived, he pushed for social and economic reforms. In the 1932 presidential election, Roosevelt stormed to victory in part because he promised to help the working men and women whose labor energized the American economy. He vowed to defeat the Great Depression by relying on plans "that build from the bottom up and not from the top down, that put their faith once more in the forgotten man at the bottom of the economic pyramid."

FDR was elected to four terms as president. During the first two terms, his New Deal programs gave hope to millions of Americans. He worked to find jobs for the unemployed and urged Congress to do more for those in need. In the process, he changed the role of government in American life.

At 39, Roosevelt contracted polio and lost the use of his legs. "If it hadn't been for his affliction, he never would have been President," noted an aide. "In those earlier years, he was just a play-boy . . . During his long illness he began to read deeply and study public questions." This statue of FDR in his wheelchair sits in the Franklin Delano Roosevelt Memorial in Washington, D.C.

◀ FDR with workers, from a 1934 mural by Conrad Albrizio

In this photograph, a Texas couple listens to one of Roosevelt's fireside chats. With his radio addresses, FDR revolutionized the relationship between the president and the people. After his first fireside chat, hundreds of thousands of letters flooded into the White House. Thereafter, FDR received about 6,000 letters a day. To manage the volume of mail, the White House increased its mailroom staff from one or two clerks to dozens of mail handlers.

33.2 The First New Deal

In 1933, some 13 million Americans—nearly one fourth of the workforce—were unemployed. FDR recognized that getting people back to work was his primary task as president. But he also understood that businesses needed help. Since 1930, thousands of banks and other companies had closed their doors. The production of goods had fallen by more than half.

FDR also knew that he must calm people's fears. To do this, he gave a series of radio addresses called "fireside chats." In these brief broadcasts, the president explained his plans and asked Americans for their support. FDR's soothing voice and upbeat tone greatly appealed to people, and he quickly gained the public's trust. They in turn backed the New Deal programs of the First Hundred Days, often called the First New Deal.

Restructuring the Financial Sector President Roosevelt first attacked problems in the financial sector—the areas of money, banking, and investment. On March 6, 1933, he ordered all banks to close temporarily. This banking holiday stopped the steady withdrawal of funds from financial institutions. Over the next few days, officials put together the Emergency Banking Act, and Congress quickly passed it into law. This law reformed the banking system and gave the federal government more power to supervise bank activities.

On March 12, with many banks set to reopen the next day, FDR gave his first fireside chat. He hoped to restore confidence in the banking system. About 60 million radio listeners tuned in to the broadcast to hear the president explain the government's efforts to halt the banking crisis. He called on Americans to do their part as well. "I can assure you," he said, "that it is safer to keep your money in a reopened bank than under the mattress." The following day, deposits began to flow back into the nation's banks.

A month later, Congress passed the Banking Act of 1933. This law created the Federal Deposit Insurance Corporation (FDIC), which guaranteed individual bank deposits up to $5,000. This guarantee helped restore public confidence in banks and stabilize the banking system. The law also limited the freedom of banks to trade in stocks and bonds. Before the stock market crash, banks had used depositors' savings for risky, speculative investments.

Speculation in stocks had helped cause the 1929 crash. Part of the problem was ignorance. Many investors lacked reliable information about investments. Together, FDR and Congress set out to reform the stock market. A key step was the creation of the Securities and Exchange Commission in 1934. The SEC required companies to publish the important facts about their business. It also regulated the activities of stockbrokers and others in the investment business.

Shoring Up the Free Enterprise System During the Great Depression, some people thought the free enterprise system had failed. They wanted to do away with it, but FDR differed—he wanted to help the system recover. As with the New Deal in general, the president did not have a master plan for economic recovery. He preferred to experiment, even though he knew that some programs would succeed and others would fail. One of his grandest experiments was the National Industrial Recovery Act (NIRA) of 1933.

The NIRA was the centerpiece of the New Deal's efforts to breathe life into the economy. It was designed to increase production while boosting wages and prices. Its goals were to make more goods available and to give consumers more money with which to buy them. The NIRA targeted the needs of three groups: business, labor unions, and the unemployed.

To help business, the law set up the National Recovery Administration (NRA). This government agency worked with business leaders to create codes of fair competition in various industries. Each industry followed its own code, which required companies in that industry to standardize products, set minimum prices, and announce any expected price increases. With the NRA, the New Deal increased government regulation and economic planning and moved away from the laissez-faire policies of the past.

To help labor unions, the NIRA guaranteed workers the right to organize and bargain collectively. It also authorized the NRA to propose codes for establishing minimum wages and maximum hours in various industries. These measures represented a new level of government support for organized labor.

To help the unemployed, the NIRA allotted $3.3 billion for various public works. It established the Public Works Administration (PWA) to oversee these construction projects. FDR hoped not only to create jobs but also to restart the economy with a large infusion of government cash. Unfortunately, the PWA spent its money so slowly that it had little effect on jobs or the economy.

Paying Farmers Not to Plant Another piece of recovery legislation created the Agricultural Adjustment Administration (AAA). This agency tried to aid farmers by reducing crop production and raising prices. Farmers had long suffered from low market prices for their products, which eroded their purchasing power—their ability to buy farm machinery and other goods. Many farmers also lost their farms because they were unable to pay their mortgages.

The aim of the AAA was to raise crop prices to reach **parity**. This is the price that gives farmers the same purchasing power they had during an earlier, more prosperous time. To raise prices, the AAA paid farmers to plant fewer crops. In theory, this would reduce crop supplies and increase market demand, thereby boosting prices. The AAA also provided loans to farmers so they could pay their mortgages and stay on their land rather than join the jobless in cities.

Support for the NRA was widespread. Here, female film industry workers march with an American flag during the National Recovery Administration Parade.

The AAA sought to reduce crop production and raise prices to help farmers. Here, an AAA worker is examining the surface of the land to find ways that can improve farming.

The New Deal funded public works projects to stimulate the economy and put people back to work. Among the largest projects were dams like those built for the Tennessee Valley Authority. Workers also built bridges and roads, planted trees, and cut trails through national forests. This Depression-era mural by artist William Gropper is titled *Construction of the Dam*.

Promoting Economic Development and Homeownership Another New Deal program worked to promote economic development in one of the poorest regions of the country, the Tennessee River valley. In 1933, at the urging of the Roosevelt administration, Congress passed a bill creating the Tennessee Valley Authority. The TVA, an independent government agency, built a series of dams on the Tennessee River and its tributaries. These dams provided flood control and hydroelectric power to seven southern states. The TVA also battled erosion and deforestation, both processes that posed serious problems in the Tennessee Valley. In addition, this far-reaching program brought badly needed jobs to the region and encouraged businesses to invest there.

The New Deal also created two new federal agencies that would deal with housing issues. Like farmers, many homeowners had lost their homes because they could not pay their debts. One agency, the Home Owners' Loan Corporation, provided loans to help people meet their mortgage payments. The other agency, the Federal Housing Administration (FHA), gave a boost to the banking and construction industries by insuring mortgage loans up to 80 percent of a home's value.

Remembering the "Forgotten Man" After FDR's inauguration, more than 450,000 Americans wrote letters to the new president. Many of them pleaded for help. During his campaign, FDR had promised to remember the "forgotten man." Now, under the First New Deal, he carried out that promise by providing relief programs designed to help ordinary Americans as they struggled to survive the Depression.

One important work-relief program was the **Civilian Conservation Corps (CCC)**, which gave young men jobs planting trees and working on other conservation projects. A much larger program, the Federal Emergency Relief Administration (FERA), took an approach different from providing people with work. Instead, it sent funds to state governments, which then distributed the cash to the needy. For the first time in American history, a federal agency provided direct relief to the unemployed. State and local agencies also pitched in with supplies of food and clothing to help the poor.

The flurry of activity during the First Hundred Days caught most Americans by surprise. Few would have predicted that so much could be done so quickly. However, while Roosevelt managed to instill hope in desperate Americans, he had not yet beaten the Depression. Unemployment remained high, and the economy remained flat. Gradually, discontent with FDR's policies surfaced.

Critics Attack the New Deal When the early New Deal failed to restore economic prosperity, critics began to question FDR's approach. Many of these critics had ideological differences with FDR. Some came from the **right wing,** those on the conservative side of the political spectrum. Others came from the **left wing,** those on the liberal side. At the two extremes existed the people with the most radical views. In the center stood the political moderates. When asked whether he was "left or right politically," FDR claimed to be part of the mainstream near the center of the spectrum. "I am going down the whole line a little left of center," he said.

Right-wing critics generally thought the New Deal had gone too far in expanding the role of the federal government. These critics included a mix of conservative politicians, wealthy industrialists, bankers, and religious leaders. Some of these critics joined forces in 1934 to form the American Liberty League. This organization attacked FDR as a leftist radical and called New Deal legislation socialist and unconstitutional. One of the league's founders was Al Smith, a former New York governor and the Democratic candidate for president in 1928. In 1936, Smith bitterly attacked the New Deal as a betrayal of Progressive ideas about good government and threw his support to the Republican candidate for president.

The Granger Collection, New York

Although the First New Deal was popular with most Americans, it sparked criticism from both the left and the right. Critics on the right complained that much of the tax money being pumped into the economy by New Deal programs was being wasted. Critics on the left argued that the New Deal was not doing enough to help those in need.

Huey Long was a powerful speaker with an emotional delivery that could cast a spell over his audience. The Louisiana senator and former governor attacked the New Deal for not doing enough to help poor Americans. He held much in common with the Populists of the 19th century.

Left-wing critics of the New Deal generally thought the New Deal should give greater aid to the needy. Robert La Follette, a progressive Republican senator, favored larger public works programs. Dr. Francis Townsend devised a plan calling for a monthly payment of $200 to everyone over the age of 60. Recipients would promise to retire and spend the money in the same month it was issued. Townsend claimed his plan would free up jobs for younger workers and boost the economy.

Socialists offered more critical views from the left. Norman Thomas, leader of the Socialist Party, found little to praise in the New Deal, except for the TVA. He likened this program to "a beautiful flower in a garden of weeds." Another socialist, the muckraker Upton Sinclair, called for a more radical New Deal. He urged California's state government to buy, rent, or seize unused land and factories and give them to jobless workers to use to produce their own food and goods. He called his program End Poverty in California (EPIC). Sinclair ran for governor of California in 1934 on the EPIC platform but was soundly defeated.

Demagogues Turn Up the Heat At the extremes of the political spectrum, **demagogues** also denounced the New Deal. A demagogue is a political leader who appeals to people's emotions and prejudices. Charles Coughlin, a Roman Catholic priest, attracted millions of listeners to his radio broadcasts. With his dynamic voice, the "radio priest" stirred up hatred against Wall Street bankers and greedy capitalists. He grew increasingly critical of Roosevelt for not doing enough to help the poor, saying that FDR had "out-Hoovered Hoover."

Huey Long, regarded by his supporters as a champion of the poor, seemed to his opponents a wild-eyed demagogue. A Louisiana senator with Populist appeal, Long colorfully portrayed himself as the hero of the common man in the fight against big business. In 1934 he launched his Share Our Wealth program with the slogan "Every Man a King." Long wanted to take money from the rich and give every American family a grant of $5,000, a guaranteed job, and an income of at least $2,500 per year. He explained the idea behind his program this way:

> It is our estimate that 4 percent of the American people own 85 percent of the wealth of America . . . Any man with a thimble-full of sense ought to know that if you take 85 percent off of that table and give it to one man that you are bound to have two thirds of the people starving because they haven't got enough to eat. How many men ever went to a barbecue and would let one man take off the table what's intended for nine tenths of the people to eat? The only way to be able to feed the balance of the people is to make that man come back and bring back some of that grub that he ain't got no business with!

> —Huey Long, "Share our wealth" speech, 1934

The WPA's Federal Art project provided jobs for more than 5,000 artists who created over 200,000 works of art. Many of the work that the WPA commissioned were murals that depict scenes from American life, like the one shown here. This mural was painted on a courthouse in Trenton, New Jersey. Many of the WPA artists were inspired by famed Mexican muralist Diego Rivera.

33.4 The Second New Deal

To meet challenges from the right and the left, Franklin Roosevelt took to the airwaves once again. In a June 1934 fireside chat, he asked Americans to judge the New Deal's progress by "the plain facts of your individual situation. Are you better off than you were last year?" The response of most Americans was loud and clear. In the November 1934 congressional elections, Democrats gained a large number of seats in both the House and the Senate.

The huge Democratic victory encouraged FDR. In 1935, he began introducing another flurry of legislation. In part to counter the demagogues, FDR shifted his focus away from recovery and toward social and economic reforms. He aimed to provide Americans with relief, stability, and security. Many historians call this round of programs the Second New Deal.

Energizing the Country with Electricity and Jobs In the spring of 1935, Congress passed FDR's Emergency Relief Appropriation Bill. FDR called it the Big Bill because it created several new agencies and called for nearly $5 billion in new spending, an unprecedented increase.

One of the new agencies was the Rural Electrification Administration (REA). In 1935, fewer than 20 percent of American farms had electricity. The REA established hundreds of publicly owned electrical cooperatives, built generating plants, and strung power lines. When it completed its work, about 90 percent of the country's farms had access to cheap power.

The Big Bill also spawned a huge agency called the **Works Progress Administration (WPA)**. The WPA, a work-relief organization, put more than 3 million Americans to work in its first year. They built hundreds of thousands of bridges, public buildings, and parks. At the urging of Eleanor Roosevelt, the WPA also established arts projects. It hired unemployed artists to paint murals in public buildings. Musicians combed the American backcountry to find and record folk music. Writers created guidebooks to the states.

The WPA generated a lot of controversy. Many conservatives denounced the program's cost, while labor unions attacked it for depressing wage rates. Despite the criticisms, the program continually expanded. By 1936, the WPA employed 7 percent of the American workforce.

The Supreme Court Attacks the New Deal Meanwhile, the Supreme Court had begun weighing in on key New Deal programs. In 1935, in the case *Schechter Poultry Corp. v. United States,* it struck down the National Industrial Recovery Act. The court ruled that the act violated the constitutional separation of powers by giving the president, rather than Congress, the power to issue "codes of fair competition" to businesses.

The next year, the Court killed the Agricultural Adjustment Act on the grounds that a law "to regulate and control agricultural production [was] a matter beyond the powers delegated to the federal government." It also struck down a New York law setting a minimum wage for workers. Roosevelt fumed that the Court had created a "no-man's land" where no government, state or federal, could act effectively.

A Bill of Rights for Workers Despite the Court's rulings, FDR continued to push for reform legislation. A month after the Supreme Court declared the NIRA unconstitutional, Congress passed a new bill to protect workers. The National Labor Relations Act, also called the **Wagner Act** for the senator who sponsored it, came to be seen as a bill of rights for organized labor.

The Wagner Act guaranteed workers "the right to self-organization, to form, join, or assist labor organizations, [and] to bargain collectively through representatives of their own choosing." To protect these rights, the act created the National Labor Relations Board (NLRB). This board had the power to supervise union elections to ensure that they were free and democratic. It could also penalize employers for "unfair labor practices," such as attempting to discourage workers from joining or forming a union.

Congress passed a related bill in 1938. The Fair Labor Standards Act regulated conditions in the workplace. It also set a minimum wage of 25 cents an hour and a maximum 44-hour workweek for most workers. In addition, the act banned "oppressive child labor." Together, the Wagner Act and the Fair Labor Standards Act met many of the longstanding demands of American workers and promised to make their lives more secure.

The National Labor Relations Board (NLRB) had the power to supervise union elections and regulate some union laws. Here, the chairman of the NLRB calls for fewer restrictions on the Wagner Act.

Economic Security for Americans FDR also addressed the long-term problems of the aged and unemployed. "Among our objectives," he told Congress in January 1935, "I place the security of the men, women, and children of the nation first." Later that month, FDR revealed his landmark **Social Security Act**. Congress passed the bill in June, and in August the president signed it into law. At the signing ceremony, FDR said,

> We can never insure one hundred percent of the population against one hundred percent of the hazards and vicissitudes [unexpected changes] of life, but we have tried to frame a law which will give some measure of protection to the average citizen and to his family against the loss of a job and against poverty-ridden old age.
>
> —Franklin Roosevelt, August 14, 1935

The Social Security Act created a social insurance program that provides two main types of benefits: retirement and disability. Retirement benefits are cash payments made to retired workers sometime after they reach the age of 62. This is the program most often associated with Social Security today. The government finances these payments by taxing current workers and their employers. Disability benefits are payments made to workers who have become too disabled to continue working, regardless of their age. Severely disabled children are eligible for Social Security disability benefits as well.

The Social Security Act also set up an unemployment insurance program for workers. This program makes payments to people who have lost their jobs and are seeking new work. Its funding comes from taxes on employers. Usually, unemployment benefits last for up to six months. However, Congress has sometimes extended benefits for longer periods during economic recessions.

Battling the Supreme Court In 1936, FDR won a second term as president with a landslide victory. He viewed this victory as a **mandate**— a grant of authority—to extend the New Deal further. But FDR feared that the Supreme Court would continue to block his efforts. By then, several Court decisions had threatened his attempts to give government a greater role in stabilizing the economy and society. FDR's frustration led him to take a controversial step.

In 1937, FDR presented Congress with legislation to redesign the Supreme Court. The bill called for adding a new justice for every sitting justice over age 70. FDR claimed that the Court was behind in its work, partly because aging justices could not keep up. But his real intention was clear. He wanted to pack the Supreme Court with liberal justices who would favor New Deal programs. Republicans and Democrats alike expressed outrage at FDR's court-packing plan. So did the American people. Congress rejected the bill.

Roosevelt's scheme to put more liberal justices on the Supreme Court backfired. Opponents accused him of threatening the independence of the judiciary and undermining the system of checks and balances. Congress rejected the court-packing plan and dealt FDR a harsh political blow.

Around this time, the Supreme Court shifted course, becoming more accepting of government regulation of the economy. In 1937, the Court upheld both the Social Security Act and the Wagner Act. In these decisions, the Court redefined its understanding of liberty. Conservatives, backed by the Court, had long equated liberty with the freedom of private enterprise to act without government interference. Chief Justice Charles Evans Hughes observed that there was no constitutional basis for this narrow definition. In fact, he said, the Constitution supported a broader definition of liberty that included "the protection of law against the evils which menace the health, safety, morals, and welfare of the people." That is, government could promote liberty by using its powers to ensure fair treatment of all Americans.

New Deal legislation supporting workers' right to organize spurred the growth of labor unions. In 1937, a sit-down strike was organized by the United Auto Workers union at the General Motors plant in Flint, Michigan. A sit-down strike occurs when workers take over their workplace by "sitting down" on the job, preventing employers from replacing strikers with scabs. Here, a striker sits down with his supportive fiance.

33.5 Social and Political Impacts

The New Deal was a bold attempt to resolve the worst economic crisis in American history. President Roosevelt wanted to use the vast power of the federal government to end the Depression. But he also wanted to create a more just society. The United States, he said, should become "a country in which no one is left out." The New Deal's sweeping reforms aimed, in part, to meet this social objective. Workers, women, and members of minorities all felt the impact of the New Deal, though some got a better deal than others.

A Good Deal for Workers The New Deal helped many workers by strengthening the labor movement. First the NIRA and then the Wagner Act guaranteed the right of workers to form unions and to bargain collectively. This change in government policy boosted the power of labor unions. They now stood on a more equal footing with employers.

As unions became stronger, they also began to grow. This growth presented a challenge to the American Federation of Labor (AFL), a large and powerful alliance of unions. From its birth in the late 1800s, the AFL had organized skilled workers according to their craft, such as welding or printing. It had left less-skilled workers to fend for themselves. During the 1930s, activists within the AFL began demanding that it organize workers not by craft but by industry. That way, all workers in an industry would belong to the same union.

John L. Lewis, head of the United Mine Workers union, became one of the strongest supporters of this idea. In 1935, Lewis helped form a group within the AFL to organize workers in mass-production industries. This group later took the name **Congress of Industrial Organizations (CIO)**. The AFL suspended Lewis's group in response to its industry-wide organizing. In 1938, the CIO formed an independent federation.

The CIO grew quickly, accepting African American workers and other laborers shunned by the AFL. It organized unions in the automobile, rubber, and steel industries. The CIO's success, aided by New Deal laws supporting labor, helped swell union membership. Less than 14 percent of workers belonged to unions in 1935. By 1940, union membership would climb to almost 28 percent of the total labor force.

A Mixed Deal for Women Women also made some advances during the New Deal. Much of this progress stemmed from the influence of Eleanor Roosevelt. The first lady played a key role in the FDR administration. Her experience working with the poor gave her insight into the needs of factory workers, tenant farmers, and others hit hard by the Depression. She traveled the country, meeting people, assessing their needs, and reporting back to the president. She pushed him to be more daring in advancing his social agenda. She especially encouraged him to place more women in government positions.

Under FDR, the government hired an unprecedented number of women— more than in any previous administration. Talented women, such as Frances Perkins, reached high positions in government for the first time. Perkins, FDR's secretary of labor, proved to be an outstanding adviser to the president. The first female member of the cabinet, she worked tirelessly to shape and administer such programs as Social Security and the Fair Labor Standards Act. Another prominent figure, Mary McLeod Bethune, served as a special adviser to the president on minority affairs. She also worked in the National Youth Administration (NYA), where she fought to increase opportunities for young African Americans.

Not all women fared as well, however. As the Depression deepened, women were pressured to leave the workforce to free up jobs for men with families to support. The Economy Act of 1932 prohibited a husband and wife from both working for the federal government. State and local governments banned the hiring of a woman whose husband earned "a living wage." Other employers simply refused to hire married women at all. Labor unions often supported the exclusion of women from the workforce. "The working wife whose husband is employed," argued one union leader, "should be barred from industry."

Eleanor Roosevelt played a key role in the New Deal. She traveled the country, acting as her husband's eyes and ears. She pushed hard for better treatment of women and minorities. One journalist called her "the most influential woman of our times."

A Disappointing Deal for African Americans The New Deal offered some hope for black Americans, a group hit especially hard by the Depression. Competition for jobs, along with discrimination in hiring, pushed the unemployment rate for blacks well above that for white Americans. Direct government relief as well as work-relief programs such as the CCC and the WPA helped many poor African Americans survive. At the same time, more educated African Americans got jobs in government. A lawyer named William Hastie rose from a position as an adviser to the president on race relations to become the first African American to serve as a federal judge.

Still, African Americans continued to suffer from oppression. Even New Deal agencies practiced racial segregation, especially in the South. FDR himself failed to confront the evil of lynching, which claimed the lives of some 60 blacks between 1930 and 1934. In 1935, a federal antilynching bill came before Congress, but FDR declined supporting it for fear of offending powerful southerners in Congress.

Eleanor Roosevelt took a more courageous stand on civil rights. In 1939, the Daughters of the American Revolution refused to allow a renowned black singer, Marian Anderson, to perform at Constitution Hall in Washington, D.C. Roosevelt arranged for her to sing outdoors, on the steps of the Lincoln Memorial. A crowd of 75,000 people, including many members of Congress, attended Anderson's performance.

In 1939, Marian Anderson sang to a crowd of 75,000 people at the Lincoln Memorial. Here, Secretary of the Interior Harold Ickes congratulates Anderson at her concert. Eleanor Roosevelt arranged this opportunity after the Daughters of the American Revolution did not allow Anderson to perform at Constitution Hall.

Who Benefited from the New Deal?

	Providing Relief	Stimulating Recovery	Promoting Reform
The Hungry and Homeless	Provided funds to state and local relief agencies: **1933** Federal Emergency Relief Administration		
The Unemployed	Created jobs: **1933** Civilian Conservation Corps (CCC) **1933** Public Works Administration (PWA) **1933** Civil Works Administration **1933** Tennessee Valley Authority (TVA) **1935** Works Progress Administration (WPA) **1935** National Youth Administration (NYA)	Built hospitals, schools, dams, power plants, and highways that stimulated economic growth: **1933** Public Works Administration (PWA) **1933** Tennessee Valley Authority (TVA) **1935** Works Progress Administration (WPA)	Created a publicly owned electric utility to compete with private utilities: **1933** Tennessee Valley Authority (TVA)
Homeowners	Helped homeowners make mortgage payments: **1934** Home Owners Loan Corporation	Guaranteed loans for home building and repairs: **1934** Federal Housing Administration (FHA)	Cleared slums and built low-cost housing: **1937** United States Housing Authority
Farmers	Provided cash and loans: **1933** Agricultural Adjustment Act **1934** Farm Mortgage Foreclosure Act	Raised crop prices by regulating crop production: **1933** Agricultural Adjustment Act	Improved rural life with electric power and better farming practices: **1936** Rural Electrification Administration (REA) **1937** Farm Security Administration (FSA)
The Elderly, Disabled, and Dependent	Aided the blind, the disabled, and dependent children: **1935** Social Security Administration	Encouraged older workers to retire to open up jobs: **1935** Social Security Administration	Provided pensions to retired workers: **1935** Social Security Administration
Workers		Recognized the right of collective bargaining: **1933** National Recovery Administration (NRA)	Protected workers' rights and set a minimum wage: **1935** National Labor Relations Board (NLRB) **1938** Fair Labor Standards Act
Businesses and Consumers		Established codes of fair competition: **1933** National Recovery Administration (NRA)	Required companies to list ingredients on products: **1938** Food, Drug, and Cosmetic Act
Banks and Depositors		Restored confidence in banks by insuring deposits: **1933** Federal Deposit Insurance Corporation (FDIC)	Regulated bank practices: **1933** Emergency Banking Act **1933** Federal Deposit Insurance Corporation (FDIC)
Investors		Increased confidence in the stock market: **1933** Securities Act	Regulated trading in the stock market: **1934** Securities and Exchange Commission (SEC)

A Better Deal for American Indians For American Indians, the New Deal had some positive results. Even before the Depression, many Indians lived in grinding poverty. Federal efforts to assimilate them into mainstream America had trampled on their cultures and traditions. FDR's commissioner of Indian affairs, John Collier, hoped to repair some of the damage with an Indian New Deal.

Collier ended the policy of forced assimilation, replacing government-run boarding schools with public schools on reservations. He also encouraged greater cultural awareness about American Indians and improved health care for them. As well, he tried to give Indian tribes more control over policies that affected their lives. Under the terms of the Indian Reorganization Act of 1934, Indian communities received the right to set up their own tribal governments.

The Indian New Deal did not lift Indians out of poverty or bring back traditional Indian ways. But it did reverse some harmful federal policies and restore some pride and hope to Indian communities.

A Tough Deal for Mexican Americans Like other ethnic minorities, Mexican Americans faced poverty and unemployment during the Depression. As the economy shrank, jobs dried up in the Southwest, where most Mexican Americans lived. Failing farms and businesses could not afford to hire laborers. The AAA, which paid farmers to cut back on planting, led to even more unemployment among farmworkers. Some jobless Mexican Americans resettled in cities. Others relied on work-relief programs for their survival.

Mexican laborers who were not American citizens could not enroll in work relief. More than a third returned to Mexico, many with their American-born children. Most went willingly, but the government deported others.

The Emergence of a New Deal Coalition in Politics Although the New Deal failed to bring concrete gains for many women and minorities, for most Americans its benefits outweighed its shortcomings. The belief that government could make a difference in voters' lives inspired many people to become more involved in politics. When they did, they often supported Democratic candidates. For example, in the 1936 election, over 70 percent of African American voters cast their ballots for Roosevelt. This marked a major shift for the black population, which had traditionally supported Republicans as the party of Lincoln and Emancipation.

The 1936 election signaled the emergence of a new political partnership known as the **New Deal Coalition**. Besides women and minority groups, the coalition included industrial workers, farmers, immigrants, reformers, southern whites, and city dwellers. What held these unlikely partners together was their loyalty to the Democratic Party and its leader, Franklin Roosevelt. For all their differences, they trusted FDR when he said, "The test of our progress is not whether we add more to the abundance of those who have much; it is whether we provide enough for those who have too little."

Even though unemployment remained high, FDR easily won a second term in 1936. Among his supporters were farmers. Here, Roosevelt visits farmers in North Dakota during his campaign. Later, Roosevelt would run for an unprecedented third and fourth term as president.

Social Security is one of the most popular and enduring legacies of the New Deal. Millions of Americans rely on Social Security benefits. Several plans have been put forward to cut back on welfare. Here, protesters resist cuts to Social Security.

If you live and work in the United States, you should have a Social Security card and Social Security number. This is the number that the federal government uses to keep track of you, your earnings, and your future benefits. You will have the same Social Security number throughout your life.

33.6 Legacy of the New Deal

New Deal policies did not end the Depression. The economy continued to struggle into the 1940s. But the New Deal did help millions of Americans cope with hard times. It also had a lasting impact on American government and society, leaving a legacy that affects all Americans today.

Unalienable Rights: Life, Liberty, and Economic Security One major legacy of the New Deal is the idea that Americans have a right to economic security. Franklin Roosevelt, who began an unprecedented fourth term as president in 1944, explained this idea in his State of the Union address that year:

> This Republic had its beginning, and grew to its present strength, under the protection of certain inalienable political rights—among them the right of free speech, free press, free worship, trial by jury, freedom from unreasonable searches and seizures . . . As our Nation has grown in size and stature, however—as our industrial economy expanded—these political rights proved inadequate to assure us equality in the pursuit of happiness. We have come to a clear realization of the fact that true individual freedom cannot exist without economic security and independence.
>
> —Franklin Roosevelt, January 11, 1944

FDR went on to list a number of rights that emerged from the New Deal, including the right to a job, adequate wages, a decent home, medical care, and a good education. Today we take many of these rights for granted. We also accept that the government is responsible for guaranteeing these rights.

Before the New Deal, private charities bore the burden of caring for the needy. But the severity of the Depression changed popular notions of charity. The crisis was so severe that it could be tackled only by using the enormous resources of the federal government. Americans began to accept the idea that many people could not survive without public assistance.

Most New Deal programs offered short-term relief to cope with the immediate effects of the Depression. The Social Security Act did something different, however. This milestone legislation established long-term assistance for those in need. By doing so, it laid the foundation for the modern **welfare state**. A welfare state is a social system in which the government takes responsibility for the economic well-being of its citizens.

Critics at the time grumbled that government assistance undermined the American principles of self-reliance and individualism. Nevertheless, government assistance continues today in various forms. It now includes a wide array of programs, from health insurance for older Americans to food stamps for the poor and parity price supports for farmers. These are known as entitlement programs, as people who meet eligibility requirements are entitled to receive certain benefits from them. All these programs owe their existence to the New Deal.

A Larger Role for Uncle Sam in People's Everyday Lives Another notable legacy of the New Deal is the expanded role of government. Traditionally, Americans have distrusted government power. A limited government, the founders said, protects against tyranny. However, to battle the Depression,

FDR actively involved the federal government in the economy. He also used it to advance his agenda of social justice. As a result, the government grew. Each federal program required a new agency to administer it, which enlarged the government bureaucracy. The cost was enormous. To meet the expense, FDR reluctantly resorted to **deficit spending,** or spending more than the government receives in revenues. He financed the deficit by borrowing money.

Conservatives reacted strongly to this growth in the size and power of government. In 1936, one critic wrote that FDR had transformed government "into a highly complex, bungling agency for throttling [strangling] business and bedeviling the private lives of free people. It is no exaggeration to say that he took the government when it was a small racket and made a large racket out of it." Today, that "large racket" is known as "big government." Conservatives complain that big government leads to burdensome regulations, higher taxes, and less local control. Liberals, however, defend the expanded role of the federal government as essential to creating a good and just society.

Government today is not just bigger as a result of the New Deal. It also continues to play a more direct role in people's lives. Americans buy power from government-built dams. They deposit money in bank accounts insured by the FDIC. They are protected from fraud by government agencies such as the SEC. They receive Social Security payments when they retire. These and many more benefits of big government are all legacies of the New Deal.

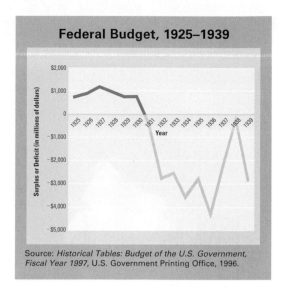

Federal Budget, 1925–1939

Source: *Historical Tables: Budget of the U.S. Government, Fiscal Year 1997,* U.S. Government Printing Office, 1996.

Federal revenues grew faster than spending during the 1920s, creating budget surpluses. During the Depression, however, spending outpaced revenues. Between 1930 and 1940, the nation's debt rose by about 250 percent.

Summary

Franklin D. Roosevelt promoted his New Deal policies to end the Great Depression and help needy Americans. The early programs of the First New Deal emphasized economic recovery and financial reform. The Second New Deal focused more on economic relief and social reform. These programs greatly expanded the role of the federal government in American life.

National Industrial Recovery Act The NIRA was aimed at shoring up the free enterprise system by helping businesses, workers, and the needy.

Agricultural Adjustment Administration The AAA sought to boost agricultural prices by paying farmers to plant fewer crops, thus reducing supply and increasing demand.

Wagner Act This law strengthened the labor movement by supporting the right of workers to organize and join unions.

Works Progress Administration The WPA organized and funded public works projects that provided jobs and wages to unemployed workers.

Social Security Act Social Security was designed to provide economic security to unemployed and retired Americans. It is a key legacy of the New Deal.

New Deal Coalition A diverse group of Americans came together to support FDR and the New Deal. This coalition helped insure FDR's reelection and the continuation of his programs.

Characteristics of Totalitarianism in the Soviet Union Under Stalin

Joseph Stalin

- Communist Party as the only authority
- State planning of the economy
- State-owned collective farms
- Brutal purges to maintain political control

Characteristics of Fascism in Italy Under Mussolini

Benito Mussolini

- Extreme nationalism
- Individual liberties crushed
- State is paramount
- Bring back glory of ancient Rome through military conquest

Hitler's violation of the Treaty of Versailles boosted his popularity in Germany. Germans hated paying war reparations, as the treaty required. They also objected to the war-guilt clause, which blamed them for World War I. The nationalistic feelings aroused by the treaty allowed Hitler to seize control and turn Germany into a dictatorship. Nationalism also helped strong leaders take power in Italy and Japan. In the Soviet Union, however, dictatorship emerged from a different source—communism.

Stalin Creates a Totalitarian Dictatorship in the Soviet Union In 1917, the Russian Revolution overthrew Czar Nicholas II. Soon afterward, the Communist Party, led by Vladimir Lenin, established itself as the sole authority in the country. In 1922, the communists formed the Union of Soviet Socialist Republics (USSR), commonly known as the Soviet Union. After Lenin's death in 1924, Joseph Stalin plotted his way to power. By the early 1930s, Stalin had established a totalitarian dictatorship. **Totalitarianism** is a system in which the government totally controls all aspects of a society, including the economy.

Stalin set two main economic goals for the Soviet Union. He wanted to raise agricultural production and to modernize industry. The two goals were linked, in that increased exports of food would bring in cash to finance industrialization.

In 1928, Stalin established a Five-Year Plan to reach his goals. This plan called for taking private land from farmers and forcing them to move onto huge collective farms. Many farmers did not want to resettle on these cooperative, state-owned farms. But those who resisted were shot or forced to do hard labor in prisonlike concentration camps. Millions of others died in the famine that followed the shift to collective farms. Stalin could have diverted food to starving farmers, but instead he sold it abroad to earn cash. The industrial part of Stalin's plan was a success. By the early 1930s, modernized factories were churning out machinery, iron and steel, and consumer goods.

Stalin also used brutal methods to strengthen his control of the Communist Party. In 1934, he started to purge party officials by having them arrested, put on trial, and executed. By 1936, the Soviet secret police were rounding up and killing enormous numbers of party leaders, military officers, industrial managers, and others. This Great Purge, which claimed millions of lives, ensured that remaining officials would be loyal to Stalin.

Mussolini Establishes a Fascist Dictatorship in Italy Serious problems plagued Italy after the First World War. Inflation and labor strikes hurt the Italian economy, and communists threatened to take over the democratic government. In addition, Italians felt insulted by the Versailles Treaty, because its grant of territory to Italy fell far short of their expectations. Benito Mussolini, a veteran of the war, took advantage of conditions in Italy to emerge as a national figure and eventually form a dictatorship.

In 1919, Mussolini founded the first fascist political movement. **Fascism** is based on an extreme nationalism in which the state comes first and individual liberty is secondary. Fascists are strongly opposed to communism and democracy. They favor military values, the use of violence, and a leader who is strong and ruthless. One fascist slogan in Italy called on youth to "believe, obey, fight." Another claimed, "A minute on the battlefield is worth a lifetime of peace." Fascism often arises during a time of crisis, promising to revive an earlier era of glory. In Italy's case, that era was ancient Rome.

Mussolini used his extraordinary skill at public speaking to promote fascism. He did not speak with the calm, soothing voice of Franklin Roosevelt in a fireside chat. Instead, Mussolini agitated crowds with emotional outbursts and dramatic gestures. At these rallies, tough young men wearing black shirts provided security. These supporters also formed violent Blackshirt squads that broke up political meetings and labor strikes, assaulted socialists and communists, and terrorized local populations.

By 1922, fascists dominated several areas of Italy, and Mussolini prepared to take control of the whole country. In October, he and thousands of Blackshirts threatened to march on Rome. Influential business and army leaders persuaded Italy's king, Emmanuel III, that Mussolini might be able to solve the nation's problems. The king asked Mussolini to form a government. As prime minister, Mussolini quickly took charge, taking the name *Il Duce,* Italian for "the leader." Within a few years, he turned Italy into a fascist dictatorship. He banned labor unions, outlawed opposing political parties, and censored the press. He also employed spies and secret police to keep an eye on the people.

Mussolini wanted to build Italy's economy, and his industrial development and public works programs had some success. He also hoped to turn Italy into a great European power, using the Roman Empire as a model. Like the ancient Romans, he sought glory through military conquest.

Hitler Leads the Rise of Nazism in Germany Like Italy, Germany also turned to fascism after World War I. In 1919, Adolf Hitler—Germany's future leader—joined a small political party that later became known as the Nazi Party. Under his leadership, this party would direct a mass movement based on a form of fascism known as Nazism. Nazis believed that Germans and other Nordic peoples—Hitler called them Aryans—were physically and morally superior to other races. Nazis wanted to purify Germany by removing other races, especially Jews.

Hitler laid out the Nazi philosophy in his book *Mein Kampf,* or "My Struggle." He started the book in 1924, while spending a year in prison for trying to overthrow the government of the German state of Bavaria. In *Mein Kampf,* Hitler said that the superior Aryan race was locked in a struggle with other races. He introduced the idea of *Lebensraum,* or "living space," declaring that Germany needed land on which Aryan settlers could raise large families. Those families, in turn, would conquer more territory, expanding the German empire. Eventually, Germany and the Aryan race would rule the world.

After Hitler gained control of the German government, he set about strengthening the Nazi party. His administration used posters to build support for Nazism. This poster calls for students to become propagandists for Hitler.

Characteristics of Nazism in Germany Under Hitler

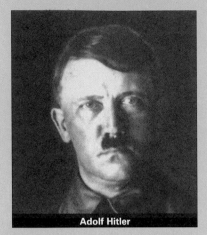

Adolf Hitler

- Extreme nationalism and racism
- Territorial expansion to create "living space"
- Civil liberties abolished
- Force used to eliminate opposition

Characteristics of Militarism in Japan Under Tojo

Hideki Tojo

- Extreme nationalism
- Military control of civilian government
- Territorial expansion to obtain raw materials

Germany's economic depression gave Hitler the opportunity to spread his ideas. The country's parliamentary government could not cope with the crisis. Hungry, unemployed Germans began looking for a leader who could save the nation from ruin. Hitler addressed large crowds, blaming the Jews for nearly every German problem, from the world war to the depression. He promised to restore Germany's economy and empire. At these Nazi rallies, bodyguards protected Hitler.

Hitler's extreme nationalism appealed to many voters. In the 1932 elections, the Nazi Party won more seats in the parliament than any other political party in Germany. As a result, Hitler was named chancellor, or prime minister. He moved quickly to dissolve the republic, replacing German democracy with a totalitarian government.

The Nazis called this government the Third Reich—the successor to two earlier German empires. They passed new laws targeting Jews, barring them from certain jobs and exposing them to persecution. Jews and other "undesirables" were shipped off to concentration camps. Hitler also centralized the government, placing Nazis in the main positions of authority. In 1934, he became both president and chancellor, giving himself the title *der Führer,* or "the leader." Hitler now had complete command of Germany. He set about building Germany's military into a powerful war machine.

The Military Takes Control of the Government in Japan Like Germany, Japan had a mixed history of military rule and democracy. Before World War I, Japan had begun to industrialize. Lacking raw materials for industry, it relied on a strong military to obtain natural resources from other countries. After the war, however, Japan became less aggressive. It helped form the League of Nations in 1920. It also signed the Kellogg-Briand Pact, joining 14 other nations in a pledge to resolve disagreements peacefully. Civilians gained more power in the government, although Japan's emperor continued to play a strong role.

In the 1930s, however, the worldwide economic depression undermined civilian rule and caused Japan to move toward a policy of **militarism**. The Japanese military began to increase its power and to play a greater role in politics.

Japan's growing militarism was combined with an extreme form of nationalism. Many Japanese turned away from Western influences and embraced traditional values and culture. Radical nationalists also called for more aggressive military action abroad to acquire territory and raw materials. Like Hitler, they wanted to expand Japan's "living space" and acquire oil and other vital resources.

Some nationalists joined with a group of army officers in efforts to overthrow the civilian government. In 1932, they assassinated the prime minister. More assassinations and upheaval followed in 1936. The government put down these rebellions and executed the rebels. Nevertheless, civilian politicians, fearing for their lives, gave up more power to the military.

Japanese militarism got another boost in 1941, when General Hideki Tojo became prime minister, replacing a civilian leader. Tojo, an aggressive militarist, continued to develop the military and prepare the nation for war.

During the early 1930s, Americans still strongly favored isolationism. With the bitter memory of the first world war and the challenge of economic problems at home, they did not want the nation to become entangled in another war. For this reason, President Franklin Roosevelt took no direct action against aggressive dictators in Asia and Europe. He did, however, speak out against aggression in principle. In his 1933 inaugural address, Roosevelt vowed that the United States would be a "good neighbor" who "respects the rights of others." This pledge was meant to send a message to aggressor nations. But it also reflected his desire to end U.S. intervention in Latin America and improve relations with that region.

At a conference later in the year, 21 nations in the Western Hemisphere signed on to Roosevelt's "Good Neighbor Policy." They declared, "No state has the right to intervene in the internal or external affairs of another." Over the next few years, the United States would encourage Japan, Germany, and Italy to abide by this principle, but it still would not back up its words with action.

Militarists Expand Japan's Empire One of the first examples of blatant aggression came in 1931, when Japan seized a portion of China. Japan and other imperialist powers had previously established spheres of influence in China, where they exploited the country's land and resources. Japan's sphere of influence was Manchuria, a region in northeastern China. When China's nationalist government threatened to expel foreign powers, the Japanese army invaded Manchuria and took control of the region.

The takeover of Manchuria had several major consequences. It gave Japan a large piece of territory that was rich in resources. In addition, it began an era in which the military dominated the Japanese government. It also isolated Japan from most other nations. In 1932, the League of Nations ordered Japan to withdraw its army from the region. Japan refused, choosing to withdraw from the League instead.

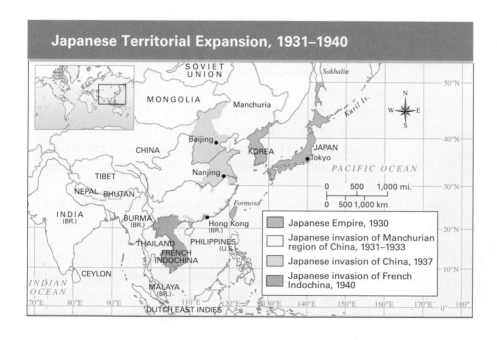

Japanese Territorial Expansion, 1931–1940

Japanese Empire, 1930

Japanese invasion of Manchurian region of China, 1931–1933

Japanese invasion of China, 1937

Japanese invasion of French Indochina, 1940

Throughout the 1930s, Japan's quest for raw materials drove its imperial expansion. In 1940, however, it still did not have a secure source of oil. Without oil, Japan could not expand, nor could it fight a war. Japan's militarists began eyeing the Dutch East Indies, which had abundant oil supplies.

As part of Mussolini's plan to create a New Roman Empire, Italy invaded and occupied Ethiopia in 1935. Italian forces also occupied Albania.

Emperor Haile Selassie fled Ethiopia just before Italy annexed his country. Selassie had pleaded with the League of Nations to take strong action against Italy. He later told the League, "It is us today. It will be you tomorrow."

More aggression followed in 1937. In July, the Japanese army clashed with Chinese forces outside Beijing, China's capital. The clash soon became a full-fledged war. The Chinese army pulled back, but the Japanese caught up with them at the city of Nanjing. After capturing the city, Japanese soldiers went on a six-week rampage known as the Rape of Nanjing. They massacred as many as 300,000 Chinese civilians and brutally raped about 20,000 Chinese women. The war did not stop there. By the end of the year, Japan's military occupied China's main cities and much of its fertile land.

Jolted by Japan's aggression, Roosevelt called on "peace-loving nations" to end the "epidemic of world lawlessness." He spoke of the need to quarantine aggressor nations. In international relations, a quarantine is a blockade or boycott. Roosevelt's "quarantine" speech did nothing to stop Japan. By 1941, Japan had added French Indochina to its Asian empire to go along with Formosa (now called Taiwan), Korea, large areas of China, and several small Pacific islands.

Europe's Dictators Test the League of Nations Japan's aggression tested the League of Nations. The League was intended to serve as an instrument of international law. In theory, it could impose boycotts and other economic sanctions or use the combined military force of its members to keep unruly nations in line. In practice, however, it was a weak organization, partly because the United States was not a member. The League failed to respond effectively to Japan's challenge. Throughout the 1930s, Germany and Italy would also test the League's will.

Like Japan, Germany pulled out of the League of Nations in 1933. At the same time, Hitler began rebuilding the German military. In 1935, he announced the formation of an air force and the start of compulsory military service. Both actions went against the Treaty of Versailles. The League of Nations lodged a formal protest, but it refused to consider sanctions against Germany. The next year, Hitler openly challenged France by sending troops into the Rhineland. This was another test of the League's resolve to stand up to aggression.

Meanwhile, Mussolini began his quest to build a New Roman Empire. In October 1935, the Italian army invaded the African nation of Ethiopia. The poorly equipped Ethiopian forces could not stop the invaders. Ethiopia appealed to the League of Nations, which voted to impose economic sanctions on the aggressor. The sanctions were mild, and few League members seriously applied them. In May 1936, Italy officially annexed Ethiopia. Hitler heartily approved of the invasion. In October, he and Mussolini joined in a treaty of friendship that forged an alliance, known as the Rome–Berlin axis, between their countries.

Events in Spain also aided the growth of fascism. In July 1936, a military rebellion started the **Spanish Civil War**. Led by General Francisco Franco, the Spanish military and its right-wing allies, known as the Nationalists, sought to overthrow Spain's democratic republic. Italy and Germany backed the rebels with supplies, weapons, and troops. Various left-wing groups, known as the Republicans, battled to save the republic, with aid from the Soviet Union and volunteer fighters from other countries. Although some 3,000 Americans volunteered, the U.S. government stayed out of the conflict. At least half a million people died in the three-year war. In the end, Franco and the Nationalists won and established a right-wing dictatorship.

Great Britain and France Seek to Appease Hitler Encouraged by events in Italy and Spain, and by his own successful occupation of the Rhineland, Hitler continued his campaign of expansion. During this time, Britain and France did little to stop him, choosing instead to follow a policy of appeasement.

Hitler next set his sights on neighboring Austria, the country of his birth. At the time, Austria had an unstable government with fascist elements. Hitler pressured its leaders to join the Third Reich. Finally, in 1938, a member of the Austrian Nazi Party took over as chancellor of Austria. On March 12 of that year, Hitler's army crossed the border into Austria without opposition. The following day he proclaimed *Anschluss,* or "political union," with Austria. Britain and France remained passive spectators to this German expansion.

Hitler next wanted to take over Czechoslovakia. By signing the Munich Pact in September 1938, he acquired the Czech region of the Sudetenland. Hitler told Chamberlain that this would be his "last territorial demand." Chamberlain chose to believe Hitler, declaring that he had achieved "peace with honor" and adding, "I believe it is peace in our time." Another member of Parliament, Winston Churchill, disagreed. He wrote, "By this time next year we shall know whether the policy of appeasement has appeased, or whether it has only stimulated a more ferocious appetite."

In 1938, Adolf Hitler's army crossed the Austrian border without opposition and joined Austria to Germany. Here, the Nazi emblem hangs beneath the Austrian flag, symbolizing unity between the two nations. The leaders of Great Britain and France stood by idly as Hitler expanded German territory. Others, like Winston Churchill, were more skeptical of Hitler's aims.

The U.S. Congress Legislates Neutrality During this period, the United States did little to thwart aggression. When Mussolini invaded Ethiopia, for example, the League of Nations considered establishing an oil embargo, or suspension of trade, against Italy. Italy's offensive would grind to a halt without oil. The League asked the United States, a major oil supplier, if it would join the embargo. Roosevelt said no, pointing out that he had just signed the Neutrality Act of 1935. This act prevented the United States from supplying "arms, ammunition, or implements of war" to nations in conflict. Because the law said nothing about oil, Roosevelt chose not to block oil shipments to Italy.

Congress passed additional **neutrality acts** in 1936 and 1937, all designed to keep the country out of conflicts brewing in Europe, such as the Spanish Civil War. Americans passionately supported this isolationism. Like Europeans, they recalled the horrors of World War I and wanted to avoid getting drawn into a new conflict. Roosevelt did, however, devote enormous energy to preserving peace. He wrote letters to the aggressors and to League members, urging them to settle their differences through negotiation.

Blitzkrieg tactics made the German army seem unstoppable. The Nazi war machine took just a month to crush Poland. When General Eisenhower visited years later, Warsaw was still in ruins.

34.4 Hitler Plunges Europe into War

Great Britain and France chose to avoid war with Germany by allowing Hitler to behave as he pleased. But Hitler had no interest in avoiding war and grew bolder with every aggressive step he took. In March 1939, he broke the Munich Pact by invading Czechoslovakia and seizing control of Prague, the Czech capital. As Churchill suspected, appeasement only made Hitler more eager to conquer new territory. The takeover of Czechoslovakia finally caused Britain and France to draw a line in the sand. They declared that if Germany made any further attacks on small states, then they would declare war.

Hitler Signs a Nonaggression Pact with Stalin Part of Hitler's plans for war involved Stalin, the communist leader of the Soviet Union. Communists and Nazis despised each other and had little reason to cooperate. Yet Hitler sought an agreement with Stalin to keep the Soviet Union neutral in the coming war. Hitler offered Stalin a nonaggression treaty, and Stalin accepted it.

The German-Soviet Nonaggression Pact, signed in August 1939, served the interests of both leaders. Hitler planned to attack Poland, an action that was likely to ignite a broader war in Europe. The geography of that war concerned him. The Soviet Union lay to the east. Britain and France lay to the west. Hitler could not afford to fight a war on two fronts, east and west, at the same time. For that reason, Soviet neutrality was vital. The pact helped Stalin, too. The Soviet dictator wanted more power and secure borders. As part of the pact, Hitler secretly promised to give Stalin part of Poland and grant him a sphere of influence in Eastern Europe.

But Hitler already had plans to attack the Soviet Union, which had vast, fertile farmlands that were a key to fulfilling the quest for *Lebensraum*. Hitler also understood that Nazi Germany could not coexist for long with the communist USSR to its east.

German Armies Roll Across Europe With the Soviet Union neutralized, Hitler sprang into action. On September 1, 1939, the German army marched east into Poland. Two days later, France and Britain—the Allied powers— declared war on Germany. World War II had begun.

In Poland, the German armed forces relied on a strategy of **blitzkrieg,** or "lightning war." Without any warning, German bombers launched attacks on railroads, airfields, communications networks, military bases, and other strategic sites. These attacks helped prevent Polish **mobilization,** the assembling of troops and equipment for war. Meanwhile, waves of infantry, supported by tanks and artillery, pushed toward key cities. Germany's method was to outflank, surround, and destroy. Motorized units quickly swept around and encircled the Polish army. Warplanes rained bombs and bullets on the enemy. Then the foot soldiers moved in to finish the job.

Ill-equipped and overwhelmed, the Polish forces quickly collapsed. On September 17, the Soviet army invaded Poland from the east. By the first of October, Germany and the USSR had complete control of the country.

How Did Germany's Blitzkrieg Tactics Work?

Germany's blitzkrieg tactics were designed to avoid the stalemate and trench warfare of World War I. The objective was to break through enemy lines at the weakest points and then rush forward to spread fear and confusion behind the lines. Pockets of enemy resistance could then be isolated and destroyed. A blitzkrieg attack unfolded in six stages.

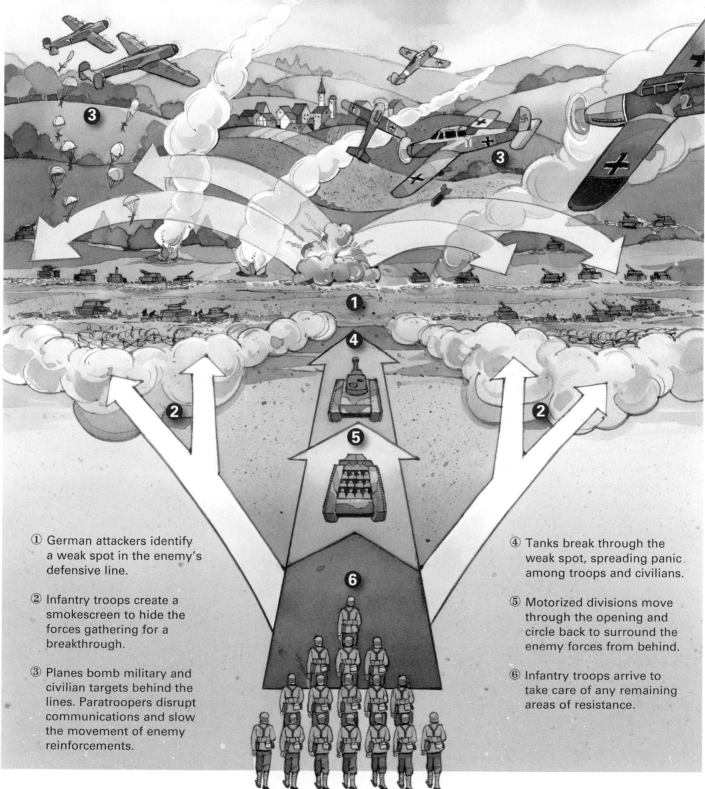

① German attackers identify a weak spot in the enemy's defensive line.

② Infantry troops create a smokescreen to hide the forces gathering for a breakthrough.

③ Planes bomb military and civilian targets behind the lines. Paratroopers disrupt communications and slow the movement of enemy reinforcements.

④ Tanks break through the weak spot, spreading panic among troops and civilians.

⑤ Motorized divisions move through the opening and circle back to surround the enemy forces from behind.

⑥ Infantry troops arrive to take care of any remaining areas of resistance.

Hitler now switched his focus to the west. He moved soldiers to Germany's border with France and the Low Countries—Belgium, the Netherlands, and Luxembourg. France relied for its main defense on the Maginot Line, a string of heavily armed fortresses along the German border. Most French troops massed here, while others gathered along the border with Belgium. British forces crossed the English Channel, prepared to aid France and the Low Countries. For the next few months, not much happened on the western front. American newspapers began referring to this as the "Phony War."

Then suddenly, in a series of lightning actions, the Germans struck. In April 1940, they launched a surprise attack on Denmark and Norway. Within a few weeks, Germany had conquered these two Scandinavian countries. Next, on May 10, the Germans invaded the Low Countries. In just 18 days, these three countries would fall into German hands.

Using blitzkrieg tactics, the main German force burst through Luxembourg and southern Belgium into France in just four days. Then it began a dramatic drive toward the French coast. Skirting the Maginot Line, the Germans sped westward, encircling defenders. Hundreds of thousands of French and British troops found themselves trapped in a shrinking pocket of French countryside. They retreated toward the port of Dunkirk on the northwest coast of France. Britain sent every boat it could find across the English Channel to evacuate the soldiers. The daring rescue saved some 338,000 men.

Meanwhile, Paris was about to fall to the Germans. Mussolini took this opportunity to declare war on Britain and France. Italy and Germany became known as the Axis powers. On June 22, France surrendered to Germany. Under the terms of the armistice, Germany would occupy three fifths of the country.

Germany had enormous success in the first year and a half of World War II. Except for neutral nations, nearly all of Europe fell under Axis control. Only Great Britain managed to hold off Hitler's invading armies.

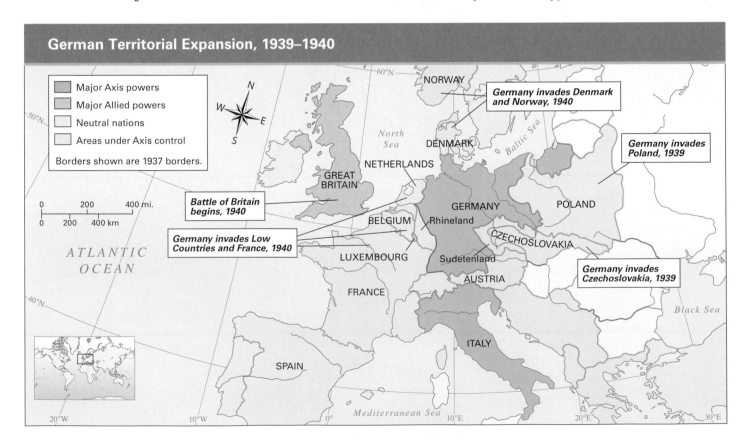

German Territorial Expansion, 1939–1940

Major Axis powers
Major Allied powers
Neutral nations
Areas under Axis control
Borders shown are 1937 borders.

0   200   400 mi.
0   200   400 km

Battle of Britain begins, 1940

Germany invades Denmark and Norway, 1940

Germany invades Poland, 1939

Germany invades Low Countries and France, 1940

Germany invades Czechoslovakia, 1939

NORWAY
North Sea
DENMARK
Baltic Sea
GREAT BRITAIN
NETHERLANDS
POLAND
BELGIUM
GERMANY
Rhineland
CZECHOSLOVAKIA
LUXEMBOURG
Sudetenland
AUSTRIA
FRANCE
ATLANTIC OCEAN
SPAIN
ITALY
Black Sea
Mediterranean Sea

During the Blitz, German bombs pounded residential areas of London. Hundreds of thousands of children were evacuated to safer rural areas. Many Londoners who stayed in the city took shelter in the subway, or the Underground, during air raids. The Underground could hold more than 170,000 people.

The southeast would become a **puppet government** known as Vichy France. A puppet government is one that is run by citizens of a conquered country who carry out the policies of the conqueror.

Britain Fights on Alone Britain, now led by Prime Minister Winston Churchill, stood alone against the Axis powers. After the evacuation from Dunkirk, Churchill had vowed to fight Germany and defend Britain with every resource at his disposal. In a speech to Parliament, he declared,

> We shall not flag [tire] nor fail. We shall go on to the end. We shall fight . . . on the seas and oceans; we shall fight with growing confidence and growing strength in the air. We shall defend our island whatever the cost may be; we shall fight on the beaches, landing grounds, in fields, in streets and on the hills. We shall never surrender.
> —Speech before the House of Commons, June 4, 1940

Hitler wanted to conquer Britain, but he knew that the large and powerful British navy could keep his army from crossing the English Channel. To defeat that navy, he had to establish dominance in the air. He set up air bases in conquered lands from France to Norway and moved in some 2,800 bombers and fighter planes.

German planes flew raids throughout the summer of 1940 and into the fall. They attacked British ships, ports, airfields, radar stations, and industrial centers. To counter this onslaught, the British sent up the fighter pilots of the Royal Air Force (RAF) in an engagement known as the Battle of Britain. The RAF pilots, flying their Spitfires and Hurricanes, proved effective against the German air campaign. By late August, they had downed more than 600 German aircraft, at a cost of 260 British planes.

In September 1940, Britain launched its first bombing raid on Berlin. Germany shifted its targets to British cities. For the next several months, bombing attacks devastated sections of London and other large cities. Londoners called this campaign the Blitz, a shortening of blitzkrieg. By the spring of 1941, the number of raids dwindled. The British had successfully defended their homeland. That victory gave the Allies reason to believe that Hitler could be stopped.

34.5 The United States Enters World War II

After war broke out in Europe, isolationism lost some of its appeal for Americans. Most now openly supported the Allies. Hoping to keep the United States out of the war, Hitler sought to expand his alliance. In September 1940, Germany, Italy, and Japan signed the Tripartite Pact, making Japan a member of the Axis powers. The three nations agreed to provide mutual support in the event of an attack by a country not yet in the war. The attacker they had in mind was the United States. If the United States entered the war, it would have to fight on two fronts—Asia and Europe. Hitler hoped that the threat of a two-front war would ensure American neutrality for a while longer.

Roosevelt Inches Away from Neutrality The start of war put the United States in a risky position. Americans feared getting drawn into the fighting, but they wanted to help the Allies. France and Great Britain needed weapons. Yet the neutrality acts banned the sale of arms to belligerent nations. In November 1939, Roosevelt pushed a bill through Congress that repealed the arms embargo. This Neutrality Act of 1939 included a "cash-and-carry" provision. Nations had to pay cash for materials and carry them away in their own ships.

After the fall of France, the United States finally began rearming itself in earnest. In September 1940, Congress enacted the first peacetime military draft in U.S. history. A month later, the Selective Training and Service Act had enrolled 16 million men. Yet during the 1940 election campaign, Roosevelt assured Americans, "Your boys are not going to be sent into any foreign wars." In November, he won an unprecedented third term as president.

In December 1940, the Battle of Britain was raging. Churchill declared that his country was nearly bankrupt. Roosevelt was determined to provide Britain "all aid short of war" and urged Congress to adopt a plan to lend, not sell, arms to Britain. This legislation, the **Lend-Lease Act,** passed in March 1941, but only after heated public and congressional debate.

In June 1941, Hitler broke the Nonaggression Pact by attacking the Soviet Union. Great Britain announced its support for the USSR, and the United States began sending supplies to the besieged country under the Lend-Lease Act.

In August, Churchill and Roosevelt met in secret aboard a warship in Canadian waters of the North Atlantic. There they prepared a declaration of common principles known as the Atlantic Charter. They promised not to use the war to expand their own territory, and they asserted the right of all peoples to self-government. Three months later, Congress voted to allow American merchant ships to arm themselves and sail to Britain.

Japan Attacks the United States From 1940 to 1941, Japan continued seeking raw materials through conquest. It occupied French Indochina, in Southeast Asia, and set its sights on the Dutch East Indies. Its goal was to push Western powers out and establish a "new order in East Asia," with

By attacking Pearl Harbor, the Japanese hoped to destroy the U.S. Pacific Fleet. Although the Japanese inflicted major damage, they failed to destroy the fuel depot that served the fleet. They also failed to sink any aircraft carriers, which were not in Pearl Harbor at the time.

Japan at the center. The United States tried to undercut Japan's aggression in several ways. It sent loans and other aid to Japan's enemy, China, and froze Japanese assets in American banks. It also blocked the export of vital resources, including oil, to Japan. Relations between the two nations steadily worsened.

By 1941, American intelligence officers had managed to intercept and decode secret messages from Japan to its foreign offices. Late in the year, officers learned of a coming attack on American territory in the Pacific Ocean. They thought the attack might target an American base in the Philippines. Instead it was aimed at Pearl Harbor, Hawaii—the home of the U.S. Pacific Fleet.

On December 7, 1941, Japanese aircraft carriers approached Hawaii. From the carriers, more than 300 bombers and fighter planes launched the attack on Pearl Harbor. In a little more than two hours, the Japanese sank or damaged 18 American ships. At nearby airfields, Japanese warplanes damaged or destroyed about 300 military aircraft. In all, the raid left more than 2,400 Americans dead and nearly 1,200 wounded. The Japanese lost just 29 planes in the attack.

The next day, Roosevelt asked Congress to declare war on Japan. "Hostilities exist," he said. "Our people, our territory, and our interests are in grave danger." Three days later, Germany and Italy declared war on the United States. Americans began to prepare for a conflict that would test the nation's strength and courage.

On December 8, 1941, President Roosevelt signed a declaration of war against Japan. In response, Germany and Italy declared war on the United States. Roosevelt, in turn, declared war on the two major Axis powers.

Summary

By the 1930s, extreme nationalists had gained power in Italy, Germany, and Japan, which became known as the Axis powers. By seeking to expand through military conquest, these countries began World War II. In 1941, the United States entered the war as one of the Allied powers.

Totalitarianism In 1924, Joseph Stalin became the dictator of the communist Soviet Union. Nazi dictator Adolf Hitler gained power by promising to restore German strength. He built up the German military and began a campaign of expansion. Similar actions took place in Italy under dictator Benito Mussolini and in Japan under Japanese militarists.

Munich Pact Great Britain and France tried to appease Hitler. In the Munich Pact, they agreed to give him part of Czechoslovakia in return for peace. But Hitler continued with territorial expansion. Germany's invasion of Poland in 1939 triggered World War II.

Neutrality Acts A series of neutrality acts in the 1930s kept the United States from being drawn into European conflicts, including the Spanish Civil War. As World War II began, however, Franklin Roosevelt and Congress revised the acts to allow arms trading with the Allies.

Lend-Lease Act Germany quickly occupied most of Europe and threatened to invade Great Britain. As German bombers ravaged British cities, the United States decided to help Britain by passing the Lend-Lease Act. This law allowed the United States to lend arms to Britain and, later, to the Soviet Union.

Attack on Pearl Harbor On December 7, 1941, Japan attacked the U.S. Pacific Fleet at Pearl Harbor. This attack caused the United States to declare war on Japan and enter World War II.

Chapter 35

The Impact of World War II on Americans

What kinds of opportunities and hardships did the war create for Americans at home and abroad?

35.1 Introduction

After the shock of the Pearl Harbor attack, many Americans wondered what would happen next. Would waves of Japanese bombers attack the West Coast? For months, rumors of an enemy invasion haunted the region. In time, the fears faded, but coastal communities remained wary.

As it turned out, the United States was not immediately endangered by an enemy invasion. Yet, as President Franklin Roosevelt warned, the threat was real. If the Allies failed to stop the Axis powers, then one day Americans could personally experience the horrors of war in their own land.

Roosevelt knew the war effort would require the enthusiastic backing of the American people in order to succeed. Millions of Americans would be needed to serve in the armed forces. Many others would help on the home front by working to expand the output of war materials. Everyone would have to make sacrifices in support of the armed forces. They would have to accept **rationing**—a system for limiting the distribution of food, gasoline, and other goods—so the military could have the weapons, equipment, and supplies it needed. As a result, life in the United States would change dramatically.

These changes were evident in many ways, even in clothing styles. The armed forces needed fabric for uniforms. In March 1942, the government announced rules aimed at saving more than 40 million pounds of wool a year. Men's suits could no longer be sold with a vest or an extra pair of pants. Cuffs were eliminated, as were patch pockets and wide lapels. The new rules also restricted the type and amount of fabric in women's clothes. Designers cooperated by using more synthetics, such as rayon, and by making skirts shorter and dresses simpler.

During the war, the entire country would endure hardships, many extending far beyond being forced to wear plainer clothes. Yet the war would also offer new opportunities to countless Americans.

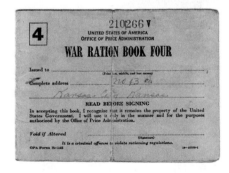

Civilians contributed to the war effort when they took part in the rationing system. The key to the system was the ration book, which contained coupons that allowed consumers to buy rationed items, such as canned goods, sugar, coffee, and dairy products.

◀ Women workers at an aircraft plant

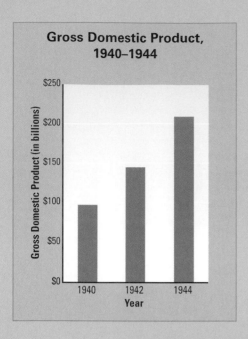

Gross Domestic Product, 1940–1944

Gross Domestic Product (in billions)

Year

As the war effort got underway, the government spent billions of dollars on military supplies and equipment. War industries worked night and day to satisfy this demand. As a result, the nation's gross domestic product rose sharply. So did the national debt, as the government borrowed heavily to cover war expenses.

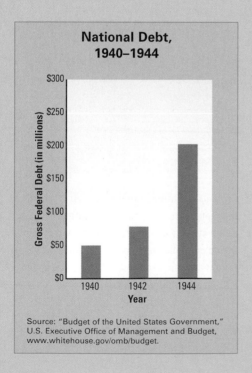

National Debt, 1940–1944

Gross Federal Debt (in millions)

Year

Source: "Budget of the United States Government," U.S. Executive Office of Management and Budget, www.whitehouse.gov/omb/budget.

35.2 Organizing the American Economy for War

The job of organizing the wartime economy fell to the **War Production Board (WPB)**. The WPB sought to meet Roosevelt's goal of making the United States the "arsenal of democracy." As with the War Industries Board of World War I, the WPB's main task was to manage the conversion of industries to military production. Some of these makeovers seemed natural. Automobile manufacturers, for example, switched from making car engines to making airplane and tank engines. Other conversions called for more dramatic changes. For example, a soft drink company might retool its machinery and retrain its workers to pack artillery shells with explosives. A maker of model trains would begin producing bomb fuses. All across the country, businesses mobilized their resources to serve the needs of the military.

A Wartime Production Boom Ends the Depression The huge demand for military supplies revived the economy. Businesses expanded and hired more workers. Farmers prospered as crop prices and farm incomes rose. The Depression ended, and a period of vigorous economic growth began.

As the economy moved into high gear, the **gross domestic product (GDP)** rose rapidly. GDP is the total value of goods and services produced in a country in a year. From 1940 to 1944, this basic measure of national output increased by 116 percent. During the same four years, the total personal income of American workers rose by more than 110 percent. Business income grew even faster, increasing by nearly 130 percent.

During the New Deal, the government had taken an active role in stimulating the economy. To meet wartime needs, it expanded that role. The WPB successfully mobilized businesses behind the war effort, leading to closer relationships between the government and large corporations. As also happened during World War I, a National War Labor Board (NWLB) was set up to mobilize labor.

The main task of the NWLB was to settle labor disputes before they disrupted the production of war goods. Immediately after the attack on Pearl Harbor, union leaders agreed to a no-strike pledge. Eight months later, the NWLB imposed limits on wage increases. The wage limits and no-strike pledge left labor leaders with very little bargaining power. In exchange, the NWLB guaranteed unions that all new employees at companies with union contracts would automatically become union members. This policy boosted union membership.

Financing the War Effort with Taxes and Bonds During the war, government spending rose to new levels. More than $175 billion worth of defense contracts went out to businesses from 1940 to 1944. The government met these costs the same way it had during World War I—through taxes and borrowing.

Taxes provided about 45 percent of the revenue needed to pay for the war. The Revenue Act of 1942 increased individual and corporate income tax rates and more than tripled the number of individuals required to pay income tax. To make tax collection easier, Congress devised a system of withholding. Employers held back a certain amount from every paycheck and sent it directly to the government. This system of payroll taxes is still in place today.

Borrowing provided much of the rest of the money to finance the war. The government borrowed from banks and other financial institutions. It also borrowed from the American people through the sale of war savings bonds. As during World War I, war bonds not only provided the government with cash but also gave people a way to show their support for the war effort. Government agencies and private companies once again produced advertisements urging Americans to buy war bonds. Campaigns to sell bonds involved a variety of Americans, from schoolchildren to glamorous celebrities.

Government Attempts to Curb Inflation and Consumption Inflation became a serious problem during the war. Americans had money to spend, but the focus on military production meant that few consumer goods were available. In a fireside chat, Roosevelt explained the supply-and-demand problem: "You do not have to be a professor of mathematics or economics to see that if people with plenty of cash start bidding against each other for scarce goods, the price of those goods goes up."

Congress gave the job of curbing inflation to the Office of Price Administration. The OPA instituted **price controls**—a system of legal restrictions on the prices charged for goods. These controls seemed to work. From 1940 to 1945, consumer prices rose only 35 percent, instead of doubling or tripling as some officials had feared.

The OPA also rationed about 20 basic consumer products, including gasoline, tires, sugar, meats, and processed foods. Each month, consumers received books of coupons that they turned in to the grocer when they bought rationed foods. When they ran out of coupons, they could buy no more until they received a new book the next month. Drivers used a different ration book to purchase gasoline. Americans grumbled about rationing, but most complied. This program succeeded in reducing the overconsumption of scarce goods and ensured that everyone would have fairly equal access to those goods.

Americans also aided the war effort in other ways. They formed car pools or rode bicycles to work. They recycled metals, paper, rubber, and other materials. One old shovel, Americans were told, contained enough iron to make four hand grenades. Children collected much of the scrap material. They also peeled the foil off cigarette packages and gum wrappers and rolled them into balls for recycling. Families also planted victory gardens to grow food. In 1943, more than 20 million gardens yielded one third of all the vegetables eaten in the country that year. Victory gardens and recycling campaigns not only boosted war production but also raised the morale of Americans on the home front. People understood they were making an important contribution to the war effort.

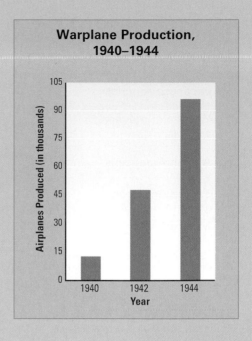

Warplane Production, 1940–1944

Warplanes and tanks were critical items for the U.S. military during the war. Production of both types of equipment increased rapidly during the early years of the war. Warplane production continued to grow through 1944, while the production of tanks was in decline.

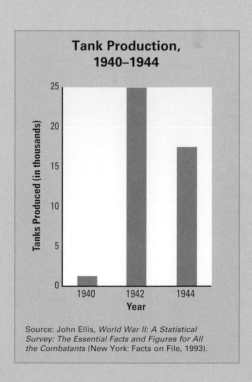

Tank Production, 1940–1944

Source: John Ellis, *World War II: A Statistical Survey: The Essential Facts and Figures for All the Combatants* (New York: Facts on File, 1993).

Service in World War II by Selected Groups	
Japanese Americans	25,000
Women in military auxiliary	350,000
African Americans	1,057,000
Jewish Americans	550,000
Mexican Americans	500,000

Sources: "A More Perfect Union," americanhistory.si.edu. National Manpower Council, *Womanpower*, 1957. *Selective Service and Victory*, 1948. "When Jews Were GIs," Fathom, University of Michigan. National Park Service.

More than 16 million Americans served in the military during World War II. These men and women represented many different ethnic groups. Members of these groups often faced racism or other forms of discrimination. Some groups were segregated. Within each combat unit, however, a bond often emerged that crossed ethnic lines.

35.3 American GIs Go to War

Many young Americans left the comforts of home to join the military. While they were in the service, the government provided all of their food and supplies. Those items were often labeled "government issue," or GI. Soldiers had GI soap, GI socks, a GI helmet, and a GI rifle. For that reason, they began referring to themselves as GI soldiers, or simply **GIs**. The name stuck, and fighting men in all the armed forces used it proudly.

Assembling a Fighting Force In 1940, more than 16 million men between the ages of 21 and 35 had registered for the draft. Later registrations expanded the age limits to include men from 18 to 44. Most draftees ended up in the army. By the time of the attack on Pearl Harbor, they had swelled the army's ranks from 300,000 to a fighting force of more than 1.5 million troops.

After the attack on Pearl Harbor, volunteers swamped military recruiting stations throughout the nation. They represented a broad range of American society, from miners and mill workers to professors and politicians. By the end of the war, nearly 6 million had enlisted, mainly in the navy or the army air corps.

For draftees and volunteers alike, the war offered an opportunity to show their patriotism by fighting for their country. Most willingly packed their bags and boarded buses and trains, not knowing whether they would ever return. Immigrants and ethnic minorities saw joining the military as an opportunity to show that they were truly Americans.

Preparing the Troops to Fight Draftees and recruits reported first to an army reception center within a huge complex, such as at Fort Dix, New Jersey, or Fort Bragg, North Carolina. Here they had their first taste of military life. They slept in barracks with no privacy and traded their civilian clothes for uniforms. They listened to lectures and submitted to medical exams. The main goal of the reception center, however, was to determine where each recruit should go for training. Various aptitude tests helped decide this.

After a couple weeks, most new soldiers were sent off to one of the many army training camps scattered across the country. Most of these young men had little experience with life outside their hometowns. Suddenly they found themselves thrown into an unfamiliar environment with fellow soldiers from all over the country. One GI from the Midwest recalled, "The first time I ever heard a New England accent was at Fort Benning . . . [and] the southerner was an exotic creature to me."

The trainers, or drill instructors, had as little as eight weeks to prepare men for combat. The job of the trainers was to turn soft civilians into rugged fighting men. Trainees followed a strict routine. They got up at 6 A.M., washed, dressed, ate, and made the long march to the training site by 8 A.M. For the next nine hours or so, they worked at becoming a soldier.

Instruction included tent pitching, map reading, guard duty, sanitation, weapons care, and endless physical training. Later, trainees took part in parachute jumping and live-ammunition exercises, which called for soldiers to crawl through the dirt while real machine gun bullets whizzed above their heads. They marched back to camp in the evening, exhausted. One draftee wrote home to his parents in May 1943: "I don't know whether I can stand to do what we have to do or not. I have to try it though." Near the end of his basic training, he wrote again: "It was 106 today and when we are out drilling we really do get hot, but I will tell you the truth, I have got so that I can stand it just as good as the next one. I sweat a lot but I go on like I was cool." The draftee had become a GI.

The GI's War: Hardships and Opportunities Training could only do so much to prepare a GI for combat. Few were ever truly ready for the intensity of the battlefield. The deafening blasts of artillery or grenades, the squeal and clatter of tanks on the move, and the billowing clouds of smoke all combined to create a surreal atmosphere.

Then there was the fear. Soldiers knew they could die at any time, especially if they were crossing an open field or storming a beach under heavy enemy fire. New soldiers, especially, tended to freeze at the first sign of danger—and they saw danger everywhere. Experienced soldiers learned to distinguish the real dangers, such as the sound of an enemy tank or incoming artillery fire, from the din of war. Yet even battle-hardened veterans often felt a heart-pounding sense of doom in the battle zone, where uncertainty ruled.

Between battles, boredom sometimes became the enemy. Soldiers with free time often felt homesick and lonely. Many men fought these feelings by writing letters. At night, they would try to put their thoughts and experiences down on paper for girlfriends, wives, or parents. A letter from home was a major event.

Under the stress of war, soldiers developed strong bonds of friendship. "The reason you storm the beaches is not patriotism or bravery," one rifleman recalled. "It's that sense of not wanting to fail your buddies."

Those who survived the war often found their lives significantly changed. Many returned physically, mentally, or emotionally wounded by their combat experiences. Amid the horrors of war, though, many gained a greater appreciation for such American ideals as liberty and came home with a new sense of pride in themselves and in their country.

Most U.S. soldiers went off to fight in World War II with a strong commitment to the Allied cause. Nevertheless, they often found the experience of war shattering. Combat was grueling and traumatic, and many soldiers came home with a new respect for the horrors of war.

Many U.S. residents of Japanese descent, including this woman and her grandchild, were moved to internment camps during World War II. This measure was intended to prevent sabotage during the war. Most of the detainees were Japanese Americans, however, and relocation violated their rights as U.S. citizens.

35.4 The Internment of Japanese Americans

When the attack on Pearl Harbor occurred, there were about 150,000 Japanese Americans living in the Hawaiian Islands. Some people questioned their loyalty, even accusing them of helping plan the surprise attack. Fearing sabotage, the War Department recommended the mass evacuation of Japanese Americans from Hawaii. But the American military governor of Hawaii urged everyone to stay calm. Businesses on the islands opposed evacuation. They noted that losing so many workers would ruin the islands' economy. The press backed this position and worked hard to keep false rumors from circulating. In the end, nearly all of the Japanese Americans in Hawaii stayed there.

Dealing with the Fear of Potential Collaborators On the mainland, concerns about disloyalty extended to people of German or Italian ancestry. They were seen as potential collaborators—people who work with an enemy to undermine a nation's security. Shortly after the Pearl Harbor attack, President Roosevelt signed proclamations declaring all German, Italian, and Japanese nationals, or non-U.S. citizens, to be "enemy aliens." These orders affected more than 314,000 people of German ancestry, 690,000 people of Italian ancestry, and 47,000 people of Japanese ancestry.

All "enemy aliens" had to register with the government and carry special identification cards. They had to turn in all firearms and cameras, as well as shortwave radios, which might be used to send information to the enemy. They also needed a travel permit to go more than 5 miles from their homes.

Government officials considered putting all "enemy aliens" into camps. However, the task of relocating all the German and Italian aliens posed huge problems. Also, politically influential groups of German Americans and Italian Americans resisted such a measure. The government did round up several thousand German and Italian aliens and sent them to **internment camps** in the middle of the country. An internment camp is a center for confining people who have been relocated for reasons of national security.

Roosevelt Authorizes the Removal of Japanese Americans The people of Japanese ancestry, in contrast, were a much smaller group with much less political power. They faced more racial discrimination than did people of German or Italian ancestry because they were of nonwhite, non-European ancestry. Their social isolation also worked against them. They had not assimilated into American culture as well as other immigrant groups had. They kept largely to themselves, in ethnic communities outside the American mainstream. In addition, they lived mainly on the West Coast, where fear of a Japanese invasion was strongest. Unlike in Hawaii, the mainland press whipped up that fear by accusing Japanese Americans of spying or of being more loyal to Japan than to the United States.

All these factors made it easier for the government to act against people of Japanese ancestry. In February 1942, Roosevelt issued **Executive Order 9066**. This order declared that large military zones could be set up to exclude current residents who were believed to be a threat to security. In March 1942, the military used this executive order to launch a mass evacuation of people of Japanese ancestry from the Pacific Coast. Evacuees had just a few weeks to sell their homes and possessions.

The order to "move out and stay out" applied not only to Japanese "enemy aliens" but also to Japanese American citizens. Of the 127,000 people of Japanese ancestry living in the mainland United States, 80,000 were native-born American citizens. As such, they were entitled to the same constitutional rights as all citizens. This was the main argument made by a Japanese American named Fred Korematsu, who did not obey the order because it would mean leaving his non-Japanese girlfriend. After two months, Korematsu was arrested and convicted with remaining in a restricted military area.

Korematsu appealed the verdict all the way to the Supreme Court. In the case *Korematsu v. United States,* the Court upheld his conviction on the grounds that a group's civil rights can be set aside in a time of war. Three of the nine justices dissented from this opinion, including Justice Robert H. Jackson. He expressed his fear that "the Court for all time has validated the principle of racial discrimination in criminal procedure and of transplanting American citizens."

Life in the Internment Camps More than 100,000 Japanese "enemy aliens" and Japanese American citizens were forced to evacuate. Families collected their belongings in a few pieces of luggage and left their homes. First they gathered at assembly centers. Then, in the summer of 1942, they boarded trains for internment camps scattered throughout the western states. They had no idea where they were headed. The typical camp, officially known as a relocation center, was in a desert region far from any town. "No houses were in sight," one internee recalled. "No trees or anything green—only scrubby sagebrush and an occasional low cactus, and mostly dry, baked earth." In this setting, internees endured extreme heat in the summer and cold in the winter.

The camps had been constructed in a hurry. They consisted of "row after row of barracks," as one surprised visitor recalled, with "high barbed wire fences" and "machine gun towers all around." The single-story, wooden barracks contained several one-room apartments. Each came with cots, blankets, and a bare light bulb. Here, an entire family tried to make a home. They shared toilets with others in the barracks and used common bathing and dining facilities. The crowded conditions meant that sanitation was often a problem.

Despite these hardships, most of the internees worked to make camp life more bearable. They built chairs and tables from scrap lumber. They grew vegetables. They set up schools, libraries, hospitals, and newspaper offices.

As early as 1942, while the camps were still filling up, the government realized that the threat of a West Coast invasion had passed. Officials began allowing certain groups of Japanese Americans to leave the camps. These included about 10,000 farm workers and 4,300 college students. Starting in 1943, thousands of young men left the camps to join the army. Most of them served in the 442nd Regimental Combat Team. This all-volunteer Japanese American unit became famous for its bravery in battle. In fact, it earned more medals than any other unit of its size in American history. In 1944, the government began letting the remaining internees return to the West Coast. Within the next year, all were free to leave the camps.

Most internment camps were located in the West. They were set up in desert areas away from the coast and far from population centers. The government referred to these camps as relocation centers, but critics called them concentration camps.

Several thousand Japanese American GIs fought with the 442nd Regimental Combat Team. This unit won many medals during the war, including the Congressional Medal of Honor. In 1946, President Harry Truman told the 442nd, "You fought for the free nations of the world. You fought not only the enemy, you fought prejudice—and you won."

Women started out in the armed forces as secretaries and clerks but soon took on more challenging tasks. Here, a woman prepares for a military career alongside men at New York University.

35.5 Women at War

In early 1942, a popular song called "Rosie the Riveter" captured the spirit of the home front:

> All the day long,
> Whether rain or shine,
> She's a part of the assembly line.
> She's making history,
> Working for victory,
> Rosie the Riveter.
> —"Rosie the Riveter," by Redd Evans
> and John Jacob Loeb, 1942

One of the country's most popular artists, Norman Rockwell, put his own version of Rosie on the cover of a national magazine, *The Saturday Evening Post*. Two films about Rosie followed. The fictional Rosie the Riveter came to represent all the real women who worked to support the war effort.

New Opportunities for Women in the Workforce The demand for workers skyrocketed during the war, as men left their jobs to serve in the armed forces. At first, industry hired unemployed men to fill those jobs. But as war production soared, businesses and the government started recruiting women, using slogans such as, "The more women at work, the sooner we win!" About 18 million women took jobs outside the home during the war, up from 12 million before the war.

Most women continued to work in occupations that were traditionally female, such as service, clerical, and sales work. Many women, however, took positions held traditionally by men. They became welders, mechanics, and lumberjacks, as well as lawyers, physicists, and architects.

Nearly 2 million women worked in shipyards and other heavy industries. Many toiled as riveters on the thousands of airplanes built during the war. Riveters operated in pairs. One woman used a heavy mechanical gun to shoot a rivet through a pair of metal sheets. The other woman stood on the opposite side to buck, or flatten, the rivet. The rivets held the metal sheets and the plane together. Tough physical labor like this increased women's self-confidence and independence, as well as their income. As one riveter explained,

> "The war years had a tremendous impact on women. I know for myself it was the first time I had a chance to get out of the kitchen and work in industry and make a few bucks . . . You came out to California, put on your pants, and took your lunch pail to a man's job . . . This was the beginning of women's feeling that they could do something more."
>
> —Sybil Lewis, quoted in *The Homefront: America During World War II*, 1984

Hardships on the Job and at Home Not everything about the workplace pleased women, though. They often faced hostility on the job, especially in male-dominated industries. African American women faced the added stress of racial hostility. Another issue was that women's wages did not increase as much as men's pay. In 1942, the NWLB ruled that women should get equal pay for "work of the same quality and quantity." However, businesses often ignored this rule. Even labor unions, whose female membership soared during the war, rarely challenged unfair wage rates.

During the war, most working women were married and were expected to keep up with their family responsibilities. Many husbands had gone off to war. As a result, women often faced the hardship of working a "double shift." They spent a full day at the plant or office and another full day cooking, cleaning, and performing other domestic duties.

By the end of the war, the typical working woman was over the age of 35. Relatively few of these women had young children at home. Those who did usually arranged for their children to stay with relatives or friends during the day. But older children were often left to fend for themselves. As a result, rates of juvenile delinquency and school truancy increased. Many teenage boys dropped out of school, lured by high-paying war-production jobs.

New Opportunities for Women in the Military Soon after the war started, military leaders realized that women could do much of the clerical and secretarial work done by male soldiers, freeing up the men for combat duty. Congress agreed. In 1942, it passed legislation creating a civilian support unit for the army known as the Women's Army Auxiliary Corps.

On the first day of registration, more than 13,000 women volunteered to serve in this unit. The following year, the unit was granted military status and was renamed the **Women's Army Corps (WAC)**. Women in the WAC became members of the military and underwent rigorous army training. "If the guys can take it," one volunteer remarked, "so can I."

In 1942, the navy and the coast guard also established their own branches for women. Navy women were called WAVES and coast guard women were SPARs. Women in all the armed forces quickly moved beyond clerical work into jobs such as truck driver, mechanic, radio operator, air traffic controller, and parachute rigger. A select few became pilots, mainly to ferry aircraft from factories to bases. Only WACs, however, served on the battlefield, working behind the lines in various support roles, including nursing. More than 200 American women died overseas as a result of enemy action.

During the war, posters and magazine ads encouraged women to fill jobs left by men who joined the armed forces. Millions of women responded—some for patriotic reasons, some for higher pay. Women made up about a third of the new workers hired during the war.

The United States was fighting in the name of democracy against Nazi Germany, which embraced an extreme form of racism based on the idea of Aryan supremacy. Yet racism was still a powerful force in American society. No one was more keenly aware of this contradiction than African Americans. After all, their participation in World War I had not helped their struggle against racism at home. As one black newspaper, the *Chicago Defender,* asked, "Why die for democracy for some foreign country when we don't even have it here?"

Other black leaders called for a battle against racism on two fronts. They wanted all citizens to join in the fight for a "double victory"—a victory for democracy both at home and abroad. This **Double V campaign** forced many white Americans to rethink their attitudes toward black Americans.

Confronting Segregation in the Military With the establishment of the draft in 1940, thousands of African Americans lined up to join the armed forces. By war's end, more than a million had served. They faced many hardships, beginning with their segregation in training camp. They ate in separate mess halls from the white troops and slept in separate barracks. Camps that had a single movie theater even made black trainees sit together in the last row.

In the early buildup to war, the marines and army air corps refused to take any African Americans. The navy limited African American duties to cooking, cleaning rooms, and shining shoes. One such "mess man" aboard the USS *Philadelphia* sent a letter to a newspaper hoping to discourage other black men from joining the navy. "All they would become," he wrote, "is seagoing bellhops, chambermaids, and dishwashers." The army accepted black GIs, but it excluded them from combat. The GIs served in segregated units led by white officers, often working in construction, supply, or other service groups.

Black leaders pressed the government to end military discrimination. In time, the armed services gave more black soldiers the opportunity to engage in combat and to become officers. The army air corps established its first black combat unit in 1941. Known as the **Tuskegee Airmen,** these pilots and their support crews showed that African Americans could handle the most demanding assignments. They served mainly as bomber escorts, engaging in direct

In 1941, the army air corps brought African Americans from around the country to train at a flying school in Tuskegee, Alabama. As one pilot recalled, "They recruited All-American athletes. They had mathematical geniuses. They had ministers, doctors, lawyers, farm boys, all down there trying to learn to fly." These men won fame as the Tuskegee Airmen.

combat with German fighter planes. The Tuskegee Airmen gained a reputation for skill and courage, shooting some 400 German attackers out of the sky. They were the only fighter group never to lose a bomber to enemy planes.

Seeking Opportunity and Equality on the Home Front Black leaders were also working to improve conditions at home. In June 1941, A. Philip Randolph, head of a powerful all-black railroad union, met with President Roosevelt at the White House. The government had done little to end discrimination in defense-related jobs. One steelmaker expressed the attitude of many in the defense industry when he said, "We have not had a Negro worker in twenty-five years, and do not plan to start now." Roosevelt sympathized with black Americans, but the war in Europe had kept him from paying much attention to civil rights—until Randolph's visit.

Randolph focused Roosevelt's attention by threatening to lead a massive march on Washington to protest discrimination. He promised that unless Roosevelt acted, tens of thousands of African Americans would swarm into the nation's capital on July 1. The threat worked. On June 25, 1941, Roosevelt signed Executive Order 8802, outlawing discrimination by defense contractors.

This executive order helped pave the way for nearly a million African Americans to work for defense industries during the war. It also triggered a migration of African Americans out of the rural South and into the industrial cities of the North and the West. From 1940 to 1945, some 500,000 black Americans, attracted by higher-paying jobs, left the South. In the process, they escaped the Jim Crow laws that legalized segregation and kept many of them from voting. In the cities, however, black Americans faced other hardships, including a lack of housing and social services, as well as ongoing racial discrimination.

They also faced a white backlash. Race riots broke out in many cities across the country as black migrants competed with white residents for housing and jobs. One of the worst riots occurred in Detroit, Michigan, in the summer of 1943. A fistfight and other minor incidents ballooned into a widespread conflict. Mobs of rioters burned automobiles, looted stores, and engaged in bloody battles in the streets. The riots resulted in the deaths of 25 blacks and 9 whites.

Challenging Racism at Home The Double V campaign's call for an end to racism and segregation received support from several African American organizations. One group, the National Urban League, had been helping black migrants since its founding in 1910. It opposed discrimination in defense plants, fought to integrate labor unions, and pushed federal officials to ensure equal opportunity for African Americans in housing and employment. Another group, the NAACP, had been fighting for equality since 1909. It focused on seeking racial justice through the courts. During the war, its membership soared.

The National Urban League and the NAACP did not want to undermine the war effort, so they avoided making strident demands. Another organization, the Congress of Racial Equality (CORE), took a tougher stance. Founded in 1942, CORE believed in confronting discrimination through nonviolent protest. Its efforts, along with the work of the NAACP and the National Urban League, helped set the stage for the postwar civil rights movement.

In wartime America, the letter V commonly stood for Allied victory. In 1942, someone wrote to the *Pittsburgh Courier,* black America's leading newspaper, suggesting that African Americans should seek victory not just abroad but also at home. On February 7, the *Courier* printed this emblem on its front page. The Double V campaign was born.

On November 9, 1938, the Nazis organized riots that killed Jews and destroyed Jewish property. So much glass littered the streets that the event became known as *Kristallnacht,* or the "night of broken glass." Franklin Roosevelt told a reporter that he "could scarcely believe that such things could occur in a twentieth-century civilization."

35.7 Jewish Americans and the War

The war brought special hardships for Jewish Americans. They not only made sacrifices like other Americans did, but they also suffered from knowing that millions of Jews were being imprisoned and murdered in Europe. Furthermore, they could do nothing to stop the slaughter.

Growing Alarm at Nazi Persecution of Jews American Jews started hearing reports of Nazi persecution in Germany shortly after Hitler took power in 1933. That year, the Nazi Party organized a nationwide boycott of Jewish businesses. Two years later, the German parliament stripped Jews of their citizenship. It also forced them to sell their property to non-Jews. Shortly after taking over Austria in March 1938, Hitler began persecuting Austrian Jews. Tens of thousands fled.

Then, on November 9, 1938, the Nazis instigated a night of anti-Jewish rioting known as *Kristallnacht,* or the "night of broken glass." Mobs smashed the windows of thousands of Jewish-owned shops, burned nearly every Jewish synagogue in Germany, and killed more than 90 Jews. Some 30,000 Jewish men were arrested and sent to concentration camps. These events received detailed coverage in the American press.

After *Kristallnacht,* thousands of Jews wanted to flee to the United States. But the 1924 National Origins Act placed severe limits on the number of immigrants from any one nation. Besides, very few Americans wanted to open the country to a flood of immigrants, especially during the Depression.

These factors, combined with widespread anti-Semitism, led to incidents such as the voyage of the steamship *St. Louis.* In 1939, the *St. Louis* carried 930 Jews from Germany across the Atlantic Ocean to Cuba. But Cuba refused to accept the refugees. The *St. Louis* next steamed north along the Florida coast. Roosevelt ignored pleas for help from the ship's passengers, however. With food and water running low, the captain decided to return to Europe. A number of passengers ended up in France and the Low Countries or back in Germany. Many would later die in concentration camps.

During the war, reports trickled out of Europe about mass killings of Jews by the Nazis. Accounts from Poland told of concentration camps that had gas chambers for killing Jews. Few American news sources passed this information along to the public, however. When they did, the stories did not make headlines. Editors failed to tie these stories together or explain that they represented a Nazi campaign to exterminate European Jews.

Jewish Americans Urge the Government to Help Jews in Europe Jewish Americans, however, were painfully aware of the mass murder of European Jews. Many had relatives and friends in Europe but felt helpless to save them. Others took action, such as boycotting German products, raising money for refugees, and holding public demonstrations. In July 1942, about 20,000 people gathered at Madison Square Garden in New York City to protest Nazi brutality. Similar rallies took place in Chicago, Los Angeles, and other cities. Jews urged officials to send food packages to concentration camps and to set up prisoner exchanges to free Jews. Jewish groups pleaded with legislators and the president to change immigration laws.

Passengers aboard the steamship *St. Louis* wave goodbye as the ship leaves Havana, Cuba, on May 3, 1939. The passengers, all Jews fleeing Nazi Germany, were refused entry to Cuba and to the United States. They ended up back in Europe, where many died at the hands of the Nazis.

Several factors kept the government from offering refuge to victims of the Nazis. Polls showed that most Americans, their views colored by anti-Semitism, were unwilling to admit large numbers of European Jews. Even many American Jews worried that massive immigration might intensify anti-Semitic feelings. Roosevelt also feared espionage and sabotage. Advisors insisted that any stream of Jewish refugees into the United States would include Nazi agents.

By the end of 1942, the government knew that Hitler was slaughtering Jews in a systematic way. Still, it was not until 1944 that Roosevelt issued an executive order creating the War Refugee Board. This agency arranged for Jewish refugees to stay at centers in Italy and North Africa, as well as in former army camps in the United States. Henry Morgenthau Jr., the only Jew in Roosevelt's cabinet, later recalled the mission of the War Refugee Board. "The stake was the Jewish population of Nazi-controlled Europe," he said. "The threat was their total obliteration. The hope was to get a few of them out."

Jewish American GIs Go to War Like other Americans, Jews did what they could to support the war effort. More than 500,000 Jewish Americans went to war, including half of all Jewish men aged 18 to 44.

The opportunity to serve in the armed forces transformed the lives of many Jewish American soldiers. Many had previously been unaware of life outside their urban neighborhoods. As GIs, they often trained in the rural South and then journeyed overseas. Both experiences opened their eyes to unfamiliar cultures.

In the armed forces, Jewish American GIs often felt the sting of prejudice. A frustrated corporal, after two years in the marines, sent a letter to the editor of a Jewish magazine. "I am the only Jewish boy in this detachment," he wrote. "I am confronted with anti-Semitism on all sides."

Other Jewish soldiers had a different experience, however, that affirmed their faith in their country and its ideals. In 1944, GI and future novelist Leon Uris wrote a letter to his father noting that he "fought beside Catholics, Protestants, and Mormons, Indians, Irish, Italians, Poles." Uris's experience convinced him that "it's not the religion we look at, but the man himself."

GIs of Mexican ancestry served with distinction in World War II. Many received medals for bravery in combat. Some of these GIs were Mexican nationals—citizens of Mexico living in the United States. Service in the armed forces gave them a better chance to gain U.S. citizenship.

35.8 Mexican Americans Leave the Fields for War Work

During the war, many Mexican Americans faced discrimination in their daily lives. Like African Americans, some wondered whether joining the armed forces made sense. "Why fight for America," one soldier asked, "when you have not been treated as an American?" Despite such doubts, many Mexican Americans enlisted in the armed forces, while others left their traditional farm jobs or segregated urban neighborhoods to join the industrial workforce. These changes opened up new opportunities for Mexican Americans.

Mexican Americans and Mexicans Join the War Effort About half a million Mexican Americans served in the armed forces during World War II. One of their slogans was "Americans All." As this suggests, many saw the war as an opportunity to prove their loyalty and become part of the mainstream.

A higher proportion of Mexican Americans fought in combat units than any other ethnic group. In addition, Mexican American soldiers suffered heavy casualties in comparison with other ethnic groups. They also received many combat awards. Fourteen Texans received the Congressional Medal of Honor for heroism in the war. Of those, five were Mexican Americans. One Mexican American leader summed up the social effects of the war this way:

> "This war . . . has shown those 'across the tracks' that we all share the same problems. It has shown them what the Mexican American will do, what responsibility he will take, and what leadership qualities he will demonstrate. After this struggle, the status of the Mexican Americans will be different."
>
> —Manuel de la Raza, quoted in Carlos Muñoz Jr.,
> *Youth, Identity, Power: The Chicano Movement,* 1989

Before the war, discrimination had barred most Mexican Americans from many high-paying industrial jobs. The war, with its labor shortages, changed that. Thousands of Mexican Americans left their rural, agricultural lives behind and migrated to industrial centers to work in the defense industry.

To replace Mexican American farm labor, the government looked south of the border. In August 1942, the United States and Mexico devised the Bracero Program. *Bracero* is the Spanish term for "manual laborer." Under the program, Mexican citizens received short-term contracts to come to the United States to work. By 1944, about 120,000 Mexican braceros were performing farm labor in 21 states. Other Mexicans did maintenance work on railroads in the West.

Prejudice Against Mexican Americans Erupts in Zoot Suit Riots Mexican Americans in major cities lived apart from whites. Their barrios, or neighborhoods, were nearly self-sufficient, with their own shops, churches, and schools. Like many immigrant communities, barrios tended to develop in poor, run-down parts of cities, where crime rates were often high. The barrio of East Los Angeles during the war was no different. Mexican Americans there had little regular contact with white Americans. Relations between the two groups were hostile. In 1943, a full-scale riot erupted in the barrio. Part of the focus of the riot was a fashion fad known as the "zoot suit."

In June 1943, groups of sailors and marines attacked young Mexican Americans in East Los Angeles—in part because the teenagers were wearing zoot suits. In general, the police left the servicemen alone and arrested the victims instead.

A zoot suit consists of a flat, broad-brimmed felt hat, a long suit coat with large shoulder pads, and baggy pants that flared at the knee. Many Mexican American teenagers, or *pachucos,* in East Los Angeles began dressing in this flashy style and wearing their hair long in the back, in the ducktail fashion. White Americans tended to associate the zoot suit with Mexican American street gangs, many of whom also adopted the style. Thus, many people saw the outlandish zoot suit as a symbol of lawlessness.

Pachucos and servicemen from the local navy base occasionally clashed. Those small-scale clashes escalated in June 1943 into the Zoot Suit Riots. For several nights, mobs of sailors and marines roamed the streets of the barrio, attacking not just gang members but also anyone wearing a zoot suit. They beat hundreds of *pachucos* and ripped off their suits.

The Los Angeles police did little to stop the servicemen. Instead, they arrested the victims and hauled them off to jail. Meanwhile, newspapers whipped up the mobs with headlines such as "Zoot Suiters Learn Lesson in Fights with Servicemen." Military police finally stepped in to end the violence. Later, an investigating committee found that the main causes of the Zoot Suit Riots were racial prejudice, police discrimination, and inflammatory articles in the press.

Summary

World War II had a great impact on Americans. Some aided the war effort by joining the armed forces. Others produced military equipment and supplies. Many tended victory gardens, recycled goods, and used ration coupons. Minority groups struggled for equal treatment.

Opportunities to serve For many young Americans, World War II provided an opportunity to fight for their country and its ideals. Members of minority groups also saw the war as an opportunity to show that they deserved the respect of white Americans.

New job opportunities Millions of workers left their jobs to join the military. The resulting labor shortage opened the doors of industry to many who had once been shut out. Women, African Americans, and Mexican Americans all found jobs in war-related industries.

Broader worldviews The war sent soldiers far from home and many to foreign lands. They came back with a broader view of the world and a new perspective on what it meant to be an American. Many civilians moved to industrial centers, where they lived and worked with different groups of people.

Hardships of war Most Americans knew little about the real hardships of war. GIs, however, faced those hardships every day as they risked their lives in battle.

Continued prejudice Racial and ethnic prejudice continued to plague American society. African Americans and Mexican Americans faced harassment at home and in the service. Japanese Americans lost their civil rights because of their ancestry. American Jews struggled against anti-Semitism that limited efforts to save European Jews from Nazi extermination.

Hardships at home Women often worked "double shifts" at a paying job and domestic jobs at home. All Americans learned to live with rationing and price controls.

Chapter 36

Fighting World War II

What military strategies did the United States and its allies pursue to defeat the Axis powers in World War II?

36.1 Introduction

After the attack on Pearl Harbor, the United States began mobilizing troops for war. Some of these soldiers would end up in Europe, fighting the German army. First, though, they had to cross the Atlantic Ocean on troop ships, braving attacks by Germany's deadly U-boat fleet.

Since the start of the war, in 1939, German U-boats had been working to disrupt and destroy Allied shipping in the Atlantic. During this phase of the war, known as the Battle of the Atlantic, U-boats sank thousands of ships carrying vital war supplies.

When the United States entered the war, its Atlantic coastal waters were relatively unprotected. Freighters and oil tankers sailed along the coast without military escort. U-boats began to prowl the area, sinking ships on the East Coast and in the Gulf of Mexico. The United States was not prepared to respond to these attacks. It did not have enough naval vessels. Nor, at this point, did it require coastal cities to observe nighttime blackouts. The city lights made it possible for U-boats to spot ships as they entered or left American ports, thus making them easy prey for German torpedoes.

During the first several months of 1942, U-boats sank dozens of American ships off the Atlantic Coast. At night, coastal residents could hear the hum of U-boats just off shore. They could even see ships burning at sea. Oil spills and debris from wrecked ships washed up on beaches all along the East Coast.

These losses would not continue, however. As in World War I, the Allies reduced their losses by using the convoy system. Destroyers and other naval vessels would surround and protect unarmed ships. In addition, the United States began a feverish period of shipbuilding. By 1943, it was churning out enough ships to replace lost vessels and to defend against U-boat attacks. This new U.S. fleet would play a key role in naval battles and in supporting ground and air forces during World War II.

Although German U-boats sank dozens of American ships in 1942, by 1943, the Allies were able to reduce their losses. One factor that helped turn the tide against the Germans was an increase in American shipbuilding.

U.S. Marines raise the American flag on Mount Suribachi during the Battle of Iwo Jima in
◀ Japan in 1945

36.2 Preparing for War in Europe

In late December 1941, Franklin Roosevelt and Winston Churchill met in Washington, D.C. Their purpose was to devise a strategy to help the **Allies** defeat the **Axis powers**. They knew they could not afford to fight an offensive war on two fronts—Europe and the Pacific—at the same time. So, at this early date, they decided on a strategy of "Europe First." They would concentrate most of their forces on winning back Europe, while initially fighting a defensive war against Japan in the Pacific.

Axis Powers Roll Across Europe into North Africa By the time the United States entered World War II, the Axis powers controlled most of Europe. Great Britain had saved itself by fighting off an intense German air attack during the Battle of Britain. But the country was running out of money and resources. On the eastern front, the Nazis had invaded the Soviet Union, using blitzkrieg tactics to overcome Soviet troops massed at the border. One large German force nearly reached Moscow before the onset of winter froze it in its tracks. Another force marched toward the Soviet Union's oil-rich Caucasus region.

Oil played a key role in Axis strategy. Hitler already controlled oil fields in Romania, but he sought more oil to keep his war machine running. He also hoped to cut off Allied oil from the Middle East. But first he had to secure North Africa by pushing the British out of Egypt. In 1941, Hitler sent Field Marshal Erwin Rommel and his Afrika Korps, a tank-based German army division, to join the Italian army already in North Africa. By June 1942, Rommel's force had taken much of the region and had driven deep into Egypt.

The Axis powers controlled much of Europe and North Africa at the start of 1942. The size of Axis-controlled territory suggests the huge task facing the Allies as they considered strategies for fighting the war.

War in Europe and North Africa, January 1942

Legend:
- Axis powers before World War II
- Extent of Axis control as of January 1942
- Allies
- Neutral nations

Europeans Suffer Under German Occupation In German-occupied Europe, many people were suffering. Some lived under puppet governments, like Vichy France. Others endured harsh military rule. The SS, a brutal military unit within the Nazi Party, forced millions of Europeans to work in the German arms industry. The SS treated Russians, Poles, and other Slavs with special contempt, partly because Hitler claimed the Slavs were subhuman. The Nazis worked them to death and killed large groups of them outright.

No group suffered more than the Jews. Hitler had long been obsessed with the "Jewish question"—how to rid Germany of Jews. He had stripped Jews of their civil rights, had them beaten or killed, and confined them to concentration camps. As Germany expanded, more Jews came under Nazi control. Thus, the "Jewish question" grew more critical. Hitler forced Jews from all over Europe into overcrowded ghettos, small sections of cities that could be walled off and guarded. The largest ghetto established by the Nazis was the Warsaw Ghetto in Poland. Thousands of people died in the ghettos from starvation and disease.

Gradually, the Nazis decided on what they called the "final solution." As part of this plan, they would systematically exterminate the Jews. The slaughter began in the Soviet Union, shortly after the invasion in 1941. Mobile killing squads rounded up and murdered thousands of Soviet Jews at a time. In early 1942, the Nazis built the first of six death camps in Poland. Jews, many from ghettos, were shipped to these camps by rail, often packed into cattle cars.

The Nazis built death camps to imprison and kill Jews and other "undesirables." The largest and most lethal of these camps was at Auschwitz, in Poland, where the Nazis used poison gas to murder more than a million people. This photograph shows bones piled up at Majdanek, another camp in Poland.

Unlike regular concentration camps, these death camps were equipped with gas chambers. Camp operators sealed groups of Jews and other prisoners inside these rooms and turned on the poison gas, usually carbon monoxide. Pregnant women, young children, the elderly, and the sick were killed soon after they arrived. Able-bodied prisoners were kept alive as long as they could work, often at a nearby factory. Each death camp could kill tens of thousands of people each month. In addition to Jews, the Nazis also gassed homosexuals, disabled people, captured Soviet soldiers, and Gypsies, among others.

Allied Leaders Debate War Strategies When Roosevelt and Churchill met in Washington in 1941, they knew nothing about the Nazis' "final solution." Their goal was to figure out how to win the war in Europe. To do this, they had to choose from a number of possible strategies.

At the time, the Allies had limited resources. For a few months at least, while the United States gathered troops and war materials, the Allies would have to focus on defending territory against the Axis powers. After that, they would go on the attack, but they had to decide where.

They had several choices. Occupied France was a possibility, because the French people would support such an invasion. Also, nearby Britain could serve as a staging area for the massing of troops and resources before the assault. But the German army had a strong presence in France that would make such an invasion extremely difficult.

Some thought a direct attack on Italy made more sense. The Italian army was fairly weak, and Italy would provide a good base for securing the rest of Europe. Sailing through the U-boat-infested waters of the Mediterranean, however, would be dangerous.

Others wanted to launch the Allied offensive in North Africa, which was not as well defended and could serve as a gateway to Europe. But it was also far from the ultimate target, Germany, so it would test the Allies' ability to transport and maintain their forces.

Another plan called for moving troops into the Soviet Union to help the Soviet Red Army push back the Germans. The USSR, now one of the Allies, greatly needed its partners' help. But transporting and supplying forces so far from home would require a massive effort.

British Prime Minister Winston Churchill and President Franklin Roosevelt met several times during the war to plan strategy. They developed a strong relationship based on mutual respect.

Britain's choice of strategy in early 1942 was clear. Already caught up in the battle against Rommel's forces, Churchill wanted the Allies to strike North Africa first. In contrast, the Soviet leader, Joseph Stalin, wanted an invasion of France to take pressure off his weakened army. Roosevelt's top military advisor, General George C. Marshall, also supported this option. But this plan had two problems. First, the U.S. Army did not have enough trained combat forces. That meant the exhausted British army would have to do most of the fighting. Second, German U-boats were sinking ships at an alarming pace in the North Atlantic. Transporting masses of soldiers and supplies to a staging area in Britain would be a dangerous, perhaps disastrous, process. In June, Roosevelt made his decision. U.S. forces would invade North Africa, starting in the fall.

Allies Invade North Africa and Italy In November 1942, Allied forces made sea landings in Morocco and Algeria. Led by the American general Dwight D. Eisenhower, they swept east into Tunisia. The Germans quickly sent reinforcements across the Mediterranean. Meanwhile, British forces stopped Rommel and forced him out of Egypt. Rommel's Afrika Korps retreated west toward Tunisia, with the British in hot pursuit.

American soldiers did their first fighting of the war in a series of battles in the winter of 1942–1943. The U.S. II Corps, which saw much of the action in North Africa, benefited from the leadership of two generals—first George Patton and then Omar Bradley. They helped the combined Allied armies launch a final offensive in May 1943. Axis resistance in the region collapsed, leaving about 250,000 German and Italian soldiers in the hands of the Allies.

Using North Africa as a staging area, the Allies crossed the Mediterranean into Sicily, a large island in southern Italy. The massive Allied assault in July 1943 met little opposition at first. The success of the invasion put a scare into Italy's political leaders. Mussolini's North Africa campaign and several other failures had caused them to lose faith in *Il Duce*. The Fascist Grand Council met on July 24 and voted to restore the king and parliament. Mussolini resigned the next day. Italy soon surrendered to the Allies. Its government signed an armistice in September and declared war on Germany the next month.

German forces were still in Italy, however. As the Allies marched north, the Germans battled them every inch of the way. By October, the Allied army had taken about a third of the Italian peninsula, but they did not get much farther that year.

The Allies carefully planned how to free Europe from Axis control. Their strategy called for massive invasions of Axis-held territory. The ultimate focus of the Allied thrust was the German capital of Berlin, where Hitler had his headquarters.

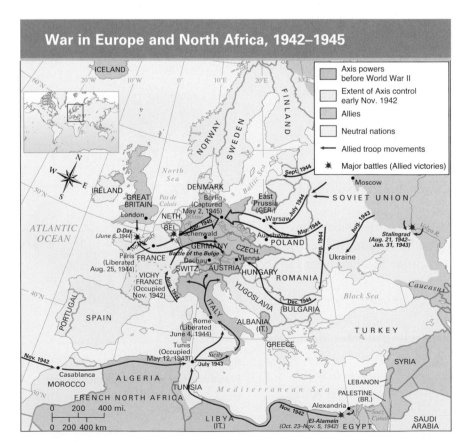

War in Europe and North Africa, 1942–1945

Legend:
- Axis powers before World War II
- Extent of Axis control early Nov. 1942
- Allies
- Neutral nations
- → Allied troop movements
- ✳ Major battles (Allied victories)

A solid German defensive line completely stopped the Allies about 60 miles south of Rome, the Italian capital.

Soviets Fight Alone at Stalingrad The decision to invade North Africa had left the Soviets on their own. Hitler now had the chance to crush the USSR with a new summer offensive. Starting in June 1942, Axis troops thrust farther into Soviet territory. Hitler split his forces so they could seize the rest of the Caucasus and also take Stalingrad, a large city on the Volga River. At Stalingrad, German firebombs set most of the city on fire, but Stalin forbade his soldiers to retreat. "Not a step back!" he ordered. By mid-September, Axis troops had a large Soviet force trapped in a strip of the city along the Volga.

Fierce street-by-street fighting followed for two months. Then, in November, the Soviet Red Army began a **counteroffensive,** launching its defensive forces against the Nazi assault. In a few days, the Soviets had encircled the German troops. Hitler insisted that his soldiers fight to the death, which most of them did. In January 1943, the remains of the German force, starving and frozen, surrendered to the Soviets.

The Battle of Stalingrad cost Germany more than 200,000 troops, while more than a million Soviet soldiers died. Nevertheless, the USSR had forced the Germans to retreat, giving up all they had gained after June 1942, including the Caucasus.

Taking the War to the Germans by Air With the loss of the Caucasus, Hitler had only one major source of oil—Romania. The Romanian oil fields became a prime target of Allied strategic bombing. Strategic bombing involves hitting vital targets to destroy the enemy's war-making capacity.

American pilots in B-24 Liberator and B-17 Flying Fortress bombers typically launched daytime raids. They favored **precision bombing** of specific targets. Flying at high altitude to avoid antiaircraft fire, they dropped bombs on oil refineries, rail yards, factories, and U-boat bases. By the end of the war, Germany's infrastructure and economy were in ruins.

British pilots relied mainly on **saturation bombing,** the rapid release of a large number of bombs over a wide area. They usually flew nighttime raids over enemy cities. The strategy behind the bombing of cities, with its appalling loss of life, was to destroy civilian morale and force a surrender. This strategy turned German cities like Dresden and Hamburg into rubble-strewn graveyards, but it did not bring an early end to the war.

In August 1944, American planes dropped more than a thousand bombs on an oil-production facility in Poland. Five miles to the west stood Auschwitz, the largest Nazi death camp. Jewish organizations, the War Refugee Board, and others urged the government to bomb Auschwitz. If the gas chambers or nearby rail lines were destroyed, they said, thousands of lives could be saved.

American military officials opposed bombing Auschwitz. They said they could not afford to divert resources from military targets. They also claimed that such bombing might kill many prisoners. Elie Wiesel, who had been a prisoner at Auschwitz, said he would have welcomed the bombs anyway. "We were no longer afraid of death; at any rate, not of that death," he recalled. "Every bomb filled us with joy and gave us new confidence in life."

The development of bombers such as the B-24 Liberator and the B-17 Flying Fortress helped the Allies gain the upperhand during the war. These planes were able to fly at higher altitudes and bomb bases in Germany.

Operation Overlord Opens a New Front in France In the end, the Allies decided not to bomb Auschwitz because doing so would not hasten the end of the war. To meet that objective, the military focused most of its efforts in 1944 on the invasion of France. They code-named this mission Operation Overlord.

General Eisenhower directed the invasion. At his command were about 1,200 warships, 800 transport ships, 4,000 landing craft, 10,000 airplanes, and hundreds of tanks. Troops would cross the English Channel by ship and land on the beaches of Normandy, in northern France. **D-Day**—the day the invasion began—was June 6, 1944. Eisenhower sent off his first wave of 156,000 troops with a message of hope: "You will bring about the destruction of the German war machine, the elimination of Nazi tyranny over the oppressed peoples of Europe, and security for ourselves in a free world." He knew that many of these men would not return.

The landing craft unloaded Allied troops on Normandy's five beaches, while warships provided covering gunfire from offshore. German gun batteries took aim at the mass of invading soldiers, who by now were wading ashore, crawling along the sand, and climbing the dunes and cliffs. One soldier later described his arrival at Omaha Beach, scene of the bloodiest fighting:

> It seemed like the whole world exploded. There was gunfire from battle-ships, destroyers, and cruisers. The bombers were still hitting the beaches. As we went in, we could see small craft from the 116th Infantry that had gone in ahead, sunk. There were bodies bobbing in the water, even out three or four miles.
> —Lt. Robert Edlin, from Gerald Astor, *June 6, 1944: The Voices of D–Day*

After the chaos of the landing, the soldiers regrouped. By the end of the first day, the Allies held the entire 59-mile section of the Normandy coast. In July, the American army, under General Bradley, and the British army, under General Bernard Montgomery, began a rapid sweep across France. In August, the Allies liberated Paris. In September, the first American GIs crossed the German border.

President Ronald Reagan later described the D-Day invasion of France as the first step in the Allied attempt to "seize back the continent of Europe." At least 2,500 American, British, and Canadian soldiers died in this effort. Their sacrifices helped turn the tide of the war and end Nazi hopes for world domination.

Allies Liberate Nazi Concentration Camps As the Americans carried out the invasion of France, the Red Army chased a retreating German force out of the Soviet Union and into Poland. SS officials frantically tried to hide evidence of concentration camps in Poland. They cleared out many of the forced-labor camps, marching prisoners westward and shooting any who fell behind. They also tried to dismantle some of the death camps, quickly killing the remaining prisoners. With the Red Army closing in on Auschwitz, the Nazis crowded about 60,000 Jews and others onto freight trains and shipped them west into Germany. The survivors ended up in camps such as Buchenwald and Dachau.

Allied soldiers fighting their way through Germany stumbled upon concentration camps. These camps, though not as grim as the death camps of Poland, shocked the soldiers. The camps held thousands of slave laborers, starved to near death. Many of these "living skeletons," too sick to even eat, died in the weeks after they were liberated. At Dachau, the smell of rotting flesh led GIs to 28 railway cars packed with dead bodies. They also uncovered evidence of medical research. SS doctors at the camp had carried out inhumane experiments on more than 3,500 prisoners.

The Nazis had committed crimes so reprehensible that no word existed to describe them. In 1944, a Polish Jew coined the term **genocide** to refer to the systematic killing of a racial, political, or cultural group. The Nazis killed some 6 million Jews, or about 40 percent of the world's Jewish population. An existing word that meant "sacrifice by fire"—*holocaust*—was capitalized and applied to this massive slaughter. The Holocaust was the systematic, state-sponsored persecution and murder of Jews and other minority groups by the Nazis.

A GI described the newly freed inmates of Dachau: "Many of them were Jews. They were wearing black and white striped prison suits and round caps. A few had shredded blanket rags draped over their shoulders . . . The prisoners struggled to their feet [and] shuffled weakly out of the compound. They were like skeletons—all skin and bones."

The War in Europe Ends with Germany's Surrender When the Allies crossed from France into Germany, they met fierce resistance. By December 1944, their offensive had stalled. Hitler made plans to burst through the Allied lines in the wooded Ardennes region of Belgium, where the American forces were weakest. He launched his counteroffensive on December 16. Eight German armored divisions smashed into the surprised Americans, creating a huge bulge in the American line. Allied air support and quick action by Patton's Third Army forced the Germans to withdraw by mid-January. The Battle of the Bulge was the last German offensive on the western front.

By April 1945, the Red Army had fought its way through Poland and into Germany to the outskirts of Berlin. On April 30, with advancing Soviet soldiers just half a mile from his Berlin bunker, Hitler killed himself. German forces quickly began surrendering, and at midnight on May 8, the war in Europe officially ended. President Roosevelt did not live to celebrate Victory in Europe Day, or V-E Day. He had died on April 12. The new president, Harry S Truman, dedicated the victory to Franklin Roosevelt.

World War II took a very different course in Asia and the Pacific. After the shock of the Pearl Harbor attack, American forces in the Pacific needed several months to regroup. During this time, Japan took control of much of the region's natural resources, including oil and rubber. Through conquest, Japan formed what it called the Greater East Asia Co-Prosperity Sphere. The "Co-Prosperity" in the title had nothing to do with sharing the wealth. Instead, Japan's goal was its own economic self-sufficiency, along with expanded political influence.

The Japanese Advance in Asia and the Pacific Japan's attack on Pearl Harbor was just the first in a series of strikes against Allied territory in the Pacific. By the end of March 1942, the Japanese had captured British Hong Kong and Singapore, the American islands of Guam and Wake, and the oil-rich Dutch East Indies. Japan had also invaded several larger possessions of the Allies, including the American-held Philippine Islands and the British colony of Burma.

In the Philippines, Americans and Filipinos under General Douglas Mac-Arthur resisted a fierce Japanese onslaught. Disease and malnutrition killed many of the defenders. In March, Roosevelt ordered MacArthur to leave the islands. Upon his departure, the general promised, "I shall return." Two months later, Japan completed its conquest of the Philippines. On the largest island, the Japanese rounded up 70,000 starving, exhausted American and Filipino prisoners and marched them up the Bataan Peninsula near Manila to a prison camp. During the brutal 63-mile march, Japanese soldiers beat and bayoneted many of the prisoners. More than 7,000 died on the infamous Bataan Death March.

The fall of the British colony of Burma, in May 1942, had serious consequences for China. Japan already controlled most of coastal China, including the main ports. No supplies could reach the Chinese army by sea. China relied on British and American supplies carried in from India over the Burma Road. Now Japan had cut this lifeline. If Japan defeated China, hundreds of thousands of Japanese soldiers would be free to fight elsewhere. To help China keep fighting, the Allies set up an airborne supply route over the Himalayas.

The Pacific War Begins in the Air and at Sea Japan's string of victories in the Pacific hurt American confidence. To boost morale, Roosevelt urged his military chiefs to strike directly at the Japanese home islands. They came up with a plan to fly B-25 bombers off an aircraft carrier. The B-25 could make a short takeoff and also had the range to presumably reach Japan and then land at Allied airfields in China.

By mid-1942, Japan had taken Southeast Asia and much of the Central and South Pacific. Japan even captured the westernmost islands of Alaska's Aleutian chain. In August 1943, Allied troops finally pushed the Japanese out of the Aleutians.

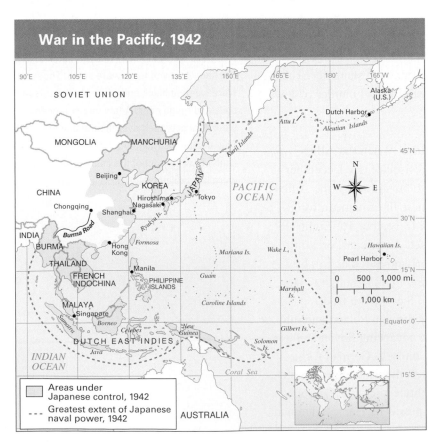

War in the Pacific, 1942

Areas under Japanese control, 1942

Greatest extent of Japanese naval power, 1942

On April 18, 1942, 16 bombers took off from the carrier *Hornet,* which had sailed to within 650 miles of Japan. Led by pilot Lieutenant Colonel James Doolittle, the bombers hit Tokyo and other Japanese cities. Although the bombs did little damage, this surprise attack thrilled Americans as much as it shocked the Japanese. Japan reacted by putting more precious resources into defending the home islands. It also decided to try to destroy the remaining American fleet, a plan that would prove disastrous.

During Doolittle's raid, American code breakers got news of enemy activity far to the south in the Coral Sea. Japan was moving into position to isolate Australia, a key American ally. To stop the Japanese, Admiral Chester Nimitz sent two aircraft carriers, several cruisers, and a few destroyers—all he could spare at the time. They would face a larger Japanese force that included three carriers.

The resulting Battle of the Coral Sea, in early May 1942, was fought entirely by carrier-based aircraft. It was the first naval battle in history in which the enemies' warships never came within sight of each other. Japanese aircraft sank the carrier *Lexington* and damaged the *Yorktown.* American planes sank one Japanese carrier and damaged the other two. Despite fairly even losses, the Americans gained a strategic victory. They blocked Japanese expansion to the south, and they learned a valuable lesson—the Japanese navy could be beaten.

When Japanese advances forced General MacArthur to leave the Phillipines in March 1942, he proclaimed, "I shall return." A little over two years later, General MacArthur was able to fulfill his promise. He returned to the Phillipines to defeat the Japanese army.

Military Leaders Consider Their Options in the Pacific The "Europe First" strategy put Pacific commanders at a disadvantage. Because they had fewer ships, planes, and soldiers than the Japanese, a defensive strategy made sense. American naval forces would try to contain the Japanese, stopping their expansion in the Central and South Pacific. Critics in the navy pointed out that this strategy allowed the Japanese to strengthen their hold on newly won territories, making those lands harder to win back later. As part of the defensive strategy, these critics advised keeping the Japanese off balance with occasional attacks.

Some navy officials wanted to go on the offensive, and they debated different strategies. One idea was to build air bases in the Aleutian Islands, the part of Alaska that extends westward toward Japan. But pilots and their crews would have had to deal with the snow, wind, and fog that afflicted this region. Also, all supplies would have had to be shipped in from the U.S. mainland.

Another idea was to build bases in China. China's coast would have made an ideal staging area for an air assault on nearby Japan. However, the fuel, bombs, and parts needed to keep bombers in the air could best be delivered by sea, and the Japanese controlled China's ports. Inland air bases might have worked, but they would have had to be supplied by planes flying over the Himalayas from India.

A third offensive option called for liberating Japanese-held territory in the Pacific. By first freeing islands far from Japan, American forces could gradually move closer to get within B-29 striking distance. This would take time, though, and Japanese resistance would stiffen the closer the Americans got to Japan. Many of the islands were well fortified, so American casualties would be high.

The Americans led the Allied forces in the Pacific and did most of the fighting. When they went on the offensive, they chose a strategy of liberating Japanese-held islands in the Pacific and using them as stepping-stones. Each captured island served as a base for assaults on other islands as the Allied forces moved closer to Japan.

One of the keys to Allied success in the Pacific was the use of secret codes. The United States trained a special group of Navajo Indian "code talkers" for this task. Because Navajo is not a written language and is understood by very few people, it made an excellent basis for a code to transmit vital information. The Navajo code talkers played a key role in the Pacific campaign. Japan was never able to break the Navajo code.

The Japanese Offensive Ends at the Battle of Midway Before the Allies could go on the offensive, they had to stop Japanese expansion. They achieved this goal at the Battle of Midway, in June 1942. The Americans intercepted a Japanese message telling of plans for a major offensive. They figured out that the target was the U.S. base at Midway, a pair of islands about 1,200 miles northwest of Pearl Harbor. With this knowledge, the navy sat in wait for the Japanese fleet.

At Midway, Japanese naval strategists hoped to destroy the U.S. Pacific Fleet, which had been their plan since Doolittle's raid on Tokyo. Instead, the U.S. Navy won a resounding victory. American planes from Midway and from three aircraft carriers demolished the enemy force, destroying all four Japanese carriers, a cruiser, and about 300 aircraft. Japan never recovered from the loss of the carriers and so many experienced pilots. The Battle of Midway was Japan's last offensive action. From then on, Japan would focus on defense.

American forces in the Pacific used a leap-frogging strategy to move steadily toward Japan. Along the way, the fighting grew more vicious as Japanese resistance increased.

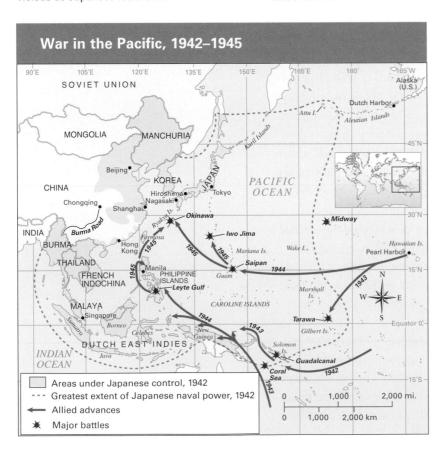

War in the Pacific, 1942–1945

- Areas under Japanese control, 1942
- - - - Greatest extent of Japanese naval power, 1942
- ◄— Allied advances
- ✷ Major battles

Liberating the Pacific Islands Proves Costly A strategy known as **leapfrogging** enabled the Americans to go on the offensive with limited resources. They would often leapfrog, or bypass, a heavily defended island and then capture a nearby island that was not well defended. The captured island was then used as an airbase to bomb the Japanese-held island and prevent ships from resupplying it. Cut off from reinforcements and supplies, the Japanese forces would be left to wither. General MacArthur described this leapfrogging approach as "hit 'em where they ain't—let 'em die on the vine."

Despite the success of leapfrogging, many of the island invasions came at a terrible cost. Thousands of soldiers died in the jungles of Guadalcanal, New Guinea, Tarawa, and Saipan. But they kept pushing the Japanese back, closer and closer to the home islands. In October 1944, MacArthur made his triumphant return to the Philippines, where his forces would battle the Japanese until the end of the war. In August 1944, the marines finished retaking the Mariana Islands. The Marianas campaign was a landmark victory. It gave the Allied Pacific force secure bases from which long-range B-29s could make strategic bombing raids on Japan.

The Final Push Toward Japan Brings Heavy Losses The Allied push through the Pacific steadily shrank the defensive perimeter that Japan had established around the home islands. That perimeter would all but disappear if the Allies could capture the key islands of Iwo Jima and Okinawa. Iwo Jima's airfields would offer a place for B-29s to land in an emergency. They would also serve as a base for fighter planes escorting bombers over Japan. Control of Okinawa, just 310 miles south of Japan, would give Americans a prime staging area for the invasion of Japan. To meet these threats, Japanese military leaders moved their best army units from Japan and China to defend the two strategic islands.

On the small volcanic island of Iwo Jima, the defenders dug caves, tunnels, and concrete-lined bunkers. Three months of Allied bombardment before the February 1945 invasion did little to soften the defense. The month-long Battle of Iwo Jima was among the bloodiest of the war. Nearly all of the 22,000 Japanese troops followed their commander's orders to fight to the death. To win the island, more than 6,800 American troops died. Admiral Nimitz noted that on Iwo Jima, "uncommon valor was a common virtue."

To take the much larger island of Okinawa, the Allies mounted a huge amphibious, or sea-to-land, invasion in April 1945. More than 1,200 American and British ships, including 40 aircraft carriers, supported a combined army-marine force of 182,000. As on Iwo Jima, the 120,000 troops defending Okinawa strongly resisted the American invaders. The bloody combat at the **Battle of Okinawa,** much of it hand-to-hand, continued for two months. It claimed the lives of some 12,000 American soldiers and more than 100,000 Japanese soldiers.

Meanwhile, another kind of combat was taking place in the surrounding waters. Earlier in the Pacific war, the Japanese had introduced a new weapon—**kamikaze** pilots. Hundreds of men flew their bomb-filled planes directly into the vessels of the Allied fleet. Kamikaze attacks sank or damaged hundreds of ships. But they failed to sink any aircraft carriers, which were their main targets.

Scientific advances helped win the war in the Pacific. New antiaircraft guns—like this one—radar, and other military technology enhanced combat operations. Improved medicines and blood products also helped save lives on the battlefield.

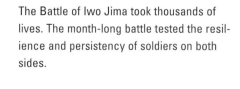

The Battle of Iwo Jima took thousands of lives. The month-long battle tested the resilience and persistency of soldiers on both sides.

The atomic bombs dropped on Japan had a devastating effect. The searing heat from the blasts turned thousands of people into ash. Birds caught fire in midflight. Clothing, trees, and wooden buildings exploded into flames. Survivors suffered from severe burns, radiation sickness, and, later, cancer.

The Manhattan Project Develops a Top Secret Weapon The stage was now set for an invasion of Japan. But the United States had its scientists working on another option. In 1939, German American scientist Albert Einstein had written to President Roosevelt explaining that scientists might soon be able to turn uranium into a new form of energy. That energy, he said, could be harnessed to build "extremely powerful bombs." Einstein expressed his fear that Germany was already engaged in experiments to create such an **atomic bomb**. The power of this explosive weapon comes from the energy suddenly released by splitting the nuclei of uranium or plutonium atoms.

Three years after Einstein sent his letter, the government established the **Manhattan Project,** a top-secret program to develop an atomic weapon. A team of scientists, many of whom had fled fascist nations in Europe, carried on the research and development. Much of the work took place at a lab in Los Alamos, New Mexico. By the summer of 1945, their efforts had produced the first atomic bomb. On July 16, that test bomb was exploded on a remote air base in the New Mexico desert. Physicist J. Robert Oppenheimer witnessed the blinding flash of light, intense heat, and violent shock wave that the bomb produced. He later said the blast reminded him of a line from Hindu scripture: "I am become Death, the destroyer of worlds."

Truman Faces a Decision to Drop the Bomb After the successful test of the atomic bomb, or A-bomb, President Truman had to decide whether to drop the bomb on Japan or to launch an invasion. After Iwo Jima and Okinawa, Truman knew an invasion would produce enormous casualties. The number of Allies killed and wounded might reach half a million, he was told.

Truman faced a stubborn enemy. American B-29s were already destroying Japan with conventional bombs, including incendiaries. These firebombs killed hundreds of thousands of people and turned large areas of major Japanese cities, with their masses of wooden buildings, into cinders. At the same time, a naval blockade cut off the supply of raw materials to Japan. The bombing and blockade had left many Japanese starving, and many of the country's leaders realized that Japan could not possibly win the war. Yet the Japanese refused to accept the unconditional surrender Truman demanded. In fact, they seemed ready to fight to the last man, woman, and child, in the spirit of the kamikaze. Oppenheimer and others believed only the shock of an atomic bomb would end the Japanese resistance.

Some officials objected to dropping the A-bomb. General Curtis LeMay insisted that his B-29 bombing campaign would soon bring Japan's surrender. General Eisenhower agreed. "It was my belief," Eisenhower wrote later, "that Japan was, at that very moment, seeking some way to surrender with a minimum loss of 'face' [honor]." Others maintained that the Japanese would give up if Truman would agree to let them keep their beloved emperor.

The United States Bombs Hiroshima and Nagasaki Truman stuck to his demand for an unconditional surrender. He told Japan that the alternative was "prompt and utter destruction." On August 6, 1945, a B-29 named the *Enola Gay* dropped an atomic bomb on Hiroshima, Japan, a city of 300,000 people.

Within seconds of the explosion, up to 80,000 people died. The blast's shock wave toppled nearly 60,000 structures, and hundreds of fires consumed the rest of the city. Three days later, the United States dropped a second atomic bomb. This one obliterated the city of Nagasaki, killing some 40,000 people instantly. As many as 250,000 Japanese may have died from the two atomic bombs, either directly or as the result of burns, radiation poisoning, or cancer.

Truman had no regrets. "Let there be no mistake about it," he said later. "I regarded the bomb as a military weapon and never had any doubt that it should be used." The destruction of Nagasaki brought a Japanese surrender. Truman received this informal surrender on August 14, Victory over Japan Day, or V-J Day. The terms of the surrender allowed the emperor to keep his office but only in a ceremonial role. The Allies officially accepted the surrender aboard the American battleship *Missouri* in Tokyo Bay.

Millions celebrated V-J Day, which marked the end of the Second World War. But they also mourned the loss of lives. About 55 million died—30 million of them civilians. The Soviet Union paid the highest human cost, with more than 20 million of its people killed. Some 400,000 Americans, nearly all in the military, gave their lives. Most Americans believed strongly that those soldiers, sailors, airmen, and others had died for a noble cause.

Summary

World War II lasted from 1939 to 1945. The United States played a major role in both main fronts of the war—Europe and the Pacific. To retake Europe, the Allies invaded North Africa, Italy, and France, and then moved on to Germany. To retake the Pacific, they fought island by island, until they closed in on Japan.

Allies versus Axis powers The Allies' strategy of "Europe First" set the United States, Britain, and the USSR against the Axis countries of Germany and Italy. In the Pacific, the United States and China battled Japan.

Battle of Stalingrad Hitler's effort to conquer the USSR ended at Stalingrad, where the Red Army forced the Nazis to retreat. The Soviets then pushed westward to Germany.

D-Day The Allies invaded France on June 6, 1944. Then they swept into Germany and took Berlin. Hitler committed suicide, and Germany surrendered.

Holocaust Moving through Poland and Germany, Allied forces liberated Jews and others from Nazi concentration camps and began to uncover the horrors of the Holocaust.

Battle of Midway The United States stopped Japanese expansion in the Pacific at the Battle of Midway. It then went on the offensive, using tactics like leapfrogging to overcome Japanese resistance.

Battle of Okinawa After the Battle of Okinawa, the Allies were poised for an invasion of Japan. Given the losses at Okinawa, however, they knew it would be a long and costly struggle.

Manhattan Project Scientists with the Manhattan Project developed an atomic bomb and tested it in July 1945. A month later, the United States dropped two bombs on Japanese cities, forcing Japan's surrender and bringing an end to World War II.

Chapter 37

The Aftermath of World War II

Did the United States learn from past mistakes at the end of World War II?

37.1 Introduction

On V-J Day, when Japan announced its surrender to the Allies, newspaper headlines in the United States screamed out the news. Factories and offices shut down, and Americans poured into the streets to celebrate. With hugs and smiles and joyful cheers, they expressed their relief that World War II had finally ended. All across the Pacific, from Pearl Harbor to Okinawa, soldiers shouted, "It's over!"

The war's end brought jubilation in the United States, but it also ushered in a period of uncertainty for the nation. One writer noted at the time that some Americans even seemed to fear "the coming of peace." Wartime productivity had lifted the country out of the Depression. Americans wondered what would happen to the economy now. When the government stopped handing out huge military contracts, would the Depression start up again? Many people recalled that after World War I, the economy had collapsed. Along with inflation and unemployment, crime and social tensions had increased. Americans now feared being hit by another wave of problems.

Foreign policy created even greater concerns. Victory brought with it the responsibility for maintaining peace. After World War I, the Senate had refused to ratify the Treaty of Versailles, and therefore the United States did not join the League of Nations. Other victorious nations had used the Treaty of Versailles to punish Germany, a course that helped lead to World War II. Would the United States now take a leading role in world affairs? If so, how would it choose to treat the defeated nations, particularly Germany and Japan?

President Franklin Roosevelt had realized the importance of these questions as early as 1943. In January of that year, he declared, "Victory in this war is the first and greatest goal before us. Victory in the peace is the next." Roosevelt did not live to see either victory, but his hard work and realistic vision of the world helped prepare the United States to meet its postwar obligations.

After the war, millions of servicemen were eager to return to civilian life. When they finally got home, many were greeted with open arms. However, the transition from wartime to peacetime also brought challenges for many Americans.

Representatives of 50 nations signed the UN Charter in San Francisco, California, on June 26, 1945. The main goal of the United Nations is to maintain peace and security. But it also takes a firm stand on issues such as human rights and social and economic development.

37.2 The End of Isolationism

In 1918, when President Woodrow Wilson proposed the League of Nations, Franklin Roosevelt—who was then assistant secretary of the navy—had high hopes for its success. If the Senate had ratified the Treaty of Versailles and the United States had become a member of the League of Nations, perhaps the League might have stood up to Germany and helped prevent the actions that led to another world war. Now that World War II had ended, would the United States slip back into isolationism, or would it take a strong part in world affairs?

The United States Leads the Creation of New World Organizations In the years leading up to World War II, Roosevelt had quietly fought against isolationism. After Pearl Harbor, more and more Americans realized the United States could no longer stand alone in the world. To be secure, the nation had to work with others to maintain peace. This shift in attitude allowed Roosevelt to move toward a policy of internationalism. Late in the war, he pushed for the creation of new worldwide organizations to help prevent future wars by promoting stronger economic and diplomatic ties between nations.

In July 1944, representatives of the United States and 43 other nations met at Bretton Woods, New Hampshire. Together, they founded the International Bank for Reconstruction and Development, or the **World Bank**. The bank was designed to provide loans to help countries recover from the war and develop their economies. Much of the bank's funding came from the United States.

The same group of nations also created the International Monetary Fund. The IMF's goal was to stabilize the world monetary system and establish uniform exchange rates for foreign currency. Making exchange rates more predictable would help international banking and trade. Three years later, 23 nations took another step to encourage trade by signing the General Agreement on Tariffs and Trade. Member nations of GATT agreed to lower tariffs and to eliminate barriers to international trade.

The United States also worked closely with its allies to design a replacement for the League of Nations. In the fall of 1944, representatives of the United States, Great Britain, China, and the Soviet Union gathered at Dumbarton Oaks, an estate in Washington, D.C. U.S. Secretary of State Cordell Hull opened the meeting: "It is our task here to help lay the foundations upon which, after victory, peace, freedom, and a growing prosperity may be built for generations to come." The product of this conference was a draft charter for a new organization called the **United Nations (UN)**. In June 1945, 50 nations signed the UN Charter.

In seeking approval for the League of Nations, President Wilson had worked hard to win public support and thought he did not need the support of Republicans in the Senate. In seeking support for the United Nations, Roosevelt did not make the same mistake. He not only spoke to the public about the need for nations to "learn to work together" for peace and security but also worked to persuade Republican senators. His efforts paid off, although he did not live to see the results. In July 1945, three months after Roosevelt's death, the Senate ratified U.S. membership in the United Nations by a vote of 89–2.

The United Nations Gets Organized The United States played a leading role in founding the United Nations. Its influence is evident in the UN Charter, which proclaims what Roosevelt called "four essential human freedoms." He had first identified those **Four Freedoms** in a speech in January 1941. In that speech, he depicted a world in which all people would have freedom of speech and expression, freedom of worship, freedom from want, and freedom from fear. "The world order which we seek," he said, "is the cooperation of free countries, working together in a friendly, civilized society." In August 1941, Roosevelt and Winston Churchill had incorporated the Four Freedoms into the Atlantic Charter, which was a major expression of the Allies' postwar goals.

Four years later, the framers of the UN Charter looked to the Atlantic Charter and the Four Freedoms when devising the framework for the United Nations. The preamble to the UN Charter states that members seek to "reaffirm faith in fundamental human rights, in the dignity and worth of the human person, in the equal rights of men and women and of nations large and small."

To reinforce these principles, the United Nations adopted the **Universal Declaration of Human Rights** in 1948. This document affirms basic **human rights,** including the rights to life, liberty, and equality before the law, as well as to freedom of religion, expression, and assembly. Eleanor Roosevelt, who was the chair of the committee that drafted the declaration, compared it with the U.S. Bill of Rights and other similar documents.

In addition to listing principles, the UN Charter lays out the structure of the United Nations. The General Assembly is the main body of the United Nations and consists of all member states. The Security Council, a much smaller but more powerful body, consists of just 15 member states. Five of these members are permanent—the United States, Britain, France, Russia, and China. Each permanent member can veto any Security Council resolution. The Security Council focuses on peace and security issues, and it can use military power to enforce its decisions.

In 1947, the United Nations faced one of its first challenges. It was drawn into a crisis in Palestine, a region on the eastern edge of the Mediterranean Sea. Jews, many of whom had migrated to the area to escape the Nazis, wanted to establish their own nation. Arabs in the region rejected that idea, and violent clashes followed. The United Nations decided to partition Palestine, dividing it into Arab and Jewish territories. In 1948, the Jews proclaimed the state of Israel. The first of several Arab-Israeli wars followed, and tensions continue in the region to this day.

37.3 Dealing with the Defeated Axis Powers

Even before World War II ended, the Allies began to face important decisions about the future of the defeated Axis powers. A generation earlier, the victors in World I had imposed a harsh peace on Germany. The Treaty of Versailles, with its war-guilt clause and excessive reparations, had caused bitter resentment among Germans. Adolf Hitler had used that resentment to help fuel his rise to power. Looking back at the mistakes made after World War I, Roosevelt was determined not to let history repeat itself.

The UN flag features a view of the globe centered on the North Pole. A wreath of olive branches, which symbolizes peace, embraces the globe.

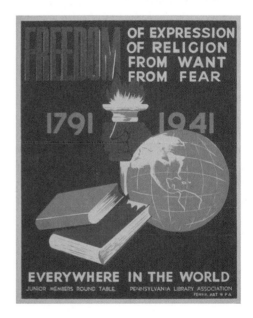

President Roosevelt's Four Freedoms became an integral influence of the Atlantic Charter and the UN Charter.

At the Nuremberg Trials, several defendants, including Nazi official Hermann Goering (shown above), claimed they were just doing their duty. "For a soldier, orders are orders!" one blurted. Another defendant said, "We were all under Hitler's shadow." The tribunal rejected these claims, saying that the defendants made a moral choice to carry out orders from their superiors.

War Crimes Trials Allied demands at the end of World War II were much less harsh than those in the Versailles Treaty. Germany and Japan did have to disarm and give up the territory they had taken. They also had to pay reparations. But the Allies did not demand a great deal of money. Instead, reparations took the form of industrial equipment and other goods and services.

Roosevelt had explained this approach in his last address to Congress, in March 1945. "By compelling reparations in kind—in plants, in machinery, in rolling stock [railroad cars], and in raw materials," he said, "we shall avoid the mistake that we and other nations made after the last war." After World War II, Allied leaders did not want to punish the people of Germany and Japan. They wanted to leave those countries enough resources to remain independent. They sought only to punish the German and Japanese leaders who had committed **war crimes**. A war crime is a violation of internationally accepted practices related to waging war.

Roosevelt made his statement shortly after returning from Yalta, a Soviet city on the Black Sea, where he had met with Churchill and Joseph Stalin. At Yalta, the Allies began discussing punishment for war criminals. Five months later, at a meeting near Potsdam, Germany, the new president, Harry Truman, agreed with the other Allies on a plan. They would give Nazi war criminals fair and open trials.

The trials took place at Nuremberg, Germany, in front of an international military tribunal. The judges and chief prosecutors of this **tribunal,** or court, came from the United States, the Soviet Union, Great Britain, and France. The American prosecutor, Robert H. Jackson, presented the opening statement of the trial:

> The wrongs which we seek to condemn and punish have been so calculated, so malignant, and so devastating that civilization cannot tolerate their being ignored, because it cannot survive their being repeated. That four great nations, flushed with victory and stung with injury, stay [stop] the hand of vengeance and voluntarily submit their captive enemies to the judgment of the law is one of the most significant tributes that power has ever paid to reason.
> —Robert H. Jackson, opening remarks, November 21, 1945

The 22 defendants at the **Nuremberg War Crimes Trials** included leaders of the Nazi Party, the military, the SS, and the Gestapo. The SS were the elite Nazi Party corps, most infamous for running the concentration camps. The Gestapo were the secret police. These leaders were charged not only with war crimes but also with crimes against humanity, such as persecution and extermination. They all pleaded not guilty. On October 1, 1946, twelve defendants were condemned to death by hanging, seven received prison terms, and three were acquitted. Other trials followed. Those convicted of war crimes included officials who ran concentration camps and doctors who carried out gruesome medical experiments on inmates.

A separate tribunal met in Tokyo in 1946 to try Japanese war criminals. The trial lasted more than two years and found 25 defendants guilty. Sixteen received life sentences, and two received lesser sentences. Seven were sentenced to death by hanging, including Hideki Tojo, Japan's leader for much of the war.

From Enemies to Allies: Rebuilding Germany and Japan The Allies also set out to restructure Germany and Japan after the war. At Yalta, they had decided to divide Germany into four military occupation zones, one each for the United States, the USSR, France, and Britain. Although Berlin lay entirely within the Soviet zone, it also was divided in four parts—one for each occupying power.

During the war, Allied bombers had destroyed many German cities. As a result, many Germans continued to suffer from famine and disease. At first, the United States did little to help rebuild Germany. It was more concerned with dismantling German factories to eliminate any war-making capacity. Only later would American policy focus on restoring Germany's economic health.

The Allies took a different approach to postwar Japan. They put an American general, Douglas MacArthur, in charge of the country. Allied soldiers occupied Japan, but they did not control the country directly as they did in Germany. Instead, the Japanese government carried out the political reforms that MacArthur and his staff prescribed.

After dissolving Japan's empire and disbanding its military, the Allies worked to bring democracy to Japan. Officials under MacArthur prepared a new constitution. It set up a parliamentary government, based on the British model, with a strong legislature and an independent judiciary. The emperor would only have ceremonial powers. Women as well as men could elect representatives to the parliament, and a lengthy bill of rights ensured civil and political liberties. The constitution also stated that "the Japanese people forever renounce war . . . and the threat or use of force as means of settling international disputes."

At first, as in Germany, the United States sought to weaken Japan's industrial economy. By 1948, however, U.S. officials had decided to promote economic growth. Japan began the difficult task of rebuilding its ruined cities. In 1951, Japan, the United States, and 47 other countries signed a peace treaty. The treaty restored Japan to full **sovereignty,** or independent authority.

After the war, the United States promoted political, economic, and social reforms in Japan. It also provided aid to the Japanese people, including food and other goods. Here, Japanese workers hand out rations of wheat flour from the United States in 1946.

37.4 Americans Adjust to Postwar Life

After World War I, the mass cancellation of government contracts had thrown many Americans out of work. Demobilization of millions of soldiers made the unemployment problem even worse. After World War II, American leaders took steps to try to ease the difficult transition from a wartime economy to a peacetime economy.

From Soldiers to Civilians: The Impact of the GI Bill In September 1942, three years before the end of the war, President Roosevelt was already planning for the peace. In a radio broadcast heard by American soldiers abroad, Roosevelt spoke of the economic crisis that followed World War I. He promised, "When you come home, we do not propose to involve you, as last time, in a domestic economic mess of our own making."

One year later, Roosevelt asked Congress to pass the Servicemen's Readjustment Act, better known as the **GI Bill of Rights**. This bill provided federal funds to help returning GIs make the transition to civilian life. Those funds would make it easier for many war veterans to continue their education and to buy a home. Congress passed the GI Bill by unanimous vote in the spring of 1944.

The GI Bill provided many benefits to war veterans. It paid up to $500 a year for college costs, enough to cover full tuition at many schools. It paid unemployment compensation of $20 a week for up to a year. It also offered housing loans up to $2,000. These loans led to a real estate boom that generated new jobs.

Five months after the war ended, the armed services had released 8.5 million men and women from duty. Several million more came home in the next year. Many veterans took advantage of the GI Bill to enhance their prospects in civilian life. With the bill's help, some 2.3 million veterans attended college and 7 million received vocational or on-the-job training. The middle class expanded, as veterans became doctors, lawyers, teachers, and other professionals.

Veterans also took advantage of low-interest federal loans to buy homes. By 1955, the government had granted 4.3 million home loans through the GI Bill. These loans enabled millions of Americans to move out of central cities into outlying neighborhoods. Instead of being renters, they became homeowners.

The GI Bill had other benefits. Returning veterans could receive unemployment compensation. They could also take out cheap federal loans to start farms or businesses. The effect of this legislation was not limited to the individuals it helped. The GI Bill also helped transform society.

African Americans Seek New Opportunities The GI Bill raised the expectations of all GIs, including African Americans. Shortly after the bill became law, the National Urban League predicted that returning black GIs would want "jobs, opportunities to complete their education, a chance to go into business, and the privilege of sharing completely in the future development and prosperity of the nation."

Not all African American GIs were able to make full use of the GI Bill. Discrimination often prevented African American veterans from buying a home, even if they had the money. Segregation kept them out of many colleges. Still, in the years following the war, many African Americans did become homeowners through the GI Bill. Thousands more received a college education, mainly by attending historically black institutions.

The end of the war did not stop the migration of African Americans from the South. Returning veterans seemed especially eager to leave. By 1947, some 75,000 black GIs had left the South in search of jobs and a better life. A total of 2.5 million black Americans migrated from the region in the 1940s and 1950s.

In general, the lives of African Americans did improve in the postwar years. From 1947 to 1952, the **median income,** or average pay, for nonwhite families rose 45 percent. Politically, though, the picture was more mixed. In national elections, most African Americans backed Truman, who in turn supported progress in the area of civil rights. In the South, however, discriminatory state regulations kept many African Americans from voting.

The Demobilization of Women: From Factory Jobs to the Service Sector By 1947, nearly all war industries had been shut down. The women who had stepped forward to work in shipyards, aircraft plants, and other war-related jobs had received their last paychecks. At the same time, millions of GIs had returned from the war. This set up a potential conflict, pitting men and women against each other for the same jobs.

In the postwar period, most female workers felt a duty to step aside for men. They had been told throughout the war that their jobs were temporary. Yet many women enjoyed the independence and self-esteem that came from holding a paying job, and they wanted to keep working. "They are the women," a reporter commented, "who feel that if they are good enough to serve in a crisis they deserve a chance to earn a living in peacetime."

They did earn a living, but not in heavy industry. Those jobs went mainly to men. Instead, many women moved into jobs in the booming **service sector,** the segment of the economy that does not produce goods. They became teachers, nurses, librarians, bank tellers, and social workers. At these jobs, they earned, on average, just over half of what men earned. For the most part, though, women accepted their new roles and economic status.

From 1940 to 1944, the number of women in the workforce jumped 37 percent, to more than 19 million. That figure declined after the war, but not to prewar levels. Then it began a steady climb. This upward trend signifies a strong economy and a shift in attitudes.

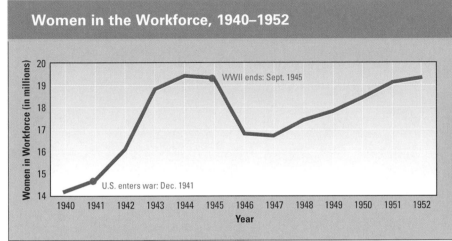

Women in the Workforce, 1940–1952

WWII ends: Sept. 1945

U.S. enters war: Dec. 1941

Source: U.S. Census Bureau, *Historical Statistics of the United States,* 1970.

Summary

At the end of World War II, the United States vowed not to repeat the mistakes of World War I. With the other Allies, it worked to establish ways of avoiding future conflicts and dealing with war crimes. At home, Congress passed legislation to help returning veterans rejoin postwar society.

Four Freedoms In 1941, Franklin Roosevelt expressed the wish that all people should have freedom of speech and expression, freedom of worship, freedom from want, and freedom from fear. These Four Freedoms became part of the charter of the United Nations.

United Nations Before the war was over, 50 nations cooperated to form the United Nations. The United States played a strong role in founding this international organization. The goals of the United Nations include world peace, security, and respect for human rights.

Nuremberg War Crimes Trials Instead of punishing all Germans, the Allies held Nazi leaders responsible at the Nuremberg Trials. A similar set of trials brought Japanese leaders to justice. Later, temporary international tribunals, as well as a permanent International Criminal Court, were formed to deal with war criminals.

GI Bill of Rights The United States sought to prevent economic and social problems at home after the war. One measure designed to accomplish this goal was the GI Bill of Rights, which provided unemployment benefits, college funds, and housing loans to veterans.

Chapter 38

Origins of the Cold War

How did the United States and the Soviet Union become Cold War adversaries?

38.1 Introduction

In spring 1945, as World War II wound down in Europe, a historic encounter took place between U.S. and Soviet troops in Germany. Up until that time, the Americans and Soviets had been allies in the war but had not actually fought together. Now the two forces prepared to meet as they moved into Germany, pressing in on the Nazis from both west and east.

As the U.S. Army advanced eastward, it sent small patrols ahead of the main force to search for Soviet troops. Lieutenant Albert L. Kotzebue, a 21-year-old officer from Texas, led one such patrol. On April 25, as his men approached the Elbe River near the German city of Torgau, they spotted a Soviet patrol on the opposite bank. Shouting and waving their arms, they caught the Soviet soldiers' attention. The men on the other side screamed, "Americanski, Americanski," pointing and waving back. Lieutenant Kotzebue found a small boat near the shore and made his way across the river. The Soviet and U.S. soldiers greeted each other warmly.

Several such meetings took place along the Elbe. Later, the senior commanders of the two armies exchanged more formal visits. Photographers recorded the historic occasion, capturing an image of a GI and a Soviet soldier shaking hands. Working together, the Allies would soon bring an end to the war in Europe. That would be an event, noted President Harry Truman, "for which all the American people, all the British people and all the Soviet people have toiled and prayed so long." Furthermore, the friendly meetings on the Elbe suggested that an ongoing partnership between the United States and the Soviet Union was possible.

However, the days of U.S. and Soviet soldiers hugging and shaking hands would not last. Before long, the United States and the Soviet Union would engage in a grim struggle for world power known as the **Cold War**. As one momentous global conflict ended, another was about to begin. The two countries would soon become bitter enemies.

The red star and the hammer and sickle were symbols of the Soviet Union. The star stood for the Communist Party. The hammer and sickle represented Soviet workers. The hammer was for industrial workers and the sickle was for agricultural workers. These symbols were featured on the Soviet flag and on propaganda designed to win support for Soviet communism.

In 1945, Churchill, Roosevelt, and Stalin met at Yalta, a resort on the Black Sea. There they discussed plans for postwar Europe. It was Roosevelt's last meeting with his World War II allies, as he died shortly afterward.

38.2 Forming an Uneasy Peace

During the war, the United States and the USSR formed an alliance based on mutual interest. Although they had differences, the two nations set these aside to focus on the shared goal of defeating Germany. The differences resurfaced, however, as the war ended and the Allies began to plan for the postwar era.

A Wartime Alliance Begins to Erode In February 1945, Franklin Roosevelt, Joseph Stalin, and Winston Churchill met in the Soviet city of Yalta for the Yalta Conference. In mostly amicable talks, they agreed to collaborate in shaping postwar Europe. They decided to divide Germany into four occupation zones, each controlled by a different Allied country. They also declared their support for self-government and free elections in Eastern Europe. Roosevelt returned from Yalta with hope that the wartime allies could maintain friendly relations. Soon, however, that relationship began to weaken.

In July, with Germany defeated, the Allied leaders met again in Potsdam, near Berlin. Harry S Truman now represented the United States, having become president after FDR's death three months earlier. Churchill, later replaced by new prime minister Clement Attlee, and Stalin also attended. At the Potsdam Conference, the Allies finalized their postwar plans for Germany, including the division of Berlin into occupation zones.

The mood at Potsdam was tense. During the conference, Truman learned that the United States had tested its first atomic bomb. He hinted to Stalin that the United States had a powerful new weapon, but he did not name it. This fueled Stalin's distrust of the United States. Truman also felt wary of Stalin. The Soviet army still occupied much of Eastern Europe, and Truman was suspicious of Soviet intentions. The Soviet leader had promised to allow free elections in Eastern Europe but had not yet fulfilled that promise. In fact, in Poland the Soviets had helped rig elections to ensure a communist win.

Truman and Stalin clearly held very different visions of postwar Europe. Security concerns drove many of Stalin's decisions. Germany had attacked the Soviet Union in two world wars, using Poland as its invasion route. Stalin wanted to create a buffer zone of friendly communist states to protect the USSR. Viewing control of Eastern Europe as critical to his nation's security, he claimed the region as a Soviet sphere of influence. Truman, on the other hand, wanted to allow Eastern European nations to determine their own form of government. He believed that given free choice, they would pick democracy.

The U.S. and the USSR Count Up the Costs of War The United States and the USSR viewed Europe's future differently in part because of their very different experiences in World War II. The USSR had suffered enormous casualties. As many as 20 million Soviet citizens died in the war, including at least 7 million soldiers. Many were killed or died of disease in German labor camps. Others starved when Nazi invasion forces stripped the Soviet countryside of crops, farm animals, and equipment and torched farms and villages. In addition, the Nazis leveled several Soviet cities, including Stalingrad and Kiev. Flying into the USSR in 1945, General Dwight D. Eisenhower noted, "I did not see a house standing between the western borders of the country and . . . Moscow."

Source: *Istoriia Velikoi Otechestvennoi Voiny*, Vol. 6, in *The Oxford Companion to World War II*, I. C. B. Dear, ed., Oxford: Oxford University Press, 1995.

	1941	1942	1943	1944	1945
Availability of Goods in the USSR, 1941–1945, as Compared to 1940					
Clothing	61%	10%	10%	11%	18%
Shoes	65%	8%	7%	10%	15%
Cloth	73%	14%	14%	19%	29%

In contrast, the United States suffered far less from the war. Approximately 290,000 U.S. soldiers died, but civilian casualties were limited to those killed or wounded at Pearl Harbor. Other than that attack, no fighting took place on U.S. soil. No cities were bombed, and no farms or factories were destroyed. In fact, the U.S. economy boomed during the war. By 1945, the United States was producing more than half of the world's total industrial output. The United States had spent at least $320 billion financing the war, but most Americans felt the money was well spent. President Truman called it "an investment in world freedom and world peace."

Like the rest of Europe, the Soviet Union hoped for aid to rebuild after the war. It asked the United States for a loan, but Truman, angered by Stalin's broken promises and disregard of the Yalta agreements, decided on a "get tough" policy toward the Soviets. Shortly after Germany fell, Truman stopped all lend-lease shipments to the Soviet Union. Even American ships already traveling to the Soviet Union returned home. Stalin called this action "brutal."

Soviet citizens suffered greatly during World War II. Some 20 million died. The survivors endured hunger, loss of land, and shortages of basic goods. The table shows the steady decline in availability of household goods as the war progressed. For example, in 1942 the Soviet Union produced only 10 percent as much clothing as it had in 1940.

Differing Ideologies Shape the U.S. and the USSR The differences between the United States and the Soviet Union resulted from more than just wartime experiences. They also represented sharp differences in ideology, or the set of beliefs that form the basis of a political and economic system.

The U.S. system centered on a belief in democratic government and capitalist economics. In capitalism, individuals and private businesses make most of the economic decisions. Business owners decide what to produce and consumers decide what to buy. Most property, factories, and equipment are privately owned. The United States hoped to see capitalist democracy spread throughout Europe.

The USSR also hoped European countries would accept its system, which was communism. Communists regard capitalism as an unjust system that produces great social inequalities and denies the **proletariat,** or working class, a fair share of society's wealth. Communism revolves around single-party rule of politics and government control of the economy. The state owns and runs most businesses and decides what goods will be produced. Such a system is also known as a command or centrally planned economy. In this type of system, small farms are often joined together in collectives, which the state and the farmers own together. This economic arrangement is known as **collectivism**.

By 1946, the balance of power in the world was shifting. Two global wars and the destruction of economic infrastructure had greatly weakened formerly strong countries such as Britain, France, and Germany. The United States and the Soviet Union now stood alone as leading powers in the world. Their size, economic strength, and military prowess enabled them to dominate global affairs. They became known as **superpowers**—nations that influence or control less powerful states. Most nations chose or were forced to align with one superpower or the other. The world was dividing into two power blocs.

Tensions Rise Between Two Superpowers In February 1946, Stalin gave a speech attacking capitalism. He declared that peace was impossible as long as capitalism existed. He said that capitalist nations would always compete with one another for raw materials and markets for their products and that such conflicts would always be settled by "armed force." War, he said, was inevitable "under the present capitalist conditions of world economic development." He seemed to suggest that communism should replace capitalism.

After the war, Truman ordered atomic tests on Bikini Atoll, a remote island in the Pacific Ocean. The island's inhabitants became casualties of the Cold War. Forced to leave in March 1946, they were never able to return because of the radiation caused by the bomb.

George Kennan, a U.S. diplomat at the American Embassy in Moscow, studied Stalin's speech and sent a long reply to the U.S. secretary of state. This "Long Telegram," as it became known, helped shape U.S. foreign policy for decades to come. In it, Kennan described the Soviets as being "committed fanatically" to the belief that the U.S. system and way of life must be destroyed "if Soviet power is to be secure." To prevent this outcome, he said, the Soviet Union must be "contained" within its present borders. After he returned to the United States, Kennan expanded on this notion in an article for a foreign policy journal. In that article, he wrote, "It is clear that . . . any United States policy toward the Soviet Union must be that of a long-term, patient but firm and vigilant containment of Russian expansive tendencies."

Kennan later pointed out that he viewed the policy of **containment**—the restriction of Soviet expansion—as a political strategy, not a military one. He did not want war. He felt that in time, containment would lead to either communism's collapse or its transformation into a milder, less hostile system.

By the time Kennan wrote his famous telegram, U.S. leaders had grown very uneasy. They feared that the USSR planned to spread communism beyond Eastern Europe to other parts of the world. These concerns deepened in March 1946, when the Soviets refused to withdraw troops from northern Iran. During the war, Britain and the Soviet Union had shared control of Iran. In refusing to leave, the Soviets ignored a 1942 agreement with Britain stating that both countries would withdraw within six months of the war's end. This action generated the first major postwar crisis. It ended peacefully after the USSR gave in to U.S. pressure and withdrew. Tensions, however, were clearly rising.

New Nuclear Technologies Raise the Stakes for Both Sides Conflicts between nations have always prompted fears of war. In the new age of the atomic bomb, the possible effects of a superpower conflict became even more frightening. The threat of a nuclear attack compelled both countries to show restraint in their use of force, but it also fueled the race to develop nuclear weapons.

After World War II, the United States continued to test and improve its nuclear capability. In the summer of 1946, American scientists conducted tests of two atomic bombs at Bikini Atoll in the Marshall Islands of the Pacific Ocean. Scientists studied the impact of atomic bombs on naval vessels, using a fleet of more than 90 battleships and aircraft carriers as targets. Many battleships were old; some were captured enemy ships. Nuclear testing on Bikini Atoll continued into the 1950s. For three years, the United States was the only country with an atomic bomb. But Soviet scientists were working hard to develop their own atomic weapon.

Turning to the United Nations to Mediate Conflicts Truman and his advisers knew the damage an atomic bomb could do, and they sought ways to control this powerful new weapon. They asked the United Nations to help limit the development and use of **atomic energy,** the power released by a nuclear reaction.

In June 1946, Truman sent a key adviser, Bernard Baruch, to the United Nations to explain U.S. goals to the **UN Atomic Energy Commission**. He told the panel that the United States wanted the United Nations to enact strict controls on raw materials used in bomb making and a ban on the making of any future bombs. Baruch's proposal, known as the Baruch Plan, would allow the United States to retain its small nuclear stockpile for the time being. However, it would deny the Soviet Union and other nations the right to build bombs. The plan called for UN inspections of nuclear plants and stiff sanctions on nations found making such weapons. Under the plan, UN Security Council members would not be allowed to use their veto power to prevent UN sanctions.

The Baruch Plan prompted strong opposition from the Soviet Union. Soviet delegate Andrei Gromyko asked why the United States should be allowed to keep its atomic bombs while denying the Soviet Union the right to develop its own weapons. He declared that further talks on international control of atomic weapons could take place only after the United States destroyed all of its atomic weapons. Until then, he refused to discuss the terms of the Baruch Plan. He also declared that the Soviet Union would not give up its veto power in the Security Council. Because neither side would budge, this early effort at nuclear arms control came to an end.

At the United Nations in 1946, presidential adviser Bernard Baruch proposed a plan for international control of atomic energy. However, the Baruch Plan failed to win Soviet support.

38.4 Confronting the Communist Threat

On March 5, 1946, Winston Churchill warned of the growing Soviet threat in a speech at Westminster College in Fulton, Missouri. As British prime minister, Churchill had earned the loyalty and respect of the Allies by standing up to Nazi aggression and holding his nation together during World War II. Having known Stalin for years, he worried about the Soviet dictator's plans for Eastern Europe. In his speech, Churchill cautioned that Stalin was cutting the region off from the rest of Europe. "From Stettin in the Baltic to Trieste in the Adriatic," the prime minister declared, "an iron curtain has descended across the continent." The term **Iron Curtain** came to symbolize this growing barrier between East and West.

The Iron Curtain Divides Europe By the time Churchill gave his speech, Stalin was already setting up Soviet-controlled governments in Poland and other countries of Eastern Europe. The Soviet Union's **hegemony** in the region had begun. Hegemony is a dominating influence of one country over others.

In Romania, for example, the Soviets forced the king to appoint a pro-communist government. Once in power, Communist Party leaders used the secret police to silence all opposition. When the United States and Britain protested, the Romanian government promised early elections. But its officials manipulated the electoral process to make sure it won a majority. Bulgaria followed a similar pattern. Backed by the Soviets, local communists used threats or violence to get rid of political leaders who opposed them. Police charged the opposition party leader with plotting to overthrow the government. A few months later, officials arrested and executed him. A similar pattern of communist takeovers occurred later in Hungary and Czechoslovakia.

Nine days after Churchill's "Iron Curtain" speech, Stalin responded. He defended the communist takeovers, explaining that his country needed loyal governments nearby "to ensure its security." He questioned how one could see "these peaceful aspirations of the Soviet Union as 'expansionist tendencies.'"

The growing division between communist and anticommunist nations manifested itself into physical barriers in Germany. Here, British officers are staking a sign to clearly mark their territory in Berlin.

Growing Prospects of Communism in Greece and Turkey Concerns about communist expansion were not limited to Eastern Europe. After the war, both Greece and Turkey also faced potential communist takeovers. In the fall of 1946, civil war began in Greece when communist rebels tried to overtake the Greek government. Yugoslavia, a communist country to the north, backed the rebels. Britain sent troops and money to support government forces.

Britain also tried to help Turkey, which faced growing pressure from the Soviet Union. The USSR sought control of a vital Turkish shipping channel, the Dardanelles, which linked Soviet ports on the Black Sea with the Mediterranean. In 1947, while facing severe economic problems of its own, Britain told the United States that it could no longer afford to help Turkey or Greece.

How Did the Iron Curtain Isolate Eastern Europe?

The Iron Curtain was both a physical and an ideological barrier. The physical barrier consisted of fences that stopped the movement of people across borders. The ideological barrier was less visible, but equally real. Communist leaders worked hard to block the flow of foreign ideas into their countries.

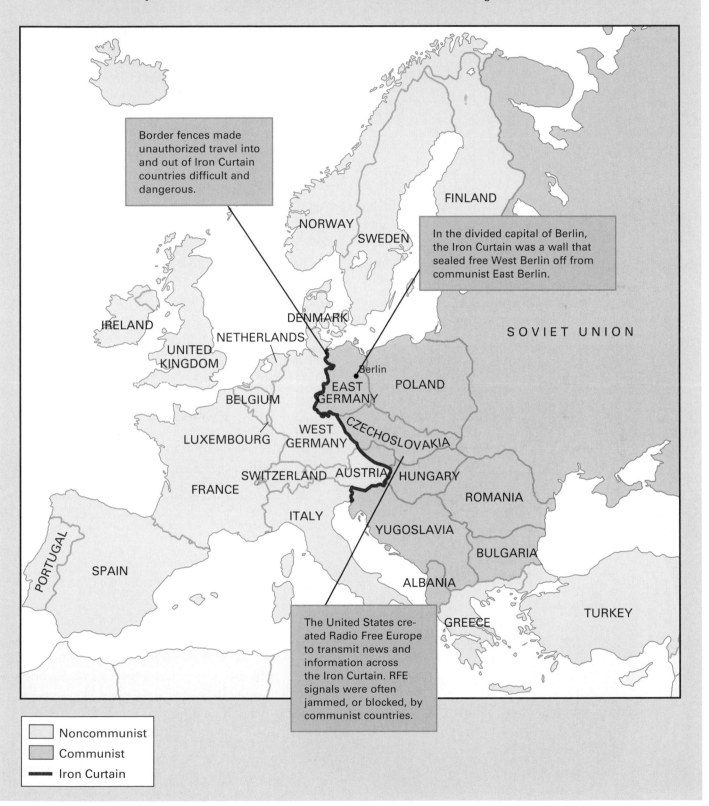

Border fences made unauthorized travel into and out of Iron Curtain countries difficult and dangerous.

In the divided capital of Berlin, the Iron Curtain was a wall that sealed free West Berlin off from communist East Berlin.

The United States created Radio Free Europe to transmit news and information across the Iron Curtain. RFE signals were often jammed, or blocked, by communist countries.

NORWAY

SWEDEN

FINLAND

DENMARK

SOVIET UNION

IRELAND

NETHERLANDS

UNITED KINGDOM

Berlin

EAST GERMANY

POLAND

BELGIUM

LUXEMBOURG

WEST GERMANY

CZECHOSLOVAKIA

FRANCE

SWITZERLAND

AUSTRIA

HUNGARY

ROMANIA

ITALY

YUGOSLAVIA

BULGARIA

PORTUGAL

SPAIN

ALBANIA

GREECE

TURKEY

Noncommunist

Communist

Iron Curtain

Truman Advocates the Containment of Communism Not long after receiving the British message, Truman addressed Congress. In that speech, he outlined a policy that became known as the **Truman Doctrine**. "It must be the policy of the United States," he declared, "to support free peoples who are resisting attempted subjugation [conquest] by armed minorities or by outside pressures." He then asked lawmakers for $400 million to use to provide aid to Greece and Turkey. He explained the importance of helping these countries resist communism:

> The seeds of totalitarian regimes are nurtured by misery and want. They spread and grow in the evil soil of poverty and strife. They reach their full growth when the hope of a people for a better life has died. We must keep that hope alive.
>
> —Harry S Truman, from a speech to Congress on March 12, 1947

Congress granted Truman's request. With U.S. aid and military equipment, the Greek government defeated the communist rebels. Turkey also resisted pressure from the Soviet Union and maintained control of the Dardanelles.

The Truman Doctrine committed the United States to a foreign policy based on Kennan's strategy of containment. Truman hoped to stop the spread of communism, limiting the system to countries in which it already existed. Underlying his policy was the assumption that the Soviet Union sought world domination. The United States believed it had to fight this effort, with aid as needed and with force if necessary.

In this American political cartoon, the octopus stretching its tentacles around the globe represents the Soviet Union. In the late 1940s, many Americans began to believe that the USSR was set on dominating the world.

Scholars still debate how well each side understood the aims and motives of the other. U.S. leaders viewed communist takeovers in Eastern Europe as brutal efforts to suppress democracy. They saw their own attempts to control nuclear weapons through the United Nations as a noble effort to keep the peace. The Soviets, on the other hand, saw the United States and its allies as hostile powers committed to destroying communism and threatening Soviet security. They viewed efforts to restrict nuclear weapons as a way to maintain a U.S. monopoly on atomic energy. Each side talked past the other, and as one superpower acted, the other reacted.

In 1947, Truman asked Congress to reorganize the government's security agencies in light of the Soviet threat. In response, Congress passed the National Security Act. This law created two new agencies, the National Security Council (NSC) and the Central Intelligence Agency (CIA). The NSC advises the president on national security issues and oversees the actions of the CIA. The CIA collects and analyzes intelligence gathered, in part, by agents operating in foreign countries.

38.5 Rebuilding European Economies

On both sides of the Iron Curtain, Europe was in terrible shape after the war. One reporter described Warsaw, Poland, as "rows of roofless, doorless, windowless walls" that looked like they had been "dug out of the earth by an army of archaeologists." Times were hard in Britain, too, which was nearly bankrupt after the war. Conditions worsened during the frigid winter of 1946–47, when Britons faced grave shortages of food, fuel, and electricity. In Italy, France, and many other European countries, conditions were even worse.

European Nations Face Widespread Devastation The challenge of rebuilding war-torn Europe was enormous. Across the continent, governments and economies barely functioned. Warfare had devastated numerous cities, leaving many of the inhabitants homeless and unemployed. It had destroyed schools, hospitals, churches, and factories, knocked out communications systems, and ruined ports. It left many roads, bridges, and railroad lines heavily damaged. Without a usable transportation system, carrying raw materials to factories and crops and goods to market was impossible. In the hardest-hit areas, deadly diseases like tuberculosis spread rapidly.

U.S. leaders feared that conditions in Europe would give rise to political and social unrest. In some countries, workers staged strikes and demonstrations to protest the hardships of daily life. Some poor and jobless people began to look to communist ideology for answers to their problems. Many recalled how local communist groups had resisted the Nazis' rise to power. In these stressful and difficult times, communism quickly gained appeal in Italy and France.

During the war, bombing raids targeted such cities as London, Dresden, and Cologne. These raids sometimes produced firestorms with heat so intense that everything in their path was incinerated. It took years for the cities to recover. Here, a young boy sits among the ruins of London after a German raid.

The U.S. Provides Aid Through the Marshall Plan As with Greece and Turkey, Truman reasoned that rebuilding shattered economies and supporting freely elected governments would be the best way to stop communism from spreading. Truman also knew that, as the strongest economic power in the world, the United States had the money and resources to help Europe rebuild. With these factors in mind, Truman and his advisers developed a plan for European recovery. In June 1947, Secretary of State George Marshall announced the plan in a speech at Harvard University. There, he described the plan as both high-minded and practical:

> It is logical that the United States should do whatever it is able to do to assist in the return of normal economic health in the world, without which there can be no political stability and no assured peace. Our policy is directed not against any country or doctrine, but against hunger, poverty, desperation and chaos.
>
> —George Marshall, June 5, 1947

Aid to European Countries Under the Marshall Plan, 1948–1952

Country	Amount of Aid (in millions of U.S. dollars)
Austria	$678
Belgium and Luxembourg	$559
Denmark	$273
France	$2,714
Greece	$707
Iceland	$29
Ireland	$148
Italy	$1,509
Netherlands	$1,084
Norway	$255
Portugal	$51
Sweden	$107
Turkey	$225
United Kingdom	$3,190
West Germany	$1,391

Source: "The Marshall Plan: Origins and Implementation," U.S. Department of State. Washington, D.C.: Bureau of Public Affairs, April 1987.

During the four years of the Marshall Plan, the United States provided over $12 billion in aid to 16 European countries. This amount was less than Congress had authorized, but the funds still gave an enormous boost to Western European economies.

This recovery plan became known as the **Marshall Plan**. It offered all European nations, including the Soviet Union, generous funding to rebuild their economies as long as the money was spent on goods made in the United States. The plan appealed to many U.S. leaders. Those who supported it hoped to promote democracy in Europe and oppose the spread of communism, thus reinforcing the Truman Doctrine and the policy of containment. They also wanted to open markets for American goods and further boost the economy of the United States.

Some Republicans in Congress did initially oppose what they called a "New Deal" for Europe. However, the Marshall Plan gained wide support in the spring of 1948 after lawmakers learned that the Communist Party had taken control of Czechoslovakia. That year, Congress approved over $13 billion in aid, to be spent over a four-year period, from 1948 to 1952. This aid would play a crucial role in stimulating economic growth and prosperity in Western Europe.

The USSR Responds with the Molotov Plan Although the United States painted the Marshall Plan as a generous effort to aid European recovery, Soviet leaders questioned its motives. They believed that its real purpose was to create a U.S. sphere of influence in Western Europe. Stalin viewed the Marshall Plan as an attempt to interfere in Soviet internal affairs. The Soviets knew that to receive aid, they would have to share information about their economy and resources with the United States and even allow U.S. inspectors into the country to see how the aid was being used. Stalin also felt that his government, in accepting American aid, would have to cede some control over economic planning and decision making. For these reasons, the Soviet Union chose not to take part.

Czechoslovakia, however, was eager to join the Marshall Plan. Czech leaders met with Stalin in Moscow to get his approval. They explained that two thirds of the raw materials Czechoslovakia needed for manufacturing came from Western countries. But Stalin denied their request, saying that they could not "cooperate in an action aimed at isolating the Soviet Union." In the end, at the urging of the Soviets, no Eastern European nations took part in the Marshall Plan.

To compete with its rival, in 1949 the Soviet Union created the **Molotov Plan,** named after Foreign Minister Vyacheslav Molotov. This plan was designed to aid economic recovery in Eastern Europe. To do this, it established a new organization, the Council for Mutual Economic Assistance. Initially, COMECON's main task was to create two-way trade agreements between the Soviet Union and other COMECON members. In the 1950s, COMECON attempted more ambitious projects. It worked to integrate Eastern European economies by encouraging member states to specialize in goods and services not produced in other states.

A Cold War Has Begun By 1949, the wartime alliance of the United States and the Soviet Union had turned into a relationship of mutual distrust and suspicion. Each side held a different vision for the world. The United States wanted to promote the growth of independent, capitalist democracies, while the Soviet Union wanted to surround itself with communist states that followed its lead.

The two superpowers had clashed over communist takeovers in Eastern Europe. They had confronted each other over Iran and, less directly, in Greece and Turkey. They had argued over atomic energy and plans for postwar economic recovery in Europe.

Although the hostility between the two superpowers and their allies often heated up, it never led to armed conflict between the United States and the Soviet Union. It was for that reason that this postwar struggle became known as the Cold War.

During the Cold War, Europe and much of the world divided into two hostile camps. The United States and the Soviet Union waged a war of words, using propaganda, diplomacy, economic and military aid, and espionage as weapons. Each superpower viewed its own motives and actions as right and good, while it cast its rival's behavior in a bad light. As the conflict grew, compromise and cooperation became greater challenges. These problems worsened with the development of atomic weapons, which in turn raised fears of a deadly arms race. Both sides knew that if the Cold War turned hot, it could result in another world war, potentially the most destructive in human history.

During the Cold War, the United States and the USSR engaged in a tug-of-war over power and influence in the world. The conflict often centered on the development of atomic weapons.

Summary

In the postwar period, clear differences between the United States and the Soviet Union soon emerged. Communist ideology and the creation of Soviet-backed states in Eastern Europe alarmed the U.S. government. The United States responded with efforts to support European democracy and limit Soviet expansion. As the rivalry intensified, Europe divided into communist-controlled Eastern Europe and mostly democratic Western Europe.

Yalta and Potsdam Conferences At Yalta, the Allied leaders met to shape postwar Europe. They divided Germany and Berlin into four occupation zones each and declared their support for self-government and free elections in Eastern Europe. At Potsdam, the leaders finalized their postwar plans for Germany. However, the relationship among the superpowers began to weaken.

Iron Curtain In a 1946 speech, Winston Churchill accused the Soviet Union of dividing Europe into East and West and drawing an "iron curtain," or barrier, across the continent.

UN Atomic Energy Commission At the United Nations, the United States offered a plan to limit the development of atomic weapons. The Soviet Union, working on its own atomic bomb, rejected U.S. efforts to retain a monopoly on atomic energy.

Truman Doctrine President Truman adopted a policy of containment as part of the Truman Doctrine. The doctrine aimed to limit the spread of communism and support democracy.

Marshall Plan This aid program reflected the Truman Doctrine's goals. It provided aid to European nations to help them recover from the war, promote stability, and limit the appeal of communism. The Soviets responded with the Molotov Plan for Eastern Europe.

Cold War The postwar struggle for power between the United States and the Soviet Union became known as the Cold War. Although this was largely a war of words and influence, it threatened to heat up and produce armed conflict between the superpowers.

Chapter 39

The Cold War Expands

Were the methods used by the United States to contain communism justified?

39.1 Introduction

By the late 1950s, the United States and the Soviet Union were deeply involved in the Cold War. A key weapon in the struggle between the superpowers was espionage. Both sides used spies and secret agents—along with hidden cameras, listening devices, and other spy gear—to gather information about the enemy.

On May 1, 1960, the Soviets shot down a U.S. spy plane flying over the USSR. The plane was a U-2, a high-altitude, black aircraft known as the Black Lady of Espionage. Special cameras aboard the U-2 could photograph Soviet military installations from heights of 60,000 feet or more. By the time of the U-2's downing, U.S. pilots working for the CIA had been flying deep into Soviet airspace for nearly five years. They had taken photographs of Soviet missile bases, airfields, rocket-engine factories, and other military facilities.

On that May Day, Francis Gary Powers was flying the U-2. Like all U-2 pilots, he carried a deadly poison that he could take if the enemy captured him. After the Soviets hit his plane, Powers parachuted to safety. However, before he could drink the poison, Soviet troops grabbed him. Soviet officials later put Powers on trial in Moscow. They sentenced him to 10 years in prison.

Soviet leader Nikita Khrushchev reacted to the U-2 incident with outrage, accusing the United States of conducting a vicious spying campaign against the Soviet Union. President Dwight D. Eisenhower first denied the charge, but later admitted that Powers had been on an intelligence-gathering mission. The president declared espionage a "distasteful necessity."

The spy plane incident set back efforts to improve U.S.-Soviet relations. It occurred just weeks before Eisenhower and Khrushchev planned to meet in Paris. At that meeting, Khrushchev demanded that the United States stop its U-2 flights and asked the United States to apologize for them. Eisenhower agreed to end the flights but insisted on the United States' right to defend its interests. The talks ended almost as soon as they began, and the Cold War intensified.

Soviet forces recovered the wreckage of a U-2 spy plane shot down over the Soviet Union in May 1960. The U-2 incident enraged Soviet leaders and caused a further chilling in U.S.-Soviet relations. It also focused world attention on the espionage taking place during the Cold War.

◀ U-2 pilot Francis Gary Powers on trial in Moscow, 1960

During the Berlin Blockade, American planes brought vital food and supplies to city residents. The planes sometimes also dropped candy to eager children in the streets below, in an operation dubbed "Little Vittles." Here, a soldier attaches a candy bar to a parachute.

39.2 Europe Feels the Heat of the Cold War

The U-2 incident came at the end of a decade marked by increasingly tense U.S.-Soviet relations. Like players in a chess game, leaders on each side studied the other's moves. Each was alert to threats to its national security and stood ready to respond to such challenges. During this period, Europe was the Cold War's main battleground. The Soviet Union tried to consolidate its control of Eastern Europe, while the United States tried to contain the USSR and limit its power.

The USSR Protests the Unification of West Germany One of the main issues causing Cold War tensions was the status of Germany. After the war, the Allies had divided Germany and its capital, Berlin, into four occupation zones. But they did not decide when and how the zones would be reunited. When three of the Allies took a step toward reunification, it prompted a Cold War crisis.

In March 1948, the United States, Great Britain, and France announced plans to merge their occupation zones to form a new country, the Federal Republic of Germany. The three Allies agreed that this reunited Germany would have a democratic government and a capitalist economy. Their decision angered the Soviets, who controlled both eastern Germany and access to the former German capital Berlin, which lay within the Soviet occupation zone.

On June 24, the Soviet Union imposed a blockade on Berlin, halting all land travel into the city from the Allied occupation zones. The Soviets believed that the **Berlin Blockade** would force the Allies to give up either Berlin or their plans for a West German state.

The United States did not respond as the Soviet Union expected. Instead, General Lucius Clay, the commander of U.S. forces in Germany, called for resistance to the Soviet blockade. "If we mean . . . to hold Europe against communism, we must not budge," he said. "The future of democracy requires us to stay." President Harry Truman agreed, fearing that the loss of Berlin would cause the fall of Germany to the communists. He ordered a massive airlift of food, fuel, and other vital supplies to defeat the Berlin Blockade.

Over the next ten and a half months, pilots made more than 270,000 flights into West Berlin, carrying nearly 2.5 million tons of supplies. The Berlin Airlift kept the hopes of the city's 2 million residents alive and became a symbol of the West's commitment to resisting communist expansion. By the spring of 1949, the Soviets saw that their policy had failed. They ended the blockade, and Germany officially became two countries: communist East Germany and democratic West Germany. Berlin also remained divided into East and West.

The Iron Curtain Falls on Czechoslovakia By the time of the Berlin crisis, the Soviet Union controlled most of Eastern Europe. Poland, Romania, Bulgaria, and Hungary had all established pro-Soviet communist governments. Just weeks before the Berlin crisis, Czechoslovakia became the last major country to fall.

After World War II, the Czechs had formed an elected government dominated by communists but also including noncommunist parties. In February 1948, Joseph Stalin amassed Soviet troops on the Czech border and demanded the formation of an all-communist government. Shortly afterward, communists seized control, ending the Czech experiment in postwar democracy.

This sudden government takeover, or **coup d'état,** alarmed Truman. It showed that Stalin would not accept a government in which power was shared with noncommunists and that he was prepared to use force to achieve his ends.

The Czech coup d'état brought drastic changes to the country's political and economic life. Czechoslovakia was now a one-party state, and communist leaders arrested, tried, and jailed all those who opposed them. They suppressed basic rights, including freedom of the press and free speech, as well. They also forced farmers to give up their land and work on state-owned collective farms.

Europe Is Divided: NATO Versus the Warsaw Pact Czechoslovakia was not the only country to feel Soviet pressure. In the late 1940s, the USSR tightened its grip on all its **satellite nations,** or countries under one nation's control.

As divisions increased in Europe, the superpowers also formed new military alliances. In 1949, the United States, Canada, and 10 countries of Western Europe formed the North Atlantic Treaty Organization (NATO). The founding European members of NATO were France, Luxembourg, Belgium, the Netherlands, Iceland, Italy, Britain, Denmark, Norway, and Portugal. Greece and Turkey joined NATO in 1952, and West Germany followed in 1955.

NATO members agreed to a plan for collective security. They pledged to consider an attack on any member as an attack on all and formed a standing army to defend Western Europe in the event of a Soviet invasion. The United States played a key role in NATO, providing money, troops, and leadership. By joining this alliance, the United States took another step away from isolationism.

The creation of NATO prompted the Soviet Union to form its own security alliance in 1955. Under the Warsaw Pact, the Soviet Union, Albania, Bulgaria, Czechoslovakia, East Germany, Hungary, Poland, and Romania joined forces for mutual defense. NATO and Warsaw Pact members began to see each other as enemies. Europe was now formally divided into two armed camps.

A Divided Europe, 1955

- NATO members
- Warsaw Pact members
- Nonmembers

By 1955, two military alliances—the Warsaw Pact and NATO—had further divided Europe. On one side were the Soviet-backed states of Eastern Europe. On the other were the non-communist states of Western Europe.

The Cold War Expands **445**

Hungary's attempt to break free of Soviet control brought a strong Soviet reaction. In November 1956, the Soviet Union invaded Hungary and crushed the rebellion. In 1958, the communist government put reform leader Imre Nagy on trial and then executed him.

Hungary Tests the Limits of Containment Not long after the signing of the Warsaw Pact, upheaval in Hungary tested the West's anticommunist resolve. In October 1956, thousands of Hungarians took part in a brief revolt against the communist government. The protesters marched through the streets of Hungary's capital, Budapest, waving flags and calling for democracy.

The leaders of the revolt formed a government led by Imre Nagy, a reform-minded communist. He aimed to free Hungary from Soviet domination. He boldly declared that Hungary would withdraw from the Warsaw Pact and become a neutral country, and he appealed to Western nations to help stave off Soviet aggression. In a speech to the Hungarian people, he said,

> This fight is the fight for freedom . . . against the Russian intervention and it is possible that I shall only be able to stay at my post for one or two hours. The whole world will see how the Russian armed forces, contrary to all treaties and conventions, are crushing the resistance of the Hungarian people . . . Today it is Hungary and tomorrow, or the day after tomorrow, it will be the turn of other countries because the imperialism of Moscow does not know borders.
>
> —Imre Nagy, November 4, 1956

Soviet leaders moved quickly to crush the revolt by sending tanks and Red Army troops into Budapest. After killing thousands of protesters, the troops put Soviet-backed leaders back into power in Hungary. Nagy stood trial before the county's communist leaders, who then put him to death.

Hungarians had counted on help from the United States. Before the revolt, many had listened faithfully to U.S.-sponsored radio broadcasts beamed into the country from Europe. There they heard speakers urging them to resist the spread of communism. Through these programs, Hungarians learned of the Eisenhower administration's goal of freeing "captive peoples."

Many Hungarians believed that the United States would support its bid for independence by sending troops and weapons to aid them in their fight against the Soviet Union. They were shocked when American forces failed to come. One Hungarian resident recalled, "People had been watching from rooftops hoping to see U.S. planes arriving." Eisenhower, however, was unwilling to risk war with the Soviet Union to free one of its satellites.

The superpowers did not confine their rivalry to Europe. Before long, Cold War conflicts erupted around the globe. Asia was one of the first affected regions. By the 1950s, both China and Korea had become arenas in the Cold War struggle.

The "Fall of China" to Communism During World War II, Chinese communists led by Mao Zedong and the Nationalists led by Chiang Kai-shek had joined forces to fight Japan. With Japan's surrender in 1945, however, the two groups turned on each other and waged a civil war for control of China. The United States backed the Nationalists, even though Chiang was not a popular leader. At times, both allies and adversaries saw him as corrupt or ineffective. In 1949, the communists defeated the Nationalists. Chiang and his followers fled to Formosa, an island off the coast of China, which they renamed Taiwan. There, Chiang led a small Nationalist holdout against communism.

The fall of China to the communists ended U.S. hopes that the country would become a powerful, noncommunist ally in Asia. Some Americans reacted to the event with anger and looked for a scapegoat. In public speeches and on the floor of Congress, they asked bitterly, "Who lost China?" Some Republican leaders pointed accusing fingers at President Truman.

U.S. Secretary of State Dean Acheson denied that the administration held responsibility for China's acceptance of communism. "Nothing this country did or could have done within the reasonable limits of its capabilities," he said, "could have changed the result." Many China scholars agreed, noting the unpopularity of Chiang and the broad public support for Mao Zedong.

Many U.S. leaders feared that China and the Soviet Union would form an alliance and pose an even greater threat to U.S. interests around the world. Most Americans viewed communist China as similar to the Soviet Union both in its attitude toward the West and its desire to spread communism around the world. Nevertheless, although China remained a key ally of the Soviet Union for years, it pursued its own interests and rejected Soviet control.

The communist takeover of China prompted the United States to seek a new ally in Asia, and Japan was the logical choice. The United States gradually lifted restrictions on industrial and economic growth imposed on Japan after World War II. Eventually, Japan became an economic powerhouse and a strong U.S. partner in the region.

In October 1949, the Chinese communist Red Army defeated Nationalist forces and took control of China. The new People's Republic of China, led by Mao Zedong, established communist rule in China. The United States viewed communist China as a major Cold War threat.

Chinese Nationalist leader Chiang Kai-shek (also known as Jiang Jieshi) fled to Taiwan after his defeat in China's civil war. The United States remained a staunch ally of Chiang's government, however, and worked to isolate communist China.

Containment by Isolation: The U.S. Ends Relations with China Meanwhile, the United States adopted a stern policy toward China. When Mao formed the People's Republic of China in 1949, the United States refused to recognize the new state. Instead, it continued to refer to the Nationalists in Taiwan as China's legitimate government. The United States also cut off all trade with China and opposed its admission to the United Nations. The U.S. government meant for these steps to contain China by isolating it from the world community.

Not all American officials favored this tough policy, however. Some felt that improving U.S. relations with China might weaken China's ties to the Soviet Union. But U.S. officials faced strong pressure from Congress and the public to treat China as an enemy. Many Americans felt that Mao and Stalin were equally reprehensible. Forging a better relationship with either one seemed unthinkable.

Until the 1970s, the United States continued to recognize Taiwan and bar China from the UN. The United States did not resume formal relations with China until 1979.

Containment by Armed Force: The Korean War Like China, Korea was freed from Japanese control when World War II ended. At that time, Soviet troops occupied the Korean Peninsula north of the 38th parallel, while U.S. troops held the area to the south. In the north, the Soviet Union put a pro-Soviet communist government in power. In the south, U.S. officials supported the existing anticommunist government. However, this arrangement masked deep tensions, which erupted in June 1950 in the **Korean War**.

The war began when North Korean troops armed with Soviet weapons invaded South Korea. Their aim was to unite all of Korea under communist rule. Truman, viewing the invasion as a test of American will, ordered U.S. forces to help South Korea repel the invaders.

Truman turned to the United Nations for support. A UN resolution condemned the North Korean invasion and called on member states to aid South Korea. Troops from 15 nations joined the UN force, with the vast majority of the soldiers coming from the United States. According to another UN resolution, the purpose of this joint force was to create a "unified, independent and democratic Korea." Officials selected American general Douglas MacArthur to lead the troops. Under his command, the army invaded North Korea and fought its way northward, nearly reaching the Chinese border along the Yalu River.

The Korean War was the first major conflict to take place during the Cold War. Several million Koreans died, along with some 54,000 American soldiers. In the end, the fighting resolved little. Korea remained divided between the communist north and the noncommunist south.

The Granger Collection, New York

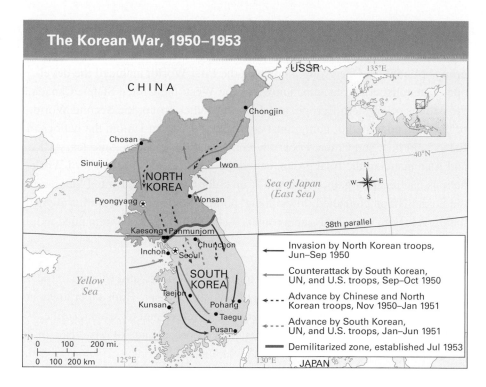

The Korean War, 1950–1953

CHINA

USSR
135°E

Chongjin

Chosan

Sinuiju

Iwon

NORTH KOREA

40°N

Sea of Japan (East Sea)

Pyongyang

Wonsan

38th parallel

Kaesong Panmunjom

Chunchon

Inchon Seoul

Yellow Sea

SOUTH KOREA

Taejon

Kunsan

Pohang

Taegu

Pusan

0   100   200 mi.
0   100   200 km
125°E

130°E

JAPAN

- ← Invasion by North Korean troops, Jun–Sep 1950
- ← Counterattack by South Korean, UN, and U.S. troops, Sep–Oct 1950
- ◄-- Advance by Chinese and North Korean troops, Nov 1950–Jan 1951
- ◄-- Advance by South Korean, UN, and U.S. troops, Jan–Jun 1951
- ── Demilitarized zone, established Jul 1953

For much of the Korean War, the fighting see-sawed back and forth across the 38th parallel, the dividing line between North and South Korea. At times, however, both sides pushed deep into the other's territory.

Alarmed by the approach of UN forces, China sent tens of thousands of soldiers streaming over the border into North Korea. An army of more than 400,000 Chinese and North Korean troops forced the UN army back to the 38th parallel. MacArthur then called for an expansion of the conflict. He wanted to blockade China's ports and bomb major Chinese industrial centers.

President Truman rejected MacArthur's plan, however. In fact, once China entered the conflict, the president began looking for a way out of it. He feared the onset of another global war. But MacArthur would not back down. In an angry letter to a friend, he wrote, "I believe we should defend every place from communism . . . I don't admit that we can't hold communism wherever it shows its head." When MacArthur publicly questioned the president's decision, Truman fired him.

The final two years of the war became a stalemate, with most of the fighting taking place near the 38th parallel. Finally, in 1953 the two sides signed an armistice ending hostilities. The agreement left the Korean Peninsula divided along the 38th parallel and created a buffer zone, called the **demilitarized zone (DMZ),** between the two countries. No military forces from either North Korea or South Korea were allowed to enter the DMZ.

The war left all of Korea ailing. It destroyed homes, factories, roads, hospitals, and schools throughout the peninsula. About 3.5 million North Korean and South Korean soldiers died or suffered injuries. As many as 2 million Korean civilians may have lost their lives. More than 54,000 American soldiers also died in the war.

After the war's end, North Korea turned inward, becoming increasingly isolated from the rest of the world. South Korea, in contrast, continued to develop strong economic and political ties with the United States. In time, South Korea's economy flourished. As the economic gap between the two Koreas widened, hopes for a "unified, independent and democratic Korea" faded away.

The United States Information Agency produced various types of propaganda during the Cold War. One of its most effective forms of propaganda was radio broadcast. The anticommunist messages of Radio Free Europe aimed to stir up anticommunist sentiment in Eastern Europe. Here, a young Czech refugee speaks during a 1952 broadcast beamed into communist Czechoslovakia.

39.4 Fighting the Cold War in Other Parts of the World

By the mid-1950s, the Cold War had effectively divided the world into three groups of nations. One group, known as the First World, included the developed, capitalist countries, also known as the West: the United States, Canada, the nations of Western Europe, and Japan. Another group, the Second World, or the East, consisted of communist countries: the Soviet Union, the nations of Eastern Europe, and China. Poor, developing nations in Latin America, Africa, and Asia made up the final group, called the Third World. Many Third World nations had recently gained freedom from colonial rule. The United States and the Soviet Union competed to win their support. Some of the countries aligned themselves with one of the superpowers. Others, such as India, remained independent and nonaligned.

United States Information Agency: Influencing Hearts and Minds In the Cold War, nations used words and persuasion as weapons. Both superpowers utilized propaganda to exert influence over their allies and to persuade others to join their side. The United States designed its propaganda to raise fears of communism and highlight the benefits of capitalist democracy. This propaganda took many forms, from books and news articles to films and radio broadcasts. To carry out this war of words, the government created the United States Information Agency, or USIA, in 1953.

One of the USIA's main jobs was to beam radio broadcasts into the Soviet bloc. It used three networks to carry out this task: Voice of America, Radio Free Europe, and Radio Liberty. The CIA funded these last two services. Radio Free Europe broadcast to Eastern Europe in Czech, Polish, and other local languages. Radio Liberty broadcast to the Soviet Union in Russian. Many of the staff members of these services had fled Eastern Europe to escape communist rule. The families they left behind often faced harsh treatment from communist governments due to their relatives' ties to the radio networks.

Soviet and Eastern European leaders tried to isolate their citizens from Western news and ideas by banning radio programs from the West. They disrupted the broadcasts by jamming the signals and filling the airwaves with mechanical shrieks, howls, and other loud noises.

Foreign Aid: Supporting Friendly Governments Nations also used foreign aid as a Cold War weapon. Both the United States and the Soviet Union gave money and assistance to other countries to gain new allies.

Some U.S. aid helped the poor by providing funds for agriculture, health care, and other social and economic programs. However, much of it took the form of military assistance to friendly Third World governments. Pro-American states such as Turkey, Pakistan, and South Korea received help, while more independent nations often did not. In some countries, such as Nicaragua and Haiti, the United States gave support to anticommunist dictators. These leaders used the aid to tighten their grip on power—often at the expense of their people. Many citizens in those countries bitterly resented the aid, which seemed to contradict the U.S. goal of promoting democracy.

At times, the United States withheld aid to punish nations that failed to support its policies. In the 1950s, Egyptian leader Gamal Abdul Nasser began building trade ties with communist nations. In 1956, Egypt bought tanks and other weapons from communist Czechoslovakia, in defiance of U.S. wishes. In response, the United States and Britain withdrew their offers to help Egypt finance the building of the much-needed Aswan Dam on the Nile River. Nasser reacted by seizing control of the Suez Canal from Britain. This led Britain, France, and Israel to invade Egypt, hoping to regain control of the canal. The Soviet Union then threatened to back up Egypt with military force. To prevent war, the United States stepped in, persuading all sides to withdraw and thus ending the crisis.

The CIA: Containing Communism Through Covert Action In the 1950s, the CIA played a growing part in the Cold War. During this period, it expanded its role from intelligence gathering to **covert action**. A covert action is a secret political, economic, or military operation that supports foreign policy. Agents try to shape events or influence affairs in foreign countries while hiding their role in those events.

During the Cold War, both superpowers used spies, satellite photography, wiretapping, and other covert methods to gather information about or influence events in other countries. Francis Gary Powers's U-2 flight was a covert CIA operation. At times, CIA agents also bribed foreign leaders, supported political parties, or funded supposedly independent radio stations.

The United States often used covert action to overthrow unfriendly or leftist governments. For example, in 1953 it helped topple Mohammed Mossadegh, Iran's premier. Mossadegh had nationalized a British oil company, establishing government control over the formerly private company. He also hinted that he might seek Soviet aid. CIA agents worked with Iran's military leaders to overthrow Mossadegh and reinstate the Iranian monarch, Shah Mohammed Reza Pahlavi. As absolute ruler with close ties to the United States, the shah ruled Iran for almost 30 years.

In Central America, the United States also relied on covert action to achieve its goals. In 1954 in Guatemala, for example, CIA agents helped overthrow the elected president, Jacobo Arbenz Guzmán. Both U.S. economic interests and Cold War concerns motivated this action. The United Fruit Company, a U.S. firm with operations in Guatemala, opposed certain social reforms laid out by the Guatemalan government. In particular, United Fruit objected to a government plan to hand over thousands of acres of company land to the country's landless peasants. Concerned that Guatemala might turn communist, the United States ordered the CIA to support a military coup. Arbenz was overthrown, and a military government took charge. It returned United Fruit lands, shelved other reforms, and jailed many of its critics. The U.S. role in Guatemala caused many Latin Americans to view the United States as an enemy of social reform.

Sometimes the United States intervened more aggressively. In 1962, voters in the Dominican Republic elected a noncommunist reformer, Juan Bosch, as president. Seven months after he had taken office, a military coup toppled Bosch. In 1965, his supporters started a civil war to return him to power. Fearing that many of his supporters were communists, the United States sent troops to crush the revolt and keep Bosch from regaining power.

During the Cold War, American troops often intervened with conflicts across the world. In 1958, American soldiers were sent to Beirut, Lebanon, to help resolve a rebellion.

Cold War Hot Spots, 1944–1965

During the Cold War, many conflicts broke out around the world. Some, like the Cuban Revolution, were guerrilla wars. Others, like the 1965 rebellions in Indonesia, were struggles between competing factions in a country. But all of them were tied, directly or indirectly, to the global struggle between East and West.

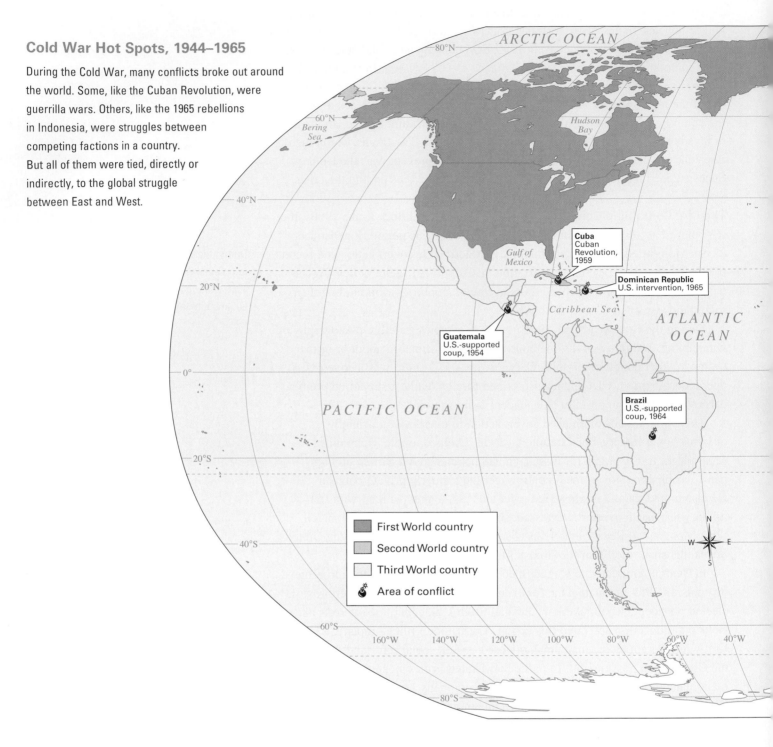

Cuba
Cuban Revolution, 1959

Dominican Republic
U.S. intervention, 1965

Guatemala
U.S.-supported coup, 1954

Brazil
U.S.-supported coup, 1964

- First World country
- Second World country
- Third World country
- Area of conflict

39.5 An Arms Race Threatens Global Destruction

On September 23, 1949, President Truman made a grim announcement. "We have evidence," he said, "that within recent weeks an atomic explosion occurred in the USSR." The statement alarmed Americans. Previously, only the United States had possessed an atomic bomb. Now that the Soviets had one as well, the United States felt the need to develop weapons with even greater destructive force. Soon the two superpowers were locked in a deadly **arms race,** or a competition to achieve weapons superiority.

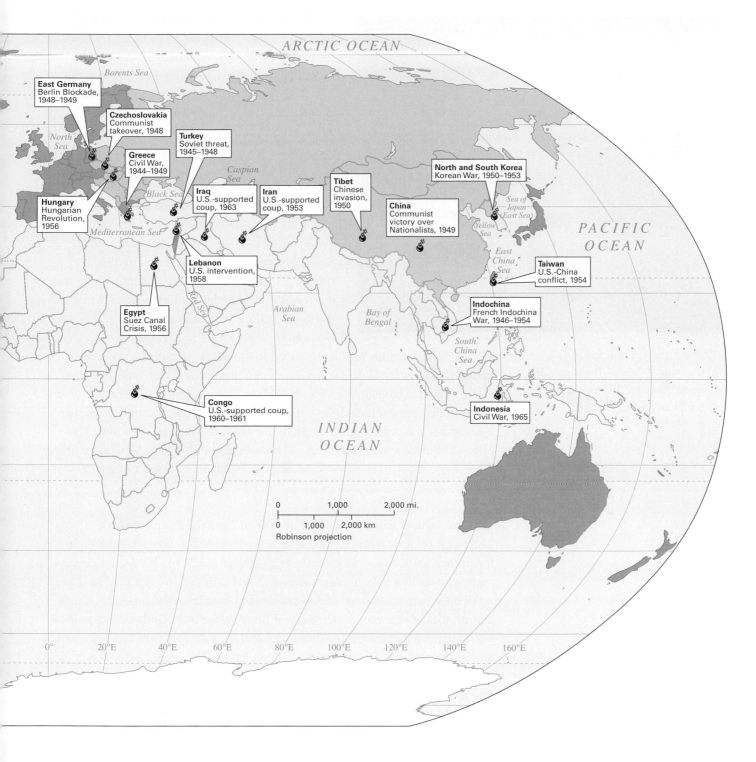

East Germany
Berlin Blockade,
1948–1949

Czechoslovakia
Communist
takeover, 1948

Turkey
Soviet threat,
1945–1948

Greece
Civil War,
1944–1949

Hungary
Hungarian
Revolution,
1956

Iraq
U.S.-supported
coup, 1963

Iran
U.S.-supported
coup, 1953

Tibet
Chinese
invasion,
1950

North and South Korea
Korean War, 1950–1953

China
Communist
victory over
Nationalists, 1949

Taiwan
U.S.-China
conflict, 1954

Lebanon
U.S. intervention,
1958

Egypt
Suez Canal
Crisis, 1956

Indochina
French Indochina
War, 1946–1954

Congo
U.S.-supported coup,
1960–1961

Indonesia
Civil War, 1965

ARCTIC OCEAN

Barents Sea

North Sea

Caspian Sea

Black Sea

Mediterranean Sea

Red Sea

Arabian Sea

Bay of Bengal

INDIAN OCEAN

Yellow Sea

Sea of Japan (East Sea)

East China Sea

South China Sea

PACIFIC OCEAN

0   1,000   2,000 mi.
0   1,000   2,000 km
Robinson projection

0°   20°E   40°E   60°E   80°E   100°E   120°E   140°E   160°E

The Race to Develop Weapons of Mass Destruction Shortly after the
Soviet atomic test, American scientists began discussing plans for a new type
of bomb. It would be based not on splitting atoms—the technology used in the
atomic bomb—but on fusing them. Known as a hydrogen bomb, or **H-bomb,**
this weapon would be far more powerful than an atomic bomb. Some scientists, including J. Robert Oppenheimer, argued against it. In a report to the
Atomic Energy Commission, they warned that the H-bomb was "not a weapon
which can be used exclusively" for military purposes, since it would have a far
greater effect on civilian populations than an atomic bomb would.

In the 1952, the United States tested its first H-bomb, codenamed "Mike." The impact of "Mike" was so great that it eliminated an island in the South Pacific.

The Joint Chiefs of Staff, the nation's top military leaders, disagreed. "The United States," they said, "would be in an intolerable position if a possible enemy possessed the bomb and the United States did not." When other scientists and Truman's advisers sided with the generals, Truman gave the green light for producing the hydrogen bomb.

In 1952, the United States tested its first H-bomb. It was smaller than the atomic bombs dropped on Japan during World War II but 500 times more powerful. A year later, the Soviet Union tested its own H-bomb. A witness at the Soviet test recalled how "the earth trembled beneath us, and our faces were struck like the lash of a whip . . . From the jolt of the shock wave it was difficult to stand on one's feet . . . Day was replaced by night."

By 1960, the arms race had also led to the development of nuclear missiles and submarines. First, the United States and the Soviet Union built long-range, intercontinental ballistic missiles, or ICBMs, which could deliver nuclear warheads to distant continents. Next, the United States developed nuclear-powered submarines that could launch up to 16 nuclear missiles from the water. The Soviet Union soon followed with its own nuclear submarines. With these new weapons, citizens of both nations faced the frightening prospect of enemy warheads raining down on their cities from far away.

Brinkmanship: Using the Threat of War to Contain Communism
The threat of nuclear war carried with it the prospect of utter annihilation, a threat the United States tried to use to its advantage. In the 1950s, the government developed a foreign policy known as **brinkmanship**—a willingness to go to the edge, or brink, of war. Brinkmanship was based on a simple, if dangerous, idea. According to Secretary of State John Foster Dulles, the Soviets had to believe that the United States would use its nuclear weapons if pushed too far. In a speech, Dulles declared, "You have to take chances for peace, just as you have to take chances in war. The ability to get to the verge without getting into the war is the necessary art . . . If you are scared to go to the brink, you are lost."

To its critics, brinkmanship seemed foolhardy. It implied that the Soviets only understood force and assumed that they would back down if faced with the prospect of nuclear war. But Dulles believed that the United States had to be ready to go to war to keep the peace.

A growing conflict in Asia soon tested this policy. In China, both communists on the mainland and Nationalists in Taiwan claimed to be the nation's legitimate rulers. In 1954, Mao decided to assert China's claim to Taiwan and ordered his troops to fire on the nearby islands of Quemoy and Matsu. The Nationalist government claimed these islands and feared that their loss to the communists would prompt an invasion of Taiwan.

Eisenhower saw the shelling of Quemoy and Matsu as a challenge to American influence in Asia. As a result, the United States signed a treaty with the Nationalist government promising to protect Taiwan in case of attack. Three years later, China resumed its assault. This time the United States threatened to launch a nuclear attack on China, causing China to back off. In the eyes of the United States, this result was a victory for brinkmanship.

Deterring Attack by Threatening Mutual Assured Destruction As the threat of nuclear war continued, Dulles developed a new strategy to reinforce brinkmanship and ensure American nuclear superiority. The strategy, called **deterrence,** revolved around developing a weapons arsenal so deadly that the Soviet Union would not dare to attack. Dulles also believed that warning the Soviets that any attack on the United States would be met with an even deadlier counterattack would reduce the threat of war.

The combination of deterrence and the willingness to use nuclear weapons came to be known as Mutual Assured Destruction (MAD). It meant that either side would respond to a nuclear attack by launching its own missiles, with devastating results for both sides. Fear of a nuclear conflict made the United States and the Soviet Union more likely to step back from all-out war. However, while MAD may have helped prevent the Cold War from turning hot, it also kept the world in a state of heightened anxiety.

Summary

During the Cold War, the superpower conflict that began in Europe expanded to China and other parts of the world. The nuclear arms race added to Cold War tensions.

Berlin Blockade In 1948, the Soviet Union set up a blockade around Berlin to force the Allies to either abandon the city or cancel plans for the creation of West Germany. The Allies launched an airlift to bring supplies into Berlin and break the blockade. In the end, Germany was split between east and west.

NATO and the Warsaw Pact In 1949, the Western powers formed the North Atlantic Treaty Organization as a military alliance to counter Soviet aggression. The Soviets responded by forming their own military alliance, the Warsaw Pact, with Eastern European countries.

Korean War After the fall of China to communism, Cold War tensions flared up in Korea. In 1950, North Korean communists invaded South Korea, prompting a war with U.S. and UN forces. The Korean War ended in 1953, but Korea remained divided.

Third World During the Cold War, the United States and the Soviet Union tried to win friends and allies in the Third World—the developing nations of Latin America, Africa, and Asia. This battle for "hearts and minds" involved propaganda, aid, covert action, and military intervention.

Mutual Assured Destruction The invention of the H-bomb fueled a deadly arms race. In response, the United States developed various policies, including brinkmanship and deterrence, to manage the nuclear threat. In the end, it relied on the policy of Mutual Assured Destruction to limit the chances of all-out war.

Chapter 40

Fighting the Cold War at Home

How did the anxieties raised by the Cold War affect life in the United States?

40.1 Introduction

Norman Finkelstein wore the "dog tag" that hung around his neck proudly. It was similar to the identification tags that members of the military wore—if soldiers were killed or injured, their dog tags revealed their name and which military outfit they belonged to. However, Finkelstein was no soldier. "I was in the fifth grade and had no intention at that time of joining the army," he remembers.

In many towns and cities during the early Cold War years, children wore dog tags like Finkelstein's, with their name and address imprinted on them. Some tags also carried their birth date, religion, and blood type. Authorities hoped the tags would help them deal with a nuclear attack if one took place. Finkelstein recalls, "In case of a nuclear attack, my body could be easily identified—that is, if the dog tag survived and there were others still alive to receive the information. It all seemed very strange at the time and even stranger today."

Children growing up during the Cold War lived with the fear that Soviet bombers—and later guided missiles—armed with nuclear weapons could attack the United States at any moment. No one could predict when a nuclear attack would occur, so people tried to remain constantly prepared. In addition to wearing dog tags, children practiced duck-and-cover drills at school. During these drills, when their teachers gave a signal, students ducked under their desks and covered their heads with their hands. Historian Doris Kearns Goodwin confesses, "I could never figure out how my flimsy desk, with its worn inkwell and its years of name-scratching, could protect me from the atomic bomb."

For Americans, the Cold War was a new and unfamiliar type of war. Like earlier conflicts, it caused fear and anxiety on the home front. It also raised concerns about how to keep the nation secure from external threats and unseen enemies within the country while also maintaining civil liberties. As in past wars, finding the right balance between freedom and security posed a challenge.

Many schoolchildren wore dog tags during the Cold War. These tags were designed to identify children in the aftermath of a nuclear attack. Americans also took other precautions, such as holding emergency drills and stockpiling goods, out of fear of nuclear war.

◀ Schoolchildren involved in a duck-and-cover nuclear attack drill, 1951

The House Un-American Activities Committee held thousands of hearings in its hunt for subversives in American society. Here the committee questions a Hollywood executive about alleged communist influence in the film industry.

40.2 Searching for Communists on the Home Front

In 1951, the federal government published a pamphlet that listed 100 questions and answers about communism in the United States. Here are three examples:

> *What is communism?*
> A system by which one small group seeks to rule the world.
>
> *What do communists want?*
> To rule your mind and your body from cradle to grave.
>
> *Where can a communist be found in everyday life?*
> Look for him in your school, your labor union, your church, or your civic club.
> —"100 Things You Should Know About Communism
> in the U.S.A.," 1951

This publication revealed that the United States fought the Cold War not only against communists in foreign countries—it also fought communism at home.

Communists Come Under Suspicion at Home Not all Americans agreed with the government's definition of communism. Some people believed that communism offered a much fairer way of organizing a society than capitalism did. Under communism, everyone would share equally in what society produced. Extremes of wealth and poverty would fade away. The result, supporters maintained, would be a great increase in human happiness.

During the Depression, this vision had attracted many followers in the United States. Some had joined the Communist Party. Others became **communist sympathizers,** or people who believed in communist ideology but did not join the party. By 1950, Communist Party membership in the United States was just 43,000. Still, as the Cold War heated up, so did fears of communist **subversion,** or plots to overthrow the government and replace it with a communist dictatorship.

To calm public anxiety, in 1947 President Truman established the Federal Employee Loyalty Program. It required government employers to take **loyalty oaths,** or pledges of loyalty to the United States. It also called for background investigations of employees who had possible connections to subversive groups. After 5 million investigations, hundreds of government workers lost their jobs for being "potentially" disloyal. Several thousand others were forced to resign.

HUAC Hunts for Communists in Hollywood and Beyond Meanwhile, Congress began its own investigation. It was led by the **House Un-American Activities Committee (HUAC),** which had been formed in 1938 to investigate subversive organizations. In 1947, HUAC turned its attention to communist influence in the film industry. "Large numbers of moving pictures that come out of Hollywood," charged one committee member, "carry the Communist line." The committee called on writers, actors, and directors to testify about their political beliefs.

Ten witnesses refused to answer the committee's questions. Called the Hollywood Ten, they argued that the Fifth Amendment gave them the right to refuse to answer on the grounds that their testimony might **incriminate** them, or cause them to look guilty. The committee disagreed and charged them with **contempt of Congress,** or willful failure to obey the authority of Congress. When the House of Representatives voted to convict the Hollywood Ten of that crime, the group issued a joint statement that warned, "The United States can keep its constitutional liberties, or it can keep the [HUAC]. It can't keep both."

The heads of Hollywood movie studios grew concerned about the impact the HUAC investigation would have on their industry. They stated that they would not hire anyone with communist sympathies. To carry out this pledge, they created a **blacklist** of people thought to be Communist Party members or communist sympathizers. Anyone whose name appeared on this blacklist could no longer find work making films.

From the film industry, HUAC moved on to other groups. In 1954, it called on labor organizer John Watkins to testify about communist influence in labor unions. When Watkins refused to answer certain questions, HUAC convicted him of contempt of Congress. Watkins appealed his conviction, arguing that the Constitution does not give Congress unlimited power to investigate the private lives of citizens. The Supreme Court agreed with him. Writing for the majority, Chief Justice Earl Warren ruled that Congress's power to investigate must be related to its business of making laws:

> There is no general authority to expose the private affairs of individuals without justification in terms of the functions of the Congress . . . Investigations conducted solely for the personal aggrandizement [glorification] of the investigators or to "punish" those investigated are indefensible.
> —*Watkins v. United States,* 1957

Spy Cases Raise New Fears Public worries about subversion deepened with news that Americans in important government posts had been charged with working as spies for the Soviet Union. The **Alger Hiss case** involved a State Department official who had served as an adviser to President Roosevelt at the Yalta Conference. A former Communist named Whittaker Chambers accused Hiss of passing secrets to the Soviet Union. In 1950, a federal grand jury convicted Hiss of **perjury,** or lying under oath. Still, he continued to proclaim his innocence. However, secret documents made public in 1995 indicate that Hiss probably had spied for the Soviet Union.

Just as shocking were charges that Americans had helped the Soviet Union test its first atomic bomb in 1949. A year later, a German-born British physicist named Klaus Fuchs confessed that he had spied for the Soviet Union while he was working on the Manhattan Project for Britain during World War II. The information Fuchs passed along to Soviet scientists may well have helped to speed their development of atomic weapons. From Fuchs, a trail of espionage led investigators to Ethel and Julius Rosenberg, whom the United States charged with passing atomic secrets to the Soviet Union. The **Rosenberg trial** concluded with death sentences for both defendants. At the time, many people protested the verdict and sentences, arguing that the evidence against the suspects was inconclusive. Nonetheless, the Rosenbergs were executed in 1953, becoming the only American civilians to be put to death for spying during the Cold War.

Ethel and Julius Rosenberg were tried, convicted, and executed for passing atomic secrets to the Soviet Union. Such well-publicized spy cases raised fears that the federal government was riddled with traitors. Soviet documents opened in the 1990s indicate that Julius had spied for the Soviet Union. Ethel was probably guilty only of keeping quiet about her husband's activities.

The Rise and Fall of Joseph McCarthy About two weeks after Fuchs confessed to spying, Senator Joseph McCarthy of Wisconsin was speaking in West Virginia. He asked his audience how communists had been so successful in taking over Eastern Europe and China. The answer, he said, could be found in "the traitorous actions" of Americans working in high government posts. Then he added, "I have here in my hand a list of 205 . . . names that were made known to the Secretary of State as being members of the Communist Party and who nevertheless are still working and shaping policy in the State Department."

McCarthy never produced this list of names. Nor did he offer evidence to back up his charges. Still, he launched a crusade against subversives that rapidly gained momentum. Widespread public support for his investigations helped the Republican Party win control of the Senate in 1952. As a result, McCarthy was named head of the Government Committee on Operations of the Senate.

Over the next two years, McCarthy used his newfound power to search for subversives. Although he never made a solid case against anyone, his accusations drove some people out of their jobs. For example, under hostile questioning by McCarthy's chief lawyer, Roy Cohn, Army Signal Corps employee Carl Greenblum broke down and cried. As Greenblum collected himself, McCarthy announced, "the witness admits he was lying." Greenblum had admitted no such thing, yet he was still fired. Such reckless persecution of innocent people became known as **McCarthyism**. Today, this term signifies the practice of publicly accusing someone of subversive activities without evidence to back up the charges.

McCarthyism made people even more fearful. Lawmakers refused to enact reforms that might be viewed as moving the country toward communism. Schools asked teachers to sign loyalty oaths, and those who objected to doing so lost their jobs. Citizens became reluctant to speak out about injustices for fear of being labeled subversive. This anxiety was often carried to extremes. When graduate students at a university circulated a petition asking for a vending machine in the physics department, some students refused to sign. They feared having their names on a list with other allegedly radical students.

Finally, McCarthy went too far. In 1954, he accused both the Army and President Dwight D. Eisenhower of being "soft on Communism." In the nationally televised Army-McCarthy hearings, spellbound Americans watched as McCarthy's brutal tactics were exposed for all to see. The climax of the hearings came when McCarthy attacked a young man who worked for Joseph Welch, the lawyer who represented the Army. An emotional Welch responded,

The more reckless Senator McCarthy's accusations became, the less believable they were. When McCarthy made false charges against a young lawyer working for Joseph Welch during the Army-McCarthy hearings, a disgusted Welch replied, "Have you no sense of decency, sir, at long last? Have you left no sense of decency?"

> Little did I dream you could be so reckless and so cruel as to do an injury to that lad. It is, I regret to say, equally true that I fear he shall always bear a scar needlessly inflicted by you. If it were in my power to forgive you for your reckless cruelty, I would do so. I like to think I'm a gentle man, but your forgiveness will have to come from someone other than me.
> —Joseph Welch, addressing Senator Joseph McCarthy, June 9, 1954

Public opinion quickly turned against McCarthy. Late in 1954, the Senate passed Resolution 301, which **censured,** or formally scolded, McCarthy for his destructive actions. His behavior, it stated, had "tended to bring the Senate into dishonor and disrepute." McCarthy soon faded from the national scene.

In addition to fear, the Atomic Age inspired excitement. In 1946, a cereal company offered children an "atomic bomb" ring for the price of 15 cents and a cereal box top. "See real atoms split to smithereens!" the advertisement gleefully claimed. About 750,000 children ordered the ring.

40.3 Living with Nuclear Anxiety

A stark white flash enveloped their world. Randy felt the heat on his neck. Peyton cried out and covered her face with her hands. In the southwest, in the direction of Tampa, St. Petersburg, and Sarasota, another unnatural sun was born, much larger and infinitely fiercer than the sun in the east . . . Peyton screamed, "I can't see! I can't see, Mommy. Mommy, where are you?"
—Pat Frank, *Alas, Babylon,* 1959

Like many novels written in the 1950s, Pat Frank's *Alas, Babylon* portrayed a world engulfed in World War III—an imagined conflict fought with weapons powerful enough to destroy all life on Earth.

The Perils and Promise of the Atomic Age Books like *Alas, Babylon* explored the perils of the **Atomic Age**. During these early Cold War years, the destruction caused by the atomic bombs dropped on Japan remained fresh in Americans' minds. People were terrified to think of such bombs raining down on American cities—yet by 1949, such an attack seemed all too possible.

Despite such fears, the promise of atomic power also excited Americans. The media ran glowing stories predicting atomic-powered cars, ships, airplanes, and power plants. One newspaper reported,

Atoms in an amount of matter spread out the size of a fingernail, say the scientists, could supply sufficient energy to propel an ocean liner across the sea and back. An automobile, with a microscopic amount of matter from which atomic energy could be released, could be driven around for a lifetime if it didn't wear out, never stopping at a gas station.
—*Milwaukee Journal,* August 7, 1945

Businesses jumped on the atomic bandwagon as well. The bar at the Washington Press Club marked the arrival of the Atomic Age with the "Atomic Cocktail." Department stores advertised "Atomic Sales." Musicians recorded songs with titles like "Atom Buster" and "Atom Polka." A French fashion designer named his new two-piece bathing suit the "bikini" in honor of the testing of an atom bomb on Bikini Atoll in the Central Pacific.

In the 1950s, atomic bomb tests moved to the Nevada desert. In Las Vegas, the Chamber of Commerce promoted atomic tourism, publishing a schedule of tests and the best places to view them. Armed with "atomic box lunches," tourists hoping to feel and see an atomic bomb's power flocked as close to ground zero—the point of a bomb's impact—as the government allowed.

Creating a Civil Defense System As the atomic arms race took off, the federal government began planning for **civil defense**—the organization and training of citizens to work with the armed forces and emergency services during a war or natural disaster. In 1951, Congress established the **Federal Civil Defense Administration (FCDA)**. The head of FCDA warned Americans that the "back yard may be the next front line." The agency distributed millions of civil defense manuals to help people prepare for a nuclear attack. These publications made it clear that Americans could not rely on the military to protect them from a surprise attack. People would have to be prepared to protect themselves as best they could.

Schools used a civil defense film, *Duck and Cover,* to teach children how to respond to a nuclear attack. This image from the film shows Bert the Turtle hiding in his shell from a dynamite blast. The film compares this situation to how children should react to an atomic bomb explosion.

Civil defense preparedness soon became part of daily life. Many communities set up bomb shelters in public buildings. Stocked with emergency food and water supplies, these shelters offered people refuge during an attack. Across the country, tests of warning sirens and emergency radio stations were carried out every week. Civil defense workers called block wardens trained their neighbors on how to fight fires and provide first aid after an attack.

Children also took part in civil defense training. The FCDA developed a film and booklet featuring a character called Bert the Turtle, who taught children how to survive an atomic explosion. Bert led the children through duck-and-cover drills to prepare them for how to react if they ever heard an emergency siren.

Some families took preparedness a step further by burying an underground shelter in their backyard. Several companies sold prefabricated "fallout shelters" for single-family use. The shelters were designed to shield families not only from an atomic explosion, but also from the radioactive dust that "falls out" of the sky afterward. Authorities advised families to remain sealed in their fallout shelters for several weeks after an attack to let this toxic dust settle.

Preparedness Versus Peace These early civil defense preparations were based on the expected impact of an atomic bomb attack. By the mid-1950s, the development of far more powerful H-bombs raised questions about the effectiveness of such methods. Faced with this new threat, the FCDA concluded that the only practical way to protect large numbers of people during an attack was to evacuate them from target cities. "It's much better to get people out, even if in the process you may kill some," said a civil defense planner, "than to have millions of Americans just stay there and be killed."

The FCDA created a large-scale civil defense drill called Operation Alert to test how quickly cities could be evacuated. On June 15, 1955, sirens began to wail across the country. The results were mixed. Some people ducked into bomb shelters. Others headed out of town. Many paid little or no attention to the drill. Had the attack been real, observed the *New York Times* in an editorial, millions of people would have died. The editorial concluded that

> This demonstration gives new emphasis to President Eisenhower's dictum [observation] that war no longer presents the possibility of victory or defeat, but only . . . varying degrees of destruction, and that there is no substitute for a just and lasting peace.
>
> —*New York Times,* June 16, 1955

The FCDA repeated Operation Alert drills throughout the 1950s. However, for a growing number of Americans, the drills became an opportunity to speak out against the nuclear arms race. In 1960, a group of young mothers in New York City organized hundreds of protesters around this simple idea: "Peace is the only defense against nuclear war."

The growing anxiety about the nuclear arms race among Americans spawned a series of protests. Many of the protesters were women. The woman pictured above marches to protest atomic bomb tests.

Summary

Like earlier wars, the Cold War created fright and anxiety on the home front. Fearful of attacks from within, the government sought to root out communist subversion. Faced with the threat of nuclear attack from the Soviet Union, it promoted civil defense and preparedness planning.

House Un-American Activities Committee HUAC investigated the loyalty of people in many areas of life. Its probe of the movie industry led movie studio heads to blacklist anyone thought to be a communist or communist sympathizer.

Spy trials Fears of subversion deepened with the Alger Hiss case and the Rosenberg trial. Hiss served a prison term, and the Rosenbergs were executed for selling atomic secrets to the USSR.

McCarthyism Senator Joseph McCarthy launched a well-publicized crusade against subversives in government. The term McCarthyism came to refer to personal attacks against innocent people with little or no evidence to support the charges.

Atomic Age Americans greeted the Atomic Age with a mixture of fear and excitement. Many people had high hopes for peaceful uses of atomic power.

Federal Civil Defense Administration Congress established the FCDA to help Americans survive a nuclear attack. The FCDA published civil defense manuals and promoted drills and other measures to protect Americans from harm. As the power of nuclear weapons increased, however, the usefulness of such precautions came into question.

Chapter 41

Peace, Prosperity, and Progress

Why are the 1950s remembered as an age of affluence?

41.1 Introduction

D. J. Waldie grew up in the 1950s in Lakewood, California, a community located 15 miles south of Los Angeles. In 1949, Lakewood was 3,500 acres of lima bean fields. A year later, houses were rising out of the farm fields at a rate of 50 homes a day. By 1953, some 90,000 people lived in Lakewood, making it the fastest-growing housing development in the world.

The Depression and World War II had greatly slowed home construction. Once the war ended, however, millions of soldiers returned home to marry and start families. The developers of Lakewood were betting that those families would soon be looking for a place to live. Still, Waldie later wrote, "No theorist or urban planner had the experience then to gauge how thirty thousand former GIs and their wives would take to frame and stucco houses on small, rectangular lots next to hog farms and dairies."

Some local businesspeople predicted that Lakewood would be an instant slum—or worse, a ghost town. They could not have been more wrong. "Buyers did not require encouragement," recalled Waldie.

> When the sales office opened on a cloudless Palm Sunday in April 1950, twenty-five thousand people were waiting . . . Salesmen sold 30 to 50 houses a day, and more than 300 during one weekend, when the first unit of the subdivision opened. At one point, salesmen sold 107 houses in an hour.
>
> —D. J. Waldie, *Holy Land: A Suburban Memoir,* 1996

For these white, middle-class homebuyers, owning a house in Lakewood was a symbol of their new affluence, or prosperity. Aided by the GI Bill of Rights, veterans could buy a home with no money down. All they needed was a steady job and a promise to keep up with the house payments. As a Lakewood salesperson said of his job, "We sell happiness in homes."

Suburbs like Lakewood, California, made it possible for many people to buy their first home. A two-bedroom house in Lakewood sold for $7,575. Every house came with up-to-date features like stainless-steel kitchen counters and an electric garbage disposal. In this photograph, prospective buyers walk along a street of model homes in 1951.

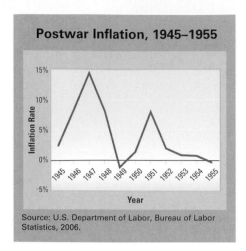

Postwar Inflation, 1945–1955

Source: U.S. Department of Labor, Bureau of Labor Statistics, 2006.

Inflation is a general rise in the price of goods and services over an extended period of time. If a worker's wages stay the same but prices go up, the worker can afford to buy fewer things. As the graph shows, inflation spiked after wartime price controls were lifted in 1946. Prices also rose because the demand for consumer goods after the war far outstripped the supply.

41.2 Postwar Politics: Readjustments and Challenges

Harry Truman had never wanted to be president. The day after he learned of Franklin Roosevelt's death on April 12, 1945, he told reporters,

> Boys, if you ever pray, pray for me now. I don't know whether you fellows ever had a load of hay fall on you, but when they told me yesterday what had happened, I felt like the moon, the stars, and all the planets had fallen on me.

—Harry Truman, 1945

Truman's first task was to bring the war to an end. Once that was done, he faced the enormous challenge of leading the country back to a peacetime economy.

A Rocky Transition to Peace Truman welcomed the war's end by announcing a package of reforms that later came to be known as the **Fair Deal**. He called on Congress to increase the minimum wage, increase aid to agriculture and education, and enact a national heath insurance program. Complaining that Truman was "out–New Dealing the New Deal," Republicans in Congress did their best to stall his reforms.

Meanwhile, the economy was going through a difficult period of adjustment. As the war came to a close, government officials canceled billions of dollars' worth of war contracts. As a result, millions of defense workers lost their jobs. In addition, once wartime price controls were lifted, prices skyrocketed.

As **inflation** soared, workers demanded wage increases. When employers refused to meet these demands, labor unions triggered the largest strike wave in U.S. history. In 1946, nearly 5 million workers walked off the job, many of them in such key industries as steel production, coal mining, and oil refining.

When railroad workers went on strike, Truman took action. In a speech to Congress, he warned, "Food, raw materials, fuel, shipping, housing, the public health, the public safety—all will be dangerously affected" if the strike were allowed to continue. Truman threatened to call out the armed forces to run the railroads. However, the strike was settled before he could carry out his threat.

Truman Battles a Republican Congress The labor unrest was still fresh in voters' minds as the 1946 congressional elections drew near. Running under the slogan "Had Enough?" Republican candidates swept to victory. For the first time since the 1920s, Republicans gained control of both houses of Congress.

One of the first actions of the new Republican Congress was passage of the Twenty-second Amendment in 1947. This amendment limits a president to two terms of office. The Republican sponsors of the amendment did not want to see another liberal president like Franklin Roosevelt seek four terms as president. They argued that without term limits, a popular president might seek to become "president for life," much like a dictator. The amendment was overwhelmingly ratified by the states and was added to the Constitution in 1951.

Congress also took aim at the labor unions by passing the **Taft-Hartley Act** in 1947. This law placed many limits on the power of unions. Among other things, it outlawed the closed shop. A closed shop is a workplace in which the employer agrees to hire only members of a particular union. It banned sympathy

These workers are on strike against the Inland Steel Company in Indiana Harbor, Indiana, in 1946. To resolve such strikes, President Harry Truman appointed fact-finding boards to hear workers' complaints. Usually, the boards recommended wage increases.

strikes, in which workers of one union walk off their jobs to show their sympathy with another striking union. It also allowed the president to impose an 80-day "cooling off" period before a union could strike in certain industries. This provision especially enraged union supporters, who called it "slave labor law." President Truman vetoed the law, but Congress passed it over his veto.

Truman also battled with Congress over civil rights. Late in 1946, he established the President's Committee on Civil Rights to investigate racial inequality in the United States. The committee issued a report calling for an end to segregation and discrimination in voting, housing, education, employment, and the military. Truman praised the report as "an American charter of human freedom." Congress, however, refused to act on its recommendations. In 1948, Truman sidestepped Congress and desegregated the armed forces by executive order.

An Upset Victory in 1948 As the election of 1948 drew near, Democrats were filled with gloom. Truman, who had been unable to get any of his reforms passed by the Republican Congress, looked like a weak candidate. Worse yet, the Democratic Party had splintered into three factions.

Left-wing Democrats, led by former U.S. vice president Henry Wallace, pulled away to form the Progressive Party. Wallace was more liberal than Truman on domestic issues. But his main difference with the president was over foreign policy. Fearing that Truman's hard-line containment policy could lead to World War III, he advocated friendlier relations with the Soviet Union.

Segregationist southern Democrats, known as Dixiecrats, left to form the States' Rights Democratic Party. The Dixiecrats nominated Strom Thurmond, the governor of South Carolina, for the presidency. Thurmond ran on a platform of complete segregation of the races.

The Republicans nominated New York governor Thomas E. Dewey to run against Truman. Dewey was heavily favored to win, despite his lackluster campaign style. One newspaper ran this parody of the typical, bland Dewey speech: "Agriculture is important. Our rivers are full of fish. You cannot have freedom without liberty. Our future lies ahead."

The 1948 election was a huge political upset for pollsters and headline writers. On election night, some newspapers printed the next day's edition before the results were final. Here, a gleeful Truman winks during a campaign stop.

Truman decided to fight for the presidency. He launched an ambitious "whistle-stop" tour of the country. A whistle-stop is a small town where a train would stop only if signaled to do so by a whistle. During his tour, Truman made 356 stops to speak directly to voters. At every one, he lambasted the "do nothing" Republican Congress. His supporters cheered him on with the slogan, "Give 'em hell, Harry!"

On election eve, opinion polls predicted a Dewey landslide. Only Truman seemed to believe he could win. The voters proved Truman right. In one of the biggest electoral upsets in history, Truman narrowly won reelection.

For the next four years, Truman regularly presented his Fair Deal programs to Congress. However, a coalition of conservative southern Democrats and midwestern Republicans blocked most of his reform efforts. Congress did agree to a modest expansion of Social Security benefits. It also agreed to increase the minimum wage and support slum clearance.

Ike Takes the Middle of the Road During the 1952 election season, the Democratic Party came together again around Adlai Stevenson, the governor of Illinois. Stevenson was much admired for his elegant speaking style and wit.

The Republicans nominated the immensely popular war hero Dwight D. Eisenhower. Eisenhower had an impressive biography. After serving as supreme commander of the Allied forces in Europe during World War II, he had gone on to become head of NATO. Moreover, people loved Eisenhower's winning smile and agreeable manner. Building on his nickname, Ike, the Republican campaign featured posters and buttons saying, "I like Ike."

Richard Nixon, a young senator from California, was chosen to be Eisenhower's running mate. A strong anticommunist, Nixon had gained prominence as a member of the House Un-American Activities Committee. In the election, Eisenhower swept to victory in 39 of the 48 states. Four years later, he again defeated Stevenson to win a second term as president.

During his presidency, Eisenhower embraced a program he described as "modern Republicanism." He promised to be "conservative when it comes to money and liberal when it comes to human beings." He resisted calls by conservatives to roll back the New Deal. "Should any political party attempt to abolish Social Security, unemployment insurance, and eliminate labor laws and farm programs," he warned, "you would not hear of that party again in our political history." Eisenhower went further and expanded Social Security. By doing so, he ensured that this popular New Deal program would survive no matter which party controlled the White House.

At the same time, Eisenhower presided over a massive peacetime arms buildup. "Our arms," he stated, "must be mighty, ready for instant action." Still, he worried about the growing power of what he called the "military-industrial complex." In his last address as president, Eisenhower warned,

This conjunction [joining] of an immense military establishment and a large arms industry is new in the American experience . . . We recognize the imperative need for this development. Yet . . . we must never let the weight of this combination endanger our liberties or democratic processes.
—Dwight D. Eisenhower, Farewell Address, 1961

41.3 Economic Growth Creates an Age of Affluence

In 1940, Dick and Mac McDonald opened a drive-in restaurant in San Bernardino, California. The restaurant was popular, but customers sometimes had to wait as long as 20 minutes for their food. Dick McDonald later recalled,

> The cars were jamming up the lot. Customers weren't demanding it, but our intuition told us they would like speed. Everything was moving faster. The supermarkets and dime stores had already converted to self-service, and it was obvious the future of drive-ins was self-service.
>
> —Dick McDonald

So the brothers decided to streamline every aspect of their business. Instead of offering hamburgers, hot dogs, and sandwiches, they narrowed the menu to hamburgers. They replaced carhops with a self-service order counter. Instead of serving food on plates and glasses that needed washing, they used paper wrappers and cups. They set up the kitchen to run like an assembly line.

Their timing could not have been better. When they reopened their restaurant as McDonald's Famous Hamburgers in 1948, the country was entering one of the greatest economic booms in its history. By the end of the 1950s, middle-class families were enjoying a level of affluence beyond anything their Depression-era parents and grandparents could have imagined.

Consumer Demand Spurs Economic Growth During World War II, Americans had saved billions of dollars. Flush with cash, they were ready to go on a spending spree as soon as factories could convert from war production to consumer goods. This surge in consumer demand encouraged businesses to expand production. By 1955, the United States, with only 6 percent of the world's population, was producing almost half of the world's goods.

As the economy grew, incomes rose. **Real income** is income measured by the amount of goods and services it will buy, regardless of inflation. By the mid-1950s, the average American family had twice as much real income to spend as the average family of the 1920s had. And spend it they did.

The McDonald brothers developed an assembly-line process to speed service and lower costs. At this Illinois branch of McDonald's, customers could receive their meal in as little as 15 seconds after placing an order.

The 1950s in America was an age of consumerism. Store displays flaunted new fashions and gadgets to their customers. American customers gladly paid for the newest items.

Not only were Americans spending more money than ever before, they were also spending it in different places. In the past, most people had bought their goods in stores lining the main street of town. By the mid-1950s, however, suburban shopping centers were luring consumers away from downtown shopping districts. Shopping centers offered customers easy parking and a wide array of shops to browse, often in air-conditioned comfort. By 1964, there were more than 7,600 shopping centers across the United States.

Businesses used methods pioneered during the 1920s to encourage consumers to keep on spending. One method was slick advertising campaigns. By 1955, businesses were spending $8 billion a year on ads that encouraged consumption.

Another method was to offer consumers easier ways to buy now and pay later. Large stores issued charge cards that allowed their customers to charge goods to an account rather than pay cash. By 1960, Sears Roebuck had more than 10 million accounts, or one for every five families. In 1958, American Express launched the first all-purpose credit card that could be used in stores, hotels, restaurants, and gas stations.

A third method used to encourage consumption was called **planned obsolescence**. Brooks Stevens, the industrial designer who popularized this term, defined it as a way to create "the desire to own something a little newer, a little better, a little sooner than is necessary." Businesses using this method looked for ways to make what a consumer bought today seem obsolete, or out-of-date, after a fixed period of time. Clothing companies did this by introducing new fashions every season. As they did so, last season's garments, although still usable, looked dated. Automobile companies did the same thing by changing the styling of their cars every year.

The Economy Begins to Shift from Goods to Services When the 1950s began, the U.S. economy was dominated by industries that produced such goods as steel, appliances, and cars. By the end of the decade, industries that provided services, rather than manufacturing goods, were growing in importance. The biggest and best-known manufacturing company was the automaker General Motors (GM). In 1955, GM became the first U.S. corporation to earn more than $1 billion a year. It accomplished this feat by producing and selling as many cars as all of its competitors produced combined.

An important factor in GM's success was an improved relationship with its workers. In 1948, GM signed a historic agreement with the United Auto Workers union. The agreement guaranteed that GM workers would receive regular wage hikes tied to a **cost-of-living index**. A cost-of-living index measures differences in the price of goods and services over time. If inflation pushes prices up, the index measures by how much prices went up. *Fortune* magazine called the agreement "the treaty of Detroit." It brought GM years of labor peace.

As the economic boom continued, new service industries began to compete for the consumer's dollar. One was the fast-food service industry. In 1954, a go-getter named Ray Kroc visited McDonald's Famous Hamburgers in San Bernardino. He was amazed by what he saw. An hour before lunch, there was already a long line of customers waiting to be served. Kroc asked people in line what they liked about the restaurant. They replied that it was clean, fast, and cheap. In addition, the burgers tasted good, and it was not necessary to tip anyone.

Kroc convinced the McDonald brothers to hire him as a franchising agent. A **franchise** is an agreement to operate a business that carries a company's name and sells its products. The next year, he opened his own franchise restaurant in Des Plains, Illinois. Like the original, Kroc's McDonald's was wildly successful. It was especially attractive to families with young children who did not feel comfortable in more formal restaurants. Under Kroc's leadership, hundreds of McDonald's soon dotted the landscape. By 1963, the fast-food chain had sold more than 1 billion hamburgers.

Another new service industry, the motel chain, was inspired by a summer driving trip. In 1951, Kemmons Wilson, a homebuilder in Tennessee, took his family on a car trip to Washington, D.C. Day after day, he faced the problem of finding a decent place for his family to spend the night. Motels at that time were independent, mom-and-pop operations. Some were clean. Others were filthy. Some charged extra for children. Others did not. The only way to find out was to go from one motel to the next.

A frustrated Wilson finally turned to his wife and announced he was going into the motel business. She asked how many motels he planned to build. "Oh, about four hundred," he answered. "That ought to cover the country." His motels would be clean, affordable, easy to find, and family-friendly. "If I never do anything else worth remembering in my life," he added, "children are going to stay free at my motels."

Wilson returned home and built his first Holiday Inn. After franchising his chain, the number of Holiday Inns grew rapidly. Other chains, such as Best Western and Howard Johnson's, also began to expand. By the 1960s, the motel chain had become a fixture on America's highways.

Gross National Product, 1945–1960

Source: U.S. Census Bureau.

At the end of World War II, many economists feared the economy would once again fall into a depression. Instead, consumer spending helped spur a long period of economic growth. The nation's productivity more than doubled from 1945 to 1960.

The Workforce Shifts from Blue- to White-Collar Jobs As the economy grew and changed, the kinds of work people did also changed. When the 1950s began, **blue-collar workers** made up the largest part of the workforce. Blue-collar workers are people who work in factories or at skilled trades, such as plumbing or auto repair. Most are paid by the hour. The name comes from the durable blue shirts that manual workers often wore to work.

By the end of the 1950s, the workforce looked different. For the first time in history, **white-collar workers** outnumbered blue-collar employees. White-collar workers include professionals such as doctors and lawyers, engineers, salespeople, managers, and office staff. Most receive a weekly or yearly salary rather than an hourly wage. Because white-collar employees worked in offices, they could wear white shirts to work without fear of getting them dirty.

Both groups prospered during the 1950s. As blue-collar workers moved up into the middle class, they began to dress, act, and consume like their white-collar neighbors. "During the war," observed a sociologist in Detroit, "you could sit on a streetcar and tell at a glance who were the [blue-collar] defense workers and who were the white collars . . . Today you just can't tell who's who."

During the 1950s, the number of people holding white-collar office jobs grew rapidly. White-collar workers were far less likely to belong to labor unions than their blue-collar neighbors.

41.4 Marriage, Families, and a Baby Boom

The year 1946 was one second old when a navy machinist's wife gave birth to a baby girl in Philadelphia. In Chicago, seconds after the new year began, a son was born to the wife of an army trombone player. For both sets of parents, these births may have been long-awaited and happy events. But for demographers who study the growth of human populations, these births marked the beginning of the largest population boom in U.S. history.

A Marriage Boom Leads to a Baby Boom During the Depression, marriage rates and birthrates had dropped as worries about the future caused people to postpone decisions that would change their lives. After World War II ended, the future looked brighter. In 1946, there were almost 2.3 million marriages in the United States, an increase of more than 600,000 from the year before. More people were marrying—and at younger ages—than during the war years. The average age of marriage in the 1950s was 20 for women and 22 for men.

Many of these newlyweds started families right away. Older couples who had delayed having children also began to start families. "It seems to me," observed a visitor from Great Britain, "that every other young housewife I see is pregnant." The result was a baby boom, a large increase in the number of babies born in proportion to the size of the population. At the peak of the baby boom, in 1957, 4.3 million births were recorded. By 1964, the last baby boom year, four Americans in ten were under the age of 20.

Economists and businesspeople were thrilled by the baby boom. Signs in New York City subway cars informed riders that

> Your future is great in a growing America.
> Every day 11,000 babies are born in America.
> This means new business, new jobs, new opportunities.

The babies overflowing maternity wards boosted sales for diaper services and baby food bottlers. Home sales boomed as young families flocked to the suburbs in search of living space. Factories worked overtime to fill these new homes with furniture and appliances and to put a car in every garage.

Schools had trouble finding room for the millions of children reaching school age each year. During the 1950s, California opened new schools at the rate of one a week to make room for the baby boomers. Older schools added temporary buildings to create more classrooms. Other schools handled the flood by running two shifts of classes, one in the morning and another in the afternoon. Despite these efforts, large classes with two students to a desk were common during the 1950s.

Family Roles: Working Dads and Stay-at-Home Moms The majority of baby boomers grew up in so-called traditional families, with dads who went to work each day and moms who stayed home. The importance of marriage and family was driven home in marriage manuals of the day. "Whether you are a man or a woman, the family is the unit to which you most genuinely belong," wrote Dr. John Schindler in *The Woman's Guide to Better Living 52 Weeks a Year*. "The family is the center of your living. If it isn't, you've gone far astray."

Getting married and starting a family was an important step for women living in the 1950s. An article in the *New York Times Magazine* warned, "A girl who hasn't a man in her sight by the time she is 20 is not altogether wrong in fearing that she may never get married."

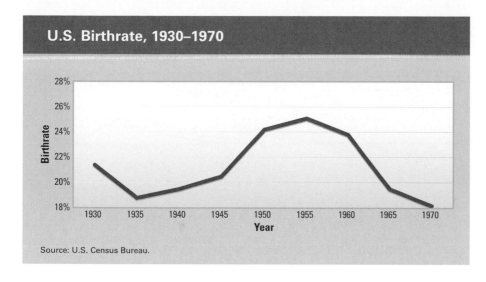

U.S. Birthrate, 1930–1970

Source: U.S. Census Bureau.

The economic prosperity that followed World War II triggered a baby boom that lasted until 1964. Then, almost as suddenly as it began, the boom ended. By 1966, the birthrate had dropped below the lowest level seen during the Depression years. In just two years, the baby boom had become a baby bust.

The belief that mothers should not work outside the home unless they had to for economic reasons was promoted by Dr. Benjamin Spock, the leading child-care expert of the day. First published in 1946, Spock's *Common Sense Book of Baby and Child Care* was a best seller for many years. Spock advised mothers to devote themselves full-time to raising their children. Any distraction from that task, such as a job or hobby, he argued, could damage a young child.

The mass media reinforced traditional family roles. Magazines, movies, and advertisements portrayed the ideal family as one in which the husband was the breadwinner while the wife stayed home. The homemaker's role was expanded to include a number of jobs. A mom became a teacher, doctor, nurse, cook, adviser, decorator, housekeeper, manager, and chauffeur all in one

A new medium called television brought this ideal family to life on screen. In *Leave It to Beaver,* June Cleaver was a stay-at-home mom who wore high heels and pearls while working in the kitchen. When asked what kind of girl her son Wally should marry, she answered, "Oh, some sensible girl from a nice family . . . who's a good cook and can keep a nice house and see that he's happy." Jim Anderson, the sensible dad in *Father Knows Best,* calmly solved his family's problems when he got home from work. In one episode, he advised his tomboy daughter Kathy to act helpless around boys. "The worst thing you can do," he told her, "is to try to beat a man at his own game."

Such television shows taught children the roles they would be expected to play as adults. Children got the message in other ways, too. Toy stores were filled with dolls and tea sets for girls and toy guns for boys. Girls were given miniature hope chests to encourage them to dream of one day getting married. Children's books reinforced traditional roles with sayings like this one, from *The Happy Family,* a Little Golden Book popular at the time: "The happiest time of the day is when Father comes home from work."

The strong emphasis on marriage led many young women to forgo a college education. College enrollment among women dropped sharply. And although some women pursued careers after college, many others dropped out early to get married or headed from graduation straight into marriage. A professor at Smith College complained of having to cancel a final class with female senior honors students because it conflicted with too many bridal showers.

In the "traditional" 1950s family, the father worked, and the mother stayed at home raising the children. In this photograph, the mother looks happy with her role as wife and mother. But not all women found full-time homemaking an ideal way of life.

With the booming success of Levittown came the equally successful Levittown shopping centers. Families that moved into their affordable houses also gained easy access to a variety of stores.

41.5 Population Shifts to Suburbs and Sunbelt States

In 1941, Bill and Alfred Levitt won a government contract to build thousands of homes for war workers in Norfolk, Virginia. At first, everything went wrong. Skilled workers were in short supply. The schedule was too tight. It looked like they would miss their deadlines and lose money. The Levitts decided to rethink how they built homes. They broke the construction process into 27 steps. Then they hired and trained 27 teams of workers, each of which specialized in just one step. By the time the project ended, they had revolutionized the process of building homes.

Middle-Class Families Move to the Suburbs No industry had suffered more during the Depression and war years than the homebuilding industry. Housing starts had dropped from more than 1 million new homes a year to fewer than 100,000. By war's end, housing was in such short supply that 250 used trolley cars were sold as homes in Chicago. Returning veterans were eager to buy homes and start families. The GI Bill was ready to assist them with home loans at low interest rates. But there were few homes to buy.

The Levitt brothers knew exactly how to help those veterans use those loans. In 1947, they began work on **Levittown,** the first planned community in the nation. It was located on Long Island, about 20 miles from New York City. By 1951, the brothers had built 17,447 homes around Levittown. They would go on to build two more Levittowns, in Pennsylvania and New Jersey, by 1960.

To keep costs down, the Levitts built small, boxy, almost identical homes with two bedrooms and one bathroom. Different work crews moved from house to house doing only one job. There were tile crews and floor crews. One team specialized in white paint while another one only applied red paint. By mass-producing their homes in this way, the Levitts greatly sped up production. By 1948, the Levitts were building 36 houses a day. They also kept their prices under $8,000.

The first Levittown in New York was a kind of suburb called a bedroom community. Most people who lived there commuted by car or public transportation to jobs in New York City. Although a commute could be tiring, countless young families jumped at the chance to live in a clean, safe, child-friendly suburb. Between 1950 and 1956, the number of Americans living in suburban communities increased by 46 percent.

As a group, these new suburbanites were overwhelmingly white and middle class. Many suburbs, including Levittown, did not sell to African Americans. Indeed, this homogeneity was part of the appeal of suburbs. "Everybody lives on the same side of the tracks," observed the *Saturday Evening Post* in 1954. "They have no slums to fret about, no families of conspicuous wealth to envy, no traditional upper crust to whet and thwart their social aspirations [ambitions]."

Weather and Wages Spur Migration to the Sunbelt Americans were not only on the move from cities to suburbs. They were also moving from the northern half of the country to the Sunbelt. This "belt" of warm-weather states stretched across the southern third of the United States from Florida to California.

After World War II, manufacturers and other businesses began locating in the Sunbelt. They were attracted by low labor costs. In addition, unions were less entrenched in the Sunbelt states than in the older industrial regions of the North. The Sunbelt tourist industry also grew, as families flocked to sunny beaches and new attractions like Disneyland.

As businesses moved south, people followed. California felt the effects of this migration as much as any state. Between 1950 and 1960, California's population grew by 50 percent, from about 10.6 million to more than 15.7 million people. Other Sunbelt states experienced similar growth.

Two advances in technology made this large population shift possible. The first was the design and construction of massive water projects in the arid Southwest. These projects involved building dams on major rivers to capture precious water in huge reservoirs. This water was then distributed through a system of canals and aqueducts to fast-growing cities such as Phoenix, Arizona; Las Vegas, Nevada; and Los Angeles, California. The second key technology was the development of room air conditioners designed for home use. Air conditioning made summers bearable in Sunbelt states like Florida and Arizona. Annual sales of room air conditioners jumped from around 30,000 in 1946 to more than a million by 1953.

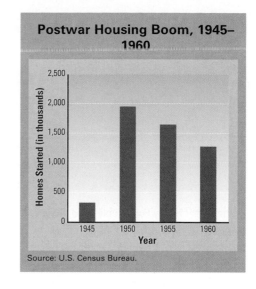

The rapid growth in housing starts was made possible by a revolution in home construction techniques. Using assembly-line methods pioneered by Henry Ford, homebuilders like the Levitt brothers were able to mass-produce homes at an astonishing rate.

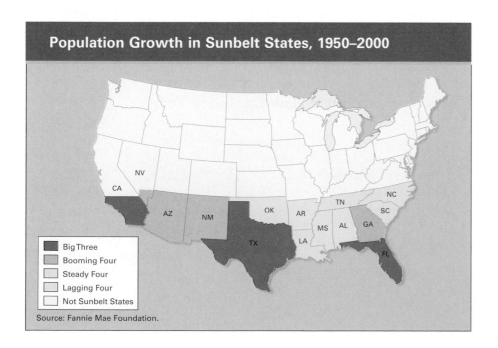

Not all Sunbelt states grew at the same rate. Each of the Big Three grew by more than 13 million people between 1950 and 2000. The Booming Four also showed large gains. The Steady Four grew at about the same rate as the rest of the country. The Lagging Four grew only half as fast as the nation as a whole.

Named after Henry Ford's only child, the Edsel failed to sell well. Only 181,000 Edsels were produced over three years. Today, the Edsel is considered a "poor man's collectors car." As Edsel historian Phil Skinner explains, "There are a lot more Edsels out there than people who love them."

41.6 The Triumph of the Automobile

On September 4, 1957, a new car called the Edsel appeared in Ford showrooms around the country. At first, consumers showed up at the dealerships in record numbers. Ford executives were thrilled. But then they realized people were looking, not buying. And most people did not like what they saw. The Edsel had been designed to be the biggest, flashiest, most luxurious Ford ever. Public response, however, was not enthusiastic. "One member of the media called it 'an Oldsmobile sucking a lemon,'" recalls a rare Edsel owner, "and another called it 'a Pontiac pushing a toilet seat.'" After three years of poor sales, Ford gave up on the Edsel. But such failures were rare in the 1950s. For most of the decade, automobile sales stayed strong as the growth of suburbs increased the demand for cars.

The Middle-Class Dream: Two Cars in Every Garage Life in the suburbs depended on access to an automobile. Because most suburbs lacked public transportation, fathers commuted by car to their jobs in nearby cities. Mothers needed cars to drive to supermarkets and suburban shopping centers. After school, children depended on the family car to get to their music lessons or sports games. Suburban families began to find they needed not just one, but two cars in their garage.

Yet cars were more than a necessity in this booming consumer culture. They became a **status symbol,** or sign of wealth and prestige. Automakers encouraged car owners to trade in last year's models for new ones to keep up with their neighbors. Buyers were also urged to "move up" to ever-more-expensive cars to show that they had become a success in life. The Edsel was introduced as "the smart car for the young executive or professional family on the way up." A 1958 ad proclaimed, "They'll know you've *arrived* when you drive up in an Edsel." That same year an Oldsmobile ad gushed,

> Obviously this is a car to attract attention. Its precedent-breaking beauty fully deserves all the applause owners are giving it. Men and women who have just recently moved up to a '58 Oldsmobile from another make are the loudest in their praise . . . proudest of their new possessions.

How Did Automakers Persuade Americans to Buy a New Car Every Year?

For many Americans in the 1950s, buying a new car was a yearly ritual. Automakers encouraged this practice in two ways. First, each year, they made changes to the style, so that each year's models looked different from those of the year before. Second, they introduced new features every year, designed to make driving more pleasurable. The combined effect was to make last year's car look and feel old long before its useful lifetime was over.

Model: 1949 Chevrolet Fleetline
Style: 2-door sedan
Base price: $1,492
New standard features: starter button, 2-speed heater
New options: white sidewall tires, AM-FM radio

Throughout the 1950s, car sales stayed mostly above 7 million a year. By 1958, more than 67 million cars were on the road. Close to 12 million families owned two or more cars. Two years later, the census reported that 65 percent of all working people drove cars to work.

Roads to Everywhere: The Interstate Highway System As the majority of Americans came to depend on cars for transportation, they demanded more and better roads. State and federal lawmakers responded by funding new highway construction programs. The most ambitious was a program authorized by Congress in 1956 to construct a nationwide **interstate highway system**. The goal of this system was to connect major cities around the country by a network of super highways.

President Eisenhower strongly supported federal funding of the interstate highway system. He remembered how useful the four-lane *autobahns,* or high-speed highways built by Germany in the 1930s, had been for moving troops during World War II. With the United States engaged in the Cold War, a system of superhighways was seen as an important aid to the nation's defense. Both troops and weapons could be transported easily and quickly with such a network of high-speed highways in place.

By 1960, about 10,000 miles of interstate highway had been constructed. Today, the system has about 45,000 miles of highway, all built to the same high standards. Interstate highways are divided, with at least two lanes in either direction. Access is controlled by the use of on-ramps and off-ramps. The flow of traffic is not interrupted by traffic lights or railroad crossings. Curves are engineered to be safe at high speeds. Rest areas are spaced along the way for the comfort of travelers.

The interstate highway system benefited the country in many ways. It made travel by road over long distances both faster and safer. It created economic opportunities as new roadside businesses, such as gas stations, motels, and restaurants, sprang up at interstate exits. By improving access to all parts of the country, the system gave people more choices as to where to live, work, shop, and vacation. For better or worse, the highways also increased Americans' dependence on cars and trucks as their main form of transportation.

Model: 1955 Chevrolet Bel Air
Style: 4-door sedan
Base price: $1,932
New standard features: electric windshield wipers, back-up lights
New options: electric clock, power windows and seats, spare tire on back bumper

Model: 1959 Chevrolet Bel Air
Style: 4-door sedan
Base price: $2,440
New standard features: vinyl interior
New options: air conditioner, leather seats, dual exhausts, cruise control

Model: 1962 Chevrolet Bel Air
Style: 4-door sedan
Base price: $2,510
New standard features: two front-seat safety belts
New options: front bucket seats, padded dash

41.7 Technological Advances Transform Everyday Life

In 1953, Charles Mee was a 14-year-old high school football player in Barrington, Illinois. One summer night, on the way to a dance, Mee fell ill. He was dizzy, unsteady on his feet, and chilled. Later that night, he could not stand up. His parents drove him to the nearest hospital. The head nurse took one look at Mee and pronounced, "This boy has polio." Mee knew that his life was changed forever.

Advances in Medicine Extend Life Expectancy It would have been small comfort to Mee to know that he was not alone. Polio, or infantile paralysis, was one of the most feared diseases of the 20th century. The first polio epidemic in the United States, in 1916, left 27,000 people paralyzed and 9,000 dead. Over the next 40 years, polio epidemics struck every summer across the country. The worst year was 1952, when almost 60,000 new polio cases were reported.

President Franklin Roosevelt was perhaps the most famous victim of polio. In 1938, he established the National Foundation for Infantile Paralysis to seek a cure for polio. Over the next 17 years, the foundation funded research to create a vaccine against polio. That research led to the development of the first **polio vaccine** by Dr. Jonas Salk. The vaccine was made up of very small parts of the polio virus. People who took the vaccine developed antibodies that protected them from infection by the actual polio virus. In 1954, some 2 million schoolchildren took part in trials of the vaccine. Statistics showed the vaccine to be as much as 90 percent effective in preventing polio. A dreaded disease had finally been conquered.

Surgical techniques advanced rapidly in the 1950s as well. The first open-heart surgery and the first kidney transplant were performed. The first pacemaker, a device designed to regulate the beating of a patient's heart, was developed. Medical researchers also began to experiment with heart transplants.

A number of diseases once viewed as killers were routinely cured in the 1950s through the use of antibiotic drugs. Penicillin, streptomycin, and other "wonder drugs" attacked bacteria that caused everything from earaches to pneumonia and tuberculosis. These advances in medicine contributed to a rise in **life expectancy** during the 1950s. A child born in 1950 could expect to live to the age of 68. By 1960, the average life expectancy had reached 69.7 years.

Peaceful Uses for Nuclear Energy During the 1950s, scientists explored peaceful uses for nuclear energy. One of the most promising was the generation of electricity. "It is not too much to expect that our children will enjoy in their homes electrical energy too cheap to meter," predicted Lewis Strauss, chair of the U.S. Atomic Energy Commission, in 1954. Three years later, the first full-scale nuclear power plant opened in Shippingport, Pennsylvania.

Medical researchers were also finding new uses for nuclear energy. Radioactive isotopes were used in the diagnosis and treatment of disease. The use of X-rays as a diagnostic tool became a general practice in the 1950s. At the same time, specialists in nuclear medicine began to use radioactive iodine to treat thyroid cancer.

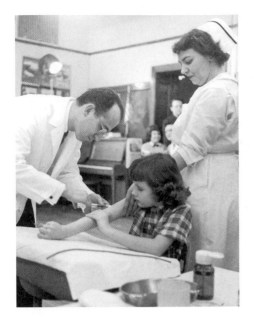

In 1953, Dr. Jonas Salk, shown here on the left, announced the development of a trial polio vaccine. Among the first to test it were his wife and sons. Later trials found the vaccine safe and effective. Salk received many honors for his work in wiping out polio. He refused cash awards, however, and continued working to improve the vaccine.

Computers Enter the Workplace In 1946, two engineers from the University of Pennsylvania built one of the earliest electronic digital computers. Called ENIAC (Electronic Numerical Integrator and Computer), it contained nearly 18,000 vacuum tubes and took up about 1,500 square feet of floor space—almost as much as two Levittown homes. It could perform 300 multiplications per second. Five years later, the same team introduced the first commercially successful computer. Called the UNIVAC, it could do more than just crunch numbers. The UNIVAC could handle letters and words. In 1952, a UNIVAC proved its power by accurately predicting the election of Eisenhower just 45 minutes after the polls closed.

The invention of the transistor in 1947 led to dramatic improvements in computer design. A transistor is a small, low-powered electronic device. By 1959, transistors had replaced the bulky and unreliable vacuum tubes. As computers shrank in size, they began to appear in more and more workplaces. The new machines revolutionized the collection and storage of data. They sped up the work of record keepers, such as librarians and tax collectors. But as the decade ended, few people could foresee a time when there would be a personal computer on almost every desk.

By today's standards, ENIAC was a 30-ton monster. But it had most of the elements of a modern computer. It could add, subtract, multiply, divide, and find square roots at amazing speeds.

Summary

The years following World War II were a time of prosperity in the United States. As the economy boomed, fears of a return to depression conditions faded. During the 1950s, millions of working-class families became affluent enough to move up into the middle class.

Fair Deal President Harry Truman guided the transition from a wartime to a peacetime economy. But he was unable to get his Fair Deal reform program approved by a Republican Congress.

Taft-Hartley Act Immediately after the war, a series of labor strikes threatened to cripple the economy. In response, Congress passed the Taft-Hartley Act, which limited the power of unions.

Baby boom As the economy improved, Americans married and had children at record rates. The result was a baby boom that lasted from 1946 to 1964.

Levittown Suburbs like Levittown attracted homebuyers by offering inexpensive houses on small lots. Suburban life revolved around the so-called traditional family, with a working dad and stay-at-home mom.

Sunbelt Besides leaving cities for suburbs, Americans were also moving from northern states to the Sunbelt. California, Texas, and Florida all grew rapidly as a result.

Interstate highway system A federally funded network of high-speed roads linked the nation as never before. Better roads encouraged the growth of suburbs and suburban shopping centers.

Polio vaccine Medical advances such as antibiotics increased life expectancy in the 1950s. But no advance was more welcomed than the polio vaccine. This vaccine ended a decades-long battle with a much-dreaded disease that caused paralysis and death among its victims.

Chapter 42

Two Americas

Why did poverty persist in the United States in an age of affluence?

42.1 Introduction

In September 1956, Vice President Richard Nixon gave a speech in which he predicted a prosperous next few years for the United States. In the "not too distant" future, he said, a four-day workweek would become the norm. The "remaining pockets of [economic] distress" would be wiped out. "These are not dreams or idle boasts," he stated confidently. "Our hope is to double everyone's standard of living in ten years."

Nixon was not alone in his optimism. Booming economic growth since World War II had led many government officials and leading intellectuals to believe that poverty would soon be eradicated. Although some voiced concern that not all Americans shared in the general prosperity, most of the public ignored the existence of poverty in the United States. *Time* magazine went so far as to forecast "the elimination of poverty as a fact of human life."

In 1962, a new book called *The Other America* jolted the nation out of its complacency. Written by social activist Michael Harrington, the book described two Americas—one affluent, the other impoverished.

Harrington's book shocked readers with details of how the impoverished population in America lived and facts of just how far-reaching poverty stretched in the country. It was a wake-up call for the American people. *The Other America* generated a national discussion about the responsibility of government to address gross inequalities in American society.

Michael Harrington was a social and political activist who became best known for writing *The Other America*. This book stunned readers with its portrayal of poverty in the midst of American affluence. It helped inspire a government antipoverty program—called the War on Poverty—in the 1960s.

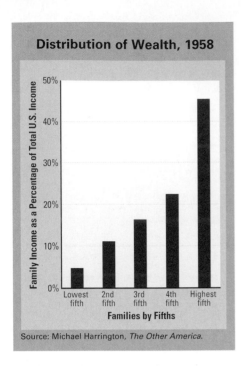

Distribution of Wealth, 1958

Family Income as a Percentage of Total U.S. Income

- 50%
- 40%
- 30%
- 20%
- 10%
- 0%

Families by Fifths: Lowest fifth, 2nd fifth, 3rd fifth, 4th fifth, Highest fifth

Source: Michael Harrington, *The Other America*.

During the 1950s, the United States prospered, but all Americans did not benefit. This graph shows that in 1958, the top fifth of American families received almost half of the nation's income. The bottom fifth received less than one twentieth of all income.

42.2 The Persistence of Poverty in an Affluent Society

Greenwood, Mississippi, was one of countless towns in which the two Americas existed side by side. During the 1950s, playwright Endesha Ida Mae Holland grew up there, raised alongside her three siblings by a hardworking single mother. Holland later wrote a memoir about her childhood in which she described the contrast between poverty and prosperity in Greenwood. The well-to-do whites, she wrote, lived on quiet, shady boulevards in houses "with many big rooms and bright, soft rugs on the floors." Each house had a neatly trimmed lawn, "with pretty flowers set in borders along the walkway." In these neighborhoods, "the streets were paved and no open window was without its screen."

Holland herself lived in the "respectable" black section of town. Her home was a small, ramshackle house infested with cockroaches. The roof leaked, the walls were plastered with newspaper, and the packed earth showed through between the floorboards. Holland was poor, but others were poorer. She wrote that "the poorest black people lived" near the railroad tracks, where "in places the tracks were almost hidden by the smelly black mud that oozed from the 'bayou,' an open cesspool that held the waste from outhouses."

Different Ways of Defining Poverty Most people understand poverty as the lack of means—money, material goods, or other resources—to live decently. But what does it mean to live decently? There has never been a single standard for measuring economic deprivation. What people think of as poor depends on where and when they live.

For much of U.S. history, many Americans felt poverty to be as much a moral condition as an economic problem. They looked down on people, known as paupers, who did not work and who lived on public charity. Many viewed **pauperism,** or dependency on public assistance, as a moral failing. "Pauperism is the consequence of willful error," wrote a leading clergyman in 1834, "of shameful indolence [laziness], of vicious habit."

At the same time, society recognized that poverty could result from misfortune. People who could not work—such as the elderly, the disabled, and children—could not help being poor. Many Americans also realized that most poor people did work, but their wages were too low to lift them out of poverty. Known today as the **working poor,** these Americans were once referred to as "the poorer sort." Although the working poor hold a more respectable place in society than did paupers, economically, there is little difference between the two.

In the late 1800s, social scientists began examining poverty more objectively, viewing it in economic rather than moral terms. For the first time, they defined poverty as a lack of income. They used the term **poverty line** to refer to the minimum amount of income one would need to meet basic needs. However, scholars disagreed about exactly where to draw the poverty line.

In 1949, the Subcommittee on Low-Income Families proposed a poverty line of $2,000 per year for families of all sizes. This unofficial line was widely used until 1958, when the government began to adjust the amount based on family size. An official poverty line was not established until 1965. It was determined by calculating a minimal family food budget and then tripling that figure, because food typically made up about one third of a family's total budget.

The Poor in Postwar America: An Invisible Class By the end of the 1950s, about one in four Americans lived below the poverty line. According to *The Other America,* this meant that about 50 million people endured an inadequate quality of life. Middle-class readers of Michael Harrington's book were shocked to discover the extent of the country's poverty. How could they not have noticed such widespread misery? Harrington suggested they had not noticed because poverty in America was camouflaged and stowed away. Factors such as where the poor lived, what they wore, and how old they were helped obscure them from affluent Americans.

Harrington contended that the movement of middle-class families to the suburbs after World War II was one reason for the general lack of knowledge about America's poor. Middle-class workers commuting to urban business districts seldom encountered the poor people left behind in old city neighborhoods. Harrington suggested that commuting workers easily overlooked the destitution in the cities and imagined that most Americans lived comfortably. The availability of inexpensive clothing also helped hide the poor from view. Their clothes may have been better than what people assumed the poor would wear, but they still lived a substandard lifestyle.

Age was another factor that made the poor hard to see. Harrington noted that over 8 million of the poor were 65 years old or older. Even more of that population was younger than 18 years old. Elderly poor people seldom strayed from their rented rooms or homes in older urban neighborhoods. Because older poor people are not very mobile, they are often ignored. Young poor people are more noticeable, but they also rarely depart too far from where they live.

In addition, the poor wielded no political power. This made it easy for others to ignore them. Harrington recognized that many poor people were not involved with unions, fraternal organizations, and political parties. They also were not involved in lobbying or with creating legislation.

42.3 The Landscape of Poverty in a "Land of Plenty"

The "other America," the land of the poor, had no geographic or cultural boundaries. It reached into cities and rural areas in every state. Its "inhabitants" belonged to every racial, ethnic, and age group in the country. In 1959, more than one fourth of the nation's poor were children, and one third were elderly. In a decade marked by prosperity, how did so many get left behind?

Left Behind in the Inner Cities As middle-class whites moved out of cities in the 1950s, poor people moved in. From 1945 to 1960, about 5 million African Americans left the South for northern cities. By 1955, nearly 700,000 Puerto Ricans migrated to the mainland, mostly to New York City. In the West, large numbers of Mexican immigrants moved to Los Angeles and other cities.

Michael Harrington argued that destitution in America is concealed. The growing availability of cheap clothing and consumer goods helped create this impression. A family with a television or a car might not appear poor. But a closer look might show telltale signs of poverty, such as poor health, a rundown home, and a decaying neighborhood.

In the 1950s, Appalachia was one of the poorest regions in the country. Many of the poor were unemployed coal miners and their families. They struggled to make ends meet through subsistence farming or by working low-wage jobs. The living conditions shown here were typical of the region's severe poverty.

Many of the new arrivals came in search of manufacturing jobs. However, as industries relocated to the suburbs, the jobs disappeared. Housing discrimination limited where minorities could live and work. "When I went . . . to look for apartments," a Puerto Rican in Philadelphia recalled, "they throw the door in my face. They don't want no colored people, you know, my skin is dark." Black and Latino populations became concentrated in decaying, inner-city areas that were being abandoned by whites. These blighted neighborhoods turned into overcrowded slums with high rates of poverty and unemployment.

To rectify this problem, Congress passed the **Housing Act of 1949**. Its goal was to provide "a decent home . . . for every American family" by funding public housing and **urban renewal** programs. Under urban renewal, the government demolished many slums and replaced them with high-rise apartments, offices, and civic buildings. Despite its lofty-sounding goal, however, the Housing Act of 1949 made urban poverty worse. Hundreds of thousands of poor people lost homes when their neighborhoods were bulldozed. The government intended low-income public housing projects to provide an alternative, but not enough housing was built to accommodate all the displaced households. In many cities, the overcrowded and impoverished "projects" became the new slums.

Trying to Live Off the Land American farmers also faced poverty. After World War II, new agricultural technology contributed to the growth of **agribusiness**—the industry of food production by large corporations or wealthy individuals. Agribusiness holdings were vast in size and produced huge quantities of food very efficiently by applying industrial production techniques to farming. Agribusiness was profitable, but its earnings accumulated at the expense of the rural poor. Small farmers could not compete with the giant corporate farms, and many sank into poverty. As a result, thousands of poor rural whites and blacks moved off the land and into cities in search of work.

On large corporate farms, migrant workers endured low pay and wretched living conditions. Many were Mexican *braceros* who came to the United States between 1942 and 1964. Other Mexicans came illegally. In 1954, the government organized Operation Wetback to expel undocumented Mexican immigrants. As a result, officials seized and deported several million Mexicans. Of the Mexican immigrants who remained in the United States in the 1950s, one in three lived below the poverty line.

Appalachia, a mountainous region in the South, was another rural outpost of poverty. Because of the steep terrain there, living off the land by farming was difficult. Coal mining, the region's once-dominant industry, declined after World War II, as the demand for coal fell. The decrease in demand and the mechanization of mining led to job losses for miners. In the 1950s, more than 2 million impoverished people left Appalachia. Harrington described those who remained as "a beaten people, sunk in their poverty and deprived of hope."

America's Poorest Citizens Perhaps the poorest U.S. citizens were American Indians. A 1949 study of conditions on American Indian reservations found "hopeless poverty and slum squalor." Indeed, those living on reservations seemed the most invisible poor of all, so much so that Michael Harrington omitted them—"quite wrongly" he later wrote—from *The Other America*.

In 1934, the Indian Reorganization Act had affirmed American Indians' right to govern themselves. It had also affirmed their status as wards of the federal government. This meant the government held responsibility for protecting their lands and providing them with economic aid and social services.

After World War II, the government wanted to end this relationship. As a practical matter, "getting out of the Indian business" would save money. Many people also thought that releasing American Indians from federal supervision would allow them to assimilate and become economically self-reliant. "Set the Indians free!" was their slogan. Others believed American Indians were not ready to be self-sufficient and would be vulnerable to exploitation. They feared that the tribes would be "freed" of the few assets—mainly land—they had left.

In 1953, Congress voted to terminate the government's responsibility for American Indians. The **termination policy** ended federal aid to tribes, withdrew federal land protection, and distributed tribal land among individuals. The **Voluntary Relocation Program** encouraged American Indians to move to cities. It provided transportation and initial help with finding housing and a job. By 1960, about 30 percent of American Indians lived in urban areas. However, many who relocated struggled to adapt to city life.

More than 100 Indian tribes and bands were eventually "terminated." Without economic aid, their poverty grew worse. Destitute tribes were forced to sell their land, resulting in the loss of more than 1 million acres of land. Termination eventually proved to be a failure, and in 1963, the policy was abandoned.

Summary

Michael Harrington's *The Other America* revealed that despite the general affluence of the 1950s, millions of "socially invisible" Americans lived in poverty. Although people's views and understanding of poverty have changed over time, the problem persists.

Defining poverty Pauperism was once considered a moral failure. Today, poverty is defined in terms of income. People below the poverty line do not have enough income to live decently.

An invisible class In *The Other America,* Michael Harrington argued that the poor were "invisible" for many reasons. They lived apart from the middle class but looked much the same. They also played no role in politics.

Urban poverty Impoverished minorities became concentrated in decaying cities when the middle class moved out. The Housing Act of 1949 launched urban renewal programs to clear out slums and build new housing. However, many of these housing projects became slums.

Rural poverty The growth of agribusiness harmed many farmers. Migrant workers on corporate farms were not paid enough to lift them out of poverty. One of the poorest rural regions, Appalachia, suffered from poor farming conditions and a declining coal industry.

American Indian policy Efforts by the federal government to "terminate" its responsibility for Indian tribes led to increased poverty among Native Americans. The Voluntary Relocation Program helped Indians move to cities, but many had trouble adapting to urban life.

Chapter 43

Segregation in the Post–World War II Period

How did segregation affect American life in the postwar period?

43.1 Introduction

For as long as she could remember, Melba Pattillo had wanted to ride the merry-go-round at Fair Park in her hometown of Little Rock, Arkansas. But whenever she asked her mother or grandmother to take her, they said it was not possible. So one day, when Melba was five, she decided to ride on her own.

Melba and her family were at Fair Park on a picnic. It was the Fourth of July. While the grownups were setting up tables of food, Melba made her escape. She later recalled, "I had had my eye on one horse in particular, Prancer, the one I had dreamed about during all those months I saved up the five pennies I needed to ride him."

Melba tried to give her money to the man working the ride. "There is no space for you here," he told her coldly. When she pointed out that Prancer's saddle was empty, the man got angry. He banged so hard on the counter that the pennies fell off. "You don't belong here!" he yelled.

Melba's knees shook. She noticed other angry faces glaring at her as though she had done something wrong. She ran back to her family. "I was so terrified," she said, "that I didn't even take the time to pick up my precious pennies. At five I learned that there was to be no space for me on that merry-go-round no matter how many saddles stood empty."

Melba Pattillo was a black child in the segregated South. In the 1940s, when this event took place, African Americans throughout the South suffered under a harsh system of racial discrimination. Jim Crow segregation laws not only kept blacks out of amusement parks like Fair Park. They also separated blacks from whites in most public facilities, including schools, libraries, and hospitals.

In this chapter, you will learn what life was like for African Americans in the postwar years in the South and the rest of the country. You will also learn how things finally began to change for the better.

Throughout the segregated South, African Americans were required to use separate waiting rooms, water fountains, and bathrooms. These facilities were labeled with signs reading "white" or "colored." Above is the "colored" entrance to a movie theater in Mississippi. Facilities for blacks and whites were supposed to be equal, but often were not.

◀ Segregated school in a Baptist church in Arkansas, 1949

In the above photo, a young black boy drinks from a water fountain designated for African Americans. Areas like these were commonplace in the South and both black and white citizens strictly followed the segregation rules.

43.2 A Nation Divided: Segregation in American Life

Racial segregation forced blacks to behave in certain ways. They were expected to accept their lesser status in society and act accordingly. W. E. B. Du Bois called this pattern of behavior "living behind the veil." In private or among other blacks, they acted normally. But around whites, they put on a "mask," hiding their true feelings and acting meek and inferior.

In practice, this meant that most blacks avoided looking white people in the eyes. When they spoke to whites, they looked at the ground. A black male could not look at a white woman or touch her accidentally. If charged with inappropriate attention to while females, a black male might face a lynch mob in many states throughout the nation. Blacks had to accept white insults and degrading names such as "boy," "girl," "auntie," or "uncle," regardless of their age. This code of rules and behavior was the product of a long history of racial discrimination in the United States. It was most evident in the South, but it extended throughout American society.

Segregation in Public Accommodations Segregation was common in public places, especially in the South. The segregation of public accommodations got a boost in 1896, when the Supreme Court ruled in *Plessy v. Ferguson* that railroad cars could be segregated as long as the accommodations were "separate but equal." This ruling gave rise to many state laws legalizing segregation in public accommodations, including theaters, restaurants, libraries, parks, and transport services.

Jim Crow laws established separate facilities for whites and blacks across the South. In waiting rooms and rest rooms, train cars and buses, theaters and restaurants, and even on park benches, blacks and whites were kept apart. One state even passed a law requiring separate telephone booths.

Often there was simply no accommodation for blacks at all. Some restaurants refused to serve African Americans. And in some places there was a bathroom for whites but none for blacks. In other cases, the facility for blacks was notably inferior. That was often the case with schools.

Segregation in Schools Jim Crow laws for schools began to appear shortly after the Civil War. By 1888, school segregation had been established in almost every southern state, along with some northern and western states.

In the South, black schools were often much worse than white schools. In the 1940s, state governments in the South spent twice as much to educate white children and four times as much on white school facilities. Many black students had to make do with poor, unheated classrooms and few books or supplies.

Although the *Plessy* decision stated that separate accommodations for the races must be equal, the reality was often quite different. Southern states spent far more on white schools than on black schools. Teachers in black schools got lower salaries and worked under more difficult conditions. They often lacked books and supplies, and their school facilities were frequently substandard. In some schools, students had to gather firewood to heat their classrooms in the winter. Although white schools had bus systems, black students often had to walk miles to get to school.

Segregation in Housing African Americans also experienced housing segregation. This came in two main forms. One was **de facto segregation,** which was established by practice and custom, rather than law. This form was found in all parts of the country. The other was **de jure segregation,** or segregation by law. De jure segregation occurred mostly in the South.

De facto segregation was common in many northern cities. When large numbers of African Americans began moving north in the 1900s, many white residents used informal measures to keep blacks out of their neighborhoods. One practice was the **restrictive covenant**. This was an agreement among neighbors not to sell or rent to African Americans or other racial minorities. Restrictive covenants often forced blacks into poor neighborhoods that were farther from jobs, public transport, or good schools.

De jure segregation was accomplished through **racial zoning**. These local laws defined where the different races could live. In the 1930s and 1940s, the federal government supported racial zoning. In 1951, however, the Supreme Court declared racial zoning unconstitutional. Yet segregated neighborhoods remained the norm in many southern cities.

Segregation in Marriage Between 1870 and 1884, eleven southern states passed laws against **miscegenation,** or interracial marriage. In the words of one historian, these were the "ultimate segregation laws." They stated that blacks were inferior to whites and that any amount of racial mixing through marriage or childbirth threatened the "purity of the white race."

Some states outside the South also banned interracial marriage. Many laws against miscegenation prohibited marriage not only between African Americans and whites but also between whites and Asians or whites and American Indians.

Segregation in the Workplace Employment and working conditions reflected widespread segregation in American society. Few blacks held white-collar jobs, or jobs that do not involve manual labor. Those who did were usually teachers or ministers. Not many blacks were employed as skilled laborers, either. Most worked in agriculture or services. Their wages were much lower than those of whites. In 1940, for example, the median income level of black men was less than half that of white men.

Discrimination in employment was a direct result of racism, but it was also the product of poor schooling for African Americans. Illiteracy and a lack of education helped trap blacks in low-level jobs, especially in the South.

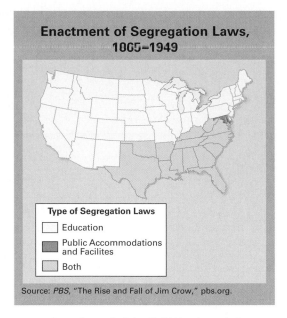

Enactment of Segregation Laws, 1865–1949

Type of Segregation Laws
- Education
- Public Accommodations and Facilites
- Both

Source: *PBS*, "The Rise and Fall of Jim Crow," pbs.org.

From the end of the Civil War through the 1940s, various states passed laws imposing segregation in public schools and accommodations. Although these laws were most common in the Jim Crow South, some northern and western states enforced segregation as well.

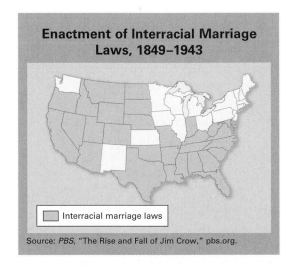

Enactment of Interracial Marriage Laws, 1849–1943

Interracial marriage laws

Source: *PBS*, "The Rise and Fall of Jim Crow," pbs.org.

More than half of all states banned interracial marriage in the 1940s. In 1967, however, the Supreme Court ruling in the case *Loving v. Virginia* declared that laws against mixed marriage are unconstitutional. Alabama was the last state to repeal its interracial marriage law.

Segregation in Politics Southern whites also found ways to **disenfranchise,** or deny voting rights to, African Americans. In the years after Reconstruction, poll taxes and literacy tests kept many blacks from voting. Many southern states also disenfranchised blacks through use of the **white primary**. This was a primary election in which only whites could participate. It was based on the domination of southern politics by the Democratic Party, which southern whites perceived as the opponent of radical Reconstruction and civil rights. The Democrats excluded blacks from party membership and thus denied them the right to vote in party primaries. As a result, the Democrats had no need to court black voters, and blacks had no political representation.

Texas was one state in which the white primary was used extensively. Between 1923 and 1944, Texas Democrats used it to limit black participation in politics. In 1944, however, the Supreme Court declared white primaries unconstitutional. As a result, more African Americans began voting in Texas, and the number of registered black voters rose substantially.

Gerrymandering was another method used to discriminate against black voters and render their votes meaningless. Gerrymandering is the practice of redrawing the lines of a voting district to give one party or group of voters an advantage. If the majority of voters in a particular voting district are African Americans, they may be able to elect a candidate who represents their interests. But if the voting district lines are gerrymandered to break up that population and place African Americans in white-majority districts, the black vote gets diluted and becomes less effective. Through gerrymandering, black voters were often denied political influence.

These methods were unlike the violent methods used in the early years after Reconstruction, when blacks were sometimes forcibly prevented from voting. But they were equally effective in denying blacks voting rights and limiting black representation in government.

Incomes varied considerably for blacks and whites in the 1940s. This graph shows the difference between white and nonwhite income in five major American cities. The median is the middle value in a set of numbers. Half of people have incomes below the median income, and half have incomes above it.

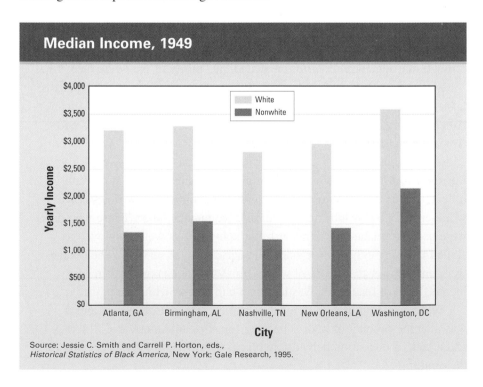

Median Income, 1949

Source: Jessie C. Smith and Carrell P. Horton, eds., *Historical Statistics of Black America,* New York: Gale Research, 1995.

43.3 Small Steps Toward Equality

Jackie Robinson would become one of the greatest baseball players in the history of the game. In 1944, however, he was a lieutenant in the army, stationed at Fort Hood, Texas. Leaving the base one day, he got on a military bus and took a seat up front. The driver ordered him to move to the back, but Robinson refused. When he got off at his stop, he was arrested. Robinson was nearly court-martialed for his actions that day. Later, he would achieve fame on the baseball diamond and become a role model for millions of Americans. Over the course of his life, Robinson came to represent both the struggles of African Americans and their gradual advances in white-dominated society.

Breaking the Color Line in Sports Jackie Robinson began his baseball career in the Negro Leagues after World War II. At the time, baseball was divided by the **color line,** a barrier created by custom, law, and economic differences that separated whites from nonwhites.

When Jackie Robinson signed a contract with the Brooklyn Dodgers in 1945, he became the first African American to cross the color line in professional baseball. He credited his black fans with helping him get through his first difficult years in the major leagues. This photo stamp was made in 1999 to commemorate Jackie Robinson's historic career.

In 1945, Robinson crossed the color line when Brooklyn Dodgers general manager Branch Rickey hired him. After briefly playing for a minor league team, Robinson took the field in a Dodgers uniform in 1947. Being the first black major league baseball player was not easy. Fans taunted him, and some of his own teammates resented playing with a black man. Players on opposing teams sometimes tried to "bean" him with the ball or spike him with their cleats. As he later recalled, "Plenty of times I wanted to haul off [and fight] when someone insulted me for the color of my skin, but I had to hold to myself. I knew I was kind of an experiment. The whole thing was bigger than me." Robinson overcame these challenges and eventually led his team to six league championships and one World Series victory.

Around the same time, other professional sports began to open up to black athletes. Football became integrated in 1946, when four black players joined the professional leagues. Four years later, the National Basketball Association accepted its first African American players. By the 1950s, the color line in professional sports was gradually disappearing.

Desegregation of the Armed Forces Another area of American life in which the color line would soon fall was the armed forces. But again, change did not come easily. Despite the valuable contributions of African American soldiers during World War II, the military remained segregated after the war.

Many GIs returning from combat continued to face segregation at home, especially in the Jim Crow South. In 1946, army veteran Isaac Woodard was traveling by bus from North Carolina to Georgia. At one stop, the driver threatened Woodard for taking too much time in the "colored" bathroom. The two men argued, and Woodard was arrested. Police officers then beat him so badly that he was permanently blinded. When President Truman learned of the incident, he was appalled and vowed to do something about segregation in the military. "I shall never approve of it," he wrote. "I am going to try to remedy it."

Truman knew that desegregation in the armed forces was necessary, not only on moral grounds but also for political reasons. Like many Americans, he recognized that it was hypocritical to fight Nazism and anti-Semitism abroad while maintaining a color line at home. Likewise, he saw that continued segregation in the United States could undermine efforts to promote freedom and democracy overseas as part of the Cold War struggle with the Soviet Union.

As the Cold War intensified in the late 1940s, political leaders began to discuss the need to rebuild the armed forces. Many African Americans said they would refuse to fight in a segregated army. Although many leaders in the armed forces opposed desegregation, Truman believed that discrimination in the military must end.

On July 26, 1948, Truman signed Executive Order 9981, which stated, "It is hereby declared to be the policy of the President that there shall be equality of treatment and opportunity for all persons in the armed services without regard to race, color, religion, or national origin." With this order, desegregation became official policy in the armed forces.

Thurgood Marshall, head of the NAACP's legal defense branch, was denied admission to the University of Maryland because he was not white. He went on to earn a law degree from Howard University. In one of Marshall's first legal victories, he sued the University of Maryland for its race-based policy. Marshall later served on the Supreme Court.

Civil Rights Organizations Challenge Discrimination The fight to end segregation would never have succeeded without the determined efforts of civil rights activists. Many Americans worked tirelessly for various organizations dedicated to achieving equal rights.

One of these organizations was the Congress of Racial Equality (CORE). Founded in Chicago in 1942 by a group of students, CORE was committed to nonviolent direct action as a means of change. Its first action—a peaceful protest at a segregated coffee shop in Chicago in 1943—gained national attention and helped CORE spread to other northern cities. It went on to assist in the desegregation of many public facilities in the North and then turned its attention to the South in the late 1950s.

Another key group, the National Urban League, formed in response to the Great Migration of blacks to northern cities in the early 1900s. The Urban League focused on helping African Americans achieve success in the North. It counseled newly arrived migrants and trained black social workers. It also promoted educational and employment opportunities for African Americans. During World War II, the Urban League helped integrate defense plants.

The National Association for the Advancement of Colored People, the oldest major civil rights organization, also remained active in the struggle for equal rights. Founded in 1909, the NAACP continued its efforts to promote civil rights legislation. In 1939, the group established a legal arm for civil rights actions, the NAACP Legal Defense and Educational Fund. The following year, Thurgood Marshall became the head of this group.

The Legal Defense and Educational Fund focused on defeating segregation through the court system. Its main weapon was the equal protection clause of the Fourteenth Amendment. This clause prohibits states from denying any person equal protection of the laws. Since the clause does not allow states to discriminate, it is crucial to the protection of civil rights.

43.4 The Courts Begin to Dismantle Segregation

In 1951, getting to school every day was hard for Linda Brown, a seven-year-old in Topeka, Kansas. First she had to walk a mile, passing through a railroad yard on her way to the bus stop. Then she had to take a long bus ride to school. All of this made no sense to Linda because there was a good school only seven blocks from her house. But the schools in Topeka were segregated. The school near Linda was for whites only, and Linda was black. Her father, Oliver Brown, decided to do something about that. With the help of the court system, Brown and other civil rights activists began to dismantle segregation.

Early Court Decisions Make Big Strides In the 1930s and 1940s, the Supreme Court began to strike down Jim Crow laws. In 1935, the Court ordered the University of Maryland to admit a black student. Later it declared white primaries unconstitutional and barred segregation on interstate transport. These were important steps in breaking down segregation.

In 1948, the Supreme Court tackled the issue of segregated housing. In *Shelley v. Kraemer,* the Court ruled that states could not enforce restrictive covenants. As a result, many city neighborhoods became desegregated. Over the next few years, for example, thousands of black families in Chicago moved into areas that had previously been restricted to whites.

In 1950, the Court handed down strong rulings against discrimination in education. In two cases, the Court declared that segregation in graduate schools and law schools was unconstitutional. It began to look as if all "separate but equal" education was on the way out.

Beginning in the 1930s, the Supreme Court began to strike down laws mandating segregation in public facilities. Several of these Court rulings had to do with public schools. The map below shows four key education cases decided by the Supreme Court between 1938 and 1950.

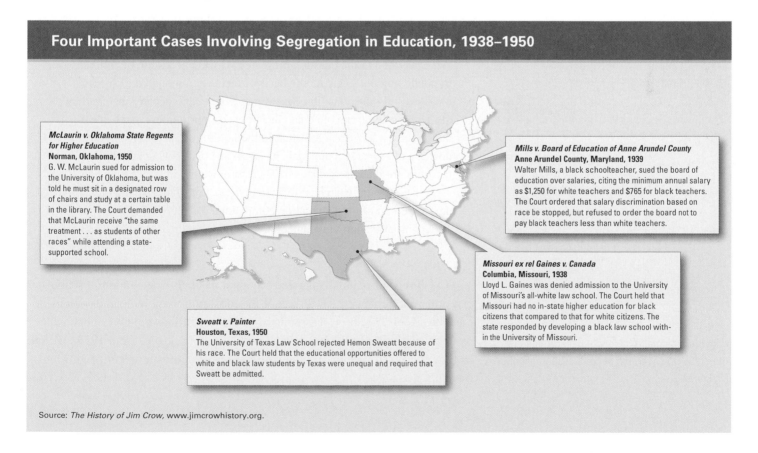

Four Important Cases Involving Segregation in Education, 1938–1950

McLaurin v. Oklahoma State Regents for Higher Education
Norman, Oklahoma, 1950
G. W. McLaurin sued for admission to the University of Oklahoma, but was told he must sit in a designated row of chairs and study at a certain table in the library. The Court demanded that McLaurin receive "the same treatment . . . as students of other races" while attending a state-supported school.

Mills v. Board of Education of Anne Arundel County
Anne Arundel County, Maryland, 1939
Walter Mills, a black schoolteacher, sued the board of education over salaries, citing the minimum annual salary as $1,250 for white teachers and $765 for black teachers. The Court ordered that salary discrimination based on race be stopped, but refused to order the board not to pay black teachers less than white teachers.

Missouri ex rel Gaines v. Canada
Columbia, Missouri, 1938
Lloyd L. Gaines was denied admission to the University of Missouri's all-white law school. The Court held that Missouri had no in-state higher education for black citizens that compared to that for white citizens. The state responded by developing a black law school within the University of Missouri.

Sweatt v. Painter
Houston, Texas, 1950
The University of Texas Law School rejected Hemon Sweatt because of his race. The Court held that the educational opportunities offered to white and black law students by Texas were unequal and required that Sweatt be admitted.

Source: *The History of Jim Crow,* www.jimcrowhistory.org.

A Landmark Ruling: *Brown v. Board of Education* Meanwhile in Topeka, Oliver Brown, Linda's father, had contacted the NAACP, which in turn gathered 12 other parents to join in efforts to desegregate the city's schools. First the parents tried to enroll their children in white schools, but all were denied admission. So in 1951 the NAACP sued the Topeka school district in court. A local court found "no willful discrimination." The NAACP appealed the case, and it went all the way to the Supreme Court.

Brown v. Board of Education was actually a set of cases from Kansas, South Carolina, Virginia, Delaware, and Washington, D.C., that had moved up through the court system at the same time. The Court decided to combine the cases because the plaintiffs were all looking for the same legal remedy. The *Brown* case was a **class-action lawsuit,** a lawsuit filed by people on behalf of themselves and a larger group who might benefit.

The NAACP's lead attorney, Thurgood Marshall, argued the case. He supplied evidence showing how segregation harms African American children. The most famous piece of evidence was the "doll test." In the test, 16 black children had been shown a white doll and a brown doll. Ten of the children chose the white doll as the "nice" doll. According to the psychologist who conducted the test, "the Negro child accepts as early as six, seven or eight the negative stereotypes about his own group."

The *Brown* case stayed in the Supreme Court for a year and a half. During this time, a new chief justice, Earl Warren, was appointed to the Court. Warren was a firm opponent of segregation. Believing that a unanimous decision in the *Brown* case would carry more weight than a divided one, he worked hard to convince all the judges to rule in favor of the plaintiffs. Finally, in May 1954, he succeeded. On May 17, he announced the Supreme Court ruling in *Brown v. Board of Education:*

> We come then to the question presented: Does segregation of children in public schools solely on the basis of race, even though the physical facilities and other "tangible" factors may be equal, deprive the children of the minority group of equal educational opportunities? We believe that it does . . . We conclude that in the field of public education the doctrine of "separate but equal" has no place. Separate educational facilities are inherently unequal. Therefore, we hold that the plaintiffs and others similarly situated for whom the actions have been brought are, by reason of the segregation complained of, deprived of the equal protection of the laws guaranteed by the Fourteenth Amendment.
>
> —*Brown v. Board of Education,* 1954

The *Brown* decision dismantled the legal basis for segregation in schools and other public places. It was one of the most important judicial decisions in the nation's history. It was also one of many key rulings on civil rights made by the Court under Earl Warren, who served as chief justice from 1953 to 1969. In fact, the **Warren Court** became known for its activism on civil rights and free speech.

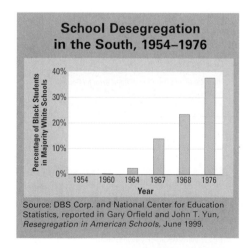

School Desegregation in the South, 1954–1976

Source: DBS Corp. and National Center for Education Statistics, reported in Gary Orfield and John T. Yun, *Resegregation in American Schools,* June 1999.

In the first 10 years after the *Brown* ruling, slow progress was made in school desegregation. After 1964, however, the pace of desegregation quickened.

All Deliberate Speed? Much of the South Resists Change A year after the *Brown* decision, the Supreme Court issued a second ruling, known as *Brown II*. This ruling instructed the states to begin desegregation "with all deliberate speed." The phrase was chosen carefully. The justices wanted desegregation to go forward as quickly as possible, but they also recognized that many obstacles stood in the way. They wanted to allow states some flexibility in desegregating their schools in accordance with *Brown*.

In some border states, desegregation took place without incident. But in parts of the South, there was greater resistance. For example, in 1955 a white citizens' council in Mississippi published a handbook called *Black Monday*, referring to the day the Supreme Court handed down the *Brown* decision. The handbook called for an end to the NAACP and public schools. It also advocated a separate state for African Americans.

Despite such opposition, the *Brown* decision inspired hopes that African Americans could achieve equal rights in American society. It served as a catalyst for the civil rights movement of the 1950s and 1960s, a time when many individuals and groups dedicated themselves to promoting equality, opportunity, and rights.

This photo shows an integrated classroom in Washington D.C., 1957. Black and white students sit side by side in the classroom.

Summary

Segregation remained widespread in the United States after World War II, especially in the South. But there were also signs of change. In the 1940s and 1950s, desegregation began in sports and the military. Civil rights organizations grew stronger. The landmark Supreme Court ruling *Brown v. Board of Education* heralded the beginning of the modern civil rights movement.

Segregated society Segregation affected every aspect of life in the Jim Crow South. De jure segregation was defined by law, while de facto segregation was determined by custom. Blacks in the North and West also experienced de facto segregation, especially in housing.

Breaking the color line Professional sports began to be integrated in the late 1940s. Most notable was Jackie Robinson's entry into major league baseball. The integration of professional football and basketball soon followed.

Executive Order 9981 President Truman was determined to integrate the armed forces. His executive order, issued in 1948, ended segregation in the military.

Civil rights groups Civil rights organizations gained strength in the postwar years. CORE was dedicated to civil rights reform through nonviolent action. The National Urban League tried to help African Americans who were living in northern cities. The NAACP began a legal branch and launched a campaign, led by Thurgood Marshall, to challenge the constitutionality of segregation.

Brown v. Board of Education The NAACP's legal campaign triumphed in 1954, when the Warren Court issued the *Brown v. Board of Education* decision. This ruling declared segregation in public schools to be unconstitutional and undermined the legal basis for segregation in other areas of American life.

Chapter 44

The Civil Rights Revolution: "Like a Mighty Stream"

How did civil rights activists advance the ideals of liberty, equality, and opportunity for African Americans?

44.1 Introduction

Four decades later, Cardell Gay still remembered the day—May 3, 1963—when hundreds of young people marched through the streets of Birmingham, Alabama, to protest segregation. "The police were there with their dogs and their hoses," he recalled. "And . . . although they had instructed us to stop, we would not stop. We continued to move closer to them. What they did, they let it fly."

What the police "let fly" was water from a high-pressure fire hose. "It knocked us on the ground," Gay said. "The hoses were so strong . . . [the water] . . . would knock us all over the place, send you tumbling." The force of the blast even rolled children down the street.

It was the second day of marches by young people in Birmingham that spring. Gay was 16 at the time. His high school teachers had influenced his decision to march. "In class, they'd say, 'Don't leave campus or you'll be expelled,'" Gay explained years later. "But in private, they'd say, 'Go on. I can't do it, I'd lose my job. But do it up. Keep it up.'"

More than a thousand young people, some as young as five, marched on May 2, the first day of the protest. Hundreds were arrested for marching without a permit. The following day, an even larger force of young blacks turned out to march. Police Chief Bull Connor ordered them to be dispersed with fire hoses. As the youngsters fled, policemen chased them down with clubs and dogs.

The Birmingham protests showed that African Americans were not going to back down in their struggle for civil rights. They would persist until they reached their goal. "I'll keep marching till I get freedom," one 12-year-old protester declared.

In this chapter, you will learn about key events in the early years of the civil rights movement. The years from 1955 to 1965 witnessed efforts to desegregate buses, schools, lunch counters, and other public places. During these years, civil rights activists also worked to secure voting rights for African Americans.

Hundreds of child marchers were arrested in a Birmingham park in May 1963. Today that park features monuments honoring those children and their fight against segregation.

◀ Children arrested during Birmingham civil rights marches

497

Public buses were rigidly segregated in the South. If a bus was full, black passengers had to make way for whites. In 1955, however, activists in Montgomery, Alabama, organized a successful bus boycott and achieved integration on city buses.

Rosa Parks was arrested for refusing to give up her seat on a bus to a white man. When told by the driver that he was going to call the police, she calmly replied, "You may go on and do so." Her action served as a catalyst for the Montgomery Bus Boycott.

44.2 A Boycott in Montgomery Inspires a Movement

Although the 1954 Supreme Court ruling in *Brown v. Board of Education* outlawed segregation in public schools, segregation continued in much of the South. Law and custom still required blacks and whites to use separate facilities, like drinking fountains and waiting rooms, and to sit separately in restaurants and on buses. In 1955, however, a boycott in Montgomery, Alabama, began to shake up the Jim Crow South.

Protesting Unfair Bus Laws In the 1950s, public buses in Montgomery were segregated, as they were throughout the South. African Americans had to sit at the back of the bus. If the bus was full, they were required to give up their seats to white riders. Furthermore, blacks could never share a row with whites.

That was about to change. On December 1, 1955, Rosa Parks, a 43-year-old African American woman, refused to give up her seat on a bus to a white passenger. Parks, a seamstress, had been active in the Alabama chapter of the National Association for the Advancement of Colored People. Years later, Parks described her motives for remaining in her seat: "This is what I wanted to know: when and how would we ever determine our rights as human beings?"

Leaders of the Montgomery chapter of the NAACP had been looking for a test case to fight segregation. Parks, who was well-spoken and had a solid reputation in the community, seemed perfect. E. D. Nixon, a local activist, asked Parks if the NAACP could build a case around her arrest, and Parks agreed.

The following evening, a group of African American ministers met to plan a strategy. They decided to hold a one-day bus boycott on December 5. Black ministers announced the boycott at Sunday services, and activists distributed leaflets asking African Americans to take part.

On December 5, a sign at a Montgomery bus stop read, "People, don't ride the bus today. Don't ride it, for freedom." On that day, 90 percent of African Americans who usually rode the bus honored the boycott.

A Young Minister Becomes a Leader
The one-day boycott was so successful that the organizers, who called themselves the Montgomery Improvement Association (MIA), decided to extend it. To lead the Montgomery Bus Boycott, the MIA chose a 26-year-old minister, Martin Luther King Jr.

King was pastor of the Dexter Avenue Baptist Church. Originally from Atlanta, King had come to Montgomery after completing a Ph.D. in theology at Boston University. He had been in town two years when the boycott began. King explained the purpose of the action in a speech to a mass meeting at Holt Street Baptist Church on the evening of December 5:

My friends, I want it to be known that we're going to work with grim and bold determination to gain justice on the buses in this city. And we are not wrong, we are not wrong in what we are doing. If we are wrong, the Supreme Court of this nation is wrong. If we are wrong, the Constitution of the United States is wrong. If we are wrong, God Almighty is wrong . . . If we are wrong, justice is a lie. And we are determined here in Montgomery to work and fight until justice runs down like water and righteousness like a mighty stream.

To make the boycott work, African Americans in Montgomery organized an elaborate carpool system to get around town. Several thousand people used the carpools daily. Others walked, rode bicycles, took taxis, or hitchhiked.

Many of Montgomery's white leaders did everything they could to stop the boycott and preserve segregation. Some business owners fired black protesters from their jobs. Other people took more drastic action. Some radical segregationists, including members of the Ku Klux Klan, attacked protesters and even set off bombs at the houses of boycott leaders. They also firebombed several churches that served the black community.

In November 1956, the Supreme Court upheld an Alabama court's ruling that segregation on buses was unconstitutional. About a month later, on December 20, the protesters voted to end the boycott, which had lasted 381 days. As a result of the Montgomery Bus Boycott, Martin Luther King Jr. earned a national reputation as a civil rights leader.

Reverend Martin Luther King Jr. quickly established himself as a leader in the struggle for civil rights. King's use of nonviolent protest—which he learned from studying the great Indian leader Mahatma Gandhi—helped shape the civil rights movement. Here he is answering questions during a press conference.

African American Churches Support the Movement After the boycott, King worked with other ministers and civil rights leaders to form the Southern Christian Leadership Conference (SCLC) in 1957. With King as its president, the SCLC would play a major role in the civil rights movement.

The SCLC pledged to use **nonviolent resistance** to redeem "the soul of America." Nonviolent resistance is peaceful protest or noncooperation with authorities that is designed to achieve social or political goals. In a public statement on January 11, 1957, the SCLC explained the strategy:

Nonviolence is not a symbol of weakness or cowardice, but as Jesus demonstrated, nonviolent resistance transforms weakness into strength and breeds courage in the face of danger. We urge . . . [African Americans], no matter how great the provocation, to dedicate themselves to this motto: "Not one hair of one head of one white person shall be harmed."
—SCLC, "A Statement to the South and Nation," January 11, 1957

Supporters of the SCLC vowed that they would not resort to violence to achieve their ends but would remain peaceful and steadfast in their pursuit of justice. This would prove to be a powerful tactic in the struggle for civil rights.

44.3 School Desegregation

After the *Brown* ruling, some districts and states in the South desegregated their schools quickly. Others, however, resisted the Supreme Court decision. Governors of several southern states staunchly maintained their opposition to integration. The governors of Arkansas and Mississippi, for example, aggressively intervened in an effort to prevent blacks from attending all-white schools. The battle to integrate public schools proved to be long and difficult.

Nine Teenagers Integrate Central High School In 1957, a federal judge ordered public schools in Little Rock, Arkansas, to begin desegregation. The Little Rock school superintendent, Virgil Blossom, hoped to postpone the change as long as possible. He set up a plan to integrate just one school, Central High School. Two thousand white students attended Central. In September 1957, nine black students were scheduled to join them. They would later be known as the Little Rock Nine.

Citing public opposition to integration in Arkansas, Governor Orval Faubus declared that he would not support desegregation in Little Rock. Faubus called out the Arkansas National Guard. On September 4, 1957, the day the nine students were to begin classes, the troops appeared at Central High as a show of force and to prevent the students from entering the building. One of the students, Elizabeth Eckford, recalled being surrounded by an angry white crowd outside the school:

> They moved closer and closer . . . I tried to see a friendly face somewhere in the crowd—someone who maybe would help. I looked into the face of an old woman and it seemed a kind face, but when I looked again, she spat on me.
> —Elizabeth Eckford, in an interview with NAACP official Daisy Bates

Another white woman later emerged from the crowd and helped to shield Eckford from harm. But Eckford and her fellow black students were kept out of school that day and for days afterward.

Finally, on September 23, the Little Rock Nine returned to Central High. Once again, an angry white mob surrounded the school. This time, though, the mayor of Little Rock sought help from President Eisenhower. Although

In 1957, nine black students, including Elizabeth Eckford (shown here), challenged segregation by enrolling at Central High School in Little Rock, Arkansas. The governor and a mob of angry citizens tried to stop them, but the federal government backed them up. Eventually all southern states integrated their public schools.

Eisenhower did not believe that integration should be accomplished by force, he could not allow defiance of federal authority. The president issued Executive Order 10730, sending in federal troops to maintain order and enforce the integration of the school. Eisenhower also put the Arkansas National Guard under federal control. The students rode to school in a convoy led by army jeeps with guns mounted on their hoods. They also had military bodyguards to protect them—at least for part of the school year.

Despite this protection, the black students were subjected to insults and acts of violence from white students. As one of the nine, Minnijean Brown, said at the time, "They throw rocks, they spill ink on your clothes . . . they bother you every minute." Melba Pattillo was another one of the students. Acid was thrown in her eyes, and only the quick action of her bodyguard saved her eyesight. The students and their families also received death threats.

Eight of the nine African American students finished out the year at Central High. The following year, however, Governor Faubus closed all the Little Rock schools rather than allow another year of integration. It was not until September 1959 that integration continued in Little Rock.

James Meredith Enrolls at the University of Mississippi Public universities were also required to integrate. In 1961, James Meredith, an African American veteran of the Korean War, applied for admission as a transfer student to the University of Mississippi, commonly known as Ole Miss. The university had traditionally been all white, and Meredith knew he would be taking a stand to integrate it.

When his application was rejected, Meredith turned to the NAACP to help him take his case through the courts. At first, a district court ruled against him. On appeal, however, a higher court ruled that the university had to admit Meredith. Refusing him admission, the court said, amounted to the state of Mississippi maintaining segregation.

Mississippi governor Ross Barnett vowed that no black student would attend Ole Miss while he was in office. On September 20, Barnett, acting as university registrar, personally refused to enroll Meredith.

But President John F. Kennedy, also known as JFK, and Attorney General Robert Kennedy were determined to uphold the law as *Brown* had defined it. Although JFK was concerned about losing Democratic support in the South, he was sympathetic to the civil rights movement. In a nationally broadcast speech, he declared, "Americans are free to disagree with the law but not to disobey it."

On Sunday, September 30, 1962, James Meredith secretly arrived on campus. When the news got out that night, a riot erupted. Angry white students burned cars and destroyed property. Before the night was over, two men had been shot and killed.

President Kennedy sent armed federal marshals to protect Meredith so he could attend classes. Meredith survived verbal taunts and threats against his life and the lives of his parents. But he had always known what was at stake. Just days before entering Ole Miss, he had written, "The price of progress is indeed high, but the price of holding back is much higher." Meredith graduated from Ole Miss in the summer of 1963.

James Meredith required protection from U.S. Marshals in order to attend classes at Ole Miss. He was the first African American to attend Ole Miss. He later wrote that the country's future "rests on . . . whether or not the Negro citizen is to be allowed to receive an education in his own state."

Across the South, protesters held sit-ins to integrate lunch counters. The demonstrators remained nonviolent, even when local residents taunted them.

44.4 Sit-Ins and Freedom Rides

The campaign to integrate public facilities in the South continued through the 1960s. During this time, a growing student movement influenced the direction of the civil rights struggle. Student protesters challenged segregation in various ways. They sat down in "whites-only" public places and refused to move, thereby causing the business to lose customers. This tactic is known as a **sit-in**. They also boycotted businesses that maintained segregation. And they rode interstate buses that many whites in the South tried to keep segregated.

Sitting Firm to Challenge Segregated Facilities

On February 1, 1960, four African American students from North Carolina's Agricultural and Technical College sat down at a lunch counter in the Woolworth's drugstore in Greensboro. They ordered food, but the waitress refused to serve them, saying that only white customers could eat at Woolworth's.

The four students stayed at the counter until the store closed. One of the four, Franklin McCain, explained later that the group did not like being denied "dignity and respect." They decided to return the next day, and about 20 other people joined them. They sat at the counter all day, but were not served.

During the 1960s, sit-ins like this one captured nationwide attention for the civil rights movement. As news of the Greensboro action spread, protesters began sit-ins in towns and cities across the South.

The Greensboro protests continued for months. In April, the city's blacks organized a boycott of Woolworth's and another local store with a segregated lunch counter. Eventually the local businesses gave in. On July 25, 1960, the first African American ate at the Woolworth's lunch counter in Greensboro.

Black students also mounted a large sit-in campaign in Nashville, Tennessee. As in Greensboro, Nashville's African American community followed up with a boycott of downtown businesses. And once again, local business owners and public officials gave in. On May 10, 1960, Nashville became the first major city in the South to begin integrating its public facilities.

Students Organize to Make a Difference The sit-ins and boycotts began to transform the segregated South and change the civil rights movement. College students took the lead in the sit-ins, and many became activists in the movement.

In April 1960, Ella Baker, a leader with the SCLC, called a meeting of student civil rights activists in Raleigh, North Carolina. Although Baker herself was 55 years old and no longer a student, she believed it was important for students to organize and run their own organization.

Under Baker's guidance, the students formed the **Student Nonviolent Coordinating Committee (SNCC)**, pronounced "snick." SNCC's Statement of Purpose, written in May 1960, affirmed the new organization's commitment to justice, peace, and nonviolence:

We affirm the philosophical or religious ideal of nonviolence as the
foundation of our purpose . . . Through nonviolence, courage displaces
fear; love transforms hate. Acceptance dissipates prejudice; hope ends
despair. Peace dominates war; faith reconciles doubt. Mutual regard
cancels enmity. Justice for all overthrows injustice.

SNCC trained students in **civil disobedience,** counseling them to deliber-
ately break laws they considered unjust. SNCC leaders emphasized that protesters must not use violence, even if they were physically attacked. One SNCC
training document explained, "You may choose to face physical assault without protecting yourself, hands at the sides, unclenched; or you may choose to
protect yourself, making plain you do not intend to hit back."

SNCC members planned and participated in **direct action** throughout the
South. Direct action refers to political acts, including protests of all types,
designed to have an immediate impact. SNCC members played a major role in
various campaigns of nonviolent direct action over the next several years.

Freedom Riders Face Violence One
direct action targeted the interstate
bus system in the South. In 1960, the
Supreme Court ruled that segregation
in interstate transport was illegal. In the
spring of 1961, the civil rights group
Congress of Racial Equality (CORE)
organized Freedom Rides to test
whether southern states were complying
with the ruling.

On May 4, 1961, seven blacks and six
whites boarded two buses in Washington,
D.C., and headed south. When the first
bus reached Anniston, Alabama, on May
14, a white mob attacked the Freedom
Riders. The mob followed the bus as it
left town, threw a firebomb through the
window, and then beat the passengers
as they fled the bus. Passengers on the
second bus were also beaten when they
arrived in Alabama.

CORE abandoned the Freedom Rides,
but SNCC continued them. Finally,
Attorney General Robert Kennedy sent

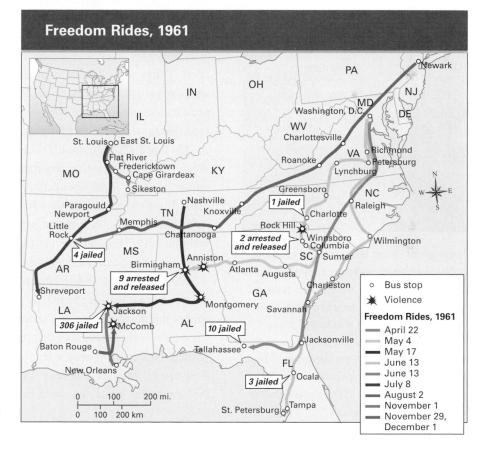

federal marshals to ensure safe passage for the riders to Jackson, Mississippi.
When the Freedom Riders arrived, however, Jackson officials arrested them.
They suffered physical abuse while in jail, but most became even more com-
mitted to ending segregation.

In late 1962, the Interstate Commerce Commission issued clear rules stating that buses and bus terminals involved in interstate travel must be integrated. CORE's leader, James Farmer, proclaimed victory for the Freedom Rides.

44.5 A Campaign in Birmingham

In the early 1960s, Birmingham, Alabama, was a steel-mill town with a long history of bigotry. Martin Luther King Jr. called it the most segregated city in the country. As a result, the SCLC decided to focus its attention there in 1963.

Taking Aim at the Nation's Most Segregated City Black residents of Birmingham experienced segregation in nearly every aspect of public life. Virtually no public facility in Birmingham allowed blacks and whites to mix.

Furthermore, Birmingham had a history of racist violence. Between 1956 and 1963, there were 18 unsolved bombings in black neighborhoods. The violence not only targeted African Americans. In 1960, the *New York Times* reported attempts to explode dynamite at two Jewish synagogues as well.

The SCLC stepped directly into this violent climate in the spring of 1963. King and the SCLC joined forces with local Birmingham activists, led by Reverend Fred L. Shuttlesworth. Together they carefully planned a series of nonviolent actions against segregation.

King Advocates Nonviolence in "Letter from a Birmingham Jail" The protests began on April 3 with lunch-counter sit-ins followed by street demonstrations. Thirty protesters were arrested for marching at Birmingham City Hall without a permit. As leader of the Birmingham campaign, King decided the protests and arrests must continue. With little money to post bail, King realized that he would most likely go to jail and stay there for a while.

On April 12, King and 50 others demonstrated and were quickly arrested. While King was in jail, many members of Birmingham's white clergy took out an ad in the local newspaper, criticizing King's tactics: "We recognize the natural impatience of people who feel that their hopes are slow in being realized," the ad said. "But we are convinced that these demonstrations are unwise and untimely." Instead, the clergy urged African Americans to abide by the law and to negotiate with whites to achieve integration.

King disagreed. While he waited in jail, he wrote a response to the ad. In "Letter from a Birmingham Jail," King explained why African Americans were using civil disobedience and other forms of direct action to protest segregation. "The answer lies in the fact that there are two types of laws: just and unjust," he wrote. "One has not only a legal but a moral responsibility to obey just laws. Conversely, one has a moral responsibility to disobey unjust laws." Concerning the charge that protesters were being "impatient," King wrote,

> We know through painful experience that freedom is never voluntarily given by the oppressor; it must be demanded by the oppressed. Frankly, I have yet to engage in a direct-action campaign that was "well-timed" in the view of those who have not suffered unduly from the disease of segregation. For years now I have heard the word "Wait!" It rings in the ear of every Negro with piercing familiarity. This "Wait!" has almost always meant "Never." We must come to see . . . that "justice too long delayed is justice denied."
>
> —Martin Luther King Jr., "Letter from a Birmingham Jail,"
> April 16, 1963

Hundreds of people were arrested and jailed during mass demonstrations in Birmingham in 1963. This photograph of protesters at the jail was taken through the bars of a paddy wagon. Martin Luther King Jr. was one of those arrested. It was at this time that he wrote his famous "Letter from a Birmingham Jail." In it he said, "Injustice anywhere is a threat to justice everywhere . . . Whatever affects one directly, affects all indirectly."

On May 3, 1963, police in Birmingham turned high-pressure fire hoses on children during a civil rights march. The force of such a blast can tear the bark from a tree and knock a grown man to the ground. Events that day horrified many Americans and helped win support for the civil rights movement.

The Nation Watches in Horror By late April, Birmingham's black leaders realized their protests were running out of steam. Few members of the black community were willing to carry out more direct action at the risk of going to jail. So the SCLC decided to turn to children. Although the decision was controversial, King argued that the children who took part in the demonstrations would develop "a sense of their own stake in freedom and justice."

On May 2, 1963, more than 1,000 African American youths marched from Birmingham's Sixteenth Street Baptist Church into the city center. The city's public safety commissioner, Bull Connor, had most of them arrested.

On May 3, more students gathered at the church, preparing to march again. This time, Connor ordered the police to barricade them in. When some students tried to leave, the police used attack dogs and high-pressure fire hoses on them.

News photographers captured scenes of peaceful protesters being knocked down by blasts of water or attacked by snarling dogs. The images in newspapers and on television shocked Americans, many of whom had never imagined that southerners would go to such brutal lengths to maintain segregation.

The protests and the national attention they attracted marked a turning point. At the urging of local business leaders, the city stepped back from confrontation, and on May 10 civil rights leaders announced a historic accord in Birmingham. Their agreement with the city called for a number of changes, including the desegregation of public facilities within 90 days. King called the deal "the most magnificent victory for justice we've seen in the Deep South."

In honor of the four African American girls killed in the bombing, CORE held a march in Washington D.C. The march brought more attention to the hostile atmosphere in Birmingham.

A racist backlash soon followed, however. The Ku Klux Klan held a rally, and bombs later went off at a motel where black leaders had been staying. In response, President Kennedy sent federal troops to a nearby military base, promising to deploy them if necessary to keep the peace.

Birmingham remained calm for several months after that, but then another violent attack occurred. On September 15, during Sunday services, a bomb exploded at the Sixteenth Street Baptist Church, killing four African American girls. Reverend King later spoke at their funeral, calling them "the martyred heroines of a holy crusade for freedom and human dignity."

On August 28th 1963, some 250,000 people marched in Washington D.C. People marched for civil rights, employment, decent housing, and voting rights.

44.6 Achieving Landmark Civil Rights Legislation

Despite the success of the Birmingham campaign, the city did not change overnight, nor did the events there bring immediate equality for African Americans. But the campaign did have important effects. It increased support for the civil rights movement around the country. More Americans came to identify with the movement's emphasis on rights, freedom, equality, and opportunity.

Following the spring protests in Birmingham, civil rights activists took their concerns to Washington, D.C. There they demonstrated for "jobs and freedom" and urged the passage of civil rights legislation.

Thousands March on Washington for Jobs and Freedom The 1963 March on Washington was a long time coming. A. Philip Randolph, the head of the Brotherhood of Sleeping Car Porters, had proposed the march in 1941. His goal was to protest unequal treatment of African Americans in the war industries. He called off that rally, however, in deference to President Roosevelt's call for unity in the war effort.

In 1963, however, the time was ripe for the long-delayed march, which was organized by leaders of the country's major civil rights organizations. On August 28, more than 250,000 people marched in Washington. It was the largest political gathering ever held in the United States. The quarter of a million protesters included about 60,000 whites as well as union members, clergy, students, entertainers, and celebrities such as Rosa Parks and Jackie Robinson.

That day, marchers listened to African American performers, like opera great Marian Anderson, who sang "He's Got the Whole World in His Hands." They also held hands and joined in as folksinger Joan Baez sang "We Shall Overcome."

King Inspires the Nation with His Dream The most notable event of the day was Martin Luther King Jr.'s "I have a dream" speech, delivered from the Lincoln Memorial. In ringing tones, King spoke of his dream for a better America:

> I have a dream that one day this nation will rise up and live out the true meaning of its creed: "We hold these truths to be self-evident; that all men are created equal . . ." When we allow freedom to ring, when we let it ring from every village and every hamlet, from every state and every city, we will be able to speed up that day when *all* God's children, black men and white men, Jews and Gentiles, Protestants and Catholics, will be able to join hands and sing in the words of the old Negro spiritual, "Free at last! Free at last! Thank God Almighty, we are free at last!"
>
> —Martin Luther King Jr., "I have a dream" speech, August 28, 1963

In his "I have a dream" speech, Martin Luther King Jr. declared, "When the architects of our republic wrote the magnificent words of the Constitution and the Declaration of Independence, they were signing a promissory note . . . that all men . . . would be guaranteed the unalienable rights of life, liberty, and the pursuit of happiness."

At the time of the march, a civil rights bill cautiously supported by President Kennedy was making its way through Congress. After Kennedy's assassination in November, President Lyndon B. Johnson continued to push for the bill. It stalled in the Senate, however, when senators opposed to the bill **filibustered,** speaking at great length to prevent legislative action. Nevertheless, the bill finally passed and was signed into law on July 2, 1964. The landmark Civil Rights Act of 1964 banned discrimination on the basis of race, sex, religion, or national origin—the most important civil rights law passed since Reconstruction.

How Did the Civil Rights Act of 1964 Affect African Americans?

The Civil Rights Act of 1964 transformed race relations in the United States. It outlawed racial discrimination in voter registration, public accomodations, public facilities, public schools and colleges, labor unions, and employment. The effects of this landmark legislation were both widespread and long term.

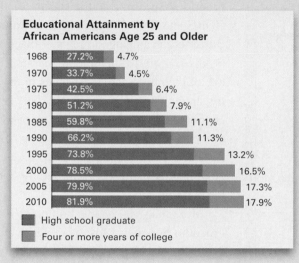

Educational Attainment by African Americans Age 25 and Older

Year	High school graduate	Four or more years of college
1968	27.2%	4.7%
1970	33.7%	4.5%
1975	42.5%	6.4%
1980	51.2%	7.9%
1985	59.8%	11.1%
1990	66.2%	11.3%
1995	73.8%	13.2%
2000	78.5%	16.5%
2005	79.9%	17.3%
2010	81.9%	17.9%

Education The Civil Rights Act gave the federal government the power to enforce school desegregation. Graduation rates for African Americans have risen ever since.

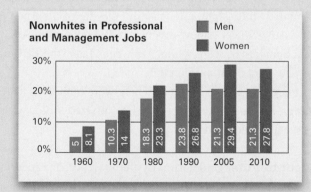

Nonwhites in Professional and Management Jobs

Legend: Men, Women

Year	Men	Women
1960	5	8.1
1970	10.3	14
1980	18.3	23.3
1990	23.8	26.8
2005	21.3	29.4
2010	21.3	27.8

Employment The Civil Rights Act opened up white-collar jobs traditionally held by whites to African Americans and other minority groups.

Income With more education and better job opporunties, African American incomes rose. Median income is the middle income in a series of incomes ranked from least to greatest.

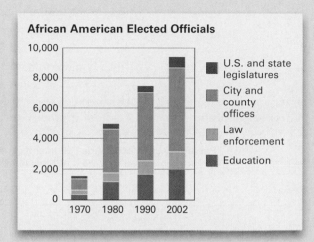

African American Elected Officials

Legend: U.S. and state legislatures; City and county offices; Law enforcement; Education

(Years: 1970, 1980, 1990, 2002; vertical scale 0 to 10,000)

Political Participation The Civil Rights Act's ban on racial dis-crimination in voter registration was strengthened by the Voting Rights Act of 1965. Since then, blacks have increased their political participation as both voters and officeholders.

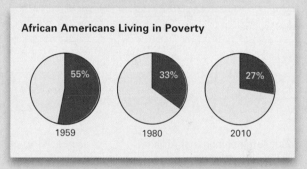

African Americans Living in Poverty

1959	1980	2010
55%	33%	27%

Poverty By banning racial discrimination in labor unions and employment, the Civil Rights Act helped pull many black families out of poverty.

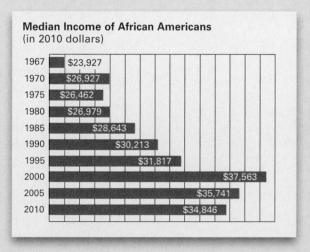

Median Income of African Americans (in 2010 dollars)

Year	Median Income
1967	$23,927
1970	$26,927
1975	$26,462
1980	$26,979
1985	$28,643
1990	$30,213
1995	$31,817
2000	$37,563
2005	$35,741
2010	$34,846

Sources: Bureau of Labor Statistics. U.S. Census Bureau. William H. Frey, *The New Great Migration: Black Americans' Return to the South, 1965–2000*, Washington, D.C.: Brookings Inst., 2004. Matthew Sobek, "New Statistics on the U.S. Labor Force," Historical Methods (2001): 71–87, in *Historical Statistics of the United States, Millennial Edition On Line*, ed. Susan B. Carter et al., 2006: Cambridge University Press.

44.7 Regaining Voting Rights

In January 1964, the Twenty-fourth Amendment to the Constitution was ratified. It stated that no U.S. citizen could be denied the right to vote "by reason of failure to pay any poll tax or other tax." Some southern states had used poll taxes to prevent blacks from voting. The Twenty-fourth Amendment was a key victory in the African American struggle for voting rights. But there was more to be done to ensure that black citizens could actually vote.

Voter Registration Rates in Selected Southern States, 1965

State	Percentage of Voting-Age Blacks Registered to Vote	Percentage of Voting-Age Whites Registered to Vote
Alabama	19.3%	69.2%
Georgia	27.4%	62.6%
Louisiana	31.6%	80.5%
Mississippi	6.7%	69.9%
North Carolina	46.8%	96.8%
South Carolina	37.3%	75.7%
Virginia	38.3%	61.1%

Source: Grofman, Handley, and Niemi, *Minority Representation and the Quest for Voting Equality*, New York: Cambridge Press, 1992, as reported at *U.S. Dept of Justice, Civil Rights Division, Voting Section*, "The Effect of the Voting Rights Act," www.usdoj.gov.

In the South, large numbers of African Americans were denied voting rights in the early 1960s. One way this was done was to limit voter registration for blacks.

Registering African American Voters in a Freedom Summer In the spring of 1964, CORE and SNCC organized Freedom Summer, a campaign to register black voters in Mississippi. At the time, Mississippi was one of the most segregated states in the country, and voting rights for blacks were severely restricted. Although they made up nearly half of the state's population, only a few African Americans were registered to vote, due in large part to restrictions imposed by state and local officials.

More than 900 people volunteered for Freedom Summer. Most were white college students from the North. They were given training in voter registration and were told to expect violent opposition to their efforts.

That prediction promptly came true. On June 21, three student activists disappeared in Neshoba County, Mississippi, after visiting the site of a burned black church. One of the activists, James Chaney, was black. The other two, Andrew Goodman and Michael Schwerner, were white. Six weeks later, the FBI discovered their bodies. They had been murdered.

Other violent acts marred Freedom Summer. There were numerous beatings, shootings, and bombings. At least three other activists suffered violent deaths. Most of these crimes went unpunished.

Marching for the Right to Vote Undeterred by the violence of Freedom Summer, activists continued their registration campaign. Early the following year, the SCLC began to register black voters in Selma, Alabama. In Dallas County, where Selma is located, only 320 of more than 15,000 eligible black voters were registered to vote at the time. For weeks, civil rights protesters held daily marches at the Dallas County Courthouse. By February, more than 3,000 had been arrested, charged with crimes such as "unlawful assembly." At that point, the SCLC called for a march from Selma to the state capital at Montgomery. The marchers planned to present the governor with a list of grievances.

On March 7, 1965, the protesters began their walk. Decades later, civil rights activist John Lewis recalled,

> As we crossed the Pettus Bridge, we saw a line of lawmen. "We should kneel and pray," I said . . . but we didn't have time. "Troopers," barked an officer, "advance!" They came at us like a human wave, a blur of blue uniforms, billy clubs, bullwhips and tear gas; one had a piece of rubber hose wrapped in barbed wire.

Once again, televised images of the violence that day outraged many Americans. The civil rights movement continued to gain support around the country.

In August, Congress passed the **Voting Rights Act of 1965**. The act outlawed literacy tests and other tactics used to deny African Americans the right to vote. The act also called for the federal government to supervise voter registration in areas where less than half of voting-age citizens were registered to vote. Federal intervention would ensure that eligible voters were not turned away.

Efforts to secure voting rights proved quite successful. In 1964, less than 7 percent of Mississippi's eligible black voters were registered to vote. By 1968, that number had risen to 59 percent. In Alabama, the numbers rose from about 20 percent to 57 percent during the same four-year period. Overall, the number of African American voters in the South increased from 1 million to 3.1 million between 1964 and 1968. The civil rights movement had made great strides in the years since the Montgomery Bus Boycott.

African Americans lined up to vote for the first time throughout the South after passage of the Voting Rights Act of 1965. The number of registered black voters grew dramatically in the late 1960s.

Summary

Between 1955 and 1965, many key events took place in the civil rights movement. African Americans made great progress in their struggle for rights and equality.

Montgomery Bus Boycott In 1955, blacks in Montgomery, Alabama, began a lengthy boycott of the city's segregated bus system. As a result, Montgomery's buses were integrated.

SCLC and SNCC These two groups helped organize nonviolent civil rights actions. The Southern Christian Leadership Conference was led by Martin Luther King Jr. It played a major role in the Birmingham campaign and other events. The Student Nonviolent Coordinating Committee organized sit-ins and engaged in other forms of civil disobedience.

Freedom Rides In 1961, black and white Freedom Riders rode buses through the South. They were testing southern compliance with laws outlawing segregation in interstate transport. The riders were subjected to violence and eventually received federal protection.

March on Washington A quarter of a million people marched in Washington, D.C., in August 1963 to demand jobs and freedom. The highlight of this event was Martin Luther King Jr.'s "I have a dream" speech.

Freedom Summer In the summer of 1964, activists led voter registration drives in the South for African Americans.

Landmark legislation The Civil Rights Act of 1964 banned discrimination on the basis of race, sex, religion, or national origin. The Voting Rights Act of 1965 outlawed literacy tests, enabling many African Americans to vote.

Chapter 45

Redefining Equality: From Black Power to Affirmative Action

How did civil rights activists change their strategies and goals in the 1960s and 1970s, and how successful were they in achieving racial equality?

45.1 Introduction

In 1966, James Meredith, the first African American graduate of the University of Mississippi, began a campaign he called his March Against Fear. He planned to walk from Memphis, Tennessee, to Jackson, Mississippi. Along the way he hoped to encourage the African Americans he met to stand up for their rights by registering to vote. Only 30 miles out of Memphis, Meredith was shot by a sniper. He survived but was hospitalized.

A number of civil rights leaders stepped up to complete Meredith's march. Among them were Dr. Martin Luther King Jr. and Stokely Carmichael, the young leader of the Student Nonviolent Coordinating Committee (SNCC). On their first day, an angry policeman knocked King down. Carmichael prepared to retaliate, only to be stopped by other marchers. Rather than thanking Carmichael, King scolded him for straying from the strategy of nonviolence. In Carmichael's view, this incident had little to do with nonviolence. "It was," he insisted, "about self-defense."

For days the marchers endured insults and threats from angry whites. When they reached Greenwood, Mississippi, Carmichael was arrested while trying to set up a tent for the night. "By the time I got out of jail," he recalled, "I was in no mood to compromise with racist arrogance." The night of his release, Carmichael addressed a rally in Greenwood. "It's time we stand up and take over," he said. "We been saying freedom for six years and we ain't got nothin'. What we gonna start saying now is **Black Power**." Again and again he asked the crowd, "What do you want?" Each time the crowd roared back, "Black Power!"

Carmichael's speech and the crowd's response reflected a turning point in the civil rights movement. For more than 10 years, the movement's leaders had favored nonviolence as their main strategy and integration as their primary goal. With his talk of Black Power, Carmichael was signaling a change in what many blacks wanted and how they would achieve these new goals.

Stokely Carmichael first spoke of Black Power in 1966. Martin Luther King Jr. had reservations about the term. "I don't believe in black separatism," he said. "But certainly if Black Power means the amassing of political and economic power in order to gain our just and legitimate goals, then we all believe in that."

◀ Fists raised in what became known as the Black Power salute

45.2 The Nation's Black Ghettos Explode

In 1963, the African American writer James Baldwin published an essay on what it was like to be black in the United States. Baldwin reminded his readers that blacks had waited far too long for equality. If the United States did not live up to its ideals soon, he warned, the result could be an eruption of violence.

> If we—and now I mean the relatively conscious whites and the relatively conscious blacks . . . do not falter in our duty now, we may be able, handful that we are, to end the racial nightmare . . . If we do not now dare everything, the fulfillment of that prophecy, re-created from the Bible in song by a slave, is upon us:
>
> *God gave Noah the rainbow sign,*
> *No more water, the fire next time!*
>
> —James Baldwin, *The Fire Next Time,* 1963

Fire did indeed erupt, as anger increased over the slow pace of progress and the federal government's weak support for civil rights. Beginning in 1964, African Americans lashed out in violent protests in cities across the country.

Riots erupted around the nation following the Watts riots in Los Angeles. This photo shows the aftermath of a riot in Washington, D.C.

From Watts to Newark: Riots in the Streets By the 1960s, almost 70 percent of African Americans lived in large cities. Urban blacks were often concentrated in ethnic **ghettos**. A ghetto is a part of a city where people belonging to a single ethnic group live. Sometimes people live in an ethnic ghetto because they want to be among people who share their culture. But often people live in such neighborhoods because social and economic conditions prevent them from moving elsewhere. This was true for African Americans. Because of job discrimination, many could not afford to live anywhere else. Even those with good jobs found it almost impossible to buy houses in white neighborhoods.

In August 1965, a race riot exploded in Watts, an African American ghetto in Los Angeles. The immediate cause of the riot was a charge of police brutality. The more long-term cause was African Americans' festering frustrations about poverty, prejudice, and police mistreatment.

The **Watts riot** lasted for six long days. During that time, 34 people died, almost 900 were injured, and nearly 4,000 were arrested. Rioters burned and looted whole neighborhoods, causing $45 million of property damage. The rioting did not end until 14,000 members of the National Guard were sent to Watts to restore order.

Over the next few years, riots erupted in other cities as well. In 1967 alone, more than 100 cities experienced violent protests. In Detroit, Michigan, 43 people died and more than 1,000 were wounded in an urban upheaval. Eventually the army quelled the riots by sending in tanks and soldiers with machine guns. Riots in Newark, New Jersey, lasted six days and resulted in many deaths and injuries.

Major Urban Riots, 1967

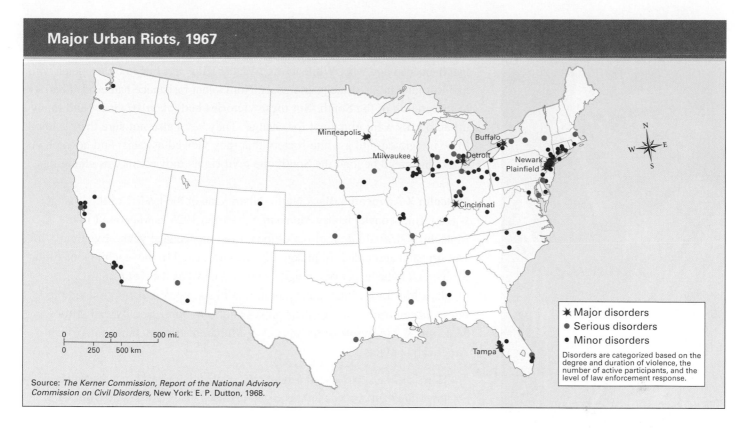

Source: *The Kerner Commission, Report of the National Advisory Commission on Civil Disorders*, New York: E. P. Dutton, 1968.

Legend:
- ✹ Major disorders
- ● Serious disorders
- • Minor disorders

Disorders are categorized based on the degree and duration of violence, the number of active participants, and the level of law enforcement response.

The Kerner Commission Report: Moving Toward Two Societies It was not until 1967, in response to the rioting that summer, that President Lyndon Johnson, also known as LBJ, established the National Advisory Commission on Civil Disorders to examine what had caused the riots. The commission came to be known as the Kerner Commission after its leader, Illinois governor Otto Kerner. Its final report, issued in 1968, concluded that "Our nation is moving toward two societies, one black, one white—separate and unequal."

Looking deeper, the report found that riots were usually triggered by a specific event that touched off a "reservoir of underlying grievances":

> Social and economic conditions in the riot cities constituted a clear pattern of severe disadvantage for Negroes compared with whites . . . Negroes had completed fewer years of education and fewer had attended high school. Negroes were twice as likely to be unemployed . . . and were more than twice as likely to be living in poverty. Although housing cost Negroes relatively more, they had worse housing—three times as likely to be overcrowded and substandard.
>
> —National Advisory Commission on Civil Disorders, 1968

The report pointed to "unfulfilled expectations" raised by the civil rights movement. When these expectations were not met, some African Americans had concluded that violence was the only way to "move the system."

The commission called on the country to address the inequalities that the riots had laid bare. "It is time now to turn with all the purpose at our command to the major unfinished business of this nation," it urged. "It is time to make good the promises of American democracy to all citizens—urban and rural, white and black, Spanish-surname, American Indian, and every minority group."

Beginning with rioting in Harlem and Rochester, New York, in 1964, racial unrest spread out of the North to cities across the nation. This map show major riots in 1967. Other disturbances also occurred that year. The murder of Martin Luther King Jr. in 1968 triggered the worst violence of the decade. After that, racial unrest subsided.

As a Black Muslim minister, Malcolm X supported black nationalism. He said, "The only way the black people who are in this society can be saved is not to integrate into this corrupt society but separate ourselves from it, reform ourselves, lift up our moral standards and try and be godly." Later he broke with the Black Muslims and made a broad, nonracial appeal for human rights.

45.3 The Rise of Black Power and Black Pride

After the Watts riot, Martin Luther King Jr. visited Los Angeles to find out what had happened and why. While touring Watts, King was booed by residents who had lost faith in his strategy and goals. Nonviolent resistance had eroded barriers to integration in the South. But these victories had taken 10 years, and many urban blacks were impatient for change. They were also not sure they wanted to be integrated into a white society that they viewed as racist and corrupt. As activism spread beyond the South, the civil rights movement was changing.

Malcolm X Advocates Black Nationalism One of the leaders of this change was a former convict named Malcolm X. Born in 1925 as Malcolm Little, Malcolm X drifted into a life of crime during his teenage years. Eventually he was arrested and jailed. In prison, he was introduced to the teachings of Elijah Muhammad, the leader of a religious group known as the **Nation of Islam,** or Black Muslims. Muhammad taught that blacks were Earth's first people but had been tricked out of their power and long oppressed by evil whites. Malcolm X later wrote of the appeal of Muhammad's teachings to African American convicts:

> Here is a black man caged behind bars, probably for years, put there by the white man . . . You let this caged up black man start thinking, the same way I did when I first heard Elijah Muhammad's teachings: let him start thinking how, with better breaks when he was young and ambitious he might have been a lawyer, a doctor, a scientist, anything . . . That's why black prisoners become Muslims so fast when Elijah Muhammad's teachings filter into their cages . . . "The white man is the devil" is a perfect echo of that black convict's lifelong experience.
>
> —Malcolm X, *The Autobiography of Malcolm X,* 1964

After Malcolm Little left prison in 1952, he joined the Nation of Islam and changed his name to Malcolm X. He said Little was the name of a white slave-owner. He chose X as his new last name because "a Negro in America can never know his true family name, or even what tribe he was descended from." He quickly became the Nation of Islam's most effective preacher. In 1959, he was featured in a weeklong television special called *The Hate That Hate Produced,* which brought widespread attention to Malcolm and the Nation of Islam.

As a Black Muslim, Malcolm X rejected the goals of the early civil rights movement. Rather than seeking integration, the Nation of Islam promoted **black nationalism,** a doctrine that called for complete separation from white society. Black Muslims worked to become independent from whites by establishing their own businesses, schools, and communities.

Malcolm X also rejected nonviolence as a strategy to bring about change. Speaking to a group of black teenagers in New York City in 1964, he said,

> If the leaders of the nonviolent movement can go to the white community and teach nonviolence, good. I'd go along with that. But as long as I see them teaching nonviolence only in the black community, we can't go along with that . . . If black people alone are going to be the ones who are nonviolent, then it's not fair. We throw ourselves off guard. In fact, we disarm ourselves and make ourselves defenseless.

By the time he made this speech, Malcolm X had split with the Nation of Islam. During a pilgrimage to the Muslim holy city of Mecca in 1964, he had met Muslims of all races, including "blonde-haired, blued-eyed men I could call my brothers." On his return home, Malcolm X converted to orthodox Islam and began to reach out to people of all races, making a broader call for human rights. His change of heart upset many Black Muslims. In 1965, three members of the Nation of Islam assassinated Malcolm X while he was speaking in New York City.

SNCC Stands Up for Black Power A year after Malcolm X's death, SNCC leader Stokely Carmichael introduced the idea of Black Power to the civil rights movement. Black Power had a variety of meanings, such as political power, economic power, and pride in being black. In a speech on Black Power, Carmichael observed that,

> This country knows what power is. It knows it very well. And it knows what Black Power is 'cause it deprived black people of it for 400 years. So it knows what Black Power is . . .
>
> We are on the move for our liberation . . . The question is, Will white people overcome their racism and allow for that to happen in this country? If that does not happen, brothers and sisters, we have no choice but to say very clearly, "Move over, or we're going to move on over you."
>
> —Stokely Carmichael, speech in Berkeley, California, 1966

Carmichael went on to convert SNCC from an integrated organization to an all-black organization. "We cannot have white people working in the black community," he argued. "Black people must be seen in positions of power, doing and articulating [speaking] for themselves."

The Black Panthers, who were militant black nationalists, called for economic and political equality for African Americans. They dressed in military-style clothing and often carried guns as a symbol of Black Power.

Black Panthers Work for Self-Determination Among the many African Americans influenced by Malcolm X were Bobby Seale and Huey Newton. In 1966, they founded the **Black Panther Party** in Oakland, California. In choosing that name, the founders were sending the world a message. An early supporter explained, "The black panther was a vicious animal, who, if he was attacked, would not back up. It was a political symbol that we were here to stay and we were going to do whatever needed to be done to survive."

The Black Panther Party developed a 10-point platform setting out its goals. The first and last points dealt with self-determination. "We want freedom," the platform began. "We want power to determine the destiny of our Black Community." Other demands included jobs, decent housing, "education that teaches our true history," and "an immediate

African Americans in Congress

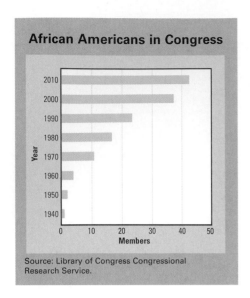

Source: Library of Congress Congressional Research Service.

The civil rights movement increased the number of black voters. It also led to increased numbers of African Americans being elected to Congress. When it was founded in 1969, the Congressional Black Caucus had 13 members. By 2010, that number had grown to 42.

In 1968, Shirley Chisholm became the first black woman elected to Congress. Chisholm was one of a growing number of African Americans elected to political office as a result of the civil rights movement. In 1972, Chisholm ran for president.

end to police brutality." Finally, the platform called on the United Nations to supervise a **plebiscite** among African Americans to determine "the will of black people as to their national destiny." A plebiscite is a vote on a question of importance.

The Black Panthers provided many services for blacks in their community, such as free breakfast programs for children, and medical clinics. But they were probably best known for their efforts to end police mistreatment of blacks. They sent observers onto the streets to watch interactions between police and black citizens. The observers carried a law book to provide information about people's rights, a tape recorder to document what was said, and a shotgun to show that they were prepared to defend themselves.

Because Black Panthers carried weapons and were willing to stand up to the police, they were viewed as dangerous radicals by law enforcement agencies. Local police and FBI agents often raided the Panthers' offices and homes. When confrontations with the police turned violent, the Panthers involved were arrested and jailed. By the mid-1970s, with its legal problems mounting, the Black Panther Party fell apart.

Black Power at the Polls Brings Political Gains For many African Americans, Black Power meant the power to shape public policy through the political process. Supported by the Voting Rights Act of 1965, civil rights groups organized voter-registration drives across the South. Between 1964 and 1968, the number of southern blacks registered to vote rose from 1 to 3.1 million.

Across the nation, African American candidates successfully competed for both black and white votes. Edward Brooke of Massachusetts was elected to the Senate in 1966, becoming the first black senator since 1881. Two years later, Shirley Chisholm of New York became the first black woman to win election to the House of Representatives. In 1969, the African American members of the House of Representatives started the Congressional Black Caucus. Over the years, the caucus has worked to address legislative concerns of African American citizens.

Black politicians were also successful at winning state and local elections. In 1967, Carl Stokes of Cleveland, Ohio, became the first black mayor of a major U.S. city. Six years later, Tom Bradley became the first black mayor of Los Angeles. Bradley won by forging a powerful coalition that included inner-city blacks, the Jewish community, and business and labor leaders. "He built bridges to whites and to other groups," noted a political scientist, "without ever losing his commitment to the black community." Bradley was reelected four times, serving as mayor for 20 years.

African Americans also rose in the judicial branch of the government. Thurgood Marshall, who had argued the *Brown v. Board of Education* case as the NAACP's lead attorney, was named the first black Supreme Court justice in 1967.

Black Pride: The Growth of Afrocentrism For many African Americans, Black Power meant taking pride in their African heritage. This focus on African history, African culture, and the achievements of African peoples and their descendants in the United States came to be known as **Afrocentrism**.

Afrocentric scholars argued that the accounts of history taught in most schools ignored the many contributions of African peoples. In their view, Afrocentrism helped to balance the Eurocentric, or European-centered, view of the past that had long been presented to American schoolchildren, both black and white.

African Americans showed pride in their heritage in many ways. College students pushed for the establishment of African and African American studies classes. Museums began to show African American history and art. On a more day-to-day basis, many blacks began to dress in traditional African clothing, wear their hair in African styles called Afros, and exchange their Eurocentric names for Afrocentric ones. In 1966, a black scholar invented an Afrocentric holiday called Kwanzaa, which takes place each year between December 26 and January 1. During Kwanzaa, black Americans celebrate seven principles of African American culture, including faith, creativity, and unity.

Black writers also expanded Afrocentric culture as they wrote about their experiences. Poets like Nikki Giovanni and playwrights like Amiri Baraka and August Wilson brought the struggles of African Americans into their poems and plays. Novelists like Maya Angelou, Toni Morrison, and Alice Walker wrote widely read novels about African American life, both past and present.

In 1977, a 12-hour television miniseries on African American life called *Roots* became one of the most highly rated shows in television history. Based on a historical novel by Alex Haley, *Roots* told the story of several generations of an enslaved black family. More than 250 colleges planned courses around the broadcasts, while more than 30 cities declared "Roots" weeks. Vernon Jordan, former president of the Urban League, called the miniseries "the single most spectacular educational experience in race relations in America."

Kwanzaa is an African American holiday created to celebrate the rich history of African culture and tradition in America. This picture displays a traditional Kwanzaa setting.

45.4 The Federal Government Confronts Racism

On March 31, 1968, Martin Luther King Jr. preached at the National Cathedral in Washington, D.C. In his sermon, King spoke frankly about racism:

> It is an unhappy truth that racism is a way of life for the vast majority of white Americans, spoken and unspoken, acknowledged and denied, subtle and sometimes not so subtle . . . Something positive must be done. Everyone must share in the guilt as individuals and as institutions . . . The hour has come for everybody, for all institutions of the public sector and the private sector to work to get rid of racism.
> —Martin Luther King Jr., "Remaining Awake Through a Great Revolution," 1968

That hour never came for King. Four days later he was assassinated in Memphis, Tennessee, where he had gone to support a sanitation workers' strike. Riots erupted in more than 100 cities, including Washington, D.C. As dawn broke on April 6, 1968, a thick pall of smoke hung over the nation's capital. In the wake of these tragedies, the federal government increased its efforts to end racism and discrimination in public life.

Banning Racial Discrimination in Housing Before his death, King had shifted his focus from integration to economic equality. As part of this campaign, he took on the issue of racial discrimination in housing. In many U.S. cities, landlords in white neighborhoods refused to rent to blacks. African Americans also found it difficult to buy houses in many neighborhoods. Even when African Americans found a home to buy, they discovered that banks were reluctant to make loans to black borrowers.

Under King's leadership, the black community joined with realtors and bankers to encourage open housing in Chicago. But very little actually changed. Then, in 1968, only days after King's assassination, Congress finally took action. Drawing on King's efforts and on the national grief over his death, Congress passed the **Civil Rights Act of 1968**. This law included a fair-housing component that banned discrimination in housing sales and rentals. It also gave the federal government the authority to file lawsuits against those who violated the law.

Desegregating Public Schools In 1954, the Supreme Court had ruled in *Brown v. Board of Education* that school segregation was unconstitutional. A year later, it had ordered schools to be desegregated "with all deliberate speed." But a decade later, only 1.2 percent of black children in the South attended integrated schools.

The Civil Rights Act of 1964 gave the federal government new powers to promote school desegregation. Government officials pushed school districts to integrate their schools by threatening to cut off federal funds if they did not. By 1968, the proportion of African American students in the South attending schools with whites had risen to 32 percent.

By this time, however, the Supreme Court was losing patience with school districts that were slow to act. In a 1969 case known as *Alexander v. Holmes County Board of Education,* the Court took another look at "with all deliberate speed." The case involved a segregated Mississippi school district that was trying to delay integration. In the Court's decision, Justice Hugo Black wrote,

Due to protests against desegregation, this newly integrated classroom was left with just African American students.

There are many places still in this country where the schools are either "white" or "Negro" and not just schools for all children as the Constitution requires. In my opinion there is no reason why such a wholesale deprivation of constitutional rights should be tolerated another minute. I fear that this long denial of constitutional rights is due in large part to the phrase "with all deliberate speed." I would do away with that phrase completely.

—*Alexander v. Holmes County Board of Education,* 1969

Three years later, the Supreme Court took another look at school segregation in *Swann v. Charlotte-Mecklenburg Board of Education*. This case raised the question of whether de facto segregation caused by housing patterns was constitutional. This was the situation in North Carolina's Charlotte-Mecklenburg School District. Because most children in the district lived in predominantly white or black neighborhoods, they also attended all-white or all-black schools. In 1970, a federal judge ordered the district to use busing to integrate its schools. Under the judge's desegregation plan, some students, including very young ones, would be bused to schools outside their neighborhoods to create more racially balanced schools.

A decade after *Brown v. Board of Education* ruled that schools must desegregate, many had not done so. These children are being bussed to a school in North Carolina.

The school district appealed to the Supreme Court, arguing that the judge had gone too far. In a unanimous decision delivered in 1971, the Court supported the judge's busing plan. "We find no basis for holding that the local school authorities may not be required to employ bus transportation as one tool for of school desegregation," wrote Chief Justice Warren Burger. "Desegregation plans cannot be limited to the walk-in school."

Using Busing to Achieve Racial Balance in Schools The Court's approval of busing to achieve racial balance in schools was controversial. Supporters argued that busing was useful for ending school segregation. They quoted studies showing that black children got higher test scores when attending integrated schools. However, many parents, both black and white, felt strongly that their children should attend schools close to home. They worried about the effects of long bus rides, especially on young children. They also feared for the safety of children bused into unfamiliar neighborhoods.

Nowhere was resistance to busing stronger than in the city of Boston, Massachusetts. In 1974, a judge ordered the busing of 17,000 Boston school children to desegregate the city's schools. Large numbers of white families opposed the judge's order. Resistance was especially strong in South Boston, a mostly white neighborhood.

When school began at South Boston High School that fall, 90 percent of its white students boycotted classes. Black students leaving the school to board buses back to their neighborhoods were pelted with rocks. Later that fall, a white student was stabbed in a racial confrontation at the school. In response, an angry white mob trapped 135 black students in the school building for four hours. A force of 500 police officers was assigned to South Boston High— which had only 400 students—to keep order.

Over the next two years, an estimated 20,000 white students left Boston's public schools to avoid busing. Some went to private schools. Others moved with their families to the suburbs. As a result, by 1976, blacks and Hispanics made up the majority of Boston's school population.

Despite public resistance, the courts continued to enforce the *Brown* decision. By 1976, almost half of black students in the South attended schools with a majority of white students. In the Northeast, only 27.5 percent of black students attended integrated schools.

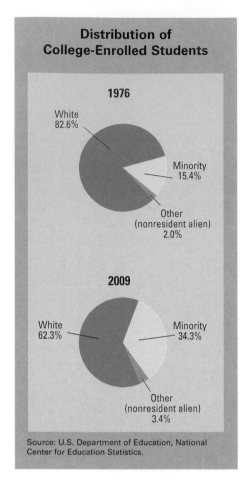

Distribution of College-Enrolled Students

1976

White 82.6%

Minority 15.4%

Other (nonresident alien) 2.0%

2009

White 62.3%

Minority 34.3%

Other (nonresident alien) 3.4%

Source: U.S. Department of Education, National Center for Education Statistics.

Affirmative action increased the number of minority students attending U.S. colleges and universities. In 1978, the Supreme Court ruled in *Regents of the University of California v. Bakke* that race could be considered in school admissions. But it could not be the only factor. The term "nonresident alien" in the graphs refers to foreign students.

Fighting Racism in the Workplace Through Affirmative Action The Civil Rights Act of 1964 had outlawed discrimination in hiring based on race, religion, gender, or national origin. However, many argued that simply "leveling the playing field" in hiring was not enough. As President Lyndon Johnson observed in a speech to graduates of Howard University,

> You do not take a person who for years has been hobbled by chains and liberate him, bring him up to the starting line of a race and then say, "you're free to compete with all the others," and still justly believe that you have been completely fair. Thus it is not enough just to open the gates of opportunity. All our citizens must have the ability to walk through those gates.
> —Lyndon Johnson, Howard University, 1965

Johnson argued that more needed to be done to counteract past discrimination that had denied minorities equal opportunities. One way to do this was through a policy known as **affirmative action**. This policy called on employers to actively seek to increase the number of minorities in their workforce.

Affirmative action was first introduced by President John F. Kennedy. In 1961, he issued an executive order that called on contractors doing business with the federal government to "take affirmative action" to hire minorities. President Johnson expanded Kennedy's policy to include women. He also required contractors to have written affirmative action plans. "This is the next and more profound stage of the battle for civil rights," Johnson said. "We seek . . . not just equality as a right and a theory, but equality as a fact and as a result."

President Richard Nixon took affirmative action a giant step further. In an executive order, he required government contractors to develop "an acceptable affirmative action program" that included "goals and timetables."

Equalizing Opportunities Through Preferential Treatment Many Americans agree with the goals of affirmative action. However, the practices used to carry out this policy have been controversial. An affirmative action plan may set specific goals, such as numbers of minority or women workers to be hired. It may include a timetable with dates for achieving those goals. It may also prescribe **preferential treatment** for some groups. This means giving preference to a minority or female job applicant because of that person's ethnicity or gender. To many people, preferential treatment looks like unfair discrimination against white males.

During the 1960s, many colleges and universities adopted affirmative action plans to attract more minority students. Members of minority groups were often given preferential treatment over white students who were equally qualified or more qualified. Such treatment was necessary, admissions officers argued, to open opportunities for minorities and to create a diverse student body.

In the late 1970s, a white male named Allan Bakke challenged preferential treatment in university admissions. Bakke had twice applied for admission to the University of California Davis Medical School. He was rejected both times. At the same time, minority candidates with lower grade point averages and test scores were admitted under a special admissions program. Bakke concluded that he had been refused admission because he was white, and he sued the school for **reverse discrimination**.

In 1977, *Regents of the University of California v. Bakke* reached the Supreme Court. After hearing arguments on both sides, the Court was left deeply divided. Four justices were firmly against any use of race in university admissions. Another four felt just as strongly that race should be used. The remaining justice, Lewis Powell, thought race could be used as a criterion in choosing students but opposed the system of preferential treatment used by the University of California. Writing for the majority, Powell cautioned, "Racial and ethnic classifications of any sort are inherently suspect and call for the most exacting judicial scrutiny."

The Court's ruling narrowly upheld affirmative action by declaring that race could be used as one of the criteria in admissions decisions. However, it also said that racial quotas were unconstitutional—that race could not be used as the only criterion. Therefore, the Court ordered the university to admit Bakke to medical school. The ruling, however, did not end the debate over affirmative action and preferential treatment for women and minorities.

Summary

The civil rights movement changed course in the mid-1960s, moving beyond the South and expanding its goals. Some activists also abandoned the strategy of nonviolence.

Black Power In 1966, civil rights activists began calling for Black Power. They wanted African Americans to have economic and political power, as well as pride in their African heritage.

Watts riot In the summer of 1965, the Watts section of Los Angeles exploded in violence. This event was followed by riots in black ghettos across the nation.

Kerner Commission This commission, established by Lyndon Johson to study the riots, concluded that their fundamental cause was pent-up resentment over historic inequalities.

Nation of Islam Also called Black Muslims, the Nation of Islam advocated black nationalism. Its members believed that blacks should live apart from whites and control their own communities.

Black Panther Party The Black Panther Party demanded economic and political rights. Unlike nonviolent civil rights leaders, the Black Panthers were prepared to fight to realize their goals.

Civil Rights Act of 1968 The most important clause in this law bans discrimination in the sale, rental, and financing of housing based on race, religion, national origin, or sex.

Swann v. Charlotte-Mecklenburg Board of Education In this decision, the Supreme Court ruled that busing is an acceptable way to achieve school integration.

Regents of the University of California v. Bakke In its first case on affirmative action, the Supreme Court ruled that race may be used as one, but not the only, factor in school admissions.

Chapter 46

The Widening Struggle

Why and how did the civil rights movement expand?

46.1 Introduction

As a schoolteacher in the 1950s, Dolores Huerta taught the children of farm-workers in California's San Joaquin Valley. Huerta had grown up in the valley and knew about the hardships endured by farmworkers and their families.

Huerta liked teaching, but she wanted to do more to help the farmworkers. So she decided to give up her teaching job. "I couldn't stand seeing kids come to class hungry and needing shoes," she explained later. "I thought I could do more by organizing farm workers than by trying to teach their hungry children."

Together with farm labor organizer Cesar Chavez, Huerta formed the National Farm Workers Association. As a small union for migrant farmworkers, the NFWA seemed powerless next to the large corporations that ran farming operations in the San Joaquin Valley. Nevertheless, in 1966 it won a major victory by negotiating a collective bargaining agreement with the Schenley Wine Company. It was the first time a farmworkers' union had signed a contract with an agricultural corporation. Later that year, the NFWA merged with another group to become the United Farm Workers (UFW).

In the decades that followed, Huerta expanded her focus. Through her UFW work, she became an advocate for Latinos. In time she joined the struggle for women's rights, too.

Many groups of Americans experienced discrimination in the 1950s and 1960s. Some of these, like farmworkers, were mounting their campaigns for equal rights while the black civil rights movement was growing in the South. That movement inspired many groups to carry on with their own struggles.

This chapter continues the story of the civil rights movement as it expanded to include more Americans. Following the example of African Americans, other groups—including women, Latinos, American Indians, and Asian Americans—fought for their rights. Disabled, gay, and older Americans began to organize for equal treatment, too.

Dolores Huerta helped to found the United Farm Workers with Cesar Chavez and other labor activists in the late 1960s. She became a powerful advocate for workers' rights. Here is Dolores Huerta in a parade celebrating Mexican Independence Day in Los Angeles, California, 2010.

◀ Poster for a United Farm Workers boycott, 1978

46.2 Women Demand Equality

Like Dolores Huerta, many women who fought for civil rights and workers' rights later became active in the movement for women's rights. More than a century before, in the 1830s and 1840s, many women abolitionists had followed a similar path. In fighting to end slavery, they had come to recognize their own status as second-class citizens. These early advocates of women's rights held the 1848 Seneca Falls Convention and launched the women's suffrage movement. In the same way, many women who were inspired by the black civil rights movement of the 1960s and 1970s went on to forge the women's movement.

One Half of America Although women make up half the American population, in the early 1960s many women felt they were being treated like a minority and denied their rights. They wanted equal opportunity and the same rights as men.

In 1963, author Betty Friedan exposed the unhappiness of many middle-class women in her book *The Feminine Mystique*. She described women who had the things they thought they wanted—marriage, home, family—but were still dissatisfied. As Friedan wrote, the typical housewife wanted something more:

> As she made the beds, shopped for groceries, matched slipcover material, ate peanut butter sandwiches with her children, chauffeured Cub Scouts and Brownies, lay beside her husband at night—she was afraid to ask even of herself the silent question—"Is this all?"
>
> —Betty Friedan, *The Feminine Mystique,* 1963

Many middle-class wives had attended college, but few had entered professions. Although the number of women in the workforce was rising, most held what were considered to be "women's jobs." They were secretaries or bank tellers, for example, while men might work as lawyers, doctors, or business executives. Because they held lower-status jobs, they earned less than men. In 1965, they made only about 60 cents for every dollar men earned. Even women in higher positions were paid less than male colleagues. Although the gap has narrowed, it remains significant. In 2009, women earned about 77 cents for every

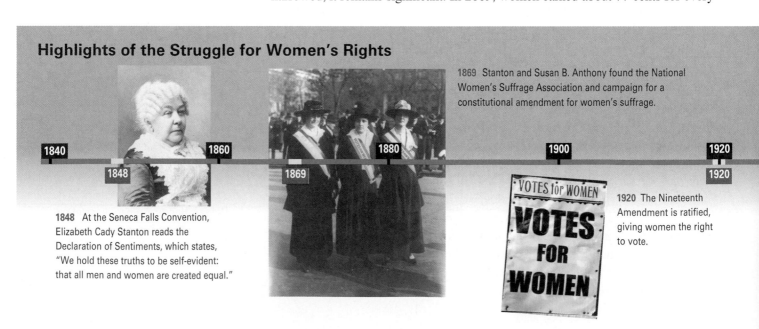

Highlights of the Struggle for Women's Rights

1840 — 1848 — 1860 — 1869 — 1880 — 1900 — 1920 — 1920

1848 At the Seneca Falls Convention, Elizabeth Cady Stanton reads the Declaration of Sentiments, which states, "We hold these truths to be self-evident: that all men and women are created equal."

1869 Stanton and Susan B. Anthony found the National Women's Suffrage Association and campaign for a constitutional amendment for women's suffrage.

1920 The Nineteenth Amendment is ratified, giving women the right to vote.

VOTES for WOMEN
VOTES FOR WOMEN

dollar men earned. Meanwhile, relatively few women have been promoted to upper management. The invisible barrier to women's professional advancement has been called the **glass ceiling**. This term has also been applied to minorities.

Organizing for Action In the early 1960s, Congress passed two laws banning sex discrimination, but neither had much impact. The first, the Equal Pay Act of 1963, outlawed "wage differentials based on sex" in industries that produced goods for commerce. This law only affected jobs that were nearly identical, however. Since women and men generally did different types of work, the law had little effect on women's wages. The second law, the Civil Rights Act of 1964, also prohibited discrimination based on sex. This law set an important precedent, but it brought few immediate benefits for women.

To advance women's rights, Betty Friedan and other activists formed the **National Organization for Women (NOW)** in 1966. This group pledged "to bring women into full participation in the mainstream of American society." NOW was made up mostly of middle-aged, middle-class women. Like the more moderate organizations of the civil rights movement, NOW placed much of its focus on legal reforms and workforce discrimination, demanding equal opportunity for women.

On August 26, 1970, NOW organized the Women's Strike for Equality. The date marked the 50th anniversary of the ratification of the Nineteenth Amendment, which granted women the right to vote. The strikers urged women not to do their usual domestic tasks that day. Their slogan was, "Don't iron while the strike is hot." That day, 50,000 women marched in New York City. Altogether, more than 100,000 people around the country took part in the strike, making it the largest action for women's rights in American history.

A more radical branch of the women's movement arose in the late 1960s. It was made up of younger women who had worked in the civil rights movement. They coined the term **sexism** to describe oppression of women in the workplace and home. They used the term **women's liberation** to describe their goal. They wanted to emancipate women from customs and laws that kept them subordinate to men. Many of these ideas became part of the broader women's movement.

1966 Betty Friedan and others form the National Organization for Women and launch the modern-day women's liberation movement.

1972 The equal rights amendment is passed by Congress, yet fails to gain the approval of three fourths of the states. Supporters continue to rally for its approval into the 21st century.

1981 Sandra Day O'Connor became the first woman to serve on the Supreme Court. She retired in 2006 and was awarded the Presidential Medal of Freedom in 2009.

1940   1960   1980   2000   2010

1960   1966   1972   1981   2008

1960 The number of women in the workforce is rising, but women are still earning substantially less than men.

2008 General Ann E. Dunwoody became the first female four-star general in the United States armed forces. General Dunwoody has commanded at every level and is currently Commanding General, U.S. Army Material Command.

Phyllis Schlafly was a key leader of the opposition to the Equal Rights Amendment. She argued that the ERA would devalue traditional roles for women and harm the American family. Some opponents also feared that women would have to serve in the military and take on other roles normally associated with men.

Despite the growing prominence of the women's movement, many Americans at the time opposed **feminism,** the movement for women's equality. They believed that feminism posed a threat to traditional values and would undermine marriage and weaken the American family. They claimed that traditional roles for women gave them a strong and respected place in society and argued that feminists wanted to make women more like men.

Working for Equal Rights One of the main goals of the women's movement was to win passage of the equal rights amendment to the Constitution, or ERA, which stated that "equality of rights under the law shall not be denied or abridged by the United States or by any state on account of sex." The ERA had been submitted to every session of Congress since 1923. In 1972, for the first time, Congress passed the ERA and sent it to the states to be ratified.

At first it seemed certain that three fourths of the states would ratify the ERA and it would become law. But the amendment provoked a backlash. Some Americans feared that the ERA would devalue the roles of mother and homemaker. Some also believed it would lead to requiring women to serve in the military. As a result, the ERA failed to achieve ratification by the 1982 deadline set by Congress, falling 3 states short of the required 38 states.

Despite that loss, women's efforts to attain equal rights succeeded on many fronts. Some clear examples came in education. Between 1969 and 1973, the number of women law students nearly quadrupled, while the number of women medical students almost doubled. By 1997, women made up the majority of college students and earned the majority of master's degrees. Women's opportunities in education were enhanced by federal legislation. A law called Title IX of the Educational Amendments of 1972 prohibited discrimination on the basis of sex in any school program receiving federal funds, including school athletics.

The Fight over Birth Control and Abortion The struggle for women's rights also focused on birth control and abortion. Many feminists believed that to control their lives, women must be able to control when, or if, they had children.

The development of the birth control pill was a major step in this direction. In 1960, the Food and Drug Administration approved the pill, and by 1965, five million women were using it. The pill had a tremendous impact on women's lives, and on society, by allowing women greater control over reproduction.

Some Americans disapproved of the pill. They favored abstinence as a form of birth control and argued that family-planning centers should not advise couples on other methods to avoid pregnancy. But in 1965, the Supreme Court ruled that married couples had a "right to privacy in marital relations" that included access to counseling on birth control, including use of the pill.

Several years later, the Supreme Court extended this right of privacy to the question of abortion. In 1973, the Court ruled in *Roe v. Wade* that the "right of privacy . . . is broad enough to encompass a woman's decision whether or not to terminate her pregnancy." Feminists considered this ruling a major advance in the struggle for women's civil rights, but the ruling has remained controversial. Opponents argue that life begins at conception and see abortion as murder. Supporters say women have the right to control their bodies and that abortion should remain legal.

46.3 Latinos Organize to Be Heard

In 1967, Rodolfo "Corky" Gonzales published a poem called "Yo Soy Joaquin" ("I Am Joaquin"). The poem describes the difficulty of retaining a Mexican identity while living in American society. Part of the poem reads,

> I am Joaquin . . .
> lost in a world of confusion,
> caught up in the whirl of a
> gringo society, confused by the rules,
> scorned by attitudes,
> suppressed by manipulation,
> and destroyed by modern society.
>
> —Rodolfo "Corky" Gonzales, "I Am Joaquin," 1967

For many Latinos, the poem struck a chord. They saw it as a cultural and political statement, and it became a rallying cry for Latino rights.

Gonzales was one of many Spanish-speaking Americans who cried out for equal rights in the 1960s. As the civil rights movement expanded around the country, Latinos also lent their voices to the struggle for equality.

Diverse People Speaking One Language Latinos, or Hispanics, are a diverse group. They include Mexican Americans, Cubans, Puerto Ricans, and people with origins in Central and South America. Some were born in the United States while others migrated here. Despite their different backgrounds, however, most share some similar cultural traits, including the Spanish language.

In the 1960s, Latinos also faced similar issues. For example, they often experienced employment discrimination. Many had low-wage jobs with few benefits. Many also struggled with language problems in school, where most classes were taught in English.

At the same time, the various Latino groups had their own distinct concerns and perspectives. In the mid-1960s, many Mexican Americans began to identify themselves as Chicanos. This term had originally been used as an insult, but young Mexican Americans embraced the name as an expression of pride in their culture.

Cuban Americans in the 1960s differed in many ways from Mexican Americans. Most lived in Florida, and they tended to be better educated and more affluent than other Latino groups. Most had fled their homeland after the Cuban Revolution and were recent arrivals in the United States.

Puerto Ricans were already U.S citizens when they came to the mainland because Puerto Rico is an American commonwealth, an unincorporated territory of the United States. However, they suffered some of the same injustices as other Spanish speakers. They sought better education and improved conditions in the cities where they lived. They also wanted to end discrimination.

Boycotting Grapes for Recognition One of the most notable campaigns for Latino rights in the 1960s was the farmworker struggle in California. Cesar Chavez, a farmworker born in Arizona, was one of the principal leaders of this effort to improve the lives of migrant workers.

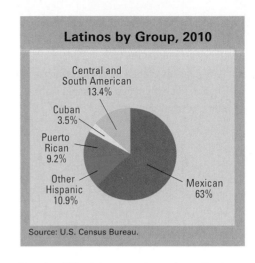

Latinos by Group, 2010

Central and South American 13.4%
Cuban 3.5%
Puerto Rican 9.2%
Other Hispanic 10.9%
Mexican 63%

Source: U.S. Census Bureau.

People of Mexican ancestry make up the largest share of the U.S. Latino population. In 2010, about two thirds of all Latinos in the country fell into this group. "Other Hispanic" refers mainly to people with roots in Spain or the Dominican Republic.

Cesar Chavez was a major figure in the struggle for farmworkers' rights. Having grown up in a family of migrant workers, he understood the hardships they faced. A skilled organizer and leader, Chavez headed the United Farm Workers for many years until his death in 1993.

Chavez helped found the United Farm Workers, along with Dolores Huerta and other labor activists. The union was made up mostly of Mexican American migrant workers. In 1965, the union—then known as the National Farm Workers Association—joined a strike against grape growers. The strike, or "La Huelga," lasted five years. During this time, Chavez organized a national boycott of table grapes that won widespread support. Finally, in 1970, grape growers agreed to a historic contract that granted most of the workers' demands, including union recognition and higher wages and benefits.

Like Martin Luther King Jr., Chavez relied on nonviolence in the struggle for equal rights. Among other tactics, he used hunger strikes as a political tool. He fasted several times over the years to draw attention to the plight of farmworkers and to pressure employers to improve working conditions.

La Raza: A People United In the late 1960s, young Chicanos also began to organize a political movement called La Raza Unida, or "The People United." They used the term *la raza,* meaning "the people" or "the race," to identify themselves and connect with their roots in ancient Mexico. They claimed this heritage, particularly their links to the Aztec people, as a common bond among Chicanos. La Raza Unida became a political party in 1970 and ran candidates in state and local elections across the Southwest.

A key issue for Chicano activists was **bilingual education,** or teaching in two languages. In 1968, President Johnson signed the Bilingual Education Act, legalizing instruction in languages other than English. The courts later ruled that schools must address the needs of non-English speakers, including teaching in students' native languages. Spanish-speaking students continued to face discrimination, though. In 1968 and 1969, Chicano students throughout the Southwest boycotted classes to protest poor education in their schools.

During this time, the Brown Berets also fought for Chicano rights. Founded in East Los Angeles, this group modeled itself on the Black Panthers. It worked to improve housing and employment and instill pride in Chicano culture.

As Mexican Americans fought for civil rights, so, too, did other groups of Latinos. Gradually, Cuban Americans, Puerto Ricans, and other Latinos began to find greater opportunity in American society.

46.4 American Indians Seek Justice

In 1968, 10 percent of the population of Minneapolis was American Indian. However, Indians made up 70 percent of the prisoners in the city's jails. Local activists believed that this imbalance reflected police harassment of Indians. To fight for their rights, Indian activists formed the **American Indian Movement (AIM)**. For much of 1968, they monitored police radios and responded to calls that involved Indians, often arriving at the scene before the police. As a result, AIM prevented the unfounded arrests of many Indians. According to AIM, the number of Indians in jail in Minneapolis decreased by 60 percent that year.

One People, Many Nations Indians come from many tribes, which they often call nations. In the late 1960s, some Indian activists believed that the Indian nations had much in common, including a shared identity as native peoples. And although they lived in different ways and different places—some on reservations, others dispersed throughout society—they shared many of the same problems.

Most American Indians lived in poverty. They suffered greater economic hardship than any other ethnic group in the country. Unemployment was 10 times higher than the national average and was especially high on reservations. The average annual family income was $1,000 less than for African Americans. Life expectancy was also much lower than the national average.

The federal government had tried to help American Indians, but with little success. In 1968, Congress passed the Indian Civil Rights Act. This law was designed to ensure equality for American Indians. It guaranteed Indians protection under the Constitution, while recognizing the authority of tribal laws. It had few concrete effects, though. In practice, American Indians still lacked equal rights and opportunity in American society, and many were losing patience.

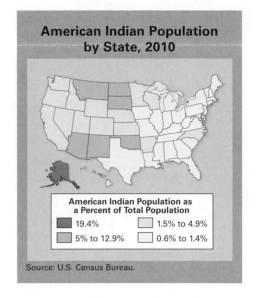

American Indian Population by State, 2010

American Indian Population as a Percent of Total Population

- 19.4%
- 5% to 12.9%
- 1.5% to 4.9%
- 0.6% to 1.4%

Source: U.S. Census Bureau.

Most American Indians, including Alaska Natives, live in the western United States. This map shows the percentage of population in each state for people who were American Indian or Alaska Native, either alone or in combination with one or more races. Note that Alaska Natives made up nearly 20 percent of that state's population in 2010.

The 2010 census reported 5.2 million American Indians and Alaska Natives in the United States, or 1.7% of the total population. This figure includes people who were either American Indian alone or who had partial American Indian ancestry. These native peoples belonged to many different tribes, or nations. This graph shows population figures for the 10 largest tribes in 2010.

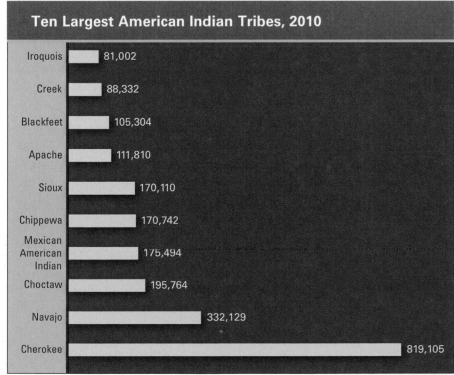

Ten Largest American Indian Tribes, 2010

Iroquois	81,002
Creek	88,332
Blackfeet	105,304
Apache	111,810
Sioux	170,110
Chippewa	170,742
Mexican American Indian	175,494
Choctaw	195,764
Navajo	332,129
Cherokee	819,105

Source: U.S. Census Bureau.

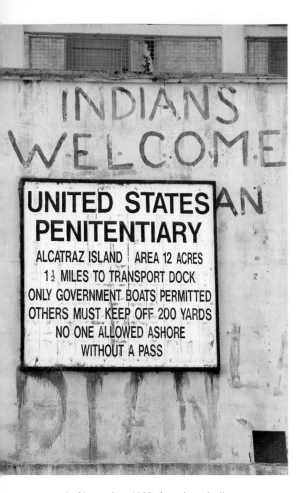

In November 1969, American Indians occupied Alcatraz Island in San Francisco Bay. They demanded Indian ownership of the island and funding for an Indian university and cultural center. The occupation lasted until June 10, 1971.

Radicals Make the Cause Known On November 20, 1969, eighty-nine Indians took over Alcatraz Island in San Francisco Bay, occupying the island's deserted prison. The group called themselves Indians of All Tribes. Their Alcatraz Proclamation declared, "We . . . reclaim the land known as Alcatraz Island in the name of all American Indians by right of discovery." In addition to the land, the group demanded that the government fund cultural and educational centers.

The U.S. government rejected the demands. But for the Indian rights movement, also called Red Power, the occupation was a success. As one participant said, "We got back our worth, our pride, our dignity, our humanity." The Indians occupied Alcatraz for more than a year and a half.

American Indians took other actions in their struggle for equality. In 1972, AIM led an event called the Trail of Broken Treaties. A caravan of protesters left the West Coast and traveled to Washington, D.C., to draw attention to Indian concerns. They brought a 20-point proposal to present to the government. The proposal focused on restoring federal recognition of Indian tribes and Indian control on reservations. It also sought protection for Indian cultures and religions.

When the caravan arrived in Washington, some protesters occupied the offices of the Bureau of Indian Affairs. After six days, they agreed to leave, on the condition that no one be prosecuted and that the federal government agree to respond to the 20 points. After studying the AIM document, however, the Nixon administration rejected its demands.

Tensions increased in February 1973, when AIM protesters occupied the town of Wounded Knee on the Pine Ridge Indian Reservation in South Dakota, the site of an 1890 massacre of American Indians. They called for changes in the governing of reservations. They also demanded that the U.S. government honor the Indian treaties it had signed over the years. After 70 days, the FBI stormed the site. Two Indians were killed, and one federal marshal was seriously injured.

In 1978, American Indian activists continued their actions with a five-month protest they called the Longest Walk. The walk started in San Francisco and ended in Washington, D.C. Its purpose was to bring attention to the many times American Indians had been forced off their land.

Courts and Legislation Bring Victories Although the actions of groups like AIM failed to bring dramatic improvements in the lives of most American Indians, they did draw attention to Indian rights and help promote some reforms. In 1975, Congress passed the Indian Self-Determination and Education Assistance Act. The law provided more federal money for Indian education. It gave Indians more control over reservations. It also placed more American Indians in jobs at the Bureau of Indian Affairs.

Indian tribes also won some legal victories. The government returned control of Blue Lake in New Mexico to the Taos Pueblo tribe, which considers the site sacred. Congress also passed the Alaska Native Land Claims Settlement Act in 1971. The law turned 40 million acres of land over to Alaska Natives. In 1980, Penobscot and Passamaquoddy Indians in Maine were awarded $81.5 million in exchange for giving up claims to their land. They used some of the money to buy back 300,000 acres. These victories raised hopes for a better life for American Indians.

46.5 Asian Americans Raise Their Voices

Asian Americans also joined the broad movement for civil rights in the 1960s. In fact, the farmworkers' strike against California grape growers was launched by Asian American activists. Larry Itliong, one of the leaders of a largely Filipino farmworkers' union, played a key role in this strike. He and other Filipino activists also helped form the United Farm Workers. They were part of a growing movement for Asian American rights.

The "Model Minority" Like Latinos, Asian Americans are a diverse group. They have ties by birth or culture to the countries of eastern and southern Asia. Asian groups with a longstanding history in the United States include Chinese, Japanese, Filipinos, and Koreans.

Starting in the 1870s, the U.S. government set limits on Asian immigration. The Immigration Act of 1965 removed those limits, and the number of Asian immigrants increased greatly. In recent decades, people from such countries as India, Vietnam, and Cambodia have added even more diversity to the Asian American population.

From the 1960s to the 1980s, many Asian Americans thrived in the United States. They were sometimes called the "model minority" because they were seen as working hard and succeeding without protesting or making demands. Some people even pointed to their progress as proof that ethnic differences were no barrier to success in American society. But these arguments, along with the "model minority" label, aroused resentment among other minorities, who sometimes felt that Asian Americans received favorable treatment.

The perceived success of Asian Americans was only partly true. Although data from 1980 show that many Asian Americans earned salaries higher than the national average, more than half lived in just three states: New York, California, and Hawaii. These states have a very high cost of living, a measure that includes the price of food, housing, and other essentials. People had to earn more to live in those states. Also, many Asian American households include several adult wage earners, a fact that was reflected in higher family incomes.

Furthermore, although many Asian Americans had attended college and entered professions, others had not. Many Asian immigrants had low-paying jobs, limited English language skills, and little education. Like other minorities, they faced discrimination because they were not white.

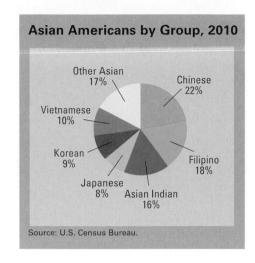

Asian Americans by Group, 2010

Other Asian 17%
Chinese 22%
Vietnamese 10%
Korean 9%
Japanese 8%
Asian Indian 16%
Filipino 18%

Source: U.S. Census Bureau.

Chinese Americans have traditionally been the largest Asian group in the United States. As this graph shows, that was still the case in 2010. Since the 1960s, however, immigrants from other parts of Asia have been arriving in increasing numbers. As a result, Asian Indians, Vietnamese, and others are making up a growing share of the Asian American population.

Although Asian Americans live throughout the United States, many are concentrated in traditional ethnic neighborhoods. New York City's Chinatown, pictured here, is the largest Chinese enclave in the Western Hemisphere. In recent years, it has also become home to other Asian groups, including Burmese, Filipinos, and Vietnamese.

College Students Unite to Be Heard Asian American students began to call for equal rights in the 1960s. On some college campuses, student activists organized a political movement. Their stated aim was to end racial oppression "through the power of a consolidated yellow people." Yellow Power became their slogan.

In 1968 and 1969, Asian American students at San Francisco State University and the University of California at Berkeley helped organize student strikes. They wanted more minority participation in university affairs. They also called for academic programs that focused on ethnic and racial issues. At the time, minority perspectives played little role in university education.

Their efforts succeeded. In 1969, San Francisco State started the country's first school of ethnic studies. Between 1968 and 1973, many other colleges and universities also set up Asian American studies programs.

These new programs had a great impact on students. Helen Zia, a Chinese American, recalled, "In college, I learned that I was an Asian American. I learned that I didn't have to call myself Oriental like a rug. It was like a light bulb going off." What Zia and many others learned about their heritage gave them a new understanding of their identity and rights in American society.

Fighting for Internment Reparations One key battle for Asian American rights focused on Japanese American internment during World War II. Executive Order 9066 had forced many into internment camps, and the Supreme Court's 1944 ruling in *Korematsu v. United States* had upheld the order. Thirty years later, many people began to demand reparations for this historic injustice.

In the 1970s, a younger generation of Japanese Americans inspired by the Black Power movement spoke out against the discrimination their families had suffered. In 1978, a group in Seattle held the first Day of Remembrance. They shared family stories and discussed the hardships of internment. One organizer described the event as a "way to reclaim our past and make it our own." The Day of Remembrance is now observed in other cities, too.

Meanwhile, the **Japanese American Citizens League (JACL)**, which was formed in 1929 to defend the rights of Japanese Americans, sought legal remedy. In 1978, it began to pursue compensation for the suffering in the internment camps. In 1988, Congress finally apologized for the internment. It also authorized payment of $20,000 to each survivor. Although the sum was relatively small compared to individual losses, this official response helped to make up for a historic wrong.

In 1978, Japanese Americans began seeking reparations for their internment during World War II. Three key activists in this effort were Fred Korematsu, Minoru Yasui, and Gordon Hirabayashi (shown here, left to right). Each had fought the internment policy in the courts during the 1940s. In 1988, the government apologized and offered $20,000 to each survivor.

46.6 More Groups Seek Civil Rights

In 1962, the University of California at Berkeley reluctantly admitted Ed Roberts as a student. Roberts had a severe **disability,** an impairment that limited his daily activities. Polio had left him paralyzed, and he needed a respirator to breathe. California's vocational rehabilitation agency had told Roberts that he would be too disabled to work. But Roberts surprised everyone. He fulfilled his degree requirements and graduated from UC Berkeley.

As a disability-rights activist, Roberts changed the way many Americans viewed people with disabilities. He helped disabled people gain the right to participate in life at the university. His achievements encouraged other disability activists around the country.

Many disabled Americans were inspired by the African American civil rights movement. So, too, were other groups, including gay Americans and older Americans. Starting in the 1960s, these groups made their own claims for equal rights.

In the 1970s, disability-rights activists began to demand equal rights and opportunity. Protesters blocked doorways and demonstrated at the Capitol building. In 1990, the Americans with Disabilities Act brought major reforms. Disabled Americans continue to hold marches and rallies to advocate civil rights for disabled people.

Disabled Americans Demand Equal Access to Opportunities Disabilities can be both physical and mental. Physical disabilities include blindness, deafness, and impaired movement. Mental disabilities include illnesses like bipolar disorder. According to the 2000 census, nearly 20 percent of Americans over the age of five have some type of disability. But this large population has often been subject to discrimination.

The first groups of disabled Americans to fight for their rights were deaf and blind people. Decades before the civil rights movement, they set up organizations to provide education and other services to those who needed them. They also asserted that blind and deaf people had a right to use their own languages: braille and American Sign Language.

In the early 1970s, after graduating from UC Berkeley, Ed Roberts started a program to make it easier for physically disabled students to attend the university. He and fellow activists pressed the school to improve **accessibility** on campus, making it easier for the physically disabled to enter university facilities. Ramps and curb cuts, for example, made the campus more accessible to people in wheelchairs.

In 1973, Congress passed the Rehabilitation Act, which some supporters compared to the 1964 Civil Rights Act. This law stated,

> No otherwise qualified individual with a disability . . . shall, solely by reason of his or her disability, be excluded from the participation in, be denied the benefits of, or be subjected to discrimination under any program or activity receiving Federal financial assistance.
>
> —Section 504, Rehabilitation Act of 1973

The law granted disabled people the same access to federally funded programs as other Americans. It took four years, however, for government officials to decide how to enforce the law. They finally did so in 1977 after protesters, many in wheelchairs, took over the offices of the Department of Health, Education, and Welfare in Washington, D.C.

Equal access applied to children, too. In 1975, Congress passed the Education for All Handicapped Children Act. This law set a new standard for educating disabled children. It said that these students must be in "the least restrictive environment possible." Wherever possible, students with disabilities were to be **mainstreamed,** or included in classrooms with nondisabled students.

The most important civil rights victory for disabled Americans came years later. In 1990, Congress passed the **Americans with Disabilities Act (ADA).** The ADA called for better public access for people with disabilities. Changes included braille signs on elevators and accessible public transportation. The ADA has also improved education for disabled children. Equal access to employment remains a problem, however. About 30 percent of people with disabilities are unemployed.

Every year, activists hold gay pride marches to mark the anniversary of the Stonewall riots of 1969. Stonewall is considered the start of the gay rights movement. The rainbow flag is a symbol of gay and lesbian community pride.

Gay Americans Stand Up for Their Rights Gay men and lesbians also began to demand equal rights in the 1960s. At the time, the police often harassed gay men and lesbians in public places. An employee could be fired for being gay or even for being perceived as gay. Many gays and lesbians felt they had to hide their sexual orientation to avoid discrimination.

A gay rights movement had begun to emerge in the late 1950s and early 1960s. By the late 1960s, gay rights activists in Philadelphia were holding an annual Fourth of July protest. Neatly dressed gays and lesbians gathered at Independence Hall, where the Constitution was signed. They pointed out to visitors that gay Americans did not enjoy many of the rights that most Americans took for granted.

It was not until the **Stonewall riots,** however, that the gay pride movement became highly visible. On June 27, 1969, New York City police raided the Stonewall Inn, a gay bar in the neighborhood of Greenwich Village. New York outlawed homosexuality at the time, and police raids were common. That night, however, the customers at the Stonewall fought back. Riots broke out and lasted for hours. The Stonewall riots marked the beginning of the gay rights movement. Since then, the anniversary of Stonewall has prompted annual gay pride events in cities around the world.

After Stonewall, more Americans began to join the gay rights movement. In March 1973, a group of parents with gay sons and daughters began meeting in New York. By 1980, the group—now known as Parents and Friends of Lesbians and Gays, or PFLAG—had members around the country.

Another key event in the history of gay rights occurred in 1977, when Harvey Milk was elected to the board of supervisors in San Francisco. Milk was the first openly gay candidate to win office in a major American city. Eleven months later, however, Milk was assassinated by a former colleague.

Older Americans Promote Productive Aging Older Americans also joined the civil rights struggle. In 1972, Maggie Kuhn and some fellow retirees in Philadelphia formed the Gray Panthers. This group spoke out against unfair treatment of older Americans. The Gray Panthers called this treatment **ageism,** or discrimination against people on the basis of age.

Other groups had formed earlier to advocate for older Americans. The largest was the American Association of Retired Persons, founded by Ethel Percy Andrus in 1958. Andrus formed AARP to help retirees get health insurance. At the time, many older Americans had no health coverage, either because it was too expensive or because private insurance companies would not insure them. They were considered too much of a risk because of their age and potential health problems.

AARP lobbied for government health insurance. In 1965, Congress responded by establishing Medicare. This program provided hospital insurance for people ages 65 and over. It also helped pay prescription drug costs and other medical expenses for seniors.

Older workers also complained about discrimination in the workplace. To remedy this problem, Congress passed the Age Discrimination in Employment Act of 1967. This law made it illegal for employers to use age as a factor in hiring or promotion. In 1978, the Gray Panthers helped persuade Congress to push back the required retirement age from 65 to 70. Seniors could now work longer and continue to enjoy the benefits of employment.

The Gray Panthers fought age-based discrimination. Most of the Panthers, like cofounder Maggie Kuhn (above), were older Americans, but they believed that many young people suffered from discrimination, too.

Summary

The civil rights movement inspired many Americans to stand up for their rights. During the 1960s and 1970s, various groups sought equal treatment under the law and in society.

Women The National Organization for Women (NOW) and other feminist groups worked for women's rights. They wanted reforms to ensure greater equality and opportunity for women.

Latinos Various groups of Latinos struggled for their rights and identity in American society. The United Farm Workers (UFW) organized migrant farmworkers and helped increase their wages and benefits. The 1968 Bilingual Education Act required public schools to provide bilingual instruction.

American Indians The American Indian Movement (AIM) protested unfair treatment of American Indians. By the mid-1970s, some tribes had won payment for lost lands.

Asian Americans Asian American students asked for university programs in ethnic studies. The Japanese Americans Citizens League (JACL) sought compensation for internment during World War II.

Other groups Disabled Americans fought for equal access and won passage of the Americans with Disabilities Act. After the Stonewall riots, gay Americans gained greater visibility in their fight for equal rights. Older Americans countered ageism by working through such groups as the Gray Panthers.

Chapter 47

The Age of Camelot

Was John F. Kennedy a great president?

47.1 Introduction

In 1961, when John F. Kennedy, the youngest man elected to the presidency, replaced Dwight Eisenhower, one of the oldest presidents, the atmosphere in the White House changed. The handsome, charming young president and his graceful wife, Jacqueline, made the house inviting and exciting to visit. On some evenings, famous musicians or opera singers performed. On others, noted actors read scenes from plays or ballet dancers performed classic works. These social events made the White House a showcase for arts and culture.

At the time of Kennedy's inauguration, a new musical called *Camelot* had recently begun its long run on Broadway. Its main character is the legendary King Arthur, who ruled Camelot, an enchanted kingdom. As the play unfolds, Arthur founds an order of knights called the Knights of the Round Table. Dedicated to doing noble deeds, the order attracts the best and bravest knights in the realm.

As Kennedy began his administration, fans of the ideals that were portrayed in *Camelot* hoped Kennedy would prove to be an equally gifted leader. Sadly, Kennedy's life ended before most people could decide whether he had lived up to expectations. In an interview after his death, Jacqueline Kennedy recalled the words of her husband's favorite song from the musical, written by Alan Jay Lerner. In that song, Lerner writes about a brief, yet dignified moment in time.

Many Americans viewed Kennedy's time in office as just such a moment. Others felt less sure that the young president had behaved with true greatness. In this chapter, you will learn how such differing opinions developed.

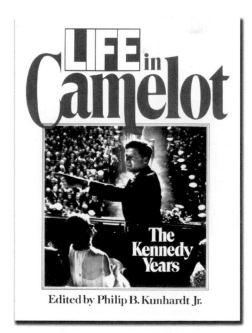

As the cover of this *Life* magazine suggests, many Americans associated the White House during the Kennedy years with the mythical kingdom of Camelot. The Broadway musical *Camelot* premiered in New York City just after Kennedy was elected president. It became an overnight hit when the public learned that the cast album was one of President Kennedy's favorite records.

During the first Kennedy-Nixon debate, Richard Nixon looked tired and uncomfortable, while Kennedy looked relaxed and confident. The debate exposed millions of voters to Kennedy's charisma. Afterward, his approval rating shot up in the opinion polls.

47.2 President Kennedy's Domestic Record

On a chilly day in Washington, D.C., with fresh snow at their feet, a large crowd gathered in front of the Capitol to watch John F. Kennedy be sworn in as the 35th U.S. president. The new leader then laid out his vision of the road ahead:

> Let the word go forth from this time and place . . . that the torch has been passed to a new generation of Americans—born in this century, tempered by war, disciplined by a hard and bitter peace . . . Let every nation know, whether it wishes us well or ill, that we shall pay any price, bear any burden, meet any hardship, support any friend, oppose any foe, in order to assure the survival and the success of liberty.
>
> —John F. Kennedy, inaugural address, January 20, 1961

The young president's dedication to the ideal of liberty touched the hearts and minds of many Americans. He closed with an appeal to his listeners' sense of idealism, urging them to make a personal commitment to public service. "And so, my fellow Americans," he said in words that would often be repeated, "ask not what your country can do for you—ask what you can do for your country."

Kennedy Takes Office with a Narrow Election Victory Kennedy's inaugural address and the dazzling festivities and balls that followed later that evening set the tone of elegance and youthful vigor that became known as the "Kennedy style." Even before Kennedy had won the race for president, people had started to talk about his charisma—a combination of charm and personal magnetism that caused others to like and support him. At campaign stops, young people had cheered him as if he were a movie star. One senator observed that Kennedy combined the "best qualities of Elvis Presley and Franklin D. Roosevelt."

During the campaign, Kennedy and his opponent, Richard Nixon, had expressed similar views on many issues. Both had vowed to get a sluggish economy moving again and to halt the spread of communism. Kennedy, however, had attacked the Eisenhower-Nixon administration for allowing a "missile gap" to open up between the United States and the Soviet Union. Unless something was done to restore American military superiority, he warned, "the periphery [edges] of the Free World will slowly be nibbled away."

The most obvious difference between the two candidates was their personal style. This contrast became clear on September 26, 1960, when they met in the first live, televised presidential debate in history. More than 70 million viewers tuned in, while others listened on the radio. For many Americans, this was their first close look at the candidates—especially Kennedy, who was less known.

Nixon, weakened by a serious knee injury and a bout of the flu, appeared nervous and uneasy. His face was pale, all the more so because he had refused to wear any stage makeup. Kennedy, in contrast, appeared relaxed and confident. Most of the people who watched the debate on television thought Kennedy had won. But those who listened on the radio thought Nixon was the winner.

On election day, Kennedy barely squeaked by Nixon in the closest election since 1888. As a result, Kennedy took office without a clear electoral mandate. This lack of a strong go-ahead from voters would put the new president at a severe disadvantage in his dealings with Congress.

An Administration of "the Best and the Brightest" Like the legendary King Arthur, Kennedy set out to surround himself with "the best and the brightest" advisers he could find. Some, like National Security Adviser McGeorge Bundy, had attended elite universities. Others, such as Secretary of Defense and former president of Ford Motor Company Robert McNamara, were top executives. To the surprise of many people, Kennedy selected his brother Robert, only 35 years old, to be attorney general. When people grumbled that Robert was too young for this position, the president joked, "I see nothing wrong with giving Robert some legal experience . . . before he goes out to practice law."

Kennedy's inaugural call to service attracted many talented young people to Washington. Those who joined his administration found public service to be exciting, even glamorous. Like their boss, they worked hard and played hard. Fueled with fresh idealism, they hoped to change the world.

Kennedy's "New Frontier" Challenges the Nation While running for president, Kennedy had already begun to lay out his vision for changing the world. In his speech accepting the Democratic presidential nomination, he had told Americans,

> We stand today on the edge of a New Frontier—the frontier of the 1960s—a frontier of unknown opportunities and perils—a frontier of unfulfilled hopes and threats . . . Beyond that frontier are the uncharted areas of science and space, unsolved problems of peace and war, unconquered pockets of ignorance and prejudice, unanswered questions of poverty and surplus.
>
> —John F. Kennedy, July 15, 1960

Once in office, Kennedy worked to translate his **New Frontier** rhetoric into a list of concrete goals. To expand opportunity, he called for an increase in aid to education, new programs to end poverty, and a tax cut to stimulate economic growth. To promote equality, he sought to raise the minimum wage, fund medical care for the elderly, and make cities more livable. To guarantee civil rights, he hoped to enact legislation banning racial discrimination. To protect liberty and democracy, he called for a large increase in defense spending.

Kennedy had trouble getting his **legislative agenda,** or list of programs to enact, through Congress, even though Democrats held a majority of seats. He did succeed in raising the minimum wage and enacting some urban development programs. However, a coalition of conservative southern Democrats and Republicans, who voted to block change, stalled much of Kennedy's agenda. After several failures, Kennedy gave up on some of his programs. "There is no sense raising hell," he observed, "and then not being successful."

Reviving the Economy Kennedy had mixed success in his effort to, as he put it, "get the economy moving again." When he took office, the nation was in a mild recession. Kennedy laid out a two-part approach to promoting economic recovery. The first part of his plan was to increase spending on defense. By this time, Kennedy knew that the "missile gap" he had referred to in his campaign was not real. In fact, the United States had far more weaponry than the Soviet Union had.

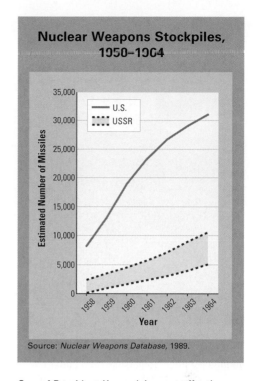

Nuclear Weapons Stockpiles, 1950–1964

Source: *Nuclear Weapons Database*, 1989.

One of President Kennedy's most effective campaign issues was what he called the "missile gap." This was a supposed difference in the number of nuclear missiles the United States and the Soviet Union held in their defense arsenals. In actuality, the United States was ahead of, not behind, the USSR in missile strength.

To the Kennedy children, Caroline and her younger brother, John (seen here under his father's desk), the White House was not the seat of government but, rather, their home. The young couple and their two playful children made the family media favorites.

On August 28, 1963, after the massive March on Washington, Kennedy invited civil rights leaders to meet with him at the White House. Martin Luther King Jr. and Roy Wilkins were among the key civil rights leaders present.

Nonetheless, Kennedy convinced Congress to boost the defense budget by nearly 20 percent in 1961. Over the next few years, the government pumped billions of dollars into the economy while increasing the nation's stockpile of missiles and other high-tech weapons, such as nuclear submarines.

The second part of Kennedy's plan was to pass a major tax cut, which he hoped would put more money in people's pockets and stimulate economic growth. Here he was less successful. Conservatives in Congress opposed any tax cut that would lead to an unbalanced federal budget. Even some liberal Democrats opposed cutting taxes when so many of the nation's needs were still unmet. As the liberal economist John Kenneth Galbraith observed,

"I am not quite sure I see what the advantage is in having a few more dollars to spend if the air is too dirty to breathe, the water too polluted to drink, the streets are filthy, and the schools so bad that the young, perhaps wisely, stay away."
—in James T. Patterson, *America in the Twentieth Century,* 1976

Even without the tax cuts, the recession did end. By the close of 1961, the economy had begun a period of growth that would last throughout the decade.

A Cautious Approach to Civil Rights On civil rights legislation, Kennedy had even less success with Congress. While campaigning, Kennedy had called for an end to racial discrimination. When authorities in Atlanta jailed Martin Luther King Jr., Kennedy had responded by asking his brother Robert to arrange King's release. Widely reported in the press, news of the brothers' work on King's behalf had helped Kennedy win the African American vote.

Once in office, however, Kennedy became more cautious. Fearing that bold action on civil rights would split the Democratic Party between the North and South, he ordered his administration to vigorously enforce existing civil rights laws. But for his first two years in office, Kennedy did not propose new laws.

In the spring of 1963, televised violence against peaceful protesters in Birmingham, Alabama, horrified much of the nation. Sickened by what he saw, President Kennedy addressed the nation on the issue of civil rights:

> We are confronted primarily with a moral issue. It is as old as the scriptures and is as clear as the American Constitution. The heart of the question is whether all Americans are to be afforded equal rights and equal opportunities, whether we are going to treat our fellow Americans as we want to be treated. If an American, because his skin is dark, cannot eat lunch in a restaurant open to the public, if he cannot send his children to the best public school available, if he cannot vote for the public officials who will represent him, if, in short, he cannot enjoy the full and free life which all of us want, then who among us would . . . be content with the counsels of patience and delay?

A week later, the president submitted a broad civil rights bill to Congress. Once again, however, a coalition of Republican and conservative southern Democratic lawmakers blocked Kennedy's proposed legislation.

Kennedy Proposes Landing a Man on the Moon Kennedy's most exciting New Frontier challenge—space exploration—developed out of a Cold War embarrassment. In 1957, the Soviet Union had surprised the world by launching the first artificial satellite into orbit around Earth. Called *Sputnik*, or "Little Traveler" in Russian, the unmanned satellite traveled at 18,000 miles per hour. A month later, the Russians launched *Sputnik II* with a dog onboard.

In contrast, delays and failed launches had plagued American efforts to send rockets into space. Around the world, newspapers ridiculed U.S. rockets as "flopniks" and "kaputniks." When asked what Americans would find if they ever reached the moon, nuclear physicist Edward Teller quipped, "Russians."

In 1958, President Eisenhower had responded to the Soviet challenge by creating the **National Aeronautics and Space Administration (NASA)**. By the time Kennedy took office, NASA had launched its first communication and weather satellites into space. But on April 12, 1961, the Soviet Union stunned the world again by sending the first human, astronaut Yuri Gagarin, into space. Six weeks later, Kennedy made a dramatic announcement:

> I believe that this nation should commit itself to . . . landing a man on the moon and returning him safely to the earth. No single space project in this period will be more impressive to mankind, or more important for the long-range exploration of space; and none will be so difficult or expensive to accomplish.
>
> —Speech to a Joint Session of Congress, May 25, 1961

NASA moved rapidly to meet the challenge. In 1961, astronaut Alan Shepard made a short spaceflight. A year later, John Glenn was the first American to orbit Earth. On July 20, 1969, just eight years after Kennedy had set the goal of a moon landing, Neil Armstrong, Michael Collins, and Edwin "Buzz" Aldrin Jr. reached the moon as part of the Apollo space program. The world watched in awe as Armstrong stepped onto the moon's surface. "That's one small step for a man," he said as he stepped onto the lunar soil, "one giant leap for mankind."

The spaceflight from Florida's Cape Kennedy Space Center to the moon took about 102 hours and 45 minutes. After stepping onto the lunar surface on July 20, 1969, Neil Armstrong and Edwin "Buzz" Aldrin Jr. erected a U.S. flag. The two astronauts also collected soil and rock samples and left behind scientific instruments.

47.3 President Kennedy's Record in Foreign Affairs

As president, Kennedy's greatest triumphs—but also his most disastrous mistakes—were in foreign affairs. U.S. relations with Cuba proved to be especially troublesome for the president. A crisis over Soviet missile sites in Cuba brought the United States and the Soviet Union to the brink of nuclear war.

Fidel Castro Establishes a Communist Regime in Cuba In 1959, communist revolutionaries, led by Fidel Castro, had ousted Cuban dictator Fulgencio Batista. As a result, the United States suddenly found that it had a communist **regime,** or government, for a neighbor, just 90 miles off the Florida coast.

Once in power, Castro established strong ties with the Soviet Union. The USSR sent advisers, weapons, and financial aid to Cuba. With this Soviet help, Castro transformed Cuba into a communist country with a **planned economy**. Government planners began to make almost all economic decisions. The government took control of U.S. oil refineries and farms on the island and seized private businesses and properties from wealthy Cubans.

Reluctant to live under a communist regime, many Cubans fled the island. Most of these **exiles,** or people who live outside their home country, settled in southern Florida. Shortly after taking office, Kennedy learned that the CIA had begun training some of these Cuban exiles in Florida and Guatemala as guerrilla fighters. The clandestine mission of these exiles was to return to Cuba and lead a popular uprising that would topple Castro and his regime.

The Bay of Pigs Fiasco Fails to Dislodge Castro The CIA officials who briefed Kennedy on the invasion plan assured the new president that the invasion would inspire Cubans to rise up and rebel against Castro. CIA director Allen Dulles told Kennedy that if he wanted to stop Castro's growing influence in Latin America, the time to act was "now or never." Eager to show he was a strong Cold War president, Kennedy allowed the plan to move forward.

On April 17, 1961, a small army of Cuban exiles sailed into the Bay of Pigs in southern Cuba. The landing was a disaster. CIA trainers had told the exiles they would come ashore on an empty beach, but their boats ran aground on a coral reef. Once the exiles reached land, Cuban troops quickly killed or captured them. Meanwhile, the expected uprising never took place. A few officials tried to persuade Kennedy to send U.S. warplanes to back up the exiles, but Kennedy did not want to involve the United States further in this poorly executed fiasco.

After the **Bay of Pigs invasion,** people throughout Latin America criticized Kennedy for interfering in another country's affairs. Shouldering the blame, Kennedy remarked, "Victory has a thousand fathers, but defeat is an orphan."

Escalating Cold War Tensions in Berlin In June 1961, not long after the Bay of Pigs disaster, Kennedy and Soviet leader Nikita Khrushchev held a **summit meeting** in Vienna, Austria. Heads of state hold such meetings to discuss important topics. In Vienna, one of the topics discussed was the future of Berlin.

Since the end of World War II, Berlin had been a divided city. East Berlin served as the capital of communist East Germany. West Berlin, although surrounded by East Germany, remained under the control of the wartime Allies.

In 1963, Cuban leader Fidel Castro visited the Soviet Union to strengthen ties with his communist ally. He is seen here with Soviet leader Nikita Khrushchev, who once told Western diplomats, "Whether you like it or not, history is on our side. We will bury you." Khrushchev provided aid and guidance to Castro in hopes of helping make that boast come true.

Havana

Bay of Pigs

CUBA

✳ Battle site

In 1963, a huge crowd in West Berlin turned out to hear Kennedy speak at the Berlin Wall. Before the wall's construction, 2.5 million East Germans had escaped into West Germany. Their loss put severe strains on the East German economy and embarrassed the Soviets by showing just how unpopular communism was.

In time, the border between Eastern and Western Europe was closed everywhere except in Berlin. As a result, Berlin became the only escape route for people trapped behind the Iron Curtain. Hundreds of thousands of East Germans took advantage of this opening to flee their country. By 1961, approximately 25,000 East German refugees were crossing into West Berlin each day. At that rate, East Germany would soon lose much of its workforce.

During the Vienna summit, Khrushchev warned Kennedy that he would not allow the flow of refugees into West Berlin to continue. Kennedy responded that he was prepared to defend West Berlin, even at the risk of war. At this point, Khrushchev decided that the only option left to East Germany was to wall itself off from West Berlin. On August 13, 1961, East German workers began building a barbed wire fence between East and West Berlin. Later, the government replaced the fence with tall concrete walls. The **Berlin Wall** made it all but impossible for East Germans to escape to freedom in West Berlin. The United States and other Western European nations reacted with outrage to the building of the Berlin Wall. To show American support for the people of West Berlin, Kennedy spoke in front of the wall:

> There are many people in the world who really don't understand, or say they don't, what is the great issue between the free world and the Communist world. Let them come to Berlin. There are some who say that communism is the wave of the future. Let them come to Berlin . . . Freedom has many difficulties and democracy is not perfect, but we have never had to put a wall up to keep our people in . . . All free men, wherever they may live, are citizens of Berlin. And, therefore, as a free man, I take pride in the words "Ich bin ein Berliner."
>
> —John F. Kennedy, June 26, 1963

Nonetheless, Kennedy was not willing to risk war to tear down the wall. Privately, he said, "A wall is a hell of a lot better than a war."

The Cuban Missile Crisis: 13 Days on the Brink of Nuclear War A little more than a year after the Bay of Pigs fiasco, President Kennedy again focused his attention on Cuba. In October 1962, a U-2 spy plane flying over Cuba discovered that the Soviet Union was building missile-launching sites on the island. From these sites, missiles carrying nuclear warheads could easily reach most major cities in the United States.

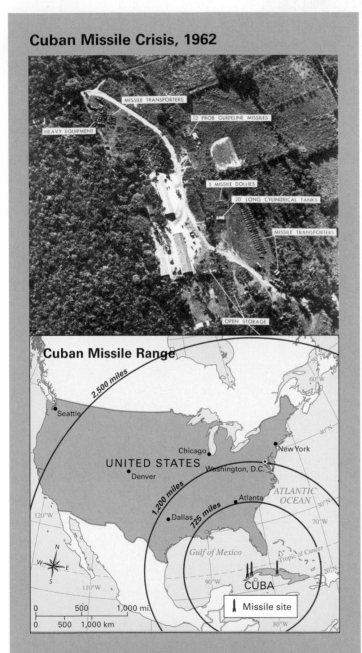

Cuban Missile Crisis, 1962

A U-2 spy plane took this aerial photograph of Cuba, revealing storage areas and launchpads for Soviet nuclear weapons. The information revealed in photographs like this one helped trigger the Cuban missile crisis. The map shows the range of Soviet missiles that could be fired from bases in Cuba. Only states in the far western United States were at a safe distance.

To discuss ways to respond to this new threat, Kennedy brought together a group of his 12 most trusted advisers. Called the Executive Committee for National Security (later known as ExCom), its members all agreed that the United States must halt construction of the Soviet missile sites. Failure to remove this threat would endanger American cities. It would also make the United States look weak to its European allies and to anti-Castro forces in Latin America.

The ExCom did not, however, agree on how to deal with the **Cuban missile crisis**. Some advisers urged the president to bomb the missile sites before they could be completed. Others suggested blockading Cuban ports to prevent Soviet ships from bringing missiles to the island. They called the blockade a "quarantine," because under international law, establishing a naval blockade is an act of war. Kennedy chose the quarantine plan.

On October 22, Kennedy announced to the nation the discovery of the missile sites and his decision to quarantine the island. He warned that the United States would view any nuclear missile launched from Cuba as an attack on the United States by the Soviet Union. He also demanded that the Soviets remove all offensive weapons from Cuba.

For the next two days, Soviet ships continued to move toward Cuba. Fearing that the nation could be on the brink of nuclear war, Kennedy put the U.S. military on high alert. "I guess this is the week I earn my salary," he nervously joked. Then, on October 24, Khrushchev ordered Soviet ships approaching Cuba to slow down or turn around. With great relief, Secretary of State Dean Rusk commented, "We're eyeball to eyeball, and I think the other fellow just blinked."

A few days later, Khrushchev sent a note to Kennedy agreeing to remove Soviet missiles from Cuba. In exchange, he demanded that Kennedy end the Cuban blockade and promise not to invade Cuba. The next day, he sent a second note. In it, he proposed removing the Cuban missiles in exchange for the United States removing missiles it had placed in Turkey, which bordered the USSR.

Kennedy had already decided to remove the U.S. missiles from Turkey, because they were outdated. However, he did not want Khrushchev to think he was bowing to

Soviet pressure. The ExCom advised him to pretend he did not receive the second note. Publicly, Kennedy accepted the first deal. Privately, he sent Robert Kennedy to the Soviet embassy to agree to the second deal as well. On October 28, Khrushchev agreed to remove all Soviet missiles from Cuba. About three months later, the United States removed its missiles from Turkey.

Easing Cold War Tensions The Cuban missile crisis led Kennedy and his advisers to rethink the doctrine of "massive retaliation" adopted during the Eisenhower years. Instead, Kennedy began to talk about the need for a flexible response to local Cold War conflicts. When communists seemed on the verge of taking over Vietnam, a small country in Southeast Asia, the president tested this new approach. He sent money and military advisers to Vietnam to build noncommunist forces in the country. By the end of 1962, more than 9,000 American military advisers were helping defend Vietnam from communism.

The missile crisis also left Kennedy and Khrushchev frightened by how close they had come to nuclear war. As a result, both men began looking for ways to ease tensions between the superpowers. As a first step, the two leaders established a **hotline** between them. This line of communication would be kept open at all times so they could contact each other instantly during a crisis. The hotline still exists today and has been tested once an hour since 1963.

Later the same year, the superpowers took another step in establishing more amicable relations. Along with Great Britain, they signed a **Test Ban Treaty**. This agreement banned nuclear testing in the atmosphere, while allowing underground nuclear weapons tests to continue. By signing, the United States and Soviet Union showed that they could cooperate on important issues.

Aiding Development in Foreign Countries President Kennedy was deeply concerned about the spread of communism to **developing countries**. Such countries are poorer and less industrialized than the wealthy **developed countries** of North America, Western Europe, and parts of Asia. In a campaign speech in San Francisco, Kennedy spoke about his vision for helping the developing world. "There is not enough money in all America to relieve the misery of the underdeveloped world in a giant . . . soup kitchen," he said. "But there is enough know-how . . . to help those nations help themselves."

To spread this "know-how," Kennedy issued an executive order creating the **Peace Corps**. This new government agency sent thousands of men and women to developing nations to support local communities in such areas as education, farming, and health care. Before moving overseas, Peace Corps volunteers learned languages and skills they could use to build and help run schools and health clinics, teach farming methods, or plant crops.

Kennedy also launched an aid program for Latin America, called the Alliance for Progress. Its goal was to provide economic and technical aid to Latin American nations while encouraging democratic reforms. The program had little impact, however. Wealthy elites in Latin American nations resisted reform efforts. In time, most Alliance for Progress funds ended up in the pockets of anticommunist dictators for use in fighting communist rebels or others who opposed their rule.

President Kennedy often conferred with his younger brother, Attorney General Robert "Bobby" Kennedy. In an effort to reduce tensions during the Cuban missile crisis, Bobby sometimes conferred secretly with Soviet diplomats.

Like the volunteer shown in this commemorative stamp, Peace Corps workers have sought to improve life for the poor in developing countries for more than 40 years. Volunteers are of all ages and from a variety of backgrounds. Most share a strong commitment to the ideal of helping to create a free and peaceful world.

47.4 The Tragic and Controversial End to Camelot

In late November 1963, President Kennedy and the first lady traveled to Texas. Kennedy wanted to build support there for his reelection campaign, since the next presidential election was a year away. Just before noon on November 22, the Kennedys joined Texas governor John Connally and his wife in a motorcade that drove through downtown Dallas. It was a sunny day, and people eager to see the presidential couple crowded the streets. Watching the cheering crowd, Mrs. Connally leaned over and told the president, "You can't say that Dallas isn't friendly to you today." Moments later, gunshots rang out.

A National Tragedy Unfolds in Dallas The motorcade took the president's car past the Texas School Book Depository. Lee Harvey Oswald, a worker in the building, stood waiting on its sixth floor. As the cars came within range, Oswald fired three shots. One bullet missed the motorcade. Two bullets hit Kennedy in the neck and head. One of those bullets also struck Governor Connally. The driver rushed both men to the hospital, and Connally survived. Doctors frantically worked to revive Kennedy, but at 1:00 p.m., they declared him dead.

Two hours after the shooting, Vice President Lyndon B. Johnson met Jacqueline Kennedy and the president's coffin at the Dallas airport. Together they would return to Washington. Before the plane took flight, however, a local Texas judge swore Johnson in as the nation's 36th president. Jacqueline Kennedy stood beside Johnson as he took the oath of office.

Dallas police quickly captured Oswald and charged him with the president's murder. Authorities knew Oswald strongly supported Fidel Castro and the Cuban revolution and had lived in the Soviet Union for three years. However, before they could learn anything about his motives for assassinating Kennedy, Oswald too was killed. This second murder occurred as police moved the prisoner from one jail to another, more secure one. With scores of newspaper and television reporters looking on, a local nightclub owner named Jack Ruby jumped out of the crowd and fired at Oswald. Television viewers watched in horror as live news cameras beamed Oswald's murder into their homes.

On November 24, a horse-drawn carriage transported Kennedy's body from the White House to the Capitol building. There, hundreds of thousands of people walked past his casket to pay their final respects. The following day, as many as a million people lined the streets of Washington as the funeral procession carried the slain president to Arlington National Cemetery. There, Kennedy's brothers and wife lit an "eternal" gas flame on his grave.

Across the nation and around the world, people mourned Kennedy's death. To this day, most Americans old enough to remember it can recall exactly where they were when they heard the news of Kennedy's assassination. A poll taken at the time reported that almost two thirds of Americans felt the death of the president as "the loss of someone very close and dear."

Questions and Conspiracy Theories Surround the Assassination
Kennedy's assassination raised many unanswered questions: Had Oswald acted alone, or was he part of a larger conspiracy to murder the president? If he did not act alone, with whom was he working? And why did Ruby murder him?

Inside a crowded Air Force One—the presidential airplane—U.S. district judge Sarah Hughes swore in Lyndon B. Johnson as president just two hours after Kennedy was shot. A somber Jacqueline Kennedy stood at Johnson's side as he took the oath of office.

Eager to know the truth, President Johnson created a special commission to investigate the assassination. Headed by Supreme Court Chief Justice Earl Warren, it became known as the Warren Commission. After a year of poring through thousands of pages of documents and listening to more than 550 witnesses, the Warren Commission reported the following in its 1964 report:

> On the basis of the evidence before the Commission it concludes that Oswald acted alone. Therefore, to determine the motives for the assassination of President Kennedy, one must look to the assassin himself. Clues to Oswald's motives can be found in his family history, his education or lack of it, his acts, his writings, and the recollections of those who had close contacts with him throughout his life.
>
> —*Report of the President's Commission on the Assassination of President John F. Kennedy, 1964*

Many Americans questioned the Warren Commission's findings. In the years since Kennedy's death, numerous conspiracy theories and assassination myths have emerged. Some involve plots by the CIA, the FBI, or organized crime groups. Others involve secret agents from Cuba, the Soviet Union, or other countries unfriendly to the United States at the time of Kennedy's death. However, because Oswald did not survive to speak for himself, the full story of the Kennedy assassination may never be known.

With Robert and Ted Kennedy at her sides, Jacqueline Kennedy and her children, Caroline and John Jr., watched President Kennedy's casket travel to Arlington National Cemetery for burial. At the funeral, an "eternal" flame was lit that still marks Kennedy's grave today.

Summary

During his brief time as president, John F. Kennedy faced many domestic and foreign challenges. His presidency began with great optimism and ended in tragedy, leaving many of his goals unfulfilled.

New Frontier Kennedy's New Frontier focused on reviving the economy, winning the space race, building the nation's defenses, and aiding developing countries.

National Aeronautics and Space Administration In 1961, Kennedy pledged to put an American on the moon by the end of the decade. In 1969, NASA achieved this bold goal.

Bay of Pigs invasion Kennedy's first foreign policy initiative, the Bay of Pigs invasion, was an attempt to remove Fidel Castro from power in Cuba. It failed miserably.

Berlin Wall In 1961, a concrete barrier dividing communist East Berlin from noncommunist West Berlin became a symbol of the deepening Cold War divide.

Cuban missile crisis One of the most frightening confrontations of the Cold War occurred when the United States discovered Soviet nuclear missile sites in Cuba. The crisis ended peacefully, partly due to Kennedy's measured response and a willingness to take the nation to the brink of war.

Test Ban Treaty Kennedy and Khrushchev, both determined to reduce Cold War tensions, signed a treaty banning nuclear weapons tests in the atmosphere.

Peace Corps Kennedy's Peace Corps gave thousands of American volunteers the chance to help people in developing nations improve their lives.

Chapter 48

The Great Society

What is the proper role of government in shaping American society?

48.1 Introduction

On November 22, 1963, the day that John Kennedy was assassinated, Vice President Lyndon Johnson took over the presidency. Most Americans knew little about Johnson and doubted his ability to take Kennedy's place as president. However, Johnson handled the crisis masterfully. "A nation stunned, shaken to its very heart, had to be reassured that the government was not in a state of paralysis," he recalled later. "I had to convince everyone everywhere that the country would go forward."

In his first address as president, Johnson sought to put people's doubts to rest. He vowed to carry on the late president's dreams for the nation. Invoking the challenge Kennedy had laid out in his inaugural address, Johnson exclaimed,

> On the 20th day of January, in 1961, John F. Kennedy told his countrymen that our national work would not be finished "in the first thousand days, nor in the life of this administration, nor even perhaps in our lifetime on this planet. But," he said, "let us begin." Today, in this moment of new resolve, I would say to all my fellow Americans, let us continue.
>
> —Lyndon B. Johnson, Joint Session of Congress, November 27, 1963

Johnson echoed his "let us continue" message the following year, when he ran for a full term as president. In his speech accepting the nomination, Johnson looked back to a long line of Democratic presidents: "I know what kind of a dream Franklin Delano Roosevelt and Harry S Truman and John F. Kennedy would dream if they were here tonight," he told the delegates at the nominating convention. "And I think I know what kind of dream you want to dream." Looking ahead to the challenge of turning that dream into a new political reality, Johnson ended with these words: "So as we conclude our labors. Let us tomorrow turn to our new task. Let us be on our way!"

In contrast to Harvard-educated Kennedy, Lyndon Johnson was a rough-hewn Texan. He served in Congress for 23 years before becoming vice president. A master of the legislative process, Johnson had far more political experience than Kennedy. Comparing the two presidents, one journalist said, "Kennedy inspired . . . Johnson delivered."

◀ The 1964 Democratic National Convention in Atlantic City, New Jersey

48.2 The 1964 Election: Debating the Role of Government

Lyndon Johnson was a man of enormous energy and big ideas. As president, he wanted to do far more than simply enact Kennedy's programs. Soon after taking office, he began developing an ambitious vision for his own presidency, should he win reelection the following year.

The Liberal View: Expanding Government to Promote Well-Being Johnson unveiled his vision in a commencement speech at the University of Michigan. "In your time," he told the graduating class, "we have the opportunity to move not only toward the rich society and the powerful society, but upward to the **Great Society**." The president explained further,

> The Great Society rests on abundance and liberty for all. It demands an end to poverty and racial injustice . . . But that is just the beginning.
>
> The Great Society is a place where every child can find knowledge to enrich his mind and to enlarge his talents. It is a place where leisure is a welcome chance to build and reflect, not a feared cause of boredom and restlessness. It is a place where the city . . . serves not only . . . the demands of commerce but the desire for beauty and the hunger for community.
>
> It is a place where man can renew contact with nature . . . a place where men are more concerned with the quality of their goals than the quantity of their goods.
>
> But most of all, the Great Society is not . . . a finished work. It is a challenge constantly renewed, beckoning us toward a destiny where the meaning of our lives matches the marvelous products of our labor.
>
> —Lyndon B. Johnson, May 22, 1964

As the election campaign continued, Democrats adopted the goals of the Great Society as their party platform. In their eyes, Johnson's vision continued a tradition of liberal reform that stretched back to Franklin Roosevelt and, before him, to the Progressive Era. Like Progressives, these liberal Democrats believed the power of government should be expanded to promote social well-being.

President Johnson once said he wanted to be president so he could "give things to people —all sorts of things to all sorts of people, especially the poor and the blacks." His vision of the Great Society reflected that desire. Johnson is shown here, signing the 1968 Civil Rights Bill to promote a fairer society for all Americans.

The Conservative View: Limiting Government to Preserve Liberty Senator Barry Goldwater of Arizona, the Republican candidate for president, held a very different view on government. An outspoken conservative, he had rejected Eisenhower's modern Republicanism as "a dime-store New Deal"—that is, a cheap version of the Democrats' famous domestic program.

Goldwater believed that government's most important role was to "preserve and extend freedom." Regulating every aspect of people's lives was not its proper role. Yet, he observed, that was exactly what it had done since the time of the New Deal. "Our defenses against the accumulation of power in Washington are in poorer shape," he warned, "than our defenses against the aggressive designs of Moscow." Like many conservatives, Goldwater longed for a presidential candidate who had the courage to say what he had said himself:

> I have little interest in streamlining government or in making it more effi-
> cient, for I mean to reduce its size. I do not undertake to promote welfare,
> for I propose to extend freedom. My aim is not to pass laws, but to repeal
> them. It is not to inaugurate new programs, but to cancel old ones that
> do violence to the Constitution, or that have failed in their purpose, or that
> impose on the people an unwarranted financial burden. I will not attempt
> to discover whether legislation is "needed" before I have first determined
> whether it is constitutionally permissible. And if I should later be attacked
> for neglecting my constituents' "interests," I shall reply that I was informed
> their main interest is liberty and that in that cause I am doing the very best
> I can.
>
> —Barry Goldwater, *The Conscience of a Conservative,* 1960

In 1964, Goldwater got his chance to be that candidate. When more moderate Republicans warned that voters would reject Goldwater's views as **extremism,** or radicalism, he answered, "Extremism in the defense of liberty is no vice. And . . . moderation in the pursuit of justice is no virtue."

Johnson Wins by a Landslide The campaign quickly turned nasty. Opponents portrayed Goldwater as a reckless extremist who, if elected, would abolish Social Security and take his anticommunist aggression toward the Soviet Union so far as starting World War III. On September 7, the Johnson campaign aired "Daisy," a television advertisement that quickly became famous. It showed a young girl counting the petals of a daisy. Suddenly her voice was drowned out first by a nuclear countdown and then by a mushroom cloud. The ad announced, "Vote for President Johnson on November 3. The stakes are too high for you to stay home." "Daisy" ran only once, but that was enough to scare voters.

Johnson beat Goldwater in a landslide, winning 44 states to Goldwater's six. Johnson won 61 percent of the popular vote, the greatest margin received by any president to that point. Democrats also gained a large majority in Congress.

However, the election gave rise to two developments that would eventually challenge the Democrats' hold on power. One was the modern conservative movement, which grew out of Goldwater's ideas. The other was the political transformation of the South. In 1964, for the first time since Reconstruction, five southern states voted Republican. This shift marked the beginning of the transformation of the South from solidly Democratic to reliably Republican.

Barry Goldwater lost his bid for the presidency in 1964. But his book, *The Conscience of a Conservative,* sold 3.5 million copies and helped inspire a new generation of conservatives. Some observers consider Goldwater to be the most influential losing candidate in the nation's history.

President Johnson and Martin Luther King Jr. are shown here discussing the Voting Rights Act legislation. President Johnson fought to end racial injustice during his presidency.

48.3 Implementing Johnson's Great Society

Johnson took his decisive election victory as a mandate to move forward with his Great Society agenda. Long before the election, he had begun work on civil rights and antipoverty programs. Now he was ready to move forward with a broad range of proposals for improving life for all Americans.

The Johnson Treatment Gets Results in Congress In contrast to Kennedy, who had trouble getting his legislative program through Congress, many of Johnson's bills passed. Having served in Congress for more than two decades, Johnson knew how to deal with legislators. He praised them publicly, sought their advice, returned their calls, and instructed his aides to do the same, "or else."

> When all else failed, the president subjected lawmakers to "the treatment." Two journalists described Johnson's persuasive powers in this way:
>
> Its tone could be supplication [pleading], accusation, cajolery [persuasion], exuberance, scorn, tears, complaint, the hint of threat . . . Johnson . . . moved in close, his face a scant millimeter from his target, his eyes widening and narrowing, his eyebrows rising and falling. From his pockets poured clippings, memos, statistics . . . The Treatment [was] an almost hypnotic experience and rendered the target stunned and helpless.
> —Rowland Evans and Robert Novak, *Lyndon B. Johnson: The Exercise of Power,* 1966

The "treatment," along with a Democrat-controlled Congress after 1965, helped Johnson compile an extraordinary legislative record. In the five years of his presidency, he shepherded more than 200 measures through Congress.

Ending Racial Injustice Johnson envisioned a society free of racial injustice. One of his first priorities as president was passage of Kennedy's civil rights legislation banning discrimination in public accommodations. "No memorial oration," Johnson said, "could more eloquently honor President Kennedy's memory than the earliest possible passage of the civil rights bill." Several months later, Johnson signed the Civil Rights Act of 1964 into law.

The new law was quickly tested in the courts. The case known as *Heart of Atlanta Motel v. United States* arose when a motel owner refused to rent rooms to blacks. He argued that the Civil Rights Act overstepped the power given to Congress to control interstate commerce. He also claimed that it violated his rights under the Fifth and Thirteenth amendments by forcing him to use his property in ways he opposed. The Supreme Court rejected these claims. It noted that much of the motel's business came from out-of-state guests. Hence, Congress had acted within its power to regulate interstate commerce.

Johnson continued to push Congress to end racial injustice. In 1965, he signed the Voting Rights Act, which guaranteed voting rights to African Americans. Three years later, he signed the Civil Rights Act of 1968, which prohibited housing discrimination. These laws helped move the country toward Johnson's vision of a color-blind society.

Declaring War on Poverty Another goal that both Kennedy and Johnson shared was the elimination of poverty. Spurred by Michael Harrington's book *The Other America,* Kennedy had asked his advisers to develop strategies for attacking poverty. Johnson expanded these ideas into an ambitious antipoverty program called the **War on Poverty**.

The centerpiece of the War on Poverty was the **Economic Opportunity Act**. Passed by Congress in August 1964, the act created dozens of federal anti-poverty programs and an Office of Economic Opportunity to oversee them. One program, the Job Corps, worked to teach disadvantaged young people job skills. Project Head Start set up programs for low-income preschool children. Volunteers in Service to America, or VISTA, was modeled on the Peace Corps. VISTA volunteers lived and worked in poor communities within the United States, providing job training or educational services.

President Johnson also hoped to reverse the decline of America's cities. In 1965, he created the Department of Housing and Urban Development (HUD) to manage federal programs aimed at revitalizing blighted urban neighbor-hoods. Its head, Robert Weaver, was the first African American to join any president's cabinet.

President Johnson's wife, Lady Bird, helped promote his Great Society programs. As part of the effort to beautify America, she helped coordinate the planting of wildflowers along highways. She also took an interest in children and education.

Improving Access to Health Care Also high on Johnson's list of Great Society goals was helping needy Americans gain access to health care. Liberals in Congress had tried for years to provide hospital insurance to retired workers as part of Social Security. Johnson made this measure a top priority.

In 1965, Congress established the **Medicare** and **Medicaid** programs. Medicare is a federal health insurance program that pays for hospital and nurs-ing home services for citizens 65 years or older. Medicaid is a health insurance program jointly financed by federal and state governments. It covers low-income people as well as older Americans whose medical needs have exceeded their Medicare benefits. With the creation of these programs, many Americans no longer had to forgo medical care for lack of health insurance.

Supporting Lifelong Learning and Culture Education, Johnson believed, was the key to a better life. He pushed several measures to improve the nation's educational system. One was the Elementary and Secondary Education Act of 1965, which provided federal aid to school districts nationwide. Because the government allocated funds to needy students rather than to schools, the act helped finance both public and parochial, or faith-based, education.

That same year, Johnson signed an act creating the National Endowment for the Arts (NEA) and the National Endowment for the Humanities (NEH). These organizations give grants to artists, musicians, writers, scholars, and researchers to promote a vibrant national culture. Johnson also spearheaded passage of the Public Broadcasting Act of 1967. "While we work every day to produce goods and create new wealth," he explained upon signing the act, "we want most of all to enrich man's spirit. That is the purpose of this act." The act established the Corporation for Public Broadcasting (CPB), which supports the development of public radio and television programs. One of the first CPB-funded shows was *Sesame Street,* which first aired on public television stations in 1969.

Senior Citizens benefited from the creation of Medicare and Medicaid. Here are some seniors protesting for the creation of afford-able health care for the elderly.

How Have Great Society Programs Saved Our History and Natural Heritage?

Among the most enduring legacies of the Great Society are four landmark laws enacted to preserve historic sites, endangered species, free-flowing rivers, and wilderness areas for generations to come.

The bald eagle was declared an endangered species in 1967. Since then the FWS has helped the eagles make a remarkable comeback.

Wilderness Act of 1964
What it did: Created the National Wilderness Preservation System to preserve areas "where earth and its community of life are untrammeled by man."
Long-term impact: Nearly 110 million acres of land were preserved as wilderness areas by the end of 2011.

At more than 9 million acres, the Wrangell–Saint Elias Wilderness in Alaska is the nation's largest wilderness area.

Opening Doors for Immigrants Johnson also supported a major overhaul of the nation's immigration policy. Since the 1920s, the government had placed quotas on immigration from every part of the world except Western Europe. Johnson, who believed this quota system was rooted in prejudice, wanted to end it.

The Immigration Act of 1965 eliminated the old quotas based on national origin. It made a person's skills and ties to family in the United States the key criteria for admission into the country. Johnson praised the act for repairing "a very deep and painful flaw in the fabric of American justice." He had no idea what an impact the law would have: in the years since its signing, immigration has quadrupled, with immigrants arriving from all over the world.

Preserving the Environment In striving toward the Great Society, Johnson hoped to improve the quality of the environment for all. In 1962, the publication of the book *Silent Spring,* by Rachel Carson, had raised public interest in **environmentalism,** or protection of the environment. The book showed how uncontrolled pesticide use was poisoning the environment. "The air we breathe, our water, our soil and wildlife," Johnson warned, "are being blighted by poisons and chemicals which are the by-products of technology and industry."

Johnson worked with Congress to pass several environmental laws. The Clean Air Act of 1963 set emission standards for factories to reduce air pollution. Other laws focused on cleaning up waterways, preserving wilderness, protecting endangered species, and beautifying the landscape.

Protecting Consumers Johnson also supported **consumerism,** or the protection of the rights of consumers. The Cigarette Labeling Act of 1965 required cigarette packages to carry labels warning that smoking could cause health problems. Other acts set standards for wholesome meat and poultry products, for truth in lending practices, and for honest labeling of food.

In 1965, the book *Unsafe at Any Speed,* written by Ralph Nader, focused public attention on auto safety. It showed how lax engineering standards in the automobile industry had put drivers at risk. The book spurred Congress to pass the National Traffic and Motor Vehicle Safety Act of 1966. This law required automobile makers to install seat belts in all cars.

Endangered Species Preservation Act of 1966
What it did: Directed the U.S. Fish and Wildlife Service (FWS) to identify and protect plants and animals that are endangered or threatened with extinction.
Long-term impact: By 2012, the FWS had listed 1,994 endangered or threatened species worldwide, of which 1,387 were in the United States. It has also brought several species back from the brink of extinction including the American Bald Eagle.

National Historic Preservation Act of 1966
What it did: Created the National Register of Historic Places, a list of sites, structures, and objects worthy of preservation.
Long-term impact: More than 80,000 places were registered as historic sites by the beginning of 2012.

The nationally registered Sixteenth Street Baptist Church, Birmingham, Alabama, is the site of the 1963 church bombing which resulted in the death of four African American girls.

Wild and Scenic Rivers Act of 1968
What it did: Created the National Wild and Scenic River System to preserve rivers of great scenic, recreational, wildlife, or historic value "in free-flowing condition."
Long-term impact: By mid 2011, the system protected 12,598 miles of river.

The Rogue River Gorge is one of the rivers protected by the 1968 Wild and Scenic Rivers Act.

Debating the Great Society By the early 1970s, the impact of Johnson's Great Society reforms could be seen in many areas of life. The poverty rate had fallen from 22.2 percent of Americans in 1960 to just 12.6 percent in 1970. High school graduation rates were rising. In 1962, only about 42 percent of black students and 69 percent of white students completed high school. By 1970, those rates had climbed to about 60 percent for blacks and 80 percent for whites. African American participation in politics was growing as well. By 1970, ten members of the House of Representatives and one Senator were black.

Despite these successes, the Great Society had its critics. The War on Poverty proved especially controversial. Left-wing opponents complained that its mix of programs was not the best approach to ending poverty. In their view, poverty resulted from social and economic forces beyond the control of the poor. The best way to help low-income people, they argued, was to give them money while trying to change the economy to create more jobs for them.

Critics on the right alleged that the War on Poverty was creating an under-class of people who were dependent on government welfare. In their view, poverty's main cause was a lack of individual responsibility on the part of the poor. The best approach to ending poverty, they argued, was to find ways to change the behaviors that kept poor people poor.

At the heart of the debate over Johnson's Great Society were age-old questions about the proper role of government in a democracy. Liberal supporters applauded the scheme's broad goals and multitude of programs aimed at improving American life. Their main concern was that many of the programs were not funded well enough to achieve those goals. Conservative critics, on the other hand, saw the Great Society as government run amok. The high cost of the many Great Society programs confirmed their belief that government should not try to solve all of society's problems.

Johnson's presidency proved to be a high point for the liberal view of government as society's problem solver. After he left office, world events caused liberals to lose ground to more conservative politicians. Still, the Great Society left a lasting imprint on American life. Few Americans today voice a desire to do away with Medicare, *Sesame Street*, or consumer protections. Many such products of the Great Society have become fixtures of American life.

Earl Warren, a Republican, was governor of California when President Eisenhower named him Chief Justice. Warren proved much more liberal than expected. Eisenhower later cited Warren's appointment as the biggest mistake he ever made. Nicknamed the "Superchief," Warren earned the ire of many conservatives with his strong leadership of the Court.

48.4 The Activist Warren Court

The Supreme Court, led by Chief Justice Earl Warren, also played a role in reshaping American society during the 1960s. By reinterpreting much of what had been settled law, the Warren Court became known as an "activist" court.

Ensuring "One Person, One Vote" The Warren Court decided two important cases that changed the political landscape. The first, *Baker v. Carr,* began when Charles Baker, a Republican citizen of Tennessee, sued Joe Carr, the secretary of state of Tennessee, because the state had not redrawn its legislative districts in five decades. During that time, many rural families had migrated to cities. As a result, Baker's urban district had many more residents than some rural districts, but the number of representatives did not reflect that increase. Baker claimed that this imbalance violated his Fourteenth Amendment right to "equal protection under the laws."

The Supreme Court had treated **reapportionment**—redrawing voting district boundaries to reflect population changes—as a matter for state legislatures to decide. But in 1962, after long deliberation, the Warren Court rejected that stance, ruling that reapportionment *was* a question for federal courts to consider.

The Court returned to reapportionment in the case of *Reynolds v. Sims.* In his majority opinion, Chief Justice Warren wrote,

> A citizen, a qualified voter, is no more nor no less so because he lives in the city or on the farm. This is the clear and strong command of our Constitution's equal protection clause . . . This is at the heart of Lincoln's vision of "government of the people, by the people, [and] for the people." The equal protection clause demands no less than substantially equal state legislative representation for all citizens, of all places as well as of all races.

As a result, legislative districts across the country were redrawn following the principle of "one person, one vote." That is, each legislator would represent the roughly same number of people, allowing each person's vote to count equally.

Ruling on Prayer in Public Schools In 1962, the Court considered the role of prayer in public schools. The case of *Engel v. Vitale* arose when state officials, including William Vitale, ordered New York schools to have students recite a morning prayer. Parents, led by Steven Engel, sued the state, claiming that the prayer violated the **establishment clause** of the First Amendment. This clause states, "Congress shall make no law respecting the establishment of religion."

The Supreme Court agreed with the parents. It found that state-sponsored prayer in school, even if voluntary, was unconstitutional because it was "wholly inconsistent with the establishment clause." This controversial decision sparked efforts to amend the Constitution to permit prayers in public schools.

Protecting the Rights of the Accused Another series of Warren Court rulings reshaped the criminal justice system. The case of *Mapp v. Ohio* involved a woman, Dollree Mapp, who had been convicted of a crime based on evidence found during an illegal police search of her home. The Court ruled in 1961 that evidence obtained illegally may not be used in court.

In *Gideon v. Wainwright,* defendant Clarence Gideon had not had the money to hire a lawyer. Forced to defend himself, he had been found guilty and sent to prison. In 1964, the Court ruled that Gideon's Sixth Amendment right to an attorney had been violated. As a result, courts now provide public defenders to people who are accused of a crime but who cannot afford a lawyer.

In another 1964 case, *Escobedo v. Illinois,* police had denied a murder suspect, Danny Escobedo, an opportunity to speak to a lawyer during questioning. Escobedo eventually confessed to the crime and was convicted. The Court overturned the conviction because Escobedo's constitutional right to be represented by a lawyer after his arrest had been violated.

In a 1966 case, *Miranda v. Arizona,* the Court ruled that the police must inform suspects of their rights before questioning. A suspect must be told, wrote Warren, "that he has the right to remain silent, that any statement he does make may be used as evidence against him, and that he has a right to the presence of an attorney." These protections are called **Miranda rights,** after the defendant.

Americans hotly debated these and other Warren Court rulings. Some critics called on Congress to impeach Chief Justice Warren. "Of all three branches of government," argued Senator Barry Goldwater, "today's Supreme Court is the least faithful to the constitutional tradition of limited government." Others praised the Warren Court for doing what Congress had failed to do: protect the rights guaranteed to every citizen by the Constitution.

Summary

In 1964, voters elected liberal Democrat Lyndon Johnson by a wide margin. Johnson used this mandate to enact a broad program of reforms he called the Great Society. With his powers of persuasion, Johnson pushed more than 200 bills through Congress.

War on Poverty Johnson's Great Society grew out of the liberal tradition of the Progressive and New Deal eras. Its centerpiece was an ambitious War on Poverty.

Economic Opportunity Act This act created a number of antipoverty measures, including the Job Corps, Project Head Start, and VISTA, which all helped cut poverty rates almost in half.

Medicare and Medicaid As part of the Great Society, Congress amended the Social Security Act to include medical health insurance for the elderly and disabled.

Immigration Act of 1965 This measure ended the national origins quota system begun in the 1920s. Entry to the United States was now based on criteria such as skills and family ties.

Silent Spring This influential book sparked a new interest in environmentalism. As a result, Congress passed several environmental laws.

"One person, one vote" The activist Warren Court changed the political landscape by insisting that states create legislative districts following the principle of "one person, one vote."

Miranda rights In a series of controversial decisions, the Warren Court expanded the rights of the accused. It ensured that people placed under arrest be informed of their rights before questioning.

WOODSTOCK
MUSIC & ART FAIR

presents

AN
AQUARIAN
EXPOSITION

in

WHITE LAKE, N.Y.

3 DAYS of PEACE & MUSIC

AUGUST
15, 16, 17

WITH

FRI., AUG. 15
Joan Baez
Arlo Guthrie
Tim Hardin
Richie Havens
Incredible String Band
Ravi Shankar
Sly And The Family Stone
Bert Sommer
Sweetwater

SAT., AUG. 16
Canned Heat
Creedence Clearwater
Grateful Dead
Keef Hartley
Janis Joplin
Jefferson Airplane
Mountain
Quill
Santana
The Who

SUN., AUG. 17
The Band
Jeff Beck Group
Blood, Sweat and Tears
Joe Cocker
Crosby, Stills and Nash
Jimi Hendrix
Iron Butterfly
Ten Years After
Johnny Winter

ART SHOW

CRAFTS BAZAAR

FOOD

HUNDREDS OF ACRES
TO ROAM ON

MUSIC STARTS AT 4:00 P.M. ON
FRIDAY, AND AT 1:00 P.M. ON
SATURDAY AND SUNDAY.

WHITE LAKE, TOWN OF BETHEL, SULLIVAN COUNTY, N.Y.

Chapter 49

The Emergence of a Counterculture

What was the impact of the counterculture on American society?

49.1 Introduction

Bob Dylan grew up listening to rock 'n' roll on the radio. As a teenager, he thought he wanted to become a rock star himself. However, while attending the University of Minnesota in 1959, he became passionate about traditional American folk music. Dylan dropped out of college, moved to New York City, and began performing as a folk singer in tiny Greenwich Village nightclubs.

Unlike many performers, Dylan was not showy or handsome, nor did he have a strong singing voice. Still, people paid attention to his music. Accompanying himself on guitar and harmonica, Dylan sang about racial injustice, nuclear war, and other serious issues that engaged people living in a time of social change. His lyrics held more in common with beat poetry than with the simple rhymes of teenage love songs. In one of his early hits, he warned of an emerging clash of values between parents and their baby boom children.

In the 1960s, the themes of Dylan's lyrics resonated with millions of young people, as well as with many of their elders. They considered the racial discrimination, riots, poverty, and political assassinations occurring in the United States and concluded that society had to change. As some people experimented with new ways of living, they redefined old ideals, such as freedom and democracy, on their own terms. They created a counterculture—a group with ideas and behaviors very different from those of the mainstream culture.

Bob Dylan became a famous folk musician in the early 1960s. In his first big hit, "Blowin' in the Wind," he protested racial discrimination, which persisted in the United States despite the civil rights movement.

◀ Poster advertising the counterculture concert that came to be known as Woodstock

49.2 Baby Boomers Launch a Cultural Revolution

The postwar baby boom created the largest generation of children in American history. By the early 1960s, the oldest baby boomers were nearing their twenties. Most looked forward to futures full of opportunities. However, some baby boomers felt guilty about growing up with advantages denied to many Americans. They believed American society was deeply flawed—rife with materialism, racism, and inequality—but they also believed it could change.

Activists on College Campuses Form a New Left Responding to the plight of the poor, small groups of student activists formed a movement called the New Left. Some members of the Depression-era "Old Left" had been radicals who supported a worldwide communist revolution. The students who made up the New Left rejected communism. Inspired by the civil rights movement, they were committed to more traditional American ideals, such as the democratic goal of allowing all people to take an active part in government.

The strongest voice in the New Left was a group called Students for a Democratic Society (SDS). In 1962, SDS founders met to craft their vision of a just society. "Freedom and equality for each individual, government of, by, and for the people—these American values we found good, principles by which we could live," they declared. "We would replace power . . . rooted in possession, privilege, or circumstance by power and uniqueness rooted in love, reflectiveness, reason, and creativity. During the first year, SDS membership grew to more than 8,000 students—a small fraction of all college students.

In 1964, a student protest at the University of California at Berkeley radicalized large numbers of students across the country. The Free Speech Movement developed in response to a university rule banning groups like SDS from using a plaza on campus to spread their ideas. Freedom of expression, declared student activist Mario Savio, "represents the very dignity of what a human being is." Comparing the university to a factory, he urged his fellow students to "put your bodies upon the gears and upon the wheels." Thousands of students joined the Free Speech Movement, shutting down the campus for weeks. Eventually, the university lifted the ban.

The student uprising at Berkeley was the first of many protests at colleges across the country. Some protests revolved around local issues. Others were reactions to the growing U.S. military presence in Vietnam. Student activists called on college officials to ban military recruiters from campuses and to end weapons-related research. In 1965, SDS held a rally in Washington, D.C., against the Vietnam War, attracting nearly 25,000 people. You will read more about this war in upcoming chapters.

An Emerging Counterculture Rejects the Establishment In another form of rebellion against social expectations, many young people dropped out of school and rejected the "rat race" of nine-to-five jobs. Known as hippies, they developed a counterculture seeking freedom of expression. Shunning conventions, hippies dressed in jeans, colorful tie-dyed T-shirts, sandals, and necklaces called love beads. They wore their hair long and gave up shaving or wearing makeup. Many lived on handouts from their parents, by begging, or by taking short-term jobs.

Mario Savio addressed a mass of students at the 1964 Free Speech Movement rally at the University of California at Berkeley. Protests against the ban on political activity on campus lasted three months. The students' success in overturning the ban is still seen as a victory for First Amendment rights on college campuses.

Although no organization united members of the counterculture, a number of beliefs did. One was distrust of the **Establishment**, their term for the people and institutions who, in their view, controlled society. Another was the sentiment embodied in the counterculture motto of "never trust anyone over 30." Members of the counterculture also shared the belief that love was more important than money.

Many members of the counterculture rejected political activism in favor of "personal liberation." As one hippie put it, "Human beings need total freedom. That's where God is at. We need to shed hypocrisy, dishonesty, and phoniness and go back to the purity of our childhood values." Hippies talked of creating a new age of peace and love in which everyone was free to "do your own thing."

In the late 1960s, counterculture members of the Youth International Party, known as yippies, tried to combine their hippie lifestyle with New Left politics. Led by Abbie Hoffman and Jerry Rubin, the yippies attracted media attention by carrying out amusing pranks. In one of them, they poked fun at the Establishment's love of money by throwing dollar bills off the balcony of the New York Stock Exchange. As the money floated down, the stock traders below dropped their work to scramble for free cash. Hoffman called such stunts "commercials for the revolution."

Hippies dreamed of a world in which peace, love, and freedom were the dominant values. They wore colorful clothing rather than conventional dress. Compared with mainstream Americans, they adopted more relaxed views regarding money, work, and the pursuit of pleasure.

A Generation Gap Opens Between Rebel Youth and Mainstream Parents
Hippies were a minority of 1960s youth. But media coverage made their values known to other young people, many of whom responded sympathetically. To their parents' distress, these youth let their hair grow long, wore hippie clothes, and criticized the Establishment, especially the war in Vietnam. The result was a growing **generation gap,** or difference in attitudes and behaviors between youth and their parents.

Adults who had lived through the Depression and World War II often dismissed "long-haired hippies" as spoiled rich kids. They resented the counterculture's focus on hedonism, or pursuit of pleasure, and its lack of concern for their future. The majority of young people, however, adhered to mainstream values. Like their parents, they wanted a good education, a decent job, a successful marriage, and their own home.

Peggy Noonan, a presidential speechwriter and newspaper columnist, was one of those mainstream youth. While hippies were dreaming of personal liberation, Noonan accepted the idea that "not everything is possible, you can't have everything, and that's not bad, that's life." Rather than chanting anti-Establishment slogans such as "Make love, not war," her motto was "Show respect, love your country, stop complaining!"

Mainstream Americans remained loyal to traditional values during the 1960s. They believed in family ties, hard work, and respect for God and country. They often viewed youth of the counterculture as irresponsible and immoral.

49.3 A Culture Clash

In San Francisco in January 1967, an event dubbed the "Human Be-In"—a fun-loving twist on a sit-in—drew together various counterculture factions. The festival attracted nearly 20,000 young people. News reports showed young men and women holding one another, using drugs, and dancing to the music of rock bands. For many young people, the gathering looked like an invitation to enjoy sex, drugs, and rock 'n' roll. For parents, stories about the Human Be-In confirmed their worst fears of a society in moral decline.

Changing Views of Love and Marriage The counterculture's openness about sexual behavior took place amid rapidly changing views toward love and marriage. The **sexual revolution** was a by-product of the introduction of the birth control pill early in the decade. More couples were living together outside of marriage, and more marriages were ending in divorce. Millions of Americans came to see a loveless marriage as worse than no marriage at all. As a result, many states eased divorce laws. Between 1960 and 1970, the annual divorce rate rose from fewer than 10 couples per 1,000 to almost 15. The number of children living in single-parent families rose along with the divorce rate.

While numbers of young people experimented with the freedom the sexual revolution brought, mainstream adults focused on problems it created. They worried that young people were being pressured to engage in sexual behavior. Adults also expressed alarm at the rapid rise in the number of children born out of wedlock. Just as shocking was an increase in sexually transmitted diseases.

Hippies experimented with new sounds in music and new styles of art. Concert posters and album covers often sought to evoke the colorful visions that counterculture artists sometimes had while high on music or drugs.

Hippies Experiment with Freer Lifestyles Many hippies created mini-societies in which they could live by their own values. Some congregated in crash pads, free and usually temporary places to stay. Others experimented with more permanent group-owned living arrangements, called **communes**. Members of communes shared responsibilities and decision making. During the 1960s, about 2,000 communes arose, most often in rural areas. Many mainstream parents reacted strongly to communal modes of living. Some parents felt that by choosing such unconventional lifestyles, their children may have been limiting their prospects for future success.

The counterculture also held changing views on the recreational use of drugs. At the 1967 Human Be-In, psychologist Timothy Leary urged the crowd to "turn on, tune in, and drop out." The casual attitude of young people toward illegal mind-altering drugs appalled mainstream adults. They pointed out that some drug users experienced "bad trips" that led to panic attacks, depression, violence, and death. Government spending on antidrug programs increased from $65 million in 1969 to $730 million in 1973.

Rock 'n' Roll Gives Voice to the Counterculture Hippies also embraced the changing music scene. Counterculture rock bands soon developed a new sound known as psychedelic rock. They experimented with free-flowing songs that used elements of jazz and Indian music, sound distortion, and light shows to create vivid musical experiences. Many mainstream adults worried this type of music promoted increased drug use.

The counterculture was at its height at Woodstock, a 1969 concert in rural upstate New York. About 400,000 people convened at the festival—far more than expected. Despite rain and food shortages, the gathering was peaceful.

Woodstock helped popularize a new generation of rock performers. It also drew media attention to the counterculture. In August 1969, *Time* magazine reported, "The festival . . . may well rank as one of the significant political and sociological events of the age." However, just a few months after Woodstock, four people died at a rock festival staged by the Rolling Stones in Altamont, California. The mainstream culture pointed to this event as an example of the dangers of rock 'n' roll.

The Impact of the Counterculture on Mainstream Media By the end of the 1960s, countercultural ideas and images appeared in mainstream magazines and movies and on television. Experimentation with new forms of expression spread to the visual arts, where abstract expressionism of the 1950s gave way to **pop art,** short for "popular art." Pop art focused on everyday life, commenting on consumer culture by elevating mundane objects into high art.

The counterculture's impact on society was reflected in a variety of media. Pop artists, such as Andy Warhol, influenced the direction of visual arts. Warhol was known for his paintings of everyday objects, particularly cans of soup.

Summary

Members of the counterculture valued individual freedom and expression over materialism. Their values created a generation gap between themselves and older, mainstream Americans.

The New Left Politically active college students formed a movement known as the New Left. In 1964, the Free Speech Movement challenged the University of California at Berkeley.

Hippies Members of the counterculture, known as hippies, believed in peace, love, and individual freedom. They shunned the Establishment and its materialistic values.

Sexual revolution As living together before marriage and getting divorced became more accepted in the 1960s, the divorce rate went up, as did the number of children living with a single parent.

Drug use Casual attitudes toward the use of illegal drugs shocked mainstream America.

Rock 'n' roll Psychedelic rock combined musical styles with light shows to create vivid experiences. The music festival Woodstock drew media attention to the counterculture.

Impact of the counterculture The media introduced countercultural values to mainstream America through television and radio, as well as art, music, and theater.

Chapter 50

The United States Gets Involved in Vietnam

Why did the United States increase its military involvement in Vietnam?

50.1 Introduction

In Washington, D.C.'s Constitution Gardens, not far from the Lincoln Memorial, sits a long, sloping wall made of polished black granite. Etched into the wall are thousands of names. Visitors file past this stark monument at a funereal pace. Here and there, some stop to touch a familiar name. Many simply stand in contemplation or quiet prayer, while others shed tears. Some leave letters, flowers, or personal objects, including medals, at the base of the wall.

The official name of this monument is the Vietnam Veterans Memorial, but it is more commonly known as "the Wall." The Wall lists the names of U.S. soldiers killed or missing in action in the Vietnam War. The first two men listed, Chester Ovnand and Dale Buis, were the first U.S. soldiers to die in Vietnam, according to official records. They were noncombat troops killed in a surprise attack on their camp in 1959. At the time, few Americans were paying any attention to this faraway conflict. Later, reporter Stanley Karnow, who had written a brief account of the soldiers' deaths, mentioned their names at a congressional hearing. He said, "I could never have imagined that these were going to be at the head of more than 58,000 names on the Wall."

Today many young people visit the Wall. Some of them wonder why a list of names carved in stone has such a strong impact on other, older visitors. They wonder why the remembrance of this war provokes not only tears but also anger. The answer is complicated. It has to do with painful memories of loss, with Cold War policies, and with social rebellion. It has to do with American GIs fighting and dying in a war far from home, for reasons many did not entirely understand.

Before the United States entered the war, politicians and their advisers argued about the wisdom of getting drawn into the conflict. During the war, Americans bitterly debated U.S. policy. The war divided the country more than any other issue since the Civil War. Today, many are still asking the question: Did the United States have good reasons for getting involved in Vietnam?

The Vietnam Veterans Memorial lists the names of 58,253 Americans killed or missing in the Vietnam War. For many Vietnam veterans, the Wall is a place for healing. Visiting the monument helps them come to terms with their experiences during the war, including the loss of close friends and family members. Above is a replica of the Wall that is part of a traveling exhibit.

Ho Chi Minh was president of North Vietnam from 1945 to 1969. He fought for an independent, unified Vietnam. At first he sought support from the United States, but his communist ideology aroused U.S. hostility. Though considered a "freedom fighter" by many, he ordered the killing of thousands of North Vietnamese landowners as "class enemies."

50.2 Three Presidents Increase Involvement in Vietnam

From the 1880s up until World War II, Vietnam was part of French Indochina, a French colony in Southeast Asia that also included Cambodia and Laos. During World War II, Japanese troops occupied part of French Indochina. But Vietnam had a 2,000-year history of resisting foreign rule. In 1941, a Vietnamese communist, Ho Chi Minh, drew on that history to stir up nationalist feelings. In northern Vietnam, he helped found a group to oppose foreign occupation. Members of this independence movement became known as the **Viet Minh**.

On September 2, 1945, the same day that Japan formally surrendered to the Allies, Vietnam declared its independence. Ho Chi Minh made the announcement. In what seemed like a bid for U.S. backing, he began his speech with words from the Declaration of Independence. "All men are created equal," he said. "They are endowed by their Creator with certain inalienable rights, that among these are Life, Liberty, and the pursuit of Happiness." Ho ended his speech with words that might have stirred the hearts of the original American patriots. "The entire Vietnamese people," he said, "are determined to mobilize all their physical and mental strength, to sacrifice their lives and property in order to safeguard their independence and liberty." Ho's followers would show their determination over the next three decades. First they fought France when it tried to reestablish colonial rule. Later they would fight the United States, which saw them as a communist enemy. In the early stages of the war, three presidents would set the pattern for deepening U.S. involvement.

Truman Chooses Sides in the First Indochina War The Viet Minh called their country the Democratic Republic of Vietnam. The northern city of Hanoi was their capital, and Ho Chi Minh was their president. France, however, refused to accept Vietnamese independence and set out to eliminate the Viet Minh. First, French troops drove the rebels out of the southern city of Saigon, the French colonial capital. Then the French launched attacks on Viet Minh strongholds in the north. In November 1946, French warships opened fire on the port city of Haiphong, killing some 6,000 Vietnamese civilians. The following month, the Viet Minh attacked French ground forces. These incidents marked the start of the **First Indochina War**. This war would continue for eight years.

Some American officials saw this conflict as a war between a colonial power and nationalists who aspired to govern themselves. They urged France to set a goal of complete independence for Vietnam. Others, including President Truman, held views of the conflict that were more colored by the Cold War. They believed that the Viet Minh intended to create a communist dictatorship. Although Truman suspected the French might be fighting to preserve their empire, he chose to see their efforts as a fight against communism.

For Truman, containing communism was more important than supporting a nationalist movement. By 1951, thousands of U.S. soldiers had already died in Korea trying to halt the spread of communism. Truman was determined to block any further communist advance in Asia. For this reason, he called for an increase in military aid to French Indochina. This aid rose from $10 million in 1950 to more than $100 million in 1951. By 1954, the United States was paying 80 percent of the cost of the war in Indochina.

Eisenhower Considers Increased American Involvement Despite U.S. aid, the First Indochina War dragged on. The French controlled the cities in both northern and southern Vietnam, but the Viet Minh dominated the countryside. The Viet Minh took control of rural villages, often by assassinating local leaders with close ties to the French. They gained the support of Vietnam's peasants, who made up around 80 percent of the population, in part by giving them land taken from the wealthy.

The decisive battle of the war began in March 1954, when the Viet Minh launched a surprise attack on a large French military base at Dien Bien Phu, in the mountains of northern Vietnam. They soon had the base surrounded. By April, the more than 12,000 French soldiers at Dien Bien Phu appeared ready to give up. Now Truman's successor, President Dwight D. Eisenhower, faced a dilemma. A loss at Dien Bien Phu might knock the French out of the war. Eisenhower briefly considered sending B-29 aircraft to bomb Viet Minh positions, but he did not want to act alone. What he really wanted was a commitment from Britain and other allies to take unified military action to stop communist expansion in Vietnam and elsewhere in Indochina.

In a news conference on April 7, Eisenhower warned that if Vietnam fell to communism, the rest of Southeast Asia would topple like a "row of dominoes." Even Japan, he said, might be lost. In the years to come, this **domino theory** would provide a strong motive for U.S. intervention in Vietnam. But for now, just months after the Korean War had ended, neither the United States nor its allies were prepared to fight another ground war in Asia. Senator John F. Kennedy reflected the mood of Congress when he said, "To pour money, materiel, and men into the jungles of Indochina without at least a remote prospect of victory would be dangerously futile and self-destructive." **Materiel** is military equipment and supplies. Other policymakers feared that direct military intervention might even trigger a war with Vietnam's communist neighbor, China.

The key battle of the First Indochina War took place between March and May 1954, when Viet Minh troops attacked the French stronghold at Dien Bien Phu. The French lost the battle and began to withdraw their forces from Vietnam.

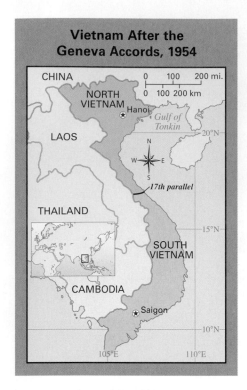

Vietnam After the Geneva Accords, 1954

CHINA

NORTH VIETNAM

Hanoi

Gulf of Tonkin

LAOS

20°N

17th parallel

THAILAND

15°N

SOUTH VIETNAM

CAMBODIA

Saigon

10°N

105°E   110°E

0   100   200 mi.

0   100   200 km

The Geneva Accords of 1954 split Vietnam temporarily at the 17th parallel. The French moved into South Vietnam, and the Viet Minh moved into North Vietnam. The Viet Minh left a political network in the south, however, in the hope of winning victory in the national unity election set for 1956. They also left weapons hidden in the south.

On May 7, 1954, the Viet Minh finally overran the French base, ending the Battle of Dien Bien Phu and shattering French morale. The French, lacking public support at home for the war, began pulling out of northern Vietnam. The final act of the First Indochina War would be played out at a peace conference in Geneva, Switzerland.

Geneva Peace Conference Splits Vietnam in Two Representatives of France and the Viet Minh began talks in Geneva the day after the French loss at Dien Bien Phu. France wanted to maintain some control over southern Vietnam. The Viet Minh demanded that France leave the country completely and that the Democratic Republic of Vietnam be recognized as an independent nation.

As negotiations dragged on, China and the Soviet Union put pressure on the Viet Minh to compromise. They did not want to antagonize the United States, fearing it would intervene militarily. Finally, in July 1954 the French and Viet Minh signed the Geneva Accords. Under this agreement, the fighting stopped, and Vietnam was split temporarily along the 17th parallel. The Viet Minh moved north of that line, while the French withdrew to the south. Under the accords, national elections to reunify Vietnam were scheduled for 1956.

As France prepared to leave Vietnam, the United States began moving in. American officials believed they could form a strong noncommunist state in South Vietnam. In 1955, the United States used its influence to put an anti-communist South Vietnamese leader, Ngo Dinh Diem, in charge. Diem began building an army. To help shape this army, Eisenhower provided some 350 U.S. **military advisers**—noncombat specialists who train and equip another nation's soldiers. Chester Ovnand and Dale Buis, the first U.S. soldiers killed in Vietnam, were military advisers.

As the election to unify north and south approached, Ho Chi Minh seemed likely to win. Diem, with U.S. approval, blocked the national vote, thus rejecting the Geneva Accords, and held elections only in the south. In October 1955, he declared himself president of South Vietnam. Diem began returning land to wealthy landlords and drafting young men from the countryside into his army. He ruthlessly attacked opponents and jailed thousands of people without putting them on trial or charging them with a crime.

Viet Minh communists still living in the south launched a guerrilla war against Diem's brutal government. Their strategy included terrorism and assassination. In 1960, the Viet Minh formed a group called the National Liberation Front and invited all opponents of Diem to join. Diem referred to the group as Viet Cong, slang for "Vietnamese communists," even though many of its members were noncommunists. By now, North Vietnam was supplying and supporting these rebels. The stage was set for the Second Indochina War, also known as the Vietnam War.

Kennedy Tries to Prop Up South Vietnam The Viet Cong **insurgency,** or rebellion, threatened to overwhelm the South Vietnamese army. Many army officers, like many leaders of South Vietnam's government, were incompetent and corrupt. Some officers even sold weapons to the Viet Cong. When Kennedy became president in 1961, he sent an inspection team to South Vietnam to evaluate the situation.

Kennedy had originally opposed U.S. military intervention to help the French. As the years passed, however, his ideas about the strategic importance of Vietnam shifted. In 1956, he offered his own version of the domino theory. JFK called Vietnam "the cornerstone of the Free World in Southeast Asia, the keystone in the arch, the finger in the dike." As president, he continued to favor a policy of containing communism.

When Kennedy's inspection team returned from Vietnam, they told the president that South Vietnam was losing the war. They recommended more economic and military aid, including the use of U.S. combat troops. However, some political advisers urged him to pull out of Vietnam completely. JFK, unsure of the best course, opted to send more weapons and equipment and more technicians and military advisers. By mid-1962, the number of military advisers had soared to around 9,000. But JFK resisted calls to send U.S. soldiers into combat. This policy was designed, according to one policy memo, to help Diem's army "win its own war."

Diem was losing not only the war but also the respect of his people. Besides being corrupt and brutal, Diem discriminated against the Buddhist majority. In May 1963, at a Buddhist rally opposing Diem's policies, South Vietnamese police killed nine demonstrators. Several Buddhist monks protested by publicly setting themselves on fire. Kennedy realized that Diem had failed as a leader. In November, a group of South Vietnamese generals staged a coup, with the tacit approval of U.S. officials. Diem was assassinated as he tried to flee Saigon.

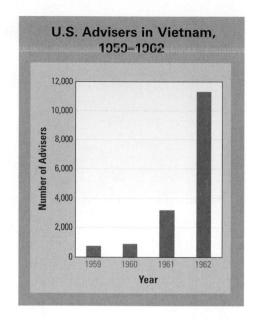

U.S. Advisers in Vietnam, 1959–1962

The United States began sending military advisers to Vietnam to help the French in the early 1950s. The number of advisers increased rapidly in the early 1960s. These advisers were not combat troops, but they played a key role in the military buildup in Southeast Asia.

The Granger Collection, New York

In 1963, photographs of Buddhist monks burning themselves to death in South Vietnam shocked the world. The monks were protesting the corruption and brutality of the Diem regime. Diem had taken power with U.S. support, but his actions embarrassed the United States and led to his overthrow.

Ho Chi Minh Trail

The Ho Chi Minh Trail was actually a network of some 12,000 miles of trails. Soldiers and supplies traveled the route on foot and by bicycle, oxcart, and truck. The trip south, through the rugged mountains of Laos and Cambodia into South Vietnam, could take as long as three months.

50.3 Johnson Inherits the Vietnam Problem

Three weeks after Diem's death, Kennedy was also assassinated. The growing problem in Vietnam thus fell into the lap of a new president, Lyndon B. Johnson. LBJ knew that Vietnam was a potential quagmire that could suck the United States into protracted conflict. But he also believed that the communists had to be stopped. In May 1964, he expressed his ambivalent feelings about Vietnam to an adviser. "I don't think it's worth fighting for," he said, "and I don't think we can get out."

LBJ was first and foremost a politician. He knew how to get things done in Congress and how to win elections. During the 1964 campaign, his opponent, Barry Goldwater, insisted that the United States should take a more active role in the war. Johnson responded, "We are not about to send American boys nine or ten thousand miles away from home to do what Asian boys ought to be doing for themselves." This moderate approach to Vietnam boosted LBJ's appeal to voters. Yet the president had already begun making plans to **escalate,** or increase, U.S. involvement in the war. In March 1964, he asked the military to begin planning for the bombing of North Vietnam.

Gulf of Tonkin Incident Riles the U.S. For years, North Vietnam had been sending weapons and supplies south to the Viet Cong over the Ho Chi Minh Trail. This network of footpaths, roads, bridges, and tunnels passed through the mountainous terrain of eastern Laos and Cambodia. In mid-1964, regular units of the North Vietnamese Army (NVA) began heading south along this route. Johnson knew that South Vietnam's weak and ineffective army would be hard-pressed to stop this new offensive. The United States had to do more, he believed, or risk losing Vietnam to communism.

In July 1964, Johnson approved covert attacks on radar stations along North Vietnam's coast. The CIA planned the operation, but South Vietnamese in speedboats carried out the raids. U.S. Navy warships used electronic **surveillance,** or close observation, to locate the radar sites. On August 2, in response to the raids, NVA patrol boats struck back. They fired machine guns and torpedoes at a U.S. destroyer in the Gulf of Tonkin, off the coast of North Vietnam. The ship was not damaged.

LBJ chose not to retaliate, but he sent a message to Hanoi warning the North Vietnamese government that further "unprovoked" attacks would bring "grave consequences." On the night of August 4, in stormy weather in the Gulf of Tonkin, American sailors thought their destroyer was again under attack. They fired back, although they never saw any enemy boats. In fact, no attack had taken place.

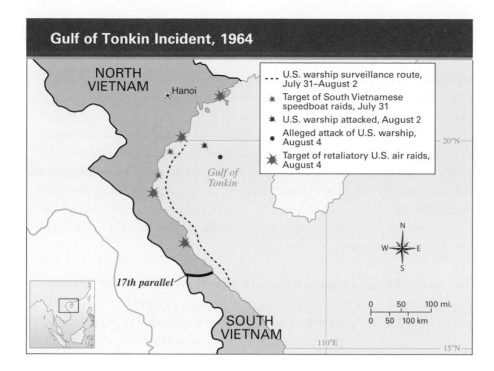

Gulf of Tonkin Incident, 1964

NORTH VIETNAM

Hanoi

Gulf of Tonkin

17th parallel

SOUTH VIETNAM

- - - - U.S. warship surveillance route, July 31–August 2
* Target of South Vietnamese speedboat raids, July 31
✳ U.S. warship attacked, August 2
● Alleged attack of U.S. warship, August 4
✳ Target of retaliatory U.S. air raids, August 4

20°N

110°E

15°N

0   50   100 mi.
0 50 100 km

The Gulf of Tonkin Incident provoked an escalation of U.S. involvement in Vietnam. On August 2, 1964, North Vietnamese boats fired on a U.S. ship, causing little damage. Two days later, false reports of a second attack prompted the United States to launch air strikes against North Vietnam.

Back in Washington, D.C., officials quickly studied accounts of the incident. Based on erroneous evidence, these officials—and the president—concluded that a second attack had occurred. LBJ immediately ordered air strikes against naval bases in North Vietnam. The next day, August 5, he asked Congress to approve those air strikes and to give him the power to deal with future threats.

Two days later, Congress passed the **Gulf of Tonkin Resolution**. This resolution allowed the president "to take all necessary measures to repel any armed attack against the forces of the United States and to prevent further aggression." The Gulf of Tonkin Resolution was not a legal declaration of war, but it did, in effect, give the president permission to expand the U.S. role in the conflict.

Only two members of Congress, both in the Senate, voted against the resolution. One of them, Ernest Gruening of Alaska, explained his opposition in a speech on the Senate floor:

> [Authorizing this measure] means sending our American boys into combat in a war in which we have no business, which is not our war, into which we have been misguidedly drawn, which is steadily being escalated. This resolution is a further authorization for escalation unlimited.
>
> —Senator Ernest Gruening, August 1964

The U.S. Reaches a Crisis Point in Vietnam The escalation that Senator Gruening feared began on February 7, 1965, after the Viet Cong attacked a U.S. air base in the south. LBJ responded by ordering the bombing of barracks and military staging areas north of the 17th parallel. "We have kept our guns over the mantel and our shells in the cupboard for a long time now," the president said of his decision. "I can't ask our American soldiers out there to continue to fight with one hand behind their backs."

U.S. Advisers in Vietnam, 1959–1964

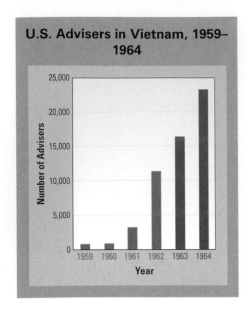

The number of U.S. military advisers in Vietnam continued to grow in the mid-1960s. By 1964, there were more than twice as many advisers in the country as there were two years before. The figure was more than 30 times the number in 1959.

The February bombing raid led to a series of massive air strikes called Operation Rolling Thunder. Most of the president's advisers believed that this action was needed to give a boost to the Army of the Republic of Vietnam (ARVN) and to avoid the collapse of South Vietnam. The government, plagued by coups and corruption, was in turmoil. It had little support outside Saigon and other large cities. The military, too, was in rough shape. Units of the ARVN rarely had success against the enemy forces that roamed the countryside. ARVN soldiers deserted by the thousands each month.

Besides attacking staging areas, U.S. planes began intensive bombing of the Ho Chi Minh Trail, hoping to cut off supplies and soldiers streaming in from the north. But the flow of men and materiel from the north continued, as did the war. In light of these results, the Johnson administration decided to reexamine U.S. policy in Vietnam.

Johnson's Advisers Debate Increased Involvement President Johnson believed in a limited war to secure South Vietnam's independence. His foreign policy team debated what actions were necessary to reach that objective.

Most of LBJ's political advisers were hawks, people who favored expanding U.S. military involvement in Vietnam. In their eyes, the defense of Vietnam was crucial in the wider struggle to contain communism. In policy debates, the hawks—a group that included Secretary of Defense Robert McNamara and Secretary of State Dean Rusk, along with top military leaders—argued in favor of escalating the war by introducing U.S. ground troops. One of their arguments had been heard many times before: the domino theory. The fall of Vietnam, they asserted, would trigger the collapse of Cambodia, Laos, and the rest of Southeast Asia. Under this scenario, communism would spread across the entire region and beyond.

The hawks also argued against a policy of appeasement. They recalled the Munich Pact of 1938, which was intended to appease Hitler but allowed for the continued aggression that led to World War II. LBJ understood their point. "The central lesson of our time," he said, "is that the appetite of aggression is never satisfied. To withdraw from one battlefield means only to prepare for the next."

A third argument of the hawks stressed American credibility. They said that allies must be able to rely on the United States, the leader of the free world, to stand by them in times of crisis. Only then, the hawks claimed, could the United States count on allied support in the worldwide battle against communism. They also argued that the United States had to make clear to the communists that it

President Johnson relied on advisers, such as Defense Secretary Robert McNamara, to help formulate Vietnam policy. Here, McNamara discusses Vietnam during a press conference in 1965. McNamara, like many of LBJ's advisers was a hawk who favored sending more troops to Vietnam. Other advisers, known as doves, urged the president to seek more peaceful means to resolve the Vietnam conflict.

572 Chapter 50

The domino theory was a key rationale for increasing U.S. military involvement in Vietnam. According to this theory, the fall of Vietnam to communism would lead to communist advances throughout Southeast Asia and the rest of the world. Presidents Truman, Eisenhower, and Kennedy, along with Johnson, were all strongly influenced by the domino theory.

would meet any challenge to its power. A related argument was purely political. During the Cold War, politicians were expected to take a hard line against the communist threat. LBJ could not afford to lose domestic support by being branded "soft on communism."

Not all of LBJ's advisers took such a hard line. Some, such as Undersecretary of State George Ball, were doves—advocates of a peaceful solution in Vietnam through negotiation and compromise. Previously they had argued against widespread bombing. Now, in policy debates, they made the case against escalating the conflict further by sending in U.S. combat troops.

The doves contended that escalating the war would not guarantee victory, arguing that the war was unwinnable. They pointed to the case of Korea, where U.S. troops had fought a costly war for three years but achieved little. Fighting a guerrilla war in the unfamiliar jungle terrain of Vietnam, the doves predicted, would prove even more difficult and deadly. In addition, the expense of such a war would undermine LBJ's top priority, his Great Society programs.

The doves also argued that involvement in the war was not in the nation's interest. They said the United States had no business becoming entangled in someone else's civil war. In addition, they questioned the strategic value of Vietnam to the United States. The huge investment the United States was making in Southeast Asia, they argued, was diverting attention from more important problems both at home and abroad.

Furthermore, the doves pointed out that direct U.S. involvement in Vietnam might draw China or even the Soviet Union into the conflict. Both countries were supplying North Vietnam with military aid, and China was building an air base just inside its border with North Vietnam. The doves feared that China might counter the entry of U.S. ground troops with combat forces of its own. Increased U.S. involvement, they claimed, would not reassure its allies but instead make them more anxious that a major war could erupt in the region.

Some critics of the Vietnam War believed that the conflict could not be managed successfully. This cartoon shows President Johnson clinging desperately to the tail of a tiger, representing Vietnam, as it whips him through space. The cartoonist is implying that Vietnam could not be controlled.

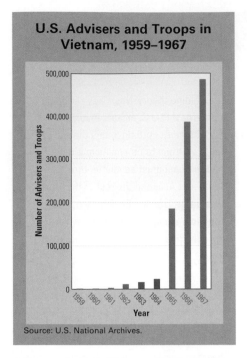

U.S. Advisers and Troops in Vietnam, 1959–1967

Source: U.S. National Archives.

U.S. troop levels in Vietnam rose rapidly after the first soldiers arrived in 1965. Four months later, the number of young men drafted into the armed forces doubled, to 35,000 a month, to meet the demand for new soldiers.

After the first U.S. combat troops arrived in Vietnam in 1965, the number of troops increased rapidly. Here, U.S. troops navigate a Vietnamese jungle in 1969. As the war became Americanized, the South Vietnamese played less and less of a role.

50.4 Johnson Americanizes the War

After weighing all the advice he received about American involvement in Vietnam, Johnson decided to send troops. On March 8, 1965, about 3,500 U.S. marines waded ashore at a beach near Da Nang, South Vietnam. This was the first time U.S. combat troops had set foot in Vietnam. The marines received a warm greeting from local officials. Several Vietnamese girls placed garlands of flowers around the soldiers' necks.

The marines knew this was no time to celebrate, though. They immediately began digging foxholes on the beach, preparing to defend against a Viet Cong attack. The next day, they continued bringing equipment and supplies ashore, including tanks equipped with flamethrowers. The marines' job was to defend the air base at Da Nang, the home base for bombers taking part in Operation Rolling Thunder. Soon their orders changed, however. They were sent on patrol to find and eliminate enemy forces. These search-and-destroy missions led to the first firefights with Viet Cong guerrillas. Until the following month, LBJ kept this shift to combat status a secret from the American people.

Johnson Dramatically Increases Troop Levels By the end of April, President Johnson had approved the dispatch of 60,000 more combat troops to Vietnam. In July, after conferring with advisers, he publicly announced that he was boosting U.S. troop levels dramatically, to 125,000 men. "We cannot be defeated by force of arms," he said. "We will stand in Vietnam." LBJ's actions and words revealed that the United States was about to undertake a full-scale war. Yet the president did not officially declare war or ask Congress for permission to expand troop levels. He based his authority to act on the Gulf of Tonkin Resolution.

In the months that followed, the air war continued to intensify, and the pace of the ground war accelerated. The first major assault by U.S. ground troops, called Operation Starlite, took place in August 1965, against 1,500 Viet Cong who were preparing to attack a U.S. air base near the coast. The battle started with bomb and artillery attacks on Viet Cong positions. Helicopters flew many of the 5,500 marines to the battle site, and others came ashore from ships. Supported by tanks and fighter planes, the marines successfully smashed the enemy force. In this American victory, marines killed more than 600 Viet Cong, while 45 U.S. soldiers died.

This pattern of delivering troops by helicopter while battering the enemy with overwhelming firepower would continue throughout the war. So would the lopsided pattern of casualties. Although many U.S. and ARVN soldiers would die in Vietnam, four times as many enemy troops would perish. Despite huge losses, however, the Viet Cong and North Vietnamese managed to produce enough new fighters to keep the war going.

The United States, too, relied on ever-increasing numbers of ground troops to sweep through jungles and rice paddies and root out the enemy. By the end of 1965, U.S. combat soldiers numbered more than 184,000. That figure more than doubled in 1966, to 385,000. By late 1967, nearly half a million Americans were serving in Vietnam, and more were streaming into the country.

An American War Starting in 1965, with the landing of the first combat forces, the conflict in Vietnam changed. The United States took over the main responsibility for fighting the war, adopting a two-phase strategy. First, U.S. marines would take key cities and other vital sites along the coast and transform them into modern military bases. They would then use those bases to launch search-and-destroy missions against the Viet Cong. From that time forward, the South Vietnamese would play only a supporting role.

This change in strategy represented the Americanization of the Vietnam War. As one of LBJ's advisers, Horace Busby, put it, "This is no longer South Vietnam's war. We are no longer advisers. The stakes are no longer South Vietnam's. The war is ours."

Summary

After World War II, nationalist and communist rebels in the French colony of Vietnam fought for their independence. A 1954 agreement ending this colonial war split the country into communist North Vietnam and democratic South Vietnam. When France pulled out the following year, the United States stepped in to prop up South Vietnam. Over the years, American involvement grew and eventually led to the introduction of U.S. ground forces.

First Indochina War In this first phase of fighting, which lasted from 1946 to 1954, Ho Chi Minh led Viet Minh insurgents in the struggle to end French rule in Vietnam.

Geneva Accords The First Indochina War ended with a 1954 agreement known as the Geneva Accords. The accords split Vietnam into north and south but called for elections to reunify the country. The United States backed South Vietnam financially and militarily.

Viet Cong Insurgents in the south, known as the Viet Cong, worked to overthrow the nominally democratic but corrupt government of South Vietnam. The Viet Cong received aid from communist North Vietnam.

Gulf of Tonkin Resolution An alleged attack on U.S. ships off the coast of North Vietnam led Congress to pass the Gulf of Tonkin Resolution. This resolution gave President Johnson broad powers to expand the U.S. role in Vietnam. Massive air strikes against North Vietnam followed.

Ho Chi Minh Trail By 1965, North Vietnamese Army troops were moving south along the Ho Chi Minh Trail to help the Viet Cong. The United States feared that South Vietnam would fall without more direct support.

Americanization In March 1965, the United States began sending ground troops to fight the Vietnam War. The war quickly became an American conflict.

Chapter 51

Facing Frustration in Vietnam

What made the Vietnam War difficult to win?

51.1 Introduction

"We seem to have a sinkhole," the new secretary of defense, Clark Clifford, told President Johnson in March 1968. "We put in more, they match it." For three years, the United States had been putting more troops, weapons, and money into Vietnam but was more bogged down than ever. While Clifford described the conflict as a sinkhole, others called it a swamp, a quagmire, or a morass. The idea was the same: the United States was stuck in Vietnam with no easy way out.

Clifford was not the only policy adviser with a negative message. The war had turned several hawkish advisers into doves. They now counseled Johnson to cut back on the bombing, reduce troop levels, and pursue negotiations.

One of LBJ's closest friends in Congress, Senator Mike Mansfield, gave him similar advice. When the president wanted to send 40,000 more troops to Vietnam, the senator objected. "You're just getting us involved deeper," he said. "You've got to offer the American people some hope . . . It's costing too much in lives. And it's going to cost you more if you don't change your opinion."

When Johnson became president in 1963, few Americans were paying much attention to the war because it did not involve U.S. combat troops. Two years later, however, the war had escalated and had become front-page news. Every day, the public learned more about U.S. soldiers fighting and dying in Vietnam. Yet most Americans still supported the president's efforts to contain communism in Southeast Asia.

By 1968, however, many of those Americans were blaming Johnson for a war that was out of control. They called it "Johnson's War." For LBJ, the burden of responsibility was heavy. He had made great strides with his Great Society agenda for social reform. But with public opinion shifting against his war policy, he feared that he would also lose public support for his civil rights and antipoverty programs. The enormous pressures and frustrations of the Vietnam War were taking a toll on Johnson and his presidency.

Even before the United States introduced combat troops to Vietnam in 1965, some U.S. soldiers were dying in the conflict. This photograph shows war dead returning home in 1962. As the number of troops increased and the death count rose, more Americans turned against the war.

◀ President Johnson in the White House, 1968

U.S. soldiers spent much of their time on patrol, seeking to engage the enemy. They trudged through dense vegetation, swamps, and other difficult terrain, carrying rifles, ammunition, and packs weighing 90 pounds or more.

To avoid detection, the Viet Cong created an elaborate system of underground tunnels to hide from the U.S. troops. Here is the entrance to one of those tunnels.

51.2 U.S. Troops Face Difficult Conditions

Initially, much of the pressure on LBJ came from hawks in Congress and from the military, who called for more troops in Vietnam. LBJ wanted to fight a limited war with a limited number of soldiers. The American public, he believed, would turn against him if he allowed troop levels—or casualties—to rise too high.

By 1968, most of the ground troops in Vietnam were not professional soldiers like the marines who first landed at Da Nang. As the war progressed, more and more of the fighting was done by men who had been drafted into the army. Many of them took a dim view of the war. In a letter home, one draftee summed up the feelings of many soldiers when he wrote, "We are the unwilling working for the unqualified to do the unnecessary for the ungrateful." This attitude toward the war reflected the difficult conditions that U.S. soldiers faced in Vietnam.

Fighting in Unfamiliar Territory One set of difficulties had to do with the geography and climate of South Vietnam. Few American GIs had ever experienced such hot and humid conditions. In some areas, temperatures rose above 90°F much of the year, and heavy monsoon rains fell from May to October. One GI recalled his reaction upon landing in Vietnam, when the plane door first opened. "The air rushed in like poison, hot and choking . . . I was not prepared for the heat." This uncomfortable tropical climate also gave rise to a host of insects and other pests, as well as diseases like malaria.

Perhaps the greatest geographic challenge for U.S. soldiers, however, was Vietnam's rugged topography. Troops had to march through soggy, lowland rice paddies and swamps and over steep, jungle-clad mountains. The heavily forested terrain often made it difficult to locate the enemy. Unlike U.S. soldiers, the Viet Cong and the **North Vietnamese Army (NVA)** knew this land intimately and were skilled at concealing themselves in the dense tropical vegetation.

In an effort to deny the enemy its forest cover, the U.S. military sprayed chemical herbicides from the air. These herbicides stripped the foliage from plants and killed many trees. The favored herbicide was **Agent Orange,** named for the color of the barrels in which it was stored. The military sprayed Agent Orange along the Ho Chi Minh Trail and in many other areas. It also used herbicides to kill crops that might feed the enemy. However, this spraying had a limited effect on enemy operations because the forest cover in Vietnam was so extensive. It also contaminated the soil and water, destroyed civilian food sources, and exposed civilians and soldiers to toxins that posed long-term health risks.

Engaging an Elusive Enemy As the United States escalated its commitment to the defense of South Vietnam in 1965, the Viet Cong and NVA realized that they could not match superior U.S. firepower. To win they had to engage in guerrilla warfare, relying on the element of surprise and their skill at disappearing into the landscape.

The ability of the insurgents to avoid detection frustrated U.S. commanders. Besides concealing themselves in the jungle, Viet Cong and NVA soldiers often hid from their American pursuers in underground tunnels. Some of these tunnels had several exits, which made escape easier. Others were even more elaborate, containing living areas, storage spaces, and even kitchens.

The Viet Cong also had the ability to "hide in plain sight." A South Vietnamese peasant tilling the soil by day might be a guerrilla killing Americans by night. GIs passing through a small village could not tell friend from foe. They could trust no one, not even women or children.

To counter these guerrilla war tactics, the commander of U.S. forces in Vietnam, General William Westmoreland, decided to fight a **war of attrition**—a military campaign designed to wear down the enemy's strength. The United States hoped to eliminate so many enemy troops that the Viet Cong and NVA could no longer fight the war.

How Did the Viet Cong Survive Underground?

The Viet Cong built underground tunnels to hide from U.S. troops and to serve as base camps for their forces. These tunnel networks were sometimes quite extensive, with many rooms and passageways in all directions.

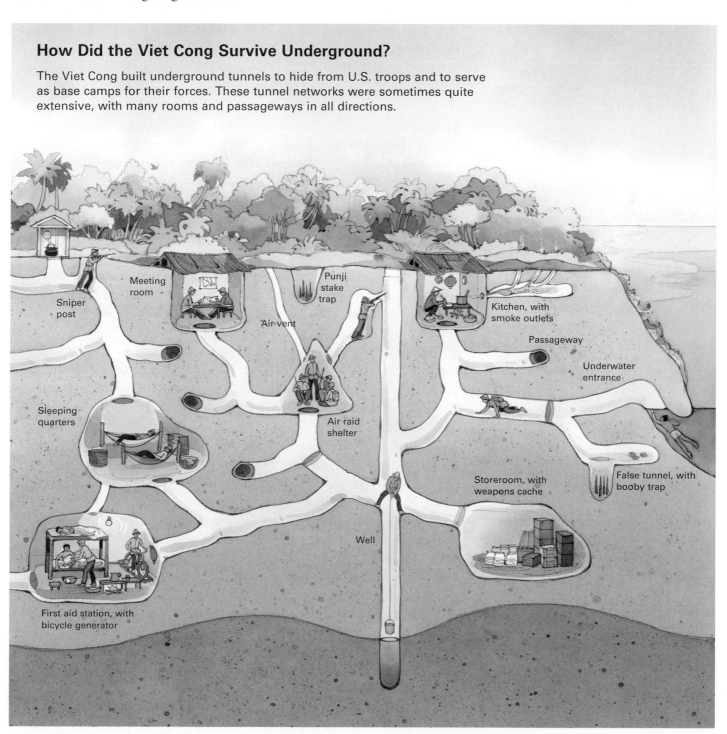

Sniper post

Meeting room

Punji stake trap

Air vent

Kitchen, with smoke outlets

Passageway

Underwater entrance

Sleeping quarters

Air raid shelter

Storeroom, with weapons cache

False tunnel, with booby trap

First aid station, with bicycle generator

Well

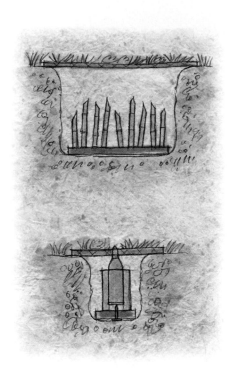

The communists laid many types of booby traps to injure or kill U.S. troops. One type was the punji stake trap, made with bamboo stakes often coated with poison. These stakes were sharp enough to pierce a soldier's boot when he stepped into the trap. Another type was the cartridge trap, in which a bullet cartridge was rigged to fire into a soldier's foot when he stepped on it.

The chief tactic in this strategy was the search-and-destroy mission. Small units of soldiers, called platoons, would search out insurgents and draw them into a fight. Then they would call in an air strike by helicopter gunships or jet fighter-bombers to destroy the enemy force. This search-and-destroy tactic appeared effective when measured by the enemy body count—the number of soldiers killed. Communist deaths far exceeded American losses. For Westmoreland, the body count became the key measure of U.S. progress in the war.

Search-and-destroy missions, however, made U.S. combat soldiers clear targets for enemy attack. Insurgents frequently ambushed platoons as they marched through the jungle. Snipers, or sharpshooters, sometimes picked off U.S. soldiers from concealed locations. Soldiers also fell prey to **land mines**—explosive devices, buried just below ground, that blew up when stepped on. Men on patrol also had to watch for booby traps, such as tripwires connected to explosives and sharpened stakes coated with poison.

Many soldiers managed to overcome these challenging circumstances. They served with distinction and carried out their combat duties as required. Others, however, became severely demoralized. During their 12-month tour of duty in Vietnam, some soldiers focused solely on survival, avoiding combat when possible. Low morale also led to increased drug use.

The Limited War Proves Ineffective The United States had reasons for pursuing a limited war. First, General Westmoreland believed that a war of attrition could achieve victory. The goal was to kill more enemy soldiers than North Vietnam or the Viet Cong could replace. If the strategy worked, the communists would have to give up eventually. Through limited war, Westmoreland thought, the United States could achieve its main goal of establishing a democratic South Vietnam.

Second, U.S. leaders saw grave dangers in pursuing a total war with no limits. Total war calls for the complete mobilization of a nation's resources to achieve victory. This approach would have meant invading North Vietnam and forcing the communists to surrender. It would likely have led to an enormous American death toll. Also, China and the Soviet Union, which were providing military aid to North Vietnam, might be provoked to intervene directly, potentially resulting in a nuclear confrontation.

The limited war proved ineffective, however, because the strategy of attrition failed. There were simply too many enemy forces to eliminate. Ho Chi Minh had once warned the French, "You can kill ten of my men for every one I kill of yours. But even at those odds, you will lose and I will win." The same held true a decade later. Some 200,000 North Vietnamese men reached draft age every year. Westmoreland's annual body counts never came close to that figure. The war continued, and antiwar sentiments began to grow in the United States. Most Americans could not tolerate a war, especially an undeclared war, that seemed to drag on endlessly at a growing cost in American lives.

Ultimately, Americans underestimated their enemy. The Viet Cong and North Vietnamese saw the United States as another colonial power that had to be expelled from their country. They were determined to fight on, no matter how long the war took or how deadly it became. The commitment of the United States to the war was much less certain.

GIs on search-and-destroy missions often burned or bombed South Vietnamese villages. Such actions were authorized if soldiers were fired upon or if the people in the village were known to support the Viet Cong. These tactics turned millions of peasants into refugees.

51.3 The War Divides the People of South Vietnam

The Vietnam War deeply divided the South Vietnamese people. Some, especially in the countryside, joined the Viet Cong or supported their cause. Others, mostly in the cities, backed the government of South Vietnam. A third group, perhaps even the majority, remained neutral in the conflict. They were often caught in the middle when fighting broke out. One of those in the middle made a plea to both sides:

> Our people no longer want to take sides in this war that is gradually but inexorably destroying us. We have no desire to be called an "outpost of the Free World" or to be praised for being "the vanguard people in the world socialist revolution." We simply want to be a people—the Vietnamese people.
>
> —Ly Qui Chung, Saigon newspaper editor, 1970

Contending for the Loyalty of the Vietnamese People American leaders knew that gaining the trust and support of people like Ly Qui Chung was a crucial element in defeating the insurgency. So, in addition to the "shooting war," the United States mounted a separate campaign to win over the Vietnamese people and undermine support for the Viet Cong. The key to this "other war" was **pacification**—a policy designed to promote security and stability in South Vietnam.

Pacification involved two main programs, both run by the Saigon government but organized by the U.S. Army and the CIA and funded by the United States. The first aimed to bring economic development to rural South Vietnam. Rural development projects ranged from supplying villages with food and other goods to building schools and bridges. This program also spread propaganda designed to persuade the Vietnamese to support the government of South Vietnam. In this way, the United States hoped to "win the hearts and minds" of the Vietnamese people.

The second pacification program sought to undermine the communist insurgency by having the **Army of the Republic of Vietnam (ARVN)** remove the Viet Cong and their sympathizers from villages. The goal was to cut off the flow of recruits to the enemy and make it safe for rural Vietnamese to support

Few Vietnamese survived napalm bomb blasts, and those who did often suffered severe burns. Napalm is a sticky gasoline gel that adheres to everything it touches and burns everything in its path. About 10 percent of all bombs dropped on Vietnam contained napalm.

the Saigon government. As one CIA officer put it, "If we were going to win the war, what we had to do was get in and eliminate the ability of the VC [Viet Cong] to control or influence the people."

The pacification campaign had many problems, though. First, the ARVN lacked the leadership, skills, and dedication to effectively provide security for villages being pacified. Some ARVN units fought with distinction, but many lacked training or the will to fight. Second, the U.S. forces in Vietnam were too busy fighting the Viet Cong to pay much attention to "the other war" for villagers' "hearts and minds."

The lack of security, in turn, made it difficult for rural development teams to carry out their mission of building roads, schools, and other basic infrastructure. In some areas, they might make progress on a project only to see it disappear when a U.S. bomb destroyed their village. In other areas, development workers were targeted by the Viet Cong. Not surprisingly, some fled. Those who stayed on risked death. During a seven-month period in 1966, the number of rural development team workers killed or kidnapped reached 3,015.

The Viet Cong Maintain Popular Support The Americanization of the war also undermined efforts to lure rural Vietnamese away from the Viet Cong. Search-and-destroy missions often created more enemies than friends among the peasants. One GI described a typical search for Viet Cong in a rural community:

> We would go through a village before dawn, rousting everybody out of bed, and kicking down doors and dragging them out if they didn't move fast enough. They all had underground bunkers inside their huts to protect themselves against bombing and shelling. But to us the bunkers were Viet Cong hiding places, and we'd blow them up with dynamite—and blow up the huts too . . . At the end of the day, the villagers would be turned loose. Their homes had been wrecked, their chickens killed, their rice confiscated—and if they weren't pro–Viet Cong before we got there, they sure as hell were by the time we left.
>
> —U.S. Marine William Ehrhart

Several other aspects of the U.S. war of attrition hurt the pacification cause. The "destroy" part of search and destroy often included air strikes. A village that had been secured by pacification workers might suddenly be bombed or shelled by U.S. forces trying to hit a Viet Cong target.

Missiles and bombs from U.S. planes leveled villages, killed thousands of civilians, and produced a steady stream of refugees. But a different kind of weapon, napalm, may have brought the greatest agony to the Vietnamese people. Napalm is jellied gasoline. It was dropped from planes as an incendiary bomb designed to burn forests and destroy enemy installations. When it hit the ground, it set fire to everything—and everyone—it touched.

The Viet Cong had significant popular support among Vietnamese nationalists. But the insurgents also used brutal means to ensure loyalty. By intimidating, kidnapping, or assassinating local leaders, including schoolteachers and religious figures, they eliminated voices of opposition. These ruthless tactics helped the Viet Cong gain control of much of South Vietnam.

51.4 Growing Opposition to the War

Before 1966, vocal opposition to the Victnam War came mainly from college students, pacifists, and a few radical groups. Most Americans considered those protesters unpatriotic. In 1966, however, criticism arose from within the U.S. Senate Committee on Foreign Relations. In early February, the committee chairman, Arkansas Democrat J. William Fulbright, began public hearings on U.S. policy in Vietnam, seeking to answer the questions, "Why are we fighting in Vietnam, and how do we plan to win?"

The committee questioned several prominent witnesses, including former ambassador George Kennan, whose ideas in the late 1940s had inspired the containment doctrine. U.S. leaders used this doctrine to justify their policies in Vietnam. At the committee hearing, Kennan spoke against those policies. He said, "If we were not already involved as we are today in Vietnam, I would know of no reason why we should wish to become so involved, and I could think of several reasons why we should wish not to."

The news media brought stark images of the Vietnam War into American homes. As the war progressed, television news and the print media increasingly displayed the grim realities of war. Here an army medic treats a wounded soldier in 1966.

The War Comes to America's Living Rooms Americans might have paid little attention to the Fulbright hearings if they had not been televised by the three major networks. Instead, millions of people across the country watched as Fulbright and other respected senators criticized Johnson administration policies. From then on, more Americans would feel free to oppose the war in Vietnam.

Television continued to play an important role in how Americans perceived the war. Night after night, news of the war was broadcast into their living rooms. At first, those news reports struck a positive note. They described U.S. successes and told upbeat stories about the courage and skill of American soldiers. As the war continued, however, television reports began to show more scenes of violence, suffering, and destruction—the human toll of the war.

Escalating Costs Raise Questions The soaring costs of the war, both human and economic, began to trouble more Americans. In 1968, troop levels rose to over 500,000 and the number of GIs killed in action exceeded 1,200 per month. During the same year, the government spent $30 billion on the war. This huge expense led to increased inflation and higher taxes for the American people.

As Americans began taking a closer look at the war, some began to question LBJ's policies. They criticized the bombing of North Vietnam and the sending of combat troops without a declaration of war. A growing number began to echo Senator Fulbright's question: "Why are we fighting in Vietnam?"

Television networks now focused most of their news coverage on the war. Viewers saw graphic images of combat and rows of body bags containing dead U.S. soldiers. In April 1968, General Westmoreland declared, "We have never been in a better relative position." Yet to many Americans, the administration's optimistic assessments of the war now seemed overblown and even deceitful. Television newscasts emphasized a **credibility gap**—the difference between the reality of the war and the Johnson administration's portrayal of it.

Many critics of the Vietnam War joined peace demonstrations around the country. In 1968, singer Eartha Kitt expressed her disapproval of the war to Lady Bird Johnson. Though her career had declined since then, protestors, such as the ones pictured above, supported Kitt's views.

Hawks and Doves Divide the Nation

Public opinion polls showed that by 1967 the American public was about evenly divided on the war. The views of hawks and doves were pulling the nation in two directions. Hawks believed in the containment doctrine. They argued that the war was morally correct and could be won by giving the military a free hand to expand the fighting. Doves regarded U.S. actions as immoral and futile. In their view, the war was a civil conflict in which the United States had no right to interfere. They wanted LBJ to seek peace.

The peace movement, or antiwar movement, blossomed on college campuses. In March 1965, faculty members at the University of Michigan held a nightlong "teach-in" and debate on Vietnam and U.S. policy. Other teach-ins followed at campuses across the nation. Sit-ins, borrowed from the civil rights movement, also became a popular way to protest the war. In February 1967, students at the University of Wisconsin at Madison occupied a campus building to protest the arrival of recruiters from the Dow Chemical Company, the maker of napalm. When the students refused to leave, police officers dragged them out. Other sit-ins followed around the country, including at Columbia University in 1968.

Younger students also took action. Three students in Des Moines, Iowa, aged 13 to 16, wore black armbands to school to protest the war. When the school suspended them for breaking school rules, they sued the school district and later took their case to the U.S. Supreme Court. In 1969, the Court ruled in *Tinker v. Des Moines* that students have a right to engage in symbolic speech—actions that express an opinion in a nonverbal manner.

Protesters also turned to civil disobedience. Some publicly burned their draft cards, while others took the more serious step of refusing induction into the armed forces. One such "draft dodger," world-champion boxer Muhammad Ali, echoed the sentiments of many when he said, "I ain't got no quarrel with no Viet Cong." Other young men between the ages of 18 and 21 complained that they could be sent off to fight even though they had no right to vote against the war. Congress took their complaint seriously. In 1971, it passed the **Twenty-sixth Amendment** to the Constitution, which lowered the voting age to 18. The states ratified the amendment just three months later.

Many young men took advantage of college deferment, a law that exempted college students from the draft. However, they could be drafted after graduation, which is partly why many students opposed the war so strenuously. Still, the draft fell disproportionately on poor Americans and minorities who were unable to attend college. This led some critics to label Vietnam a "rich man's war and a poor man's fight." Citing the large proportion of African Americans in Vietnam, Martin Luther King Jr. called it "a white man's war, a black man's fight."

51.5 1968: A Year of Crisis

By 1967, antiwar protesters had turned on President Johnson. Demonstrators chanted, "Hey, hey, LBJ. How many kids did you kill today?" To counter growing opposition to the war, the Johnson administration tried to persuade Americans that there was "light at the end of the tunnel." Officials presented statistics and reports to show that the United States was winning the war. They showed journalists' captured enemy documents that implied the insurgency was failing. LBJ visited military bases, where he touted U.S. prospects in Vietnam.

LBJ's campaign to restore confidence worked. American support for the war effort increased—at least for a few months. Then in January 1968, the Viet Cong and NVA started a campaign of their own, also aimed at influencing American public opinion.

Tet Offensive Changes Americans' View of the War In the summer of 1967, North Vietnamese military planners decided on a risky new strategy. They would launch attacks on cities in South Vietnam, while staging an uprising in the countryside. Communist leaders hoped this strategy would reveal the failure of pacification efforts and turn Americans even more against the war. They planned the attack to coincide with the Vietnamese holiday known as Tet. This holiday marked the lunar New Year, when many ARVN troops would be home on leave.

On January 31, 1968, the Tet Offensive began. Like a shockwave rolling through South Vietnam, some 85,000 Viet Cong and NVA soldiers attacked cities, villages, military bases, and airfields. In Saigon, North Vietnamese commandos blew a hole in the wall surrounding the U.S. embassy, but U.S. military police fought them off. The North Vietnamese succeeded in holding the city of Hue for nearly a month, but that was their only real military success. In battle after battle, South Vietnamese and U.S. forces pushed back the attackers. As many as 45,000 enemy soldiers, mostly Viet Cong, were killed. In the countryside, no uprising occurred. In fact, the brutality of the communist assault boosted rural support for the South Vietnamese government.

Although it was a military disaster for the communists, the Tet Offensive shocked the American people and became a psychological defeat for the United States. On their TV screens, Americans saw enemy soldiers inside the walls of the U.S. embassy. They saw U.S. bases under attack. They heard journalists' startled reports about the enemy's ability to penetrate American strongholds. No amount of positive analysis from the administration could persuade reporters or the public that this was a U.S. victory. Instead, many Americans saw these statements as another example of a widening credibility gap.

In 1968, during the Tet holiday, Viet Cong and NVA soldiers launched a major offensive across South Vietnam. Key battles took place in and around Hue and Saigon. Viet Cong guerrillas did most of the fighting and suffered most of the casualties. Some were also captured. In fact, after Tet, the NVA had to handle most of the combat in the war.

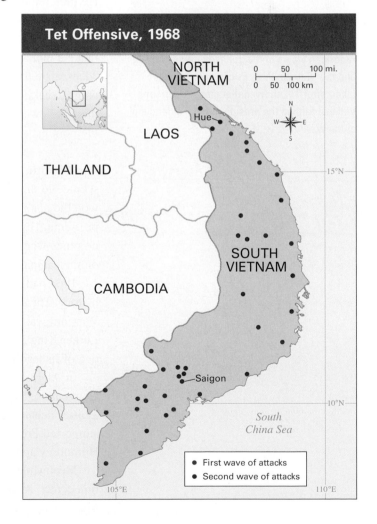

Tet Offensive, 1968

NORTH VIETNAM

0 50 100 mi.
0 50 100 km

Hue

LAOS

THAILAND

15°N

SOUTH VIETNAM

CAMBODIA

Saigon

10°N

South China Sea

• First wave of attacks
• Second wave of attacks

105°E

110°E

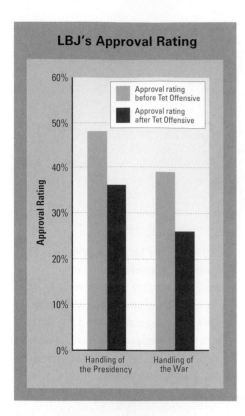

LBJ's Approval Rating

Approval rating before Tet Offensive
Approval rating after Tet Offensive

The Tet Offensive had a major impact on American views of the Johnson presidency and the Vietnam War. Public opinion polls taken after Tet showed that many Americans had lost faith in the president and his handling of the war.

Johnson Decides Not to Run for Reelection As public confidence in Johnson fell, the president suffered another sharp blow. This time it came from the nation's most respected television news anchor, Walter Cronkite. Cronkite, who had traveled to Vietnam to cover the Tet Offensive, delivered an on-camera editorial expressing his view that Johnson had misled the American people. In a solemn voice, he said, "It seems more certain than ever that the bloody experience of Vietnam is to end in a stalemate." Hearing this editorial, LBJ remarked, "That's it. If I've lost Cronkite, I've lost America."

After Tet, polls showed that only 26 percent of Americans approved of LBJ's conduct of the war. Two Democratic senators thought they could do better. Eugene McCarthy of Minnesota, a fierce critic of the war, had already entered the race for the Democratic presidential nomination. Now Robert Kennedy of New York, a favorite of civil rights and antiwar activists, announced he would also run against Johnson.

LBJ saw Tet as a political catastrophe. But General Westmoreland saw it as an opportunity to finish off the communists. He asked the president for 206,000 more troops. Secretary of Defense Clark Clifford told LBJ that even "double or triple that quantity" would not be enough to destroy the enemy forces. LBJ decided to reject the increase, leaving U.S. troop levels at around 500,000. He then removed Westmoreland as commander of U.S. forces in Vietnam. The president also considered Clifford's advice to try to open peace talks.

On March 31, 1968, Johnson stood before national television cameras to make a momentous announcement. The United States, he said, would try to "deescalate the conflict" by cutting back on the bombing of North Vietnam and by seeking a negotiated settlement of the war. An even bigger announcement followed. LBJ told Americans, "I shall not seek, and I will not accept, the nomination of my party for another term as your president."

The Chaotic Election of 1968 The war had exhausted the president, and he seemed to think he had lost his political influence. Although LBJ might have won the nomination if he had chosen to run, he threw his weight behind his vice president, Hubert H. Humphrey. In June 1968, Humphrey became the likely nominee when his most experienced rival, Robert Kennedy, was assassinated on the campaign trail by a lone gunman.

1968 had already been one of the most turbulent years in recent American history. The country was reeling from the combined effects of the Vietnam War, antiwar protests and other social unrest, and the assassination of Martin Luther King Jr. Now it was stunned by yet another assassination, this time of one of its leading political figures. And there was more upheaval to come.

In August, delegates gathered in Chicago for the Democratic National Convention. Many of them backed the antiwar views of McCarthy. Following a bitter debate, however, the convention endorsed a campaign platform that supported President Johnson's Vietnam policy. Under pressure from LBJ, Humphrey approved the platform and won the Democratic nomination.

Meanwhile, thousands of antiwar protesters rallied in parks near the convention center. At times they confronted police and national guardsmen called in by Mayor Richard Daley. On August 28, the violence escalated. A clash occurred between Chicago police and a group of rowdy protesters trying to march into the convention center. Some protesters threw rocks and bottles at the police, and police fired tear gas and beat protesters and onlookers with batons and rifle butts. Americans watching the spectacle on television were appalled.

In contrast, the Republican National Convention was a tidy affair. Delegates chose Richard M. Nixon, Eisenhower's vice president, as their candidate for president. Nixon's speech accepting the nomination blasted LBJ and the Democrats:

> When the strongest nation in the world can be tied up for four years in a war in Vietnam with no end in sight, when the richest nation in the world can't manage its own economy, when the nation with the greatest tradition of the rule of law is plagued by unprecedented lawlessness . . . then it's time for new leadership for the United States of America.
> —Richard M. Nixon, August 8, 1968

Humphrey and the Democrats never quite recovered from their disastrous convention. Nixon connected with voters by promising to maintain "law and order" at home and secure "peace with honor" in Vietnam. In November 1968, Americans voted for change, electing Nixon as their new president.

Violence erupted at the 1968 Democratic National Convention in Chicago. The police attacked antiwar protesters, and the protesters fought back. During a violent clash on August 28, some 100 demonstrators were injured while 175 were arrested.

Summary

The United States decided to wage a limited war in Vietnam, with limited troop strength. Fighting an elusive enemy on unfamiliar terrain frustrated U.S. soldiers. The South Vietnamese people themselves were unsure whom to support: the Saigon government or the communist-backed Viet Cong. As the war dragged on, American antiwar protests grew. Opposition to the war greatly affected the 1968 elections.

War of attrition The U.S. military waged a war of attrition, hoping to wear down the enemy by inflicting heavy losses. Increasing the enemy body count became a key military goal.

Opposing Vietnamese armies Regular troops of the North Vietnamese Army (NVA) joined forces with Viet Cong insurgents. The United States trained the Army of the Republic of Vietnam (ARVN) to defend South Vietnam.

New weapons of war The United States sprayed the herbicide Agent Orange to clear forest vegetation and expose the enemy. It dropped napalm firebombs that burned forests and buildings and caused widespread destruction. Both weapons had devastating effects on the Vietnamese population.

Credibility gap The Johnson administration's optimistic public assessments of the war did not match reality. This created a credibility gap, and many Americans lost faith in the president.

Protest movement Antiwar protesters on college campuses and elsewhere held demonstrations and carried out acts of civil disobedience. The protesters called for peace negotiations and an end to the war.

Tet Offensive Some 45,000 Viet Cong and NVA soldiers died after launching a major offensive in 1968. But the Tet Offensive also boosted U.S. opposition to the war and undermined the Johnson presidency, helping to pave the way for Richard Nixon's election in 1968.

Chapter 52

Getting Out of Vietnam

What lessons for Americans emerged from the Vietnam War?

52.1 Introduction

In 1968, Richard Nixon had promised to end the war in Vietnam. Seven years later, on April 29, 1975, all American personnel were ordered to leave South Vietnam immediately. U.S. combat troops had pulled out two years before, and since then the South Vietnamese army had lost ground to the North Vietnamese. By mid-April, most of South Vietnam had fallen to the communists, and the enemy was bearing down on Saigon.

The scene in Saigon that day was chaotic. The streets were filled with South Vietnamese trying to flee the invading communist army. Some climbed into small boats and headed out to sea, hoping to board U.S. ships. Others flocked to the U.S. embassy in the hope of getting a place on one of the helicopters ferrying American personnel to safety.

Several thousand Vietnamese were allowed to evacuate that day, but most were turned away for lack of space. Even for those who did manage to get out, the experience was often traumatic. One evacuee described the fate of her family:

> When we got the signal that we could leave, my family divided into two. My four brothers went with my uncle's family. My three sisters and I went with my parents. We left by boat, my brothers and my uncle went by helicopter. We've never found them. My parents tried to find them through the American Red Cross. They looked everywhere but have never found them. My parents lost four sons. It was a very painful experience. We still aren't over it . . . and probably never will be.
> —Anne Pham, in "Memories of the Fall of Saigon," CBS News

President Nixon had hoped to arrange a peaceful end to the Vietnam War that would leave South Vietnam free and independent. Why did the United States fail to achieve that goal? This chapter examines the final years of the war and some views of lessons that emerged from the conflict.

Many South Vietnamese tried to flee Saigon during the evacuation of April 29, 1975. Here, evacuees board a helicopter perched on a Saigon rooftop. Many others were unable to escape. Several hundred people were left at the U.S. embassy, for example, waiting for helicopters that never arrived.

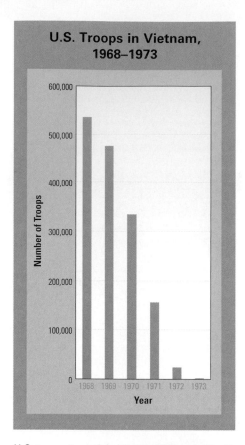

U.S. Troops in Vietnam, 1968–1973

U.S. troop strength in Vietnam fell dramatically under President Nixon. In place of U.S. soldiers, ARVN forces took up the battle against the insurgents. Better training programs and equipment helped, but low morale and poor leadership continued to hinder the South Vietnamese military.

52.2 Nixon's Dilemma: Achieving "Peace with Honor"

President Nixon entered the White House with a mandate to change the course of the Vietnam War. To that end, he relied heavily on his national security adviser, Henry Kissinger. Nixon and Kissinger drew two basic conclusions about Vietnam. First, they agreed that the war was not winnable, at least in the conventional sense. U.S. forces could not fight their way into Hanoi the way the Allies had entered Berlin in World War II. The political costs, and the cost in American lives, would be too great. Second, they decided that the United States could not just "cut and run." An abrupt withdrawal from Vietnam would damage U.S. credibility by showing both friends and foes that the United States could not be trusted to stand by its allies.

Instead, Nixon sought to achieve "peace with honor." He wanted to end the war in a way that left the reputation of the United States intact. Nixon decided on a carrot-and-stick approach—a tactic that combines actions that reward (the "carrot") with actions that punish (the "stick"). Using this approach, he hoped to persuade the North Vietnamese to accept a negotiated end to the war.

The Carrot: Peace Talks and Vietnamization Peace talks had begun in Paris in May 1968, but little progress had been made. In 1969, Nixon sent Kissinger to Paris to reopen talks with North Vietnamese diplomats. Kissinger proposed ending the bombing of the North—the "carrot"—in exchange for an agreement by both sides to withdraw their troops from South Vietnam. But he insisted that South Vietnam remain independent. The North Vietnamese rejected this offer as a "farce," saying they were prepared to remain in Paris "until the chairs rot."

When diplomacy failed to bring about "peace with honor," Nixon decided to try another approach known as **Vietnamization**. South Vietnam, he said, would gradually take over conduct of the war, while American GIs would steadily be withdrawn. In this way, Nixon could offer the "carrot" of troop reductions to North Vietnam, while easing antiwar tensions at home.

Vietnamization was part of a broader Asian policy that called for each American ally to accept primary responsibility for providing soldiers for its own defense. The number of U.S. troops in Vietnam peaked in March 1969 at 543,000. By the end of the year, more than 60,000 of those soldiers would be withdrawn.

The plan for Vietnamization set three main goals for South Vietnam: self-government, self-development, and self-defense. According to this plan, political reforms, including local elections, would increase popular participation in government and provide for essential public services. Rural development would bring economic opportunity to the countryside, while pacification would create local self-defense forces to take charge of village security.

U.S. officials believed that strengthening South Vietnam's military forces was key to making Vietnamization work. Training schools were expanded. Pay for soldiers in South Vietnam's army (ARVN) was increased. Living conditions in military camps were improved. So many U.S. ships, planes, helicopters, and vehicles were shipped to Vietnam that one Congressman wondered whether the goal of Vietnamization was to "put every South Vietnamese soldier behind the wheel."

In a television address on April 30, 1970, President Nixon announced the U.S. invasion of Cambodia, which he described as a haven for communist forces. "The time has come for action," he said. "We will not be humiliated. We will not be defeated." He did not reveal that B-52s had already been bombing Cambodia for a year.

The Stick: Widening the Air War and Invading Cambodia Vietnamization would be a long process, and many American officials were pessimistic about its prospects. Meanwhile, negotiations in Paris were proving fruitless. The "carrot" offered by the United States—U.S. troop withdrawals and an end to bombing—did not satisfy the North Vietnamese.

Nixon considered several military options to pressure North Vietnam to negotiate, including bombing its industrial areas, mining its harbors, and invading its territory. His strategy, which he called the "madman theory," was to make North Vietnam's leaders and their allies, the Soviet Union and China, believe that he would do anything to win the war. He even briefly put nuclear forces on alert as a bluff that he might use tactical nuclear weapons, small but highly destructive nuclear bombs.

Nixon had already shown a willingness to expand the war. In March 1969, he had secretly ordered B-52s to begin bombing Cambodia, a neutral nation on Vietnam's western border. For the next four years, U.S. bombers would strike communist base camps and supply lines in Cambodia.

With Vietnamization, U.S. ground forces began focusing more on intercepting supplies from the north and less on fighting guerrillas in the south. Nixon also decided to give those ground forces another mission. In April 1970, he ordered U.S. troops to invade Cambodia. The military goal of the invading U.S. force was to destroy enemy "safe havens" from which North Vietnamese Army (NVA) and Viet Cong forces could launch assaults into South Vietnam. The political goal, said Nixon, was to "show the enemy that we were still serious about our commitment in Vietnam."

The invasion was a partial success. The GIs destroyed enemy bases and relieved pressure on ARVN forces fighting in the south. But the invasion did not help the peace process. The communists boycotted the Paris talks until U.S. troops left Cambodia three months later.

In February 1971, Nixon launched a similar invasion of Laos, another neighboring country, after years of bombing had failed to dislodge the communists. By now, the steady withdrawal of GIs had left fewer than 175,000 U.S. combat soldiers in Vietnam. ARVN troops carried out the ground fighting in Laos, with U.S. air support. However, a large, well-equipped NVA force easily defeated the ARVN, forcing them to retreat. So far, Vietnamization had failed to prove its worth on the battlefield.

52.3 The Expanded War Sparks Increased Protest

Vietnamization dampened antiwar protests for a while. On November 12, 1969, journalist Seymour Hersh published an article describing a grisly killing spree at My Lai, a village in South Vietnam. The **My Lai massacre** had taken place in March 1968 but had been covered up by the military. U.S. soldiers, believing My Lai to be a Viet Cong stronghold, had gone there on a search-and-destroy mission. To their surprise, they found no armed Viet Cong in the village, just women, children, and old men. Nevertheless, one morning the soldiers rounded up and executed about 500 of these civilians. Only a handful of villagers survived.

News of the massacre shocked Americans, though many doubted that such an atrocity could occur. Others believed the soldiers were just following orders or that their actions were justified. Enough Americans expressed outrage, though, that Nixon decided to accelerate the withdrawal of troops from Vietnam.

Demonstrations Increase on City Streets and College Campuses The news of My Lai added fuel to an already growing antiwar movement. About a month before, on October 15, 1969, peace activists had staged the biggest antiwar demonstration in U.S. history: the nationwide Vietnam Moratorium Day. A **moratorium** is a suspension of activity. Organizers asked Americans to take the day off to reflect on the war. More than 2 million people—not only students but also older, middle-class Americans—responded in a day of dramatic and widespread protest. They took part in rallies and marches, attended church services, and engaged in discussions. About 250,000 demonstrators came to the nation's capital. In one of the protest activities, tens of thousands of them marched from the Washington Monument to the White House, where they held a candlelight vigil.

Nixon responded to this outpouring of antiwar sentiment with a televised speech on November 3. He reminded viewers of his Vietnamization policy and his plan for withdrawing U.S. troops. He ended with an appeal for support from "the great silent majority of my fellow Americans." And he warned that "the more divided we are at home, the less likely the enemy is to negotiate at Paris." Nixon's speech quieted the antiwar movement for a time.

The invasion of Cambodia in 1970, however, brought another upsurge in protests. Students held mass rallies and demonstrations, some of which turned violent. The **Kent State shootings** were the most shocking example. On May 4, students at Kent State University in Ohio were holding a peace rally after several days of violent unrest, which included the burning of the army's Reserve Officers' Training Corps (ROTC) building on campus. National Guard troops, called out to quell the protests, ordered the crowd to

In the My Lai massacre, U.S. troops slaughtered hundreds of Vietnamese civilians. Twenty or so officers were later charged with crimes, but only the unit leader, Lieutenant William Calley, was found guilty. He received a life sentence but won parole after serving three and a half years.

Escalation of the Vietnam War prompted renewed protests across the nation. These protesters in Des Moines, Iowa, are calling for U.S. withdrawal from Vietnam. Their posters also indicate a link between antiwar protests and the civil rights movement.

disperse. After some students began chanting slogans and throwing rocks, the troops opened fire. Four students were killed and nine were wounded.

Ten days later, a similar incident took place at Jackson State College in Mississippi. Protesters threw debris at police, and the officers responded with shotgun and machine-gun fire that left two students dead.

Reactions to these incidents varied. Many Americans were stunned, and protests erupted on college campuses and in cities across the nation. Vietnam veterans took part in some of these protests, as did several labor unions. Nevertheless, only a small percentage of Americans ever demonstrated publicly. In fact, many Americans rejected antiwar protests, seeing them as unpatriotic and disruptive. In May 1970, construction workers in New York City showed their disgust with antiwar demonstrators by holding marches in support of the war. Some soldiers also wrote home asking for public support. An army nurse wrote her parents, saying, "Display the flag, Mom and Dad . . . And tell your friends to do the same. It means so much to us to know we're supported, to know not everyone feels we're making a mistake being here."

Throughout the Vietnam War, Americans had been protesting for and against the war. Though prowar supporters were not as vocal as the antiwar protesters, there were prowar demonstrations, such as the one pictured above in 1967.

The Pentagon Papers Raise New Questions About the War Nixon soon had other problems to contend with. In 1971, a former Department of Defense official, Daniel Ellsberg, leaked a top-secret study known as the **Pentagon Papers** to the *New York Times*. This study revealed how previous administrations had deceived Congress and the public about Vietnam. Nixon feared that release of this document might lead to questions about his own policies and the secret actions he was taking in Vietnam.

Government lawyers won a temporary restraining order to stop further publication of the Pentagon Papers. Their appeal for a permanent injunction went to the Supreme Court. On June 30, 1971, in the case *New York Times Co. v. United States,* the Court ruled 6–3 against the government and in favor of free speech. In their opinion, the government had not proved the need for **prior restraint,** the prevention of speech or expression before publication.

Congress Responds to Widening War After the invasion of Cambodia, antiwar members of Congress intensified their efforts. By the end of 1970, they had repealed the Gulf of Tonkin Resolution, which had allowed Johnson and Nixon to escalate the conflict without a formal declaration of war. In February 1971, Congress passed legislation forbidding U.S. troops from operating outside the borders of South Vietnam.

Two years later, when Congress learned that Nixon had secretly bombed Cambodia without congressional approval, it passed the **War Powers Resolution.** This law placed strict limits on a president's power to use the armed forces in hostilities without congressional authorization. By then, support in Congress for the war had greatly declined.

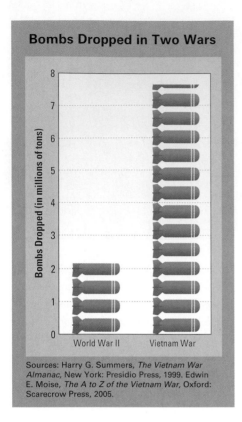

Bombs Dropped in Two Wars

Sources: Harry G. Summers, *The Vietnam War Almanac*, New York: Presidio Press, 1999. Edwin E. Moise, *The A to Z of the Vietnam War*, Oxford: Scarecrow Press, 2005.

Airpower played a huge role in the Vietnam War. By the war's end, the United States had dropped nearly 8 million tons of bombs. This was more than three times the tonnage it had dropped in World War II. Partly as a result of this massive bombing, more than 2 million Vietnamese died in the war.

52.4 American Involvement in the War Ends

By the time Nixon entered office in 1969, some 30,000 Americans had already died in Vietnam. During his first year as president, 11,500 more died and 55,000 were wounded. Over the next three years, however, Vietnamization drastically cut U.S. casualties, as more and more soldiers came home. Their ARVN replacements, though, had not yet shown they could stand up to an NVA assault. They got another chance in the spring of 1972.

On March 30, North Vietnamese troops backed by tanks and artillery invaded South Vietnam. They smashed through the ARVN defenders at the border. The U.S. military, with just 6,000 soldiers left in the country, provided airpower to counter the invasion. Then Nixon took a bolder step. In April, for the first time since 1969, he unleashed U.S. bombers on North Vietnam. He also ordered the mining of Haiphong and other North Vietnamese ports, where war supplies from the Soviet Union and China arrived. His stated goal was to "destroy the enemy's war-making capacity." By mid-June, the North's offensive had been shut down, and ARVN forces had begun pushing the invaders back.

Nixon Declares "Peace Is at Hand" North Vietnam's failed invasion caused it to soften its stand at the secret Paris peace talks. North Vietnamese negotiators withdrew their demand that South Vietnam's government share power with the Viet Cong. For its part, the United States stopped its bombing and agreed that some NVA forces could stay in the south. These compromises allowed Henry Kissinger to reach an agreement with Hanoi's diplomats. At a news conference less than two weeks before the 1972 presidential election, Kissinger announced, "We believe that peace is at hand." By that time, polls showed that Nixon already had a large lead over Democratic candidate George McGovern, an antiwar senator. Nixon went on to win a second term in a landslide.

But peace was not at hand. South Vietnam's president, Nguyen Van Thieu, feared that the United States was abandoning his country to the communists. He insisted on dozens of changes to the Paris agreement. Learning of the changes, Hanoi's leaders backed out, and the peace talks collapsed.

Frustrated by the failed talks, Nixon decided to punish the north. On December 14, he ordered a series of B-52 and fighter-bomber attacks on Hanoi and Haiphong. Known as the Christmas bombings, this aerial campaign reached an intensity not previously seen in the war. One NVA leader said it was "like living through a typhoon with trees crashing down and lightning transforming night into day." Nixon hoped to destroy North Vietnam's will to fight. He also wanted to show President Thieu that after peace came, the United States would use its might to enforce the terms of the treaty.

North Vietnam returned to the bargaining table, and South Vietnam agreed to the earlier proposals. By late January, the negotiators had a final treaty ready to sign. On January 27, 1973, representatives of the United States, South Vietnam, North Vietnam, and the Viet Cong signed the Paris Peace Accords. This treaty set the goal of "ending the war and restoring peace in Vietnam." To that end, it established a cease-fire and kept the dividing line between North and South Vietnam at the 17th parallel. It also called for the withdrawal of all U.S. troops and the release of all U.S. prisoners of war.

Senator John McCain was a former prisoner of war. He and other POWs were released after the signing of the Paris Peace Accords in January 1973. Here, McCain gives an interview about his experience three months after his release.

Veterans and Prisoners of War Return Home By March 29, 1973, the United States had withdrawn all combat forces from Vietnam. Arriving home, many soldiers were dismayed to find themselves the victims of their country's bitter debate over the war. Unlike soldiers returning from World War II, most Vietnam veterans were not treated like heroes. Few communities welcomed their soldiers back with parades or celebrations. Instead, Vietnam veterans were often shunned or simply ignored by the general public. As a result, they did not receive the support and understanding they deserved for their service and sacrifices.

For combat veterans especially, the Vietnam War had been a harrowing experience. Many soldiers were haunted by their fears in battle and by the death and destruction they had witnessed. They rarely talked about their combat experiences, except with other veterans. Of the 2.6 million Americans who served in Vietnam, nearly a half million suffered from **post-traumatic stress disorder**. Symptoms of this mental illness include anxiety, irritability, nightmares, and depression.

More than 760 Americans were taken prisoner by the North Vietnamese. Of these prisoners of war, or **POWs,** at least 110 died in captivity. The typical POW was a pilot whose plane had been shot down. POWs lived in miserable conditions, often in solitary confinement, and they faced regular interrogations and torture. One former POW described his experience in a Hanoi prison:

> From the moment you enter a political prison, you are told and forced to act as though you are subhuman—a dreg of society. And there's every effort made . . . to remind you daily that they're looking at you: You're not to look at the sky. That's enough to give you a left hook to the jaw. You're to bow down. You have no rights. You have no name. You have no nationality. You are a criminal. You are a worm.
>
> —Navy pilot James Stockdale, shot down in 1965

North Vietnam had released all POWs by April 1, 1973. Another 2,600 Americans were **MIA,** or missing in action. Some 1,800 MIAs are still unaccounted for today. Few, if any, are thought to be alive.

These POWs were released from a prison in North Vietnam. Although some POWs were able to leave, many died in captivity. Prisoners of war had to endure difficult conditions both physically and mentally.

52.5 The War in Vietnam Comes to an End

After the withdrawal of U.S. ground forces from Vietnam, President Thieu and the ARVN continued to depend on U.S. airpower. American bombers and fighter jets had played a critical part in the war, and the South Vietnamese relied on Nixon's promise to "respond with full force" if North Vietnam violated the cease-fire. "You can be sure," Nixon said to Thieu in April 1973, "that we stand with you as we continue to work together to build a lasting peace."

South Vietnam Falls to the Communist North The cease-fire did not hold for long. In 1973 and 1974, fierce fighting between insurgents and the ARVN left some 50,000 ARVN soldiers dead. Meanwhile, North Vietnam readied a final invasion of the south by rebuilding its army and military apparatus. In March 1975, the NVA launched an all-out offensive.

As ARVN forces scattered in the face of the assault, Thieu pleaded with the United States for help. President Gerald Ford, who succeeded Nixon in 1974, urged Congress to boost military aid. But he did not demand that U.S. forces return to Vietnam. In a speech on April 23, 1975, Ford said, "America can regain the sense of pride that existed before Vietnam. But it cannot be achieved by refighting a war that is finished as far as America is concerned."

Four days after Ford's speech, the NVA had surrounded Saigon. As panic gripped the city, U.S. embassy personnel worked frantically to evacuate more than a thousand Americans and several thousand frantic South Vietnamese. Helicopters airlifted most of them from the embassy rooftop to U.S. ships waiting offshore.

Early on April 30, NVA tanks and troops entered Saigon unopposed. President Thieu had resigned and fled nine days earlier. His replacement, Duong Van Minh, surrendered unconditionally. "I declare that the Saigon government, from central to local level, has been completely dissolved," he said. The Vietnam War, and South Vietnam itself, had come to an end.

The Aftermath of the War in Southeast Asia The end of the war did not bring an end to suffering in Vietnam. Nor did it end the suffering in Cambodia and Laos, where separate communist revolts had occurred. Local communist insurgents took over in both of those countries and worked to convert the people to communism.

In Vietnam, communists seized private property and nationalized businesses. Many anticommunists had feared a bloodbath, but instead the communists sent hundreds of thousands of people—including ARVN officers, government officials, scholars, and religious leaders—to "reeducation camps," where they were subjected to hard labor. They also relocated hundreds of thousands of city residents to rural "economic zones" to toil on collective farms. Faced with these circumstances, more than a million South Vietnamese have fled the country since 1975. Because many left by boat, they became known as the boat people. A great majority of these refugees eventually settled in the United States.

A similar period of turmoil followed the communist takeover in Laos. This social upheaval produced some 350,000 refugees. But Cambodians had the worst experience by far. The communist

After the communist victory in Vietnam, many South Vietnamese sought to escape communism by fleeing the country. Half a million left in boats. More than 50,000 boat people died at sea. The rest found refuge in other countries or returned to Vietnam.

regime there, called the Khmer Rouge, immediately cleared out all urban areas, forcing about 3 million city dwellers to work at hard labor on farms. Nearly 1.7 million Cambodian officials, merchants, members of minority groups, and others were worked to death, starved to death, or killed outright.

The Aftermath of the War in the United States The Vietnam War left the United States in a state of shock. More than 58,000 soldiers died in the war and another 300,000 were wounded, many of them losing limbs. To some Americans, the soldiers' sacrifices seemed pointless. The United States, after all, had lost the war—a war that could have been avoided. To others, failure to win the war suggested that the nation lacked the will to be a world leader.

For several years after the war, Americans tried to forget about Vietnam. The memories were too painful. Yet those memories also led to changes. The country reduced, for a while, its involvement in global conflicts. Also, because of the credibility gap fostered by government officials, Americans no longer automatically trusted what their leaders told them.

A monument erected in 1982 helped many Americans—especially Vietnam veterans—come to terms with the war. The Wall, part of the Vietnam Veterans Memorial in Washington, D.C., encouraged Americans to reflect on the conflict and thus heal some of the war's wounds. Many veterans, after seeing the Wall, finally felt they had come home.

Summary

In 1969, President Nixon began withdrawing U.S. troops from Vietnam, but the war continued throughout his time in office. He carried on peace talks with the North Vietnamese but also ordered massive bombing of North Vietnam, Cambodia, and Laos. He faced ongoing protests from the antiwar movement and criticism from Congress. In 1973, the last U.S. combat forces came home. North Vietnam swept to victory over the South in 1975.

Vietnamization Nixon's Vietnamization of the war allowed for the withdrawal of U.S. troops and prepared South Vietnam to take over responsibility for the war.

My Lai massacre In 1968, U.S. soldiers slaughtered hundreds of Vietnamese civilians in the village of My Lai. Reports of the massacre shocked Americans and increased antiwar protests.

Kent State shootings The invasion of Cambodia in April 1970 sparked an increase in antiwar protests. The most violent one occurred the following month at Kent State University in Ohio, where National Guard troops fired into an angry crowd, killing four students.

War Powers Resolution Congress reacted to Nixon's activities in Cambodia by passing the War Powers Resolution. This resolution limits a president's ability to send armed forces into combat.

Pentagon Papers In 1971, Daniel Ellsberg leaked to the press a top-secret study of the U.S. role in Indochina. This study, the Pentagon Papers, revealed secrecy and deceit on the part of U.S. presidents.

Boat people The North Vietnamese defeated South Vietnam and took control in 1975. This prompted an exodus of refugees from Indochina, many of whom fled by boat.

Chapter 53

The Rise and Fall of Richard Nixon

What events influenced Richard Nixon's rise to and fall from power?

53.1 Introduction

On September 23, 1952, California senator Richard Nixon reserved time on national television to make the most important speech of his career. He hoped to silence claims that he had accepted $18,000 in illegal political contributions to help cover personal expenses. The Republicans had recently nominated Nixon to run for vice president, alongside Dwight D. Eisenhower. When the charges became public, Eisenhower remained noncommittal. He did not drop Nixon from the ticket, but he also did not come to the defense of his running mate.

In his speech, Nixon told Americans, "Not one cent of the $18,000 or any other money of that type ever went to me for my personal use. Every penny of it was used to pay for political expenses that I did not think should be charged to the taxpayers of the United States." He did, however, confess to having accepted one personal gift from a contributor:

> A man down in Texas heard [my wife] Pat on the radio mention the fact that our two youngsters would like to have a dog. And, believe it or not, the day before we left on this campaign trip, we got a message from Union Station in Baltimore saying they had a package for us. We went down to get it. You know what it was. It was a little cocker spaniel dog in a crate he'd sent all the way from Texas. Black and white spotted. And our little girl—Tricia, the 6-year-old—named it Checkers. And you know, the kids, like all kids, love the dog, and I just want to say this right now, that regardless of what they say about it, we're gonna keep it.
>
> —Senator Richard Nixon, "Checkers" speech, September 23, 1952

Nixon's "Checkers" speech was a high point in a tumultuous career that culminated in his election to the presidency in 1968. In the years that followed, President Nixon would engineer stunning successes in both domestic and foreign affairs. He would also set in motion a humiliating fall from power.

This 1952 photograph shows vice presidential candidate Richard Nixon relaxing with his pet dog, Checkers. In his famous "Checkers" speech, Nixon defended himself against charges that he had misused campaign contributions. He made it clear that his family did not live lavishly, emphasizing that his wife, Pat, wore not a mink coat but "a respectable Republican cloth coat."

◄ President Richard Nixon tossing a ball at a Senators' baseball game, April 1969

In his 1968 presidential election campaign, Nixon reached out to moderate, middle-of-the-road voters. In a pamphlet titled "The Nixon Stand," he outlined his position on five key issues facing the country. He defined these issues as winning the peace, fighting rising crime, progress with order, preventing runaway government, and respect for America.

53.2 Richard Nixon's Rise to the Presidency

Born in California in 1913, Richard Nixon was one of five brothers. He worked to pay his way through college and law school. After serving in the Navy during World War II, he was elected to the House of Representatives and, later, to the Senate. From 1953 to 1960, he served as vice president to Dwight Eisenhower.

In 1960, Nixon ran for president. He lost to John F. Kennedy in a very close election. Two years later, he ran for governor of California and lost that race as well. In his concession speech, Nixon announced his retirement from politics. "You won't have Richard Nixon to kick around any more," he told reporters. In reality, however, Nixon's political career was far from over.

A Bumpy Road to the White House In 1968, Nixon made a spectacular political comeback by winning the Republican nomination for president. In what had been a troubled election year, the choice of Nixon as a candidate was one of many surprises and shocks. First, President Lyndon Johnson had unexpectedly decided not to run for reelection. Soon thereafter had followed the stunning assassinations of Martin Luther King Jr. and Robert Kennedy.

To add to the surprises, Alabama governor George Wallace mounted a strong campaign for president on the American Independent Party ticket. During civil rights struggles in his state, Wallace had been an ardent segregationist. His resistance to integration won him support from white voters in the South. Wallace also appealed to "the average man on the street" by attacking the "liberals, intellectuals, and long hairs [who] have run the country for too long."

A final shock to the nation came with the outbreak of violence in Chicago, Illinois, during the Democratic National Convention. Outside the convention, protesters opposed to the Vietnam War clashed with police, while inside, Vice President Hubert Humphrey won the Democratic nomination on a prowar platform. The Democratic Party left the convention anything but united.

These troubling events left many Americans fearful that the country was falling apart. Recognizing this concern, Nixon made it central to his campaign. As he put it, "We live in a deeply troubled and profoundly unsettled time. Drugs, crime, campus revolts, racial discord, draft resistance—on every hand we find old standards violated, old values discarded." In his campaign, he depicted himself as the champion of the many ordinary people who worked hard, paid their taxes, and loved their country. Nixon appealed to their desire for stability by promising a renewed commitment to "law and order."

To win votes in what had long been the solidly Democratic South, Nixon implemented a "southern strategy." For a running mate, he chose a southern governor, Spiro T. Agnew, of Maryland. Agnew was known for his tough stand against racial violence and urban crime. Nixon also reached out to conservative southern voters with talk of respect for states' rights and a smaller federal government, which were traditionally valued by southern Democrats.

The election proved to be very close. Nixon won with just 43.4 percent of the popular vote. In five Southern states, Wallace won a **plurality** of votes—not a majority but more than any other candidate. Democrats also maintained control of Congress. Because Nixon lacked both a strong electoral mandate and a Republican majority in Congress, it was not clear whether he would be able to lead the country the way he wanted.

Nixon's Domestic Policies: A Conservative and Liberal Blend Having won the presidency by a narrow margin, Nixon tried to appeal to conservatives and liberals once in office. He reached out to conservatives with a plan, called **New Federalism,** to reduce the size and power of the federal government. "After a third of a century of power flowing from the people and the states to Washington," Nixon explained, "it is time for a New Federalism in which power, funds, and responsibility will flow from Washington to the people."

The centerpiece of Nixon's New Federalism was a proposal called **revenue sharing**. Under revenue sharing, the federal government distributed tax revenues to states and local governments to spend as they saw fit. State and local leaders liked the practice because it gave them more funds as well as the power to spend those funds where most needed. Revenue sharing proved to be popular with conservatives.

However, Nixon was less successful at shrinking the federal government. He did do away with some of Lyndon Johnson's Great Society bureaucracy, including the Office of Economic Opportunity. At the same time, though, Nixon expanded several social benefit programs. He increased Social Security and enlarged the Food Stamp Program.

Nixon went on to increase the size and power of the government by signing new federal agencies into existence. One was the **Occupational Safety and Health Administration (OSHA)**. He charged OSHA with protecting workers on the job. He also established the **Environmental Protection Agency (EPA)** in order "to protect human health and to safeguard the natural environment."

Nixon's most surprising initiative was the **Family Assistance Plan**. Under this proposed plan, the government would support every poor family with a minimum annual income. To get this support, family members able to work would be required to seek employment. The Family Assistance Plan would have greatly expanded the number of families eligible for public assistance.

Nixon thought this program would appeal to liberals. He also hoped the increased responsibility for running welfare programs that it gave the states would interest conservatives. Instead, conservatives attacked the plan as a reward for laziness. Liberals denounced its proposed guaranteed income as too little to live on. After much debate, Congress rejected the plan.

A Mixed Record on Civil Rights Nixon's civil rights policies were as mixed as the rest of his domestic agenda. In pursuit of his "southern strategy," he sought to appoint conservative southern judges to the Supreme Court. His first two choices had records of supporting segregation. The Senate rejected them both. Nixon also called for changes to the Voting Rights Act when it came up for renewal in 1970. Congress rejected his proposals, which would have reduced federal oversight of voting officials in the South. Nonetheless, he resigned the Voting Rights Act into law.

At the same time, Nixon sought to increase economic opportunities for African Americans by expanding affirmative action. Under the Philadelphia Plan, he required construction companies working on federally funded projects to hire specific numbers of minority workers. He also encouraged "black capitalism" by providing federal assistance to black-owned businesses.

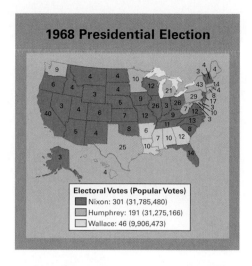

When Lyndon Johnson signed the Civil Rights Act of 1964, he commented, "I think we just delivered the South to the Republicans for a long time to come." In 1968, his prediction began to prove true. Democrat Hubert Humphrey won only one southern state. Segregationist George Wallace won five, and Republican Richard Nixon carried the rest of the southern states.

The Nixon administration founded the Occupational Safety and Health Administration. Today, this organization continues to work to ensure safe workplaces for Americans.

In response to the 1973 oil embargo, Congress enacted the National Maximum Speed Law. This law required states to impose a 55 mph speed limit on all roads if they wanted to receive federal highway funds. At first the lower speed limit seemed to increase highway safety, but this effect was short-lived. In 1995, Congress returned control of highway speed limits to the states.

Struggling with a Stagnant Economy Throughout his presidency, Nixon struggled with the nation's economic problems. In 1970, the United States entered a recession. Normally, during a recession, unemployment rises, wages drop, and consumers spend less money. To encourage people to buy goods, companies lower their prices. As prices drop, people start spending again. Then business activity picks up, and eventually the recession ends. However, this is not what happened in the early 1970s. Instead, the nation experienced an economic condition known as **stagflation**. Unemployment rose, just as it would in a normal recession. But prices also increased at an alarming rate. Americans found themselves living with both a stagnant economy and rapid inflation.

Nixon responded to stagflation in two ways. First, he attacked inflation with a three-phase program. In Phase I, he froze wages and prices for 90 days. In Phase II, he authorized a new federal agency to strictly limit future wage and price increases. He then turned to unemployment. He increased government spending to put more money into the economy. As a result, joblessness fell. Nixon then moved to Phase III of his inflation plan, replacing strict wage and price controls with voluntary guidelines. Unfortunately, with controls lifted, the nation suffered its most rapid rise in cost of living since World War II's end.

To make matters even worse, in the fall of 1973, oil-exporting nations in the Middle East stopped shipping oil to the United States. They established this oil embargo to protest U.S. support for Israel in conflicts between Israel and Arab nations. The result was a nationwide energy crisis. To conserve dwindling supplies, the government urged homeowners to lower their thermostats. It also reduced highway speed limits to 55 miles per hour. The crisis did not ease until the Middle Eastern nations lifted the ban the following year.

53.3 President Nixon's Foreign Policy Record

Early in his political career, Richard Nixon had made a name for himself as a staunch opponent of communism. As president, however, he was determined to reshape America's containment policy. He hoped to replace endless conflict with a stable world order in which the superpowers could coexist peacefully.

Nixon's Realistic Approach to Foreign Affairs Nixon based his foreign policy on **realpolitik,** a German term that means "the politics of reality." It refers to politics based on practical rather than idealistic concerns. Nixon's top foreign policy adviser, Henry Kissinger, backed him in this realistic approach.

As part of their realpolitik approach, Nixon and Kissinger concluded that the United States could no longer bear the full burden of defending the free world. Addressing the nation in 1969, the president laid out his plan, which became known as the Nixon Doctrine. He promised that the United States would continue to protect its allies from Soviet or Chinese nuclear attacks. In other cases of aggression, however, the United States would expect the nation at risk to do more to help itself. The president's plan for Vietnamization of the war in Southeast Asia was an early application of the new Nixon Doctrine.

The president also applied the Nixon Doctrine in the Persian Gulf region of the Middle East. With their vast deposits of oil, Persian Gulf nations had become increasingly important to the United States. However, the United

States had no military forces stationed in the region. Rather than try to move troops in, Nixon sent military aid to Iran and Saudi Arabia. With this aid, he hoped these allies would take on the responsibility of keeping the region peaceful and stable. At the same time, the United States continued to support its closest ally in the Middle East, Israel, with both military and financial aid.

The limits of the Nixon Doctrine became clear when Israel was attacked by a coalition of Arab countries led by Egypt and Syria during the Yom Kippur holy days in October 1973. The Yom Kippur War lasted just three weeks, but that was long enough to trigger the oil embargo. Despite receiving American aid, Saudi Arabia backed the embargo to punish the United States for its long-standing support of Israel.

In dealings with the Soviet Union and communist China, Nixon and Kissinger pursued a policy of **détente**. Détente is a French word that means a relaxation of tension or hostility. To many conservatives, détente seemed inconsistent with Nixon's earlier anticommunism. Some also saw it as a sellout of U.S. interests and ideals. Most liberals, however, applauded any policy that had the potential to prevent a nuclear holocaust.

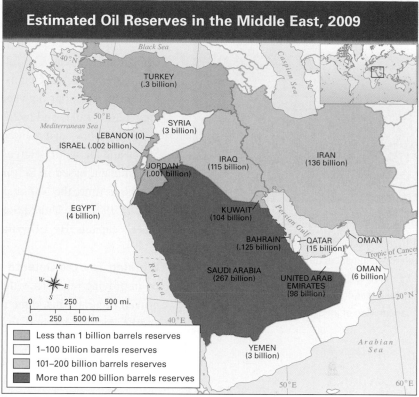

Estimated Oil Reserves in the Middle East, 2009

Less than 1 billion barrels reserves
1–100 billion barrels reserves
101–200 billion barrels reserves
More than 200 billion barrels reserves

Source: Energy Information Administration, www.eia.doe.gov, 2009.

More than half of the world's proven crude oil reserves lie in the Middle East. Proven reserves are known deposits of petroleum that can be pumped at a reasonable cost.

Opening Diplomatic Relations with China The policy of détente brought a dramatic change in U.S. interactions with China. When Nixon took office in 1969, the United States did not engage in diplomatic relations with China. Nor did it officially recognize the communist government that had ruled mainland China since 1949. Nixon believed that the policy of isolating China had worn out its usefulness. In 1970, he reported to Congress that it was in America's national interest to improve "practical relations with Peking [Beijing]."

The president had several reasons for wanting better relations with China. One was the sheer size of that nation—one fifth of the world's population lived in China. In addition, Nixon had watched the relationship between China and the Soviet Union change from one of communist comrades to one of hostile neighbors. He believed that establishing friendly diplomatic relations with China might pressure Soviet leaders, who feared Chinese power, to cooperate more with the United States.

In April 1971, a sporting event opened the way for détente. The Chinese government had invited a U.S. table tennis team to play in Beijing. The 15 team members were the first Americans to visit Beijing since the communists took power. Chinese leaders treated the American athletes as though they were ambassadors. At a meeting with the team, Chinese Premier Chou En-lai stated that the athletes' arrival in China marked a new chapter in U.S.-China relations.

President Nixon's historic trip to China in 1972 marked the first visit by a U.S. president to a communist country. While there, Nixon attempted to establish friendly relations with Chinese leaders. Here, Nixon converses with Madam Mao at an opera.

Shortly after the table tennis competition, Nixon announced proposals to begin trade and travel between the two countries. Two months later, Kissinger secretly traveled to China. In July 1971, Nixon announced that he would visit China the next year. The following February, Nixon and his wife, Pat, made an official state visit to China. While there, Nixon pledged to establish formal diplomatic relations between the two countries. He described the trip as bridging "12,000 miles and twenty-two years of noncommunication and hostility."

The historic visit marked a turning point in relations between the United States and the world's largest communist nation. The trip led to the communist government, based in Beijing, taking over China's seat in the United Nations. Until that time, the Nationalist government of Taiwan had occupied China's seat. In 1973, the United States and China opened information offices in each other's capitals. By 1979, the two countries engaged in full diplomatic relations.

Working Toward Détente with the Soviet Union Nixon's expectation that by improving relations with China he could push the USSR toward détente proved accurate. Just three months after visiting China, Nixon embarked on another historic journey. In May 1972, he became the first American president to visit Moscow, the capital of the USSR. Soviet leader Leonid Brezhnev had invited Nixon partly in response to Soviet concerns about U.S. involvement with China. The invitation had also revealed Brezhnev's desire to receive U.S. economic and technological aid.

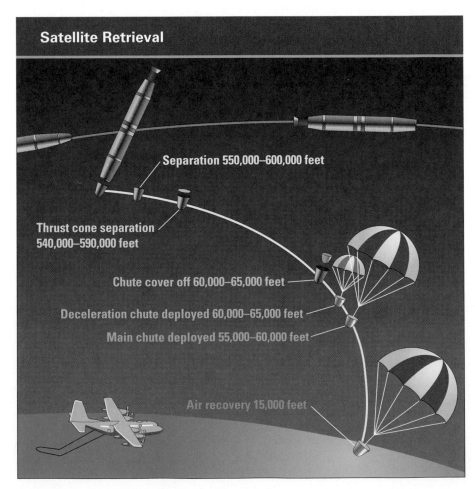

Satellite Retrieval

Separation 550,000–600,000 feet

Thrust cone separation 540,000–590,000 feet

Chute cover off 60,000–65,000 feet

Deceleration chute deployed 60,000–65,000 feet

Main chute deployed 55,000–60,000 feet

Air recovery 15,000 feet

During the 1960s, U.S. and Soviet engineers equipped satellites with long-range cameras to create "spies in the sky." The spy satellites would eject canisters of undeveloped film back toward Earth. When a canister reached the upper atmosphere, a parachute on it opened. An airplane would catch the canister in midair.

Brezhnev and Nixon were able to negotiate a trade deal that benefited both countries. The United States agreed to sell to the USSR at least $750 million worth of grain over a three-year period. The grain deal helped the people of the Soviet Union, which was not growing enough grain to feed its population. It also helped American farmers, who were happy to sell their surplus grain.

The two leaders then negotiated a much more difficult agreement—to limit the number of nuclear missiles in their arsenals. Such an agreement had been made possible by the development of spy satellites in the 1960s. Cameras mounted on these satellites took photographs that, when sent back to Earth, allowed the two countries to monitor each other's missile sites. The **Strategic Arms Limitation Talks (SALT)**, later called SALT I, was a five-year agreement. The treaty limited the USSR to 1,618 missiles and the United States to 1,054. The United States accepted the smaller number because its missiles were more advanced. The deal applied to both ground-based intercontinental ballistic missiles (ICBMs) and submarine-launched ballistic missiles (SLBMs). In addition, Nixon and Brezhnev signed a statement of "basic principles," which called on both of the superpowers to "do their utmost to avoid military confrontations."

Nixon was pleased with this first agreement to halt the arms race. "The historians of some future age," he predicted, "will write . . . that this was the year when America helped to lead the world up out of the lowlands of constant war, and to the high plateau of lasting peace." Over time, however, hope that détente would lead to an era of cooperation between the superpowers began to fade. The USSR continued to support armed struggles in the Third World. It also began arming its missiles with multiple warheads in order to work around the treaty's limits. As a result, conservative critics of détente concluded that the Soviet Union should never be trusted again.

53.4 Watergate Ends Nixon's Career

On June 17, 1972, five men broke into the offices of the Democratic National Committee in Washington, D.C. A security guard at the Watergate building, where the offices were located, caught the men. But the burglars were unusual —they wore suits and carried bugging, or wiretapping, devices. Further investigation showed that they had ties to Nixon's reelection campaign.

Early news reports of the break-in did not stop Nixon from winning the 1972 presidential election by a landslide. But the bungled burglary and attempts to cover it up would eventually lead to Nixon's fall from power.

Abusing Power to Limit Dissent At first, the Watergate burglars' intentions were unclear. Their actions, however, were part of a larger pattern of abuse of presidential power. Nixon tended to view critics of his policies as a threat to national security. Once elected, he developed an "enemies list" that included reporters, politicians, activists, and celebrities whom he viewed as being unfriendly to his administration. He authorized the FBI to tap the phones of news reporters whom he felt were biased against him. He even ordered phone tapping of members of his own staff whom he distrusted. All these wiretaps were unconstitutional, and thus an abuse of power, because a judge had not properly authorized them.

At the height of the scandal, Nixon released recordings of the White House conversations on the break-in. On one tape, a conversation between Nixon and an aide was replaced by 18.5 minutes of silence. This revelation caused many Americans to grow skeptical of political leaders. Here, a demonstrator calls for the impeachment of Nixon.

Rather than face impeachment, Richard Nixon resigned from the presidency in August 1974. Most Americans felt that his fall from power showed that the Constitution works. The legislative branch led the way by investigating Nixon's role in the Watergate cover-up. The judicial branch did its part by forcing Nixon to release his Oval Office tapes.

The president also showed grave concern for secrecy. He set up his own White House security operation to investigate leaks of damaging information to the press. The group received the nickname "the plumbers," because their main job was to "plug" leaks. In 1971, the plumbers had broken into the office of a psychiatrist whose clients included Daniel Ellsberg, a former defense analyst. Nixon had suspected Ellsberg of leaking the Pentagon Papers, a set of secret military documents on the Vietnam War, to the *New York Times*. A year later, it was the White House plumbers who carried out the botched Watergate burglary.

The Watergate Scandal Unfolds The break-in might have been forgotten after Nixon's reelection if not for the work of two *Washington Post* reporters. Bob Woodward and Carl Bernstein would not let the matter drop. With the help of an anonymous source, whom they called Deep Throat, they discovered that Nixon's reelection campaign had paid the plumbers to bug the Democrats' offices. More details came out when the plumbers faced trial in 1973. During the legal proceedings, one of them implicated the Nixon administration in a cover-up. He reported that the defendants had been paid to lie to protect government officials.

At this point, what the White House had tried to dismiss as a "third-rate burglary" had turned into the Watergate scandal. Pressure to thoroughly investigate the scandal increased. The Justice Department appointed Archibald Cox, a respected law professor, to serve as **special prosecutor** in the case. A special prosecutor is a lawyer from outside the government whom the attorney general or Congress appoints to investigate a federal official for misconduct while in office.

After the plumbers' trial, the Senate formed a committee to investigate the Watergate affair. In televised hearings, former White House counsel John Dean testified that Nixon had been involved in efforts to cover up White House links to the Watergate break-in. Another former Nixon aide revealed that President Nixon had installed a recording system in the White House Oval Office that taped every conversation Nixon had there. If the committee could hear those tapes, it would find out whether the president had ordered a cover-up.

In July 1973, the Senate Watergate Committee issued a **subpoena,** or court order, compelling Nixon to turn over several tapes. Nixon refused, invoking a right to withhold information known as **executive privilege**. The concept of executive privilege is based in the constitutional separation of powers. Presidents since George Washington's day have argued that separation of powers gives the executive branch the right to operate without having to reveal to the other branches the details of every conversation or working document.

Over the next few months, Nixon battled both Special Prosecutor Cox and the Senate Committee over the release of the White House tapes. In October 1973, in what became known as the "Saturday Night Massacre," Nixon fired Cox. Nixon's own attorney general then resigned in protest.

That same month, for reasons unrelated to Watergate, Vice President Spiro Agnew resigned. He left office to avoid facing trial on charges of accepting bribes and evading taxes while governor of Maryland. Nixon appointed Gerald Ford, Republican minority leader in the House of Representatives, to be Agnew's successor as vice president.

In July 1974, in the case of *United States v. Nixon,* the Supreme Court ruled that the president must release his tapes to the Senate. Once released, the recordings proved beyond a doubt that he had ordered a Watergate cover-up.

Nixon Resigns in Disgrace Late in July, the House Judiciary Committee approved three articles of impeachment against Nixon. The articles accused him of obstruction of justice, abuse of power, and contempt of Congress. Rather than face trial and almost certain conviction in the Senate, Nixon announced his resignation on August 8, 1974. On August 9, Vice President Gerald Ford was sworn in as president. "Our Constitution works," Ford said. "Our long national nightmare is over."

In September, Ford issued Nixon a presidential pardon. Ford hoped the pardon would help unify the country by putting the Watergate mess to rest. Instead, it aroused controversy. Some Americans wanted to see Nixon tried for his alleged crimes. Others preferred to move on from Watergate. Despite Ford's efforts to close this unhappy chapter of presidential history, the nation remained deeply disillusioned with political leadership.

Summary

Richard Nixon won the presidency in 1968. While in office, he made strides toward easing the tensions of the Cold War. He also saw many of his domestic policies enacted. However, scandal forced him to resign in disgrace in 1974.

New Federalism Nixon came into office determined to revive federalism. He hoped to reduce the power of the federal government and return power to the states. Revenue sharing, central to his plan, allowed state and local governments to spend tax revenues as they saw fit.

Occupational Safety and Health Administration Despite his promise to shrink the federal government, Nixon created OSHA, which works to improve health and safety in the workplace.

Environmental Protection Agency Another new agency, the EPA, was created to protect Americans' health and the natural environment.

Energy crisis Nixon tried to revive a stagnant economy with increased spending while fighting inflation with wage and price controls. However, an energy crisis made a bad situation worse.

Détente Nixon tried to encourage détente, or a relaxation of Cold War tensions. In 1972, he visited both communist China and the Soviet Union.

Strategic Arms Limitation Treaty In 1972, Nixon and Soviet leader Leonid Brezhnev signed SALT I, the first superpower treaty to place limits on the arms race.

Watergate scandal In 1972, burglars broke into Democratic headquarters in the Watergate building. The scandal over the cover-up that followed the break-in led to Richard Nixon's resignation in 1974.

Chapter 54

Politics and Society in the "Me Decade"

How should historians characterize the 1970s?

54.1 Introduction

On July 4, 1976, the United States celebrated the **bicentennial**—or 200th anniversary—of the signing of the Declaration of Independence. Across the nation, Americans marked the day with parades, picnics, and fireworks displays. But the celebration surpassed the usual Independence Day events. It lasted most of the year. The U.S. Mint issued coins with bicentennial designs. Television networks featured programs that explored the events of the nation's first two centuries. A flag with a special bicentennial logo flew throughout the year.

To many Americans, the bicentennial year brought a welcome sense of national pride. The celebrations, with their focus on the nation's founding ideals, helped them move past the trauma of Vietnam and the disillusionment of Watergate. Others, however, reacted differently. As they looked back on the nation's founding, they worried that the United States had lost its sense of purpose.

In the bicentennial year, a journalist named Tom Wolfe captured such concerns in his essay, "The Me Decade and the Third Great Awakening." In it, Wolfe wrote of changes he had seen in American life since the end of the 1960s. In that decade, he noted, idealistic Americans had worked hard to end racism, fight poverty, and create a more just society. During the 1970s, however, the drive for social change had been replaced with a quest for self-improvement and personal fulfillment. "We are now in the Me Decade," he wrote, "seeing the upward roll of . . . the third great religious wave in American history." The focus of this latest "great awakening," Wolfe observed, was "the most fascinating subject on earth: Me."

Wolfe's characterization of the 1970s as the "Me Decade" stuck. Today, however, most historians view the 1970s as being much more complex than the label "Me Decade" suggests.

The U.S. Mint released coins with bicentennial designs in 1976. Many of the designs inspired a sense of national pride. The design on the quarter, pictured above, features a colonial drummer.

◀ A bicentennial celebration at Independence Hall in Philadelphia

In 1979, gas prices soared. Like in 1973, drivers would wait in long lines at gas stations for fuel. Some motorists would pick fights with each other when their patience wore thin.

54.2 A Time of Economic and Political Malaise

When Gerald Ford took office as president in 1974, he inherited a number of political problems. Although the United States had withdrawn from Vietnam, the war there raged on. Ford's decision to pardon Richard Nixon had divided the nation. In addition, the economy continued to suffer from stagflation. In a speech to Congress, Ford explained just how dire the situation was. "Inflation, our public enemy number one, will, unless whipped," he stated, "destroy our country, our homes, our liberties, our property, and finally our national pride, as surely as any well-armed wartime enemy."

President Ford Tries to "Whip Inflation Now" The inflation that dragged down the economy in the 1970s had many causes. One was President Johnson's decision to escalate the war in Vietnam while also launching a War on Poverty. Both military and welfare spending tend to be inflationary, because they put more money into people's pockets without increasing the supply of goods those dollars can buy. When too many dollars chase too few goods, prices rise.

The **Organization of the Petroleum Exporting Countries (OPEC)** made matters worse. Formed in 1960, OPEC is an association of nations that depend on oil sales for their national income. In its early years, OPEC priced oil at $2 to $3 per barrel. The 1973 oil embargo, however, revealed the dependence of many countries on imported oil. As a result, OPEC began to increase oil prices. By 1976, the price of a barrel of oil had jumped to $12.

Soaring oil prices hurt the U.S. economy. Products that used oil as a raw material became more costly to produce. As fuel prices went up, so did the cost of moving goods from farm or factory to consumers. Stunned by high gas prices, drivers stopped buying American-made gas-guzzlers for a while. As sales plummeted, auto manufacturers laid off more than 225,000 workers in 1974.

Ford tried to beat down rising prices with a crusade called Whip Inflation Now (WIN). He cut federal spending while urging Americans to conserve energy and practice thrift. "Clean up your plate before you leave the table," the president advised. "Guard your health." Unfortunately, WIN was not effective. Prices continued to rise, growing 11 percent in 1975. The unemployment rate grew more than 8 percent—the highest it had been since the Depression's end.

An Outsider in the White House: Jimmy Carter The 1976 presidential election pitted Ford against former Georgia governor Jimmy Carter. Carter appealed to voters as a Washington outsider untouched by scandal. He promised Americans, "I will never lie to you."

Neither candidate generated much excitement. As Election Day neared, people talked of a "clothespin vote," a phrase that implies "hold your nose and vote for one or the other." Only 53 percent of eligible voters went to the polls—the lowest turnout since 1948. Carter won, but by a narrow margin.

Once in the White House, Carter maintained his outsider status. Rather than hiring experienced Washington insiders, he surrounded himself with staff from Georgia. Nor did he establish close relations with Congress. As a result, his efforts to enact such reforms as a national health insurance system went nowhere.

Carter's Energy Program: "The Moral Equivalent of War" Convinced that the era of cheap energy had ended, the new president called on Americans to "face the fact that the energy shortage is permanent." Soon after taking office in 1977, Carter put forward a plan to end the nation's dependence on imported oil. He called this effort the "moral equivalent of war."

Carter's energy plan centered on conservation. "It is the cheapest, most practical way to meet our energy needs," he told Congress, "and to reduce our dependence on foreign oil." His plan would penalize energy waste while encouraging energy efficiency. Lawmakers, however, were slow to respond to it. Reporters began to refer to Carter's "moral equivalent of war" as MEOW, revealing their feeling that Congress would not take it seriously.

Late in 1978, Congress finally passed a watered-down version of Carter's original plan. This **National Energy Act** offered **tax credits** as incentives to people who conserved energy by insulating their homes or investing in alternative energy sources, such as solar energy panels. Tax credits reduce the amount of taxes a taxpayer owes to the government.

While the National Energy Act helped make the nation more energy efficient, it did not end U.S. dependence on foreign oil. In 1979, a second energy crisis disrupted life across the country. This energy shortage was triggered by a revolution in Iran that led that country to stop exporting oil. Over the next year, oil prices rose to a staggering $39.50 per barrel. Long lines reappeared at gas stations, and fistfights broke out among some motorists who were waiting in line for gas.

Americans Face a "Crisis of Confidence" With his approval rating low, at 25 percent, Carter planned to speak to the nation once more about conserving energy. However, after a week of discussions with various advisers, he changed his mind. "I want to speak to you first tonight about a subject even more serious than energy or inflation," Carter told the nation in a televised address.

> I want to talk to you right now about a fundamental threat to American democracy . . . It is a crisis of confidence. It is a crisis that strikes at the very heart and soul and spirit of our national will. We see this crisis in the growing doubt about the meaning of our own lives and in the loss of unity of purpose for our Nation . . .
>
> In a nation that was proud of hard work, strong families, close-knit communities, and our faith in God, too many of us now tend to worship self-indulgence and consumption. Human identity is no longer defined by what one does, but by what one owns. But we've discovered that owning things and consuming things does not satisfy our longing for meaning. We've learned that piling up material goods cannot fill the emptiness of lives which have no confidence or purpose.
>
> —Jimmy Carter, "Crisis of Confidence" speech, July 15, 1979

Carter's address, which the media called his "malaise speech"—malaise meaning "a feeling of general unease"—backfired. "There's nothing wrong with the American people," responded newspaper editorials. "Maybe the problem's in the White House, maybe we need new leadership to guide us."

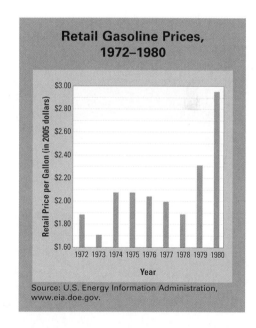

Retail Gasoline Prices, 1972–1980

Source: U.S. Energy Information Administration, www.eia.doe.gov.

The effects of the first energy crisis in 1973–1974 and of a second one in 1979 can be seen on this graph. As the supply of imported oil dropped, the price of gasoline spiked upward. Automakers began equipping automobile gas tanks with locks to prevent theft during such fuel shortages.

54.3 President Carter's Approach to Foreign Policy

Once Carter took office in 1976, it was clear that his approach to foreign policy differed sharply from Richard Nixon's realpolitik. Whereas Nixon had prided himself on his realism, Carter applied his idealism to foreign affairs. He insisted that the government not separate foreign policy from "questions of justice, equity, and human rights." "Fairness, and not force," he urged, "should lie at the heart of our dealings with nations of the world."

Promoting Justice, Equity, and Human Rights Carter worked hard to put his ideals into practice. In some areas, he saw success. For example, he established a more equitable relationship with the nation of Panama. Panamanians had long regarded a 1903 treaty between the two countries as unjust, as it gave the United States permanent control of the Panama Canal. In 1977, Carter negotiated a new treaty that would return control of the canal to Panama in 1999. Despite strong objections, the Senate ratified the Panama Canal Treaty in 1978.

In the area of human rights, Carter's record proved to be more mixed. He came into office determined to end the Cold War policy of supporting dictators who opposed communism even if they abused human rights. When leftist rebels ousted an anticommunist dictator from Nicaragua in 1979, Carter stood by his new policy and did not intervene. However, he did continue to support dictators with poor human rights records in other parts of the world—such as the Philippines and Indonesia—that he viewed as vital to American interests.

A Step Toward Middle East Peace: The Camp David Accords Carter achieved his greatest foreign policy success in the Middle East. In 1978, he invited the leaders of Egypt and Israel to peace talks at Camp David, the presidential retreat in Maryland. Just five years earlier, Egypt and Israel had been adversaries in the Yom Kippur War. During that conflict, Israel had gained control of lands that had previously belonged to its neighbors. These occupied territories included Egypt's Sinai Peninsula.

Israeli Prime Minister Menachem Begin and Egyptian President Anwar el-Sadat conversed for 13 tense days. Finally, they reached an agreement known as the **Camp David Accords**. The Accords provided a framework for peace between the two countries. Israel agreed to return the Sinai Peninsula to Egypt, while Egypt agreed to establish normal diplomatic relations with Israel. This made Egypt the first Arab country to formally recognize Israel's right to exist, which Arab nations had opposed since Israel's establishment in 1948.

In 1979, Sadat and Begin together received the Nobel Peace Prize for their efforts to end hostilities between their countries. When presenting the award, the chairman of the Nobel Committee spoke of Carter's contribution. Carter, he said, was "the master builder responsible for the bridge" that brought "two one-time enemies" together to talk of peace.

The Camp David Accords ended hostilities between Egypt and Israel. Israel agreed to return the Sinai Peninsula to Egypt over the course of four years. In exhange, Egypt agreed to recognize Israel's right to exist.

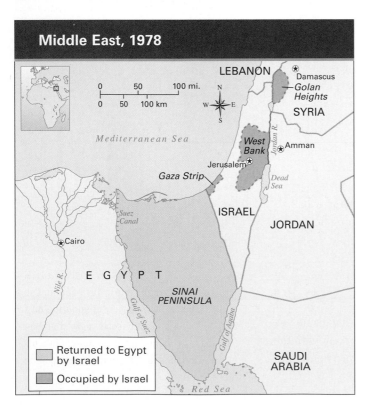

Middle East, 1978

Mediterranean Sea

LEBANON
Damascus
Golan Heights
SYRIA
West Bank
Jordan R.
Amman
Jerusalem
Gaza Strip
Dead Sea
ISRAEL
JORDAN
Suez Canal
Cairo
Nile R.
E G Y P T
SINAI PENINSULA
Gulf of Suez
Gulf of Aqaba
SAUDI ARABIA
Red Sea

0 50 100 mi.
0 50 100 km

Returned to Egypt by Israel

Occupied by Israel

The Death of Détente Between the U.S. and USSR Both presidents Nixon and Ford had pursued a policy of détente toward the USSR. In contrast, Carter openly criticized the Soviet Union's human rights record. Still, he cooperated with Soviet leaders enough to negotiate a second Strategic Arms Limitation Treaty (SALT II). "Peace will not be assured," he said in a speech before the United Nations, "until the weapons of war are finally put away."

Any remnants of détente vanished in 1979, when Soviet troops marched into Afghanistan. The USSR invaded this neighbor to help its failing communist government handle a rebellion. Calling the invasion the "most serious threat to world peace since World War II," Carter responded by promoting a boycott of the Olympic Games that would be held in Moscow the following summer.

A Hostage Crisis in Iran Under Carter, the Nixon Doctrine fared little better than did détente. Early in the 1970s, as part of that policy, the United States had increased military aid to Iran. In return, it had expected Iran's royal ruler, Shah Mohammed Reza Pahlavi, to help maintain stability in the Persian Gulf region. Carter continued to support the Shah, despite the leader's poor human rights record. However, in January 1979, a revolution swept through Iran. Under a religious leader, the Ayatollah Ruholla Khomeini, the revolutionary army declared Iran a republic. It forced the Shah from the throne and into exile. Khomeini established a new government based on a strict understanding of Islamic principles.

Later that year, Carter allowed the exiled Shah to enter the United States for medical treatment. This decision enraged many Iranians. On November 4, 1979, militant students stormed the U.S. embassy in Tehran, Iran's capital. In violation of international law, which protects diplomats, the students took 66 Americans hostage. They paraded the hostages through the streets of Tehran, while the angry crowd shouted, "Death to Carter!"

For more than a year, Carter struggled to bring the hostages home. Appeals to the United Nations and U.S. allies for help in securing the hostages' release accomplished little. In April 1980, Carter attempted a military rescue. The mission failed when two helicopters had engine trouble, a third was damaged while landing, and a fourth crashed, killing eight Americans.

The hostage crisis angered Americans. Some directed their outrage at Iran. Texans displayed signs urging, "Don't buy Iranian oil." Other Americans blamed Carter's "fairness, not force" approach to foreign policy. "Wild as he is," stated former energy secretary James Schlesinger, "the Ayatollah Khomeini would not have touched the Soviet embassy." Fifty-two of the hostages were not released until Carter left office in January 1981. By then, they had endured 444 days in captivity.

Congress applauds Menachem Begin of Israel and Anwar el-Sadat of Egypt after President Jimmy Carter announces the signing of the Camp David Accords. The agreement marked a high point in Carter's efforts to bring peace to the Middle East.

The Iran hostage crisis began when Iranian students seized Americans working in the U.S. embassy in Tehran. As the crisis wore on, many Americans criticized Carter for not bringing the hostages home. To them, his inability to free the hostages symbolized a loss of U.S. power.

Many Americans participated in the first Earth Day in 1970 by cleaning up trash and holding marches. Senator Gaylord Nelson, who organized the event, commented, "Earth Day worked because of the spontaneous response at the grassroots level...That was the remarkable thing about Earth Day. It organized itself." Earth Day is still celebrated each year.

54.4 Protecting the Environment

On April 22, 1970, Americans celebrated the first **Earth Day**. Across the country, nearly 20 million people came together to show their concern for a healthy environment. Some held marches. Others organized cleanup projects. "The Establishment sees this as a great big antilitter campaign," observed George Brown, a congressman from California. But Earth Day was far more than that. By 1970, polls showed that for many Americans, the condition of the environment had become the nation's most pressing domestic issue.

An Environmental Movement Emerges The success of Earth Day signaled the emergence of a grassroots environmental movement. Some groups, such as the Audubon Society and the Sierra Club, had existed for many years. The Sierra Club had come into being in 1892 under the leadership of John Muir and other conservationists. The club's original purpose was to enjoy and protect the mountains of the West. Over time, it expanded this mission to include preserving wilderness and protecting the environment across the nation. As a result, the club's membership grew. In 1970, the Sierra Club had 100,000 members. By the end of the decade, membership had swelled to nearly 200,000.

New organizations also sprang up in response to environmental concerns. Some dealt with local issues, such as cleaning up rivers or starting recycling programs. Others dealt with national and even global issues. A group called Zero Population Growth (ZPG) that formed in 1968 aimed to raise awareness of the connection between rapid population growth and environmental destruction. With its slogan "Stop at Two," ZPG encouraged families to stay small.

A Decade of Environmental Legislation In response to growing public concern, Congress enacted a number of environmental laws during the 1970s. Soon after the first Earth Day in 1970, it approved legislation to create the Environmental Protection Agency (EPA). This agency's mission was to repair damage already done to the natural environment and to prevent new problems. The EPA grew quickly. By the end of the decade, it had become the government's largest regulatory agency, with more than 10,000 employees.

Air pollution was a major concern during this decade. In 1970, Congress amended the Clean Air Act of 1963. The updated act set stricter standards for emissions from automobiles, factories, and power plants. In 1977, lawmakers amended the act once more. This time they strengthened air-quality standards.

Congress also dealt with water pollution. In 1969, Americans had been shocked when the polluted Cuyahoga River burst into flames in Cleveland, Ohio. The **Clean Water Act** of 1972 limited the amount of sewage and other pollutants flowing into waterways. The **Safe Drinking Water Act** of 1974 allowed the EPA to regulate the quality of public drinking water.

The EPA also took steps to deal with another source of water pollution, **acid rain**. Acid rain is precipitation that contains acid as a result of water vapor mixing with molecules of sulfur dioxide and oxides of nitrogen in the atmosphere. These pollutants are released into the atmosphere by automobiles, factories, and power plants that burn fossil fuels. Acid rain can harm plants and animals. It also corrodes buildings and other stone structures.

During the 1970s, the EPA began requiring cars to have reduced pollution. By 1975, manufacturers were equipping each car with a catalytic converter, a device that removes pollutants from the car's exhaust. By 1979, the EPA had also required the use of smokestack scrubbers. These removed pollutants from the exhaust of coal-fired power plants. This technology was widely adopted during the 1980s.

Environmental Disasters Fuel Public Concern Two well-publicized disasters underscored public concern about environmental hazards during the 1970s. The first occurred in Love Canal, a neighborhood in Niagara, New York. People in Love Canal unknowingly resided atop a chemical waste dump, which exposed them to poisons. As a result, residents developed unusually high rates of cancer and birth defects. When officials discovered the cause of the health problems in 1978, Love Canal became a media event. Eventually, the federal government relocated 800 families to safer areas. Meanwhile, Congress passed laws requiring companies to clean up their toxic waste areas.

The second disaster of the decade occurred at Pennsylvania's Three Mile Island Nuclear Generating Station. On March 28, 1979, the nuclear power plant suffered a partial meltdown. The situation was brought under control. However, some radioactive gases did escape into the atmosphere. The **Three Mile Island accident** convinced many Americans that nuclear power plants posed an unacceptable risk to people and the natural environment. As a result, no new nuclear power plants have been built in the United States since 1979.

Clean drinking water is essential for human health. By the 1970s, however, the water supply in some areas had become so polluted by chemicals, sewage, or pesticides that it was unsafe to drink. The Safe Drinking Water Act of 1974 was designed to protect public health by setting national standards for safe drinking water. Since 1974, the law has been amended to protect drinking water at its sources, such as rivers, lakes, springs, and wells.

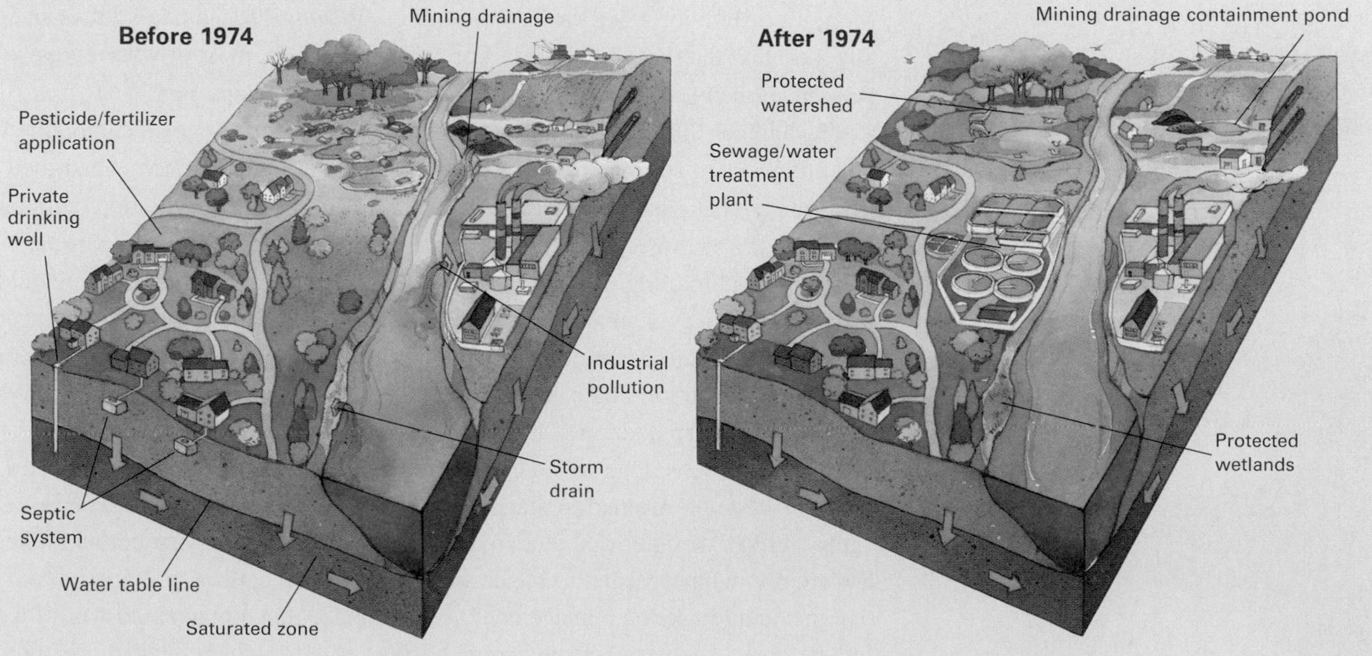

Before 1974

Mining drainage
Pesticide/fertilizer application
Private drinking well
Industrial pollution
Storm drain
Septic system
Water table line
Saturated zone

After 1974

Mining drainage containment pond
Protected watershed
Sewage/water treatment plant
Protected wetlands

During the 1970s, more and more women embarked on careers in fields that had previously been considered "men's work." By the end of the decade, it was no longer surprising to see women working at construction sites, delivering weather reports on television, or defending clients in the courtroom.

54.5 Women Continue Their Struggle for Equality

On September 20, 1973, professional tennis player Billie Jean King took on an aging former Wimbledon champion named Bobby Riggs. Billed as "The Battle of the Sexes," this was no ordinary tennis match. Riggs proudly admitted to being a **male chauvinist,** a person who believes men are superior to women. He boasted that at age 55, he could beat King, who was, after all, only a woman. In a match that 50 million people watched on television, King proved Riggs wrong and easily won the match. To many viewers, King's victory symbolized the gains women were making not only in sports but also in many other realms.

Women Challenge Gender Segregation in the Workplace During the 1970s, record numbers of women entered professions that men had traditionally dominated. The decade saw a 144 percent increase in the number of female accountants and a doubling of female chemists. In 1972, only 4 percent of the nation's lawyers were women. By 1980, that figure had risen to 13 percent. By the same year, one in five medical students was female.

As encouraging as these numbers were, they did not tell the whole story. In the 1970s, most women still toiled in a workplace segregated by gender. Men did certain jobs, and women did others. In addition, women's jobs usually paid less than men's jobs did. For example, nurses, most of whom were women, earned less than truck drivers, most of whom were men.

To address this inequality, feminists in the late 1970s began a campaign for what they called **comparable worth**. Advocates of comparable worth argued that jobs typically held by women, such as nursing positions, should command as much pay as those jobs typically held by men that required comparable education and training. If this change took place, a highly trained nurse would make more money than a less-skilled truck driver. These arguments convinced many employers to examine their pay practices. Some agreed to increase pay for certain jobs traditionally held by women.

Feminists also addressed barriers that prevented women from entering higher-paying jobs. One was the reluctance of men who controlled most workplaces to promote women to management. Women described this barrier as a "glass ceiling" that allowed them to rise only so far in a company but no higher. Eventually, women began to break through this glass ceiling, proving not only that they could take on management tasks, but also that a man could work for a female boss. Another obstacle was a shortage of affordable childcare. Without such care, many women took on part-time or less-demanding jobs in order to have time to watch over their children. Such jobs usually paid less than full-time or more demanding work. Feminists lobbied for employers and government officials to establish and help fund childcare centers for working parents.

The lack of affordable childcare was part of a larger problem referred to as the "feminization of poverty." Poverty rates for all Americans had declined during the 1960s. However, the decline was more dramatic for men than for women. By the 1970s, women were much more likely to be poor than men were. This was especially true for single mothers with children to support.

Feminists addressed this problem in a number of ways. For example, they worked to achieve better treatment of divorced women and their children. They did so by pushing government officials to ensure that divorced mothers received child-support payments that they had been awarded as part of their divorce settlements. They also sought stricter penalties for divorced fathers who did not meet financial obligations to their families.

Women Increase Their Political Clout To bring about such reforms, many women threw themselves into politics. During the 1970s, a growing number of women voted, sought public office, and worked for changes in public policy. The National Women's Political Caucus (NWPC), formed in 1971 by feminist leaders, encouraged such activism. The new organization raised money to get more women elected to office. The NWPC also helped fund male candidates who took a strong stand on women's issues.

Women quickly became more active and influential in their political parties. In 1968, only 13 percent of the delegates at the Democratic National Convention were women. By 1972, due to the efforts of the NWPC, women accounted for 40 percent of delegates. Women in the Republican Party also increased their representation at national conventions—from 17 percent of delegates in 1968 to 30 percent by 1972.

Women also gained influence with elected officials by voting in larger numbers than men did. As a result, a candidate running for office could no longer risk failing to address women's concerns. In addition, at the national level, Congress in 1972 voted to prohibit discrimination against women in the armed services. Under pressure from female voters, state legislatures reformed laws that had made it nearly impossible to prosecute cases involving sexual assaults against women. Women also worked with local governments and school boards to ensure that their daughters had the same opportunities to grow and thrive as their sons had.

Voter Turnout in Presidential Elections, 1964–1980

Year	Eligible Adults Who Voted (in millions)	
	Women	Men
1964	39.2	37.5
1968	41.0	38.0
1972	44.9	40.9
1976	45.6	41.1
1980	49.3	43.8

Source: Center for the American Woman and Politics. *Sex Differences in Voter Turnout Fact Sheet.* July 1989.

In 1964, the gender gap between women and men at the ballot box was less than 2 percent. By 1980, that gap had stretched to over 5 percent. By voting in greater numbers than men did, women increased their political influence with elected officials.

Gloria Steinem founded NWPC along with Bella Azbug, Betty Friedan, and Shirley Chisholm. In 1972, Representative Shirley Chisholm made a historic bid for the Democratic presidential nomination. In announcing her candidacy, Chisholm said, "I am not the candidate of black America, although I am black and proud. I am not the candidate of the women's movement of this country, although I am a woman, and I am equally proud of that...I am the candidate of the people."

Steve Jobs cofounded Apple Computers in 1976. Two years later, his company released the Apple II—an affordable personal computer that revolutionized how people used computers at home and at work. Over the next 35 years, Jobs continued advancing computing devices for personal use.

In 1977, the first installment of the Star Wars epic opened in movie theaters. With its dazzling computer-generated special effects and fast-paced action, the film was a blockbuster hit. *Star Wars* was so popular with moviegoers of all ages that it revived the science-fiction film genre. In addition, the movie showcased new uses of computer technology. By the 1970s, innovations in technology were changing everything from movies to medicine.

The Microprocessor Shrinks Computing Devices Computing machines began to change the ways Americans worked as early as the 1950s. However, the first computers were large and complicated to use. During the 1970s, new technologies that replaced bulky vacuum tubes and transistors with tiny silicon chips inspired a revolution in computing. For the first time, it became practical for ordinary Americans to buy and use a personal computer, or PC.

The introduction of microprocessors in 1971 made the PC possible. The processor is like the computer's brain—it performs all the basic operations that enable a computer to do work. A microprocessor integrates all the elements of a processor on a piece of silicon called a chip. As silicon chips shrank in size, so did computers and other computing devices.

The microprocessor inspired an array of new products that people today often take for granted. One was the pocket-sized calculator. The first of these, called the Bowmar Brain, hit the U.S. market in 1971. Unlike bulky adding machines, this mini number-cruncher was only a little more than 5 inches high and 3 inches wide. At a cost of $245, it initially was a luxury item. However, as demand for pocket calculators grew and more companies began to make them, prices dropped significantly.

Another favorite new product based on microprocessor technology was the video game. The first successful video game was a ball-and-paddle game called Pong. It appeared in game arcades in 1972. In 1975, its manufacturer, Atari, released a home version in the form of a video game console that connected to a television. To the surprise of company executives, Atari sold 150,000 units that year. During the 1975 holiday season, people waited in lines for hours to purchase a "pong on chip"-powered video game to play at home.

In 1977, a California-based company called Apple Computer introduced a computer that was small enough and cheap enough to use at home. By today's standards, the Apple II was slow and had a minuscule amount of memory. But selling at a price that middle-class families could afford, the Apple II launched the personal computer revolution. Families, businesses, and schools purchased more than two million Apple IIs between 1977 and the end of the computer's production in 1993.

Medical Advances Advances in medical technology improved health care in the 1970s. Inspired by the success of the polio vaccine in preventing that disease, researchers developed vaccines for other childhood plagues. By 1971, scientists had introduced a combination vaccine to prevent measles, mumps, and rubella, or German measles.

The microprocessor soon found its way into a new imaging device that enabled doctors to look inside a person's body for problems. The computed tomography (CT) scanner was introduced in 1974. This device uses X-rays and a computer to construct detailed three-dimensional images of a patient's internal organs. Doctors use CT scanners to spot tumors, bone breaks, and other problems that less-advanced technologies leave invisible.

Other medical advances created new options for women who had difficulty getting pregnant. In 1978, the first "test-tube baby" was born in England. In such cases, a woman's egg is fertilized outside of her body. This type of fertilization is called in vitro, meaning "in glass," because it takes place in a glass test tube or dish. A doctor then implants the fertilized egg in the woman's womb, and pregnancy proceeds as normal. The first American test-tube baby was born in 1981. Although the technique remains controversial, more than 40,000 babies are born in the United States each year using in vitro fertilization.

Microwaves and Movies at Home Two electronic devices reshaped Americans' home lives in the 1970s. The first was the microwave oven. Microwave technology had existed since the 1940s, but it was not until the late 1960s that Raytheon produced a microwave oven for home use. Microwave ovens work by bombarding food with radio waves. As the waves pass through the food, they set molecules of water, fat, sugar, and other elements into rapid motion. This rapid motion causes friction, which creates heat. Foods that take an hour to cook in a conventional oven heat in minutes in a microwave—an attribute that appealed to the growing number of working women.

The second electronic device to change life at home was the videocassette recorder, or VCR. The VCR allowed people to record TV programs on videotape and replay the shows later. VCR users could also play prerecorded tapes of movies and videotapes they had made themselves using video cameras called camcorders. VCRs changed the way Americans entertained themselves. In the past, people had seen movies at theaters or watched them at home when broadcast on television. The VCR changed those viewing habits. Movie fans could rent or buy videotapes of movies to watch whenever they wanted. In addition, fans of television shows no longer had to plan their schedule around broadcast times.

The invention of the microprocessor in 1971 contributed to the development of pocket calculators, personal computers, and CT scanners. This tiny chip shrunk down the size of these devices.

When an American businessman bought London Bridge and relocated it to the Arizona desert in 1971, some people thought he was a bit crazy. Today, however, the bridge is the state's third most visited attraction. Retirees are drawn to Sunbelt states like Arizona to pursue an active lifestyle in a warm climate.

U.S. Birthrate, 1960–1975

Source: *Vital Statistics of the United States* 2000, Volume 1.

After a long baby boom, birthrates began to decline in the mid-1960s. This change represented a change to a longer-term trend—having smaller families.

54.7 The Baby Bust and Retirement Boom

In 1971, a new landmark appeared in the Arizona desert. It was London Bridge, the old English bridge that was always falling down in nursery rhymes. Built in 1831, London Bridge had become a victim of its own great weight. In 1962, London officials announced that it was sinking into the Thames River and would have to be torn down. An American businessman named Robert McCulloch had a different idea. McCulloch purchased the bridge and had it transported, stone by stone, to Arizona. Workers reassembled it in tiny Lake Havasu City, a new resort community that McCulloch was planning in the Arizona desert.

As McCulloch had hoped, the relocated London Bridge drew people to his real estate development. Many of the visitors were older people who chose to retire there. Lake Havasu City became one of numerous Sunbelt cities to benefit from the aging of the U.S. population that began in the 1970s.

A Baby Bust Begins the Aging of America During the baby boom that followed World War II, the average age of the U.S. population decreased year by year. In the 1970s, this trend reversed itself. Rather than getting younger, the U.S. population began growing older.

One cause of this shift was a drop in the birthrate. At the peak of the baby boom in 1957, the average American woman had three to four children. Between 1975 and 1980, that statistic slipped to between one and two children. Newspapers referred to this sharp decline in fertility as the "baby bust" or **birth dearth**.

Many factors contributed to this dearth, or lack, of births. One was the decision that a growing number of women made to enter the workforce. In 1950, one third of adult women worked outside the home. By 1978, fully half of adult women were part of the labor force. Those who chose to enter demanding professions, such as law, medicine, or teaching, often postponed having children to pursue their careers. Once they did begin families, most of those women gave birth to fewer children than their mothers had.

Another key factor in the aging of America was a rise in life expectancy. A person born in 1900 could expect to live an average of 49 years. In contrast, a person born in 1980 had a life expectancy of almost 74 years. This change meant that there were more older people than ever before.

With Longer Lives, Americans Redefine Retirement Longer life expectancies meant Americans who retired in the 1970s could look forward to more retirement years than earlier generations had. In addition, the economic boom that followed World War II had left many Americans with enough money to enjoy their last years. Many retirees owned their own homes. Most had pensions from years of working for one employer. Retirees also benefited from the expansion of Social Security and Medicare benefits in the 1960s and 1970s. Whereas in 1950, approximately 33 percent of older Americans lived in poverty, by 1978, only 14 percent were poor.

With these changes, older Americans began to redefine retirement as a time for fun, travel, and relocation. A growing number of older Americans, especially those living in northern states, sold their homes and moved to the Sunbelt. Other retirees, called "snowbirds," traveled from place to place according to the season. Resort communities like Lake Havasu City attracted mobile retirees who visited there to boat and golf during the winter months.

Population and Power Shift from the Rustbelt to the Sunbelt The movement of people from northern to southern states caused shifts in economic and political power. Fast-growing Sunbelt states saw their economies grow with the influx of people and new businesses. In contrast, the Northeast and the Midwest suffered economically. Parts of these regions were known together as the **Rustbelt** because of the rusting factories that declining industries left behind. Even well-established Rustbelt industries, such as steel milling and automobile assembly, struggled to survive the stagflation of the 1970s. Many laid-off workers then migrated to the Sunbelt in search of work.

The Sunbelt states saw their political clout grow along with their populations. After each census, seats in the House of Representatives are reapportioned to reflect population changes. States with expanded populations gain seats in the House and, with those seats, votes in the Electoral College. Since the 1970s, Sunbelt states have gained more than 35 electoral votes at the expense of Rustbelt states. Between 1964 and 2004, every successful candidate for president came from a Sunbelt state.

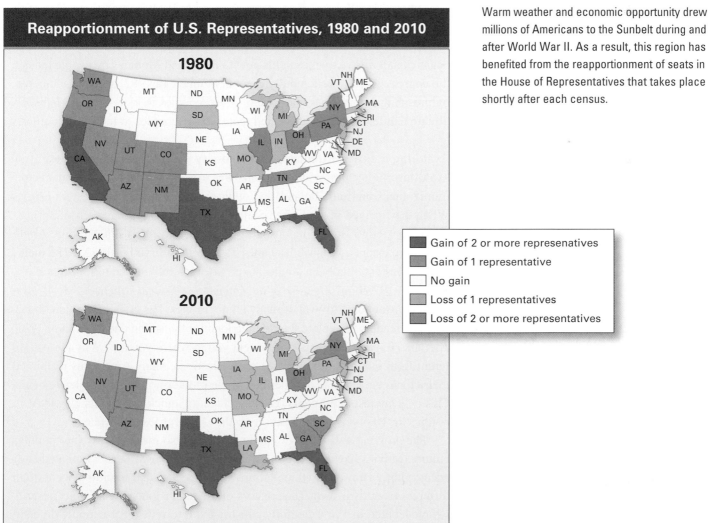

Reapportionment of U.S. Representatives, 1980 and 2010

1980

2010

Gain of 2 or more represenatives

Gain of 1 representative

No gain

Loss of 1 representatives

Loss of 2 or more representatives

Warm weather and economic opportunity drew millions of Americans to the Sunbelt during and after World War II. As a result, this region has benefited from the reapportionment of seats in the House of Representatives that takes place shortly after each census.

One way people achieved self-improvement in the 1970s was through fitness. Jogging became a popular fad. For joggers in the 1970s, running was not only a physical exercise. It was also strongly connected to spiritual improvement.

54.8 Looking for Meaning and Fun in Daily Life

For some Americans, the 1970s were a time to look inward to explore who they were and what they believed. Others found joy in fads and fashions.

The Third Great Awakening: Self-Improvement and Spirituality When Tom Wolfe wrote of the Third Great Awakening in the 1970s, he had in mind two broad movements. He called the first the "therapeutic movement." Its focus was on self-improvement through some kind of therapy, or treatment. A variety of self-improvement activities emerged during the decade. The common goal, observed Wolfe, was to change "one's personality—remaking, remodeling, elevating, and polishing one's very self."

The second broad movement was more spiritual in nature. The 1970s saw an explosion of new religious groups. Some were based on Eastern religious traditions, mainly Buddhism and Hinduism. Buddhist meditation and the Hindu practice of Yoga both gained many followers. One new group, the International Society for Krishna Consciousness, originated in India. Members of this group regularly chant a mantra, or set of sacred words, to bring about a higher spiritual awareness. Because the mantra begins with the phrase "Hare Krishna," or "Oh, Lord Krishna," the group is more commonly known as the Hare Krishnas.

Other new religious groups drew more from Western traditions. One of the most successful was the Unification Church, founded by a Korean religious leader named Sun Myung Moon. In 1972, Moon moved to the United States and began a major drive to expand his new faith. Called Moonies by people outside the church, his followers rapidly grew in number. In 1982, Moon made news by presiding over a mass marriage of 2,075 couples in New York's Madison Square Garden. Moon had selected many of the couples to marry each other.

Exploring Identity, Ethnicity, and Diversity For some, turning inward meant exploring one's cultural identity. This was especially true for descendants of immigrants from Italy, Poland, and other parts of southern and eastern Europe. When they arrived in the United States, these immigrants and their offspring were expected to "melt" into a society dominated by **WASPs,** or white Anglo-Saxon Protestants. As novelist James T. Farrell observed in 1972, "The melting pot was essentially an Anglo-Saxon effort to rub out the past of others."

In his 1973 book *The Rise of the Unmeltable Ethnics,* Michael Novak wrote about the stubborn survival of many ethnic groups. His goal, he explained, was to invite readers to explore their ethnic identity by asking questions like, "Who, after all, are you? What history brought you to where you are? Why are you different from others?" In answering such questions, many Americans reclaimed their ethnic background as a heritage to be proud of, not a past to leave behind. This new interest in **ethnicity,** or ethnic identity, quickly found its way into politics. In 1974, President Ford set up the Office of Ethnic Affairs.

The growing awareness of ethnic diversity also made its way into popular culture. Movies like *The Godfather* and *Saturday Night Fever* fascinated audiences with portrayals of ethnic groups whose values and traditions were often different from their own. The creators of the television show *Sesame Street,* which debuted in 1969, carefully constructed it to reflect the nation's diversity.

The program took place on a fictional street on which people of different backgrounds lived and worked. The puppets on the show interacted with an African American couple, a Latina woman, and people with disabilities.

Fun, Fads, and Funky Fashions The 1970s also had a less serious side. Disco, a form of dance music loved by some and loathed by others, drew young people to dance clubs called discotheques. Disc jockeys at these clubs kept records spinning and dancers dancing long into the night. As one disco fan later wrote, "With its driving beats, [disco] almost had a hypnotic feel that makes you wanna dance . . . It's really hard to sit still when you hear a good disco tune."

The decade also saw its share of silly fads, such as the pet rock craze. A pet rock was a rock packed in a box that looked like a pet carrying case. Streaking, another fad, involved running naked through public places. In 1974, a streaker ran across the stage during the Academy Awards ceremony.

The 1970s also saw a flowering of funky fashions. Platform shoes, polyester leisure suits, and hot pants came and went. Bell-bottom pants moved from hippies to housewives. Also popular were mood rings, which supposedly changed color to match the wearer's mood. A black ring signaled stress. Blue meant the wearer was relaxed or in a romantic frame of mind.

Summary

During the 1970s, the U.S. economy suffered from stagflation as the nation faced a number of crises. The decade was also a time of changing views about everything from the environment and ethnicity to retirement and gender equality.

Organization of Petroleum Exporting Countries A major cause of inflation was OPEC's decision to raise the price of oil. This led to rising prices for many goods.

National Energy Act In 1978, Congress tried to reduce U.S. dependence on imported oil. The National Energy Act offered incentives for conserving energy or using alternative energy sources.

Camp David Accords In 1978, Jimmy Carter brokered a peace agreement between Israel and Egypt. The Camp David Accords ended the long state of war between these two countries.

Earth Day The first Earth Day celebration in 1970 signaled the emergence of a new environmental movement. Followers worked to clean up and protect the environment locally and globally. Congress passed antipollution laws such as the Clean Water Act and the Safe Drinking Water Act.

Three Mile Island accident An accident at the Three Mile Island Nuclear Generating Station in 1978 highlighted the potential dangers of nuclear energy.

Searching for meaning During the 1970s, many Americans turned inward to search for meaning. Some explored self-help movements, others new religions, and others their ethnic identity.

Population changes Fewer births and longer life expectancies led to an aging of the U.S. population. The population also shifted south, as people migrated from the Rustbelt to the Sunbelt.

Gender equality Women worked to gain greater equality in the workplace and politics. In growing numbers, women entered professions that had once been dominated by males.

Chapter 55

A Shift to the Right Under Reagan

How did the Reagan Revolution impact the nation?

55.1 Introduction

When Ronald Reagan took office on January 20, 1981, he was almost 70 years old—the oldest man ever to become president of the United States. A little over two months later, his presidency—and his life—nearly came to an abrupt end. As he emerged from a Washington, D.C., hotel, a gunman attempted to assassinate him. The would-be killer was 25-year-old John Hinckley Jr.

Timothy McCarthy was one of the Secret Service agents guarding Reagan. He had thought it would be a routine day. Everything was going as planned until Reagan left the hotel and headed for the presidential motorcade. "Just before the president got to the car," McCarthy recalled, "Hinckley pushed himself forward and fired six rounds in about one and a half seconds." McCarthy threw himself in front of Reagan, taking one of the bullets himself. Another bullet hit Reagan in the chest.

Hinckley also shot Reagan's press secretary, James Brady, and a police officer. Reagan and the other injured men were immediately transported to the hospital, while police grabbed Hinckley and took him to jail. Hinckley later confessed that he had shot the president to get the attention of a famous movie actress. At his trial, he was declared not guilty by reason of insanity and sent to a mental institution for life.

At the hospital, Reagan joked with the doctors before going into surgery. As they wheeled him into the operating room, he looked around, smiled, and said, "I hope you are all Republicans."

When Reagan was elected president, some people wondered whether he had the energy and stamina to carry out such a demanding job. However, he survived the shooting and went on to lead the country for two terms as president. His conservative agenda calling for lower taxes, reduced government regulation of business, and cuts in spending on social programs ushered in an era of political and economic change known as the **Reagan Revolution**.

Press Secretary James Brady and police officer Thomas Delahaney lie wounded on the sidewalk after the attempt on Reagan's life. President Reagan and Officer Delahaney both made full recoveries, but the shooting left Brady permanently paralyzed.

◀ President Reagan and First Lady Nancy Reagan wave to crowds after the new president was sworn into office in 1981.

Ronald Reagan, a former movie actor and Republican governor of California, made an appealing presidential candidate. His friendly manner and positive, "can-do" attitude won the support of voters across the country, including some moderate Democrats.

55.2 The Triumph of the Conservative Coalition

Two years after the assassination attempt, Ronald Reagan appeared before a gathering of conservative Christian organizations. They were part of a broad coalition of diverse groups of Americans who favored traditional social values. In his speech, Reagan touched on many of the points that had helped him win the support of conservatives. He also spoke of the importance of religion in the founding of the nation. "Freedom prospers when religion is vibrant and the rule of law under God is acknowledged," he said.

Evangelical Christians Gain a Political Voice Reagan's audience that day was made up of evangelical Christians, or evangelicals. These are Christians who emphasize the authority of the Bible, believe strongly in spreading their faith, and seek a direct, personal experience of God. Many describe their conversion to evangelical faith as being "born again." By the late 1970s, evangelicals had become a significant force in both religion and politics.

Many evangelicals, particularly conservative fundamentalists, were upset by what they saw as declining moral and religious values in American society. They were distressed by rising divorce rates, drug use, gay rights, and feminism. They were also angered by Supreme Court decisions legalizing abortion and banning prayer in public schools. They feared that the nation was turning away from religion and becoming a "godless culture."

In 1979, evangelical leaders joined forces to form the **Moral Majority,** a political lobbying group led by the Reverend Jerry Falwell. Falwell wanted to train Christian activists who could make their voices "heard in the halls of Congress." He also called on Christians to elect public officials who were "pro-life, pro-family, pro-moral, and pro-America." The Moral Majority was succeeded by an even larger group, the Christian Coalition, led by the Reverend Pat Robertson.

These groups formed part of a political movement known as the **New Right**. This movement comprised various special-interest groups and activists who worked for conservative causes. New Right groups lobbied Congress and raised money for political campaigns. They supported the growth of conservative "think tanks" like the Heritage Foundation, where scholars wrote policy papers and opinion pieces for newspapers and journals. The New Right influenced the public debate on many issues and helped bring about the Reagan Revolution of the 1980s.

Reagan Wins the 1980 Election As the 1980 election drew near, conditions at home and abroad were prompting many Americans to look for a change in leadership. The nation faced high inflation, high unemployment, and soaring energy prices. Overseas, the Iran hostage crisis continued, and the United States seemed to be losing ground to the Soviet Union in the Cold War.

For many voters, Ronald Reagan offered an appealing alternative to President Jimmy Carter. Before starting his political career, Reagan had been a movie actor and the host of a popular TV show. He had served two terms as governor of California before running for president. On the campaign trail, he showed a natural gift for public speaking, a skill that earned him the nickname "the Great Communicator." He knew how to make a point or gently attack his opponent with a joke. One of his most memorable jabs came when he poked fun at Carter's handling of the economy. "A recession is when your neighbor loses his job," Reagan said. "A depression is when you lose yours. And recovery is when Jimmy Carter loses his."

During a television debate with President Carter in October 1980, Reagan delivered the most famous line of the campaign when he asked viewers, "Are you better off than you were four years ago?" For millions of Americans, the answer was no. Reagan promised to pull the nation out of its slump and restore its standing in the world. His optimism appealed to many Americans, making them feel more confident about the nation's future.

On election day, Reagan defeated Carter by more than 8 million votes. Part of his success was due to the Republican Party's effective use of databases to identify potential supporters and get out the vote. Reagan won the support of the religious right, most Republicans, many business leaders, and many moderate Democrats. Republicans also won control of the Senate for the first time since 1955. Democrats managed to retain their majority within the House of Representatives, but Republicans made significant gains there, too.

Reagan in the White House In his inaugural speech, Reagan introduced many of the themes he would return to as president. Recognizing that many Americans had become disillusioned with government in the aftermath of the Vietnam War and the Watergate scandal, he called on his listeners to have faith in themselves and in their ability to solve the country's problems. "After all," he said, "why shouldn't we believe that? We are Americans." Minutes after Reagan took the oath of office, Iran freed the American hostages as a result of previous negotiations. Across the country, Americans celebrated their release. Reagan's first term was off to a good start.

As president, Reagan used speeches on television and in public to build support for his programs. He sometimes recalled scenes from old movies to explain his ideas in ways that made sense to his listeners. Charming and friendly, he was often liked even by those who disagreed with his policies. Reagan's advisers soon learned, however, that the president rarely involved himself with policy details or the day-to-day tasks of governing. He provided a general overview of what he wanted done and relied on his advisers and staff to carry out his wishes.

1980 Presidential Election

Electoral Votes (Popular Votes)
Reagan: 489 (43.9 million)
Carter: 49 (35.5 million)
Anderson: 0 (5.7 million)

Reagan carried nearly every state in the 1980 election and won the Electoral College vote by a landslide. He also claimed the popular vote by a wide margin. This overwhelming victory gave the new president a strong mandate to carry out his policies.

Reagan was a talented orator, and he effectively used public and televised speeches to win support for his political causes. His skill earned him the title "the Great Communicator." Here Reagan explains his tax reduction policies in a 1981 speech televised from the Oval Office.

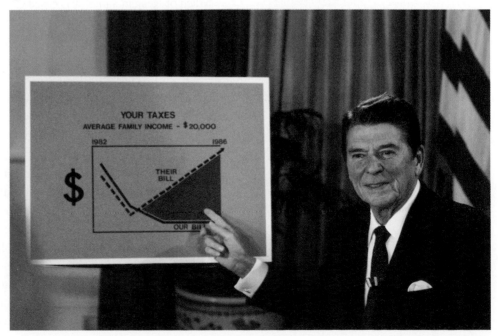

Supporters claimed that Reagan's tax cuts would promote economic growth and create more jobs. Critics charged that the cuts helped only the rich, while poor and middle-class Americans had to wait for the benefits to "trickle down" from above.

55.3 Reagan's Economic Policies

Ronald Reagan came into office promising to change government. He had won support from voters who believed that government taxed them too much and wasted their tax dollars. Pledging to get government "off their backs," he set out to reduce the power of the federal government. "Government is not the solution to our problem," he said. "Government is the problem."

The Evolution of the New Federalism As part of his assault on "big government," Reagan expanded the policy of New Federalism begun by Richard Nixon. Like Nixon, Reagan wanted to shift power from the federal government to the states. Nixon had used revenue sharing to distribute federal tax dollars to the states. Reagan went a step further by handing responsibility for many programs in health, education, and welfare to the states themselves.

Reagan helped states pay for these social programs with block grants from the federal treasury. These were lump-sum payments that states could use as they wished. This system gave the states more flexibility, allowing them to design programs and allocate resources to suit their needs. However, these block grants generally provided less funding than the federal programs they replaced. Some liberal critics charged that the block grant system was really a way to reduce federal spending on social programs.

Supply-Side Economics Leads to Tax Cuts When Reagan took office, the economy was burdened by inflation. According to the law of supply and demand, inflation occurs when demand exceeds supply. Inflation often occurs in times of low unemployment, when more workers are trying to buy goods and services, thereby driving up prices. However, when Reagan took office, he faced both inflation and high unemployment, partly as a result of soaring oil prices. To meet this challenge, he promised to stimulate the economy by cutting taxes and promoting private enterprise. His economic plan quickly became known as Reaganomics.

Much of Reagan's plan was based on a theory called **supply-side economics**. According to this theory, economic growth depends on increasing the supply of goods and services. The way to increase supply is to cut taxes. Lower tax rates will leave more money in the hands of individuals and businesses, providing an incentive for them to save and invest. Individuals will then work harder, save more, and spend more. Companies can hire more workers and increase the supply of goods and services. As businesses create more jobs, new workers will pay taxes, which will replace at least some of the revenues lost through lower tax rates.

Critics called this theory "voodoo economics," saying it was unrealistic to believe that lowering tax rates would increase revenues. But Reagan and his advisers believed it was the route to economic growth. In August 1981, Reagan signed a bill that cut federal taxes by 25 percent over a three-year period. However, the economy continued to lag for another two years, with even greater unemployment.

Gradually, though, the inflation picture began to improve. By the end of 1983, the economy was making a strong comeback. The following year, the gross national product grew by 7.1 percent. The stock market also rose.

The recovery created 18.4 million new jobs. Economists still debate what role the tax cuts played in the resurgence. However, many agree that a major factor was a large increase in defense spending. Military purchases pumped billions of dollars into the economy.

Not everyone fared equally well, though. While personal income grew at all levels of society in the 1980s, the income gap between rich and poor widened. The rich saw their incomes rise, while those with lower incomes saw fewer benefits. Liberals charged that Reaganomics helped the rich and hurt the poor. One economist noted that tax cuts had redistributed "income, wealth and power—from government to private enterprise, . . . from poor to rich." One Reagan official acknowledged that the tax cuts were intended to produce wealth at the upper levels that would "trickle down" to all Americans.

The economic boom made Reagan an even more popular candidate in the 1984 election. He built his campaign around the theme "It's Morning Again in America," suggesting a new era of pride and prosperity. A Reagan adviser noted the difficulties that the Democratic challenger, Walter Mondale, faced. "It's like running against America," he said. Reagan won by a landslide.

Reagan Calls for Deregulation Another key element of Reagan's economic plan was **deregulation**. Deregulation is the reduction or removal of government controls on business in order to promote economic efficiency and stimulate free enterprise. Reagan saw deregulation as another way to limit the power of government. Like many conservatives, he believed that deregulation would make businesses more efficient and competitive, thereby allowing them to pass the savings on to consumers. In the 1970s, under President Carter, Congress had lifted many regulations on the airline, railroad, and trucking industries that had determined what they could haul, where, and at what price. Reagan felt that further deregulation would increase business activity in other industries and boost the economy even more.

Some deregulation efforts focused on getting rid of laws designed to curb pollution and ensure safety in the workplace. Many companies found such regulations a costly obstacle. A Reagan task force on deregulation delayed or blocked rules on the handling of hazardous waste and the exposure of workers to toxic chemicals. Under Reagan's guidelines, the Environmental Protection Agency also began to lower federal standards on air and water quality.

Reagan chose officials to lead government agencies who shared his belief in deregulation. For example, Secretary of the Interior James Watt removed many environmental regulations, arguing that these laws prevented industry from creating jobs and expanding the economy. He opened up more national forest land to logging operations and gave oil and gas companies offshore drilling rights. He also approved the sale of public lands at low prices to oil and mining companies.

Many public-interest groups fought efforts to revise environmental laws and workplace safety rules. They charged that the proposed changes endangered workers and the general public. In some cases, court decisions and actions by Congress slowed efforts by Reagan officials to drop environmental regulations.

President Reagan campaigned for reelection in 1984 and easily defeated Democratic challenger Walter Mondale. The president's election campaign emphasized renewed American optimism and pride. Reagan's popularity was also boosted by the fact that the American economy was booming.

Deficits and Debt Grow Under Reagan Despite Reagan's efforts to control government spending, **federal budget deficits** soared during his two terms in office. A budget deficit is the shortfall that results when government spending exceeds government revenues in a given year. Before Reagan, budget deficits remained below $75 billion. From 1982 to the end of Reagan's second term, however, annual deficits exceeded $100 billion. In 1986, the annual deficit reached a new record of $221 billion.

One reason for these soaring deficits was tax cuts and the resulting fall in government revenues. Another was high military spending. During Reagan's first term, the annual budget of the Department of Defense increased nearly 85 percent. Budget deficits also grew as the cost of Social Security and Medicare rose.

Federal budget deficits caused the **national debt** to soar. The national debt is the sum of all loans taken out by the government to finance its annual deficits. During the Reagan years, the national debt nearly tripled from $908 billion in 1980 to $2.6 trillion in 1988. This sum was far greater than the debt accumulated by all former presidents combined. The government had to borrow hundreds of billions of dollars each year just to pay the interest on this debt.

Conservatives and liberals held different views on the problem of deficits and debt. Although both favored a balanced budget, each said debt could be justified for the right reasons. Conservatives believed that low taxes and a strong defense were good reasons. Liberals argued that debt was acceptable if it came from investing in transportation, education, health care, and other social and economic improvements. Analysts called this the "guns or butter" debate, with conservatives favoring "guns" and liberals favoring "butter."

Under Reagan, federal budget deficits skyrocketed. These annual deficits, in turn, caused the national debt to swell. In less than a decade, the United States went from being the world's largest creditor, or lending, nation to one of the world's biggest debtor nations. Democrats had often been called "tax-and-spend liberals." Now liberals called Republicans "borrow-and-spend conservatives."

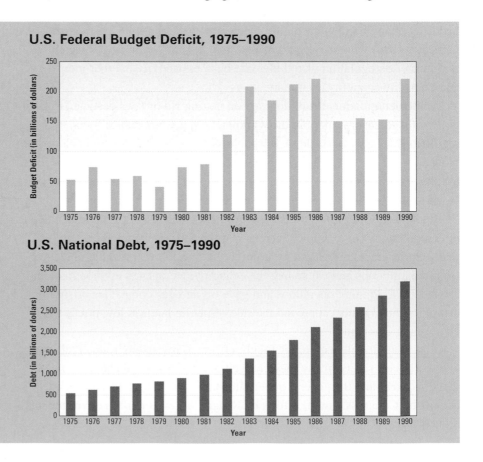

U.S. Federal Budget Deficit, 1975–1990

U.S. National Debt, 1975–1990

55.4 Reagan's Social Policies

Ronald Reagan liked to compare the United States to a "shining city upon a hill." This phrase was adapted from a sermon by John Winthrop, a founder of the Massachusetts Bay Colony. Winthrop hoped the new colony would become a model Christian society, a "city upon a hill" that would serve as an example to the world. In his farewell address, Reagan said,

> The past few days, I've thought a bit of the "shining city upon a hill." . . . In my mind it was a tall, proud city . . . God-blessed and teeming with people of all kinds living in harmony and peace, open to anyone with the will and the heart to get here.
> —Ronald Reagan, Farewell Address, January 11, 1989

Had Reagan's social policies helped to create such a model society? His admirers and critics disagree.

Social Welfare Spending Is Reduced Reagan and other conservatives opposed most government spending on social welfare. They believed that social programs stifled personal initiative and produced a dependence on government aid, thus trapping people in a cycle of poverty. At Reagan's urging, Congress slashed funds for many of Lyndon Johnson's antipoverty programs, including food stamps and aid to the elderly, poor, and disabled. Other cuts targeted student loans and subsidized-housing programs that helped low-income families pay their rent.

Liberals protested that these cuts harmed the poor and forced cities to reduce services to those in need. Cuts fell most heavily on single women with young children and on young adults with few job skills and little education. In the 1980s, the number of children living in poverty grew by 25 percent. The number of homeless people also increased dramatically.

Panels of the AIDS Memorial Quilt, which honors those who have died from AIDS, were displayed in New York City in 1988. The quilt had around 2,000 panels at its first exhibit, in Washington, D.C., the year before. Thousands more have since been added in the quilt's various tours of the country. These tours have helped raise millions of dollars for AIDS organizations.

HIV/AIDS Emerges In the 1980s, the United States also faced a grim health crisis brought on by a previously unknown disease called **HIV/AIDS**. This disease attacks the immune system, making it much harder for the body to fight illness. Many AIDS patients die from infections, such as pneumonia, that their weakened immune systems cannot fight.

In the United States, many of the first AIDS cases were among gay men, which led to the mistaken belief that AIDS was largely a "gay disease." In the mid-1980s, however, AIDS began to appear in patients who had received blood transfusions. This led to the discovery that AIDS was transmitted mainly through contact with the blood or other bodily fluids of an infected person. This type of transmission also explained why many drug users who shared needles got AIDS.

At the end of Reagan's first term, statistics showed over 8,700 confirmed U.S. deaths from AIDS. Four years later, that number had grown to over 46,000. AIDS activists urged Reagan to speak out on AIDS and fund AIDS research. At first he resisted, but by the end of his second term he had declared AIDS "public health enemy number one." Still, he put little effort into fighting the epidemic.

First Lady Nancy Reagan promoted drug and alcohol prevention programs, such as the DARE (Drug Abuse Resistance Education) program, whose slogan was "Just Say No." The program was designed to educate students on the dangers of drug use. Some critics felt that funds for DARE might have been better spent on drug treatment programs or on efforts to combat drug-related crime.

The Reagans Urge Americans to "Just Say No" to Drugs Like AIDS, drug-related violence in inner-city neighborhoods was also a concern in the 1980s. With his wife, Nancy, the president initiated a "Just Say No" media campaign that urged youths to "just say no to drugs." The Reagan administration also funded a drug education program known as Drug Abuse Resistance Education (DARE). This program sent police officers into schools to teach students about the dangers of drug use.

Reagan advisers labeled DARE a success, citing studies that showed reduced drug use among high school seniors. By the mid-1990s, however, longer-term studies showed little or no effect from the program. In addition, critics of Reagan's drug-intervention policy pointed to studies showing increased use of cocaine among the urban poor and minority youths.

Although many conservatives favored teaching students about the dangers of drug use, they opposed government programs to provide treatment for drug addicts. Critics of this approach argued that helping people overcome addiction is also an essential part of the effort to reduce drug-related crime and unemployment.

The Supreme Court took a turn to the right under Ronald Reagan, who appointed conservative justices Sandra Day O'Connor, Antonin Scalia, and Anthony Kennedy. Presidential appointments can have a great influence on Court rulings.

Conservatism Dominates the Supreme Court In the legal arena, Reagan's judicial appointments helped move the Supreme Court in a more conservative direction. He appointed three new justices to the Court. Sandra Day O'Connor, the first female justice, was followed by two more conservatives, Antonin Scalia and Anthony Kennedy.

The Court's more conservative makeup was evident in a 1985 case, *New Jersey v. T.L.O.,* which considered the privacy rights of high school students. The case focused on a 14-year-old girl, identified as T.L.O., whose purse was searched at school and found to contain marijuana. As a result, she was charged with delinquency and sent to juvenile court. Her lawyers argued that the evidence against T.L.O. was gained in violation of the Fourth Amendment's protection against unreasonable search and seizure. The Supreme Court disagreed. It ruled that a search without a warrant by school officials did not violate the Fourth Amendment as long as "there are reasonable grounds for suspecting that the search will turn up evidence that the student has violated or is violating either the law or the rules of the school."

A decade later, the Court—still dominated by Reagan-era conservatives—ruled against privacy rights again in *Vernonia School District v. Acton.* In that case, the Court said that schools have a right to impose random drug testing on student athletes, despite objections that such tests violate the students' rights.

Civil Rights Groups Feel Alienated With respect to civil rights, Reagan believed the federal government should be less involved in enforcement. He was reluctant to support an extension of the 1965 Voting Rights Act and was against the use of school busing as a means to achieve integration. He also called for an end to affirmative action, which he considered a form of reverse discrimination that was unfair to the white population. They also claimed that such efforts infringed on the rights of state and local governments. But civil rights groups contended that Reagan was simply trying to appeal to southern white voters by turning back the clock on civil rights.

Civil rights activist Jesse Jackson was one of the strongest critics of Reagan's policies. In the 1980s, he twice sought the Democratic nomination for president. In 1984, he formed the National Rainbow Coalition, a political organization that advocated social progress and equal rights for people of color, women, and gays and lesbians.

Civil rights leader Jesse Jackson ran for president twice, in 1984 and 1988. Jackson strongly criticized Reagan-era policies that he believed harmed the poor and disadvantaged. He formed the National Rainbow Coalition to fight for progressive reform.

In a speech at the 1984 Democratic National Convention, Jackson blamed worsening conditions in the inner cities on cuts in social programs for the poor and elderly. Quoting a common saying in economics that "a rising tide lifts all boats," Jackson disputed the claim that the economic expansion under Reagan would eventually benefit all Americans. "Rising tides don't lift all boats," he said, "particularly those stuck at the bottom. For the boats stuck at the bottom there's a misery index . . . Under Mr. Reagan, the misery index has risen for the poor." Jackson called for renewed efforts to advance civil rights and help the poor.

Reagan Supports Immigration Reform Immigration laws were another focus of domestic policy during the Reagan years. The last major immigration reform, the Immigration Act of 1965, had opened the doors to a new wave of immigration. By the 1980s, large numbers of immigrants from Asia and Latin America had come to the United States. Some of these were **undocumented immigrants** who entered the country illegally, without a visa. Many of these undocumented immigrants were Latin Americans who crossed the U.S.–Mexico border. As a result, the impact of illegal immigration was most keenly felt in the southwestern border states, from Texas to California.

Some Americans showed their opposition to increased immigration by joining the "English-only movement." Members of this group advocated laws to make English the official language of the United States and to limit the use of other languages by government agencies. Most English-only supporters opposed bilingual education in schools, believing that it kept immigrants from learning English. In the 1980s, several states passed laws making English the official language.

In 1986, Reagan signed the Immigration Reform and Control Act. This act called for increased immigration controls on the U.S.–Mexico border and provided stiff penalties for employers who hire undocumented workers. At the same time, it offered amnesty for 2.8 million immigrants who had entered the country illegally, thus putting them on the road to citizenship.

When George H. W. Bush became president in January 1989, he had already had a long career of public service. In World War II, he was the youngest fighter pilot in the Navy. He later represented Texas in the House of Representatives for two terms, served as ambassador to the United Nations, directed the Central Intelligence Agency, and was Reagan's vice president.

55.5 George H. W. Bush: Continuing Reagan's Policies

The election of 1988 was a test of both old and new party loyalties. The Republican candidate was Reagan's vice president, George H. W. Bush. Bush promised to continue the Reagan Revolution. His campaign appealed to evangelicals and voters who had benefited most from Reaganomics. Bush's Democratic opponent, Massachusetts Governor Michael Dukakis, tried to rally the fraying Democratic coalition by focusing on weaknesses in the economy. Dukakis appealed to liberals and to poor and middle-class voters who had not shared in the Reagan recovery.

When the votes were tallied on election night, Bush was the clear winner. He captured 40 states and 53 percent of the popular vote. Most alarming to Democratic Party leaders, Bush had even won key industrial states, including Michigan and Ohio.

Legislative Wins and Losses In his acceptance speech at the Republican National Convention, Bush had made a number of campaign promises. He had pledged to expand the economy by creating "30 in 8—Thirty million jobs in the next eight years." He had promised to hold the line on taxes. "Read my lips," he had declared, "no new taxes!" And he had talked of creating a "kinder, gentler nation." He made a pledge "to do whatever it takes to make sure the disabled are included in the mainstream," explaining that "for too long they've been left out. But they're not gonna be left out anymore."

Bush succeeded in carrying out this last campaign promise. In 1990, Congress passed the **Americans with Disabilities Act (ADA)**. This law banned discrimination in employment against people with disabilities. It also required employers to make "reasonable accommodation" to help disabled employees. This might mean building a ramp to enable a person in a wheelchair to enter a workplace. Or it could entail ordering special equipment to help workers with limited vision or hearing perform their jobs.

The president was less successful in carrying out his pledge to create 30 million new jobs. One reason for this was a financial mess, known as the **savings and loan crisis,** which he inherited from the Reagan administration. Savings and loan associations, or S&Ls, are financial institutions that were originally set up to provide low-cost home loans to the public. During the Depression, the Federal Savings and Loan Insurance Company (FSLIC) had encouraged people to deposit money in S&Ls by guaranteeing their deposits up to a fixed amount. In return for this guarantee, S&Ls were limited by regulation to making low-risk loans.

During the 1980s, the Reagan administration deregulated the S&L industry. Some S&Ls began making risky loans in the hopes of earning higher profits. More than a thousand of these S&Ls stumbled into financial troubles and went bankrupt. A slowdown in lending and home sales resulted, hurting the economy. By 1990, the nation was moving into a recession, and unemployment was on the rise.

Bush worked with Congress to clean up the S&L mess by repaying depositors who had lost their savings. But the cost of their plan, borne partly by taxpayers, was more than $150 billion. The resulting drain on the federal treasury contributed to another economic problem—soaring budget deficits.

In 1990, Bush sat down with leaders in Congress to forge a budget compromise that would reduce the deficit. Congress agreed to cut spending, but only after Bush agreed to raise taxes. This violation of Bush's "Read my lips" pledge upset his conservative backers. Journalist Tom Wicker later wrote,

> [Bush] had broken one of the most ironclad political pledges ever made—offered . . . before a national television audience—a promise without which he might conceivably not have been able to win the presidential election. With that one action . . . the president of the United States brought into question both his personal reliability and his political judgment.
> —Tom Wicker, *George Herbert Walker Bush*, 2004

Economic Problems and Social Tensions Increase   Despite the budget compromise, the deficit and debt continued to rise. In late 1990, the economy entered a recession. Economic growth slowed, and unemployment shot up. Working-class Americans were hit especially hard.

At the same time, social tensions were mounting, especially in urban areas. In April 1992, rioting broke out in a poor Los Angeles neighborhood after a jury acquitted four police officers in the videotaped beating of Rodney King, a black resident. The Rodney King riots, as they were called, soon spread across the city. They caused more than 50 deaths and millions of dollars in damages. Smaller riots also broke out in other U.S. cities. For many Americans, the riots were a sign of continued social and economic tensions in the country.

A man walks by burning storefronts during riots in Los Angeles in April 1992. During the riots, violence, arson, and looting caused widespread damage. The unrest resulted from tensions between the Los Angeles police and the African American community in Los Angeles.

Summary

In the 1980s, Ronald Reagan's political skills and conservative support won him two terms in office. During his presidency, the economy revived, but the federal budget deficit soared. Reagan approached serious social problems in ways that reflected his conservative ideals.

Reagan Revolution   Reagan helped spark a conservative revolution in American politics. He worked to shrink government, promote free enterprise, and reduce spending on social programs. He also called for fewer regulations related to business and the environment.

The New Right   Reagan's strongest support came from the New Right, a movement of conservative activists and organizations. This movement included evangelical Christian organizations like the Moral Majority.

Supply-side economics   Reagan's economic plan was based on supply-side economics. He cut taxes to stimulate business activity, arguing that this would boost the economy and produce jobs. Tax cuts and increased defense spending, however, led to large budget deficits and a huge national debt.

A conservative Court   The Supreme Court moved to the right under Reagan. This shift was evident in such cases as New Jersey v. T.L.O., which limited privacy rights for students.

George H. W. Bush   In 1988, Bush appealed to Reagan Republicans with his campaign pledges to expand the economy, not raise taxes, and create a "kinder, gentler" America. After a costly bailout to deal with the savings and loans crisis, he broke his no-taxes pledge in an effort to balance the federal budget.

Chapter 56

Ending the Cold War

What were the effects of Ronald Reagan's and George H.W. Bush's foreign policy actions?

56.1 Introduction

On June 12, 1987, President Ronald Reagan stood on a platform in front of the Berlin Wall. Behind him loomed the Brandenburg Gate, a symbol of the divided German capital. The president was visibly angry. He had just been told that police had driven off East Germans who had gathered on the other side of the wall to hear him speak. "General Secretary Gorbachev," he said, knowing that his words would reach the Soviet leader in Moscow. "If you seek peace, if you seek prosperity for the Soviet Union and Eastern Europe, if you seek liberalization: Come here to this gate! Mr. Gorbachev, open this gate!" Reagan continued, his last four words loud and clear, "Mr. Gorbachev, tear down this wall!"

It was a ringing challenge from one superpower to the other. The wall was by far the most well-known symbol of the Cold War. Twelve feet tall and over 100 miles long, it encircled West Berlin. Thousands of well-armed guards, aided by hundreds of tracking dogs, patrolled the wall with orders to shoot anyone who tried to escape to the West. Despite the risks, however, as many as 10,000 East Germans tried to cross the wall over the years. About half of them succeeded, while the rest were captured or lost their lives. Some died jumping out of windows. Others were shot. Some drowned as they tried to swim across lakes or rivers along the border.

On the night of November 9, 1989, however, a little more than two years after Reagan's speech, the gates of the Berlin Wall finally opened. As the news spread, hundreds of thousands of people rushed to the wall. Strangers hugged and kissed, while others cheered, danced, and set off fireworks. Then the crowd began to dismantle the wall by hand. The noise level grew "louder and louder," reported one journalist, "as hundreds of hammers and chisels attack[ed] the wall, taking it down chip by chip." It was a celebration of freedom after decades of anxiety, fear, and oppression. As one young East German put it, "I don't feel like I'm in prison anymore."

In 1987, Reagan gave his famous "tear down this wall" speech in front of West Berlin's Brandenburg Gate. The 200-year-old gate was closed in 1961 when the Berlin Wall was built. Just before he spoke, Reagan learned that East German police had forcibly removed a crowd of East Germans gathered on the other side of the wall to hear his speech.

◀ Celebrating the opening of the Berlin Wall, November 10, 1989

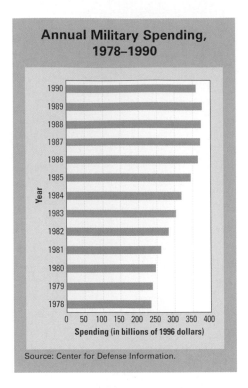

Annual Military Spending, 1978–1990

Year | Spending (in billions of 1996 dollars)

Source: Center for Defense Information.

Defense spending rose considerably over the course of Reagan's two terms in office. This increase was designed to counter the Soviet military threat and undermine the Soviet economy.

In his February 1985 State of the Union address, President Reagan declared that it was America's mission to "nourish and defend freedom and democracy" throughout the world. To do this, Reagan proposed that the United States needed to more actively support anticommunist movements in foreign countries. This policy came to be known as the Reagan Doctrine.

56.2 Anticommunism Guides Reagan's Foreign Policy

Reagan had strong views on the dangers of communism. He believed that the Soviet Union posed an ongoing threat to freedom and democracy. In a speech in March 1983, he described the Soviet Union as the "evil empire." Reagan's tough talk pleased conservatives but alarmed other Americans who feared an escalation of Cold War tensions.

An Ardent Cold Warrior Reagan believed that the Soviet Union was bent on world domination. To counter the Soviet threat and undermine communism, he increased defense spending. The result was the largest peacetime military buildup in U.S. history.

In 1983, Reagan announced plans for a new arms program, the Strategic Defense Initiative (SDI). This program would create a "missile shield" designed to protect the United States from nuclear attack. It would include land-based and space-based weapons, which could in theory knock down incoming missiles. Reagan argued that SDI would be a deterrent to war and make nuclear weapons "impotent and obsolete."

Critics of the SDI program nicknamed it Star Wars after the title of a popular science fiction movie of the time. They claimed that SDI would provoke a new arms race and undermine arms control agreements. Many scientists expressed doubts that an effective missile shield could ever be built, while members of Congress also voiced concerns about SDI's enormous cost. The program went ahead anyway, although technical problems hampered its development.

To further undermine the Soviets, Reagan called for the United States to openly support anticommunist insurgents and movements around the world. Under this policy, which became known as the Reagan Doctrine, the United States provided aid to rebels fighting Soviet-backed governments in Asia, Africa, and Latin America. Reagan called these groups "freedom fighters."

Battling Communism in Central America and the Caribbean Central America was one of the first places where the Reagan Doctrine was applied. In Nicaragua, leftist rebels known as Sandinistas had overthrown the country's dictator, Anastasio Somoza, in 1979. The Sandinista government then acquired Soviet arms and forged close ties with communist Cuba.

Reagan saw events in Nicaragua, along with a growing insurgency in El Salvador, as evidence of Soviet and Cuban efforts to spread communism in Central America and throughout the Western Hemisphere. In a speech to Congress in 1983, he warned that these events threatened U.S. interests. "The national security of all the Americas is at stake in Central America," he warned. "If we cannot defend ourselves there, we cannot expect to prevail elsewhere."

In the early 1980s, the Reagan administration began funding covert operations to overthrow the Sandinista government. U.S. advisers armed and trained over 10,000 Nicaraguan rebels. This U.S.-backed force, known as the Contras, attacked the Sandinistas from bases in neighboring countries.

Congress questioned Reagan's policy. In 1984, after lawmakers learned that the CIA had been illegally placing mines in Nicaraguan harbors, they banned further U.S. military aid to the Contras. Covert operations continued, however, and would later embroil the Reagan administration in its most serious scandal.

In the 1980s, the United States funded and trained Contra rebels fighting to oust Nicaragua's leftist government. Reagan praised the Contras as "the moral equivalent of our Founding Fathers." In 1984, however, Congress voted to end all military aid to the Contras.

Meanwhile, the administration was also providing economic and military aid to El Salvador, which was battling its own leftist rebellion. Reagan argued that this aid would counter communist influence and support the country's struggling democratic government. But most U.S. aid went to the Salvadoran military, which compiled a brutal human rights record. The civil war lasted for 12 years and left at least 70,000 Salvadorans dead, before ending in 1992.

The Reagan Doctrine also led the United States to invade the tiny Caribbean island of Grenada. In 1983, a military coup brought a communist leader to power in Grenada. He invited Cuban workers to the island and signed military agreements with several communist countries. Alarmed by these events, Reagan sent an invasion force of U.S. Marines to Grenada to oust the regime, expel the Cubans, and install a new government. The people of Grenada and nearby islands supported the U.S. invasion. But many countries around the world condemned the action as unlawful interference in another nation's affairs.

Although the United States saw their troops as peacekeepers, their presence disgruntled Israeli radicals and incited terrorist bombings. In April 1983, terrorists attacked the U.S. embassy. Here, U.S. marines work with members of a multinational peacekeeping force to deal with the aftermath.

Key Events of the Iran-Contra Affair

1984–1985
Several Americans are kidnapped in Lebanon.

1985–1986
In exchange for help in securing the release of the hostages, the Reagan administration sells missiles to Iran.

1986
Reagan administration officials send millions of dollars from the Iran arms deal to Contras in Nicaragua.

56.3 On Shaky Ground in the Middle East

The Reagan administration also got involved in the Middle East. The United States provided aid to Israel as well as to moderate Arab states in the region, such as Egypt, Jordan, and Lebanon. In 1975, a civil war broke out in Lebanon when various ethnic and religious groups, both Christian and Muslim, began to struggle for power. This conflict included factions tied to Syria and Iran, as well as elements of the **Palestine Liberation Organization (PLO),** a group fighting for an Arab Palestinian state that would include land claimed by Israel. In the early 1980s, the United States intervened in this war in an effort to bring peace.

Hopes of Peace in Lebanon Shattered Just before the U.S. entry into Lebanon, the conflict took a turn for the worse. Angry over repeated PLO raids from southern Lebanon, Israel set out to secure its northern border. In June 1982, Israeli troops crossed into Lebanon and destroyed PLO bases. In heavy fighting, they pushed the PLO north to Beirut, Lebanon's capital. Syria condemned the Israeli invasion and sent its own troops to support the PLO.

Reagan feared that Syrian involvement in the conflict might lead to a wider war in the Middle East. Hoping to end the fighting, Reagan sent a diplomat to Beirut to negotiate a settlement. An agreement was reached to create a multinational force consisting of troops from the United States, France, and Italy. These troops would enforce a cease-fire in Lebanon and give the PLO time to withdraw from Beirut. After that, Israel would leave, too.

The United States saw its troops as peacekeepers, but many Muslim groups did not. The U.S. presence in Lebanon angered Islamic radicals and provoked terrorist attacks against U.S. forces. In April 1983, terrorists bombed the U.S. embassy in Beirut, killing 63 people, including 17 Americans.

The following September, Israel began withdrawing its troops from Lebanon. But this did not bring peace. A month later, on October 23, a suicide bombing took place at the marine barracks at Beirut International Airport. The suicide bomber drove a truck filled with explosives into the barracks, killing 241 Americans. At the same time a few miles away, a similar explosion left at least 58 French troops dead. Unwilling to risk more American lives, Reagan withdrew all U.S. troops from Lebanon in February 1984. French and Italian troops left as well. It was a grim setback for U.S. peacekeeping efforts in the Middle East.

Despite the U.S. withdrawal from Lebanon, terrorist attacks on Americans continued. In June 1985, Lebanese terrorists hijacked an airliner flying out of Athens, Greece. Most of the 153 passengers on board were Americans. The plane landed in Beirut, where one passenger was killed. Another 39 passengers were held captive in Lebanon for 17 days before they were released. This incident, along with other events in the Middle East, underscored a growing trend in Third World conflicts. Increasingly, insurgent groups with little political power relied on terrorism to advance their goals.

The Iran-Contra Affair A year later, in 1986, Reagan faced the most serious crisis of his presidency, a scandal known as the **Iran-Contra Affair.** In November, a Lebanese magazine reported that the United States had been secretly selling

Why was the Iran-Contra Affair damaging to Reagan's presidency?

Broken promise Despite Reagan's vows to "never deal with terrorists," his officials sold weapons to Iranian-backed terrorists.

Illegal funding Ignoring a congressional ban, Reagan officials sent money from arms sales to the Contras in Nicaragua.

Lying to Congress Administration officials tried to cover up illegal activities during congressional investigations.

Abuse of executive power These actions violated the constitutional separation of powers and system of checks and balances between the executive and legislative branches of government.

arms to Iran. The public then learned that the weapons had been sold to Iran to help gain the release of U.S. hostages held by Iranian-backed terrorists in Lebanon.

This news shocked Americans. Reagan had repeatedly vowed that he would "never deal with terrorists." Yet his administration had supplied arms to Iran, a country that had once held Americans hostage and that was known to support terrorism. By the time the weapon sales were uncovered, more than 1,500 missiles had been shipped to Iran. The weapons deal had not made Lebanon safer for Americans, though. Three U.S. hostages were freed, only to be replaced by three more. Secretary of State George Schulz called the exchange "a hostage bazaar."

Over the next several months, the scandal widened. Investigations by Congress and a special commission appointed by Reagan discovered that millions of dollars from the Iranian arms sales had been passed along to the Contras in Nicaragua, in violation of U.S. law. Investigators learned that top administration officials had backed this operation and lied to Congress.

The "point man" for the Iran-Contra operation was Lieutenant Colonel Oliver North, a staff member at the National Security Council. During special hearings in Congress, North told investigators that his superiors at the NSC had approved his actions, even though they violated the 1984 law banning aid to the Contras. He also admitted that he had helped to mislead Congress with statements that were "evasive and wrong." North's boss, Admiral John Poindexter, justified such deceptive practices as necessary to avoid "leaks" of information to the press. Both men were convicted of crimes related to the Iran-Contra Affair, but their convictions were overturned on appeal for technical reasons.

Meanwhile, the Tower Commission, an independent group set up to investigate the Iran-Contra Affair, later found that Reagan "did not seem to be aware" of the illegal operation. But it said that the president's disengagement from White House affairs had made the deception possible. It also found fault with the president for his failure to "take care that the laws be faithfully executed."

Reagan's approval ratings dropped sharply as a result of the Iran-Contra Affair, and some people wondered if his presidency would survive. In the end, however, the scandal didn't "stick" to the president, and his popularity rebounded.

Lieutenant Colonel Oliver North testified before Congress in the Iran-Contra Affair. A decorated Vietnam veteran, North ran the covert operation that funneled millions of dollars to the Contras. North defended his actions and claimed that he was following orders. Some Americans hailed him as a patriot, while others called him a criminal.

As the Soviet economy declined in the 1980s, many Soviet citizens suffered great hardship. Economic mismanagement of the Soviet planned economy caused shortages of consumer goods starting in the mid-1980s. Often store shelves were simply empty, as in the Moscow grocery store shown here.

56.4 The Cold War Winds Down

In 1985, Mikhail Gorbachev became the head of the Soviet Union. At 54, he was the youngest Soviet leader in decades. The son of peasants, Gorbachev had risen rapidly to the top ranks of the Communist Party. Energetic and confident, he took office with bold plans for reform. The changes he made would help bring the Cold War to an end.

A Changing Soviet Union By the time Gorbachev came to power, the Soviet economy was in deep trouble. Production on farms and in factories was in decline. Centralized planning had left local managers little freedom to increase output or improve the quality of goods. Soviet workers also had little incentive to work harder and produce more.

The Soviet Union faced shortages of all kinds. Consumer goods such as shoes, clothing, and soap were in short supply. So were many foods. Families sometimes spent hours in line waiting to buy necessities. When scarce goods did appear in stores, shoppers often bought as much as they could afford. Such hoarding only made shortages worse. Eventually, rationing was imposed on many products. In addition, the country had a severe housing crisis, especially in the cities. Many families had to wait for years to get a tiny, cramped apartment.

Gorbachev knew that the Soviet economy had to change. Soon after taking office, he announced a program of economic reforms called *perestroika*, or restructuring. He closed many unprofitable state-run factories and allowed some private businesses to operate. He also cut the defense budget to make more money available for domestic needs.

Along with economic reforms, Gorbachev announced a policy of *glasnost*, or openness. He called for an honest discussion of the nation's political and social problems. He also allowed the Soviet media greater freedom to criticize the government. Gorbachev hoped that this new climate of openness would help win public support for his reforms. At the same time, however, he made it clear that he did not intend to do away with the communist system.

Negotiating with the "Evil Empire" When Gorbachev took office, the Cold War was intensifying. In the early 1980s, both the Soviet Union and the United States had increased the number of nuclear missiles deployed in Europe. This arms buildup, as well as the Reagan administration's hostile references to the Soviet Union as an "evil empire," revived fears of nuclear war.

In the United States and Western Europe, these fears gave rise to the **nuclear freeze movement**. This movement called for a moratorium, or "freeze," on the production, testing, and deployment of nuclear weapons by the superpowers. Freeze advocates held parades and rallies, lobbied Congress, and raised money for antinuclear political candidates.

Despite these efforts, the likelihood of a thaw in U.S.-Soviet relations seemed slight during Reagan's first term in office. With Gorbachev in power, however, the prospects for ending the Cold War began to improve. Gorbachev knew that continuing the arms race would jeopardize his efforts to bring economic reform. The economy was already weakened further by a lengthy war in Afghanistan, where Soviet forces were fighting a rebellion against a Soviet-backed government. Gorbachev also feared that the development of SDI and other U.S. weapons systems would leave the Soviet Union more vulnerable to attack. As a result, he was prepared to negotiate new arms control agreements with the United States.

Surprising both his supporters and his critics, Reagan agreed to meet with Gorbachev in Geneva, Switzerland, in 1985. It was the first of four summit meetings between the two leaders. Although they made little progress on arms control in Geneva, the men discovered that they liked each other. Reagan later described Gorbachev as having "warmth in his face and his style, not the coldness bordering on hatred I'd seen in most senior Soviet officials."

In 1986, the two leaders met again in Reykjavik, Iceland. They discussed removing missiles from Europe and reducing nuclear stockpiles. The talks stalled, however, when Gorbachev insisted that Reagan cancel the SDI program, a demand that Reagan refused.

Negotiations got back on track the following year when Gorbachev agreed to discuss missile reductions without an end to SDI. At a summit in Washington in December 1987, the two leaders signed the **Intermediate-Range Nuclear Forces Treaty,** more commonly called the **INF Treaty.** They agreed to remove and destroy all missiles with a range of between 300 and 3,400 miles. It was the first arms treaty that required both sides to destroy missiles. It also allowed both sides to inspect each other's missile bases to verify that the weapons had been withdrawn and destroyed.

Five months later, the fourth and final summit took place in Moscow. By that time, the two leaders had become friends. In his farewell address to the nation in 1989, Reagan told Americans that the United States had "forged a satisfying new closeness with the Soviet Union." It was a far cry from the anti-Soviet views Reagan had voiced just a few years before.

Reagan and Gorbachev held four summit meetings on arms control, developing a warm friendship in the process. At their final meeting in Moscow, a reporter asked Reagan if he still thought the Soviet Union was an evil empire. "No," he replied, "I was talking about another time, another era."

Iraqi dictator Saddam Hussein built one of the most powerful armies in the Middle East. After he invaded Kuwait in 1990, the United States formed an international coalition to force Saddam to withdraw. Iraq suffered defeat in the Persian Gulf War, but Saddam remained in power.

56.5 Confronting Dictators

As the Cold War wound down, the United States carried out several military actions against foreign dictators. In the past, fear of provoking a superpower conflict or losing an anticommunist ally might have inhibited such actions. But with the Cold War ending, the United States had more freedom to act.

Removing a Dictator in Panama The first military intervention took place in Panama, which General Manuel Noriega had ruled since 1983. Although Noriega was a ruthless dictator, he had close ties to the United States. He had helped the Reagan administration by aiding the Contras in their battle against the Nicaraguan government.

U.S. relations with Noriega soured under Reagan's successor, George H. W. Bush. In 1988, before Bush took office, the United States had indicted Noriega on drug trafficking charges. The following year, Panamanians began protesting against Noriega after he voided national elections. At that point, Bush withdrew U.S. support from Noriega, emphasizing Noriega's violations of human rights and democratic rule.

Bush decided to intervene. On December 20, 1989, he sent into Panama an invasion force of more than 20,000 U.S. troops. Two weeks later, they captured Noriega and took him to Miami. In 1992, a U.S. federal court convicted him of drug trafficking and sent him to prison.

Halting Iraqi Aggression Bush faced his next foreign crisis in the Middle East. In August 1990, Iraq invaded Kuwait, its much smaller neighbor to the south. Iraqi dictator Saddam Hussein coveted Kuwait's reserves of oil. He tried to justify this invasion by claiming that Kuwait was rightfully part of Iraq. Shortly after the invasion, Saddam announced plans to annex Kuwait.

President Bush condemned the invasion and called for an international coalition to force Saddam out of Kuwait. Thirty-four countries, including most of the Arab nations, joined the UN-sponsored coalition. The Soviet Union agreed to collaborate with the coalition, despite the USSR's previously friendly relations with Iraq.

As a first step, the coalition sent nearly 700,000 troops to Saudi Arabia's border with Kuwait. This force included more than 400,000 U.S. soldiers. The United Nations also imposed economic sanctions on Iraq in hopes of forcing Saddam's withdrawal without going to war. But Saddam refused to budge. On January 12, Congress approved the use of "all necessary means" to free Kuwait from Iraqi occupation.

Four days later, the **Persian Gulf War** began. The first phase consisted of six weeks of air strikes against Iraq. On February 24, the ground war began. But as coalition forces chased Saddam's fleeing troops into Iraq, they encountered little resistance. Just four days later, Iraq agreed to a cease-fire.

The coalition forces chose not to force Saddam Hussein from power. Nevertheless, for the United States and its partners, the Persian Gulf War was a success. They had shown that international cooperation could be marshaled against a common enemy for the purpose of opposing aggression.

56.6 The Soviet Union Falls While Communism Struggles On

In August 1991, crowds in Moscow's Lubyanka Square cheered as a huge bronze statue of Felix Dzerzhinsky toppled to the ground. Dzerzhinsky was the founder of the Soviet Union's hated secret police, the KGB. Protesters used giant cranes to pull the statue down as millions of startled Soviet citizens watched on television. This incident became a symbol of the Soviet Union's collapse.

The Breakup of the Soviet Bloc By the late 1980s, the Soviet economy was in tatters and the future of Soviet communism was in doubt. The new openness of glasnost had made more people in the Soviet bloc aware of the success of free-market economies and the failure of central planning. Many demanded greater freedom and independence.

In 1989, Mikhail Gorbachev announced that the Soviet Union would no longer interfere in the internal affairs of other communist countries. "Any nation," he said, "has the right to decide its fate by itself." With the threat of a Soviet invasion removed, communism collapsed across Eastern Europe.

Most governments fell peacefully, as leaders resigned or agreed to reforms. One exception was Romania, where an angry mob rose up to drive dictator Nicolae Ceausescu and his wife from power. In East Germany, desperate communist officials tried to hold on to power by opening the Berlin Wall and promising other changes. But East German citizens took to the streets, calling for democratic rule. Free elections followed, and in October 1990, East and West Germany were reunited.

The Soviet Union itself grew weaker, as power flowed to its constituent republics and away from the central government. In July 1991, Eastern European leaders disbanded the Warsaw Pact. This and other signs of Soviet collapse angered communist hardliners. In August, they attempted to overthrow Gorbachev by taking him prisoner. The coup failed after just four days. However, it shifted the political winds toward democratic rule and introduced a new leader, Boris Yeltsin.

Yeltsin, the president of the Russian republic, had defied the coup leaders and called for Gorbachev's return to power. Standing on top of army tanks in front of the Russian parliament building in Moscow, he rallied the Soviet people against the coup. Yeltsin continued to gain influence and power as the Soviet Union broke apart in the months that followed.

In August 1991, when communist hardliners led a coup against Gorbachev, Yeltsin called for resistance. Here, Yeltsin (holding paper) rallies people against the coup in front of the Russian Parliament building. When the attempt failed a few days later, Yeltsin emerged as the most powerful political figure in the country. He went on to lead Russia's transition from communism to a free-market system.

In June 1989, Chinese authorities broke up pro-democracy protests in Beijing's Tiananmen Square. One protester risked his life by standing in front of army tanks as they rolled through the city. His action was a symbolic gesture of defiance against China's communist state.

By the fall of 1991, the Baltic republics of Latvia, Estonia, and Lithuania had achieved independence. Ukraine and the other republics soon followed. All 15 Soviet republics became separate nation-states. A **nation-state** is an independent country populated mainly by citizens who share a common culture, history, and language. Most of the former republics turned away from their Soviet past and toward the West. In December, Gorbachev resigned as the Soviet leader and declared the Soviet Union officially dissolved. The Cold War was finally over.

Communism Survives in Other Countries While communism was disappearing in Eastern Europe, communist governments remained in power in Cuba, Vietnam, North Korea, and China. With the fall of the Soviet Union, however, most communist countries lost a key sponsor. For decades, Cuba had relied on the Soviet Union for trade and economic aid. Without Soviet help, Cuba's economy faced serious problems. Nevertheless, Cuba's communist government remained in power.

In the late 1980s, Vietnam's communist government began to carry out reforms. It allowed some private businesses to operate and sought foreign investment to boost its economy. By the 1990s, Vietnam's **mixed economy**— one combining elements of free enterprise and central planning—was growing rapidly, offering more opportunities to the Vietnamese people. Relations with the United States and other Western nations also improved.

Unlike Vietnam, communist North Korea remained isolated. With the fall of the Soviet bloc, North Korea lost a major source of economic support. It turned increasingly to China as an ally and remained a closed, rigidly controlled communist society.

The changes that rocked Eastern Europe and the Soviet Union also touched China. The Chinese were already pursuing economic reforms. By the mid-1980s, they were moving toward a market-oriented economy, with a robust private sector. But the fall of Soviet communism prompted many Chinese to call for greater political freedom as well. In May 1989, thousands of students joined pro-democracy protests in Beijing's Tiananmen Square. After several weeks of demonstrations, Chinese leaders finally decided to act. On June 3 and 4, government troops and tanks moved into the square to crush the protest. The protesters were dispersed and an unknown number were killed. By repressing the protest, the Chinese government signaled that it was not ready to accept political change.

Summary

Reagan's foreign policy emphasized anticommunism and support for democracy and freedom. His efforts to undermine Soviet power, along with changes in the Soviet Union itself, helped end the Cold War. The winding down of the Cold War allowed Reagan's successor, George H. W. Bush, more freedom to confront dictators.

Strategic Defense Initiative (SDI) Reagan increased military spending to counter the Soviet threat. One program, the Strategic Defense Initiative, was designed to create a "missile shield" to defend the United States from nuclear attack.

Reagan Doctrine The president backed anticommunist movements around the world as part of the Reagan Doctrine. He gave aid to rebels like the Contras, who were fighting to overthrow the Sandinista government of Nicaragua.

Middle East policy Reagan sent U.S. peacekeeping forces to Lebanon. These troops helped secure the withdrawal of the Palestine Liberation Organization. But terrorist attacks later forced Reagan to pull the soldiers out.

Iran-Contra Affair The Reagan administration faced a scandal over arms sales to Iran and the diversion of funds to the Contras. Several top officials were convicted of illegal actions in the Iran-Contra Affair.

Nuclear freeze movement Rising tensions with the Soviet Union increased fears of nuclear war. The nuclear freeze movement called for an end to the spread of nuclear weapons.

Intermediate-Range Nuclear Forces Treaty Reagan and Soviet leader Mikhail Gorbachev signed the Intermediate-Range Nuclear Forces Treaty, reducing nuclear missiles in Europe. U.S. pressure, along with economic and political problems at home, eventually caused the collapse of the Soviet Union and the end of the Cold War.

Persian Gulf War The United States fought alongside other nations to force Iraqi dictator Saddam Hussein out of Kuwait.

Chapter 57

U.S. Domestic Politics at the Turn of the 21st Century

To what extent did Bill Clinton, George W. Bush, and Barack Obama fulfill their domestic policy goals?

57.1 Introduction

George H. W. Bush did not serve a second term as president. He lost the 1992 election to Bill Clinton. Clinton won, in part, by focusing on economic issues. The recession that had begun in 1990 ended less than a year later. But the sluggish economy still worried Americans. Clinton believed that promoting economic growth should be his main theme. A sign posted in his campaign headquarters made that clear. The sign said, "It's the economy, stupid."

The economy has always been a major political issue. Modern presidents know that to be successful, they must keep the economy strong. But doing so has proved to be a difficult task.

The economy boomed under Clinton. The stock market climbed to record heights, thanks largely to the computer revolution. Internet-based businesses, often called dot-coms, multiplied rapidly. Economists refer to the too-rapid expansion of a sector of the economy as a "bubble." Around the time George W. Bush, son of George H. W. Bush, took office in 2001, the dot-com bubble burst. Stock prices plunged, and the economy went into a recession.

The economy roared back early in Bush's second term, only to take a nosedive again late in 2007. Home prices had soared, thanks in part to questionable lending practices by banks. When the housing bubble burst, home prices fell, and the economy fell with them. In 2009, Barack Obama took office as president. He had to devote much of his presidency to trying to restore the nation's economic health.

The economy is a key domestic issue. But it has never been the only one. All three of these presidents came into office with several goals they expected to achieve. In a country deeply divided in its party loyalties, none of them would accomplish all they had hoped. In this chapter, you will examine how well those three presidents—Bill Clinton, George W. Bush, and Barack Obama—met their domestic policy goals after entering the Oval Office.

President Obama inherited a struggling economy. Early in his presidency, Obama sponsored a $787 billion stimulus package that aimed to fund economic recovery. In February 2009, Obama travelled to an Illinois tractor factory to explain his policies and to show his support for creating jobs in the American industrial sector.

◀ President-elect Barack Obama, accompanied by First Lady Michelle Obama, takes the oath of office on January 20, 2009.

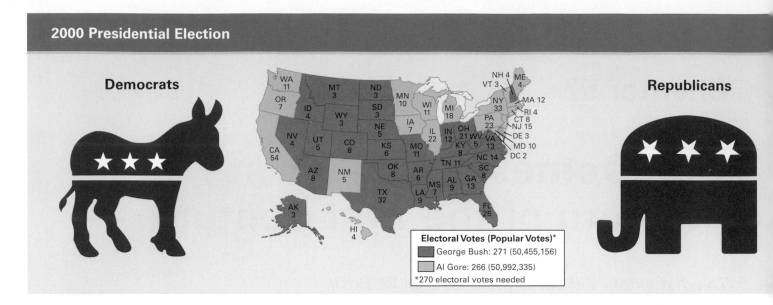

Democrats

Republicans

WA 11
MT 3
ND 3
MN 10
NH 4
ME 4
VT 3
NY 33
MA 12
RI 4
CT 8
NJ 15
PA 23
DE 3
MD 10
DC 2
OR 7
ID 4
WY 3
SD 3
WI 11
MI 18
CA 54
NV 4
UT 5
CO 8
NE 5
IA 7
IL 22
IN 12
OH 21
WV 5
VA 13
KY 8
NC 14
SC 8
AZ 8
NM 5
KS 6
MO 11
TN 11
AR 6
MS 7
AL 9
GA 13
TX 32
LA 9
FL 25
AK 3
HI 4

Electoral Votes (Popular Votes)*

George Bush: 271 (50,455,156)
Al Gore: 266 (50,992,335)

*270 electoral votes needed

The terms *red state* and *blue state* originated with the 2000 presidential election map. Red states are states in which the majority votes Republican. In blue states, the majority votes Democratic. Although the red states cover more territory, the blue states are usually more densely populated. The result was a very close election in 2000.

57.2 Parties and Politics at the Turn of the Century

At the turn of the 21st century, American politics was taking a new shape. Many observers believed that the nation had splintered politically into two main camps. On election night in 2000, the major television networks gave this split a color code. They all used the same two colors to shade their election maps. Red represented states in which a majority voted for Republican George W. Bush. Blue signified states that favored Democrat Al Gore. By evening's end, there seemed to be two Americas—red and blue. However, a closer look at recent elections reveals a more complex picture.

Red America vs. Blue America   The voters who made so many states red in 2000 generally supported a conservative agenda. They believed in reducing the size of government, lowering taxes, maintaining a strong military, and promoting traditional social values. This agenda appealed to many evangelical Christians and people living in small towns. It also attracted blue-collar workers, veterans, and businesspeople. These groups made up the Republican Party's **political base,** or core of supporters.

The voters in blue states in the 2000 election represented two groups of Democrats. The first included those who had long been loyal to the party—liberals, African Americans, immigrants, and union members. They were united by their belief in government's power to improve life for ordinary people. The second group were moderates. They embraced welfare reform, a balanced budget, expanded trade, and a tough stand on crime.

Not everyone accepted the red vs. blue split. In a speech delivered at the 2004 Democratic National Convention, a state senator from Illinois named Barack Obama said,

> [T]here's not a liberal America and a conservative America—there's the United States of America. There's not a black America and white America and Latino America and Asian America—there's the United States of America. The pundits [self-appointed experts] like to slice-and-dice our

country into Red States and Blue States; Red States for Republicans, Blue States for Democrats. But I've got news for them, too. . . . We are one people, all of us pledging allegiance to the stars and stripes, all of us defending the United States of America.

—Barack Obama, speech at the Democratic National Convention, 2004

Obama's stirring speech brought him national recognition. It was the first step on the road that would lead him to the presidency five years later.

Neither Red Nor Blue: Independents and Third-Party Voters   About 30 to 35 percent of registered voters define themselves as independents. As a result, neither Democrats nor Republicans can claim that their party represents a majority of the **electorate**, or the officially qualified voters. To win elections, both parties must also appeal to independent voters.

This new political arithmetic drove Bill Clinton's decision in 1992 to campaign as a moderate, or what Democratic party leaders called a **New Democrat**. It also helped motivate Republican George W. Bush in 2000 to promote more caring social policies, which he called "compassionate conservatism." Even so, in both of those elections, millions of voters rejected the major party nominees. Instead, they cast their ballots for third-party presidential candidates.

The most successful third-party candidate in recent elections was Texas billionaire Ross Perot. In 1992, Perot ran for president as an independent candidate. On election day, Perot received 19 percent of the votes cast. This was the best showing for a third-party candidate since Theodore Roosevelt ran for president as a Progressive in 1912.

In 2000, consumer advocate Ralph Nader ran for president on the Green Party ticket. The roughly 2.9 million votes cast for Nader amounted to only 2.7 percent of the vote. But that election was so close that many Democrats accused Nader of acting as a "spoiler" whose campaign cost their candidate, Al Gore, the White House.

A young supporter of the Green Party holds a sign for presidential candidate Ralph Nader in the 2000 presidential election. The Green Party platform focused on the need for universal health care, environmental and consumer protections, and campaign finance reform. However, the Green Party failed to attract a significant number of people away from the traditional two party system, and won only 2.7 percent of the vote in the 2000 election.

The Republican and Democratic parties have always appealed to different groups of voters. In the early 21st century, however, both parties struggled to adapt to a decrease in party loyalty and an increase in independent voters.

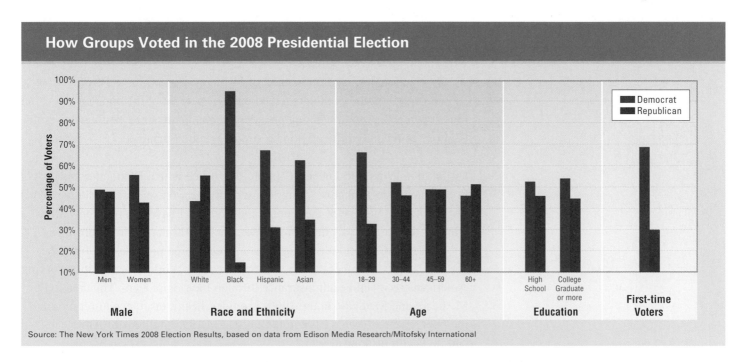

How Groups Voted in the 2008 Presidential Election

Percentage of Voters

- ■ Democrat
- ■ Republican

Male: Men, Women

Race and Ethnicity: White, Black, Hispanic, Asian

Age: 18–29, 30–44, 45–59, 60+

Education: High School, College Graduate or more

First-time Voters

Source: The New York Times 2008 Election Results, based on data from Edison Media Research/Mitofsky International

In 1992, Ross Perot became the first third-party candidate to participate in televised presidential debates. "Look at all three of us," Perot advised viewers. "Decide who you think will do the job, pick that person in November, because believe me, as I've said before, the party's over, and it's time for the cleanup crew."

57.3 Bill Clinton: A New Democrat in the White House

As Democrats approached the 1992 presidential election, they had to confront some unpleasant realities. The New Deal coalition was broken. The Reagan Revolution had moved the nation to the right. And George H. W. Bush, running for a second term, began the campaign with high approval ratings. To overcome these obstacles, the party needed an appealing candidate with a fresh message. It found both traits in the young, five-term governor of Arkansas, Bill Clinton.

The Election of 1992 Leaves Clinton Without a Mandate Clinton reached out to voters as a New Democrat who cared deeply about the struggles and concerns of ordinary Americans. When he accepted the Democratic nomination, he spoke of creating a new style of government, which he described as

> a government that is leaner, not meaner; a government that expands opportunity, not bureaucracy; a government that understands that jobs must come from growth in a vibrant and vital system of free enterprise. . . . We offer opportunity. We demand responsibility. We will build an American community again. The choice we offer is not conservative or liberal. In many ways, it is not even Republican or Democratic. It is different. It is new. And it will work.
>
> — Bill Clinton, speech accepting the nomination for president at the Democratic National Convention, 1992

Opportunity, responsibility, and community became the central themes of Clinton's campaign.

Two factors helped Clinton overcome Bush's early lead. The first was the recession that began in 1990. As the months passed and the economy continued to limp along, Bush's popularity sank. Clinton gained ground by focusing on how to get the economy moving again. The second factor was the third-party candidacy of Ross Perot. The Texas billionaire promised to restore prosperity by balancing the federal budget and paying off the national debt. His frank talk about the economy attracted voters who felt dissatisfied by the two main parties. Most of Perot's supporters, however, were conservatives who otherwise might have voted for Bush.

On election day, Clinton won 32 of 50 states. But owing to Perot's strong showing at the polls, Clinton received only 43 percent of the popular vote—the lowest percentage for a winning presidential candidate since 1912. As a result, Clinton would enter office lacking a strong electoral mandate.

Legislative Wins and Losses Clinton took office with a Democratic majority in both houses of Congress. With this support, he won several legislative victories, including passage of the Family and Medical Leave Act. This law allowed workers to take time off for family emergencies without risking their jobs.

However, Clinton failed to deliver on a campaign promise to reform the nation's health insurance system. Since the end of World War II, most working Americans received health insurance through their employers. The creation of Medicare and Medicaid in the 1960s provided health insurance to retirees and the poor. Even so, when Clinton took office in 1993, millions of Americans had no health insurance.

In 1993, Clinton sent to Congress a plan for sweeping reform of the nation's health care system. The plan sought to provide **universal health care**, or health care for all Americans. But the plan proved overly complex, and it faced fierce criticism by Republicans. Many health care providers opposed it, fearing increased government regulation. After much debate, Congress chose not to act on the plan. When Clinton left office in 2000, about 40 million Americans still lacked health insurance.

Republicans Take Control of Congress Every two years, congressional elections take place. When they occur in the middle of a president's term, they are known as **midterm elections**. As the 1994 midterm elections approached, Republicans aimed to gain control of Congress. Led by Georgia Representative Newt Gingrich, Republican candidates appealed to voters with a 10-point plan called the Contract with America. The contract promised that, if elected, Republicans would strive to balance the federal budget, combat crime, reform the welfare system, cut taxes, create jobs, and minimize lawsuits. The contract captured many voters' imaginations. When Congress met in 1995, Republicans had gained a majority in both the House and the Senate for the first time since 1955.

Flush with victory, House Republicans set out to balance the federal budget. They called for major cutbacks in government spending on education, welfare, and Medicare. Clinton rejected their plan, claiming the reductions were too steep. Both sides refused to alter their stances. Without a budget to authorize expenditures, the government prepared to close down in mid-November 1995. On the eve of the shutdown, Clinton met with Republican leaders. "I am not going to sign your budget," he told them. "It is wrong. It is wrong for the country."

The next day, the federal government came to a standstill. Most Americans blamed Congress for the shutdown. The government did not reopen until early 1996, after Congress approved a budget that Clinton would accept.

Reforming the Welfare System Republicans in Congress next turned to welfare reform. The U.S. welfare system included a federal program known as Aid to Families with Dependent Children (AFDC). Initiated during the Depression as part of the Social Security system, this program gave money to unemployed single mothers. By 1996, nearly 5 million women and 9 million children were receiving public assistance under AFDC.

Critics of the welfare system charged that instead of serving as a temporary safety net to help families through hard times, AFDC had created a culture of poverty that continued from one generation to the next. They pointed out that if welfare recipients married or found work, they would lose their welfare benefits. Such eligibility rules, they claimed, discouraged mothers from making changes that might help them gain economic stability. The program's opponents also observed that children raised in homes with no working parent were more likely to need welfare as adults.

During his 1992 campaign, Clinton had pledged to "end welfare as we know it." Democrats took this to mean reforming AFDC. Instead, the Republican-controlled Congress abolished AFDC and created a new system, called **Temporary Assistance to Needy Families (TANF)**. TANF limited the

President Clinton appointed his wife, Hillary Rodham Clinton, to lead a committee charged with developing a plan for universal health care. The committee's proposal was widely criticized and died in Congress. In 2000, Hillary Clinton was elected to serve as a U.S. senator from New York. When Barack Obama took office as president in 2009, he appointed Clinton secretary of state.

amount of time a family could receive welfare payments to five years. Its goal was to get mothers off welfare and into the workforce as quickly as possible.

Despite protests from Democrats that the new law would increase poverty and hunger, Clinton signed the welfare reform bill. It soon made a significant impact. Employment of single mothers increased dramatically. As it did, the child poverty rate decreased from 20.2 percent in 1995 to 15.8 percent in 2001.

A Balanced Budget and an Economic Boom Clinton's support for welfare reform, coupled with an improving economy, boosted his popularity as president. In 1996, he easily won reelection. The victory made Clinton the first Democratic president since Franklin Roosevelt to secure a second term.

Clinton began his second term determined to avoid another budget impasse. Over the next year, Republicans and Democrats worked together to craft a tax-cut bill and the Balanced Budget Act of 1997. "This legislation represents an historic compromise," said Clinton, "a monument to the progress that people of goodwill can make when they put aside partisan [political party] interests to work together for the common good and our common future."

In 1998, the federal budget did not just balance. It ran its first surplus in nearly 30 years. A **budget surplus** occurs when the government takes in more money than it spends. Clinton's efforts to slow federal spending contributed to the surplus. A surge in tax revenues, however, had an even greater impact.

By 1998, the country was enjoying a period of prosperity. It was largely driven by new business opportunities related to the Internet. By linking computers all over the world, the Internet gave businesses instant access to distant markets. It made today's global economy possible. The Internet also gave rise to a host of online businesses. Their Web addresses ended in .com—short for *commercial*. As the dot-com boom continued, unemployment dropped to less than 4 percent, the lowest it had been in 30 years. Inflation also remained low, while stock prices soared.

In 1998, President Clinton lied under oath about his relationship with a White House intern. The House of Representatives impeached Clinton for perjury and obstruction of justice. The Senate, however, chose not to remove him from office.

As the amount of money people earned, spent, and invested increased, tax revenues poured into the federal treasury, helping put the federal budget in surplus. The budget surplus continued through the year 2001. "If we maintain our fiscal discipline," Clinton declared, "America will entirely pay off the national debt by 2015." Republicans argued that the government should return some of the surplus to taxpayers in the form of tax cuts.

Surviving Scandal and Impeachment Rumors of scandals dogged Clinton from the start of his presidency. The primary charge was that he had illegally profited from an investment in an Arkansas real estate development called Whitewater. Accusations also surfaced of his having had numerous affairs while he was governor of Arkansas. In May 1994, a former Arkansas state employee filed a lawsuit accusing Clinton of sexual harassment.

Attorney General Janet Reno appointed lawyer Kenneth Starr to investigate the Whitewater claims. In January 1998, Starr also obtained evidence that Clinton had engaged in an affair with a

White House intern, Monica Lewinsky, which contradicted Clinton's sworn testimony in the Arkansas sexual harassment case. In September, Starr submitted to Congress a report that accused the president of committing perjury, or lying under oath. It also recommended that Clinton be impeached.

On December 19, 1998, the House voted along party lines to impeach President Clinton on two counts: (1) he had committed perjury, and (2) he had obstructed justice by lying under oath. In January 1999, the Senate tried Clinton on both counts. At the close of the trial, senators voted along party lines. As a result, the votes on both charges fell far short of the two thirds needed to remove Clinton from office. After the trial Clinton asserted, "I want to say again to the American people how profoundly sorry I am for what I said and did to trigger these events and the great burden they have imposed on the Congress and on the American people."

Clinton not only survived the scandal but also ended his presidency with a remarkably high 65 percent approval rating. This was the best "end-of-career" showing of any president since the end of World War II.

Bill Clinton's Domestic Agenda

Issue	Goals	Progress and Setbacks
Crime	Increase public safety and reduce gun violence	**Violent Crime Control and Law Enforcement Act of 1994** Banned sales of some assault weapons, increased penalties for many crimes against women, and funded the hiring of 100,000 new police officers
		Brady Handgun Violence Prevention Act of 1993 Required a waiting period and background check before purchase of a handgun
		Hate Crimes Prevention Act of 1999 Expanded hate crimes to include those based on gender, sexual orientation, or disability (supported by Clinton but failed to pass Congress)
Trade	Expand trade across U.S. borders	**North American Free Trade Agreement (NAFTA; 1992)** Reduced trade barriers, such as tariffs, among the United States, Canada, and Mexico
Civil Rights	Continue Affirmative Action	**"Mend it, don't end it"** Fought off attempt to end affirmative action while improving how it works
	Promote equal rights for homosexuals	**Appointments of gays** Appointed more than 150 openly gay men and women to key executive and judicial positions
		"Don't Ask, Don't Tell" Policy Allowed homosexuals to serve in the military as long as they kept their sexual preference a secret
Education	Improve education and job opportunities for young people	**Corporation for National and Community Service (1993)** Launched AmeriCorps, which put young people to work on community projects in exchange for financial aid to help pay for college
		School-to-Work Opportunities Act (1994) Funded state programs designed to help high school students develop job skills
Liberal Values	Create a more liberal Supreme Court	**Supreme Court** Appointed Stephen Breyer and Ruth Bader Ginsburg, both liberals, to the Supreme Court

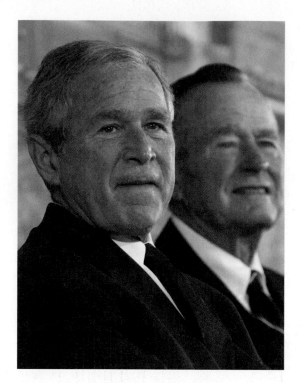

George W. Bush was the 43rd president, and his father, George H. W. Bush, was the 41st. They are the second father-and-son pair to win the White House. The first was John Adams and John Quincy Adams.

57.4 George W. Bush: Conservatism in Action

To win the presidential election of 2000, Republicans needed a candidate who could unite Republicans while appealing to moderate Democrats. That task fell to the governor of Texas, George W. Bush. He would face Vice President Al Gore, a strong and seasoned campaigner. Gore could point to a soaring economy and years of peace as Democratic achievements. Bush's chances of beating him seemed slim at first. But as the months passed, Bush's theme of "compassionate conservatism" attracted voters. His promise of a more caring Republican Party became a central issue of his campaign.

The Supreme Court Decides the 2000 Presidential Election On election day in 2000, Americans were stunned to see how close the presidential vote was. Gore led Bush in the popular vote by one half of 1 percent. The all-important Electoral College vote came out similarly close. With 270 votes needed to win, Gore had 266 and Bush 246. Florida's 25 electoral votes would decide the election. But the Florida vote proved too close to call. An initial count had Bush ahead by 1,784 votes out of nearly 6 million. The next day, a recount by machine reduced his lead to just 327 votes.

In some counties, officials raised questions about confusing ballots or ballots that may not have been properly counted by voting machines. Gore demanded that those counties recount their votes by hand. To stop the recount, Bush filed a lawsuit known as ***Bush v. Gore***. When the Florida Supreme Court ruled against Bush, he appealed its decision to the Supreme Court. On December 12, 2000, the Court voted 5–4 to stop the recount. The majority reasoned that without clear legal standards for evaluating the ballots in question, a hand recount violated the equal protection clause of the Fourteenth Amendment. This decision gave Florida's 25 electoral votes to Bush. On January 20, 2001, George W. Bush took the oath of office as the 43rd U.S. president.

The Supreme Court decision cast a cloud of doubt over Bush's **legitimacy,** or right to exercise power, as president. These doubts were largely dispelled when he ran for reelection in 2004. That year he became the first candidate since his father in 1988 to win more than 50 percent of the popular vote.

Legislative Wins and Losses For six of his eight years in office, Bush was backed by a Republican majority in Congress. With this support, he was able to enact much, but not all, of his domestic agenda. He did succeed in winning passage of an education reform bill known as the **No Child Left Behind Act (NCLB).** Bush outlined the need for such reform in his speech accepting the Republican nomination in 2000:

> Too many American children are segregated into schools without standards, shuffled from grade-to-grade because of their age, regardless of their knowledge. This is discrimination, pure and simple—the soft bigotry of low expectations. . . . When a school district receives federal funds to teach poor children, we expect them to learn.
> —George W. Bush, speech accepting the nomination for president at the Republican National Convention, 2000

NCLB ushered in a new era of **accountability** for public schools. Accountability is based on the principle that individuals or organizations are responsible for their actions and should be able to show how well they are doing at achieving their goals. NCLB required schools receiving federal funds to test their students' progress in reading and math and to share the results.

Bush's efforts to reform the Social Security system were less successful. Many political leaders agreed that the system was heading for trouble. With baby boomers moving into retirement, there would soon be too few workers to support the growing number of retirees at the current levels of benefits.

Bush proposed reforming the system by allowing workers to invest part of their Social Security tax payments in retirement accounts. He argued that personal accounts would provide workers with better pensions than the current system. It would also leave them with funds to pass on to their children. Critics complained that Bush's plan could leave some workers worse off. Also, it would be an expensive approach.

"Social Security has been called the third rail of American politics," Bush once observed, "the one you're not supposed to touch because it might shock you." Bush's efforts seemed to prove this true. His plan never generated widespread support. By the end of 2005, Bush had dropped Social Security reform from his domestic agenda.

Reviving the Economy with Tax Cuts Bush had made cutting taxes a key element of his 2000 campaign. His pledge took on new urgency because the dot-com bubble began to burst in 2000. To spur an economic recovery, Bush pushed through Congress a plan that cut income tax rates for most Americans. But the economy received a second shock in 2001. Terrorists attacked the World Trade Center in New York City and the Pentagon on September 11, or what became known as **9/11**. Unsure of what would happen next, Americans sharply reduced their spending. By the end of 2003, the U.S. economy had suffered a loss of more than 2 million jobs.

Bush responded by pushing Congress to reduce tax rates on earnings from savings and investments. He argued that lower tax rates would encourage people to work harder, save more, and invest in new enterprises. His opponents charged that his tax cuts would mainly enrich the wealthy. They predicted that cutting tax rates would also lead to falling tax revenues and a string of budget deficits.

The federal budget did fall from a surplus of $128 billion in 2001 to a deficit of $158 billion in 2002. But the shift from surplus to deficit was not entirely due to the recession and tax cuts. The events of 9/11—which you will read more about in the next two chapters—also played a part. In response to the attacks, Bush persuaded Congress to create a new cabinet-level agency, the Department of Homeland Security (DHS), to protect the country from terrorists. He also launched a war on terrorism in Afghanistan and, later, in Iraq. As spending to fight terrorism soared, so did budget deficits, surpassing $400 billion by 2004.

Fortunately, as Bush had predicted, the tax cuts helped stimulate an economic recovery. As the economy rebounded, tax revenues rose rapidly. To the surprise of Bush's critics, tax revenues in 2005 were higher than in any year since the peak of the dot-com boom in 2000. In addition, the share of income taxes paid by the wealthiest taxpayers was on the rise.

Many Florida voters in 2000 did not punch a tiny rectangle, called a "chad," completely off their ballots. As a result, voting machines did not count their ballots. The Supreme Court denied Al Gore's request for a hand count of such ballots.

George W. Bush's No Child Left Behind Act increased federal funds to public schools. In exchange for these funds, schools were expected to show that their students were learning basic reading and math skills.

Large, new housing developments, which generated great wealth during the housing bubble, were especially affected by the downturn in the real estate market. In some areas, such as this development outside Las Vegas, Nevada, multiple homes on each street were repossessed by banks. Some homes were simply abandoned by owners who could no longer afford to live in them.

Start of the Great Recession The economic expansion did not last long. A sharp decline in the housing market cut it short. For many years, house prices had been increasing rapidly. From 1985 to 2006, the average sale price of a house rose from $100,000 to $300,000, and it was still climbing. A housing bubble had formed. In 2006, the bubble burst.

Owning a home has long been part of the American dream. But for many people, that dream turned into a nightmare. The government was partly to blame. So were builders and bankers. Federal policies encouraged people to buy homes. Construction firms built too many houses. Banks approved too many subprime mortgages. A mortgage is a loan used to finance the purchase of a house. A subprime mortgage is a loan made to someone who may not be able to repay the loan.

As a result of these actions, home values crashed. Many homeowners now owed more money to their mortgage lender than their house was worth. Foreclosures followed. A foreclosure is the legal process by which a bank can take over a mortgaged property when the borrower cannot pay back the loan.

The housing slump led to a severe economic downturn beginning in December 2007. Shocked by their homes' falling values, homeowners slowed their spending. With sales decreasing, businesses laid off workers. Rising unemployment cut consumption further. The downturn—the nation's worst since the Great Depression—would become known as the Great Recession.

Meanwhile, many big banks and other financial institutions had poured money into what are called mortgage-backed securities. These often included bundles of subprime mortgages. Banks believed that these risky investments would bring great profits in the booming housing market. When the boom went bust, so did their investments. Suddenly, a number of the nation's largest and richest firms were facing bankruptcy. By 2008, the entire financial system was on the brink of collapse.

Bailouts The federal government came to the rescue. President Bush and Congress put together legislation to bail out the failing banks and other huge investment firms. Those firms were declared "too big to fail." That is, if any one of them went bankrupt, it could start a domino effect that would topple even those firms that were financially sound. The rescue package was called the Troubled Asset Relief Program, or TARP. Congress allocated $700 billion to the program.

The Treasury Department used TARP funds to make loans to banks and also to buy from banks their "toxic assets." These included mortgage-backed securities and other investments that had lost money and that nobody else was willing to buy. Using TARP funds, the Treasury Department also bought shares in the nation's nine largest banks. The government—and therefore the people of the United States—thus became part owners of those banks.

The federal government also bailed out the American auto industry. Bush approved the use of TARP funds to loan some $17 billion to auto makers General Motors and Chrysler. Additional funds went to auto parts suppliers and other sectors of the industry.

Falling Approval Ratings After 9/11, the nation rallied behind President Bush. His approval rating soared to 90 percent. But during his second term, Americans' opinions of the president began to plummet. The economic crisis was just one of the factors behind Bush's falling popularity.

Another was the federal government's reaction to Hurricane Katrina in 2005. The hurricane devastated New Orleans and other Gulf Coast towns, leaving tens of thousands of people homeless. Yet the response by the Federal Emergency Management Agency (FEMA) seemed slow and disorganized.

A third factor was the war on terrorism. Some Americans believed that the expansive powers given to the Department of Homeland Security undermined their civil liberties. Also, hundreds of Americans were dying each year in wars in Iraq and Afghanistan. Those wars were also sapping the treasury, adding to mounting budget deficits.

During the 2006 midterm elections, many voters used their ballots to express dissatisfaction with Bush's policies. For the first time since 1994, Democrats won control of the House and the Senate. As you will learn in the next section, voters would also elect a Democratic president in 2008.

Hurricane Katrina devastated New Orleans, especially the Ninth Ward section, shown here. The Bush administration took a lot of blame for the catastrophe. A House bipartisan committee investigating preparation for and response to the disaster identified failures at all levels of government. It also stated bluntly, "Critical elements of the National Response Plan were executed late, ineffectively, or not at all."

George W. Bush's Domestic Agenda

Issue	Goals	Progress and Setbacks
Social Welfare	Encourage community and faith-based groups to help the needy	**Office of Faith-Based and Community Initiatives (2001)** Assisted religious and community groups seeking federal funds to combat social problems such as homelessness and drug addiction
Immigration	Secure borders, create a guest worker program, and provide a path for undocumented immigrants to earn citizenship	**Comprehensive Immigration Reform Act** Proposed reforms in line with Bush's goals (approved by the Senate but rejected by the House) **Secure Fence Act of 2006** Authorized construction of hundreds of miles of fencing to reduce illegal immigration from Mexico
Health	Help elderly pay for drugs and protect the sanctity of life	**Medicare Prescription Drug Benefit (2003)** Helped retirees and people with disabilities pay for needed prescription drugs **Embryonic stem cell research ban** Limited federal funding of stem cell research to halt the use of human embryos in medical research
Conservative Values	Strengthen and support marriage and families	**"Marriage penalty"** Ended income tax provisions, resulting in some married people paying more taxes than if they had remained single **Federal marriage amendment** Defined marriage as "the union of a man and a woman" (not approved by Congress)
	Create a more conservative Supreme Court	**Supreme Court** Appointed John Roberts and Samuel Alito, both conservatives, to the Supreme Court

Many Americans, especially young people and minorities, were inspired by Barack Obama's run for president, and his theme of bringing change to the established political system. Obama attracted enthusiastic crowds throughout his campaign. His personal charisma and stirring speeches helped him win the presidency.

57.5 Barack Obama: Working for Change

The election of 2008 pitted a young Democratic senator from Illinois, Barack Obama, against a much more experienced senator from Arizona, John McCain. Obama, a Democrat, called for change. He criticized President Bush's tax-cut policies and his pursuit of the war in Iraq. To the question "Can we make America great again?" he answered with the campaign slogan "Yes, we can!"

Voters Are Drawn to Obama's Vision of Change In 2008, in the midst of the election campaign, a book written by Barack Obama was published. The book laid out the candidate's plan for restoring the economy and America's leadership position in the world. In it, he said,

We stand at a moment of great challenge and great opportunity. All across America, a chorus of voices is swelling in a demand for change. The American people want the simple things that—for eight years—Washington hasn't delivered: an economy that honors the efforts of those who work hard, a national security policy that rallies the world to meet our shared threats and makes America safer, a politics that focuses on bringing people together across party lines to work for the common good. It's not too much to ask for. It is the change that the American people deserve.

—Barack Obama, *Change We Can Believe In,* 2008

Voters responded favorably to Obama's ideas. He won the presidency with 365 electoral votes to McCain's 173, becoming the nation's first African American president. This landslide victory gave Obama a mandate to pursue his plan for moving the country in a new direction. Once in office, however, Obama would discover that real change can be difficult to bring about.

The Great Recession Continues Polls conducted before and after the election made it clear that the economy was the most important issue in the minds of voters. They had good reason to be concerned. The financial system, centered on investment firms located in New York City, was still unstable. Home sales—a key indicator of economic health—remained sluggish, and housing prices slipped steadily lower. Companies continued to lay off workers. The recession showed no signs of ending.

Soon after his election, Obama began working with the Democratic leaders of Congress on ways to bring about an economic recovery. One result was an economic stimulus package. A **stimulus** is an attempt by the government to inject money into the economy to encourage growth. With input from Republicans, the Democrats pushed the package through Congress. The final bill, passed in February 2009, contained $787 billion in spending and tax cuts. It included money for public works projects and tax credits for middle-class families. In March, Obama announced a second auto bailout to prevent the auto industry from collapsing. The government provided some $60 billion in aid to General Motors and Chrysler.

The recession officially ended in June 2009, five months after Obama took the oath of office. The economy began to grow again, but very slowly. Most economists credit the TARP bailout, begun under President Bush, with breathing life back into the banking system. They also agree that Obama's economic stimulus and auto bailout saved jobs and gave the economy a needed boost.

However, at the time, economists continued to warn of the possibility of a second downturn—a "double-dip" recession. Nervous about the future of the economy, consumers continued to limit their spending. With demand for goods low, businesses continued to limit their hiring. The unemployment rate hovered around 9 percent from early 2009 into 2012.

Health Care Reform In 2009, some 30 million Americans had no health insurance. Most others worried about the steadily rising cost of health care. Republicans and Democrats agreed that something had to be done. But they disagreed about the best way to do it.

In September 2009, President Obama outlined his plan for overhauling the nation's health care system. His plan, he said, would lower health costs, secure and stabilize health care for those who already had health insurance, and expand coverage to the millions who had none. A key element of Obama's plan was the "individual mandate"—the requirement that all Americans must buy health insurance.

The president urged Congress—where Democrats held a majority in both houses—to work out the details together, in a bipartisan way. That did not happen. Democrats made a few compromises to try to fashion a bill acceptable to Republicans. But in the end, the Affordable Care Act passed without a single Republican vote in favor of it. On March 23, 2010, Obama signed the bill into law.

Republicans called the reform law a government takeover of health care. They claimed that its estimated $930 billion cost over 10 years was too high and that it would add to budget deficits. Referring to the law as "Obamacare," they vowed to repeal it. By 2012, lawsuits alleging that the health care law was unconstitutional were working their way toward a Supreme Court decision. The lawsuits focused mainly on the individual mandate.

The Tea Party The Affordable Care Act also faced harsh criticism from a new group on the political scene—the Tea Party. The group, which took its name from the Boston Tea Party of 1773, had no official leaders. It was a conservative, populist protest movement that arose in reaction to what it saw as too much government involvement in the economy.

Tea Party activists used Facebook and other social media Web sites to organize protest rallies. There they denounced "big government" and the taxes that supported it. Its members condemned the bailout of big Wall Street banks, and they called for overturning the new health care law.

The Tea Party was not an organized political party, but it had significant political influence. Many Republicans sought to align themselves with this growing movement. Candidates backed by the Tea Party—mainly conservative Republicans—won races across the country.

The Tea Party, which emerged in 2009, was a conservative, populist movement that opposed excessive taxation and government intervention in the private sector. On April 15, 2009, the day taxes traditionally fall due, the Tea Party staged a series of anti-tax rallies across the nation that drew more than 250,000 people.

Gridlock In the 2010 midterm elections, with Tea Party help, Republicans made solid gains. When all the votes were counted, they had taken away the Democrats' majority in the House and had cut into their majority in the Senate. President Obama would now find it harder to meet his domestic policy goals. In fact, the new Congress would work to block his agenda.

Two episodes exemplify the **gridlock**—the inability to make progress—that plagued the national legislature. The first involved the raising of the debt ceiling. The second involved an attempt to increase employment.

President Obama negotiates with congressional leaders, July 13, 2011. In the summer of 2011, the federal government became embroiled in a contentious battle over the raising of the debt ceiling. Although a grudging compromise was eventually reached, many Americans were angered by the quarrel and saw it as a sign of the dysfunction of the national government.

The **debt ceiling** is the maximum amount of debt that the federal government is, by law, allowed to accumulate. If the federal budget for the year has a deficit—more money paid out than taken in—the deficit adds to the debt. If the total debt would then exceed the legal limit Congress has to vote to raise the debt ceiling.

The raising of the debt ceiling had become a routine event—but not in 2010. Republicans in Congress, encouraged by the Tea Party, refused to increase the national debt unless progress was made toward deficit reduction. They demanded large cuts in programs such as Medicare and Medicaid. Democrats wanted to balance any cuts with tax increases for the wealthy.

Barack Obama's Domestic Agenda

Issue	Goals	Progress and Setbacks
Education	Provide a high-quality education for all children to enable them to succeed in a global economy	**"Race to the Top"** Offered grants to states and school districts that made notable advances in educational reform and innovation **"Education to Innovate"** Aimed at improving the participation and performance of students in science and technology
Energy and the Environment	Reduce dependence on oil, promote energy efficiency, and invest in a clean energy future	**Cap and trade** Effort to reduce greenhouse gases and thus global warming by setting a cap, or limit, on carbon emissions (approved by the House but rejected by the Senate) **New national fuel efficiency standards** Aimed at raising average fuel economy to 54.5 miles per gallon by 2025
Health	Find cures to various diseases and conditions	**Embryonic stem cell research** Removed barriers that prevented the federal funding of scientific research involving human stem cells
Liberal Values	Create a more liberal Supreme Court	**Supreme Court** Appointed Sonia Sotomayor and Elena Kagan, both liberals, to the Supreme Court

After a series of often-heated negotiations, the president and the leaders of Congress came to an agreement. They would raise the debt ceiling in two steps. The first was a short-term increase of $900 billion. Domestic and defense spending would be cut over the next 10 years to balance the increase. The second step called for a congressional "super committee" of six Democrats and six Republicans to reduce the deficit by $1.2 billion more. If they failed to agree on what should be cut, automatic reductions would be made to defense and non-defense spending. The super committee, succumbing to gridlock, did fail. It remained to be seen whether Congress would allow the automatic cuts, especially to the defense budget.

The second example of gridlock involved jobs. In September 2011, to boost employment, President Obama submitted the American Jobs Act to Congress. The bill aimed to reduce the payroll taxes paid by workers and smaller businesses. Payroll taxes consist of money withheld from a worker's check, plus an equal amount paid by the employer. The bill also included new spending for building schools and repairing roads and bridges. Together, these parts of the bill were intended to put extra money in workers' pockets and encourage companies to hire more workers.

Obama planned to pay for this jobs bill mainly through tax changes that would affect Americans making more than $200,000 per year. Democrats in Congress replaced this with a "millionaires tax"—a tax of 5.6 percent on income over a million dollars. Republicans, in charge of Congress, refused to consider any new taxes. They would not let the jobs bill to come to a vote. Wrangling over the bill, and how to pay for it, continued.

Summary

Democratic Presidents Bill Clinton and Barack Obama and Republican President George W. Bush struggled to meet their domestic policy goals.

Bill Clinton As a moderate New Democrat, Clinton breathed new life into the Democratic coalition. One of his main legacies is welfare reform. Clinton failed to enact universal health care, however. In his second term, Clinton was impeached but not removed from office.

Contract with America In the 1994 midterm elections, Republicans won control of Congress with their 10-point Contract with America.

Bush v. Gore In the 2000 election, Al Gore led George W. Bush in the popular vote by a very thin margin. The Supreme Court decided the outcome, denying Gore's demand for a recount in Florida.

George W. Bush As a candidate, Bush reached out to moderates with his compassionate conservatism. One of his main legacies is education reform. However, Bush failed to reform the Social Security system.

Barack Obama Faced with a slow-growing economy and high unemployment, Obama pushed an economic stimulus package through Congress. However, his jobs bill faced tough Republican opposition, as did his comprehensive health-care reform law.

Chapter 58

U.S. Foreign Policy in a Global Age

How well have U.S. foreign policy decisions met the challenges of the global age?

58.1 Introduction

The Cold War ended with the collapse of the Soviet Union. Democracy had triumphed. Finally, the world would now know peace and stability. At least, that was what some Americans predicted and what most Americans hoped. Instead, the post-Cold War world presented the United States with new and often dangerous challenges. To meet those challenges, U.S. leaders have had to rethink American foreign policy.

A driving force in the post-Cold War world is the trend toward globalization, or the increasing interdependence of nations. As organizations, groups, and companies have expanded their use of the Internet, the pace of globalization has intensified. Globalization has created networks of connections among countries.

Much of that interconnectedness is economic. For example, the United States has entered into several trade pacts with other countries, and its banks do business internationally. But the globalization of trade and finance also carries risks. Today, a crisis in one part of the world might not affect just a single country or region. It could spread across the globe. This presents a foreign policy challenge—how intricately should the U.S. economy be linked to other economies?

Another challenge of the global age is military. After the Cold War, the United States stood apart as the world's only superpower. It could choose to act alone, in a unilateral ("one-sided") fashion, to pursue its political objectives. Or it could take a multilateral ("many-sided") approach, working with other countries. This presents another foreign policy challenge—how should the United States handle foreign crises that call for military action?

This rapidly changing world is full of other potential challenges, from terrorism to ethnic clashes to natural disasters. The United States is still trying to determine the best ways to deal with them. This chapter will examine how well U.S. foreign policy decisions have met those challenges so far.

In December 2011, President Obama gave a speech at Fort Bragg military base in North Carolina to mark the withdrawal of all U.S. forces from Iraq. The war lasted nearly nine years, and a majority of the American public was relieved to see it end. Ending the Iraq war had been one of Obama's chief campaign promises.

◀ The last convoy of U.S. troops leaving Iraq, December 2011

58.2 The End of the Cold War Intensifies Globalization

Although people around the world welcomed the end of the Cold War, the sense of celebration was short-lived. Many crucial issues still had to be dealt with, and many difficult questions about the future had to be answered. For example, the United States and Western Europe had to reformulate their relationships with Russia and the other former Soviet republics. The pressures of globalization demanded it.

Negotiating with the Former Soviet Union Despite the tensions and dangers of the Cold War era, a certain predictable order characterized those years. The United States and the Soviet Union had largely dominated world affairs. When the Cold War ended, so did that predictability. Instead of dealing with one major adversary—the Soviet Union—the United States now faced a host of potential rivals. Some were solely economic rivals, like the European Union. Some were economic and military rivals, like China.

U.S. Secretary of State Hillary Clinton and Russian Foreign Minister Sergey Lavrov exchange documents after finalizing the New START treaty. The new treaty called on both countries to reduce their nuclear stockpiles by 30 percent, compared with previous limits.

An immediate set of problems concerned nuclear weapons in the former Soviet Union. In mid-1991, before the Soviet collapse, the United States and the USSR had signed the Strategic Arms Reduction Treaty, or START. This agreement called for both countries to reduce their nuclear stockpiles. Attempts to further lower each side's number of warheads, missiles, and bombers fell victim to Russian concerns over various U.S. foreign policy decisions. The 2009 round of talks, between President Obama and Russian leader Dmitry Medvedev, did prove fruitful. In April 2010, they signed New START, which would significantly limit offensive nuclear weapons.

Other former Soviet republics also possessed nuclear arms. After the fall of the Soviet Union, the United States tried to persuade them to place their stockpiles under Russian control. The United States feared that deadly nuclear materials might end up in the hands of terrorists or be sold to potential nuclear states such as Iran or North Korea. Eventually, all the republics agreed. However, the security of the Russian arsenal remained in doubt.

Economic problems also challenged peace and democracy in the former Soviet Union. Several republics had formed democratic governments. However, economic difficulties threatened to undermine their political stability. In October 1992, after much debate, Congress approved a foreign-aid package to help stimulate economic growth and support democracy in Russia and the newly independent states. Over the next decade, the United States provided them with billions of dollars in assistance to support the transition to a market economy and the development of civil society.

In 1999, Vladimir Putin succeeded Boris Yeltsin as president of Russia. Putin's strong leadership brought stability, but the nation continued to suffer from economic woes and political corruption. Putin also restricted rights and freedoms in Russia and tried to exert influence over the former Soviet republics. When Medvedev succeeded Putin as president of Russia, he made Putin his prime minister. Putin, who still seemed to hold the reins of power in Russia, announced plans to run for the top office again in 2012. In spite of Putin's aggressive style, the United States and Russia maintained a cooperative relationship.

Building New Ties in Europe During the Cold War, the Iron Curtain divided Europe in many ways. After the Cold War ended, however, new political, military, and economic alliances developed in Europe. They included the expansion of NATO and the European Common Market.

One set of changes revolved around the collapse of the Soviet military alliance—the Warsaw Pact. Several former Warsaw Pact nations hoped to join NATO as a way to develop closer ties to Western Europe and the United States. NATO saw the addition of countries that were previously enemies as a way to increase global stability and security. Russia, however, feared that an expansion of NATO might isolate it and threaten its interests. After careful consideration, NATO agreed to enlarge its membership. It would also seek to appease Russia by giving it a voice in NATO policy. From 1999 to 2009, NATO added 12 new members from Eastern Europe.

Europe changed in political and economic terms as well. In 1992, 12 countries in Western Europe agreed to form the **European Union (EU)**. The EU was an expanded version of the 40-year-old Common Market. The goal of the EU was to advance Europe's economic integration and unify European laws and foreign policies. In 1999, most of the EU countries adopted a shared currency, the euro. Ten new member states joined the EU in 2004 and two more in 2007. Most of them came from the former Soviet bloc.

The European Union brought together the original members of the Common Market, formed in 1952, with other European nations. The EU admitted 10 new members and in 2004. Most of these countries came from the former Soviet bloc. Two more countries joined the EU in 2007, for a total of 27.

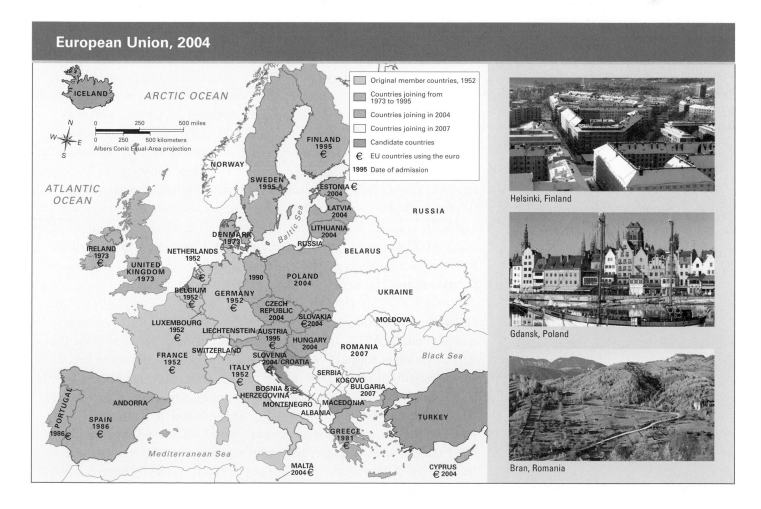

European Union, 2004

Helsinki, Finland

Gdansk, Poland

Bran, Romania

In July 1995, more than 7,000 Bosnian Muslim boys and men were murdered by Bosnian Serb forces in the town of Srebrenica. This was the worst episode of mass murder in Europe since World War II. Widows and mothers of the victims of Srebrenica continue to organize protests to remind people of those who were murdered, and of the thousands who are still missing as a result of the Bosnian Serb military occupation.

58.3 Responding to Ethnic Conflicts and Genocide

In the post-Cold War era, the rise of ethnic conflict posed a challenge to the United States. In parts of the former Soviet Union and Eastern Europe, ethnic and national tensions that communist rulers had suppressed for decades were suddenly unleashed. Some of the worst violence occurred in the former Yugoslavia. At the same time, mass killings took place in Africa.

Ending Ethnic Cleansing in Yugoslavia During the Cold War, Yugoslavia consisted of six republics held together under communist rule. Diverse ethnic and religious groups populated these republics. Most Serbs were Orthodox Christians. Most Slovenes and Croats were Catholics. And most Bosnians and ethnic Albanians were Muslims. Tensions simmered among these groups, but the communist system kept the situation from boiling over.

When communism collapsed in Eastern Europe, Yugoslavia fell apart. Four of its republics declared independence, and civil war broke out in Bosnia. The fighting pitted Bosnian Serbs against the majority Muslim population. The conflict was stoked by neighboring Serbia, whose president, Slobodan Milosevic, hoped to hold Yugoslavia together under Serbian leadership.

Bosnian Serbs carried out a policy that they called **ethnic cleansing**—the forced removal and murder of certain ethnic groups, in this case, non-Serbian peoples. They rounded up Muslims, Croats, and ethnic Albanians. The Serbs burned villages, tortured and raped their victims, and committed other atrocities. They killed at least 200,000 people and caused some 2 million Bosnians to flee.

In 1995, the conflict expanded. Croats and Muslims began fighting back against the Serbs. NATO decided to support these attacks by bombing Serbian forces and installations. With the conflict widening, the United States was finally able to bring the warring factions to the peace table. Negotiations held in Dayton, Ohio, led to a peace plan called the Dayton Accords. In 1996, with a cease-fire in place, U.S. troops joined NATO forces in the region. They separated the warring factions, protected civilians, and provided economic aid.

The Serbs, however, launched another round of ethnic cleansing in the Serbian province of Kosovo. The Muslim victims in Kosovo were ethnic Albanians. At the urging of President Clinton, NATO intervened. In March 1999, NATO fighter-bombers attacked the Serbian military in Kosovo. The bombing lasted until June, when Serbian forces began to retreat.

Failing to Halt Genocide in Africa Ethnic violence also took place on a massive scale in Africa. In the 1990s, hundreds of thousands died in the East African nation of Rwanda. Many more were uprooted and forced to flee. A similar tragedy struck the northeastern African nation of Sudan in the 2000s. In both cases, the United States failed to take military action to stop the violence.

In Rwanda, two rival ethnic groups, the Hutus and the Tutsis, vied for power. In 1994, the Hutu-led government lashed out at the Tutsi minority. In about three months, Hutu forces slaughtered more than 800,000 Rwandan men, women, and children, most of them Tutsis. France eventually intervened—but too late to stop the genocide. Not long afterward, Tutsi rebels managed to take control of the country.

The government of Sudan is controlled by Arabs. The western Sudan region of Darfur is populated mainly by black Africans. Long-running disputes between the two ethnic groups escalated into warfare in 2003. Sudanese troops and local Arab militias fought rebel groups in Darfur. The militias made a point of attacking civilians. According to reports from Darfur, they executed men and boys and raped and kidnapped women and girls. They often burned entire villages.

Peacekeepers from the African Union and the UN (none of whom were Americans) tried to prevent more violence. A peace treaty was signed in 2006, but not all rebel groups had agreed to it. Six years later, in spite of diplomatic efforts by the United States and other countries, hundreds of thousands of Darfuris remained in refugee camps, and fighting continued. By 2012, the conflict had killed an estimated 300,000 people, and more than 2 million civilians had fled their homes.

The United States did not take military action in Rwanda and Sudan for several reasons. In general, countries try to avoid interfering in other nations' internal affairs, which are usually best left to the individual countries to resolve. Also, although rich and powerful, the United States could not afford to get involved in every civil war around the world. But critics of U.S. inaction in Rwanda and Sudan argue that in the face of genocide, the United States had a moral responsibility to intervene in a case when human rights were being violated on such an enormous scale. They suggest that the United States would have done so if it had regarded those African nations as crucial to its own interests. Evidently, they say, it did not. Another powerful reason for ignoring the conflicts in Rwanda and Sudan relates to an earlier—and unsuccessful—intervention in the East African nation of Somalia.

In 1994, ethnic conflict and genocide forced millions of Rwandans to flee their homes. Many ended up in refugee camps in neighboring nations. UN Secretary General Kofi Annan later apologized for the world's failure to act. "The world must deeply repent this failure," he remarked. "Rwanda's tragedy was the world's tragedy."

Hasty Withdrawal from Somalia Somalia in the early 1990s was a failed state. That is, its government was ineffective, or incapable of maintaining law and order or providing public services. Civil war had led to economic collapse and famine. After the government fell, numerous rival groups fought one another for power.

Into this chaos, the United States led a multinational force to try to restore order and provide Somalis with food. In 1993, the deaths of 18 U.S. soldiers in a firefight, followed by the dragging of a dead soldier's body through the streets of the Somali capital, outraged the American public. The United States decided to pull its troops out, and the UN mission ended shortly thereafter. When later tragedies unfolded in Rwanda and Sudan, the disastrous intervention in Somalia was still fresh in the memories of U.S. policy makers—and it would remain so for years.

58.4 Supplying Humanitarian Aid

The United States hesitated to get involved militarily in Africa, but along with the rest of the world's wealthiest countries, it shipped generous amounts of food and supplies to Somalia, Rwanda, Sudan, and other African countries. The U.S. government remained committed to providing humanitarian aid wherever it was needed. **Humanitarian aid** includes money, food, and other forms of assistance given to people who are suffering and in need. U.S. aid agencies often worked through the UN to combat famine, disease, and natural disasters.

Countering Famine in North Korea During the Cold War, North Korea had relied on the Soviet Union for trade and aid, including food shipments and farm equipment. After the Soviet Union collapsed, communist North Korea did not seek new global partners. Instead, it largely closed itself off from the outside world. Within a few years, famine gripped the country.

Natural disasters made the situation worse. Between 1995 and 1998, severe floods and periods of drought destroyed crops. As many as 3 million North Koreans died of starvation. In spite of its policy of isolation, in 1995 North Korea began to accept aid from the World Food Program (WFP), a branch of the United Nations. Over the next few years, the WFP oversaw the delivery of millions of tons of food to North Korea, including large shipments from the United States.

In the years that followed, North Korea's harvests rarely produced enough food to feed all of people. It relied heavily on U.S. food aid. Critics claimed that much of the food went to government officials and the army, never reaching the starving peasants it was meant to help. In 2011, three years after halting large-scale shipments of food and fertilizer to North Korea, the United States considered restarting those shipments. It hoped to link food aid to a key foreign policy goal—the resumption of stalled talks aimed at limiting North Korea's nuclear weapons program.

Dealing with AIDS in Africa In the 1990s, another humanitarian crisis emerged in Africa: the HIV/AIDS epidemic. By the end of the decade, more than 20 million Africans were infected with HIV, the virus that causes AIDS. Several million were dying every year. The United States responded slowly to the crisis. Although President Clinton offered sympathy, his administration did little to combat the AIDS epidemic.

In 2003, President George W. Bush signed a bill allocating $15 billion over a five-year period to combat AIDS in Africa and the Caribbean. It was called the President's Emergency Plan for AIDS Relief (PEPFAR). At the signing ceremony, Bush declared that the United States had a moral duty to take action and urged other rich nations to do the same.

PEPFAR was the most ambitious attempt by any one country to combat a single disease. By 2008, the U.S. government had spent $18 billion, treated some 2 million people, and provided medical care to more than 10 million others. Under President Obama, PEPFAR funding continued. Its new goals included expanding prevention, care, and treatment.

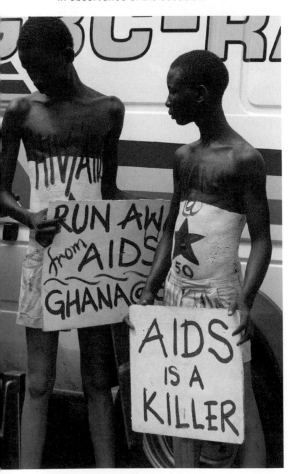

Two young Ghanaians do their part to call attention to the problem of AIDS in Ghana. Every December 1 since 1988, World AIDS Day has been observed throughout the world. The event aims to prevent future infections by increasing awareness of the disease. Each year, the U.S. president issues a proclamation in observance of the occasion.

Supporting Earthquake Victims in Haiti On January 12, 2010, a huge earthquake unleashed its destructive forces on the Caribbean island nation of Haiti. Buildings collapsed in the capital city of Port-au-Prince and throughout the surrounding region. Houses, schools, hospitals, and even Haiti's parliament building were turned to rubble. At least 230,000 people died and another 1.5 million were left homeless.

President Obama immediately called for a "swift, coordinated, and aggressive effort to save lives." A disaster team arrived the next day to begin planning the U.S. response, as did members of a search-and-rescue team. In the coming days, weeks, and months, various U.S. agencies provided food, water, shelter, medical care, and other humanitarian aid. Some 20,000 Americans worked alongside teams from other countries, from the United Nations, and from numerous **nongovernmental organizations (NGOs),** such as the Red Cross. An NGO is a group formed by private individuals in order to provide a service or pursue a public policy.

Two years after the earthquake, in spite of the multinational efforts, Haiti had not yet fully recovered. Around half a million people were still living in camps under rough conditions. Millions had no steady job. Rebuilding was going slowly in part because Haiti's government was weak and ineffective.

Helping Japan Recover from an Earthquake and Tsunami In March 2011, an earthquake some 200 miles off the east coast of Japan generated a tsunami, a huge and powerful ocean wave. This wall of water, moving at 50 miles per hour, smashed into Japan's northern coastline and rolled several miles inland, carrying boats, cars, and houses with it. Some small towns were washed away completely. The tsunami killed more than 20,000 people.

The tsunami caused a catastrophe at the Fukushima Daiichi nuclear power plant, located 150 miles north of Tokyo. After explosions in three nuclear reactors at the plant, radioactive gas leaked into the atmosphere and settled on farmlands, forests, and houses. Water used to cool the reactors carried radioactive material into the ocean. Japan's government evacuated around 90,000 residents from the surrounding "hot zone." It was uncertain whether they would ever be able to return to their homes. Months later, Japanese technicians were still trying to stabilize the reactors. Cleanup crews were working to remove contaminated topsoil from an area the size of Connecticut.

Unlike Haiti, Japan had significant economic and technical resources. Yet it still needed help dealing with this huge natural disaster. Shortly after the earthquake and tsunami struck, disaster response teams from the United States and other countries, as well as from various NGOs, went to Japan. But much of the international aid to Japan came in the form of donations of money. Just a month after the event, Americans had already given $246 million to the relief effort.

Two Haitian women sit amid the rubble of the capital city of Port-au-Prince. The catastrophe in Haiti galvanized the American public to donate millions of dollars to relief organizations, such as the Red Cross.

After the catastrophe at the Fukushima Daiichi nuclear power plant, the Japanese government established a restricted zone around the plant and evacuated residents from the area. Months after the disaster, former residents of the town of Okuma, located within the restricted zone, returned in protective gear to attend a memorial service for victims of the tsunami.

One effect of economic globalization is off-shore outsourcing, in which companies use overseas workers to make their products. Here, workers in China assemble laptops for U.S. corporations. Outsourcing opponents say that the practice takes jobs away from American workers. Supporters of outsourcing argue that it benefits the U.S. economy by employing people in other countries who will use their incomes to buy American products.

58.5 Competing in a Global Economy

The United States confronted new economic challenges in the post-Cold War era. At the height of the Cold War, the world had been divided into two main spheres of influence that fractured along ideological lines. In issues of trade and economic development, as in other realms, the world split between communism and capitalism. With the collapse of the Soviet Union, the world moved quickly toward a more diverse, global economy. As a result, the United States had to find new ways to compete in the global marketplace.

Promoting Free Trade At the end of the Cold War, the United States had the largest economy in the world. However, it ran a high **trade deficit** with economic powers such as China, Japan, and the European Union. A trade deficit occurs when the value of a country's imports exceeds the value of its exports. One way U.S. leaders hoped to correct the trade imbalance was through free trade.

To that end, in 1993, Congress passed the **North American Free Trade Agreement (NAFTA)**. NAFTA created a **free-trade zone** among the United States, Mexico, and Canada. A free-trade zone is a defined geographic area in which governments lower or eliminate tariffs and other barriers to international trade. Supporters of NAFTA claimed that it would increase the market for American exports and would create new, high-wage jobs for American workers. They also maintained that by boosting Mexico's economy, NAFTA would help curtail limit illegal immigration from Mexico. Opponents argued that NAFTA would cost jobs by encouraging American factories to move to Mexico, where labor costs were lower.

Whether or not NAFTA has been good for the U.S. economy is open to debate. Trade among the United States, Canada, and Mexico has increased, but the U.S. trade deficit has continued to grow. Many U.S. factories have moved out of the country, taking jobs with them, but more jobs have gone to China than to Mexico. Employment continued to rise after NAFTA, although an economic downturn starting in 2007 began a lengthy period of high unemployment.

Whatever the impact of NAFTA might be, the United States has continued to pursue free trade. In 1994, the U.S. government participated in a major overhaul of the General Agreement on Tariffs and Trade (GATT). The first GATT, signed after World War II, had required its members to reduce barriers to trade. The updated GATT called for further reductions. It also established the **World Trade Organization (WTO)**. The main function of the WTO is to set trade policies and mediate disputes among its more than 150 member nations. In the years that followed, the government made more than a dozen other trade pacts. These include a 2006 free-trade agreement with the Dominican Republic and five Central American countries. It is known as CAFTA-DR.

Challenges and Opportunities of Economic Globalization The creation of the WTO and the sharp increase in free-trade deals indicated that economic globalization during the post-Cold War era was on the rise. Several factors have contributed to its growth. Trade pacts like GATT and NAFTA have certainly spurred the expansion of the global marketplace. But advances in transportation and communications technology have been just as important. The Internet, for

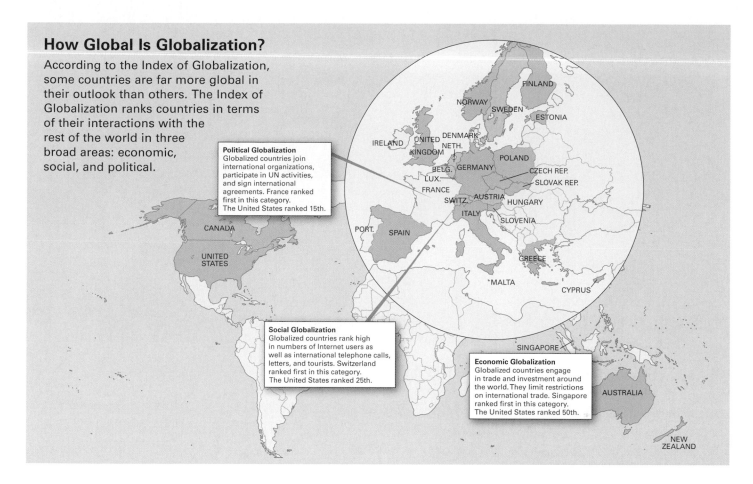

How Global Is Globalization?

According to the Index of Globalization, some countries are far more global in their outlook than others. The Index of Globalization ranks countries in terms of their interactions with the rest of the world in three broad areas: economic, social, and political.

Political Globalization
Globalized countries join international organizations, participate in UN activities, and sign international agreements. France ranked first in this category. The United States ranked 15th.

Social Globalization
Globalized countries rank high in numbers of Internet users as well as international telephone calls, letters, and tourists. Switzerland ranked first in this category. The United States ranked 25th.

Economic Globalization
Globalized countries engage in trade and investment around the world. They limit restrictions on international trade. Singapore ranked first in this category. The United States ranked 50th.

example, has helped "shrink" the globe, making it possible for people in distant parts of the world to communicate and work together almost instantaneously.

Globalization has produced many benefits. It has given more people access to goods and services from around the world. It has helped promote economic development and create new opportunities in poor countries. It has also stimulated cultural diffusion, or the sharing of ideas and customs among nations.

But globalization has also raised concerns. Environmentalists argue that the rapid growth of the world economy is adding to environmental problems such as global warming. Labor leaders worry about the transfer of jobs to low-wage countries. Many people are also concerned that globalization may result in a loss of cultural diversity. They fear that modern, Western values will take the place of more traditional customs. In addition, some critics argue that globalization amounts to a new type of colonialism by helping concentrate wealth in the hands of economically advanced nations and large, multinational corporations. A **multinational corporation** has facilities—offices, factories, stores, warehouses—in more than one nation.

The Great Recession, discussed in the previous chapter, showed just how perilous globalization can be. It began in the United States when the housing bubble burst and banks faced collapse. Through the financial networks that link economies around the world, the recession quickly became a global phenomenon. Clearly, the globalization that allows the free and rapid flow of goods, ideas, and money across borders can also spread financial chaos worldwide. It may create opportunities, but it also poses new and complex challenges.

The Global Top 30 in 2008

1. Belgium
2. Austria
3. Netherlands
4. Sweden
5. Switzerland
6. Denmark
7. France
8. Hungary
9. Portugal
10. Ireland
11. Finland
12. Czech Republic
13. Canada
14. Luxembourg
15. Slovak Republic
16. Germany
17. Spain
18. Singapore
19. Norway
20. Cyprus
21. United Kingdom
22. Australia
23. Italy
24. Estonia
25. New Zealand
26. Slovenia
27. United States
28. Poland
29. Greece
30. Malta

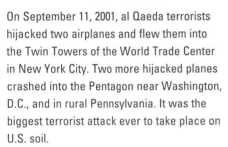

On September 11, 2001, al Qaeda terrorists hijacked two airplanes and flew them into the Twin Towers of the World Trade Center in New York City. Two more hijacked planes crashed into the Pentagon near Washington, D.C., and in rural Pennsylvania. It was the biggest terrorist attack ever to take place on U.S. soil.

58.6 Fighting Terrorism

Among the most critical security concerns is terrorism. For decades, terrorists have used violence to try to achieve their political goals. After the Cold War, groups emerged to carry out terrorist acts in previously unaffected parts of the world, including the United States.

Terrorists Strike the United States A series of terrorist attacks took place during the Clinton administration. In 1993, Muslim terrorists set off a bomb beneath the World Trade Center in New York City. In 1998, the U.S. embassies in the East African nations of Kenya and Tanzania were bombed. Then, in 2000, terrorists attacked the USS *Cole,* a Navy destroyer anchored off the coast of the Arab nation of Yemen. In response, the United States arrested and prosecuted suspects. It also launched missile strikes against terrorist camps overseas.

Such actions did not deter terrorists. The next attack occurred during George W. Bush's presidency and was by far the worst in U.S. history. On September 11, 2001, terrorists hijacked four commercial airplanes. They flew two of the planes into the Twin Towers of New York City's World Trade Center, causing both towers to collapse. The third airplane hit the Pentagon, the Defense Department's headquarters just outside of Washington, D.C. The fourth crashed in a Pennsylvania field after passengers fought with the hijackers. This last plane had been heading for either the White House or the Capitol building. Altogether, about 3,000 people died in the terrorist acts of 9/11.

In the days that followed, Americans learned that an international terrorist network called **al Qaeda** had carried out the 9/11 attacks. The organization's leader was Osama bin Laden, a wealthy Saudi Arabian and Muslim extremist. Al Qaeda sought to rid Muslim countries of Western influence and establish a "pan-Islamic caliphate"—a kind of kingdom ruled according to fundamentalist Islamic principles. Al Qaeda had also carried out the U.S. embassy attacks in Africa and the assault on the USS *Cole.*

Bin Laden ran al Qaeda from Afghanistan, but local al Qaeda cells, or groups, operated all over the world. They often took refuge in failed states, where the government was weak. To coordinate activities, they used modern communications technologies—cell phones, the Internet, encrypted e-mail, and laser disks. Electronic transfers of money financed those activities.

In 1998, bin Laden had declared that all Muslims had a duty "to kill the Americans and their allies—civilian or military." Bin Laden was not representing the feelings of the vast majority of Muslims, who reject terrorism as being counter to Islamic values. But he did speak to a general feeling among some Muslims that the United States did not respect Islam or support Muslim interests. These Muslims resented having thousands of U.S. soldiers stationed in Saudi Arabia years after the Persian Gulf War's end. They also resented U.S. support for Israel in its struggle with the Arab Palestinians. Bin Laden used those bitter feelings to promote his cause and to recruit terrorists.

President Bush reacted to al Qaeda's attacks on September 11, 2001, by declaring a **war on terror**. In a speech to Congress he stated, "Our war on terror begins with al Qaeda, but it does not end there. It will not end until every terrorist group of global reach has been found, stopped, and defeated." This war would be waged not only against the terrorists themselves, Bush explained, but also against any governments that sponsored them.

Ending Taliban Rule in Afghanistan The war on terror began in 2001 in Afghanistan, al Qaeda's main base of operations. At the time, a radical Muslim group called the **Taliban** controlled the nation. The ultraconservative Taliban were known for their harsh punishments and their rules barring women from working, receiving an education, or enjoying other basic rights. The Taliban also permitted al Qaeda to operate terrorist training camps on Afghan soil.

After 9/11, President Bush asked the Taliban to turn bin Laden over to the United States. The Afghan leaders refused. The United States formed an international coalition to overthrow the Taliban and capture bin Laden. In early October 2001, U.S. and British forces began bombing al Qaeda camps and Taliban military sites. U.S. ground troops and anti-Taliban Afghan militias also joined the fighting. By mid-November, Afghanistan's capital, Kabul, and other major cities had fallen. U.S. Marines took on the task of subduing the remaining Taliban fighters. The U.S forces then began to hunt for bin Laden, who had gone into hiding.

Toppling the Iraqi Regime After the victory in Afghanistan, President Bush turned his attention to another Southwest Asian country—Iraq. In his State of the Union address in January 2002, Bush referred to Iraq, Iran, and North Korea as an "axis of evil." These nations, he said, all had **weapons of mass destruction (WMD)**. WMD include chemical, biological, and nuclear weapons. Bush feared that Iraq, in particular, might provide such weapons to terrorists.

Since taking power in 1979, Iraq's dictator, Saddam Hussein, had compiled a horrific human-rights record. He brutally tortured and killed his opponents. In the late 1980s, he used chemical weapons against the Kurds, an ethnic group in northern Iraq. At least 50,000 Kurds died. After the Persian Gulf War, Saddam—a Sunni Muslim—crushed a rebellion by Shi'a Muslims in southern Iraq.

U.S. military troops departed from Iraq in late 2011, ending nearly nine years of American military operations in the Iraq War. Shown here are troops from the Third Brigade, First Cavalry Division, part of the last U.S. combat units to depart from Iraq, arriving at their home base in Fort Hood, Texas.

The Sunni and Shi'a branches of Islam have a long-standing rivalry in the Muslim world. In putting down the rebellion, Saddam murdered many thousands of Shi'ites and other Iraqis. He also blocked UN inspectors in their search for WMD, which the victorious coalition forces had banned in Iraq after the Gulf War.

After 9/11, President Bush accused Saddam of aiding terrorists and hiding WMD. Bush thus urged an extension of the war on terror to Iraq. Iraq had taken no direct action against the United States. Yet Bush insisted that Saddam had WMD and that a real threat existed. He was ready to act unilaterally, without the approval of U.S. allies or the UN. The president's foreign policy of taking action to head off trouble became known as the Bush Doctrine. In October 2002, persuaded by Bush's arguments, Congress authorized the president to send troops to Iraq if necessary.

In March 2003, the United States launched an invasion of Iraq. President Bush did seek to enlist the support of the international community, as he had said he would. He put together a "coalition of the willing" that consisted of some three dozen nations that agreed to send troops. But several European allies, including France and Germany, opposed the invasion, and the UN failed to approve it.

Within a month, coalition forces had seized Iraq's capital, Baghdad, and toppled the government. Saddam escaped, only to be captured eight months later, tried in an Iraqi court, and executed. Meanwhile, U.S. inspection teams began the search for banned weapons. However, they would later find that Iraq had no significant weapons of mass destruction.

The Second Phase of the Iraq War After a quick victory, the United States struggled to bring peace to Iraq. It undertook a mission of **nation building**—the construction of political institutions and a stable government in a country. Although most Iraqis welcomed the end of Saddam's regime, some resented having foreign troops in their country. An armed resistance, including insurgent forces from both inside and outside Iraq, soon rose up to battle the coalition forces. The Iraq War entered a second, much longer phase.

Attempting to destabilize the new government, insurgents used guerrilla warfare and terror tactics, such as the assassination of Iraqi leaders. They ambushed coalition troops, often employing roadside bombs that could be detonated from a distance. Meanwhile, armed conflicts between rival Sunni and Shi'a militias increased, especially in Baghdad. Many analysts began calling the conflict in Iraq a civil war.

In January 2007, President Bush announced that 30,000 more troops would be sent to Iraq. This "troop surge" helped U.S. and Iraqi forces get better control of the country. Over the next several years, U.S. forces remained a prime target of the violence. But that violence slowly diminished. Meanwhile, the Iraqi government grew more stable, and with the help of U.S. trainers, the Iraqi army and police gained the skills and experience needed to keep order in the country.

In August 2010, President Obama announced that all U.S. troops would leave Iraq by the end of the following year. The withdrawal went according to plan. The last U.S. troops left Iraq in December 2011.

Nearly 4,500 U.S. soldiers were killed in the Iraq War. Neither the United States nor the Iraqi government provided an official count of Iraqi civilian deaths over the nine-year war. Estimates of civilian deaths reported by private organizations and the UN varied widely and were greatly disputed. One U.S.-British independent group run by peace activists estimated between about 90,000 and 100,000 civilian deaths. In 2010, an independent organization called WikiLeaks released an archive of several hundred secret Pentagon reports on the Iraq War. The reports were posted online and were made available to several major news organizations. According to these reports, most civilians were killed by other Iraqis.

War Continues in Afghanistan In Afghanistan, the Taliban resurfaced as an armed force. Its fighters regularly attacked the Afghan army and the coalition forces, which were now under NATO command and made up largely of American soldiers. The Taliban, along with a limited number of al Qaeda advisers, launched its attacks largely from the mountainous border region of Afghanistan and neighboring Pakistan. They were able to take back territory that they had earlier lost. In late 2009, following the strategy that worked in Iraq, Obama announced a surge of 33,000 U.S. troops into Afghanistan. As in Iraq, the surge helped NATO forces blunt the Taliban assaults.

Meanwhile, the U.S. military launched a successful campaign to weaken al Qaeda by killing some of its leaders. It owed its success largely to the use of drones, remotely piloted aircraft whose missiles could be directed at targets on the ground. Drone attacks killed a number of al Qaeda officials in Pakistan, causing the Pakistani government to protest that U.S. strikes were violating their sovereignty. The United States provoked a harsher protest from Pakistan in May 2011, when an American assault force on the ground in Pakistan finally located and killed Osama bin Laden.

With bin Laden dead and the Taliban no longer in control, Obama decided to begin withdrawing U.S. soldiers from Afghanistan. According to his timetable, the troops would gradually pull out of the country, the last leaving in 2014. However, some military leaders believed that U.S. forces would have to stay longer to ensure that the Taliban would not retake control.

Soldiers in Apache Company 2-28 of the U.S. Army prepare for a patrol in Afghanistan. More than 2 million U.S. troops served in Afghanistan and Iraq since the 9/11 attacks, deployed from the Army, Navy, Marine Corps, Air Force, and Coast Guard.

In 2005, Iraqis took advantage of their new democratic rights to elect a national assembly. Many proudly showed off their ink-stained fingers—proof that they had voted in the election.

58.7 Challenges and Progress

One of the United States' foreign policy goals is to promote freedom and democracy around the world. U.S. military actions in Afghanistan and Iraq were intended to support that goal. In 2011, however, a movement to achieve democratic government in several countries in North Africa and the Middle East came not from the United States but arose within that region. People in North Africa and the Middle East sought democratic rule in a series of uprisings against authoritarian rulers.

Afghanistan and Iraq The United States and the United Nations worked with Afghan opposition groups to establish a democratically elected government. By 2005, the nation had a new president and a constitution. The constitution included rights and freedoms found in many Western democracies. It made Afghanistan an Islamic republic, but it also guaranteed freedom of religion. In addition, it ensured that women would have the same legal rights as men. A second round of national and provincial elections took place in 2009. These elections—the first post-Taliban elections run by the Afghan government— were marred by incidents of violence and widespread charges of voter fraud.

Afghanistan continued to experience serious problems as it struggled to recover from decades of war. Although the U.S.-led invasion of Afghanistan removed the Taliban from power in 2001, Taliban leaders continued to act against the Afghan government and U.S. forces. The resurgence raised concerns both in the United States and in Afghanistan that women's rights would once again be threatened.

The United States also supported efforts to build democracy in Iraq. In October 2005, Iraqis voted by a large majority to approve a new constitution. As in Afghanistan, Islam would play a role in the nation's laws, but Iraqis would enjoy most of the rights and freedoms of other democracies. Two months later, Iraqi voters cast ballots to elect a national assembly. In 2010, Iraq again held an election that led to a national government in which the country's major political parties agreed to share power. Despite progress, Iraq continued to suffer from political violence. Attempting to destabilize the new government, insurgents used guerrilla warfare and terror tactics, such as the assassination of Iraqi leaders. Meanwhile, armed conflicts between rival Sunni and Shi'a militias continued, especially in Baghdad.

The Arab Spring In 2011, a remarkable wave of democratization swept across North Africa and the Middle East. It consisted of a series of popular revolts against oppressive rulers in this largely Arab region. Together, they became known as the **Arab Spring**.

The Arab Spring began in the North African country of Tunisia in late 2010. Tunisians, many of them young and unemployed, took to the streets to protest the lack of jobs, poverty, and government corruption. After just a few weeks, the growing demonstrations caused Tunisia's president to flee the country.

Tunisia's outburst of democratic action triggered other civil unrest. At the end of January 2011, pro-democracy demonstrations broke out in several Egyptian cities. By April, huge protests in the capital city of Cairo led to the downfall of the government and the arrest of Egypt's president, Hosni Mubarak. Similar protests, most of them peaceful, followed in Algeria, Yemen, Lebanon, Iran, Bahrain, and elsewhere.

In Libya, however, it took an armed rebellion to overthrow dictator Muammar al-Gaddafi. The rebels relied on NATO air strikes, some of which were carried out by U.S. aircraft.

Beginning in early 2011, rebels also fought for democracy in Syria. Syria's dictatorship government responded with with heavy military force, leading to thousands of civilian deaths. The United States supported the rebels with trade sanctions, and a call for Syria's president to resign. In early 2012, it was too soon to know if the Arab Spring countries would achieve fully democratic rule.

Gauging Future Foreign Policy Challenges As the second decade of the 21st century began, several areas of the world posed ongoing challenges for the United States. Iran's capacity to build a nuclear weapon remained a key issue. The Israeli-Palestinian peace process had to be revived. Iraq and Afghanistan, as well as Pakistan, needed support to maintain stability and democratic rule.

As U.S. military operations in Iraq ended, the United States began focusing more attention on Asia. India and China, both with robust economies, have increased military spending, especially on their navies. U.S. officials viewed India's naval buildup as a way to add stability to the region, while helping balance power on a continent dominated more and more by China.

The United States also began to reassert its power in Asia. In 2011, it opened a new military base in Australia, not far from the vital shipping lanes of the South China Sea. This move showed that the United States was serious about looking after old allies such as Japan and South Korea and making new friends in Asia.

In 2011, Libyans celebrated the official declaration of their country's liberation from 42 years of dictatorship under Muammar al-Gaddafi. Revolutionary leaders set up a Transitional National Council that pledged to lead the country to a democratically elected government.

Summary

The beginning of the 21st century brought hopes for a new era of peace and cooperation in the world. Nevertheless, the United States faced many challenges.

Ethnic cleansing and genocide Ethnic conflicts in various countries prompted mixed responses from the United States. In the former Yugoslavia, the United States backed NATO military actions against ethnic cleansing. However, it failed to stop genocide in Rwanda and Sudan.

Humanitarian aid The United States offered humanitarian aid in a number of countries, including Somalia, North Korea, Haiti, and Japan. To combat the rise of HIV/AIDS in Africa, the United States funded a program of prevention, care, and treatment.

Free trade The United States promoted free trade as part of a growing trend toward economic globalization. The North American Free Trade Agreement linked Mexico, Canada, and the United States.

Fighting terrorists The al Qaeda terrorist attacks of September 11, 2001, prompted the United States to declare a war on terror in Afghanistan and Iraq.

Building democracy The United States worked with Afghans and Iraqis to try to build stable democracies in their countries. It also supported, although less directly, the Arab Spring uprisings.

Chapter 59

9/11 and Its Aftermath: Debating America's Founding Ideals

What debates have arisen since 9/11 about how to balance security while preserving American ideals?

59.1 Introduction

On the morning of September 11, 2001, a series of delays made Richard Moller late to work. His office was on the 100th floor of the North Tower of the World Trade Center in New York City. Before Moller reached his office, an airplane hijacked by terrorists smashed into the North Tower. Moller realized that the delays that morning had saved his life. "If I had gotten an elevator just a few minutes earlier," he recalled, "I would be dead."

The aircraft that hit the North Tower, a Boeing 767 jetliner, carried a full load of fuel. Most Americans can recall exactly where they were when they heard the news. Many people turned on their televisions just in time to see a second passenger plane slam into the South Tower 17 minutes after the first. As fire began consuming the upper floors of both buildings, most people in the towers managed to escape down stairwells. But many did not. Shock turned to horror as the Twin Towers collapsed. The South Tower was the first to fall at 9:59 A.M. The North Tower collapsed at 10:28 A.M. Less than an hour before, a third hijacked passenger jet had crashed into the Pentagon building near Washington, D.C. Soon after came news that a fourth hijacked plane had crashed in Pennsylvania.

As Americans watched the tragedy unfold, they reacted with emotions ranging from bewilderment and dismay to anger and outrage. And most sensed that life had suddenly changed. The deaths provoked both an outpouring of grief and tremendous anxiety as Americans all around the country asked one another, "Are you all right?" In just two hours, nearly 3,000 people lost their lives—more than had died when Japanese bombers attacked Pearl Harbor in December 1941.

The terrorist attacks of 9/11 had not only shattered Americans' sense of security. In the months and years ahead, they would also significantly influence the nation's approach to preserving its founding ideals.

On 9/11, one of four hijacked airplanes smashed into the Pentagon, killing 125 people. As the headquarters of the Department of Defense and the U.S. armed forces, the Pentagon is a symbol of American power.

◀ An annual "Tribute in Light" memorializes the victims at Ground Zero.

New York City's police and firefighters worked tirelessly to save victims of the 9/11 attacks. In the process, more than 400 rescue workers lost their lives. Many others suffered medical problems from inhaling toxic fumes at Ground Zero, as the site of the World Trade Center disaster is sometimes called.

59.2 The Immediate Impact of 9/11

On the evening of 9/11, President George W. Bush spoke to the nation about the horrific events of the day. He began by calling the terrorist attacks an assault on the nation's values. "Today," he said, "our way of life, our very freedom came under attack." He went on to reassure Americans that the government was taking action not only to help with rescue efforts in New York but also to find those "behind these evil acts." The president ended by saying,

> This is a day when all Americans from every walk of life unite in our resolve for justice and peace. America has stood down enemies before, and we will do so this time. None of us will ever forget this day. Yet, we go forward to defend freedom and all that is good and just in our world.

A New Sense of Vulnerability In the days following the attacks, shock gave way to a mixture of stunned disbelief and fear. It seemed incomprehensible to many people that terrorists could launch such a devastating attack on U.S. soil. After all, the United States had the most powerful military in the world. Most Americans believed the nation to be secure from outside threats. But after 9/11, no one knew how many terrorists might still be in the country, prepared to strike again at any time. As one Florida resident commented, "I realize now that we are as vulnerable as all of those nations [in] Europe [and] the Middle East."

In the aftermath of the 9/11 attacks, many normal activities came to a halt. One journalist wrote, "It was as though life as we knew it had stopped, to be replaced by an anxious emptiness, a national stillness, immobility." The stock markets stayed closed for nearly a week, and officials shut down the tunnels and bridges leading into Manhattan until they were secured. Airlines canceled flights. They did not resume service for several days. When they did, most planes flew virtually empty. In towns and cities across the nation, heightened security measures caused delays and disrupted everyday life. Authorities around the country warned Americans to be vigilant and report suspicious activities.

Drawing Together to Defend Our Way of Life Despite the mood of fear and vulnerability, 9/11 also drew Americans together. For weeks after the attacks, strangers greeted one another on the streets. Friends who had not spoken in years phoned to talk. A New Jersey woman who lost her husband at the World Trade Center found anonymous gifts of food at her front door every morning. "The kindness of people is what is getting me through this," she said. "It's enlightening to know that I'm not entirely alone."

Americans also came together in groups, holding candlelight vigils and memorial services for the victims of 9/11. Schools and other local organizations raised money for victims' families. The country mourned together for those who died in the attack and for the police, firefighters, and other heroic first responders who gave their lives in the rescue effort.

Firefighters across the nation expressed their solidarity with the New York City Fire Department. Some took time off to travel to Manhattan to help with the recovery effort. A group of Indiana firefighters ran the distance from Indiana to New York City, an effort that raised $170,000 for victims of the attacks. And the Wisconsin-based company that supplied New York's fire trucks quickly began work on replacing the trucks lost in the disaster. Similar stories of individual and group actions of support recurred all over the nation.

The Administration Takes Action In the meantime, the Bush administration devised a two-pronged strategy to cope with the threat of terrorism and keep the country safe. First, it rolled out the war on terror, which called for aggressive military action abroad to combat perceived terrorist threats. This approach led to lengthy and controversial wars in Afghanistan and Iraq. Second, the administration focused on measures to prevent future terrorist attacks at home. Like the wars abroad, these domestic security measures aroused controversy.

At the heart of the often-heated debates that followed 9/11 lay a question that Americans have confronted before, during times of national peril: How can we balance such ideals as equality and liberty with our desire for security? In the years since 9/11, both the U.S. government and the American people have worked to review and, at times, revise domestic and foreign policy choices in hopes of ensuring that they achieve just that balance.

In the immediate aftermath of the terrorist attacks in New York City, family members of those in and around the Twin Towers hoped their loved ones had somehow survived. Near the ruins of the World Trade Center, they posted pictures and descriptions of missing persons. Thousands of such fliers were attached to walls, lampposts, and mailboxes.

In the first year and a half after 9/11, the FBI investigated more than 400 hate crimes against Arab Americans. The perpetrators of these crimes attacked innocent people and vandalized mosques and Muslim-owned businesses.

After 9/11, airports increased security to try to prevent future terrorist acts. Security officials carried out more rigorous searches, including the use of full-body scanners. These scanners, which produce detailed images of a person's body in order to check for concealed weapons, raised questions about a person's right to privacy.

59.3 Safeguarding Equality

The 9/11 attacks reminded many Americans of Japan's attack on Pearl Harbor 60 years earlier. After that assault, the government forced more than 100,000 Japanese Americans to live in internment camps. After learning that the 9/11 terrorists were Arab Muslims, many people of Middle Eastern and North African descent worried that they might suffer a similar fate. Bush reassured American Muslims that they would be treated the same way as other citizens. "America counts millions of Muslims amongst our citizens," he declared. "In our anger and emotion, our fellow Americans must treat each other with respect."

Balancing Safety and Equality: Profiling The question of how best to protect the ideal of equality in the new, post-9/11 era first arose in airports. Airline officials began paying special attention to young men who looked like the 9/11 terrorists or had names similar to those of the terrorists. These travelers faced more rigorous searches than others did. The practice of using physical traits to decide whether to investigate or arrest someone is known as **racial profiling**.

Some Americans strongly supported racial profiling. They viewed terrorism as an extreme threat that justified the use of special security strategies. The principle of equality, they argued, should not be allowed to jeopardize public safety. Others viewed racial profiling as discrimination. They insisted that all travelers should go through the same search procedures. Norman Mineta, the U.S. secretary of transportation and a Japanese American, agreed. As a child, he had been sent to an internment camp.

Mineta banned racial profiling in airports. He also helped develop new procedures to prevent air travelers from carrying weapons or other devices that pose a security risk. Before people could board a plane, they had to take off their shoes, empty their pockets, and walk through a metal detector. These rules irritated a few air travelers, but most Americans were willing to suffer some inconvenience to ensure their safety.

One procedure, however, triggered much stronger complaints. Travelers who could not pass through a metal detector without setting off the alarm had to go through a pat-down. Critics argued that the equal treatment of travelers had gone too far when a 6-year-old child or a 96-year-old grandmother could be frisked.

Opposing Economic Inequality After 9/11 and again in 2007, recession slowed the U.S. economy. In stressful times like these, economic inequality—the huge gap in income between rich and poor—becomes an issue. The Great Recession officially ended in 2009, but the economy remained weak. Many people blamed overly greedy, corrupt Wall Street bankers for the nation's economic woes. In September 2011, a group of Americans gathered on Wall Street to demonstrate. Some decided to camp out on the site, launching a protest movement known as Occupy Wall Street.

The Occupy movement spread to hundreds of other towns and cities. Economic inequality was one of the protesters' key concerns. They noted that just 1 percent of Americans owned more than 30 percent of the nation's wealth. Cold weather and evictions by police weakened the movement, but its slogan, "We are the 99 percent," resonated with many Americans.

59.4 Preserving Opportunity

The United States has long appealed to immigrants as a land of opportunity. But after 9/11, the government put in place tougher immigration policies in an effort to keep terrorists out of the country. The new laws also made it harder for some foreign students, workers, and tourists to enter or stay in the country. The result has been a loss of opportunity for foreigners and for the schools and businesses that cater to them.

Balancing Security and Opportunity: Foreign Visitors Nonresidents make some 50 million visits to the United States each year. Some arrive as permanent immigrants, but the vast majority comes as short-term visitors. Citizens of Canada and 36 selected countries can enter the United States with just a passport. Others need a passport and a visa. A **passport** is a document issued by a person's home government to verify his or her identity. A **visa** is an authorization from a government for a foreigner to enter its country. The 9/11 terrorists all entered the country legally, with valid passports and visas.

After 9/11, Congress passed new laws to make the country's borders more secure. They included new procedures to make visas harder to obtain. As part of the process, officials now check each applicant's identity against a "watch list" of known or suspected terrorists. This check can lead to delays or denials of visas to applicants with Muslim names similar to those on the list. Some people contend that the new security procedures violate visitors' privacy. Others see them as a legitimate way of protecting the nation from terrorists.

The Immigration Debate Heats Up The U.S. government must also secure the nation's borders against foreigners who try to enter the country illegally. Some could be terrorists. Concern about how to deal with illegal, or undocumented, immigrants has led to a heated debate in the United States.

Most of the 10 million or more undocumented immigrants now in the United States are Mexicans. They came mainly to find work. Some entered the country legally but stayed beyond the terms of their visas. Others came into the country illegally. Many U.S. employers rely heavily on these workers and may overlook or not be aware of their employees' illegal status.

After 9/11, the federal government took steps to slow illegal immigration. By 2011, it had doubled the number of border patrol agents and had built some 650 miles of fencing along the U.S.-Mexico border. The Obama administration also cracked down on undocumented immigrants living in the United States. From 2009 to 2011, nearly 400,000 were deported each year.

In addition, some states took it upon themselves to find and arrest undocumented immigrants. In 2011, Arizona and Alabama both enacted laws that were stricter than federal law. Critics complained that enforcing these laws might call for police to use racial profiling to identify immigrants.

Many Americans think it is improper and unsafe to allow anyone to be in the country illegally. Yet, as the government has sharpened its focus on border security, critics have pointed out that the reasons for illegal immigration—the need for work and for workers—persist. The question of whether the flow of undocumented migrants can or should be stopped remains a heated one.

Passports are issued by a country's government as a form of identification for legal citizens of that country. They have always been important documents for international travelers, but they have become essential in the post-9/11 world.

59.5 Securing Liberty

The events of 9/11 left many Americans anxious about the future. A week after the attacks, President Bush addressed their worries in a speech to the nation:

> After all that has just passed . . . it is natural to wonder if America's future is one of fear. . . . But this country will define our times, not be defined by them. As long as the United States of America is determined and strong, this will not be an age of terror; this will be an age of liberty, here and across the world.

Balancing Safety and Freedom: The Department of Homeland Security

Bush's words highlighted an immediate reaction that many Americans had to 9/11. Was it safe to travel anywhere? Should people limit public events and activities until the situation came under control? That is, would Americans have to give up their freedoms of movement and expression, among many others, to feel safe?

A key role of government is to keep the nation secure. The 9/11 terrorist attacks represented a breach of national security, caused in part by poor communication. Before 9/11, key federal agencies often failed to share intelligence that they had gathered. After the attacks, Congress took action to fix this problem. It created the cabinet-level **Department of Homeland Security (DHS)**, which centralized and coordinated the functions of 22 existing agencies. The mission of DHS is to "prevent and deter terrorist attacks and protect against and respond to threats and hazards to the nation."

The Department of Homeland Security launched the "If You See Something Say Something" campaign in 2010. The campaign relied on citizens to help prevent terrorism. Posters like the one shown here called on Americans to report suspicious activities to local law enforcement.

Improving National Security

In 2002, Bush also set up a commission to investigate the circumstances surrounding the 9/11 attacks and suggest lessons to be learned. The commission published its findings in 2004 and made 37 recommendations to improve national security. Since then, DHS has made many changes in how the government protects its people and secures their liberty.

DHS has expanded and improved how information is shared. Threat-related intelligence is gathered and analyzed in DHS centers and distributed to law enforcement and other partners at the state and local level. Citizens, too, are kept informed. In 2011, DHS launched a new alert system, which includes two **threat levels.** One warns Americans that a credible terrorist threat exists. The other warns that a specific terrorist action is about to take place.

In addition, DHS has increased the security of all modes of transportation. It works with shippers to keep the global supply chain safe. It also helps maintain global standards of air travel safety. This includes screening passengers at airline terminals and using new technologies to check all baggage and cargo for explosives. DHS tries to do all this without undercutting privacy and civil liberties protections. In this way, it seeks to strengthen national security while preserving individual freedoms.

59.6 Protecting Rights

After 9/11, the Bush administration asked Congress for new powers to fight terrorism. Just 45 days after the attacks, Congress passed the **USA Patriot Act**. This act loosened many restrictions on intelligence gathering by U.S. security and law enforcement agencies. As details became public, Americans began debating the act's impact on their constitutional rights.

Balancing Security and Privacy Rights: The Patriot Act The most controversial sections of the Patriot Act involve privacy rights protected by the Fourth Amendment. This amendment bans unreasonable searches and seizures by government officials. It defines as reasonable only those searches and seizures that are authorized by a search warrant from a judge. To gain a warrant, agents must show probable cause. That is, they must show that there is reason to believe a crime has already been committed.

The Fourth Amendment applies to "persons, houses, papers, and effects." That includes modern communications devices. For example, federal agents cannot place wiretaps on telephones without a search warrant. However, the Patriot Act allows judges to approve a single warrant for tapping all phones a suspect uses. That means a wiretap can "rove" from phone to phone to follow a suspect's communications.

Some Americans opposed these roving wiretaps, arguing that their use could easily violate the privacy rights of people who talk unknowingly to a suspected terrorist. But law enforcement officials contend that agents need roving wiretaps to track down terrorists who move from phone to phone.

The Patriot Act also allows agents with a warrant to search a suspect's home or business in secret. Agents may break in, take photographs, examine computers, and remove evidence without alerting the suspect. Officials argue that this freedom allows them to carry out a lawful search without giving suspects a chance to flee or destroy evidence. Critics view the use of these "sneak and peek" warrants as a clear violation of privacy rights. The Patriot Act was reauthorized by Congress in 2005 and in 2009.

National Security Letters Long before 9/11, Congress created a way for the government to gain access to communications and financial records. It gave the FBI the authority to demand customer information from a bank or phone company via a **national security letter (NSL)**. But the FBI could issue such an order only when investigating a foreign power or its agents, or spies.

The Patriot Act broadened the scope of the NSL. It gave a number of intelligence agencies the right to use NSLs. They could secretly acquire personal records not just from banks and phone companies but also from credit agencies, hotels, Internet providers, and other sources. And they did not need to get a search warrant to do so. Since 9/11, hundreds of thousands of NSLs have been issued and billions of records accessed—many of them generated by law-abiding U.S. citizens.

Critics claimed that national security letters invade people's privacy and are too prone to abuse by the government. There is not enough congressional oversight or judicial review of NSLs, they said. Supporters of the law argued that the use of NSLs is critical to preventing additional terrorist attacks.

The Patriot Act gives the FBI and other federal security agencies broad powers to prevent terrorism, such as roving wiretaps on phones. Critics claimed that some of those powers violate privacy rights spelled out in the Fourth Amendment. Despite these concerns, President Bush renewed the Patriot Act in 2006.

In 2009, President Obama vowed to close the detention facility in Guantánamo Bay. However, his attempts were ineffective, and the United States resumed military trials there in 2011. By 2012, the facility still held over 150 prisoners.

59.7 Defending Democracy

The war on terror, conducted by President George W. Bush and later by President Barack Obama, was in part a war in defense of democracy. Yet it also tested the ideals upon which that democracy was founded. One such test involved the U.S. treatment of prisoners captured in the fighting in Afghanistan.

Debating the Limits of Presidential Power: Military Commissions Most of the prisoners taken during the 2001 invasion of Afghanistan stayed in that country. But Bush ordered that 660 of them, from 42 nations, be detained at the U.S. military base in Guantánamo Bay, Cuba. Held as suspected terrorists, these detainees were described as **unlawful enemy combatants,** or enemy fighters who were not part of a regular army.

The detainees, most of who had been turned over to the U.S. military by its Afghan or Pakistani allies, had little hope of being released. They were not accused of any crime and were not given the chance to present their case before a judge or jury. The detainees were also interrogated regularly. The government's goal was to obtain timely information about terrorists and terror plots. So-called "enhanced interrogation techniques"- were designed to force prisoners to reveal what they knew. One, waterboarding, involved pouring water over the prisoner's nose and mouth to simulate drowning.

Bush's critics argued that detainees should be treated as prisoners of war (POWs) under the terms of the Geneva Conventions. A series of international agreements made between 1864 and 1949, the Geneva Conventions set rules for proper conduct toward civilians, sick and wounded soldiers, and prisoners of war in times of armed conflict. Under the Geneva Conventions, POWs have certain rights. They may not be tortured or subjected to humiliating treatment. They may petition for a writ of habeas corpus—an order compelling a prison official to take a prisoner in front of a court to assess whether the person is imprisoned lawfully. Bush claimed that these rights did not apply to unlawful enemy combatants.

In 2004, the Supreme Court ruled that the detainees did have the right to challenge their imprisonment in court. Bush responded by establishing **military commissions** to try detainees. These are courts set up by the armed forces to try enemy soldiers during wartime. Two years later, the Supreme Court ruled that Bush did not have the constitutional authority to set up military courts. Only Congress had that power.

In September 2006, at Bush's request, Congress passed the **Military Commissions Act of 2006**. This act authorized the use of military commissions to try enemy combatants, and it set out rules for such trials. However, this act failed to grant detainees basic legal rights, including habeas corpus. In 2009, President Obama halted the military commission trials and ordered a review of the whole process. Out of that came an amended law, the Military Commissions Act of 2009. It increased the rights of the accused to bring them more into line with regular military courts and federal criminal courts.

Earlier that year, in one of his first acts as president, Obama had ordered the closure of the detention facility at Guantánamo Bay. But Congress blocked his attempts to have detainees tried in U.S. civilian courts or transferred to U.S. prisons. The Guantánamo camp stayed open, and in 2011, Obama resumed military commission trials there.

Critics continued to decry the U.S. detention policy. Elizabeth Goitein, an expert on national security policies, summed up their feelings. "Requiring the continued detention of individuals based solely on the fact that they were at one time suspected of terrorism is profoundly wrong," she wrote. "It is not the behavior of a nation that abides by principles of justice and the rule of law." Clearly the debate over the treatment of suspected terrorists was far from over.

Pursuing America's Founding Ideals Writing in 1776, Thomas Jefferson could not have even dimly imagined the complex world in which we live today. Nonetheless, the ideals he set forth for our nation have endured, as points of pride and prods to progress. In the troubled times since 9/11, they have also led us to consider new ways—at times successful, at others not—to uphold them.

Building a nation based on ideals has never been easy. Being human, we are bound to disagree about what our founding ideals mean. We are even more likely to disagree about how they should be applied to the complex business of governing a nation of hundreds of millions of people. Nevertheless, it is our commitment to these ideals that binds us together as Americans. Like our founders, we know that a nation built on ideals is never finished—it is always becoming. Just what it is to become, however, is up to each generation to decide.

To honor the tenth anniversary of 9/11, President Barack Obama, First Lady Michelle Obama, former President George W. Bush, and former First Lady Laura Bush (not shown) visited the World Trade Center site in New York City. There, two memorial pools placed in the imprints of the World Trade Center towers commemorate those who lost their lives during the attack.

Summary

The attacks of 9/11 left Americans with a new sense of vulnerability and prompted a war to eliminate the threat of terrorism. The war on terror—at home and abroad—posed the challenge of balancing our founding ideals with our desire for security.

Equality After 9/11, Americans debated these questions: Should all airline passengers be treated equally? Or should those fitting the profile of the 9/11 terrorists face special scrutiny? The nation chose equality over racial profiling, but racial profiling persists. The Occupy Wall Street protests pointed out another equality issue—the income gap between rich and poor.

Opportunity Congress struggled to preserve the United States as a land of opportunity while tightening visa requirements and border control to keep terrorists out of the country.

Liberty Congress created the Department of Homeland Security to improve the ability of U.S. security agencies to keep the country safe from terrorists. DHS worked to improve communication among its agencies and the public and otherwise secure Americans' liberty.

Rights Congress enacted the Patriot Act after 9/11 to help government agencies track down terrorists. The act sparked a long debate over what some saw as assaults on privacy rights.

Democracy U.S. policies toward unlawful enemy combatants raised questions about how to treat suspected terrorists in a democracy. Could they be detained indefinitely? Should they be tried by military commissions or by civilian courts? Is "enhanced interrogation" appropriate?

Resources

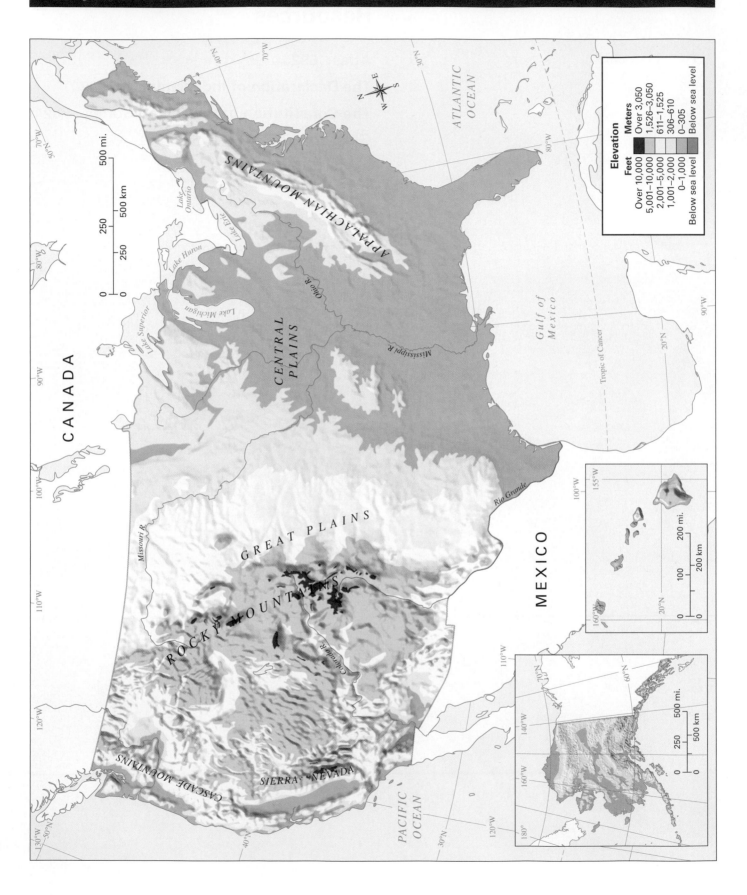

Elevation

Feet	Meters
Over 10,000	Over 3,050
5,001–10,000	1,526–3,050
2,001–5,000	611–1,525
1,001–2,000	306–610
0–1,000	0–305
Below sea level	Below sea level

ATLANTIC OCEAN

Gulf of Mexico

Tropic of Cancer

CANADA

MEXICO

PACIFIC OCEAN

APPALACHIAN MOUNTAINS

CENTRAL PLAINS

GREAT PLAINS

ROCKY MOUNTAINS

CASCADE MOUNTAINS

SIERRA NEVADA

Lake Ontario

Lake Erie

Lake Huron

Lake Michigan

Lake Superior

Ohio R.

Mississippi R.

Missouri R.

Colorado R.

Rio Grande

500 mi.

500 km

250

250

0

0

200 mi.

200 km

100

0

500 mi.

500 km

250

0

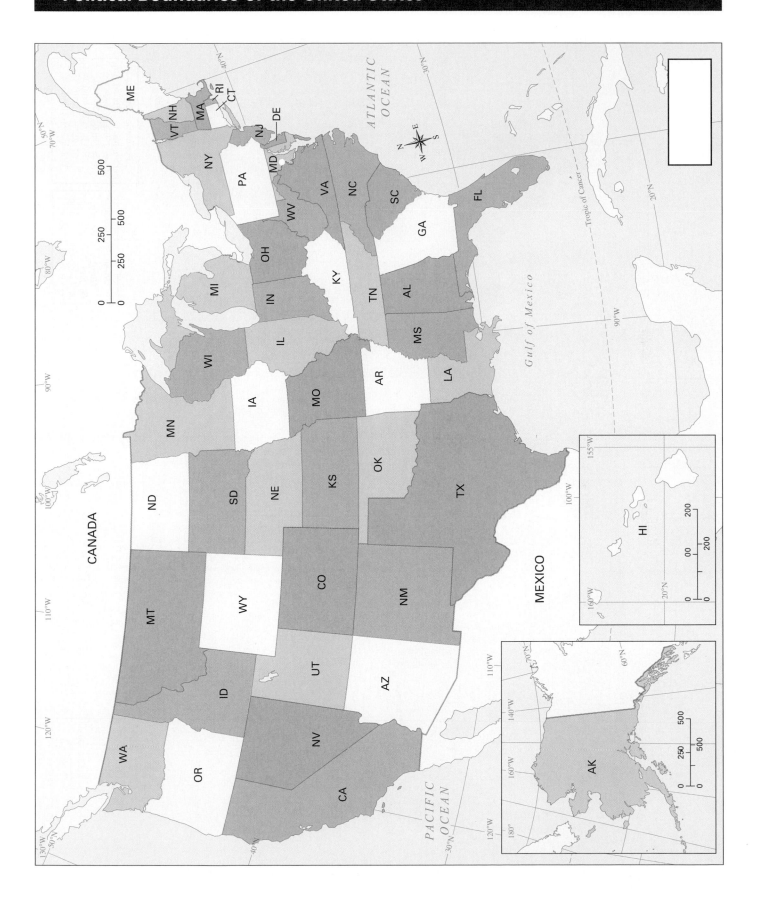

CANADA

MEXICO

ATLANTIC OCEAN

Gulf of Mexico

PACIFIC OCEAN

Tropic of Cancer

ME
NH
VT
MA
RI
CT
NY
NJ
DE
PA
MD
WV
VA
NC
SC
GA
FL
OH
KY
TN
AL
MS
IN
IL
MI
WI
AR
LA
MO
IA
MN
OK
KS
TX
ND
SD
NE
CO
NM
WY
MT
UT
AZ
ID
NV
CA
WA
OR

HI

AK

Population Density of the United States

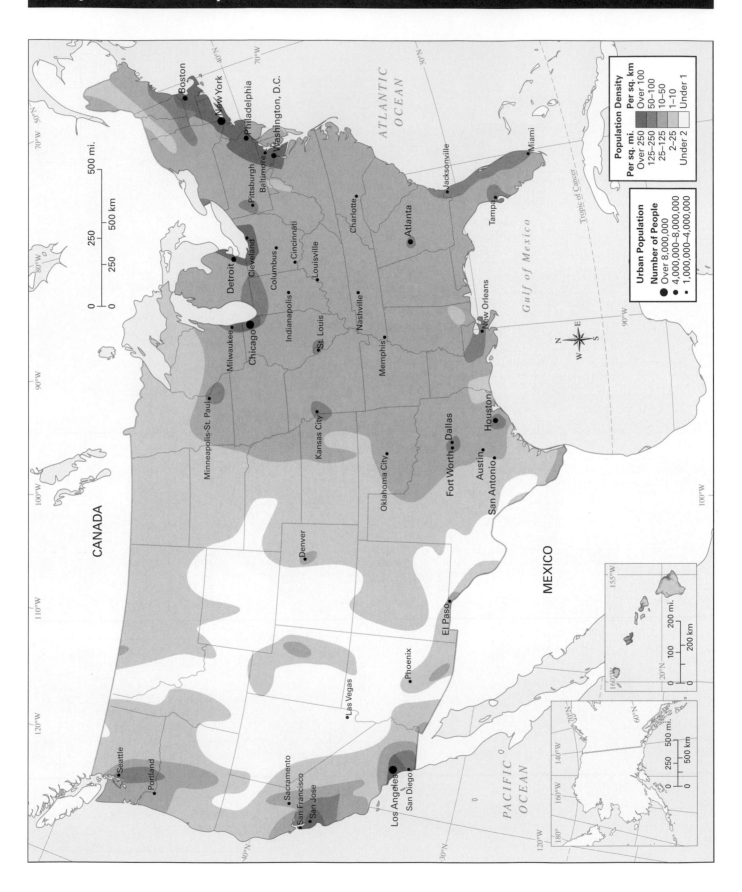

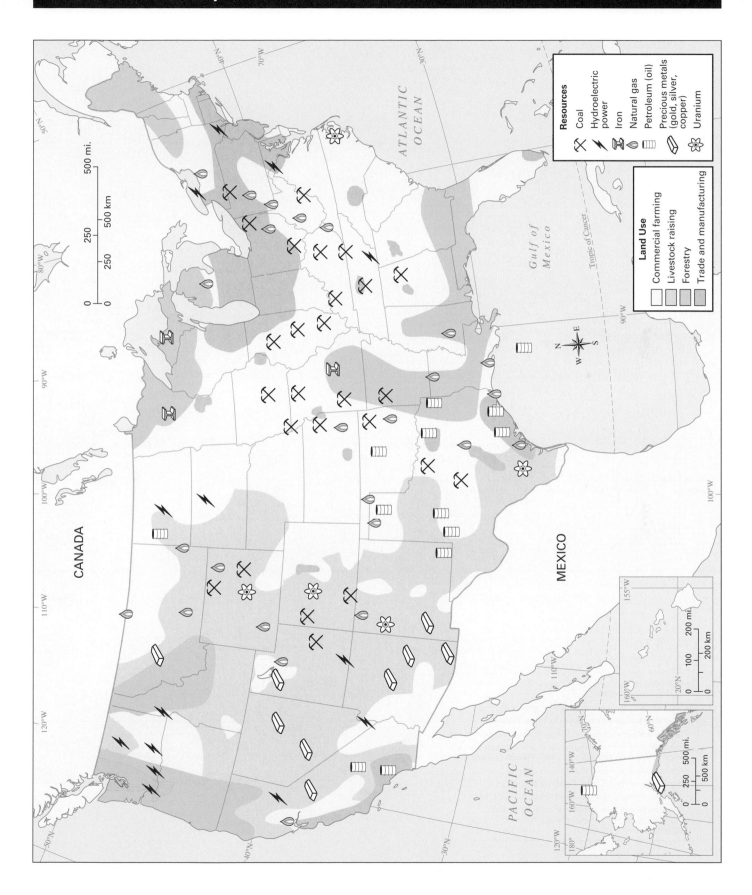

Resources

Coal
Hydroelectric power
Iron
Natural gas
Petroleum (oil)
Precious metals (gold, silver, copper)
Uranium

Land Use

Commercial farming
Livestock raising
Forestry
Trade and manufacturing

ATLANTIC OCEAN

Gulf of Mexico

Tropic of Cancer

CANADA

MEXICO

PACIFIC OCEAN

500 mi.
500 km
250
250

Political Boundaries of the World

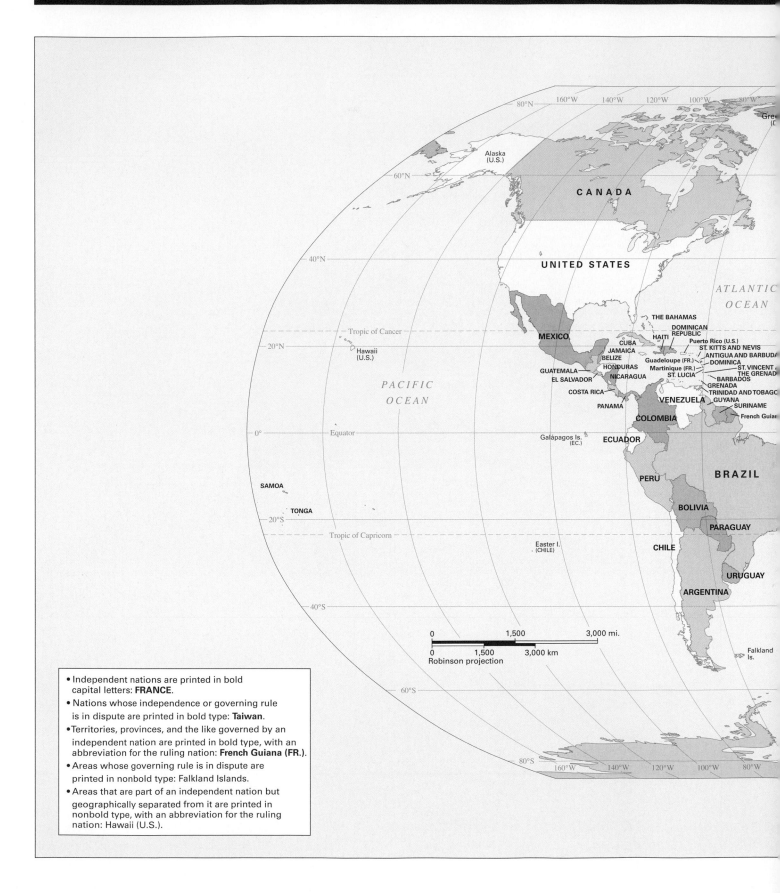

80°N
160°W 140°W 120°W 100°W 80°W

Gre
(C

Alaska
(U.S.)

60°N

C A N A D A

40°N

UNITED STATES

ATLANTIC
OCEAN

Tropic of Cancer

20°N

Hawaii
(U.S.)

THE BAHAMAS

DOMINICAN
REPUBLIC

MEXICO

CUBA

HAITI

Puerto Rico (U.S.)

JAMAICA

ST. KITTS AND NEVIS

BELIZE

ANTIGUA AND BARBUD

Guadeloupe (FR.)

DOMINICA

ST. VINCENT

PACIFIC
OCEAN

GUATEMALA

HONDURAS

Martinique (FR.)

THE GRENAD

EL SALVADOR

NICARAGUA

ST. LUCIA

BARBADOS

GRENADA

COSTA RICA

TRINIDAD AND TOBAG

PANAMA

VENEZUELA

GUYANA

SURINAME

COLOMBIA

French Guiar

0°
Equator

Galápagos Is.
(EC.)

ECUADOR

SAMOA

PERU

B R A Z I L

BOLIVIA

TONGA

20°S

PARAGUAY

Tropic of Capricorn

Easter I.
(CHILE)

CHILE

URUGUAY

ARGENTINA

40°S

0   1,500   3,000 mi.

0   1,500   3,000 km
Robinson projection

Falkland
Is.

60°S

80°S
160°W 140°W 120°W 100°W 80°W

- Independent nations are printed in bold
  capital letters: **FRANCE**.
- Nations whose independence or governing rule
  is in dispute are printed in bold type: **Taiwan**.
- Territories, provinces, and the like governed by an
  independent nation are printed in bold type, with an
  abbreviation for the ruling nation: **French Guiana (FR.)**.
- Areas whose governing rule is in dispute are
  printed in nonbold type: Falkland Islands.
- Areas that are part of an independent nation but
  geographically separated from it are printed in
  nonbold type, with an abbreviation for the ruling
  nation: Hawaii (U.S.).

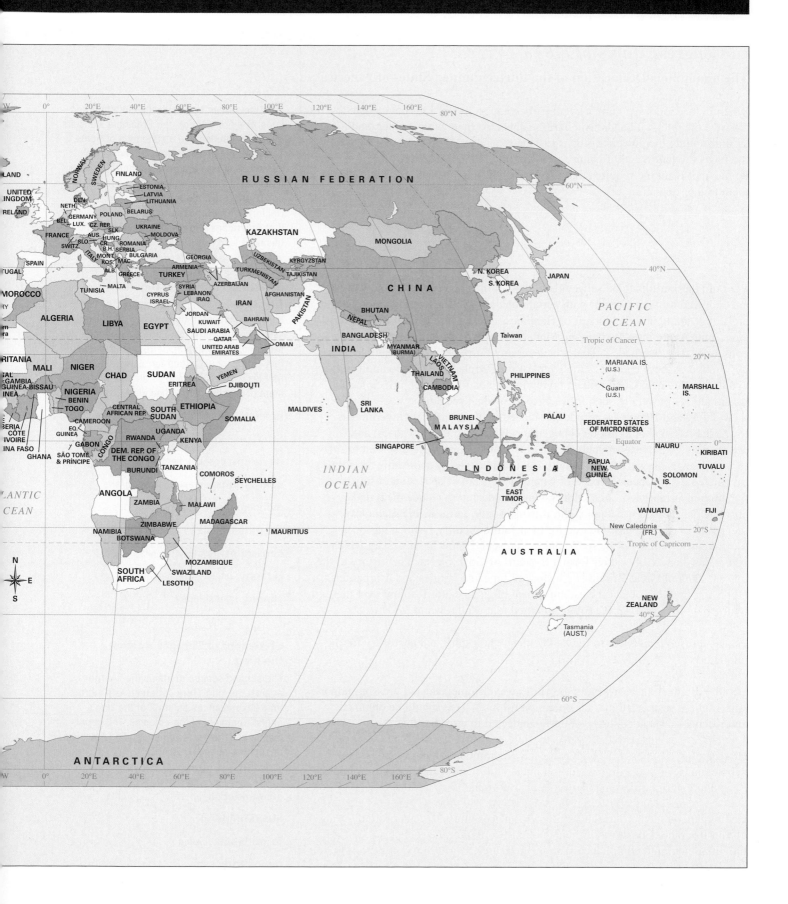

W 0° 20°E 40°E 60°E 80°E 100°E 120°E 140°E 160°E 80°N

LAND
UNITED
KINGDOM
IRELAND

NORWAY
SWEDEN
FINLAND
ESTONIA
LATVIA
LITHUANIA

RUSSIAN FEDERATION

60°N

DEN.
NETH.
BEL. GERMANY POLAND
LUX. CZ. REP. BELARUS
FRANCE SLK.
HUNG.
SWITZ. SLO. CR.
ITALY MONT. B.H. SERBIA
KOS. MAC.
ALB.
GREECE
MALTA
ARMENIA
AZERBAIJAN

UKRAINE
MOLDOVA
ROMANIA
BULGARIA
GEORGIA

KAZAKHSTAN

MONGOLIA

N. KOREA
S. KOREA
JAPAN

40°N

SPAIN
TUGAL
GAL
MOROCCO
ra

TUNISIA

TURKEY
CYPRUS
ISRAEL
SYRIA
LEBANON
JORDAN
IRAQ

UZBEKISTAN
TURKMENISTAN
KYRGYZSTAN
TAJIKISTAN

AFGHANISTAN

IRAN
KUWAIT
BAHRAIN

PAKISTAN

CHINA

TAIWAN

PACIFIC
OCEAN

Tropic of Cancer

ALGERIA
LIBYA
EGYPT

SAUDI ARABIA
QATAR
UNITED ARAB
EMIRATES
OMAN

INDIA

BHUTAN
NEPAL
BANGLADESH

MYANMAR
(BURMA)
LAOS
VIETNAM

20°N

RITANIA
GAL
GAMBIA
GUINEA-BISSAU
NEA

MALI
NIGER
CHAD
SUDAN

ERITREA

YEMEN
DJIBOUTI

THAILAND
CAMBODIA

MARIANA IS.
(U.S.)
Guam
(U.S.)

MARSHALL
IS.

NIGERIA
BENIN
TOGO
CENTRAL
AFRICAN REP.
SOUTH
SUDAN
ETHIOPIA

SOMALIA

MALDIVES

SRI
LANKA

PHILIPPINES

BERIA
CÔTE
IVOIRE
INA FASO
GHANA
CAMEROON
EQ.
GUINEA
GABON
CONGO
SÃO TOMÉ
& PRÍNCIPE
RWANDA
UGANDA
KENYA
DEM. REP. OF
THE CONGO
BURUNDI
TANZANIA

BRUNEI
MALAYSIA

SINGAPORE

PALAU

FEDERATED STATES
OF MICRONESIA

Equator

NAURU

KIRIBATI

INDONESIA

PAPUA
NEW
GUINEA

TUVALU
SOLOMON
IS.

0°

COMOROS
SEYCHELLES

INDIAN
OCEAN

EAST
TIMOR

VANUATU

FIJI

ANGOLA
ZAMBIA
MALAWI

ANTIC
CEAN

NAMIBIA
BOTSWANA
ZIMBABWE

MADAGASCAR
MAURITIUS

New Caledonia
(FR.)

20°S

Tropic of Capricorn

SOUTH
AFRICA
MOZAMBIQUE
SWAZILAND
LESOTHO

AUSTRALIA

N
W E
S

NEW
ZEALAND

40°S

Tasmania
(AUST.)

60°S

ANTARCTICA

W 0° 20°E 40°E 60°E 80°E 100°E 120°E 140°E 160°E 80°S

In Congress, July 4, 1776

The unanimous Declaration of the thirteen united States of America

When in the Course of human events it becomes necessary for one people to dissolve the political bands which have connected them with another, and to assume among the powers of the earth, the separate and equal station to which the Laws of Nature and of Nature's God entitle them, a decent respect to the opinions of mankind requires that they should declare the causes which impel them to the separation.

We hold these truths to be self-evident, that all men are created equal, that they are endowed by their Creator with certain unalienable Rights, that among these are Life, Liberty and the pursuit of Happiness. —That to secure these rights, Governments are instituted among Men, deriving their just powers from the consent of the governed, —That whenever any Form of Government becomes destructive of these ends, it is the Right of the People to alter or to abolish it, and to institute new Government, laying its foundation on such principles and organizing its powers in such form, as to them shall seem most likely to effect their Safety and Happiness. Prudence, indeed, will dictate that Governments long established should not be changed for light and transient causes; and accordingly all experience hath shewn, that mankind are more disposed to suffer, while evils are sufferable, than to right themselves by abolishing the forms to which they are accustomed. But when a long train of abuses and usurpations, pursuing invariably the same Object evinces a design to reduce them under absolute Despotism, it is their right, it is their duty, to throw off such Government, and to provide new Guards for their future security. —Such has been the patient sufferance of these Colonies; and such is now the necessity which constrains them to alter their former Systems of Government. The history of the present King of Great Britain is a history of repeated injuries and usurpations, all having in direct object the establishment of an absolute Tyranny over these States. To prove this, let Facts be submitted to a candid world.

He has refused his Assent to Laws, the most wholesome and necessary for the public good.

He has forbidden his Governors to pass Laws of immediate and pressing importance, unless suspended in their operation till his Assent should be obtained; and when so suspended, he has utterly neglected to attend to them.

He has refused to pass other Laws for the accommodation of large districts of people, unless those people would relinquish the right of Representation in the Legislature, a right inestimable to them and formidable to tyrants only.

He has called together legislative bodies at places unusual, uncomfortable, and distant from the depository of their Public Records, for the sole purpose of fatiguing them into compliance with his measures.

The Declaration can be divided into four sections. The first section, the Preamble, consists of an introduction and a statement of rights. The introduction explains the document's purpose and sets a principled tone. The idea that people had the right to rebel against an oppressive government was not new. The Declaration's purpose was to show the world that Americans were justified in exercising this right.

Statement of Human Rights

The statement of rights is constructed like a logical argument. It begins with what it calls "self-evident truths" and proceeds logically to the need for revolution. Jefferson expressed this argument with such force and eloquence that his words still stand as an enduring statement of America's founding ideals.

unalienable: undeniable

prudence: common sense

transient: passing, fleeting

usurpations: unlawful power grabs

evinces: shows evidence of

despotism: rule by a dictator

constrains: forces, compels

tyranny: unjust government

candid: honest, open

Statement of Charges Against the King

The second section contains the charges against the king. Here Jefferson lists more than 20 grievances as proof of the king's unjust treatment of the colonies. This proof was needed to persuade undecided colonists to support independence.

assent: approval

suspended: temporarily stopped

inestimable: invaluable

formidable: alarming

depository: storage site

He has dissolved Representative Houses repeatedly, for opposing with manly firmness his invasions on the rights of the people.

He has refused for a long time, after such dissolutions, to cause others to be elected, whereby the Legislative Powers, incapable of Annihilation, have returned to the People at large for their exercise; the State remaining in the mean time exposed to all the dangers of invasion from without, and convulsions within.

He has endeavoured to prevent the population of these States; for that purpose obstructing the Laws for Naturalization of Foreigners; refusing to pass others to encourage their migrations hither, and raising the conditions of new Appropriations of Lands.

He has obstructed the Administration of Justice, by refusing his Assent to Laws for establishing Judiciary Powers.

He has made Judges dependent on his Will alone, for the tenure of their offices, and the amount and payment of their salaries.

He has erected a multitude of New Offices, and sent hither swarms of Officers to harass our people and eat out their substance.

He has kept among us, in times of peace, Standing Armies without the Consent of our legislatures.

He has affected to render the Military independent of and superior to the Civil Power.

He has combined with others to subject us to a jurisdiction foreign to our constitution, and unacknowledged by our laws; giving his Assent to their Acts of pretended Legislation:

For Quartering large bodies of armed troops among us:

For protecting them, by a mock Trial, from punishment for any Murders which they should commit on the Inhabitants of these States:

For cutting off our Trade with all parts of the world:

For imposing Taxes on us without our Consent:

For depriving us in many cases, of the benefit of Trial by Jury:

For transporting us beyond Seas to be tried for pretended offences:

For abolishing the free System of English Laws in a neighbouring Province, establishing therein an Arbitrary government, and enlarging its Boundaries so as to render it at once an example and fit instrument for introducing the same absolute rule into these Colonies:

For taking away our Charters, abolishing our most valuable Laws, and altering fundamentally the Forms of our Governments:

For suspending our own Legislatures, and declaring themselves invested with power to legislate for us in all cases whatsoever.

---

dissolved: disbanded, broken up

annihilation: destruction

convulsions: disturbances

endeavoured: tried
naturalization: becoming a citizen
appropriations: distributions
obstructed: blocked
judiciary powers: courts of law
tenure: right to hold
offices: government jobs

combined with others: worked with Parliament
jurisdiction: authority
quartering: housing
mock: fake

neighbouring province: Canada
arbitrary: with unlimited power

He has abdicated Government here, by declaring us out of his Protection and waging War against us.

He has plundered our seas, ravaged our Coasts, burnt our towns, and destroyed the lives of our people.

He is at this time transporting large Armies of foreign Mercenaries to compleat the works of death, desolation and tyranny, already begun with circumstances of Cruelty & perfidy scarcely paralleled in the most barbarous ages, and totally unworthy the Head of a civilized nation.

He has constrained our fellow Citizens taken Captive on the high Seas to bear Arms against their Country, to become the executioners of their friends and Brethren, or to fall themselves by their Hands.

He has excited domestic insurrections amongst us, and has endeavoured to bring on the inhabitants of our frontiers, the merciless Indian Savages, whose known rule of warfare, is an undistinguished destruction of all ages, sexes and conditions.

In every stage of these Oppressions We have Petitioned for Redress in the most humble terms: Our repeated Petitions have been answered only by repeated injury. A Prince whose character is thus marked by every act which may define a Tyrant, is unfit to be the ruler of a free people.

Nor have We been wanting in attentions to our British brethren. We have warned them from time to time of attempts by their legislature to extend an unwarrantable jurisdiction over us. We have reminded them of the circumstances of our emigration and settlement here. We have appealed to their native justice and magnanimity, and we have conjured them by the ties of our common kindred, to disavow these usurpations, which, would inevitably interrupt our connections and correspondence. They too have been deaf to the voice of justice and of consanguinity. We must, therefore, acquiesce in the necessity, which denounces our Separation, and hold them, as we hold the rest of mankind, Enemies in War, in Peace Friends.

We, therefore, the Representatives of the united States of America, in General Congress, Assembled, appealing to the Supreme Judge of the world for the rectitude of our intentions, do, in the Name, and by Authority of the good People of these Colonies, solemnly publish and declare, That these United Colonies are, and of Right ought to be Free and Independent States; that they are Absolved from all Allegiance to the British Crown, and that all political connection between them and the State of Great Britain, is and ought to be totally dissolved; and that as Free and Independent States, they have full Power to levy War, conclude Peace, contract Alliances, establish Commerce, and to do all other Acts and Things which Independent States may of right do. —And for the support of this Declaration, with a firm reliance on the protection of divine Providence, we mutually pledge to each other our Lives, our Fortunes and our sacred Honor.

The foregoing Declaration was, by order of Congress, engrossed on parchment, and signed by the 56 members.

abdicated: abandoned

mercenaries: hired soldiers

perfidy: deceit, treachery

The Government's Failure to Answer the Colonists' Complaints
The third section is a denunciation of the British people for their indifference to the colonists' plight. American leaders had petitioned the king and Parliament, but their efforts to advance their cause had met with little sympathy among their "British brethren."

insurrections: rebellions

petitioned: asked in writing

redress: the righting of wrongs

unwarrantable: unjustified

magnanimity: generosity

conjured: pleaded with

kindred: family relationships

disavow: publicly condemn

consanguinity: blood ties

acquiesce: agree

denounces: formally announces

Statement of Independence
In the fourth section, the conclusion, Congress formally declares independence on behalf of the people of the colonies. The signers' final pledge of their "sacred Honor" was a most solemn vow at a time when honor was highly prized.

rectitude: righteousness

absolved: released

engrossed: copied in large, clear handwriting

New Hampshire

Josiah Bartlett, William Whipple, Matthew Thornton

Massachusetts

John Hancock, Samuel Adams, John Adams, Robert Treat Paine, Elbridge Gerry

Rhode Island

Stephen Hopkins, William Ellery

Connecticut

Roger Sherman, Samuel Huntington, William Williams, Oliver Wolcott

New York

William Floyd, Philip Livingston, Francis Lewis, Lewis Morris

New Jersey

Richard Stockton, John Witherspoon, Francis Hopkinson, John Hart, Abraham Clark

Pennsylvania

Robert Morris, Benjamin Rush, Benjamin Franklin, John Morton, George Clymer, James Smith, George Taylor, James Wilson, George Ross

Delaware

Caesar Rodney, George Read, Thomas McKean

Maryland

Samuel Chase, William Paca, Thomas Stone, Charles Carroll of Carrollton

Virginia

George Wythe, Richard Henry Lee, Thomas Jefferson, Benjamin Harrison, Thomas Nelson Jr., Francis Lightfoot Lee, Carter Braxton

North Carolina

William Hooper, Joseph Hewes, John Penn

South Carolina

Edward Rutledge, Thomas Heyward Jr., Thomas Lynch Jr., Arthur Middleton

Georgia

Button Gwinnett, Lyman Hall, George Walton

Delegates to the Constitutional Convention, 1787

John Hancock, a revolutionary leader from Massachusetts, was the first person to sign the engrossed Declaration of Independence. His bold signature is so widely known that when people today sign a document, they are said to be adding their "John Hancock."

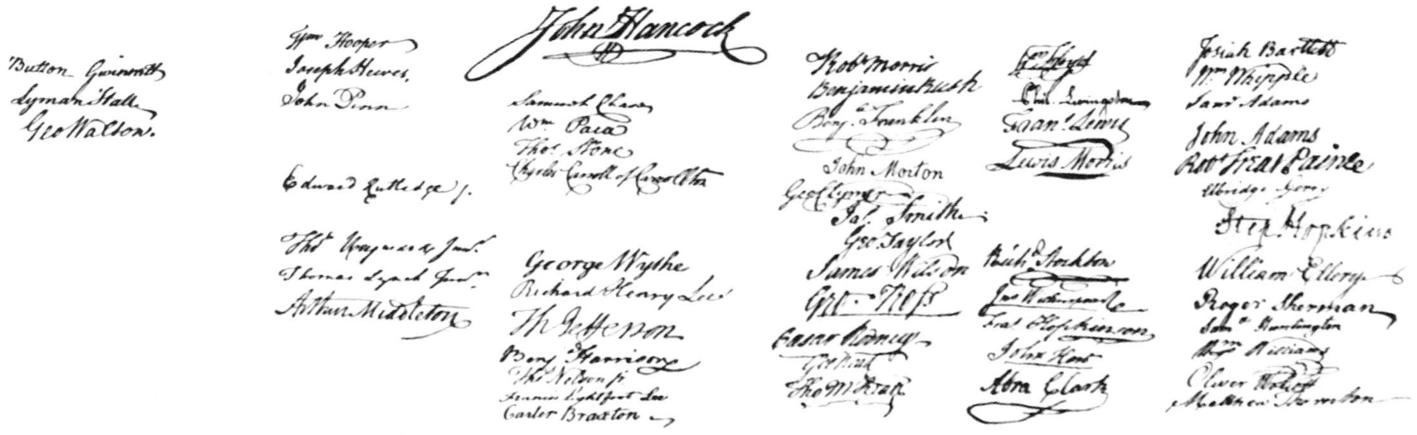

This version of the Constitution retains the original text, spellings, and capitalizations. Parts of the Constitution that have been changed through amendment have been crossed out.

We the People of the United States, in Order to form a more perfect Union, establish Justice, insure domestic Tranquility, provide for the common defence, promote the general Welfare, and secure the Blessings of Liberty to ourselves and our Posterity, do ordain and establish this Constitution for the United States of America.

Article I.

Section 1.

All legislative Powers herein granted shall be vested in a Congress of the United States, which shall consist of a Senate and House of Representatives.

Section 2.

The House of Representatives shall be composed of Members chosen every second Year by the People of the several States, and the Electors in each State shall have the Qualifications requisite for Electors of the most numerous Branch of the State Legislature.

No Person shall be a Representative who shall not have attained to the Age of twenty five Years, and been seven Years a Citizen of the United States, and who shall not, when elected, be an Inhabitant of that State in which he shall be chosen.

Representatives ~~and direct Taxes~~ shall be apportioned among the several States which may be included within this Union, according to their respective Numbers, ~~which shall be determined by adding to the whole Number of free Persons, including those bound to Service for a Term of Years, and excluding Indians not taxed, three fifths of all other Persons~~. The actual Enumeration shall be made within three Years after the first Meeting of the Congress of the United States, and within every subsequent Term of ten Years, in such Manner as they shall by Law direct. The Number of Representatives shall not exceed one for every thirty Thousand, but each State shall have at Least one Representative; and until such enumeration shall be made, the State of New Hampshire shall be entitled to chuse [choose] three, Massachusetts eight, Rhode Island and Providence Plantations one, Connecticut five, New York six, New Jersey four, Pennsylvania eight, Delaware one, Maryland six, Virginia ten, North Carolina five, South Carolina five, and Georgia three.

When vacancies happen in the Representation from any State, the Executive Authority thereof shall issue Writs of Election to fill such Vacancies.

These annotations will help you understand the Consitiution.

Preamble

The Preamble establishes that the federal government gains its power from the people, not the states. It also lists the purposes of the government: to maintain peace at home, to protect the nation from enemies, to promote the well-being of the people, and to secure the people's rights and freedoms.

Article I: Legislative Branch

Section 1: Two-Part Congress

The power to make laws is granted to Congress, which consists of the Senate and the House of Representatives.

Section 2: House of Representatives

Clause 1: Election Members of the House of Representatives are elected by the people every two years. *Electors* refers to voters.

Clause 2: Qualifications A member of the House must be at least 25 years old, must have been an American citizen for seven years, and must live in the state he or she represents.

Clause 3: Apportionment The number of Representatives from each state is based on the state's population. An *enumeration*, or census, must be taken every 10 years to determine that population. The total number of Representatives in the House is now fixed at 435. This clause contains the infamous Three-fifths Compromise, which specified that slaves ("all other Persons") were to be counted as three-fifths of a citizen when determining population. This provision was rendered meaningless by the Thirteenth Amendment (1865), which ended slavery.

Clause 4: Vacancies If a representative resigns or dies in office, the governor of that state can issue a "Writ of Election," calling for a special election to fill the vacancy.

The House of Representatives shall chuse [choose] their Speaker and other Officers; and shall have the sole Power of Impeachment.

Clause 5: Officers and Impeachment Power The House elects a speaker, who normally comes from the majority party. Only the House has the power to impeach, or accuse, a federal official of wrongdoing.

Section 3.

Section 3: Senate

The Senate of the United States shall be composed of two Senators from each State, ~~chosen by the Legislature thereof~~, for six Years; and each Senator shall have one Vote.

Clause 1: Election Each state is represented by two senators. Senators were elected by state legislatures until 1913, when the Seventeenth Amendment was ratified. It provides for the direct election of senators by the people. Senators serve six-year terms.

Immediately after they shall be assembled in Consequence of the first Election, they shall be divided as equally as may be into three Classes. The Seats of the Senators of the first Class shall be vacated at the Expiration of the second Year, of the second Class at the Expiration of the fourth Year, and of the third Class at the Expiration of the sixth Year, so that one-third may be chosen every second Year; ~~and if Vacancies happen by Resignation, or otherwise, during the Recess of the Legislature of any State, the Executive thereof may make temporary Appointments until the next Meeting of the Legislature, which shall then fill such Vacancies~~.

Clause 2: Terms and Classification To ensure continuity in the Senate, one-third of the senators run for reelection every two years. To establish this system, the first senators, elected in 1788, were divided into three groups. One group served for two years, the second group for four years, and the third group for a full six years.

No Person shall be a Senator who shall not have attained to the Age of thirty Years, and been nine Years a Citizen of the United States, and who shall not, when elected, be an Inhabitant of that State for which he shall be chosen.

Clause 3: Qualifications A senator must be at least 30 years old, must have been an American citizen for nine years, and must live in the state he or she represents.

The Vice President of the United States shall be President of the Senate, but shall have no Vote, unless they be equally divided.

Clause 4: President of the Senate The vice president presides over the Senate but votes only in event of a tie.

The Senate shall chuse [choose] their other Officers, and also a President pro tempore, in the Absence of the Vice President, or when he shall exercise the Office of President of the United States.

Clause 5: Other Officers The Senate selects its other leaders and may also select a temporary ("pro tempore") president to preside if the vice president is absent.

The Senate shall have the sole Power to try all Impeachments. When sitting for that Purpose, they shall be on Oath or Affirmation. When the President of the United States is tried, the Chief Justice shall preside: And no Person shall be convicted without the Concurrence of two thirds of the Members present.

Clause 6: Impeachment Trials Only the Senate has the power to put impeached federal officials on trial. When an impeached president is tried, the chief justice of the Supreme Court acts as the trial judge. A two-thirds vote of the senators present is required to convict. Congress has used its impeachment power sparingly. Only two presidents have ever been impeached by the House and tried in the Senate. In 1868, the Senate acquitted President Andrew Johnson of charges of violating federal laws. In 1999, President Bill Clinton was acquitted of perjury charges. Facing impeachment in 1974, President Richard Nixon resigned from office.

Judgment in Cases of Impeachment shall not extend further than to removal from Office, and disqualification to hold and enjoy any Office of honor, Trust or Profit under the United States: but the Party convicted shall nevertheless be liable and subject to Indictment, Trial, Judgment and Punishment, according to Law.

Clause 7: Penalty Upon Conviction A federal official convicted by the Senate is removed from office. The Senate may bar him or her from future office but may not impose further punishment.

Section 4.

The Times, Places and Manner of holding Elections for Senators and Representatives, shall be prescribed in each State by the Legislature thereof; but the Congress may at any time by Law make or alter such Regulations, except as to the Places of chusing [choosing] Senators.

The Congress shall assemble at least once in every Year, ~~and such Meeting shall be on the first Monday in December,~~ unless they shall by Law appoint a different Day.

Section 5.

Each House shall be the Judge of the Elections, Returns and Qualifications of its own Members, and a Majority of each shall constitute a Quorum to do Business, but a smaller Number may adjourn from day to day, and may be authorized to compel the Attendance of absent Members, in such Manner, and under such Penalties as each House may provide.

Each House may determine the Rules of its Proceedings, punish its Members for disorderly Behaviour, and, with the Concurrence of two thirds, expel a Member.

Each House shall keep a Journal of its Proceedings, and from time to time publish the same, excepting such Parts as may in their Judgment require Secrecy; and the Yeas and Nays of the Members of either House on any question shall, at the Desire of one fifth of those Present, be entered on the Journal.

Neither House, during the Session of Congress, shall, without the Consent of the other, adjourn for more than three days, nor to any other Place than that in which the two Houses shall be sitting.

Section 6.

The Senators and Representatives shall receive a Compensation for their Services, to be ascertained by Law, and paid out of the Treasury of the United States. They shall in all Cases, except Treason, Felony and Breach of the Peace, be privileged from Arrest during their Attendance at the Session of their respective Houses, and in going to and returning from the same; and for any Speech or Debate in either House, they shall not be questioned in any other Place.

No Senator or Representative shall, during the Time for which he was elected, be appointed to any civil Office under the Authority of the United States, which shall have been created, or the Emoluments whereof shall have been encreased during such time; and no Person holding any Office under the United States, shall be a Member of either House during his Continuance in Office.

Section 7.

All Bills for raising Revenue shall originate in the House of Representatives; but the Senate may propose or concur with Amendments as on other Bills.

Section 4: Elections and Meetings

Clause 1: Elections States regulate their own congressional elections, but Congress may make laws changing the regulations.

Clause 2: Sessions Congress must meet at least once a year. The Twentieth Amendment (1933) moved the opening day of Congress to January 3.

Section 5: Congressional Proceedings

Clause 1: Attendance Each house judges whether its members are qualified and have been elected fairly. A majority of members of either house must be present for that house to conduct legislative business. This minimum required number is called a *quorum*.

Clause 2: Rules Each house makes its own rules of conduct for its members.

Clause 3: Records Both houses keep a journal of their proceedings. It is published as the *Congressional Record*.

Clause 4: Adjournment During a session, neither house can close down or hold meetings elsewhere for a period of more than three days without the approval of the other house.

Section 6: Compensation, Immunity, and Restrictions

Clause 1: Salaries and Immunity Members of Congress set their own pay and are paid out of the U.S. Treasury. Legislators may not be sued or prosecuted for their speeches and actions on the floor of Congress. This privilege protects free expression and fosters open debate.

Clause 2: Employment Restrictions To ensure separation of powers, members of Congress may not hold any other federal office during their terms as legislators.

Section 7: Making Laws

Clause 1: Revenue Bills Only the House can propose a law raising taxes, though the Senate can offer changes. This provision ensures that people are not taxed without their consent.

Every Bill which shall have passed the House of Representatives and the Senate, shall, before it become a Law, be presented to the President of the United States; If he approve he shall sign it, but if not he shall return it, with his Objections to that House in which it shall have originated, who shall enter the Objections at large on their Journal, and proceed to reconsider it. If after such Reconsideration two thirds of that House shall agree to pass the Bill, it shall be sent, together with the Objections, to the other House, by which it shall likewise be reconsidered, and if approved by two thirds of that House, it shall become a Law. But in all such Cases the Votes of both Houses shall be determined by Yeas and Nays, and the Names of the Persons voting for and against the Bill shall be entered on the Journal of each House respectively. If any Bill shall not be returned by the President within ten Days (Sundays excepted) after it shall have been presented to him, the Same shall be a Law, in like Manner as if he had signed it, unless the Congress by their Adjournment prevent its Return, in which Case it shall not be a Law.

Every Order, Resolution, or Vote to which the Concurrence of the Senate and House of Representatives may be necessary (except on a question of Adjournment) shall be presented to the President of the United States; and before the Same shall take Effect, shall be approved by him, or being disapproved by him, shall be repassed by two thirds of the Senate and House of Representatives, according to the Rules and Limitations prescribed in the Case of a Bill.

Section 8.

The Congress shall have Power

To lay and collect Taxes, Duties, Imposts and Excises, to pay the Debts and provide for the common Defence and general Welfare of the United States; but all Duties, Imposts and Excises shall be uniform throughout the United States;

To borrow Money on the credit of the United States;

To regulate Commerce with foreign Nations, and among the several States, and with the Indian Tribes;

To establish an uniform Rule of Naturalization, and uniform Laws on the subject of Bankruptcies throughout the United States;

To coin Money, regulate the Value thereof, and of foreign Coin, and fix the Standard of Weights and Measures;

Clause 2: Submitting Bills to the President A *bill* is a proposed law. A bill passed by a majority of both houses becomes law when the president signs it. If the president *vetoes*, or rejects, a bill, Congress can overrule the veto by a two-thirds vote of both houses.

Clause 3: Submitting Other Measures Other measures approved by Congress also require the president's approval or may also be passed over the president's veto.

Section 8: Powers of Congress Congress has the specific powers listed in this section.

Clause 1: Taxation Congress has the power to levy taxes. This power was challenged early in the Republic's history by the Whiskey Rebellion. In 1797, Pennsylvania farmers attacked federal officials collecting an unpopular tax on whiskey. The government sent in the militia to arrest the rebels. This show of force demonstrated beyond a doubt the federal government's power to tax.

Clause 2: Borrowing Congress borrows money by issuing bonds, which create a debt that must be repaid.

Clause 3: Trade Regulation Congress regulates foreign trade and interstate commerce.

Clause 4: Naturalization and Bankruptcy Congress makes naturalization and bankruptcy laws. *Naturalization* is the process by which an immigrant becomes a U.S. citizen. *Bankruptcy* applies to individuals or companies that are unable to pay their debts.

Clause 5: Currency Congress establishes the national *currency*, or system of money.

To provide for the Punishment of counterfeiting the Securities and current Coin of the United States;

To establish Post Offices and post Roads;

To promote the Progress of Science and useful Arts, by securing for limited Times to Authors and Inventors the exclusive Right to their respective Writings and Discoveries;

To constitute Tribunals inferior to the supreme Court;

To define and punish Piracies and Felonies committed on the high Seas, and Offences against the Law of Nations;

To declare War, grant Letters of Marque and Reprisal, and make Rules concerning Captures on Land and Water;

To raise and support Armies, but no Appropriation of Money to that Use shall be for a longer Term than two Years;

To provide and maintain a Navy;

To make Rules for the Government and Regulation of the land and naval Forces;

To provide for calling forth the Militia to execute the Laws of the Union, suppress Insurrections and repel Invasions;

To provide for organizing, arming, and disciplining, the Militia, and for governing such Part of them as may be employed in the Service of the United States, reserving to the States respectively, the Appointment of the Officers, and the Authority of training the Militia according to the discipline prescribed by Congress;

Clause 6: Punishment for Counterfeiting Congress punishes counterfeiting, or the making of imitation money.

Clause 7: Postal Service Congress sets up the mail system.

Clause 8: Copyrights and Patents Congress passes copyright and patent laws to encourage creativity and invention. *Copyrights* protect authors and *patents* protect inventors so their work cannot be stolen.

Clause 9: Court System Congress has the power to create a federal court system. *Inferior* means lower.

Clause 10: Crimes at Sea Congress punishes crimes at sea. Piracy was a key concern when the Constitution was written.

Clause 11: Declaring War Congress declares war. World War II was the last time Congress formally declared war. Since then Congress has usually passed resolutions giving the president the authority to use military force where necessary. Such resolutions empowered presidents to send troops to fight the Vietnam War, the Persian Gulf War, and wars in Afghanistan and Iraq. Letters of Marque and Reprisal authorize *privateers*, or private ships, to attack and seize enemy vessels during times of war. The United States ceased issuing such letters during the Civil War.

Clause 12: Raising an Army Congress *appropriates*, or sets aside, funds for the military, usually on a yearly basis but never for more than two years. It also regulates the armed forces.

Clause 13: Maintaining a Navy

Clause 14: Regulating Armed Forces

Clause 15: Calling Up the Militia Congress has the power to call up *militias*, or armies of citizen soldiers, in times of emergency. Each state has its own militia, known today as the National Guard. Over the years, the National Guard has been called to respond to a variety of crises and natural disasters. In 2003, President Bush sent National Guard troops into combat in Iraq.

Clause 16: Regulating the Militia Congress regulates militias but leaves training to the states, under federal guidelines.

To exercise exclusive Legislation in all Cases whatsoever, over such District (not exceeding ten Miles square) as may, by Cession of particular States, and the Acceptance of Congress, become the Seat of the Government of the United States, and to exercise like Authority over all Places purchased by the Consent of the Legislature of the State in which the Same shall be, for the Erection of Forts, Magazines, Arsenals, dock-Yards and other needful Buildings;—And

To make all Laws which shall be necessary and proper for carrying into Execution the foregoing Powers, and all other Powers vested by this Constitution in the Government of the United States, or in any Department or Officer thereof.

Section 9.

~~The Migration or Importation of such Persons as any of the States now existing shall think proper to admit, shall not be prohibited by the Congress prior to the Year one thousand eight hundred and eight, but a Tax or duty may be imposed on such Importation, not exceeding ten dollars for each Person.~~

The Privilege of the Writ of Habeas Corpus shall not be suspended, unless when in Cases of Rebellion or Invasion the public Safety may require it.

No Bill of Attainder or ex post facto Law shall be passed.

~~No Capitation, or other direct, Tax shall be laid, unless in Proportion to the Census or Enumeration herein before directed to be taken.~~

No Tax or Duty shall be laid on Articles exported from any State.

No Preference shall be given by any Regulation of Commerce or Revenue to the Ports of one State over those of another; nor shall Vessels bound to, or from, one State, be obliged to enter, clear, or pay Duties in another.

No Money shall be drawn from the Treasury, but in Consequence of Appropriations made by Law; and a regular Statement and Account of the Receipts and Expenditures of all public Money shall be published from time to time.

Clause 17: Control of Federal Property Congress controls the District of Columbia and all other federal land. Congress governed Washington, D.C., until 1973, when an elected municipal government was established.

Clause 18: Elastic Clause This "necessary and proper" clause is known as the "elastic clause" because it gives Congress the flexibility to pass laws to carry out its functions and deal with new problems as they arise.

Section 9: Limits on the Power of Congress

Clause 1: Slave Trade This clause became obsolete after 1808, when the Constitution permitted Congress to outlaw the slave trade.

Clause 2: Writ of Habeas Corpus A *writ of habeas corpus* gives prisoners the right to challenge their imprisonment in court. Congress may not suspend this right except in extreme emergencies. Habeas corpus has been suspended only rarely in the nation's history. Since September 11, 2001, a debate has raged over whether this right applies to people detained on suspicion of terrorism. In 2004, the Supreme Court ruled that the writ must be extended to U.S. citizens imprisoned at Guantánamo, Cuba.

Clause 3: Unfair Laws This clause protects individuals from unfair laws. Congress cannot pass a law declaring a person or group guilty of a crime *(bill of attainder)*, nor can it pass a law making an act illegal after it has been committed (*ex post facto* law).

Clause 4: Individual Taxes This clause prohibiting direct taxes on individuals was voided by the Sixteenth Amendment (1913), which permits Congress to tax individual income.

Clause 5: Taxes on Exports This clause prohibits the taxation of exported goods.

Clause 6: Trade Preferences Congress may not favor one port over another and must ensure free trade between the states.

Clause 7: Spending The government cannot spend public money unless Congress has passed a law appropriating it. Congressional "power of the purse" acts as a check on the executive branch by controlling how much it can spend.

No Title of Nobility shall be granted by the United States: And no Person holding any Office of Profit or Trust under them, shall, without the Consent of the Congress, accept of any present, Emolument, Office, or Title, of any kind whatever, from any King, Prince, or foreign State.

Section 10.

No State shall enter into any Treaty, Alliance, or Confederation; grant Letters of Marque and Reprisal; coin Money; emit Bills of Credit; make any Thing but gold and silver Coin a Tender in Payment of Debts; pass any Bill of Attainder, ex post facto Law, or Law impairing the Obligation of Contracts, or grant any Title of Nobility.

No State shall, without the Consent of the Congress, lay any Imposts or Duties on Imports or Exports, except what may be absolutely necessary for executing its inspection Laws: and the net Produce of all Duties and Imposts, laid by any State on Imports or Exports, shall be for the Use of the Treasury of the United States; and all such Laws shall be subject to the Revision and Control of the Congress.

No State shall, without the Consent of Congress, lay any Duty of Tonnage, keep Troops, or Ships of War in time of Peace, enter into any Agreement or Compact with another State, or with a foreign Power, or engage in War, unless actually invaded, or in such imminent Danger as will not admit of delay.

Article II.

Section 1.

The executive Power shall be vested in a President of the United States of America. He shall hold his Office during the Term of four Years, and, together with the Vice President, chosen for the same Term, be elected, as follows:

Each State shall appoint, in such Manner as the Legislature thereof may direct, a Number of Electors, equal to the whole Number of Senators and Representatives to which the State may be entitled in the Congress: but no Senator or Representative, or Person holding an Office of Trust or Profit under the United States, shall be appointed an Elector.

The Electors shall meet in their respective States, and vote by Ballot for two Persons, of whom one at least shall not be an Inhabitant of the same State with themselves. And they shall make a List of all the Persons voted for, and of the Number of Votes for each; which List they shall sign and certify, and transmit sealed to the Seat of the Government of the United States, directed to the President of the Senate. The President of the Senate shall, in the Presence of the Senate and House of Representatives, open all the Certificates, and the Votes shall then be counted. The Person having the greatest Number of Votes shall be

Clause 8: Titles of Nobility Congress may not establish titles of nobility, nor may federal officials accept such titles, or any gifts, from a foreign nation without congressional approval.

Section 10: Limits on the Power of the States

Clause 1: Forbidden Actions The states cannot exercise certain powers granted to Congress or the president. These include negotiating treaties with foreign nations and creating their own money. They also may not tax imports or maintain armies without the approval of Congress.

Clause 2: Prohibition on Taxing Trade

Clause 3. Prohibition on Foreign Relations

Article II: Executive Branch

Section 1: President and Vice President

Clause 1: Term of Office The power to *execute*, or carry out, the laws passed by Congress rests with the president. A president and vice president are elected every four years. The Twenty-second Amendment (1951) limits the president to two terms in office.

Clause 2: Electoral College This clause establishes the Electoral College, which elects the president and vice president. The Electoral College is a group of citizens, called *electors*, chosen from each state to cast votes for president and vice president. Each state gets as many electors as it has members of the House and Senate combined. Before 1800, electors were usually elected by state legislatures. Today electors are chosen by the voters of each state.

Clause 3: Method of Election The original electoral method described here was modified by the Twelfth Amendment (1804). The revised method, which still operates today, calls for each elector to cast one vote for president and one vote for vice president. Most states give their entire slate of electoral votes to whichever candidate wins the most popular votes in the state. If no candidate for

the President, if such Number be a Majority of the whole Number of Electors appointed; and if there be more than one who have such Majority, and have an equal Number of Votes, then the House of Representatives shall immediately chuse by Ballot one of them for President; and if no Person have a Majority, then from the five highest on the List the said House shall in like Manner chuse the President. But in chusing the President, the Votes shall be taken by States, the Representation from each State having one Vote; A quorum for this Purpose shall consist of a Member or Members from two thirds of the States, and a Majority of all the States shall be necessary to a Choice. In every Case, after the Choice of the President, the Person having the greatest Number of Votes of the Electors shall be the Vice President. But if there should remain two or more who have equal Votes, the Senate shall chuse from them by Ballot the Vice President.

The Congress may determine the Time of chusing the Electors, and the Day on which they shall give their Votes; which Day shall be the same throughout the United States.

No Person except a natural born Citizen, or a Citizen of the United States, at the time of the Adoption of this Constitution, shall be eligible to the Office of President; neither shall any person be eligible to that Office who shall not have attained to the Age of thirty five Years, and been fourteen Years a Resident within the United States.

In Case of the Removal of the President from Office, or of his Death, Resignation, or Inability to discharge the Powers and Duties of the said Office, the Same shall devolve on the Vice President, and the Congress may by Law provide for the Case of Removal, Death, Resignation or Inability, both of the President and Vice President, declaring what Officer shall then act as President, and such Officer shall act accordingly, until the Disability be removed, or a President shall be elected.

The President shall, at stated Times, receive for his Services, a Compensation, which shall neither be increased nor diminished during the Period for which he shall have been elected, and he shall not receive within that Period any other Emolument from the United States, or any of them.

Before he enter on the Execution of his Office, he shall take the following Oath or Affirmation:—"I do solemnly swear (or affirm) that I will faithfully execute the Office of President of the United States, and will to the best of my Ability, preserve, protect and defend the Constitution of the United States."

Section 2.

The President shall be Commander in Chief of the Army and Navy of the United States, and of the Militia of the several States, when called into the actual Service of the United States; he may require the Opinion, in writing, of the principal Officer in each of the executive Departments, upon any Subject relating to the Duties of their respective Offices, and he shall have Power to grant Reprieves and Pardons for Offenses against the United States, except in Cases of Impeachment.

president gets a majority of electoral votes, then the House of Representatives chooses the president. The Electoral College is controversial because it has the potential to elect a candidate who did not win the popular vote.

Clause 4: Time of Elections Presidential elections are held on the Tuesday that follows the first Monday in November, every four years. Electors cast their votes more than a month later, on the Monday following the second Wednesday in December.

Clause 5: Qualifications The president must be an American citizen born in the United States, must be at least 35 years old, and must have resided in the United States for 14 years.

Clause 6: Presidential Succession If the president dies or leaves office before the end of his or her term, the vice president becomes president. The ambiguous wording of this clause was clarified by the Twenty-fifth Amendment (1967). Congress decides who succeeds to the presidency if both the president and the vice president are incapacitated.

Clause 7: Salary Congress sets the president's salary and cannot change it during a presidential term. The president cannot accept *emoluments*, or other compensation, while in office.

Clause 8: Oath of Office The oath taken by the president is administered by a judicial officer, typically the chief justice of the Supreme Court.

Section 2: Powers of the President
Clause 1: Military and Executive Powers The president is commander-in-chief of the armed forces of the United States. This puts the military under civilian control. The president can grant pardons for federal crimes, except in cases of impeachment.

He shall have Power, by and with the Advice and Consent of the Senate, to make Treaties, provided two thirds of the Senators present concur; and he shall nominate, and by and with the Advice and Consent of the Senate, shall appoint Ambassadors, other public Ministers and Consuls, Judges of the supreme Court, and all other Officers of the United States, whose Appointments are not herein otherwise provided for, and which shall be established by Law: but the Congress may by law vest the Appointment of such inferior Officers, as they think proper, in the President alone, in the Courts of Law, or in the Heads of Departments.

The President shall have Power to fill up all Vacancies that may happen during the Recess of the Senate, by granting Commissions which shall expire at the End of their next Session.

Clause 2: Treaties and Appointments
The president has the power to make treaties with other nations, but the Senate must approve them by a two-thirds vote. The "advice and consent" of the Senate act as a check on presidential power. The president can name certain officials and federal judges, but a majority of the Senate must approve the president's choices.

Clause 3: Temporary Appointments
If the Senate is not in session, the president can make appointments without Senate approval. Such "recess" appointments expire at the end of the next Senate session. Presidents sometimes use recess appointments to avoid the Senate confirmation process.

Section 3.

He shall from time to time give to the Congress Information of the State of the Union, and recommend to their Consideration such Measures as he shall judge necessary and expedient; he may, on extraordinary Occasions, convene both Houses, or either of them, and in Case of Disagreement between them, with Respect to the Time of Adjournment, he may adjourn them to such Time as he shall think proper; he shall receive Ambassadors and other public Ministers; he shall take Care that the Laws be faithfully executed, and shall Commission all the Officers of the United States.

Section 3: Duties of the President
The president can propose ideas for new laws. The president also reports to Congress, usually every year, on the State of the Union. In emergencies, the president can call Congress into special session.

Section 4.

The President, Vice President and all civil Officers of the United States, shall be removed from Office on Impeachment for, and Conviction of, Treason, Bribery, or other high Crimes and Misdemeanors.

Section 4: Impeachment
Presidents and federal officials can be removed from office if they abuse their powers or commit other "high crimes."

Article III.

Article III: Judicial Branch

Section 1.

The judicial Power of the United States, shall be vested in one supreme Court, and in such inferior Courts as the Congress may from time to time ordain and establish. The Judges, both of the supreme and inferior Courts, shall hold their Offices during good Behaviour, and shall, at stated Times, receive for their Services a Compensation, which shall not be diminished during their Continuance in Office.

Section 1: Federal Courts Judicial power is the power to decide legal cases in a court of law. This power is given to the Supreme Court and lower federal courts established by Congress. Federal judges hold office for life and their salaries cannot be reduced, thereby assuring the independence of the judiciary. Congress has set the number of Supreme Court justices at nine.

Section 2

The judicial Power shall extend to all Cases, in Law and Equity, arising under this Constitution, the Laws of the United States, and Treaties made, or which shall be made, under their Authority; —to all Cases affecting Ambassadors, other public Ministers and Consuls; —to all Cases of admiralty and maritime Jurisdiction; —to Controversies to which the United States shall be a Party; —to Controversies between two or more States, —between a State and Citizens of another State; —between Citizens of different States, —between Citizens of the same State claiming Lands under Grants of different States, and between a State, or the Citizens thereof, and foreign States, Citizens or Subjects.

Section 2: Jurisdiction
Clause 1: Types of Cases *Jurisdiction* is the right of a court to hear a case. The federal courts have jurisdiction in cases pertaining to the Constitution, federal law, treaties, ambassadors, and maritime law. Federal courts can decide disputes between states, between states and the federal government, and between citizens of different states. In *Marbury v. Madison* (1803), the Supreme Court determined that it had the power to decide whether a law is constitutional.

In all Cases affecting Ambassadors, other public Ministers and Consuls, and those in which a State shall be Party, the supreme Court shall have original Jurisdiction. In all the other Cases before mentioned, the supreme Court shall have appellate Jurisdiction, both as to Law and Fact, with such Exceptions, and under such Regulations as the Congress shall make.

The Trial of all Crimes, except in Cases of Impeachment; shall be by Jury; and such Trial shall be held in the State where the said Crimes shall have been committed; but when not committed within any State, the Trial shall be at such Place or Places as the Congress may by Law have directed.

Section 3.

Treason against the United States, shall consist only in levying War against them, or in adhering to their Enemies, giving them Aid and Comfort. No Person shall be convicted of Treason unless on the Testimony of two Witnesses to the same overt Act, or on Confession in open Court.

The Congress shall have Power to declare the Punishment of Treason, but no Attainder of Treason shall work Corruption of Blood, or Forfeiture except during the Life of the Person attainted.

Article IV.

Section 1.

Full Faith and Credit shall be given in each State to the public Acts, Records, and judicial Proceedings of every other State; And the Congress may by general Laws prescribe the Manner in which such Acts, Records and Proceedings shall be proved, and the Effect thereof.

Section 2.

The Citizens of each State shall be entitled to all Privileges and Immunities of Citizens in the several States.

A Person charged in any State with Treason, Felony, or other Crime, who shall flee from Justice, and be found in another State, shall on Demand of the executive Authority of the State from which he fled, be delivered up, to be removed to the State having Jurisdiction of the Crime.

No Person held to Service or Labour in one State, under the Laws thereof, escaping into another, shall, in Consequence of any Law or Regulation therein, be discharged from such Service or Labour, but shall be delivered up on Claim of the Party to whom such Service or Labour may be due.

Section 3.

New States may be admitted by the Congress into this Union; but no new State shall be formed or erected within the Jurisdiction of any other State; nor any State be formed by the Junction of two or more States, or Parts of States, without the Consent of the Legislatures of the States concerned as well as of the Congress.

Clause 2: Role of Supreme Court
The Supreme Court has "original jurisdiction"—the power to hear cases for the first time, not on appeal from a lower court—only in limited circumstances. Most of the time, the Court functions as an appeals court, deciding whether a case was properly tried in a lower court and reviewing its decision.

Clause 3: Trial by Jury
All defendants accused of a federal crime, except in cases of impeachment, have the right to a jury trial.

Section 3: Treason
Clause 1: Definition Treason, the only crime defined in the Constitution, is described as waging war against the United States or aiding its enemies. Criticism of the government, even in times of war, is protected by the First Amendment.

Clause 2: Punishment Congress has the power to decide how to punish convicted traitors. Punishment cannot be directed at the guilty person's relatives or friends.

Article IV: Relations Among the States

Section 1: Full Faith and Credit Each state must honor the laws and authority of other states. For example, an adoption legally performed in one state must be recognized as legal in other states.

Section 2: Treatment of Citizens
Clause 1: Equal Privileges States may not discriminate against citizens of other states.

Clause 2: Extradition States must honor extradition orders. *Extradition* is the return of a suspected criminal or escaped convict to the state where he or she is wanted.

Clause 3: Fugitive Slaves This clause required states to return runaway slaves to their owners in other states. The Thirteenth Amendment (1965) voided this provision.

Section 3: New States and Territories
Clause 1: New States A new state cannot be carved out of an existing state or formed by the merger of existing states without the consent of the states or of Congress.

The Congress shall have Power to dispose of and make all needful Rules and Regulations respecting the Territory or other Property belonging to the United States; and nothing in this Constitution shall be construed as to Prejudice any Claims of the United States, or of any particular State.

Section 4.

The United States shall guarantee to every State in this Union a Republican Form of Government, and shall protect each of them against Invasion; and on Application of the Legislature, or of the Executive (when the Legislature cannot be convened), against domestic Violence.

Article V.

The Congress, whenever two thirds of both Houses shall deem it necessary, shall propose Amendments to this Constitution, or, on the Application of the Legislatures of two thirds of the several States, shall call a Convention for proposing Amendments, which, in either Case, shall be valid to all Intents and Purposes, as Part of this Constitution, when ratified by the Legislatures of three fourths of the several States, or by Conventions in three fourths thereof, as the one or the other Mode of Ratification may be proposed by the Congress; Provided that no Amendment which may be made prior to the Year One thousand eight hundred and eight shall in any Manner affect the first and fourth Clauses in the Ninth Section of the first Article; and that no State, without its Consent, shall be deprived of its equal Suffrage in the Senate.

Article VI.

All Debts contracted and Engagements entered into, before the Adoption of this Constitution, shall be as valid against the United States under this Constitution, as under the Confederation.

This Constitution, and the Laws of the United States which shall be made in Pursuance thereof; and all Treaties made, or which shall be made, under the Authority of the United States, shall be the supreme Law of the Land; and the Judges in every State shall be bound thereby, any Thing in the Constitution or Laws of any State to the Contrary notwithstanding.

The Senators and Representatives before mentioned, and the Members of the several State Legislatures, and all executive and judicial Officers, both of the United States and of the several States, shall be bound by Oath or Affirmation, to support this Constitution; but no religious Test shall ever be required as a Qualification to any Office or public Trust under the United States.

Article VII.

The Ratification of the Conventions of nine States, shall be sufficient for the Establishment of this Constitution between the States so ratifying the Same.

Done in Convention by the Unanimous Consent of the States present the Seventeenth Day of September in the Year of our Lord one thousand seven hundred and Eighty seven and of the Independence of the United States of America the Twelfth In Witness whereof We have hereunto subscribed our Names.

Clause 2: Federal Territory Congress has power over all federal territories and property. This means that it can regulate public lands, such as national parks and forests, and make laws for overseas possessions, such as Guam and Puerto Rico.

Section 4: Protection of States
Known as the "guarantee clause," this provision ensures that each state has a representative democratic government. The federal government is obliged to protect the states from invasion and from internal, or *domestic*, riots or other violence.

Article V: Amending the Constitution

The Constitution can be *amended*, or changed. Amendments must first be proposed either by a two-thirds vote of both houses of Congress or by a national convention of two-thirds of the states. A proposed amendment must then be ratified by three-quarters of the states, either in special conventions or in the state legislatures. The amendment process was made difficult so that the Constitution would not be amended too frequently or lightly. The Constitution has been amended only 27 times.

Article VI: National Supremacy

Clause 1: National Debts This clause recognizes debts incurred by the previous government under the Articles of Confederation.

Clause 2: Supremacy of National Law
The so-called "supremacy clause" makes the Constitution and federal law the supreme, or highest, law of the land. If a state law and a federal law conflict, the federal law takes precedence. Federal courts can overturn state laws deemed to be unconstitutional or in conflict with federal law.

Clause 3: Oaths of Office Federal and state officials must swear allegiance to the Constitution. Public officials cannot be required to adopt or practice any particular religion.

Article VII: Ratification of the Constitution

To take effect, the Constitution had to be ratified by nine of the original 13 states. On June 21, 1788, the ninth state (New Hampshire) ratified. New York and Virginia ratified soon afterward. Rhode Island and North Carolina waited until the Bill of Rights was added to ratify. The Constitution went into effect on April 30, 1789.

Amendments

The Bill of Rights, or first 10 amendments, was passed by Congress on September 25, 1789, and ratified on December 15, 1791. Later amendments were proposed and ratified one at a time. The year of ratification appears in parentheses.

First Amendment

Congress shall make no law respecting an establishment of religion, or prohibiting the free exercise thereof; or abridging the freedom of speech, or of the press, or the right of the people peaceably to assemble, and to petition the Government for a redress of grievances.

Second Amendment

A well regulated Militia, being necessary to the security of a free State, the right of the people to keep and bear Arms, shall not be infringed.

Third Amendment

No Soldier shall, in time of peace be quartered in any house, without the consent of the Owner, nor in time of war, but in a manner to be prescribed by law.

Fourth Amendment

The right of the people to be secure in their persons, houses, papers, and effects, against unreasonable searches and seizures, shall not be violated, and no Warrants shall issue, but upon probable cause, supported by Oath or affirmation, and particularly describing the place to be searched, and the persons or things to be seized.

First Amendment (1791)
Basic Freedoms

This amendment protects five freedoms that lie at the heart of American democracy: freedom of religion, freedom of speech, freedom of the press, freedom of assembly, and the freedom to *petition*, or ask, the government to correct wrongs.

Second Amendment (1791)
Right to Bear Arms

The right to bear arms guaranteed in this amendment is controversial. Americans are divided as to whether it applies to individuals or only to militias. The courts have ruled that individuals do have the right to bear arms, but that it is not an unlimited right. The Supreme Court has upheld some federal gun control laws, such as those requiring gun registration and waiting periods, but has ruled that other gun control measures should be left to the states.

Third Amendment (1791)
Quartering of Soldiers

In the turbulent years leading up to the American Revolution, American colonists were compelled to *quarter*, or house, British soldiers in their homes. This amendment bars the government from using private homes as military quarters, except in wartime and in a lawful way.

Fourth Amendment (1791)
Search and Seizure

Like the Third Amendment, this amendment protects citizens against government intrusions into their property. Government officials cannot search citizens or their property, or seize citizens or their belongings, without good reason. Searches and seizures generally require a *warrant*, or written order approved by a judge. The Supreme Court has ruled that the Fourth Amendment also applies to electronic searches and wiretapping.

Fifth Amendment

No person shall be held to answer for a capital, or otherwise infamous crime, unless on a presentment or indictment of a Grand Jury, except in cases arising in the land or naval forces, or in the Militia, when in actual service in time of War or public danger; nor shall any person be subject for the same offence to be twice put in jeopardy of life or limb; nor shall be compelled in any criminal case to be a witness against himself, nor be deprived of life, liberty, or property, without due process of law; nor shall private property be taken for public use, without just compensation.

Sixth Amendment

In all criminal prosecutions, the accused shall enjoy the right to a speedy and public trial, by an impartial jury of the State and district wherein the crime shall have been committed, which district shall have been previously ascertained by law, and to be informed of the nature and cause of the accusation; to be confronted with the witnesses against him; to have compulsory process for obtaining witnesses in his favor, and to have the Assistance of Counsel for his defence.

Seventh Amendment

In Suits at common law, where the value in controversy shall exceed twenty dollars, the right of trial by jury shall be preserved, and no fact tried by a jury shall be otherwise re-examined in any Court of the United States, than according to the rules of the common law.

Eighth Amendment

Excessive bail shall not be required, nor excessive fines imposed, nor cruel and unusual punishments inflicted.

Fifth Amendment (1791)
Rights of the Accused

This amendment guarantees basic rights to people accused of crimes. A *capital* crime is punishable by death. *Infamous* crimes are punishable by imprisonment. A *grand jury* is a group of citizens who hear evidence of a crime and decide if the evidence warrants a trial. An *indictment* is their formal accusation. These procedures are intended to prevent the government from prosecuting people unfairly. In addition, accused persons cannot be tried twice for the same crime, known as *double jeopardy*. They cannot be forced to *testify*, or give evidence, against themselves. They cannot be jailed or have their property taken without *due process of law*, or a fair court hearing or trial. The government cannot take away private property without paying a fair price for it.

Sixth Amendment (1791)
Right to a Fair Trial

A citizen accused of a crime has the right to a jury trial that is both public and "speedy," or that takes place as quickly as circumstances allow. An *impartial* jury does not favor either side. An accused person has the right to question witnesses and has the right to a lawyer. Both federal and state courts must provide a lawyer if the accused cannot afford to hire one.

Seventh Amendment (1791)
Civil Trials

Citizens have the right to a jury trial to settle lawsuits over money or property worth more than $20. *Common law* refers to the rules of law established by previous judicial decisions.

Eighth Amendment (1791)
Bail and Punishment

Bail is money that an accused person pays in order to get out of jail while awaiting trial. The money is returned when the accused appears at trial; it is confiscated if he or she doesn't appear. Bail and fines that are set by a court must be reasonable. Punishments for crimes cannot be "cruel and unusual." The meaning of this phrase has broadened to include punishment considered too harsh for a particular crime. In 2005, the Supreme Court ruled that laws that apply the death penalty to people 17 and younger constitute "cruel and unusual" punishment and are unconstitutional.

Ninth Amendment

The enumeration in the Constitution, of certain rights, shall not be construed to deny or disparage others retained by the people.

Tenth Amendment

The powers not delegated to the United States by the Constitution, nor prohibited by it to the States, are reserved to the States respectively, or to the people.

Later Amendments

Eleventh Amendment

The Judicial power of the United States shall not be construed to extend to any suit in law or equity, commenced or prosecuted against one of the United States by Citizens of another State, or by Citizens or Subjects of any Foreign State.

Twelfth Amendment

The Electors shall meet in their respective states, and vote by ballot for President and Vice President, one of whom, at least, shall not be an inhabitant of the same state with themselves; they shall name in their ballots the person voted for as President, and in distinct ballots the person voted for as Vice President, and they shall make distinct lists of all persons voted for as President, and of all persons voted for as Vice President, and of the number of votes for each, which lists they shall sign and certify, and transmit sealed to the seat of the government of the United States, directed to the President of the Senate;—The President of the Senate shall, in the presence of the Senate and House of Representatives, open all the certificates and the votes shall then be counted;—The person having the greatest number of votes for President, shall be the President, if such number be a majority of the whole number of Electors appointed; and if no person have such majority, then from the persons having the highest numbers not exceeding three on the list of those voted for as President, the House of Representatives shall choose immediately, by ballot, the President. But in choosing the President, the votes shall be taken by states, the representation from each state having one vote; a quorum for this purpose shall consist of a member or members from two-thirds of the states, and a majority of all the states shall be necessary to a choice. And if the House of Representatives shall not choose a President whenever the right of choice shall devolve upon them, before the fourth day of March next following, then the Vice President shall act as President, as in the case of the death or other constitutional disability of the President. The person having the greatest number of votes as Vice

---

Ninth Amendment (1791)
Rights Retained by the People

Americans have fundamental rights beyond the rights listed in the Constitution. The government cannot deny these rights just because they are not specified. This amendment was added out of fear that the Bill of Rights would be interpreted as limiting people's rights to those listed.

Tenth Amendment (1791)
States' Rights

This amendment attempts to balance power between the federal government and the states. It gives to the states and to the people any powers not specifically granted to the federal government. States' rights and the scope of federal power have been the subject of intense debate since the founding of the Republic. Slavery was perhaps the most significant issue over which this conflict played out, eventually plunging the nation into civil war.

Eleventh Amendment (1795)
Lawsuits Against States

People cannot sue a state in federal court if they are citizens of a different state or of a foreign country. The courts have interpreted this to mean that states may not be sued in federal courts without their consent.

Twelfth Amendment (1804)
Presidential Elections

This amendment modifies the electoral process so that the president and vice president are elected separately. In the original Constitution, the candidate who finished second in the voting for president automatically became vice president. In 1800, this resulted in a tie for president between Thomas Jefferson and Aaron Burr. It took the House of Representatives 36 ballots to elect Jefferson president and Burr vice president. The Twelfth Amendment was added to prevent another tie vote.

President, shall be the Vice President, if such number be a majority of the whole number of Electors appointed, and if no person have a majority, then from the two highest numbers on the list, the Senate shall choose the Vice President; a quorum for the purpose shall consist of two-thirds of the whole number of Senators, and a majority of the whole number shall be necessary to a choice. But no person constitutionally ineligible to the office of President shall be eligible to that of Vice President of the United States.

Thirteenth Amendment

Section 1.
Neither slavery nor involuntary servitude, except as a punishment for crime whereof the party shall have been duly convicted, shall exist within the United States, or any place subject to their jurisdiction.

Section 2.
Congress shall have power to enforce these articles by appropriate legislation.

Fourteenth Amendment

Section 1.
All persons born or naturalized in the United States, and subject to the jurisdiction thereof, are citizens of the United States and of the State wherein they reside. No State shall make or enforce any law which shall abridge the privileges or immunities of citizens of the United States; nor shall any State deprive any person of life, liberty, or property, without due process of law; nor deny to any person within its jurisdiction the equal protection of the laws.

Section 2.
Representatives shall be apportioned among the several States according to their respective numbers, counting the whole number of persons in each State, excluding Indians not taxed. But when the right to vote at any election for the choice of electors for President and Vice President of the United States, Representatives in Congress, the Executive and Judicial officers of a State, or the members of the Legislature thereof, is denied to any of the male inhabitants of such State, being twenty-one years of age, and citizens of the United States, or in any way abridged, except for participation in rebellion, or other crime, the basis of representation therein shall be reduced in the proportion which the number of such male citizens shall bear to the whole number of male citizens twenty-one years of age in such State.

Section 3.
No person shall be a Senator or Representative in Congress, or elector of President and Vice President, or hold any office, civil or military, under the United States, or under any State, who, having previously taken an oath, as a member of Congress, or as an officer of the United States, or as a member of any State legislature, or as an executive or judicial officer of any State, to support the Constitution of the United States, shall have engaged in insurrection or rebellion against the same, or given aid or comfort to the enemies thereof. But Congress may by a vote of two-thirds of each House, remove such disability.

Thirteenth Amendment (1865) Abolition of Slavery

Section 1: Abolition
This amendment bans slavery throughout the United States. *Involuntary servitude* is work done against one's will. No person can be forced to work against his or her will except as a legal punishment for a crime.

Section 2: Enforcement

Fourteenth Amendment (1868) Rights of Citizens
This amendment was originally designed to resolve issues that arose after the Civil War ended and slavery was abolished.

Section 1: Citizenship
By defining as a citizen anyone born in the United States, this section extends citizenship to blacks. It prohibits the states from denying rights, due process, and equal protection of the law to their citizens. Despite these guarantees, it took nearly a century for the Supreme Court to decide that racial segregation violated the "equal protection" provision. In *Brown v. Board of Education* (1954), the Court struck down school segregation, ruling that separate schools for whites and blacks were inherently unequal.

Section 2: Representation and Voting
This section nullifies the "three-fifths clause" of the original Constitution. It guarantees equal representation to all citizens. The reference to "male inhabitants" upset women's rights leaders who felt that equality for women was being pushed aside in favor of equality for blacks. In time, the "equal protection" provision would be expanded to include women, minorities, and noncitizens.

Section 3: Former Confederate Leaders
Any member of government who took an oath to uphold the Constitution before the Civil War and who then joined the Confederate cause cannot be elected to any federal or state office.

Section 4.

The validity of the public debt of the United States, authorized by law, including debts incurred for payment of pensions and bounties for services in suppressing insurrection or rebellion, shall not be questioned. But neither the United States nor any State shall assume or pay any debt or obligation incurred in aid of insurrection or rebellion against the United States, or any claim for the loss or emancipation of any slave; but all such debts, obligations and claims shall be held illegal and void.

Section 5.

The Congress shall have the power to enforce, by appropriate legislation, the provisions of this article.

Fifteenth Amendment

Section 1.

The right of citizens of the United States to vote shall not be denied or abridged by the United States or by any State on account of race, color, or previous condition of servitude

Section 2.

The Congress shall have the power to enforce this article by appropriate legislation.

Sixteenth Amendment

The Congress shall have power to lay and collect taxes on incomes, from whatever source derived, without apportionment among the several States, and without regard to any census or enumeration

.

Seventeenth Amendment

Section 1.

The Senate of the United States shall be composed of two Senators from each State, elected by the people thereof, for six years; and each Senator shall have one vote. The electors in each State shall have the qualifications requisite for electors of the most numerous branch of the State legislature.

Section 2.

When vacancies happen in the representation of any State in the Senate, the executive authority of such State shall issue writs of election to fill such vacancies: Provided, That the legislature of any State may empower the executive thereof to make temporary appointments until the people fill the vacancies by election as the legislature may direct.

Section 3.

This amendment shall not be so construed as to affect the election or term of any Senator chosen before it becomes valid as part of the Constitution.

Section 4: Public Debts
By voiding all Confederate debts, this section ensured that people who had lent money to Confederate states would not be paid back, nor would former slave owners be paid for the loss of their emancipated slaves.

Section 5: Enforcement
Congress can make laws to enforce this amendment. Beginning in the 1960s, Congress used this enforcement provision to pass new civil rights legislation, including the Civil Rights Act, the Voting Rights Act, and the Americans with Disabilities Act.

Fifteenth Amendment (1870)
Voting Rights

Section 1: The Right to Vote
States cannot deny voting rights to citizens on the basis of race, color, or previous enslavement.

Section 2: Enforcement

Sixteenth Amendment (1913)
Income Tax

The income tax amendment allows Congress to tax the earnings and income of individuals. At first only the very wealthy were taxed, but eventually the tax was extended to almost all wage earners.

Seventeenth Amendment (1913)
Election of Senators

Section 1: Elections
This amendment provides for the direct election of senators by popular vote. Previously, senators were elected by state legislatures, but deadlocked votes in state legislatures resulted in many Senate seats remaining vacant for long periods. By 1911, public demand for direct senatorial elections forced Congress to pass the Seventeenth Amendment.

Section 2: Vacancies
If a Senate seat becomes vacant, and if the legislature of that state approves, the governor of that state may appoint a replacement senator until an election can be held.

Section 3: Previously Elected Senators

Eighteenth Amendment

Section 1.
~~After one year from the ratification of this article, the manufacture, sale, or transportation of intoxicating liquors within, the importation thereof into, or the exportation thereof from the United States and all territory subject to the jurisdiction thereof for beverage purposes is hereby prohibited.~~

Section 2.
~~The Congress and the several States shall have concurrent power to enforce this article by appropriate legislation.~~

Section 3.
~~This article shall be inoperative unless it shall have been ratified as an amendment to the Constitution by the legislatures of the several States, as provided in the Constitution, within seven years from the date of the submission hereof to the States by the Congress.~~

Nineteenth Amendment

Section 1.
The right of citizens of the United States to vote shall not be denied or abridged by the United States or by any State on account of sex.

Section 2.
Congress shall have power to enforce this article by appropriate legislation.

Twentieth Amendment

Section 1.
The terms of the President and Vice President shall end at noon on the 20th day of January, and the terms of Senators and Representatives at noon on the 3d day of January, of the years in which such terms would have ended if this article had not been ratified; and the terms of their successors shall then begin.

Section 2.
The Congress shall assemble at least once in every year, and such meeting shall begin at noon on the 3d day of January, unless they shall by law appoint a different day.

Eighteenth Amendment (1919)
Prohibition of Liquor

Section 1: Ban on Alcohol
This amendment outlawed the production, sale, and transport of alcoholic beverages within the United States. It was the culmination of a decades-long reform effort to end the problems associated with alcohol abuse. This sweeping ban proved impossible to enforce. Prohibition led to a rise in lawlessness and organized crime as the alcohol business flourished illegally. Prohibition ended when the Twenty-first Amendment *repealed*, or canceled, this amendment.

Section 2: Enforcement

Section 3: Ratification

Nineteenth Amendment (1920)
Women's Suffrage

Section 1: Right to Vote
This amendment guaranteed women the right to vote. The women's suffrage movement had sought this right since 1848. Although some western states already allowed women to vote, activists argued that a constitutional amendment was needed to guarantee the vote to all women. The Nineteenth Amendment is sometimes called the Susan B. Anthony amendment after its most prominent and persistent advocate.

Section 2: Enforcement

Twentieth Amendment (1933)
Terms of Office

Section 1: Beginning of Terms
The president and vice president take office on January 20. Members of Congress begin their terms on January 3. Prior to this amendment, these terms of office began on March 3. These calendar changes shortened the period during which a "lame duck"—an incumbent who was not reelected or did not run for reelection—remained in office.

Section 2: Congressional Session

Section 3.

If, at the time fixed for the beginning of the term of the President, the President elect shall have died, the Vice President elect shall become President. If a President shall not have been chosen before the time fixed for the beginning of his term, or if the President elect shall have failed to qualify, then the Vice President elect shall act as President until a President shall have qualified; and the Congress may by law provide for the case wherein neither a President elect nor a Vice President shall have qualified, declaring who shall then act as President, or the manner in which one who is to act shall be selected, and such person shall act accordingly until a President or Vice President shall have qualified.

Section 4.

The Congress may by law provide for the case of the death of any of the persons from whom the House of Representatives may choose a President whenever the right of choice shall have devolved upon them, and for the case of the death of any of the persons from whom the Senate may choose a Vice President whenever the right of choice shall have devolved upon them.

Section 5.

Sections 1 and 2 shall take effect on the 15th day of October following the ratification of this article.

Section 6.

This article shall be inoperative unless it shall have been ratified as an amendment to the Constitution by the legislatures of three-fourths of the several States within seven years from the date of its submission.

Twenty-first Amendment

Section 1.

The eighteenth article of amendment to the Constitution of the United States is hereby repealed.

Section 2.

The transportation or importation into any State, Territory, or Possession of the United States for delivery or use therein of intoxicating liquors, in violation of the laws thereof, is hereby prohibited.

Section 3.

This article shall be inoperative unless it shall have been ratified as an amendment to the Constitution by conventions in the several States, as provided in the Constitution, within seven years from the date of the submission hereof to the States by the Congress.

Twenty-second Amendment

Section 1.

No person shall be elected to the office of the President more than twice, and no person who has held the office of President, or acted as President, for more than two years of a term to which some other person was elected President shall be elected to the office of the President more than once. But this Article shall not apply to any person holding the office of President when this Article was proposed by Congress, and shall not prevent any person who may be holding the office of President, or acting as President, during the term within which this Article becomes operative from holding the office of President or acting as President during the remainder of such term.

Section 3: Presidential Succession This and Section 4 provide for succession if a newly elected president should die or be unable to take office before the start of his or her term.

Section 4: Congress Decides Succession

Section 5: Date of Implementation

Section 6: Ratification

Twenty-first Amendment (1933) End of Prohibition

Section 1: Repeal
This amendment ended national prohibition, leaving it to states to ban alcohol if they wished.

Section 2: State Laws
Alcoholic beverages may not be brought into a state where they are still banned.

Section 3: Ratification
This amendment was the only one ratified by special state conventions rather than state legislatures. Most Americans were eager to end prohibition, and this method was quicker.

Twenty-second Amendment (1951) Term Limits for the Presidency

Section 1: Two-Term Limit
The Constitution did not specify how many terms a president could serve, but George Washington stepped down after two terms, and succeeding presidents followed his example. In 1940, with World War II looming, Democratic president Franklin D. Roosevelt broke precedent by running for a third term. He was elected in 1940 and again in 1944. After his death in 1945, Republicans in Congress proposed this amendment to limit future presidents to two terms.

Section 2.

This article shall be inoperative unless it shall have been ratified as an amendment to the Constitution by the legislatures of three-fourths of the several States within seven years from the date of its submission to the States by the Congress.

Twenty-third Amendment

Section 1.

The District constituting the seat of government of the United States shall appoint in such manner as the Congress may direct:

A number of electors of President and Vice President equal to the whole number of Senators and Representatives in Congress to which the District would be entitled if it were a state, but in no event more than the least populous State; they shall be in addition to those appointed by the States, but they shall be considered, for the purposes of the election of President and Vice President, to be electors appointed by a State; and they shall meet in the District and perform such duties as provided by the twelfth article of amendment.

Section 2.

The Congress shall have power to enforce this article by appropriate legislation.

Twenty-fourth Amendment

Section 1.

The right of citizens of the United States to vote in any primary or other election for President or Vice President, for electors for President or Vice President, or for Senator or Representative in Congress, shall not be denied or abridged by the United States or any State by reason of failure to pay any poll tax or other tax.

Section 2.

The Congress shall have power to enforce this article by appropriate legislation.

Twenty-fifth Amendment

Section 1.

In case of the removal of the President from office or of his death or resignation, the Vice President shall become President.

Section 2.

Whenever there is a vacancy in the office of the Vice President, the President shall nominate a Vice President who shall take office upon confirmation by a majority vote of both Houses of Congress.

Twenty-third Amendment (1961)
Electors for Washington, D.C.

Section 1: Number of Electors
This amendment gives the citizens of Washington, D.C., the right to vote in presidential elections. It allots to the District of Columbia the same number of presidential electors it would have if it were a state. Until this amendment was enacted, District of Columbia residents could not vote for president, even though they had all the obligations of citizenship, including taxation. In 1978, Congress passed a constitutional amendment that would have made the District a state, but the states failed to ratify it.

Section 2: Enforcement

Twenty-fourth Amendment (1964)
Abolition of Poll Tax

Section 1: Ban on Poll Taxes
A *poll tax* is a fee that a voter must pay in order to vote. This amendment bans poll taxes, which some states imposed to prevent African Americans from voting.

Section 2: Enforcement

Twenty-fifth Amendment (1967)
Presidential Succession

Section 1: President's Death or Removal
If the president dies, resigns, or is removed from office, the vice president becomes president.

Section 2: Vice Presidential Vacancy
If the vice presidency becomes vacant, the president can appoint a vice president, who must be confirmed by Congress. This amendment was first applied in 1973, when Vice President Spiro Agnew resigned in the face of bribery and corruption charges. President Nixon appointed Gerald Ford to be vice president. Within a year, Nixon himself resigned over the Watergate scandal. Ford became president and appointed Nelson Rockefeller vice president. Ford and Rockefeller became the nation's only unelected president and vice president.

Section 3.

Whenever the President transmits to the President pro tempore of the Senate and the Speaker of the House of Representatives his written declaration that he is unable to discharge the powers and duties of his office, and until he transmits to them a written declaration to the contrary, such powers and duties shall be discharged by the Vice President as Acting President.

Section 4.

Whenever the Vice President and a majority of either the principal officers of the executive departments or of such other body as Congress may by law provide, transmit to the President pro tempore of the Senate and the Speaker of the House of Representatives their written declaration that the President is unable to discharge the powers and duties of his office, the Vice President shall immediately assume the powers and duties of the office as Acting President.

Thereafter, when the President transmits to the President pro tempore of the Senate and the Speaker of the House of Representatives his written declaration that no inability exists, he shall resume the powers and duties of his office unless the Vice President and a majority of either the principal officers of the executive department or of such other body as Congress may by law provide, transmit within four days to the President pro tempore of the Senate and the Speaker of the House of Representatives their written declaration that the President is unable to discharge the powers and duties of his office. Thereupon Congress shall decide the issue, assembling within forty-eight hours for that purpose if not in session. If the Congress, within twenty-one days after receipt of the latter written declaration, or, if Congress is not in session, within twenty-one days after Congress is required to assemble, determines by two-thirds vote of both Houses that the President is unable to discharge the powers and duties of his office, the Vice President shall continue to discharge the same as Acting President; otherwise, the President shall resume the powers and duties of his office.

Twenty-sixth Amendment

Section 1.

The right of citizens of the United States, who are eighteen years of age or older, to vote shall not be denied or abridged by the United States or by any State on account of age.

Section 2.

The Congress shall have power to enforce this article by appropriate legislation.

Twenty-seventh Amendment

No law, varying the compensation for the services of the Senators and Representatives, shall take effect, until an election of Representatives shall have intervened.

Section 3: President Incapacitated
The "disability clause" provides for the vice president to act as president if the president informs Congress that he or she is too ill to perform the duties of office.

Section 4: Vice President as Acting President
This section spells out the process by which the vice president takes over as president if the president is unconscious or unable or unwilling to admit that he or she is incapacitated.

Twenty-sixth Amendment (1971) Voting Age

Section 1: The Right to Vote

This amendment lowered the voting age to 18. Previously, the voting age was 21. The amendment was passed and ratified during the Vietnam War, when Americans questioned the fairness of drafting 18-year-olds to fight a war, but not allowing them to vote for the leaders who make decisions about war.

Section 2: Enforcement

Twenty-seventh Amendment (1992) Congressional Pay
If members of Congress vote to raise their own pay, the pay increase cannot go into effect until after the next congressional election. James Madison introduced this amendment in 1789 along with the Bill of Rights. It took over 200 years for it to be ratified by the required number of states.

Glossary

Key Content Terms are in blue type. Social studies terms are in black type.

A

abolition the official end to the practice of slavery

accessibility access for physically disabled people to facilities

accountability the principle that individuals or organizations are responsible for their actions and should be able to show how well they are achieving their goals

acid rain precipitation that contains acid as a result of water vapor mixing with molecules of sulfur dioxide and nitrogen oxide in the atmosphere and that causes water pollution

activist a person dedicated to the cause of reform and prepared to use political action toward that goal

Act of Religious Toleration a law enacted in Maryland in 1649 declaring that all Christian denominations have a right to practice their faith

affirmative action a policy that calls on employers to actively seek to increase the number of minorities in their workforce

Afrocentrism a focus on African history, culture, and achievements of African peoples and their descendants in the United States

ageism discrimination against people on the basis of age

Agent Orange an herbicide used by the U.S. military in Vietnam to kill foliage in an effort to deny cover to the enemy

agitator someone who tries to stir up public feelings about a controversial issue

agribusiness the part of a nation's economy in which agricultural products are produced on a large scale, generally by large corporations or wealthy individuals

Agricultural Adjustment Administration (AAA) as part of the New Deal, a federal agency created by Congress in 1933 to help reduce farmers' crop production and restore the prices of their goods to a reasonable level

Albany Plan of Union a proposal drafted in 1754 by Benjamin Franklin calling for an alliance of the English colonies for their own defense

Alger Hiss case a court case involving Alger Hiss, a U.S. State Department official accused of passing secrets to the Soviet Union, that contributed to a growing fear of subversion during the early Cold War; in 1950 a federal grand jury convicted Hiss of perjury, but his guilt in regard to espionage was not proven

Allied powers the World War I coalition, headed by France, Britain, and Russia and later including Portugal, Japan, and Italy, that opposed the Central powers

Allies the countries that fought against the Central Powers during World War I and the countries that fought against the Axis Powers during World War II

al Qaeda an international terrorist network led until 2011 by Osama bin Laden and that coordinated the attacks on the World Trade Center and the Pentagon on September 11, 2001, the USS *Cole* in 2000, and two U.S. embassies in Africa in 1998, among other activities

America letters letters from immigrants in the United States to friends and relatives in the old country, which spurred further immigration

American Civil Liberties Union (ACLU) an organization founded in 1920 to defend Americans' rights and freedoms as given in the Constitution

American Expeditionary Force (AEF) in World War I, the first U.S. military force to be deployed to France

American Federation of Labor (AFL) a national labor organization, founded in 1886, that consisted mainly of skilled workers and focused on higher wages and shorter workdays

American Indian Movement (AIM) a movement formed in 1968 by Indian activists to protest unfair treatment

Americanization the assimilation of immigrants into American society, a goal of some patriotic groups who feared that increased immigration threatened American society and values

Americans with Disabilities Act (ADA) a law passed by Congress in 1990 requiring better public access and improved education for people with disabilities

amnesty a general pardon for a crime, usual a political one, issued by a government to a specific group of people

Anaconda Plan Civil War strategy devised by President Abraham Lincoln and General Winfield Scott by which Union forces would establish a naval blockade of southern ports and take control of the Mississippi River in order to squeeze in on the South from the east and west and defeat it

anarchist a person who rejects all forms of government

Angel Island Immigration Station the port of entry for most Asian immigrants arriving in San Francisco between 1910 and 1940

annexation the taking control of a territory and adding it to a country

Anti-Defamation League (ADL) an organization founded in 1913 to halt the defamation, or attack on a person's or group's reputation or character, of the Jewish people and to ensure the fair treatment of all Americans

Anti-Imperialist League an organization formed during the Spanish-American War to oppose the establishment of U.S. colonies

anti-Semitism policies, views, and actions that discriminate against Jewish people

Appalachia a mountainous region in the southeastern United States

appeasement yielding to an enemy's demands in order to maintain peace

arable suitable for growing crops

Arab Spring a series of popular revolts against oppressive rulers in North Africa and the Middle East

arbitration a legal process in which a neutral outside party helps resolve a dispute

armament a weapon or piece of equipment used in war

armistice a cessation of hostilities

arms race a competition between nations to achieve the more powerful weapons arsenal

Army of the Republic of Vietnam (ARVN) the army of the government of South Vietnam

arsenal a stockpile of weapons and military equipment or the building in which they are stored

Articles of Confederation the nation's first constitution, which was drafted in 1777 and created a framework for a loose confederation of states

artifact an object made by a human being

assimilation the absorption of people into the dominant culture

Atomic Age the era in which atomic weapons have been used, beginning in 1945 with the first use of the atomic bomb and lasting to the present time

atomic bomb a bomb with explosive power that comes from the energy suddenly released by splitting the nuclei of uranium or plutonium atoms

atomic energy the power released by a nuclear reaction

Axis Powers the alliance between Germany, Italy, and Japan during World War II

baby boom the large increase in the number of babies born in proportion to the size of the population that took place after World War II and lasted until 1964

Back-to-Africa movement a movement, led by Marcus Garvey during the 1910s and 1920s, that promoted the return of blacks living all over the world to Africa

bank run a financial crisis in which a large number of customers simultaneously attempt to withdraw their money from a bank out of fear that the bank will close

Battle of Midway the U.S. naval victory in the Pacific during World War II that stopped Japanese expansion and forced Japan to focus on defense

Battle of Okinawa the U.S. victory in World War II that positioned the Allies for an invasion of Japan

Battle of Saratoga the decisive American victory in 1777 that was a major turning point in the revolution, prompting France and Spain to enter the war against Britain

Battle of Stalingrad a key Soviet victory during World War II that ended Hitler's effort to conquer the USSR

Battle of Yorktown the American victory in 1781 that ended the revolution

battleship the largest and most heavily armored type of warship

Bay of Pigs invasion an invasion of Cuba in 1961, which was authorized by John F. Kennedy for the purpose of overthrowing Castro's regime, organized by the CIA, executed by Cuban exiles, and defeated by Castro's forces

bear market a period in which stock prices are steadily decreasing

belligerent taking part in war

Berlin Blockade the Soviet blockade of the German city of Berlin, implemented from 1948 to 1949 to halt land travel into the city in hopes of forcing the United States, Great Britain, and France to give up their plan to combine their occupation zones into a single, democratic West German state; the Allied nations resisted the blockade by airlifting food and supplies into Berlin

Berlin Wall a concrete wall that the communist East German government erected in 1961 to cut off West Berlin from the rest of East Germany and prevent East Germans from escaping into democratic West Berlin; the wall stood until 1989

Bessemer process a method of steelmaking invented in 1855 that enabled steel to be made more cheaply and quickly

bias a personal leaning or a preference for a particular outlook

bicameral legislature a lawmaking body made up of two houses

bicentennial a 200th anniversary

Big Four at the Paris peace conference, the nickname for the leaders of the four largest victorious nations of World War I, including U.S. president Woodrow Wilson, British prime minister David Lloyd George, French prime minister Georges Clemenceau, and Italian prime minister Vittorio Orlando

Big Stick Policy President Theodore Roosevelt's strong-arm approach to foreign affairs, emphasizing diplomacy backed by force

bilingual education teaching in two languages

birth dearth the drop in the birth rate that resulted when, during the period from 1975 to 1980, many American women began having one or two children instead of three or four children

black blizzard a severe dust storm

black codes laws enacted in 1865 and 1866 in the former Confederate states to restrict freedom and opportunities for African Americans

blacklist a list of people or groups who are under suspicion for something and are thus excluded from certain opportunities

black nationalism a doctrine, promoted by the Nation of Islam, calling for complete separation from white society

Black Panther Party a group founded in 1966 that demanded economic and political rights and was prepared to take violent action

black power the call by many civil rights activists, beginning in the mid-1960s, for African Americans to have economic and political power, with an emphasis on not relying on nonviolent protest

Black Tuesday October 29, 1929; the worst day of plunging stock market prices during the stock market crash that helped initiate the Great Depression

blitzkrieg "lightning war," the German military strategy during World War II of attacking without warning

blue-collar worker a person who works in a factory or at a skilled trade, usually for an hourly wage

bond a certificate issued by a government or company that promises to pay back borrowed money at a fixed rate of interest on a specific date

Bonus Army a group of thousands of World War I veterans who traveled to Washington, D.C., in 1932 to request early payment of a retirement bonus to help them through the hard economic times of the Great Depression

bootlegging the production, transport, and sale of illegal alcohol

Boston Tea Party the dumping of tea in Boston harbor in 1773 to protest the Tea Act

boycott a peaceful protest in which people refuse to buy or use certain goods

breadline a line of needy people waiting for handouts of free food

bread riot during the Civil War, a riot involving hundreds of women in Richmond, Virginia, who sought food and other goods that were becoming scarce in the South as Union forces cut off key parts of the region's economy

brinkmanship a foreign policy characterized by a willingness to push a dangerous situation to the brink, or edge, of war rather than give in to an opponent

broker a person who buys and sells stocks for clients

Brown v. Board of Education the 1954 Supreme Court ruling declaring that segregation in public schools was unconstitutional

budget surplus an excess of income over expenditures

bull market a period in which stock prices are steadily rising

Bush v. Gore immediately after the 2000 election, a lawsuit filed by George W. Bush to halt the recount of votes that opponent Al Gore demanded; the Florida Supreme Court ruled against Bush, but the U.S. Supreme Court ruled in his favor, making him president

business cycle in a capitalist economic system, a recurring cycle of economic growth, decline, panic, and recovery

buying on margin buying stock by paying a percentage of a stock's price and borrowing the rest of the money from a broker, allowing one to make greater profits if the stock does well

C

Camp David Accords brokered by President Jimmy Carter, a 1978 peace agreement between Israeli prime minister Menachem Begin and Egyptian president Anwar el-Sadat in which Israel, which had taken control of the Sinai Peninsula during the Yom Kippur War, agreed to return the land to Egypt, and Egypt agreed to establish normal diplomatic relations with Israel, making it the first Arab country to formally recognize Israel's right to exist

capital any financial asset—including money, machines, and buildings—used in production

capitalism an economic system in which factories, equipment, and other means of production are privately owned rather than controlled by government

cede to give up or grant land to another country, typically by treaty

censure to formally scold someone

census an official count of a population conducted at set time intervals

Central powers the World War I coalition, headed by Germany and Austria-Hungary and later including the Ottoman Empire and Bulgaria, that opposed the Allied powers

Charleston a dance that originated as an African American folk dance in the South and became popular throughout the United States and Europe during the Roaring Twenties

checks and balances the system by which each branch of the federal government can limit, or check, the power of the others

chemical weapon a weapon that contains a poisonous substance

chief executive the president and the head of the executive branch

child labor the practice of using children as manual laborers

Chinese Exclusion Act an 1882 law prohibiting immigration of Chinese laborers for 10 years and preventing Chinese already in the country from becoming citizens; the first U.S. immigration restriction based solely on nationality or race

Chisholm Trail the cattle-drive trail from San Antonio, Texas, to Abilene, Kansas

chronicle an account of events listed in chronological order

chronology the order in which events occur, or the arrangement of events in the order in which they occur

civil defense the organization and training of citizens to work with the armed forces and emergency services during a war or natural disaster

civil disobedience the nonviolent refusal to obey a law that the protester considers to be unjust

Civilian Conservation Corps (CCC) a work-relief program established in 1933, as part of the First Hundred Days of the New Deal, to provide work for unemployed Americans during the Great Depression

civil liberty a basic right guaranteed to individual citizens by law

civil right a right that is guaranteed to all citizens of a country

Civil Rights Act of 1964 a landmark act that banned discrimination on the basis of race, sex, religion, or national origin; the most important civil rights law since Reconstruction

Civil Rights Act of 1968 a law that included a ban on discrimination in the sale, rental, and financing of housing based on race, religion, national origin, or sex

civil service nonmilitary government employees

class-action lawsuit a lawsuit filed by people on behalf of themselves and a larger group who might benefit

Clean Water Act a law passed by Congress in 1972 to limit the amount of sewage and other pollutants flowing into waterways

clemency the act of lessening a punishment

Cold War the hostile but nonviolent struggle for power between the United States and the Soviet Union, as well as their respective allies, from the end of World War II to the collapse of the Soviet Union in 1991

collective bargaining negotiations between employers and employees concerning wages, working conditions, and other terms of employment

collective security a system in which a group of countries commit to jointly dealing with a nation that threatens the peace or security of any one of the countries

collectivism an economic system in which the people, often under supervision of the state, jointly own the means of production and distribution

color line a barrier—created by custom, law, and economic differences—that separated whites from nonwhites

combatant a person who physically fights a war

Committee on Public Information (CPI) a government agency created by President Woodrow Wilson in 1917, during World War I, to promote pro-war propaganda to the American public

committees of correspondence groups of letter writers who spread news about British actions throughout the colonies

Common Sense a pamphlet written by Thomas Paine in 1776 making an influential argument for independence

commune in U.S. history, a group-owned living arrangement in which members share responsibilities and decision making, which became popular in the 1960s

communism an economic or political system in which the state or the community owns all property and the means of production, and all citizens share the wealth

communist sympathizer a person who believes in communist ideology but is not a member of the Communist Party

comparable worth the argument that jobs typically held by women should command as much pay as jobs typically held by men that require comparable education and training

Compromise of 1850 measures passed by Congress in 1850 to admit California into the Union as a free state, to divide the rest of the Southwest into the New Mexico and Utah territories, with the people there determining for themselves through popular sovereignty whether or not to accept slavery, to ban slavery in Washington, D.C., and to establish a new, stronger fugitive slave law

concurrent power a power that the Constitution delegates, or grants, to Congress but does not deny to the states

confederation an alliance of independent governments

Congress the legislative branch of the federal government, consisting of the Senate and House of Representatives

Congress of Industrial Organizations (CIO) a labor organization established in 1938 to organize workers by industry rather than by occupation or skill

Congress of Racial Equality (CORE) an organization founded in 1942 that was dedicated to civil rights reform through nonviolent action

conscientious objector a person who opposes war for religious or moral reasons and therefore refuses to serve in the armed forces

conservation the limited use of natural resources

conservative someone who cherishes and seeks to preserve traditional customs and values

consolidation the merging of two businesses

Constitutional Convention the convention held in Philadelphia in 1787 to draft the Constitution of the United States

Constitution of the United States the plan of government of the United States, drafted by the Constitutional Convention in 1787 to replace the Articles of Confederation

consumer culture a culture that views the consumption of large quantities of goods as beneficial to the economy and a source of personal happiness

consumerism the protection of the rights of consumers

consumer price index a measure of the cost of basic necessities, such as food and housing

containment after World War II, the U.S. foreign policy practice of attempting to restrict the expansion of Soviet influence around the world

contempt of Congress willful failure to obey the authority of Congress

contract laborer an immigrant who signed a contract in Europe to work for an American employer, often to replace a striking worker

Contract with America during the 1994 midterm election campaign, the Republicans' promise that, if elected, they would strive to balance the federal budget, combat crime, reform the welfare system, cut taxes, create jobs, and minimize lawsuits

Contras U.S.-backed rebels who were attempting to overthrow the leftist Sandinista government of Nicaragua

convoy a group of vessels or vehicles that travel together, often under the protection of an armed escort

Copperhead during the Civil War, a nickname Republicans used to describe those Northerners, mostly Democrats, who opposed the war and were sympathetic to the South

corporation a company recognized by law to exist independently from its owners, with the ability to own property, borrow money, sue, or be sued

cost-of-living index a measure of the differences in the price of goods and services over time

cotton gin invented by Eli Whitney in 1793, a machine that removes the seeds from cotton

counterculture a group in society with ideas and behaviors very different from those of the larger mainstream culture

counteroffensive a large-scale military counterattack by a force that was previously on the defensive

coup d'état the sudden overthrow of a government by violent force

covert action a secret political, economic, or military operation that aims to shape events or influence affairs in a foreign country in order to support the initiating nation's foreign policy

creationism the belief that God created the universe

credibility gap the difference between the reality of the Vietnam War and the Johnson administration's positive portrayal of it

credit an arrangement for buying something now with borrowed money and paying off the loan over time

Cuban missile crisis a confrontation between the United States and the Soviet Union in fall 1962 over the building of Soviet missile-launching sites in Cuba, in response to which the United States established a quarantine to prevent Soviet ships from transporting missiles to Cuba and to demand withdrawal of all Soviet weapons from the island; after a few days, the Soviet Union agreed to withdraw its missiles and President John Kennedy agreed not to invade

D

Dawes Act an 1887 federal law distributing land to individual Indians rather than to tribes, thereby encouraging Indians to become assimilated

Dawes Plan developed by banker Charles Dawes, a plan for Germany to pay reparations after World War I by receiving loans from the United States

D-Day June 6, 1944, the day that the Allied invasion of German-occupied France began

debt ceiling legal limit on the amount of money that the federal government can borrow

debt peonage a system of servitude in which debtors are forced to work for the person to whom they owe money until they pay off the debt

Declaration of Independence the document approved in 1776 by the Second Continental Congress declaring that the 13 former colonies were free and independent states

de facto segregation segregation established by practice and custom, rather than by law

deficit spending a government's practice of spending more money than it receives in revenue, the difference being made up by borrowing

de jure segregation segregation by law

delegated power a power that the Constitution delegates, or grants, to Congress and therefore to the national government

demagogue a political leader who gains power by appealing to people's emotions and prejudices rather than relying on rational argument

demilitarized zone (DMZ) an area, often along the border between two military powers, that no military forces are allowed to enter

demobilization the act of discharging forces from military service or use

democracy a system of government in which the power to rule comes from the consent of the governed

Democratic Party one of the two major U.S. political parties; founded in 1828 by Andrew Jackson to support a decentralized government and states' rights

Department of Homeland Security (DHS) a cabinet-level department of the federal government that Congress created after the September 11, 2001, terrorist attacks to coordinate 22 security-related federal agencies in order to prevent terrorist attacks and protect Americans in case of threats

depopulation the loss of residents from an area

deportation a forced return of immigrants to their home country

deregulation the reduction or removal of government regulations on business to promote economic efficiency and free enterprise

desertification a process by which land becomes increasingly dry and desert-like

détente the relaxation of Cold War tensions between the United States and the Soviet Union and between the United States and China that began under President Richard Nixon

deterrence a foreign policy in which a nation develops a weapons arsenal so deadly that another nation will not dare attack

developed country a country this is wealthy and has extensive industrialization

developing country a country that is poor and has little or no industrialization

dictatorship a system of government in which power is seized and exercised by force

diplomacy the art of conducting negotiations with other nations

direct action political acts, including protests of all types, designed to have an immediate impact

disability an impairment that limits a person's daily activities

disarmament the process of reducing the number of weapons in a nation's arsenal or the size of its armed forces

discount rate the rate of interest at which banks that belong to the Federal Reserve System can borrow money from Federal Reserve banks

disenfranchise to deny voting rights

division of labor a method in which factory production is divided into separate tasks, with one task assigned to each worker

Dollar Diplomacy President William Howard Taft's approach to foreign policy, focusing on encouraging and protecting U.S. trade and investment in Latin America and Asia

domino theory the belief that if Vietnam fell to the communists, the rest of Southeast Asia would fall like "a row of dominoes"

Double V campaign a campaign in which black leaders called for all citizens to fight against racism by seeking a "double victory"—a victory for democracy at home and abroad

Dow Jones Industrial Average a commonly used daily measure of stock prices

draft riots a series of deadly riots that took place in U.S. cities in 1863 to protest the newly established military draft

Dred Scott decision the 1857 ruling of the Supreme Court in the case Scott v. Sandford that legalized slavery in the territories and declared the Missouri Compromise unconstitutional

due process of law a system in which government cannot deprive a person of life, liberty, or property except according to rules established by law

Dust Bowl an area of the Great Plains of the United States that suffered severely from wind erosion during the 1930s

E

Earth Day an annual holiday to bring people together to show their concern for a healthful environment, the establishment of which in 1970 signaled the emergence of a new environmental movement

economic depression a drastic decline in the economy, marked by business failures and unemployment

Economic Opportunity Act a law passed by Congress in 1964 to create dozens of federal antipoverty programs, including the Job Corps and VISTA, and the Office of Economic Opportunity to oversee them

Eighteenth Amendment a constitutional change ratified in 1919 prohibiting the manufacture, sale, or transportation of alcoholic beverages; repealed by the Twenty-first Amendment in 1933

elastic clause the constitutional clause that gives Congress authority to "make all laws which shall be necessary and proper" to carry out its powers

Electoral College a body made up of electors from each state who cast votes to elect the president and vice president

electorate the body of officially qualified voters in a country or other voting area

Ellis Island Immigration Station the port of entry for most European immigrants arriving in New York between 1892 and 1954

emancipation the act of freeing slaves from bondage

Emancipation Proclamation an edict issued by President Abraham Lincoln on January 1, 1863, to free the slaves in the Confederate states

embargo a government order that restricts or prohibits trade of a particular good or with a particular nation

empathy the ability to imagine oneself in another's place in order to understand the person's feelings, desire, ideas, and actions

energy crisis an energy shortage in fall 1973 that resulted from oil-exporting nations of the Middle East halting their shipping of oil to the United States to protest U.S. support of Israel in its conflict with its Arab neighbors

English Bill of Rights an act passed by Parliament in 1689 further limiting the monarch's power by giving Parliament the sole power to tax and specifying citizens' rights, such as trial by jury and protection from cruel and unusual punishment

entrepreneur a bold, ambitious person who establishes a new business

environmentalism a movement that works to protect the environment from harmful human activities

Environmental Protection Agency (EPA) a government agency created by Congress in 1970 to protect Americans' health and the natural environment by setting and enforcing pollution standards

equality the state of having the same privileges, rights, status, and opportunities as others

equal rights amendment (ERA) a proposed but unratified Constitutional amendment first introduced in 1923 by Alice Paul for the purpose of guaranteeing equal rights for all Americans regardless of gender

escalate increase, as in to increase military involvement

espionage the use of spying to gather information

Espionage Act a law passed by Congress in 1917 to make it illegal to spy, interfere with government foreign policy, or resist the military draft

Establishment a term used by members of the counterculture of the 1960s to describe the people and institutions who, in their view, controlled society

establishment clause a clause within the First Amendment to the Constitution that states that "Congress shall make no law respecting the establishment of religion"

ethnic cleansing the forced removal and murder of ethnic groups from a region

ethnicity a person's ethnic identity, which may be shaped by such criteria as language, religion, and history

eugenics the idea that the human species should be improved by permitting only people with characteristics judged desirable to reproduce

European Union (EU) established in 1992 by 12 Western European countries, this alliance was designed to advance Europe's economic integration and unify its laws and foreign policies; expansions in 2004 and 2007 added 12 new members, mainly nations from the former Soviet bloc

eviction the legal process by which a landlord removes a tenant from his or her property, usually because the tenant has failed to pay rent

evidence information that can be used to prove a statement or support a conclusion

Executive Order 9066 an executive order issued by FDR in 1942 allowing internment camps to be set up to exclude current residents believed to be a threat to security

Executive Order 9981 an executive order issued by President Harry S. Truman in 1948 ending segregation in the military

executive privilege a president's right to withhold information under certain circumstances

exile a person who, for personal or political reasons, lives outside his or her home country, either by choice or by order of the home country's government

Exodusters African Americans who migrated from the South to the Great Plains following the Civil War

extractive industry businesses that take mineral resources from the earth

extremism the advocacy of radical measures

faction a group of people who form a minority within a larger group and that have interests or beliefs that do not entirely agree with those of the larger group

factors of production land, labor, and capital

factory system a manufacturing system in which products are created on a large scale by using machines in factories, rather than by individuals

Fair Deal President Harry S. Truman's domestic program, which he began promoting in 1945 with such intentions as increasing the minimum wage, increasing aid to agriculture and education, and enacting a national heath insurance program, only some of which Congress approved

Family Assistance Plan a proposal by President Richard Nixon, which was rejected by Congress, under which the government would have supported every poor family with a minimum annual income

fascism a political movement based on an extreme nationalism in which the state comes first and individual liberty is secondary

federal budget deficit a shortfall that results when federal spending exceeds federal tax revenues in a given year

Federal Civil Defense Administration (FCDA) a federal agency established by Congress in 1951 to plan for civil defense during the arms race by preparing Americans to survive a nuclear attack

federal judiciary the federal court system, consisting of the Supreme Court and lower federal courts

Federal Reserve System the central banking authority of the United States, which manages the nation's money supply

federalism the division of power between the federal and state governments

feminism the movement for women's equality

Fifteenth Amendment a constitutional change ratified in 1870 granting black males the right to vote

54th Massachusetts Regiment in the Civil War, the first entirely African American regiment of the Union Army

filibuster a tactic in which a member of a legislature speaks at great length to prevent legislative action

First Hundred Days the first three months of Franklin D. Roosevelt's presidency, during which Congress passed a record number of bills in order to implement the New Deal and provide relief, recovery, and reform from the Great Depression

First Indochina War the war between the Viet Minh and the French from 1946 to 1954

fiscal policy the approach of a government to taxes and government spending

flapper during the Roaring Twenties, a young woman who broke with traditional expectations for how women should dress and behave

Florida Land Boom a 1920s get-rich-quick scheme in which real estate developers sold many Florida coast lots, some undesirable, to speculators in other parts of the country, causing prices to raise rapidly

foreclosure the legal process by which a lender takes over a property it has helped a borrower buy, usually because the buyer has failed to make payments

foreign policy the set of guidelines and practices that a nation follows in its relations with other nations

Fort Sumter a federal fort in the harbor of Charleston, South Carolina, at which the first battle of the Civil War took place on April 12, 1861

fossil fuel a fuel that contains carbon and is derived from the decomposed remains of prehistoric plants and animals

Four Freedoms essential freedoms identified by FDR in a 1941 speech and later incorporated into the UN charter: freedom of speech and expression, freedom of worship, freedom from want, and freedom from fear

Fourteen Points at the end of World War I, a 14-part plan for peace presented by President Woodrow Wilson to Congress on January 8, 1918

Fourteenth Amendment a constitutional change ratified in 1868 granting citizenship to all former slaves by declaring that anyone born in the United States is a citizen; it also extended to blacks the rights of due process of law and equal protection under the law

franchise an agreement to operate a business that carries a company's name and sells its products

freedman a man who has been freed from slavery

Freedmen's Bureau a federal agency established in 1865, at the end of the Civil War, to help and protect the 4 million newly freed black Americans as they transitioned out of enslavement

freedom of the seas the principle that merchant ships have a right to travel freely and unthreatened in international waters in times of peace and war

Freedom Rides civil rights protests in which blacks and whites rode interstate buses together in 1961 to test whether southern states were complying with the Supreme Court ruling against segregation on interstate transport

Freedom Summer a 1964 campaign by CORE and SNCC to register black voters in Mississippi

free enterprise system an economic system that relies on private ownership of property, competition for profits, and the forces of supply and demand to produce needed goods and services and that discourages government regulation; also known as capitalism

Free Speech Movement a student movement that developed in 1964 at University of California at Berkeley in protest of a university rule that banned political activities on campus and that eventually persuaded the university to overturn the ban

free-trade zone a defined geographic area in which governments lower or eliminate tariffs and other barriers to international trade

Fugitive Slave Law a law first passed by Congress in 1793 to allow the seizure and return of slaves who escaped into another state or a federal territory; Congress passed a second version of the law in 1850 to establish fines on federal officials who refused to enforce the law or from whom a runaway slave escaped, to establish fines on individuals who helped slaves escape, to ban runaway slaves from testifying on their own behalf in court, and to give special commissioners power to enforce the law

fundamentalism the belief that scripture should be read as the literal word of God and followed without question

general strike a strike, or work stoppage intended to achieve a particular objective, conducted by the majority of workers in all of a region's industries

generation gap a difference in attitudes and behaviors between youth and their parents

Geneva Accords the 1954 agreement between France and the Viet Minh to split Vietnam along the 17th parallel and to schedule national elections in 1956 to reunify Vietnam

Geneva Conventions a series of international agreements that set rules for proper conduct toward sick and wounded enemy soldiers and the civilians who take care of them

genocide the systematic killing of a racial, political, or cultural group

gerrymandering the practice of redrawing the lines of a voting district to give one party or group of voters an unfair advantage

Gettysburg Address an inspirational speech given by President Abraham Lincoln on November 19, 1863, at the Civil War battle site of Gettysburg, Pennsylvania, in memory of the Union soldiers who died there trying, in Lincoln's words, to protect the ideal of freedom upon which the United States had been founded

ghetto a part of a city where people belonging to a single ethnic group live

GI a nickname for U.S. soldiers during World War II, derived from the GI ("government issue") label on many of their supplies

GI Bill of Rights a law passed in 1994 to provide federal funds to help returning GIs make the transition to civilian life

glass ceiling an invisible barrier to professional advancement of women and minorities

globalization the integration of the cultures, economies, and politics of nations around the world

gold standard a monetary policy requiring that every paper dollar in circulation be backed by a dollar's worth of gold in the U.S. Treasury

graduated income tax an income tax requiring people with higher incomes to pay a larger percentage of their earnings than people with lower incomes

grandfather clause a provision in a law that exempts anyone already involved in a certain activity from any new restrictions on the activity that are established by the law

The Grapes of Wrath a novel, written by John Steinbeck and published in 1939, that won acclaim for its description of the experience of Dust Bowl migrants during the Great Depression

grassroots organization an organization created and run by its members, as opposed to a strong central leader

Gray Panthers an organization formed in 1972 to speak out against unfair treatment of older Americans

Great Awakening a period of religious revival during the early 1700s that encouraged people to question authority and to think freely about religious matters

Great Compromise the compromise reached during the Constitutional Convention on representation in Congress, with each state represented equally in the Senate and with representation in the House based on state population

Great Flood of 1936 devastating flooding in New England that resulted from a series of record-breaking storms that pounded the region daily between March 9 and March 22, 1936

Great Migration beginning during World War I, the mass movement of millions of African Americans from the rural South to cities in the North and Midwest in order to take jobs in industry

Great Society President Lyndon Johnson's domestic reform program from 1965 to 1969, which focused on social welfare improvements, with the War on Poverty at its centerpiece, and almost all of which Congress passed

gridlock the inability to make progress; in political terms, especially related to lack of progress of legislation in Congress

gross domestic product (GDP) the total value of the goods and services produced in a country in a year

gross national product (GNP) the total value of goods and services produced in a country in a year

guerrilla warfare hit-and-run attacks by small, mobile groups of soldiers

Gulf of Tonkin Resolution the resolution passed by Congress in 1964 giving President Lyndon Johnson broad powers to expand the U.S. role in Vietnam

H

habeas corpus the right of a person being detained to appear in court so that a judge may determine whether the person has been imprisoned lawfully

Hamdan v. Rumsfeld a 2006 Supreme Court case that declared that President George W. Bush did not have constitutional authority to set up military commissions

Harlem Renaissance an era of heightened creativity among African American writers, artists, and musicians who gathered in Harlem during the 1920s

Hawley-Smoot Tariff Act a law passed by Congress in 1930 to raise the tariffs on imported goods in order to protect U.S. businesses and farmers

Haymarket Affair a violent clash in 1886 between union supporters and Chicago police that divided and weakened the labor movement

H-bomb a hydrogen bomb, or a bomb created by fusing atoms; more powerful than an atomic bomb, a weapon of mass destruction that the United States first tested in 1952 as part of the arms race

hegemony the dominating influence of one country or group over others

hippie in the 1960s, a young person who took part in a counterculture that rebelled against the social expectations of the older generation and that supported love, peace, and freedom

historical interpretation the process of finding the meaning or significance of historical events

HIV/AIDS a disease that attacks the immune system, making it much harder for the body to fight illness

holding company a corporation that owns or controls other companies by buying up their stock

Holocaust the systematic, state-sponsored persecution and murder of Jews and other minority groups by the Nazis

Homestead Act an 1862 federal law that granted tracts of land called homesteads to western settlers who agreed to work the land and live on it for five years

Homestead Strike an 1892 Carnegie Steel plant workers' strike that was broken by the state militia and resulted in the union being shut out of the plant for four decades

Hooverville during the Great Depression, a shantytown of makeshift dwellings

horizontal integration a corporate expansion strategy that involves joining together as many firms from the same industry as possible

hotline a communication line between the United States and the Soviet Union that is kept open at all times so they can contact each other instantly during a crisis

House of Burgesses the first legislature in the English colonies in America, formed in 1619

House Un-American Activities Committee (HUAC) formed in 1938, a committee of the U.S. House of Representatives that investigated subversive organizations in the United States until 1975

Housing Act of 1949 a law passed by Congress in 1949 to create public housing and urban renewal programs in order to help all Americans live in decent conditions

howitzer a type of cannon

Hull House the first settlement house in Chicago, founded by Jane Addams

humanitarian aid money, food, and other forms of assistance given to people in need

human rights rights that are regarded as belonging to all people, such as the right to life, liberty, and equality before the law, as well as freedom of religion, expression, and assembly

ideal a principle or standard of perfection that a person or group consistently tries to achieve

idealism in foreign policy, the belief that moral values should influence international relations

ideology a set of basic ideas, beliefs, and values that form the basis of a social, economic, or political philosophy or program

Immigration Act of 1965 a law passed by Congress in 1965 to eliminate immigration quotas based on country of origin and to make a person's skills and ties to family in the United States the key criteria for admission into the country

impeach to charge a government official with an offense committed while in office

imperialism empire building

improvisation a process by which musicians make up music as they play rather than relying solely on printed scores

incriminate to provide evidence that makes someone appear guilty

indentured servant a settler who voluntarily gave up freedom for five to seven years in exchange for passage to America

independent judiciary a system in which judges cannot be removed or have their salaries reduced for making unpopular decisions

Indian Removal Act a law passed by Congress in 1830 to authorize the forced resettlement of Indian tribes living east of the Mississippi River in an area west of the Mississippi known as Indian Territory (later to become Oklahoma)

industrialization the transformation from producing goods by hand to producing goods by machine

infantry soldiers who fight on foot

inflation an increase in the supply of money or credit relative to the availability of goods and services, resulting in generally higher prices

infrastructure the facilities or equipment required for an organization or community to function, including roads, sewage and power systems, and transportation

INF Treaty See **Intermediate-Range Nuclear Forces Treaty**

inheritance tax a tax charged on assets inherited from someone who has died

initiative a lawmaking reform enabling citizens to propose and pass a law directly without the state legislature

installment buying an arrangement in which a buyer makes a down payment on a product to be purchased and the seller loans the remainder of the purchase price to the buyer; the purchaser must pay back the loan over time, in monthly installments, or the seller can reclaim the product

insurgency rebellion

insurrection a rebellion

intelligent design a theory that states that some features of the natural world are too complex to have evolved by means of natural selection, so they must have been designed by an intelligent agent, but does not state who or what that intelligent agent might be

interest the charge made by a bank for the use of money deposited in an account

Intermediate-Range Nuclear Forces Treaty (INF Treaty) the treaty signed by Reagan and Gorbachev in 1987, in which the two leaders agreed to remove and destroy all missiles with a range between 300 and 3,400 miles

International Criminal Court (ICC) a permanent international tribunal established in 1998, with the power to try people accused of genocide, crimes against humanity, war crimes, and the crime of aggression. More than half of the world's nations, including the United States, have not joined the ICC.

internationalist at the close of World War I, one of the Democratic senators who strongly supported the Treaty of Versailles

internment camp a center for confining people who have been relocated for reasons of national security

interstate commerce trade between states

interstate highway system authorized by Congress in 1956, a network of highways that connect major cities around the country; all highways are built under the same guidelines, so that each has at least two lanes in each direction, periodic rest areas for travelers, and no traffic lights or railroad crossings

Intolerable Acts laws passed by Parliament in 1774 to punish Massachusetts for the Boston Tea Party by closing Boston harbor, shutting shown civilian courts, forcing colonists to house British troops, and placing the colony under the rule of an appointed governor

Iran-Contra Affair a scandal in which officials in the Reagan administration sold arms to Iran to help gain the release of U.S. hostages and sent money from the arms sales to the Contras in Nicaragua

Iron Curtain the ideological barrier that existed between Eastern and Western Europe from 1945 to 1990

irreconcilable at the close of World War I, one of 16 Republican senators who opposed the Treaty of Versailles

isolationism a government policy of not taking part in economic and political alliances or relations with other countries

J

Japanese American Citizens League (JACL) an organization formed in 1929 to defend the rights of Japanese Americans

jazz a music form developed by African Americans beginning in the 1910s and influenced by blues, ragtime, and European and African musical traditions

Jazz Age the era during the 1920s in which jazz became increasingly popular in the United States

Jim Crow law any of the laws legalizing racial segregation of blacks and whites that were enacted in Southern states beginning in the 1880s and enforced through the 1950s

John Brown's raid a raid led by abolitionist John Brown in 1856 in hopes of seizing the federal arsenal at Harper's Ferry, Virginia, in order to distribute the weapons to slaves in the area and spark a slave revolt; the attempt failed when federal troops captured the men, leading to Brown's execution for treason

judicial review the power of the Supreme Court to review an action of the legislative or executive branch and declare it unconstitutional

The Jungle Upton Sinclair's 1906 novel about unsanitary conditions in meatpacking plants

K

kamikaze a Japanese strategy during World War II, in which suicide pilots flew bomb-filled planes directly into the vessels of the Allied fleet

Kansas-Nebraska Act a law passed by Congress in 1854 to establish Kansas and Nebraska as territories with popular sovereignty

Kellogg-Briand Pact an agreement made among most nations of the world in 1928 to try to settle international disputes by peaceful means rather than war

Kent State shootings the killing of four protesters at Kent State University in 1970 by National Guard troops; reports of the shootings led to increased antiwar protests

Kerner Commission the National Advisory Commission on Civil Disorders that concluded that white racism was the fundamental cause of the Watts riot

Korean War a war fought on the Korean Peninsula from 1950 to 1953 after troops from communist North Korea, armed with Soviet weapons, invaded democratic South Korea, prompting the United States and the United Nations to send forces to support South Korea and fight to unify the Korean Peninsula into one democratic nation, which in turn prompted China to join the war on North Korea's side; at war's end, the peninsula remained divided into two nations

Korematsu v. United States the 1944 Supreme Court decision declaring that the government had the right to keep Japanese Americans in internment camps

Ku Klux Klan established in 1866, a secret, white supremacist terrorist group that resisted Reconstruction by tormenting black Americans

L

labor union a group of workers organized to protect the interests of its members

laissez-faire the idea that the free market, through supply and demand, will regulate itself if government does not interfere

landform a natural feature of Earth's surface, such as a mountain or valley

land mine an explosive device buried just below the ground, designed to blow up when stepped on

League of Nations an international organization established by the Allied powers at the close of World War I to promote international peace and security

League of Women Voters formed in 1920, a grassroots organization created to influence government and public policy by educating voters about public issues

leapfrogging an American strategy in the Pacific during World War II in which islands heavily defended by the Japanese were bypassed in order to capture nearby islands that were not well defended

left wing the liberal side of the political spectrum

legacy a person's impact on future generations

legislative agenda the list of programs a president hopes to enact while in office

legislature a group of people chosen to make laws

legitimacy the right to exercise power

Lemon test instituted by the Supreme Court in the 1971 case Lemon v. Kurtzman, a three-point assessment used to determine whether a government action violates the First Amendment's ban on any "law respecting an establishment of religion"; the assessment states that to be constitutional, a government action must (1) have a nonreligious purpose, (2) neither help nor hurt religion, and (3) not result in an "excessive entanglement" of government and religion

Lend-Lease Act legislation passed by Congress in 1941 adopting a plan to lend arms to Britain

Levittown the first planned community in the nation, built between 1947 and 1951 in Long Island, New York, to relieve the housing shortage of the Great Depression and World War II years

liberal someone committed to the expansion of liberty

liberty freedom

Liberty Bond a government-issued bond sold during World War I to raise money for the Allied war effort

life expectancy the average age that a person in a given population can expect to live

literacy test a test of one's ability to read and write

living wage a wage high enough to provide an acceptable standard of living

lobbyist a person who tries to persuade legislators to pass laws favorable to a particular group

Lost Generation a group of young Americans—including E. E. Cummings, Ernest Hemingway, F. Scott Fitzgerald, John Dos Passos, and Sherwood Anderson—who established themselves as prominent postwar writers during the 1920s

loyalty oath a pledge of loyalty to a group, such as an organization or a nation

Lusitania an unarmed British ocean liner whose sinking by a German U-boat on May 7, 1915, influenced the U.S. decision to enter World War I

lynch to kill someone without approval by law, often by hanging and by a mob of people

M

Magna Carta the agreement made in 1215 between King John and his barons listing rights granted by the monarch to all free men of the kingdom

mainstreamed included in classrooms with nondisabled students

male chauvinist a person who believes that men are superior to women

malnutrition a physical condition that results from a person not eating an adequately healthful diet

mandate the authority bestowed on a government or candidate by an electoral victory

mandates the former colonies given over by the League of Nations to France and Britain to administer

Manhattan Project the top-secret U.S. government project that developed the atomic bomb

manifest destiny the belief, held by many Americans in the 1840s, that the United States was destined to spread across the North American continent and beyond

March on Washington a 1963 protest in which more than 250,000 people demonstrated in the nation's capital for "jobs and freedom" and the passage of civil rights legislation

market economy a type of economy in which prices and wages are determined mainly by supply and demand

market revolution the transition of a society from having a traditional economy to a market economy

Marshall Court the Supreme Court during John Marshall's term as chief justice, from 1801 to 1835

Marshall Plan a U.S. plan, initiated by Secretary of State George Marshall and implemented from 1948 to 1951, to aid in the economic recovery of Europe after World War II by offering certain European countries substantial funds

mass media newspapers, magazines, and other methods of communicating to a mass audience

mass production the manufacturing of goods on a large scale in factories

materiel military equipment and supplies

Mayflower Compact the first written framework for self-government in what is now the United States, made by the Mayflower passengers in 1620

McCarthyism the practice of publicly accusing people of subversive activities without evidence to back up the charges; named for Senator Joseph McCarthy, who began such a practice in the early 1950s as part of the search for communists in the United States during the early Cold War

median income average pay

Medicaid a health insurance program that is jointly financed by federal and state governments and that covers low-income people as well as older Americans who have used up their Medicare benefits

Medicare a federal health insurance program that pays for hospital and nursing home services for U.S. citizens 65 years or older

mercenary a professional soldier for hire

Meuse-Argonne Offensive in World War I, the final Allied offensive that brought about the end of the war

Mexican War the war with Mexico from 1846 to 1847, resulting in Mexico ceding to the United States a huge region from Texas to California

MIA missing in action

midterm election an election that takes place halfway between presidential elections to select members of Congress, state legislatures, and governors

militarism the glorification of military power and values

military adviser a noncombat specialist who trains and equips another nation's soldiers

military commission a court set up by the armed forces to try enemy forces during wartime

Military Commissions Act of 2006 a law passed by Congress to authorize the use of military commissions to try enemy combatants and set out rules for such trials; amended in 2009 to increase the rights of the accused to bring them more into line with regular military courts and federal criminal courts

military draft a system of requiring by law that all people who meet certain criteria, such as age and gender, report for military duty

militias groups of citizens who volunteer to be soldiers during emergencies

Miranda rights the rights of a person accused of a crime to remain silent and to have a lawyer present when being questioned

miscegenation interracial marriage

Missouri Compromise measures passed by Congress in 1820 to admit Missouri into the Union as a slave state and Maine as a free state while also setting a line at latitude 36°30′ (Missouri's southern border) north of which all Louisiana Purchase territory would be free

mixed economy an economy combining elements of free enterprise and central planning

mobilization the assembling of troops and equipment for war

mobilize to organize people or resources for action, such as war

modernist a person who embraces new ideas, styles, and social trends

Molotov Plan a Soviet plan, initiated by Soviet foreign minister Vyacheslav Molotov in 1949, to aid in the economic recovery of Eastern Europe after World War II by establishing the Council for Mutual Economic Assistance to create two-way trade agreements between the Soviet Union and other COMECON members and to integrate members' economies

monarchy a system of government in which the ruler inherits the right to rule and has power for life

monetary policy government policy aimed at controlling the supply and value of a country's currency

monopoly a company that completely dominates a particular industry

Monroe Doctrine the declaration by President James Monroe in 1823 warning European powers against future colonization in the Western Hemisphere or interference in Latin American republics

Montgomery Bus Boycott a 1955 boycott that resulted in the integration of Montgomery, Alabama's bus system

Moral Diplomacy President Woodrow Wilson's approach to foreign policy, focusing on promoting democratic ideals abroad

Moral Majority a lobbying group founded by Reverend Jerry Falwell in 1979 to give evangelical Christians a stronger political voice

moratorium a suspension of activity

muckraker a journalist who wrote about social, environmental, and political problems Americans faced in the early 1900s

multinational corporation a company with facilities in more than one country

Munich Pact the 1938 agreement in which Britain and France appeased Hitler by agreeing that Germany could annex the Sudetenland, a German-speaking region of Czechoslovakia

Mutual Assured Destruction (MAD) during the arms race between the United States and the Soviet Union, the principle that either side would respond to a nuclear attack by launching its own missiles, which helped prevent the Cold War from becoming a hot war

My Lai Massacre a massacre of hundreds of Vietnamese civilians in 1968; reports of the killings shocked Americans and increased opposition to the war

N

napalm jellied gasoline dropped from U.S. planes during the Vietnam War as an incendiary bomb designed to burn forests and destroy enemy installations

National Aeronautics and Space Administration (NASA) a U.S. government agency established in 1958 for the research and development of space exploration vehicles and projects

National American Woman Suffrage Association (NAWSA) a group formed by leading suffragists in the late 1800s to organize the women's suffrage movement

National Association for the Advancement of Colored People (NAACP) a group formed in 1909 to fight through the courts to end segregation and ensure that African American men could exercise voting rights under the Fifteenth Amendment

National Child Labor Committee a progressive organization formed in 1904 to promote laws restricting or banning child labor

national debt the sum of all loans taken out by the federal government to finance its annual deficits

National Energy Act a law passed by Congress in 1978 to offer tax credits to people who conserved energy by insulating their homes or investing in alternative energy sources, such as solar energy, in hopes of reducing U.S. dependence on imported oil

National Industrial Recovery Act (NIRA) as part of the New Deal, a law passed by Congress in 1933 to increase production while boosting wages and prices; it created the National Recovery Administration

national interest the political, economic, military, and cultural goals that a nation considers important

nationalism a strong feeling of pride in and loyalty to one's nation

National Organization for Women (NOW) a group formed in 1966 to advance women's rights

national security letter (NSL) a document that allows federal agencies, when pursuing a terrorism-related investigation, to secretly gain access to a variety of records held by "third party" sources such as banks, phone companies, and Internet providers

National Women's Political Caucus (NWPC) formed in 1971 by feminist leaders, an influential organization that worked to get more women elected to office and supported male candidates who took a strong stand on women's issues

nation building the process of constructing political institutions and a stable government in a country

Nation of Islam a religious group, also known as the Black Muslims, that promoted complete separation from white society by establishing black businesses, schools, and communities

nation-state an independent country populated mainly by citizens who share a common culture, history, and language

nativism the policy of favoring the interests of native-born Americans over those of immigrants

natural resource a substance found in nature, such as iron or water, that can be used by people

natural right a power or privilege held to be common to all people and granted at birth by nature, not by society

naval blockade a military maneuver in which one side sets up a line of ships to block entry into or departure from the ports of the opposing side

Nazism a form of fascism that promoted the belief that Germans and other Nordic peoples were superior to other races

neoconservative a person who began to hold economically, socially, and politically conservative views during the 1980s, in response to the liberalism of the 1960s and 1970s

neutrality the policy of not taking sides in wars between other nations

neutrality acts legislation passed by Congress in 1936 and 1937 designed to keep the United States out of European conflicts, such as the Spanish Civil War

New Deal President Franklin D. Roosevelt's domestic program from 1933 to 1939, which aimed to bring about immediate economic relief from the Great Depression

New Deal Coalition a political partnership formed during the 1930s among various social and political groups in support of the New Deal, the Democratic Party, and Franklin D. Roosevelt

New Democrat a political moderate attracted to the Democratic Party in the 1990s

New Federalism President Richard Nixon's plan to reduce the size and power of the federal government and return power to the states, the centerpiece of which was a proposal for revenue sharing

New Freedom President Woodrow Wilson's reform program that focused on transferring power from the trusts to small businesses and average citizens, restricting corporate influence, and reducing corruption in the federal government

New Frontier President John F. Kennedy's domestic program from 1961 to 1963, which aimed to increase support for education, antipoverty programs, and medical care for the elderly; cut taxes; raise the minimum wage; ban racial discrimination; and increase defense spending

New Jersey v. T.L.O. a 1985 decision that limited privacy rights for students, reflecting the Supreme Court's shift to the right under President Ronald Reagan

New Left a political movement formed by student activists in the 1960s to promote traditional American ideals such as allowing all people to take an active role in government

New Right a political movement comprising evangelical Christian organizations and other groups and activists who worked for conservative causes

9/11 an attack launched against the United States on September 11, 2001, in which planes flown by terrorists destroyed the World Trade Center in New York City, damaged the Pentagon, and crashed into a field in Pennsylvania, killing nearly 3,000 people

Nineteenth Amendment a constitutional change ratified in 1920 declaring that women have the right to vote in state and national elections

No Child Left Behind Act (NCLB) an education reform bill, initiated by President George W. Bush and passed by Congress in 2002, that holds schools accountable for students' educational success by requiring that schools receiving federal funds test students' progress in reading and math and share the results

non-colonization President James Monroe's policy of warning European powers against future colonization in the Western Hemisphere

nonconformity rebellion against conventional behavior

nongovernmental organization (NGO) a group formed by private individuals in order to provide a service or pursue a public policy

non-interference President James Monroe's policy of warning European powers against interference in Latin American republics

nonviolent resistance peaceful protest or noncooperation with authorities to achieve social or political goals

normalcy the concept of life as it was before World War I, when the nation could focus on its own domestic prosperity, which Republican candidate Warren G. Harding promoted during the 1920 presidential election campaign and which helped him win the presidency

North American Free Trade Agreement (NAFTA) a 1993 agreement of the United States, Canada, and Mexico to create a free trade zone to encourage trade among them

North Atlantic Treaty Organization (NATO) as part of the Cold War, a military alliance formed in 1949 among the United States, Canada, France, Luxembourg, Belgium, the Netherlands, Iceland, Italy, Britain, Denmark, Norway, and Portugal—and expanded to include Greece and Turkey in 1952 and West Germany in 1955—to establish collective security against the Soviet Union

North Vietnamese Army (NVA) the army of communist North Vietnam, which supported the Viet Cong in South Vietnam with troops and supplies

Northwest Ordinance a law passed by Congress in 1787 specifying how western lands would be governed

nuclear freeze movement a movement in the United States and Western Europe calling for a moratorium, or "freeze," on the production, testing, and deployment of nuclear weapons by the superpowers

nullification the act of making something legally invalid

Nuremberg War Crimes Trials a series of trials in 1945 and 1946 in Nuremberg, Germany, in which an international military tribunal convicted former Nazi leaders of war crimes

O

Occupational Safety and Health Administration (OSHA) a government agency created by Congress in 1971 to protect workers on the job

Okie a nickname for a person who migrated from the Dust Bowl to California during the Great Depression

Open Door Policy a U.S. policy issued in 1899 stating that foreign nations must allow free trade in China

opportunity the chance for advancement or progress

ordinance a law that sets local regulations

Organization of Petroleum Exporting Countries (OPEC) formed in 1960 by Saudi Arabia, Iran, Iraq, Kuwait, and Venezuela, a worldwide association of nations that depend on oil sales for their national income and that sets oil prices; today Qatar, Indonesia, Libya, Algeria, Nigeria, and the United Arab Emirates are also members

overproduction a situation in which more goods are being produced than people can afford to buy

pacification a U.S. policy designed to promote security and stability in South Vietnam

pacifist a person who opposes all wars, usually on moral or religious grounds

Palestine Liberation Organization (PLO) a group fighting for the formation of an Arab state that would include land claimed by Israel

Palmer Raids conducted by Justice Department attorney J. Edgar Hoover at the instruction of U.S. Attorney General Mitchell Palmer, a series of unauthorized raids on homes, businesses, and meeting places of suspected subversives that resulted in the arrest of 6,000 radicals, often without any evidence against them

Panama Canal the canal built by the United States through the Isthmus of Panama to connect the Atlantic and Pacific oceans

parity in U.S. agricultural economics, the price that gives farmers the same purchasing power they had during an earlier, more prosperous time

Parliament the lawmaking body of England

partisanship rivalry between political parties based on strong disagreement about political principles

passport a document issued by a person's home government to verify his or her identity for the purpose of traveling outside the country

Patriot Act See **USA Patriot Act**

patronage the practice of politicians giving jobs to friends and supporters

pauperism the state of being impoverished and dependent on public assistance for survival

Peace Corps a government agency created by President John F. Kennedy in 1961 to send skilled volunteers to developing nations to support their local communities in areas such as education, agriculture, health, technology, and community development

Pendleton Act an 1883 federal law that limited patronage by creating a civil service commission to administer exams for certain nonmilitary government jobs

Pentagon Papers a top-secret Pentagon study of the U.S. role in Vietnam that was leaked to the press in 1971, revealing that previous administrations had deceived Congress and the public about the war

perjury willfully lying while under oath to tell the truth

Persian Gulf War a 1991 international conflict in which UN forces, led by the United States, attacked Iraq over the course of two months and successfully forced its troops out of neighboring Kuwait, which Iraq had invaded in 1990

philanthropist a person who gives money to support worthy causes

physical feature a natural feature of Earth's surface, such as a mountain or valley

planned economy a type of economy in which government planners make all economic decisions

planned obsolescence a method of encouraging the purchase of products in which businesses try to make what a consumer buys today seem obsolete, or out-of-date, after a fixed period of time

plantation a huge farm requiring a large labor force to grow crops for profit

Platt Amendment provisions in the Cuban constitution, added as a condition for the withdrawal of U.S. troops in 1902, allowing the United States to intervene in Cuban affairs and to buy or lease land for naval bases

plebiscite a vote on a question of importance

Plessy v. Ferguson the 1896 Supreme Court case that established the controversial "separate but equal" doctrine by which segregation became legal as long as the facilities provided to blacks were equivalent to those provided to whites

plurality the greatest number of votes a candidate receives in an election when none of the candidates receives a majority, or more than 50 percent, of the vote

pogroms organized anti-Jewish attacks that forced many Jews to leave Russia

point of view a person's way of thinking about or approaching a subject, as shaped by his or her character, experience, culture, and history

polio vaccine a vaccine, for the often deadly disease polio, developed by Dr. Jonas Salk and released for use in the United States in 1955

political base the core group of supporters of a political party

political bosses powerful leaders who ran local politics in many cities, providing jobs and social services to immigrants in exchange for political support

political machine an organization consisting of full-time politicians whose main goal was to retain political power and the money and influence that went with it

poll tax a tax of a set rate that is imposed on each person in a population

pop art short for "popular art," an art form of the 1950s and 1960s that focused on everyday objects that came mostly from popular culture

popular culture the culture of ordinary people, including music, visual art, literature, and entertainment, that is shaped by industries that spread information and ideas, especially the mass media

popular sovereignty a political practice, common in the United States before the Civil War, in which the people living in a newly organized territory had the right to vote on whether to allow slavery in the territory

populism a political philosophy that favors the common person's interests over those of wealthy people or business interests

Populist Party a political party founded in 1892 calling for policies to help working people, such as government ownership of railroads and coinage of silver

post-traumatic stress disorder a mental illness suffered by about half a million Vietnam veterans, with symptoms including anxiety, irritability, nightmares, and depression

Potsdam Conference in July and August 1945 in the German city of Potsdam, a conference of the main Allied leaders—U.S. president Harry S. Truman, British prime minister Winston Churchill and later his successor Clement Atlee, and Soviet premier Joseph Stalin—to finalize post–World War II plans for Europe

poverty line the minimum amount of income one needs to meet basic needs

poverty rate the percentage of people living in poverty

POW a prisoner of war

Preamble the first part of the Constitution, which states the purposes of the new plan of government

precedent a court decision used as a guideline in deciding similar cases

precision bombing the bombing of specific targets

preferential treatment giving preference to a minority or female job applicant because of that person's ethnicity or gender

preparedness movement beginning in 1915, before U.S. entry into World War I, a movement led by former president Theodore Roosevelt that called on the government to increase U.S. military strength and convince Americans of the need for U.S. involvement in the war

preservation the protection of wilderness lands from development

price controls a system of legal restrictions on the prices charged for goods

primary source a document or other record of past events created by someone who was present during the events or the time period in which they occurred

prior restraint the prevention of speech or expression before publication

productivity the rate at which goods are produced

progressive a member of a social and political movement of the early 1900s committed to improving conditions in American life

prohibition a ban on the production and sale of alcoholic beverages

proletariat the working class in a society

propaganda information or rumors spread by a group or government to promote its cause or ideas or to damage an opposing cause or idea

property value the worth of a piece of real estate on the market

proprietor a person who owned a colony as a result of receiving a land grant from the king

protectorate a nation protected and controlled by a stronger nation

protocol a first draft of a treaty to be submitted for ratification

public assistance aid, in the form of money, goods, or services, that a government provides to those in need

public works government-funded construction projects for public benefit

pull factor an attraction that draws immigrants to another place

Pullman Strike an 1894 railway workers' strike that was broken by federal troops, weakening the labor movement

puppet government a government that is run by citizens of a conquered country who carry out the policies of the conqueror

Pure Food and Drug Act a 1906 federal law that established the Food and Drug Administration to test and approve drugs before they go to market

push factor a problem that causes people to immigrate to another place

Q

quota system established by the Emergency Immigration Act of 1921, a system limiting immigration to the United States by permitting no more immigrants from a country than 3 percent of the number of that country's residents living in the United States in 1910; the Immigration Act of 1924 reduced the quota to 2 percent of the number of a country's residents living in the United States in 1890

R

racial profiling using physical traits to decide whether to investigate or arrest someone

racial zoning local laws that defined where the different races could live

racism the belief that one race of people is superior to another

radical someone who wants to make sweeping social, political, or economical changes in a society

radicalism a point of view favoring extreme change, especially in social or economic structure

Radical Republican during and after the Civil War, a member of the Republican Party who believed in and fought for the emancipation of slaves and, later, the equal rights of American blacks

Rasul v. Bush a 2005 Supreme Court case that determined that detainees held by the United States at a military base in Guantánamo Bay, Cuba, had the right to challenge their imprisonment in court

ratification the approval of a plan of government or of a constitutional amendment

rationing a system for limiting the distribution of food, gasoline, and other goods so that the military can have the weapons, equipment, and supplies it needs

Reagan Doctrine President Ronald Reagan's policy of openly supporting anticommunist insurgents and movements around the world

Reagan Revolution an era of political and economic change marked by President Ronald Reagan's conservative agenda calling for lower taxes, reduced government regulation of business, and cuts in spending on social programs

real income income measured by the amount of goods and services it will buy, regardless of inflation

realism in foreign policy, the belief that international relations should be guided by pragmatic self-interest—practical goals such as national defense and access to resources

realpolitik a political policy based on practical rather than idealistic concerns

reapportionment redrawing voting-district boundaries to reflect population changes

recall the process by which voters can remove an elected official before his or her term expires

recession a period in which there is a decline in economic activity and prosperity

Reconstruction Finance Corporation (RFC) a government agency created by Congress in 1932 to provide loans to banks, railroads, and big businesses and later also to farmers and public works projects

Red Scare lasting from 1919 to 1920, a campaign launched by U.S. attorney general Mitchell Palmer and implemented by Justice Department attorney H. Edgar Hoover to arrest communists and other radicals who promoted the overthrow of the U.S. government; revived during the Cold War by Senator Joseph McCarthy during a period of anticommunism lasting from 1950 to 1957

referendum a lawmaking reform that allows a law passed by a state legislature to be placed on the ballot for approval or rejection by the voters

Regents of the University of California v. Bakke a 1978 Supreme Court ruling that narrowly upheld affirmative action, declaring that race may be one factor, but not the sole criterion, in school admissions

regime a government

region a geographic area defined by one or more characteristics that set it apart from other areas

reparation a payment demanded of a nation defeated in war by a victorious nation

Republican Party one of the two major U.S. political parties; founded in 1854 by antislavery opponents of the Kansas-Nebraska Act

reservation an area of federal land reserved for Indian tribes

reservationist at the close of World War I, one of the Republican senators who agreed to approve the Treaty of Versailles only if changes were made in response to their concerns about the document

reserved power a power that the Constitution does not delegate to Congress or deny to the states and is therefore reserved to the states or the people

resolution a formal statement by a government about a course of action

restrictive covenant an agreement among neighbors not to sell or rent to African Americans or other racial minorities

revenue sharing a practice initiated under President Richard Nixon in which the federal government distributed revenues to states and local governments to spend as they saw fit

reverse discrimination discrimination against whites or males

rifled musket a type of gun used during the Civil War that had improved power and accuracy

right a power or privilege granted by an agreement among people or by law

right wing the conservative side of the political spectrum

Roaring Twenties a nickname given to the 1920s because of the decade's prosperity, technological advances, and cultural boom

Roosevelt Corollary President Theodore Roosevelt's assertion that, as a direct corollary of the Monroe Doctrine, the United States could intervene to preserve peace and order in the Western Hemisphere and protect U.S. interests

Rosenberg trial the controversial 1951 trial of two Americans, Ethel and Julius Rosenberg, charged with passing atomic secrets to the Soviet Union; the two were sentenced to death and executed in 1953, making them the only American civilians to be put to death for spying during the Cold War

Rough Riders a volunteer cavalry regiment recruited by Theodore Roosevelt to fight in Cuba in the Spanish-American War

Rustbelt the area in parts of the Northeast and Midwest that suffered economically because of rusting factories left behind by declining industries as a large part of the population moved to Sunbelt states in the 1970s

S

Sacco and Vanzetti trial a hotly protested criminal trial, held from 1920 to 1927, in which Italian immigrants Nicola Sacco and Bartolomeo Vanzetti were convicted of robbing and murdering two men and sentenced to death; many people believed that the trial was unfair and that the defendants were prosecuted because they were anarchists, not because they were guilty

Safe Drinking Water Act a law passed by Congress in 1974 to allow the Environmental Protection Agency to regulate the quality of public drinking water

Sandinistas leftist rebels who overthrew the dictator of Nicaragua in 1979 and established a government with close ties to the Soviet Union and Cuba

San Juan Hill the key battle in Cuba during the Spanish-American War

satellite nation a country under another country's control

saturation bombing the rapid release of a large number of bombs over a wide area

savings and loans crisis a financial crisis during the 1980s in which over 1,000 savings and loans associations, after being deregulated by President Ronald Reagan, made risky loans and went bankrupt, causing a slowdown in lending and home sales and significantly hurting the economy

Schenck v. United States the 1919 Supreme Court case that declared that Charles Schenck's propaganda efforts against the military draft were illegal under the Espionage Act of 1918 and were not protected by his First Amendment right to freedom of speech

Scopes trial a criminal trial, held in Dayton, Ohio, in 1925, that tested the constitutionality of a Tennessee law that banned the teaching of Darwin's theory of evolution in schools; science teacher John Scopes was found guilty and fined for his conduct, leaving the Tennessee law intact

secession formal withdrawal from a group; in U.S. history, the formal withdrawal of 11 Southern states from the Union in 1860–1861, leading to the Civil War

secondary source a document or other record of past events created by someone who was not present during the events or the time period in which they occurred

Second Great Awakening from about 1795 to 1835, a period of renewed religious fervor among Christians in the United States

sectionalism strong concern for local interests

Sedition Act a law passed by Congress in 1918 to make it illegal to say anything disloyal, profane, or abusive about the government or the war effort

segregation the forced separation of races in public places

Selective Service Act a law passed by Congress in 1917 to create a national draft

self-determination the right of people of other nations to determine their own government, free of outside influence

self-evident obvious without explanation or proof

Seneca Falls Convention held on July 19 and 20, 1848, the gathering of supporters of women's rights that launched the women's suffrage movement

separation of powers the division of government power into executive, legislative, and judicial branches

service sector the segment of the economy that does not produce goods

settlement house a community center that provided a variety of services to the poor, especially to immigrants

Seventeenth Amendment a constitutional change ratified in 1913 requiring the direct election of senators by popular vote

sexism oppression of women in the workplace

sexual revolution a shift in attitudes about sex and marriage that occurred during the 1960s as hippies espoused a more permissive outlook on sexual behavior than members of the mainstream did

sharecropping a form of tenant farming in which the land owner provides a tenant not only with land but also with the money needed to purchase equipment and supplies and possibly also food, clothing, and supervision

Sherman Antitrust Act an 1890 federal law that outlawed trusts, monopolies, and other forms of business that restricted trade

Sherman's March to the Sea during the Civil War, a devastating total war military campaign, led by Union general William Tecumseh Sherman, that involved marching 60,000 Union troops through Georgia from Atlanta to Savannah and destroying everything along the way

Silent Spring a 1962 book by Rachel Carson that raised public interest in environmentalism by revealing how uncontrolled pesticide use was poisoning the environment

sit-in a civil rights protest in which protesters sit down in a public place and refuse to move, thereby causing the business to lose customers

Sixteenth Amendment a constitutional change ratified in 1913 allowing the federal government to impose an income tax

social class a group of people within a society who possess similar socioeconomic status

social Darwinism an idea, based on Charles Darwin's theory of evolution, that the best-run businesses led by the most capable people will survive and prosper

Social Gospel a religious movement of the late 1800s based on the idea that social reform and Christianity go hand in hand

socialism a political theory that advocates ownership of the means of production, such as factories and farms, by the people rather than by capitalists and landowners

Social Security Act a law passed by Congress in 1935 to establish federal programs to offer old-age assistance and benefits, unemployment compensation, and aid to needy mothers, children, and the blind

social welfare government or private social services intended to aid disadvantaged groups

soup kitchen a place that serves free meals to the needy

Southern Christian Leadership Conference (SCLC) an organization formed by Martin Luther King Jr. and other civil rights leaders in 1957 to use nonviolent resistance to achieve social and political goals

sovereignty a nation's independent authority

Spanish Civil War a civil war from 1936 to 1939 in which the Spanish military and its right-wing allies, known as the Nationalists, overthrew Spain's democratic republic

speakeasy a secret club that sold alcohol during the era of prohibition

special interest group an organization whose members share an interest or concern and want to influence policymaking

special prosecutor a lawyer from outside the government whom the attorney general or Congress appoints to investigate a federal official for misconduct while in office

spectator sport a sport that attracts large numbers of fans

speculative bubble an unrealistic or unfounded rise in economic values

speculator a person who takes the risk of buying something in the hope of reselling it for a higher price

spheres of influence areas in which a single nation controlled trading rights, as foreign powers did in China during the 1890s

spoils system the practice of giving appointed positions in government to people loyal to the party in power

Square Deal President Theodore Roosevelt's reform program, focused on regulating big business, protecting workers and consumers, and preserving the environment

stagflation an economic condition in which prices and the rate of unemployment increase at the same time

stalemate a situation in a contest or conflict in which neither side can make a useful move

Stamp Act an act passed by Parliament in 1765 requiring colonists to pay a stamp tax on newspapers and documents; the first direct tax imposed on the colonies, prompting protests of "no taxation without representation"

status quo the condition or states of affairs that currently exist

status symbol a possession that serves as a sign of wealth and prestige

steerage the open area below a steamship's main deck, where most immigrants lived during the Atlantic crossing

stimulus an attempt by the government to inject money into the economy to encourage growth

stock market crash in October 1929, the period of plunging stock market prices that helped initiate the Great Depression

Stonewall riots riots in 1969 by customers of a gay bar in New York in response to a police raid; the clash marked the beginning of the gay rights movement

Strategic Arms Limitation Talks (SALT) a five-year agreement between the United States and the Soviet Union to limit the number of nuclear missiles in their arsenals; the treaty limited the Soviet Union to 1,618 missiles and the United States to 1,054, including both ground-based intercontinental ballistic missiles (ICBMs) and submarine-launched ballistic missiles (SLBMs)

Strategic Defense Initiative (SDI) an arms program announced by President Ronald Reagan to create a "missile shield" designed to protect the United States from nuclear attack

strike a labor action in which workers refuse to go to work

Student Nonviolent Coordinating Committee (SNCC) a civil rights organization formed in 1960 by college students, who organized sit-ins and other nonviolent protests

subpoena a written legal order used to summon a witness to court or require certain evidence be submitted to court

subversion a plot or an action intended to overthrow a government

suffrage the right to vote

summit meeting a meeting of heads of state to discuss matters important to their nations

Sunbelt the "belt" of warm-weather states that stretches across the southern third of the United States, from Florida to California

superpower a nation that is so powerful that it influences or controls less powerful states

supply-side economics the theory that economic growth depends on increasing the supply of goods and services through tax cuts

supremacy clause the constitutional clause affirming that the Constitution and federal laws are the supreme law of the land

surveillance close observation

Sussex pledge during World War I, a German promise in 1916 to begin giving advance warning of submarine attacks on ocean liners and to spare the lives of passengers and crew

Swann v. Charlotte-Mecklenburg Board of Education the 1971 Supreme Court ruling that busing was an acceptable way to achieve school integration

sweatshop a small factory where employees work long hours under poor conditions for low wages

symbolic speech conduct that conveys a message without the use of words

Taft-Hartley Act a law passed by Congress, though President Harry S. Truman vetoed it, in 1947 to limit the power of unions

Taliban a radical and ultraconservative Muslim group that supported al Qaeda and ruled Afghanistan from 1996 to 2001, when U.S.-led forces ousted it in retaliation for its unwillingness to turn over Osama bin Laden after al Qaeda's September 11, 2001, terrorist attacks

Tammany Hall a political machine in New York City

tariff a tax on imported goods

tax credit a reduction in the amount a taxpayer must pay to the government

Teapot Dome Scandal a political scandal in which U.S. secretary of the interior Albert Fall leased national oil reserves in Elk Hills, California, and Teapot Dome, Wyoming, to two companies that had bribed him

temperance movement a reform movement calling for moderation in drinking alcohol

Temporary Assistance to Needy Families (TANF) a new welfare system created by Congress in 1996 to limit the amount of time a family can receive welfare payments to five years

tenant farming a system of agriculture in which landowners rent plots of land to workers, who pay for the use of the land in cash, with a share of the crop raised, or both

tenement a run-down apartment building

termination policy during the 1940s and 1950s, a federal policy focused on ending the special status of American Indian tribes and integrating Indians into mainstream American culture

territorial integrity a diplomatic principle in which nations respect one another's borders and do not try to gain one another's territory by force

Test Ban Treaty an agreement signed by the United States, the Soviet Union, and Great Britain in 1963 to ban nuclear testing in the atmosphere but allow underground testing

Tet Offensive a major offensive in 1968 by Viet Cong and NVA soldiers that resulted in growing opposition among Americans to the war

Texas Revolution the 1836 rebellion of Texans against Mexican rule

theory of evolution developed by naturalist Charles Darwin in the mid-1800s, a scientific theory that all plants and animals, including humans, evolved from simpler forms of life over thousands or millions of years

third party a political party outside the two-party system

Third World originally, the group of nations that had recently gained independence from colonial rule and were not aligned with the West (First World) or the East (Second World) after World War II; more broadly, the developing nations of the world

Thirteenth Amendment a constitutional change ratified in 1865 abolishing slavery in the United States

threat level one of two levels of danger established by the Department of Homeland Security to inform the public about terrorist threats

Three Mile Island accident a disaster that occurred at Pennsylvania's Three Mile Island Nuclear Generating Station on March 28, 1979, when the nuclear power plant suffered a partial meltdown, allowing radioactive gases to escape into the atmosphere and highlighting the potential danger of nuclear power plants

369th Regiment in World War I, an African American regiment of the U.S. Army

totalitarianism a system in which the government totally controls all aspects of a society, including the economy

total war a military policy in which one side in a conflict decides it is willing to make any sacrifice necessary to completely defeat the opposing side

trade deficit an economic situation in which the value of a country's imports exceeds the value of its exports

traditional economy a type of economy in which resources are used for purposes established by long-standing custom and goods are bartered or informally exchanged

traditionalist a person who has deep respect for long-held cultural and religious values

transcontinental railroad a railroad that spans the continent

Treaty of Versailles a peace treaty signed by the Allied powers and Germany on June 18, 1919, at the Paris peace conference at the Palace of Versailles in France; it assigned Germany responsibility for the war, required Germany to pay reparations to the Allied countries, reduced Germany's territory, and included the covenant for the League of Nations

trench warfare a form of warfare in which armies conduct attacks on each other from opposition positions in fortified trenches

tribunal a court

trickle-down theory an economic policy in which the government attempts to indirectly aid the needy by promoting economic growth at the business level in the hope that it will influence prosperity at all levels

Truman Doctrine a U.S. foreign policy, established in 1947 by President Harry S. Truman, of providing economic and military aid to countries—initially Greece and Turkey—that were attempting to resist communism

trust a set of companies managed by a small group known as trustees, who can prevent companies in the trust from competing with each other

Tuskegee Airmen a group of Army Air Corps pilots and support crews, established in 1941 as the first black combat unit

Tuskegee Institute a vocational college for African Americans in Alabama, founded by Booker T. Washington

Twenty-sixth Amendment the constitutional change ratified in 1971 lowering the voting age to 18

tyranny the unjust use of government power

U-boat a German submarine that was the first submarine employed in warfare, initially used during World War I

UN Atomic Energy Commission a panel established by the United Nations in 1946 to propose ways to control atomic energy and restrict the development of nuclear weapons

Uncle Tom's Cabin an 1852 novel by Harriet Beecher Stowe that described the cruelties of slavery so clearly that it increased the fervor with which both proslavery and antislavery Americans supported their causes

underconsumption a situation in which people are purchasing fewer goods than the economy is producing

undocumented immigrant an immigrant who enters the country illegally

unilateralism a policy of not seeking military or political alliances with foreign powers

United Farm Workers (UFW) a small union for migrant farmworkers, founded in the late 1960s

United Nations (UN) an international organization founded in 1945 to further the causes of peace, prosperity, and human rights

Universal Declaration of Human Rights a document adopted by the United Nations in 1948 affirming basic human rights, including the right to life, liberty, and equality before the law, as well as freedom of religion, expression, and assembly

universal health care health care that is provided to all citizens of a country

unlawful enemy combatants fighters in armed conflict with the United States who are not part of a regular army

unrestricted submarine warfare during World War I, a German military policy of staging submarine attacks on Allied and neutral nations' unarmed ocean liners without advance warning

urban characteristic of or relating to a city

urbanization the growth of cities

urban renewal the redevelopment of impoverished urban areas by such means as demolishing or renovating existing buildings and constructing new ones, improving sanitation systems and transportation, and combating crime

USA Patriot Act standing for "Uniting and Strengthening America by Providing Appropriate Tools Required to Intercept and Obstruct Terrorism," a law passed by Congress in 2001 to loosen restrictions on intelligence gathering by U.S. security and law enforcement agencies after the September 11, 2001, terrorist attacks; questions about the constitutionality of parts of the law have since raised controversy

USS Maine a battleship sunk in Havana harbor in 1898, an event that helped rouse public support for war with Spain

vaquero a Mexican cowboy

vertical integration a corporate expansion strategy that involves controlling each step in the production and distribution of a product, from acquiring raw materials to manufacturing, packaging, and shipping

Viet Cong communist insurgents in South Vietnam

Viet Minh the Vietnamese movement led by Ho Chi Minh against foreign occupation, first against the Japanese during World War II and then against the French occupation

Vietnamization President Richard Nixon's policy of having the government of South Vietnam gradually take over the conduct of the war, especially ground combat

Vietnam syndrome the reluctance of many Americans to the United States becoming involved in a military conflict unless assured of a quick victory

visa a document from a government that authorizes a foreigner to enter its country

Volstead Act a law passed by Congress in 1919 to enforce the Eighteenth Amendment, which prohibited the manufacture and sale of alcoholic beverages

Voluntary Relocation Program during the 1950s and 1960s, a federal program that worked to relocate American Indians from reservations to cities

Voting Rights Act of 1965 an act of Congress outlawing literacy tests and other tactics that had long been used to deny African Americans the right to vote

Wagner Act officially the National Labor Relations Act, a law passed by Congress in 1935 to protect workers' right to organize into unions; it created the National Labor Relations Board

war crime a violation of internationally accepted practices related to waging war

war-guilt clause a clause included in the Treaty of Versailles that held Germany responsible for World War I and required it to make reparations to the Allied nations to pay for losses and damage they suffered during the war

war of attrition a military campaign designed to wear down the enemy's strength

War of 1812 the war between the United States and Britain from 1812 to 1814, prompted mainly by anger at British seizures of U.S. ships and sailors and ending in a draw

War on Poverty President Lyndon Johnson's extensive antipoverty program from 1964 to 1969, the centerpiece of which was the Economic Opportunity Act of 1964

war on terror declared by President George W. Bush after the September 11, 2001, terrorist attacks, an international war aimed at finding and defeating every terrorist organization in the world, beginning with U.S.-led invasions of Afghanistan and Iraq

War Powers Resolution a resolution passed by Congress in 1973 placing strict limits on a president's powers to use armed forces in hostilities without congressional approval

War Production Board the federal agency set up to manage the conversion of industries to military production during World War II

War Refugee Board an agency created in 1944 that arranged for Jewish refugees to stay at centers in Italy and North Africa, as well as in former army camps in the United States

Warren Court the Supreme Court under Chief Justice Earl Warren from 1953 to 1969, known for its activism on civil rights and free speech

Warsaw Pact as part of the Cold War and in response to the formation of the North Atlantic Treaty Organization, an agreement signed in 1955 by the Soviet Union, Albania, Bulgaria, Czechoslovakia, East Germany, Hungary, Poland, and Romania to establish a military alliance for mutual defense

Washington Naval Conference a 1921 international conference, including representatives of Britain, France, Italy, and Japan and hosted by the United States in Washington, D.C., to discuss naval disarmament and resulting in agreements to discuss power conflicts in the Pacific, to reduce or limit the size of each nation's navy, to regulate submarine use, and to ban poison gas use

Washington's Farewell Address President George Washington's final message to the nation, which primarily covered domestic issues but also recommended avoiding alliances with other nations

WASP an acronym used to describe a white Anglo-Saxon protestant

Watergate scandal a political scandal from 1972 to 1975 in which President Richard Nixon and members of his staff organized a burglary of the Democratic National Committee's headquarters in the Watergate building and then attempted to cover up their illegal activities, leading to prison terms for many involved and Nixon's impeachment

Watts riot a 1965 race riot in Watts, a black ghetto in Los Angeles, caused by frustrations about poverty, prejudice, and police mistreatment

weapons of mass destruction (WMD) chemical, biological, and nuclear weapons that can inflict extremely severe damage on a very large scale

welfare state a social system in which the government takes responsibility for the economic well being of its citizens by providing programs and direct assistance

white-collar worker a person who works in an office-based profession that does not involve manual labor and that requires a certain amount of formal dress, usually for a set salary

white primary a primary election in which only whites could participate

Wobblies a nickname for members of the Industrial Workers of the World (IWW), an anticapitalist labor organization founded in 1905

Woman's Peace Party an organization, established by a group of pacifist women in 1915 in response to World War I beginning in Europe, that called for arms limitations and mediation to take the place of combat in Europe

Women's Army Corps (WAC) a women's unit of the U.S. Army, established in 1942

women's liberation the goal of emancipating women from customs and laws that keep them subordinate to men

Woodstock a three-day music festival in 1969 that was held at a farm in upstate New York, was attended by 400,000 people, and helped popularize a new generation of rock performers

workers' compensation the legal right of workers who are injured at work to receive some pay, even if their injuries prevent them from working

working class people who work for wages in factories, mills, mines, and other businesses, usually performing manual labor

working poor people in society who work but earn wages too low to lift them out of poverty

Works Progress Administration (WPA) a work-relief organization established in 1939, as part of the New Deal, to provide work for unemployed Americans during the Great Depression

World Bank a bank founded in 1944 by the United States and 43 other nations in order to provide loans to help countries recover from World War II and develop their economies

World Trade Organization (WTO) established by the 1994 General Agreement on Tariffs and Trade, an international organization that sets trade policies and mediates disputes among its 153 member nations

Yalta Conference held in February 1945 in the Soviet city of Yalta, a conference of the main Allied leaders—U.S. president Franklin D. Roosevelt, British prime minister Winston Churchill, and Soviet premier Joseph Stalin—to plan the future of post–World War II Europe

yellow journalism the exaggerated style of newspaper reporting during the 1890s that was sparked by the rivalry between two New York City newspapers and helped inflame public support for war with Spain

Zenger trial a trial that helped promote the idea that the freedom of the press is a right that should be protected

Zimmermann note during World War I, a coded telegram that German foreign minister Arthur Zimmermann sent to the German minister in Mexico proposing that if the United States entered the war, Mexico and Germany should become allies; it helped influence the United States to declare war on Germany five weeks later

Zoot Suit Riots racial clashes in Los Angeles in 1943 between mobs of sailors and marines and Mexican American youths who wore zoot suits

Index

Page numbers in **bold** type indicate definitions.

A

accessibility, **533**

accountability, **657**

acid rain, **614**

activists, **196**

Adams, John, 9, 42, 45, 56, 81, 86, 217

Adams, John Quincy, 85–86, 95

Adams, Samuel, 41, 56

Addams, Jane, 159, 195, 198, 232, 268

advertising and advertisements, 310–311

affirmative action, **520**–521, 633

affluence, age of (1950s)

    and the automobile, 476–477

    and economic growth, 469–471

    marriage, families, and baby boom, 472–473

    political readjustments and challenges, 466–468

    population shifts, 474–475

    and poverty, 482–563

    and technology, 478–479

Affordable Care Act, 661

Afghanistan, 613, 675, 678, 679

Afghanistan War, 659, 677, 683

Africa, 31, 281, 668–670

African Americans. *See also* slavery

    affirmative action, 520–521, 633

    black codes, 121

    civil rights. *See* civil rights movement

    cowboys, 133

    discrimination against, 115, 128, 296, 402–403, 428

    education, 120, 125, 127, 129, 193, 488–489

    Emancipation Proclamation, effect of, 114

    equal rights demonstrations, 10

    folk dancing, 309

    and GI Bill of Rights, 428

    and Great Depression, 352

    and jazz, 318–319

    labor unions, 291, 372

    leaders' response to WWI, 272

    life in 1900, 191

    migration to northern cities, 191, 272, 319, 428, 483–484

    military service, 114–115, 231, 259, 402–403

    and the New Deal, 373

    occupations, 129, 489

    post-WWII life, 475, 481–560, 486–495

    and racism, 115, 139

    and segregation, 486–495

    struggle for equality, 202–203

    testing freedom during Reconstruction, 120–121

    in U.S. Congress, 124, 126, 516

    voting rights, 14, 52, 124–125, 127–128, 191, 490, 516, 601

    westward migration, 139

    writers, 320

Afrocentrism, **516**–517

ageism, **535**

Agent Orange, **578**

Age of Innovation and Industry

    big business and government, 151–153

    The Gilded Age, 153–155

    industrial growth explosion, 148–150

    inventions and technologies, 144–147

agitators, **100**

Agnew, Spiro T., 600, 606–607

agribusiness, **484**

Agricultural Adjustment Act (AAA), 348–349, **365,** 370, 375

agriculture. *See* farming and farmers

Aguinaldo, Emilio, 230, 242

AIDS, **631**

    in Africa, 670

Aid to Families with Dependent Children (AFDC), 653

airplanes, 145, 262–263, 304–305, 312, 389, 395

air travel safety, 686

Alabama, 94, 508–509

Alaska, 218–219

Albany Plan of Union, **35**

al-Gaddafi, Muammar, 679

Alger Hiss case, **459**

Algeria, 679

Allen, Frederick Lewis, 289, 304, 313

Alliance for Progress, 545

Allied powers, **248**–253, 258–259, 264, 341, **410,** 410–421

al Qaeda, **674**–675, 677

America letters, **169**

American Civil Liberties Union (ACLU), 77, **295, 332**

American Expeditionary Force (AEF), **258,** 259, 264

American Federation of Labor (AFL), **161,** 290–291, 372

American Indian Movement (AIM), **529**–530

American Indians

    assimilation efforts, 137

    and civil rights, 529–530

    colonization's effect on, 31

    English arms supply, 54

    forced westward migration, 84

    French and Indian War, 40

    land losses (1850–1900), 135

    military service in WWII, 418

    and the New Deal, 375

    Plains wars, 136–137

    population by state (2010), 529

Meuse-Argonne Offensive, **264**

Mexican Americans, 375, 406–407, 527

Mexicans, 685

Mexican War, 83, **221**

Mexico, 83, 220–254, 240, 302

Mexico border, 633, 685

MIA (missing in action), **595**

middle class, 190–191, 483–484

Middle East, 612

    Islam. *See* Islam

    Reagan's policies in, 640–641

    terrorism. *See* terrorism

midterm elections, **653**

migrant workers' rights, 523, 527–528, 531

militarism, **249, 382**–384

military advisers, **568**

military commissions, **688**–689

Military Commissions Act(s), **688**

military draft, **110,** 115, 258, 390, 396, 584

military weapons, 112–113, 260–263, 395, 419, 452–455, 539

militias, **43**

"millionaires tax," 663

Milosevic, Slobodan, 668

Mineta, Norman, 684

mining, 132, 158–159, 178, 187

Miranda rights, **557**

miscegenation, **489**

"misery index," 633

Mississippi, 94, 106–108, 353, 500–501, 508, 518

Mississippi River, 18, 22, 94, 106–108

Missouri, 94, 106, 358

Missouri Compromise, **94**–95

mixed economy, **646**

mobilization, **386**

mobilized, **267**

Moderates, 39

modernists, **325**–327

Molotov Plan, **440**

monarchy, **14**

Mondale, Walter, 629

monetary policy, **140**

money, 54, 72, 340

money supply, 140–141

monopoly, **150**–151

Monroe Doctrine, **218,** 236–237

Montesquieu, Baron de, 56, 58

Montgomery, Alabama, 498–499

Montgomery Bus Boycott, **498**–499

Moral Diplomacy, **237**

Moral Majority, **626**

moratorium, **592**

Morgan, J. P., 144, 205

motion pictures, 315, 328–329, 458, 622

Mubarak, Hosni, 679

muckrakers, **181,** 185

Muir, John, 210, 614

multinational corporations, **673**

Munich Pact, **379,** 386

Mussolini, Benito "Il Duce," 380–381, 384, 388, 412

Mutual Assured Destruction (MAD), **455**

My Lai massacre, **592**

N

Nader, Ralph, 554, 651

napalm, **582**

Nashville, Tennessee, 154, 174, 502, 582

National Aeronautics and Space Administration (NASA), 68, 541

National Association for the Advancement of Colored People (NAACP), **203,** 403, 492, 498, 501

National Child Labor Committee, **198**

national debt, 394, **630**

    under Reagan, 630

    reduction of, 662–663

national defense, 54, 64, 394–395, 400–401, 403, 406, 539–540

National Energy Act, **611**

national government

    and big business, 151–153

    confederation in crisis, 54–55

    constitutional convention, 56–59

    delegated powers, 65, **72**

    formation by Continental Congress, 52–53

    and Great Depression, 340–341

    and labor unions, 164–165

    limits on powers, 86

    and political corruption, 189

    popular participation in, 76–77

    powers shared with states, 73

    progressive reforms, 211–213

    purposes of, 64

    ratification of constitution, 60–61

    role in everyday life, 376–377

    size of, 271

    WWI agencies, 271

National Industrial Recovery Act (NIRA), 348, **365,** 370, 372

national interest, **236**

nationalism, **248**

National Organization for Women (NOW), **525**

National Rainbow Coalition, 633

national security after 9/11, 683–689

national security letters (NSLs), **687**

National Urban League, 403, 428, 492

National War Labor Board, 271, 290, 394

National Women's Political Caucus (NWPC), **617**

nation building, **676**

Nation of Islam, **514**–515

nation-states, **646**

nativism, **174,** 294

Notes

Chapter 1

1: Abraham Lincoln, Gettysburg Address, Nov. 18, 1863, at 100 Milestone Documents, www.ourdocuments.gov. Martin Luther King Jr., "I Have a Dream," reprinted by arrangement with The Heirs to the Estate of Martin Luther King Jr., c/o Writers House as agent for the proprietor New York, NY. Copyright 1963 Martin Luther King Jr., copyright renewed 1991 Coretta Scott King. **4:** Frederick Jackson Turner, "The Significance of History," 1891, at www.teachingamericanhistory.org. **6:** Henry Ford, in *Chicago Tribune,* May 25, 1916, at www.quotationspages.com. Henry Ford, 1916, at Albert Castel, "Henry Ford's Time Machine: Michigan's Ford Museum and Greenfield Village" (Primedia Publications), away.com. Robert Penn Warren, *The Legacy of the Civil War: Meditations on the Centennial* (New York: Vintage Books, 1961). Arnold Toynbee, History News Network, "Quotes About History," www.hnn.us. **7:** George Santayana, 1905, at www.bartleby.com. Maya Angelou, "On the Pulse of Morning: The Inaugural Poem" (1993), at PBS, www.pbs.org. Stephen Schiff, "Scurvy Rascal Sees It Through," *New York Times,* May 4, 1986, www.nytimes.com.

Chapter 2

9: Page Smith, *A New Age Now Begins: A People's History of the American Revolution,* Vol. 1 (New York: McGraw-Hill, 1976). Thomas Jefferson, in David Hackett Fischer, *Liberty and Freedom: A Visual History of America's Founding Ideas* (New York: Oxford Univ. Press, 2005). **10:** Eric Foner, *The Story of American Freedom* (New York: W. W. Norton, 1998). **11:** Arthur Szyk, in "The Artist," www.szyk.org/artist.html. **12:** Foner, *Story.* **13:** Smith, *New Age.* John Smith, in Foner, *Story.* **14:** "Return of the Town of Dorchester on the Proposed Massachusetts Constitution, 1778," at www.vindicatingthefounders.com/library. **15:** Carl Schurz, 1859, at www.bartleby.com.

Chapter 3

17: Michael Drayton, *Odes,* "To the Virginian Voyage," 1619, at www.bartleby.com. Richard B. Morris, ed., *The New World,* Vol. 1 (New York: Time-Life Books, 1969). John Smith, in "First Hand Accounts of Virginia, 1575–1705," at www.virtualjamestown.org. **20:** Thomas D. Clark, *Frontier America: The Story of the Westward Movement,* 2d ed. (New York: Charles Scribner's Sons, 1969). **22:** Arthur M. Schlesinger, "The City in American Civilization," in Alexander B. Callow Jr., ed., *American Urban History: An Interpretive Reader with Commentaries* (New York: Oxford Univ. Press, 1969). **26:** George Washington, Farewell Address, Sep. 19, 1796, at www.ourdocuments.gov.

Chapter 4

30: Eric Foner, *Give Me Liberty! An American History,* Vol. 1 (New York: W. W. Norton, 2005). **31:** Virginia General Assembly declaration, 1705, at "Africans in America," www.pbs.org. Phillis Wheatley, in Andrew Carroll, ed., *Letters of a Nation* (New York: Kodansha America, 1997). **34:** Alexander Hamilton, *Hamilton's Itinerarium; Being a Narrative of a Journey from Annapolis, Maryland, Through Delaware, Pennsylvania, New York, New Jersey, Connecticut, Rhode Island, Massachusetts and New Hampshire, from May to September, 1744* (Saint Louis: W. K. Bixby, 1907). **35:** Roger Williams, in Carroll, ed., *Letters.* **36:** Henry Steele Commager, *Documents of American History* (Englewood Cliffs, NJ: Prentice Hall, 1975). Andrew Hamilton, in Doug Linder, "The Trial of John Peter Zenger: An Account," Univ. of Missouri-Kansas City School of Law, www.law.umkc.edu. **37:** Curtis P. Nettels, *The Roots of American Civilization* (New York: Crofts, 1963).

Chapter 5

40: Patrick Henry, in Thomas Fleming, *Liberty! The American Revolution* (New York: Viking, 1997). **44:** King George III, "Proclamation for Suppressing Rebellion and Sedition," 1775, at www.ushistory.org. Thomas Paine, *Common Sense,* 1776, at www.ushistory.org. Thomas Paine, in Thomas A. Bailey and David M. Kennedy, eds., *The American Spirit: United States History as Seen by Contemporaries* (Lexington, MA: D.C. Heath, 1984). **46:** Nathanael Greene, in David McCullough, *1776* (New York: Simon and Schuster, 2005).

Chapter 6

51: George Washington, in Carroll, *Letters.* Smith, *New Age.* **54:** George Washington, at U.S. Department of State International Information Programs, usinfo.state.gov. **56:** James McGregor Burns, *The Vineyard of Liberty* (New York: Alfred A. Knoph, 1982). Thomas Jefferson, in Catherine Drinker Bowen, *Miracle at Philadelphia: The Story of the Constitutional Convention* (Boston: Little Brown, 1986). Patrick Henry, in Bowen, *Miracle.* **60:** James Madison, *The Federalist* No. 51, 1788, at www.ourdocuments.gov. **61:** Thomas Jefferson, at www.usconstitution.net.

Chapter 7

63: George W. Bush, 2003, at the National Archives Experience, www.archives.gov. John W. Carlin, 2003, at www.archives.gov. **64:** Benjamin Franklin, 1789, at "The Quotable Franklin," www.ushistory.org. **70:** Charles Evans Hughes, at Columbia250, c250.columbia.edu. **74:** Thomas Jefferson, in a letter to James Madison, 1789, in Philip B. Kurland and Ralph Lerner, eds., *The Founders' Constitution* (Univ. of Chicago Press, 2000), press-pubs.uchicago.edu/founders.

Chapter 8

79: Page Smith, *The Nation Comes of Age: A People's History of the Ante-Bellum Years* (New York: McGraw-Hill, 1981). **80:** George Washington, Inaugural Address, Apr. 16, 1789, at www.ourdocuments.gov. **81:** Washington, Inaugural Address, www.ourdocuments.gov. Thomas Jefferson, at "Thomas Jefferson to Walter Jones," The Founders' Constitution, press-pubs.uchicago.edu/founders, credited to Andrew A. Lipscomb and Albert Ellery Bergh, eds., *The Writings of Thomas Jefferson* (Washington: Thomas Jefferson Memorial Assoc., 1905). George Washington, Farewell Address, www.ourdocuments.gov. **82:** Thomas Jefferson, at "Louisiana Purchase Treaty (1802)," www.ourdocuments.gov, credited to Stacey Bredhoff, *American Originals* (Seattle: Univ. of Washington Press, 2001). **83:** "Freedom: A History of Us," www.pbs.org. **84:** Andrew Jackson, "Message to Congress 'On Indian Removal,'" Dec. 6, 1830, at www.ourdocuments.gov. **85:** Smith, *Nation Comes.* **90:** Sojourner Truth, in Joy Hakim, *Freedom: A History of Us* (New York: Oxford Univ. Press, 2003).

Chapter 9

93: Charles Sumner, "The Crime Against Kansas," May 18, 1856, at Furman Univ., facweb.furman.edu. Preston Brooks, in Smith, *Nation Comes.* **95:** John Quincy Adams, in David Colbert, ed., *Eyewitness to America: 500 Years of American History in the Words of Those Who Saw It Happen* (New York: Vintage Books, 1998). **97:** David Wilmot, *The American Civil War* (New York: Palgrave MacMillan), at www.palgrave.com. **98:** Daniel Webster, in Hakim, *Liberty.* **100:** "Bleeding Kansas," Encyclopaedia Britannica Online, www.britannica.com. John Brown, in Hakim, *Liberty.* "Bleeding Kansas," www.britannica.com. **101:** Smith, *Nation Comes.* **102:** Ralph Waldo Emerson, at Douglas O. Linder, "The Trial of John Brown: A Commentary," Univ. of Missouri-Kansas City School of Law, www.law.umkc.edu. "John Brown's Body," at "Lyrical Legacy," the Library of Congress, www.loc.gov. Abraham Lincoln, at "The Lincoln-Douglas Debates of 1858," National Park Service, www.nps.gov. Robert Anderson, "Telegram Announcing the Surrender at Fort Sumter," Apr. 13, 1861, at www.ourdocuments.gov. **103:** Abraham Lincoln, in Smith, *Nation Comes.* Horace Greeley, in *Tribune,* Apr. 15, 1861.

Chapter 10

105: Geoffrey C. Ward, Ric Burns, and Ken Burns, *The Civil War: An Illustrated History* (New York: Knopf, 1990). **107:** Ward et al., *Civil War.* Abraham Lincoln, letter to Horace Greeley, Aug. 22, 1862, at www.bartleby.com, credited to Roy P. Basler, ed., *The Collected Works of Abraham Lincoln,* Vol. 5 (Abraham Lincoln Assoc., 1953). *New York Times,* at "Mathew B. Brady—Biographical Note," Selected Civil War Photographs, memory.loc.gov/ammem/cwphtml. **108:** Abraham Lincoln, Gettysburg Address, at www.ourdocuments.gov. **109:** William Tecumseh Sherman, in Ward et al., *Civil War.* William Tecumseh Sherman, in Bruce Catton, *The American Heritage Picture History of the Civil War* (New York: Gramercy, 1994). Wilmer McLean, 1865, at Civil War History, www.trivia-library.com. Terms of the surrender at Appomattox, in Catton, *Picture History.* William Tecumseh Sherman, in Ward et al., *Civil War.* **111:** Page Smith, *Trial by Fire: A People's History of the Civil War and Reconstruction Period,* Vol. 1 (New York: Penguin, 1990). Robert K. Sutton, ed., *Rally on the High Ground: The National Park Service Symposium on the Civil War* (2001), at www.cr.nps.gov. Catton, *Picture History.* Jefferson Davis, in Ward et al., *Civil War.* **112:** Ward et al., *Civil War.* Catton, *Picture History.* **113:** Ward et al., *Civil War.* Bell Irvin Wiley, *The Life of Johnny Reb: The Common Soldier of the Confederacy* (Baton Rouge: Louisiana State Univ. Press, 1994). Henry Tucker and Charles C. Sawyer, "Weeping Sad and Lonely, or, When This Cruel War Is Over," in Bell Irvin Wiley, *The Life of Billy Yank: The Common Soldier of the Union* (Baton Rouge: Louisiana State Univ. Press, 1979). **114:** Frederick Douglass, in Ward et al., *Civil War.* Henry M. Turner, *The Negro in Slavery, War, and Peace* (1913), in James M. McPherson, *The Negro's Civil War: How American Blacks Felt and Acted During the War for the Union* (New York: Vintage Books, 2003). Frederick Douglass, at Civil War: Black Soldiers, www.mrlincolnandfreedom.org, attributed to Susan-Mary Grant and Brian Holden Reid, eds., *The American Civil War: Explorations and Reconsiderations* (New York: Longman, 2000). **115:** War Department General Order 143: Creation of the U.S. Colored Troops, at www.ourdocuments.gov. Ward et al., *Civil War.* McPherson, *Negro's Civil War.* Ward et al., *Civil War.* **116:** Clara Barton, in Ward et al., *Civil War.* Augusta Morris, at "Rose O'Neal Greenhow," americancivilwar.com.

Chapter 11

119: Abraham Lincoln, Second Inaugural Address, Mar. 4, 1865, www.ourdocuments.gov. Caroline Cowles Richard, at "The War Ends—A Small Town's Reaction, 1865," EyeWitness to History, www.eyewitnesstohistory.com. **120:** Shelby Cullom, "The Impeachment of Andrew Johnson (1868)," Great Epochs in American History, www.usgennet.org. Andrew Johnson, in Eric Foner, *Forever Free: The Story of Emancipation and Reconstruction* (New York: Knopf, 2005). Booker T. Washington, *Up from Slavery: An Autobiography* (New York: Doubleday,

Page, 1901), at American Studies at the Univ. of Virginia, xroads.virginia.edu. **120:** Thaddeus Stevens, "Reconstruction Speech" to the House of Representatives, Dec. 18, 1865, at "Thaddeus Stevens Papers Online," Furman Univ., history.furman.edu. Benjamin Flanders, in Foner, *Forever.* Sidney Andrews, at Furman Univ., facweb.furman.edu, attributed to "Three Months Among the Reconstructionists," *Atlantic Monthly* 17, no. 100 (Feb. 1866). **122:** *Chicago Tribune,* in Foner, *Forever.* Andrew Johnson, in Foner, *Forever.* Thaddeus Stevens, in Foner, *Forever.* **123:** Tenure of Office Act, in Kenneth Stampp, *The Era of Reconstruction: 1865–1877* (New York: Knopf, 1966). John Hope Franklin, *Reconstruction After the Civil War* (Chicago: Univ. of Chicago, 1994). Lyman Trumbull, at "The Impeachment Trial of President Andrew Johnson," DCBA Brief Online, www.dcba.org. **124:** Foner, *Forever.* William Lloyd Garrison, in Foner, *Forever.* **125:** Foner, *Forever.* **126:** Thomas Miller, in Foner, *Forever.* Stampp, *Era.* Ulysses S. Grant, in Franklin, *Reconstruction.* **127:** Foner, *Forever.* Frederick W. M. Holliday, at The Library of Virginia, www.lva.lib.va.us. **128:** Charleston News and Courier (1898), in C. Vann Woodward, *The Strange Career of Jim Crow* (New York: Oxford Univ. Press, 1974).

Chapter 12

131: Sandra L. Myres, *Westering Women and the Frontier Experience, 1800–1915* (Albuquerque: Univ. of New Mexico Press, 1982). **136:** Vincent P. de Santis et al., *America Past and Present: An Interpretation with Readings,* Vol. 2 (Boston: Allyn and Bacon, 1968). Rutherford B. Hayes, 1877, in Foster Rhea Dulles, *The United States Since 1865* (Ann Arbor: Univ. of Michigan Press, 1971). **137:** Frederick E. Hoxie, ed., *Encyclopedia of North American Indians* (Boston: Houghton Mifflin, 1996). **141:** William Jennings Bryan, in Isidore Starr, Lewis Paul Todd, and Merle Curti, eds., *Living American Documents* (New York: Harcourt, 1961). Omaha Platform, in Foner, *Give.*

Chapter 13

145: Alexander Graham Bell, "The Alexander Graham Bell Family Papers," at www.loc.gov. **150:** John D. Rockefeller, in Ralph K. Andrist, ed., *The American Heritage History of the Confident Years* (New York: American Heritage, 1973). **152:** Lincoln Steffens, "Enemies of the Republic," 1904, at the School of Cooperative Individualism, www.cooperativeindividualism.org. **154:** Andrew Carnegie, "Wealth," *North American Review,* 1889, in *Encyclopedia Britannica Ultimate Reference Suite,* 2004, CD-ROM.

Chapter 14

157: Rose Schneiderman, Apr. 2, 1911, "Triangle Factory Fire Documents," at Cornell Univ. ILR School, www.ilr.cornell.edu. **158:** Henry George, 1879, in de Santis, *America Past.* Page

Smith, *The Rise of Industrial America: A People's History of the Post-Reconstruction Era* (New York: McGraw-Hill, 1984). **159:** Mary Harris Jones, in Smith, *Rise.* Jane Addams, *Twenty Years at Hull-House* (1910), in Oscar Handlin, ed., *Readings in American History* (New York: Alfred A. Knopf, 1963). Esmond Wright, *The American Dream: From Reconstruction to Reagan* (Cambridge, MA: Blackwell, 1996). **164:** Mary Harris Jones, *The Autobiography of Mother Jones,* 3d ed. (Chicago: Charles H. Kerr, 1974).

Chapter 15

167: Edward Corsi, *In the Shadow of Liberty: The Chronicle of Ellis Island* (New York: Macmillan, 1935), in Oscar Handlin, *Statue of Liberty* (New York: Newsweek, 1971). Emma Lazarus, "The New Colossus" (1883) in John Higham, *Send These to Me: Immigrants in Urban America* (Baltimore: Johns Hopkins Univ. Press, 1984). **172:** Constantine M. Panunzio, *The Soul of an Immigrant* (New York: Arno Press, 1969), in Handlin, *Statue.* Riis, *How the Other.* **176:** Ronald Takaki, *Strangers from a Different Shore: A History of Asian Americans* (Boston: Little, Brown, 1989). **179:** Massachusetts Bureau of Statistics of Labor, *Twelfth Annual Report* (1881) in Charles W. Calhoun, ed., *The Gilded Age: Essays on the Origins of Modern America* (Wilmington, DE: Scholarly Resources, 1996).

Chapter 16

181: Riis, *How the Other.* Theodore Roosevelt, in John Mack Faragher et al., *Out of Many: A History of the American People,* Vol. 2, 5th ed. (Englewood Cliffs, NJ: Prentice Hall, 2005). **184:** Riis, *How the Other.* **185:** Faragher, *Out.* Upton Sinclair, *The Jungle* (New York: Doubleday, Page, 1906), online edition, Berkeley Digital Library SunSITE, sunsite.berkeley.edu. **186:** Alexis de Tocqueville, in Mary Beth Norton, et al., *A People and a Nation: A History of the United States,* 6th ed. (Boston: Houghton Mifflin, 2001). **187:** David E. Nye, *America as Second Creation: Technology and Narratives of New Beginnings* (Cambridge: MIT Press, 2003). Otto L. Bettmann, *The Good Old Days—They Were Terrible!* (New York: Random House, 1974). **188:** Lincoln Steffens, *The Shame of the Cities,* reprint ed. (New York: Amereon, 1957). Big Tim Sullivan, in Faragher, *Out.*

Chapter 17

195: Donald Miller, *City of the Century: The Epic of Chicago and the Making of America* (New York: Simon and Schuster, 1996). Jane Addams, in Miller, *City.* **196:** Woodrow Wilson, Inaugural Address, Mar. 4, 1913, in Richard Hofstadter, ed., *The Progressive Movement, 1900–1915* (Englewood Cliffs, NJ: Prentice Hall, 1963). **197:** Walter Rauschenbusch, *Christianity and the Social Crisis* (New York: Macmillan, 1907), in Hofstadter, *Progressive.* **198:** Robert Hunter, *Poverty* (New York: Macmillan, 1904), in Hofstadter, *Progressive.* Jacob Riis, *A Ten*

Years' War: An Account of the Battle with the Slum in New York (New York: Books for Libraries, 1969), at "New York City at the Turn of the Century," www.loc.gov. **200:** Steffens, Shame. **202:** Inez Haynes Irwin, Angels and Amazons: A Hundred Years of American Women, reprint ed. (New York: Arno Press, 1974). Elizabeth Cady Stanton, Seneca Falls Convention, at Smithsonian National Portrait Gallery, www.npg.si.edu. **203:** Ida B. Wells-Barnett, in Faragher, Out.

Chapter 18
205: J. P. Morgan and Theodore Roosevelt, in John Milton Cooper Jr., The Warrior and the Priest: Woodrow Wilson and Theodore Roosevelt (Cambridge, MA: Belknap Press, 1983). **206:** Theodore Roosevelt, in John Morton Blum, The Republican Roosevelt (New York: Athenaeum, 1965). Theodore Roosevelt, in James Chace, 1912: Wilson, Roosevelt, Taft, and Debs—The Election That Changed the Country (New York: Simon and Schuster, 2004). **207:** Theodore Roosevelt, in Chace, 1912. Eugene V. Debs, in James West Davidson et al., Nation of Nations: A Concise Narrative of the American Republic (New York: McGraw-Hill, 2005). Woodrow Wilson, in Arthur S. Link, Woodrow Wilson and the Progressive Era, 1900–1917 (New York: Harper Torchbooks, 1954). **208:** Theodore Roosevelt, in Chace, 1912. Theodore Roosevelt, in Richard B. Morris, Encyclopedia of American History, 7th ed. (New York: HarperCollins, 1996). **209:** Sinclair, Jungle. Upton Sinclair, in Paul S. Boyer et al., The Enduring Vision: A History of the American People to 1877, 5th ed. (Boston: Houghton Mifflin, 2002). William Taft, at "The Children's Bureau," Social Security Online History, www.ssa.gov. **210:** John Muir, The Story of My Boyhood and Youth (Boston, New York: Houghton Mifflin, 1913), at "John Muir Exhibit," Sierra Club, www.sierraclub.org. Theodore Roosevelt, in Norton, People. **213:** Theodore Roosevelt, in Thomas A. Bailey and David M. Kennedy, eds., The American Pageant: A History of the Republic, 9th ed. (Lexington, MA: Heath, 1991).

Chapter 19
216: George Washington, Farewell Address, 1796, at usinfo.state.gov. **217:** George Washington, Proclamation of Neutrality, 1793, in Bailey and Kennedy, American Pageant. Washington, Farewell Address. **218:** James Monroe, Monroe Doctrine, 1823, at usinfo.state.gov. Henry Cabot Lodge, "England, Venezuela, and the Monroe Doctrine," North American Review 160, no. 463 (June 1895), at "Making of America," cdl.library.cornell.edu. Chicago Journal, in Julius William Pratt, A History of United States Foreign Policy (New York: Prentice-Hall, 1955). **219:** James Knox Polk, Inaugural Address, 1845, at Yale Law School, www.yale.edu. **221:** James Knox Polk, May 11, 1846, at www.yale.edu.

Chapter 20
226: José Martí, in Carlos Ripoll, "José Martí: Thoughts," Oct. 31, 2005, Florida International Univ., www.fiu.edu. **228:** Enrique Dupuy de Lôme, in Bailey and Kennedy, American Spirit. **229:** Charles D. Sigsbee, at "An On-Line History of the United States," Public History Resource Center, www.publichistory.org. Redfield Proctor, Mar. 17, 1898, in Bailey and Kennedy, American Spirit. **230:** John Hay, July 27, 1898, at www.nytimes.com. **231:** John J. Pershing, in Melvin Sylvester, "African American Freedom Fighters: Soldiers for Liberty," Long Island Univ., www.liu.edu. **232:** Anti-Imperialist League platform, 1899, at "Modern History Sourcebook," Fordham Univ., www.fordham.edu. Henry Cabot Lodge, in John A. Garraty, Henry Cabot Lodge: A Biography (New York: Alfred A. Knopf, 1953).

Chapter 21
236: Theodore Roosevelt, in Nathan Miller, Theodore Roosevelt: A Life (New York: Harper Perennial, 1994). **237:** Woodrow Wilson, "Address Before the Southern Commercial Congress in Mobile, Alabama, Oct. 27, 1913," at www.presidency.ucsb.edu. **238:** "Building the Canal: Old World Failure," Dec. 8, 1999, BBC News, news.bbc.co.uk. **239:** Theodore Roosevelt: An Autobiography (New York: Da Capo Press, 1985; orig. pub. by Macmillan, 1913). **240:** Woodrow Wilson, at "American President: An Online Reference Resource," Miller Ctr. of Public Affairs, Univ. of Virginia, www.millercenter.virginia.edu. **242:** William McKinley, at "America at the Turn of the Century: A Look at the Historical Context," www.loc.gov. Mark Twain, in Howard Zinn, A People's History of the United States: 1492–Present (New York: HarperCollins, 1980). **244:** John Hay, Mar. 20, 1900, in Bailey and Kennedy, American Pageant. **245:** "The Boxer Rebellion and the U.S. Navy, 1900–1901," Naval Historical Center, www.history.navy.mil.

Chapter 22
247: Edward House, in Reader's Digest Assoc., Our Glorious Century (Pleasantville, NY: Reader's Digest Assoc., 1994). Blaine Baggett, Jay M. Winter, and Joseph Angier, "The Cruel Knock," The Great War and the Shaping of the Twentieth Century, www.neh.gov. **248:** Theodore Roosevelt, in Page Smith, America Enters the World: A People's History of the Progressive Era and World War I, Vol. 7 (New York: Penguin Books, 1991). **249:** Woodrow Wilson, Declaration of Neutrality, Aug. 19, 1914, at World War I, net.lib.byu.edu. Woodrow Wilson, State of the Union Address, Dec. 18, 1914, at stateoftheunion.onetwothree.net. James T. Patterson, America in the Twentieth Century: A History, 4th ed. (New York: Harcourt Brace Jovanovich, 1976). **250:** Ralph Raico, "American Foreign Policy—The Turning Point, 1898–1919," Freedom Daily, www.fff.org. Woodrow Wilson, First Warning to the Germans, Feb. 10, 1915, at The World War I Document Archive, net.lib.byu.edu. Theodore Roosevelt, May 11, 1915, "An American Time Capsule: Three Centuries of Broadsides and Other Printed Ephemera," American Memory, memory.loc.gov. **251:** William Jennings Bryan, in Harold Evans, The American Century (New York: Alfred A. Knopf, 2000). Robert Lansing, in Patterson, America. **252:** Woodrow Wilson, May 10, 1915, at www.bartleby.com. Woodrow Wilson, in Evans, American Century. "American Foreign Policy," www.fff.org. Kenneth W. Thompson, ed., Lessons from Defeated Presidential Candidates (Lanham, MD: Univ. Press of America, 1994), at webstorage1.mcpa.virginia.edu/library. **253:** Lord James Bryce, in Alan McDougall, "Dirty Hands: Atrocities of World War I," www.channel4.com/history. **254:** Woodrow Wilson, Address to the Senate, Jan. 22, 1917, at firstworldwar.com. Woodrow Wilson, "Joint Address to Congress Leading to a Declaration of War Against Germany," Apr. 2, 1917, at www.ourdocuments.gov. Woodrow Wilson, Joint Address to Congress, www.ourdocuments.gov. **255:** Woodrow Wilson, in Joseph P. Tumulty, Woodrow Wilson As I Know Him, www.gutenberg.org. George Norris, "Speech Against Declaration of War, April 4, 1917," www.iath.virginia.edu. Robert LaFollette, in Evans, American Century.

Chapter 23
257: William Langer, in David M. Kennedy, Over Here: The First World War and American Society (New York: Oxford Univ. Press, 2004). Henry Villard, in Peter Jennings and Todd Brewster, The Century: America's Time (New York: Doubleday, 1998). **258:** Thomas Martin, in Kennedy, Over Here. Newton Baker, in Kennedy, Over Here. David Lloyd George, in Kennedy, Over Here. **262:** Harold Saunders, at "Memoirs and Diaries: Trenches at Vimy Ridge," www.firstworldwar.com, attributed to C. B. Purdom, Everyman at War (London: J. M. Dent, 1930). **263:** John Jellicoe, in Byron Farwell, Over There: The United States in the Great War, 1917–1918 (New York: W. W. Norton, 1999). **264:** Erich Ludendorff, in Reader's Digest, Glorious. Erich Ludendorff, at "World War I: The Western Front, March–September 1918," www.brittanica.com. Siegfried Sassoon, "Does It Matter?" at www.bartleby.com. **265:** John Raws, Aug. 4, 1916, at www.spartacus.schoolnet.co.uk. Ezra Pound, "Hugh Selwyn Mauberly," 1920, at The Norton Anthology of English Literature, www2.wwnorton.com.

Chapter 24
267: Elsie Janis, "Ohioana Authors," WOSU, www.ohioana-authors.org. **268:** George M. Cohan, in Farwell, Over There. **269:** Woodrow Wilson, in Reader's Digest, Glorious. **270:** Farwell, Over There. "Seattle General Strike Program," faculty.washington.edu/gregoryj, attributed

to "Protecting the Working Mothers," *Seattle Union Record,* Apr. 24, 1918. **271:** Herbert Hoover, in *Reader's Digest, Glorious.* David Houston, in Ida Clyde Clarke, *American Women and the World War* (New York: D. Appleton, 1918), at "The World War I Document Archive," net.lib.byu.edu. **272:** Woodrow Wilson, Joint Address to Congress, at www.ourdocuments.gov. W. E. B. Du Bois, in John Hope Franklin, *From Slavery to Freedom: A History of African Americans* (New York: Knopf, 2000). Ronald Takaki, *A Different Mirror: A History of Multicultural America* (Boston: Little, Brown, 1993). "Jean Toomer's Washington and the Politics of Class: From 'Blue Veins' to Seventh-Street Rebels," at andromeda.rutgers.edu, attributed to Lee E. Williams, *Post-War Riots in America 1919 and 1946: How the Pressures of War Exacerbated American Urban Tensions to the Breaking Point* (Lewiston, NY: Edwin Mellen, 1992). Franklin, *From Slavery.* **273:** "Spies and Lies," Univ. of California, Davis, historyproject.ucdavis.edu. John Milton Cooper, *The Pivotal Decades: The United States, 1900–1920* (New York: W. W. Norton, 1990). Hiram Johnson, in Arthur Schlesinger, *War and the American Presidency* (New York: W. W. Norton, 2004). **274:** Eugene Debs, June 16, 1918, at "The Canton, Ohio, Speech," *International Socialist Review,* no. 20 (2001). Howard Zinn, *A People's History of the United States* (New York: HarperCollins, 1999). Oliver Wendell Holmes Jr., in Cooper, *Pivotal.*

Chapter 25

277: Thomas A. Bailey, *A Diplomatic History of the American People* (Englewood Cliffs, NJ: Prentice-Hall, 1980). Margaret MacMillan, *Paris 1919: Six Months That Changed the World* (New York: Random House, 2002). **278:** Woodrow Wilson, "Fourteen Points Speech," Jan. 8, 1918, at usinfo.state.gov. William Taft, in Thomas A. Bailey, "Woodrow Wilson Wouldn't Yield," *American Heritage Magazine,* www.americanheritage.com. **279:** "President Woodrow Wilson's Fourteen Points," at www.ourdocuments.gov. **280:** "International Relations," www.britannica.com. Woodrow Wilson, Address to the Senate, Jan. 22, 1917, at firstworldwar.com. Harold Nicolson, at William R. Keylor, "A Re-evaluation of the Versailles Peace," The Great War Society, www.worldwar1.com/tgws. **282:** John Pyne and Gloria Sesso, "Woodrow Wilson and the U.S. Ratification of the Treaty of Versailles," Organization of American Historians, www.oah.org. Henry Cabot Lodge, "On the League of Nations," Aug. 12, 1919, at www.firstworldwar.com. Henry Cabot Lodge, in "George A. Sanderson, Secretary of State," www.senate.gov. **283:** William Borah, in Patterson, *America.* William Borah, at Pyne and Sesso, www.oah.org, attributed to *Congressional Record,* Nov. 10, 1919, 66th Congress, First Session. Woodrow Wilson, in William D. Miller, *Pretty Bubbles in the Air: America in 1919*

(Chicago: Univ. of Illinois, 1991). **284:** "Edith Wilson," www.britannica.com. Edith Wilson, at "American President: Edith Wilson," www.millercenter.virginia.edu. Woodrow Wilson, at Bailey, "Woodrow Wilson Wouldn't Yield," www.americanheritage.com. Woodrow Wilson, in George Brown Tindall and David E. Shi, *America: A Narrative History* (New York: W. W. Norton, 2003). Franklin Roosevelt, at "United Nations and Human Rights," www.san.beck.org, attributed to *Franklin D. Roosevelt's Own Story, Told in His Own Words from His Private and Public Papers as Selected by Donald Day* (Boston: Little, Brown, 1951). "Republican Party Platform of 1920," at www.presidency.ucsb.edu. Edith Wilson, www.millercenter.virginia.edu. **285:** Woodrow Wilson, www.britannica.com. Robert Lansing, in Smith, *America Enters.* Joseph Tumulty, in Bailey, *Diplomatic History.*

Chapter 26

287: "Woody Guthrie: Ballads of Sacco and Vanzetti," at www.geocities.com, attributed to Felix Frankfurter, "The Case of Sacco and Vanzetti," *Atlantic Monthly* (Mar. 1927). **289:** Frederick Lewis Allen, *Only Yesterday: An Informal History of the 1920s* (New York: Harper and Row, 1964). **290:** "Preamble to the IWW Constitution," Industrial Workers of the World, www.iww.org. Bill Haywood, at "Minutes of the IWW's Founding Convention," www.iww.org. Ole Hanson, in Zinn, *People's History.* **291:** Calvin Coolidge, at "Boston Police Strike," www.britannica.com. **292:** Bartolomeo Vanzetti, in Judy Monroe, *The Sacco and Vanzetti Controversial Murder Trial: A Headline Court Case* (Berkeley Heights, NJ: Enslow, 2000). George Weston, in Daniel Gross, "Previous Terror on Wall Street: A Look at a 1920 Bombing," Sep. 20, 2001, www.thestreet.com. **293:** Walter Lippmann, in Nathan Miller, *New World Coming: The 1920s and the Making of Modern America* (New York: Scribner, 2003). **294:** Alan Brinkley, *American History: A Survey,* 10th ed. (New York: McGraw-Hill College, 2005). **295:** Hiram Wesley Evans, in Patterson, *America.* **296:** Bartolomeo Vanzetti, in "Sacco and Vanzetti," *Time,* Apr. 18, 1927, at www.time.com. Claude McKay, "If We Must Die," at Representative Poetry Online, rpo.library.utoronto.ca, attributed to Claude McKay, *Harlem Shadows: The Poems of Claude McKay* (New York: Harcourt, Brace, 1922). Marcus Garvey, at "UNIA History," www.unia-acl.org. Marcus Garvey, at "Religion and Ethics," www.bbc.co.uk.

Chapter 27

299: Warren G. Harding, at www.whitehouse.gov. Boies Penrose, in Miller, *New World.* Harding, at www.whitehouse.gov. Miller, *New World.* **300:** Harry Daugherty, at "Warren Gamaliel Harding," The American Presidency, ap.grolier.com. Warren G. Harding, at "Politics During the 1920s," Digital History, www.digitalhistory.uh.edu. **301:** Warren

G. Harding, in Miller, *New World.* Calvin Coolidge, at "Politics During the 1920s," www.digitalhistory.uh.edu. Calvin Coolidge, in Miller, *New World.* Herbert Hoover, in Miller, *New World.* Herbert Hoover, at "Oh Yeah?: Herbert Hoover Predicts Prosperity," historymatters.gmu.edu, attributed to Edward Angly, *Oh Yeah! Compiled from Newspapers and Public Records by Edward Angly* (New York: Viking Press, 1931). **302:** Warren G. Harding, at "Inaugural Address of Warren G. Harding," The Avalon Project, www.yale.edu. Kellogg-Briand Pact, 1928, at www.yale.edu, attributed to United States Statutes at Large, Vol. 46, Pt. 2. Bailey, *Diplomatic History.* "Isolationism," www.digitalhistory.uh.edu. **303:** Herbert Hoover, at "Statement on the President's Commission for the Study and Review of Conditions in the Republic of Haiti," Feb. 4, 1930, www.presidency.ucsb.edu. **304:** Lincoln Steffens, in Eric Foner, *Give Me Liberty! An American History,* Vol. 2 (New York: W. W. Norton, 2004). Henry Ford, in Frederick Lewis Allen, *The Big Change: America Transforms Itself, 1900–1950* (New York: Harper, 1952). Allen, *Big Change.* **306:** "Charles Ponzi," www.digital.history.uh.edu.

Chapter 28

309: Bee Jackson, "Keep Working: Hey! Hey! Charleston," *National Weekly,* Dec. 10, 1917. Gilbert Seldes, "Shake Your Feet," *The New Republic,* Nov. 4, 1925. **311:** Stuart Chase, "The Tragedy of Waste," *Atlantic Monthly* (1925), in Patterson, *America.* Bruce Barton, *The Man Nobody Knows* (New York: Collier Books, 1987). Bruce Barton, at "BBDO," Center for Interactive Advertising, www.ciadvertising.org. **312:** "Lindberg Flies the Atlantic, 1927," Charles Lindbergh: American Aviator, www.charleslindbergh.com. Amelia Earhart, at www.ameliaearhart.com. **313:** "The Twenties: The Rise of the Automobile," A Biography of America, www.learner.org. Allen, *Big Change.* **315:** David Sarnoff, at "The Time 100," www.time.com. "Radio Pioneers Enter Story of Wire," www.rwonline.com. Donald R. McCoy, *Coming of Age: The United States During the 1920s and 1930s* (Baltimore, MD: Penguin Books, 1973). **316:** Carrie Chapman Catt, in Eleanor Flexner, *Century of Struggle: The Woman's Rights Movement in the United States* (Cambridge, MA: Belknap Press, 1996). "The ERA: A Brief Introduction," www.equalrightsamendment.org. Jeannette Rankin, in Gail Collins, *America's Women: 400 Years of Dolls, Drudges, Helpmates, and Heroines* (New York: HarperCollins, 2003). **317:** Margaret Sanger, *Woman and the New Race* (1920), at "Margaret Sanger's Fight for Women's Reproductive Rights," Margaret Sanger Papers Project, www.nyu.edu/projects. Alice Paul, at www.alicepaul.org. **318:** Geoffrey C. Ward and Ken Burns, *Jazz: A History of America's Music* (New York: Knopf, 2000). Louis Armstrong, at www.music-with-ease.com. Duke Ellington, at www.bartleby.com, attributed to "On Jazz," *Herald Tribune,* July 9, 1961. Paul Williams, in Ward and Burns, *Jazz.* Wynton Marsalis, in Ward and Burns, *Jazz.* Mahalia Jackson, in Ward and Burns, *Jazz.* **318:** Duke Ellington, in Ward and Burns, *Jazz.* **320:** Langston Hughes, *The Big Sea: An Autobiography* (New York: Hill and Wang, 1963). Langston Hughes, "The Negro Speaks of Rivers," at www.poets.org, attributed to *The Collected Poems of Langston Hughes* (New York: Alfred A. Knopf, 1994). Langston Hughes, "A Brief Guide to the Harlem Renaissance," www.poets.org. **321:** F. Scott Fitzgerald, *Tender Is the Night* (New York: Scribner, 1996). Georgia O'Keeffe, at "Inspiring Visions: Artists' Views of the American West," www.cartermuseum.org, attributed to *Georgia O'Keeffe* (New York: Viking Press, 1976).

Chapter 29
325: Norman Rockwell, at "A Brief Biography," The Norman Rockwell Museum, www.nrm.org. **326:** Joe Young and Sam Lewis, "How Ya' Gonna Keep 'Em Down on the Farm? (After They've Seen Paree)," at www.firstworldwar.com. **327:** Calvin Coolidge, in William E. Leuchtenburg, *The Perils of Prosperity, 1914–1932,* 2d ed. (Chicago: Univ. of Chicago Press, 1993). Sinclair Lewis, *Main Street* (1920), at www.americanliterature.com. Billy Sunday, in "Billy Sunday Again Hits the Trail Here," *New York Times,* Apr. 16, 1925. **329:** Zelda Fitzgerald, in Miller, *New World Coming.* Allen, *Only Yesterday.* Edna St. Vincent Millay, "First Fig," *A Few Figs from Thistles* (New York: Harper and Brothers, 1922), at "A Celebration of Women Writers," digital.library.upenn.edu. George E. Mowry and Blaine A. Brownell, *The Urban Nation, 1920–1980,* rev. ed. (New York: Hill and Wang, 1981). Herbert Hoover, in Leuchtenburg, *Perils.* Al Capone, in Andrew Sinclair, *Era of Excess: A Social History of the Prohibition Movement* (New York: Harper and Row, 1962). **331:** H. L. Mencken, in Paul Johnson, *A History of the American People* (New York: Harper Perennial, 1997). David Walsh, in Leuchtenburg, *Perils.* *Variety* (Oct. 16, 1929), at "New York in the 1920s," www.americanheritage.com. Will Rogers, in Edward Behr, *Prohibition: Thirteen Years That Changed America* (New York: Arcade, 1996). Leuchtenburg, *Perils.* **332:** Public Acts of the State of Tennessee, House Bill No. 185, 1925, at "Tennessee Anti-evolution Statutes," www.law.umkc.edu. Foner, *Give.* **333:** William Jennings Bryan, in Edward Caudill, *The Scopes Trial: A Photographic History* (Knoxville, TN: Univ. of Tennessee Press, 1999). George Rappelyea, at Doug Linder, "George Rappelyea," www.law.umkc.edu. Doug Linder, "State v. John Scopes ('The Monkey Trial')," www.law.umkc.edu. "Between the Wars: The Scopes Trial," Center for History and New Media, chnm.gmu.edu. John Scopes, at Doug Linder, "John Scopes," www.law.umkc.edu.

Chapter 30
335: Herbert Hoover, in David Kennedy, *Freedom from Fear: The American People in Depression and War, 1929–1945* (New York: Oxford Univ. Press, 1999).

Chapter 31
343: Walter Waters, in William C. White, *B.E.F.: The Whole Story of the Bonus Army* (New York: John Day, 1933). **344:** Franklin Roosevelt, in William Safire, *Safire's New Political Dictionary* (New York: Random House, 1993). **346:** Herbert Hoover, at "Great Depression in the United States," MSN Encarta, encarta.msn.com. **347:** Herbert Hoover, in T. H. Watkins, *The Hungry Years: A Narrative History of the Great Depression in America* (New York: Henry Holt, 1999). Franklin Roosevelt, in Robert S. McElvaine, ed., *Encyclopedia of the Great Depression* (New York: Thomson Gale, 2004). Franklin Roosevelt, in E. J. Dionne Jr., "Roosevelt, America's Original Man from Hope," May 1, 1997, at The Washington Post, www.washingtonpost.com. **349:** Franklin Roosevelt, Mar. 4, 1933, in *Encarta Encyclopedia Deluxe 2003,* CD-ROM.

Chapter 32
351: Harry Hopkins, in Richard Lowitt and Maurine Beasley, eds., *One Third of a Nation: Lorena Hickok Reports on the Great Depression* (Urbana: Univ. of Illinois Press, 1981). **352:** E. Y. Harburg, in "The Song," in Studs Terkel, *Hard Times: An Oral History of the Great Depression* (New York: Pantheon Books, 1970). **353:** Mirra Komarovsky, *The Unemployed Man and His Family: The Effects of Unemployment Upon the Status of the Man in Fifty-nine Families* (New York: Dryden Press, 1940). "American Experience: Riding the Rails," www.pbs.org. **354:** Franklin Roosevelt, Second Inaugural Address, Jan. 20, 1937, at www.bartleby.com. William E. Leuchtenburg, *The FDR Years: On Roosevelt and His Legacy* (New York: Columbia Univ. Press, 1995). "American Experience: Riding the Rails," www.pbs.org. **355:** Robert Cohen, ed., *Dear Mrs. Roosevelt: Letters from Children of the Great Depression* (Chapel Hill: Univ. of North Carolina Press, 2002). Louis Adamic, *My America, 1928–1938* (New York: Harper and Brothers, 1938). **356:** "Surviving the Dust Bowl: Enhanced Transcript," www.pbs.org. **357:** Ibid. **359:** "After the Deluge," *New York Times* (Mar. 22, 1936), in Joseph L. Arnold, *The Evolution of the 1936 Flood Control Act* (Fort Belvoir, VA: U.S. Army Corps of Engineers, 1988). "City Water Fails; 45 Dead, 350 Hurt," *Pittsburg Sun-Telegraph* (Mar. 20, 1936), at Carnegie Library of Pittsburgh, clpgh.org. *Business Week* (Apr. 1936), in Arnold, *Evolution.* **360:** Jerry Siegel, in David Michael Petrou, "Superman, the Legend," at theages.superman.ws. Daniel Aaron and Robert Bendiner, eds., *The Strenuous Decade: A Social and Intellectual Record of the 1930s* (New York: Anchor Books, 1970), attributed to Robert Carter, *The New*

Republic LXXIV (Mar. 8, 1933). Lorena Hickok, in Kennedy, *Freedom.* **361:** Kennedy, *Freedom.* Harry Hopkins, in H. H. Adams, *Harry Hopkins: A Biography* (New York: G.P. Putnam's Sons, 1977).

Chapter 33
363: Franklin Roosevelt, in "Eleanor Roosevelt: Enhanced Transcript," www.pbs.org. Franklin Roosevelt, radio broadcast, in "Smith 1; Roosevelt 154," Apr. 18, 1932, www.time.com. **364:** Franklin Roosevelt, "On the Bank Crisis" fireside chat, Mar. 12, 1933, at New Deal Network, newdeal.feri.org. **367:** Franklin Roosevelt, in Safire, *Dictionary.* **368:** Franklin Roosevelt, in "Dead Flower," *Time Magazine,* Nov. 12, 1934, at Time, jcgi.pathfinder.com/time. Charles Coughlin, in Kennedy, *Freedom.* Huey Long, "Share our wealth" speech, Dec. 11, 1934, at "Historical Speeches," John C. Stennis Institute of Government, Mississippi State Univ., www.msgovt.org. **369:** Franklin Roosevelt, in Kennedy, *Freedom.* **370:** Franklin Roosevelt, message to Congress, Jan. 1, 1935, in Kennedy, *Freedom.* Franklin Roosevelt, Aug. 14, 1935, in "Social Security: A Primer" (Congressional Budget Office, www.cbo.gov, Sep. 2001), attributed to *Project on the Federal Social Role: The Report of the Committee on Economic Security of 1935* (Washington, DC: National Conference on Social Welfare, 1985). **371:** Charles Evans Hughes, in Foner, *Give.* **372:** Franklin Roosevelt, in Kennedy, *Freedom.* **373:** Foner, *Give.* Leuchtenburg, *FDR Years.* **375:** Franklin Roosevelt, Second Inaugural Address, at newdeal.feri.org. **376:** Franklin Roosevelt, address to Congress, Jan. 11, 1944, in Leuchtenburg, *FDR Years.* **377:** Richard M. Ebeling, "Monetary Central Planning and the State, Part 14: The New Deal and Its Critics," Feb. 1998, Future of Freedom Foundation, www.fff.org, attributed to Howard E. Kershner, *The Menace of Roosevelt and His Policies* (New York: Greenberg, 1936).

Chapter 34
379: Neville Chamberlain, in Norman Moss, *Nineteen Weeks: America, Britain, and the Fateful Summer of 1940* (Boston: Houghton Mifflin, 2003). **381:** "Fascism: Military Values," www.britannica.com. **383:** Franklin Roosevelt, at "First Inaugural Address," Mar. 4, 1933, American Rhetoric, www.americanrhetoric.com. *Peace and War: U.S. Foreign Policy, 1931–1941* (Washington, D.C.: U.S. Government Printing Office). **384:** Franklin Roosevelt, "Quarantine the Aggressor," Oct. 15, 1937, www.presidentialrhetoric.com. Haile Selassie, in Barbara Bryant, "The Largest Event: Library of Congress Resource Guide for the Study of World War II," www.loc.gov. **385:** Adolf Hitler, "The Triumph of Hitler Nazis Take Czechoslovakia," The History Place, www.historyplace.com. Winston Churchill, *The Second World War, Vol. I: The Gathering Storm* (Boston: Houghton-Mifflin, 1948). **388:** "'The Phony War:' Oct. 1939–

Apr. 1940," www.worldwar2database.com. **389:** Winston Churchill, "Speech Before Commons (June 4, 1940)," Hanover College, history.hanover.edu. **390:** Franklin Roosevelt, at "President and Public Pressure: 'For a Redress of Grievances,'" The White House Historical Assoc., www.whitehousehistory.org. "Japanese Foreign Minister Togo Shigenori's Address to the Imperial Diet, November 17, 1941," *New York Times,* Nov. 18, 1941, at WWII Resources, www.ibiblio.org/pha. **391:** Franklin Roosevelt, Joint Address to Congress Leading to a Declaration of War Against Japan, Dec. 8, 1941, at www.ourdocuments.gov.

Chapter 35

394: Franklin Roosevelt, "Arsenal of Democracy" speech, Dec. 29, 1940, at International Relations Program, www.mtholyoke.edu. **395:** Franklin Roosevelt, fireside chat, Apr. 28, 1942, at www.presidency.ucsb.edu. **396:** "A More Perfect Union," americanhistory.si.edu. National Manpower Council, Womanpower (New York: Columbia Univ. Press, 1957). Selective Service and Victory: The 4th Report of the Director of Selective Service (Washington: Government Printing Office, 1948), at "Minority Groups in World War II," www.army.mil. "The Battle to Enlist: Anti-Semitism in the Armed Forces," When Jews Were GIs: World War II and the Remaking of America, FATHOM: The Univ. of Michigan, www.fathom.com. "Five Views: An Ethnic Historic Site for California," www.cr.nps.gov. **397:** James West Davidson, Nation of Nations: A Narrative History of the American Republic, 5th ed. (New York: McGraw-Hill, 2004). Lee Kennett, G.I.: The American Soldier in World War II (Norman: Univ. of Oklahoma Press, 1987). Studs Terkel, The Good War: An Oral History of World War II (New York: Pantheon, 1984). **399:** Robert H. Jackson, in Kermit L. Hall, ed., The Oxford Companion to the Supreme Court of the United States, 2d ed. (New York: Oxford Univ. Press, 2005). Takaki, Different. **400:** Redd Evans and John Jacob Loeb, "Rosie the Riveter," at Sheridan Harvey, "Rosie the Riveter: Real Women Workers in World War II," www.loc.gov. "Rosie The Riveter" written by John Jacob Loeb and Redd Evans. © Copyright Secured Fred Ahlert Music Group (ASCAP)/Flojan Music (ASCAP). Administered by Bug/Music Sales Corp. (ASCAP). All Rights Reserved. Used By Permission. ROSIE THE RIVETER. Words and Music by Redd Evans and John Jacob Loeb. Copyright © 1942 (Renewed) by Music Sales Corporation (ASCAP) and Fred Ahlert Music Corporation. International Copyright Secured. All Rights Reserved. Reprinted by Permission. Penny Colman, Rosie the Riveter: Women Working on the Home Front in World War II (New York: Crown, 1995). **401:** Sybil Lewis, in Mark Jonathan Harris, Franklin D. Mitchell, and Steven J. Schechter, eds., The Homefront:

America During World War II (New York: Putnam, 1984). John W. Jeffries, Wartime America: The World War II Home Front (Chicago: Ivan R. Dee, 1996). Ronald H. Bailey, The Home Front: U.S.A. (Alexandria, VA: Time-Life Books, 1978). **402:** Takaki, Different. Doris Kearns Goodwin, No Ordinary Time: Franklin and Eleanor Roosevelt: The Home Front in World War II (New York: Simon and Schuster, 1994). Terkel, Good War. **403:** David M. Kennedy, Freedom from Fear: The American People in the Depression and War, 1929–1945 (New York: Oxford Univ. Press, 1999). **404:** Franklin Roosevelt, in Kennedy, Freedom. **405:** Henry Morgenthau Jr., in John Morton Blum, V Was for Victory: Politics and American Culture During World War II (New York: Harcourt, 1976). David S. Wyman, The Abandonment of the Jews (New York: Pantheon, 1984). Leon Uris, at "Jewish Empowerment in Response to the War," When Jews Were GIs, www.fathom.com. **406:** Takaki, Different. **407:** "Los Angeles Zoot Suit Riots," Los Angeles Almanac, www.laalmanac.com.

Chapter 36

410: Simon Appleby, "Churchill, Roosevelt, and the Casablanca Conference, January 1943," The Casablanca Conference, www.casablancaconference.com. **413:** Joseph Stalin, at "The Tide Turns: Stalingrad and the Advances in the Pacific," World War II, www.history.com. Elie Wiesel, in Michael Berenbaum, "Why Wasn't Auschwitz Bombed?" www.britannica.com. **414:** Dwight Eisenhower, "Order of the Day," June 6, 1944, at www.ourdocuments.gov. Robert Edlin, in Colbert, *Eyewitness to America.* Ronald Reagan, in "Remembering Reagan," *U.S. News and World Report,* June 6, 2005. **415:** Takaki, *Different.* **416:** Douglas MacArthur, at "The Philippines, Dec. 8 1941–May 8, 1942," www.worldwar2database.com. **418:** Douglas MacArthur, *Reminiscences* (New York: McGraw-Hill, 1964), in William Manchester, *American Caesar: Douglas MacArthur (1880–1964)* (Boston: Little, Brown, 1978). **419:** Nimitz, in Williamson Murray and Allan R. Millett, *A War to Be Won: Fighting the Second World War* (Cambridge, MA: Belknap Press of Harvard Univ. Press, 2000). **420:** Albert Einstein, at "Einstein's Letters to Roosevelt," Aug. 2, 1939, hypertextbook.com. J. Robert Oppenheimer, at Atomic Archive, www.atomicarchive.com. Dwight Eisenhower, in "President Truman: Using Atomic Bombs Against Japan, 1945," www.digitalhistory.uh.edu. Harry Truman, in Stephen Walker, *Shockwave: Countdown to Hiroshima* (New York: HarperCollins, 2005). **421:** Harry S. Truman, *Memoirs,* Vol. 1 (New York: Doubleday, 1955)

Chapter 37

423: Calder M. Pickett, *Voices of the Past: Key Documents in the History of American Journalism* (Columbus, OH: Grid, 1977).

James T. Patterson, *Grand Expectations: The United States, 1945–1974* (New York: Oxford Univ. Press, 1996). Franklin Roosevelt, in Georg Schild, *Bretton Woods and Dumbarton Oaks: American Economic and Political Postwar Planning in the Summer of 1944* (New York: St. Martin's, 1995). **424:** Cordell Hull, in Schild, *Bretton.* **425:** Franklin Roosevelt, Address on the Signing of the Agreement Establishing the U.N.R.R.A., Nov. 9, 1943, at www.presidency.ucsb.edu. Franklin Roosevelt, "Four Freedoms Speech," Jan. 6, 1941, at www.ourdocuments.gov. **426:** Franklin Roosevelt, Address to Congress on the Yalta Conference, Mar. 1, 1945, at www.presidency.ucsb.edu. Robert H. Jackson, at "Nuremberg Trial Proceedings, Vol. 2," www.yale.edu. G. M. Gilbert, *Nuremberg Diary* (New York: Da Capo Press, 1995). **427:** Franklin Roosevelt, Address to the International Student Assembly, Sep. 3, 1942, at www.presidency.ucsb.edu. **429:** Alice Kessler-Harris, *Women Have Always Worked: A Historical Overview* (Old Westbury, NY: The Feminist Press/McGraw-Hill, 1981).

Chapter 38

431: Harry Truman, in "Russians and Americans Link at Elbe," Apr. 27, 1945, news.bbc.co.uk. **432:** Dwight D. Eisenhower, in J. T. Dykman, "The Soviet Experience in World War Two," The Eisenhower Institute, www.eisenhowerinstitute.org, attributed to Dwight Eisenhower, *Crusade in Europe* (Garden City, NY: Doubleday, 1948). **433:** Harry S. Truman, Truman Doctrine, Mar. 12, 1947, at www.yale.edu. **434:** Joseph Stalin, Feb. 9, 1946, in "Speech Delivered by J. V. Stalin at a Meeting of Voters of the Stalin Electoral District, Moscow," from the pamphlet collection at the Foreign Languages Publishing House, Moscow, 1950, at The Cold War Files: Interpreting History Through Documents, www.coldwarfiles.org. George Kennan, Long Telegram, Feb. 22, 1946, at The National Security Archive, George Washington Univ., www.gwu.edu~nsarchiv/. George Kennan, "The Sources of Soviet Conduct," *Foreign Affairs* (July 1947), at "Cold War: A CNN Perspectives Series," CNN Interactive, www.cnn.com. **436:** Winston Churchill, in "Winston Churchill, Iron Curtain Speech, Mar. 5, 1946," at "Modern History Sourcebook," www.fordham.edu. Joseph Stalin, in "Joseph Stalin: Reply to Churchill, 1946," at www.fordham.edu. **438:** Harry S. Truman, Truman Doctrine, www.yale.edu. **439:** Irving Brant, in Richard C. Lukas, *Bitter Legacy: Polish-American Relations in the Wake of World War II* (Lexington, KY: Univ. Press of Kentucky, 1983). George Marshall, June 5, 1947, at usinfo.state.gov. **440:** Joseph Stalin, in David Reynolds, "Marshall Plan Commemorative Section: The European Response: Primacy of Politics," *Foreign Affairs* (May/June 1997), at www.foreignaffairs.com.

Chapter 39

443: Dwight Eisenhower, May 11, 1960, in "'Our First Line of Defense': Presidential Reflections on US Intelligence," Center for the Study of Intelligence, www.cia.gov/csi. **444:** Lucius Clay, in Ernest May, ed., *Anxiety and Affluence: 1945–1965* (New York: McGraw-Hill, 1966). **446:** Imre Nagy, Nov. 4, 1956, in "Hungary 1956," at www.fordham.edu. James T. Patterson, *Grand*. Douglas Brinkley, *American Heritage History of the United States* (New York: Penguin Group, 1998). **449:** Dean Acheson, in Patterson, *America*. Douglas MacArthur, in Alan Brinkley, *American History*, 11th ed. (New York: McGraw-Hill Higher Education, 2003). **454:** Harry S. Truman, Sep. 23, 1949, at "American Experience: Race for the Superbomb," www.pbs.org. Report to the Atomic Energy Commission, Joint Chiefs of Staff, at "American Experience: Race for the Superbomb," www.pbs.org. **454:** John Foster Dulles, in Reader's Digest Assoc., *Glorious*.

Chapter 40

457: Norman H. Finkelstein, *The Way Things Never Were: The Truth About the "Good Old Days"* (New York: Atheneum, 1999). Doris Kearns Goodwin, in Kenneth Rose, *One Nation Underground: The Fallout Shelter in American Culture* (New York: New York Univ. Press, 2001). **458:** "100 Things You Should Know About Communism in the U.S.A.: The First of a Series on the Communist Conspiracy and Its Influence in This Country as a Whole, on Religion, on Education, on Labor and on Our Government," U.S. House of Representatives' Committee on Un-American Activities (1951). J. Parnell Thomas, House Un-American Activities Committee, 1947. **459:** Jay Walz, "Ten Film Men Cited for Contempt in Overwhelming Votes by House," *New York Times*, Nov. 25, 1947, reprinted in Richard Halworth Rovere and Gene Brown, *Loyalty and Security in a Democratic State: The Great Contemporary Issues* (New York: Arno Press, 1977). **460:** Joseph McCarthy, at "'Enemies from Within': Senator Joseph R. McCarthy's Accusations of Disloyalty," historymatters.gmu.edu. Joseph Welch, June 9, 1954, in "Have You No Sense of Decency?," www.senate.gov. **461:** Pat Frank, *Alas, Babylon*, reprint ed. (New York: HarperCollins, 2005). *Milwaukee Journal*, Aug. 7, 1945, in Paul Boyer, *By the Bomb's Early Light: American Thought and Culture at the Dawn of the Atomic Age* (Chapel Hill: Univ. of North Carolina Press, 1994). **462:** Millard Caldwell, in "Women Defend the Nation," The Cold War Museum, www.coldwar.org, attributed to Federal Civil Defense Administration, "Can Americans Take It?," *The Civil Defense Alert*, Apr. 1951. Val Peterson, Mar. 11, 1955, in "Infrastructure: Civil Defense, 1955," U.S. Department of Transportation, Federal Highway Administration, www.fhwa.dot.gov.

Chapter 41

465: D. J. Waldie, *Holy Land: A Suburban Memoir* (New York: W. W. Norton, 2005). **466:** Harry Truman, in Paul Boller Jr., *Presidential Anecdotes* (Philadelphia: Running Press, 2007). Foner, *Give*. Harry Truman, at "'Word Has Just Been Received:' Truman Speaks on the Railroad Strike," historymatters.gmu.edu. **467:** "Pamphlets in the Fights Against Taft-Hartley, 1947–1948," Labor Studies and Radical History, www.holtlaborlibrary.com. Harry Truman, at "Statement by the President Making Public a Report on the Civil Rights Committee," Oct. 29, 1947, www.presidency.ucsb.edu. "U.S. Presidential Election, 1948," www.fact-index.com, attributed to Gary A. Donaldson, *Truman Defeats Dewey* (Louisville: The Univ. Press of Kentucky, 1999), quoting the *Louisville Courier Journal*, Nov. 18, 1948. **468:** Harry Truman, "Whistle-Stop Tour," Sep. 18, 1948, at www.millercenter.virginia.edu. Mowry and Brownell, *Urban Nation*. Dwight Eisenhower, The White House, www.whitehouse.gov. Dwight Eisenhower, at "Chapter 12: Postwar America," usinfo.state.gov. Dwight Eisenhower, at Louis Galambos and Daun van Ee, "A President's First Term: Eisenhower's Pursuit of '"The Middle Way,'" www.neh.gov, adapted from *The Papers of Dwight David Eisenhower: The Presidency: The Middle Way* (Baltimore, MD: Johns Hopkins Univ. Press). Dwight Eisenhower, Farewell Address, Jan. 17, 1861, at The Dwight D. Eisenhower Library, www.eisenhower.archives.gov. Foner, *Give*. **469:** Dick McDonald, in David Halberstam, *The Fifties*, copyright © 1993 by The Amateurs Limited. Used by permission of Villard Books, a division of Random House, Inc. **470:** Brooks Stevens, at "Industrial Strength Design: How Brooks Stevens Shaped Your World," Milwaukee Art Museum, www.mam.org. **471:** Kemmons Wilson, in *Half Luck and Half Brains: The Kemmons Wilson, Holiday Inn Story* (Nashville, TN: Hambleton-Hill, 1996). **472:** Landon Y. Jones, *Great Expectations: America and the Baby Boom Generation* (New York: Coward, McCann and Geoghegan, 1980). John Schindler, *The Woman's Guide to Better Living 52 Weeks a Year* (Englewood Cliffs, NJ: Prentice-Hall, 1957), in Douglas T. Miller and Marion Nowak, *The Fifties: The Way We Really Were* (Garden City, NY: Doubleday, 1977). Halberstam, *Fifties*. **473:** "School Sweater," Reoccurring Themes, www.leaveittobeaver.org. Stephanie Coontz, *The Way We Really Are: Coming to Terms with America's Changing Families* (New York: Basic Books, 1997), at www.questia.com, attributed to Susan Douglas, *Where the Girls Are: Growing Up Female with the Mass Media* (New York: Times Books, 1994). *The Happy Family* (New York: Simon and Schuster, 1947). **475:** *Saturday Evening Post*, 1954, at "Becoming a Levittowner," Levittown: Building the

Suburban Dream, The State Museum of Pennsylvania, www.statemuseumpa.org. **476:** Kathleen A. Ervin, "*Failure* Examines the History of the Edsel," *Auto Biography*, *Failure Magazine*, www.failuremag.com. Miller and Nowak, *Fifties*. Phil Skinner, in Ervin, www.failuremag.com. **478:** Charles Mee, *A Nearly Normal Life: A Memoir* (Boston: Little, Brown, 1999). Lewis Strauss, at J. Rothwell, *Cold Fusion and the Future* (2004), lenr-canr.org, attributed to "Speech to the National Association of Science Writers," New York, 1954.

Chapter 42

481: Richard Nixon, in "Nixon Foresees a Four-Day Work Week," *New York Times*, Sep. 22, 1956. "Prosperity and Expansion: A Business Review and Forecast," *Time*, Dec. 31, 1956. **482:** Endesha Ida Mae Holland, *From the Mississippi Delta: A Memoir* (New York: Simon and Schuster, 1997). Charles Burroughs (1834), in John Iceland, *Poverty in America: A Handbook* (Berkeley: Univ. of California Press, 2003). **484:** Carmen Whalen, *From Puerto Rico to Philadelphia: Puerto Rican Workers and Postwar Economics* (Philadelphia: Temple Univ. Press, 2001). "Midwest Indians Found in Squalor," *New York Times*, Sep. 1, 1949. Peter Iverson, *"We Are Still Here": American Indians in the Twentieth Century* (Wheeling, IL: Harlan Davidson, 1998).

Chapter 43

487: Melba Pattillo Beals, *Warriors Don't Cry: A Searing Memoir of the Battle to Integrate Little Rock's Central High* (New York: Simon and Schuster, 1994). **488:** W. E. B. Du Bois, in "Communities 'Behind the Veil,'" Remembering Jim Crow, americanradioworks.publicradio.org. **489:** Ronald L. F. Davis, "Creating Jim Crow: In-Depth Essay," The History of Jim Crow, www.jimcrowhistory.org. **491:** Jackie Robinson, in "Guide to Black History," www.britannica.online. Harry S. Truman, in Philip P. Klinkner and Rogers M. Smith, *The Unsteady March: The Rise and Decline of Racial Equality in America* (Chicago: Univ. of Chicago Press, 2002).

Chapter 44

497: Cardell Gay, in "1963 Civil Right Activist Welcomed Back to Birmingham, Alabama," www.cnn.com. Cardell Gay, in Len Holt, "Eyewitness: The Police Terror at Birmingham," *The National Guardian* (May 16, 1963), reprinted in Clayborne Carson et al., *Reporting Civil Rights, Part One: American Journalism 1941–1963* (New York: Library of America, 2003). Cardell Gay, in David M. Halbfinger. "Birmingham Recalls a Time When Children Led the Fight," *New York Times* (May 2, 2003), at www.nytimes.com. Sanford Wexler, *An Eyewitness History of The Civil Rights Movement* (New York: Checkmark Books, 1993). **498:** Rosa Parks, in Wexler, *Eyewitness*. Reprinted by arrangement with The Heirs to the Estate of Martin Luther King Jr., c/o Writers

House as agent for the proprietor New York, NY. Copyright 1969 the Estate of Martin Luther King Jr., copyright renewed 1997 Coretta Scott King. Rosa Parks, in Rita Dove, "Rosa Parks: Her Simple Act of Protest Galvanized America's Civil Rights Revolution," June 14, 1999, www.time.com. **499:** Southern Christian Leadership Conference, "A Statement to the South and Nation," Jan. 11, 1957, in Clayborne Carson et al., *The Papers of Martin Luther King Jr.,* Vol. 4 (Berkeley: Univ. of California Press, 2000), at www.stanford.edu. **500:** Elizabeth Eckford, in Herb Boyd, *We Shall Overcome* (Naperville, IL: Sourcebooks, 2004). **501:** Minnijean Brown, in Beals, *Warriors*. John F. Kennedy, Sep. 30, 1962, in Wexler, *Eyewitness*. James Meredith, Sep. 26, 1962, in Wexler, *Eyewitness*. James Meredith, *Three Years in Mississippi* (Bloomington: Indiana Univ. Press, 1966), in Peter B. Levy, ed., *Let Freedom Ring: A Documentary History of the Modern Civil Rights Movement* (Westport, CT: Praeger, 1992). **502:** Franklin McCain, in Boyd, *We Shall*. Student Nonviolent Coordinating Committee, Statement of Purpose (May 1960), in Boyd, *We Shall*. **503:** Student Nonviolent Coordinating Committee, in Wexler, *Eyewitness*. **504:** "Letter to Dr. King," *Birmingham News* (Apr. 12, 1963), in William Dudley, ed., *The Civil Rights Movement: Opposing Viewpoints* (San Diego: Greenhaven Press, 1996). Martin Luther King Jr., "Letter from a Birmingham Jail" (Apr. 16, 1963). Reprinted by arrangement with The Heirs to the Estate of Martin Luther King Jr., c/o Writers House as agent for the proprietor New York, NY. Copyright 1963 Martin Luther King Jr., copyright renewed 1991 Coretta Scott King. **505:** Martin Luther King Jr., in "The Children's Crusade," The Martin Luther King, Jr., Research and Education Institute, www.liberationcurriculum.org. Martin Luther King Jr., in Wexler, *Eyewitness*. Martin Luther King Jr., in Boyd, *We Shall*. **506:** Martin Luther King Jr., "I have a dream" (Aug. 28, 1963). Reprinted by arrangement with The Heirs to the Estate of Martin Luther King Jr., c/o Writers House as agent for the proprietor New York, NY. Copyright 1963 Martin Luther King Jr., copyright renewed 1991 Coretta Scott King. **509:** John Lewis, "We Marched to Be Counted," *Newsweek* (Dec. 11, 2000).

Chapter 45

511: Stokely Carmichael, in Boyd, *We Shall*. Martin Luther King Jr., in Boyd, *We Shall*. **512:** James Baldwin, *The Fire Next Time* (New York: Dial Press, 1963). **514:** Malcolm X, in Alex Haley and Malcolm X, *The Autobiography of Malcolm X (As Told to Alex Haley)* (New York: Ballantine, 1999). Malcolm X, in Wade Hudson, *Powerful Words: More Than 200 Years of Extraordinary Writings by African Americans* (New York: Scholastic, 2004). **515:** Stokely Carmichael, Oct. 1966, at "Stokely Carmichael: 'Black Power,'"

www.americanrhetoric.com. John Huelett, in Boyd, *We Shall*. **516:** Raphael J. Sonenshein, "Tom Bradley: Mayor Who Reshaped L.A., 1917–1998," Los Angeles Unified School District, www.lausd.k12.ca.us. Vernon Jordan, at "Roots: U.S. Serial Drama," Museum of Broadcast Communications, www.museum.tv. **517:** Martin Luther King Jr., "Remaining Awake Through a Great Revolution," 1968. Reprinted by arrangement with the Estate of Martin Luther King Jr., c/o Writers House as agent for the proprietor New York, NY. Copyright 1968 the Estate of Martin Luther King Jr., copyright renewed 1996. **518:** Ruth Baston, in Jeanne F. Theoharis, "'We Saved the City': Black Struggles for Educational Equality in Boston, 1960–1976," *Radical History Review* 81 (Fall 2001), at Project MUSE, muse.jhu.edu. **520:** Lyndon Johnson, at "President Lyndon B. Johnson's Commencement Address at Howard University: 'To Fulfill These Rights,' June 4, 1965," at Lyndon Baines Johnson Library and Museum, National Archives and Records Admin., www.lbjlib.utexas.edu. Lyndon Johnson, at "The Origins of Affirmative Action," National Organization for Women, www.now.org.

Chapter 46

523: Dolores Huerta, at United Farm Workers, www.ufw.org. **524:** Betty Friedan, *The Feminine Mystique,* 1963, reprint ed. (New York: W. W. Norton, 2001). **527:** Rodolfo "Corky" Gonzales, "I Am Joaquin," 1967. **532:** Helen Zia, at "Becoming American: The Chinese Experience," www.pbs.org. "A Day of Remembrance: Learning from the Past," at King County, Washington, www.metrokc.gov.

Chapter 47

538: John F. Kennedy, Inaugural Address, Jan. 20, 1961, at www.ourdocuments.gov. Tindall and Shi, *America*. John F. Kennedy, in Frederick Siegel, *Troubled Journey: From Pearl Harbor to Ronald Reagan* (New York: Hill and Wang, 1984). John F. Kennedy, at The Future of Freedom Foundation, www.fff.org, attributed to John F. Kennedy and Bill Adler, *Complete Kennedy Wit* (New York: Citadel Press, 1967). John F. Kennedy, in Reader's Digest Assoc., *Glorious*. John F. Kennedy, in Boyer et al., *Enduring*. **540:** John Kenneth Galbraith, in Patterson, *America*. **542:** John F. Kennedy, "Civil Rights Message," June 11, 1963, at www.americanrhetoric.com. Edward Teller, in Herbert F. York, *Race to Oblivion: A Participant's View of the Arms Race* (New York: Simon and Schuster, 1970), at Denuclearization, www.learnworld.com. John F. Kennedy, Special Message to Congress on Urgent National Needs, May 25, 1961, John F. Kennedy Presidential Library and Museum, www.jfklibrary.org. Neil Armstrong, at "Launching NASA," A Brief History of NASA, www.hq.nasa.gov. Allen Dulles, in Patterson, *America*. Nikita Krushchev, at "We Will Bury You," Nov. 26,

1956, *Time,* www.time.com. **543:** John F. Kennedy, "Remarks at the Rudolph Wilde Platz," June 26, 1963, www.jfklibrary.org. John F. Kennedy, at "American Experience: The Kennedys," www.pbs.org. **544:** John F. Kennedy, in Reader's Digest Assoc., *Glorious*. Dean Rusk, at Thomas Blanton, "Annals of Blinksmanship," The National Security Archive, George Washington Univ., www.gwu.edu, attributed to *The Wilson Quarterly* (Woodrow Wilson International Center for Scholars). **545:** John F. Kennedy, "Staffing a Foreign Policy for Peace," Nov. 2, 1960, JFK Link, www.jfklink.com. **546:** Nellie Connally, at "JFK: A Forty-Year Reflection," John F. Kennedy Exhibit at the President Benjamin Harrison Home, www.presidentbenjaminharrison.org. **547:** William Chafe, *The Unfinished Journey: America Since World War II* (New York: Oxford Univ. Press, 2003). Report of the President's Commission on the Assassination of President Kennedy (1964), JFK Assassination Records, National Archives, www.archives.gov.

Chapter 48

549: Lyndon B. Johnson, in Robert Dallek, *Flawed Giant: Lyndon Johnson and His Times, 1961–1973* (New York: Oxford Univ. Press, 1998). Lyndon B. Johnson, Address Before a Joint Session of Congress, Nov. 27, 1963, www.lbjlib.utexas.edu. Lyndon B. Johnson, Remarks Before the National Convention upon Accepting the Nomination, Aug. 27, 1964, www.lbjlib.utexas.edu. **550:** Lyndon B. Johnson, Remarks at the Univ. of Michigan, May 22, 1964, www.lbjlib.utexas.edu. Lyndon B. Johnson, in Dallek, *Flawed*. **551:** Barry Goldwater, in Bart Barnes, "Barry Goldwater, GOP Hero, Dies," Washington Post Online, www.washingtonpost.com. Barry Goldwater, *The Conscience of a Conservative* (Shepherdsville, KY: Victor Publishing, 1960). Barry Goldwater, at "Goldwater's 1964 Acceptance Speech," Washington Post Online, www.washingtonpost.com, attributed to The Arizona Historical Society. "The Daisy Spot," Eagleton Digital Archive of American Politics, Eagleton Institute of Politics, www.eagleton.rutgers.edu. **552:** Dallek, *Flawed*. Rowland Evans and Robert Novak, *Lyndon B. Johnson: The Exercise of Power, A Political Biography* (New York: New American Library, 1966). Lyndon B. Johnson, Address Before a Joint Session of Congress, Nov. 27, 1963, www.lbjlib.utexas.edu. **553:** Lyndon B. Johnson, Remarks Upon Signing the Public Broadcasting Act of 1967, at www.presidency.ucsb.edu. **554:** Lyndon B. Johnson, in Dallek, *Flawed*. Lyndon B. Johnson, Special Message to the Congress on Conservation and Restoration of Natural Beauty, Feb. 8, 1965, www.lbjlib.utexas.edu. **557:** Barry Goldwater, in "The Limits That Create Liberty and the Liberty That Creates Limits," *Time,* Oct. 9, 1964, www.time.com.

Chapter 49

560: Students for a Democratic Society, Port Huron Statement, June 15, 1962, in Foner, *Give.* Mario Savio, at Free Speech Movement Archives, www.fsm-a.org. **561:** Hunter S. Thompson, "The Hippies," at Microsoft Encarta 2004. Abbie Hoffman in Ken Goffman and Dan Joy, *Counterculture Through the Ages: From Abraham to Acid House* (New York: Villard, 2004). Patterson, *Grand.* Peggy Noonan, in Paul Lyons, "Another Sixties: The New Right," *Nobody Gets Off the Bus: The Viet Nam Generation Big Book,* The Sixties Project, lists.village.virginia.edu. **563:** "The Message of History's Biggest Happening," *Time,* Aug. 29, 1969, www.time.com.

Chapter 50

565: Stanley Karnow, at Vietnam Veterans Memorial Fund, www.vvmf.org. **566:** Ho Chi Minh, in "Viet Nam Documents," Australian National Univ., coombs.anu.edu.au. **567:** John F. Kennedy, Apr. 6, 1954, in "Should the U.S. Intervene in Indochina?," encarta.msn.com. **569:** John F. Kennedy, in George C. Herring, *America's Longest War: The United States and Vietnam, 1950–1975* (New York: Wiley, 1979). **570:** Lyndon B. Johnson, in William Appleton Williams, et al., eds., *America in Vietnam: A Documentary History* (New York: Doubleday, 1985). **571:** Ernest Gruening, Aug. 6–7, 1964, at "The Senate Debates the Tonkin Gulf Resolution," Vassar College, vietnam.vassar.edu. Lyndon B. Johnson, in Herring, *Longest War.* **572:** Lyndon B. Johnson, at "President Lyndon B. Johnson's Address at Johns Hopkins Univ.: 'Peace Without Conquest,' April 7, 1965," www.lbjlib.utexas.edu. **574:** Lyndon B. Johnson, in Loren Baritz, *Backfire: A History of How American Culture Led Us into Vietnam and Made Us Fight the Way We Did* (New York: Morrow, 1985). **575:** Horace Busby, July 21, 1965, at "The War in Vietnam: Escalation Phase," www.presidency.ucsb.edu.

Chapter 51

577: Clark Clifford, in Robert Mann, *A Grand Delusion: America's Descent into Vietnam* (New York: Basic Books, 2001). Mike Mansfield, in Mann, *Delusion.* **578:** Peter Goldman and Tony Fuller, *Charlie Company: What Vietnam Did to Us* (New York: Morrow, 1983). Christian G. Appy, *Working-Class War: American Combat Soldiers and Vietnam* (Chapel Hill, NC: Univ. of North Carolina Press, 1993). **580:** Ho Chi Minh, in Stanley Karnow, *Vietnam: A History* (New York: Viking Press, 1983). **581:** Ly Qui Chung, ed., *Between Two Fires: The Unheard Voices of Vietnam* (New York: Praeger, 1970). **582:** Al Santoli, ed., *Everything We Had: An Oral History of the Vietnam War by Thirty-three American Soldiers Who Fought It* (New York: Random House, 1981). William Ehrhart, in Barry Denenberg, *Voices from Vietnam* (New York: Scholastic, 1995). **583:** George Kennan, in *Encarta Encyclopedia Deluxe 2003*. William Westmoreland, in Clyde Edwin Pettit, *The Experts* (Secaucus, NJ: Lyle Stuart, 1975). **584:** Muhammad Ali, in Brian Duffy, "Truth Tellers: Muhammad Ali," *U.S. News and World Report,* Aug. 27, 2001. Martin Luther King Jr., in "Martin Luther King: Beyond Vietnam—A Time to Break Silence," www.americanrhetoric.com. **586:** Walter Cronkite, in Patterson, *Grand.* Lyndon B. Johnson, in "Pacifica Radio/UC Berkeley Social Activism Sound Recording Project," Univ. of California Berkeley Library, www.lib.berkeley.edu. Clark Clifford, in *Encyclopedia Britannica Ultimate Reference Suite, 2006,* CD-ROM. Lyndon B. Johnson, Mar. 31, 1968, in "President Lyndon B. Johnson's Address to the Nation Announcing Steps to Limit the War in Vietnam and Reporting His Decision Not to Seek Reelection," www.lbjlib.utexas.edu. **587:** Richard M. Nixon, Aug. 8, 1968, in "Nixon's Acceptance of the Republican Party Nomination for President," watergate.info.

Chapter 52

589: Anne Pham, in "Memories of the Fall of Saigon," CBS News, www.cbsnews.com. **590:** Herring, *Longest War.* **591:** Richard Nixon, Apr. 30, 1970, in Michael A. Genovese, *The Nixon Presidency: Power and Politics in Turbulent Times* (New York: Greenwood Press, 1990). **592:** Richard Nixon, Nov. 3, 1969, "The Great Silent Majority," www.americanrhetoric.com. **593:** Bernard Edelman, ed., *Dear America: Letters Home from Vietnam* (New York: Pocket Books, 1985). **594:** Richard Nixon, in Larry Berman, *No Peace, No Honor: Nixon, Kissinger, and Betrayal in Vietnam* (New York: Touchstone, 2002). Henry Kissinger, Oct. 26, 1972, "American Experience: Vietnam Online," www.pbs.org. Berman, *No Peace.* **595:** James Stockdale, in Kim Willenson et al., *The Bad War: An Oral History of the Vietnam War* (New York: New American Library, 1987). **596:** Richard Nixon, Jan. 5, 1973, in "Letter from President Nixon to President Nguyen Van Thieu," TeachingAmericanHistory.com. "Richard Nixon: Remarks at the Conclusion of Discussions with President Thieu of the Republic of Vietnam," at www.presidency.ucsb.edu. Gerald Ford, in Harry G. Summers, *Historical Atlas of the Vietnam War* (Boston: Houghton Mifflin, 1995). Duong Van Minh, "American Experience: Vietnam Online," www.pbs.org.

Chapter 53

599: Richard Nixon, "Checkers" speech, Sep. 23, 1952, at www.watergateinfo.com. **600:** Richard Nixon, "American Experience: Nixon's China Game," www.pbs.org. George Wallace, at Grace Pietrocarlo, "The Political Legacies of the Vietnam War Era," Consortium for Innovative Environments in Learning, www.cielearn.org. Richard Nixon, in Johnathan Schell, *The Time of Illusion* (New York: Knopf, 1976). "Richard Nixon for President 1968 Campaign Brochures: 'The Nixon Stand,'" www.4president.org.

601: Lyndon B. Johnson, at Bill Moyers, "Second Thoughts: Reflections on the Great Society," *New Perspectives Quarterly* 4, no. 1, digitalnpq.org. **602:** Richard Nixon, First Annual Report to the Congress on United States Foreign Policy for the 1970s, Feb. 18, 1970, at www.presidency.ucsb.edu. **604:** Richard Nixon, Remarks at Andrews Air Force Base on Returning from the People's Republic of China, Feb. 28, 1972, at www.presidency.ucsb.edu. Richard Nixon, Exchange with Reporters at the Great Wall of China, Feb. 24, 1972, at www.presidency.ucsb.edu. **605:** "Basic Principles of Relations Between the United States and the Union of Soviet Socialist Republics," at www.presidency.ucsb.edu. Richard Nixon, in Siegel, *Troubled.* **606:** Ron Ziegler, at "Nixon Press Secretary Ziegler Dead at 63," The Nixon Era Times, www.watergate.com. **607:** "Watergate Chronology," *Washington Post,* www.washingtonpost.com. Gerald Ford, Remarks on Taking the Oath of Office as President, Aug. 9, 1974, at Gerald R. Ford Presidential Library and Museum, www.ford.utexas.edu.

Chapter 54

609: Tom Wolfe, "The Me Decade and the Third Great Awakening," at Dept. of History, Univ. of Warwick, www2.warwick.ac.uk. **610:** Gerald Ford, "Whip Inflation Now," Oct. 8, 1974, Miller Center of Public Affairs, Univ. of Virginia, www.millercenter.virginia.edu. Gerald Ford, in Peter Carroll, *It Seemed Like Nothing Happened: America in the 1970s* (New Brunswick, NJ: Rutgers Univ. Press, 1990). Jimmy Carter, in Foner, *Give.* Patterson, *America.* **611:** Jimmy Carter, in Carroll, *Seemed.* Jimmy Carter, National Energy Plan, Address Delivered Before a Joint Session of the Congress, Apr. 20, 1977, at www.presidency.ucsb.edu. Jimmy Carter, "Primary Sources: The 'Crisis of Confidence' Speech," July 15, 1979, www.pbs.org. "People and Events: Carter's 'Crisis of Confidence' Speech," www.pbs.org. **612:** Jimmy Carter, in Foner, *Give.* Jimmy Carter, in Carroll, *Seemed.* Aase Lionaes, "Presentation Speech," Dec. 10, 1978, The Nobel Peace Prize 1978, nobelprize.virtual.museum. **613:** Jimmy Carter, in Carroll, *Seemed.* Jimmy Carter, in *Patterson,* America. Carroll, *Seemed.* Patterson, *America.* James Schlesinger, in Carroll, *Seemed.* **614:** George Brown, in Carroll, *Seemed.* Nina Rao, "Population Connection History," Population Connection, www.populationconnection.org. Gaylord Nelson, "How the First Earth Day Came About," EnviroLink, www.earthday.envirolink.org. **617:** Shirley Chisholm, "Women's History," The Democratic Party, www.democrats.org. **622:** Wolfe, "The Me Decade," at www2.warwick.ac.uk. James T. Farrell, in Michael Novak, *Unmeltable Ethnics: Politics and Culture in American Life,* 2d ed. (Piscataway, NJ: Transaction, 1995). "The Disco History Page," www.disco-disco.com.

Chapter 55

625: Timothy McCarthy, in "He Took a Bullet for Reagan," June 11, 2004, www.cbsnews.com. Ronald Reagan, at www.britannica.online. **626:** Ibid. Jerry Falwell, in Ross K. Baker, "'Values' and U.S. History: We've Been Here Before," Jan. 26, 2004, *USA Today,* www.usatoday.com. **627:** Ronald Reagan, in Tindall and Shi, *America.* **628:** Ronald Reagan, Inaugural Address, Jan. 20, 1981, Ronald Reagan Presidential Library and Foundation, www.reaganlibrary.com. **629:** William H. Chafe, *The Unfinished Journey: America Since World War II* (New York: Oxford Univ. Press, 1991). **631:** Ronald Reagan, Farewell Address, Jan. 11, 1989, www.reaganlibrary.com. Ronald Reagan, "Remarks at a Luncheon for Members of the College of Physicians in Philadelphia," Apr. 1, 1987, www.reaganlibrary.com. **633:** Jesse Jackson, "Address before the Democratic National Convention," July 18, 1984, www.pbs.org. **634:** George W. Bush, Republican National Convention Acceptance Speech, Aug. 3, 2000, at www.presidency.ucsb. edu. **635:** Tom Wicker, George Herbert Walker Bush (New York: Penguin, 2004).

Chapter 56

637: Ronald Reagan, "Tear Down This Wall," Great Speeches Collection, www.historyplace.com. "Eyewitness: The Night the Wall Came Down," www.bbc.co.uk. George J. Church, "Freedom! The Wall Crumbles Overnight, Berliners Embrace in Joy, and a Stunned World Ponders the Consequences," *Time,* Nov. 20, 1989. **639:** Ronald Reagan, Apr. 27, 1983, "Address Before a Joint Session of the Congress on Central America," www.reaganlibrary.com. Ronald Reagan, in "American Experience: The Iran-Contra Affair," www.pbs.org. **641:** George Schulz, in Julie Wolf, "The Iran-Contra Affair," www.pbs.org. **643:** Ronald Reagan, in Douglas Brinkley, *American Heritage History of the United States* (New York: Penguin , 1998). Ronald Reagan, Farewell Address, Jan. 11, 1989, www.reaganlibrary.com. Ronald Reagan, in Evans, *American Century.* **645:** Mikhail Gorbachev, in Reader's Digest Assoc., *Glorious.*

Chapter 57

650–651: Barack Obama, Keynote Address at the 2004 Democratic National Convention, at www.pbs.org. **652:** Bill Clinton, Acceptance Speech to the Democratic National Convention, July 16, 1992, at www.presidency.ucsb.edu. **653:** Bill Clinton, in John F. Harris, *The Survivor: Bill Clinton in the White House* (New York: Random House, 2005). **654:** Bill Clinton, Statement on Signing the Balanced Budget Act of 1997, Aug. 5, 1997, at www.presidency.ucsb.edu. Bill Clinton, in "Clinton: Pay Debt by 2015," June 28, 1999, at CNNMoney, www.money.cnn.com. **656:** George W. Bush, Aug. 3, 2000, at www.presidency.ucsb.edu. George W. Bush, in "Bush Stumps for 'No Child Left Behind'," Jan. 6, 2004, at www.cnn.com. George W. Bush, Aug. 3, 2000, at www.presidency.ucsb.edu. **660:** Barack Obama, in Barack Obama, *Change We Can Believe In.* (New York: Three Rivers Press, 2008).

Chapter 58

669: Kofi Annan, Address to the Parliament of Rwanda, May 7, 1998, at Frontline, www.pbs.org/wgbh/pages/frontline. **675:** Osama Bin Laden, at "Mind of Bin Laden Transcript," Sep. 26, 2001, BBC Newsnight, news.bbc.co.uk. George W. Bush, Address to a Joint Session of Congress and the American People, Sep. 20, 2001, at www.whitehouse.gov. George W. Bush, State of the Union, Jan. 29, 2002, at www.whitehouse.gov.

Chapter 59

681: Richard Moller, in Dean E. Murphy, *September 11: An Oral History* (New York: Doubleday, 2002). **682:** George W. Bush, Sep. 11, 2001, at www.whitehouse.gov. Roger Simon, "One Year," *U.S. News and World Report* (Nov. 11, 2002), at www.usnews.com. Richard Bernstein and the staff of *The New York Times,* eds., *Out of the Blue: The Story of September 11, 2001, from Jihad to Ground Zero* (New York: Times Books/Henry Holt, 2002). **683:** Bernstein et al., *Out.* **684:** George W. Bush, Sep. 17, 2001, at "Remarks by the President at the Islamic Center of Washington," www.americanrhetoric.com. "Arab Americans," Caught in the Crossfire, www.pbs.org. **686:** George W. Bush, Sep. 20, 2001, at www.whitehouse.gov. **689:** Elizabeth Goitein, "President Obama: It's not too late to reject bad detainee law," at The Hill, www.thehill.com.

Credits

Photographs

Front Cover
Katrin Solansky/iStockphoto.

Front Matter
i: Katrin Solansky/iStockphoto.
iv: Katrin Solansky/iStockphoto.
xv: Katrin Solansky/iStockphoto.

Chapter 1
xviii: Flip Schulke/Corbis. 1: Mawhyyouare/shutterstock. 2 r: Library of Congress. 2 c: Library of Congress. 2 l: Library of Congress. 3 l: FPG/Getty Images. 3 c: Library of Congress. 3 r: Library of Congress 4 c: Andrew F. Kazmierski/Shutterstock.com. 4 l: TCI. 4 c: Andrew F. Kazmierski / Shutterstock.com. 4 r: TCI. 5 tl: Cheryl Fenton. 5 lc: Library of Congress. 5 br: Daniel M. Silva/Shutterstock. 5 bl: Library of Congress. 5 bc: Letters from Jon Adams, 1777-1778. 5 tr: Time & Life Pictures/Getty Images. 6 l: Jose Gil/Shutterstock.com. 7 r: TCI.

Chapter 2
8: Corbis. 9 r: The Granger Collection, New York. 10 l: Library of Congress. 10 c: Library of Congress. 11 r: Library of Congress. 12 l: Michael Thompson/Dreamstime.com. 13 tr: Library of Congress. 13 br: Library of Congress. 14 tl: Library of Congress. 15 r: Library of Congress.

Chapter 3
16: Steve Brigman/Shutterstock. 17 r: Ivy Close Images/Alamy. 18 tl: Robert Kyllo/Shutterstock. 18 lc: Christopher Jackson/Shutterstock. 18 bc: Benkrut./ Dreamstime.com 20 tr: Lou Oates/Shutterstock. 20 bl: Library of Congress. 21 r: Library of Congress. 22 tl: RF/Getty. 22 br: lofoto/Shutterstock. 23 tl: Greg Kieca/Shutterstock. 25 tc: Shutterstock. 25 br: Linda Johnsonbaugh/Dreamstime.com. 25 tcl: Gmeyerle/Dreamstime.com. 25 bc: Terry W. Ryder/Shutterstock. 25 bl: Paul B. Moore/Shutterstock. 25 tl: Paul Yates/Shutterstock 25 tr: Jixue Yang/Dreamstime.com.

Chapter 4
28: Library of Congress. 29 r: Library of Congress. 30 l: Library of Congress. 31 l: Library of Congress. 34 l: 1000 Words/ Shutterstock.com. 35 br: Schlesinger Library-Radcliffe Institute/Harvard University/The Bridgeman Art Library. 35 tr: Library of Congress. 36 bc: Library of Congress. 37 r: Library of Congress.

Chapter 5
38: Library of Congress. 39 r: Keith Reicher/iStockphoto. 40 l: Library of Congress. 41 r: Library of Congress. 44 l: Library of Congress. 45 l: Library of Congress. 46 l: Library of Congress, Prints & Photographs Division, Detroit Publishing Company Collection. 48 c: Library of Congress. 49 r: Library of Congress.

Chapter 6
50: Tetra Images/Getty Images. 51 r: RF/Getty. 52 l: The Granger Collection, New York. 54 l: The Granger Collection, New York. 54 bl: The Granger Collection, New York. 55 l: Bettmann/Corbis. 56 l: Library of Congress. 57 tr: Library of Congress. 57 tl: Library of Congress. 57 tcl: Library of Congress. 57 tcr: Library of Congress. 58 l: Library of Congress. 59 l: The Granger Collection, New York. 60 l: Library of Congress.

Chapter 7
62: Library of Congress. 63 cr: Vacclav/Shutterstock. 63 br: TCI # 27. 63 tr: Getty Images. 64 tl: Library of Congress. 64 bl: Denis Jr. Tangney/iStockphoto 64 cl: Visions of America, LLC/Alam. 65 bc: Vacclav/Shutterstock. 65 br: TCI. 65 bl: Getty Images. 67 c: Getty Images. 68 bl: Ed Stock/iStockphoto. 69 c: Vacclav/Shutterstock. 70 bl: Steven Wynn/iStockphoto. 70 tl: Richard Gunion/Dreamstime.com. 71 c: TCI. 72 l: Matthias Haas/iStockphoto. 73 bl: P_Wei/iStockphoto. 73 tr: Ilene MacDonald/ Alamy. 75 br: Visions of America, LLC/Alamy. 75 tr: Library of Congress. 76 br: Richard Gunion/Dreamstime. 76 tl: Getty Images. 77 r: Library of Congress.

Chapter 8
78 tc: The Granger Collection, New York. 78 bc: The Granger Collection, New York. 79 r: Library of Congress. 81 r: Library of Congress. 82 c: Library of Congress. 84 l: Library of Congress. 85 br: Library of Congress. 86 l: Library of Congress. 88 l: Library of Congress. 89 r: Library of Congress. 90 l: Library of Congress. 91 l: Library of Congress.

Chapter 9
92: The Granger Collection, New York. 93 cr: DC State Historic Preservation Office. 93 tc: Library of Congress. 95 c: Library of Congress. 97 r: Library of Congress. 99 r: Bettmann/Corbis. 100 c: Library of Congress. 101 r: Library of Congress. 102 br: Library of Congress. 102 bl: National Archives.

Chapter 10
104: Ivy Close Images/ Alamy. 105 r: Library of Congress. 107 r: Library of Congress. 109 r: Library of Congress. 111 br: Library of Congress. 111 tr: Library of Congress. 112 c: Library of Congress. 113 r: Library of Congress. 114 c: Library of Congress. 115 l: Library of Congress. 116 tl: The Granger Collection, New York. 116 bl: Library of Congress. 116 tl: Library of Congress.

Chapter 11
118: Library of Congress. 119 r: Library of Congress. 120 l: Library of Congress. 121 r: Library of Congress. 122 l: Library of Congress. 124 bl: Library of Congress. 124 tl: Library of Congress. 125 r: Library of Congress. 126 tl: Library of Congress. 127 r: Library of Congress. 128: Library of Congress

Chapter 12
130: The Granger Collection, New York. 131 r: Library of Congress. 132 l: Library of Congress. 133 l: Library of Congress. 135 r: Library of Congress. 135 br: Library of Congress. 136 l: Library of Congress. 137 tr: Library of Congress. 138 tl: Library of Congress. 138 bl: Library of Congress. 139 c: Library of Congress. 140 l: Library of Congress. 141 r: Library of Congress.

Chapter 13
142: The Granger Collection, New York. 143 r: The Library of Congress. 144 l: Library of Congress. 145 r: Library of Congress. 146 c: Corbis. 147 l: Library of Congress. 148 l: Library of Congress. 150 l: Library of Congress. 152 c: Library of Congress. 153 l: Mikhail Kusayev/Dreamstime.com. 155 r: Library of Congress.

Chapter 14
156: Keystone/Getty Images. 157 r: Library of Congress. 158 c: Library of Congress. 159 tr: Library of Congress. 159 br: Library of Congress. 160 l: Library of Congress. 162 l: Library of Congress. 163 tr: Library of Congress. 163 tl: Library of Congress. 164 br: Library of Congress. 164 bcl: Library of Congress. 164 bcr: Library of Congress. 164 bl: Library of Congress.

Chapter 15
166: Edwin Levick/Getty Images.] 167 l: Library of Congress 167 r: Library of Congress. 168 l: The Granger Collection, New York. 169 r: Library of Congress. 170 c: Library of Congress. 170 cl: Library of Congress. 171 c: The Granger Collection, New York. 172 l: Library of Congress. 173 l: Library of Congress. 174 l: Library of Congress. 175 r: Library of Congress. 176 bl: Library of Congress 176 l: National Archives. 176 br: Library of Congress. 177 l: Bettmann/CORBIS. 178 l: Library of Congress.

Chapter 16
180: The Granger Collection, New York. 181 l: Library of Congress. 182 r: Library of Congress. 185 r: Corbis. 187 r: Library of Congress. 188 l: Library of Congress. 189 l: Library of Congress. 191 r: Library of Congress. 192 br: Library of Congress. 192 tl: Library of Congress.

Chapter 17
194: Library of Congress. 195 r: Library of Congress. 196 c: Library of Congress. 197 r: Library of Congress. 198 r: Library of Congress. 200 l: Library of Congress. 201 r: The Granger Collection, New York. 201 bl: Library of Congress.

Chapter 58

664: Associated Press. **665:** Logan Mock-Bunting/Zuma Press/Corbis. **666:** Sebastian Zwez/Xinhua Press/Corbis. **667 b:** Cristi111/Dreamstime.com. **667 t:** Dainis Derics/Dreamstime.com. **667 c:** Artur Bogacki/Dreamstime.com. **668:** AFP/Getty Images. **669:** Abdelhak Senna-AFP/Getty images. **670:** David Snyder/Dreamstime.com. **671 t:** Niko Guido/iStockphoto. **671 b:** STR/AFP/Getty Images. **672:** AFP/AFP/Getty Images. **674:** Sean Adair-Reuters/Corbis. **676:** Joe Raedle/Getty Images. **677:** Getty Images. **678:** Muhannad Fala'ah/Getty Images. **679:** MOHAMED MESSARA/epe/Corbis.

Chapter 59

680: Leungphotography/Dreamstime.com. **681:** Super Nova Images/Alamy. **682:** Neville Elder/Sygma/Corbis. **683:** Reuters/CORBIS. **684 t:** Ed Kashi/Corbis. **684 b:** Getty Images. **685 cr:** Christy Uyeno Collection. **685 b:** Kelly Shafsky Collection. **685 cl:** Vicki Philp Collection. **685 t:** Ronan Mohan Collection. **686 t:** John Marshall Mantel/ZUMA Press/Corbis. **687:** Jim Young/Reuters/Corbis. **688:** Alamy. **689:** Kristoffer Tripplaar/Pool/Corbis.

Back Matter

690-691: Ocean/Corbis. **691:** Katrin Solansky/iStockphoto. **701:** Corbis.

Art

Chapter 5
42–43: Len Ebert.

Chapter 7
65: Qin Zhong Yu. **66:** Qin Zhong Yu. **67:** Gary Undercuffler. **69:** Gary Undercuffler. **71:** Gary Undercuffler. **74:** Qin Zhong Yu.

Chapter 8
87: Phong Saechao.

Chapter 10
106: Phong Saechao.

Chapter 11
126: Phong Saechao.

Chapter 13
148–149: Len Ebert. **151:** Qin Zhong Yu. **154:** Qin Zhong Yu.

Chapter 14
161: Phong Saechao. **165:** Qin Zhong Yu.

Chapter 16
182: Phong Saechao. **183:** Phong Saechao. **184:** Len Ebert.

Chapter 17
203: Phong Saechao.

Chapter 21
239: Len Ebert. **244:** Phong Saechao.

Chapter 22
250: Phong Saechao.

Chapter 23
261: Len Ebert.

Chapter 25
279: Rosiland Solomon.

Chapter 26
294: Phong Saechao.

Chapter 27
306: Phong Saechao.

Chapter 29
327: Phong Saechao.

Chapter 30
340: Len Ebert.

Chapter 31
344: Phong Saechao.

Chapter 32
352: Phong Saechao. **357:** Len Ebert.

Chapter 33
377: Phong Saechao.

Chapter 34
387: Len Ebert

Chapter 35
394–395: Phong Saechao. **403:** Phong Saechao.

Chapter 37
429: Phong Saechao.

Chapter 41
466: Phong Saechao. **471:** Phong Saechao. **473:** Phong Saechao. **475:** Phong Saechao. **476-477:** Phong Saechao.

Chapter 42
482: Phong Saechao.

Chapter 43
490: Phong Saechao. **494:** Phong Saechao.

Chapter 44
507: Don Taka

Chapter 45
516: Phong Saechao. **520:** Phong Saechao.

Chapter 46
524-525: Phong Saechao. **527:** Phong Saechao. **529:** Phong Saechao. **531:** Phong Saechao.

Chapter 47
539: Phong Saechao.

Chapter 49
560: Phong Saechao.

Chapter 50
569: Phong Saechao. **572:** Phong Saechao. **573:** Scott Willis. **574:** Phong Saechao.

Chapter 51
579: Len Ebert. **580:** Gary Undercuffler. **586:** Phong Saechao.

Chapter 52
590: Phong Saechao. **594:** Phong Saechao.

Chapter 53
604: Qin Zhong Yu.

Chapter 54
611: Phong Saechao. **615:** Len Ebert. **620:** Phong Saechao.

Chapter 55
630: Phong Saechao.

Chapter 56
638 t: Phong Saechao.

Chapter 57
650: Phong Saechao. **651:** Phong Saechao.

Chapter 58
673: Phong Saechao.